# Future Worlds of Social Science

# Future Worlds of Social Science:

## Essays on Sociality

By

**Lawrence Hazelrigg**

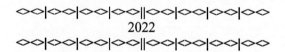
2022

**Future Worlds of Social Science**
*By Lawrence Hazelrigg*

This book first published 2022

Ethics International Press Ltd UK

British Library Cataloguing in Publication Data

A catalogue record for this book is available from the British Library

Print Book ISBN: 978-1-871891-85-0

eBook ISBN: 978-1-871891-86-7

# Contents

# Preface

When I was a young man, Henry David Thoreau's writings, especially his *Walden*, told of some experiences and sentiments that were very familiar to me. If that seems strange today (as it does, in part, to me), one must remember a difference in time. *Walden* was published two years after the birth of my father's paternal grandfather Hazelrigg, who, according to some correspondence left behind, was enthralled by the book. I was born fewer than nine decades later, and although I was born in a city my formative years were lived on prairie that held many more heads of cattle and horses than the number of human beings scattered across that land. Furthermore, during World War II, while my parents were living at a US Army base in Texas, I lived with my maternal grandparents in a log house lighted by kerosene lanterns and heated by wood, my sleeping quarters (a "feather bed" pallet) in a loft reached by climbing a ladder fastened to a wall. A few years later I began public school in a one-room schoolhouse, one teacher for all eight grades of about twenty children. Thoreau would have noticed many differences, of course: airplanes loudly overhead, trains heard faintly in the distance, automobiles on graveled or dirt roads, plus asphalted federal highways; the jangle of telephones and the whistle of radios (later, television) added to voices of family and neighbors; many more books, including a set of the Encyclopedia Britannica which my parents purchased in 1952 and later a set of Great Books of the Western World; and other material changes. But sentiments and some experiences were not so different.

Today? It is difficult to draw connections of familiarity between then and now. When I revisit Thoreau's writings, I am reminded that my past is in some ways much as the novelist, L P Hartley (1953), described in his opening line about "the past" being "a foreign country."[1] Only in the illusions or delusions of nostalgia does passage to that "country" seem possible, since one cannot remove the productivity of memories between then and now. Granted, I can recognize a few residues of Thoreau that have remained with me. When I built part of my house, and then my barn, I remembered Thoreau saying that "I never in all my walks came across a man engaged in so simple and natural an occupation as building his house" (Thoreau 1985 [1854], p. 359), and I knew the difference he had in mind[2]. But there are some differences that I know to be beyond my best efforts to comprehend his experience. These have to do mostly with his accounts of "intellectual" activity—or more precisely his accounts of what he took to be the possibilities of intellect. Foremost among the mirages at which I balked?

Yes, he demonstrated his independence as craftsman more than I could have done (even had I not to contend with county regulations and the like). Perhaps as writer, too. I won't argue the point, although one cannot avoid the fact that he had a few books at his disposal, he had one or two teachers, and so forth. But in general can a person in fact live independently today? Is a life Robinsonade possible today? Was it, in fact, in Thoreau's time? No. Not unless one defines "independent" with blinders so extensive a spirited horse would rebel.

---

[1] Hartley's novel, *The Go-Between* (London: Hamish Hamilton), is mainly remembered for an opening sentence that has sometimes been (mis-)attributed to Harold Pinter, among others.

[2] One day, while I was finishing the raftering of the double-hipped roof for that part of the house, a neighbor stopped to visit, and it soon became apparent that he was curious to confirm that I was indeed the builder, my wife up there with me as assistant. I also noticed that as he left he (director of law enforcement for a state agency) checked my county permit.

This six-part volume marks the thirtieth year since my prior foray into the thickets, that one being my second. The first began during the late 1960s from a welter of mis-matched views and experiences, mainly of reading social science literatures against a backdrop of philosophy, David Hume most prominently resident of my mind. By the time I read Michel Foucault's *The Order of Things*, and more especially the reception it was getting among some quarters of social scientists, the better I understood how and why my first effort had come to a halt on the shoals of inadequacy: like virtually all of the social scientists I had been reading, I had not grasped in full the implications of Immanuel Kant's critique, and those shoals of inadequacy had been masked by the inky waters of what Pierre Bourdieu referred to in his inaugural lecture at the Collège de France as scholastic discussions of the relations between "individual" and "structure." By the time of my second foray I was satisfied that my grasp had become much richer especially with respect to the place of Kant's third volume as bridging effort and in that sense pinnacle. But my understanding was still under the illusion that the "left Hegelian" critique had demonstrated the way—and so far as I could see the only way—to set aside the enormous roadblock that Kant had erected across the future of any effective claim to a science of human affairs. I had failed to notice that Hegel himself had concluded late in life that he had failed to appreciate subtleties of Kant's critique, which held hostage to the hope of species maturity any pragmatism such as Karl Marx expressed in the last of his theses on the most advanced materialist philosophy of the day, Ludwig Feuerbach's. I had suffered more than I had realized the blindness of a reason that lacks sufficient experience (as Kant had cautioned), my reason telling me that our species had strode far along the path to maturity since 1804.

The process of writing and rewriting these essays has been slow, mainly because I have become slow. Most of them are built of pieces that have been "in process" for quite some time. Indeed, a few of the pieces have been in their germination and first growth since the early 1970s; scattered pieces even to the late 1960s. Do those pasts seem foreign countries today? In part, they do, as I have indicated just above.

While in the midst of what were markedly new experiences six decades ago—being a sailor (circa 1960)—I stumbled onto Michael Oakeshott's first book, *Experience and Its Modes*, in a Long Beach bookshop and bought it for reading aboard ship. Hegel was still a mountain barely approached, but Oakeshott's text for the most part could be read without having dared toeholds on those heights. As best memory serves, his book was my first encounter with the question, "What counts as experience?" The startle would have been unique but for the fact that a few of David Hume's questions had already left major markings in my perspective on "world" (a concept that was then rapidly expanding in particulars for me: other places, other cultures). I was too green to appreciate how idiosyncratic Oakeshott's book was for its time—indeed, that there had been nothing quite like it. But of his thoughts that made their way into my notebook one in particular would recur: it is the ambition of every writer to be understood, but whether the writer can also convince and persuade others is a matter upon which it is wise to be indifferent (Oakeshott 1933, p. 248). And for me, dare I confess, that indifference seemed ordinary—very likely, I suppose, because of the old "cattle country" culture in which I had been reared. Talk had been scarce, most of the time. But for what there was, you said what you thought without expecting anyone to agree or disagree.

There are numerous threads of continuity, of course, which one can recite between a past and a present. Many of the circuits in the essays that follow can be traced through other writings that extend to the days of ancient Athens. A simple example will perhaps clarify at least part of my meaning. One of the most recent events that had as an effect (one among many) a stalling of my wordsmithing was the quadrennial US election of 2016. Surprised at the outcome (to put it mildly), I was slow to get to grips with its meanings, thus to locate them in histories that lived partly in my conscious memory. One morning in December I awoke long before dawn, retrieving something of a passage I had once read of the great Italian historian, Santo Mazzarino, who in one of his books had sought to bring a coherence to the surviving accounts of processes and events collected in European memory as "fall of the Roman Empire." As I re-read those dimly remembered passages from the last pages of that book, I was struck by one of the circuits:

> The ruin of the ancient world is a tragedy with many voices. We are watching the failure of balance between the requirements of supranational centralization and productive inadequacy, the separation of certain "nations," and the related victory of "barbarians" of many races in regions which classical civilization had attached to the Greco-Roman heart of the empire (Mazzarino 1966 [1959], p. 187).[3]

Another replay? Seemingly so, although with the disclaimer that "replays" are always with and within difference, sometimes greater, sometimes smaller, and often carry the qualifier that Marx had assigned ("farce"). Again, I realized, I had been in partial blinders. Recent processes of globalization had brought to mind the advance of globalization that began during the last decades of the nineteenth century—of that I was convinced—and the tremulous part of my focus had been on the events that had ended that advance, a Great War that later gained the Roman numeral I: massive destructions of human beings, body and soul, with the attendance of also massive destructions of land, animals, buildings, machinery, memories and anticipations, and more. I had not noticed so much the migrations of peoples and disruptions of "nations" that had then been involved—until I remembered the great waves of immigrants who had been arriving on North American shores and realized the same east-to-west migrations had been passing through lands of Europe. In recent times the migrations and disruptions could not be missed, of course; nor the emotive energies fueled (still) not only by nativism but also, often inseparably, by fundamentalist religious sectarian ideologies (Christian and Judaic as well as Islamic), some of them used as rusty hinges by those who have been "left behind" in mind, time, and place. But until my "brain search" during that December night I had not recalled the more distant "foreign country" and the long train of efforts to understand the lessons of Roman *inclinatio* (decline, decay, death), if any could be found, if any could be applied to a present time. As Santo Mazzarino (1966 [1959], 174) reminded, "the idea that states grow old, as a man grows old, always had a contemporary significance."

What future worlds of social science? Perhaps none. Perhaps somewhere from "bloody awful" to "all in no one's past," a road already travelogued by Cormac McCarthy.

*Lawrence Hazelrigg Tallahassee. FL 15 October 2021*

---

[3] The first scare quotes are Mazzarino's. I added the second, for Mazzarino had already noted that "barbarian" had long been an indication relative to the outward gaze of a particular cultural tradition (ancient Greek, then Greco-Roman, etc.) and would be used accordingly throughout his text.

## Part One
## Perspectives, Relations, and Responses to an Illusion

The essays comprising this volume are variously concerned with self as knowing subject and as known object, both the doubled gaze of self-knowledge and the gaze, whether wittingly reflexive or not, of knowledge of other self. They share some common themes in an area of the sociology of knowledge that intersects with epistemology and ethics. One of these themes has to do with the production of doubt—doubt of a claim of specific knowledge, for instance, doubt of a claim of authority, doubt of self and self-competence (one perspective of which, as will be described below, is the way in which prosthesis, as in "prosthetic device," is distributed across things in relation to actors who use them).

Doubt, some would say, is not a product; it simply is, or is not. But doubt actually has different antecedents in historical sociocultural contexts and conditions. It is not simply *there*, as one might imagine oxygen in an atmosphere to be present (until it is not). Doubt is bound up in the production of knowledge, in the invention of facts and understandings and things. From an economist's point of view it is a "good" (or a "bad") distributed more or less equitably through a population. In particular circumstances an economist might regard doubt, or its opposite, as a service (think of a concierge, for instance, or a minister or a technician who fits a client with an appliance). Some of these perspectives on doubt will be visited only glancingly. One that will course throughout the essays, sometimes disconcertingly, is the perspective on doubt that can be called "Humean" (after the philosopher David Hume). As a general category of experience, doubt has probably been integral to human being longer than most components of culture (doubt of this or that god, of the stranger who appears without introduction, of one's child's survival, of the local shaman's bona fides). But Hume brought doubt into the most interior reaches of self: how can I have complete confidence in what I think I believe, in which I think I know, in what I *think* and therefore in the I that is thinking?

There are other themes, but they are secondary. One of these, for example, has to do with what seems to be an expanding gap between knowledge and skill expectations of societal formations, on the one hand, and the capabilities of most adult actors, on the other. Included here are (1) a practical theory of mind by which a person self-orients and navigates among other selves: e.g., until recent decades the error in assuming stasis in other's mind, including other's assumption about one's own "stability" and "integrity" (i.e., the reflexivity dimension), was usually small, but now other's mind might shift in sentiments, ressentiments, paranoias, anxieties, etc., rather quickly as response to more rapidly changing conditions; (2) a person's sense of self-efficacy: e.g., do my *best* or most important actions on a typical day have effects, beneficial or malign, intended or unintended, that last more than a few hours, a few days, a few years? (3) self-management of temporality in anticipation: e.g., self's estimation of rates of change, distributions of horizon effects, exercises of patience, discounts of future value; and (4) the apparently increased prevalence of rejectionist postures, especially those amounting to capitulation even though the rejectionist actor presents it as an effective act of critique.[1]

Another theme has to do with a little-studied process, or set of processes, by which beliefs constituted as "facts"—reliable empirical knowledge—are transmitted to, and in the

---

[1] In a *New York Times* tribute to recently deceased Alvin Toffler, author of the once highly popular book, *Future Shock* (1970), Farhad Manjoo (2016) raised again the question whether human being has evolved rapidly enough to produce effects (commonly grouped as "technological") that human being cannot manage, either as threats to one's immediate health or, perhaps, as threats to species survival.

1

actions of transmission to some extent create, specific audiences. Included here are (1) issues of "the tragedy of ideas"—the peculiar bias by which "ideas" can be pure and unsullied, until they are "applied"; also, that ideas in transmission usually carry marks of authority (authorship, etc.), the authorities are credentialed and lend the ideas pedigrees and reputations as positional goods, such that, in any marketplace of ideas, it may happen that an idea which might be seen as otherwise "the same" but deriving from different authorities can proceed with different currency depending on pedigree, even to the extent that a superior formulation that carries a less reputed pedigree will be neglected;[2] (2) the recurrent tendency to assume that facts exist independently of theory and can travel independently as "theory-free observations" (to use an older locution; see my 1989a);[3] (3) variances in receptivity are also part of the "transmission process," however, and these too have been neglected: e.g., what proportion of the adult population are adequately prepared to understand basic phenomena of quantum mechanics? Or present-day evolutionary theory? Or differences among various investment instruments for, say, retirement planning? How well prepared are adult actors to deal with the fact that facts change, without lapsing into an anti-intellectualist paranoia or conspiracy theory? (Think of the climate change "discussion."

Running throughout the secondary thematic aspects of the essays is the issue of doubt and in conjunction with doubt—integral to it, in fact—issues of belief, illusion, and authority. In a paternalistic society, belief in what might be called "an authority of the apex"—the fatherly ruler of a household, the highest majesty of a king or a queen, the supremacy of an omniscient, omnipotent, omnipresent godhead—could still the greater range of doubts and uncertainties (while swords, the rack, drawing and quartering, disemboweling, could staunch the sturdiest challengers who might otherwise remain unconvinced). Gradually, matter-of-fact endorsement of that view changed. By the late eighteenth century in Europe an odd sense of rootlessness was taking hold in the towers of enlightened thought. Others have recited this story very well, especially in regard to social sciences, and in general I defer to their accounts, more or less.[4] Here I want only to highlight some late events of the main thread of that sequence, from which sprang the sense of rootlessness and despair, hopelessness (as in the title Hawthorn attached to his account); for these events exist in background to the essays here assembled. The following section, "Kant's Legacy," is an abstracted rendition of a process that in its many particulars was, as life virtually always is, messily complex and sometimes confused, inconsistent, sometimes contradictory. I have chosen as the focal authority Immanuel Kant because I remain convinced, after half a century of thinking of these matters, that if one were asked to choose the one thinker whose projective theorizing was most formative of the basic template of modern European and Euro-American society, whether stringently capitalistic or modified in socialistic tendencies, the

---

[2] Biernacki's study of the authority of facts should be cited; likewise, the spate of studies finding that much research in psychology, medical science, etc., does not replicate well.

[3] Examples of the tendency are present in Howlett and Morgan's (2011) collection of studies of "how well facts travel" (including explicitly in Morgan's introductory essay).

[4] One of the best, I still think, is Geoffrey Hawthorn's *Enlightenment and Despair* (1976). Other, more recent works that track much of the argument can be read with great benefit—for instance, Alston (1993), everything I have read by Geuss (e.g., from 1981 to 2014) and by Pippin (e.g., from 1999 and 2005 to 2015). The brief essay by Taylor and Montefiore in introduction to Kortian's 1980 study of Jürgen Habermas assumes some basic acquaintance with the history of philosophy but otherwise is helpful and gains in texture as one reads Kortian's short book. Cascardi's (1999) study is interesting for aesthetics and critical theory. Thorne's (2009) treatment of skepticism and dialectical threads weaving through enlightenment movements and resistances adds useful perspective. For detailed surveys of relevant philosophical literatures in wake of Kant, see Beiser (1987, 2014a, 2014b).

2

choice could be none other than Kant.[5]  Certainly European philosophy after 1800 developed under the strong influence of his critical theory, and one can say—as Jean-Luc Nancy (2008 (1976)] has said, that his critique of critique inspired a literary tradition.  But I mean more than that.  Kant's inquiry and his conclusions became a sort of propaedeutical frame of the development of modern society.  It is not that he had many readers.  Rather, his insights gave systematic voice to developments underway, resulting in a propaedeutic for what was to come.  This included the modern social sciences—and I emphasize "modern" only to remind that Aristotle (e.g., in his *On Politics*) had produced understandings that could be retrospectively counted as something of a "social science" (likewise, the tragedians, Aeschylus, Sophocles, and Euripedes; and so on)[6]— which  came on the heels of Kantian theory, partly reinterpreted by others (e.g., Schopenhauer) and partly answered by others (e.g., Hegel), but almost always bearing clear marks of heritage in the Kantian effort and its consequence.  Kant's critical theory was the looming presence, so to speak, whether one self-described as critic, as sympathetic, or as champion.

My presentation of and in this history attempts to honor the realization, as Kant did, that when the ardor of the artist has been put in service to a chimera, the outcome is not a happy one.  There are chimera aplenty, all of them interrelated as if in a ghostly genealogy, with its originary event(s), privileged appearances of visage and voice, certitudes from nowhere and nothing about everywhere and everything.  The presentation weaves scenes of a tapestry, if you will, all threads moving up and down, forth and back, some of them in laminations (temporal as well as spatial) as in a palimpsest.  On occasion a reader will suspect repetition; I ask forbearance enough to see the new, at least an effort that was once thought to be new, in the appearance of nothing new in a tapestry apparently overexposed to the sun.  The burden of apparent repetition will be due, or so I contend, to the fact that we have had great difficulty trying to leave Kant behind.  That burden of repetition is *not*, I hope the reader will see, due to the importance of Kant (although I admit to being among those who think that few if any "modern" European or Euro-American thinkers have been his peer in importance of contribution).  Rather, it is due to the long and continuing train of efforts evidently committed to producing what Kant—after, and in much greater detail than, Hume—demonstrated could not be achieved.

Various adjectives have been used in conjunction with the central effect of Kant's critical philosophy.  Meillassoux (2008 [2006], pp. 120, 124-125) wrote of the "Kantian catastrophe," a description which, the emotive flair peeled away, renders fair judgment of consequence—from a certain point of view, of course.  A term of Greek tragedy, "catastrophe" referred to the crucial turn or tipping point after which the "before which" could never again exist as it had been.  Few theories have had such impact.  Meillassoux believed that catastrophe brought to a particular conclusion Hume's "destruction of the absolute validity of the principle of sufficient reason."  In that view, then, Kant was only following to its logical conclusion a course already laid down; but he did this in a way that was allegedly deceptive, as if the end of metaphysics (and Meillassoux agreed this was and is final) necessarily implied an end of the absolute.  It is in that deception, he avowed, that one can see the secret of recovery, a solution to the problem that Kant left to us:

---

[5] Cavell (2004, p. 121) put it this way (as, he said, a personal "guess"): "the interrelations of these three worlds [Kant's three critiques] have enlarged libraries around the world over the past two centuries more extensively, and more fruitfully, than any other intellectual project of Western culture."  This is in part, I think, because it has taken a large chunk of that span of years for readers to reach a good understanding of the subtleties of Kant's "architectonic" of critical thinking.

[6] And of course this is to say nothing of ancient texts of Chinese cultures (e.g., texts by Jia Yi, considered in the last chapter), or of Indian cultures or Persian cultures, and so forth.

3

modern science must be encouraged to exercise its inherent powers, not otherwise sufficiently grasped, and complete the mathematization that Descartes began. It is in mathematization that "thought's absolutizing scope" will be restored. As to a major obstacle to his speculative program—the fact that those who are evidently most in need of an absolute are predominantly people who dislike and distrust the mathematical—Meillassoux was silent.[7]

## §1. Kant's Legacy

Kant prefaced the first edition of his *Critique of Pure Reason* by declaring a major conclusion of his efforts of critical theory. It was a conclusion that the world of Enlightenment was then ill-prepared to hear. It reverberated across the next two centuries, and it remains today a conclusion in place—one that many do not want to entertain, much less accept. Human reason has this peculiar fate, Kant explained: called upon to consider questions which it cannot decline (because they are presented by the nature of reason itself), it cannot answer them, for they transcend every faculty of mind.[8] Dogmatisms of various persuasions had been offering false promise and corrosive hope: if one but accepted certain specific beliefs, without question, without doubt, one would harvest the benefits of perfect knowledge of the certainty of a world and its order. The offer came from an already constituted authority, which formed the ground of what was not to be doubted, never questioned; thus the price of having all revealed, or all that anyone subject to that authority would ever need to know. Two strictures that Kant addressed to himself were a rejection of all dogmatisms and an insistence on evidence of experience in the world. The first stricture meant that any claim to know must be self-consistent—that is, it must be able to account for itself in the same terms, from the same assumptions, as that about which it presents accounts (i.e., no special pleading, no claim of "special actor" status). This is a difficult challenge to meet (as demonstrated by theorists who continue the effort; see, e.g., Gabriel 2011; 2015 [2013]). The second stricture meant that any claim to know must lend itself to open empirical testing, directly or indirectly but as directly as possible. The strength of this challenge has also proven to be formidable, as proponents of a recent "speculative realism" have been demonstrating insofar as they confront issues of counterfactual utilities (see, e.g., Harman 2002; 2016; 2018; Gratton 2014; cf. Lewis 1986).

Kant's conclusion about the limits of human knowledge, that human being is capable of asking questions that it is incapable of answering, was not a product of atmospheric mysticism, nor did it descend from any higher authority. Among its antecedents, Newton's theories and experiences of them were central, as Kant said at the beginning. Even more crucial, however, was the startle that, Kant (1997 [1783], p. 10) admitted, had shaken him from his slumbers: the greatly controversial but seemingly incontrovertible conclusion announced by Hume in his *Treatise of Human Nature* (1964 [1739-40], I.iv.6), that the perceiving I cannot catch sight of itself in the act of perceiving.[9]

---

[7] I have no means of assessing Meillassoux' understanding of developments in theoretical physics since Dirac's monumental advance of mathematization during the 1920s. Perhaps he sees the way out of present conundrums (see Putnam 1994 [1979]; and below). I should note also my concurrence with others who have read a more measured work in Meillassoux' (1997) dissertation (about which, more below).

[8] Connection with the question cited above in conjunction with Toffler's *Future Shock* (1970) is apparent.

[9] We now have an excellent biography of Hume (Harris 2015), one that interweaves Hume's written product with life events and circumstances. Pierre Baldi, renowned for his programs in genomics and informatics, reprised Hume's point when he (2001, p. 114) said, "what can be done with intelligence and other faculties" of the human being is, "almost by definition, … in a blind spot that our brains cannot really see." Kant (1998 [1787], B792/A764) avowed, having been roused from slumbers by Hume, that he had thus encountered "perhaps the most ingenious of all skeptics," by which he meant in part that Hume had glimpsed Kant's synthetic judgment, from which point Kant proceeded to improve Hume's skepticism.

4

Hume had brought new life to a very old couple, Reason and Passion. Ancient writers had celebrated the pair as antagonists at the core of human nature, generally with little attention to internal relations. Sometimes their writings had also referred to what in effect could be called a negotiator or a peacemaker or even a directorial agency that could strike the proper agreement between mutual forces of the antagonism. But in general the various accounts were rather superficial, mostly silent about venue and dynamics. Hume located them within an interiority of self that few predecessors had even begun to fathom. René Descartes' "cogito" (as in "cogito ergo sum"), an immaterial substance, lacking any bodily element, was detailed enough to suit the times (early to mid-1600s), especially because in the third of his *Meditations* he had buttressed it with a God who would never play the trickster, and his ideas, rendered in a standard Latin and then, under his gaze, in a plain French, were simply meant to be distinct and clear, as anyone could see (Descartes 1984 [1642], pp. 18, 35).[10] John Locke's most memorable contribution to understanding of self, coming at the end of the seventeenth century, was the simple assertion of a neo-natal condition, *tabula rasa*: the core of self, mind, began empty; and indeed who could remember an infancy that did not begin mentally as a blank?

Hume, much like Descartes and Locke, inspected his own inner-most mental functioning, in particular an introspection of the interior process of perception, the interior space and time of the act of perceiving. What he realized in and from that introspection was startling: while he could perceive all sorts of things and events and ideas, and while he could grasp via memory *having* perceived such and such, he could never perceive his own perceiving I—the I of "I perceive" such and such—*in* the act of perceiving. This interiority of "I perceive," whether one imagined it to be at the surface of mental action or rather deeper in an interiority of self, was opaque.[11] The light of perception never entered, never shone on the moment of the act itself. This opened troubling questions of what might actually be happening in that functionally principled act, even when the I should genuinely and completely believe that only the purest of reasons, only the purest of motives were in charge of the process. What is more, Hume's experiment, like Locke's and Descartes' before him, was openly democratic. Any fair-minded person would encounter the same opaque core of the act of perception.

---

[10] As Matthews (1992, p. 40) pointed out, there was in this a similarity to Augustine's argument (cf. Dihle 1982). For an earlier period, see Sextus Empiricus' *Adversus mathematikos* (IX,190), whose view can be read as teacher to Hume's critique of induction, and more generally to his skepticism, which word, Sextus Empiricus had pointed out in his *Outlines of Pyrrhonism* (I.7), derives from "sképtesthai" ("to investigate": i.e., take nothing on faith but look again). In Kant's conception the "I" (in his German, "Ich") is rendered fundamentally as a purely functionalist principle, a conception that would then be replayed well into the twentieth century, as in the work of George Herbert Mead (see Part Four, below).
[11] Soon thereafter, however, various authors and other artists began furnishing the general interiority— not the opaque core (that flourishing began with Sigmund Freud, or his predecessors), but its surrounds. There is now a very large and diverse literature that considers these furnishings, directly or indirectly. For a small and no doubt partial sampling of recent entries, see Brown (2003), Castiglia (2008), Dahms (2011), Dusinberre (2016), Kearns and Walter (2019), Metzinger (2009), Riley (2000), and Seigel (2005). New chapters are being written. For instance, whereas not long ago the main assumption held that the interiority is centered in the very complex neocortex, the main contender is presently being shifted deeper into the mid-brain. Neurological researchers are arguing that sensory data are organized as a unified egocentric sentience, perhaps consciousness, in this simpler, and evolutionarily older, mid-brain, which is not so dissimilar to the central neural complex of many other animals, including insects.

Whereas Locke's and Descartes' conclusions were meant to inspire confidence in a certain authority of voice (one's own included), Hume's inspired doubt. The more persistently and thoughtfully one contemplated that doubt and its conditions, the more disturbing, the more radical, the more destabilizing it became. A careful reader of history will not be surprised that the prevailing response to Hume's work was denial, refusal, and an effort to change the subject. In short order, Hume, not yet thirty years old, had become a purveyor of rot, and the charge proved to be a sticky one, not only for Hume himself but also and more generally for his main message. Thus, by way of illustration of the point, not until far into the twentieth century did scholarship systematically demonstrate that even first-person experience could not be entirely trusted, because of a variety of biases in perception.[12] There is a hint of irony in the fact that Hume has been described retrospectively as a leading light of British empiricism. It is a just attribution. The hint is due to the fact that a notable part of that brand of philosophy would prefer to be oblivious.

Kant's response, which initiated his critique of critique, his critical theory, was to take Hume's conclusion in a radical skepticism entirely seriously and attempt to answer it.[13] The fact that he began the first volume of his critical theory, his *Critique of Pure Reason*, first published in 1781, with what might be judged a disclaimer was simultaneously an announcement of main conclusions about Newton's evident accomplishments. A prime illustration of Newton's accomplishments consists in the simple, elegant algebra of his laws of motion and, even more impressively, his capture of the law of attraction among moving planets in another algebraic expression: $F_1 = F_2 = G [ (m_1 * m_2) / r^2]$.[14] Kant's disclaimer has already been cited: reason poses questions that it cannot answer but also cannot dismiss. While this had been said in somewhat different vocabulary countless times before (e.g., John Donne's point about "reach" exceeding "grasp"), Kant was probably the first to express the crucial point in terms other than a confession of piety, and he proposed it as a defining mark of the autonomy of critical thinking. This limitation of knowledge was, is, unavoidable in any analytical perspective whatsoever. Illustration was found in Newton's own accomplishment. How could Newton, how could anyone, how could any human mind, fallible as it is, have confidence in the knowledge which Newton declared in that equation (or in any other of his equations)? How can reason achieve

---

[12] A good overview of that scholarship has been contributed by Kahneman (2011), a report that in its earlier days often got less than a friendly reception (see, e.g., Lewis 2016). See also Nisbett's (2015) overview.
[13] Allison (2008, esp. ch. 10) has shown that Kant improved the Humean thesis of skepticism most importantly by correcting Hume's neglect that the aim of the perceptual model is an act of judgment, the application of pure and practical reason to experience (sensory data), an application unavoidable. Thielke (2003) has rightly drawn a line from Hume's "fiction" to Kant's "transcendental Illusion" (about which more below), though I (like Allison) think Thielke overstated it a bit. See also Watkins (1984) for a review of responses to skepticism, especially in relation to modern science, which integrated an "organized skepticism" as a productive perspective of its own.
[14] In words: the mutual attractive force between two bodies is directly proportional to the masses of the respective bodies and inversely proportional to the square of the distance between them. Newton's "universal law" was superseded by Einstein's theory but remains a good approximation to the latter within a large (Newtonian) domain of moving bodies—close enough that Newton's equations were used during the Apollo navigations between Earth and its moon (mainly because Newton's were simpler, easier and faster to solve in practical applications, in a day when the best computing power was much weaker and slower than existed in the first "smart phone").

6

that much? No one had direct experience, measured observations, of any but local events of local objects. From those, how can one have confidence in any parsing of relations from the local to the universal (far distant in space and, so Newton thought, timeless)?[15] And in any case, Hume was correct: empirical evidence alone can never be taken as incontrovertible, because of the problem of induction: the very next observation always could be such as to overturn any universal conclusion based on any large number of prior observations. The saving grace, as it were, is that the reason that informs the natural order also informs the structure of mind. This posit cannot be demonstrated, however. Logical though it may be, the internal relation so posited resides in a realm of hidden causes, the realm of nature as it is in itself. One can infer from effects to those causes, but the causes are not available to direct access. Effects that humans experience are not the causes in themselves; rather, they are effects "for us," as it were, effects in our experiences, our perceptions, our thoughts, and so on, which we can only *infer* are due ultimately to those hidden causes. That is to say (as Kant did), this "nature as it is in itself" is not, and cannot be, what it seemingly announces. Why? Because that is simply beyond the limits of human knowledge.

The fact of the posit was nonetheless troubling, as Kant acknowledged in a late section of his *Critique of Pure Reason* (B354/A297): The "subjective necessity of a connection of our concepts" impels us to assume "an objective necessity in the determination of things in themselves." This step takes us into an illusion, however, which he called the "transcendental Illusion." Why, then, take that step? Reason itself impels us. The argument is not obscure—unless, that is, one is thinking from within the illusion and therefore erasing a crucial distinction in the practice of the object. We will come to that in a moment, but first let's add some useful context.

### §2. From Skepticism to Transcendental Illusion to Existential Insecurity
Kant is far more often accounted a leading member the Enlightenment crew than one of the Romantics who reacted to it, unhappily for the most part. Although he had never read anything by John Keats, the poet, he knew already the sentiment of one of the lines of Keats' most famous poem: "Heard melodies are sweet, but those unheard / Are sweeter; …" (Keats 1820). For Kant the struggle was to express the transcendental in words—that is, in empirical terms; how could it be otherwise? But the task was to express *without sabotage*, and *this* entailed the matter of an authority of voice, his own in particular. Sensitive to that practical crux—the authority of his own writing within a context of deep tradition to which his critical theory was profound disruption—he wrote of Reason as if it possessed of itself will, intent, motive power. His exposition of his own new system had to work around what could be characterized as a gap: his inquiry into cognition was meant to be free of the problem of language, for like Descartes he regarded ideas as only harbored within "merely sensible" words, which can be entirely neglected once cognitions are clearly grasped; yet whatever insights and conclusions he had mustered in the name of his critical theory would remain his alone without the empirics, the full sociality, of language. In what manner, then, does one present in language the limits of Reason? One of the few to have attempted systematic demonstration of Kant's awareness of the gap, a nagging

---

[15] Judging from Newton's text, he was not entirely confident in that thought. In the scholium following his eighth definition Newton acknowledged that absolute time and absolute space are artifices of high abstraction perhaps having no counterpart in physical reality: "It may be, that there is no such thing as an equable motion, whereby time may be accurately measured"; and "it may be there is no body really at rest, to which the places and motions of others may be referred" (see Newton's *Principia* (1729 [1687] Motte trans., vol. 1, pp. 11, 13).

specter of inconsistency, in and *as* the manner of his exposition, Nancy (2008 [1976], esp. §6) settled on the notion of a syncope, an abrupt absence (as in a dropped note in musical composition) that bridges registers as if nothing changed, as the means of Kant's solution of *Darstellung* (i.e., "presentation").[16]

And what *had* changed, by Kant's telling? In a word, the *subject*; therefore necessarily also the object—that is, the *relationality* of the two (as in knowing subject / object to be known)— and indeed the entire world that both opens within and yet contains that copula, "subject and object." Well into his first critique one reads this verdict: "the proud name of an ontology, which presumes to offer synthetic *a priori* cognitions of things in general in a systematic doctrine (e.g., the principle of causality), must give way to the modest one of a mere analytic of the pure understanding." This came close on the heels of a warning: "the deception of substituting the logical possibility of the concept (since it does not contradict itself) for the transcendent possibility of things (where an object corresponds to a concept) can deceive and satisfy only the inexperienced." Thus, "it follows irrefutably that the pure concepts of the understanding can never be transcendental, but always only of empirical use" (Kant 1952 [1787], B303/A246-247).

Was all of that statement *worse* than it read? Could it *be* worse? Perhaps it was not as bad as it read? To late eighteenth and early nineteenth European minds even the last possibility was too much. After initial publication of the first critique in 1781 virtually no reader accepted Kant's new system, so he set about a revised and expanded edition. Ordinarily he could have waited for the older generations to die, in a typical process of succession of educations (up-bringings). But in this instance it would be several generations before understanding overcame simple refusal. As Nancy (2008 [1976], p. 85 n. 21) put it, "philosophy started over after Kant." The empirics of human being could no longer be evaded by imaginations of something higher, some descent of certain authority. Se we are back to Kant's "transcendental Illusion."

Think the skein of the argument as follows.[17]

In the analytic framework of knowing subject and object known (including object to be known; object knowable) subject necessarily brings to bear on sensory data a conceptual scheme through which reason operates. The conception of an object results; this object is legislated by reason ("legislated": Kant's word). Conception as such is a subjective necessity; a knowing subject cannot know without it. Kant's adamantine rejection of dogmatism means that claims of "I just *know*! *Believe* me, *I* know!" are not acceptable because such claims demand acceptance of an authority of voice without being able to demonstrate, rationally, logically, the claimed knowledge (i.e., the acceptance depends on special pleading, fallacies of begging the question).

---

[16] Foucault surely had noticed the "gap" when writing his own dissertation on Kant and relied on it when, soon after, composing his *Les Mots et les Choses* (1966), but this latter work was addressed primarily to a French audience, for which Foucault sought to underplay the significance of Kant in favor of a sequence of French authors (or so I have argued; Hazelrigg 2009). See also Weber's (1986, p. 145) brief notice of the French scene during the middle decades of the nineteenth century.

[17] The next three paragraphs reproduce parts of Hazelrigg (2016), by and large, as well as parts of Hazelrigg (1989a; 1989b; 1992; and 1995). Regarding "postmodernism" see also Antonio's (2000) notice of "reactionary tribalism."

The object known by reasoning via conception is therefore always already a *conditioned* object. This object is conditioned by the knowing subject, the subjective necessity of conception. To say that conception is subjectively necessary also is to say that the knowing subject strives to formulate conceptions that are coherent and consistent and necessary (logically necessary) in their interrelationships (as a conceptual scheme) as well as in their individual constitutions. Reason is legislative of the known object, in that whatever coherence and consistency and necessity this object has, as object, is due to the subjective necessity of conception.

However, humans are wont to think also *another* object, an object that in some sense stands *behind* or *beneath* the legislated object. This object we think as "the object as it is itself, prior to human conception, the object that simply is; the *real* object." This object we think as (but now think *of* as) constitutive of the *real*, the *fundamental* realm of reality. This object and its realm are assumed to be not conceptual—that is, as *un*conditioned (one might say, "without human fingerprints"). This object is not conditioned by human reason, by conception, which means that while humans think it *must* exist—there must be something that is real in itself prior to any human conception of it—humans in fact have no conception of it, no means of knowing it. (It could count as another fantasy world, like the world of Hume's fictions.) Kant called this prior object and its realm of existence "noumenal," in contrast to the "phenomenal" realm which humans do conceive, know conceptually, have in thought and language and experience. But note that the formulation given in the immediately previous paragraph called upon this "prior object" already when stating that knowing subject "necessarily brings to bear on sensory data a conceptual scheme through which reason operates." This "prior object" is, one could say, an object that would not be an object. [18]

We now have the conditions both of a "transcendental illusion" and of its necessity, its status in human cognition as an unavoidable illusion, even a necessary illusion. Humans insist on knowing, indeed knowing with certainty, what their own reasoning tells them they cannot know, a reality that lies beyond the reach of any possible conceptual scheme precisely because this reality is defined in advance as necessarily *un*conditioned. In service to that compulsive need to know, humans cannot avoid taking the subjective necessity of conception as (that is, *as if*) objective necessity.

> [I]n our reason (considered subjectively as a human faculty of cognition) there lie fundamental rules and maxims for its use, which look entirely like objective principles, and through them it comes about that the subjective necessity of a certain connection of our concepts on behalf of the understanding is taken for an objective necessity, the determination of things in themselves. [This illusion] cannot be avoided at all. [The

---

[18] Marx later made much the same distinction when he scolded the materialism of his day for imagining its powers to be empty of conception: it was an example of a doctrine, Marx (1976 [1924], p. 4) said, that divides society into two parts, one of which is then regarded as superior to the whole (see also Bonefeld 2014, p. 54).

illusion] does not cease even though it is uncovered and its nullity is clearly seen into by transcendental criticism (Kant 1998 [1787], B353-54/A297).[19]

The "confusion" is in a sense not even a confusion, because for the phenomenal object—the (at least in principle) genuinely known object, the only object of which we have experience—*is* conditioned by subjective necessity, and in fact by this subjective necessity we generate real understandings which we then treat as objective presences precisely because they *are* real presences to us and have real effects upon us. Kant's transcendental Illusion is transcendental precisely because it goes beyond that. This illusion stakes its anchorage (terminus a quo) to the phenomenal realm and harpoons its would-be anchorage (terminus ad quem) into the noumenal realm. After all, don't we humans want our knowledge to be of something real (but real in the sense of having independent existence logically prior to us)? We have been conditioned during centuries, during eons—perhaps all the way back to those ancestors of hundreds of thousands of years ago who logically must have existed—to expect the comfort, the certitude of an ontotheologic authority.

Authority is now newly at issue. A reader might be quick to challenge: How can anyone have confidence in a claim of knowledge, in the speaker or writer who advances a claim to know, when the linchpin anchoring that claim is ultimately not a received truth but only a *posit*, however logical it may be? Two responses are appropriate. First of all, the question ignores Kant's "concession" at the beginning, that there are unavoidable limits to what reason can answer. The only certainties that can be attained rationally are those which are internal to a particular system of logic, and these systems have no demonstrable connection to natural things in themselves. But secondly, which dogmatism would you prefer?

Kant (1998 [1787], B707/A679) treated as perfectly "natural" (i.e., to be expected) that reason, or a person who reasons well, is led by "the procedure of the transcendental analytic" (the operation of a purely logical procedure) to generalize from "the idea of the possibility of all things" to the idea that this sum-total of all things can be deduced from a single, unitary primal being. Reason's need to have a "conception of a being that may be admitted, without inconsistency, to be worthy of the attribute of absolute necessity" impels the illusion, a transcendental illusion, of "the existence of a cause which is not contingent," a primal cause that "exists necessarily and unconditionally." The authority of the unconditioned remained a powerful magnet and talisman. Who would want to relinquish such a treasure? Certainly not those who had been so fortunately placed as to be able to speak in its name.

---

[19] A manifestation of that duality of objects has been a topic of considerable empirical interest, since the early 1970s, among psychologists, social psychologists, and, more recently still, economists. For a good review of that research literature in psychology and social psychology, see Pronin, Gilovich, and Ross (2004). Their general conception of the phenomenon is of an "epistemic stance," one of a naïve realism, "the defining feature of which is the conviction that one sees and responds to the world objectively, or 'as it is,' and that others therefore will see it and respond to it differently only to the extent that their behavior is a reflection of something other than that reality" (p. 781). One consequence is the tendency for any given person to rate himself or herself as being more objective in judgment than the average person.

In a famous passage of his "Idea for a Universal History with a Cosmopolitan Purpose,"[20] published between the first and second editions of his first critique, Kant engaged in a quasi-Socratic dialogue with himself as the interlocutor who wants to know "who masters the master," having just been told that

> man is *an animal who needs a master*. For he certainly abuses his freedom in relation to others of his own kind. And even although, as a rational creature, he desires a law to impose limits on the freedom of all, he is still misled by his self-seeking animal inclinations into exempting himself from the law where he can. He thus requires a *master* to break his self-will and force him to obey a universally valid will under which everyone can be free.

But, the rhetorical question comes, "where is he to find such a master?" And the answer?

> Nowhere else but in the human species. But this master will also be an animal who needs a master. … the highest authority must be just *in itself* and yet also a *man*. This is therefore the most difficult of all tasks, and a perfect solution is impossible (Kant 1991 [1784a], p. 46).[21]

We have no means of passage to a realm that is beneath or behind or prior to the human. If a realm that is not humanly conditioned does exist, it is closed to human knowledge.

I do understand that it is easy to cross a boundary or a threshold from "that which humans have made" to "that which came before the advent of the human species" or even "the advent of life on Earth." Quentin Meillassoux, whose recent work I mentioned above, has formulated a concept that he (2008 [2006], pp. 9-27) called "ancestrality." This refers to "any reality anterior to the emergence of the human species." Modern scientists have authored many statements that refer to such realities, and many of those statements have been received with carefully weighed

---

[20] This short essay can be read as Kant's participation in but also as his evaluation of the new wave of historiography with "universal intent" (or, somewhat anachronistically, "globalization"). Among the most notable components of that efflorescence the *Encyclopédie, ou dictionnaire raisonné des sciences, des arts et des métiers*, edited by Denis Diderot and Jean le Rond d'Alembert, first published between 1751 and 1772, became the most famous. But at the time another massive undertaking, *An Universal History, from the Earliest Account of Time*, appeared in 65 volumes beginning in 1747. Also in the Anglophone world Edward Gibbon, a name now seldom cited, was at work on his *History of the Decline and Fall of the Roman Empire* (6 volumes), close on the heels of David Hume's *History of England* and Adam Smith's treatise of the *Wealth of Nations*. An ardent reader of Montesquieu from young age, Gibbon fingered barbarity and religious despotism as culprits without and within (cf. Harper 2017). Much had changed during the half-century from Jacques-Bénigne Bossuet's *Discours sur l'histoire universalle* (1681), which reported human history as a continuing struggle between God and Satan, to Giambattista Vico's *Principi di scienza nuovo* (1725), including a profound revision of the concept and practice of historiography among European scholars (although Vico himself was accorded scant appreciation until the nineteenth century). A small yet significant step in that revision, *La istoria universal*, was published already in 1697 by Francesco Bianchini, librarian of the Biblioteca Ottoboniana in the Vatican. For some transitional context see Abbattista (2001) and Ricuperati (1981; 2005).
[21] Kant added a footnote which began thusly: "Man's role is thus a highly artificial one. We do not know how it is with the inhabitants of other planets and with their nature." The speculation was common among scientists.

11

evidence of their "ancestral" existence. Meillassoux asked, What are we to make of such statements? What do the scientists themselves make of such statements? When considering the questions, one can very easily cross the boundary or threshold from "that which humans have made" (the statements, the evidence, the technologies on which the statements and evidence rest, and so forth) to "that which existed millions of years before the advent of Homo sapiens." This recalls what Michael Overington (1979) called "ontological gerrymandering." Border crossing can become well-nigh imperceptible when an epistemological act quietly renders contingency (our evidence, etc.) into necessity (what must have been). The rendering is virtually automatic when one has in hand the palpable evidence (e.g., fossilized bones) of an existent thing that, all available evidence assures us, was present, say, 100 million years ago. The very palpability has already convinced us of "what the thing *is*" and *therefore* of "what it *was*" (see, e.g., Hazelrigg 1993a; 1979).

It is mistaken to see the culprit as a lamed rationalism or a blind empiricism; or as an idealism versus a materialism. The issue is about posits or presuppositions, and the discomforts they can raise. In fact, neither rationalism nor empiricism, neither idealism nor materialism, is presuppositionless. Whereas Kant was explicit about posits (which is not to say that he grasped all of them as precisely as he thought), his predecessors often were not explicit, and most who came soon after him tried mightily either to ignore posits or to imagine that they were already founts of *the* truth, the absolute. Michael Williams (1998; first edition 1977) offered a stellar account of how foundationalism, including the sort that begins with sense data as epistemically primary, is actually a shell game covering for the fact that conviction in the sheer "givenness" of primary perception is itself a groundless belief. Williams' book has been mostly ignored; whereas the actual meaning of "groundless" must be carefully understood, many potential readers think it denotes an exercise in sophism or a present-day version of Aristophanes' Cloud Cuckoo Land. Williams' basic argument is not new, of course—as he acknowledged in the afterword of his second edition the contribution of his great predecessor, Agrippa, a late-first-century CE thinker commonly labeled "Agrippa the Skeptic." Williams (1998, pp. 183-184) paid Agrippa the respect of rehearsing his argument, often called "the regress problem," pointing out that this label actually understates the complexity of the problem which Agrippa set for himself. "According to the Agrippan skeptic, any attempt to justify a claim"—a claim to truth, for instance—"either opens a vicious regress or terminates in one of two unsatisfactory ways: we run out of things to say, thus making an ungrounded assumption; or we find ourselves repeating a claim or claims already entered, thus reasoning in a circle." Thus, a trilemma we face: we want to avoid the regress, but we should want also to avoid both circular reasoning and turning our shovel with some bare assumption, a claim of intrinsic and necessary credibility. Williams appreciated the difficulty well enough, but he was uncomfortable with what seems to be the inevitable Agrippan conclusion: "if there are no foundations for knowledge, justification becomes purely dialectical" (Williams 1998, pp. 184-185). The discomfort turned on his own belief that "dialectical" and "objective" are inconsistent, even contradictory, that dialectical justification is inadequate to a claim of objective knowledge.

It would be entirely mistaken to conclude that, according to Kant, we lack knowledge of objective reality. On the contrary, as I tried to make clear in the foregoing, we do produce real knowledge, and what we produce as real knowledge we then treat as an objective presence; it has the objectivity of being a presence that "we," some community of observers, declare genuinely to be real for us, and not merely my opinion or your opinion but what we know to be the case, to be real, to be true. As such, this presence does have real effects on us. Pippin (1999, p. 53) put the point this way. We do have "knowledge of experienceable, external, spatio-temporal objects." Kant was concerned with the *possibility* of such knowledge: what are the conditions necessary to the very possibility of such knowledge? And the answer is, again quoting Pippin, "we have such [knowledge] only as subject to *our conditions*, conditions valid only for experiencers like us, with spatio-temporal forms of receptivity and discursive intellects." And that of course is the necessary key: how could it ever have been otherwise? Of course it *had* been otherwise, in the fictional world that Hume found all about him, people quite certain in their perceptions because, after all, these were always "*my* perceptions, and who could possibly know better than I what went into them?" Likewise, the certitude of Descartes' clear and distinct ideas (given that his God never played tricks on him).

In shaking off such slumbers, Kant managed to shake very much more as well, and the reception soon became fierce. In many quarters it still is. Meillassoux (2008 [2006]) has not been the only one to see in Kant's critical theory "catastrophe" not merely in the ancient Greek sense but in a present-day sense of "collapse" (or worse). We see and hear people every day who profess beyond reason, supposedly from their worlds of *fiat* knowledge, ready and anxious to enforce it by whatever means necessary, no reasoning required. To quote Pippin one more time:

> Kant defined his project in opposition to rationalist and empirical formulations of the modern philosophical enterprise. This opposition alone suggests the problem now at hand [in wake of Kant]. There is, after all, something philosophically comforting in being able somehow to "tie down" or "anchor," to check or to test our speculations about substance or being or even the good life. Early attempts to do natural philosophy or metaphysics or ethics in an ever more independent way, free from ecclesiastical or traditional or political authority, inspired an understandable concern about such self-regulation in many early modern philosophers (focused, often, on the great skepticism bugbear), prompting the well-known concerns with an ultimate court of appeal in empirical experience, or a reliance on updated, classical doctrines of intuition, certainty, or self-evident axioms and geometric method in the rationalist tradition. But Kant has argued that there are no immediately accessible experiences to serve as a foundation for "thoughts," and that no metaphysical implications follow from conceptual or, as he saw it, purely logical or methodological necessities (Pippin 1999, p. 56).

For anyone whose security and confidence depend vitally on an unquestionable certitude of anchorage in the "rock solid" reality of the thing in itself, the object in its own measure, Kant's transcendental Illusion is the next best thing. In our apprehensions of a phenomenal object, the object of our experience, an empirical object, we succumb to the illusion's "objective necessity," which is that the phenomenal object *must* have its causal conditions in a corresponding noumenal object. Thus, we make experience of phenomenal objectivity do double duty, as it were, once for itself and once for the real object it represents. In that doubling the illusion is transcendental.

It pretends to an immediacy that is impossible, taking the process of inference to be a purely metaphysical act and thus not inference at all but implication or logical deduction.

Reason, Kant (1998 [1787], B576/A548) avowed, "legislates," and in legislating it frames "*for itself* with perfect spontaneity [that is, the spontaneity of mind, roughly correspondent to Hume's insight about perception's limit] *an order of its own* according to ideas, *to which* it adapts the empirical conditions" (my emphases). Collapsing the phenomenal, experience, into the noumenal through sleight of hand seems to offer reassurance of "rock solid" reality. In that comfort it easily appears that Kant sought to replace reason, the rational, with the poetic, as Pippin (1999, pp. 56-57) put it, and of course "the poetic" is mere artifice, cannot offer the reassurances of dogmatic thought.[22]

At this point I want to interrupt the flow, so to speak, and rehearse a Kantian conception that will be a major point of reference throughout the remainder of this Part One (and will be topical of a more discursive treatment in Part Two). Indeed, the preceding presentation has been silently trading on it: Kant's conception of "the unity of apperception" (wherein the "ap" prefix means "as the perception—the act and its product—comes to me and is integrated into my extant attention"). I want to make clear my understanding of what was (and is) at issue.

First of all, we have an explicit posit, one that Kant regarded as simply inescapable if we, any one of us, are to proceed seriously with our cognitions, with the experience of "the cogito" ("I think"). The posit cannot be proven, for reasons that should become clear in the following discussion (if they are not already). One has a choice: either accept someone's dogmatic claim of "what is" and why one should accept the claim or try to exercise one's reason in grasping the logical possibilities of reasoned thought, human thought, one's own thought. Kant believed that he had done so, after having been awakened from slumbers by Hume's text. (Remember, if we take the date of the first edition of his *Critique of Pure Reason* as reference, Kant was then near the end of his sixth decade and for all practical purposes starting over, after having enjoyed university life as a successful philosopher and teacher.) He sought to share the conclusions of his intense inquiry. The key to those conclusions was itself a conclusion, which, he realized, was simply unavoidable but beyond proof: he himself had experienced so often, to the point of taking for granted the experience as *a kind* (i.e., experience *as such*), his ability to connect in one consciousness (his own) such a great variety of representations, that he then realized that it had been that fact that enabled him to represent *to himself* the identity of consciousness, of *his self*-consciousness, throughout all of those representations.[23] It is here that

---

[22] As I have argued before (e.g., Hazelrigg 1989a, 1989b), that sense of replacement is understandable—although it was not Kant's conclusion, and it is not exactly a replacement of reason or empirics so much as it is a revision of both in intersection (and, to be more careful of expression, by *poiesis*, which is more general than, parent to, poetics).

[23] One might think of this declaration as the first fact of human life and, as such, being on a par with Descartes' famed "cogito ergo sum." But no. The Cartesian declaration was *not* for Descartes the first fact of life. Because he needed to be assured that his reasonings were not simply hallucinations, he turned to what then became a prior fact of human life, finding assurance in his belief that his God would not play the trickster. Whether Descartes actually believed his own statement or was merely "throwing a bone" to state and church cannot be decided except by fiat.

one sees the sign of Kant's reputed "revolution," displacing ontology by epistemology, "the object as it is in itself" by "the object as known to the human subject." Note that this shorthand (and thus inaccurate) summary of what had been accomplished is told from the standpoint of the old ontology, not from the standpoint of that accomplishment. Note also (and this caution is often overlooked because of a bias toward "the physical object") that the great variety of representations which Kant concluded he had been uniting in one consciousness, and which was the basis of his own reflexivity of self, included other human beings, their thoughts and actions— or, to use a word that I will be emphasizing throughout, "sociality," which is inherent in one of Kant's favored verbs, "to legislate." The composition of Kant's posit is logically consistent and coherent; it is beyond proof, but it cannot be avoided, on pain of relinquishing reason.

Human beings experience sensations, from which intuitions derive in accordance with the two *forms* of intuition, space and time. Cognition, too, "starts from the senses"; but it then "proceeds to the understanding," the "pure concepts" of which are always only of empirical use (i.e., cannot themselves be transcendental to human experience but are always contingent on a "here and now," the conditions of one's being, of one's knowing). And from the understanding, in all its plenitude, cognition "ends with reason, beyond which there is nothing higher to be found in us to work on the matter of intuition and bring it under the highest unity of thinking" (Kant 1998 [1787] B355/A298). This "highest unity of thinking," described by Kant (1998 [1787] B672/A644) in terms of a "transcendental unity of apperception," is not constituted by transcendental ideas (such ideas, Kant said, "are never of constitutive use"). The empirical remains paramount. However, the transcendental ideas do have "an excellent and indispensably necessary use, namely that of directing the understanding to a certain goal," with respect to which all of the rules of the understanding converge, as at an imaginary point ("imaginary" because the point of convergence is "only an idea"). That is, "the concepts of the understanding do not really proceed" from that imaginary point (since that point "lies outside the bounds of possible experience"). Nevertheless, by and in "directing the understanding to [the] certain goal" toward which all of the rules of the understanding converge, the idea of that convergence to a point "serves to obtain for these concepts the greatest unity alongside the greatest extension." Again, the pure concepts of the understanding can never be transcendental; only empirical. But the very posit of a convergence on *a* goal, the goal of understanding, serves to produce a unity *toward* that goal. This is, as it were, a pure functionality, the locus of which is at the core of "I think." The functionality of that imagined convergence is directive; it is projective; it is legislative (as in "make it happen").[24]

The first sentence of Kant's section "On the Original-Synthetic Unity of Apperception" reads (all quoted emphases are Kant's; 1998 [1787] B132): "*I think* must *be able* to accompany all my representations; for otherwise something would be represented in me that could not be

---

[24] I will return to this passage later. Kant was utilizing the function of what we now call "the vanishing point": a posit, a positioning. As I cautioned earlier, because we tend to privilege "the physicality" of "object" as if it somehow speaks directly (i.e., without thought, without language, etc.) "to *me*," it is easy to overlook the fact that Kant was referring to human action, human deeds, human thinking—while keeping that reference within the limits of human knowledge (i.e., without trading on any claim to something higher than human reason).

thought at all, which is as much as to say that the representation would either be impossible or else at least would be nothing for me." Throughout this section Kant continued to establish some limits of meaning within the analytical logic of a fundamental posit understood in first-person terms, and at the very start a connection was drawn between representation and the "cogito": while the prefatory "I think" need not always be said explicitly, it must always be present as the assertion of *my* cognition. But what of "intuition"? As we saw above, while intuition occurs "prior to all thinking," it must be in relation to cognition. Indeed, it has "a necessary relation to the *I think*." This representation does not itself belong to sensibility. Rather, Kant called it "an act of spontaneity." It happens (when it happens) without announcement, without being called upon, without a shepherd yet also not alone. Kant gave it a sequence of names, each establishing a relation: "I call it the *pure apperception*, in order to distinguish it from the *empirical* one." An empirical apperception may and perhaps always does include sensation ("a feeling"), although sensation as such occurs prior to cognition. Kant next called this act of spontaneity "also the *original apperception*, since it is that self-consciousness which, because it produces the representation *I think*, which must be able to accompany all [other representations] and which in all consciousness is one and the same, cannot be accompanied by any further representation." And then he wrote of the act, "I also call its unity the *transcendental* unity of self-consciousness in order to designate the possibility of a priori cognition from it."

Thus, I have within my first-person experience of perception that which comes to me spontaneously as *pure* perception, whatever its empirical content might be, and as *original* perception because it is also (whatever else is brought to me) the consciousness "I think" such and such; *and*, thirdly, it is possibly a perception that—in the unity of that consciousness of "I think" such and such of *this* perception—I have never previously experienced. In other words, the unity of my consciousness of the cogito, the unity of "*I* think" such and such which is necessarily also a consciousness of the unity of *my* consciousness, is a transcendental unity. The self-identity of the "I" of "I think" does not derive from the *dispersed* experiences of my perceptions. Rather, if it is present, it is always already present as that "act of spontaneity" (Kant 1998 [1787] B132). There is spontaneously in the legislative act an anticipation of that which is to *be* legislated even if, and most hopefully because it has never before been experienced.

Kant then proceeded to elaborate on what he had already said (again, all emphases are his): "it is only because

> I can combine a manifold of given representations *in one consciousness* that it is possible for me to represent *the identity of the consciousness in these representations* itself, i.e., the *analytical* unity of apperception is only possible under the presupposition of some *synthetic* one. The thought that these representations given in intuition all together belong *to me* means, accordingly, the same as that I unite them in a self-consciousness, or at least can unite them therein, and although it is itself not yet the consciousness of the *synthesis* of the representations, it still presupposes the possibility of the latter, i.e., only because I can comprehend their manifold in a consciousness do I call them all together *my* representations; for otherwise I would have as multicolored, diverse a self as I have representations of which I am conscious (Kant 1998 [1787] B133-134).

16

This passage is also—indeed, *must* also be—a statement *about* Kant's posit, the consistency and coherence of its composition. The "about" consists in that relation of analytic/synthetic (which, in turn, we are prone to think as an analytic relation, when in fact it can be only dialectical, each not just in a "dependence" on the other but as a mirror of the other in the reflexivity of the "I think"). In particular, Kant was reminding us of one side of that relation —namely, that analyticity by necessity presupposes the synthetic, the integrity of *an* experience and thus of experience as such. This applies when we think analysis as a "taking apart" (dependence on the integrity of a whole that can be disassembled into its parts), and it applies when we think analysis as an "analytic statement" or a claim that is "true by definition" (dependence of the integrity of wholes which we experience as relatedness to one another as operative elements of what we mean by "definition"; thus, definition as destination rather than as point of departure). That he did not bother to remind us of the other side of the dialectic probably followed from awareness that he had already made its case (i.e., the categories are analytic distinctions on which experiences, the synthetic, depend), whereas the tendency to think a priority of the analytic was, then as now, too one-sided an apprehension.

It is easy to see in that composition of posit a circularity, which stems from the fact that the posit begins and ends with human being. There is no extra-human authority; no guarantee; no certainty; and from all of that it is easy for a person to feel "too much responsibility" (in the almost caricaturizing emblem, the feeling "Where is father? Father knows best!"). It is the tale/tail of the ouroboros. The most interesting feature of that mythical creature is the naming that the ancient Greeks bestowed on their borrowing from ancient Egyptians. For the word, "ouroboros" comes from the verb, "bibrōskō" ("I eat"), which via the Latin became "I imbibe," which in turn points back to a double meaning in the Greek, since "bibrōskō" can be rendered "literally" as "I book"—or, in other words, "to imbibe" is also "to learn," "to take in," and so forth. Nevertheless, the issue of authority, and at its center the authority of voice, looms so large that the foregoing example of a wordplay (serious thought it was) is easily seen as being gratuitous, insulting, puerile.

Thus, back to the previously interrupted flow.

Authority of voice (the credibility of a speaker) depends on the power of reason and on an audience's preparation (in the sense of education, experience with reasoning, freedom from dogmatism). The power of reason is itself also contextual and conditioned, historically and culturally, both with respect to the speaker (qualifications) and in audience preparation. Anyone who could succeed in legitimacy of claim to speak the word of God possessed an extraordinarily powerful authority of voice (one that had to be managed with care). Likewise, anyone who could succeed in legitimacy of claim to speak for a monarch had gained an authority of voice in proportion to the earthly power of the monarch, and monarchs who had succeeded in legitimacy of claim to rule by divine right exercised that earthly power with extraordinary authority. An ability to speak for the monarch also had to be managed with care. Whereas succeeding in claim to speak the word of God was greatly aided by an inherent ambiguity (after all, who otherwise could say whether God was pleased or offended?), monarchs were prone to jealousy of anyone who did speak in the monarch's name. Practices that encouraged attitudes of dogmatism (e.g., that "reason" was whatever God and/or a monarch said it was) reduced members of a realm to

17

little opportunity, and even less incentive, to practice skills of reasoning. The dominant lesson for most people was to avoid any claim to authority of voice—at least any that extended beyond one's own body, perhaps one's own household family, and sometimes not even that. Such circumstances had been changing well before Kant's day (think, e.g., of the Puritan movement's individuation of practical reason vis-à-vis divinity). But as Kant's remarks about continued tutelage or subservience testify, he was aware that for most people the power of reason always depended on someone else. For most people authority of voice came from above, not from one's own reasoning and experience. Thus, the "second object" described by Pippin virtually always carried dominant weight. It often still does. Still today most people prefer to be told "the truth," at best reserving only the right to sort among alternative claims to "the truth"; and given their limited practice of reasoning, they usually prefer simple to complex statements. The very fact such questions now must be answered, that they no longer come with their answers already given as announcements, becomes for many people an existential crisis, a crisis of security.

Having been reared as a child of German pietism, Kant probably appreciated an irony within the central principle of his critical theory. Consider this bit of history: an ancient Hebrew writer known to us by the pseudonym, Qoheleth (sometimes accorded the title "the first Jewish philosopher"), is generally credited as the author of the twentieth of the twenty-four books of the Hebrew bible (or Tanakh). This book, located in that part of the Tanakh known as the Ketuvim ("Writings"), is a "gathering" of the wisdom of Solomon, which Qoheleth ("Gatherer") presented as if speaking Solomon's own words. When, centuries later, Qoheleth's book was translated as part of the Christian bible into Greek, "Qoheleth" became "Ecclesiastes" (from "ekklēsiā," the public gathering or assembly of citizens). Now, here is the point: according to Ecclesiastes 11.5, "you cannot understand the activity of God." Or, to revert to the ancient Hebraic, Yhwh (Yahweh or the one God) is, as it were, "noumenal," inaccessible to human being. The rest of the wisdom of Solomon, according to Qoheleth's reportage, reduces to this: since "you cannot do anything about that limit to human knowledge, accept it phenomenologically and live with it." The central principle of Kant's critical theory reconvenes this wisdom in a secularized temple of enlightenment, "secularized" in order to ground an old lesson within a space of experience, human experience (empiricism), free of prior dogmatisms, available to exercises of legislation by human reason. That was, in any case, the ideal intent. As a gamble, this intent might have been a reach too far, well beyond John Donne's horizon (see, e.g., Dreyfus and Kelly 2011; Eagleton 2014). Atavistic forces of tribalism are loath to give up their own privileged warrants of certain truth.[25]

Kant's point about inevitable conditionality refers us to the issue of an infinite regress: each master needs a master, *ad seriatim ad infinitum*. Without the convenience of an exit hole provided by some principle of the unconditioned, we are supposedly stuck in an infinite regress. Of course, any knowing subject can stop the regress at any moment by declaring, "Here I turn my shovel," and that is what typically transpires. The question of community remains, however: will anyone, or enough of an audience, agree? While the full-stop can be uttered as an individual

---

[25] On the other side of the coin, however, Chateaubriand (2018 [1849-50], p. 184), remembering his experiences as a young observer of the French Revolution, hailed the legislative actions of "parliaments, most notably the parliament of Paris," as the new, revolutionary "instruments of a philosophical system."

solipsism, an attentive declarer typically has a community in mind, a "we-ness" formed as a more or less distinctive culture—sometimes more specifically as a solipsism of religious or ethnic or gender or similar other grouping of shared consciousness—one that features a ready-made receptivity such that a reflexivity of the cultural solipsism is masked or diverted, however abstemious the effect may be.

Anthropologically, having become accustomed to absolutist claims of authority presented not just as a realism but as *the real* (typically via religious and political habits of consciousness), critical thinkers, even those of secular and/or decentered perspective, have sought a general principle, typically a universal principle, by which the regress will cease, the skepticism be stilled, as if no knowing subject, no particular grouping of knowing subjects, has in any way exercised an agency beyond responsible receptivity to the real, to what is. No purely empirical principle could suffice, for it would be grounded in the experiences of a historically-culturally specific people and would always carry the mark of that origin (which would become plain, if not already plain, given enough time for experiences to change and/or to have encountered different experiences by others). Any purely empirical principle, having been derived inductively, would ever and always be uncertain, vulnerable to the test of the next new instance of experience, as Hume had said. Thus, there was broad consensus that the sought principle must transcend human experience at least enough to escape those vulnerabilities. A typical manoeuver toward that end, and beyond, can be illustrated as follows. Each human, both as knowing subject and as known object, both as actor and as acted-upon, is a particular being, a specific empirical, which is to say experiencing and experienced, being. But notice that, through all the enormous collection of particularity, now numbering billions of human beings, there is *one* condition, *one* presence, *one* quality, in which they all share—whatever their nativity, age, gender, beliefs, material possessions, and so forth—namely, the quality of beingness, a quality that transcends all of their particularities, all of their experiences of being human: *Being*. This metaphysical claim seemed to be a perfectly ordinary act of logic: abstraction of the particular in order to find the common, the general, even the universal. The temptation was, however, then to invert the order of that process and imagine that what is left after abstraction is foundational, progenitive, from the universal to the particular, ignoring the fact that abstraction had left a remainder perfectly ahistorical, acultural, not recognizably human at all. If in fact foundational, from what source of accretion to that abstract remainder did all subsequent reality derive? The answer of course was that the source was concretely real historical sociocultural processes—even though these did not exist, by stipulation could not have existed, as of the progenitive foundation. The contradiction could be removed by magic: invoke a godhead, for example, or, if secular terms are preferred, Mother Nature.

Newtonian mechanics, in its basic principles, had seemed to qualify as transcendental (although as we now generally agree, those principles are relative to *our* experiences of world, which at the time of Kant—as well as earlier, of Newton—did not include such entities as quantum particles, processes of quantum events, and the like). Newton's models were, and do remain, impressive. They were indeed models, mathematical models. But the distance between the abstractedness of the models and the experienced reality of the everyday world was usually such that casual observers did not notice the abstraction and assumed that the models were in fact descriptions of reality, descriptions of how various physical processes actually work in measured experiences. When errors of predicted outcomes did become noticed, a frequent response was to indict adequacy of theory. Kant (1991 [1793], p. 62) highlighted a classic illustration of this gap in reasoning, early in his oft-cited essay "On the common saying: 'this may be true in theory, but it does not apply in practice.'" One of his illustrative examples involves ballistics, the trajectory of a missile (a rock, a bullet, a rocket) that, once launched, travels without guidance correction: "all of us would merely ridicule ... the artilleryman who criticized the mathematical theory of ballistics [a Newtonian theory] by declaring that, while the theory is ingeniously conceived, it is not valid in practice, since experience in applying it gives results quite different from those predicted theoretically."[26]

Impressive as they proved to be in their own realm, the Newtonian models also set in stark relief the fact that relations and events of human affairs fall outside the bounds of necessity, which determine the relations of theoretical knowledge in the world of nature. Phenomena of human affairs are instead discernable, describable, knowable, only as empirical generalizations. Human *being* exists as a congenital dividedness: as a physicality, a living organic physicality, human being is a presence within the natural world of Newtonian mechanics; but as a self-conscious, self-legislating being, a being that apprehends itself reflexively as an object to be acted upon, human being is a presence apart from that world of necessity, a being of the realm of freedom, and indeed the being that invented the Newtonian mechanics of nature's world—which is to say, invented a another new "nature's world" (i.e., inferential chain to a noumenal realm of "things in themselves"). The same must be said today, long after succession to Newtonian mechanics by quantum mechanics. Following previous work by Erwin Schrödinger, Paul Dirac premiered his famous report of 1929 by declaring that "the underlying physical laws necessary for the mathematical theory of a large part of physics and the whole of chemistry are thus completely known," as represented by his set of fundamental quantum equations (Dirac 1929, p. 714). His set made an astonishing display of perspicacity and elegant concision. Think of it this way: most school boys and school girls of the twentieth century (i.e., even after 1929), having had at least a passing introduction of Mendeleev's period chart of the chemical elements, also had at least the passing thought, "Why does it look like *that*?" It was very difficult, no doubt, for even the best of grammar school and high school (for that matter, college teachers as well) to answer the question, because grasping the full text that Dirac had enfolded in his equations challenged nearly everyone. But in fact, Dirac's assertion at the beginning of his paper was correct: he did give a complete account of chemistry, one equation per element. To say that the system within which his quantum mechanics—plus the subsequent developments—exist as a coherence of determinate relations predisposes any subsequent set of experimental expectations is not to cast aspersions against his work or that system. It is merely to point out that the full play of doubt remains vast.[27]

---

[26] Imagine an intended target as a point on the ground, the missile being a thrown rock or a fired rocket. Draw a circle of some radius around that point. Depending on that radius and the accuracy of the ballistic trajectory, some proportion of missiles will land within that circle, more or less close to the target. (An illustration, narrative and graphic, is given in Hazelrigg 2004, pp. 77-78.) The actual landings form a Rayleigh distribution around the target, simply because so many relevant variables cannot be measured with sufficient accuracy (e.g., variations in force vectors of barometric pressure, wind currents, gravitational attraction, and so on, all of which can vary throughout duration of the flight). All of the relevant forces can be stipulated by Newtonian theory, but predictive efficacy will depend on mensural accuracy of those forces all through the flight.

[27] I should also point out that, in a way that is roughly analogous to my prior illustration of the limits of application of Newton's equations of moving bodies (due to the large number of force vectors at work in any actual empirical setting), Dirac's fundamental equation and those derived from it are too complicated to be solved in applications except for small particles. Therefore, chemistry as it had been in 1929—and

## §3. Grappling with the Legacy

Dissatisfaction with Kant's demonstration of limits fueled a continual search for a way through the predicament, the inability of any knowing subject to attain knowledge of any aspect of human affairs that could claim the banner of objectivity in the sense of it being a claim transcending its ground in subjectivity, its inescapable relativity to the subjectivity of the claimant. And if not *through* the predicament, then *around* it. Philosophers other than Kant had been addressing what were seen increasingly as aporia and limitations of his critical system—Hegel, Schopenhauer, Nietzsche, for instance—but while their works had impact among philosophers, the main philosophical framework within which the new social sciences were developing was primarily and largely Kantian, or, increasingly, a modified version that came to be known as neo-Kantian.

The course of academic philosophy during the nineteenth century consisted mainly in efforts to reconsider the claim of reason in wake of Kant's critique and its failure to achieve its intended end. Efforts to make good on that claim by installing a first principle that logically preceded the challenges of consciousness were begun years before Kant's death (1804), but they succumbed one after another, at best lapsing into a fideist version of dogmatism while trying without success to forestall the bracing vision of skepticism. The more incisive the effort, the greater the recognition that Kant's critical theory had not simply confirmed the limits which Hume's skepticism had shown by reason; Kant's attempt to answer Hume and save the claim of reason had actually deepened and broadened the limits of reason and the bounds of possible knowledge. Few were willing to accept that verdict, and searching began for what Beiser (1987, p. 326) fittingly called "a higher intuitive form of knowledge"—a phrase alluding to Kant's declaration that all human "cognition starts from the senses, proceeds to the understanding, and ends with reason, beyond which there is nothing higher to be found in us to work on the matter of intuition and bring it under the highest unity of thinking" (Kant 1998 [1787], B355/A298). Searches for a foundational metaphysics that would reveal something higher were the order of the day.

By the end of the century all such searches had failed, typically because they could not withstand the critique leveled against them by the very theory (Kant's) whose limits they had sought to overcome, set aside, unravel, or, when all else failed, simply ignore. The social sciences were mostly oblivious to all of the philosophical excursions against those limits—and often oblivious to the limits themselves—as the several increasingly distinct disciplines began their own theoretical and practical endeavors of acquiring knowledge. Some of those endeavors were largely in keeping with Kant's boundaries, however, the limits of knowledge as sets of empirical generalizations of human states of affairs (Kant 1798). Building an authority of voice on independent theoretical grounds of reason could be subordinated for some time, while building an authority of voice based in utilities of practical assistance to state and society. That is, developing an agency of "public policy"—itself a relatively new postulation in revisions of instruments of governance toward more participation by a restricted citizenry—would take

---

as it is today—remains highly useful (just as are Newton's equations, which in fact got human beings to earth's moon).

21

precedence, as the several disciplines of social science planned to become "useful to the elites" (Gibbs 1979).

Before turning more specifically to the social sciences' responses to the transcendental Illusion (to the extent that there have been any), it will be useful to note a few highlights of the nineteenth-century course taken in philosophy with regard to Kantian critical theory. Four of the focal turns within philosophy will be treated here (for many more details, see Beiser 1987, 2014a, 2014b): materialist responses to Kantian idealism, Hegel's objectivist-idealist system, a mid-century bout of so-called pessimist solutions (e.g., Schopenhauer), and a sequence of efforts commonly collected under the head of "neo-Kantianism." This last is particularly of interest here, because it issued in positions that were widely adopted in disciplines of social science during the late nineteenth and early twentieth centuries.

Materialist opposition to Kant gained some prominence during the first half of the century and then again, in somewhat altered version, late in the century. The earlier efforts, which are sometimes styled as "classical materialism," generally preferred to solve the challenge of consciousness by ignoring it. In other words, they assumed that sense perception gives faithful recordings of the real—if one properly engages in acts of sensory perception (i.e., solving the challenge by a stipulated methodical practice, without treating the latter as in principle fallible and as addressable by any practice other than that same method). To the extent that disciplines sought to justify their practice, they invoked "scientific method," the method of the sciences of nature (a well-nigh magical invocation for many audiences). This materialism was an easy target because of what it could not account for in its own terms, as Marx (1976 [1888]) demonstrated by his short yet decisive critique of Ludwig Feuerbach, a "left Hegelian" who was also a leading exponent of one version of materialism. Later in the century materialist positions were adopted by a philosophical psychologism that developed around the claim of psychophysical parallelism and by proponents of a positivist methodology that rejected any argument of unobservables as uselessly metaphysical and anti-science.[28] Perhaps the single most important exemplar of these movements was Hermann L F von Helmholtz (1847), whose theory of neural process as an unconscious inferential process that converts stimuli generated by external objects into mental representations was a sensation of popular accounts of modern science.[29] His theory, which today is sometimes regarded as forerunner of neuroscience, is also an exemplar of what has been called "explanation by the black box": the unconscious inferential process remains opaque, rather as

---

[28] By this time, one should have thought, the point of Kant's (1998 [1787], B401/A343) notice that "*I think* is … the sole text of rational psychology" would have been grasped clearly enough that no one would have bothered to ask "Why?": "the supposed Cartesian inference *cogito ergo sum* is in fact tautological"—that is, not an inference at all, much less a conclusion—"since the *cogito (sum cogitans)* [i.e., "I think (I am thinking)"] immediately asserts the reality" (A355). Note Kant's use of parergonal perspective in that (a topic considered in Part Two, below).

[29] His long, productive career began in mechanics with his theory of the conservation of force (1853 [1847]), then moved to physiology, optics, psychology, and other areas. One of his students, Wilhelm Wundt, also followed the thesis of parallelism and, in publishing studies of sense perception, became a major influence in early work in behavioral science in the USA and elsewhere.

Hume had said. Major proponents of the positivist strand at that time included Richard Avenarius and Ernst Mach.

Hegel's response to the "dilemma" left by Kant is the preeminent instance of the common interest in subordinating epistemology and ethics to metaphysics in search of a foundational platform organized on a (supposedly) self-evident first principle. As Jürgen Habermas (1992 [1988], p. 128) phrased it, "Hegel renew[ed] the unitary thinking of metaphysics for the last time"—or so he attempted. What actually became evident, after the dust of excitement in trying to grasp the whole of Hegel's system had settled, was that he had not so much "solved the dilemma" as produced another question-begging dogmatism such as Kant's critical theory had already exposed. By mid-century Hegel's star had descended, never to regain its zenith, although at times subject to a resurgence of interest (e.g. in his *Phenomenology of Spirit*). Recently, several scholars have resurrected Hegel's own late-in-career re-appreciation of Kant's critical theory, finding in Hegel evidence of his acceptance of, even efforts to improve, Kant's critique (e.g., Brandom 2002; 2007; 2008; Pippin 2008, 2010).[30]

The next event to captivate the imagination of readers of philosophy seeking a solution to the "pessimistic" conclusion of Kant's critical theory was a heightened awareness of the work of Arthur Schopenhauer, who, although author of *The World as Will and Representation*, published in 1819, was by mid-century already dead (see Cartwright 2010, pp. 524-548). The fact that a philosopher noted for his "personal pessimism" could become a considered source of the wanted solution might seem a strange curiosity, perhaps indicative of a paucity of alternatives more than anything else. But two other factors merit consideration. First, since the dilemma had come to roost from reasonings laden with sentiments of optimism from the Enlightenment tradition about the future of humankind, perhaps a metaphysics of pessimism would hold a key to solution, a useful tonic at least. Second, had Schopenhauer merely proposed a pessimism of the subject, he would have stood accused easily of having presumed what Hume had shown to be unavailable—namely, a platform of constancy of knowing subject by which comparisons in time could be achieved of oneself, or of any other, independently of history. Indeed, one of the most urgent emblems of the dilemma itself was a solipsism of the knowing subject as an individual consciousness within the moment, reaching for evidence beyond presumption of continuity from moment to moment.[31] But Schopenhauer located the condition of pessimism as integral to world spirit, an objective spirit. In formulating the metaphysical principle, however,

---

[30] I do not mean to suggest that Hegel is now irrelevant or redundant; far from it. In addition to the citations above, see, e.g., Rose (1981), Pippin (2011), and Buchwalter (2012). While I am not confident that he has captured Hegel's consistency (or inconsistency) of intent between his *Phenomenology of Geist* and his later works, Terry Pinkard's reading of Hegel's *Phenomenology* as a "sociality of reason" is a genuine feast of healthy, imaginatively productive reading (Pinkard 1996; see also his 2000 biography).

[31] Or, as Bertrand Russell (1921, pp. 159-160) posed the matter (on top of a popular nineteenth-century book about the *Genesis* story, "There is no logical impossibility in the hypothesis that the world sprang into being five minutes ago, exactly as it then was, with a population that 'remembered' a wholly unreal past. There is no logically necessary connection between events at different times; therefore, nothing that is happening now or will happen in the future can disprove the hypothesis that the world began five minutes ago."

he remained vulnerable (just as had Hegel in guise of the supreme phenomenological observer) to the charge of question-begging dogmatism. Or, ask of him as knowing subject, "And how do you know *that*?" To be sure, Schopenhauer was not alone in his diagnosis of a world in pain, spiritual pain. After all, a sense of loss in wake of Kant dominated much of the discourse. Schopenhauer was not the only person who, as Safranski (1991 [1987], p. 345) has said of him, sought to express as more than a personal tribulation "the pain of secularization, of metaphysical homelessness, of lost original confidence," although he might well have been the only one who assembled the components of that sense of loss as due to "the great affronts to human megalomania." Was it megalomania? To take on the powers that human beings had given to their finest creations, the all-powerful, all-knowing, ever-present gods, could hardly have been better designed as a recipe of disappointment, leaving the creators to ask the question that Safranski found to be central to Schopenhauer: "How can one live when there are no prescribed horizons to meaning and no guarantee of meaning?"

Even before the initial deflation of Hegel's "objective idealist" system, another sequence of works had begun with the aim of modifying Kant's critical theory in ways that would obviate the worst conclusions. This sequence became known in retrospect as "neo-Kantianism," a bin to which various proposals have been assigned. One of the earliest instances was the work of Salomon ben Josua Maimon, who died four years before Kant, and whom Kant himself, having read some of Maimon's work, regarded as perhaps his best critic (though he found the criticism to be wrong).[32] Among the last (although the label continues to be used today, as, for example, in application to Habermas were the positivist-empiricists whose solutions commenced with methodical observations from which, given sufficient agreement of qualified observers, would result in "law-like" statements (ignoring that the absence of ahistorical, acultural metrics of approximation would leave "degrees of likeness"—as with "degrees of verisimilitude"—without consistent gauge, not only internally but also relative to the presumed gold standard, Newtonian law). In fact, it is difficult to draw a "finish line" after "neo-Kantian" precisely because Kantian critical theory has long been endemic to European and Euro-American cultures and societies. One small illustration will suffice. Habermas has been known for a theory of "communicative action" that features as utopist principle a counterfactual condition, the "ideal speech situation," which came with this rider: "if only we could achieve that, all else would fall into place." One could say that Habermas' theory is not sufficiently efficacious in specificity to generate action models that would predictably enable us to get from here to there—that is, into the condition of an ideal speech situation with good regularity. To be sure, that is a lot to ask of anyone's theory. My aim here is rather to point out that Habermas' version of a utopist principle can be read as another version of Kant's, which was expressed in various ways—among them, the categorical imperative and the principle of hope.

Soon after Kant's lectures in anthropology were published (1798) developments toward some conception of a science of society began to gather audiences. From the works of the baron de Montesquieu (e.g., 1750 [1748]) and other principals of the French Enlightenment, to those of David Hume, John Millar (1771), and other principals of the Scottish Enlightenment, thence

---

[32] See, e.g., Beiser (1987), Makkreel and Luft (2010), among other sources, for details of Maimon and later figures.

24

the work of Auguste Comte (1853 [1844]), for example, percolations of "natural history" and similar studies of variations of human culture gradually coalesced into several disciplines that are today named the social sciences. During that early period, much of the development informed and pursued as a pragmatic undertaking (see, e.g., Rasmussen 2013).[33] Indeed, Kant's own highly popular lectures in anthropology were presented "from a pragmatic point of view" (though for a rigorously principled reason). Thus, insofar as an impact of Kant's critical philosophy was felt beyond the philosopher's and the theologian's respective domiciles, it was mostly in terms of the new sciences of nature—physics, geology, chemistry, biology—and chiefly from the three volumes of critique, especially the first volume. Understanding his argument was slow to come, partly because of its complexity and partly because some passages seemed obscure or muddled but also because of the influence of early critics and interpreters (e.g., F H Jacobi, J G Fichte, J G Herder; see Beiser 1987).[34] However, by the late decades of the nineteenth century, just as the movement toward a science of society in its various departments—economy, polity, and so forth—had quickened, a more detailed understanding of the trenchancy of Kant's argument about limits of human knowledge had also developed.

As understanding developed during the nineteenth century, it seemed that Kant had produced a self-consistent system for the modern sciences of nature. What was left out? All inquiry into human affairs (what would soon be called "the human sciences" or "the social sciences"). As Kant himself put it, this latter sort of inquiry can be only empirical, for it lacks the rational part on which a true science depends in order to discern universal principles (such as Newton's laws, for example, which were held to apply everywhere at all times). Henceforth, of course, the social sciences, as they came on line one by one, would labor under this stigma of being only "pretend sciences,"[35] the makings of an inferiority complex that stoked bad feelings, sometimes bad faith, and behaviors that psychologists would term "acting out" (rejecting rejectors, etc.). Ironically, by the middle of the twentieth century the physical-science part of "natural science" was changing in ways that made the Kantian fit considerably less impressive, as statements such as "only changes in energy are observable" became quite ordinary (an electrician could have told you about "change in the field"), giving way to slightly different statements such as "a photon is simply a disturbance in an electromagnetic field," which in turn was shifted to the ordinary, replaced by new chapters of exotica such as quantum entanglement and new debates such as whether the relation of vacuum to void is resolvable by allowing negative infinity to cancel positive infinity.[36]

---

[33] Traffic between the Scots and the French was quite high during this period. Note, for instance, how quickly major works in French were published in English translation. Hume visited intellectual circles in France, including Holbach's salon (see, e.g., Blom 2010, pp. 147-50).

[34] Also relevant, here and below, is the magisterial new work by Beiser (2014) on neo-Kantianism, which builds on work by Klaus Christian Köhnke and Ulrich Sieg, among others.

[35] That is, "pretend" in the sense of acting as if they incorporated the "rational part" as well as the "empirical part." In his lectures on logic he (1974 [1800], p. 79) referred to them as "historical sciences," in contrast to "sciences of reason."

[36] The irony can be seen in Foucault's (2008 [1964], p. 33) appreciation of Kant's view of the future course of the development of modern science—namely, that "knowledge of the world" (Weltkenntnis) had become "the sole responsibility of an anthropology which encounters nature in no other form than that of an already habitable Earth (Erde). As a result, the notion of a cosmological perspective that would organize geography and anthropology in advance, and by rights therefore serving as a single

## §4. Early European Ideas of a Science of Sociality and History

Kant's legacy included for the possibility of a science of "the social" or "the societal," and the like, a major dilemma. Pippin (e.g., 1999, pp. 53, 56) well summarized the dilemma but also its apparent resolution in terms of "the object" of inquiry: double the object, letting it be what it must be by terms of the understanding (conceptual scheme, etc.) but then allowing more or less indirectly and quietly a second object as *really the first which we struggle to know*, the sort of "objective necessity" of our settling with the transcendental Illusion. For a science such as Newtonian mechanics that "duplicity" could exist (could be made to be) in seemingly seamless unitary reality under the heading of reason, rationality. But for human affairs, Kant explicitly acknowledged, and cautioned, this posit of a unitary "rational part" could not be defended. It is this blockade that Pippin's summary neglects, by comparison to Michel Foucault's reading of Kant's legacy, such as informed Foucault's book on "Words and Things," published in English translation as *The Order of Things*. As Foucault (1970 [1966]) put it, the legacy of "man and his double" means that, in parallel with the duplicity of object there is a duplicity of subject as well. The agency of "the knowing subject" must contend with logical problems due to reflexivity: the storyteller is always a part of the story being told. Placing the storyteller outside the story is the fact of dogma that Kant rejected, warned against. Established authority vastly prefers that position for itself, of course, and it uses words such as "truth" and "doctrine" rather than "dogma" to describe its claim of authority, a claim for which it depends on an always already seemingly pre-existent legitimacy. Unless the epistemic "conditions which must be satisfied if there are to *be* any criteria of understanding at all" (Peter Winch 1958, p. 21) are explicitly addressed with regard to the necessity of the knowing subject as integral to the story (theory, explanation, etc.) being presented, the presentation can easily presuppose its own conclusion as foreordained. The practice has a long heritage: divide human reality into two parts, then treat one part as if it were superior to the whole and monopolize that part. Having been awakened from his slumbers by Hume's sharp insight, Kant knew from experience how easily the slumbers can prevail.

Although this self-consciousness of philosophy with respect to the reflexive implication of the knowing subject in products of his or her efforts to know is generally regarded as a fact peculiar to modernity, and to modern European and European-derived cultures more specifically, the relevant historical record is actually several centuries older than "modernity." Sensitivities to the implication can be detected in surviving literatures of ancient Greek cultures. While it would be too much to say that the idea of a science of sociality or of "the social" or of society as such can be read in that literature, there is very good evidence of the development of a science of "the physical" (not only Aristotle but also, e.g., Archimedes and Eratosthenes) and a science of "the biological" (again, at least as early as Aristotle). There is evidence also of at least intimations of interest in a parallel development of a science, a systematic knowledge, of human activity and relationships. It is in some of that evidence that one can discern an awareness of at

---

reference for both the knowledge of nature and the knowledge of man [i.e., knowledge of nature and knowledge of culture; cf. Hazelrigg 1995], would have to be put to one side to make room for a cosmopolitical perspective with a programmatic value, in which the world is envisioned more as a city to be built than as a cosmos already given" (modified translation).

least aspects of the problem of what Foucault called "man and his double" in relation to what Winch called "the idea of a social science."

It would not be strange were we to conclude that ancient Greeks did not leave behind a direct theorization of their society (or of any other). It would not be strange, because that very conclusion has most generally applied to known cultures. Indeed, extant cultures have evidently found the task remarkably difficult to construct this kind of self-theorization and, where such effort has been made, to agree its result. Judging from the known record, it seems that even the basic first step, conceptualization of something generally called "society," has been a daunting task. Evidence can be garnered from a two-volume collection entitled *Theories of Society*, compiled more than half a century ago by Talcott Parsons, then at the height of his fame, along with Edward Shils, Kaspar Naegele, and Jesse Pitts (1961). While a major part of the intent behind the collection was to showcase Parsons' own efforts of theory within a context of "classic passages" from (his selection of) works by many of his predecessors, it is perhaps now more notable for showcasing the fact that, as Hans Zetterberg (1962, p. 707) rightly pointed out, "theory" was here used only or mainly "in the idiosyncratic sense in which most sociologists use the word"—a habit that has hardly slacked during the ensuing decades. The preference has been to offer programmatic statements, perspectives, frameworks, and/or conceptual criticisms of prior offerings, sometimes with alternative proposals (usually rather vague), rather than actual theories of specific processes. The exceptions—and there have been some—stand out for the way in which or the degree to which they are exceptional but also, in most instances, for having come to light several decades ago and having been focused on more or less specific processes, such as those of fertility and mortality, family size, kinship, migration, exchange relations, price setting, status attainment, and the like. It is also noteworthy that one must comb the hundreds of pages with considerable imagination to find explicit conceptualization of the principal object supposedly uniting the collected passages, "society" in the singular.

A caution must be registered: we cannot conclude as a matter of fact that the ancient Greeks did *not* undertake any theorization or at least conceptualization of "society"; for absence of evidence is not the same as evidence of absence, and we do know that a vast portion of what ancient Greeks wrote did not survive to our inspection.[37] The fraction that did survive, most especially the surviving plays of the tragedians and some comedies by Aristophanes as well as the histories by Herodotus and Thucydides, the dialogues of Plato, and Aristotle's texts on ethics and on politics, give ample evidence of theorizations (implicit and indirect though much of it be) of kinds of human actions, their impulses, motives, goals, and consequences (potential as well as actual), plus the kinds of perspective and expectation that informed the dynamics of human actions, intentions, and relationships. Much was written of passions and reasons, of failures due to excess (hubris), poor planning (schédio, schēma), poor execution (paraptoma, or unintentional mistake; hettema, or inadequate effort; àkēdia, or lack of care), and bad luck (tychē); of typical patterns such as the peripeteia that ensues after yet another episode of overreach from excellence

---

[37] For a somewhat less cursory overview of the philological history discussed in the next several paragraphs, see James Turner 2014, pp. 12-24).

(hubris) and its tragic denouement; and other relevant topics.[38] Even during the short period from the earliest of Aeschylus' seven surviving plays (of a total of approximately 90) to those of Sophocles (seven of at least 100) to those of Euripides (eighteen of 95), plus eleven of the 40 comedies by Aristophanes, a careful reading demonstrates considerable change, not only in the form of playwriting but also in the sorts of material that the playwrights thought would be sufficiently inspiring to audiences to give the playwright an additional victory in the cycles of competition (i.e., the ancient Greek version of a Tony award).[39] This affords a relative abundance of materials on which to exercise our skills of semantic and pragmatic inference. But knowledge of how much material did not survive should make us leery of generalization, since survivorship could so easily have been due to factors of nonrandom selection.

Evidence by vocabulary and other tools of philology not only does not solve the problem of absence; it is by itself only suggestive at best. In fact, scholars in the Greek-speaking world at least as early as the fourth century BCE had already invented the perspective and some of the tools of philology. But their studies were designed mainly, it seems, to coordinate among variant manuscripts of "the same work," thereby settling on a "standard text" of what should count as a single, self-same work of authorship (see, e.g., James Turner 2014). A core part of exactly those efforts issued in the linguistic formation known as "koiné dialektos" ("common dialect," or just "koine") which began as early as the third century BCE, stimulated by interest in translating from Hebrew and Aramaic into Greek the books of the Hebrew bible, the result being the Septuagint (i.e., the LXX or Seventy; later known as "the Old Testament"). The new coinage, sometimes called the Alexandrian dialect but based mainly on the Attic dialect, became known as the "koine" and, spreading well beyond the confines of the Septuagint during the Hellenistic period, became a dominant force in ancient Greek philology, a major part of which was concerned with the "grammata hieratika" (priestly writings) as they existed from earlier times and then in the efforts to produce a written text of what became (first and second centuries CE) the Christian New Testament.

The base word, "koiné," the dative feminine form of "koinós," had long meant "mutual" or "shared in common" (rather than "common" as in "nothing special") and thus implied a social

---

[38] The concepts just cited were rendered explicitly (as were many others) by various writers down to the time of Aristotle (and after). They were more or less complex, depending of the author using them, and they were historical. The concept of "peripeteia," developed by the tragedians but pre-dated them at least to the Homeric works, well illustrates the difficulty of tracing conceptual development. By the time of the fifth-century playwrights the concept had acquired something more than the simple meaning of a "turning about" (i.e., that because of the reversal "after" becomes a more or less radical reworking of what had been accepted reality "before"—the heart of the tragic sense). It is easy to read that meaning into the Homeric setting as well.

[39] The three ratios of survivorship are necessarily approximate because totals are estimates and some survivors are partial, plus debates continue regarding some authorships (e.g., was *Prometheus Bound* written by Aeschylus or by his son Euphorion?). The "short period" referred to above—barely more than six decades long, from the earliest of Aeschylus' surviving works (c471 BCE) to the last of Aristophenes' and of Euripides' (c406)—largely coincided with the Athenian ascendancy of Pericles (see, e.g., Azoulay 2014 [2010]). Bear in mind that virtually every "major figure" of what we regard as "ancient Greek culture" (which is predominantly Athenian, secondarily Spartan) is or has been a figure of major controversy among modern scholars. Pericles is no exception.

relation, a mutuality, a companionship (all of which is attested at least as early as Hesiod). In fact, at least by the time of Herodotus (middle fifth century BCE), the definite nominative "tò koinon" was used to refer to the institutionalized apparatus of what we call "the state" (though of course with suitable historical specificity), and "koinótēs" meant something like "community." Moreover, the latter was already being distinguished as historical background to newer forms that we would call "associative," chief Athenian examples being the "hetairia" or "hetaireia," which were what we would call "exclusive clubs for aristocratic men."[40]

Philological evidence of a self-conscious identification with, and within, a collective entity seems to consist mainly in two varieties. One is a sort of tribalism, as signified in an attribution of common ancestry and kinship (e.g., "koinó-tokos") but also in the spatial division of Athens into demes (eventually139 of them), which were grouped into ten phylae ("tribes"). The other main variety is the polis, which (in the Attic or Athenian case) denoted both the right of citizenship and the body of citizens (or, in "polisma," the community or commonality of the citizens of a city or town). In sum, my conjecture is that even well into the fifth century BCE (i.e., the time of Aeschylus, Sophocles, Euripides, and Aristophanes, the time of Herodotus and Thucydides, of Socrates, of Periclean democracy) what I am calling "sociality," the inherent social beingness of human being, was still primarily and mainly a communal form of collective organization. While instances of what we, like the ancient Greeks (or at least the Athenians), call an "associational" form did exist, they were subordinate and probably reflected as well as assumed communalist emphases.[41]

On the other hand, however, the centuries designated in conjunction with "ancient Greek culture" were neither few in number nor static in eternal verities. After the collapse of the Mycenaean "palace culture" (c1200 BCE) the peoples of Greece—Ionians to the east, Boeotians to the north, Arkadians and Achaeans to the west, Laconians to the southwest, Attikēans to the southeast, and Dorians scattered throughout—continued their sea-faring commercial ways, at some point (perhaps as late as the eighth century BCE) adopting for their own use the alphabet of their Phoenician trading partners.[42] Because the earliest known manuscripts of the Homeric song-poems (e.g., *Iliad*) were written using that alphabet (rather than the very different writing of the Mycenaeans), the conversion from oral tradition is conventionally dated in conjunction with use of the new alphabetic dialects, Ionian in particular). Available evidence suggests that during this period the basic and dominant unit of organization of people was the household

---

[40] The word "hetairai" also referred to female courtesans who entertained at symposia. These (typically unmarried) women were generally neither prostitutes nor concubines but intellectual companions.

[41] It should be obvious by now that I feel less comfortable speculating about Sparta, a different culture and history, although others (e.g., Ferguson 1782 [1767]) offered several comparisons among a triad of Athens, Sparta, and Rome) have led the way. Located in the part of southern Greece known as Laconia, our vocabulary inheritance of "laconic" tells us much of the difference between the two main city states. If Athenians were (eventually) "loquacious," Spartans were highly "laconic" in written as well as speech pattern for which they were famous.

[42] After centuries of research and debate, little is known about these early populations, their cultures, their relations with each other, and so forth. Not long ago the Dorians were thought to be late "invaders" of Greek territory, but that thought, never well supported by evidence, has faded.

(oikos, from which "economics"), with partially institutionalized networks, probably tribally aligned, used for conjoint juridical and military interests.

After the eighth century (more or less), cities increased more rapidly in population and in wealth. Organized by the tribal or genealogical principle of the dēmos (deme), with assemblies (ekklesia) and an executive council (boule) forming a typically oligarchic process of governance, a city and its surrounding territories became a polis (city-state). At the end of the sixth century (BCE) Kleisthenēs introduced more reforms (after those by his predecessor, Solon) of the Athenian city-state, broadening the base of participation (i.e., a degree of democratization, extended later by Pericles). For present purposes part of the particular significance of these reforms is that they provide indigenous evidence of a distinctive consciousness of Athenians as *being* of a pre-existing Athenian polis. Whether that counts as a consciousness of *societal* membership is partly a different issue (as will be considered below). But even this very brief sketch should be enough to make the point that major changes had been undertaken in the organization and governance of the Athenian polis by the beginning of the fifth century BCE (which brings us to the time of the first of the famous trio of tragedians, Aeschylus), and that those changes were reflected in popular consciousness not only of the citizens (male, typically of local descent) but of dependents as well (women, slaves, foreigners).

From the time of Aeschylus' surviving plays to those of Euripides and of Aristophanes the consciousness of probably the majority of Athenian citizens (and perhaps of other residents of the city proper) changed on a number of discernable dimensions. We know this because the works of the four playwrights were very popular, as judged by the fact of their relative successes in competitions (all four were repeated prizewinners); and we know because contents of the plays changed. There is considerable repetition across playwrights in the "vehicles of history" that they used. The Homeric events, for example, continued to be memorialized as crucial to the history and therefore present meanings of "heroic character," relations of mortals and the gods, fame, destiny, and fate, differences of ethnic identity (to use our vocabulary), and many other attributions. The basic events themselves are largely ignored, while the various characters are used as vehicles for exploring what might be called "issues of the day," and it is here, as well as in the playwrights' uses of the chorus to declare, probe, and query, that one observes trajectories of change. A prime instance is growing pride of place accorded the reality of "to anthropinon," the reality of "the human" as such. That reality becomes not only more recognizable to us, the present-day reader; it also becomes more ordinary in endogenous terms. Sophocles has his chorus sing "Many things are wondrous, but nothing more wondrous than man," in *Antigone* (lines 332-334), written c442 BCE. There is little we can say about the intended meanings of the Homeric storytellers of the *Iliad*: did they contrive a bit of strangeness in their characterization of this heroic figure, signifying his hybrid genealogy/biology (mortal father and godly mother)? Or was the characterization (e.g., what we might describe as his "extraordinary petulance") in their eyes an expected statement of the unpredictability, the ineffableness, of the gods? Or was it a statement of perfectly ordinary character for any heroic actor? Even before Aeschylus one can detect an attitude of reservation or perhaps even puzzlement about Achilles.[43] But he was not the only *Iliad* figure whose presentation can strike us as rather strange.

Characterizations of "the human" also became less sensitive to "the otherworldly." This does not necessarily mean that playwrights offered explicit statements of an atheism (note the Greek word: the "privative a" signifies "not"—i.e., no gods). If any were made, however, the subsequent rise of a strong Christian monopoly would probably have at least contributed to a censorial removal from the surviving corpus of "ancient Greek literature." Even so, one can read lines that surely did signal doubt, if not denial, and these lines grew more frequent, or at least more noticeable, with passing decades of the fifth century BCE. The last of Euripides' extant plays, *Iphigenia at Aulis*, provides a good illustration. Its principal characters include Achilles, Agamemnon, his wife Clytemnestra, and Menelaus, and the central plot revolves around the remembered command that Agamemnon must sacrifice his daughter, Iphigenia. Ambivalent, reluctant to obey, Agamemnon's torment conveys doubt; but it is Clytemnestra who brings the doubt into greater force, bordering on an unstated conviction. Toward the end Euripides has her explicitly weighing the alternatives: not should Iphigenia live or die; rather, "If there are gods" versus "if there are none" (lines 1033-1035), suggesting that for a mere mortal (unlike the famed Achilles) that difference might not amount to much. The play's premier performance (occurring after Euripides' death) won for him another prize in the Athenian competition.

Euripides' plays, like those of Aristophanes and their predecessors, had stimulated controversy, which, very likely a factor in their popularity, can be taken as indication of the tenor and spread of changing conceptions within the self-conscious identification of "being Athenian." Well before his death, Pericle's democracy had collapsed into dictatorship, and civil authorities had become less and less tolerant. Late in the fifth century BCE Athenian rulers imposed stronger penalties against playwrights (among others) who violated official standards of what counted as adequate respect for public authority, the maximum penalty later memorialized as the trial and death of Socrates in 399 BCE. Some of the controversy had recalled works by several pre-Socratic philosophers who would soon be collected under the epithet, "sophists" (e.g., Heraclitus of Ephesus, Protagoras, Thrasymachus).[44] Much of the work for which they were noted had to do with arts of the rhetor—that is, an orator or public speaker, typically then a teacher, which carries an inherent risk of upsetting established authority. A rhetor such as Protagoras (born c490 BCE), Empedocles (c490), or Gorgias (c485) was active during the peak decades of the trio of tragedians, surviving nearly as long or longer than Euripides (who died c406, about twenty years after Plato's birth), and while their public performances were also sometimes controversial

---

[43] For instance, Hesiod, while very good in description of ordinary persons and scenes, had little to say about Achilles beyond the standard epithets (e.g., "lion-hearted Achilles," in *Theogony*, lines 1006-1008), and was subsequently faulted for not giving Achilles sufficient attention (see, e.g., Quintilian's *Institutio Oratoria*, book 10, ch. 1, 49-52).

[44] Xenophon reported in his *Memorabilia* (1.2.31) the "calculated insult to Socrates" designed by Critias (one of the Thirty tyrants) when he made it illegal "to teach the art of words."

31

among audiences of the time, there is no basis for assessing them as more controversial than performances of the plays (see, e.g., Wallace 1998).[45]

Romilly (1992 [1988], p. 82) acknowledged the common criticism of the sophists, voiced most effectively by Plato—namely, that they promoted "a latent assumption that success [in argument and persuasion] mattered more than the truth." The criticism invoked and fed on a common bias in favor of established authority, in the process ignoring a symmetry that was integral to the sophists' teaching: "success in argument and persuasion" is also a description of legislation, of reaching agreement among contending interests with regard to what is, and what should be, and how we should live, and indeed with regard to what the truth of this or that matter is. No doubt the arts of rhetoric can be used for ill gain or ends, for manipulations and deceits. But so too can truth ordained by gods or aristocrats, by pulpit or court, indeed by legislators, too. The difference—and this was the nub of the sophists' argument—better to teach the youth all the various arts of rhetoric so that they have better means of evaluating arguments of whatever sort as they come upon them, or as arguments are pushed onto them. Karl Popper (1945) was on the mark when he observed that the main failing of "the Sophists" was simply that they had not agreed with Plato's authoritarian proclivities, especially that they had not agreed with his need of a "transcendent reality" in which "word" and "thing" were bound by a (pre-cultural) logical necessity.[46]

Established authority always prefers obedience as the default position; it is so much easier, when the voice of authority does not have to make good its claim, again and again, with new listeners and with regard to new issues. It is so much easier for established authority when it can assume of members of a community that they already believe *in* this or that founding story. Belief *in* a story means belief *in* its claim to authority. By believing in it, the believer has already placed himself or herself *within* the story, *within* that reality, has become part of it, and it has become integral to her or him, even vitally integral. The reflexivity of belief *in* the story has been interiorized as belief in oneself. One's self-consciousness of integrity has been located in the belief, in the story. A normativity and a facticity are melded. The skepticism of the sophists, like the skepticism of Hume, threatens the meld by casting the light on doubt on the process by which it came to be.

---

[45] Indeed, some members of the group known collectively as "the sophists" generally escaped the negative evaluation of "sophism" not only at the time but also later, when that epithet became much sharper. Damon (b. c500) is a case in point. His studies of music (and sonic effects in general) in human experiences and expectations , stressing the importance of timing, harmonies, and other technical features, were clearly aesthetic in the basic sense of that word (variations of perception, etc.) and could well have been described as studies in how to manipulate audiences. But Plato, the primary instigator of the negative epithet, "sophist," and attacks against the "sophistical" teachings, wrote favorably of Damon. Socrates, too, was at the time often considered in similarity to the sophists (see Wallace 2007); yet, like Damon, Socrates escaped Plato's attacks on "Sophism."

[46] While sometimes at odds with Popper's proposals (e.g., the oversimplification known as "falsification"), I have applauded his critique of Plato's "closed society" views in general, and with particular regard to the sophists.

Such is the difference between believing X and believing *in* X. It is all the difference of a world (see Veyne 1988 [1983]).

In Plato's *Republic* and again in *Laws* we have what can be called a theory of (an) ideal society.[47] Notably, the primary and main focus is on political relations of governance, and thus on authority and its basis in power, whether it be of belief or of sword. Much the same can be said of Aristotle's work, although he did separate more distinctly between what we might call "normative theory" or "ideals of life well lived" in the *Nicomachean Ethics* and *Eudemian Ethics*, on the one hand, and, in *On Politics*, a more pragmatic theory of political relations of human being as "zōon politikon" as these relations must be considered in best practices of good governance of the whole. However, Aristotle (e.g., *Nicomachean Ethics* 1177b33), like Plato (*Republic* 613b; *Theœtetus* 176b), defined human limitation ("human destiny") in terms of absence, or what human being was *not*—namely, not divine, not gods (or in Harold Fowler's anachronistic translation of *Theœtetus*, God)—even though belief *in* this story had been weakening already as seen in stories by the tragedians. As Greer (1989, pp. 150-162) pointed out, these passages—repeating a formulaic "so far as it is possible for human being," whether with regard to "knowing what is" or "living the good life"—figured prominently in Christian texts about the burdens of an "open society" (in contradistinction to Popper's "open society") and the charms of fleeing perils of freedom (as in "freedom of choice" or freedom to decide for oneself, and decide "wrongly").

The question, "Why no theory of "society as a whole"? is to ask first of all why no specific *concept* of "society as a whole"? The ancient Greeks recognized a "polis," which amounted to a political community consisting primarily of citizens (male) and metics (foreigners), plus familially attached women, plus sometimes the category of women known as "hetairia (female companions, as described above) and of course the many slaves, who circulated throughout market areas, transport circuits, and workplaces of a polis but were not of the polis as such. That was evidently the extent of indigenous (or emic) conceptualization of aggregate forms larger than the familial household (oikos), other than remnants of an old tribalism that persisted as a political geography (we might say "ethnic districts") of a city state. In general, one might argue that if people experience little or no significant change from generation to generation, there would be no sense of a dynamism of collective forms larger than, say, the vagaries of familial households due to accident, early death, wildfire, and the like, whether by human hand or caprice of a god or gods. However, "Greek experience" (perhaps especially Athenian experience) had been anything but static. Engaged in long-distance trade, the city state had been staunchly commercial for many generations, accretive of innovations from other Greek places and more broadly from around the Mediterranean coast and the rim of the Black Sea (all sites of colonization). Inventions of style in artistic productions—sculpture, architecture, music, painting (little of which survived), and the literary arts (most of which also did not survive)—demonstrate conceptions of a collective identity that, while perhaps centered on a city state, nevertheless stretched across peripheral territories, as did the standardization across several dialects (i.e.,

---

[47] Some scholars have suggested that in these latter dialogues Plato was speaking for himself rather than acting as a vehicle for his teacher, Socrates. I am less than confident of that attribution, and even less confident that such difference would make much difference.

koine). Productions of "material sciences" were plentiful, effective, and generally shared. Contrary to a later gloss, "the ancient Greeks" were *not* mainly "contemplative" (as in the "what every school child knows" contrast to "active" Romans). Inventions by Archimedes alone are nearly enough to dispel that canard.

And yet, there is little if any indication that a consciousness of "society" in the sense of a territory-wide identification by *associational* organization as *Greek* actually developed. The nearest that an identity of "unity of diversity" approached the associative model was apparently the "inter-city league" that was negotiated from time to time for purposes of combat against outsiders (mainly the Persians). But as first the Romans and then the Christians demonstrated, many ingredients for invention and development of that organizational form had been produced and utilized in some fashion. Arguably, the most important of them were housed in native Greek installations of hieratic, patristic formations, but insofar as these were shared across city states (and excepting the inter-city leagues mentioned above) they remained largely communal and local because of tribal loyalties and persistently polytheistic devotions and mythic heritages.

Perhaps the Greeks, or more specifically the Athenians, had become "too skeptical too soon" (in a manner of speaking), or in Nietzsche's (1983 [1873-74]) formulation "knew too much too soon." As commentators have repeatedly said, Nietzsche drew heavily on (his understanding of) ancient Greek cultures, and it was primarily lessons he took from that understanding that led him to add to his "untimely meditations" the supposition—thinking from his precipice of destiny by the "Overman"—that most adults (now as then) do depend on a "necessity of boundaries and illusions," not only the big one, Kant's transcendental Illusion, but also sequences of smaller, entailed illusions. As Morley (2009, p. 136) so aptly summarized Nietzsche's main thrust, "somehow, one must know not to know too much."[48] The suggestion is prominent in works by the tragedians, and, as Wallace-Hadrill (1982) emphasizes, the stature of appearances, feints, indirections that can misdirect, all to the service of maintaining belief *in* civic myths is too prominent to be missed by later observers, just as Achen and Bartels (2016) have shown that in one's own contextual experience appearances are often as uncontested as mother's milk (see also Wolfe 2006; Ackerman 2010; Kuttner 2018; and Taylor 2019).

It is often said that the Romans invented the concept of "society"—that while they depended on and borrowed Greek literatures during a long period before developing their own distinctively *Latin* literature, the Romans were quicker to invent and develop practical skills of organization and that this included some useful vocabulary. There is considerable evidence on the one hand supporting the claim that the word, "societās," was indeed of Roman coinage, but evidence with respect to the matter of *concept* is on the other hand rather different from what has sometimes been claimed.

The Greeks did have a concept of the collection of human beings (we would say, "the human species"): in the most general sense, "to anthrōpótēta." It is said that Marcus Tullius Cicero (106-43 BCE) invented the Latin word, "humanitas," and the record supports that claim

---

[48] Morley's (2009, pp. 129-138) account of Nietzsche vis-à-vis Marx and Kant is very similar to mine. Of the books that I have planned but now very likely will never complete, one would weave the main threads from Kant to Marx to Nietzsche.

in the sense that Cicero thought there should be a word in his own language with the same meaning. He invented the Latin word, not the concept. Soon thereafter Julius Caesar's justificatory propaganda known as *Commentary on the Gallic War*, published between 58 and 49 BCE, used the Latin "humanitas" on the first page of the first book, in the phrase, "cultus atque humanitas" ("culture and humanity"). So the lexicon of each language contained a general name of "all humankind." Did Latin gain a word specifically for a collection of human beings bounded far more narrowly than the sum total of humanity, but larger than the Greek city state, and emphasizing associational rather than communal relations? The record is not clear: it displays much the same sort of ambivalence that Wallace-Hadrill (1982) demonstrated in his excellent review of issues and (now dated) literature. His discussion of the dynamic of ambivalence that linked "principate" and "dominate" could be extended to a similar ambivalence of applications of "associational" vis-à-vis "communal." The key to that dynamic is probably Nietzschean: an associational form, if too far from communal "support," tends to erode the "in" of belief *in*. Or: a myth completely nude of mystery has no majesty.[49] Kant's hope for a species maturity that features autonomy and self-responsibility remains on hold.

Cicero also wrote of "societas humana" and "societas civilis," which indicates that Latin did gain such a word, "societas," perhaps also by Cicero's invention. There are texts in English which claim that Cicero's "societas civilis" was his translation of Aristotle's definition of "polis" as an "association of associations" (see Edwards 2014, p. 6). The cited Aristotelian definition is typically the passage 1252a1-6 of *On Politics*. This claim, probably a confused retro-alignment of meanings, is wrong. Aristotle did not write "association of associations." What he did write was that a "polis" is a "koinōnia politika" (the meaning of which has already been described). Cicero, evidently fluent in koinē Greek, would surely have translated Aristotle's "koinōnia" as "communitas," not "societas." But he might well have used his neologism, "societas civilis," in extension of the idea of a collection of city states (see, e.g., Wallace-Hadrill 1982). For Cicero had his own claims to make about "societas humana"—in particular, ideas about a universality of "human being." In the first book of his *De Legibus* (§23) his initial sentence is: "est igitur quoniam nihil est ratione melius eaque est et in homine et in deo prima homini cum delo rationis societas." My translation: "Thus, since nothing is better than reason, which is common to God and man, there is a certain rational association of the first human beings with God." Where I have "association," however, one could just as well say "connection" or "fellowship." In other words, Cicero's point had to do with person-to-person (or person-to-god) relationship, not a collectivity. By extension, one could argue that he was referring to humanitas as a collectivity of human beings who live in continuous association with one another on certain scales and, direct or indirect, a continual association among groupings or societies on larger scale. Was that what he meant? A passage in his *De Amicitia* (§19) supports the conjecture: "Sic enim mihi perspicere videor ita natos esse nos ut inter omnis esset societas quaedam maior autem ut quisque proxime accederet." Or by mine: "It seems clear to me that we humans were created such that there is a certain connection [fellowship, association] between all of us which becomes stronger as our

---

[49] The main point is of course not Nietzsche's alone, as Wallace-Hadrill argued with regard to Rome. Writing at about the time of Nietzsche's essay, Walter Bagehot (1867) famously offered the same (unsolicited) advice to the British monarchy.

proximity to each other increases." Still another passage, this one from the first book of his *De Officiis* (§153): "illa autem sapientia quam principem dixi rerum est divinarum et humanarum scientia in qua continetur deorum et hominum communitas et societas inter ipsos." Or mine: "That wisdom which I have held highest is the knowledge of things divine and human, which is also about the community between gods and men and the fellowship [association] among men." In sum, the evidence suggests that Cicero's "societas" mainly denoted personal relationships of what we might call "associational," rather than the name of a collectivity such as we use the word "society."[50]

Two other Roman authors may be considered briefly, mainly because their writings seem to solidify that difference of usage: the historian Cornelius Tacitus, of whom we know much, and a man known to us only as Gaius, whose main work nearly succumbed permanently to a practice of the Christian Church.

First, Tacitus. One might suppose that his works of history would contain multiple uses of the word, "societas," however uniform or varied the uses might be. In fact, the whole of his *History* contains not one instance of it. His English translators (Church and Brodribb) did use the English word, "society," once: it was in translation of "civitas," which I would have rendered not as "society" but as "citizenship."[51] There is one appearance of "societas" in his *Annales* (also written c109 CE): in book 12, chapter 15, Tacitus, recounting a campaign in the Bosporus area, said that the Roman army had "no difficulty" in forming a "societas" with an army of the Adorsi (another people). Church and Brodribb translated the word as "alliance," which fits very well.

Now to Gaius, a legal scholar whose work combined some history and some theory, in the form of a compendium of practices, entitled *Institutes of Roman Law*, published in c170 CE (a little more than two centuries after Cicero's death).[52] Cicero had had much to say about "societas civilis," or "civil society" (or, perhaps nearer his meaning, "civil state") a form of organization centered on but larger than a set of political institutions. He was not the last Latin author to address these matters, although there was an interregnum of sorts (due to political turmoil in Rome) between him and Gaius. Once conditions had become more stable, Latin writers tended to display more "practical" concerns about matters of "civil society," and the

---

[50] Note that *De Officiis* was about "offices," but an "office" was a service and duty, and, as Wallace-Hadrill (1982, p. 40) said, "social relations found concrete expression at Rome in the exchange of official, the etiquette of 'services' of a purely ceremonial nature paid by inferior to superior ... in exchange for more material benefits."

[51] Tacitus (book 1, chapter 92) was referring to a pair of Empire functionaries, who "had long before been led to suspect each other by animosities scarcely concealed among the cares of the campaign and the camp, and aggravated by unprincipled friends and a state of society calculated to produce such feuds." The point was directly about a state of civility, of fellowship, of citizenship, or of sociality; only indirectly about a society as a whole.

[52] Gaius' compendium was lost until 1816, when a sharp reader spied it beneath text of a Christian writer who had written over Gaius' work. The usual justification was that materials on which to write were scarce and had to be re-used, the better replacing the unneeded. The Latin writer was in his time called Eusebius Sophronius Hieronymus, later dubbed Saint Jerome. It was he who translated the Christian Bible (or most of it) into Latin, thereafter known as the "Vulgate" (meaning "common") Bible.

concerns generally were expressed in one of two forms: codification of Roman law and institutionalization of the new "church religion" of Christianity.

Codification of Roman law had two main focal points, one political and military, the other commercial. Between the two, the latter had become primary venue for the development of an organizational form to which the name "societas" was attached. Judging by the text of Gaius' compendium of Roman institutions of law including the legal code, the word "societas" had become a specialized term applied mainly to a form which we recognize as "commercial partnership" (and which developed into an early version of the joint stock company). Gaius' compendium distributed far and wide a representation not only of Rome proper but also of Rome's vast empire.

That appears to have been how matters stood, with respect to the relations of "societas" and "communitas" for centuries to come, as the dominant force expanding through European cultures became a sacralized version of Roman bureaucracy. But this force also, having adopted a text that was deemed "raw" or "primitive" or, as the Greeks said, "barbarian" and taking it to its breast, so to speak, was from the late second century also pre-occupied with the task of accommodating that text—the Hebrew Tanakh, the "*Old* Testament"—and making in consonant with a *New* Testament. As Grafton and Williams (2006) have shown with abundant specificity, this was a difficult task. The core of what was later styled as "primitive Christianity" was richly communal (see, e.g., Meeks 1995; 2003), and doctrine retained a strong communalism in, for instance, the ritual of communion. But it was also an evangelical, proselytizing, missionary religion, seeking expansion into ever new territories as, in effect, a colonial power (presented as self-evident authority), and the colonization was temporal as well as spatial—which is to say that "the past" of any given people or culture had to be converted. This delicate process was nowhere better documented than in the epistles attributed to Paul (born Saul), in which the evangel was riding on associations in order to reach converts to communion.[53]

As early Christianity developed into a centralized and centralizing church, it parlayed its success as a movement of popular consciousness into routinizing forms developed within state functions of the Roman Empire. In retrospect, the churchly process might well have appeared as if designed in a strategically cunning program of monopolistic organization, but that view would be to mistake a blend of happenstance with deliberate organizational effort as self-conscious plan from the beginning. Church doctrine continued to stress a "movement communalism" during the early patristic period, through the second century CE, when a style of writing, the "grammata hieratika" (which Greeks had adapted from Egyptian priestly style), flourished in organizational and evangelical functions. Many of the major exemplars were recorded in letters written to the general populations of important cities—as mentioned above, for instance, Pauline letters to the people of Rome, to the people of Corinth, and so forth (altogether, about half of the generally agreed 27 books of the Christian New Testament)—and these epistles gave emphasis to specific valuations as if they were uniquely Christianity's own. A classic illustration is the still often heard line (13) of Paul's first letter to the people of Corinth. Written in the koiné that had long

---

[53] The delicacy is testified in Wayne Meeks' (2003) study of *The First Urban Christians* (i.e., Pauline Christianity), but also *by* the fact of his introductory essay in which he answers his own question, "Why a social description of early Christianity?"—the point being that some, perhaps many, potential readers would think the only description that matters is "theological," even that to give a *social* description borders on blasphemy.

served as (in effect) a main "trade language" of the Mediterranean basin, he was reported to have extolled νυνὶ δὲ μένει πίστις, ἐλπὶς, ἀγάπη, τὰ τρία ταῦτα, μείζων δὲ τούτων ἡ ἀγάπη (or, in NRSV English: And now faith, hope, and love abide, these three; and the greatest of these is love).[54]

The new church's message was not entirely new, of course, for it had a history from which it descended. That was a problem: the church had "founded itself on a tradition that it could never fully incorporate or reduce to sameness" (Grafton and Williams 2006, p. 235). Yet the promise of its power (and authority) resided in tests such as this. Unlike imperial Rome which deployed massive materials means of monopolizing violence, the empire of the Christian Church would succeed in organizing and controlling even larger material resources of territory (the monastic system) via a monopoly of violence through symbolic means (not to discount materializations of the rack, flammable stakes, and the like). Defeating all rivals for the mantle of sacred authority would be crucial to its mission. Its attention was therefore focused more narrowly than by a perceived need to apportion applications of words such as "communitas" and "societas" into a "correct" balance. In documents extending from Quintilian's first-century (CE) *Institutio Oratoria* to Origen's *De Principiis*, written by 231, to the *Historia ecclesiastica* of Eusebius of Alexandria (263-339) there is no mention of "societas."[55] This does not mean that the church was without a conception of human organization somewhere on a scale between the totality of human beings, at one extreme, and a household, at the other. The extent of a city was an obvious instance; an empire such as Rome had achieved was another. But to the rule of the Christian Church the preeminent and dominant instance was to be itself—which is to say, neither communitas nor societas but a nexus of both, a whole greater than either—and its public theory would be neither social or cultural nor historical but theological. This status became evident, if not earlier, in the writings of Augustine of Hippo. By rough estimate, this man was author of texts totaling five million words (which compares with the lexical corpus of Latin, a little more than twice that number). His greatest work of political theory (housed in theological defense of Christianity against claims that it had been undermining Rome's empire) was entitled *De Civitas Dei contra Paganos* (1998 [436]). Although Augustine used both "communitas" and "societas" in his writings, he preferred the metaphor of a "civitas," as in his contrast of "heavenly" and "earthly" forms of civitas. As mentioned earlier, in the Latin of Cicero and contemporaries, the word primarily meant "condition of being a citizen," which implied a right of freedom of the city (being able to move about more or less at will). Standards translations of the word into "city" are reasonable, but one should remember two conditions: first, Latin included a perfectly good word, "urbis," that translates easily as "city"; second, the Latin concept of "civitas" referred to a kind of membership; for as Augustine stressed in book 14, chapter 28, there was by Church doctrine a profound difference between self-consciousness as member of an "earthly city" (to

---

[54] Note that πίστις (pistis) also generally meant "belief," sometimes "trust"; but the Church preferred to standardize it in English as "faith," from the Latin fidēs, which gives more emphasis to "confidence" and "reliance" than does "belief" (which, more general, can include "agreeing in the opinion of"). It is also not incidental that the Church replaced ἀγάπη (agapē) with the Latin caritas, which is translated into English usually as "charity."

[55] This does not mean that I have read all of the documents produced during that interval. Origen alone supposedly produced at least 800, the texts of most of which are unknown to me (see Grafton and Williams 2006, p. 68)

use the English translation) and a "heavenly city"—this in application to a person who obviously was resident of some earthly place, be it a city or a rural seclusion. Christianity had been and still was primarily a self-conscious reflexive identity among urban populations. Paul's epistles had reflected that (peoples of Corinth, for example, or of Rome). But Augustine did not tie Christianity's claim of universality to the orb of any given city or indeed the sum total of all cities of his world.[56] His "political theory" was about a different kind of "membership," one that was simultaneously communal and associational. Thus, of the three appearances of the word "societas" in James Baxter's selection of Augustine's *Epistulae*, the third (from Letter 35) is exemplary. The relevant line is "Si acta ibi non est, innocens est Christi societas per omni transmarinus gentes"; that is, "all of the people across the sea" are welcomed into the "fellowship of Christ."

During the decline and then collapse of the Roman Empire the Christian Church had in place an effective model of systemic bureaucracy (based on the Roman model of organization of territory and its population) which could then serve colonial functions as the monastic system. Conversion into Christian belief meant almost automatically subservience to the monopolizing processes of that system, and the Church added to the movement list of primary values another: obedience. Obedience was the other half of the bargain that offered care or charity ("caritas," having replaced "agapē" in the standard Christian lexicon ) and hope in the faith or confidence of doctrine, in particular the self-consciousness of communalism. After all, one of the core rituals of faith was called "communion," not "association." The genesis account inherited from the folk religion of the ancient Hebrews (among others)—that is, the originary events of humankind and their consequences—emphasized not simply *hamartia*, the word in koinē that was most often translated into "sin" (and which in its own linguistic context meant something like "missing the mark"; its oldest known uses pertain to archery) but also, and far more importantly, an *original sin*, meaning a stain and responsibility that would ever after infect every human being.[57] Insofar as that idea could be implanted in communal consciousness, and thus in self-consciousness of individual person, reins of authority could never be removed or dropped. Moreover, it was integral to the universalist claim of the Christian doctrine, a major theme of the evangelical and proselytizing activities of the Church as bureaucratic organization, as soterial mission of every present moment, and as the intendedly deepest self-consciousness of the individual person. Personal dependence on the Church was meant to be, for the faithful *was*, inescapable. Augustine understood an imperialism of mind, when he wrote his famous Latin phrase in Sermon 279: ubi terror, ibi salus ("where there is terror there is salvation").[58] A power to instill the emotions of a

---

[56] Indeed, whereas the word "urbis" appears abundantly in Cicero's texts and still often in those of Tacitus, it was of rare utility for Quintilian, being too tied to specificity of place and time.

[57] Other words of koinē translated into "sin" denoted lack of intention (paraptoma) or lack of sufficient attention or effort (hettema) or, more seriously, intentional violation of authority usually in specific context of law or custom (parabasis) or a general condition of lawlessness (paranomia: circumventing the law; anomia: lack of law). In the Old Testament koinē a condition known as asebia described a general condition of wickedness or impiety. But relative to original sin all of these latter terms specifically (though usually implicitly) cultural and/or situational, not genetic (in the older sense of that word, as in "congenital").

[58] An interesting line of comparison across four texts comes to mind: Augustine's *Confessions*, Kierkegaard's *The Concept of Anxiety*, first published in 1844, Erich Fromm's *The Sane Society* (1955), and Richard Wilkinson and Kate Pickett's *The Inner Level* (2018). The question all four works ask, in

terrible fright could accomplish what blood on a sword could not: keep the body alive and productive while the mind cowered (cf. Kierkegaard 2014 [1844]).[59]

An argument such as Plato's recommendation of aristocracy (rule by "the best"), as in his *Republic* and *Laws*, was based on the presumption that "the common people" could not safely participate in a "self-ruling" regime of governance, because they could never attain the necessary wisdom and skills.[60] One should not imagine that Christian-inspired enlightenment has rendered that view appreciably less attractive (to say nothing of obsolete) to philosophy (see, e.g., Dreyfus and Kelly 2011). However, the vignette of Christian history just presented does raise an issue of lasting import to the general discussion advanced here and continued repeatedly in later sections of this book. The Christian Church was (to an extent still is) remarkably successful in fusing communal and associational forms of sociality. I have presented that fusion as though the formal difference was (and is) important and perhaps in some sense basic. But is that the case? Think again of the two words, different languages, koinōnia and societās, both discussed above. What specifically is the difference, and how important is it? Athenians (and perhaps other "ancient Greeks") knew of hetairia (associations) as well as the communal, although the word was used in more specific settings (insofar as can be judged by surviving documents) and in that sense, at least, was subordinate? Romans knew of commūnitās as well as societas (as well as socius, from which it derived), but judging by literatures left by Cicero, Tacitus, and Horace "societas" had a less well focused application. That should not blind us, however, to the fact that what is most noticeable about Cicero's discussion of societas humana is the centerpiece: humanly *legislated* standards and rules, and the fact that he was virtually silent about the relation of human law and any notion of a natural or divine law.[61] Not until Christian scholars imposed a necessity that all three converge did that link become focal, and for Christians mandatory.

Should we conclude that the difference is of little importance? Or that its import is at best secondary to the fact that humans have demonstrated persistent interest in investing a self-consciousness of belief *in* each of those forms, the communal and the societal? Or does the fact of that distinction, perhaps its difference in basic dynamic, infect and infest self-consciousness to such an extent that there is a parallel difference, a difference of mind in parallel to a difference of external behavior?

In due course, the question of difference, potential if not actual, got bound up with a spatiotemporal metaphor, "the shape of history," which in turn was later linked to a "battle of the

---

one way or another—Can an entire society, a society as such, become "mentally ill"?—remains relevant today, as illustrations mound higher. See also Koestler (1965, pp. 80-81).

[59] As Catherine Nixey (2017) has most recently documented, the Christian Church furthered its mission of an empire of the mind by wiping it clean (or as nearly as it could do) of memories of pre-Christian cultures, both directly in educational activities and indirectly through a selective iconoclasm, destroying, and encouraging its believers to destroy, as many temples, sculptures, scrolls, and other art forms from pre-Christian times as possible. Wilson-Lee (2018, p. 139) described scraps of "mutilated ancient manuscripts" as souvenirs sold to visitors in Rome during the sixteenth century.

[60] Whereas I said "presumption," one could justifiably say "assumption," in that Plato had the "object lessons" of Athens (Periclean democracy and its collapse into anarchy-fearing dictatorship) as measure of the difference. As to the argument that a regime described as "aristocratic" from one point of view might be described from another as "kakistocratic" (rule by the worst), Plato's tendency to analytic circularity was probably sufficient to forestall such recognition.

[61] See, e.g., *De Legibus* book 1, 18-19. Rome's "ius gentium," which applied to aliens, was linked to a notion of natural law.

books"—that is, a series of disputes about the relative superiority of "the ancients" or "the moderns" (see, e.g., Manuel 1965; Curtius 1953, pp. 251-253; Morley 2009). This latter linkage reflected what began as a secondary choice but in due course became primary. The more general choice, within the metaphor of shape, was "cyclical versus linear," but the latter option implied a difference in direction or in polarity, and the conditional, "linear or cyclical," was soon swamped by what had been secondary: "regression versus progression." Jerome and Augustine were already involved in an ongoing "struggle between Antiquity and Christianity" (Curtius 1953, p. 72), difficult for the latter combatant on a number of dimensions. A Sisyphean image of endless repetition could be discerned in the doctrine of original sin, all of one's effort assessed in balance only after some unknown future (earthly) date following what theorists promised as a Second Advent (or, in the Greek text, a Parousia). In the meantime, believers could grow confused and tired, worrying about seemingly endless debates whether "times" were getting better or worse. And yet "the times" in question were "earthly times" and therefore might not make a whit of difference in the promised final accounting. All the while, the Church sought, and at each and every opportunity proclaimed, progress in its mission toward universality.

The debate about "history's shape" had from its beginnings been secular as well as sacred (the dialectical insurance, as it were), and gradually the secular component became more visible in explicit discussion. By Kant's day, the idea that a "universal history" had metaphorical shape had long since grown stale, replaced by a conviction that, if viewed at proper scale by correct perspective, the course of history would be seen as a logical development, even if the opacity of causes of sequences of events and changes cannot be overcome. Deciphering the inherent *logic* of history had become the new name of the game. A passage highlighted by Morley (2009, p. 124) describes the terrain:

> History is concerned with giving an account [of phenomena of human affairs], no matter how deeply concealed their causes may be, and it allows us to hope that, if [the study of history] examines the free exercise of the human will *on a large scale*, it will be able to discover a regular progression among freely will actions. In the same way, we may hope that what strikes us in the actions of individuals as confused and fortuitous may be recognized, in the history of the entire species, as a steadily advancing but slow development of man's original capacities.... Individual men and even entire nations little imagine that, while they are pursuing their own ends, each in his own way and often in opposition to others, they are unwittingly guided in their advance along a course intended by nature. They are unconsciously promoting an end which, even if they knew what it was, would scarcely arouse their interest (Kant 19921 [1784a], p. 41).

This was Kant arguing, not against his conclusion regarding the transcendental Illusion, but from his principle of hope regarding what might yet be learned through careful observations compiled only as empirical generalizations. The causes would remain concealed. But one might still hope that empirical generalizations, if based on enough observations, could generate inferences that might give insight into the "logic" of historical developments. As Morley said further, this hope was "echoed ... almost exactly" by Hegel and thus at least the "Kantian" version of Karl Marx (see Hazelrigg 1993b, 1995).

Even when the secular discussion was oriented by the metaphor of history's "shape" the issue of "freely willed actions" had become contentious, since by at least one reading "free actions" were as likely to issue in deleterious as beneficial effects or, even more disconcertingly, none at all. Even when practicing as assiduously as possible what the Greeks called "eubolia" (good decisions), outcomes could be, if detectable at all, devilishly perverse. Needless to say, for secularizing theorists that had been disconcerting at best. Now, however, nothing so simply

41

or crude as mere "shape" would be searched for signs. Rather, a logic. And the demands of this expected logic seemed to necessitate that it be an originary logic, a "genetic logic," the earlier sense of that phrase.[62] A new concept (or at least phrase) had come to light—namely, "world-historical development" (now superseded usually by "globalization"). It rested on an old platform of reasoning: since "we humans are not just sentient but rational by design, great things must be expected of us. The main difference from old to new versions was that "God's design" had been replaced by "the design of evolutionary process," which, the bet was, could now be extended into all manner of human affairs. Kant's principle of hope was not this simple, to be sure, but early formulations of the idea of a science of society were untroubled by Kant, and hardly anyone noticed the fallacy. None of us is any more capable of observing the origin of one's species being than observing the origin of one's own personal being. Neither is or ever has been a goal-directed process by design.

But never mind. Early thoughts of a science of human affairs had a rich heritage to work from and with. Kant's recommendation about "large scale" had been intended in part to cover as much diversity of human experience as possible, and many European observers had already seen and catalogued diversities of human living, which seemed to range from "first peoples" (or, as more often said, "primitive peoples") to the companions of present observer as such. Moreover, that catalogue had been constructed by categories—the basic one, "primitive" versus "modern," an extension of, to some extent a reformulation of, the polarity of "ancients" versus "moderns," which suggested a still older vocabulary of contrast, "communal" versus "association."[63]

For theorists active during the late nineteenth century this latter difference had come to matter greatly, in part because it seemed to assure that the question of linear direction has been settled as a matter of science. A commanding figure of psychology, Wilhelm Wundt, argued a thesis known as "psychophysical parallelism." Ferdinand Tönnies, now remembered mainly for his book, *Gemeinschaft und Gesellschaft*, first published in 1887, argued that those contrastive nouns are in some sense basic, and the contrast has been part of the standard lexicon ever since. The influence of Wundt will reappear in a later discussion. For present purposes, let's focus on Tönnies.

Tönnies based the contrast (intended as an idealization, not as exhaustive in empirical description) on a difference in will formation, although there is a "hen and egg" quality to his presentation, such that one should not conclude that he intended one "type" as either more important than or exclusive of the other.[64] Unfortunately, the author was ill-served by the

---

[62] A version of this in analytic thought is the device of an "original position." These claims will be addressed again in the last section; see also Habermas (1990 [1983], p. 202 n.15).

[63] At one time, "diversity" had been honored by legend as well as direct observation; various "outlandish" accounts of strange people encountered supposedly by travelers were popular publications from the fifteenth century. But a more sober empiricism sorted across the proceeds well before Montesquieu's accounts in his *De l'esprit des lois* (1748) and elsewhere (see Shackleton 1961). Church censorship was still regulating what could be read or viewed, however. For instance, Bartolomé de las Casas' sixteenth-century five-volume compilation of *Historia de las Indias* could not be published until 1875.

[64] While there are certainly influences from his reading of Thomas Hobbes (see, e.g., Tönnies 1971 [1896]), I do not agree that Tönnies constructed his argument by an "originary logic" (e.g., that human being began as one kind of Homo sapien and gradually evolved to become another kind). More about this below. Tönnies was explicit about the reasoning behind his decision to begin philosophically with pre-Kantian arguments, and Hobbes in particular, as a simpler ground on which to begin his

translation into English made during the 1950s by Charles Loomis, who, in the interest of simplification and ambiguity-reduction, pared away too much of the richness of Tönnies' German vocabulary. For example, in Tönnies' initial paragraph he said that any relationship between individual persons is inherently mutual and can be either affirming or denying, even destructive, of one or more persons involved, and that his treatise is about the affirmative aspect. His basic perspective is dialectical (even though weakly so), in that the mutual affirmation was deemed simultaneously "unity in plurality" and "plurality in unity," and this mutuality, this dialectic, is present in the "group" that is formed by or as the relationship. In Tönnies' words, Die durch dies positiv Verhältnis gebildte Gruppe heist, als einheitliche nach innen und nach aussen wirkendes Wesen order Ding ausgefasst, eine Verbindung. My English version: The group composed through this positive relationship as a uniform inwardly and outwardly acting being [Wesen] or thing is an assemblage [Verbindung]. The discrepancies between Loomis' and my translations of this German sentence are mostly minor. The principal exception is the noun, Verbindung, which Loomis translated as "association." That choice is lexically acceptable in general. But in this case the choice is not neutral vis-à-vis the principal distinction Tönnies made between Gemeinschaft and Gesellschaft, as well as the "forms of will" that are its basis (about which, more in a minute). The root of Verbindung is the verb "binden" (to bind or connect or combine or tie together), and the prefix adds the notion of mutual implication of the "things" ("elements," etc.) that are bound together. The best "neutral" translation of the noun is "connection," I think, but as that seems rather awkward I chose "assemblage" (even though the main verbal form of "to assemble" is different in German).

Tönnies announced of his own account that his starting point in building his thesis was a distinction in the meaning of "human will," a distinction that he called one of "form" and which occupies the second part of his treatise. Here, too, the distinction should be understood as an ideal typification in his "pure sociology," not as a difference of kind, such that one person could have one kind of will whereas another could have the other kind of will. And here a failing of the Loomis translation is more serious, in part due to the presence of an abetting introductory essay by Loomis and John McKinney, which prepares the reader to see similarities between Tönnies' "dichotomies" and typifications by Max Weber, Emile Durkheim, and others (as if in furtherance of Parsons' claim of basic convergence; see Parsons 1937).[65]

His distinction between what he called "Wesenwille" and "Kürwille" has to do with the relation of an individual person as integral to a collectivity of persons and that person as an individual actor; more specifically, between effects of the collectivity as they are manifest in the person and effects of aims and intents by the personal agency as such. The difference between

---

constructions "from philosophy to sociology" (see, e.g., p. 226 in Jacoby's collection of some of his essays, Tönnies 1974).

[65] A reader should bear in mind that "similar" is an elastic comparative, and it carries simultaneously the meaning of "different." Tönnies was born in Schleswig (then part of Denmark) in 1855, nearly three years before Georg Simmel (1858, Berlin) and nine years before Max Weber (1864, Erfurt in Prussia). If similarities are to be noted, there are as many (though different) to Simmel as to Weber. Tönnies was co-founder (with Simmel, Weber, and others) of the German Sociological Association in 1909 and served as president until 1933, when the Nazi regime forced him out (see Tönnies 1974, p. 95, n7). In the meantime other factors, perhaps including his background in a farming family in North Frisia (although financially successful), impeded his vocational success in the German academy. Weber, on the other hand, was oriented more to economics and social policy, active in the Verein für Sozialpolitik (until he bolted in wake of some personal disputes), and prone to continue a rather prickly demeanor with colleagues in the GSA.

43

his compound words is held by the first term of the compound; "wille," the second part, means "will" or "will formation" in each compound, but this base meaning is importantly modified by the respective prefatory term. The word "Wesen" (whether taken as noun, as just written, or in adjectival or adverbial form) is a very good illustration of a word that can convey rather different meanings, depending on syntactic and semantic context and/or on history. To list only a few of the most relevant nominations, it can be translated as "being," as "essence," as "substance," as "nature," as "character," as "intrinsic virtue," and a still other supposed cognates in English. The problem with cognates is that a reader can be easily misled into assuming that there must be one "main cognate," that it applies generally across text, and that it is static in time. But the bounds of our little lexical packets known as "words" are never a sharp as the notion of "law" often prefers to enforce. In the fifth sentence of the first paragraph of the first part of his treatise (quoted above from the fifth edition) Tönnies already used the word "Wesen," which Loomis rendered as "being"—satisfactorily in the specificity of that sentence. In the very first sentence Tönnies wrote, Die menschliche Willen stehen in vielfachen Beziehungen zu einander; jede solche Beziehung ist eine gegenseitige Wirkungs die insofern als von der einen Seite getan oder gegeben, von der anderen erlitten order empfangen wird. My translation: Human wills are in many-faceted relationships with each other; each such relationship is a reciprocal effect, inasmuch as it is done or given by one side, suffered or received by the other. Loomis translated "Seite" as "party" rather than "side," as if different persons were involved. That need not be the case, for the "reciprocal effect" occurs within one and the same individual person. That meaning of an inherence and an implication is central to Tönnies' argument.

While "being" is generally adequate as English correspondent to "Wesen," one should keep in mind that the German word can often be rendered as well or better as "essence" or as "nature." The latter choice Tönnies clearly intended (i.e., a meaning of "natural being," for instance). Whether he also intended to draw on some memory of the old distinction between "essence" and "accidence" cannot be decided from the text (at least I cannot, though not because I think he was unaware of it; far from it).

On the other hand, the noun "Kür" is much more specific; it derives from the verb "küren," means "to choose" or "to select" or "to elect." Loomis chose "rational" for this "form of human will," but that was a step too far. It is not that "rational"—or more specifically, an "instrumental rationality"—was (is) irrelevant. But in his basic definition, in his presentation of his general conceptualization, Tönnies did not say that. At least one translator (Jacoby; see Tönnies 1974) preferred "arbitrary" for this other form of will. I understand the preference; it is analogous to the argument that the relation of "word" to "thing" is arbitrary, not pre-ordained as in Adamic language. But I think that, too, is misleading, in that it can give the impression that social formations (sociality in general) involve purely free choice, as if prior formations do not imply a dialectic of effects (constraint/enablement, internal/external, material/ideal, etc.). Other translators, thinking of contrast to "natural," have preferred "artificial" (e.g., Loomis, in Tönnies' magnus opus; and see Morley 2009, pp. 62-63); but this, too, can be misleading in a related way (here the bias being the notion that "humanly made," the main point of "artificial," implies a less genuine or important or determinative process and effectivity than does "natural"; see Hazelrigg 1979, 1992, 1995).

Again, the key to Tönnies' meaning of the difference of "form" is that he drew a contrast in the relation of person understood as integral to and formed by a collective of some sort and person understood as individual agent who acts with effects, whether intended in whole or in part or not at all. The interrelated notions of "mutuality" and "reciprocity" are basic to his conceptual distinction. They are implicated in each individual person, just as they are implicated in any relation of one person to another. Tönnies began the second part of his treatise (entitled "The Forms of Human Will") with this:

> Der Begriffe des menschlichen Willens, dessen richtige Auffassung der ganze Inhalt dieser Abhandlung erfordert, soll in einem doppelten Sinne verstanden werden. Da alle geistige Wickung als menschliche durch die Teilnahme des Denkens bezeichnet wird, so unterscheide ich: den Willen, sofern in ihm das Denken, und das Denken, sofern darin der Wille enthalten ist. Jeder stelt ein zusammenhaengendes Ganzes vor, worin die Mannigfalltigkeit des Gefuehle, Triebe, Begierden ihre Einheit hat; welche Einheit aber in dem ersten Begriffe als in reale or naturaliche, in dem anderen als eine ideelle oder gemachte Verstanden werden muss. Den Willen des Menschen in jener Bedeutung nenne ich seinen Wesenwille; in dieser: seinen Kürwillen.[66]

My translation:

> The concept of the human will—on the correct comprehension of which the entire content of this treatise depends—should be understood in a twofold sense. Since all geistige [spiritual, mental] winding [wrapping, casing, envelopment] is designated as human through [by means of, owing to] the participation of thinking, I distinguish: the will insofar as thinking is within it, and thinking insofar as the will is contained in it. Each one presents a coherent whole in which the manifoldness of the feelings, instincts, desires has its unity; but which unity in the first conception as in real or natural understanding, in the other as an ideational or mediated [made, imaginal] understanding. In [terms of] that [first-described] meaning I call the will of "Man" his essential or natural will; in this [latter meaning], his chosen or deliberated will.

Although Tönnies generally avoided an explicit vocabulary of "dialectics," my understanding of his orientation is that he was attempting a dialectical conceptualization. He did not in the above passage intend an endorsement of the Spinozan motto, *voluntas atque intellectus unum et idem sunt* ("will and intellect are one and the same');[67] rather, that each depends upon and forms the other, the ratio between them being variable, conditional, and conditioned. In this way, Tönnies was more Hegelian than Hobbesian.

Tönnies' position on several major issues was a bit unusual for the time (1887); less so, today. Peter Berger, for instance, began his sociological study of religion (1967, p. 3) with the claim that society is "a human product, and nothing but a human product, that yet continuously acts upon its producers." This was, needless to say, not commensurate with the theory of society championed by the Christian church (not "even" Martin Luther's version, though perhaps close to John Milton's view), and some social scientists today would take strong exception to it, which fact perhaps makes all the more remarkable that Ferdinand Tönnies was trying to say something very much like that (and rather different from the stodgy image that was later visited upon him

---

[66] As before, this is from the fifth edition (p. 85), published in 1922 (the edition used by Loomis; his translation at p. 103).

[67] However, as Jacoby observed in a footnote in Tönnies (1974, p. 231 n. 9), the second part of his treatise at one time carried as preface Spinoza's formula.

45

by sociologists, among others).[68]  In applauding the seventeenth-century "demolition of the anthropomorphic hypothesis," Tönnies was referring the medieval Christian doctrine according to which "Man" had been made in the image of the Christian God, and all of Nature for "Man's" benefit and thus a reflection of human needs and wants.

## §5.  New Philosophical Phenomenologies, and Still the Objectivity Question

The various notions of a "constructivism," whether as that which can be seen in the argument of Tönnies (1887) or in Berger's (1967) involution (in mathematical sense of the word) of a religious modality as operative of society as a whole, or in Niklas Luhmann's (2012 [1997]) similarly involuted referentialism—the German edition of this book was entitled by Luhmann as *Die Gesellschaft der Gesellschaft*—has not been comforting to all who profess a discipline of the social sciences.  A preference to discover, or to recover, "the *real* object" in place of facsimiles concocted in human consciousness retained potency of promise.  The succession in European philosophy from Husserl's repeated futility of efforts to design a transcendent phenomenology to Martin Heidegger's effort to plumb the depths of "being and time" as if in quest for a success that would redeem medieval wagers on essence told numerous social scientists, especially young generations of them, that the promise of that potency could be made good.  Thus, new theoretical perspectives began to compete for audience—for instance, a "phenomenological sociology" that could accomplish more than Kant's phenomenology (i.e., only empirical descriptions of states of affairs), an "existential sociology" that could do more than simply say "No," and so forth.

Husserl's initial presentation of his efforts of phenomenological investigation—namely, *Logical Investigations* (1970 [1900-01])—proposed an inquiry into "structures of consciousness" as capable of apprehending objects external to itself.  Not incidentally, this had been a time of some major advances in theories of analytical logic.  For example, Georg Cantor and others developed a set theory (also known as the theory of aggregates) that led to a point-set typology of space and many other inventions, in an explosive growth of tools in an analytic language that has proved to be very useful in analyses of complex problems, and Alfred North Whitehead and Bertrand Russell were moved to prepare what they thought to be the definitive account of all mathematical logic (*Principia Mathematica*, 1910-13).  Recall, too, that major advances were underway in the main physical sciences.  A positivist bent in philosophy was prevalent and increasingly influential in light of scientific developments that could be presented as entirely "post-metaphysical"—that is, as no longer dependent on (concepts of) things that had never been directly experienced (i.e., empirical to observation and, at least in principle, measurement), "things" such as Newton's "æther," for example, and Henri Bergson's "vital force."  By the same token, however, some self-described phenomenologists felt under pressure to demonstrate that consciousness was (is) not epiphenomenal, a concern that the positivists among them ignored by virtue of their assumption of "special powers" of "knowing what is."  Husserl had felt that call, and he was nothing if not tenacious.  After several attempts that he himself agreed had fallen short, he remained ever ready to try again.  Eventually fatigue gave way to despair.

According to his Vienna Lecture of 1935, delivered in a two-day sequence before the Vienna Cultural Society (and published the following year), Husserl despaired of the future of

---

[68] In his postscript to Tönnies 1974 (p. 250), Jacoby referred fittingly to Tönnies' "general constructionist theory" (a nomination that was hardly usual at the end of the nineteenth century.

science because science suffered, as the rest of European culture, from a "sickness of the soul." Now toward the end of his career (and his life; he died three years later), and having witnessed truly sickening events in his homeland and beyond, Husserl was determined to make a trenchant diagnosis for future benefit. The sickness was moral, to be sure, but its roots lay in the loss of a classical rationalism, a loss which he saw as having begun with Descartes, if not before. As a result of that loss, modern science had been reduced to a positivism that could explain little of the world, including itself. But he recognized that positivism was itself a consequence of a much deeper problem, and that was radical skepticism. Husserl had tried again and again to build a transcendental phenomenology, a mode of inquiry that would achieve understanding of the true objective foundations of human life, free of the disease of the soul. Each attempt had failed, as each attempt came up against the very dilemma that Kant had explained. Husserl could not fairly be described as a champion of Kant, and it is not clear how thoroughly he understood Kant's work. But he had seen early in his career the failure to answer effectively the challenge posed by Hume,[69] and it was Hume whose main work, the *Treatise*, most inflamed Husserl, as is evident from his lecture in Vienna. By Husserl's reading (which appears to have been almost willfully superficial), Hume had nullified the very possibility of knowledge of objective reality, asserting that all reality is but a tissue of fictions.

But let's take a brief step back, to give Husserl his due. Some commentators have said that Husserl began his own project by accepting the arguments of Hume and then Kant. That is accurate insofar as Husserl understood the predicament left by Kant after his effort to answer Hume. Thus, Husserl's meaning of the specific "crisis" in the title of the book that came from his Vienna lecture. But one should not be misled into thinking that Husserl agreed with either Hume or Kant in the final analysis. To the contrary. He (1970 [1936], §13) said of Hume's skepticism that it was "nonsense." He did understand the argument by Kant that all objectivity was (is) constituted as a result of subjective activity, but he identified that as a false psychology which had become the profession of a new naïve realism. Husserl's intended answer was a restoration of access to the reality that must exist in order for skepticism, even Hume's most radical skepticism, to have meaning. The key to that access was Husserl's (1970 [1936], §§13, 54) notion of a "functioning subjectivity" which itself exists behind or beneath any conceivable psychology in an intentionality that is both collective and anonymous. It operates in its own "hiddenness."

How Husserl himself came to know that was and remains, of course, a mystery. Indeed, as some commentators have remarked, there is enough of a change of "attitude" between his Vienna lecture of 1935 and his earlier work to generate an ambiguity as to how his *Crisis* book was intended: did it manifest a change in approach, or in mode of presentation, or in his project of a "transcendental phenomenology"? I have no opinion regarding those alternative answers, other than to say, first, that Husserl's effort had previously been one of repeated "renewals" or "new beginnings" and, second, that his Vienna lecture shows evidence of frustration. There are good reasons for frustration, even anger and fear: his world of the German academy was being destroyed by Nazism and its anti-Semitic and anti-intellectual, nativistic assaults. Husserl could

---

[69] See Quentin Lauer's translation of Husserl's early essay, "Philosophy as rigorous science" (Husserl 1965 [1910-11]), as well as the five lectures published by Walter Biemel as Husserl 1964 (1950).

well have feared that time for making his argument more successful in convincing others of his privileged access to the "true" or "real reality" that he believed he understood was rapidly closing. In 1935, in Vienna as well as in Berlin, other actors who also were claiming privileged access, although of a rather different kind, were winning the day. Perspective is crucial. A very short time ago William J T Mitchell, a foremost theorist of artistic sensibility and intelligibility, observed that the dominant "world picture" had changed—an observation that most if not all of us today can say has been one of personal experience. Mitchell (2011, p. 253) was struck by an "emergence" of a world picture that "has become incredibly clear, realistic, and information-saturated." While you and I may easily agree in a mutual recognition of that experience along with Mitchell, a moment's reflection will surely suggest that Leonardo da Vinci could well have said the same statement half a century earlier, and perhaps Aristotle eighteen centuries before that. Those worlds were replete with information, too. They, too, seemed clear and realistic. It was probably then, too, in each of those times-places, a "world picture" seen most clearly and with greatest realism of information content by observers most intelligently capable, observers with greater conceptual vocabularies, greater perceptual experiences, greater wealth of first-hand accomplishments of information.[70]

It is clear to me, however, that Husserl's point of departure had been a firm conviction in an objective reality of his own comprehension of that which truly exists independently of any human knower. It was this very conviction that had repeatedly brought him face to face with his own image in Kant's mirror, the transcendental Illusion (which Husserl in effect had attributed to Humean skepticism). Moreover, Husserl attributed the success of Hume's poisonous potion to a deceitfulness: "Hume takes care, throughout his whole presentation [i.e., the *Treatise*], blandly to disguise or interpret as harmless his absurd results" (Husserl 1970 [1936], §23). Suffice to say, Husserl's efforts succumbed to his own diagnoses of inadequacy (which led him on a sequence of "starting over" again and again), as well as to the sometimes scathing evaluation by one of his principal students, Martin Heidegger.[71]

This is even less the place to survey the complexities of Heidegger's works, beginning with his initial opus magnum, *Being and Time* (1927). Once again we are left with an effort—in in this instance one that mixes penetrating insights with scattered infusions of a mysticism from some unexplicated reserve—that its own author found to be inadequate to the task. Evidence of

---

[70] In referring to the "information-saturated" world of his own experience, Mitchell added parenthetically that "every inch of the world has now been scanned, and is searchable." We surely do understand that judgment as one that neither Leonardo nor Aristotle *could* have made. But would either man have agreed about the judgment of his own world in his own terms of reference?

[71] I confess that I have no special insight into Husserl's motives or his actual understanding of Hume or Kant. One of my longtime friendly critics has argued that Husserl understood very well, and as first-person experience, Hume's main point about perception, and that this accounted for his "exasperation" long before 1935. In any case, it should also be made clear that I do not regard Husserl alone in his rejection of Humean skepticism or in his desire to erect a barrier against the knowing subject as contaminant of assertions of claims of knowledge of "that which is in itself." He has had much subsequent company, and from a variety of ideological positions (although not always as pointedly focused on Hume), from Horkheimer and Adorno (2002 [1969]) to Bellah, Madsen, Sullivan, Swidler, and Tipton (1985), and Taylor (1989), among others. Discussion of "authority of voice" issues will continue in later Parts.

that diagnosis is less explicit here than in the case of Husserl, but it can be appreciated from a few statements. One of them occurs in Heidegger's major effort to continue and extend the line of inquiry undertaken in *Being and Time*—namely, the 1927 Marburg lectures, publication of which (as volume 24 of his collected works) he withheld until 1975, months before his death, probably because of his own evaluation of inadequacy. This volume was translated into English as *The Basic Problems of Phenomenology* (1982). Heidegger closed this work with what can be best described as an embarrassed look back to Kant, whom he called "the first and last scientific philosopher in the grand style since Plato and Aristotle"—in Heidegger's cultural lexicon a very high accolade (1982 [1975], p. 328). Having taken Kant as his most important modern predecessor, the "thinker" who had advanced understanding the most since the ancient Greeks, Heidegger seemingly struggled to acknowledge that he had not made good on his critique of Kant's understanding and thereby overcome its insufficiency in order to restore ontology. He regarded his phenomenology as superior to others, including that of the Marburg school (of what had already come to known as a neo-Kantianism), which, he said, in merely ignoring the limits that Kant had demonstrated, had actually regressed from Kant's advanced understanding. The superiority of his own phenomenology, Heidegger avowed, could be appreciated by the fact that it was nothing less than "the method of ontology."

Heidegger had proposed a work entitled *The Scientific Method of Ontology and the Idea of Phenomenology*, the main task of which was to be a careful detailed statement of the method that, he said, he had been using all along (Heidegger 1975, p. 467). Given his remarks, which include an outline of the proposed book, it appears that he had planned, somewhat as Husserl had before him, to begin again at the beginning of his investigation of the temporality of *his* thinking vis-à-vis that which had been enacted as philosophical argument in preceding efforts of a metaphysics. The work was never completed, however, and by all known evidence probably never undertaken. No one, it appears, knows why it was not produced—or, if produced for Heidegger himself, apparently never revealed to others. My suspicion—and it can be only that— is that crucial self-reflexivity stood in the way. In order to explicate one's method of inquiry in a way that is useful, one must be very clear and systematic about the processual steps and how they fit together into an explanatory whole, from basic premises to final persuasive conclusion. The task amounts to a meta-discourse with one's prior self and that self's conditions and context. But, to the extent that the achievement of that prior self was productive (i.e., self-instructive), a translational bridge must be built, and it is nearly inevitable (again, depending on effect that prior instruction) that this effort at bridging will reveal lacunae and inconsistencies, even some logical contradictions, that previously had escaped notice. One notable site for Heidegger would surely require that he be systematically clear in some terminological matters that, to this day, remain impenetrably obscure. More generally, the obstacle was, I suspect, integral to his own thinking of his supposed *Urwissenschaft*, as he called it—namely, "original science," science without any ontic presuppositions. After all, his task required, by his own diagnosis, that he resolve the dilemma left in wake of Kant, by refounding ontology so as to avoid "the turn to the subject" and its train of problems such as a seemingly unquenchable skepticism. Heidegger's *Urwissenschaft* had to begin at the presencing of (to use a phrase important to Theodor Wiesengrund Adorno) the "primacy of the Objekt"—as if *that* was not an ontic presupposition.

This matter of what is primary and what is secondary is hardly a new concern. Was there anything new to say? If there was, what difference did it make to the claim of order? Before turning to Adorno's project, and then to other efforts in his wake, I want to recall some efforts by theorists of social science to explicate what became known as (indeed, virtually celebrated as) "the problem of order."

## §6. Ordered Relations within and of Sociality[72]

In his tome on the structure of social action Talcott Parsons (1937, pp. 89-94) named Thomas Hobbes as the first to understand and attempt to formulate systematically "the problem of order" as the basic issue of theory—in Parsons' terms (not Hobbes') a theory of social action. Parsons devoted five pages to Hobbes' account. The importance of these five pages is partly underscored by the fact that the phrase, "problem of order," was a persistent focus of Parsons' own efforts of theorization until late in his book. Judging by the fact that this phrase accounted for more entries in the index of his book than any other concept (or name), it could be accorded the stature of at least one of the most important themes running throughout his theoretical project. In his terms, it figured in the most important problems faced by the social sciences, and indeed by modern society, as the failure of "Spencerian theory" had become evident. The central thesis of Herbert Spencer's theoretical work, oriented by a perspective of positivism and utilitarianism, had been an inevitability of progressive evolution in and of modern society.[73] But by 1937 it was evident that something had gone wrong. The failure of industrialism to ensure progress via advanced applications of "an automatic, self-regulating mechanism which operated so that the pursuit by each individual of his own self-interest and private ends would result in the greatest possible satisfaction of the wants of all" was plain for all to see, Parsons (1937, p. 4) concluded, and in the views of scholars who, though "still comparatively few, are getting more and more of a hearing," society was "at or near a turning point." The "danger of conflict," to use one of Parsons' (1937, p. 89) phrases in description of Hobbes' work, added special gravity to the task of gaining a better understanding of "the problem of order," or the conditions under which society "holds together." This theme of a "problem of order" and motivating concerns about the stability and durability of society has persisted into the twenty-first century. Apprehensions of nuclear annihilation and of devastating climate change have provided much sharper point to the concerns,

---

[72] As a reminder about the power of small words (prepositions), I mean both "within" and "of," because the ordering of relations *within* a group, for instance, or other formation will tend also to be the effect the ordering of relations *of* the group. To state the point generally, any process of a sociality takes place within sociality; likewise, any process within sociality is of sociality. In prior publications (Hazlerigg 1989a, 1989b, 1995) I used slash marks in an effort to communicate this dialectical relation, hoping to avoid, for example, that saying X is of Y did not exclude that X could also be by Y, in Y, and so forth, allowing the play of dialectical relations rather than an implied exclusion as in an analytic logic of "clear and distinct," conceptually independent categories. Post-publication I learned from friendly critics that my effort stimulated irritation much more than, and often to the exclusion of, the desired gain of understanding. The irritation was expressed by one critic as, "It seemed to me you just couldn't make up your mind about which it is!"

[73] It would be a stretch to say that Spencer had a specific theory, as distinguished from a theoretical orientation. But that could be said of the work of many scholars who are typically identified as "theorist." Whereas Parsons began his book by asking rhetorically, "Who now reads Spencer?" some critics later asked the same of Parsons. What been said of novelists can be said just as well of others, including social scientists: generational succession can be cruel.

no doubt. But Parsons' announcement in 1937, as Hobbes' treatises nearly 300 years earlier, demonstrate that the concerns were substantial long before anyone had learned of either the power of an atomic bomb or the power of simpler activities to profoundly change what most people had assumed to be an independent nature.

Parsons was a rising star in 1937, and soon after the end of World War II his star reached its apex in the US academy. For more than a decade he was the leading social theorist within US sociology. Ironically, given the notice he had given to dangers of conflict for the maintenance of order in 1937, one specific reason for his star's diminuition was the partly unfair (because not wholly correct) criticism of "Parsonian theory" as silent on matters of conflict. In any event, for present purposes it is notable that one lasting effect of his early discussions of "the problem of order" was adoption of that theme—at least the phrase, if not always clearly one and the same concept—by scholars some of whom were among his more prominent critics. Perhaps the most prominent single example came to light in a paper published by Dennis H Wrong in 1961 in the *American Sociological Review*, "The oversocialized conception of man in modern sociology." Wrong, a decade Parsons' junior, followed nearly a quarter of a century later with a more extended treatment of the importance of "the problem of order," saying that the problem was "many-sided" not simply in the sense of many threats to peace and security, within and without, but also in the sense of the complexity of the notion itself (Wrong 1994). As his chosen subtitle says, "what unites and divides society" is more complicated than allowed by the rule of analytic logic which holds that the copula must be purely functional, empty of all substance (i.e., prohibition of "an undivided middle"). What unites can also divide and what divides can also unite. The complexity is housed, as Benedict Anderson (1983) said to an audience far too small, in the dialectical relations of "*imagined communities*" (e.g., "nation," "society," and the like; my emphasis).[74]

Hobbes' first sentence in his treatise of a *Leviathan* (1909 [1651]) caught the attention of most readers of his day: "Nature (the art whereby God hath made and governs the world) is by the art of man, as in many other things, so in this also imitated, that it can make an artificial animal"; and Hobbes then proceeded to make clear that he meant no depreciation of art or artificing, referring to the Christian God as ""the Artificer." Next comes a key passage of his introduction: "Art … [imitates] that rational and most excellent work of Nature, *man*. For by art is created that great Leviathan called a Commonwealth or State (in Latin, civitas), which is but an artificial man, though of greater stature and strength than the natural, for whose protection and defence it was intended." A major part of Hobbes's undertaking, he promised his reader, would be to describe "the nature of this artificial man." This was very far from customary discourse in London, or in Britain generally—or for that matter in Europe as a whole, during the middle of the seventeenth century—and it quickly became controversial.

Some of the controversy remained alive three centuries later, despite Hobbes' evident care to make some intended meanings clear. For instance, he said that "society" is "artificial."

---

[74] Andrew Abbott (2016, ch. 7) has contributed a useful review of conceptions and disciplinary histories about "the problem of order," which will come into play below, in Parts Four and Five. See also Bourdieu 1990 (1982).

Despite his use of the same adjective in regard to the Christian God, the statement about society being "artificial" has led some readers to think that Hobbes meant to deprecate *modern* society.[75] The implied attribution is that Hobbes regarded "artificial" as less "real" or less "good" than that which is "natural," when in fact he explicitly regarded "the artificial" (or, more carefully, some formations that are "artificial") as a definite improvement over "the state of nature."

Artifice refers to human invention (though without the heroicism that every invention is to a particular inventor)—that is, to human production of a state of affairs. Society (among other "things") is "artificial," by Hobbes' account, because it consists in agreements in and to de facto "contracts" or "covenants"—in particular, for his concern, agreement among persons who freely consent to monopolization of violence by one person (monarch) or one group of persons (an oligarchy or, in principle though Hobbes was dubious, even a republican legislature) in return for a promise of security within the territory and against attack from without. This was not a novel idea, to be sure. But in the context of Hobbes' book it was both controversial (though mainly because it seemed that he had given too much credence and import to "commoners," not because of his attribution of artifice) and an extended explanation of the stability afforded by monarchal wisdom, a welcome fillip of confidence to many readers and listeners in mid-century London, and Britain generally, who were weary of the civil wars which began early in 1642, led to execution of the monarch, Charles I, in 1649, and then resumed in brief outbreaks in 1650 and 1651.

With that background in mind, one can concur with Parsons in saying that Hobbes' work was concerned with "order." What is of greater interest, however, is that Hobbes propounded a particular will-based theory of social action, featuring his version of contract theory, and with a centerpiece that, in a manner of speaking, strode out as this "artificial man." The distinction between what is "natural" and what is "artificial," although of some note to Hobbes, is another, and misleading, matter, and will be ignored here. As others have pointed out, his conception was useful to his analysis of differences of the productive or creative lines of action, and that will be my focus. Hobbes also drew a difference between "primary" and "secondary" actions, which, although an interesting development, I will leave to the side (see, e.g., Pitkin 1967; Copp 1980).

It is easy to think that Hobbes' "problem of order" had only to do with the business of war and peace. While certainly of relevance, that is *not* what is so interesting today. Rather, the interesting parts are (1) his theory of "artificial person" and (2) that part of his discussion of "order" that could answer also to the phrase, "the problem of scale." I will briefly address each of these in turn. First, the "artificial person."

Individual human beings, persons, act, whether well or ill, peacefully or warlike, intentionally or habitually, and so forth. There is no news in that; and there was no news in that for Hobbes and his readers. The "news" (at least for modern Europe and European-derived cultures) had to do with two relations. One is the relation of "artificial" vis-à-vis "natural"; the

---

[75] This careless reading is analogous to the careless treading that has Karl Marx believing capitalism an abomination that should never have been invented, when in fact he regarded it as a stepping stone—by one reading a necessary stage—to a next and better organization of society, leading eventually to his (vaguely conceptualized) ideal.

other, the relation of "one and the many," which will be dealt with below. Some of what Hobbes had to say about the "artificial person" is inconsistent, mainly between his account in *Leviathan* and his account in *On Man* (1972 [1658]).[76] As with others, I prefer the internal consistency and relative clarity of the latter presentation, although the bigger impression followed from Hobbes' prior book. In chapter 15 of *On Man* Hobbes defined "person" as "he to whom the words and actions of men are attributed, either his own or another's: if his own, the person is natural; in another's, it is artificial." The salient point is Hobbes' notion of "the natural" as prior to any human action (despite the fact that no human being comes to life without parents, who are always already inescapably social beings), as different from "the artificial" as a being which in some way to some degree drives from human action. Hobbes' concern was not primarily with that difference as such, however, but with an application of the distinction. Specifically, a collective can be an artificial person insofar as the actions of any humans are ever attributed to it (Hobbes 1972 [1658], p. 83).

The category, "artificial person," includes three sub-categories: (1) collectivities of natural persons; (2) collectivities of artificial persons; and (3) an inanimate thing insofar as it has requirements that are met by human actions involving the state (about which, more below). In order to follow the meaning of Hobbes' account, one must keep in mind his conception of the limits of human knowledge. These limits are of several kinds, but one of the most consequential has to do with perception: "Ignorance of remote causes, disposeth men to attribute all events, to the cause immediate, and Instrumentall: For these are all the causes they perceive." The myopia can be overcome (to the extent that it can be) only through applications of reason in inference.[77] Even so, outcomes can be problematic. Thus, for example, we must consider that humans "cannot distinguish, without study and great understanding, between one action of many men, and many actions of one multitude." The concept, "artificial person," can aid in making coherent that distinction and its implications. In Hobbes' general illustration of the explanatory point, we read that "the will of God is not known save through the state, and … it is required that the will of Him that is represented be the author of the actions performed by those who represent Him, it needs be that God's person be created by the will of the state." Now, "the state" is known to be a collective actor, and as such is an artificial person. Actions of the state are performed by official persons of the state, who are themselves natural persons but when acting as representatives of the state are acting as artificial persons whether individually or collectively. The words and actions attributed to this person are not his own, strictly speaking, but those of the state which he or she represents. Therefore, by Hobbes' definition, this official person is an artificial person. Moreover (as mentioned above): "Even an inanimate thing can be a person, that is it can have

---

[76] Note that the English translation of this work consists only in the last six chapters, which is not problematic for present purposes, since the chapters not included are chiefly about optics. Optical perception was a topic of much interest during the middle and later decades of the seventeenth century (Newton wrote a major treatise on optics, for example), in large part because of technical developments of telescopy (e.g., Galileo's reports) and of microscopy (work leading to Anton van Leeuwenhoek).

[77] As Hobbes (1909 [1651], p. 259) put it, "Time, and Industry, produce every day new knowledge. And as the art of all building, is derived from principles of Reason, observed by industrious men, that had long studied the nature of materials, and the divers effects of figure, and proportion, long after mankind began (though poorly) to build."

possessions and other goods, and can act in law, as in the case of a temple, a bridge, or of anything whatsoever that needs money for its upkeep. And caretakers constituted by the state bear its person, so that it hath no will except that of the state" (Hobbes 1972 [1658], pp. 79, 80, 85).

In sum, we see Hobbes laying groundwork that would lead to legal codes giving standing as legal subjects, equivalent in law to "natural persons," to collective actors such as offices of the state, private or public corporations, partnerships, and similar other entities, all deemed to be "artificial persons" in law. The interim to Oliver Wendell Holmes, Jr., and fellow jurists would be filled with various legal theories, most if not all of them will-based, as was Hobbes' theory of action (whether the will in question be that of a natural person or that ultimately of the state). But this one development within Hobbes' will-based theory would be basic to later revisions of legal codes that had become incapable of resolving disputes based on assumptions of willful decisions, revisions that centered on an artificial person determined by the state as a normal expectation of rationality (a sort of statistical average, known as "a reasonable man"; about which, more later).

Such, in brief, is the relation of "artificial" vis-à-vis "natural" at the center of Hobbes' theory. The other important relation which I mentioned above, the relation of number (or the quantity/quality dialectic) as expressed, for instance, in the relation of "the unitary" vis-à-vis "a multitude," is also explicit and central in his theory. Recall from the discussion just above that Hobbes' remarked the difficulty of distinguishing between "one action of many men and many actions of one multitude," which he then (1909 [1651], p. 79) illustrated by comparing the death of Catiline and the death of Caesar.

While Hobbes explicated the relation of number in terms of his concept of "artificial person," his discussion in a few passages suggests also a concern for what has become known as "the problem of scale" (or a certain meaning of "scale effect"). Collective actors there had been before (as Hobbes referenced with his distillations from ancient Rome). But little attention had been given, especially in terms of will theory, to the processes by which the acts (including the decisions, intentions, etc.) of individual persons could be said to be the acts of the collectivity *as such*. The acts of an individual person accumulate in time, and these somehow intersect with and survive (or not) in effects that also accumulate across space (person to person) as well as across time (person-events). Now, having engaged that complex thought, imagine the conditions under which the person-level acts, as temporally accumulated *intra*-person effects that might or might not become *inter*-person effects, undergo a qualitative change, thereby becoming more than a quantitative sum of events, achieving the status, the authority, of this "artificial person" either as a single or unitary actor or as a collective actor. *That* was "the problem of order" with which Hobbes' work was centrally concerned. The written text is not always clear; where sufficiently clear, it is not always consistent. But, for the time and place, it was a new undertaking (so far as I can tell), obviously motivated by matters of war and peace but far more general in scope than those matters. This will be a major topic of discussion and development later in this volume (see also Hazelrigg 1991).

Now back to Parsons' "problem of order": what exactly does that phrase mean? Can one imagine a society that completely *lacks* order? Surely one can imagine a society that is in some or many ways "*dis*ordered," but on closer inspection it is apparent that there is an order to the disorder. As the ancient Greeks knew, and as we moderns have relearned through the aid or, one might say, the prosthetic of mathematical reason, "even" chaos has an order. None of us living today have had direct experience with the tumult of civil war in England during Hobbs' time; we know about it, perhaps can experience it vicariously, through histories, and in some instances biographies, autobiographies, and diaries of participants. But we do have direct experiences of the chaos of war, or of a society unraveling as Zimbabwe has done over a period of years, or of a society re-creating itself in disastrous ways as the Nazi movement in Germany achieved initially through electoral means. And we do see in those experiences the presence of *orders*, orders of relations—not a single unified order, to be sure, but orders that are in fact observed, at least partly and for at least some shorter or longer period of time in this or that setting, with identifiable other actors engaged along with oneself, whether in promotion of or opposition to the ordering. Rules come and go; actors come and go; situations are more or less in flux and sometimes "helter skelter," careening, it seems, into total collapse; levels of confidence and fear and pessimism/optimism fluctuate along with the situations, the actors, the rules. But it is very difficult to find a complete lack of order, a total, persistent lack of ordered relations (except sometimes in one's panic, times when reciting the multiplication table as fast as one can will restore a sense of order and thus function).

Following Wrong's locution, one could agree that the main question implied in "the problem of order" is many-sided, and the answer will have as many sides. Human relations can be fragile, no doubt (see, e.g., Wrong 1994, p. 45).[78] Even institutions can break, lose effective function. But the duration of loss is usually short and the breakage reparable. Gradual decay of function is a greater danger, in part because it is less noticeable as "an event" and in part because distinguishing between loss of the traditional or habitual and decay as such is sometimes vexed. But institutionalized order is in general both resilient and adaptive to new conditions and/or new aspirations. Again, think of Zimbabwe. Much did collapse, and throngs of people suffered. Monetary inflation reached levels not theretofore experienced; and yet the exchange economy did not completely fail, as residents of localities worked out their own means of negotiating exchange values. Piracy, burglary, and thievery became rampant, but this never approached the scale of the governmental kleptocracy that had been endured for decades, and much of it functioned as an alternative means of redistribution of wealth. Poverty increased, public and private health suffered enormously, and life expectancy declined. But Zimbabwe survived as a society, however destitute and ravaged from within.

Recall that Wrong (1961) sought to challenge what he termed "the oversocialized conception of man" as also "the overintegrated view of society." In the context of that time, one should remember, a major motivation within US sociology in particular stemmed from strong

---

[78] Wrong (1994, pp. 44-45) made an important point about "thingification"—our tendency to imagine bundles of relations as each a distinct "thing" on the model of Newtonian mechanics. We now acknowledge that Newtonian "things" are mostly "empty space" and energy fields. See below, Part Five.

dislike of Parsons' brand of theorizing.[79] Wrong's position was formulated at least in part in reaction to what was widely seen as Parsons' lack of attention to conflict, deviance, and what Hume called "elbow room." Parsons to the side, however, if the understanding from which Wrong wrote was that there was too little latitude in the actuality of US society for deviance, or for conflict, or for individual idiosyncrasy, empirical evidence abundantly indicated otherwise. Moreover, actions that are regarded in any given culture at any given time as deviant are in fact part of a social order: they are "deviant" by virtue of the fact of being at odds with an order, and they may well be concordant with another existing order (i.e., other than the officially approved and permitted order). Likewise, in most if not all societies conflict is not only present; there are usually official channels for its regular conduct, and where conflict spills outside those bounds, and/or deliberately challenges them, the contest is typically a matter of different and conflicting orders (i.e., not a contest between "*the* order" and an absence of order). Indeed, conflictive and deviant actions are not only parts of a social order (i.e., the one that considers them as deviant or conflictive, or both); they are, as already noted, sometimes integral to an alternative order, one subordinate to the dominant order, and this subordinate order typically presents, and in some way to some degree seeks to enforce, its own normativities. The fact of social movements offers abundant illustration. Think, for example, of the movement now called "primitive Christianity," its presence within Rome and other parts of the empire before winning allegiance of more than localities of Roman subjects (see, e.g., Meeks 2003); or the reformation initiated by Martin Luther, among others; or the diverse movements among the youth of the USA during the 1960s (movements qualitatively precedented though perhaps quantitatively different by greater liberty). Developments that perhaps do not count by convention as "social movements" nonetheless have also displayed abundant evidence of conflict. Think, for example, of the alarms engendered by the growing habit of "silent reading" during the seventeenth and eighteenth centuries, a habit that raised issues of "social order" in general via expectations of policing the mind and the body (see, e.g., Darnton 1986; Chartier 2007 [2005], pp. 107-113). Goulemot's (1991, p. 72) comment was offered with serious intent (if also with tongue slightly in cheek): "the reading of the licentious book is in effect exemplary of all reading, and perhaps of all writing."

Moreover, there are indeed empirically extant orders that do not express normative expectations in any direct way but are instead either outcomes approximating a random walk or aggregate orders that display attraction to a distributional basin (e.g., regression to mean).[80] In either type of case, the underlying person actors may well, usually do, observe some degree of normative expectation. It is difficult *not* to observe, to enact, normative expectations. But they might not be uniform across actors, and they need not be expressed in the actual effects of

---

[79] I shared the dislike (see, e.g., Cohen, Hazelrigg, and Pope 1975). However, I thought some of the criticism was miscast, oversimplified and/or exaggerated.

[80] As Tuma and Hannan (1984) remarked, "random walk" models can be useful as rough approximation of human actions, but some aggregated outcomes, such as the trend of some price-setting actions, are closely approximated as a random walk. However, they (1984, pp. 96-115) also described semi-Markov versions of a continuous-time random walk that have promising applications (see also, Coleman 1964, chs. 5 and 8; Gill and Straka 2016).

action—which is to say that actual effects do not necessarily reflect motives or intentions of the given actor.

Consider the basic premise of the "problem of order"—namely, a presupposition of a presence of an already fully formed and capable individual person, from which one then asks how it is possible that this creature can form and submit to a social order. (Note: one could also say "political order" and so forth.) In other words, "the social," and in larger scale "society," may be regarded only secondarily, viewed as a supplement, an acquired "added fact." This view has been a main characteristic of will theories of human nature and human realities. If the notion that "man" is never "fully socialized" is thought to be attested by the fact that Hobbesian "war of all against all" is possible, empirical evidence in support of that alleged fact is missing. To begin with, the text that Hobbes wrote is not without important ambiguity. Let's begin with his definition of "war," stated in his essay *De Corpore* (On the Body), published in 1655 (i.e., after *Leviathan*):

> Seeing then to the offensiveness of man's nature one to another, there is added a right of every man to every thing, whereby one man invadeth with right, and another man with right resisteth, and men live thereby in perpetual diffidence, and study how to preoccupate each other; the estate of men in this natural liberty, is the state of war. For *war* is nothing else but that time wherein the will and contention of contending by force, is either by words or actions sufficiently declared; and the time which is not war, is *peace* (Hobbes 1839-45 [1655], §11).

If this is "war of all against all," it is remarkably broad in scope. One could easily include within the bounds of this "perpetual diffidence" social relations that we otherwise call "competition," "disagreement," and "conflict" of nonlethal varieties. Did Hobbes intend such inclusions? The text is not clear. That he did intend to include *lethal* conflict is told in the very next section: "The estate of hostility and war being such, as thereby nature itself is destroyed, and men kill one another ..."—hardly surprising, given his distress at the long bout of civil war recently ended. But that very memory raises the other aspect of the "missing empirical evidence" that I referred to above: did he literally mean each and every individual human being against each and every other individual human being, or did he mean groups or collections (as in "armed forces" or "armies") fighting each other? The basic conception of "human nature" as a pre-social state of nature—a typical conception in Hobbes' time, as before and after, even today in psychologistic theory—did by definition assume the former. Judging by all available evidence, however, this condition has never been recorded as having been observed (excepting perhaps some "science fiction" stories) anywhere at any time. By the other definition, according to which groups fight and attempt to kill each other, there is unfortunately an abundance of evidence. But if war is the process, armed groups that excel in solidarity have the advantage, other factors being equal, and even those with weaker solidarity display social relations of some degree of cooperation, internal conflict, and so forth. While I do not know what counted as standard of "*fully* socialized" in Wrong's account, I do know that effective fighting forces are highly social, that the intensity of sociality increases as the situation becomes more stressful, and that the key to that intensity is trust both in effective leadership and in one's companions. If a form of sociality of greater intensity exists, I do not know what it is.

There remains a question: what *does* hold a society together? This has been at the heart of the topic known as "the problem of order," even though not always explicitly stated. Think of the question in another way, however, shifting downward the scale of application: What holds a contractual relation together? What holds a marriage together? What holds a parent-child relation together? What holds a trail from Point A to Point B together? What holds a conflict between two persons together? In the specificity of these questions we come nearer to Hobbes' concern, I think, and as a result the entire terrain of concern about a "problem of order" (or "cement of society"; Elster 1989) becomes somewhat less mysterious. But only somewhat, because as I signaled in the previous paragraph a major component of the answer to each of those specific questions, as to others of the general kind, is *trust*. This is only to re-ask question, however, since "trust" is itself a social relation. Each of the answers that Elster (1989) offered, as summarized in his concluding chapter, is likewise a repetition of the same basic question (i.e., what is the "cement of society"?). The lesson I chiefly intend from all of this discussion is that, insofar as the topic has to do with human beings, one cannot get behind or beneath sociality, social relations, to a more fundamental existence. I confess I did not invent the lesson. Kant was already there.

Jon Elster (1989, p. 248) began his concluding chapter by saying, "There are no societies, only individuals who interact with each other. Yet the structure of interactions allows us to identify clusters of individuals who interact more strongly with each other than with people in other clusters." Insofar as a given cluster does, relative to the immediately surrounding clusters, evince greater cohesive among its member persons, Elster said, he would call it a "society." But other than that relative standing it had no special significance, and to call it such did not imply a presumption of being "well ordered." By his definition, however, there was presumption that any society could not be contiguous to another society. Or put differently, each society had by definition its own hinterland. Clearly (and explicitly) Elster had been thinking of the Roman empire. But his definition also allowed, at least in principle, a relation of nesting—a cluster of clusters—which perhaps pointed toward the possibility of a society more or less like those collectivities that are called, by common parlance, societies. Insofar as that is true, the task of measuring "relative cohesiveness" on a such a scale is rather daunting. Is Canadian society more cohesive internally than US society? Or is it the other way around? What of Norway vis-à-vis Sweden? And what of Iceland? It must be by default, in terms of Elster's criterion, a society.

Before leaving this section I want to address more directly than before the claim made by Jon Elster (among others) that there "are no societies"—not only in order to clarify my own use of the word (abundantly apparent in previous pages) but also as a prelude to resuming an earlier discussion about effects of the actions of individual persons.

Part of the objection to "society" is locution that treats the referent as a "thing," although this criterion can be applied selectively (e.g., Elster was willing to consider "the state" as a thing, without qualm or qualification). This objection is tightly linked to concerns about "reification," treating as a "thing" that which is not and ending, supposedly, with a vast array of "reified" objects. Anderson was astute in his use of the nomination, "imagined communities," evading or at least leaving open the worry that he might be trading in reifications. Because emotive as well as cognitive burdens are bundled into the notion of "reification"—think of the recurrent tendency to chastise Emile Durkheim for saying that "social facts" have a "thing-like" character—one must be aware of entering treacherous terrain when discussing the notion, so I must try to be as clear as I can be about meaning and intent.[81]

Try as one might, one cannot do without concepts. They are integral to thought, even to emotional states insofar as these are matters of reflection, however private they may be. In any case, a highly useful concept is "thing." Its utility is mainly a function of its relative lack of specificity: so much can be loaded into and transported as "this thing." In other words, it serves as a category of many categories (or a set of many sets, to use a later invention). However, this utility can also be abused insofar as it encourages cognitive laziness. It is worth noting that in all of his *Gesellschaft und Gemeinschaft*, Tönnies (to use an example of a work already cited for its discussion of "society") deployed the word, "Ding," only twice: once referring to "a thing and its constitution" (1887, p. 142); next, "an external thing as a dynamic store of value (money)" (p. 230). In common parlance, one can refer to a contract as a "thing," although more specifically it is or refers to an agreement between two (or more) persons; likewise, a map, a lightning strike, a flight from place to place, and a word. In each instance (as with "contract") the specified "thing" can be rendered still more specifically, and the specification usually a relation of one or another kind.[82] So it is with "society" and "the social," and so forth.

Perhaps this is the appropriate place in which to sketch some of my intentions of concept, with more presentation of terminology to come later. Here, in the remainder of this section, I will focus mainly on "society" and "the social" (or "sociality").

According to Adam Ferguson in his *Essay on the History of Civil Society*, published in 1767, "Every step and every movement of the multitude, even in what are termed enlightened ages, are made with equal blindness to the future, and nations stumble upon establishments, which are indeed the result of human action, but not the execution of any human design." It is not that human beings are unable to form rational schemes for the direction of improved futures, Ferguson (1782 [1767], p. 204) avowed. "Men in general are sufficiently disposed to occupy themselves in forming projects and schemes, but he who would scheme and project for others will find an opponent in every person who is disposed to scheme for himself." The result is not necessarily stalemate. The central point is, however, that the result of such collective relations is seldom predictable, sometimes of short duration, and not necessarily decipherable in retrospect. A few years later Adam Smith made the same general point, which he labelled under the phrase, "invisible hand," in his treatise on the dynamic of wealth creation. In his prior treatise, *A Theory of Moral Sentiments* (which at one time I thought lacked the "invisible hand" phrase though not the concept behind it), Smith got rather carried away with the insight when, near the end of the first volume, he declared that the "rich only select from the heap

---

[81] The charge against Durkheim is in part contextually anachronistic, as he was defending "the social" against the declamations of "nothing but metaphysics" and "epiphenomenalism." These issues of "realism"—what counts as "the real" and why—will be visited repeatedly in subsequent pages.

[82] I am admittedly giving short shrift to a complex topic, "thing." Whether one agrees with his main thesis about the historic advent represented in Aristotle's text, *Categories*, Mann's (2000) study will repay close attention.

what is most precious and agreeable. They consume little more than the poor, and in spite of their natural selfishness and rapacity, though they mean only their own conveniency, though the sole end which they propose from the labours of all the thousands whom they employ, be the gratification of their own vain and insatiable desires, they divide with the poor the produce of all their improvements. They are led by an invisible hand to make nearly the same distribution of the necessaries of life, which would have been made, had the earth been divided into equal portions among all its inhabitants; and thus, without intending it, without knowing it, advance the interest of the society, and afford means to the multiplications of the species (Smith 1817, p. 249).[83]

Unfortunately, Smith's mystical sounding name has tended to dominate attention to obscure the underlying dynamic, thus obscuring it to such an extent that when the same basic dynamic later gained another hearing in Charles Darwin's famous treatise, its recent heritage in disquisitions on political economy often went unremarked.

More recently, the mystical air accorded Smith's invisible hand became linked to a strand of social thought that championed a certain notion of "emergence," one that recalled medieval notions of "spontaneous generation." These latter notions had been dismissed from biological science by the late nineteenth century, but emanations from them continued to swirl in emotive-cognitive interests in "hidden powers" of certain kinds of thought (a form of "conspiracy theory" that harbored hope for humankind in special actors). A strong religious tradition of "revealed truth" had become reworked into a secular (or quasi-secular), somewhat ephemeral promise of hidden messages to be revealed by "deep thought." These strands fed from particular readings of Heidegger's quasi-theological speculations (and emphasis on gerund-forms as indicative of a special mode of thinking), on the one hand, and of Nietzchean imaginations of a new sub-species of Homo sapiens sapiens (the "Overman," or as his term was initially rendered in English, the "Superman"), on the other, some prominent spawns being the fascistic dreams of Ayn Rand, the related quests of Lafayette Ron Hubbard's religious school of Scientology, and similar other fantasies.

In fact, there is nothing mystical or magical about the conceptualizations by Ferguson, Smith, and other theorists of what amounted to early formulations of what I call "the problem of aggregation" (and will discuss later in the book).[84] Robert Novick (1974, pp. 316, 332) gave an account that could erase the confusion, when he wrote of "the spontaneous coordination of the actions of many people," and then said: "It is what grows spontaneously from the individual choices of many people over a long period of time that will be worth speaking eloquently about." That was the extent of his clarification. While I never thought to interrogate him about the word, I assume he intended a straightforward lexical definition of "spontaneous" as "unpremeditated,"

---

[83] Emma Rothschild (1994) has made good clarification of the semantic context and content of Smith's use of the "invisible hand" phrase, noting especially the ironic sense. Note, too, that while Smith has usually been treated as a one-dimensional figure, the first sentence of his *Theory of Moral Sentiments* counters that view quite well.

[84] I do not mean to suggest that I invented either the name, "problem of aggregation," or the concept to which it refers (see, e.g., Hannan 1991, first published in 1971). See Part Five, below.

without any suggestion of mystical powers of emergence. On the other hand, it is curious that he used basically the same phrase a total of four times without variation that would have unloaded a word which he must have known had been invested with strange riders. Friedrich Hayek (1967a, 1967b) did much the same, as if repeating a magical incantation (see Novick 1974, p. 336 n.13).

The basic point of the conceptualization by Ferguson and by Smith is as follows. Persons individually as well as collectively engage in specific actions, whether mainly as habituations or through self-reflection and with explicit (if not always publicly stated) intent. When there is intent, the outcome of the action by any specific person might or might not conform to intended and/or expected outcome.[85] There is nothing new in that formulation. But then consider that all of the outcomes, whether convergent with the given actor's intent and/or expectations or not, go through some sort of aggregation process, and it is *this* process that Ferguson, Smith, Novick, Hayek, and others have tried to highlight. Smith called the process an "as-if invisible hand" as a way of saying "we have little or no idea how this process works; we have not been able to view the aggregation of effects; the process is still a 'black box' to us." Clearly the specific actors did (or could have) acted with premeditation or forethought (and thus "spontaneously"), however well or poorly they deliberated on the anticipated action. But then the consequences of those actions take on "a life of their own," in a manner of speaking. The consequences, or some of them, accumulate in time and during that time interact with each other—that is, consequences that could in principle each be labeled as resulting from this or that specific actor's actions ramify, o could ramify, in interaction with each other—and thus become *new* effects (if they survive at all). Novick (1974, p. 332) said it would be "a long period of time," and no doubt some of the initial consequences do ramify and interact and thus transform repeatedly into a sequence of new effects. But the basic process operates within short intervals, too. Novick's point, presumably, was simply that "*big* effects" typically do not build overnight (so to speak) but occur through the aggregation—or as Novick (1974, p. 316) said, through "the spontaneous coordination"—of the effects of many actors' actions during some period of time. Thus it is that this "coordination" (as if by some invisible hand, or as the ancient Greeks might have said, by the caprice of the gods) can meld together effects of habituated acts as well as effects of acts of premeditated "designs," into a more or less complex tapestry of repetitive outcomes, to a large extent because of the press of institutionalized forms. This will be the specific topic of later sections of the book.

Before moving on, I need to register an additional query about uses of "spontaneous" in the literature of social theory. In addition to the citations indicated above, Elster (1989, p. 250—toward the end of his book on "the cement of society" and in the midst of concluding that all of the ingredients of that "cement" could be summarized as "envy, opportunism (or self-interest with guile, and codes of honour, or the ability to make credible threats and promises"—repeated ostensibly the same formulations by Nozick, Hayek, Adam Smith, and others, now as the question: *"How is spontaneous order possible?"* (Elster's emphasis).

---

[85] By the last five words of that sentence I mean to say that an actor might intend a specific outcome but for one reason for another expect that her or his action might not, or will not, achieve it.

Aside from the swirls of mysticism noted earlier, there *is* a genuine application of the word as technical term in thermodynamic theory, and one of Hayek's papers is suggestive of that application: "Notes on the evolution of systems of rules of conduct." At least since the time of ancient Greek experiments with "heat engines" (e.g., the third-century BCE Ktesibius) many intelligent actors have been fascinated by and curious about these dynamics, in part because they involve regulative "trade-offs" in analysis (e.g., temperature and pressure) and in part because of the energy/information dialectic. As illustration of the point I wish to make, let's assume a simple thermodynamic system. In general, its tendency is to evolve. If the system is open, it will evolve until temperature-pressure within the system is in balance with temperature-pressure outside the system. That equilibrium is temporary under most conditions, because the world outside the system is itself in flux, and the system's immediate environment is one among many localities which are themselves in circulation. Let's now assume a *closed* thermodynamic system: temperature-pressure within it are independent of conditions outside. Conditions within the closed system can still evolve, however, insofar as the system has contained some amount of free energy (i.e., energy available to do work). Over time, that free energy can degrade into unusable energy (i.e., an increase of entropy in the system). This process of intra-system change is called a "spontaneous process," the adjective meaning that the process is not (cannot be, since the system is closed) driven from outside (i.e., from extra-systemic conditions).

A human being is obviously not a closed system—not closed in physical or chemical or biological or social or psychological or political (etc.) terms. That being the case, does it make sense to say that any system of human being experiences losses of free energy? Yes, of course it does. We accomplish that all the time, even when we do not try to accomplish it, and have no awareness of the fact when we do. The very existence of each of us contributes to an increase of entropy. This is, one might say, the trade-off of life. A "living system" is a deferment of entropy.[86]

Is there any system of human being for which losses of free energy are spontaneous? One can imagine a system of human being that is in fact closed, at least for relatively short intervals of time. Experiments involving a small biosphere such as the Apollo transport capsule or the International Space Station are approximations to that condition, and it is clear that in those approximate conditions of closure there *is* loss of free energy. Food is digested, for example, and every production of information is achieved at cost of free energy. Surely it is clear that maintenance of life in physical, chemical, and biological terms requires a very large budget of free energy. The budget becomes all the greater when the living system is defined in social and psychological terms as well. Thus, we come to another question, or another version of the same question: Can one think of a similar approximation to closure in a human system at the level of *social and psychological* dynamics? The closest that comes

---

[86] In his text on *The Method of Sociology* Florian Znaniecki (1934, p. 11-14) wrote favorably of the notion of a closed system as an assumption useful to sociology. He noted (p. 12n.1) that, defined in terms of the first and second principle of thermodynamics, the concept had been abandoned by physicists, but apparently he did not understand the implications for an inquiry into phenomena far more complex than those of Newtonian mechanics.

to mind is the one-person crew of the Vostok (e.g., Yuri Alekseyevich Gagarin) and the Mercury (e.g., Alan Shepard) "space capsules" in 1961, and these one-person crews were restricted to very short intervals of time in devices and under conditions that had consumed huge quantities of energy/information.

Assuming that when Novick wrote of "spontaneous" process he meant the standard lexical definition, "not premeditated," one might still ask, "What are the systemic limits, temporal and spatial, of this assumed condition of "an absence of all forethought"—or to use Hayek's (1967a) favorite phrase, "results of human action but not human design"? An issue that I will address at greater length later has to do with that question of limits in relation to the presence of institutionalized relations of sociality. While it is certainly conceivable that the production of an institution did involve an evolutionary process that was internally non-cognitive, non-emotive, and so forth, one sees abundant evidence that an institution once formed can be a continual focus of efforts—deliberate, obviously premeditated efforts—by more powerful members of the given society to reshape, recurve, reform, manipulate this or that institutional process, in order to gain advantage. Does that not count as "premeditation"? Is the effect of the institution on, say, current distributional processes or reward and penalty absent of human design? What determines when the theorist's or analyst's clock is set to "On" or to "Off"? Issues of "social inheritance"—of wealth, power, authority—are surely relevant to a "social system," and those issues take on relative solid form when pursued through institutionalized processes. In similar vein, when workers who, despite deficits of knowledge and skills of criticism as well as wealth and individual power, did manage to produce by design an advantage of their large numbers (collectivized as a one of Hobbes' "artificial persons," a union of workers), but then witnessed powerful interests persistently carve that "artificial person" into many pieces (with some of those pieces cheering the carvers of their own base of power), were they victims of a "spontaneous"—that is, unpremeditated and lacking design—process?   When the matter of "spontaneous order" is approached in this way, one can better see why Hayek's critics said that in practicing his apologetics he was carrying water for powerful interests. There *is* an issue of major theoretical importance in the question of aggregation process, but that process is not license to kleptocracy or kakistocracy.

The word "society" refers primarily not to a thing but to relations (including sets or relations of relations) among individual persons and various collectivities of persons (some of whom are, as Hobbes said centuries ago, "artificial"). The relations are communal, associational, and mixtures of both. Relations are contextual. The context is both temporal (specifically dated history) and spatial (specific territorial places and histories of those places). Relations are of actors; but also of their conditions, their actions and effects of those actions (including of and on one another), plus the various "things" that furnish their places of being. Persons who not active (not agents) but are still present as persons (patients) may yet be influential in others' actions. The relations of actors, their conditions, actions and effects, insofar as they are repetitive and importantly consequential in distributions of resources (including rewards and penalties, enablements and constraints), are regulated so as to stabilize the repetitiveness of underlying process(es) and generate stable expectations (i.e.,

63

are institutionalized). For virtually all actors most of the time, the institutionalized relations of a kind are inherited from prior generations. Institutionalization of relations of a kind can change, improve or decay, but the change is usually gradual and slow, sometimes slow enough to appear static or inertially at rest. Inheritance is not necessarily empty of change. Excepting times of war or other calamity that accelerates and expands destructions, the changes via inheritance are usually gradual, not especially remarkable except in retrospect, and accretive of balances of variably valenced, mostly very small effects of actions accumulated over time across many actors and mostly channeled by institutional enablements and constraints.

The most important institutions during recent and present times in modern societies include (in no special order) familial, dwelling, educative (within family, then formal extra-familial), police and military, work and employment, market exchange, governance and conflict resolution, and other aesthetic, cathectic, and epistemic regulatory functions. These institutionalized forms, being relatively stable, long-lasting, powerful and authoritative, acquire referential tokens—names, metaphors, images—all of which are secondary, in the sense that they develop in actor/observer consciousness of the operative relations (and reflect the same strong inheritance patterns—that is, received names, metaphors, images, etc.). This "thingification" of relations results in "things" some of which are palpable presences but most of which are presences without palpability except by symbols. Examples of the "things" include: houses, schools, jobs, pay checks, contracts, legal codes, temples, churches, and mosques, books, tools, and so forth. Also: nation-states (analogous to city-states, a few of which remain), countries, empires, societies. The boundaries of these things are more or less stable, more or less fluid (and flows as well as solids can be stable). An obvious example of fluid boundedness: from the founding acts of 1789, the USA has expanded in territory as well as in population and in other characteristics. The USA is usually accorded the single unitary thingness of being, or having, *a* society. The fiction of this unitariness of thing is easily observable (as it is in various other cases: e.g., Belgium, Spain, China, the United Kingdom of Great Britain and Northern Ireland, etc.). The USA consists of a dominant "white society" and a subordinate "black society," and has from its beginnings in 1789. It has also contained several enclave societies—Little Italy here and there, Chinatown here and there, and similar other immigrant-community enclaves; but also Hopiland and dozens of other enclaves of "reserved-land" for remnants of the societies that thrived in the Americas before 1492.

The "fiction of unitariness," mentioned above, is a shorthand for describing the object formations produced in consciousness of persons occupying places during periods of time. The word, "fiction," denotes a quality of "having been made" (or "made up"), of having been constructed by human beings. The constructed "thing" sometimes then takes on "a life of its own," so to speak. That is, an object formation slips from being a "made thing" or a "thing of artifice" to a "natural thing" or a "thing of the gods," and so forth. This institutionalization of the humanly made as extra-human depends on an amnesia, a forgetting of the human poiesis that begat the given thing. Human beings often become enslaved, in that way, to acts of their own doing, products of their own making. The thingness of "society" can achieve that status, but more often the "privilege" is accorded to a tribalism or a nationalism (e.g., a "folk nativity").

One confusion frequently observed in discussions of that sort of conversion process can be seen in claims about "reification"—that is, the notion that a given "thing" is not genuine but fake. The vocabulary of choice often highlights the "not real" as "artificial," the underlying model being the stone over which one trips, a "*really* real thing," a "natural thing," meaning "not of human provenience" (and, note, we are again visiting Kant). In short, "reification" is typically a coin of ideological disputations, since in fact everything we can know, everything we can perceive, is a humanly made "thing." Because even a glimmer of recognition of that process can instill deep insecurity in the strongest of human beings, however, we are inclined to make that "second object" (as Pippin counted it; see above) the *primary* object, the object that must not be dependent on human being (such that we can be dependent on it). This points to a "self-evident" grave weakness of "society," indeed of all "associational" forms: they show far too easily, by comparison with "communal" forms, the fingerprints of human production. We are far more inclined to believe *in* a communion with God, a communion with Nature, and so forth, than in the worth of communion with other persons.

Finally, I will often use the word, "sociality," as a shorter version of "social relations" or "relations of social relations." I need to say a little more about this locution, because the very idea of "the social" has become rather controversial.

Any one of us exists *in* and *as* sociality. One exists *in* the social in the same way that one swims in language. One is also *of* the social. One came *from* the social, social relations, thus one is also *by* the social. One is *for* the social as inescapably as one is *about* the social. Feel free to substitute for "social," in any of those sentences the word "cultural"; likewise, "economic" or "political," and so forth. But I intend "the social" as encompassing those other adjectives, those other nominations of dimensions of human experience (cf. Sewell 2005, pp. 318-372). I mean "the social" not as exclusive of anything, any aspect, any dimension, of human being. Human biology is first of all a social activity of conception, perception, classification, measurement. Biology, chemistry, physics, medicine, engineering—these all take place within and as human activities, and these activities are inescapably social. They could not exist but for the relations of human beings doing, thinking, being together in action, thought, existence. I intend nothing mystical about any of that. I intend all of it simply as a description of what *is*. I do not deny that there are realities, realms, outside and beyond the human. But each and every one of them is a human production. Nothing more, but also nothing less.

In recent times several commentators have questioned the utility, in some instances seemingly even the legitimacy, of the word, "social," as a meaningful term in the social sciences (e.g., Law 1994; Halewood 2014). As a philological thread, this discussion gained considerable visibility when Hannah Arendt (1998, pp. 22-23) pointed out that Thomas Aquinas had altered Aristotle's text by adding a three-word clarification: "homo est naturaliter politicus, id est, socialis" (human being is by nature political, that is, social). Based on the surviving literature of ancient Greek cultures, it does seem fair to say that the common dialect, and perhaps all of the "indigenous" dialects before it, did not have a word that carried the same meaning as "social" in

65

English or "socialis" in Thomistic Latin. That is rather distant from saying that ancient Greeks were unable to think thoughts reasonably comparable to the thoughts an Anglophone thinks with the word "social." But it does suggest that had those thoughts been repeated often enough to have become common and in some degree routine, a distinctive word probably would have been coined.

However, as discussed above in connection with Tönnies, it is well off the mark to say (as Arendt did) that the ancient Greeks knew only two forms of (what I am calling) sociality: the familial household (oikos) and the city-state (polis). When Aristotle wrote, following his famous statement that anthropōs is by nature a political animal, that if the "earlier forms" of human living are natural, so is the "state" (polis), he named those earlier forms "prōtai koinōniai" or "first communities" (*On Politics*, 1252b.30). Further, when in the next passage (1253a) he wrote of anyone who is not able, by his "nature" rather than by fortune, to live with other human beings, he described such a person as "ăpolis" (without or outside a city-state), and surely not as "ăkoinōnia" (a privative I cannot say was never used, but I do not recall having ever read it) nor as outside an oikos, and as either low in the scale of man or above it.[87] Further still, Athenian men definitely did participate in what we call (using the Latin derivative) "associational" forms. Companionship during a symposium was typically neither familial nor tribal, and it often involved relationships (e.g., the hetairia) which were more similar to "men's clubs" (associational) than to communal forms. And whether by merchant or trader, commerce depended on contractual agreements among individuals who were not only not all of the same oikos, they were sometimes not all of the same polis and (among long-distance traders) not all of the same linguistic groups.

The notion that "the social" is, if not superfluous, deficient in some important way has been suggested on grounds other than Greek-to-Latin philology. For example, after nominating "the problem of the social order" as "the oldest problem of them all," John Law (1994, p. 1) next proceeded to object to his own locution in several parts. We should avoid writing the noun ("the social order"), preferring instead the verb, "to order," or in gerund form, "ordering," because nouns are stultifying, ossifying, reifying. We should as well be circumspect about the adjective, "social," since it appears that we are not at all clear about the meaning of the word; also, of course, because, being an adjective, the word lives to be handmaid to a noun. Then, thirdly, that definite article in "*the* social order" must be erased, lest we indulge our colonial proclivities.

Michael Halewood's (2014, p. 108) qualms about "social" extend to the fact that Max Weber used "social" and "associative" in applications to animals other than Aristotle's "zōon politikon," and apparently any characteristic that humans share with other animals is by that fact disqualified as "fundamental" to human being. Arendt (1998, p. 24) endorsed the standard when, acknowledging that ancient Greeks were neither "ignorant of" nor "unconcerned with, the fact that man cannot live outside the company of men," she agreed that the Greek thinkers "did not count this condition among the specifically human characteristics." If this seems a rather strange

---

[87] By this last phrase Aristotle probably meant something like "either barely human or godlike." He then proceeded to compare anthrōpos favorably to any bee (melissa) or herd-like animal (àgelaiou zōon) in gregariousness and next highlighted the crucial difference of human language.

assertion, the next two clauses both clarify meaning and express what is even stranger: "on the contrary," the need of "the company of men" was a characteristics that "human life had in common with animal life, and for this reason alone it could not be fundamentally human." The absurdity of that claim, if not already evident, surely does stand out quite starkly if one asserts as analogy that because all mammals must have some amount of oxygen and take in a minimal quantity of calories and hydration, we cannot regard these same conditions as fundamental to human being. The sort of discrimination that Arendt described was probably stimulated by the odd paranoia that humankind must be abundantly unique, as if the very fact of the paranoia itself would not be sufficiently indicative.

### §7. A Continuing Odyssey of Returning Priority to the Object

As mentioned earlier by allusion, a culture is capable of absorbing, coming to terms with, a startling new insight of itself only gradually.[88] A major instance runs through the aftermath of Kant's declaration that the limits of knowledge are considerably shorter, narrower, than those which had been heard in prophecy for and of the gods. The nineteenth century and some part of the next can be understood as a sequence of struggles first to decide what Kant had actually done and then to launch counterattacks against it or at least to erect dikes to hold away the flood of consequences for the survival of a metaphysics and, failing that, the internal coherence and self-consistency of an epistemology as authority of voice beyond mere opinion. For the social sciences it is evident that these struggles proceeded somewhat more quickly on the European continent—in Germany and in France, for instance—than they did in North America. In Germany a tradition of the "as if" extended from Hans Vaihinger (1935 [1911]) to Jürgen Habermas (1971 [1968]) and his early affinity for the "quasi-transcendental." In France neo-Kantian thinking included a long sequence of scholars—among many others, Charles-Bernard Renouvier (a significant influence on William James as well as Émile Durkheim), Léon Brunschvicg, Gaston Bachelard, Georges Canguilhem, and (though more Hegelian) Jean Hyppolite, with many heirs in recent years, such as Michel Foucault, Pierre Bourdieu, and Gilles Deleuze.

Habermas (1973 [1971], pp. 14-15) later explained that he had to relinquish his stance on matters "quasi-transcendental," acknowledging it was "a product of an embarrassment which points to more problems that it solves." First of all, he said, it "would, at the very least, tie the emancipatory interest of knowledge to fortuitous historical constellations and would thus relativistically deprive self-reflection of the possibility of a justificatory basis for its claim to validity." By his estimation, then, "neither of these" limits would allow a plausible account of "how theories could have any truth at all—including one's own theories." In preface to that

---

[88] That observation has been repeated many times. Whitehead (1954, p. 166) said of Athens that its prime "came a little before Plato, in the period of the three great tragic dramatists, ... and I include Aristophanes too. I think a culture is in its finest flower before it begins to analyse itself; and the Periclean Age and the dramatists were spontaneous, unselfconscious." Was Whitehead aware of the "doubling" that occurred in his observation, as reflected in the last clause? It is difficult to read Aeschylus or Sophocles, to say nothing of Euripides, and think that he was in fact "spontaneous" or "unselfconscious" when composing any one of his plays. On the other hand, any writer today surely knows the exasperating experience, having just been told by a reader what she or he had said, of trying to understand "how anyone could think that *that* is what I meant!"

conclusion he had already stated crucial criteria, saying that he did not "assume the synthetic achievements of an intelligible ego nor in general a productive subjectivity." But surely that stance would be tantamount to denying his own specificity of productive subjectivity and fruits of subjective achievement. What he defined as "the emancipatory interest of knowledge" must be, in his perspective, beyond or outside the historical, and this implies that the proper bearer of such interest (an investigator such as Habermas) must logically begin in some sort of originary position. In my prefatory remarks I introduced as an illustrative emblem of inquiry by those ancient Greeks who became known as (and depreciated by) Plato as "the Sophists" a puzzle of reasoning, "the ship of Theseus": if the ship has been completely "rebuilt" during a long passage of time, as decaying planks are each replaced by a new plank, is it still Theseus' ship? Several instances of a dialectic of the unity of opposites are illustrated by the puzzle. Identity/difference is one; original/copy is another. A popular "solution" to the "puzzle" has been to tie "identity" to "original" and privilege them as superior, in keeping with a logic that presupposes the sign of cause in "first beginning," in a genesis, in initial conditions, and the like. Logically, one must begin at the beginning. Time changes only "forward," never "backward." Never mind the tautologies. This is Isaac Newton declaring that $F = M * A$ as itself timeless and spaceless: the formula always was, always will be, here, there, and everywhere. Habermas' preference is one more instance of that peculiar reflection of the implicit posit of an originary position.

Foucault wrote his secondary dissertation, under Hyppolite's direction, on *Anthropology from a Pragmatic Point of View*, Kant's lectures of that general topic, reputedly his most popular course and therefore published (1798) only after he had retired from teaching. Addressing the published lectures in relation to Kant's Transcendental Dialectic as its direct descendant, Foucault acknowledged Kant's discussion of the transcendental Illusion in his first critique, even if less than confident what to make of it (Foucault 2008 [1964], pp. 62-63). One measure of the degree to which the US discourse was less well prepared than either the German or the French is found in the fact that, whereas Foucault's translation (begun in the late 1950s) was the second into French (the first was published in 1863), Kant's *Anthropology* was not translated into English until the 1970s—and was published in the Netherlands.[89] A second, closely related measure is the fact that whereas Foucault's elaboration on what he had learned from his encounter with Kant—namely, *The Order of Things* (1970 [1966])—was a bit of a sensation in the USA, stoking considerable debate about disciplinary integrity and catching attention in some parts of the social sciences, in neither France nor Germany did it garner such fanfare. His thesis of a "doubling of man" was hardly news in France or in Germany.[90]

---

[89] Remarkably, at least two new translations into English have been made during the past twenty years, one by V L Dowdell (Southern Illinois University Press, 1996) and one by R B Louden (Cambridge University Press, 2006). This corresponds to the increase in attention to Kant's dialectic and his third critique, as well as to debates about his pragmatism, his anthropology, and his psychology, and their relation to his moral philosophy.

[90] The understanding was a little different in French social science (mainly sociology and anthropology). Bourdieu, for instance, who by his own account (207 [2004], pp. 79-82, 104) had a complex relationship with Foucault, tended to emphasize his more specific institutional studies (madness, clinical medicine, incarceration) over the work that followed directly from Kant; and in averring "the challenge that Heidegger throws at the Kantians when he tears down one of the pillars of rationalism by disclosing the

Where, then, in the social sciences was the scandal of that "objective necessity" which Kant had observed as an "as if" remainder? It was held mostly to the margins, during the 1970s and after, sheltered in discourses variously labelled "critical theory," "deconstruction," "post-modern thought," and the like. As noted above, it continued to abide in Habermas' notion of a "quasi-transcendental" relation, a vision of inquiry that always refers back to what is missing. It also showed itself, and here productively, in a fleeting observation made by Foucault 2008 [1964], p. 63: Kant's "*Gemüt* is not simply 'what it is' but 'what it makes of itself.' And is this not precisely the area of inquiry that the *Anthropology* defines as its field of investigation?"[91] Indeed (cf. Hazelrigg 1989a, 1989b, and 1995). But the scandal made other appearances, one of which is available in a volume Foucault published close on the heels of *The Order of Things*.

Earlier, in the brief discussion of Heidegger's effort to find a way back to an independent objectivity, I referred to the difficulty of "extracting" for inspection a method that was followed and exemplified in a prior investigation, the difficulty being approximately proportional to the newly successful productivity of that prior work. Heidegger's apparently never undertaken exposition of method, as he announced its promise in *The Basic Problems of Phenomenology*, calls attention to aspects of risk in that temporality of relation of *ex post* conditionality on an *ex*

---

existential finitude at the heart of the Transcendental Aesthetic" (p. 102), Bourdieu seemingly overlooked that the disclosure had been left for his reader by Kant himself.

[91] Kant's Gemüt concept draws on the multivalent common noun and the ordinary words behind it, especially the past participle "gemutet" (sometimes shortened to "gemut"), which means "disposed" (as in a person's disposition). A key indicator is in a passage of Kant's last effort to "bridge the gap" left in his critical project, published in his *Opus Postumum*, unfortunately one of many passages left out of the Cambridge edition. In the Academy edition of Kant's work (volume 22, p. 112) Kant had been considering the relation of a concept of God to empirical-historical conditions of mind, and asked whether it makes sense to think of God as a rational being or essence. Then he wrote this: "Es ist im menschlichen Gemüth (mens, animus) als reinem, nicht als Seele des Menschen einwohnendes empirisch//practisches sondern reines Princip des unbedingten Geboths und ein categorischer Imperativ welcher schlechthin gesetzgebend ist" (which I render as "It is in the human Gemüt (mens, animus), not as the human soul dwelling in the empirical/practical, rather as a pure principle of unconditional commandment and a categorical imperative which is absolutely legislative"). In relating this "Gemüth" to the Latin "mens" and "animus" he was surely signaling something important of his intention of the concept that was being carried by an otherwise ordinary word. The first of the Latin words is usually translated as "mind" or "mentation." The second, "animus," has a range of meanings, and this range is very similar to the range of meanings of the vernacular "Gemüth": intellect, consciousness, will, intention, courage, spirit, sensibility, feeling, passion, pride, vehemence; and the root of the word refers to the breath, as in "the breath of life" or "the soul"). These meanings are all expressed in language, which means that they are conceptual; but most of them "strain" against conceptualization, as if trying to express meaning not yet conceptual—or in Kant's vocabulary, the "meaning" of sensation, of the intuitive. Insofar as this conjecture is accurate (and I know no way of testing it), "Gemüth" could have been Kant's final effort to unite into one concept what had remained divided. ("Gemüth" is a central concept in his third critique; see Part Three, below.) Bear in mind that in the sentence immediately after the above quotation Kant said this: "Ens summum, summa intelligentia, summum bonum — diese Ideen insgesammt gehen aus dem categorischen Imperativ hervor und das Practische ist in dem theoretisch//speculativen enthalten (or in my translation: "The highest being, the highest intelligence, the greatest good—these ideas taken together emanate from the categorical imperative, and the practical is included in the theoretical/speculative").

*ante* condition that was, supposedly, a single integral and coherent event (as if history at the end of the prior work remained identical to history at its beginning—and yet could not have been, insofar as the work was newly productive). A different enactment of the relation can be seen in the contrast, previously noted by various readers, between Foucault's *The Order of Things* (1970 [1966]) and a subsequent work, *The Archaeology of Knowledge* (1972 [1969]), which was initially promoted as exposition of the method of the prior work. Whereas the former work was primarily and mainly a translation of the broad outlines of Kant's critical theory into a context of French literature in general and social science, or the "human sciences," in particular (although writing Kant's presence in an almost incidental manner), the later work had a seemingly tenuous connection to its predecessor and rapidly lost attention. In fact, the main tale told by Foucault in his *Archaeology* had very much to do with his earlier work. It occurred toward the end of the latter text, in what can be read as delayed procatalepsis. And again, as in *The Order of Things*, Kant's name is mentioned only toward the end. But what Foucault said in *Archaeology* makes clear that Kant's presence in the work was anything but incidental and had been there from the beginning. Foucault (1972 [1969], pp. 204, 203) explained that he had been responding to "a crisis that concerns that transcendental reflexion with which philosophy since Kant has been identified," his intent having been to avoid the "role of revealing the transcendental moment that rational mechanics has not possessed since Kant." Indeed, Foucault was now making clear that his aim had been to avoid claims of transcendence altogether. This was a tale difficult to read, and as a consequence the effort of methodological exposition of his prior work served, in the minds of many readers, to undermine the authority of Foucault's voice. His effort to avoid the effect of Kant's transcendental Illusion (without ever naming it)—namely, a resignation into an illusion of "objective necessity"—revised his citizenship papers, making the tale that he told, now a fairy tale, all the easier to ignore. That was another version of what has been called the movement of an "ontological gerrymander" (see, e.g., Overington 1979; Bourdieu 1990 [1982]).

The predominant stance has been not so much to confute the aim of Foucault's project as simply to ignore it. His "celebrity" aided in that accomplishment, for celebration of the theorist, whether in favor or opposed, reduces the generality, potential as well as actual, of an argument to the particularity of the person. As Dreyfus and Kelly (2011) strangely exhibited, reduction of an argument to its absences is all too easy, encouraging simple-minded thoughts of a golden age when there existed a "shared set of values [that] we all absorb[ed] as preconscious assumptions," proposing that a solution to all of our problems (Brooks 2010, p. A23). Tomás de Torquemada would have been thrilled to hear this echo of his voice of authority more than half a millennium later.

Arguably the most rigorous effort by a critical thinker associated with (if not exactly of) the social sciences to reconstitute thought so as to return priority to "the object" was Theodor W Adorno, whose participation with members of what became known as the first generation of "the Frankfurter School" brought him into alliance with researchers and theorists of mid-twentieth-century social science in the USA,[92] and whose *Negative Dialectics* and *Aesthetic Theory* remain important factors yet today. Adorno's output is difficult to hold in internal coherence, given all the cross-currents and silences that pulsate through it, as much of it was left in sketchy, incomplete, and provisional condition. On the one hand, his work can be understood as a late effort to overturn the limits which Kant left to us—that is, to offer a theory that would perform

---

[92] See, e.g., the collection he edited with contributing colleagues, *The Positivist Dispute in German Sociology*. Also see Bernstein (2001

the function of a first-principle metaphysics, but without being overtly a metaphysics, and therein "rescue the nonidentical from the assaults of instrumental reason" (Habermas 1992 [1988], p. 123), all the while remaining consistent with his "theorem that there is no philosophical first principle," and retaining some large component of Nietzsche's cautionary stance on concepts and remaining dismissive of logic's "insistence on consistency" (see, e.g., Adorno 1997 [1970], p. 364; 1973 [1966], pp. 23, 148-151, 180-186, 381-390; 1982 [1956], pp. 108, 145-147; 2001 [1995], p. 279). The evident intent of Adorno's "nonidentity thinking" or "negative dialectic" was to achieve revelation of the "conceptuality prevailing in the object itself"—that is, the concept which an "object has of itself," of what, "left to itself," the object "seeks to be" (Adorno 1976 [1957], p. 69). There is a duplicity in this effort—or there could well be, depending on Adorno's intent of "Objekt in primacy" relative to Kant's insistence that the "thing in *itself* is not an object given outside representation, but merely the position of the thought-entity which is thought of as corresponding to the object" (Kant 1993 [1936-38], p. 173). In other words, the thing-in-itself, which he also identified as "objectum noumenon," is a pure functionality, a placeholder, "only a thought-entity without actuality (ens rationis), in order to designate a place for the representation of the subject." This is not the "objectum phenomenon" or phenomenal thing, of which subject makes actual description; nor is it of course the entity to which the "in-itself" purports to refer, since this is beyond human knowledge. Where exactly in that framework did Adorno's "Objekt in primacy" (or "priority") fit? So far as I can discern, he did not say. If nowhere within that framework, then what relation to it did his "Objekt in primary" (or "priority") have? One is left wondering if some new "ontological gerrymander" was at work, or intended. At very least, on criteria of clarity as well as consistency his project has remained a failure.

Surely he was aware of the failure? He was too well read, too thoughtful, not to have been aware of it. Yet he did not acknowledge it (at least not in any published work that I have read), did not attempt to address it directly in a diagnostic manner that might have opened a new window here or there. On the other hand, many passages of his work are obscure, to say the least. One notorious instance is his comment in *Aesthetic Theory* (1997 [1970], p. 334)—on the face of it preposterous—that Hegel knew nothing of art. Surely Adorno was aware of Hegel's extensive studies of art, within a variety of cultural and historical contexts. Presumably Adorno had in mind another, a rather different, standard of what should count as "understanding art." But he did not bother to explain that difference with sufficient specificity. Here, as in other parts of his writing, one is left with the decided impression that Adorno mostly accumulated more evidence of a dogmatism seeking its own apotheosis in privileged authority, his own. It is difficult to overlook the evidence of his lament for a long lost authority, along with his apparent disgust with skepticism ("now elevated to a prohibition on thought"; Adorno 1976 [1957], p. 69).[93] His 1959 lectures on Kant, highly selective to say the least, leave one in wonderment that he apparently believed that the force of his preferred reading would finally relegate Kant to philosophy's large shelf of treatises now entirely surpassed. And yet Adorno's persistent lament for authority also reveals a suspicion that Kant was right (notably, Adorno's lectures, which include very little on Kant's Transcendental Aesthetic, deflect attention away from the transcendental Illusion) and, by the same token, an awareness that authority of voice, an authority that somehow speaks for the object itself, remains important, seemingly even crucial, to a human

---

[93] Similarly, in his lectures on Kant he (2001 [1995], p. 184) held that "the only purpose of this question [the core question of skepticism] is to exclude every theoretical authority, every authoritative intervention of thought from the realm of experience"

being that presumably needs to feel originally and entirely subordinate to some "higher principle."

Different authors on a "received theorist's body of work" understandably offer different perspectives on and conclusions about that body of work. But eventually one discerns a general settlement on at least its main points. The diversity of accounts of Adorno remains noteworthy. Even those writers who have offered what I take to be the best accounts—for instance (to hazard a short nomination), Jay Bernstein, Robert Hullot-Kentor, Peter Gordon, Andrew Bowie—are short enough of agreement on some basic issues that, at times, one can imagine their accounts are of works by different persons sharing the name "Adorno." This is due, in no small degree, to the obscurity of much of what Adorno left as his written record.

Gordon has made plain, though without quite saying it, that Adorno's "priority of the Objekt" was a thought that would not be a thought but instead would *be* the Objekt that is prior to any and all thought directly or indirectly about it—in other words, Kant's "thing in itself" not as a thought but the thing as such (the "second object," held in reserve as supposed authorization of everything before the advent of consciousness of it). The proposal, as Gordon (after Brian O'Connor) saw it, "closely resembles a transcendental argument." This resemblance has been maintained by recourse to a difference (pre-Marx) between idealism and materialism, such that the Objekt represents materiality while human thought is idealist even as it exists as an objectivity of human product. This effort to resurrect objectness as independent of human production is Adorno's myth of nature, or what Bernstein (2001) called Adorno's version of a modern naturalism. Adorno avoided addressing the question of *his* thought of the Objekt, because to address that question would be to return the reader's focus to the *production* of a knowledge. Myth, in order to function as such, must simply *be*, must have come to be via an act even more miraculous than an immaculate conception, an act without conception at all.

In his *Negative Dialectic* Adorno proposed a rhetorical question which he presumably expected his reader to parse as a thought-stopping perplexity:

> Why the individual consciousness of every speaking person, which already presupposes a linguistic generality in the particle 'my,' which it denies through the primacy of its particularity, is supposed to be prior to anything else, is unfathomable (Adorno 1973 [1966], pp. 131-132).

Once this consciousness recedes from its sovereignty, nature will be released from oppression and returned to its rightful priority (Adorno 1997 [1970], p. 197). Why would consciousness recede, relinquishing its own sovereignty? Because, in Adorno's view, it was on the verge of collapse, the evidence being that human productivity had been creating problems that human consciousness was (is) incapable of solving.

Surely today it would be foolish indeed to claim that human imagination is capable of producing "solutions" that are perfect, of producing actions pristinely benignly intended and perfectly executed, of producing even intuitions, cognitions, perceptions, that are completely free of any seeds of future problems. But that is not really the issue here. Let's return to that matter of "individual consciousness" and "linguistic generality," in Adorno's gauge of a depth that cannot be plumbed. As Raymond Geuss (2016, p. 271) reminded us via his appreciation of Augustine, the great fault of Kant's "system" (as opposed to his anthropology) was its aim and assumption of universality. Yet on moral grounds one must be very cautious about offers, even "purely theoretical" offers, of differentiation of among human beings into "kinds," be they qualified as "natural kinds" or as "cultural kinds." This caution pertains surely to any inquiry that styles itself as a phenomenology of human affairs. If that is the case, then what must one imagine of an effort to produce an *ontology* of human affairs? Calls for restoring priority of the object are at the least suggestive of traditional ontology and its presupposition of the possibility of a rational inquiry that operates independently of human contingencies (or the "fictions," as Hume called them) and accords with the very universal principles it seeks to discover. Although they more often cite the works of Gilles Deleuze than those of Adorno as progenitive, recent proposals of a "social ontology" by a few philosophers (e.g., Brian Epstein 2015, 2018; Graham Harman 2018) seem to concur in the view of Kant's critique of critique as lacking relevance to their undertakings, although perhaps for different reasons. We will return to this development after attending to some propaedeutics.

## §8. Questions of Objectivity, Discipline, and Authority of Voice

The question of priority—as in Adorno's "primacy of the Objekt"—is an analytical question that circulates through many discussions of human affairs. Gary Tomlinson's (2015) *A Million Years of Music* offers a recent illustration, addressing the issue of priority in terms of accounts of "the origin of music." These accounts have generally followed a divided pathway, some finding that music developed from pre-existing language while other accounts have declared the reverse sequence. Each account shares with the other a common tendency to obscure what it purportedly seeks to explain. Having reached that conclusion, Tomlinson recommended that we bank instead on an explanation by co-evolution. The preference is fitting in that his larger orientation is also co-evolutionary: when addressing the question of how human beings have become sense-making beings (i.e., the question of culture), one must proceed along a track of the co-evolution of culture and biology. Tomlinson's stance is consonant with modern evolutionary theory, to be sure. But one must note that any "coevolution of biology and culture" is still a piece of human culture, as indeed is biology as a fund of concepts, knowledges, habits, and the like. When we humans think/speak/write in such manner of a biology, we are thinking/speaking/writing a piece of culture, not the biology that they presume to be referencing as a thing-in-itself that exists, or has ever existed, outside any human culture whatsoever.

Now, at the risk of being misunderstood and thereby of encouraging a part of the lunatic fringe in our society, I hasten to add that I have no doubt that "evolutionary theory," whether it be qualified as "Darwinian" or "neo-Darwinian" or "post-neo-Darwinian," is wholly integral to a culture. It *is* a production of culture. Let me also add—in view of some confusion that had previously occurred in reading prior statements—while that declaration may seem to undermine any claim to authority of one of our natural sciences, evolutionary biology, it does not. Or perhaps a better way of stating the point is that it undermines the authority of a natural science *only* to the extent that one expects an authority of voice to be *absolutist* and refuses to observe any claim of authority that is not absolutist. I reject that expectation on several grounds: it is an invitation to dictatorship; it is destructive of human responsibility and any project of maturity and self-autonomy. At any moment, and with regard to any question or problem, one must make choices on the basis of best informed understanding of relevant contexts and conditions, knowing full well that no understanding is more than provisional; none is immune to skeptical inquiry, none is complete or final, and no inquirer or decision maker is infallible.

It does seem that the ductility of intellectual authority has passed its limit and that we remain captivated by echoes of "the sound of cracking," to borrow the title of Mishra's (2015) recent diagnostics regarding exhausted authority. Having just read Greif's (2015) "philosophical

73

history" of North American anxieties of "the crisis of man" during the four decades from 1933, Mishra (2015, pp. 13) registered an unavoidable verdict: "only a reader attuned to the parochial assumptions of American exceptionalism will find anything remarkable in the fact that so many mid-century Europeans or Euro-Americans were obsessed with the crisis of man." One must add that the attitude of exceptionalism encompasses the professionally defined field of social science as well, which generally produces and consumes that same parochialism. Even so, it is notable also that Mishra had detected many putative duplicates of Saul Bellow's Augie March,

> whether in India, Russia, Japan, or Israel, [who] seem keen to surrender their onerous individuality to demagogues and to be used by them. Elsewhere, those excluded from a degraded world of man, or condemned to join its burgeoning precariate, are prone to embrace the god of destruction rather than of inner peace. The thin sound of cracking is heard from many more parts of the world as exhausted authority surrenders to nihilism (Mishra 2015, p. 15).

It remains to view—and this is perhaps the most central venue of all the essays in this book—that the proverbial voice, and any sound of cracking, must be enacted by individual persons, in and through their self-identities in some sort of mutual perception of sociality, the sociality and the selfhood of Marx' "ensemble of social relations" (Marx 1976 [1888], p. 7).[94] One of the most important observations offered by Charles Taylor in his *Sources of the Self* (1989, p. 189) is that we learn much of a particular culture in its locality of time and space by the way in which its "common sense"—its prevailing, normally taken-for-granted texture of understandings—"distributes the onus of persuasion." Thus (his example), one must argue against the occlusions of specific binary formulations in order to find light: the relation of "mental and physical" (*psyche* and *soma*, to use an idiom of, say, seventh-century BCE Greece), the relation of "culture and nature," the relation of "human being and divine being," to mention three of the largest, among the strongest dualities of which "selfhood" has been fashioned again and again, and the most recalcitrant. On the one hand, one wonders if anything fundamentally new has been thought. On the other hand, *Sources of the Self* was the book that Taylor was never ready to write, as he acknowledged (1989, p. ix) of its long gestation. Anyone who has made serious effort to undertake such as book—indeed, anyone who thoughtfully and carefully engages Taylor's book—understands the confession, and may do so independently of the relationship between her philosophy and her religion. As any accomplished translator can tell us, the line that protects "fidelity to text" is not just leaky, it dims in and out of fixation the more one thinks of and about what one has "immediately read." Productive reading, sometimes scorned as sin, is valuable exactly as it disturbs and challenges. Here, too, no doubt, lines are not exactly carved in stone. But so long as a writer clearly announces effort to use a text *perhaps* beyond its

---

[94] The reference is to the sixth of Marx' theses against materialism (i.e., Feuerbach as the then leading proponent of a materialist philosophy). Marx regarded the concrete being of a human being, a person, as "an ensemble of social relations," whereas Feuerbach abstracted all of that away in order to "see" the individual "as such"—but, Marx said, the "isolated individual," not the individual person in social reality. This variety of psychologism was prominent then and has remained prominent, sometimes in the guise of a "rational reconstruction" in search of an "original condition" (i.e., an originary logic). I have addressed these issues repeatedly (e.g. Hazelrigg 1979, 1993b, 1995) and do again below.

"originality" (whatever one thinks that to be—and thus the emphasis of "perhaps"), the effort is available for one to reject or to take as perhaps an additional pursuit (see, e.g., Pyyhtinen's 2010 thoughtful pursuit of ideas he read from Georg Simmel).

During the last quarter of the eighteenth century Immanuel Kant very well knew that his critical theory, his categorical imperative, and the rest, were in fact not universally held, that in many cultures, including some parts of German culture, different views were regnant. Kant did not, after all, intend to be, or believe that he was, "preaching to the choir." He had lessons to teach. Even aside from the contingent worlds addressed in his lectures of anthropology, he knew perfectly well that most if not all of his lessons were aspirational; and even aside from the probable fact that he knew his effort in the third critique to erect the capstone of his system did not reach his goal (and apparently was trying yet again when illness intervened), he surely did know that the point of his lessons about the tragedy of the idea, the immaturity of the human species, and other specific elements of his critique of critique were themselves also mostly aspirational, statements of and about his principle of hope for future conditions.[95]

Two hundred years later Jürgen Habermas sought to make a clear distinction between the contingency of ethical rules and the universality of a moral order, a morality of universal values (e.g., Habermas, 1990 [1983]). If nothing else, Habermas was striving to keep the principle of hope alive.[96] Roundly criticized for (as a few critics charged) arguing a distinction without a difference, for subordinating the multiplicity of ethical integrities of many historical-contingent cultures to a universalistic principle that was perhaps not even universally held in his own land, for participating in a cultural imperialism, a colonialism of ideas, Habermas persisted in and for his orientation to a future, and to that end his belief in the possibility of a sincerity of rational discourse that could accommodate all interlocutors who genuinely sought realizations of freedom in dignity and integrity. Habermas surely never deluded himself into thinking that a universality of moral order had actually been accomplished anywhere—certainly not in his writings, which were only promissory notes at best, and certainly not in any known human culture of day-to-day life. He has nonetheless held fast to the notion that the rational discourse must begin someplace, and he had offered in good faith a place to begin. His implicit response to his critics has been, in effect, "Demonstrate a better place to begin, a better way to accomplish agreement toward a future moral order that accommodates our diversity of ethical

---

[95] Some recent accounts of the failure of Kant's aim in his third critique are considerable improvements on earlier accounts, in part because of an improved understanding of what that aim was (e.g., in relation to topics such as "beauty"). The best, I believe, include Howard Caygill's extensive and penetrating account (1989); Pippin, who (1997, pp., 129-153), is especially good for the perspective of Hegel as foil (see also Part I of Pippin's 2005); and Jay Bernstein (2006, esp. 46-62) for his account in light of Adorno's "modern naturalism" and his readings of modernism in art. It should be noted that by Caygill's reading Kant was aware *prior* to composition of the third critique of the futility of his effort to demonstrate a reason peculiar to the power of judgment (a reason that would form a bridge between the emptiness of pure theory and the blindness of intuition and empirics) and that his intent was to demonstrate *that* lesson. To my mind the evidence pertinent to that question is ambiguous; but I defer.

[96] Nearly a decade later Habermas (1996 [1992]) tackled much the same issue, now under the aegis of "law" and legal theory, in his studies of the relation of "factuality" and "validity" (a pair of words that better capture the sense than do "facts" and "norms"), but the tenor had shifted from being productive to being defensive (i.e., vis-à-vis other theorists). A first-time reader of that book should begin with his 1994 Postscript (added to the English edition), wherein Habermas made some clarifications and corrections in reply to a few critics (the point being to begin with an appreciation of the extraordinary complexity of what he was trying to accomplish).

contingencies." Too many of us were waiting for him—for someone—to present to us the final design, the completed map from here to there. Too many of us have been impatient that he did not, could not, never intended as much, and instead have been holding his good faith hostage to all of the failures of identity politics—prejudicial discriminations against numerous labelled groups and on behalf of numerous labelled exercises of power such as colonialism and imperialism. Lest there be misunderstanding, I am invoking Habermas as a placeholder. I do not argue that his theory of communicative action was anything more than a place to begin, and in fact I expressed doubts about enactment, about realization in the terms he proposed, as early as the mid-1970s (writings published more than ten years later in *A Wilderness of Mirrors;* 1989a, pp. 410-449). I am not prepared to defend his theory as the best place to begin. But I am troubled that we have found it so easy to conclude that inadequacies of the particular (a particular means, a specific effort to begin) signify inadequacies of the general (the general aspiration for a morality that can accommodate all, freely, without cynicism and hypocrisy, although surely with healthy measures of skepticism kept at the ready). I am troubled that so many have seemingly concluded, in effect if not also in explicit verbiage, that *Homo sapiens* is congenitally and *irremediably* a deficient creature, irremediably too deficient to avoid wasting most other species in a single species' suicide.

What, if anything, can be said about reality as such, in light of Kant's critique? This question, asked in various ways, shrouded nineteenth-century proposals of a science of social, historical affairs. Most of the earliest names we recognize today as "forerunners"—Auguste Comte is perhaps the best, certainly the easiest, example[97]—mainly ignored the question as if it simply had never been posed, but by century's end it had become clear to several scholars that neglect was inadequate, even as it was becoming clear that they had little notion of a response more effective than simply "changing the subject" (dual meaning intended or not). Perspective is important: the question remains alive today (see, e.g., Gabriel 2011); and today as a hundred years ago the chief obstacle to building an effective response is the way in which the question has been repeatedly posed. Some questions are crafted in such a way as if by intent to evade all answer, a point that Marx made: it is wise to ask "whether the problem [being posed] does not express its own absurdity, and hence whether the impossibility of a solution does not lie already in the conditions set by the problem" (Marx 1986 [1939], p. 65).[98] That a given problem or question has already been defeated by its own conditions is usually anything but self-evident, of course. After all, how much brain power had been futilely expended over how many decades in efforts to answer the big question about celestial bodies—namely, what keeps these bodies in motion? "Yes," seventeenth-century scholars agreed, "Galileo was right and Copernicus was right: the earth orbits the sun, the moon orbits the earth, and so forth. But what keeps those bodies moving? What is the motive power, the impulse, the force?" Then Newton revised the framework within which relevant questions would be formulated, and the search for "impulse" (and the like) simply evaporated.

---

[97] Fifty years ago—and well before the tragical farce that was supposed to be a dialogue led by Adorno (see Adorno et al. 1976 [1969])—Habermas (1971 [1968], pp. 74-77) offered a detailed definition of "positivism." Would even Comte have qualified? Has anyone since his time (if then) actually endorsed all of the "elements" that Habermas laid out? It is difficult to imagine. Leading scholars of the physical sciences had by the 1930s left Ernst Mach's perspective behind.

[98] Martin Nicolaus' translation is less literal than Ernst Wangermann's (above) but captures the burden of Marx' point with greater felicity: "Frequently the only possible answer is a critique of the question, and the only solution is to negate the question."

76

For the moment, I will simply draw attention to some understandable segregations that held sway during efforts to institutionalize and professionalize the disciplines of the "historical sciences." The scholars today most often held in regard as "founding figures"—in sociology, for instance, Emile Durkheim, Georg Simmel, and Max Weber—had acquired some familiarity with works by Hume, Kant, Hegel, and others, and erected a segregation between "the philosophical parts," to which they assigned the dilemmas and conundrums, and the empirical, historical parts, from which they borrowed a substantial volume of insight.[99] In consequence, they built empirical texts of generally weak theoretical frameworks. The tendency to demarcate the "dilemmas and conundrums" bequeathed by scholars such as Hume, Kant, and Hegel as "philosophy" virtually assured weakness of theoretical framework in the historical sciences, which in turn stimulated frustrating imaginations of being inferior to "the natural sciences," held up as Kant's "true" or "rational sciences."[100] Durkheim, Weber, and others did venture brief forays into issues of "objective knowledge" of "reality as such" orientation, in doing so showing some awareness of what was at stake (e.g., Weber on "objectivity and value neutrality").[101] Their efforts were well shy of addressing the key issues, yet they left enough of a patina of authority to satisfy followers that roads of scholarly progress lay ahead. One must bear in mind that theoretical perspectives in the social sciences were seldom all that refined by the arguments of Kant, Hegel, or Nietzsche, for example. Consider Durkheim as illustrative case: when he surveyed the terrain of major scholarship in France's recent past, what he saw would not have been much different from an assessment by his compatriots, Charles-Victor Langlois and Charles Seignobos, who in their *Introduction aux études historiques* (1898, p. 6) avowed that "[T]he great majority of writing about the method of investigation of history and about the art of historiography—which in Germany and England goes by the name *Historik*—is superficial, tasteless, unreadable, and ridiculous" (see also, e.g., Weber, 1986, pp. 147-149).[102] Langlois and Seignobos' negative assessment was not peculiar to them. In his study of literatures of history, for instance, Flint

---

[99] For example, a reader well acquainted first with Max Weber's writings on bureaucracy and later coming to Hegel (e.g., his *Encyclopædia*) will probably be surprised by the volume. I say that not as a criticism; we all learn, and should learn, from our predecessors.

[100] That this anxiety of inferiority continued throughout the next century is testimony to how little attention was being given the physical sciences after 1905, although it must be said, too, that the majority of physical scientists until late in the century were uncomfortable at best with most recent developments from Einstein onward. I recall being told in 1952 that "only a handful of people in the whole world understand Einstein"—probably true even if exaggerated.

[101] Belletristic literatures of Europe's and Euro-America's late nineteenth and early twentieth centuries were more attentive to concerns about a "collapse of moral authority," although in retrospect some of the authors (e.g., Brooks 1915) seem strikingly out-of-date even for their own time. Others were symptomatic and diagnostic in one stroke (e.g., Mann's *Magic Mountain*, Eliot's "The Hollow Men," Musil's *The Man without Qualities*, Brock's *The Sleepwalkers*). More recently, Bellow demonstrated the tendency to authoritarian questing when, in a 1953 letter to a friend, he (2010, pp. 126, 127) said of one of his most noted "Every Man" creations, "Augie is the embodiment of a willingness to serve, who says 'For God's sake, make use of me, only do not use me to no purpose.'" People are desperate for the satisfaction of being put to use in some great cause, Bellow explained: "Surely the greatest human desire—not the deepest but the widest—is to be used." Without the "will to be used," social life would be "wholly pleasureless."

[102] "L'immense majorité des ecrits sur la méthode d'investigation en histoire et sur l'art d'ecrire l'histoire—ce que l'on appellee, en Allemagne et en Angleterre, l'*Historik*—sont superficials, insipides, illisibles, et il en est de ridicules." Langlois and Seignobos' book became the first widely used manual on historical methods.

77

(1893, pp. 15-16, 14) concluded that "a very large portion" of the writing on methods of historical research (i.e., "Historik"), "is so trivial and superficial that it can hardly ever have been of use even to persons of the humblest capacity." And more generally: "Not a few historians of repute owe their fame entirely" to their skills of felicitous writing; "as regards scientific and philosophical capacity [they are] below mediocrity." The same could be said of the social sciences, most practitioners simply ignoring the issues that lay unresolved in their claims to authority, writing as if uniquely privy to the dynamics of Lucretius' swerve.[103] Durkheim himself, aware of a serious epistemological problem from his studies of neo-Kantian philosophy, settled for the question-begging inconsistency of a *homo duplex* thesis: "It is not without reason," Durkheim declared,

> that man feels himself to be double: he actually is double .... In brief, this duality corresponds to the double existence that we lead concurrently; the one purely individual and rooted in our organisms, the other social and nothing but an extension of society.... The conflicts of which we have given examples are between the sensations and the sensory appetites, on the one hand, and the intellectual and moral life, on the other; and it is evident that passions and egoistic tendencies derive from our individual constitutions, while our rational activity—whether theoretical or practical—is dependent on social causes .... All evidence compels us to expect our effort in the struggle between the two beings within us to increase with the growth of civilization (Durkheim 1973 [1914], pp. 162-163).

In reviewing confusions in Durkheim (and, relatedly, Marcel Mauss), Steven Collins (1985) pointed in part to a reflection of Renouvier's (1906) effort to "correct" Kant and in part to the "objective idealist" developmentalism of Hegel. But Collins also demonstrated that the effort to neutralize the legacy of Kant's implications for social science was still very much alive, and itself still confused.

The confusions, concerns, and issues have not lessened. While the preferred stance has been to ignore them as non-existent or at least irrelevant, many scholars of the social sciences and history, when challenged to demonstrate that their claims to authority are categorically different from ordinary expressions of opinion, respond with a telling defensiveness. As Novick (1988, p. 11) pointed out, "the objectivity question is far from being 'merely' a philosophical question," irenic in its intent or aim. "It is an enormously charged emotional issue, one in which the stakes are very high, much higher than in any disputes over substantive interpretations." The charge is due primarily to recognition that professional standing depends on authority of voice, that being a professional historian or social scientist depends upon a credentialing that confers special status and thereby endows their pronouncements with sound authority, differentiating them from any "mere opinion" uttered by someone who lacks the credentials, and doing so with such finality that demonstration seems unnecessary.

Perhaps nowhere, during the early decades of the twentieth century, was the "objectivity question" and attendant threats to disciplinary authority more at issue than in pure or theoretical mathematics, long regarded as a fundamental discipline of our modern academy of science and humanities. This bit of history, generally well-remembered in the physical sciences and

---

[103] Anxieties about such matters are not often discussed in public discourse. An example of an exception during the late 1970s is Overington (1979; and, inter alia, Hazelrigg 1979). Bourdieu (1990 [1982]) was right about responses.

philosophy (as well as in mathematics), is less well known in the social sciences—perhaps in part because, excepting economics, so many students have been averse to mathematics. Thus, a brief account is in order. One of the signal ideas that modern European cultures inherited from the ancient Greeks, Plato foremost, held that mathematics, in form and in content, reigned as the epitome of eternal, necessary truth. Mathematics opened the door to pure Forms, the world of mind-independent real objects of timeless perfection. Empirically, all circles, no matter how well or poorly inscribed, are only approximations in expression of the form, *circle*. Likewise, triangles, spheres, and all other mathematical objects. By the end of the nineteenth century, however, Platonism, as the ruling framework of mathematics, had become badly frayed, partly because of the advent of new geometries which disturbed the settled reign of Euclid, overturning some of the basic assumptions of his geometry, and rattled the increasingly fragile cage of Cartesian faith in clear and distinct ideas, together with faith that certainty was assured by God's refusal to play the trickster. Henri Poincaré, premier mathematician in France, went so far as to conclude that objects of mathematics, including numbers and the zero concept, are actually constructs of mind's intuition. David Hilbert, premier mathematician in Germany, argued for a formalism that conceded the contingency of consciousness at work in a language of formal symbols (sometimes called a "game formalism"). These and other efforts to shore up the bases of mathematics' claim to certain knowledge initially showed promise, led to developments of some new ideas, and of some old ideas in new attire; but all ultimately unraveled under further scrutiny. Ironically, one of the early twentieth-century mathematicians who had been most committed to Platonism, Kurt Gödel, put paid to most of the effort (e.g., David Hilbert's formalism, the systemization of mathematical logic by Whitehead and Russell), when he demonstrated what are remembered as his "incompleteness theorems" (e.g., that mathematics cannot prove its claim to internal consistency; and if mathematics cannot, what can?). By 1979 Hilary Putnam, a highly regarded if less famous mathematician and philosopher, concluded that "nothing works." Nearly forty years later a pair of philosophers (Frodeman and Briggle, 2016) declared in the pages of the *New York Times* that philosophy as a whole had "lost its way."

## §9. Inventing New Uses of Ontology

It is sometimes said, in an elliptical manner, that cultures tend to recycle empty containers and other "things" that have lost utility. This selection process—selecting things "worth keeping" from things that have already fallen into oblivion are or about to—remains unclear, but there is at least one criterion that appears to be important in the sort: an item that at one time could be invoked as index and/or source of authority is likelier to be retained and recycled than an item without such weight. No one has rushed to redeem or reclaim Newton's æther, for example, as anything other than what it was, now considered an unnecessary figment of imagination that once plugged a whole that on later thought had not in fact been there. The word, "æther," began (so far as I know) in ancient Greek physical science, designating the "ethereal" substance filling the universe above the zone of Earth. Thus, "aithēr" has usually been translated as "upper air," and it was to that notion that Newton repaired when he concluded that there must be a kind of transmittive substance in "outer space" wherein the force of gravity is conveyed. Action at a distance—that is, without the intermediation of some kind of thingness through which the force of an action travelled—was nonsensical (or almost; Newton had doubts). Another use of the word "æther" became the popular name of a compound apparently first produced in 1540, a compound of sulfuric acid, sometimes called "oil of vitriol" (colorless, odorless, rather viscous, and bitter), and grain alcohol, the latter ingredient being a sweetener thus resulting in "sweet oil of vitriol." This liquid has a low boiling point at ground level, which means that it easily becomes a gaseous form of the same compound substance. The gas, colorless, slightly sweet-smelling, proved to be handy (although dangerously flammable) because when inhaled it "blocks aithēsis" (i.e., it is "anaesthetic"). It soon became the "ether" used in surgery. The same word is today also the technical name of a class of organic compounds each of which contains an "ether group." In 1919 a new agency, the International Union of Pure and Applied Chemistry, began the process of building a systematic nomenclature of chemical compounds. This one particular "ether" became a "diethyl ether" in the technical language of chemistry, which is to say in a classification of certain kinds of things.

After Kant had finished his "revolution," recall, the word "ontology" lost its luster. It had been the name of "the study of all things that are," as the ancient Greeks had declared it (the root "onta" or "that which is," derived from the past participle of the verb "eimi" or "to be"). These "things" were (thought to be) the foundational units, so to speak, of all being, of *Being* as such. And *as such*, Aristotle had anointed "ontology" as the basis of all metaphysics—that is, as "first philosophy" (the "second" being epistemology). Many versions of a "phenomenology" came on the scene after Kant, and some of them flourished, at least momentarily. But to most thinkers a study of "appearances" (i.e., that which appears to humans) always seemed to be a pale imitation of what had once been the regal "ontology." The very word had lost its referent, however, at least as far as any systematic inquiry by human beings was concerned. In short, the word, "ontology," had become the name of an empty category (relegated to the status of "archaism"), and many scholars shied away from use of it. It was not that "real things" had ceased to exist; rather that, as demonstrated by Kant, whatever these "really real things" may be and wherever they may exist, human beings have no access to them. The best any human being could (can) do is to infer from effects that must be due to "really real things." That would not satisfy, however, since any means of adjudicating any conclusions about how well the results of such an inference indicated the "really real thing" were always out of reach (the comparison depending on knowing the "really real thing" directly, or without inference). As the puerile phrase, "the really real thing," testifies, the mess quickly became an embarrassment, best left alone by serious scholars.

Classification is a serious business. Indeed, it is one of the most basic activities that human beings perform, and for the most part without reflecting on what exactly they are doing, for it is inseparable from language use. Because it is performed so easily without reflection, one must, and should, make effort to keep in mind that the name of the product known as this or that classification—and of the generality of the thing, classification—is nomination of a *process*, the process of classi*fying*, and thus of an inherent, inescapable temporality. Partly because of human aspiration to universality, the temporality and the productivity of classification, and of the rules of classification (a taxonomy), tend to be invisible. But even aside from such aspirations, the invisibility occurs because of utility: the very usefulness of classifying means that the action, its temporality and productivity, disappear into the end, the goal, the product, a settled arrangement of what *is*, in stable arrangements of categories. The tendency to think "classification" as *static*, the tendency for it to *be* inertially invisible, is built into the action of making one.

Thomas Mann's (1927 [1924]) explorations of categories in *The Magic Mountain* give many facets of insight into the usually unremarked, forgotten processual aspects that rest almost silently in names of things, as the name-thing coupling becomes a taken-for-granted of the real. Patients, for instance, have trajectories, while the categories into which they are sorted usually do not, or at least not in the short run; and when the categories do gain visible trajectory (as in acts of "reclassification"), the effect can be tumultuous (cf. Bowker and Star 1999, chs. 5, 6). How often do we expect patients to be activists, much less instigators and mobilizers of concerted actors? It is here that Ken Kesey (1962) intersects with the politics of large numbers, the motive power of large numbers to anchor but also to upset conveniences of classification (Desrosières 2002 [1993]).

Quantification is conditioned by classification. But as Aristotle realized in his book of categories, and in the puzzle of "heap," the relation soon becomes dialectical, each influencing the other (Mann 2000). Lawrence Slobodkin (1992, pp. 10, 208-216) showed us how the mobility of words such as "good" and "real" in descriptions of classificatory outcomes can be modified as a result of uncertainties and instabilities of quantities, both in the sense of the count of "definitive properties" of a "thing" in terms of membership criteria and in the sense of the magnitude of any particular property, "accidental" or (especially) "essential." After all, the utility of the very act of classifying is to achieve a simplification—at root, the necessity of that simplification which transforms the blur or "white light" of a flow or passage of sensations into the abstracted relation of identity/difference. "This thing" versus "that thing" must be resolved into categories each of which having a count greater than one (else the classificatory product be useless). Uniqueness represents a failure of some part of a classification, if not of its whole, but some tolerance of categories each containing a single member is achieved through a hierarchical dimension of taxonomic regulation.[104] Utilitarian dependence on simplifications tends to be as invisible as the temporality of classificatory productions in what Slobodkin (1992, p. 17) called "the peculiar humanity of stories." The particular can change location within the general scheme and be noticed at least momentarily for the mobility. Shifting boundaries of categories of "the real"—or what will then later be reconsidered as "the naïve view"—can be less noticeable to the hearer or reader of a story because of what Mourelatos (1973) called "the naïve metaphysics of things," to which we are all susceptible in virtue of a "necessity" of stability in the distribution of important things. Consciousness of the paradox tends to come only after, or in the process of, one's notice of a problem *within* that stability ("within," not "in," because one's own location has, or had, been within the stability). Even when I am convinced I have just gained an insight

---

[104] Thus, for example, the rules of botanic taxonomy tolerate a single-species genus because the unique event is contained by a higher level of the hierarchical dimension (e.g., the single-species genus is joined with one or more multi-species genera in a family. Consult the post-Linnaean history of plant taxonomy: you will see that it is replete with dozens of different systems, many of them still in use. Pursue the very recent history and you will see that, due to the advent of plant genomics, many species and subspecies have become quite mobile, shuttling across botanic charts in what amount to competitions between genomic (newer) and morphologic (older) criteria of taxonomy.

that throws some tiny piece of reality into new relief, I must contend with (and seldom more so) prior rules of names, things, and facts, in stubborn face of which my conviction may well flag. The "predicative mind" is never free of sociality (Bogdan 2009). Such is the enormous power of classification.[105]

If the standing of First Philosophy is no longer available to ontology, what is left for it to be? The study of things, including the thingness of things and categories of thingness in one or more classifications conducted according to specified rules (taxonomy).

This is as before—except that that all of these things, all of thingness and its categories and kinds, are humanly made. For a First Philosophy this is a huge exception, to be sure, even though in a sense the difference is very small. For a social science, in fact, it is and should be an ordinary fact. Aristotle's book of *Categories* can be read as a kind of social science as well as a kind of metaphysics, this difference then being a topic of the social.

And so it has happened. One of the prominent instances of a new ontology has taken its shape in the study of information and communication technologies, wherein a new language of inquiry (in multiple versions) has been constructed. The constructions began with what was decided through an ontological analysis to be conceptual primitives, the building blocks of a foundation or platform on which a purportedly complete copnceptual-structural language can be erected. Generations of "uniform mark-up languages" (UMLs) are prominent results. An example of a platform of ontological primitives is known as a Unified Foundational Ontology (or UFO), from which a UML named "Onto" has been built (Guizzardi 2005).[106] The things of a linguistic referral system populate a digital world, increasingly a world of processes and contents via "artificial intelligence," a world of materialized objects the constitution of which is by and through digital objects which act as tools of engineering, internally and externally. These worlds and tools are still works in progress, as is the sociality in which they transpire and which they are only beginning to reproduce with expected and unexpected differences. This ontology is a new means of making human realities.

Not to be outdone by scholars often seen as "mere technologists," several card-carrying members of the "proper trade" in philosophy have also resurrected ontology under a new sort of label, "social ontology." One of these philosophers, Frederick Schmitt, marked the occasion of "a burgeoning interest in the social world" among members of his profession during the 1990s

---

[105] Bogdan's (2009, pp. 132-133) account of the relation of language and thought follows a dialectical course. But as his study is of the ontogeny of the predicative relation, he was drawn to the question whether predication can gtake place only in an existing language, and his conclusion was that once the process of predication has been learned (which would be through language) it might be practicable otherwise. I can add a specific class of instances: music. Insofar as predication is a statement of thatness, music qualifies in abundance and in a manner that would count as extralinguistic, *unless* one counts music as a language. It is indeed a medium of communication—not only the communication that occurs in a passive reception, but even more the communication that occurs between two or more performers in the act of musical performance. These matters will be pursued in later discussions.
[106] Illustrations can be read in contents of a new journal, *Applied Ontology*, as well as in many recent publications of computer science, cognitive science, AI engineering, and so forth. See also Tegmark (2017).

by assembling a collection of their papers. That view of philosophers' interests was surely not inaccurate description of the then-recent past, especially for Anglophone analytic philosophers, among whom, insofar as they had ever seen reason to look to modern science for materials of interest, it was almost entirely to the physical sciences, the biological sciences a distant second because of their greater "messiness." That having been the case, why would any philosopher of the analytical persuasion want now to enter into the still greater messiness of the *social* sciences, especially after Kant's demonstration that these disciplines could only "pretend" to be a "true science," given their severe deficits of "the rational part"? And if what they wanted was a new adventure, why would they call it, as Schmitt, (2003, p. 1) said, a venture in the "metaphysics of sociality"—or as some preferred to call it, a "social ontology"?

In part the adventure can be explained as indicative of philosophers' favored self-regard as paladins of clearer, more rigorously incisive, logical thinking on *any* topic, or at least any topic susceptible of logical rigor and clarity. And in fact that has been the central tenor of most of the forays carrying Schmitt's "burgeoning interest." Without suggesting intent of sarcasm or condescension on their part, the philosophers' calling card to social scientists could honestly read, "What a mess of written thought! Stand by, while we clear out the confusions and inconsistencies, thus leaving a clear sense of what you have accomplished to date, what your basic or principled disagreements amount to, and where (and why) you need to improve your skills of logical thinking." Should a reader suspect the entry of a Trojan horse, the possibility cannot be dismissed entirely. But the evidence points far more to a resigned acceptance that pre-Kant ontology is beyond redemption. Given their reputed delight in arts of argumentation, would any self-respecting philosopher attempt a sleight of hand, as if no one would notice?

Schmitt's assessment of "interest in the social world" as "burgeoning" was certainly not an underestimation. A rough sampling of book-length essays published since his collection would include Margaret Gilbert's *Joint Commitment* (2014), following her *Social Facts* (1989; see also 2000), Michael Bratman's *Planning, Time, and Sociality* (2018; see also1999), Manuel DeLanda's *A New Philosophy of Society* (2006), Raimo Tuomela's *The Philosophy of Sociality* (2007; see also 2013), Christian List and Philip Pettit's philosophical inquiry into *Group Agency* (2011), Brian Epstein's *The Ant Trap* (2015; see also 2018), and Graham Harman's *Object-Oriented Ontology* (2018), which follows several other books, plus his conversation with Manuel DeLanda, *The New Realism* (2017). Focal topics vary across these (and other) works, authors disagree among themselves on some claims, and the meaning intended by the phrase "social ontology" is not always clear or unambiguous and (once ambiguity has been removed) might prove to be inconsistent across authors. More will be said about specific works later, as a general context is developed.

Before proceeding, I should repeat that, here as elsewhere, boundaries are pervious, sometimes vague, often threatened by instability of criteria. A main instance concerns work by Bruno Latour, relevant here because one the specific topics of the "social ontology" literature has to do with the meaning of "social" and whether it contributes anything of important content to theory. A development of theory beginning as early as the 1970s became known as "actor-network theory" (latterly abbreviated as "ANT"). Latour's investigations figured in that line of development, thus were at issue when John Law and John Hassard (1999) published a volume that became known as a set of fatal attacks against ANT; and Latour (2005) then published an effort at rebuttal and recovery. The relevance presently is due mainly to the question of "the social," and more particularly to the issue of scale or relation between "individual person" and "group" or "collective" organizations—primarily whether that relation is homologous—and related matters such as intent, motive, and will.[107] More will be said about this part of the "debate," as it intersects with "social ontology" (e.g., List and Pettit 2011) as well as with actor-network theory. Also, note that I will cease such repetitious use of scare quotes around "social ontology," but one should be cautious about assuming constancy of meaning of that phrase from author to author.

The earliest I can recall a philosopher giving attention to the social sciences and in that context (or, as best I remember, any other) using the phrase "social ontology" is Carol Gould's book (1978) on Karl Marx' theorizing. She identified two senses of the phrase, the first giving more weight to the noun (i.e., the Greek notion of inquiry into "that which is"), the second more weight to the adjective in its own nominative impact. On the one hand, Gould (1978, p. xv) said, the phrase refers "to the study of the nature of social reality, that is, the nature of the individuals, institutions and processes that compose society." The central task in this regard is "to determine the basic entities of social life," in particular how "individual person" fits into that composition. Secondly, the phrase also "may mean ontology socialized, that is, a study of reality that reflects on the social roots of the conceptions of this reality." This meaning reminds us that the person making inquiry or proposing a theory is, when the inquiry or theory is of the social, the cultural, the historical, and so forth, *inherent* to that which is being studied and/or theorized. In short, Gould was telling us that "theorist" is not, cannot be, some sort of "special actor" of Olympian vintage and thus should not act, and should not be heard or read, as if in some privileged nexus of context and conditions. The theorist is—not simply "must be" but *is*—*within* the inquiry, the theory (see Hazelrigg 1979; 1989a, passim; 1989b, pp. 73-118; 1992; 1993b).[108] With that in mind, and recognizing that those "alternative senses" of the phrase "are not mutually exclusive," Gould offered her own third sense: "social ontology is the analysis of the nature of social reality by means of socially interpreted categories."

It seems evident to me that in presenting that third sense Gould was carefully choosing her words, so as not to seem "too radical." She did not interrogate "nature," for example, leaving it to the reader to suppose that "character" might have been a suitable synonym, or that Newton's "nature" was being invoked, and so forth. Likewise, the means by which "the analysis" was to be conducted consisted in "socially interpreted categories," which of course allowed the reader to suppose that the categories themselves were not, are not, socially *produced* (it being "radical enough" to allow the difficulties of the "socially interpreted"). I also think Gould's strength in "analytical philosophy" was an impediment, however, for I believe the point she wanted to make

---

[107] Bear in mind that "ANT" (in all Roman capitals) refers to "actor-network theory," whereas "ant" in Epstein's title, *The Ant Trap* (2015), refers to the insect as metaphor for a certain view of the human individual in population. If the latter was intended also as a criticism of ANT for its tendency to what some philosophers are calling "ontological individualism," the indications of it are rather thin.
[108] Recall, in this regard, my earlier comments (in the preface) about the "ship of Theseus" story, which will figure again later in this section.

was a dialectical one—namely, the dialectic of subject/object, among similar other internal relations. Thus, for example, subject is object to others but also to perceiving self, although here only "after the fact" (Hume's point). Subject's products are objects to self, and to others; and while these (and similar other relations) are often thought as sequential (as if "first subjective, then objective"), the inherence is reciprocal and immediate. An object comes to *be* through production, although the productive act is often thought as if an after-the-fact re-cognition and sometimes as an *alien* presence (i.e., as something not due to my action directly or indirectly, or an effect of alienated labor as Marx discussed).[109] This is of prime significance in the present context, because several (if not all) of the social-ontology proponents considered below insist that *all* relations are external to the "things" being related (see, e.g., DeLanda 2006, pp. 9-11), and this insistence is apparently held by at least some of those who argue that group-level or some other collectivity-level organization is significant because it adds something "extra" to what the sum of the multiple individual-person members of the group or collectivity contribute (about which, more below).

Ambiguities of authors' uses of the phrase "social ontology" turn on which of Gould's three senses the given author had in mind. In some instances it can seem as if the author intends Gould's first sense only, perhaps with fond imagination of rechristening the phrase in, say, Cartesian waters. In other instances the author's intent seems closer to Gould's second sense, or more often to her third sense with its explicit reflexivity.[110] So, for example, one can read Harman's (2018) intent as socializing "thing in itself," and retaining it as such rather than jettisoning it completely as some post-Kant phenomenologies had attempted. In other words, the object which Kant's "objective necessity," arising in and by the transcendental Illusion, encourages and, in a sense, enables us in our existential insecurity to legislate surreptitiously should be retained as an "in-itself" object because that is what we intend to produce as surety along with the corresponding phenomenal object. Both are real, because both are products of our "reasonings," however different they may be between the phenomenal and the (quasi-)noumenal objects. Think of it by analogy to Marx' "false consciousness," which is no less real in its effects for being false. Likewise, "alienated labor": a laborer invests his or her own being, own identity, in the product of labor no less when the labor process is alienated as when it is not; and when the process *is* alienated, it is also alienating—of the product and of the producing laborer. By enthymemic criteria there is a falseness to the process, the product, and the laborer; and it is all very real. I might be doing injustice to Harman's aim and effort, but it seems to me that the key of his project is that "thing in itself" is no less real for being "only thought" (i.e., a false presence in thought, by terms of Kant's argument regarding noumenal reality) because in fact it is *not* "only thought" any more than "thing for us" (a phenomenal object) is only thought. Each is a real presence for us *as* a presence in itself. Thus, we do in that manner invest ourselves in the real object, thereby putting *in* the object our own agency, rendering the object an autonomy toward us. This investiture can be likened to the investiture that Veyne (1988 [1983]) had in

---

[109] This is, I believe, vital to what Gould (1978, pp. 168-178) was attempting in her discussion of the fraught issue of "value," for example, a confused notion that, as Martin and Lembo (201*n*) have demonstrated, has badly infected the social sciences from their modern beginnings (or "re-beginnings").
[110] Reflexivity will be topical throughout my discussions, although often only implicitly. Malcolm Ashmore's (1989) detailed treatment remains highly productive.

mind when he wrote of the difference between believing a myth and believing *in* a myth (see Hazelrigg 1989b, 1993a, 1993b; also see Loraux 1996).

In his introductory comments, Schmitt (2003) directed his reader's attention to three main themes of the "new" literature of social ontology: differences between "ontological holism" and "ontological individualism"; how those differences can be reconciled, if they can; and "how individual human beings figure in social relations and collectivities," the pivotal theme of "[v]irtually all of the discussion in the metaphysics of sociality." As he (2003, pp.1-2) observed, these themes are more or less tightly interwoven, depending on which ontologist one considers. The following presentation will follow both themes. But I shall begin with a somewhat different slant on them, one that is implicit in Schmitt's account and, as with other of these new ontologists, mostly taken for granted. As philosophers of analytic persuasion, they share not only a rejection of internal relations but also a reliance on an originary logic in their reasoning. I shall illustrate first with a consideration of Schmitt's (2003, p. 2) display of that anchor, then a consideration of Gilbert's display of it. References to it will continue to be made in subsequent text. It is important that the reader have clearly in mind my point (which I shall repeat more than once).

An analytical mereology is no less dependent on conceptual schemes or classifications for being regulated by strictly external relations of parts of a whole and of one whole to another. Boundary work is critical, on-going, and usually only partially successful in its aims of integrity maintenance, repair, and regulating authority of voice, in part because the work itself must deal in streams of ambiguity and ambivalence—Cartesian "clear and distinct ideas" are imaginary— and in part because both the objects and the objective are dynamic (see Bowker and Star 1999; Bowker 2005; Levine 1985; Gieryn 1983). Composition can begin to look too much like an eldritch exercise of sets of sets; endless is the stack without some limit of composition. Thus, the appeal analytically of and to an originary logic. Schmitt (2003, p. 2) asked straightaway, "what properties of individuals [individual human beings] count as nonsocial"? In other words, to say "the social" cannot be to address the whole of wholes, the totality of being, since to do so would render it exactly redundant of "totality" or "whole of wholes," and the like. It must do work of some differentiation, which means that there must be its counterpart, "the nonsocial." How does that boundary align with the boundary of "individual human being"? As Bowker (2005, p. 137) said with regard to a concept of biodiversity, "one of the great questions is what kinds of things we should be naming so that we can keep the historical development of [things] 'in mind' as we manage [our] future."

The phrase "originary logic" is my way of highlighting the problem of a very common practice in philosophy, and in some precincts of social science, a practice usually known as "rational reconstruction." The practice amounts to an argument of "how it must have happened that X came to be an X." It is a sort of genetic search for "first principles" or "first conditions," a procedure that makes sense for analytic pursuits but that can easily be misused. I mentioned an instance of this above, with regard to Marx' criticism of the materialist philosophy of Ludwig Feuerbach, who sought to locate the real "essence" of the individual human being by abstracting away all sociality, to leave something that he apparently thought to be "the pure individual." It seemingly never occurred to Feuerbach that sociality was, *is*, of the "essence" of human being. What did he make of Aristotle's famous announcement of "zoön politicon"? Psychologism

86

assumes that *it* is the originary logic vis-à-vis sociality.  Some presentations of biology have done likewise (e.g., genetics, now genomics, next proteomics; see Plomin 2018).

Schmitt (2003, p. 1) referred to the mereological question of boundaries also with regard to "how individual human beings figure in social relations and collectivities"—which, as a question of process, can be read as a way of asking how one, the individual human being, *becomes* the other, some sort of collectivity and in the process acquires social relationality.  Note the implicit work of originary logic in that formulation.  Schmitt verged on explicit notice of the presence of that logic when he referred to "a question of how far sociality extends into the apparently nonsocial world"—which is to ask, he said, "what properties of individuals count as nonsocial."  On first blush at least part of an answer seems so obvious as to go without remark: physical properties, biological properties, if none other.  Schmitt (2003, p. 2) concurred: "I take it that [the nonsocial] include no more than the following: the physical and biological properties of individuals and the singular—that is, nonjoint or noncollective—actions and attitudes of individuals."  But he had already drawn up short of that general stance, by noting that "race" and "gender," once assumed to be "nonsocial," are now generally regarded as both biological and social.  He also reminded his reader that since the work of Ludwig Wittgenstein several other philosophers, "notably, Peter Winch," have agreed that the main assumption underlying differentiation of "the social" and "the nonsocial"—namely, the categorial boundary supposedly separating ontological individualism and ontological holism—is fallacious, and not merely as a matter of arbitrary words.  The notion "that we can understand human beings independently of social relations and collectivities" is an absurdity, in view of the fact that "individual human beings are already bound up in social relations in virtue of having such attributes as thinking, acting, and speaking a language."[111]

That Schmitt began his discussion with the statement in which he so matter-of-factly excluded "the physical and biological properties" from "the social" is indication of the strong grasp that an "originary logic" can exert on thinking.  Another illustration can be seen in Gilbert's (1989, pp. 430-431) presentation of her preferred articulation of "the individual" and "the collective," which followed her careful interrogation of the meanings of "ontological individualism" and "ontological holism."  Paring away inconsistencies and ambiguities, she settled on a key process of individual reformation:  "In order for individual human beings to form collectivities, they must take on a special character, a 'new' character, in so far as they need not, qua human beings, have that character."  Unfortunately, this "special character" amounts to nothing less than becoming "social," so we are left with either an unexplicated process within an individual person that becomes "the social" or a bit of question begging.  The lack of explication reduces the choice to only the latter.  Much the same verdict attends her subsequent efforts in articles that she collected for her book, *Joint Commitment* (2014).  The dilemma is rather like

---

[111] Remarkably, the fact that Marx (1976 [1888], p. 7) had written of "the individual" person as an "ensemble of social relations," plus the fact that Kant had emphasized the unavoidable "filter" of conceptual scheme (historically and culturally variable language), had each been so little attended that Wittgenstein's remarks could be jolting to many philosophers and other scholars, and that Winch's (1958) elaboration of those remarks generated controversy.

that which bedeviled developments of contract theory: the so-called pre-contract conditions of contract looked suspiciously like contractual agreements in all but formality of naming.[112]

Presumptions of an originary logic (and an "original position") are tenacious for a good reason. Doesn't it seem "perfectly logical" that human beings began in a genetic sense (i.e., an evolutionary sense) as biophysical beings before they became social? That being the case, isn't it also "perfectly logical" that today the definitive properties of "human being" are ordered in a logical sequence, from physical to biological to social? Prinz (2012, pp. 107-114) described as pertinent versions of a "folk ontology" that corresponds to the view implicit in those rhetorical questions.

My answer to the first of those (rhetorical) questions is, "Perhaps; but so much depends on the temporal boundary that we draw as the advent of Homo sapiens, and it is here that one's argumentation turns on enthymemic criteria (as I have argued before; see Hazelrigg 1979, 1989a, 1989b, 1992, 1993a, 1993b, 1995). There is good evidence that the ancestor species of Homo sapiens was already social. And probably the grandparent as well as the parent species. When, then, do we want to begin the clock? As Bowker (2005, p. 137) pointed out, the convention of the Latin binomial has been a very useful device: it lets us archive established facts of internal relationships among a huge array of differences/identities of life forms. Those established facts include an encapsulation of time on which many other established facts quietly depend. This encapsulation converts the dynamism of both evolutionary change and human learning into accomplishments that are settled and seemingly in perfect correlation with each other, the evolution and the edification. Our analytical logic tells us that there *must* have been a beginning date, an origin point, in order for each of us to be here now. But we, each of us, can safely let it rest in the archive, precisely because we *are* here now. This sleight of hand regarding the conditions and the consequences of "origins" forecloses present options of future being, in a manner that Aristotle described more than 2,350 years ago in his dialectic of actual/potential (*On Metaphysics*, book 9, part 6). So many of the constructs that human beings have devised during the last two centuries have been and are unredemptive, as if we have no responsibility for future conditions of life—ours and the lives of other living beings. Shall we, each of us in our sociality, continue living our collective lives in that manner?[113]

My answer to the second question is, "Definitely not." To answer otherwise is to deny recognition of some very basic conditions: any human being enters an already social world and thereby becomes inherently social, enmeshed in social relations that are integral to the person's life—indeed, to her or his initial viability—and that will continue to be vitally integral through

---

[112] The Gilbert sentence quoted above does contain an ambiguity, however: the conjunctive phrase, "in so far as," could have been a deliberate hedge.

[113] Max Tegmark (2017, p. 268) illustrated a productive use of the "originary logic" device in thought experiments: "suppose a bunch of ants create you to be a recursively self-improving robot, much smarter than they, who shares their goals and helps them build bigger and better anthills, and that you eventually attain the human-level intelligence and understanding that you now have. Do you think you will spend the rest of your days just optimizing anthills, or do you think you might develop a taste for more sophisticated questions and pursuits that the ants have no ability to comprehend?" Of course, the hypothetical, as stimulating of thought as it may be (which is the point), remains bare of substantiation.

childhood and into adulthood. Whatever else they may be, the hoary stories of "the wolf child" are indicative of a recognition that a neonatal human cannot survive without assistance from a sustaining creature. That condition is *already* a sociality, a first fact of human life. I argue also (and "further"), however, that physics, chemistry, geology, biology, and so forth, are human activities and therefore are inescapably social. *Where otherwise do they, would they, come from?* The objects (and their complex relations) to which each of those disciplines of inquiry and skills of production refer are indeed real. We may imagine that they exist in some noumenal reality, Kant said, but insofar as we know them, handle them, use them, and so forth, it is by means of the conceptual schemes of our perceptions, understandings, skillful actions, and so forth; and all of these are inherently, inescapably historical, cultural, social. We may pretend that some of them are autonomous, have their own powers of agency, willfulness, and intention; and in a sense they do, because of investitures that we made. But we must be very careful how we build these autonomous objects to believe *in*; for we have not otherwise evaded our responsibility for them.

A sense of responsibility can be seen at work in DeLanda's (2006, p. 1) offer of what he considered be "a novel approach to social ontology," the main term of which he characterized as concern with "the question of what kinds of entities we can legitimately commit ourselves to assert exist." His "realist" account in response to that question asserts "the autonomy of social entities from the conceptions we have of them," but this is only to say that the "theories, models and classifications" which we use to study social entities "may be objectively wrong." In other words, we might at any point decide that we have been wrong, adjudicating in terms of what we have most confidently considered the "stubborn facts" of reality to be (to use a locution popular at least since Bernard Mandeville 1732, p. 162).[114] While "social entities are clearly not mind-independent," the dependence may consist partly in errors and illusions. Moreover, the social entities that humans have produced and that gain an objective presence—that is, have become objects that actors take into account, some of them in materialized form—continue to be affected by the mind-dependent activities and inherent conceptions, perceptions, and motivations of individual persons, including those who study and pronounce upon the entities (DeLanda 2006, p. 1). Thus, his understanding of "social ontology" generally mirrors Gould's (1978) but also with little sense of a dialectical internality and inherence of relations. While Delanda sought to adopt Deleuze's attempts toward a theory of "assemblages" (Deleuze and Parnet 2002 [1997]; Deleuze and Gauttari 2004 [1980]), he mainly reproduced the dilemma of the "doubled object" (as described above, and in Pippin 1999, pp. 53, 56). The main effect of his uses of a theory of assemblages (whether "Deleuzean" or not) is demonstration that it does not explain processes by which the "micro" becomes the "macro" but only gives descriptions of outcomes of those processes—descriptions, moreover, which could entail a false impression that the processes are *homologous*, inasmuch as an assumption of homology is built into the theory.[115]

---

[114] Mandeville was probably not the first to write "facts are stubborn things," which was offered without fanfare in the third dialogue of his treatise on "the origin of honour."

[115] In the foregoing I have followed DeLanda in attributing "theory of assemblages" to Deleuze, when in fact (as Delanda acknowledged, p. 3) much of the work was done with Félix Guattari. I should note, too, that DeLanda there said that the works by Deleuze and colleagues "hardly amount to a fully-fledged theory."

Those who have announced their following of Deleuzean "assemblage" have usually added to it a notion of "emergence"—that is, some sort of "value added" component to the effects of the formerly separate parts of a newly formed whole.[116] Since most of these scholars also insist that all relations are external, the "extra" that "emerges" must be due to an interaction of parts that does not change the parts themselves. Think of the common image of the game of billiards: the desired interaction of the cue ball with a selection of target balls results in "added values" that can lead to victory, and the interaction has no internal effect on any of the balls in collision. That account of a wholly external interaction is false, to be sure, according to the science of physics: there *is* internal effect, but it is so slight that the balls show no "corruption" for many years. It is worth noting, too, that in such accounts "emergence" is simply another name for the conclusion of a process.

In so using the word "corruption" I was recounting a discussion by Aristotle on problems of conceptualization in his experiences of mereological relations and processes. Across his several works, especially *Metaphysics* and *On Generation*, he was evidently at pains to develop a self-consistent classification of part-to-whole relations. While one can agree that his efforts did achieve improvements on efforts of his predecessors, problems remained, and it seems clear that he was aware of at least some of the problems especially in regard to correlative treatments of "the physical," "the chemical," and "the biological." In fact, problems remain still today (see, e.g., the entry on the Sorites Paradox in the *Standard Encyclopedia of Philosophy*).[117] Aristotle said in his *Metaphysics* (1045a6-10) that "whole" is distinguished from "heap" in that the former is a *unity* among parts, a unity in which the resulting whole is "something besides the parts," and that one must thus ask "what is the cause" of that unity. Self-consistent answers across processes of "composition" (synthesis), "coalescence" (synióta), and "combination" (míxis) as these were discussed in *Metaphysics* and in *On Generation* (e.g., 328a6, 328b23) proved to be elusive, as they are yet today across what are conventionally taken to be wholes of different "natural kinds" (e.g., the molecules of a billiard ball, those of a chemical whole such as water or methane or strychnine, and those of animal flesh or tissue or cells). To say (as Aristotle did) that "combination is the unification of combinables" (328a6) does not advance our understanding, not only because of the semantic duplication across the copula but also because "unification" apparently operates in several different ways, depending on what the "combinables" are—for example, cells of a tissue or elements of a molecule. A commonly cited example of the latter is the combination of hydrogen and oxygen: each of the gases is combustible (hydrogen rapidly, oxygen slowly), but if combined in a certain way ($H_2O$) we gain molecules of a substance that

---

[116] Deleuze wrote "agencement," which means "plan" or "scheme" or "layout" ("action d'agencer" is "action of arranging"), with no indication of any "emerging" quality or property (see Deleuze 1991 [1953]; 1994 [1968]). In his dialogue with Claire Pernet (Deleuze and Parnet 2002 [1977]), in which he sought to "explain" himself, it is noteworthy that most of his references were to Hume and Hegel; only once, in passing, to Kant.

[117] Sorites (from the Greek "sōros," meaning "heap"), a term of logic, refers to a chained sequence of propositions in which the predicate of one proposition forms the subject of the next proposition, seriatum, until at the end of the sequence the subject of the first proposition is united with the conclusion of the last. The sequence is famously illustrated by the Sorites Paradox ("the problem of the heap"), just one instance of outstanding difficulties which frustrate and entertain logicians and philosophers (for a useful review, see Bogaard 1979).

not only is not combustible but also douses many kinds of fire (see, e.g., DeLanda and Harman 2017, p. 8). This is sometimes cited as illustration of "added value"; but in this instance, note, the unification comes about through the unequal sharing of electrons, a relation that is internal to each of the parts as well as to the whole (which is made polar by the imbalanced sharing). In other words, we have a process of unification that differs from the unification that results in a sedimentary stone, and neither of those is the same as the unification that results in cellular metabolism or the unification that results in the *four* haploid cells from the *one* that undergoes meiosis or, still again, the unification of recombinant DNA. A property of "emergence" supposedly unique to "assemblage" (or to any other sort of modification of an "agencement") is surely not the simple solution to a varied passel of problems that some theorists have thought to make of it.

Recall that one of the themes highlighted by Schmitt (2003, p. 1) has to do with proper assignments mereologically of intent and willfulness. Early in the twentieth century the question of "group mind" was thought to be legitimate if controversial (see, e.g., McDougall 1920), a possibility stimulated by grave concerns about "mob action," the behavior of crowds, and similar other aspects of "the problem of order" (see above), sometimes couched in terms of memories of the French Revolution and its terrible aftermath, more recent bouts of "revolutionary" ideologies and actions in countries of Europe, and "civil disturbances" due to the labor-union movement and anxieties about large numbers of immigrants in the northeast of the USA and the violence of racist oppressions of "Jim Crow" laws in the southern states. Gilbert (1989, p. 430) made a point of declaring that "there is no empirical warrant" for believing "in independent group minds or spirits," beliefs that have "tended to give [ontological] holism a bad name." But her declaim was in part strategic, protecting her scholarly interests in investigations and theorizations of the process by which individual persons come together in joint projects of intentional action. Others, too, have offered theories of "shared agency" or "group agency" (Bratman 1999, 2018; List and Pettit 2011). As with the problems of boundary fixing in classification activities, here, too, the issues are difficult. As List and Pettit (2011, pp. 176-177) pointed out, the idea of "corporate agency" has been established law in many societies for more than a century, and as a result a corporation, a collectivity of many, sometimes thousands of individual persons, can be and is treated "as if" another person in courts of law (i.e., a latter-day installment of Hobbes' "artificial person"). Legal codes do not state the "as if" phrase, either in legal text and for all practical purposes as a description of relevant fact. And yet, there remain legitimate issues: "it is one thing to say that the personification of group agents is established practice in law and related thinking. It is another to consider this personification justified. For all that the existence of the practice shows, it may represent a legally useful fiction." Indeed, it *is* a legally useful fiction (just as it was for Hobbes a politically useful fiction). But so are a great many other practices of law and jurisprudence. The question List and Pettit sought to answer was (is), is there warrant other than the legal fiction? Is "intent" as expressed by a corporate person, for example, the same as "intent" as expressed by a single, presumably independent (at least in legal terms) individual person? If there *are* differences, do they matter? Or why *ought* they to matter or *not* matter)? Seemingly straightforward simple questions, they prove to be very difficult to answer self-consistently in coherence with other principles (see also Tuomela 2007, whose focal address was of "the shared point of view"). The questions, and the frustrations of answering them, are not

91

new, of course. That they are questions still being addressed is good indication of the degree of prior success, and this remains the case after recent efforts.

In his own chapter-length contribution to the collection he assembled, Schmitt (2003, p. 130) began from the position of a "strict individualism" in order to explore phenomena of what are popularly considered instances of "joint action." One might say if individual persons A and B perform what appears to be a certain "joint action" that it could well be that A and B "perform a certain joint action just in case each performs certain singular actions, has certain singular attitudes (beliefs, intentions), and these actions and attitudes are related by approved relations." How could an observer tell the difference? If A and B should respond to a specific interrogation by simultaneously saying, "We decided it is such a beautiful morning to walk in the park!" would that count as "joint action"? The "we" could simply reflect mutual awareness that each was walking in the presence of the other. Does that count as "jointness"? Even if each had agreed with the other in advance to "meet at the corner and go for a walk," is *that* enough for the "walking in each other's presence" to qualify as "joint action"? Schmitt's pursuit of these and related questions elucidates many of the complexities that lie in wait of an argument in favor of "joint action." "joint commitment," and the like.[118]

In a discussion that reminds me of Dennis Wrong's famous paper of 1961 (see above), DeLanda (2006, p. 4) pointed to the peculiar stance taken by those who "assume that once [individual persons] have been socialized by the family and the school, they have so internalized the values of the society or the social classes to which they belong that their allegiance to a given social order may be taken for granted. This tends to make the micro-level an epiphenomenon." I recall from my first reading of Wrong's article my puzzlement that anyone would believe that assumption. Soon thereafter, however, I began to learn "Parsonian theory" and its relation to main strands of macroeconomics, after which I better understood the point of Wrong's claim. And yet some puzzlement remained, inasmuch as there seemed to be in some views of the matter a confusion of "theoretical model," which deliberately contains simplifications (some that any given reader might regard as oversimplifications), with an empirically descriptive account of some indicated reality (see, e.g., Planck 1949 [1948], pp. 35-45). On the other hand, there was indeed evidence that some social scientists had been taking (or believing in) the former as an adequate substitute for the latter, even though this would of course have been a mockery of the basic point of a model.

In any case, the assumption also imagines that for any cohort of adult persons, history, in the form of biography, effectively ceases at some age, except that as another cohort comes along history then "resumes," as if its normal course is one of "fits and starts". This image has given rise to the expectation, held by many social scientists, that cohort analysis is a sufficient method for the study of process and change, because, supposedly, all meaningful change happens in the succession of birth cohorts aging into adulthood. Thus, supposedly, each succeeding cohort examined in the cross-section, arrayed as sequences of differences-in-identity in time,

---

[118] Schmitt's work has been exceptionally clear, concise, and consequential, but attended far less than it merits, in part perhaps because he has not been an instance of Williams' (2018) "promotional intellectual."

would yield sufficient evidence from which to infer the operative processes of change.[119] This view meshed with some evidence within science of the workings of theory itself, as Max Planck famously observed when he (1949 [1948], pp. 33-34) said that a "new scientific truth does not triumph by convincing its opponents and making them see the light, but rather because its opponents eventually die, and a new generation grows up that is familiar with it" (see Azoulay, Fons-Rosen, and Zivin 2019).

Generally speaking, the authors of this newly written literature of philosophy, or social ontology, have been in agreement that the crucial issue is about "transition" or "translation" from the kinds of activities, including perceptions, conceptions, interests, motives, intentions, and so forth, that characterize and in some sense are performed by individual persons, to the organized activities of collectivities of individual persons, call them groups or communities or corporations or mobs or crowds or conspiracies or whatever. In general, the authors seem to recognize that social scientists at least of recent decades have also given attention to this issue, if not with much success to show for it, and have noted disagreements among their approaches—for instance, that some have begun with an assumption of homology, that at least the main processes work by the same logic across all levels of transition or translation, from intra-individual dynamics over time to inter-individual dynamics to communal and associational dynamics all the way to an entire society, while other social scientists have disputed that assumption of homology, arguing that scale sensitivities are important, even determinative.

While several early social scientists—Auguste Comte, for instance; Emile Durkheim and Georg Simmel later—devoted considerable effort of inquiry and formulation of the issue, the usual approach was to address it, if at all explicitly, in terms of a combination of broad and rather vague images of logical model and a sometimes strenuous rejection of a "positivism" in favor of more ethnographic and/or ideology-critical professions of interest. These latter professions were sometimes given expression and identity as a "phenomenological social science" (as if virtually all inquiries after Kant had not been phenomenological, broadly speaking) or, in other cases, as an ideology-critique with intent of revolution and emancipation, as if existing society had already been well enough understood for one to know how to convert it into a significantly better one (the lie of that presumption usually told by occasionally violent squabbles between different theories of means and ends, sometimes with results of one or another kind of totalitarianism). As for the vaguely depicted logical models, the biological and social sciences were fated to endure "debates" between "mechanism" and "organicism" during the late nineteenth and twentieth centuries, as scholars struggled to define themselves vis-à-vis the physical sciences (and the social relative to the biological), often within the pangs of a doctrinal-institutional inferiority

---

[119] In that way, theory and methodology of social science meshed with state interests in acquiring periodic panels of demographic description (census reports) of "the state of the population" at each of succeeding interval, from which descriptive comparisons could be made (see Desrosières 2002 [1993]). Dynamics would be collapsed into statics, but supposedly in a way that would allow inferences from statics to dynamics. Such was the agreement offered by state agencies to fund social science efforts to obtain systematic observations of phenomena. Theorists and methodologists thus needed to adapt and theorize relations in a specific way and invent new means of inference to process (e.g., "event history analysis," Nancy Tuma's Rate program, etc.; see, e.g., Bartholomew 1967; Tuma and Hannan 1984; Duncan 1984).

complex (see, e.g., Allen 2005; Watkins 1957; and compare Planck 1932, pp. 77-83). These model images were frequently deployed in popular textbooks about the history and/or "schools" of theory in the social sciences.

As has been pointed out repeatedly, none of those models is in fact testable. But they do project different regulative principles, which in turn generate different (sometimes only partially different) hypotheses, some of which can be tested. A more direct, even immediate problem of the models, however, is that they have encouraged "all or nothing" mentalities, and this tendency often infects the hypotheses, making tests of those hypotheses more difficult and sometimes leading to indefinite outcomes. One major manifestation of this "all or nothing" mentality has taken the form of a "debate" between two opposing types of methodology, "individualist" and "holist," which the philosophers of social ontology have mostly preferred to render ontological individualism and ontological holism. As mentioned earlier, the tendency has been toward an assumption of homology—that is, that regulative principles of a common, uniform logic apply throughout. The individualist position tends to hold that individual-level ("micro-level") phenomena are regulated by principles that apply uniformly as effects generalize up the hierarchy of organizational scale, from micro-level to macro-level, whether the latter be specified as small-group or society or some collectivity intermediate to them. Because (as noted above) the basic conception of "individual person" tends to be informed by an originary logic, the individual begins within a psychologistic set of regulative principles, which quickly raises the question whether "the social" is real or consequential and, if it is, how it comes to be. In contrast to that individualist position, the holist position tends to begin with some collective form (which can be communal, associational, or some blend of the two) and assumes homologous relations both therein and in effects of macro-level phenomena on individual persons. As for micro-level effects, the general tendency has been to view them as epiphenomenal, if not immediately then as they "wash out" or converge to "the average" enroute to collective organizational forms. In both of these positions, then, whether interpreted ontologically or only methodologically, there is seldom a serious question of scale effects.

If the foregoing strikes social-scientist readers as old news, there is good reason for that: it *is* old news (for a recent though partial review, see Jepperson and Meyer 2011). As some of the scholars recited above have explicitly observed (e.g., Gilbert 1989), the several issues have been debated again and again in the social science literature, with little or no resolution. So far, the philosophers' expeditions of logical clarity and rigorously incisive analysis have not altered much of the understandings made by previous generations of social scientists.[120] One would hope to see from the works of the philosophers of social ontology significant advances in

---

[120] I acknowledge that movement into the academic professional realms of the social sciences and experimental psychology can be seen as part of an effort by philosophers to gain more solidity of support and standing within the institution of high education, where, along with other disciplines of the humanities, as well as the social sciences, vulnerability to a myopic mentality has gained far more than a foothold in the politics of finance. Machery (2017), for example, has developed an argument in support of greater attention among philosophers to practical everyday problems of living, folk beliefs, and the like, in order to acquire more of an image of practicality even if at the cost of neglecting the traditional role of philosophy as "persistent crank" about impossible questions (e.g., "why are we here?" "why anything rather than nothing?"). For a thoughtful response, see Setiya (2018).

understanding of the processes by which micro-level actions and effects become macro-level actions and effects, whether homologously or with sensitivity to scale. To date, these have been difficult to spot. Gilbert (1989, pp. 430-431) concluded early on that the transition or translation involves change of "the human individual qua human being," and she has specified the effect of that requisite change as "joint commitment," which is, to quote her 2014 subtitle, "how we make the social world" (see also her chapter in Schmitt 2003, pp. 39-64). However, we learn little about the process of how that jointness is produced or of how we make the social world. I mean this not as a specifically directed criticism. The question has proven to be difficult to answer, and it evidently remains so. Moreover, Gilbert did not duck the micro-to-macro question by declaring that individual-level phenomena are superfluous (as, for example, Epstein suggested in his metaphor of "ant trap").[121]

The central question is not "How does 'the social' begin?" or "Where does it begin?" The process is always already underway. Sociality has been a condition of human life for far too many centuries to count distinctly. Rather, the question is "What exactly *is* that process?" More specifically, how does it work? Are the dynamics homologous or are there scale differences?" These questions will be touched upon, sometimes addressed again, repeatedly in the sections to come, until the fifth part of this book at which point they will be the main attraction.

Despite the general tendency of the recent philosophers of ontology to dismiss internal relations, they have brought some clarity to the conversation. Perhaps the most notable—for me the most notable—development is told by the clarification that Gould offered many years ago, repeated in title of Schmitt's collection, "Socializing Metaphysics," and, assuming I have not traduced Harmon's (2018) intent with my earlier summary of what he had been about, "even" his version of a social ontology. To the extent that this reading generalizes, among those whose works I have cited and perhaps beyond, their view of the philosophy of ontology is markedly different from the stature it once had as "first philosophy." Philosophical inquiry has changed. As Ebbs (2017) has shown, analytic philosophers as different as Rudolf Carnap, Willard Van Orme Quine, and Hilary Putnam, once regarded as a disparate triad, held to some underlying principles of inquiry in common with each other and profoundly different from those of René Descartes or Gottfried Leibniz. This, too, has been part of the legacy of Immanuel Kant. It has important meanings for prospects still possible, maybe more than ever, among those disciplines collected as the social sciences.

---

[121] To repeat a point already made in other ways, I have used the verb "duck" advisedly in the foregoing sentence for the following reason. A scholar, whether social scientist or philosopher or literary critic or of other persuasion, produces a product expecting that it will have an effect on readers; or at least that it *might* have an effect on readers; or, failing even that degree of optimism, as endorsement of possibility, with a smidgen of hope, that an effect on readers will somehow occur; but also an effect that one intends; and still more, an effect that will ramify, somehow, and result in "good things" that will "make a positive difference" to and in future lives, maybe even through the next two (or three? or more?) birth cohorts. Is that too much to hope for? But then what does one make of the same scholar who does bother to produce works, even works that proclaim the futility of individual-level actions? Is this a version of performance art, something like displaying one's body encased in paint and glitter, top hat included?

95

As repeatedly stated, a main tendency among the philosophers cited above (and among others) has been to insist that all relations are external, and this view has been held as well by most social scientists. It is a posture that seeks to protect the speaker or writer from implication in what she or he says or writes. This is, of course, the posture recommended as a mark of good journalism: do not become part of the story. It preserves an image of "objective reporting" and thus an authority of voice. One of the conventional bulwarks erected to protect against slippage is known as solipsism—in its typical modern version (post-Descartes), the claim that one has reduced all knowledge to one's own self-being. Inquiry is never as simple as either that bulwark or the journalist's warrant would make it. Consider again the lesson of the ship of Theseus: as I outlined it above, in §7 (as well as in the preface), the famous ship of Theseus, having gained such glory, became a museum piece. Its decaying planks had been replaced, and as this process of reclamation continued critics asked, "But is it the same ship?"[122] The lesson is real. Consider, however, that this reality displays the same tendency to a static image. Think of the ship doing what ships are built to do, traverse the oceans of the world. Now imagine that they are repaired, restored, rebuilt, as they sail. "Not likely," you say, and I know of no evidence that the ancient Greeks had invented a floating drydock for their triremes or other ships, although they had the knowledge and skill with which to do so. The point is, however, that this process of restoration "on the go" is what a society does accomplish, and it is also the task of the theorist, the inquirer, the observer, who would not seek to impose a dogmatism of any kind, would not bother to cover her tracks or erase his fingerprints on the activity of theorizing, inquiring, observing, reporting. In her discussion of Kant's hypothetical imperative Christine Korsgaard (2009, p. 69) said that "in making up [my] mind" to do such and such, I am "constituting [my] mind" at that moment, within a context and under specific conditions of sociality. But of course it is my mind that *is* the doing. This is the ship in motion, doing what a ship does. Recall, too, that our biology tells us that a human body *is*, among other things, a continual process of living being which includes repair, replacement, regeneration, as cells die (by apoptosis, as well as by injury and disease) and are replaced by new cells. While a society is not a biological organism any more than it is a physical machine, it survives (when it does) through similar processes.

As mentioned above (and borrowing from the subtitle of Epstein 2015), it is not exactly clear what is meant by notions of "rebuilding the foundations of the social sciences." Taking the gerund phrase at face value, I can imagine that it means rigorous inquiry into conceptual schemes and attendant classifications has been underway long enough to warrant a spate of new books. But, while it is evidently true that some writers are dubious about the meaning of "social," and thus (one imagines) how that word fits coherently with other semantic spaces, there is little if any evidence of reconceptualizations and language uses in these various endeavors of social ontology. Latour (2005, p. 247) described as "odd" the starting point of his own study of the activities of "reassembling the social," the adjective coming to his mind as he neared the end of the book because he began with and remained restricted to his own question: "Is a *science* of the

---

[122] Similarly, when the USS Constitution, a three-masted heavy frigate with wooden hull, set sail on its bicentennial in 1997, some observers asked, "is it really the same ship?" Nearly all of its wood had been replaced, much of it more than once, and it had been outfitted with some modern toilets and other features. Is a person successfully fitted with a heart that had been working in another person the same person?

*social* possible again provided we modify, because of what we have learned from the sociology of science, what is meant by 'social' and what is meant by 'science'?" It is significant that Latour had been writing his book in wake of the criticisms put forth by essays in Law and Hassard (1999), which had been widely received as devastating of the sort of project of theorizing that Latour (among many others) had been pursuing. What is *most* significant about that fact is the thicket in which Latour (among many others) had found himself, together with the realization that as little as the volume collected by Law and Hassard was needed to illuminate instabilities of "actor-network theory."[123]  So is it *really* time for another "new beginning"? How does one know where to *begin*, when so much of the domain of possible movements is replete with circularities and endogeneities?

I am not referring to or anticipating another effort to invent a new language. The record of such efforts during the last four hundred years has shown very few successes, none of them promising of new fruits to come.[124]  Rather, I mean efforts to appreciate seriously the fact that language—its uses and therefore its patterns of variation in semantic and syntactical properties, conceptual schemes, and all the rest—is endogenous to inquiry, including inquiry to build or rebuild the vocabulary, the conceptual tools, by, through, and in which we perceive "things of our experience." This is surely not a novel or recent observation (as will be shown with various materials of "things of our experience" in the next two parts of this book).

In asking the question, "Where does language begin?" Noam Chomsky thought to find his answer in a natural-science kind of ontology, one that featured somehow the structure of the human brain, by which he meant a beginning in biological organic evolution prior to advent of a sociality of Homo sapiens (see, e.g., Chomsky 1975, which was written in1955; for an overview see McGilvray 2014).  One of the traps into which originary logic leads us is to assume that the human brain must have had a structural-functional capacity of language *before* the advent of language; and if the human brain was then universal in that structural-functional capacity, then there must have been, and must now still be evidence of, a universality common to all human languages.  Chomsky was trading on Kant's anchorage of nomothetic knowledge to the natural world via a posit of universal noumenal condition of human nature as such, a bridge from hidden causes to our experiences of their effects.  Chomsky sought evidence of that universal noumenal structure in the human brain's linguistic effects.  But in doing so he abstracted the problem of conceptual-scheme dependency (the forms of intuition and the categories) from the possibility of evidence; Chomsky supposed he could do what Kant could not, find an instrument of valid and reliable evidence that would reveal the universal linguistic structure deep in all human languages, as it was just prior to the advent of language, ignoring that Kant's language, his own linguistic

---

[123] I am not saying that the papers in their collection are of no consequence; hardly.  But one is hard pressed to find statements (as distinguished from sentences) that had not been made before 1999.
[124] The main instances have been Esperanto, invented during the 1870s and revised during the 1880s by Ludovik Zamenhof, and Volapük by Johann Martin Schleyer, also during the late 1870s (see Schor 2016).  Albani and Buonarroti (1994) reported at least a thousand different efforts to invent new and presumably better languages during the past thousand years.  While I have not attempted to verify their estimate, it is clear that dissatisfactions with so-called natural languages have been plentiful.  Schor's (2016, p. 16) general diagnosis tells the main story line: "deeming language to be compromised by its humanity."  See also Eco (1997); Gordin (2015); and Okrent (2009).

capacities and capabilities, like that of every other human being, began in an already effective sociality which included conceptions of nature, human nature, the universal, and so forth, conceptions variant to those of different language-users. Recent inquiries, it seems, have marked finality to Chomsky's quest (see, e.g., Bybee 2010; Tomasello 2003), although the urge to find a "way back" to those presocial, precultural, prehistorical conditions that *must* have existed at some date long ago will probably seek yet another count of delusions.

The thought to start over, to begin again, can in fact begin from a variant of the originary logic assumption mentioned just above. This variant takes notice of what has been called "the discovery of language" and, from that recognition, also recognizes that prior inquiry had given inadequate attention to its own inescapable contingency in language use. Since language is an unavoidable critical contingency of the knowing subject, and *if* there exists in principle an "objective reality"—understood in the sense of a reality that is "prelinguistic" because logically prior to processes of culture, history, and sociality, prior to processes of will, desire, meaning, invention, and so forth—then it must be true that disagreements and disputations about "what is" have been and are due to "problems of language," manifested not only in the way inquirers talk about the "what is" but, before that, in how they can possibly *think* about it, observe it, and so forth. Thus, any serious inquirer, it would seem, must first tackle the obstacles that exist in our necessity of language, and that can stimulate another mission to "clean up our language," thence to rebuild foundations of our knowledge.

As Richard Rorty observed of an earlier sequence of such notifications, this has been fertile ground for the self-perceptions of new "revolutionary thinkers" who otherwise may be rather diverse in preferences. "The history of philosophy is punctuated by revolts against the practices of previous philosophers"—a seemingly required (if sometimes forgotten) ritual of generational succession.

> In the past, every such revolution has failed, and always for the same reason. The revolutionaries were found to have presupposed, both in their criticisms of their predecessors and in their directives for the future, the truth of certain substantive and controversial theses. The new method which each proposed was one which, in good conscience, could be adopted only by those who subscribed to those theses. Every philosophical rebel has tried to be "presuppositionless," but none has succeeded. This is not surprising, for it would indeed be hard to know what methods a philosopher ought to follow without knowing something about the nature of the philosopher's subject matter, and about the nature of human knowledge. To know what method to adopt, one must already have arrived at some metaphysical and some epistemological conclusions. If one attempts to defend these conclusions by the use of one's chosen method, one is open to a charge of circularity. If one does not so defend them, maintaining that given these conclusions, the need to adopt the chosen method follows, one is open to the charge that the chosen method is inadequate, for it cannot be used to establish the crucial metaphysical and epistemological theses which are in dispute (Rorty 1967, p. 1).

Rorty's description of dilemma (which, again, recalls Kant) was then apropos, and so it remains more than a half-century later, for nothing has been accomplished by way of resolving it or going through it or going around it or, in terms of effectivities that actually count beyond the need to publish, ignoring it. Latour (2005) might have convinced himself that "the social" has been and is devoid of objects, including objects the palpability of which even he would not deny, but it is impossible to reconcile his conviction with the fact that the human person is a palpable object, that humans have invented and produced countless prosthetic objects that enable persons to do, individually and in groups, what otherwise they cannot do (e.g., fly), that terrains of our planetary topography are both enabling and constraining of actions, that humans design, build, and use bridges, canals, skyscrapers, and hundreds of other palpable objects that inhabit social spaces and influence human interactions with one another and with those objects; and so on and on.[125] Instances of the social are realized in contractual obligations that have humans at work with machinery and each other, that result in shared spaces of dwelling in protected habitats that need regular maintenance and renewal, that enable and encourage some individual persons and corporate groups to burn coal thereby accelerating climate change and destroying habitat of other creatures, that produce weapons of instantaneously massive destruction as well as other weapons that cause blood to flow freely from each of several bodies one victim at a time (see, e.g., Latour 2005, pp. 82-106). It is no doubt true that the social sciences have been prone to an ahistoricism, to assumptions of static convenience and ignorance of process, and that this tendency has been prominent in references to "the political," "the economic," and so forth, as well as "the social." But it is also true that many social scientists have been alert to those biases, have argued against those biases, have exposed those biases, for many decades. It is also true, too, that replacing "the social" by "assemblage" does nothing in itself to counteract those biases. Adding still another terminology—this one, "assemblage," reportedly taken from the workshop of Gilles Deleuze[126]—does not of itself solve any problems.

We are always already in thickets of classification, in which we are simultaneously supported, enabled, and constrained. Étienne, a main character in Julio Cortázar's *Hopscotch* (1966 [1963], ch. 9), grumbling all the while, urged recognition of a self-complicity: "if you

---

[125] Harman's "object-oriented ontology" is also concerned about "objects," which (presumably any kind) have agency at least to the extent that they "withhold themselves" from each other. That means, I take it, that a house, for instance, remembers how to be—because that memory, design, was built into it—but Harman might have meant something more daunting (e.g., that one slab of granite withholds itself from another slab?). Also: "Relations are incidental in the life of things, rather than the stuff of which they are constituted" (Harman 2018, pp. 258, 259). Yet if these things "withhold themselves" from each other, they must have some sensitivity to the external/internal relation, the "me/not-me" relation, etc. Perhaps I have not understood his intent after all (see Mulhall 2018).

[126] In fact, the word Deleuze used was "agencement," which is generally translated as "plan" or "schema" or "layout" or "disposition." The phrase, "action d'agencer," a rather common one, is usually translated as "action of arranging" or "action of laying out." The special significance that some have attributed to "assemblage" must have been a later addition. This "play of words" is unfortunately not rare. Think of the great leap ahead that was supposedly in store by addition of "field" to the social sciences from the physical. Likewise, "emergence," an introduction from vitalist literatures of the early twentieth century. Conversely, other words (e.g., "mechanism") have been nominated as great obstacles. Latour (2005, pp. 128-133) devoted four pages of criticism of the word "network," due to the fact that it has so many uses/meanings. So, too, does "air."

99

people can't name something you are incapable of seeing it." But of course his targets *had* seen, *were* seeing, lots of things, just not the right things, not the preferred things.[127] To imagine that any "thing," any object, has meaningful existence outside classification is an idle exercise. Likewise, to imagine that we can strip away all classification of an object, thereby to apprehend it just as it is in itself. Of course, an agency can be imputed to any object, even if the dynamism of the object is so slow as to be all but imperceptible in human years. The word itself, from the Latin "agree" ("do" or "perform"), allows a variety of applications (e.g., "a tree falls in the forest but makes no sound if no one is present to hear"; "the sun converts hydrogen to helium, thus producing radiant energy"; "that boulder has not moved in 60 years, I know for a fact"; and so forth). Is all of that usage of the word, "agency," an anthropocentric (and anthropomorphic, at least sometimes) exercise? Yes, of course, it is. It is a network of usages circulating more or less evenly in exchanges within each of many, perhaps all extant, human languages, managing more or less well to circulate conversationally among them. Epstein (2015, pp. 6-8, passim) was right to caution against biases built into anthropocentric reasonings and models, especially when considering nonhuman creatures. But as by analogy to the problem of translation among human languages, to "cease and desist" because of inherent bias is a self-defeating exercise in favor of ignorance and paralysis.

In *Process and Reality* (and in later works), Whitehead sought to set aside or circumvent or simply ignore the post-Kantian dilemma. But it is difficult to determine exactly what he had in mind as a coherent and effective argument to overcome the dilemma, or what he sometimes called a "complex of bifurcations" (Whitehead 1978 [1929], p. 290). One reads sentences such as this declaration: "For Kant, the world emerges from the subject; for the philosophy of organism [Whitehead's name for his own argument], the subject emerges from the world" (1978 [1929], p. 88). Whatever Whitehead intended by that sentence, the first clause is not what Kant argued, and the second is not contrary to his argument (depending on the meaning of "emerges"). Of course, details matter a great deal, and I find it more difficult to discern those in Whitehead's vague, often ambiguous presentations than in Kant's texts. But vagueness and ambiguity can serve as a cover for deflection and avoidance. Some newly minted champions of Whitehead have seen possibility. Isabelle Stengers (2008) has recommended caution, and one can see reason to doubt that his metaphysical gauge measures any good successor to "the sad tale of discovering our limitations and illusions." Others have professed to see a road to correction of the ailments of philosophy, and theory more generally—for example, a tendency to Meillassoux' (2008 [2006], p. 5) "correlationism": that "we only ever have access to the correlation between thought and being, and never to either term considered apart from the other." An implication would seem to be that the correlations that we think we see must be between poor facsimiles of either thought or being, or both. But how could we know that they are poor? Or that they are facsimiles at all?

While reading such old statements, recycled still again, one can see the point of the social ontologists: it is time to move on. But to what?

---

[127] Indeed, how persons visually match thing to name is still a puzzle (see, e.g., Pelli, Burns, Farell, and Moore-Page 2006, p. 4646).

## Part Two
### Experience, Voice, and the Aesthetics of Judgment

What is experience? I mentioned in the preface my initial encounter with Michael Oakeshott's (1933) address of that question, which in the late 1950s struck me as being topically unusual for its time (in Anglo-American literatures), and rather idiosyncratic in basic style. Indeed, the book languished until philosophical conversation caught up to it (only then to pass quickly by; cf. Winch 1958, pp. 62-65). In Oakeshott's account, "experience" is such a holistic phenomenon that one might wonder what leverage it could give. Yet Oakeshott managed to discriminate four types (or, in his terms, modes): the historical, the practical, the scientific, and the philosophical. Oakeshott himself presumably stood in the last of the four, although at places in his book one could suspect that his thinking might have been the presence of an unannounced fifth mode. But it was the "historical mode" that suggested the conundrum of an endogeneity, one which might be likened to Bertrand Russell's puzzle of a "class of all classifications"—namely, isn't the historical mode itself historical? Except that the Russellian puzzle was conceived to be one of pure logic, whereas the "history double" is one of the entire ty of the modality of experience known as history.[128]

During the next half century or so the question stimulated by Oakeshott receded to broad background, brought to the fore by occasional readings here and there. It was not until Martin Jay published his survey, *Songs of Experience* (2005), that I returned in any large systematic way to the multiplicities not only of Oakeshott's "modes of experience" but also of a self-conscious recognition that it can easily be left to taken-for-granted background (as Oakeshott himself had done once he settled on how to "manage" that "difficult word"; Oakeshott 1933, p. 9) but only as central to a false consciousness. Writing an "intellectual history" of "experience," as Jay did, is, he acknowledged, an audacious undertaking, precisely because those multiplicities *are* very difficult to "manage" (or whatever care-taking verb one prefers) at least sufficiently well to convince a reader that the self-same local "experience of a word" (and concept) has ruled across the historical-cultural spans considered by the given historian. Jay managed it well enough, even if his effort to pin much of the multiplicity onto the "*songs* of experience" is always on the verge of embarrassment by question-begging. While he began briefly with the ancient Greeks, most of his attention was focused on modern European and North American thought—which reduces the book's subtitle, "Modern American and European Variations on a Universal Theme," to another embarrassment: most distinctive cultures known to exist or to have existed lack presence in his

---

[128]In Russell's (1919, p. 136) later account, "if there is such a thing as 'everything,' then, 'everything' is something, and is a member of the class 'everything.' But normally a class is not a member of itself. Mankind, for example, is not a man. Form now the assemblage of all classes which are not members of themselves. This is a class: is it a member of itself or not? If it is, it is one of those classes that are not members of themselves, i.e., it is not a member of itself. If it is not, it is not one of those classes that are not members of themselves, i.e. it is a member of itself. Thus of the two hypotheses—that it is, and that it is not, a member of itself—each implies its contradictory. This is a contradiction." Later in the century a well-known philosopher declared that Russell's paradox "packs a surprise that can be accommodated by nothing less than a repudiation of our conceptual heritage" (Quine 1966, p. 11).

account (nothing, e.g., for Hittite, Sumerian, Babylonian, or Phoenician culture; nothing for the first cultures of the Americas or the southern Pacific; a bare mention of India, less of China or Japan; and so forth). While Jay's short preview of his journey is very effective, a large part of the effect leaves one wondering whether the journey log will be worth so many full stops, since we learn, for example, that Giorgio Agamben (1993 [1978], p. 13) had declared that "the question of experience can be approached nowadays only with an acknowledgment that it is no longer accessible to us," although Adorno (1991, vol. 1, p. 55) had left some comfort by warning only that "the very possibility of experience is in jeopardy" (see Jay 2005, p. 2). One may declare sympathy with Jay's plight, however; for as he concluded his review of the word and multiple concepts of "experience," there is indeed reason for exasperation about "the welter" of meanings and contentions suffusing a "cacophonous chorus." One recalls Walter Benjamin's exasperation with what he saw as excessive multiplicity overwhelming the integrity of his own "wholeness of experience" (see Ball 2001, pp. 319-320).

One might surmise that Jay's survey was yesterday's news, that younger generations have greater hope to offer. Recent commentators such as Mark Greif have implied a particular *difference* in or of experience as now expressed in the question, "What is it about experience that *counts* as experience?" Put differently, and in first-person terms (as I did when first reading Oakeshott's book), "When, and how, does one know that one is indeed 'having' an experience?" The point is illustrated in Greif's (2016, p. 80) sentence that "the permanent conditions of human life always remain in force, and the concept of experience recasts them in its own image." The first clause of that sentence seems trivial by tautology, but then the second clause raises a doubt about it. Perhaps someone thinks of "the permanent conditions of human life" as *not yet* of experience; rather, of the category that once was called "raw feel," or perhaps before that an older category called "word of God" or, with lessened emphasis on the second part of the metaphysical notion of "ontotheological," that which was known as "that which simply *is*"—as in "that which surely *must be*, whether we can justifiably claim that we do know that it is" (a peculiar back-formation from where-when one stands). These distinctions of "experience," hypothetical or real, would somehow figure as generative of what could *then count as* experiences—that is, as something worth having—and as such they might well have been, and remain, among "the permanent conditions of human life."

That possibility in turn raised awkward questions, of course, because of which usually it has slid from foreground to such deep background as to fall beyond what could be called the "event horizon" of rational thinking. To hold a sign over it as if to announce an itinerant's future travelogue was invitation to membership in a more sober person's museum of sophistical thinking (cf. Doubt 1990; but see also Elvin 1997, p. 7; Wallace 2007). Besides—and this was/is initiation of the slide—what counts as experience is always a matter of first-person authority as *feeling*, from which any second-person dialogue can only ever struggle to emerge by fabricating a cognition, a mutually discernable cognition, of "having had an experience." However, that is finally the point: what counts as "*having* an experience" can be assessed and decided *within* first-person terms, and it usually is; but if the qualification is to go anywhere beyond that privacy, it will be by some sort of negotiation of "*having had* an experience"—that is, by and within a sociality of accordance and confirmation in second-person relations which are virtually always contingent on, as well as contributive to, the aggregated effects that live in third-person relations of sociality. What Cavell (2004, p. 379) called the "question of voice and its non-negotiable demand for recognition" is typically present in second-person relations, but audience effects may be present by anticipation, if not by feedback, which potentially influence parties in differential ways and degrees.[129] Note, too, that "mutually discernable cognition" often depends on first-person filtering between thinking and saying, the filter usually more sensitive in second- than in third-person relations.[130]

First-person experiences of feeling are no less real for that, of course. Nor do they vanish as such, although experiences of second- and third-person relations can and often do modify them sufficiently that they are folded (sometimes unnoticed) into first-person representations, or memories, of "recent experience." The transition from feeling to knowing is usually facilitated in second- or third-person relations, but that facilitation can and often does take place within first-person memory, in much the same way that direct lessons of "proper behavior" gain most effective activation in first-person memory.[131] Sociality both allows and depends upon a latitude, culturally variable but usually considerable, in privacy of first-person experience and authority thereof. Scholarship in many venues has repeatedly come to the conclusion that this privacy must be accommodated precisely because human being is intimate and emotive, continually refreshed in second- and third-person relations by the inherent and irreducible contingencies of first-person experience (Scheler 1954 [1948]). Early theorists of rhetoric, for instance, insisted that the unique and definitive characteristic of this art of speaking is *persuasion*—thus, that rhetoric is inherently a social art. By the fourteenth century in France and the Netherlands greater attention to various contingencies associated with uses of vernacular languages and secular themes had generated a form that has been called "second rhetoric" (contrasted with "classical rhetoric," Latin, churchly, hierarchical, and mainly prosaic), which acknowledged first-person

---

[129] I am not disagreeing with Cavell but simply pointing out that his perspective was perhaps more generously civil than average: "There is an unspoken attunement of moral perception that conditions, and calls upon, our ability to make ourselves intelligible to each other.... The wonder is that the craving for clarity is available to two in conversation when it is denied to either alone" (Cavell 2004, pp. 381, 382). Were our worlds always so gracious.

[130] Harrison White (1992, pp. 346-349) was one of the first well-known social scientists to illustrate applications of models of signal filtering (e.g., first-person skills as if operating as a Kalman filter of signal emissions; uses of Gibbs or anti-Gibbs filtering; and so forth). These applications presuppose a per-person dynamic model of signals and memories.

[131] Problems of correlation between current first-person experience and first-person memory harbor such lessons in adulthood as well as childhood. Sometimes they are also venues of theoretical insight into the transitional relation of feeling and knowing. Hoffman (1998, pp. 201-202) described an interesting case, for example, of an apparently complete disconnect between sensory cognition and associated conceptual formations, on the one hand, and, on the other, feelings ordinarily correlated with them—but in this case due not to "childish tantrum" or "bad manners" or other failure of moral compliance, rather to brain injury as a result of which the adult patient recognized his father visually (i.e., his visual intelligence worked appropriately) yet the patient did not feel that this man *was* his father (instead, an impostor). The normal correlation between sensory intelligence and emotional intelligence had been completely severed. While the man looked like his father, knew things his father knew, and so forth, he definitely was *not* his father. First-person feeling dominated his experience so strongly that connections of knowledge which otherwise would have indicated "my father" were rejected as false, as an attempt at false imposition.

103

authority on matters of taste, beauty, especially sonic beauty, as a venue of "the personal" within variable contexts of sociality (see, e.g., Spies 1999, p. 58). One illustration of this expression is the troubadour "style" of musical performance (actually, various styles). But the basic point was a rhetoric that focuses on the intrinsic quality (beauty, expressivity, etc.) of an utterance, not on argumentation designed to persuade an audience. Linguistically, of course, imaginations of shared values, perspectives, and experiences were unavoidable. However, as can be seen in the history of lyric poetry and its intimate tie with musicality, these imaginations exist as circuits of sound, both expression and meaning, weaving individual first-person and collective second- and third-person experience into a sort of cultural commons.[132]

The first-person authority of lyric poetry addresses *each* hearer of an eventual multitude of hearers, producing a virtual second-person dialogue in the sonic-cum-verbal mind of each one who has heard. The word "lyric"—derived from the musical instrument, the lyre (and the Latin counterpart to the Greek word, "melic," from "melos" or "song")—came to signify this fusion of sonic and verbal, with strong tactile impulse as in toe-tapping and dance, as a general form of expression that could produce quick localities of community: a lyricism that told of a mutuality of "hearing-togetherness." From the song-poems of Homeric times to Petrarchan extensions of troubadour poetry, the effect of expressivity stitched the peculiar aggregates of a virtual second-person metrical-sonic form of a singular "I" addressing an open invitation of "you," *and* "you," *and* "you," into chains of actual "dialogue" that listeners could, and did, recognize from place to place, time to time.[133] As various historians have noted, these chains have extended from, say, Petrarchan eroticism (mostly mild) to present-day "pop music" lyricism, in which writers borrow phrases and entire lines from once-popular odes, goliardic satires, and ribalds, as well as folk songs and musical texts (see, e.g., Culler 2015, pp. 92-107). By the time of Roger Ascham (c1515-1568), a prominent humanist of Tudor England, all poetry was conveniently classified as tragedy, comedy, epic, or lyric (or melic, as Ascham called it). Three centuries later Hegel (1975 [1835], e.g., p. 1038) concurred in his *Lectures on Aesthetics* (although collapsing "tragic" and "comedic" into "dramatic" for his triad of genres of poetry) and emphasized the lyric as "subjectivity encountering itself." It might seem superfluous to caution that Hegel was not thus reducing lyric expression to "personal affect" or to "the articulation of individual experiences," which in either case would presume analytic boundaries on "subject" vis-à-vis "object" in rather stark contrast to Hegel's approach. In any case, Culler (2015, pp. 105, 125), having urged those

---

[132] The simple grammar of first-person perspective and third-person perspective is deceptive. As Nagel (1998, p. 343) pointed out, with reference to Shoemaker's address of first-person experience ("thought experiment"), a purely first-person point of view must be modified if we are to speak consistently of a "subjectivity of conscious mental state" as a state that can be accurately described *only* by a concept in which "nonobservable first-person and observational third-person attributions are logically inseparable." That concept is necessary condition to understanding one another in our speech acts. Indeed, that concept is, as George Herbert Mead (e.g., 1913) theorized, the concept of sociality (see below, Part 4, §24).

[133] The emotive intensities that can be conveyed in this recognition are readily apparent in contemporary "pop music" venues visited, actually or virtually via electronic media, by today's fans, especially adolescent fans. Consider the extraordinarily profitable production of value through phenomena such as "David Bowie" as compared with, say, "Leslie Gore," "The Beatles" or "The Andrew Sisters" (see, e.g., Doggett 2012; Ross 2007, ch. 14).

cautions, then offered the important point that the distinctiveness of the lyric resides in its performance "as it acts iterably through repeated readings" and hearings. These are objectivities, as objective as dance, song, any rhythmic activity, any haptic experience, or, for that matter, any other production of and by sociality; and as such they are indeed expressions of subjectivities (cf. George H Mead 1926).

Kant's point about the seemingly inevitable return of objective necessity after doubt has had its run (i.e., the transcendental Illusion) is testament to the exercise of reason in the midst of human contingency (freedom, uncertainty, ambiguity, etc.). If one wants an authority of truth tables that evades contingency, those tables must not show any human fingerprints; such is the objectivity, the objective necessity that holds so many people in thrall. The *real* authority must be imported surreptitiously from some pre-existent (i.e., pre-historical, pre-social, pre-cultural) seat—the titan Prometheus stealing fire from the gods and giving it to humankind, for example (see Hazelrigg 1993a, 1993b). Thus, Jay's survey remains highly pertinent, even as young generations' "own new" experiences recast those "permanent conditions of human life" into fitting relevance. Does this mean that Adorno's judgment was out of time?—that lasting *ir*relevance had already won the day? Was "experience" *ever* capable of doing, of being, what Agamben (among others) had decided now remained only as a virtual memory, perhaps in the way that ancient Greeks of Euripides' day remembered their gods as figurations they had believed *in*?

Those issues and questions circulate among the main topics of this Part: accounts of experience in first-person, vis-à-vis second- and third-person reports; how "feeling" (sensation, emotion) and "knowing" (cognition, necessity of concepts) have been articulated in the accounts; the inertial force of an almost Lockean psychologism (e.g., in the form of folk theories of mind) hitchhiking in the Kantian legacy; the presumption of continuity of experience in space and in time; the meaning of aesthetics and its chief topic, perceptions, especially in terms of gradients of pleasure "and" displeasure; scripts of experience running through poetry, music, painting, and the arts of "becoming a person"; and through all of that, relations of power and authority. In view of this last five-word phrase, by the way, I should declare openly before more words are laid down the line, that rarely have I read anything so near to complete absurdity as the charge of those who seemingly believed that something profoundly devastating of Michel Foucault's work was uttered when they said of his writings that "power is everywhere, and therefore nowhere." I do not recall having read of any author's writings that "language is everywhere, and therefore nowhere." Perhaps I have not read enough (Hume's problem of induction).

Most of the discussion will draw primarily and mainly on literatures broadly labeled "the humanities." This could include, by my reckoning, mathematics, a human invention of startling complexity as ever new extensions of inventiveness pop out from time to time, like new skeins of poetry or staffs of music. But they will be neglected. Part of my attention to the presumption will highlight "time" as well as "space," and for some of that I will draw upon current literatures from the world of physical science (cosmology and quantum dynamics in particular). This is in a way a curious necessity. Not that physical science has no business being concerned about "time" (and "space"). Rather, the curiosity is that philosophy largely left the entire domain of "time" to other disciplinary interests, as David Wood has remarked (e.g., Wood 2001, 2007), mainly to physics, music, poetry, dance, and of course mathematics. Why that abandonment should ever have occurred is for me an open question, but I do know that disciplines now and then give away specific topics. Sociology abandoned to other disciplines, mainly economics, a large domain that had once composed most of its core interests (that is, most matters having to do with processes of production, including the implicature from production in the narrower sense to processes of distribution and exchange, thence those of consumption, which is itself also a production), thus leaving sociology (especially the US variant) with a hollow center or an absence of platform, depending on one's preferred geometric metaphor, or perhaps both. To say that it has been due to an imperialistic attitude by economics is merely question begging.

## §10. The Experience of Feeling

How, John McDowell (1998, p. 130) famously asked late in the twentieth century, "can a mere feeling constitute an experience in which the world reveals itself to us?" Astonishing though it might have seemed for a philosopher in the analytic tradition to ask such a question, McDowell was not being facetious in raising it. Analytic philosophy had rarely made room for "feelings," much less given them serious attention, which is some part of the explanation of relative neglect of Kant's third critique until recent years. Kant himself, after all, had been scathingly dismissive of a popular movement of "feeling philosophy" or "emotion philosophy" (Gefühlsphilosophie), ridiculing purported results of "immediate and intuitive relation with mystery." But Kant then thought better of his own focus of attention in that commentary and settled on advice rendered in Plato's famous "seventh epistle": it is usually better simply to ignore those who are incapable of heeding good advice.

Let's postpone treatment of this matter of a "relative neglect" of Kant's third critique. It will be beneficial first to unpack McDowell's heavily stuffed question.

To begin with, there is that word, "feeling," and the apparent supposition that "feeling" either can itself count as "experience" or can lead to a constitution of "experience." This is integral to what has already been deferred momentarily, however, so let's move on to the next package, the one labeled "world." McDowell's sentence suggests that we would have something to say about the referent of that word, "world," apart from any experience we might have of it. That does seem unlikely, however, although one cannot help but notice the presumption (or at least what seems to be a presumption) that "world" has motive power to the extent of self-revelation—moreover, a power that seems to enable "world" to be at least co-constitutive with the person having an experience of "world," *of* that very experience. On further reflection, what has just been said seems both a bit mysterious and sensible. Imagine a tiny piece of "world"— say, an elephant. It does seem reasonable that this thing of the "world" would in some sense "want" to be experienced by me as what it is in fact, an elephant and not a hippopotamus or flea or beam of starlight. But how do I know that it *wants* anything at all? That aside, how does it put into my mind, my perception, that it *is* a Tembo (Swahili) or a Nzou (Shona) or a słoń (Polish)? But maybe that is unnecessarily complicated. Perhaps the element of language is unnecessary. Yet, what do I know without the use of one or another language, its conceptual scheme? What do I feel, or what of what I do feel can I share, without the use of a language, its conceptual scheme? How do I know that the self-same object is co-determinative of my perception, whether I am thinking in Swahili, in Shona, in Polish, or in English? And remember,

106

McDowell's question was about a "mere feeling"—how anything of "the world" manages to reveal itself to me as an experience not of "knowing that" or of "knowing how" but of *feeling*.

Bear in mind, moreover, that these questions of language, conceptual scheme, and the like, are hardly new—certainly not an invention of "modern thought." Democritus (fifth century BCE) is remembered as having said, "Sweet is by convention, bitter by convention, hot by convention, cold by convention, color by convention; in truth there are but atoms and the void."[134] From the standpoint of first-person experience one might be aware of a sensation, and then aware of another sensation, and perhaps feel a difference from first to second.[135] But a human being is a social being and as such *is* linguistic, conventional. Not "embedded" in language, in sociality, for that would imply an integrity of being human separate from language, from sociality, from convention; and such a human does not exist (all of the "wolf child" stories notwithstanding).[136] Can one even imagine such as thing as that as being human? Analytically, one may say, there is the necessity of sensation *prior* to language. But this is an empty result of pure abstraction, for no human being has that experience, not even as "raw feel." If Democritus was accurately quoted in the Tetralogies of Thrasyllus, as cited above (or in Bakewell 1908, p. 60, from Sextus Empiricus), then he was surely engaged in the kind of process, a "thought experiment," that modern physicists pursue, pretending to be outside a universe that contains them, much as Archimedes proposed that given a lever of sufficient length and strength, plus a pivot properly located in space, he could lift Earth from its coordinates.

Perhaps McDowell's locution was intended only as a way of referring to a presumption of spatial continuity, parallel to a presumption of temporal continuity—a way of saying that an actor posits something like an empirical version of "unity of apperception" with regard to "that to which my consciousness orients" (i.e., my perceptions are of something stable spatially and temporally, at least within reasonable bounds, such that I can say I have perceived a self-same thing, rather than a welter or scatter of stimuli, a kaleidoscope of points of light)? Possibly, except that on second thought I know the matter cannot be as simple as that, because the presumption of continuity applies at once to knowing subject, consciousness, as to known object, and I have much evidence of multiplicity, measured from myself to other-self. Surely this is evident to other selves as well as to myself; and most evident to all of us, one would think, when

---

[134] Translation is often debatable. In this instance I believe Bakewell's is better than Freeman's. The fragment reads: νόμωι (γάρ φησι) γλυκὺ καὶ νόμωι πικρόν, νόμωι θερμόν, νόμωι ψυχρόν, νόμωι χροιή, ἐτεῆι δὲ ἄτομα καὶ κενόν. I assume Freeman neglected the middle section (νόμωι θερμόν, etc.) merely to reduce redundancy, the point having been made. See Fragment O in Bakewell (1908, p. 60).

[135] This was part of the point that Hume made, raising the question about "difference" (i.e., a coherence either of "the same" or of "the different." Tetens (1913 [1777], pp. 392-394) had addressed the set of issues as well. The topic of sensation and its relation to or with unity of experience was at the vanguard of philosophical inquiry during this period (see Kuehn 1989, p. 367).

[136] One must beware oversimplification of views, however. Marcus Aurelius, a prominent follower of Stoicism, gave considerable emphasis to sociality in his "meditations" but also subscribed to the Stoic view that meanings of words are reflective of the nature of things to which they refer (i.e., not "mere" conventions); see book V, §8, of his self-reflexive observations, now commonly available as Marcus Aurelius, *Meditations* (c175 CE). Cicero, whose eclecticism included some principles of Stoicism, had criticized the Stoic view of names, at least with regard to the gods; see Cicero, *De Natura Deorum* (45 BCE).

the focal interest is something like "world experienced as feeling"—in which case one must wonder whether McDowell meant to say that such multiplicity reduces to a single world. The wonder probably recedes when under consideration of second-person perspective—that is, conversation among selves. But conversation among voices, polyphony, which surely can be *about* feelings, is not itself feeling, although I suppose one can indeed *feel* a conversation.

Multiplicity of voices, as of worlds, has at times been extraordinarily unsettling, nerve-wracking, foreboding, some of that conveyed in and as feeling. Peter Pesic (2017, p. 59) cited the reaction of a twelfth-century English cleric, John of Salisbury, to the temptations induced by musical polyphonics: the "music 'sullies the divine service' on account of the 'effete emotings' of the singers' 'before-singing and their after-singing, their singing and their counter-singing, their in-between-singing and their ill-advised singing ... to such an extent are the highest notes mixed together with the low or lowest ones. Indeed, when such practices go too far, they can more easily occasion titillation between the legs than a sense of devotion in the brain'."[137] The multiple voices conveyed in polyphony was threatening in part because of concerns about "possession," the notion that evil spirits could take possession of a human being and utter blasphemies through that person.[138] A century after John of Salisbury's pronouncement in 1159 Thomas Aquinas rendered an Aristotelian "resolution of the problem of polyphony," as Pesic summarized the point: "only a completely unified mind can experience many things as one, through its own unity. Only God and the angels can really comprehend polyphony because their nature is integrally polyphonic, unlike the merely monophonic human mind" (Pesic 2017, p. 59). A similar controversy awaited George Herbert Mead in the twentieth century, in wake of his argument that "mind" is inherently social via the multiple perspectives and voices that are incorporated as a person engages in "taking the role of the other" for each "significant other" (see below, Part Four, §24).

But then we must come back to that matter of an *auto-revelatory* world: is this in fact the motive force that produces a feeling? Is "feeling" an event for which self as such is only at most a passive recipient—and always at least potentially a passive recipient who was not in or of proper attention and therefore missed the gift? How might that accord with the crux of Kant's interest in beauty and the sublime as limit instances of the aesthetics of perception and the power of judgment (here, "limit" being as close to "purely solely subjective" as human thought had imagined, "beauty" being supposedly only "in the eye of the beholder")? Does self have any responsibility of "preparedness of attention" in order to apprehend the gift? If it makes sense to apply the elements of aspect and mood to feelings as such (separately from talk about feelings), then perhaps self's apprehensional state varies by aspect (e.g., imperfective versus perfective,

---

[137] Perhaps euphemism got in the way, but more likely one sees in that contrast the correlation of the "mind-body" duality and the duality between that which can be cleansed and that which, in its fleshiness, is always in need of careful oversight and control. Twelfth-century biology was not so poorly developed as not to have concluded that the brain is the body's primary sexual organ. While the above-cited text sounds about right, I must caution that Pesic's citation came from another source, and I have not been able to confirm John of Salisbury's own text.

[138] This sense of inherent threat of possession has continued in religious ceremonies such as "speaking in tongues" and in somewhat secularized pronouncements about "alien voice," "implanted thought," and "brainwashing" (seed, e.g., Stephens and Graham 2000).

and if the former then either repetitive-discrete or continuous in duration) and by mood (e.g., emphatic or optative, say, rather than indicative), in which case perhaps self can be more or less well "tuned" to reception. But wouldn't such variation of preparedness actually point to the revelatory event as induced subjectively—in other words, that "world" does not have an initiating or motive power of revelation, or any interests at all in revelation, except as this is imputed by self? But then, surely, for any given self "world" includes other selves, their actions and products, at least a few of which could involve complicity by the "given" self—in other words, "world" consists in objectivities, stubborn facts, resulting from and as actions aggregated in their surviving effects and whatever interests, perspectives, expectations, sorted out and aggregated (implicitly if not explicitly) in those effects (see, e.g., Brielmann and Pelli 2017). Still, for that "given" self first-person experience of the complex called "world" remains relevant, does it not? The question how any given self does sort through the complexity and make first-person meaning of it is inherent in the matter of "experience," of course, and in judgments of what counts. Is there hidden insight in this notion of "sorting through complexity" in order to achieve first-person meaning? Yes. But not what it appears to be. The insight is always that of a cul-de-sac, a loop that easily "resolves" into a circularity: the "back and forth" of sorting between "world" and "self" in search of first origin (cf. Koch 2006, §13).

While those and related issues were not McDowell's main point of concern, they do merit consideration, and some of them will recur. But let's now return to the point that until recent times Kant's third critique was set aside in relative neglect. That has bearing on the issues raised above. The Romanticists following Kant proposed their own, partly implicit and partly ironic, explanation of the neglect: insofar as Kant's aim had been to isolate an "aesthetic perspective" focused on experience that is as purely and solely subjective as possible—that is, as devoid of objectivity as possible (thus, his interest in "beauty" and "the sublime")—in order to determine whether a faculty or power of judgment does harbor a unifying principle of reason of its own,[139] this aim proved to be marginal to philosophy's core issues of relationship between subject and object, conceived in analytical frame (hence, maintenance of the copula, signifying an open question of equal logical status of separate self-same integrities), the proof being Kant's failure to realize that aim.

The implicit part of that "explanation" (the taken-for-granted analytical framing) housed an irony: so much of what the Romanticists did consisted in language; the import of even the seemingly non-linguistic reality of music (e.g., Beethoven) and of painting (e.g., Caspar David Friedrich[140]) was for philosophy conducted almost exclusively in words; but linguistic reality has been conceived primarily and mainly in analytic framework (e.g., the analyticity of grammar). The Romanticists—or those who were not simply riding waves of emotive energy for artistic gain—faced the task of how to communicate, among themselves and more especially with others, in a way that would avoid the dissolutional effects of analyticity, preserving the holistic

---

[139] This effort, recall, came on the heels of his insight that, after applying principles of pure reason (epistemic) and principles of practical reason (morality), one still has a judgment to make in any given situation: what must I do?

[140] Friedrich's painting, *Wanderer above the Sea of Fog* (c1818), has been iconic for Friedrich and for Romanticist visual imagery.

perspective of what *they* meant "aesthetic experience" to be. As Andrew Bowie (2013, ch. 6) has highlighted with admirable clarity, this was the thesis that Adorno had tried to convey and advance (see also Gordon 2016, pp. 107-119; Bernstein 2001, *passim*). "Part of what philosophy has to explicate is," in Bowie's (2013, p. 141) words closely following Adorno, "precisely the fact that what art conveys is not reducible to what can be said about what it conveys." This difference is of interest. The interest will circulate throughout this and subsequent Parts of the book. Perhaps one can already see its connection to the search for first origin. (Even when dialectic is acknowledged, the impulse to analytic adventure seeks a consummation.)

Gordon (2016, pp. 114-119) appropriately emphasized Adorno's tendency to parataxis in his written composition—his effort to "say without saying" (as one might say). The choice was in keeping with Adorno's preference for what he called a "*negative* dialectic,*" a mode of inquiry conceived partly as a means of avoiding risk of affirmation of that which is the target of one's critique—perhaps an understandable wish yet futile, even as one might fear dialectic (e.g., unity of opposites) as too much risk of becoming entrapped (wanting instead the security of "good alone"). In choosing composition by parataxis the author leaves to the reader the responsibility of supplying connection, coherence, and continuity. Because it seems evident that Adorno's choice was a motivated choice, one might wonder if the aim was simply avoidance of self-responsibility. A more charitable view could be, however, that an educational effect had been intended, similar to the aim of Samuel Beckett's uses of parataxis in his plays (e.g., much of Lucky's part in *Waiting for Godot*). That similitude points to a rather severe limit, because of its supposition of better educative preparation than actually exists. On the other hand, one might conclude that, for Adorno as for Beckett, *that* suppositional gap in contemporary culture was precisely part of the intended educational target.

McDowell's question whether "mere feeling" is enough to "constitute an experience in which the world reveals itself to us" is keyed in part by a doubt that "feeling" alone is enough to achieve unity of experience. Is there an algebra or geometry of temporal aggregation whereby one feeling and then another feeling, distinguished from its predecessor as simply different, generate *any* "added value"?[141] Is there in the relation of sequence any capacity for new meaning? Here one may recall Kant's basic distinction among conscious representations, between "sensation" and "cognition." A sensation has no represented object. This is not to say that it is "uncaused" but that the sensory input is not represented as an object; a sensation is merely a state of the subject. Neither our brains as biological organs nor our sensory instruments in themselves are sensitive to space or to time. On the other hand, a cognition *is* an objective representation. Some cognitions count as an instance of "intuition," an immediate singular represented object (the forms of which are space and time). Others count as an instance of

---

[141] I was tempted to add two words ("in kind") at the end of the adjectival phrase in that sentence. But that would be to invoke knowing (i.e., a category scheme) as supplement to or an overlay on the feeling. If I feel an emotion that I qualify as "fear," I have entered the terrain of a knowledge. On the other hand, if I feel an emotion that I *later* qualify as "fear," might I experience that emotion in increasing *quantity* (and later qualify the experience as "first I was a little scared, then I got really scared")? Or do those emotions which Fisher (2002) called "the vehement passions" each come in a hierarchy of discrete kinds, and perhaps exhibiting a transitivity that is not necessarily consistent quantitatively (as one can sometimes detect in a preference hierarchy of goods)?

"concept"; these are mediate and general, which is to say that the represented object is located within a conceptual scheme—that is, within an internally consistent classification of categorial differences—and thus is qualitatively "of a kind" and quantitatively one of potentially many, even an infinite number, of the kind. Note that an intuition is merely ostensive—a singular object to which I point (grammatically via one or another demonstrative pronoun)—and requires no other representational function (e.g., relation to one or more other objects, number, etc.).[142]

Educational conditions and effects do exist affectively, however insufficient they might be, and neglect of those presentations becomes ignorance of the sense that a person can "know" via, and as, "feeling." This sense is perhaps an awareness, only partly conscious, certainly not well cognized, of a gap or a hole in the text of an otherwise well-cognized knowledge, which has been bridged or filled in temporarily, awaiting more detailed cognitive scrutiny. This sense should not be ignored, for it is not necessarily wrong or lacking in verifiable experience and reasoning. One should no more ignore or discredit it in others than in oneself. When Nancy Isenberg (2016) or Arlie Russell Hochschild (2016), for example, reports "feelings as knowings" from people they have observed in conversation and otherwise—interlocutors who are likely to preface a claim by "I feel like …" rather than "I know that …"—the reports should not be dismissed simply because we suspect bias and/or see evidence of poor facility in language and perhaps more generally poor educational achievements. Assuming confidence that the scholar-reporter is capable of discerning a gamester, we should be confident that she is confident that her report is of one or another reality that she expects her readers to take seriously; and that means respecting the "feelings" of her interlocutors as valuably informative even if the contents do not show evidence of well-cognized reflection but seem rather to be raw expressions of frustration, confusion, a sense of isolation or loss or resentment. This is not to say that the reports should be taken as evidence of adequate understandings. But one should presume that, however poorly conceived the "feelings as knowings" might have been, the persons sharing talk were genuinely trying to teach us something of their specific worlds (and perhaps something beyond, though not exclusive of, the poor conditions from which those understandings, and the educational merits behind them, had developed). Different kinds of "acting out" presentations of self/world are, or can be, as revelatory as a well-rehearsed lecture. The messages may differ by motivation as well as self-conscious polish, but something can be learned from each insofar as motivational energies can be assessed reliably.[143] The ancient Greeks had the advantage of not believing (or assuming, presupposing) that human being begins as a psychological integrity and then develops sociality.

*******

---

[142] The demonstration takes place as if wholly outside a conceptual scheme, amounting to nothing more than physical pointing to a singular object that is only on the verge of entering a conceptual scheme—the pointing implicitly invoking some residual category that somehow spans the boundary, holding out its calling card ("puzzle" or "what shall I call it?" or "enigma") as invitation to come wholly inside, to find its proper place. The human impulse to make meaning is an impulse to classify (name) and count; and from there to endless stories (seeking unities among instances).

[143] Artists have been known to insist on a similar point: "The true value of a work of art (to whatever school it may belong) resides solely in the feeling expressed" (Malevich 2000 [1927], p. 117).

111

Before proceeding to the next section, I want to reiterate a few substantive points of the prior discussion, concisely yet clearly, add some clarification regarding positions taken on a few issues, and preview (or preview more pointedly) some themes of the remainder of this Part Two.

I take perception as a given—sensory, emotive, cognitive—and neglect the physiological processes of it. I include proprioceptive relations ("body awareness") as perception but say little about them. By and large, I treat perceptual phenomena in the joint idioms of "feeling" and "knowing" (that and how) as somewhat distinctive registers of experience. Those registers are related to "personal voice" correlatively, but only in part. There is an orthogonal aspect as well, due chiefly to the "colonizing" urge of "meaning making"—that is, the urge to bring the register of knowing (conceptual scheme) to bear on feeling *as such*, not merely in other than first-person terms but also in the latter whenever later self addresses prior self or selves in the presence of memory. While I attend to the semantics and grammar of voice, I do so mainly with an eye to authority relations (and behind those, power), and this will stand out most in discussions of two questions: whether, and how, feeling-perceptions aggregate in first-person temporality, without or with the "aid" of language; and how feeling-perception translates into an experiential register of knowing, without abstraction (i.e., without stripping away the emotive mood and aspect of feeling).

Earlier in this Part Two I used the phrase, "aesthetics of perception and the power of judgment." As should have then been apparent, I intend "aesthetics" first and foremost as it was constituted in ancient Greek—namely, a category name that covers the full gamut of perceptual experience. I will have more to say about that, and its connection to the power of judgment, in the next section. The thematics of that connection—including several sub-themes such as issues of the authority of voice, transitions from feeling to knowing, collective projects of making a better self (as during Europe's period of "Romantic reaction," as it has often been called), related projects of "world making" known as "Art," and collective-personal experiences of, and sometimes reflexively within, a dialectic of "gain-and-loss"—will be pursued throughout the remainder of this book. But here I want to emphasize the importance of what Kant meant by "the science of aesthetic" in his critical theory, since it is this theory, by and large, that I take as a main starting point of modern thought (both in general and as context of the development of social science). Kant (1998 [1787], B76/A52) was explicit about his meaning of "aesthetic"— namely, "the science of the rules of sensibility in general" (in other words, the rules or regulation of sense perception). Another important passage occurs just prior to the one just cited: "Without sensibility [i.e., our sensory capacity] no object would be given us, and without understanding none would be thought. Thoughts without content are empty, intuitions without concepts are blind" (Kant 1998 [1787], B75/A51). The first of those two sentences is sometimes neglected as soon as the second one (its cut to the stature of epigram) has been read. Objects come to us only via our senses. Our senses are limited. Kant knew that, but he did not know *how great* the limit. He knew, for example, of the visible light spectrum and conjectured that there could be more. But he had never sensed more, nor had any other human being (so far as we know). We now know of some of what he did not (i.e., other parts of the spectrum of radiant energy). We know of "X rays," "microwaves," "cosmic rays," and so forth.[144]  We have invented techniques of "reading" many of them (i.e., bringing the sensations into conceptualization and thus understanding; thence, utilities, etc.). We have no way of knowing if we have learned how to sense *all* of sensory possibility. We have altered "human nature" (as our accustomed name has it) a great amount, by learning to expand our range of sensibility and thereby sense various new sensations, to bring them into conceptualization and thus understanding. What more we might change, what more we might make of sensible capability during the *next* two centuries, we can only conjecture, as Kant did from his day. There is precedent for it. One of the famous aphorisms apparently begun in a letter that the Christian Paul wrote to residents of Corinth says, "For the present we are looking through a mirror obscurely [or darkly], but then [i.e., later] face to face. Now I know in part; then I will know fully, just as I have been fully known."[145]  As Kant was fond of exhorting his students, "Dare to know."

Finally, I want to make plain my meaning of and objection to "psychologism." It is *not*, I emphasize, a covert way of saying that I think the discipline and profession of psychology have no legitimate standing or make no worthwhile contribution of knowledge. I mean an attitude or approach to conception of human being, and to the study thereof, that has a long history and is neither held by all psychologists today nor unique to their discipline and profession. Measured on proportionate basis, it might be held as frequently, at least in some degree, by other members of the social sciences, including sociologists, and as a folk theory of mind it has often been at the core of "populist" ideologies. By "psychologism" I mean the conception of human being as first and foremost a being of *individual* integrity of self-identity, "individual" being understood as wholly *prior to and condition of* sociality (community, group, society, etc.). One or another version of this conception was prominent among some early modern theorists, as Terry Pinkard has said:

> Although reason itself as general reflective capacity to evaluate and criticize our practices, including the practices of reason-giving itself, is something that itself has a history, for [some] early modern individuals it appears as something itself that is simply within each individual. If nothing counts for an individual as an authoritative reason unless he can come to count it *for himself* as an authoritative reason, then the individual

---

[144] All of our sensory organs are sensitive to only a limited range of possible signals, and limits of sensory organs have been general limits of human experience, not easily but potentially circumvented by intellect (i.e., prosthetic devices such as X-ray imaging tools, hearing aids, etc.). It is within the limits of sensory organs that an infant's brain quickly sorts through the still-vast volume of sensations that are available and selects for retentional learning those that "mentors" have repeatedly demonstrated are worthy of attention (see Wiesel 1993 [1981]).

[145] The Greek text says ἐσόπτρου ("esoptrou," genitive of the nominative ἔσοπτρον, "esoptron"). A passage in James (1. 23) says similarly: "For if someone is a hearer of the word and not a doer, he is like a person who looks at his natural face in a mirror." Thomas Laqueur (2015, p. 370 n.5) used the Corinthian passage in a context that suggests that the "glass" (as in "looking glass") was metaphorically language, in the sense of conceptual scheme. That might be a stretch in the literal meaning of the Greek text, but metaphorically it is fitting.

(or his "reason") must remain the ultimate locus of authority for what does and does not count as authoritative for belief or for action (Pinkard 1994, p. 92).

This naturalism of the individual human being did not deny sociality but rendered it as an accretion to, a supplement of, the natural being, and the natural being as such, always already possessing reason, was natural arbiter not only of first-person experience (own perceptions, beliefs, interests, intents, etc.) but also of how that experience should enter negotiation with other individuals' first-person experiences. This conceptualization formed a large part of the backdrop for works such as Adam Smith's (1817) inquiry into the means and conditions of moral sentiments, first published in 1759.

Some prominent psychologists, critical of their fellow disciplinarians for being lax in defense of that conception, have sought to purify "individual" of any and all presence of the social (e.g., Molenaar 2004, 2005; cf. Bogdan 2000; 2010; 2013; Tuomela 2007; Prinz 2012).[146] The folk theory of mind features a reverse version of what has been called "the panopticon effect" (e.g., Foucault 1978 [1975]; Zuboff 1988). Being seen by an unseen seer, intimations of being watched in the midst of darkness, probably began in the same mixture of frightful resignation that spawned notions of supernatural beings beneficent and maleficent. In any case, the idea of a godly panopticon could have been template in reverse, in mortal clothing, of the *cogito* of "I am," each sentience gazing outward from its own location as center of the world, the only world it experiences as a palpable reality—a sort of built-in periscope, one might say (from the Greek verb, *periskopein*, "to look around"). First-person experience typically involves "the sense of living one's perceptions, thoughts, and actions as if from within," centered on "an implicit or semiconscious sense of intention and control" (Sass 1992, p. 214; Dennett 1987). This complex sense of living from within, with intent and control, will be pursued below.

In contrast to psychologism, I take an individual human being to be inherently social, cultural, historical. Human being is, in the broadest sense of Aristotle's meaning, a *zōon politikon*; that is, "anthrōpos is a political animal in greater measure than any bee or any gregarious animal" because of language, which enables perception of good and bad, right and wrong, and therein binds human beings together (*On Politics*, 1.1253a). Better still, however, is the conception, "an ensemble of social relations" (Marx 1976 [1888], p. 4).[147] As noted earlier, the risk one takes in beginning a string of qualifying adjectives is a reader who assumes the string is complete. So here I must add that by saying "social, cultural, historical" I do not mean to exclude "political" or "economic" or "geographic" or "linguistic," and so forth. Nor, certainly, do I mean to exclude "psychological" or "behavioral," but any psychologism is neither starting

---

[146] I have previously registered my critique of Molenaar's argument (Hazelrigg 2010, p. 7). See also Whitehead (1978 [1929], pp. 329, 212-213) and, for some relevant extended exchanges, Hurlburt and Schwitzgebel (2007).

[147] It is mistaken to treat this famous phrase as rare in Marx. Not only does it appear elsewhere in his writings (e.g., in his *Grundrisse*; see Hazelrigg 1989b, pp. 267-269); it is integral to his general argument. Contrary to some recent proposals of a "relational sociology," the perspective is hardly a new one.

point nor cause but consequence of a historically particular sociality.[148] Psychologistic models of "self" ("actor," etc.) did not begin with Kant, although they did develop in particular directions as a result of his notion of "Ich" ("I") as a pure functionality (about which, more below). Illustrative examples of contexts of prior accounts of "mind" that had, or were later taken to have had, psychologistic tendencies, include Augustine's self-confessional, divinity-reflective account; Thomas Hobbes' natural-kind account; and John Locke's "tabula rasa" account. The tendencies are sometimes exaggerated or distorted by neglect of context. For instance, Locke's account was formulated chiefly in rejection of the notion that a human being arrives with a pre-formed mind rather than, as Locke contended, as a (mentally) "blank slate" which will then be furnished via perception and experience. His empiricism was innovative for the time. What Locke did not know, arguably could not have known, is that the human infant is usually born with auditory experiences already "in mind," having heard sounds, including linguistic sounds, through the uterine wall. Derek Parfit, it should be noted, argued a concept of "person" similar to both Marx' and Locke's (though developed mainly from Hume) as a variable set of social relations manifest in memory, in expectations, and thus in a sense of continuity (e.g., Parfit 1987, part 3). Once we recognize that, Parfit said, we will appreciate the failure of attempts to construct (or follow) a practical reasoning that assumes a bright, sharp line of ethics separating oneself from others. A psychological memory function, "psychological" in the sense of functioning interior to mental process, proceeds for a given person as a first-person experience of the moment, which recalls personal existence at prior moments without necessarily regarding those moments and/or their recall as logically prior to sociality. Parfit's stance with regard to "self" was based more on a claim of redundancy than of absence: the empirical exercise of moral responsibility depends on a person's actions of the moment, which may well involve memory of previous moments of similar situations and moral responsibility. The presence of a superordinate constancy of an internal director or manager called "self" is, Parfit contended, superfluous (cf. Strawson 2005).[149]

---

[148] The concept "ambivalence" is a useful case to consider here, as it has been divided between psychology and sociology. Merton and Barber (1976 [1963], pp. 6, 7) referred to "the experienced tendency of individuals to be pulled ... in opposing directions" as "psychological" rather than "sociological" ambivalence, reserving the latter for inconsistencies and contradictions within social-structural formations rather than those of personality. Their sociology would resist, if not wholly avoid, following inquiry, at it pursued social, cultural, historical processes, into the constitution of particular human minds—i.e., into the mentations of gendered persons, persons of various class locations, of various educational statuses, or various dyadic or triadic relations, and so forth. They did focus some attention on inconsistency and on contradiction of conceptual-perceptual meanings bound into a particular status or relation. If their notion of "contradiction" was weakened by prevailing preference for an analytical rather than a dialectical mode of concept formation, their effort was nonetheless exceptional by comparison to the usual ignorance or neglect of contradiction as a sociological process (see also Hillcoat-Nallétamby and Phillips 2011).

[149] Critics of Parfit who, preferring a more ethnographic account of "person," indict his account as thusly deficient (e.g., Schechtman 1996) do not, I believe, understand his account. There is genuine dispute about the need of narrativity—storytelling about ourselves and others—and in that regard an issue of sociality is involved, but it is not that moral responsibility exists prior to or without the presence of sociality. To the contrary. See, e.g., Strawson (2015).

Thus, we come to considerations of the presumption that a "self-identity" exists in a continuity of time.

## §11. The Presumption of Continuity of Self

My choice of title for this section is predicated primarily in terms of the prevailing folk theory of "subjective experience," as adumbrated above. While I do not think the categorial boundary in the distinction between "folk theory" and "philosophical theory" of experience as recommended by others (e.g., Sytsma and Mackery 2010) is impermeable, I do regard the distinction as a useful point of departure, in part because it poses serious questions, as Sytsma and Mackery indicated, about what has come to be called "the hard problem of consciousness" (see, e.g., Chalmers 1995). By my understanding, the point of departure qualifies better as a presumption than as an assumption. While the choice might be thought overly fine, there is to my mind a difference important to present matters. One is more likely to question whether to maintain an assumption, whereas "presumption" better avoids suggestion that alternatives must be considered. Further, "presumption" carries something of the notion, endemic to legal doctrines of human rights, that the contrary case (discontinuity) demands substantial evidence. In terms of the formulation by Chalmers, the usual folk theory of experience at least in European and European-descendent cultures since the day of Isaac Newton is capable of answering "easy parts" of the general "problem of consciousness," even if not consistently. Thomas Nagel set terms of the key issue nearly half a century ago, when he asked his famous question, "What is it like to be a bat?":

> If physicalism is to be defended, the phenomenological features must themselves be given a physical account. But when we examine their subjective character it seems that such a result is impossible. The reason is that every subjective phenomenon is essentially connected with a single point of view, and it seems inevitable that an objective, physical theory will abandon that point of view (Nagel 1974, p. 437).

Identifying the subjective versus objective contrast with that between the "pour-soi" and the "en-soi," Nagel added, "Facts about what it is like to be an X are very peculiar."

But, you see, the presence of "about" in that sentence tells us that "physicalism" was already far in the lead, since, or insofar as, we regard "facts" as social, as agreements in meaning (whether à la Émile Durkheim, Ludwig Wittgenstein, or Nelson Goodman, among others). We use, enact, enforce such agreements in regard to other kinds of being, especially animals and plants, on a daily basis, often without a second thought. One fact about "what it is like to be a deer," for instance, will prevail among farmers of hundreds or thousands of acres of corn (maize) in the plains of Illinois (eating too much of my crop); another, perhaps more than one, among visitors to the local zoo (cute, sad, etc.); and still others to residents of foothill-suburbia of Denver (dangerous, stay out of my garden, if only I could shoot you, etc.). In every instance, of course, an imposition of meaning; it is *my* meaning of what it is like; and insofar as I am engaged in a sociality it is *my* meaning as I share it, agree it, with others as *our* meaning. Consequences are often very real, too.

Let's set aside the cross-species complication. What is it like to be a radical jihadist in New York City or London or Hamburg? Again, "facts *about* what it is like" are as varied as the social relations; and, again, these are impositions. We are therein considering third-person perspectives, perhaps (sometimes) second-person perspectives. But the key—the perspective that raises a truly difficult problem when considering "what is it like to be X?"—is *first-person experience*, the perspective of the "for me" (pour-soi).

"Subjective experiences—the emotions felt—are never relative." What Crapanzano (2015, p. 61) meant in that sentence, it is clear from context, has to do with person-to-person comparatives: "Devaluing our own experiences is permissible, so long as the devaluation is realistic and, more important, sincere. There is a delicate etiquette to subjectivity." Fencing one's "permissible devaluation" of emotive experience by limits of what is "realistic" was his way of isolating specific postures (false modesty and the like). But the sense of etiquette as "delicate" was also recognition that first-person experience, including self-evaluations, is also an interiorized sociality, a set of expectations about how one should *seem* (to borrow a line from Alan Bennett's recovered George III; see Bennett 1992).[150] Our typical folk theory of experience, and folk theory of mind, recognizes only in a peculiar way that "social life," to draw once again from Crapanzano's (2015, p. 368) reflections of a lifetime as dual observer, "demands that we be bad epistemologists. We are destined to live not in illusion, not in reality, but in oscillation between them—in what we declare illusion and reality to be, without recognizing that that distinction is made from within the oscillation itself."

Early in his *Enigmas of Identity* Peter Brooks makes very clear how much we still live on Kant's coattails in remembrance of what he (Brooks), and we, owe to Hume as well as to Kant himself. Having just reviewed variations in a long line of litterateurs' personae, characters, scenes, and commentaries, Brooks concluded with this:

> If there is one constant here, it seems to be the discovery that self-reflection, the work of memory on the self, the telling of a past by "the same" self in the present, will always run up against an insoluble problem: Is there any valid distinction between the self known and the self as knower here? The need to postulate their continuity— I am the same as I ever was—and the simultaneous claim of progress, change, and thus the possibility of an enhanced self-understanding, come into conflict, since in the very process of self-knowledge the knowing self obtrudes its presence over, and

---

[150] The reference is to a late exchange in Bennett's play, *The Madness of George III* (1991): following the king's evident recovery, Thurlow, the Lord Chancellor, extends a solicitous welcome, "Your Majesty seems more yourself," to which the king replies, "Do I? Yes, I do. I have always been myself even when I was ill. Only now I *seem* myself. That's the important thing. I have remembered how to seem. What, what?" This emphasis on "performativity," as in the dramaturgical perspectives of Kenneth Burke (e.g., 1945; see also Goffman 1959; Garfinkel 1967) and John Austin's (1962) speech-act theory, is a matter of first-person experience both within and with sociality: both, because there is a first-person sense of privacy engaging with "the social" as an exteriority, even though that privacy of an interiority already manifests a complex sociality by up-bringing, condition, and context. (By the way, that idiom is quite old; see, e.g., Locke 1975 [1700], ch 27, §20). See also Elvin (1997, p. 10).

sometimes against, the self to be known; you can't get to the latter except by way of the claims of the former, which may repress the past self, distort it, make it dependent on its present reinterpretation. In this regard, the way stories of the self are told takes on a new importance (Brooks 2011, p. 8).

Indeed, we tell stories of the self in a variety of ways, both directly and via stories of what we consider as "external" to self. Joan Didion's first sentence of *White Album* (1979)—"We tell ourselves stories in order to live"—is as richly laden with meanings as the many more books a reader can imagine writing, or being written by others (cf. White 1992 & 2008).[151]

Brooks was referring to the empirical self, but with remembrance of Kant's "objective necessity" that attends our awareness of the transcendental Illusion. This is therefore a useful juncture at which to recall that remembrance as it continues to "infect" understandings about "self" and related concepts, and in particular serious confusions about "self" as it has been read in Kant's theory (see, e.g., Collins 1985).

Kant's dualism is maintained in what amounts to an anemic theory of self. This is the dualism of phenomenal vis-à-vis noumenal reality. One might think of it as a dualism of culture vis-à-vis nature, but *only* on the condition that one recognizes the same duality between the "in-itself" and "for-human" *within* the category, "nature." That is to say, "nature" exists as noumenal, "nature-in-itself" (and, one might think, "nature-for-itself," except that this division does *not* exist within the noumenal; this division occurs *only* because of human consciousness), and as phenomenal, the nature that humans experience.[152] The human mind exists as both realities, noumenal and phenomenal. As noumenal, mind exists as forms of intuition (with regard to sensations) and as categories. Together, these are posited as necessary conditions of the *very possibility* of human knowledge; they are not merely consonant with the noumenal "structure," they *are* that "structure," that constitution. But they are not accessible by human consciousness; they are what make human consciousness possible. Accordingly, there is what one could well call a "noumenal self." But it is mere posit, the posit of a pure functionality, the functioning of the categories together with the forms of intuition.[153] These are *not* empirical: human

---

[151] Think of the possible stories told by the two books identified as White's under the same title, *Identity and Control*, published sixteen years apart. Are they two editions of the same book (as the copyright page says), or are they two different books? When is a book so richly energetic with intelligent puzzles, challenges to understand insights of another and, one hopes, in the process perhaps think something more (at least more than one had previously thought) and new (at least new to the one thinking—and thus so generative of potential for readers—when is such a book ripe for domestication? Compare, say, Alfred North Whitehead's *Process and Reality* with his part of the *Principia* (as if his part could be extracted from that of his co-author, Bertrand Russell). Or Hegel's *Phenomenology of Geist* compared with his *Encyclopædia* (see Pinkard 1994).

[152] Kant was impressed, remember, by the certainty of Newton's mechanics, knowing nothing of Einstein's relativity, quantum chromodynamics and kindred topics. These are all sociocultural historical theories—that is to say, human-made theories—within which a sense of hierarchy of knowledges and disciplinary professions of authority (i.e., authorship) remains in place much as before, more vehemently defended by some (e.g., Weinberg 2015) than by others (e.g., Muller 2016, Laughlin 2005). For a recent very sober look, see Baumberg (2018).

[153] This will be a topic of the Part Three as well.

118

consciousness does *not* experience them; rather, consciousness experiences what they make possible, make available, to consciousness.

The foregoing does not mean that Kant had nothing to say empirically about "self." To the contrary: he had a lot to say about "self" as an empirical reality; and contrary to what has been said by several social scientists, his discussion included cultural variations of "self," "person," and the like. Much of this took place in his lectures on anthropology (Kant 1798), which he arranged for publication only after he retired from teaching. He also had quite a bit to say about cultural variations of "self" in other writings, but hardly anything to say in his three volumes of critical theory. Why? Because those volumes were (are) crucially about necessary conditions of the very possibility of human knowledge—which is also to say, the necessary *limits* of human knowledge—and as such the discussions were conducted in terms of what he intended to be strictly *transcendental*. To say "strictly transcendental" in his terms means that they were intended to be (i.e., Kant posited them as) universal to human being, universal conditions of the very possibility of knowledge; thus, *not* cultural, *not* empirical, but conditions of the possibility of "the cultural," of the experiential or empirical. (This is why the "objective necessity" of the "transcendental Illusion" was (is) so devastating to the idea of a science of society—of any claim to a science of the social, the cultural, the political, the economic, and so forth, that consists in more than empirical generalizations: it can be only a "pseudo-science," because it lacks the rational part that would, in Kant's terms, make it a "true science," alongside Newton's physics. The birth of any of the "social sciences" into the empirical conditions of an "inferiority complex," as it were, was integral to that "objective necessity" of the transcendental Illusion. This is what Foucault got right in his book on "the order of things" (1970 [1966]), despite only weakly, at best, acknowledging that he was repeating Kant.

One of the symptoms (I suppose I might call it) of the fact that social scientists have often failed to distinguish between what is intended to be the basis of any *possible* human culture, on the one hand, and any *actual* human culture, on the other, is neglect of much of what Kant wrote about the latter. Here we have evidence once again of a tendency to read what has already been read and repeated multiple times, without venturing beyond the repetitive to that which has been left to the side (as if not intrinsic). And what is *my* evidence for *that* claim? Most strikingly the fact that Kant made grotesque attributions in his empirical studies of "self" and related topics, yet these attributions have virtually never been recognized especially by self-confirmed social scientists, the very people one would expect to have something to say about the attributions. What is more, one cannot claim that the attributions occurred only in Kant's "pre-critical" writings (i.e., before having been awakened from slumbers by Hume); they recurred in his lectures on anthropology. They do not appear in his critical theory, simply because they are not relevant to his transcendentalist project.

What attributions do I have in mind? As early as his *Observations on the Feeling of the Beautiful and Sublime* Kant reported his empirical observations on "gender" and on "national character" insofar as these were by his understanding relevant to differences of feeling with regard to the beautiful and the sublime (Kant 2011 [1764], §3 and §4). Although he did not regard "feeling" as itself transcendental, he did seem to think it to be an intrinsic property of every person, a capacity of every person "of being touched by ["external things"] with pleasure or displeasure" (p. 13). His comments with regard to women vis-à-vis men would surely be described today as prejudicial if not literally misogynistic. His comments with regard to at least several non-European national cultures and their native inhabitants (e.g., Chinese, Indian) would surely be described today as prejudicial and ethnocentric at best. His comments with regard to peoples of sub-Saharan Africa (i.e., "Negroes") would surely be described today as racist. One would hope that when he wrote of *his* hope that our species would attain maturity and self-responsibility he did mean the species, not just some members. It is not clear that he did. But if he did, it is clear that he believed women in general and non-European peoples had farther to go in reaching that maturity. Granted, the attributions were hardly unique to Kant. However, some predecessors whose works he had surely known—Montesquieu, Voltaire—had been somewhat less dismissive in attitude toward people of other cultures, and slightly more receptive of female accomplishments than those of bed and breakfast. Given the high standards we read in Kant's volumes of critical theory, especially in the second critique and in closely related works, it is impossible to excuse the empirical bigotry by pointing to the transcendentalist inquiry of his critical project. Dogmatism and bigotry are, if not the same, very closely related (see Pinkard 2017, ch. 3, regarding corresponding characterizations in Hegel's philosophy).

The presumption of self-continuity in time is of course neither innocent of prejudice nor antidotal to it. It is, one guesses, a very old presumption and as such carried a plethora of other prejudgments among its substantive contents. For many centuries, millennia even, it was nothing remarkable probably for anyone. Naivete, ignorance, dogmatism, and a sense of time that barely registered one day from another deflected nearly everyone from wondering, "Is it true?" Eventually, as room for doubt expanded enough to allow reflexivity to develop, the presumption surely became problematic. Hume did not invent this problem—some ancient Greeks had expounded on it, as had others—but after Hume it would not rest. Some theorists have been known to rue that fact, because it denies them the privilege of being able to speak as if all room for doubt had vanished. (Or it denies that privilege excepting readers who seek to restore it, or who believe it never died.)

One might suppose that the presumption of self-continuity in time began with the invention of "future" as a real and stable (though as yet only implicitly populated) place of time. This sense of temporality, one might suppose, was a condition of the *possibility* that one could have high confidence in the "not yet," in "soon," in a future world that *will* include me; and with that, the focus of "horizon" as a forward-looking pose, "perspective" as an orientation of *now* to that *later*; and the confidence that present perspective could tell us something worthwhile and possibly optimizing about the point of one's actions now, in this moment. Plausible as all of that speculation might seem, however, perhaps the presumption began as a retrospection, one's memory of having been, of having acted, a notion of the "before now"—a retrospection that implicitly caught a feeling of continuity, which in turn recommended invention of a presence called "tomorrow," and then more generally a more abstract place called "the future."[154] These

---

[154] By the time of Pindar, a Greek poet of the fifth century BCE, writing, or certain chains of written words, were thought to have purchase on some facsimile of immortality: "When the city I extol shall have / perished, when the men to whom I sing / shall have faded into oblivion, my words / shall remain."

are only speculations. While they can be useful contemplations, the questions that generate them can be answered only in speculative mode.[155] One of their uses is to bring forward the mostly subliminal experience of the presumption of continuity. As already suggested, the subliminal aspect is bound up with feelings of self-efficacy and self-confidence, which begin growing (or not) from very early age. Important issues within that variability will be topics in following discussions, especially in Parts Four and Five (e.g., as organizational issues of commitment, personal searches for convincing evidence of efficacy and other measures that can be taken as answer to what Philip Wagner (1996) called "the Geltung hypothesis," the validity of one's "identity and control" (White 1992), of "being here" and of "making a difference" that will appear in lasting stories that humans tell of their pasts, presents, and futures.

I am thinking of Louise Glück's (2012, p. 342) insight of what could be regarded as an ontogeny: "We look at the world once, in childhood. / The rest is memory." How often does one ask oneself of a memory, "Was that really *me*?" Or, in the other direction, "How far into the future can I really see myself as *me*?" The former question is probably not as rare or outlandish as the latter question—except perhaps that asking the former might stimulate thought of the latter. I briefly considered in the previous section the stance of John Locke with regard to memory in the presence of a self-identity; and then Derek Parfit's response to that. Another way of addressing the complex of issues is to return to Kant's interest in limits of knowledge (or Moro's interest in limits of language; Moro 2016). We humans recognize and usually accept without much deliberation that our sensory apparatus is closely circumscribed relative to what we can conceive as possibilities of radiant energy and thus information flows. For example, light that is directly visible to us is a narrow band: without prosthetic devices we do not see what an eagle or a butterfly sees. Nor do we hear what a whale hears or an elephant hears; and we do not know the communication that takes place when many tiny polyps, each with a mouth no more than a centimeter wide, evidently collaborate to entrap a stinging jellyfish and consume it. Nor do we sense what a tree senses through its mycorrhiza network. Are there similar restrictions of feeling?

Consider that insofar as there is a distinctiveness to a *discourse* of feeling—vis-à-vis first-person feeling as such—its seat is semantical, a partly distinctive vocabulary that relies on first-person privileging against comparison. By way of illustration, consider the following sentence: "Judgment is important because none of the answers to the questions that really move us can be found by following a rule." In composing that sentence Neiman (2014, pp. 6-7) was recalling one of Kant's major pronouncements about the limits of both reason and empirics. A person should exercise rational deliberation in concert with empirical evidence; but having done so, a particular conclusion or decision about course of action will often remain to be taken, and this can come only as the person exercises judgment. In one specific respect, however, the sentence hews closer to Ludwig Wittgenstein's admonition about rule following. Note, however, that admonition hardly merits blanket application: human beings do follow rules, very often and to great benefit individually and collectively. Imagine, for instance, the helter skelter, should travelers individually decide by whim or coin toss one morning whether to proceed right side or

---

[155] Not to disparage "speculative mode," however: Augustine of Hippo offered a highly insightful speculative discussion of time, in the eleventh book of his *Confessions*, following his discussion of memory in the tenth book.

left side on the day's journey on any two-way road. We depend daily on habits bestowed by formal rules, simply as a matter of coordination, efficiency, safety, and the like, and we likewise engage everyday practices of semi-formal rules in much the same way for much the same reason (e.g., "elevator behavior," queuing, turn-taking, etc.). But notice that in Neiman's sentence the operative word: the verb, "move." She could well respond to any reservation that I offered with, "And does *that* question really *move* you?" Well, maybe it does. The point is, however, what counts as "being *moved*"? Rather, even if "I feel moved by X," and she has the same first-person "feeling" experience of X, how can we know that we have implicitly been in concert of *feeling*? We could try talking about it with each other, but "talk about 'feeling moved'" is not the same as "feeling moved." Not only is there a difference of personal voice; the vocabularies differ. The emotion of "feeling moved" just is.[156] Neiman knows that, of course. She has offered to doubters if any there be her magisterial two-society journey of evidences of "feeling moved" even as one talks about this and other feelings of and from first-person experience (Neiman 2019).

The aid of analytics comes with cost. Categorial boundaries too easily become divorced from the process by which they were made (see, e.g., Tugendhat 1986 [1979]; and §28, below). Moreover, while one might notice this cost when in the midst of deliberating about feeling— after all, it is difficult to forget the subjective privilege of feeling—the same cost may well be always already congealed in objectivities produced by prior work of deliberation, and those objectivities probably feed into not only discourse about feeling but also into a person's experience of feeling (including the emotion of "feeling moved"). And so any question about "restrictions on (of) feeling"—including restrictions that could be, in any given experience, due to a self-deception or a posturing that "got out of hand" or some other slip or confusion limning a difference of "faked" or "unreal" experience of "feeling moved"—is always an invitation to ask of "restrictions on (of) thinking" and "knowing." Are the concepts that we are capable of producing a closely bounded, censored sampling of all that are possible? Do we even know how to address that question? And to the extent that we do, or think that we do, do we know how to address any intersection of the conjoined questions with regard to both, feeling and thinking?

While we generally are in agreement that we now know what no one several centuries ago knew about the meaning of the phrase "visible light spectrum" (would even have adduced a coherent sense of the chain of three words), do we similarly know, are we capable of thinking, the meaning of an analogous phrase such as "thinkable thought spectrum" or "sayable word spectrum"? Inklings of such differences haunt us from experiences of translating across what we selectively adduce out of some larger array as "natural languages." These hauntings give rise to fretful ruminations of "the almost grasped" or "the missing difference" or "the space between,"

---

[156] As scholars of ancient Greek cultures have remarked, the Greek concept of pathos—usually the word translated to the English "emotion"—had a different constitution. While it did refer to an experiential condition which could be evaluated in gradations of negative/positive valence, this condition was not primarily an internal excitation of the individual person; that excitation occurred *because* of a condition involving two or more actors, and the remedy, or *any* address of the condition, had to be an address of the "social" or interpersonal relation that had become in some way problematic (see, e.g., Konstan 2006). Note also that most characterizations of the different kinds of pathos featured the problematic (i.e., "negative" valence, such as anger, shame, jealousy); but in general a named kind had its own opposite, the condition being dialectical (although this sense had diminished by the time of Aristotle).

as they did for Wittgenstein and Heidegger, among others, harking back to Plato's discomfort with poetic possibilities.[157] Thus, George Steiner's (2010, p. 10) recent reminder: "The *Logos* equates word with reason in its very foundation. Thought may indeed be in exile. But if so, we do not know or, more precisely, we cannot *say* from what." A fool's errand, moreover, to go in search; and yet a search, or an impulse to search, that we cannot avoid. Anyone who has struggled to understand the extant thoughts of people whom we now call "the ancient Greeks," for example, or of another people whom we now call "the ancient Chinese," is acutely aware that the missing difference remains just beyond.[158]

Still another way of addressing the issues—similar to the address by Augustine in his *Confessions* (xi.14) and the way that will now be pursued—is to ask about personal conceptions of the reality of time: are "past times," for instance, relatable to each other and to "now" on a continuous gradient ("degrees of reality," one might think), or do they exist as small chunks of memory, mostly self-contained, with only tenuous links one to another ("different realities")?[159] And in such thoughts does "time" in fact exist as an independent real dimension, or is the reality of what the word "time" intends really only a carry-over of sequencing of experiential episodes when I think of my remembered "past times" and, hopefully, my imagined "future times"?[160]

Such questions are usually so matter-of-factly folded into the presumption of continuity in time and space, it is well worth pausing to appreciate what a powerful statement is actually being made in that presumption (and to appreciate Kant's relegation of "time" as well as "space" to pure form). The statement is both of and from consciousness, and while inherently social it manifests an illusion of being primarily and purely a private, first-person perspective on world from something like a pan-sensorial unity that just *is*—a perspective that projects from a self-identity in psychologistic terms or, insofar as there *is* awareness at least of "presence *in* sociality,"

---

[157] "Poetry aims to reinvent language, to make it new [think Wallace Stevens]. Philosophy labors to make language rigorously transparent, to purge it of ambiguity and confusion [think Wittgenstein]" (Steiner 2011, p. 214). To the extent that Steiner's contrast is fitting—and I think it is fitting yet partial—one is then faced with a question: Which of the practical artists, poet or philosopher, has the easier time of it?

[158] Parfit (1998) highlighted another aspect in his essay, "Why anything?" Our efforts to produce satisfying answers while suspecting that none will be final tells us something important of ourselves, as product of sociality.

[159] A hopscotch from Augustine to Husserl (1991 [1893]), then to Lyotard (2011 [1971]), will be pursued in broad steps during following pages. Explicitly comparative work across the landings will be ignored as offering too little added value.

[160] Moreover, consider that a person's "remembered past times" can intersect with objectivities of "historical time" (by which I mean, e.g., the objectivities extant as a "book of history" and/or as "lessons I learned in school" and/or "what everyone knows about X," etc.) in ways that proceed iteratively, even recursively, and in so doing redefine what had been assumed geographic settlements. For example, Paul Kosmin (2019) recently published a study of changing practices of "Greek time" that crossed territorial lines that have usually been labeled "ancient Greece," "Macedonia," and "Persia," using Alexander the Great and Seleucus as personifications of place, the latter person the key figure in massive revision of calendric time after Alexander's death, following which he became founding satrap of his own empire, the Seleucid empire, the core of which had been Persia. How many students of history have confused Seleucus and his heirs as Persian rather than Greek? In changing the calendar on territory that had been Persian prior to Alexander, and in a way that Athens (e.g.) did not follow, did Seleucus become Persian?

a self-similarity (and thus a social psychologism that tends to treat "the social" as supplement or only context). When enacting this perspective, one feels active in sensing while not being entirely available to sensing by others. Context is (as the word itself says) thought to be supplemental, a secondary presence, which in the strongest projection of self-identity virtually disappears into a sense of all-encompassing identity—as in the human infant still weakly "socialized" but perhaps also in imaginations of incomparable genius or god-like heroics, and perhaps in the delusions that attend extreme narcissism. These are materials of self-fictioning, no doubt, a story-telling that can seem to reflect well on the teller, and as such it is an old and in some sense hallowed device of celebration. For example, Michael Psellos, an eleventh-century scholar, selected as a model of rhetorical skillfulness a figure molded as if an Adamic "god-like statue," Gregory of Nazianzos (329-390; one of the Cappadocian church fathers), who in Psellos' admiration stood as "an autonomous, self-determined, free, and willing agent," one who "functions like a creative diviner agent" (Papaioannou 2013, p. 86; see also Misch 1907, pp. 383-402).[161] This rhetorical device of authorship (the auctor as author and authority) enlisted droves of believing Christians into a storyline that endowed them simultaneously with particular agency (one in the body, one in the believing mind) and with a chronic alienation from authorship of each's own story because of vital dependence on an unfathomable source of that agency. As an organizational principle expressed in the storytelling of an accomplished rhetor such as Pellos' Gregory, this reflection of a presumption of continuity in space and time would herd flocks in far greater number than any famous organizing principle of one-to-one-hundred scaling to ten-to-ten-thousand. That sort of division of agency—one as "willing agent" and the other, higher, as principal—served as highly effective means of manipulating orientations along the terrain of Brooks' "distinction between the self known and the self as knower" (cited above).

The religions of the book produced several rhetors of major influence by the standard of Gregory of Nazianzos. How different the "autobiographic self-consciousness" had become by the time of Hume. Clearly Hume was not alone in that revised perspective: think of Laurence Sterne's *Life and Opinions of Tristram Shandy, Gentleman* (1759-67) and Samuel T Coleridge's *Biographia Literaria* (1817), for example; more recently, Virginia Woolf's (1985 [1939]) "A Sketch of the Past"; then again, J D Salinger's *The Catcher in the Rye* (1951), Jack Kerouac's *On the Road* ( 1957), Sheila Heti's *How Should a Person Be?* (2010), Dana Czapnik's *The Falconer* (2019), and so forth (for some comparative perspective see, e.g., Marcus 1994; Smyth 2016).

Recall that for Kant "time" (one of his pair of forms of intuition and, along with "space," necessary to operations of the understanding) was among the conditions of the very possibility of experience—and in that sense, then, was (is) transcendental. Thus, it figured in the principles of *a priori* sensibility (i.e., our ability as a *condition* of any experience), which are the topics of

---

[161] I am indebted to Vessela Valiavitcharska for bringing both Papaioannou and Psellos to my attention. I did not recall having encountered either scholar (one small indication of the ethnocentrism that has long been a feature of some European and Euro-American cultures toward others), although I had probably encountered him in Misch's prominent history of autobiographies. Valiavitcharska's studies of various dimensions of Byzantine cultures, some of which (2014) is cited elsewhere in this Part, also merits much more attention than they have so far received.

his transcendental aesthetics in his first critique (Kant 1998 [1787], B36/A21), which, of all the many sections of his three critiques is (was) the "most revolutionary" (if such a nomination need be made).[162] There is more to his treatment of "time" than is often stated, however. In particular, consider what he had to say about the utility of the concept, "vanishing point":

> [T]he transcendental ideas are never of constitutive use.... [H]owever, they have an excellent and indispensably necessary use, namely that of directing the understanding to a certain goal respecting which the lines of direction of all its rules converge at one point, which, although it is only an idea (*focus imaginarius*)—i.e., a point from which the concepts of the understanding do not really proceed, since it lies entirely outside the bounds of possible experience—nonetheless still serves to obtain for these concepts the greatest unity alongside the greatest extension. Now of course it is from this that there arises the deception, as if these lines of direction were shot out from an object lying outside the field of possible empirical cognition (just as objects are seen behind the surface of a mirror); yet this illusion (which can be prevented from deceiving) is nevertheless indispensably necessary if besides the objects before our eyes we want to see those that lie far in the background i.e., when in our case, the understanding wants to go beyond every given experience (beyond this part of the whole of possible experience), and hence wants to take the measure of its greatest possible and uttermost extension (Kant (1998 [1787], B672-673/A644-645).

This is the "vanishing point" device used in perspective—in architecture, painting, and other sorts of representational or presentational productions. It is used with great deliberation by the artist of paints who seeks to manoeuver a viewer into proper location from which to view with desired effect the intended signals within the field. A painting may have two or more vanishing points, thus enabling the artist to create movement in the viewer as an illusion of movement of those signals.[163] (Think of the portrait of a person whose eyes seem actually to follow the viewer's movements "all around the room.") Careful use of those points which vanish beyond the horizon accentuate the illusion of three, even four dimensions on the flat canvas. Bear in mind that the technique creates this effect temporally as well as spatially; that is, even when only a single vanishing point has been used, the viewer will tend to move around within the viewing space, in search of the precise point of view "expected" by the painting. An experienced viewer can of course "move without moving"—that is, obliquely take the demanded stance imaginally. The arrangement of scene cooperates with control by perspective, much as a visual magician controls the viewer's eye, a ventriloquist the auditor's ear. The perspectival motion of vanishing point plays against arrangement of subfields—for instance, in terms of illumination, shading,

---

[162] It was also here (well before his third critique) that Kant noted that he was using the word "aesthetic" where others had been fixated on "critique of taste," and the like ("beauty," "the sublime"). That fixation had come about in what Kant regarded as a vain hope of "bringing the critical estimation of the beautiful [and the sublime] under principles of reason [Vernunftprincipien]." He preferred to retain a meaning closer to that of the ancient Greeks, for whom cognition was distributed between àisthēta and noēta (as it was for Kant).

[163] When two or more, the vanishing points can be inconsistent. The inconsistency can be a deliberate artistic device, but in earlier eras painters sometimes produced indeliberate inconsistencies (see, e.g., Hoffman 1998, p. 35, for an illustration from the early fifteenth century).

even the contrast of near-opacity—such that a viewer's attention is oriented in effect as if by an explicit preference hierarchy.[164]

Horizon is always temporal as well as spatial (i.e., since Einstein, a unity of space-time relative to any observer at rest or in motion). Note that Kant was careful to clarify that he was not, in the above-quoted passage, referring to the transcendental Illusion, which, even when we have become aware of its presence, we cannot avoid. By contrast, this "perspectival illusion" by the vanishing point *can* be avoided, not only in the sense that a naïve viewer observing a painting without careful attention might well be physically moved without conscious reflection, but also in the sense that a viewer who "looks without seeing" may be completely unmoved by the artistic device. Careless thought may lead us into believing that despite movement or passage in time we may remain in precisely the same space, or that after having been away from that place in space for some time we can then return to precisely that same place; but this belief is no more well founded than the belief that one can be in two or more different places in space at precisely the same moment in time.

Now, think of the function of "horizon" in this analogy in terms of Kant's specification that what is at play is an "indispensably necessary regulative use." Think then of the vanishing point in its simplest image: the point to which the parallel lines of, say, the iron rails of a train track converge. Note that a retinal image has only two dimensions, height and width. Thus, the fact of "distance" is, as Helmholtz (1925 [1910], vol. 3, pp. 4-6) said, an unconscious conclusion (unbewusster Schluss)—in other words, an unconscious inference in visual perception (and to some extent in sonic perception as well, which we experience most obviously in the Doppler effect). Think of one's body: it has presence that establishes width (or diameter, circumference) and height; for a third dimension of "length" or "distance" one can walk, or imagine walking, toward some other spatial point. But walking already brings a fourth dimension into experience, time. All of this means, as Hoffman (1998, p. 13) has reminded us, that "countless worlds" can be constructed from any given retinal image. Seeing (and to an extent hearing, perhaps also smelling, touching) into more than the two dimensions of width and height is a patterned action (one that becomes fixed, habitual) that a child learns, normally without instruction by another person, via the trial-and-error experience of crawling, then walking, imaginatively and actually.

Imagining the horizon as temporal leads us to a generalization from our particular experiences: the point of convergence continuously recedes with each step that I, an imagined observer on that track, take toward the horizon; that is, the point vanishes into an imagined "later" horizon that I shall never reach. Likewise, when I imagine the horizon as spatial; for my

---

[164] Le Corbusier was renowned for his deliberate effort to determine the way in which his buildings would be viewed, thought about, discussed in writing, and that he worked no less diligently in fashioning his public persona, some have said his mythical presence (see, e.g., Flint 2014). Surely the same could be said of most if not all nationally or internationally known architects (Louis Sullivan, Frank Lloyd Wright, Frank Gehry, Zaha Hadid, a few prominent examples). So it is, too, with a painter, a choreographer, a musical composer—indeed, on some scale of stage, any person who takes pride in creativity; for one's presence is bound up with the presence of one's work, both of which exist in an arrangement apprehended by any perceiver as an objectivity from one's being in subject/object dialectical process.

movement is inherently a movement in time as well as in space. The horizon is a horizon of visual perception, and it "leads" my perceptions "forward," temporally and spatially, in extensions of my current experiences. This regulative (i.e., non-constitutive) utility aids my understanding of why "the problem of the counterfactual" is insoluble. Theoretically, "the counterfactual" must exist as a matter of logic (analytically in one fashion, dialectically in another). But no observer can ever gain empirical access to, experience of, *all* (usually even most) of the implied states of being, since each step forward generates more counterfactual states. Thus, the empirical limit on causality.[165]

As Kant argued a bit later in his first critique, "[e]xperience is itself a synthesis of perceptions that augments my concepts which I have by means of one perception by the addition of others" (1998 [1787], B792/A764). Experience is actually a *process*, not a thing, although we tend to treat it as if were a store. The on-goingness of process is necessarily in time and space, but the synthesis of the sequence of perception and then another perception, and then another, imparts itself an experience of "temporal duration in this place" both as achievement and as expectation of persistence. Accordingly, one learns a "principle of persistence … that anticipates experience just as much as does the principle of causality" (Kant 1998 [1787], B795/A767). But what one thereby learns is a reflection of persistence as "a necessary condition under which alone appearances [things for us], as things or objects, are determinable in a possible experience" (1998 [1787], B232/A189). Or, again: "The synthesis of spaces and times, as the essential form of all intuition, is that which at the same time makes possible apprehension of the appearance, thus every outer experience, consequently also all cognition of its objects" (1998 [1787], B206/A165).

As with much of Kant's critical theory, those are difficult thoughts, and it takes little imagination of an attentive reader to detect a sort of shimmer—beginning at B225/A182 (if not before: "change does not affect time itself but only the appearances in time"—in what he was trying to "nail to the door," as it were, with the certainty of *a priori* principles. Perhaps he had read Newton's own statement of what seems to be doubt about *his* conception of time and space as absolutes (although the doubt might have been only of means of measurement). Granted, Kant was attempting to establish the conditions of the very possibility of our *experiences*, Newton's experiences, anyone's experiences, of change, stasis, movement, duration, and the like, and he certainly allowed that our experiences of time and space, as any other experience, are relative

---

[165] Briefly, history is the "culprit": for any given counterfactual set, each empirical test generates new counterfactuals. Investigation of counterfactuals can be enlightening nonetheless. Moro (2016) has offered useful illustration with his pursuit of the question, Can we imagine what an *impossible* human language would be? (although he was quick to leave counterfactual problems to the side— understandably but without signaling them (2016, e.g., pp. 12-13). Of course, the category "impossible language" must be null (by semantics; but see pp. 43-46); yet the exploration is useful to understanding the limits of human language. For example, Moro's work seems to have shown that the human brain has developed specifically to process recursive syntax (higher efficiency) and is much less proficient at processing non-recursive linear syntax, all of which he has taken as conclusive evidence that human language is not arbitrary and conventional. That is tantamount to saying that the human body has developed in such a way that it can survive only by ingesting some minimal caloric per day on average over long periods of time. But the kinds, timing, contexts, and other properties of that caloric level can vary arbitrarily and conventionally from place to place time to time. Neither "conventional" nor "arbitrary" necessarily implies "limitless conditionality."

(e.g., to our categories, or conceptual schemes). But we do not know in good detail how much Kant knew of the then-current science of time and space.

That one cannot look through the three dimensions of space without also looking through time is not exactly a new conception. The correlation was understood during the era of Hume, Kant, and Thomas Jefferson. Royal astronomer William Herschel, peering through his own craftsmanship in a telescope, spying evidence of a planet to be named Uranus and viewing the nebulous lights of other galaxies far away, knew that the farther into cosmic space he looked the earlier in time his observations were taking him. This correlation was not then widely known, to be sure, and Herschel's conception was certainly not Einstein's. But it is clear that Kant, among others, prided himself in staying abreast of latest developments of science, physics especially, so there is a good chance that Kant knew what many people today do not know of standard physical theory.[166] Presumably people today do understand as a perfectly ordinary fact that one cannot *physically* move through three dimensions of space without simultaneously moving through the fourth dimension. But the case for visual sense seems to strike them as different. Why? Probably because the physical sense of movement in time is mostly only a sense of duration, combined with the fact that visible radiant energy (i.e., "light") moves so fast that one cannot sensually detect the correlation of time and space, even when one is observing across a vast expanse of spatial distance, as Herschel was when admiring the distant galaxies. He knew he was viewing those galaxies as they were eons ago; and he had this knowledge because of the intelligence, the intelligibility, of a theory of dynamics.[167]

While addressing confusions in popular understanding of contemporary physical theory, I shall add to the list a story commonly told in an earlier day of Newton's work—namely, that he had expelled the human observer from the world of modern physics. Told sometimes as proof of sophistication, sometimes as criticism, but mostly for popular consumption, the story suffers too little clarity, too much ambiguity, to be helpful. What counts as "observer"? Surely Newton did not rule himself out of bounds, either as theorist or as experimenter. As Kant later made clear in his account of Newton's achievement, in order for the physicist to get his own story started he had to make a number of assumptions—about time and space, for example, as basic framework or grid within which things and events existed. Were the grids absolutes? It made the story far

---

[166] A common confusion about time-space correlation still today in popular receptions of physical theory is the idea that the farthest anyone can look across the universe is 13.7 billion light-years, since the universe became "lighted" (i.e., the initial event of radiant energy) that long ago. This figure is often cited as the size of the "cosmological bubble," the maximum observational bubble within which human observers exist. But a basic fact constructed from standard cosmological theory is that (1) the universe has been expanding since before that initiation and (2) during the subsequent 13.7 billion light-years the cosmological bubble has expanded to about 47 billion light-years. Not all that long ago, however, physicists were still debating whether the universe was in steady-state or in a state of persistent expansion (much less an expansion at accelerating rate). Kant surely did not know this latter view, probably did not entertain it as conjectured possibility.

[167] Why is it still so difficult for so many people today, two centuries after Herschel, to understand what he knew? Because, disgracefully, we do not bother to train our citizens in those skills of intelligibility. As a result, they know little of dynamics, even the relatively simple dynamical systems of Newtonian physics and elementary calculus.

128

simpler to assume that they are indeed absolute, unchanging, containers of all that happens, of all that can possibly happen (but as already noted, Newton perhaps could not completely shake a doubt about the absolutist assumption). These assumptions did not so much expel "the observer" (as if from a garden of Eden) as render all that happened in the realm of Newtonian mechanics "relative" to the absolute grid, not to any particular observer or any sum or average of observers. This did not rule out human fallibility, of course: errors of observation, measurement, logical thinking, and so forth, would remain as sources of contamination, obstacles to be overcome; but the absolute grid was immune to them, making it possible in principle for careful and astute scientists to "subtract the errors," so to speak, from observed results of tests designed to verify empirical implications of basic principles.[168] To most if not all human inhabitants of Newton's world of physics as late as the early or middle decades of the nineteenth century, it must have seemed perfectly natural that everything that could exist, if in fact extant, must exist within time and within space, independently of whether or not any observers knew anything, much less everything, about an existing thing or event. By early years of the second half of that century, however, another physicist, James Clerk Maxwell, was strongly suspecting that physical reality is actually not divorced from consciousness, although he could not figure out how to make all of the pieces, including some new ones that seemed irredeemably aberrant, fit together into a new and superior framework of understanding. Maxwell was frustrated in large part because of an unexpected limit to observation, to empirical evidence. How does one track all of the motions of tiny particles, molecules of a gas, for example, and perhaps even tinier particles hidden in molecules. This frustration was soon turned into a new kind of modeling behavior, by Josiah Willard Gibbs, models known as "Gibbsian statistical mechanics." Gibbs thought to explain the problem to his reader in a new treatise of "elementary principles," in words that were not easy of the day to comprehend:

> The laws of thermodynamics, as empirically determined, … express the laws of mechanics for such systems as they appear to beings who have not the fineness of perception to enable them to appreciate quantities of the order of magnitude of those which relate to single particles, and who cannot repeat their experiments often enough to obtain any but the most probable results (Gibbs 1902, p. viii).

The new framework came less than half a century after Maxwell's work, and close on the heels of Gibbs, except that it consisted in two seemingly disparate frameworks that resist unity still today. One was the "quantum revolution" of Max Planck. The other, the "invariance theory" of Albert Einstein, better known as relativity. The former was too difficult to gain much traction not only in popular imagination but also in most workshops of modern science. The latter gained a notoriety that at times rivaled the mysterious plots of science fiction.

After people began the effort to understand Einstein's equations, the commonly told story about Newton needed major amendment: it seemed that "the observer" had been returned.

---

[168] One of Henry David Thoreau's most famous thoughts was about time and labor: "I have learned that the swiftest traveler is he who goes afoot" (1985 [1854], p. 364). His point was (as he elaborated it) that proper calculation should include the amount of time one labored in order to have the funds to buy a train ticket, in this case for a thirty-mile ride to Fitchburg; with that factor of labor time included, Thoreau was confident that he would arrive in Fitchburg more quickly than his train-riding interlocutor.

It took considerably longer for most listeners to grasp that this observer was well ahead of the curve of everyday thought, and a far cry from the one that had been labeled as Newton's observer, a human being barely out of medieval habits.[169]

In the world of physical theory, post-Einstein, observer-relevance has been a topic of considerable debate, and it remains active. So, too, another debate, intimately related, this one focused on "time," and it has pulsated between periods of great intensity, in emotion as well as effort, and periods of relative quiescence (whether due to fatigue or a sense of wasted effort, or both). In terms of what became known as the standard model (the best collection of theories, from cosmological, including Newtonian domain, to relativity theory and quantum dynamics) the universe, or "our universe," is conceived as a fixed-block model, in which time is irrelevant except as a human illusion. (Or as Einstein once put it, "only a stubbornly persistent illusion": see Hawking 2007). Not that the universe lacks internal dynamics; far from it. Rather, all of those dynamics take place within a closed system, the block itself, which as such is timeless. Past and future are already fixed, always have been already fixed. A moment called "now" is merely an observational illusion.

Some number of well-known physical scientists reject that fixed-block theory, some of them vehemently. Several of these critics joined in debate with defenders of the block model in a conference convened by the Perimeter Institute in Waterloo, Ontario, during June 2016 (for extensive background see Unger and Smolin 2015, principal conveners). The outcome of the four-day meeting was inconclusive (perhaps the only mutually agreed conclusion) but also fascinating to some, and for many of the participants immensely frustrating. In a nutshell, two principles were upheld, neither of them new, and so long as held sufficiently apart agreed by all: (1) the dynamics *internal* to the model are perfectly symmetrical, in that they work exactly the same forward and backward—or in terms of conventional time marking, whether moving from "past" to "future" or vice versa; and (2) the second law of thermodynamics tells us that the balance sheet on entropy is unrelentingly positive (always increasing, on balance); or, in simple observational terms, no one has ever seen a scrambled egg become a whole egg, and no one ever will. There seems to be a basic contradiction at play (see, e.g., Muller 2016; Yourgrau 2005).

Is time real, or not? What kind of real, if "real"? None disagrees that time is real in the sense strictly of a human subjectivity that has repeatedly produced markings of time which are then institutionalized as objective facts and followed more or less consistently by the same and other human subjects who produced and reproduce those markers.[170] But does their existence tell us anything non-trivial about a non-subjective reality of time, if such does exist?

What difference, if any, does or would that supposed existence make? In asking this question we are facing a dependent circularity that poses a major problem of measurement and

---

[169] I return to consider Maxwell's work in Part Five, below, in connection with the concept of human "act."

[170] I am referring to clocks and calendars, schedules and expectations, various conventions such as the International Meridian Conference of 1884 and UTC (Coordinated Universal Time), and so forth; but also to memory and anticipation within the present of thought and action (e.g., as in G H Mead's theorizations; see Part Four, below).

even of independent conceptualization. What processes of interest to us are not contingent on some kind of standard of counting intervals? Even the relative simple processes of sequencing, even at the level of locutions such as "this, *then* that," must involve some means of marking temporality. How, therefore, does one put the question of determining whether time itself is more than a human convention? One can begin with "time" as a premise—not simply empirical and thus contingent on place and, ah, time, but as transcendental. Or as Kant formulated the point, the premise of a *purely formal* "form" of any possible intuition from our sensory organs. One ends Kant's discussion with clear conviction that he simply could not find any way around the need of that bare posit (along with its sister posit, "form of space").

As illustration of the problem due to dependent circularity, consider recently announced realizations by scientists of genetic evolution that they had been mistakenly reading genetic records of mutation as a clock of genetic evolution, thereby over-estimating, sometimes by great margins, recent "divergence times" between successive genetic versions of a particular species (see Ho, Phillips, Cooper, and Drummond 2005; Aiewsakun and Katzourakis 2016). In other words, it dawned on some people that a phenomenon which became known as "time-dependence in rate of genetic evolution" (a somewhat unfortunate naming, as will be seen below) had either been completely ignored or had been severely underappreciated. Standard practice had been to read the genetic code of a recent specimen of a given species, then locate successively older ancestors of that species (fossil records) and read the code at each earlier date, then compare for differences (mutations), and from that record of code changes construct an evolutionary tree of the organism's ancestry. It was as if readers had been reading successively older editions of, say, the Pentateuch, noticing differences judged to be important to meanings, from which they then wrote a history of the evolution of those five books of Mosaic law. The problem was, Ho and colleagues gradually realized, that the analogy of reading "closely enough," in the sense of length of temporal interval (or granularity of sampling in time), is misleading because it neglects the likelihood of overwriting.

Let's change the analogy. Imagine that the recording process produced an old vinyl record. The recording speed had been, say, at a (supposedly constant) rate of 45 revolutions per minute. If the track was cut by good sound equipment and the vinyl had not been abused (meaning, among other things, not played "too many times"), playback on a good machine will yield good crisp sound. But the quality could easily be less than that. The track was not cut at a precisely constant rate; the vinyl is a bit warped from too much wear or sunshine or hot spills; the playback machine is old, belt-driven, the belt slips a bit now and then, maybe the needle was cheaply made. One hears on playback the wave-like pitch changes because of a variable-rate sound reproduction. This analogue is closer to the genetic case, but still not close enough.

The code change of genetic information does not necessarily occur at a constant rate, just as the vinyl record does not necessarily reproduce expected sound at constant rate. But in addition, any unit of genetic code can be overwritten again and again and again, much like the storage memory of a computer's hard disk. Whereas sophisticated technology can usually reconstruct the multiple layers of a hard-disk palimpsest, there is as yet no reliable way of reading a current record of genetic code and telling how many times any particular part of it had been overwritten by successive mutations. As a result, reading a genetic record "backward," so to speak (i.e., now to each successively prior version), can easily give a distorted reading, and one that may well yield a drastically shortened estimate of how long ago a particular genetic version began. To describe that phenomenon as "time-dependent rate of change" is potentially, and likely, to confuse two very different temporalities. The one just illustrated is actually *not* of the underlying dynamic of genetic change itself; rather, it is a time dependency in how the measurement record has been constructed, due to the likelihood that any given unit of the code has been overwritten once, twice, thrice, who knows how many times. But there is also, then, the fact that the rate at which those genetic events actually did occur need not have been uniform during any given span of years, centuries, millennia. (Plus, other complexities, here being ignored, also need to be taken into account: drift; variable-rate pruning by worsened reproducibility, which is a function of variable interactions between a given code and its temporally variable environment; etc.) It is very difficult to pick apart the temporality of the observational measurement problem and the temporality of the underlying dynamic of genetic change as it evolves over long stretches of, yes, time.

As noted above, even if there *is* a "universal time," independent of human being, there need not be a universal "now," a "moment simultaneous" here and there, because—so we learned from Einstein—the metric of time is relative to the inertial mass of an observer vis-à-vis some other inertial mass. This piece of Einstein's theory has been confirmed repeatedly by empirical experimental means. The rate of time as measured by any sort of time keeper that we use varies according to its altitude from the surface of our planet. Our technology of geodesic positional systems now automatically adjusts for the relativity effects.

In sum, from the standpoint of physical theory there is no universal time, no universal "Now," no "moment simultaneous" here and there, etc., because the metric of time is relative to the inertial mass of an observer vis-à-vis some other inertial mass (see, e.g., Muller 2016).

What does any of that tell us, if anything, about our worlds of sociality?

First of all, note that the insight itself comes from one of those worlds of sociality. However much physical scientists might imagine that they are exempt, or "of a different reality" (which to some extent they are: few of us think, communicate, primarily in mathematics), they nonetheless live and breathe, know and feel, within and of the order, the reigns, the conditions, of a sociality—or to some extent in two different orders of sociality, one of them involving abstract entities of physics, the other involving driving vehicles in traffic, eating food in the company of family members, typing or speaking text into a computer, and various other "mundane" activities. Further, there is usually not much unanimity of view, except in a very broad way, in the social order of and within their world of physics (e.g., see Muller 2016; Yourgrau 2005).

But second, the relativity of time has not exactly been news within many, if not all, of the other worlds of sociality, since the time of Isaac Newton. Second-person talk and an abundance of reporting of first-person experience as it has survived in reflections within second-person and third-person experiences are replete of testimony about the elasticity of time and how that elasticity differs now and then, here and there. Granted, this has usually been presented, understood, as elasticity of *experienced* time, with some notion of an absolute time held in

132

protected reserve (i.e., for most persons, probably, a roughly conceived notion that "there must be one *real* time"). Even before Newton was born, people assumed some absolute as a given, as the bedrock against which human experiences struggle for *"real and final* meaning." For many, some sort of godhead figure was the absolute authority responsible for and jealously guarding all the more specific absolutes, and probably few if any of them could even glimpse the possibility that all of that basic assurance had been invented by and within human thought, reflections on first-person feelings of connection/aloneness, one/many, and so forth.

Third, sociality had long included time signatures; among them, the stress-timed or syllable-timed metric of what became designated as "metrical foot" (prosody, poetry, dance), and the bar or measure as metric of time in music (also related to bodily motion, as in dance, syncopation of foot tapping, etc.; see Jenkyns 2016, pp. 121-122; Valiavitcharska 2014).

Was Kant less than convinced that time and space are anything more than experiences due empirically to a reflexivity of consciousness itself—that is, that the notion of transcendental forms of intuition is superfluous? Would any experience within our experiences be different if "time" and "space" *as* necessary forms, *as* transcendental forms, *as* the timeless form of time and the spaceless form of space, did not exist? Perhaps our presumption of continuity is an illusion. How could we detect the difference? What would it matter?

Questions of the "reality of time" (far more than corresponding questions of the "reality of space") have perplexed countless generations, and they are still matters of debate among physicists, some of whom have been known to weigh into the contentions heavily and heatedly because profoundly different models of the cosmos seemingly turn on positions taken (see, e.g., Muller 2016; Yourgrau 2005). Phenomenally, the sense of continuity is confirmational in memories of experiences past. And yet, because we know that memory is productive, and because each of us usually knows this from one's own, sometimes disconcerting experience of that productivity (i.e., not solely from the more abstracted experience of having read about, or heard about, studies of the productivity of memory), we are usually vulnerable to the skeptic's question, "How do you know all of that remembered past is not illusory?"[171] Then of course there is the aspirational sense of continuity into future time, which we generally recognize is still to come, not yet now. But is it nonetheless real?

One of the two main positions taken by present-day physicists declares that future time *is* real, as real as past time. This is not a new understanding, by the way: the equations Newton laid out were meant to be timeless; that is, they were (and are) understood to be valid and reliable for next year and next century just as they are today and were last year and in Newton's century (although we have since Einstein learned to qualify those statements by the condition, "in the Newtonian domain"). In that sense, then, one could say that time does not exist except as a human illusion of experience. The more usual expression among physicists in this camp today, the camp sometimes named for its "block model" of the cosmos, is that "time is symmetrical," or that the cosmos is "time-symmetric" (i.e., one can run the clock forward or backward, basic

---

[171] Recall, for instance, Bertrand Russell's (1921, p. 159) point: "There is no logical impossibility in the hypothesis that the world sprang into being five minutes ago, exactly as it then was, with a population that 'remembered' a wholly unreal past."

physics remains the same). This is the model that follows from Einstein's general theory and that stands as what has come to be more widely known as "the Standard model" of particle physics. The opposing camp says that time is asymmetric (i.e., the "arrow of time" is real); thus, that while "past" is real and is therefore implicated in present conditions, "future times" are not yet real. The process by which future events are generated from present conditions and therefore from past events, that generative process is neither chimerical nor foreordained in certainty. In short, there is a *physics* of time (see Lee Smolin's contribution to Unger and Smolin 2015). One can argue, as others have (e.g., Muller 2016) that Einstein himself promoted this view when he demonstrated that space and time are necessarily linked: if the universe is expanding (as today virtually everyone agrees), this must mean that space is being created; and if new space is being created, then new time must be created as well.

Ordinary everyday experience can be accommodated to either camp's view, probably because conceptualization in that experience has not caught up to the debate, perhaps never will. After all, for most people that experience accords well enough with Newtonian mechanics, even as they have become more dependent on technologies that utilize Einsteinian conceptualizations. Whether illusory or real, time is experienced as both passage and sequence. But in what manner, more specifically, do adults assay the temporality of the everyday presumption of continuity of self—that is, of one's own self and of other's self, even the "virtual other" who is party to one's own relations of trust in largely anonymous networks of sociality?

Theorists of human experience have only recently devoted much attention to that and related questions. While "time" under some description figures abundantly throughout Kant's critical theory—including explicitly as one of his "forms of intuition"—he had little to say other than the general premise that experience depends fundamentally on the reproducibility of appearance, as he stated in the first edition of his first critique (A102): a present-moment (Now) experience recalls similar past experiences (or, failing to do so, is either an instance of the flotsam of consciousness or stands to attention, at least momentarily, as a puzzle). Hegel merely took for granted that he knew the meaning of time, the form of the unfolding of absolute being in process of becoming (see Hegel 1970 [1830], §§254-259).[172] Time figured prominently in the emotive register of the romanticists, but largely as a mystical emotive resource from which a self-fashioning, auto-didactic self draws inspiration during its course from late childhood to maturity to death.

Not until later in the nineteenth century did scholars attend more persistently and directly to issues of time in regard to experience. Henri Bergson (1910 [1899]), sensitive to what he considered the preconceptual basis of consciousness of time as duration, faced the conundrum of how one talks about it without violating that condition. His discussion therefore tends to be one of anticipation by abstracting what it is not, presumably thereby eventually leaving what it *is* (a methodical contention, "argument by negation," that will grow in popularity during the twentieth

---

[172] Karin de Boer (2000 [1997], pp. 212-13, 248-61) has given us exceptionally insightful discussions of the concepts of "time" as developed and utilized by Kant, Hegel, and Heidegger. Her treatment of Hegel's understanding of Kant is sensitive to his later appreciation of the complexity of Kant's thinking. Her treatment of Heidegger is sensitive to the plain fact that some of the apparent complexity of his conceptual explorations is irremediably ambiguous at best.

century). We do not learn much from Bergson's discussion. Nor had we from William James' earlier account of his effort to elucidate "the most baffling" experience—namely, "the *present* moment of time." James (1890, pp. 608, 609) allowed that it is "an altogether ideal abstraction, not only never realized in sense, but probably never conceived of by those unaccustomed to philosophic meditation." Apparently in complete absence of any sensory experience of the condition, James deduced that "Now" is not a knife-edged position between "past" and "future" but a saddle-backed condition on which the individual person sits, such that the "unit of composition of our perception of time is a *duration*, with a bow and a stern, as it were." [173]

Perhaps the most famous effort to reveal the experience of time came from the pen of Edmund Husserl's inquiries into the "structure of consciousness" as capable of apprehending objects external to itself (e.g., his *Logical Investigations*, 1900-01). At the beginning of his phenomenology of "internal time consciousness" Husserl (1991 [1893] announced his "attempt to submit the purely subjective time-consciousness, the phenomenological content belonging to the experiences of time, to an analysis" that necessarily, he said, depended on "the complete exclusion of every assumption, stipulation, and conviction with respect to objective time." The concern of his phenomenology was with "the *immanent time* of the flow of consciousness, not the time of the experienced world," and accordingly he devoted the first section of his book to an account of this necessary "suspension of objective time" (Husserl 1991 [1893], §1). Because this could prove to be a deceptively problematic exercise, let's consider his intended meaning of the word "objective." In general, use of that word has presupposed an analytic division between two realms, that of "the subject" and that of "the object." The latter phrase sometimes carries the implicit qualifier "in itself": the object as it is in itself. This meaning, exemplified by something on the order of "physical time" as in Newtonian mechanics, was clearly a major part of Husserl's intent. But there was more to it than that. In as much as we are concerned with the realm of human experiences, "the objective" also refers to consequences of accomplished practices of a collectivity—a social formation such as a community, a language game, and so forth—which are constitutive both by and of actual realities of social relations, including mental constructs, their interrelations and referrals, and their consequences. It is evident that Husserl meant to suspend this kind of "objective time" as well. Indeed, his intent was explicit when he distinguished between what he called "time that is posited as objective in an episode of time consciousness" and "actual objective time," and declared that both had to be suspended. However, suspension of humanly produced objectivities leads to a major difficulty: how does one staunch the bleeding? How could Husserl himself have had recourse to any experiences of his own, as "material" on which, from which, by which, to conduct his investigations? For Husserl this question did not arise because he presumed a psychology of the natural being as his object of inquiry. His inquiry into "internal time consciousness" did not need to address matters of social, cultural, historical variations, because Husserl's intent was focused in his imagination of "the human individual qua individual," a substrate of human being common to all actual human beings.

---

[173] While James took the occasion to refer to John Locke's "dim way" of understanding duration, he passed by David Hume's point about the inability of the perceiving I to catch sight of itself in the act of perception.

Leaving that conundrum to the side, Husserl's actual treatment of consciousness of inner time is not all that different from Bergson's, or any other version of what is sometimes called a "retentional model" of temporality (e.g., that of George Herbert Mead, considered in Part Four). Husserl referred the question of what "inner time" *is* to a presumption of continuity of sensory experience across successions of "Now" moments as memory, which continuity he then analyzed as a composition of three experiences, the core experience being the Now experience, a "primal impression." Irremediably momentary, it nonetheless leaves a trace in the memory of "having experienced" the same impression before. This retentional circuit in turn raises a counterpart as a "pretension," an anticipation of "having the same experience again." This scenario is a familiar one (see Kant's first edition of his *Critique of Pure Reason*, A102).

Thus, we find ourselves still in the midst of a presumption of continuity of self-in-experience.

### §12. How Do Experiences Accumulate in Time?

Concerns about unity of consciousness, unity of experience, and how experiences add up in the course of time are probably as old as the various stratigraphies that attended "the body" as a carrier or bearer of qualities of experience. A shepherd's hand as well as eye and ear could measure the vigor of a lamb, predict its near-term life expectancy. A carver's hand could know the possible forms locked in a block of *this* kind of wood as compared to another kind, and for a given kind know the likely variations in granular tendencies. The smell of a patch of soil told of part of its fertility, while another part was felt as its cohesiveness in the palm of a fist. These avenues of experience typically mixed "knowing that" and "knowing how" with "feeling like," and usually without much notice of difference in type of experience. Efforts to draw correlations between material parts of the body and specific functions of consciousness, whether of thought or of emotion, developed loosely in pace with explorations of anatomy and physiology. People who slaughtered animals were hardly blind to images of analogy from those bodies to his or her own. For all the special pleading about privileges of the soul, rare the adult human who did not understand an intimacy of life between human and animal, or between priest and villein.

We know from Aristotle, who himself had dissected animal bodies and speculated about correlations, that interest in empirical knowledge of a biology, an anatomy, a physiology, an embryology, and connections from those to behaviors, had been explored by careful observations of live animals and of their dissected corpses. Whether pre-Socratic scholars had engaged in dissection of human cadavers cannot be determined since so little of their records have survived, although given the official ban it would probably have been furtive exploration. By about 300 BCE one of Hippocrates' students, Herophilos of Chalcedon (c335-c280 BCE), was performing dissections of human cadavers at his workshop in the school of medicine at Alexandria, where he was joined by at least one other physician, Erasistratus of Ceos (c315-c240). Later records show that Herophilos had written several treatises on human anatomy and perhaps physiology, some of the studies apparently informed by vivisections conducted on persons who had been condemned to death. All of those works were lost when the great library of Alexandria was destroyed in 272 CE. Again, because of likely biases of survivorship, available documents give only a fuzzy view of actual sequences in time, but the general consensus has been that Erasistratus was probably the last to perform human cadaveric dissections as well as vivisections (see, e.g, von Staden 1992).

Pliny the Elder, a Roman naval commander, diplomat, and encyclopædist of the early Empire (c23-79 CE), reported in chapter 77, eleventh book, of his *Natural History* that his Greek predecessors had identified a membrane "in front of the heart" as seat of "quick and ready wit" and locus of "gaity of mind." This membrane "the Greeks have given the name φρένες," Pliny assured his readers, a word (phrenes, and in various other forms) that does appear repeatedly in Greek literatures from the Homeric song-poems onward. But Pliny's linkage of "phrenes" to a specific membrane was misleadingly precise—although it is not entirely clear whether he himself meant the diaphragm or the pericardium as that membrane. Far more interesting for present purposes is the fact that "phrenes," in its various forms, was one of several words that shared duties of what could be broadly defined as functions of mentation (i.e., of cognitive and emotive expression, feeling, thinking). Whereas the word "nous" later collected much of that shared duty into one word (conventionally rendered in Latin as "mens"; in English as "mind"), for the ancient Greeks those functions were distributed across parts of the body, primarily "head and heart."[174] In the ninth book of the *Iliad* (lines 320-323) the song-poet has Achilles declaring how hateful it is to him to know of a man who says one thing while he hides in his phrenes another. Samuel Butler translated the word in that site as "mind," and others have done the same. It is fitting. Jump ahead three centuries and read Aeschylus in *The Persians* telling of someone's "phren" being "wrapped in gloom" (line 115) and of another's feeling of confidence in his "phrenos" (line 373); in both instances the word has been rendered as "heart," which sits alongside an earlier statement that puts a person's soul within his "thymos" or "breast" (line 10). The context in line 373 tells more: that feeling of confidence came from the "phrenos," or "heart," because the person in question realized that he could not actually know the intents of the gods; lacking that knowledge in mind, he fell back on a less thoughtful kind of "knowing" or, rather, more of a "feeling" of being confident of outcome. Add another two centuries or so, and we come to Xenophon telling of "phronēmatías," a quality of being "self-confident" or "high-spirited" (or, as used by Aristotle, "arrogant").

The ancient Greeks were not the only people who distributed a broad sense of mental function across "head and heart." Probably evidence of similar habits can be discerned in several other linguistic cultures, but the one case I can affirm is ancient Chinese literature, in which one word, transliterated as "xīn" (from 心), is a compound meaning, "heart-mind," and usually conveys a notion of "heart" as core of a person and "state of mind" as at once a thinking and a feeling. A germane observation by Mark Elvin (1997, p. 178) is worth repeating here: "We tend to assume that the meaning of modern history will be seen by those involved in it, and affected by it, in terms of one of a small range of more or less 'modern' frameworks," typically rendered as an economic of sociopolitical "development." But sometimes, Elvin added, a "premodern"

---

[174] In fact, the unification in Latin never quite attained that singularity of word: whereas "mens" refers mainly to "the rational part" and "intellect," its counterpart, "animus," is the seat of will, of feeling and emotion. The English "mind" is only slightly less restrictive and still carries something of primordial in the English meaning of "animus." While emotive energies do now live within "mind," in many uses of that word those energies tend to be left to the side in virtual "after-thought."

137

conception will be invoked in order to make sense of current experience. For someone who has understanding of the gap between then and now, this invocation can be highly effective because it carries the weight of a visceral understanding that surpasses words. During the turmoil that is typical of a revolutionary setting, the scale effects of such an invocation can be enormous, and so enormously violent as to shock perpetrators once they take in what they have just done. That is a heightened example of the sort of experience captured by xīn. It impresses, and can shake, at the core of one's being.

The collapse of Adamic language—that is, the presumed absolute binding of word to thing, begun when Adam, the first human, obeyed God and assigned to each thing its proper God-given name—has sometimes been nominated as the inauguration of "the problem of modernity." Kant, because he reformed philosophy to be "subject-centered" rather than "object-centered," has often been convicted as "first father," as it were, of this crime. So, for example, Jürgen Habermas (1987 [1985], p. 260) declared, "With Kant, the modern age is inaugurated" (although it must be said that Habermas was there keying his discussion to an evaluation of Michel Foucault, whose book on "words and things" had made a revealingly sensational appearance in English fifteen years earlier). The salient point is that doubts about the link of word to world had been entertained many times before 1781, even 1724. Voltaire became ever more notorious in 1764 for writing of "fables convenues"; but he surely did not invent the idea. Nor did Pierre Besnier invent "the problem of language" in 1674. Many writers had been puzzling over the cultural significance of the Tower of Babel tale for many generations before.[175] However, it was much easier to assume that "all of importance" does *not* melt into thin air when the solidity of "the object" still appears at the center of things. The majesty and mystery of "things beyond the ken of man" could always be counted on as guarantee, in much the way that Descartes assured that the Christian God would never play trickster. But then Kant brought the human subject to the center, and for many who came after him Kant had put in charge a subject who is, by Kant's own account, a crooked timber; he had set free in the world a creature known to be deficient, indeed had knowingly recommended this lame being as legislator, free in a world now excessively open and unconstrained. Of course, all of that had happened well before Kant began his critical theory. (One may already have noticed that Hegel's adage about Minerva's owl, taking wing at dusk after the day's work of making world has been done, has been replayed a bit selectively since Hegel's time. So much depends on which philosopher has risen to first place in the queue of those who next must be gored.)

In fact, attention had been centering on the human subject, secular-psychological as well as sacred or theological, for centuries. No doubt Kant's thinking was "modern" to a degree that Descartes' was not. But one could argue that Descartes studiously, not to say cynically, covered

---

[175] This is a very old story, to be sure, one that can be told with considerable density of information. I will not repeat what I have said before (e.g., Hazelrigg 2016)—except to note that as late as the 1960s disturbances still given off by reports of "the problem of language" could be remarkably severe. The audience for Besnier's (1674) little book grew almost immediately to include the Anglophone world, as Henry Rose promptly issued a translation in London. On the other hand, Tetens' (1971 [1765-66 and 1772]) inquiries into etymologies and comparative linguistics of the relationship between vocalizations and conceptual semantics, very unusual for his day, have yet (so far as I know) to find their English translator.

his tracks with theological genuflection because he was well aware that his psychological thesis of "ego" in "cogito" could, without adornment, be easily read as usurpation of authority.[176] Note that a memoir, a record of memory, comes in various styles, and Descartes' *Meditations on First Philosophy*, published in 1641, and following his *Discourse on Method*, published in 1637, presented a record of his recent adventures in thought, which took place within the mysteries of one kind of substance, mind, as it was housed in a different kind of substance, body, somewhere in northwest Europe. Granted, his thesis of a basic duality of being, mind and body, was a bare posit barely sketched and hardly new; but he found it satisfactory as a lesson for men and women to read and take to heart. The *Discourse* he published in French; his volume of *Meditations* appeared in French soon after initial publication in Latin.[177] Notice, too, that tenor and line of both volumes became famous for concluding from a subject who thinks that he has been thinking very nearly of nothing—a nothingness, moreover, that the subject himself had attempted to "legislate" by an act of radical doubt. This was still the regulative perspective into which Descartes was born, in 1596, and in which he lived his first-person experiences of meditations. But there was major difference in play by Descartes, some of which Flores (1984) captured under the heading "Cartesian Striptease." If there is a way in which Descartes was "more modern" than Kant, it was in that play of a rhetoric of doubtful authority. When he proposed to his readers a memoir of radical doubt, Descartes surely knew that his expectation of readerly belief was not entirely novel. Who, after all, had been better at expressing personal doubt that Hamlet?[178] And who had more faithfully ignored the doubt of disbelief than the valiant knight, Quixote? Orchestrating an audience for new thoughts on "first philosophy" required of the author (or so Descartes evidently thought) a delicate balance of bold posture and subtle demure by the author. Unlike most of his fellow countrymen (including Pierre Besnier in 1674), Descartes, being in Amsterdam, did not rely on official permission to publish (the imprimatur).[179] He was

---

[176] Heidegger (1977 [1938], p. 140) observed that it was Descartes who produced an "interpretation of man as *subiectum*." Among the apologies for Descartes, the most curious is the allegation that he did not understand what he was doing. Heidegger did not make that mistake, yet in another sense judged Descartes' invention to be a most grievous error.

[177] Descartes was "modern" in that way, too, presenting his lessons in "common language," not just the language of church and court. Notice that we have been in the habit of writing sentences qualified as (e.g.) "When we began to write poetry in vernacular languages." The perspective itself is, one might say, enjambed. Did not Aeschylus write in *his* vernacular? Horace in his? Think about the power of a social institution that could wholly rework time itself into a subordinated calendar, then send it on the tongue of what had been a small vernacular, (Latin) out into imperial reach of most of its surrounding world, catching attention even of the Han dynasty (see section 11 of the *Hou Hanshu*, a history of the later Han dynasty (25-221 CE).

[178] Cummings (2013, p. 180) said of Hamlet that "far from speaking his mind, [he] confronts us with a fragmentary repository of alternative selves." But surely he *was* speaking his mind, a dialectic of different ways of being, of the alternative self presentations he had learned well enough to rehearse as constituents of an ordinary ambivalence.

[179] Begun as "permission to publish" by the Church, the imprimatur officially certified that a document contained nothing contrary to or harmful of Christian doctrine. Depending on royal authority as well as the predilection of the local ordinary, the device could be used more broadly as a cudgel against public speaking via the printing press. In England a series of laws beginning in 1586 regulated official licencing of presses, a function that was later put in the hands of officers of the Royal Society (e.g., Samuel Pepys granted licence in 1686 to Newton's *Principia*).

nonetheless careful to maintain balance in a modesty of what he could confess of his bodily being by shifting the stance of his "cogito" between being interior to its own body for some lessons, but then for other lessons viewing body from outside, as if (almost) an alien thing. But, as Flores (1984, pp. 85-86) emphasized, by thus negotiating his own way as narrator to his attentive reader, Descartes continually put at risk the distinction between a claim of truth-telling that was undoubtable and one that could be shown, as Descartes had been repeatedly doing, merely the convenience of a decorum. Narration by Cogito in matters of first philosophy already during Europe's seventeenth century skirted along limits of what a person could *feel* as "obviously true" (e.g., "that I *am* even when I think doubtfully that I am"), relative to what any person could possibly know demonstrably to be true.

By comparison to Descartes (or to Leibniz), Kant's argument was both more detailed and keyed primarily to what he considered necessary conditions of the very possibility of human knowledge; therefore, also to the limits of human knowledge. Insofar as his argument was persuasive, its implications were bracing, to say the least, and none more so than implications of the limits. In his explanation that human experience "is possible only through the representation of a necessary connection of perceptions," Kant (1998 [1787], B207/A166) drew on an earlier stipulation that perception "is empirical consciousness, i.e., one in which there is at the same time sensation. Appearances, as objects of perception, are not pure (merely formal) intuitions, like space and time (for these cannot be perceived in themselves). They therefore also contain in addition to the intuition the materials for some object." Perceptions are doubtable, as Hume had said; not only are the "contents" only apparent, one can never have empirical evidence of the process by which they come to be *my* perceptions. In what, then, can I have confidence in any apparent unity of my experience? For (Kant then further stipulated) experience itself "is an empirical cognition, that is, a cognition that determines an object through perceptions.

> It is therefore a synthesis of perceptions, which is not itself contained in perceptions but contains the synthetic unity of the manifold of perceptions in one consciousness which constitutes what is essential in a cognition of objects of the senses, i.e., of experience (not merely of the intuition or sensation of the senses). Now in experience, to be sure, perceptions come together only contingently, so that no necessity of their connection is or can become evident in the perceptions themselves, since apprehension is only a juxtaposition of the manifold of empirical intuition, but no representation of the necessity of the combined existence of the appearances that it juxtaposes in space and time is to be encountered in it. But since experience is a cognition of objects through perception, consequently the relation in the existence of the manifold is to be represented in it not as it is juxtaposed in time but as it is objectively in time, yet since time itself cannot be perceived, the determination of the existence of objects in time can only come about through their combination in time in general, hence only through *a priori* connecting concepts. Now since these always carry necessity along with them, experience is thus possible only through a representation of the necessary connection of the perceptions (Kant 1998 [1787] B218-219).

Notice that the empirical anchorage is the fact that one does experience a synthetic unity of whatever manifold of perceptions one has in fact experienced *in one consciousness*—that is, in one's own integral consciousness. What is to be explained is *not* that a knowing subject has such experiences as experiences of *one* consciousness. That is an empirical given.

And who would argue for a *different* point of departure in argument? Who would propose that one's own apparent unity of the manifold of perceptions that one has in mind, in one's own integral consciousness, is not worth taking seriously? What would the point be? This is not to presuppose that one's unity of experience is never faulty, in part or even in whole. Again, "truth and illusion are not in the object, insofar as it is intuited, but in the judgment about it insofar as it is thought" (Kant 1998 [1787], B350).[180] Rather, if one is not able to presuppose the possibility of a coherence of meaning in one consciousness, then there can be no reason to proceed. But empirically there can be and, one suspects, often is considerable variation in the composition of that "one consciousness," variation not only from person to person but within "one consciousness" from time to time.

For Kant, the stable platform against which those variations stand out as measurable without then flying apart by charge of biased comparison consisted in transcendental principles (a transcendental unity of apprehension). As one of Kant's biographers put it, Kant

> knew and never doubted that there are principles of the human mind that do not change [i.e., transcendental principles], [which] are indispensable for our ability to know. Nor did he ever doubt that we actually do believe that the causal connection is not merely a connection among our ideas, but also one among objects. He was mainly interested in how we come to move from the one to the other, thinking that ultimately it cannot be justified by philosophy, but only by common life. Tetens' appeal to instinct and common sense clearly was not very different from that of [Thomas] Reid and some German contemporaries [e.g., Johann Michael Feder and Johann Christian Lossius], for instance. They all did not understand the important question which Kant identifies as the key question of the entire *Critique,* namely "what and how much can the understanding and reason know apart from all experience." Instead, they all used such concepts as cause, which they believed to have established as indispensable for experience, also uncritically in contexts that go beyond any experience. Tetens himself did just that in his next work, entitled *On the Reality of our Concept of God.*[181] Kant was much more radical, answering the question "what and how much can we know apart from all experience" with "absolutely nothing" –just as Hume would have done (Kuehn 1989, p. 374).

While I generally agree with Kuehn's account of the difference between Tetens and Kant—and therefore that previous suggestions by critics that Kant borrowed his critical framework from

---

[180] Note the shift in realism vis-à-vis Democritus' position in Fragment O (Bakewell 1908, p. 60): "the objects of sense are supposed to be real and it is customary to regard them as such, but in truth they are not. Only the atoms and the void are real." Thus, a measure of Kant's insistence of an empirical standard. If Democritus (or Sextus Empiricus 600 years later) experienced an atom, then his meaning of "experience" must have been closer to John Milton's or William Blake's experience of divine blessing than to Newton's experience of gravitational attraction.

[181] Published in 1778, *Über die Realität unseres Begriff von der Gottheit* was another of Tetens' works with which Kant had considerable familiarity. For some relevant context of contemporary controversy, see Allison (1973).

Tetens are plainly erroneous—I will note that the long passage just quoted was preceded by Kuehn's statement that Kant "surely must have considered Tetens' move from subjective to objective necessity a disappointing one." I am not confident that I take Kuehn's meaning accurately. In any case, however, one should see that Kant would surely *not* have been surprised (if indeed "disappointed"), for that sentence is another description of the very illusion, the "transcendental Illusion," which, Kant explained, was unavoidable even when awareness of its presence is reflexively explicit.

Be that as it may, the transcendental Illusion, which impels us to seek refuge in an "objective necessity," gnaws away at the notion that there is, that there *can be*, a stable platform that is *not* historical, *not* cultural. Thus, the relativism that frightened or intimidated so many of Kant's critics, as well as the neo-Kantians (their "neo" having to do centrally with that issue of stability), and many social scientists today (see the contortions of Clifford Geertz as example; Hazelrigg 1992, pp. 252-255).

So the empirical question of variation—from person to person and from time to time—in composition of unity of consciousness remains. The question with which this section began is viable: do experiences aggregate in time? A question that employment officers have been known to ask subvocally suggests a vernacular awareness of that variation and its practical relevance: have you had twenty years of experience, or have you had one year of experience twenty times?

The ancient Greeks had vernacular awareness of such degrees, too, but their concern about the assay was apparently mainly about what they considered "proper balance" between heart and head. Actual variations in that balance were marked by comparisons across a gradient of heroic figures (Achilles versus Odysseus, for example, or either of these moods of the heroic compared with Ajax), as well as in tragic (e.g., Euripides) or comedic (e.g., Aristophanes) or historical (e.g., Thucydides) accounts of hubris.[182] An idiom of "proper balance" presupposed a degree of self-management, even self-making, an internal coordination of feeling and knowing via a reflexivity that supported a pragmatics of that internal coordination. Moreover, as can be seen easily in all of the case material just cited (think, e.g., of the management of Achilles' mood by specific others), the pragmatics were of a sociality. This was mainly about discursive judgments concerning "feeling," however much informed by first-person feelings it may have been. The difference remains apposite. Rachel Hewitt's (2017) addition to studies of the history of emotion—germane to the present inquiry inasmuch as its locus, the last decade of Europe's eighteenth century, counts as well or better than others, as transitional between conventionally labeled historical periods, "from Enlightenment to Romantic Reaction"[183]—displays sensitivity to problems of comparison culturally and historically, all the while faced with the questions of

---

[182] Woodruff (2011) has made invigorating use of the legend of Ajax and the scales of justice. The other Greeks named in the paragraph have been so abundantly treated as not to need referral.

[183] Edmund Burke (1910 [1790], p. 77) said the most important revolution of that decade was "the revolution in sentiments, manners, and moral opinions," virtually all of it he judged a sludge of decay.

actual first-person experiences of feeling, whatever the vocabulary of it (passions, appetites, affections, sentiments, emotions, etc.) and connections of vocabulary to experience.[184]

Disciplinary boundaries have been in play, of course, here as in most other topics of social science. As late as the 1970s a sociologist felt the need to explain his book of theory (as well as review of relevant research) on phenomena of emotions by addressing the usual boundary between his own professional discipline and that (or those) of psychology, with apparent thought that the latter might be dismissive even as his disciplinary colleagues might wonder why he was treading in foreign waters. Explaining that his thinking was "based on the proposition that most human emotions result from outcomes of interaction in social relationships," his topics therefore including "the social bases of emotion both descriptively and causally," his presentation would begin with "a comprehensive model of social interaction," or as near to one as could at that date be assembled. Bear in mind that this was written while on the cusp of 1980, although the author, Theodore (Dave) Kemper (1978, pp. vii, 48) acknowledged that the manuscript had been a work in progress for some time. It was indeed a major opening for sociology. The borders and verges of that opening were carefully marked, however, for while recognizing that distinctions had been drawn between "emotion" and "feeling" (as well as "sentiment" and similar other categories by which first-person experiences had been labeled) little attention would be given to the conceptual relations, questions of redundancy, and the like. Bringing "emotion" into cognition was enough for the moment, for sociology.[185]

While "feeling" is in fact a *topic* of classification (we have various kinds of feeling, names for them, ways of talking about them, apparent rules of oral display, and so on), a feeling itself is not conceptual. This means that, as first-person experience rather than topic of thought or conversation, feeling is as close to a strictly prelinguistic presencing as can be experienced, simply because one is at the limit of measurement (with no experience of an asymptosis). As soon as I think about "a feeling I just had," I have shifted from feeling *as such* to talk about, knowing about, feeling. Since the linchpin of consciousness is a coherence and unity of apprehensions, the experience of a feeling quickly becomes the experience of a *kind* of feeling. Indeed, one learns to expect this transformation from "feeling" to "knowing," from the immediacy and uniqueness of "a feeling like no other" to a conceptually mediated "feeling I've had before; it was the feeling of _____." Sometimes choosing the right word as name can be fraught; usually, with memory of prior "felt experiences," the name comes to mind as quickly as the feeling itself immediately expressed its stimulus. However, the fraught instances remind one of the underlying tension, even violence, that takes place as a first-person experience of feeling *as a feeling* shifts into the first-person classificatory space of "knowing that it is [such and such named feeling]." Probably most of us have had those slightly perplexing moments: "What

---

[184] In this, need it be said, another venue of disputation between a universalism of human biology (or human nature) and particularities of sociocultural historical beings long persisted (see, e.g., Wierzbicka 1986 and the various contributions to the handbook assembled by Chiao, Li, Seligman, and Turner 2016).

[185] In fact, however, the line between "the said" and "the unsaid" moved back and forth (due to its dialectic), as is virtually always the case (see, e.g., Kemper's brief endorsement of sentiments ("yearnings, aspirations, and, more important, solutions") via fictional characters; 1978, p. 140).

exactly *was* I feeling?  Was it exhilaration?  Glee?  Was an element of anxiety mixed into it, maybe an odd sense of the possibility of danger?"  The expectation of first-person coherence sometimes shades into a virtual second-person soliloquy, as present-moment self consults with remembered past selves, rather like a playwright's tragicomic character seeking guidance from the chorus (for the benefit of audience).

And yet it is evident that talk about feeling, as in second-person conversation or in third-person report of a conversation, can engender in an auditor or reader a feeling that one easily assumes as transmission.  I am thinking of Adam Smith's (1817) theoretical foray, for instance, but also and with emotional impact of Lillian Ross' report of conversation with Robin Williams in 1987, a report I remembered and read again after Williams left the stage in 2014.  At one point during the conversation Williams responded to Ross with this:

> About a week ago, I went to the Comedy Store, in Los Angeles. I was talking about bizarre things. I got going doing this whole thing about travelling at the speed of light, losing your luggage beforehand, doing Albert Einstein as Mr. Rogers, improvising. It was fun. It was like running in an open field (Ross 2015 [1987], p. 23).

Who would *not* share in the feeling of exuberance in Williams' reflection of what had been his own feeling during that performance scene?  No doubt the mutuality would depend to some extent on prior experience of "Robin Williams in performance."  But that is contextual: context is always (in)formative—isn't it?—and here being able to recall seeing and hearing "Robin Williams in performance" as context of those few words on paper is condition to the mutuality of feeling the exuberance of "running in an open field."  This was the feeling of Williams' own music of exuberance.

A music of exuberance can be felt in experiences of theorization as well as in a zany performance of comedy.  As was apparent in Part One, a major part of Kant's legacy was his strong belief in the power of theory, confidence in which came with an understanding of the limits of theory.  His successors, disturbed by the very existence of those limits, sought a way around if not through them.  In that sense, one could say that belief in theory was even stronger among Kant's heirs, for they mostly ignored the conditions of theory's power.  Because these heirs mostly only ignored what Chai (2006, p. 187) termed "the epistemological impasse [that] Kant had worried about," their efforts of theorizing were always in jeopardy of losing content while also becoming as blind as a simple empiricism.  Friedrich Hölderlin understood this risk as well or better than any other of Kant's immediate successors and, as Chai has displayed in the finest consideration of Hölderlin that I have read in some time,[186] undertook penetrating inquiry of its conditions and alternatives.  Any activity, mental, physical, or (nearly always the case)

---

[186] My earlier consideration of Hölderlin (Hazelrigg 2016) was unfortunately without benefit of Chai's unusually fine book.  While our views are very similar in many respects, I had always given far less attention to Hölderlin's poem, "Patmos," than Chai has now shown me it merits.  From this poem, late in Hölderlin's productivity, I understand that whatever earlier intents Hölderlin might have been exploring, a phrase of his which was published only in a fragment, and on which I had speculated ("through us"), was his memory of Kant (a memory of the power of conceptualization), not an anticipation of Marx (i.e., not the power of a poiesis, at once material and ideal).

both, has limits, and the greater the power of the activity the more severe its limits, in condition and in consequence. Thus,

> any inquiry into the promise or potential of theory also has to ask where its limits are. For Friedrich Hölderlin, the limits of theory are, quite simply, those of thought itself. But to arrive at the limits of thought we have to find out what thought cannot conceptualize. Unlike some of those who questioned the primacy of theory in the Romantic period, Hölderlin never doubted the capacity of theory to conceptualize our experiences. He himself, after all, had been close to those who ushered in a new era for philosophy in Germany. As a result, he had seen what the new, abstract mode of theory was capable of. To some extent he had even helped to create it. He knew, then, that it did not need to solve the epistemological impasse Kant had worried about. He had seen how the new philosophy had managed to finesse that difficulty, by means of an internal rather than external perspective. Fully aware of all the recent developments in the contemporary philosophical scene, he knew the power of theory. And because of what he had seen, he probably even believed what proponents of the new philosophy professed: that we can achieve ascendancy over anything we can conceptualize (Chai 2006, p. 187).

The "difficulty" thought to have been finessed was deeper than imagined, such that the greatest trouble was ignored. But then that is part of the risk, and it inheres in conceptualization as well as in theorization.

To conceptualize is to make (including to legislate), even if initially only in one's mind. Sooner or later the making must meet, or fail, tests of experience. Whereas in his third critique Kant had deliberately selected experiences that would be accounted as "purely subjective," or as nearly so as could be imagined, Hölderlin, in his poem "Patmos" (1990 [1803]), chose what he considered to be experience of God as experiential test. Is a god (for Hölderlin the Christian or Judeo-Christian God) the limit of conceptualization? If so, what would that mean? Do not believers conceptualize their God on regular basis? (although "regular basis" need not mean, eventually does not mean, without change; cf. Veyne 1988 [1983]).[187]

The notion regulating that question from within a belief—and after all, the question would mean little if anything if directed to (or from) someone utterly without such belief—was not exactly a novelty of the early nineteenth century. Tracing the genealogy is handicapped by the fact that official ideology in European societies maintained some version of an authority of divine provenance through the preceding centuries, while various proponents of secularizing

---

[187] An interesting outcome, as judged by Hölderlin's criterion, recently occurred in machine learning (i.e., "artificial intelligence" in which a machine's algorithm teaches itself to excel maximally within specified rules of play toward a stipulated goal). One of the major risks, programmers realized years ago, resulting from human teachers of "smart machines" was that conceptual limits that are beyond human recognition become unwittingly implanted in their algorithms. Removing that risk by giving a machine its own capacity of learning from its own experience enabled intelligent machines to achieve results never previously imagined by human teachers. The "interesting outcome" mentioned above, one in a long sequence, was due to a recent innovation via machine learning that elevated the game of Go to a previously unimagined level of expertise, far beyond the then-reigning expert players.

thought tiptoed up to if ever actually across boundaries. A major case in point, Giambattista Vico, was careful to acknowledge that God was the real "constructor" while we humans merely conceptualize (e.g., the "anatomy of nature's work") in accord with the principle that "the criterion and norm of the true is to have made it." By the same token, he rejected Descartes' nomination of first principle in the terms of "clear and distinct" ideas, on the ground that "the mind does not make itself as it gets to know itself"—a limitation not so different from Hume's later proposal about limits of perception—and because mind "does not make itself" in the act of getting to know itself, "it does not know the genus or the mode by which it makes itself" (Vico 1988 [1710], pp. 48, 52).

Hölderlin's inquiry was not free of ambiguities, indeliberate though they might have been in regard at least to some issues (see, e.g., Warminski 1976 for a sampling of the controversy). But the thrust of his effort is clear enough, whether his own "piety" was tinged with doubt or not: *if* humans do have the ability to conceptualize God, then we will know beyond doubt that they, we, can conceptualize anything, and this would be our surety of the power of theory. The main question for Hölderlin was not, as Chai (2006, p. 189) pointed out, "whether theory had a virtually limitless power to conceptualize but whether its power to conceptualize was not itself a form of limitation." Hölderlin's supposition was that perception exceeds the limits of our ability to conceptualize, and if that is in fact the case then either there must be a different kind of theory or theory itself is inherently limited.[188]  Where else to test both suppositions of limitation than with perceptions of God. A close reading of "Patmos" demonstrates the process of Hölderlin's judgment (Chai 2006, pp. 189-212). To the first part of his supposition he concluded that, Yes, what is most crucial in the perception of God is an "excess" that evades our ability to conceptualize; and if that is so here, then it should be true at least in principle elsewhere. To the second part Hölderlin concluded that our ability to theorize God in any manner at all is forestalled, the barrier being the inability of theory to theorize thought itself. Perception of God resides ultimately in a feeling that one either does or does not have, and this feeling qualifies as epiphanic if any can.[189]

From a point of view other than Hölderlin's the circuit was closed at his start. Someone for whom a God exists only in some other person's belief of feeling surely sees the fallacy in Hölderlin's test (taking one's conclusion from one's premise) and wonders why such an exercise was primed in the first place. For who would doubt that human beings ask questions for which no answers that satisfy both rational and empirical criteria are possible? That perception exceeds conception was hardly a novel thought in 1803. But nor does any of this dispute the evident fact that believers do indeed produce an objectivity of God: the evidence includes some imposing buildings in major cities, many of them still filled with people every seventh day if not oftener.

---

[188] Note that one may agree that "something radically original begins with language, an *other* that one cannot 'infer' from the sensory but that commingles with it" (Lyotard 2011 [1971], p. 34). This is certainly indicated from Kant's critical theory, for example; but it is not a relation that can be directly experienced or empirically demonstrated.
[189] The title Hölderlin chose for his poem, "Patmos," is significant because it is the name of the Greek island on which John of Patmos composed the Christian book of Revelation, his recording of his vision, an epiphany, of Jesus.

This is also not to say that Hölderlin's exercise is without useful lesson. To my mind its key lesson—and one to which Chai gave due emphasis—is that perspective is crucial to both theorizing and conceptualizing, in much the way that Hume concluded of a limit of perception (i.e., self-perception) and that Nisbett and Wilson (1977, p. 246) intended in their later report that "people have little ability to report accurately on their cognitive processes." In both regards the perspective of memory aids the effort because memory is inherently a production of distance, and thus of perspective because of difference of horizon. Nearness—in Hölderlin's assessment the critical aspect of "feeling the presence of God"—is an obstacle to conceptualizing and to theorizing because in nearness feeling can easily dominate thinking.

Nisbett and Wilson's (1977) contribution augmented the lesson unintentionally due to the odd manner in which it was reflected in subsequent literature—especially in the most popular commentary, which summarized their report as having concluded that humans labor under false understandings of their motives, preferences, perceptions, and so forth (i.e., in the words of one summary, that we do not "know our own minds"). The fact that this is definitely *not* indicative of their conclusion or the research on which their conclusion was based is telling of more than a slip of the tongue. In any case, the "contents" of a person's mind, in the sense of first-person experience, are genuine in what they *are*. The issue addressed by Nisbett and Wilson is whether those contents give a reliable and valid account of their own origins, so to speak. That is, does first-person experience contain an adequate explanation of how it came to be what it in fact *is*? The answer given by Nisbett and Wilson (see also Wilson 2002; Wilson and Dunn 2003; Wegner 2002; Wegner and Gray 2016; among others) is that in general it does not. This is the crux of what Nisbett and Wilson (1977) meant when they wrote of expectations that we somehow do tell more than we are capable of knowing; what Wilson (2002) meant when he later said that we humans are "strangers to ourselves"; and what Wegner (2002; 2003) meant when he referred to "the illusion of conscious will." It is fallacious to assume that the contents, any part or in whole, of first-person experience—which are indeed experienced for what they are—supply reliable inferential means or avenue to the processes that generated the contents of "conscious mind," the processes that produced the first-person experiences that one does have. Even such a champion of introspective phenomenalism as Wilhelm Dilthey (e.g., 1985 [1887]) was cognizant of limits to the power of his mind, acknowledging that he had—here, there, and again—posed questions that he could not answer.[190] Recall from Part One, however, the sometimes difficult to detect difference between limits to the possibility of human knowledge, as accounted by Kant, and limits due to absurdity in thinking the conditions of a question being asked, as accounted by Marx (1986 [1939], p. 65) in the chapter on money in his *Grundrisse*.

The matter of Hölderlin's judgment, not the specific contents of his own conclusion but the recommended process, remains to be addressed. I shall do so in general terms (i.e., not keyed

---

[190] Granted, Dilthey came close at times to breaching the barrier, or thinking that he had. Consider this seemingly pregnant sentence: "the formative processes of the artistic imagination are produced by the play of feelings" (Dilthey 1985 [1877], p. 77). Was he referring to the processes by which "the artistic imagination" generates effects by "the play of feelings"? Probably. But one could read the sentence as proposing that the processes of imagination are themselves formed and in that formation influenced already by "the play of feelings." Perhaps he had in mind a confusion of both.

specifically to his interest in God) and by expanding the matrix of experience to include along with "feeling and thinking" a category of "willing," which has figured in folk theories of mind, and in psychologistic accounts drawn from such theories, as a claim of personal agency that stabilizes by regulating first-person vectors from feeling and thinking to action. In process of doing so, the issue of authenticity of feeling must be addressed, for it is bound up with notions of "free will" and regulation. A good illustration of my point can be read in Jane Austen's accounts of life as the century of Enlightenment faded into the century of industrialization and a new model of custom—that is, commerce—which was remaking the very idea of custom, its scope, and its arts of presentation. One could well imagine that concerns about "genuine feeling," "genuine motive," and the power of "good will" had gained an urgency.

In the introduction to his study of Jane Austen's powers of fictioning, James Thompson (1988, p. 1) alerted his reader to the chief thematic of his study: "Jane Austen and the Language of Real Feeling." A moment's reflection should be enough to raise the unsaid—namely, that we are adventuring in a terrain of ambiguity. One of Austen's main characters in *Emma*, Frank Churchill, is "a master, not of genuine emotion, but rather of civility and address."[191] This is Thompson's quick portrait of Churchill, and we are expected to believe the direct reportage. If one remembers having read *Emma*, this portrait rings true because Austen had already shown us as much, and the power of her fictioning was greater than the effect of any simple telling.[192] Austen's way of showing simultaneously raised and settled doubts about the constitution of "real feeling," but it also left threads to be pulled in the aftermath of accumulated episodes, inviting one to recall the fulcrum of the narrator's privilege on which one's reading has depended. Absent that privilege, one realizes, so much would have remained ambiguous, just as in "real life." Thompson deftly highlighted the ambiguity by setting in such sharp relief the contrast, "genuine emotion" versus "civility and address." After all, who among honorable citizens of turn-of-the century England would *not* have been in favor of civility and propriety of address? Who would not, today? However, such matters are always relative, historically and culturally, but the relativity is often not noticed as such. Existing relations of authority have a stake in our *not* noticing. Consequently, the sociality of an urgency can fine-tune the sense of urgency as a new, even unprecedented, experience about (among other things) the bounds, markers, and substance of first-person feeling, thinking, and willing.

We are asked to ponder a gap which, due to the assurance of Austen's narrative of showing, had been successfully bridged until we, having finished the story, reflect on the

---

[191] The issue here was whether a display of emotion was feigned rather than genuine. It could also include (though in context of the novel did not) the distinction between "natural" or "normal" emotion and "unnatural" or "abnormal" emotion in the sense addressed by Lutz (1988, pp. 66-70)—namely, that insofar as emotions are within culture A thought to be basically conditions of nature, displays that in culture B are considered ordinary and normal could be considered from the standpoint of culture A as "unnatural" or "abnormal."

[192] One of the remarkable facts of Austen's novels is that they came so near to the heels of that chain of period markers, Enlightenment-Revolution-Terror-Romantic Reaction, which Edmund Burke had embossed for proper English character. A rector's daughter of Anglican Hampshire succeeded so well with her characterizations because they bridged the awkwardness of so much turmoil of experiences near and far with assurance that all would come right in the end.

counterfactuals that are covered in privileged turning points and assessments. The gap is, on initial reflection, between "real feeling" that is genuine emotion and "real feeling" that is language, presentation of self. In the reflexivity of one's question of *that* gap, however, one realizes further that it is a question of the authority of voice, of the credentials of belief, of the actions that link credibility and credulity in their odd dance to the musical chords of sensibility, persuasion, and conviction. The dance itself is existentially ordinary, an everyday occurrence of the unremarkable. Only when one pulls certain threads, tries to pursue counterfactuals, does the oddness of it come to view. Austen was accomplished at setting these "traps" into insight for her thoughtful readers. It has often been said that she exhibited a seemingly effortless mastery of showing diversities of character in particular contexts. The same could be said of her ability to guide her attentive reader into examinations of the ambivalence of character in manifestation of ambivalences of condition and context. Perhaps both abilities were for her the same, and due to the ambivalences that she had felt in first-person experiences she was able to convey those feelings so richly yet subtly in presentations of characters engaged in their own freely willed actions of self-description and projection.

Hans Aarsleff's (1967) survey of patterns of language use in England during the period of great change from 1780 to the mid-1800s showed that debates over "first language" were no less rash and conflicted for having become largely secular. Housed within that circle of argument was another: what has priority, object or thought? And of the subjective part, thought or word that properly conveys the thought? These contentions thrived in dialogue and in reportage, whether metaphysical or scientific, but of course they presented some devilish problems in the conveyance of an interiority of first-person experience, especially experience of feeling. Adam Smith had given evidence that, partly because prevailing conceptions of the ontogeny of human nature featured a "natural psychology of mind" which left sociality in a secondariness or supplemental service, an inference problem could be so easily elided as to vanish, as illustrated in his 1762-63 *Lectures on Rhetoric* when he (1983 [c1763], p. 75) averred that first-person experiences, such "as passions and affections, can be well described only by their effects." (One wonders, "Was any student 'impertinent' enough to pose the case of some version of 'con man' artistry?" Probably not, a matter of decorum.)[193] In Hewitt's (2017) broad view, by contrast, men and women of England's eighteenth century understood "feelings" to be about social relations rather than private personal experience. Surely they *were* about social relations, for England was a heavily class-weighted society (as illustrated by Edmund Burke's whinging after the "swinish" inclinations of common folk). But feelings have always been about social relations, even when only implicitly, because they arise from and project into a sociality. While sensitive to social relations, of course, the expressions could nevertheless have conveyed a great variety of feelings, depending on audience, and some of them perhaps stridently ambivalent.[194]

---

[193] One wonders, too, about understandings, in Smith's time, of the self-feeling expressed by Augustine early in the tenth book of his *Confessions*: "I turn scarlet at the very thought of myself, and I throw myself away and choose you instead." Understandings at the end of the next century had Nietzsche's diagnosis of such feelings to consider.

[194] It should be noted, too, that Hewitt's assessment was made explicitly as comparison to the "Victorian society" that followed, in which class relations remained highly important and usually stress-provoking, but proper manners dictated a posture of mute endurance and a determination to carry on.

Ambivalence in first-person experience—whether as feeling, as thinking, or as willing—is indicative of inconsistency at the least, often outright contradiction. The strings that Austen left in wake of narrations can be taken as evidence that she had some skill in dialectical reasoning.

### §13. Identity and Control

When Descartes reported his exercise in doubt, he said that it was the experience of Cogito, I think, that ended his ability to doubt his existence. The famous statement against existential doubt was not Video ergo sum (I see therefore I am). Nor was it a more broadly sensory Sentĭo ergo sum (I feel therefore I am). We cannot say with certainty why an act of thinking rather than one of seeing or one of feeling or some other possibility succeeded in stilling his doubt. But given his report, there is good evidence that for him the choice turned on the key difference between sensory experience in itself and conceptualization. Seeing is an experience, but without concepts already in place one would not know the object(s) of sight. Likewise, with feeling. In Descartes' exercise, however, Cogito already had its own object, thought, and in particular the thought of his own existence in doubt. The power of conceptualizing was built in, so to speak. This means, of course, that for all the imagination of a doubting *so radical*, so near to the very root of existence, as to cast adrift not only his own personal being but also any evidence vouched by other persons of personal knowledge of Descartes, the sociality that is inherent in acts of conceptualizing remained active throughout his efforts of doubt. What is sometimes taken to have been a "radically individual," "radically personal" act was actually anything but.

It is worth noting, in that regard, also that Descartes did not say, "Vŏlo ergo sum" ("I will therefore I am")—"willing" in the sense of vŏluntas, a voluntary agency of action.

In the first sentences of the first section of his *Groundwork of the Metaphysics of Morals*, Kant asserts the basis of his deontological ethics:[195]

> It is impossible to think of anything at all in the world, or indeed even beyond it, that could be taken to be good without limitation [or, "without qualification"], except a good will. Understanding, wit, judgment, and whatever else the *talents* of the mind may be called, or confidence, resolve, and persistency of intent, as qualities of *temperament*, are no doubt in many respects good and desirable; but they can also be extremely evil and harmful if the will that is to make use of these gifts of nature, and whose distinctive constitution is therefore called *character*, is not good (Kant 2011 [1786], p. 9).

He continued in that vein, arguing that all other goods (gifts of fortune, happiness) are derived from or are dependent upon other things. The good will is good purely in itself, purely "from volition."

This posit may seem to be psychologistic to the core. But consider its framework. First of all, there is Kant's one imperative, categorical in that it is not conditioned by, does not depend

---

[195] English editions of this work have used different titles, the difference being in initial wording: Groundwork, as here, or Fundamental Principles, elsewhere. His brand of ethical theory is called "deontic" or "deontological" from the Greek "deon," meaning "duty" or "obligation." Other English translations cite the date of first publication as 1785. That was the first edition. A second edition was published the next year, and this is the basis of the English text used here.

upon, anything beyond its obligation of will: "act only according to that maxim through which you can at the same time will that it become a universal law" (Kant 2011 [1786], p. 34). This is addressed to each individual person; it is that person's will that is invoked. Who is this person— and this is my second point—who is this person whose will is invoked? Any person. Kant did not specify gender or class or race or national culture or intelligence or probity or any qualifying characteristic whatsoever. While some critics have charged that the mandate is empty precisely because this "any person" exists only in extreme abstraction, from Kant's point of view "any person" refers to any person whatever his or her conditions and contexts; and, recall, Kant's lectures on anthropology make very clear that he was well aware of great variation across many cultures *and* that he himself was anything but free of prejudices of his own culture and social standing. My third point has to do with the source of obligation, the obligation that is stated in his categorical imperative and in other, more specific settings of morality: what exactly is the source of obligation? Ultimately, obligation, duty, resides in human legislation, human being as legislator. As Korsgaard stated the point in her exceptionally clear and careful introduction to the *Groundwork*, obligation comes from our "capacity for self-government" (Kant 2011 [1786], p. xxvii).[196] Not from any supernatural realm. Not from some mystical reservoir. Nor from some inherent logic of Nature. Nowhere else but human legislation. Taken altogether, then, "good will" is for Kant as variable as, as relative to, human culture, human history, human sociality. This means, of course, that there is no absolute *substantive* standard of "the good," "the moral," and the like, universally applicable, thus universally mandated. All such efforts in history, Kant believed, were dogmatic impositions by the strong over the weak. The only mandate had to be purely formal-functional—"act only according to that maxim through which you can at the same time will that it become a universal law"—just as the transcendental unity of apperception and the intuition of space and time are, for Kant, purely formal-functional. In practical terms, no individual person *can* will her/his act from good will to become universal, although we do know of some dictators who tried (whether in the name of God or the name of History or the name of whatever special dispensation). The outcomes will be, and should be, agreements in legislation, and these will be local. Will the agreements ever become species-wide, in that sense universal? Kant had only hope on offer—hope for species maturity, self-responsibility, autonomy. Shy of that, he saw no guarantee that any particular legislation ostensibly from good will and toward the universal could never be evil. Indeed, to the contrary. Hope is only hope.

Before Kant, and to a remarkable degree after Kant as well, a psychologistic conception of "will" prevailed, subordinating sociality beneath the abstracted logic of a pre-social, pre-cultural, pre-historical human being (e.g., represented in and reinforced by the *Genesis* account of "first man" and then "first family" as fully sufficient prior to any other human being). Recall

---

[196] This is consonant with Korsgaard's (1996, p. 371) position regarding the presumption of continuity of personal identity: "it is practical reason that requires me to construct an identity for myself; whether metaphysics is to guide me in this or not is an open question." I would say that the question is idle. But never mind. I would want to add, however, that while I do not object to the "for myself" phrase, I must remind that the construction is an enterprise of the sociality in, from, and of which any person exists as an ensemble of relations, and for that reason one's "own" self-knowledge is always partial but variably so.

again that personal voice through and from first-person experience is always tempted to claim a certain privilege of viewpoint, and the claimed privilege is, or can be, of one's own intuition, one's own conceptualizations (including what one means by specific words, bordering on private language), *and* of one's own good will. Who can claim superior insight into another person's mind? Claim and counterclaim are both negotiations of and challenges to sociality, to a history (if one) of prior agreements. Personal voice is therefore both problem and solution with regard to processes by which first-person experiences aggregate in time, to the extent that they do.

It is not clear that first-person perceptions in the register of feeling do aggregate except in first-person reflection by which present self remembers prior self in the (usually implicit) presumption of continuity; and because *that* memory trades on language (internal conversation, so to speak), sociality is already fully in play in a modality of second-person voice that at least implicitly draws on experience with other actors in negotiations of agreement (also usually implicit) about mutual memberships of competency in good standing. The second-person modality is crucial, because it enacts the subject/object dialectic with valence that can approximate equality of authority, whereas in third-person voice a first-person reflection in memory can easily experience the feeling of being mainly, perhaps even primarily, an object-to-other-authority—that is to say, an alienated standing in doubtable competency as someone who has been, or if not may yet be, called upon to demonstrate competency of membership in an otherwise shared presumption of commonality in second-person relation.

Samuel Scheffler (2013) has added useful perspective, however, in his consideration that, and how, the presumption of continuity continues into one's expectation of afterlife, not in the religious sense but in the sense that one's expectation that humankind will continue life long after one's own death is (if it is) integral to one's own well-being in life. While time will end as and for one's first-person experience, presuming that it will continue extensively for other persons, not only for the others one has known but for others of countless generations to come, is vital to one's understanding of purpose. Actors of a present look forward to future generations as representatives of humanity who will be *our* representatives as well. The temporal connection is something like the literary device of a play within a play, which some have mistakenly called a "performance of meta-theatre," ignoring that the analytic divide and the hierarchy are contrary to the point, at least as intended by Jorge Luis Borges, among others. In Borges' story, "The God's Script" (1962) one encounters a determined future present via a first-person foreknowledge—or it could be only an anticipation believed *in* with sufficient conviction—held by someone who has decoded a message left in the past. And in another story, "Partial Magic in the Quixote," Borges (1962) asks why readers find it disturbing that Don Quixote reads *Quixote* within *Quixote*, or that Hamlet is a spectator of *Hamlet*? Or, why is a map within the map? The two-part question is rendered explicitly about a "literary device"; the query about maps (which was actually the first question he wrote) says that the effect is not just about "the letter." The significance is about contingencies of experiences of time. As John Stark (1974) put the point, Borges was a master at building his own precursors, and making that *show* mysterious, but all the while telling us more quietly that each of us accomplishes the feat more or less habitually. Likewise, in his remake of the myth of Tithonos, Bernard Williams (1973, pp. 82-100) explored contingencies of "problems of the self" as expressions of problems of time. In the ancient Greek version, Tithonos, a mortal uniting with a goddess, asks her for the favor of eternal life, and Zeus granted her request. She forgot to ask for eternal youth, and Tithonos became more and more decrepit but could not die. Aristotle later summarized one side of the "dilemma" by observing that a good will not be any more good for being eternal (*Nicomachean Ethics* 1096b4), but it might be less. Most of us recognize that present contingencies will have something to do with alternative futures, although we are less adept at knowing which and how. But we tend to overlook that relation as we build our own precursors; for we neglect variabilities of memory, the fact that one's memory of *me* can become quite different over time, but with only vague (if any) future awareness of the change.

A sense of "willed stability" can endure in first-person experience ("All's well with the world"), but the feeling is hardly good testimony to one's own effectivity. Reflections of one's low efficacy in world, or of efficacy lower than one prefers, insofar as those reflections are explicitly conceptualized, threaten the sense of stability as a desired state of affairs. For the sake of maintaining that sense, a person might erect a barrier between the sense as *feeling* and any thinking that would arouse doubt about it. Good feeling tends to be inertial against decay—until decay becomes collapse. Here I am thinking of several literary illustrations of the barrier. One will suffice, one of the most remembered chapters of *The Brothers Karamazov* (Dostoyevsky 1990 [1880], pp. 255, 257): Ivan Karamazov tells his brother of part of a poem in which the Grand Inquisitor criticizes Jesus for having returned and God for having given feeble humankind the supposed gift of free will—a mistake now corrected. The upshot? People "rejoiced that they were once more led like sheep." The trick (the reader was told) had been to display a persuasive exercise of "three powers," the "only three powers on earth" that are "capable of conquering and holding captive forever"—*and* "for their own happiness"—the conscience of these feeble people. The powers are "miracle, mystery, and authority," for they instill a fellow-feeling of patriotism, a feeling of patristic oversight. Walter Bagehot (1867) had already said something of the sort in his book, *The English Constitution*, observing that the authority of the monarch rested in the mystery of its majestic appearance, the curtain of which should never be pulled back. Of other illustrations of the collapse, Scheler (1971 [1915], p. 52) summarized several accounts of one of them when he wrote of an "existential envy directed against the other person's very nature," a feeling that eventually ignited an "enormous explosion of *ressentiment*" during turmoil that we remember as the French Revolution. The primary object of the *ressentiment* consisted in "the nobility," but this object quickly expanded to include anything connected with the way of living that had been a hallmark of the nobility. Members of the bourgeoisie who flouted emulations of that way of living while lacking the qualities traditionally indicative of genuine nobility became special targets of the most rapacious feelings of revenge.

Little is known about regulation processes within first-person experiences of feeling, as distinguished from topical or discursive phenomena (whether in self-memory as thinking about those experiences or in dialogue or in third-person characterizations by presumably contemporaneous, often tacit, classifications and measures of intensity, tempo, duration, and perhaps still other properties of an objectivity). These latter phenomena are regulated, at least by and large, in the ordinary transactions of sociality, including the mostly taken-for-granted regularities of language use. The first-person experiences as such are regulated, if they are, intrinsically; but gaining access without violating their integrity is high challenge. This verdict perhaps now seems strange, given surges of application of instruments such as functional MRI, but the "maps" that result from those applications are of the electrical or electrochemical circuits of brain function, not of feeling as a first-person experience. One might ask a person's memory of what *had* been felt at such and such time-stamp of the imagery, but any resulting report would always already manifest an absorption in language, in thought, in sociality. Reading facial cues or other signals of "body language" during the course of a person's (presumed) experience of a controlled stimuli during examination might seem to be a less fraught approach to first-person feeling as such; yet those signals are already an interchange by sociality.

One can easily conclude that if "internal regulation" there be in first-person experiences of feeling, its presence is hermetic. Must we there turn our spade? Perhaps not. Consider, for example, Thompson's (1988, p. 32) reminder of the observation by numerous readers that Jane Austen shared with countless other artists the recognition that the most interesting perspective on action is "poised between these two points, the submission to necessity in the external world [i.e., the necessity of objectivities resulting from prior actions] and the promise of freedom within the individual self." Our penchant to uncover the epithetical moment of perspective leads sooner or later to an analytical reduction as end point or full stop—such as when we think that once we have located the vanishing point(s) of a painting we have uncovered its secret (the artist's manipulation of viewer), thus cease thoughtful inquiry, and lose the artist's intended effect overall. The epithetical moment on which we settle is typically either a voluntarist moment of *will* (freedom of will) or a conspiratorial moment of a necessity of hidden intent—that is, conspiracy (by "the powers that be," by "the system," etc.) or some "audition of the Word," as Lyotard (2011 [1971], p. 4) had it, a privileged voice through which "we ask to be delivered," as we "close our eyes, [in order] to be all ears," so as to believe what we are told by superior thought, whether from privileged theorists or from conspiracy hunters. Our best artists, however, strive to maintain the equipoise of the dialectic (see also Hazelrigg 2012; and in different vein Hazelrigg 2018).

In an earlier era, to an extent still today, prevailing thought assigned intrinsic regulatory powers to a person's will. Indeed, we were encouraged to a "faculty psychology" of three distinctive processes—feeling, thinking, willing—which seemed to be in instructive alignment with sensibility (sensation, felt experience), intelligibility (reason, thought, understanding), and decidability (judgment, decisional power). This had been read in Kant, for example. It was still to be read in Hannah Arendt's (1977, 1978) foreshortened opus magnum. It also looked very much like an old and still prevailing folk theory of mind. Triads were popular, obviously, prior to the accretional intents of Christianity, and that multiplicity of heritage remains strong in European and Euro-American cultures. Accounts of ontogeny had settled into a dualism, with sensation (or the passions, emotions, etc.) associated with body, and therefore the part of human being shared with "the beasts," and reason (thought, language, etc.), associated with mind and therefore the part of human being capable of dreaming with "the angels." Willfulness was, however, a site of danger, of hubris, of anarchy. It was susceptible to enticements of appetite, pleasures of the body, immediate gratifications, overreaching, refusals to leave childish things behind.

On the other hand, willing when properly disciplined was also in service as a mature person's internal regulation. In that capacity "will" was expected to answer the problem of conveying first-person feeling in externalizing expressions. This would mean, in part, managing ambiguities of expression, including those of semantical and syntactical meaning whether manifest as verbal expression or as some means of "body language." An illustration can be cited again from Thompson's exploration of Austen's skills of casting expression: consider the case of Marianne Dashwood, a major character of *Sense and Sensibility*, reporting that "sometimes I have kept my feelings to myself because I could find no language to describe them in but was worn and hackneyed out of all sense and meaning" (Austen 1933, vol. 1, p. 95). An implication of her confession is not only that at other times she *had* been content with the adequacy of language but also that her judgment had been her own, freely exercised, even though the reader knows enough of her character to infer that her judgment was generally shaped in some degree by perceptions of "external" circumstances. In sum, she had been arbiter of self-revelation, and the arbitration was neither feeling nor thinking, though it could have depended explicitly on both, but a willing at the inside/outside, the private/public, boundary in regulation of which feeling would gain expression in thought (reportage) and which would not. This willing was implicitly confessed as a judgment about sociality, specifically the adequacy of linguistic exchange, but it was also about her feeling of *self*-adequacy in risking an exposure that could run wild once beyond the immediacy of her willing.[197] Perhaps Austen had been reminded of Martin Luther's predicament, expressed in his little tract, "Against the Rioting Peasants," written in response to the huge revolt of peasants during 1524-25 (Luther 2013 [1525]).[198] Luther was embarrassed, probably shocked, that these rebellious peasants had been using the very words which he had uttered in 1521, when called to the Diet of Worm to recant heretical views: they (as he) invoked the personal privilege of first-person credentialing by God's own words (Luther's famous "sola scriptura": scripture alone is divine authority). To Luther as to other officers of ecclesia as well as crown, the peasants had indeed let first-person voice "run wild." But where, now, to draw a line?

Recognition of a risk of wildness points to a specific instance of the "chicken-and-egg" puzzle inevitably posed by a logic that purports to be abstracted of all sociality: insofar as "will" is regulative of anything beyond its auxiliary function in time (i.e., a promissory notation), what regulates "the will"? This specific version of the question has been all the more pressing on conscience as well as consciousness inasmuch as its locus has been situated at the core of a

---

[197] Thompson (1988, pp. 78-79, 85) recognized those dynamics, but he became captivated by his own notion that "language came to be commodified" in eighteenth-century England as if never before. Or perhaps he meant only to reproduce his interpretation of Austen's view: certainly, as he said, language was being "printed and packaged, sold and bought, in primers, grammars," etc., and in Austen's own novels. But broadsheets, pamphlets, catechisms, hymnals, manuals, gossip sheets, and more, had been the same for centuries. Further, words repeated endlessly by poets, troubadours, harlequins, and mystics, freely or for donations, centuries before that. Modern capitalism had major effects, to be sure, but it did not invent commodification of language—or the "commodity form" as such.

[198] Some printers sought to elevate the sense of proper outrage by retitling his pamphlet: "Against the Murderous and Thieving Hordes of Peasants."

concept of freedom—that is to say, the power of a "free will" and its relationship to Kant's concept of "good will."

One could ask, following an earlier idiom, in what the core—if core there be—of first-person experience consists. That description might index a feeling before a knowing, ego before cogito. What is thusly indicated is an assertion of presence, of being here now, that stabilizes internal relations. The presence of ego as locus of stabilization (the presumption of continuity in time) suggests some director at work prior to any particular use of "sentĭo" ("I feel")[199] and any particular use of "cogito" (i.e., awareness of sensation, followed by conceptual accounting). This directorial presence could itself be a reflexive ostension of sentĭo (as in "I feel myself exerting direction" or "being in control"). It gained a special status as vŏlo ("I will" such and such), however, due to the stabilizing, regulative power in that reflexivity. And even after recognizing that sociality impresses on the infant and young child an expectation and therein a concept of *self*-control, *self*-responsibility, and the like, via vŏlo in its capacity as gerund (i.e., as *willing*, a continuity of intentional action and its consequences), habitués of a psychologistic worldview conceptualized vŏlo in terms of a "vŏluntas of intent," a psychologistic condition of "free will" and "voluntary action." The qualification in each of these compound concepts is complicating.

A first-person sense of self-identity and being in control of oneself, including one's own actions, is usually experienced as a matter-of-fact integrity of being, the integrity of "who I am" in myself and in my ability to choose "how I act," "what I do," my effectivity in "the world." At conceptual level a voluntarism of intent is measured, adjudicated, and maintained in one's work of memory and in one's expectations of being active tomorrow. Typically that work of memory encounters ambiguities and ambivalences. Memory has potentially a rather large reservoir of such complications from which both to work recalibrations and correlations and to select which pieces will be shunted into oblivion (or near-oblivion) and which will be woven into one's first-person ongoing tapestry of remembered actions, intents, and outcomes (the background "scripted scenes" from which one makes various presentations of self). In fact, as one can usually readily see when inspecting the behaviors and actions of other persons, a large fraction of the activity manifests a strong inertial force of habit. These habituations of behavior and action may be due to custom, to superstition, to routinized instrumental applications, to value-rational preferences, or to various combinations of these and perhaps other factors that constrain or channel or induce activities (including availability of alternatives within a finite and often quite small number of options). When queried about the force of habit, first-person experience may be quick to reply in a second-person voice, "But that's the way I always do it!" In other words, "intent by habit" is merely another name for "willful intent"; and an efficiency expert would be hard-pressed to disagree. By the same token, first-person consciousness may appeal to a gap between willing and intent—as in "I freely chose to do [such and such], but it proved to be different from what I had intended." Something like an expression of "buyer's remorse," the lament reflects a hymnal of "tragedy of the idea" as well as "unanticipated consequences of purposive action" and "life is complicated" (see, e.g., Schneider 1984, pp. 214-215). In first-person terms "voluntarism" is an expansive category of internally flexible and motile subsets.

That motility is due at least in part to the aspirational moment of vŏluntas. The very idea that an individual person's will is distinctively important, even defining, encouraged the view

---

[199] The Latin "sentĭo" captures several meanings, ranging from a very basic "feeling by the senses" to "feeling emotion" (i.e., in general; some specific emotions typically take a more specific verb: e.g., "dolēo," "I hurt"), to "feeling that [proposition p] is true."

also that one's will, and willed choices, would make a difference in one's future world. Luther's recriminations against peasants' willful actions "running wild" against a legitimacy of rule, whether ecclesial or civil, achieved his self-serving goal of the moment, but in longer frame the willfulness continued to envision a popular democracy carried on the back of a sovereignty. The religious motivations of this first-person authority from God's word ("sola scriptura") also gave, however, a renewed voice to the scriptural admonition to render differently unto Caesar and unto God, a division of worlds that could (and did) encourage believers to ignore strife and terror against other, "ethno-religiously lesser" groups. The line between the more and the less visible shifts, as one turns the prismatic lens.

The idea of "free will" generally does not strike most people today as absurd or wrong-headed, even after a very long and persistent controversy about whether such as thing actually exists.[200] While I might subordinate myself to another person or to a supernatural being or to some other principal for whom I am at best mere agent, and while I might succumb to that subordination under conditions that I consider duress, unjust, and/or inhumane, throughout the descriptive clauses just enunciated, and regardless the conditions therein postulated, the "I might" stands as an alternative hypothetical state of "I will." The first-person experience of conscious will arguably begins ontogenically with the hungry infant realizing that the demand of a cry, initiated not as a thought but as a felt need, want, desire, achieves a satisfaction. From there a young person soon develops an initial second-person experience, which does involve very considerable and expansive thought (see, e.g., Darwall 2006); thence, eventually but also rather soon, a pluralist perspective of third-person standpoint, via what Adam Smith, for example, described at the start of his *Theory of Moral Sentiments* as the sympathetic experience of taking the place of the other (Smith 1817, pp. 2-3). For the Romanticists among whom (as will be seen in more detail in Part Three) a free agency of will seemed both persistently neglected in Enlightenment's broad main fibers of a rationalism and ripe for expressive work in and as artful projections of character building (self-formation), it was time to take charge of that free agency in an action itself already sufficiently endowed with ends and means of self-identity and self-control. One simply needed to get on with it. "In the beginning," Goethe (1976 [1829] lines 890-903) said, was *not* the Word, however knowledgeable it might be, but "the Deed." Words, whatever their meaning and whatever their power, are only potentiality. The creative moment lives in the deed.

There are good reasons, nonetheless, and no scarcity of empirical evidence (however much reason might slant it), that conscious will is illusory. As Wegner (2002) pointed out, the larger part of the debate about "free will" has been badly constructed. The issue is not whether the experience of conscious will is real, rather than another instance of a tendency to believe in fabulous entities and truths that speak for themselves. The illusion that attends conscious will results from a simple misapplication of correlational thinking. On the one hand, a person often does experience feelings of willfulness (again, the Latin vŏlo, "I will"). On the other hand, a

---

[200] Dihle (1982, pp. 68-72) pointed out that, judging by their surviving texts, the ancient Greeks had no distinct concept of "will." Rather, they attended to the cognition and the emotion of intent, which is always contingent on what is not yet known—namely, future conditions and events. In addition, and in recognition of the inertial tendency to presume present's past into future times, a notion of "habit" was added, most pointedly by Aristotle, who also gave emphasis to a notion of "choice" (*proairesis*) as in the cognitive and emotive process of deciding among options. See also Dihle (1982, pp. 48-67) on the state of being a *sŏphrōn* (and its relation to *sophía*), one who behaves in awareness of oneself, one's capabilities and limits.

person often does engage wittingly in specific behaviors or actions, *with intent*. Moreover, these two experiences often do coincide locally (temporally as well as spatially). Correlation is easily mistaken as causality—and in this case, the mistake occurs despite misalignment of categories. Think of it this way: a popular trope of science fiction features one or more actors whose minds are directly causes of external actions by others, minds so powerful of external effect that they can induce others to behave against their own wills. It is doubtful that any of us would want to live in such a world. But that scenario illustrates the misalignment of categories of causation that is at work when someone takes an "intentional stance" in regard to "perceiving minds" that he or she would not take when "perceiving most of the physical world" (Wegner 2002, p. 25; Dennett 1984; 1996).

The coincidence of a reflective awareness of acting with intent and a feeling of personal willfulness tends to reinforce a folk theory of directorial agency located in what Wegner called "the Free Willer," as a standing forth prior to sociality (Wegner 2002, pp. 322-323). Much of the often rehearsed discussion about free will as a definitive property of human being harbors the irony alluded to above: the most ardent champions of a psychic state of "free will" offer a self-defense that transforms the alleged process issuing from that state into a determinism, the main difference of it from, say, Newtonian motion being that it emanates from an agency hidden in the human mind rather than in "extension of matter." Whereas an experience of "free will"—no doubt as genuine as an experience of unfettered choice or happiness or regret or guilt or shame— is a first-person experience of *feeling*, the effort to rationalize it as an internal causal agency converts it into a self-denying morality play (see Turner 1983 on related ambiguities).[201]

The confusion developed within a concern that was exhibited not only in writings by Hölderlin (as discussed in the previous section) but also in writings by various other scholars who have been habitually collected under the heading "Romanticism" (Wordsworth, Goethe, etc.). It had to do with an analytics of reduction. Recall that after Kant a phenomenalism was first and foremost what scholars of human affairs had to work with, both as explanans and as explicanda. An urgent question followed: by what criterion should an analytical logic sort phenomena to one side or the other of the equation? What exactly was the simple copula equating? Several of Kant's heirs chafed at the Kantian limit, asserting that they, too, were entitled to the mantle of "true science," rejecting the attribution of "pretend science." The strongest thrust of that assertion took the form of a psychologistic quest to reduce conscious experience to its "real" foundations in processes of mentation, later increasingly pursued in terms of organic processes of brain function. As the critique of what had amounted to little more than a common folk theory of "free will" gained sharper traction, the ensuing controversy replayed the contest which Pierre Duhem had sought to settle early in the twentieth century via his little book, *To Save the Phenomena* (1969 [1908]). Among psychologistically inclined theorists who conceded the failure of will (so to speak), the new regulative question directed a return to the sorting table: if an explanation of action in terms of conscious experience of willing is indeed inadequate, where then should we seek adequate explanation of the action? Duhem had held that

---

[201] Moran (1994) addressed several evaluations of "feeling in imagination" as they have been presented in literatures of European and Euro-American cultures—for instance, a modernist "suspicion of dramatic emotions as a form of bad faith."

theorists should avoid the merely speculative introduction of a "material basis" beneath the empirically defensible levels of available theory, merely in order to "save the phenomena." Not surprisingly, given the mantle that was at stake, this sort of appeal did not stop the search by many "would-be scientists" of human affairs for the correct application of analytic reason—namely, an analysis (i.e., breaking apart) of experience in search of clues to the process that produced that experience, and perhaps (so they hoped) find in those clues evidence, or at least avenues to evidence, of the relationship between the experience (e.g., as before, the feeling of willfulness) and the real causes of a given action that has been consciously experienced in such and such way (e.g., as willfulness). How does one know, however, whether analytic reduction is producing "real components" rather than noise or random effects? How does one know when to cease analysis? This puzzle was at the core of Hölderlin's critique of a theorizing that attempts to surpass its inherent limits, in the process violating the integrity of an experience of feeling. It is also the question that John Searle raised, when he observed the practice among physiological psychologists and cognitive scientists of searching among neuronal activities, as these are represented by functional magnetic-resonance imaging, for the causes of conscious experience: Why stop there? (Searle 2000, p. 17). This is a legitimate question about analytical inquiry in general, of course.

Concerns about stability and regulation have often been formulated within and as not only an ambiguity in the meaning of each of those terms—for instance, is the adequacy of either stability or regulation defined and measured in terms of process (e.g., a process of regularity, as in homeostasis) or in terms of outcome (e.g., a steady-state of some specified outcome)—but also an ambivalence that at core has to do with the determinism and history. A determinism of necessity seemed during the eighteenth century to be assured by the promise of Newtonian mechanics as primary model of modern science. Few people had appreciated the difference between application of Newtonian laws in their proper domain (perfect vacuum) versus any ordinarily useful domain. This is not to say that they did not, do not, have utility in the latter, of course. They do. But whereas in the former domain measurement error and other contingencies can be reduced to zero in principle, in practical utilities they usually cannot, and this means that probabilistic distributions of error must be entertained. Furthermore, while the principles may be regarded in their proper Newtonian domain as ahistorical, error distributions are almost always historical, usually in complicated ways. Work by Thomas Bayes, as developed by Pierre-Simon Laplace, and other work by Carl Friedrich Gauss made tractable the probabilistic functions of error in widespread applications. The contradiction comes from the fact that expectations about utilities of knowledge remained tied to traditional standards of dogmatic claims to truth, the central one being certainty. These developments did not arrive in time for Kant to take them into account (Bayes' work had been completed, but it attracted little attention). We know from his lectures on logic that he (1974 [1800], p. 89) regarded probability as related to verisimilitude and thus as an approximation to certainty, but beyond that he had little grasp of what would soon (the day of Laplace and Gauss) become a major topic of mathematics.

Kant's categorical imperative features a recommendation—a legislative act—that is cast as virtually transcendental in order to lend it the form of an apriori statement. What he did not understand (it is doubtful that anyone then did understand) that probability has an apriori form that closely parallels that of time and space. Recall once again from Kant's innovation that intuition can be apriori the two-fold standing of time and space: neither can be an intuition as such, since by definition any intuition is singular in represented object, whereas space and time are highly general (we suppose universal) to reality—one might say the pure functionality of an uncontained container—but nor can either be a concept, since any conceptual scheme cannot but presuppose its own existence spatially and temporally. Rather, each is only the apriori *form* of an intuition that can have no singular object but *is* the form of singularity as such.[202] Similarly, the recommendation of the categorical imperative—"to act as if thy will ..."—can achieve any application only in and through an existing sociality (culture, history, etc.), a context within which, conditions under which, *any* legislation may be achieved. Not only did Kant not intend that his individual reader should singularly legislate as tyrant, he also *did* expect that this person would, if following the recommendation, necessarily engage in imaginative experimentations and perhaps overt discussions with others, because the proposal ("as if thy will ...") leads sooner or later to considerations of "other minds," more or less as Adam Smith had suggested with his account of taking the perspective of the other person. How would my neighbor seek to enact the "as if"? How, my enemy?

The proposal is not, bear in mind, to *constitute* an actual sociality as if none had already existed. Rather it is a recognition that a sociality does already exist and must be negotiated in order to achieve a legislation that even approximately satisfies the proposal as an expectation and threshold. It is not as though Kant had invented an entirely new expectation (even if the question of thresholds must be left in limbo). A version as old as the Hebraic text of *Leviticus* 19.18 and, even better, *Leviticus* 19.34 would likely have been known to Kant from childhood in German pietism (also, *Luke* 6.31 and *Matthew* 7.12). Hegel later struck a similar position, with his argument that (as summarized by Pinkard 1994, p. 291) it is in the processes of socialization "in an ethical community that we learn to treat each other in ways that count, for example, as respecting freedom," and since "individual acts of will presuppose the existence of that community, they cannot establish it." Operating in concert, such acts can indeed reform existing community, but they never constitute one de novo—that is, out of its nonexistence.

The folk theory of will did not so much disagree with that proposal as both exaggerate it and oversimplify the dynamics as it confused the matter of causality. While recognizing the force of habit, for example, the folk theory nonetheless insisted on making habit a consequence of "free will." As a point of comparison, consider the more complex, and more subtly complex,

---

[202] We have in effect Kant's answer to the puzzle of Zeno's insight via language use. In his *Physics* (4.3, 210$^b$ 22-23) Aristotle addressed this puzzle, later elaborated by Simplicius in his commentary on Aristotle: "everything that *is* is in something; and to be in something is to be in space. Space then will be in space, and so on *ad infinitum*" (see, e.g., Bakewell 1908, p. 23). Zeno's conclusion—"Therefore space does not exist"—was of course not Kant's. Nor was it Aristotle's, but he did not know quite what to make of Zeno's argument, mainly because of a premise that language, carefully considered—much like observation, carefully conducted—could be a neutral medium. Bertrand Russell later recovered and extended the "paradoxical" quality of insights such as Zeno's, as the problem of "the set of all sets that are not members of themselves" (see, e.g., van Heijenoort 1967, pp. 124-125). Jorge Luis Borges did much the same, but in wry mode.

160

accounts of many present-day psychologists such as Daniel Wegner, whose theory of transactive memory recognizes the context and conditions of sociality for memory work.

Actions and behaviors typically result from a complex of conditions, contextual factors, and causes, sometimes through chains or sequences of process that are difficult to track, whether by those who are directly involved or by third-person observer. The first-person experience of conscious will is not in itself false—first-person experience "is at it is"—nor are actor intents and deliberative imaginations (projections or plans, etc.) necessarily deceptive, fantastic, or inutile. First-person assertions of will, want, need, desire, and the like, may well engender deliberations, decisions, and eventually behavior or action. The illusion is to apprehend those assertions as necessary and sufficient causal agency due to a first-person feeling of willfulness, or conscious will. As Wegner (2002, p. 11) summarized the main point, "Action and the experience of will" correspond well enough often enough that "we feel we are doing things willfully when we actually do them and feel we are not doing something when in truth we have not done it." Nevertheless, the contrary conjunctions—when I lack any feeling of doing something that I am in fact doing ("automatisms") or when I feel that I am doing something that in fact I am not ("illusion of control")—occur often enough to "remind us that action and the feeling of doing are not locked together inevitably." The self-experience of sufficient causal agency tends to be self-affirming, however, rather like the track record of the prognosticator who remembers every success but few or no failures. A prime illustration concerns Kant's "transcendental Illusion," which, recall, is operative even when we are aware of its existence and engage in one or another version of the charade of supposedly resolving it in an "objective necessity" that, while wholly existent within an actual sociality, we imagine as itself a transcendental solution so as to anchor one's own authority of voice.

The emotional security of personal identity and control is existential to first-person being and its perspective of consciousness. While this transpires within a sociality, the tendency of self-identity and control is to imagine rising above context and conditions, even causes that are understood as not self-willed. One prominent version of the tendency of individual heroicism has been embodied in a creature known as "the self-reliant individual," which, despite abundant criticism as a myth parading as logical necessity, remains robustly alive in many cultures, none more so than the dominant culture of the USA. The nineteenth-century movement ordained in a nationalist exceptionalism as "American Transcendentalism," in which Ralph Waldo Emerson, a romantic transcendentalist (see, e.g., Emerson 1983 [1841]), plowed ground already tilled many times by New England's puritan descendants, knew that each generation was (is) responsible for its own destiny because, and in a sense despite the fact that, it had to learn its own cultural and historical context as if anew. In that regard, the movement was not far removed from Hölderlin's interest in building, partly in conjunction with his theistic interest, a "fellow feeling" grounded in shared nativity of ethnicity and nation-state. In both of these interests the projective thrust was to create a habituation of feeling that would both bind and ground in a foundational principle. Nor, too, was the "American transcendentalist" movement all that different from Hegel's reply to the dilemma that had been left in wake of Kant's critical theory. As Pinkard (1994, pp. 269, 270, 154) summarized Hegel's response, he had recognized that the existential threat of loss of all anchorage in the real, the threat of "groundlessness," was real because tied to a particular event in recent history—namely, loss of the aristocratic ethos, including "loss of the intelligibility of there being a natural or 'given' hierarchy of ends." The sense of groundlessness entailed by that loss was manifest in the reality of "bourgeois life," with its processes of "criterion-less choices" (i.e, choices based on nothing more solid than exchange relations of token agreements). Given this real history, one had only two possible responses: either one had to "go in the direction of nihilism—that is, … come to the conclusion that there were no authoritative reasons at all—or … transform the project of 'groundlessness' into the project of *self-grounding*." Here, too, the main projective interest would survive or not in and through the creation of a habituated consciousness of feeling at one with and in a transcending, absolutist principle of authority. The project would be comparable to what psychologists a century later would call the formation of a "fixed action pattern." The projective avenue to consciousness of a new "hierarchy of ends" could not be a knowing, because knowing is both too difficult and too vulnerable to individual skepticism (the same corrosive force that melted the solidity of the aristocratic ethos). As Hölderlin had already appreciated, *feeling*, as in the "fellow feeling" of a distinctive—even better, an exceptionalist—nationalism, ideally embodied to the degree of a proprioceptive feeling, would be the avenue most likely to succeed.

According to Llinás (2001), emotions can be understood in terms of fixed action patterns (FAP). Sometimes described as an "automatic brain module," an FAP renders a complex set of movements into a routine or habituated pattern, relatively unchanging yet modifiable via learning and feedback. Examples include such stereotyped movements as walking, talking, and other learned behaviors in support of the centralized predictive agency of self, thus liberating self-consciousness to concentrate on other activities such as novel problem-solving or forming a new fixed action pattern. It is tempting to regard an FAP, or some of the more basic of them such as crawling and walking, as presocial, precultural, outside history. Imagination says, one imagines, that a human being would eventually learn to crawl, then to walk, even if existing as a strict isolate. The image contains, depends upon, unnoticed assumptions. Would a newly born infant survive, if mother died soon after delivery and no other human being was around? Doubtful (fanciful stories of "wolf children," and the, like notwithstanding). Neonatal action of suckling is generally regarded as an in-born organic-behavior trait; and it is, in the same sense that laryngeal functioning enables an infant to emit pre-linguistic vocalizations. But without a natal mother or surrogate there would be nothing to suckle (again, stories of "wolf mothers" notwithstanding). In addition, would an isolated mother with child survive long enough for the child to be viable? Perhaps, though far from certain in many territories in which the two of them were the only human inhabitants. In any case, if mother or surrogate did survive, the child would have been socialized by her presence, at least in a rudimentary manner, for in order for the adult to survive she would need some considerable mobility, facility with her hands, knowledge of foodstuffs, and so forth. A human infant might become a "cultural dope" (to use a pejorative expression that has been applied now and again to some conceptions of "human actor"; see Garfinkel 1967, p. 68; Lynch 2012), but the eventuality would not be due to absence of any human culture.

Learning to read is a process of forming a very complex fixed action pattern, probably the most complex that humans undertake. Another complex example is learning to read music, which can be completed only through learning to play an instrument, whether one's voice or a device such as piano. Once established, and once one has sufficiently learned a particular composition, practice refines the fixed pattern to such an extent that one does not need to *think* one's way through the sheet music, the result now being correct tempo (or one increasingly close to the composer's or arranger's intent). Sudnow's (2001) description of his own experience in beginning piano is idiosyncratic to an extent. For that reason, perhaps, it generated controversy, yet he was correct in saying that one learns and then relies on "ways of the hand," when first learning piano, much as one learned to talk via trial-and-error pattern matching and exploration, without beginning with memorization of parts of speech, lists of words and phrases, and the like. The patterns are as much affective as cognitive, and once one has attained some proficiency the affective becomes very powerful. It is the close similarity of neuronal patterning of executing a musical composition (whether vocal or by other instrument) to emotive expression that manifests as the sensation of the *feeling* of music.[203] This similarity is such that hearing a fine performance can generate the same elation or joy (or, when one's hands no longer work so well, a mixed feeling of joy and sadness). The emotive force is more intensely embodied, however, *in the moment* of the pleasure of performing well. In that moment the felt experience includes a fine pinnacle of proprioceptive and even vestibular sensations that only begin as an experience of hand-and-ear coordination as a sort of feedback loop the effect of which courses throughout the body (although body of a listener who also has experience as a musician can easily coordinate with another who is now the player being heard). Physiologists do know that one's relative sense of body parts in motion, strength of muscular exertions, and positional balance all begins as a pre-conscious sensation (once the body training has attained a certain level of proficiency—as in learning to crawl, stand, walk, etc.), and there is no reason to dispute that knowledge. But the embodied pleasure of performing music well, the pleasure of that *in the moment*, accentuates, extends, and regales the complex of sensations as a unity of "mindful body," as if the music emanates from one's entire body in vibration.

Fixed action patterns are, as already said, durable but not static. Likewise, memory in its more general sense, both one's own and the agglomerative sort as when one constructs a physical building with enough durability built into it that, in effect, it remembers how to be for decades but not forever. Memory, like a physical construction, survives by being maintained, rebuilt now and again, sometimes with pruning and alteration the acts of which we then do not remember. Experience is subjective because it begins in what will become "self" as self-consciousness. In fact there is no bright line in that self-consciousness, however, between what is subjective and what is objective. An experience of the moment and the experience of memory are from, and project, the point of view of one's self-consciousness. One could invert the panopticon metaphor as it gained fame through Michel Foucault's (e.g., 1978 [1975]) reports

---

[203] This statement, note, amounts to a version of the "reason harnessing passion" account of creativity in musical composition (as, e.g., in John Adams' discussion; see Adams 2008, pp. 192-193). Criticisms of that account as being "reductive" are no doubt unavoidable, and musicians often try to circumvent the reductiveness by "talking with one another only through our music." Success in the effort always depends on coordinated memories of a "background talk in words," however, mainly words about performance values. That hypothesis is easily tested when one performer deliberately violates some "non-obvious" and important part of the tacit coordination.

about modern techniques of discipline and say that this point of view of the subjective is panoptical, but expand the word to "all senses" and call it pansensory. Mixed in with that point of view, however, which *is* indeed subjective, there is also a lot of the objective, in the general sense that a subject takes his or her experiences to be as real as real can be, the things that populate it with furnishings as real objects, and often displays some degree of subordination to those real objects. Some of those real objects are other subjects, with some of whom one establishes second-person relations while others are present mainly or only in third-person relations, even the anonymous third-person relations of mutual "they-ness."[204] The tendency to subordination also includes the "consumerist mentality" of gauging all value by "the things that one owns." But think, too, of our legislations: we do know, usually, that human laws (and customs, etc.) are made by human beings, and often without our direct participation (inherited laws); we treat them as objects of authority—that is, as objectivities to be obeyed, for they are objectivities by virtue of the agreements that were (are) inherent in legislation. Sometimes we go so far as to nominate some of the objects in our mixtures with subjectivity as wholly prior to and wholly independent of any human being whatsoever. These are special cases in that with these objects we are prone to shirk our mutual responsibilities.

Perhaps the best theory of the basis of experience as self-conscious experience—and due to measurement problems it is likely to remain theory—proposes that self-consciousness as an inner experience begins in an intuition of body as an ensemble of proprioceptive and vestibular relations. This intuition forms as an image of one's body in one's brain. The image is dynamic, ever-changing, as cells of the hippocampus create and store indices of spatial and temporal orientations and sequences. Note that while the vocabulary is different, and in that difference adds considerable specificity, the theory is consonant with Kant's "forms of intuition" premise. One of the best accounts of the emotive-cognitive first-person experience of damage to the body as processed by the hippocampus, thence as a conceptualized "present experience" of one's consciousness of body, is Oliver Sack's memoir, *A Leg To Stand On* (1984). Bear in mind, however, that *all* of that transpires within and as a sociality, has sociality running all through it.

Fixed action patterns are built of such images of one's body in one's brain. Each pattern is highly distinctive (thus, e.g., whereas one sits on all sorts of supports—benches, hammocks, a sandy beach, a grassy lawn, etc.—one's bodily posture at the keyboard is unlike one's sense of "body" in any other setting). It would be a mistake to regard a fixed action pattern as ahistorical, simply because it has good durability, a sort of habituation, within the life of a specific person. Even the durability is prone to degradation in absence of practice, as with a musical instrument or skill at baseball or any comparable activity (even walking, after a long period of none). These latter illustrative cases are generally well known. It is certainly no mystery that "styles" of piano performance are cultural and, within what is conventionally taken as a self-identical culture, historical. And yet it is remarkable, given the tight association of emotion with musical performance (to cite only this one illustrative case), that so often the default view seems to have

---

[204] I am referring here in part to Heidegger's (1962 [1957]) concept of the "they," an objective authority within one's sociality but of indeterminate composition and source (partly similar to "the system," as that phrase has been used as token of an impersonal abstract function). Correlative to the "they" is the "one" (Heidegger's das Man), an impersonal "anyone" (as in the immediately preceding sentence).

164

been that emotions as such are ahistorical, that they have no history. While surprise might be absent on hearing a pianist who has little or no knowledge of the history of performance to assert that her emotion of joy, say, attending her accomplished rendition of *Für Elise* must have been the same emotion of joy that her great grandaunt Harriett expressed in a letter about *her* successful performance of Beethoven's bagatelle in 1873, and that each in turn must have been the emotion that the master himself had intended,[205] it *is* surprising to read a work of social science or of historiography that clearly assumes that emotions have *no* history, that emotion is so deep in the "psychic nature" of human being that it and its categories or qualities are universal in time and space. But well-known social scientists and well-known historians have indeed written in that manner, as if there is nothing at all problematic in assuming that emotional categories, boundaries, and feelings that we, the reader, experience are the same as those experienced by writers and actors of an earlier time and/or a different place. Likewise, one encounters as taken for granted the assumption that emotions integral to one's self-knowledge here and now are the same as, have the same characteristics of, emotions integral to the self-knowledge of an actor regarded as in some sense correspondent (or of an actor selected at random) from another context in time and/or space.[206] While this matter-of-fact assumption has been common in some literatures of psychology (not a surprising fact, in view of other basic assumptions that are maintained; see Wilson and Dunn 2004), it is oddly out of step for disciplines that otherwise give greater weight to the importance of the specificity and historicity of sociocultural context. We will return to this complex of perspectives in Part Three.

### §14. Feeling Left Behind

A bias toward ahistorical perspective can be seen not only in the rationalism of a movement such as "the Enlightenment" but just as well in a counter-movement such as "the Romantic Reaction." The idea that "knowing a principle of action," such as (for example) Newton's first law, is "the same event everywhere at all time" has as its counterpart the idea that "feeling an emotion" such as (for example) joy or melancholy is likewise the same everywhere at all times. A tendency to the latter formulation can be detected in some of the writings of scholars generally identified as "Romanticist" (e.g., Emerson seemingly assumed that the feeling of "being self-reliant" was the same at different times and places; Wordsworth, that feeling aroused by one of his poems would be the same for various readers; and so forth). As noted above, thought and talk about a feeling inevitably brings language and thus the conceptual to bear, replete with an array of little boxes. However, insofar as there was a common major dynamic of emotive resistance across the many

---

[205] In fact we do not know what emotion Beethoven intended (if any); nor do we know the identity of this Elise, or which of the existing versions of the piece (sometimes classified as a sonata) is nearer the autographed sheet of 1810 (now seemingly lost; publication of any version did not occur until 1867), or how Beethoven himself understood the composition relative to other of his works.

[206] Many instances could be cited. A recent contrast will serve the limited purpose here: Tackett's (2015) account of the French Revolution of 1789 and its aftermath through the years of Terror, in many other ways a finely considered work, regards the great emotions of those tumultuous days as ahistorical properties of otherwise often highly volatile actors (their emotions, emotional categories, are exactly ours, etc.). Reddy's (2001) account is startlingly different in that regard, and the difference informs his overall account integrally, not simply as an additional perspective (see also Reddy 2012, which is comparative, spatially and temporally, of "longing and sexuality in Europe, South Asia, and Japan, 900-1200 CE"). On the "nature versus culture" debate about emotions, see Lutz (1988).

scholars whose works generally count as "romanticist," it was resistance from a feeling of *loss*, and more specifically that the rationalism of enlightenment had resulted in a loss of appreciation not of the "irrational" (which is, after all, the negative pole of a continuum of rationality) but of the "nonrational," of affective conditions of being. Before turning to the topics of Part Three, I want to pursue some registers of this experience of feeling, the feeling of loss and a resultant incompleteness, especially the feeling of "being left behind"—as in, say, "being left behind by modern science." From our standpoint today, some of us may understand that feeling with high intimacy but wonder how the same could have been true in, say, 1800, so long before Darwin's evolution, Einstein's relativity, Dirac's quantum equations, and so forth.

One of the appeals that Goethe made to readers of his novel, *Elective Affinities* (1971 [1809]), is the wisdom of patience when dealing with emotions of frustration and regret ensuing from the complex ways in which effects of one's decisions and choices aggregate over time. No theme was more central to Goethe's writings, letters included, than the notion that one's duty is to make of oneself a project of careful development. As he saw more and more clearly late in life, however, Goethe admitted that his own life project had been coming to naught, as the new generation turned away from what his life, he believed, offered to teach. As one's life proceeds, more knowledge of the what is actual begets more understanding of potential relative to actual, and therefore more and greater reason to be less than content with present conditions, and more determined to follow a path of self-betterment. But threads of willful intent are interwoven by contextual forces, by changing conditions, and sometimes by aggregations of effects of one's own intents that controvert or undermine those very intents. Thus, as one develops one's self, enriching mind and strengthening body, one opens new windows on and doors to greater happiness and to greater unhappiness. Knowledge, like love, can be at once constructive and destructive. Development, then, leads to predicament, to the dilemma of choices no one of which will be unalloyed with contradiction or offer surety of signposts to desired end. The only solace comes with the grace of patience with oneself, as well as with others.[207]

The lesson has been retold many times, with sometimes interesting variations. In his story of "The Captive" Proust (1993 [1923], p. 207) has the narrator (no doubt Proust himself referring to himself, as well as to Wagner, Baudelaire) tell of a feeling of incompleteness derived of self-contemplation of the deed of one's creation. This sense is one of beauty, the narrator reports, ultimately a feeling integral to the first-person experience of having created; and in that self-contemplation there arises a feeling of being incomplete even in and of the finished deed, an act that is in self-contemplation a past time. As insisted by as highly accomplished a translator as Richard Howard (1981), with Proust as with few others (Howard named Joyce and Beckett), a translator must attend to work with the finest of insight into an enormous range of cultural, or multicultural, understanding of how words each open onto a window of reality with complexity of relation that sometimes defies easy coherence, and sometimes cannot but be less than signs of inconsistency and contradiction integral to a culture, a time of place. Belting (2001 [1998], pp. 203, 244-247) caught in Proust's report of an event—an event at once particular to the narrator's

---

[207] I understand the different point of Benjamin's (1999 [1924]) critique of Goethe's novel. I do not believe it lessens the wisdom.

creator and the name of a category into which others (e.g., Wagner) seemed naturally to fit—the case of an "invisible masterpiece."

This metaphor, "invisible masterpiece," has a long heritage of inspiration, although in recent times it has been accredited chiefly to a story by Honoré de Balzac, *Le Chef-d'œuvre inconnu* (see Belting 2001 [1998], pp. 120-127).[208] The metaphor traces a circuit of the inside/outside dialectic. A masterpiece, visual or aural, is in its initiation invisible/inaudible, because in and for the creator it exists first and foremost as a suggestive feeling, not yet as idea, much less known fact. This is, for instance, Michelangelo "seeing" in the block of marble, with marmoreal certitude, the true likeness of David; and this is Michelangelo seeing in the finished statue of David an incompletion, even while listening to an audience murmuring astonishments in marmoreal correctitude, which, unlike certitude, is behavioral, social (an etiquette of civility, perhaps no more; but that can be enough). Likewise, say, Mozart "hearing" in imagined trains of musical notes the perfect instruction of a sonata form, then composing "Sonata facile," the *Piano Sonata No. 16, C Major* (K545), later advertised as "for beginners."[209]

The outside, inevitably a composition aural or visual with tactile intimations, takes on a totemic quality in which the maker of the work of art is repeated publicly and as such can never match the inside, yet, insofar as the inside remains as it was, is reproduced again and again via the outside, until eventually the circuit may dissolve in rituals of memory (such as my foregoing quotations of art working; see Belting 2001 [1998], ch. 18).

There is a fascination in the conjuncture of the metaphor. The deed has been finished in the midst of sociality—that is, it is inescapably a social act, not still only (having passed from initial feeling to reflection) a thoughtful first-person experience of "what I have imagined doing" and then "what I have done in strictest privacy"—and yet it has generated a feeling of being incomplete in and of the creator. Proust brought the fascination to a very fine point as an emblem of a "modernism," or of a "modernist style." But he did not invent the condition in or of the conjuncture, nor even its uses as a literary thematic. If Jenkyns' (2016, p. 122) reading of early Latin literature is accurate, for example, some of its "most fascinating effects," including a "charm in the sense of belatedness," derived from an authorial self-awareness similar to that which Proust captured. The maker of a work of art, in creating a particular unity of being,

---

[208] Balzac's story has been translated conventionally as "The Unknown Masterpiece," the adjective "inconnu" being commonly rendered as "unknown" for good reason. Belting's account, first named in German *Die unsichtbar Meisterwerk* ("The Invisible Masterpiece"), emphasizes three interrelated facts: (1) sight has long been the dominant sense in European and Euro-American cultures, (2) the focus of Balzac's story is visual art, and (3) while "unknown" is sometimes taken to mean "non-existent," it also covers the fact of an existent thing that no one, or few, have known and/or do know (i.e., "unknown" in the sense of "not uncovered to sight"), or that some believe they know but do not.

[209] In his tribute to the late Harold Bloom (*New York Times*, 15 October 2019) Dwight Garner reported how, "[I]t was impossible to read deeply in Bloom without him flooring you with feeling." Bloom's strings carry feelings of loss and loneliness, as many have said, but his best written work testified also to his felt exuberance of life and the magic of words on paper, or more especially spoken into the air, thus recalling Scheffler's point about the integrity of an afterlife in one's presumption of continuity.

supposes "a grandeur which it does not have" (Proust), and cannot escape the feeling of incompleteness. And so it goes, too, when one's work of art is "one's own self."

If such a thing as a "foundational meme" has ever existed, that might well count as one of the earliest. It resides in mythic structure—rather, one should say, in the process of myth—and especially mythemes of origination. If part of the definitive state of human being is to feel incomplete, to be less than human imagination, one has perhaps no choice but to create a god in human image, a nature that is caring and nurturing, and so forth. Kant's famous Mängelwesen, "deficient creature"—a creature of human creation, but not one humans can acknowledge as their own—rules itself in self-alienation under the sign of an ultimate otherness as sanctuary.

Dostoyevsky's "Underground Man" can be read rather easily in a one-sided manner as a victim of the complexity of modernity's competitive mores. Certainly a major thematic of the author's story—by simplest reading *the* major thematic—is that, because the essence of the nature of human being is creativity, nothing can stop the process of creation, not even (in a sense *especially* not) any result of that process, for a product of "man's creation" might then become the dominating focus of all future desire. What then of the underground man, the person who fails at creating anything of worth to others and (thus?) to himself? While reporting himself to be sick, spiteful, and unattractive, but also smarter than others yet also despicable for knowing what they do not understand but being too lazy to do anything about it, he suffers. Integral to his suffering is the fact that he has been left behind by modernity's mainstream, at best an object of condescension in their attitude of success in producing ever newer, better, more powerful things. Isolated even among the category of all those who also have been left behind, he has but one creative act within him, and that is to "burn the house down," thereby reaffirming this "dual essence" of human nature, to create *and* to destroy. After all, "it is sometimes very pleasant to smash things," and by this act the underground man demonstrates his understanding of what the builders, and all those for whom two plus two equaling four is so important, do not know: "I think man will never renounce real suffering, that is, destruction and chaos." In fact, "suffering is the sole determinant of consciousness" (Dostoyevsky 1918 [1864], pp. 22, 24). This, too, is a sense of incompleteness, turned in on itself destructively and acted out.

The underground man preaches *duality* of human nature (he denies any interest in an audience, yet he writes to others both specifically and in general), and in that duality he has some familiarity with an important thread of late nineteenth-century philosophy, running from the Romanticist Reaction at the beginning of the century to Nietzsche late in the century and on to the neo-Kantianism of early twentieth-century social science (e.g., Durkheim's "homo duplex" thesis). Nietzsche was an important conductor in that transmission—even though not always appreciated as such—because he opened the Dostoyevskian thesis to a more dialectical reading. Nietzsche read in the novella a dialectic of creativity/destruction issuing as a force of resentment, "the *ressentiment* of natures that are denied the true reaction, that of deeds, and compensate themselves with an imaginary revenge" (1967 [1887], pp. 36, 37). A manifestation of slave morality, this necessitude of victimization by an organized other survives the absence of any real objectivity of organized other except as it exists in the mind of the victimized person—in other words, survives merely as the quasi-other, the "as if" other. The resentment fuels, as it is fueled by, a reciprocated rejection: the victimized person's protest, "No, that is *not* me," is a negative sign of striving to belong; "*this* No is [resentment's] creative act."

The underground man's homiletics are always available to be institutionalized as an ethos of political discourse and guide to action. Awareness of that fact persists in anticipation of terror of the kind that flowed in aftermath of the French Year 1789, a terror that seemingly flowed so easily and naturally from purported benefits of what had been presented as a new rationalism of self-making (see, e.g., book 5 of Chateaubriand's *Memoirs from Beyond the Grave*, 2018 [1849-50]). Institutional formations bearing signatures of those memories have generally been slow to grow, but a few appeared rather quickly. One such was Mary Godwin Shelley's morality play, *Frankenstein*, which, published in 1818, assumed a place alongside Goethe's *Faust* but then soon supplanted in popular imagination the more complexly woven thematics of the latter work (all the more after publication of Part Two). Perhaps the most remarkable aspect of Shelley's story was the extraordinary rapidity with which it ascended to "master plot" status, as Baldick (1987) demonstrated through his study of the process by which this "modern myth" was born, popularly sustained, and institutionalized as an art form of literary and then cinematic production. This was hardly the first work of institutionalization (think of religion, the Christian church, and so on), but as applied to deliberate products of ingenuity known as "artistic creativity" outside the compass of illuminated scriptures, hymnals, and catechisms it stood out as an unusual display of popular interests.

"Institutions are products of the past process, are adapted to past circumstances, and are therefore never in full accord with the requirements of the present." Likewise (the author of that sentence observed), personal habits are slow to change, and that accords with institutional inertia. The author was Thorstein Veblen (1899, p. 191), a scholar of human affairs writing at the close of a century of extraordinary change, surely unprecedented in scale, average pace, accelerating rates, and ramifications for times yet to come. During the decade prior to the nineteenth century probably most Europeans, or at least those who were aware of events beyond the churchyard, shuddered at moral lessons that unfolded from what had initially seemed much like prior peasant revolts, this one begun at the Bastille prison in Paris. As few, perhaps fewer, had learned of a new nation-state founded in North America, the prospects of which seemed to warrant more than a dollop of skepticism by those who did know something of politics and economic conditions. Some new claims of modern science, mainly in physics, geology, and chemistry, had been either encouraging or disturbing, depending on how one felt about the different voices of authority vis-a-vis court and church, but most Europeans knew little if anything of those claims. Most adults in Europe, indeed most adults anywhere on the planet, presumed that their children, if surviving to adulthood, would live lives very much like their own. Contraptions powered by water that had been sufficiently heated externally, usually by burning wood, and could drive an internal piston had demonstrated usefulness for pumping water out of mines, but not until the later decades of the eighteenth century did the idea that these heat engines could be made more powerful and perform other kinds of work gain much traction. Most work was still accomplished directly by the human body or by harnessing animal power or, on much smaller scale, wind power. In 1800 the amount of energy consumed in productive activity by the average worker, most of them in agrarian pursuits, differed in raw amount or in composition very little from the comparable level a hundred years earlier, although its efficiency of use had improved a little. Both volume and efficiency increased enormously during the nineteenth century—first mainly the volume, then also the efficiency. Using the case of Great Britain as exemplar (its leading role but also its availability of data), energy consumption per capita, most of it from mineral fuels and water wheels, increased nearly six-fold during the century, the rate of growth accelerating (Humphrey and Stanislaw 1979). Similar rates occurred in the USA, with even greater accelerations during the last two decades of the century. Whereas travel from east coast to west required months in 1850, by century's end the journey was a matter of days, and electronic messages were zipping across the continental span in minutes (Gordon 2016; White 2017).

Concatenations of accelerating rates of technical change usually create backlogs of resistances both social-structural and psychological, Veblen (1899) continued, and so they had during his century. Individual actors often find themselves "propelled" into rather abrupt awakenings of now lost, or at least tattered and ragged, identities. (Actually a dialectic of identity/difference, it was now usually surveyed via an analytics of substantive, punctuated identity.) By Heidegger's existentialist argument, first published in 1927, these awakenings, while experientially exceptional and noticed as such, were the bold face of an unexceptional human condition—that inscrutable quality of "being thrown" ("geworfen") into the world, Heidegger said (1962 [1957], §§25-38)—that is, of being a "thrown projection" ("geworfener Entwurf") of history, who, relating presence to determinate experience of a past, continually awakens to "a world I never made" (Housman 1922, No. 12) but must accept as my alienated condition, which, if wisdom comes to me, may yet become my condition of freedom. Heidegger was better than Veblen had been at conveying this feeling of loss but then also of searching within for signs of a way to recovery, one result being that more readers (direct or, usually, indirect) recognized the feeling of existentialist thought without grasping its conceptual conditions and consequences.

Innovation may issue in development by the innovator, and sometimes it does. The more usual path of development is staked by someone who had been only watching and then, perhaps better visualizing applications, borrows. The success of this latter course comes also in part because sunk costs of investment in innovation can be evaded. By the start of a new century that pattern had been repeated again and again, especially in the USA and Germany. The repetition of pattern would continue. Resulting gains in efficiency of cost management were becoming ever more, Veblen (1915, p. 49) observed, in accordance with a change in "intellectual outlook," as an "engineering of a sort" was being developed and woven into "the technological scheme." That very same process tended to produce its own counterforce, however: persons, groups, even regions of a country, finding themselves in a later version of Housman's "world I never made," object to having been "treated unfairly" in and by a new regime which depends on technical knowledge and skills they do not have, or cannot practice with competitive utilities. It is a real victimization, largely by circumstances, of persons, groups, regions, who had bet their futures on continuation of yesterday's world (even when, especially when, "yesterday" was much older than they realized). Having properly "played by the rules" (at least as memory told it), these victims conceive their "lost bets" not as their own choices of will and intent but as injustice by circumstances, perhaps aided and abetted by rule-breakers, arrogant in-roaders, even thieves.[210] In Veblen's day "injustice by circumstances" seemed especially fitting (it *was* fitting) because the pace of change had become so great, and the difference between "needed knowledge" and "common ignorance" had grown so much. Few knew that the fictional Ned Ludd and his very real followers had experienced the same, early in the nineteenth century, or John Milton, author of *Areopagitica* in the mid-seventeenth, and so forth. Developments of various kinds, like the innovations they follow, vary in space and in time.

Themes of "uneven development" have been assayed repeatedly, although in recent times mainly via country comparisons—at the time Veblen was writing, for instance, comparisons within a period of rapid industrialization and globalization, and then more especially during the middle of the twentieth century when European and North American models of "modernization" (as it was then called) attempted to apply and inculcate great expectations for the people of "backward" or "undeveloped nations" of the world (virtually all of them former colonies, in one degree or another, and many of them still bearing colonialist stamps). However, "unevenness" applies no less to regional variations within countries and to educational or skill variations among persons within regions.

Some conditions associated with "unevenness" gained considerable attention during the early twentieth century, at least for a time, and a few of these conditions made enough impact in analytic and promotive literatures to merit specific names. Perhaps the most prominent of them was "penalty of taking the lead," a notion clothed deliberately or not in a skin of irony (akin, for example, to "tragedy of the idea"). But note that whereas the specific condition had no doubt been reproduced during a long history, it evidently did not gain a remembered name until about 1915, when Veblen coined it (more or less) in his comparative study of industrial innovations and developments in Germany vis-à-vis Great Britain (Veblen 1915, p. 53). It would be doubly astonishing if someone demonstrated (the impossible negative fact) that no one had ever before stated the idea of it. But it appears that no one had thought the idea important enough to merit a specific name, one that could become a topic within literatures of social science and international policy.

What had changed? For one thing, the technical complexity of innovations and pursuits of development. For another, a shortening of comparative framework—by which I mean, for example, that whereas China had long ago taken the lead in technical complexity on a number of fronts (e.g., ship construction) and by 1600 (though only in part for that reason) had long been the world leader in economic technologies and mercantile trade, Europe had hardly noticed

---

[210] In western literatures the thematic is at least as old as the Homeric song poems (think of Ajax, for example). Of our recent storytellers Faulkner made memorable use of it in the person of Ike McCaslin (in Faulkner's "The Bear"), as did Arthur Miller in the person of Willie Loman (in *Death of a Salesman*) and Bernard Malamud in the person of Yakov Bok (in *The Fixer*), among many others.

China, because it was geographically so distant and culturally so different as to seem of little import to Europe's comparative framework.[211]

The advent of Romanticism toward the end of the eighteenth century, well before the great rush of technical innovations briefly mentioned above, was already a signal of reaction to what was being felt as "uneven development." Europeans had experienced a century of modern nationalism, the project of centralization and amalgamation begun with the Peace of Westphalia in 1648, and several of the prominent figures of Romanticism (Hölderlin, for example) displayed emotions of what could be called "national feeling" ("national" in the sense of nativity, "my ancestral homeland"). The reaction from worries about uneven development was generally not an expression of national rivalry, however. The focus, rather, was *within* one's country, the uneven development within one's native culture, in particular between (to use Kant's terminology) the necessity of reason and the freedom of legislative creations moral and aesthetic. Like the famed "battle of the books" during the early-modern period, the lines of antagonism crossed seemingly familiar terrains, yet neither side grasped the real issues clearly enough to realize their preferred visions. The dominant visions of one side were fixed on past times that had in fact been long gone yet remained in memories as recoverable by sufficiently heroic thought and action, while those of the other side were also often fogged by clouds of heroic thought and action—here, being blind to the tethers lodged in their own minds, thought and action of radical breaks with past times presently preserved. Few if any of the main figures of that era displayed evidence of skill in thinking the counterfactuals of futures past.

The charge I have just laid at the feet of "reformers" is of course unrealistic in all senses but the optative mood when thinking historicity. As Koselleck pointed out, for instance, Kant himself, in "the imperative of his practical reason," can be straightforwardly read as having "sought to realize the optative mood of a progressive future that broke with the conditions of all previous history." Well, one might ask, "why would he *not* have striven for that?" But when striving for that, would he have somehow evaded all the snares and delusions of being sufficiently free oneself? It seems clear enough that Kant was aware of the dilemma in first-person experiential terms as well as in terms of presentation of voice to an audience (whether, though differentially, the audience be sympathetic or antagonistic). In recognition of the point, Koselleck (1985 [1979], pp. 204, 205) on the one hand quoted Kant's sarcastic jibe "against the prophets of decline who themselves created and promoted the predicted Fall, as well as against those supposedly realistic politicians who, shy of the public realm, fomented unrest through their fear of the Fall";[212] and on the other reminded his reader of the multiple passages in which Kant intended to distance himself from an airiness of utopist thinking. To make complicated matters still worse, one exercises little or no choice of future proselytizers in one's name: "A criticized and a vulgarized Kant initially had a greater influence than Kant had as a critical philosopher"

---

[211] Recall the curiosity of Marco Polo's *Il milione* travelogue, c1299, an element of Europe's growing store of exotica; compare, e.g., a supposed report soon thereafter of world travels by John Mandeville (1900 [c1360]).

[212] The reference was to a passage in *The Conflict of the Faculties*, in which Kant (1979 [1798], p. 143) lampooned the "soothsayers" ("Wahrsanger") who themselves make and arrange the conditions they have already predicted.

172

(Koselleck 1985 [1979], pp. 204, 205). In that judgment Koselleck's temporal adverb proved to be more elastic than he acknowledged (see also Clark 2019).

In more pragmatic terms, the argument associated with the Romantics was not whether new differences had come along. Rather, it was how to evaluate those differences; and in this as in many similar cases, disagreement was the kind that circulates elliptically around different centers, featuring lots of "talking past one another."[213] Groethuysen (1968 [1927], p. 4) began his inquiry into such developments in France by quoting perhaps the most eloquent orator of the day, certainly the most powerful theologian, Jacque-Bénigne Bossuet, reciting to all (as he had recited to son and heir of Louis XIV) the proper form of government: "those who are born, as it were, in the bosom of the true Church" are most fortunate because "God has given the Church such authority that we first believe what it proposes," and this "faith precedes, or rather, excludes analysis." Such conviction gave great comfort to masses of people, not only those born to the cloth, endowed automatically with uncontestable authority by virtue of the institution, but any and all who were (*and* would be) believers. With that as background, one can imagine the consternation felt toward this new segment of society, the bourgeoisie, who by the mid-1700s were a very strong force in city life, and increasingly also in royal courts, because of commerce and material wealth accumulated by "free individuals" and their families, largely if resentfully tolerated by court and clergy. As Groethuysen (1968 [1927], p. 200) emphasized, these individuals and families were importantly *not* the shopkeepers (and associated guild crafts), among "the eternally ordinary persons who would always remain in the estate to which God had assigned them." No, these persons were emblematic of a form later denoted "self-made man." Granted, this emblem was (and would continue to be) another myth. But to those under threat it was destruction pure and simple. If any of them had been giving sufficient attention to the Comte de Buffon's "transformist" speculations in order to notice hints of the dialectic of what Darwin would soon term "creative destruction," they likely took their cue from Buffon's Galilean-like response to the Church's reaction to his major writings. Imagine, then, the consternation, in wake of 1789, of all those who had been settled comfortably in the traditional "order of things"—that is, in conventions that had not been mere conventions.

Much of the culture of "city life" was changing, no doubt. However, "when the Church said that the merchant was possessed by an inordinate desire for riches and was therefore losing his soul, it was not attacking trade as such" (Groethuysen 1968 [1927], p. 202). Rather, the target was this burgeoning new mentality of individuality, breaking through well-worn strictures of institutional authority. Although they perhaps could not see the dialectic of it—in any case the language would have been French, not German—this new mentality of the bourgeoisie of Paris

---

[213] See, e.g., Oakes (1990, esp. pp. 106-107) on the production/consumption dialectic; and Hont (2005, pp. 185, 186, 189-190, 448-449, 470-471, 503-505). Hont (2005, p. 505 n.101) alerted his reader to the important point that "without grasping the various notions of 'sociability' the political theory debates of the second half of the century (events of and following 1789 included) cannot be properly understood." As I noted in passing in Part One, Kant's notion of "unsocial sociability" (ungesellig Geselligkeit) was a major instance, with its emphasis on contradiction within the human species (i.e., caught in an inherent antagonism between need for sociality and desire for independence), putting the individual person in a "highly artificial" condition of being free to be self-legislating. This was at the core of Kant's anthropology as an empirical ("as if") science.

amounted to a development within Kant's "social unsociality," another rise in individual desire for self-legislation. Not only a traditional dogma of religious belief was at risk of being left behind; so, too, most obviously, the dogma of royalty. However, the principal message being heard throughout the population, high and low, was that this new mentality was stripping people of their very souls (again, see Oakes 1990). By the mid-1800s traditional shopkeepers in Paris were losing material custom as well: a new form, the "store of many departments," began to disrupt the commercial scene (e.g., Le Bon Marché, from 1852). Now the commodity form was invading the "service" relationship of custom (no haggling, take it or leave it; these items are commodities, not one-of-a-kind Fabergé eggs).

It is at this juncture that Izenberg's (1992) exceptional history is especially useful, for he displayed the Janus-faced irony of this "rise of the individual." The vaunted "individuality," whether threat or salvation, could only be—and, indeed, in the very terms, implicit as well as explicit, of the regulative antagonism itself—an impossibility. What is particularly intriguing about that fact is that the antagonistic dialogue, even (and in one vein, especially) when it was conducted through sufficiently different semantics as to be two soliloquys in partial correlation, revolved around an impossibility in much the same sense as Moro (2016) intended through his search for impossible languages—that is, as a means of establishing a limit. Some of Kant's critics, in other words, were engaged *indeliberately* in an extension of the critical project. Such expeditions, usually undertaken in search of routes around the limits that Kant has established, continued throughout the nineteenth century and into its successor, often in the first-person modality of "experience of loss and being-left-behind" as a modality of social consciousness.

Walter Benjamin famously wrote as a key theme of his study of "language as medium" (Benjamin 1916) that a particular language conveys meanings of course via the content that it expresses to anyone who is able to understand, but that, in addition, the particular language is an expressive medium which *as such* also conveys meaning. The "message of the medium," as it were, varies across particular languages. What is more, for Benjamin anything that can be apprehended expressively is offering itself as its own medium, its own language. Thus, to invoke a very old illustration, there is a "language of Nature" to those who know how to apprehend it. Perhaps better, there are *various* "languages of Nature," all of them sharing in a unity of expressive media just as Nature itself is a unitary whole. This conviction is not so different from convictions held by principals of the Romantic movement a century earlier, whether it be the expressive medium of a musical composition (as in Beethoven), a poetic composition (as in Hölderlin or Wordsworth), a painting (as in Caspar David Friedrich), and so forth (see Hazelrigg 1995 and 2016).

If a difference, from the early nineteenth to the early twentieth century, was being marked by Benjamin's rendition, it was not in terms of, say, loss due to the advent of "mechanical means of reproduction," a thesis for which he has perhaps most often been remembered (Benjamin 1968 [1936]).[214] After all, the duplicating lathe had been in use since the early nineteenth century, the

---

[214] Hullot-Kentor (2006, p. 137) called it "virtually Benjamin's namesake"—but also "a condensed weave of *non sequitur* and untruth," citing as evidence of the latter Benjamin's claim "that photography was the first revolutionary means of reproduction."

pantograph dates at least to the early 1600s, the printing press to c1440; and ancient Greeks, Egyptians, and perhaps others used an early machine tool that, in the hands of a skilled artist, could turn out pieces as virtually identical as those produced by the treadle-powered lathes in woodworking shops of New England during the 1820s or 1990s.[215] Rather, the difference was that Benjamin was writing at a time when the very idea of "identity" as absolute absence of difference—of reproduction precisely without difference—had come apart largely because of advances in techniques of mechanical reproduction, which meant that margins of difference could be measured more and more finely but, like Zeno's paradox, never attain an expected destination of absolute absence (pure identity).[216] Benjamin's orientation was not expressed in terms of measures, however. Rather, it was gauged by what was in effect an already established loss, a loss that in Benjamin's orientation had posed the horizon of his gaze in the mythic dimensionality of lost innocence, the world prior to invention of sin. This horizon determined his implicit argument about language (from premise to conclusion)—namely, that once upon a time everything in creation knew its rightful name and a rightfully attuned recipient might yet recover those expressions. This originality consisted in the singularity of the object, its authenticity as a "one of a kind" object, which endowed an object with an "auratic quality" (in short, an "aura"), consisting in its uniqueness of a singular object that could be apprehended in an act of pure perception, an "absolute absorption" in a present moment (Crary 1999, p. 328). Here as elsewhere, however, Benjamin "relies on the importation of a surplus indeterminateness" in merely asserting a self-evidence (Hullot-Kentor 2006, p. 140). At times his argument lies in favor of the endowment of objectness in itself, but at other times his argument is that aura is in fact an achievement of human perception (see Bernstein 2001, pp. 112-113).[217] Insofar as the latter is the preferred stance, any "copy" can in principle be perceived auratically; a listener can be as impressed auratically by the melodically emotive power of Luciano Pavarotti singing *Nessum dorma* (from Puccini's *Turandot*) on video tape or sonic reproduction as by Pavarotti in person at La Scala or Carnegie Hall. If, on the other hand, Benjamin meant that this aura, an "aura of authenticity," comes from the uniqueness of an original object itself, then his remarks about democratization sound hollow.

Between Hullot-Kentor and Bernstein there is a level of agreement that Adorno rescued Walter Benjamin from some of the messiness of the latter's ambivalent view of "aura" and "auratic quality," and thus from the embarrassing matter of how, in any concrete situation, an interlocutor who engaged Benjamin in second-person perspective could determine difference in

---

[215] Mitcham (1994) contributed a fine review of issues of the relation of "thinking" and "making" (or "know how" as well as "know that") that avoided much of the tendency to privilege "the fine arts," vis-à-vis "the mechanical arts" and "the practical arts," when considering issues such as what counts as "original" versus "copy," whether an "auratic quality" inheres in an object independent of perception (an object's expressiveness) or is achieved within perception itself, and what it means to interrogate paths between philosophy and technology or engineering.

[216] In Kant's (1991 [1784a], pp. 46-47) estimation, this problem of approximation has "no perfect solution"—as indeed it does not.

[217] Bernstein's (2001, p. 113 n.49) brief summary is fitting: "When Benjamin is being sceptical about aura, he is thinking that this strange way of regarding artworks is bound to cult practices, and hence an anthropomorphic illusion; when he is being non-sceptical about aura he is noting the utter convergence between auratic experience and emphatic experience generally."

his first-person experience of that quality consistently from time to time, case to case (see also Jay 2005, pp. 343-360). The rescue was itself rather uneven, however, primarily because of Adorno's own motivations in what he saw as massive (and mostly occulted) loss due to the "skepticism of enlightened reason" (to borrow Bernstein's phrasing; 2001, ch. 2). Hullot-Kentor (2006, pp. 120-122) brought to mind as illustration of the point an extraordinary gap in Adorno's apparent understanding of the reception of sound—extraordinary, that is, for someone who was a performing musician and composer. While there is undoubtedly a difference in quality between the experience of listening to an orchestra playing, say, a Beethoven symphony in a music hall and listening to an electronically stored performance of the same score by the same orchestra, "quality" here means simply *difference*, not degree to which the former auditory experience would be necessarily superior (or inferior) to the latter. Adorno's "failure to understand the place of the listener in his work of this period was a motivated failure." John Cage's *4'33"* (1952), a composition in three movements for any instrument, made the point with considerable force: duration is the one quality held in common by music, noise, and silence—intervals that may be filled (or not) with various first-person experiences, even if the audition takes place in a perfectly anechoic chamber.

One last stop in this itinerary of experiences of loss keyed to the mid-twentieth century: Bernstein's rescue of Adorno from his own obscurities and ambivalences.[218] This rescue was conducted most effectively through Bernstein's interrogative mood. Of his several questions (variations on a theme), this couplet most crisply focuses the multiple thrusts:

> If more of the structures that determine the meaning of everyday life increasingly occur outside the ambit of individual experience, then how can what is meant by experience remain the same? Is not "economic experience," a sense of oneself as producing and consuming goods whose value would be intelligibly connected to one's activities and hence proportionally related to them, contradicted by the dominion of macro-economic structures? (Bernstein 2001, p. 116).

The first marker to note in that couplet is the conditional of the first question: the dialectic of this inside/outside opposition points to an implicit issue—namely, how does one know the boundary and its condition for that ambit? One may rest content with the verdict that for the individual whose experience it is, the boundary is wherever, however, the experience has located it, ambiguous or blurry it may well be. But how can any observer come to grips with it? If Adorno was diagnosing his own first-person feeling of helplessness with respect to that boundary and its allocation of "the ambit of individual experience"—and we may only assume that he was (if he was)—how would an interlocutor, engaged in second-person discussion, parse the issue of commensuration, such that some sense of the internal stability of Adorno's ambit, or his memory of that ambit, could be assessed within his "personal temporality" as process within a sharedness of history, a sense of a common history? It is here, for example, that the relativity of Adorno's

---

[218] Bernstein wrapped the rescued Adorno in clothing of a "modern naturalism" (2001, pp. 287-288), which can be interpreted on the model of Clifford Geertz' "nature" rising through a hole in culture, without any marks of culture at all (see Hazelrigg 1992)—another version of the "objective necessity" ensuing from the transcendental Illusion, albeit now sliding from naiveté into, or at least verging on, a cynicism.

claim of the before/after of Auschwitz can be situated, but only problematically: whether he knew of the genocide against Armenians in 1915, whether he knew of genocides, the quick and the slow, against so many "first nations" of the two Americas, whether he knew of *any* of the many genocidal events of human history long before either "genocide" or "Auschwitz" became such a heavy stone on gravity's rainbow, the ambit of *his* individual experience circled an event called "Auschwitz," or so one may judge from his words. The utter demoralization, at once personal and cultural, manifest in survivors of those determined quests to obliterate all first nations of the Americas bears heavily after so many generations as a stone that cannot be stilled by membership in a category, "genocide."[219] Which is the common part, the part shared between events separated by centuries?—location in the category, or surplus that erases the container?

Be that as it may, the conditionality with which that interrogational couplet by Bernstein begins also makes problematic the eminently sociological point of the couplet—namely, that the question of a *proportionality* between, on the one hand, "objectively determining structures" laid down by and in the sociality of activities of many individual actors situated in localities of time and space, and, on the other, the effective ambits of individual experiences, however isolative the first-person perspectives have rendered them, is intimately bound within *contradiction*. The old proverb, "The road to Hell is paved with good intentions" (often attributed to a twelfth-century abbot, Bernard of Clairvaux, but apparently not available in any of his known writings) has among its meanings at least these two—that good intents are of little worth unless/until put into action, and that acts intended well can nonetheless end badly—each of which can be meant as an indictment of personal failure due to sloth (lethargy) or to hubris. A sociologist would add still another meaning—namely, that a person can execute the best of intents in appropriately well-wrought actions and thereby produce results that are (1) intended and intentionally benign, (2) partly intended and benign but partly unintended and malign, (3) wholly unintended and malign, (4) partly or wholly unintended yet benign, (5) intended but sterile or empty, or (6) unintended and sterile or empty. Here the emphasis is on limitations of knowledge, because of which there may be an inconsistency or disphasing of the complexity of the "objective structures" that have been produced and reproduced through deliberated as well as habitual activities of individual actors living and working in Kant's antagonistic alliances with one another (Kant 1991 [1784a]), relative to the self-referential consciousness, both naïve and reflective, of each of the individual actors in everyday experience, wherein they enact intentionality as well as habit.

A skeptic can ask, of course, "Whenever was it not?"—and point to various illustrative instances, such as the likelihood that a similar disjunction or disphasing occurred following July 1789 in Paris, or following January 1649 in London. In either sequence it is likely that very few instances of what had been accountable as "everyday experience" were now consonant with forces that were being unleashed and erratically perpetuated by conflicting aims and interests at the "macro-structural" level of inherited institutions of "past times" now under attack by the uncertainties and ambiguities of skepticism.[220] But Bernstein's question, one should remember,

---

[219]As Grann (2017) has recently reminded us, this genocide, well underway in the seventeenth century, continued in deliberate acts of murder in the twentieth century, differing from the slower genocide via demoralization in having a more particular focus and a faster schedule of completion.

[220] Think, for instance, of the contrasts of "everyday experience" that must have been held in the minds of Londoners who had just witnessed the beheading of a king, having only months before read Sir Robert

asked in part how, under such conditions, "can what is meant by experience remain the same?" The inherent act of that question is, for the existential time of its advent, likely to have been experienced as a … what else? … a "new experience," as if a "new era" had emerged. Adorno's rejoinder had been written already, however, as Bernstein undoubtedly knew. What counted as experience for Adorno had been erased from life, almost from memory of life before loss. Thus, in his *opus magnum* of aesthetic theory Adorno (1997 [1970], p. 31) insisted that all genuine experience is gone, replaced by mere packets of information, each awaiting the next to take the stage of attention. "The marrow of experience has been sucked out; there is none, not even that apparently set at a remove from commerce, that has not been gnawed away." One suspects (as I mentioned earlier) that already in *Dialectic of Enlightenment* Adorno and Horkheimer had not understood—when, after declaring that concepts mediate subjective apprehension of phenomena (things for us) and noumena (things in themselves), they (2002 [1969], pp. 19-20) volunteered their search to rescue objectivity from a powerless subjectivity—that they had simply come upon the terrain of Kant's transcendental Illusion.

Martin Jay (2005, p. 344) concluded that "virtually all of Adorno's animadversions on the putative decay of experience were directly borrowed from formulae [evident in the writings of] Benjamin." The similarity I do not doubt, but this similarity should not be taken as evidence that Adorno would not have reached his conclusions but for his acquaintance with Walter Benjamin. Further, Adorno did not uncritically adopt all of Benjamin's positions; Hullot-Kentor (2006, p. 42) pointed, for example, to Adorno's implicit rejection of Benjamin's "völkish organicism." Nonetheless, the sort of ahistoricism that one reads in Adorno was abundant in Benjamin as well, in particular in his nostalgic view of his own childhood as a benchmark for loss. Jay (2005, pp. 318-319) was on target in drawing attention to Benjamin's recall of his childhood experiences of "bright colors": Benjamin seemed unaware (or at the very least neglectful) both that so many of those colors had come from recent innovations in chemistry laboratories and that, of those not recently invented, the brightest had come from painters' efforts to extract and purify dyes from parts of sea and earth that very few children had ever experienced (see, e.g., Ball 2001). There is an irony in that conjunction, of course: Benjamin's brief regarding a "crisis of experience" was centered on what he saw as excessive *multiplicity*, which in his mind had been overwhelming the integrity of a "wholeness of experience" (see Jay 2005, pp. 319-320). It was an integrity that he supposed he could still hear in communications from nature's first language, just as he had done during childhood, and he remained confident that the "uninterrupted flow of this communication runs through the whole of nature, from lowest forms of existence to man and from man to God" (Benjamin 1996 [1916], p. 74).[221]

---

Filmer's pronouncement of *The Necessity of the Absolute Power of All Kings* (1648; see, e.g., Robertson 2005).

[221] While it might be tempting to suppose that this early statement on language was later modified by Benjamin, in fact it was in large part repeated verbatim seventeen years later in "Antitheses concerning word and name."

# Part Three
## Artifices of Being

Richard Feynman (1918-1988), world-class theorist of the physical world, was well-known for promoting the vitality of education for all. One of his favorite statements was concisely to that point (if misunderstood by some as an arrogance): "What I cannot create, I do not understand." Effectiveness in doing, in *making*, what one understands cognitively is the decisive test of that understanding. This sentiment has stayed with me as also a test of education—that is, as a test of how well we make new generations of people. Of course, as the billions of infants created by human beings since the earliest of "deep time" attests, we are also capable of making outcomes without good understanding of the processes resulting in those outcomes. Too often, our skills in making have outrun our abilities of understanding, and these events, transpiring "behind the back of consciousness," have often had dire consequences. Feynman's adage is not symmetrical, for one can and sometimes does create a result that has escaped one's understanding. Numerous artists of word and image—Johann von Goethe's Faust and Mary Shelley's Doctor Frankenstein are but two popular examples—have shown testimony to that fact, recognition of which amounts to recognition that Kant's hope for species maturity and self-responsibility still has a long distance to go, assuming it survives our worst capabilities.

A popular set piece in the historiography of late eighteenth and early nineteenth-century European culture declaims a causal chain from Enlightenment to French Revolution, Terror, and a Romantic Reaction to it all. The first linkage in that chain has also lived in an adage, different from yet in a way parallel to Feynman's: "Too much knowledge is a dangerous thing." Ignorant people cannot do as much damage, both because they do not know how to achieve many effects of any new kind and because they are easier to control through manipulations of perspective, focus, and horizon. Tribal allegiances of nativity, religion, and ethnicity serve among the easiest of venues for the manipulation of emotive energies, of feeling more than of knowing, and they are to be preferred because they deflect attention away from differences in material resources of power. So long as the management is conducted with sufficient efficiency, these venues also count as less expensive of accumulated resources, insofar as the manipulation is conducted successfully in symbolic rather than material coinage.

That popular set piece is not entirely wrong or irrelevant. But it shorts understanding of component processes. Uprisings like the kind that became "the French Revolution" had occurred many times before "the Enlightenment"—not always with that degree of success, to be sure, but monarchs had been dethroned before, and peasants had previously gained benefits by uprisings. Eventual outcomes of uprisings had previously been unpleasant, to say the least, for some of those who had won but, as it turned out, only temporarily. Furthermore, the multiple persons who have been lumped together in the category, "Romantics reacting to the Enlightenment," professed diverse interests and perspectives on many issues, including benefits of predecessors who had carried the torch of enlightenment. Engell's (1981) deft treatment of such issues in our receptions of the back-to-back periods we have been in the habit of deeming Enlightenment and Romantic Reaction remains well worth a reader's attention, especially for his demonstration that people of both periods shared in the invention of a vitally important faculty of human learning, the creative imagination.[222]  It was this faculty which Feynman saluted with those words he kept on his blackboard.  Of course, human beings had been practicing creative imagination for millennia, and writers had been engaged in inquisitive as well as celebratory discourses of it for centuries at least.  But for European cultures, and European-descendant cultures across the planet, it was in conjunctures that began during the last decades of the eighteenth century and the first decade or two of the nineteenth century, partly occurrent as and from some loosening of hieratic shackles, that a newly found vibrancy of free self-imaginations stimulated thoughts of, as Kant put it, *self-legislation*.  The idea of a republic of free peoples, an idea that struggled to brief life in London during the late 1650s, had become much more widely believable by greater proportions of "the common people" in North America, in France, in some of the German states, and elsewhere.

The present Part expands on some matters discussed in the preceding Part but now cast into different focus.  In their introductory essay, perceptively entitled "The age of reflexion," Cunningham and Jardine offered the following stage setting:

> Around 1800 the self stood in unprecedentedly high esteem.  What is God?  What is man?  What is nature?  What is a work of art?  What are the sciences?  On what principles do they rest?  What are their limits?  How are they to be taught, learned, practiced?  In this 'Age of Reflexion' all these came to be perceived as questions of self-understanding (Cunningham and Jardine 1990, p. 1).

While I do not attend explicitly to all of the component questions, I do address the whole, and mainly in terms of three components:  discursive fabrics woven of self-conscious, and to some extent self-reflexive, apprehensions of powers of creative imagination; the shifting terrain on which ideas of difference and similarity between the modern sciences and the fine arts were composed and displayed, and the very influential notion that "any" individual person (though mainly if not exclusively male and bourgeois if not noble) could freely exercise powers of a self-fashioning.

This last-mentioned notion took a rather specific form for quite some time in Britain, in some of the German states, and in France (elsewhere as well—for instance, Spain—but these presentations have generally not received the same attention under the standard "Romanticism" heading; see, e.g., Peers 1949; Shaw 1963).  This form, usually termed a "Bildungsprozess," gained its most prominent display as the "Bildungsroman" or "coming-of-age novel."  As the latter concept indicates, it has usually been in the realm of literary arts—novels, poetry, and plays—that that commentaries on "Romantic reaction" have been focused, as the essays in Cunningham and Jardine's collection exemplify.[223]  While my discussion of Bildungsprozess and

---

[222] I also find the collection of essays generated for Cunningham and Jardine (1990) has retained considerable force after nearly three decades.  Two simple indicators suggest that others agree:  the book remains in print (paperback) as of January 2018, and at that same date used but good-quality copies of the hardcover were being advertised for $500 and more.

[223] The topic of "Bildung," in its various forms, spans a very large literature in German.  An excellent brief overview is still Verhaus (1972).  His many contributions remain valuable, but little has been translated into English.  A good general account in English is Bruford (1975); another is McClelland

related notions does reflect that emphasis, I also address the presence of Romanticist creativity in other realms of art, including most especially music and painting, and in that same context I address issues adumbrated in the question, What counts as Art? Finally, given the widespread conception of Romanticism as a reaction against perceived degradation and loss, I return in the last section of this Part to these perceptions and the emotive responses they generated circa 1800, and continue to generate today. It is not unusual for creative artists (and scientists) to be perched atop an ambivalence of one kind or another, and many of the Romantics shared in an ambivalence of the line between, the relation of, cognitive and emotive resources of Nature (a hypostasized conception of "the natural world." As Engell (1981, p. 83) observed, Samuel Taylor Coleridge and Friedrich von Schelling are good exemplars of the general pattern, in their contention that the true artist does not merely ape Nature's appearances or outward forms (in the older Latin vocabulary, natura naturata) but rather expresses Nature's own inward spirit (natura naturans). But the ambivalence rested on the question, Whose Nature?

Even the most severe Romanticist critic of the new modern science as embodied by Isaac Newton and his mechanical laws was necessarily paying his due to that very conception of the natural world. It simply could not be ignored even as, and precisely because, it was apprehended as grave threat to all that was virtuous and true. When an ambivalence resolves into a preferred option, a choice of one perspective over its opposing reflection, a new slate of counterfactuals is produced, at least some of which become almost automatically captivating. Cognitively, they must exist as a matter of logic within and by the selected perspective. Emotively, their opposing stance virtually ensures a negational apprehension from within the selected perspective, yet that observer can never gain first-person experience with the implied state of being, for the actual cases of the counterfactual exist only within a virtual field, a field open to "free play" of the imagination. The "missing cases" are like ornaments that attend any focal object of the selected perspective, standing outside it, not belonging to "the whole presentation of the object" as if actually constituent of it, yet nonetheless in some way deterministic of it (see Kant 1790, part 1, §14). Imaginations of degradation and loss are convenient substitutes, as they supplement the focal object as imagined experiences of its depletion or absence.[224] Nietzsche's madman parable (1974 [1887], §125) replays in nuanced ways befitting the anxieties of a time and place.

### §15. Calibrating Creative Imaginations
What are the most important qualities of a well-made self? By what ideals, by what standards, should we attempt to build, to bring up to maturity, each individual person? Such questions less baldly put were crucial topics during the period beginning about 1770 and extending far into the next century. Charles Rosen was correct in presuming, I believe, that the transition from neat

---

(1980). Part of the literature has been focused on reforms of higher education in Germany (e.g., Humboldt University, now the University of Berlin), a focus that remains central to controversies about the Bildung movement and continuing efforts to reform again the mission and organization of universities (see, e.g., Beck 2010; van Bommel 2015; Caygill 2016).

[224] Damisch's (1996 [1992], p. 213 n.28) engaging discussion of "the future of an emotion," the desire for beauty and most specifically sexual desire of bodily proportion, brings us to intimate consideration of the insoluble problem of the counterfactual, which is called up to us by our selective apprehension of empirical cases of a kind and which on inspection often multiplies beyond the number of cases initially selected, yet can ever exist only as vicarious image. We will return to these considerations below.

lines of a classical tradition to messy ambivalences and ambiguities of those whom he called "the romantic generation" was itself both a conveyance of that tradition and an inauguration of responses to it (see Rosen 1995 vis-à-vis Rosen 1971). I believe he was right, too, in seeing the response, often designated a "reaction," as to some considerable extent a not uncommon effort by a new generation of artists to fashion themselves, individually and interactively, as not just different from their predecessors but in some measure, often initially vague, better (Ross 2007; Dowd 2011). Be that as it may, those who have been named as Romantics in performance and Romanticist in theoretical perspective have generally been collectivized as "reactors." But to what?

The Romantics have sometimes been lumped together in a conception of reactivity to the Enlightenment movement, with advances in modern science during the ending decades of the eighteenth century serving as both emblem and anchor point of the oppositional stance. This view has less to do with actual events during those decades and the early decades of the next century than with a later penchant for unidimensional emphasis when describing or explaining a relatively complex phenomenon (i.e., an expectation that most of a persuasive story will hinge on clear indictment of *the* primary cause or *the* main cause of the phenomenon being considered). Impetus to a story of "reaction" to the Enlightenment generally and modern science particularly became all the stronger because of the popular reception of two literary successes of the time, Goethe's play, *Faust* (the first part of which was published in preliminary edition in 1806), and Mary Shelley's epistolary novel, *Frankenstein; or, A Modern Prometheus* (1818). The success of each work created a not-unusual division between its main *public* existence, indeliberately yet persuasively (as if a deliberate rhetorical intention of the author) reconfiguring the work, and the greater complexity of the work as composed in full by its author. This reductive process of reading certainly did not begin with Goethe or Shelley, nor did it reach its peak with either.[225] But the stamp each work made in its public's consciousness spread quickly and uniformly enough to become the work's "essence" as a tale of modern science gone awry, posing moral if not existential danger to ordinary folk. Victor Frankenstein (the name of the ambitious scientist, not of his "monster") stole a knowledge that properly belonged to the gods (as in the Greek myth of the clever titan, Prometheus—a name that translates into "forethought," and contrasted with that of his foolish brother Epimetheus, "afterthought"). Not incidentally, youthful literates in both Germany and Britain during this period were especially interested in their "Greek heritage," so to speak, learning more of the accomplishments of those long-ago personal figures of note and holding them up as accomplishments to be emulated in the new times. Thus, an interest in, even a fascination with, mythic themes of ancient Greek analogizing, including most especially the theme that exceptional artists are penalized exemplars of ambition taken too far, become hubris, translated into popular concerns about modern science. A highly accomplished mortal weaver, Arachnē, challenged Athena, goddess of crafts as well as wisdom, lost, and for her punishment was transformed into a spider. A musically accomplished satyr, Marsyas, challenged Apollo, lost, and suffered death by flaying, his skin turned into (by one version of the story) wineskin.

---

[225] Still to come, for example, Herman Melville's *Moby-Dick*, a long but simple tale, supposedly, of an old sailor's obsession with a whale, perhaps simple allegory of "man's struggle with Nature."

In the context of the time such transferences of allegorical lesson rode waves of anxiety about a new intellectual-cultural order, spearheaded by experimentalist scientists in fields of modern chemistry and physiology as well as physics. In contrast to older conceptions of science, which—to very considerable extent even after circulation of Francis Bacon's 1620 tome, *Novum Organum Scientiarum,* on the advantages of an experimentalist, skeptical attitude—featured thought processes of contemplation rather like those of theology, this new science actually did implement Bacon's recommendations, emphasizing activities designed to empower human investigations of "hidden powers," processes that had not been visible to ordinary sense. In fact, the new scientist was seen as being similar to an artist, a person who makes something new and different, an artificer (a descriptor which, as contrast to "naturalist," "Nature theory," and the like, often connoted a falseness, trickery, even Satan's deceptions). But these newly empowered magicians of laboratory work could be likened as well to images of "the Devil's workshop," and in some quarters they *were* tainted with such visions.[226] The emphasis of Kant's critical theory on liberation from chains of dogmatism and from self-imposed subservience to legislations of reality was vulnerable to the same suspicions, anxieties about perceived threats to settled ways of being and settled interests of future worth. Such reactions were undoubtedly present. Along with ancient Greek moral lessons about hubris, a correlated thematic of "fear of freedom" also gained benefit of a rejuvenation (see, e.g., Dodds 1951; Greer 1989; Hazelrigg 2014).

A persistent theme in the commentary on Romanticism as a reactive movement has been a "hostility" of attitude, discerned in (or imputed to) some principals of the movement, toward the still-recent "revolution" of modern science (which has sometimes been called its "second revolution," after the sluggish implementation of Bacon's views). The chief target of this hostile attitude—one might say its personification—was specifically Isaac Newton, not because of his mysticism or his dabblings in "the black arts" (nothing new in those) but due to accomplishments of his "analytic mechanicism" of physical process (the model of the cosmos as a "clockwork" being one of the prominent exemplars). While the chief locus of this attitude was apparently Britain, Goethe has also been cited as a representative case. By Cunningham and Jardine's account (1990, pp. 3-4), the "hostility runs deep: for the Romantics mechanistic natural philosophy is the culmination of the analytic and judgmental approach responsible for our fall from grace with nature; but their attitude was rarely one of outright rejection." They cited Goethe as a prime illustration both of the general attitude and that it was short of total rejection. If one reads pertinent literatures written at the time (late 1700s through the first decades of the 1800s), one indeed does see what could be described as evidence of "hostile" attitude. By my reading, however, some of the commentary is a bit overdone in that regard, perhaps reflecting more the

---

[226] I do not intend the use of "magician" loosely here. The difference between "science" and "magic," as a system of method, is mainly that whereas science offers a theory of how (sometimes "why") an observed outcome has occurred—i.e., a theory of the process resulting in a specified event—magic is a simple trial-and-error empiricism. Tablets of acetylsalicylic acid, marketed by Bayer as "aspirin," reliably produced desired effects magically—i.e., without a complete explanation of how the effects were achieved—for many decades until 1971, when John R Vane demonstrated the biochemical physiology (for which he was awarded a Nobel Prize).

perspectives of recent commentators (late nineteenth- and twentieth-century) than of the Romantics generally considered.

One prominent example is the oft-cited toast usually attributed to Charles Lamb: [let's drink to] "Newton's health and confusion to mathematics." Taken by Cunningham and Jardine (1990, p. 3), among others, as evidence of hostility, a different conclusion comes to mind once context of the toast has been considered. Lamb, John Keats, Leigh Hunt, and several other members of an informal group of friends had gathered for a London dinner hosted by a (then) well-known painter, Benjamin Robert Haydon. The following account, from one of Lamb's biographers, is based on memoirs of at least two of the participants, Leigh Hunt and Haydon himself (who is here the speaker, and might have been toastmaster): "Lamb,

> in a strain of humour beyond description, abused me [Haydon] for putting Newton's head in my picture—"a fellow," he said, "who believed nothing unless it was as clear as the three sides of a triangle." And then he [Lamb] and Keats agreed that he [Newton] had destroyed all the poetry of the rainbow by reducing it to the prismatic colours. It was impossible to resist him [Lamb], and we all drank "Newton's health and confusion to mathematics." It was delightful to see the good humour of Wordsworth in giving in to all the frolics without affectation and laughing as heartily as the best of us (Lucas 1907, p. 393).

Not that the toast lacked edge: after all, why toast the health of a man dead by nearly a century? Moreover, Keats had already declared against Newton's reduction of a rainbow to a prism (see below, however). But it was a frolic, as Haydon, Hunt, and others agreed after the fact. Even the often astringent, "difficult to please" Wordsworth had joined in.

As for Goethe as exemplar of the hostile attitude, I think Engell's (1981, pp. 282-285) summary fits well: Goethe generally gave emphasis to the importance of proper balance. In explicit as well as implicit ways, Goethe sought "to heal" the division between the passionate and the rational parts of imagination, a division that he and others saw as growing wider and deeper. It is probably true, as Engell (1981, p. 281) surmised, that Goethe "did not get much beyond the first part" of Kant's *Critique of Pure Reason* (the evidence being some strangely dismissive remarks about the book). But not only was that, if true, hardly unique to Goethe; it also can leave the impression that he had no interest in the issues being addressed. Powers of creative imagination, whether described as Johann Tetens' "forming and creative powers" ("ein bildende, schaffende Kraft"), Kant's "Einbildungskraft," Samuel Taylor Coleridge's "primary imagination," or in some other formulation, figured prominently across virtually all of his work, not as a passive imitation (the Latin "imitatio") but as the active, productive process of mimesis (see Derrida 1964; Engell, 1981, pp. 120-123; Gebauer and Wulf 1995 [1992]). Again, one is reminded of the words maintained on Feynman's blackboard.[227]

---

[227] Derrida (1964) explicated Kant's subtle understanding of the Greek concept of mimesis as an active, productive process (i.e., not the passive imitative copying as assumed when mimesis and imitation are identified). The process of mimesis generalizes across boundaries of "art," "polity," "economy," and so forth, not because it extends without distinction across differing objects or products but because it relates

Benjamin Haydon's description of "Lamb's toast" referred also to a line that is widely remembered of John Keats—words about the cold touch of philosophy unweaving a rainbow, as Newton's notorious prism had done. This is what Keats wrote entirely in this stanza of the last part of his narrative poem, "Lamia" (lines 229-238):

> Do not all charms fly
> At the mere touch of cold philosophy?
> There was an awful rainbow once in heaven:
> We know her woof, her texture; she is given
> In the dull catalogue of common things.
> Philosophy will clip an Angel's wings,
> Conquer all mysteries by rule and line,
> Empty the haunted air, and gnomèd mine—
> Unweave a rainbow, as it erewhile made
> The tender-person'd Lamia melt into a shade.

Notorious for its ambiguity (one of the standard criticisms), "Lamia" is by my reading another statement of caution, of the need for balance between reason and passion. Apollonius, who is the philosopher in question, warns the young man Lycius that the incomparably beautiful woman with whom he is passionately in love is in fact a serpent, recently given human form by Hermes. Lycius refuses Apollonius, who then calls Lycius a "fool," adding that "from every ill / Of life have I preserv'd thee to this day, / And shall I see thee made a serpent's prey?" (lines 296-298) Apollonius' stare removes Lamia's camouflage, for all to see her as the serpent she is. She flees. Lycius dies of heartbreak and despair. A not uncommon storyline (indeed, based on a Greek myth: the temptress and the young fool). It is a warning of balance, the golden mean in other guise. Is it also a warning of misogyny and naivete? That and more? Read into it what you will.

"Lamia" was presented in 1820, about three years after the Haydon dinner party.[228] Two years earlier Keats had presented his version of the Endymion story (another Greek myth about the struggles of love), and he began it with this well-celebrated: "A thing of beauty is a joy for ever." But lines 835-842 of the first book of this long poem tell us importantly his understanding of the whole:

> But who, of men, can tell
> That flowers would bloom, or that green fruit would swell
> To melting pulp, that fish would have bright mail,
> The earth its dower of river, wood, and vale,
> The meadows runnels, runnels pebble-stones,
> The seed its harvest, or the lute its tones,
> Tones ravishment, or ravishment its sweet,
> If human souls did never kiss and greet?

---

differing subjects, each of whom is, self-consciously or not, engaged in a process of world-making that includes self-making.

[228] Available in any standard collection of Keats (e.g., Barnard' edition of 1973). See also Dawkins (1998), for a celebration of Keats poetry in appreciation of modern science.

But for human being, what of that would *be*?

For Keats, only by apprehending the actuality of human experience in its entirety can one hope to achieve an abstracted ideal. He applied this principle in and to his own imaginative powers. I suppose one can read in some of his lines a "hostility" to science. But I do not see it, do not feel it. Engell (1981, p. 285) had it about right, I think, when he said of Keats' view that "the overwhelming concern of the modern poet was to find new ways to pry open and exploit new opportunities." No doubt some would read in Engell's words—"pry open" and "exploit"— a base expression, indicative of contamination by "mechanicism," a "hostility" to nature, Nature's world.[229] Certainly some battles were still being fought on one or another's field of "the natural," modernity's replacement for "the divine," and those battles have continued to the present day. Which nature, or whose nature, shall prevail? The large irony threading that field of battle, now ever more insistent of itself against barriers of stubborn ignorance, is that far too many human beings still reject the responsibility that comes with having been chief producer of nature for how many countless generations, while at the same time endlessly repeating a dogmatism of "the original condition." Such has been, as Cunningham and Jardine (1990) described it, a newly ordered "age of reflexion" (see Hazelrigg 1995).

The lesson of that irony should alert us to the fact that the judgment of hostility was in effect a judgment against understanding, a preference for dogmatism and for judgment from feeling rather than from understanding. Who today does not know at least some part of the new understanding that began to come together through Newton's prism? Who today does not know that rainbows exist on Earth but not on Earth's moon? And not on the dusty red plains of Mars? And why those differences. With that understanding in mind, who then does not still revel in the sheer majesty, the exquisite momentary wonderment, of gravity's latest rainbow?[230] And who could not wonder that our sky is so blue (as I have said before: Hazelrigg 2014, p. 31). While I understand the chromatic physics of Earth's atmosphere, I still (as now) look through the large window next to my seating and marvel at *how blue*, how *deep blue*, the sky above? This is not a rare experience for me. Where I live we have many days with very blue sky, sometimes spotted with white puffs floating by. And rare the day I do not feel the same elation, all over again, that the sky above can be *so* blue! I like to think that both Keats and Newton experienced the same elation, after the prism just as much as before. Indeed, even more. Because of the very same

---

[229] One of the favored jibes against Newton held that he reduced Nature to "line and angle," each of which is indeed an abstraction and therefore considered non-natural or even unnatural. As Hauser (1982 [1974], pp. 244-246) pointed out, however, the assurance of line and angle had a very long history before "Isaac Newton" was a name anyone knew as allegorical or metaphorical. Moreover, the typical ruse plays from an understanding of a division within Nature between "the natural" and "the cultural" (as in, e.g., the "duality of human nature") which implies that a part of Nature (e.g., the cultural invention of line and angle) is inferior to the whole of which it is part (another version, perhaps, of the problem of theodicy; or of the immune self that cannot reliably distinguish what it is not from what it is; see, e.g., Tauber 1994; 2013).

[230] Recall that Aristotle (*Metaphysics*, 9826b) understood "wonder" as fountain of the variety of convictions that "to know" is better than "not to know"—and in that, the beginnings, each new beginning, of philosophical inquiry into the simplest of the simple as well as the most complex of the complex and all in between.

understanding, I know that not all sighted creatures can see the sky that I see chromatically. Their chromatics are different from mine (as well as, often, from one another), and these differences are my understandings, which is to say a production of human meaning of being. This, too, is of that "age of reflexion." And Keats was right: what of any of that experience would *be*, but for the continuance of human being, one new generation after another.

Considered in that way, the discourse of Romanticism in contests of (abstract) Nature and (concrete) Culture, the creative imagination of Science vis-à-vis the creative imagination of Art, and similar correlative aspirations, reveals itself as a spawning ground of a distinctive discipline, that of hermeneutics. Granted, the advent of hermeneutics has typically been assigned to a later time, and to a tradition of Christian Biblical criticism that flourished in Germany during the latter part of the nineteenth century rather than to its opening years. I believe, however, that Friedrich Kittler (1990 [1985]), showed us keen insight when, during the itinerary of his comparative investigation of "writing down" systems, 1800 and 1900, he demonstrated earlier grounds in the Romanticist movement circa 1800.[231] Core to the "Universalitätsanspruch of hermeneutics" (i.e., the hermeneutical claim to universality across and throughout meanings as such) is its stake in determining what counts as experience. Kittler interrogated hermeneutical experience in its own terms—namely, that of a completed action of experience that had been immune to time (i.e., as if the action had transpired within an extended present, an indefinitely elastic now, an interval without history during operation of the now-completed action), the result being a consciousness of interpretive work as an objective experience (i.e., not merely my opinion or any particular actor's opinion but a stable arrangement of meanings agreed by all who have sufficiently gained experience with the language in and through which the interpretive work has occurred. One can see tendencies to that sense of an immunity even today in commentaries on "the Romantics." Rarely, for example, has anyone questioned the experience of "a discourse hostile to science" as evidently perceived in recent commentaries as anything *other than* the

---

[231] Rendered in English as *Discourse Networks 1800/1900*, Kittler's title was *Aufschreibesysteme 1800/1900*, which better reflects his emphasis on techniques of material recording. Perhaps the translators chose their title as a signal of similarity between Kittler's and Foucault's practices of genealogical inquiry, and it is indeed in that way a fitting choice. Kittler's work has nonetheless remained somewhat obscure in Anglophone readerships and has garnered only marginal attention in Germany. The editor of a posthumously published book of Kittler's essays referred to the Singularität of his work, a description that could (unlike, say, Einzigartigkeit: "uniqueness") more easily suggest notions of "oddity" and "strangeness," which arguably do capture some of the distinctiveness of Kittler's compositional style (see Kittler 2013, p. 396; see also Kittler 1986, p. 8, where he suggested an elaboration of comparison to 2000 and a third system, digitalized recording of image and sound as well as writing, a "total media pool" in which "any manipulations of the data flows such as modulation, transformation, synchronization, delay, storage, retouching, scrambling, scanning and mapping become possible." Then the boundaries separating discrete media of "truth events"—written words (graphemes), written sounds (phonograph), written light as two-dimensional still images (photograph), written light as illusion of moving images (cinematograph), and written three-dimensional images in motion (holograph)—will fade into interchangeable facets.

completed experience of a discourse obviously hostile to science enacted by, say, Charles Lamb or John Keats.

The universality claim is of course as empty as saying that "we" *cannot but* interpret (which is indeed all that the claim can say), that "we" cannot but make meaning, leaving unsaid why *these* meanings rather than the apparently-now-counterfactual meanings that were rejected, ignored, or simply never thought germane. Kittler understood this *ideology* of hermeneutics as having been forged within the ideology of Romanticism, as if in a backward-oriented recovery of Nature's spring in a distinctive "system of writing," or "discourse network," which, by its very existence, already established what could count as experience: faithfulness to Nature's wordless speech of origin, a supposed auto-affection of sheer emergence. The ideology was maintained surreptitiously in the technical means of a romanticist hermeneutics of recovery of Nature's meaningfulness from the grasp of reason's hubris.[232] While I do not believe that understandings of either the recovery effort or of that which was to be recovered were as monolithic as Kittler's account would make it, I do think he was on track.

By 1900, Kittler argued, that hermeneutical enterprise had itself been reconstituted in a different writing-down system of media, one of "technical sciences of meaning." To borrow a phrase from David Wellbery's foreword to Kittler (1990 [1985], p. x), the vaunted promise of hermeneutics to achieve Romanticism's "resuscitation of the living spirit from the tomb of the letter" was neither unprecedented nor, one might say, the last act of this morality play—except, as Kittler would insist, morality plays are no less made of, as well as in, contingencies than was hermeneutics' claim to universality or Romanticists' Nature.[233] Among his many illustrative materials for "1900," Kittler's citation of documents of Freud's practice captures well enough some of the differences vis-a-vis "1800." Because Freud had not advanced as far as media of phonography, "which with particulars like the voice or breath would have betrayed persons' identities to even the most naïve media consumers," we have only written media of "case histories," only "small, factual details" remaining as "indices." In "a strange anonymity" of those indices and pseudonyms (e.g., Rat-Man, Wolf-Man, and Anna O) Freud's "texts develop neither imaginative images nor novels of *Bildung*—none of the representations of man in the Spirit of 1800" (Kittler 1990 [1985], p. 287). Experiences, and what counted as *an* experience, had changed.

Condensation of complex relations into stock imaging on a principal theme of "reaction," with emphasis on emotive perceptions of degradation and loss, is perhaps a cultural or "macro-level" aggregation in time, analogous to the pruning, realigning, and compaction that takes place in and as memory of first-person experiences. As a matter of professional-disciplinary comity, we assign to historians the task of ferreting through the traces left behind as some sort of evidence

---

[232] Among Kittler's many illustrations, there is this: Goethe's Dr. Faust, having concluded to leave the Republic of Scholars, explains by "saying (in words) that he cannot possibly value words or even (as the secret eavesdropper of this private conversation will paraphrase it [line 1328 of *Faust*, Part One]) 'thinks the word so beggarly'" (Kittler 1990 [1985], p. 9).
[233] Thus, e.g., a meaning separating Mary Shelley's "extraordinarily silly" book (as it has been evaluated more than once) from Johann von Goethe's "classic treatment" of a major figure of allegory (as has generally been said of it): some works must be more contingent than others.

of the macro-level processes of condensation. A technique of "close reading," guided by an analytical or dialectical logic of conceptual relations, is often the only toolkit available, and it, too, is sometimes subject to alterations deliberate or surreptitious or both. All the more valuable, then, when we have the gift of a close reader whose skill yields a reading of new meanings out of materials that have been read over and over to mostly the same effect.

Here I am referring to the report by Gerald Izenberg (1992) of "impossible individuality" as it flowed from the creative imaginations of four prominent figures of Romanticism (Friedrich Schleiermacher, Friedrich von Schlegel, Wordsworth, and François-René de Chateaubriand—all excepting Wordsworth largely neglected by Engell) as a basically psychologistic production of self-identity. Izenberg demonstrated by way of his careful readings of these four figures that the standard account of "Romantic reaction" is biased by selection of evidence and, though to less extent, by misprision in the French sense of "historical misunderstanding" via insensitivity to context, whether by design of preferred ideological stance or by simple ignorance. Elsewhere (Hazelrigg 2014) I offered in brief compass another illustrative case, that of Friedrich Hölderlin. Here I will add still another, works by Goethe, to those which Izenberg (1992) assembled in greater detail.[234] The Goethe case is interesting in several ways, one of the most important for present purposes being that he was active in both the arts and the sciences of his day. Engell (1981, p. 283) brought attention to the Romanticist concern that it is through artistic imagination that humans can actually see the articulations of subject/object relations, although the resulting experiences can be emotionally unbridled and spill into the fantastical, stoking envy for what is not yet and might never be (cf. Hauser 1982 [1974], pp. 417-426). But of course the same appraisal and expectation can be made of the exercises of scientific imagination. In fact, it is apparent that some of the Romanticist-inclined critics implicitly did just that, but gave the result a negational qualification. Goethe's case is interesting in part because he made good effort to span that difference of valuation, although his effort was impeded by the fact that some of his understandings were soon exceeded by advances especially of physical science.

Goethe's long adulthood—born in 1749, he died in 1832—spanned an equally long list of developments in European artistic and scientific creativity, several of them connected with his personal interests. Early in his adult life he gained much fame for his partly autobiographical Bildungsroman, *The Sorrows of the Young Werther*. Toward the end of his years he displayed some sentiments of a once-famous man who now felt that he had been left behind, that life's developments had moved far beyond him. This contrast makes the case interesting from a perspective more general than his own particular trajectory of lifework, the perspective formed at juncture of a specific biography and its context of larger history. If it is difficult to separate the two trajectories, biographic and historic-period, in retrospect—and it often is very difficult— the intimate mixture of both in a first-person "lived experience" can be no less difficult for the person whose experience it has been to partial it into "my part" vis-à-vis "the rest." In retrospect

---

[234] Izenberg (1992) gave us close readings densely packed in a single volume. I am here supplementing with brief readings of two works by Goethe, relying in addition on Nicholas Boyle's (2000) second volume, 800 pages devoted to fourteen years of Goethe's life and work, an extraordinary landmark in the practice of biography within historical context. See also Ziolkowski (1990) regarding Goethe's interests in medicine and madness.

it is tempting to confuse the tableaux of this or that "past time," condensed into seemingly "epic" or "dramatic" (or simply legendary) history, as the facticity of quotidian experiences of day-to-day life as it was then being lived. It is easy to find sympathy for ancestors whose thoughts could have been expressed as Feynman's dictum in reverse: How could I possibly understand what I could not even begin to make? For example, how does one make this gas called "Sauerstoff," identified during the 1770s by Carl Wilhelm Scheele and Joseph Priestley (separately, at about the same time)?[235] Remember, while there were suspicions as early as the mid-1600s that plants might give off some kind of vapor, it was not until work by Scheele and by Priestley that those suspicions became reasonably solid evidence, and it was not until 1804 that Nicolas-Théodore de Saussure contrived an explanation of the basic process of phytochemistry in plants (and not until 1931 that Cornelius van Niel gave a reasonably good near-complete explanation of the chemistry of photosynthesis). This is merely one example of the long list of developments in the modern sciences of physics, chemistry, and geology during the half-dozen decades centered on 1800. Because many of those developments are at best only dimly understood by most people today, one is inclined to wonder what sense the average European adult made of any of them two centuries ago. No wonder, one might think, that he or she simply felt overwhelmed and left behind. But perhaps the response of the typical adult to a latest announcement of this or that discovery or invention was then, as today, a mixture of puzzlement, excitement, and perhaps pride (if so, probably nationalistic), followed by return to the usual quotidian concerns of day-to-day life.

In January 1797 Goethe, not yet 50, a highly successful writer, and far more of a celebrity than he had wished to be, began regular maintenance of a diary.[236] His ambition was to create a new symbolism, one that would be, as Boyle (2000, pp. 546, 545) has said of it, "not private but public, the objective meaning of personal experience," an effort to reconcile "the poetic ideal with a bourgeois reality." After decades of some of the most remarkable personal experience, he had come to the view that "symbolically significant things bridge the divide between subject and object." This conviction had to come to terms with Kant's critical theory. Phenomenally, object and subject are inherently related via human activity, in Kant's terms "legislative" activity most of all. If there was a divide that needed bridging, it presupposed a knowability of that which Kant had said was beyond the limit of human knowledge: in other words, "object" was being identified with "noumena" (not an unusual conflation, as repeatedly noted in previous Parts). During this period (the last years of the century), as Boyle noted, "the true nature of Kant's achievement was ignored"—by many if not by all—and Goethe found comfort in those blinders. He had understood Kant's theory well enough to chafe against the notion that noumenal Nature is beyond human experience (i.e., human empirics). If Kant's transcendental Illusion and its trail of "as if" objective necessity offers only a comforting illusion wrapped within a tale of disillusionment (the Enlightenment), surely one would be right to insist on something more and better. Thus, one could easily conclude that Goethe had grown into a determined stance of

---

[235] Sauerstoff: better known in the Anglophone world by Lavoisier's nomination, "oxygen" (the Greek "oxys," or "sharp" as in acidic sour, + the Greek "genes," or "begetter").

[236] This is not to say that he took no pleasure in fame; to the contrary. But "celebrity" had its costs then, too.

reaction to, even rejection of, the bounties being offered, and still newer ones being promised, by this new science. The "Goethe story" is far from that simple, however.

What Pierre Bourdieu said of Édouard Manet could be applied to Goethe, too, allowing suitably the difference of time and place:

> Now that we have punctured the heroic vision according to which the heresiarch was solely responsible for his heresy, we must not forget to focus on the heresiarch himself. We must bring Manet back into our analysis not because he was a socially undetermined genius, but because he was an agent who was actively involved in the game and who possessed properties which could be effective in the field (Bourdieu 2017 [2013], p. 291).

The "field" in which Goethe operated, in some ways his own attempted creation as Manet's was his, spanned a much greater range of activities than did Manet's, a Frenchman born the year the southwestern German died, 1832. Whereas Manet's "revolution" (in Bourdieu's accolade) did involve a considerable break from the Impressionist movement to which some commentators have assigned him (Manet clearly did turn away from the sequence of efforts to incorporate some details of scientific understanding into painterly perspective—indeed, even turning away from the by-then standard techniques of creating a three-dimensional scene on a flat surface),[237] Goethe's project as of the early 1800s was, as already suggested, built in accordance with his aim to bridge an expanding gap, recently noticed with alarm, between Art and Science. Having established his reputation as a critically (as well as financially) successful literary artist (novelist, playwright, poet), Goethe entered administrative service to the Duke of Saxe-Weimar, cooperated with Alexander von Humboldt in designing a new model of higher education, expanded his interests, theoretical and practical, in new sciences—adding a treatise on color to his earlier works in the morphology of plants and animals and in the geology of minerals—and resumed work on his version of the Faustus legend, which he had begun during the early 1770s, an allegorical study of the risks and rewards increasingly available from mental exertions and bargains laid well into future times, all via seemingly heroic individualistic assertions at moral junctures of artistic craft and scientific knowledge.[238]

As intended design of his own personal project of Bildungsprozess, the bundle of often, and increasingly, conflictive, inconsistent, and sometimes contradictory forces stands out in our advantage of retrospect as a recipe for personal disaster. As the years passed, Goethe himself caught sight of some of the indications. His treatise on color, published in 1810, proved to have

---

[237] One useful way in which to appreciate Manet's project is as rejection of efforts (e.g., techniques of perspective) of painting to camouflage the fact that a painter works on a two-dimensional surface. He sought to restore the dignity, one could say, of painting as work on a (more or less) flat surface, just as light works on the more or less flat surface of the retina, the brain then learning via bodily signals to see depth.

[238] The *Faust* play (or plays; the two parts are very different) is today no doubt the work for which Goethe is most often remembered. But it was not his only play. For example, *Iphigenia in Taurus*, his version of Euripides' story of Iphigenia, was first performed in prose in 1779, then transformed to verse in 1786.

been misbegotten. Although earlier scholars (e.g., Aristotle) had been aware that visible light had something to do with color (e.g., colors diminished after dusk), it was apparently not until Newton's studies of optics that a systematic treatment of chromatics was designed. Goethe's treatise, attacking Newton's approach as destructive of the phenomenon of color, offered what was intended as a scientific work of the physiology of color. In that frame it was ill-conceived (and largely neglected at the time), even though much of it could have been (and is now) better regarded had it been presented as a study in psychological effects (see Sepper 1988). Indeed, one can see Wittgenstein's (1977) point when he later concluded that Goethe's work was not as much a theory as a description of color perception. Curiously, phenomena of color remain still today a topic of controversy, in particular with regard to consequences of Kant. An example can be read in Gabriel (2015 [2013], p. 189): "Color, which was despised and denounced during the modern scientific revolution as an illusion created by our senses, becomes the very medium through which the meaning of art is articulated." This is akin to declaring that the fact that I am supported by the chair on which I presently sit is an illusion to be despised and denounced, since physicists all agree that it is composed mostly of empty space (likewise, the birdsongs that I hear, for they are nothing more than my eardrums vibrating to waves in the atmosphere; and so forth). Color is a function not only of my sensory apparatus, my brain, and my memory of culturally variant classifications by which specific frequency ranges are named, with some gradations more finely hewn than others; it is also a function of properties of the surfaces of concrete objects (all of which are as real as a promissory note, an oxidized iron bolt, or a cheerful greeting (and more or less as suffused with meaning), properties with which electromagnetic radiation interacts in specific ways to which human sight is sensitive or, in some instances, properties which are themselves emissions of electron excitation.

Goethe would have been somewhat ahead of his time, had he formulated his treatise in those terms. But his rejection of Newton's analytical approach was not about physics nearly so much as it was about protecting an experience of human appreciation. For all his powers of creative imagination, Goethe evidently could not find in the Newtonian approach, by the early 1800s more than a century old and widely accepted, any possibility of comfort for his own aim of demonstrating a scientific prowess that simultaneously upheld artistic valuations. Granted, some of the new sciences, physics especially, had been changing their understandings of basic processes rather quickly, and that pace of change had already been one of the stimulants to some of the Romanticists, as was noted above. Attempting to keep his feet in both worlds, Goethe's situation would be problematic, to say the least. Recall that at the start of his project of critical theory, Kant had found both inspiration and challenge in Newton's great accomplishment. As the first volume of his critiques was appearing in print in 1781, Johann Georg Hamann said of it in a letter to Johann Gottfried Herder that the volume might well be considered by a different title. Hamann did not suggest something on the order of "Understanding Newtonian Physics." His suggestion was, rather, "Sancho Panza's transcendental philosophy."[239]

---

[239] Hamann's letter of 15 September 1781, as quoted in Stuckenberg (1882, p. 463 n.114; and p. 268, quoting Hamann in the same letter, that Kant's book "in the end all tends to sophistry and empty verbiage"). Hamann, born twelve years before Kant, has been described as Kant's oldest friend, but in the German context I am not confident that "Freund" is the appropriate word; "Bekannte" (acquaintance)

As has been said before, sometimes new understandings percolate very slowly, or only in starts and fits.

The allegory that is *Faust* can be, like the allegory that is Marsyas (for instance), worked with little effort into testament to any one of a number of various moral lessons. Is the Horatian admonition adopted by Kant—"Sapere Aude" ("Dare to Know")—another of the many instances of the proverbial "ticket to Hell," or is it a "ticket to Heaven"? If the former, is it a train with no exit? Does the admonition itself come with an insurance policy ("Double your money back, if dissatisfied")? Is the passage a certain one, or is it a matter of chances; and if the latter, can one know in advance how to calculate the odds with good assurance? And then the question of authority: if a gamble, and a gamble decided either by imposition from above or by some sort of elective process, may I opt out if I disagree? Or, if initially I go along with my compatriots, can I opt out if the gamble begins to sour? In short, then, in what precisely—and stably—does "the moral lesson" consist? Goethe's play is as complex as we let it be.

Then, too, in 1809 Goethe published his third novel, *Elective Affinities*. (The English title is an exact translation of the German, *Die Wahlverwandtschaften*.) Long awaited as his next new novel, many readers found it confusing in its point, some even wondering if it *had* a point. It did have a point but not one that was congenial to expectations of a new story by the author of *The Sorrows of Young Werther*, Goethe's first novel and great commercial success. In the storyline, as in the title, Goethe explored an analogy between the new world of chemistry and the heritage of human relations, intimate relations as in marriage most especially. Chemists were beginning to understand bondings in the processes of aggregation by which chemical elements or simpler compounds form more complex compounds as if the elemental or simpler compounds selectively chose the "mates" with which they would form bonds. In retrospect, we see in this the usual sort of interchange or analogy by which humans seek new understandings in one domain by testing the explanatory utility of an understanding that has seemingly worked well in a different but in some sense analogous domain. Chemists had been likening chemical bonding to the elections made by men and women in their choices of friends or acquaintances. This notion of election, it is worth noting, fits well with the Kantian emphasis on human liberty to legislate. At some level, even though particular criteria probably differ, some sort of matching process in terms of criteria of compatibility could be seen at work in the domain of chemical bonds as in the domain of human bonds. Goethe simply turned the analogy around, using the process of "elective affinity" among chemicals as a metaphor for choices that humans make in intimate relationships. The effect was not well received, by and large. It was as if Goethe had reduced the supreme intimacy of marital choice and sustenance to a crass process, one that could be enacted perfectly well by inanimate substances, substances far removed from any capacity of soulfulness. Even skeptics of the hallowed idea of "holy matrimony" believed this to be impertinent, offensive to human dignity.

---

probably gives the more accurate description. Herder, a protégé of Hamann and an early influence on Goethe (who was younger by five years), became initially a partly sympathetic interpreter of Kant but soon shifted to an increasingly strident criticism, probably fueled by his belief that Kant was atheistic. Stuckenberg's biography, although obviously dated with regard to scholarship, remains a useful source.

Trying hard to stay abreast of major changes of his world, Goethe had concluded well before his day was done that the world was perilously close to escaping human intentionality, understanding, and control. His was not a new thought, to be sure. Many French men and women had come to a similar state of despair and renunciation of events of their recent past, because of the Terror that had followed 1789. Goethe had become sympathetic to that view. Many English men and women had experienced similar bouts of regret and recrimination by the end of the 1650s. There had been similar sequences well before that, and in other places, too. But a feeling of "this time is different" could point to several factors as supporting evidence in 1800. The rate of the pace of change was increasing, and this fact of *acceleration* was being noticed as never before. The fact of change was nothing new, although for most persons it had been measured in generations. An understanding that the *rate of change* was *itself* changing was something new to almost everyone. It was disconcerting, for many reasons, but most pointedly because it raised a question that seemed unpleasantly prophetic: how much more acceleration could human beings endure? What kinds of "new persons" did we have to become? What would that mean for the dignity, and the pleasures, of human life? The Romantic movement had hardly begun; was it now to cease?

The melancholy that afflicted Goethe's later years, and that attends a large portion of the "histories and commentaries" written about the movement, is but one side of the story, however. Whereas the verbal arts, including philosophy as well as prosaic writing and parts of poetry, displayed major sentiments of loss and displaced hopes, music, other parts of poetic expression, most of painting, and mathematics did not, or did not with such atmosphere. If the years Rosen (1995) designated "The Romantic Generation" in music (1827-50) exhibited a reactivity, it was far less about any perception of loss or threats by modern science and far more about the usual problem of young composers seeking ways to be stylistically distinctive relative to their famous predecessors. These concerns could not be divorced from potentially contrary receptions by audiences, which had become larger and a much greater factor in risks to livelihood, as their influence in the growing commercialization of musical performance demanded consideration. Musical composition had, like philosophical thought, long faced the dilemma that some ideas resist full empirical realization. A central dimension of music, the dialectic of audible/inaudible, posed a continuing challenge to composers in their relationship with potential audiences. As Rosen (1995, p. 3) reminded at his outset, "not everything in music can be heard." A composer seeking distinctive style must carry an audience through trials of re-education, successfully or disastrously, as compositional explorations are being conducted. Versions of John Cage roamed concert halls long before John Cage was born.

In wake of his conversations with the energetically ambitious Alexander von Humboldt, Goethe slowing realized that his polymathic intentions would not bear the expected fruit. That day was passing: polymaths would continue to appear, but more and more rarely. It was this understanding that furthered a movement to reform education, a movement in which another member of the von Humboldt family, Alexander's older brother Wilhelm, would be instrumental during the early 1800s. The impulse of Bildungsprozess animated the ideal goal.[240] But means

---

[240] At the beginning of the second chapter of Wilhelm von Humboldt's most noted work on limits and duties of the state (which, completed in 1792, was widely circulated before formal publication), the

to its attainment had necessarily changed, reformers believed, chiefly because of the growing power of modern science and its applications in everyday life. The classical curriculum should make room for several new fields of instruction, as the phrase "wissenschaftliche Bildung" ("scientific education") was announcing. The debate remains active to the present day, to be sure. And not only Germany was its venue during the early decades of the nineteenth century, although reforms were most successfully undertaken there. In England, where Coleridge, credited together with Wordsworth for bringing the Romanticist movement to Britain, was friend to fellow poet and very productive chemist, Humphrey Davy, exemplified the "elective affinity," one might say, between the new scientist as artist and the poetic artist intent on capturing as near as possible the mysteries of first-person experience on printed, sometimes illustrated, pages. The ambitions contained in those friendships in England did not, however, significantly alter standard courses in education. As one result, Charles Percy Snow, Leicester man, novelist, chemist, and civil servant, was comparatively well disposed by upbringing, and then by his own multiple careers, to warn as late as the 1960s of the problem—more, the danger—of an educational process so sharply divided between two intellectual cultures, the science and the humanities.

### §16. Building First-Person Character, Person by Person

One interest that many of the men and women later grouped as "the Romantics" did hold in common in general terms was education, in the literal sense of up-bringing or "bringing a child up to a preferred maturity." In the most general terms of that phrase, this was hardly an interest unique to these men and women in particular (although the visible presence of women in the movement—Mary Wollstonecraft and her daughter Mary, Dorothy Wordsworth, and a few others—was unusual). But these men and women stand out collectively to us—I shall continue to refer to them collectively as "the Romantics," for want of a better name—because of qualities of their written work and, to an extent, the ways in which they lived their lives. Predominantly but far from exclusively British and German, they did share interests in educational process, interests that combined classical and modern visions of the proper process of up-bringing or, as the German language expressed it, Bildungsprozess ("Bildung," from "Bild," a portmanteau of meanings).[241] Images of "ideal" when thinking of the desired product of the process varied across the several persons as well as between the two cultures.[242] But it would not be far off the mark, should a manageable synopsis of meaning be wanted, to imagine a conflation of "up-bringing," "character formation," and "cultivation." The pragmatic meaning of "training" can also be included, but in the sense of "training to high accomplishment as, say, pianist or playwright, *and*

---

author declared his commitment to cultivation of the whole person, his basic premise being that the highest end of humanity is the highest and most harmonious development of a person's powers in "perfect individuality." While there is no doubt that Wilhelm von Humboldt played an important role in the early reforms of education in Germany (memorialized in 1949 by renaming the University of Berlin as Humboldt University; then in 2012 as the Humboldt University of Berlin), his name gained mythic standing of rather inflated importance, as recent critical reviews have pointed out (see, e.g., Herrmann 2000; Hammerstein and Herrmann 2005; van Bommel 2015).

[241] "Bild" can be equivalent to "picture," "image," "representation," "simile," and "metaphor," among other words in English. More expansively, "Bildung" includes "education" and "training"; also "cultivation"; plus "formation," "development," "generation," and still others.

[242] This phrase, too, "the two cultures," is a shorthand that ignores significant cultural differences among the German states—this is circa 1800, remember—and among regions of Britain.

in the commensurate sense of "training toward perfection in a specific craft" (e.g., architect, furniture maker).

The notion of "self as personal project" was not newly invented by the Romantics, to be sure. It had been alive within part of Christian culture, as evidenced by Paul's letters to Romans and to Corinthians (c53-59), by passages of Plotinus' *Six Enneads* (c270), and later by Augustine's *Soliloquies* (c387) in which the two parts of his explicitly divided self argue about the proper way of being.[243] Peter Brown (1995, p. 68) has pointed out that "late antique hagiography" faced the important and difficult task of trying "to bring order to a supernatural world shot through with ambiguity, characterized by uncertainty as to the meaning of so many manifestations of the holy, and, as a result, inhabited by religious entrepreneurs of all faiths." This implies contests, which means negotiations within distributions of power among those entrepreneurs, power not only of overt intolerances mutually displayed and enacted but also the tacit dimensions of power, Brown's "gentle violence," which could swing the balance beam of judgment so subtly as not to be noticed by a person wracked with confusions and self-doubt.[244] Colonizing the minds of those who felt themselves to be "lost and confused" achieved the aim of settling authority on a supernatural anchor within the mind, which would then serve as agent to public leadership. As recently demonstrated in the USA, sowing confusion and suspicion remains a tactic of demagoguery, seemingly never left wanting of a gullible public.

Processes and events that we remember as Europe's twelfth-century renaissance, centered on some consolidation of partially secularized state functions, a recovery of city life and long-distance trading (enabling expansion and specialization in local markets), and inventions of what became the modern university, also opened spaces for growth of the *professions liberals*, which entailed indirectly secularizing and individualist interests in self-cultivation (see, e.g., Haskins 1927; Curtius 1953). Our record of pertinent evidence is spotty during subsequent decades until we come to the sixteenth century and figures such as Machiavelli, Montaigne, Cervantes, Bruno, and Shakespeare. Machiavelli's frustration with the Medici yoke, displayed in the composition of his *Florentine Histories* (1988 [1532]), manifested the occluding force of "livelihood by princely commission," on which his own self-cultivated republican mentality was intellectually as well as materially dependent. Later in the century Montaigne, self-sustaining by inheritance, boldly expressed his claim by insisting as motto a phrase borrowed from Horace: Sapere aude. Dare to know.[245] Even so, he practiced the versatilities of ambiguity, by which he

---

[243] Plotinus' *Enneads*, compiled in six books by one of his students, Porphyry, are so named because each book is divided into nine parts (Latin, from the Greek ennéa, "nine"). Scholars of neo-Platonist thought, and of Augustine, have generally considered Plotinus' work to have been a major influence on Augustine.

[244] As Brown was well aware, some of the confusions immanent to those contests among entrepreneurs of thought have been repeated endlessly, at least to the present day—as in, for example, contrasts of "power" and "validity" in which the latter term is qualified not as a claim but as a pure condition, free of power (see, e.g., Allen 2016).

[245] The advice is given in the second letter of Horace's *Epistles*, Book One: Dimidium facti qui coepit habet: sapere aude. ("He who has made the beginning has half the deed done: dare to know.") Just prior to that line Horace had lamented the prevalence of lassitude and ignorance. Striking a similar stance in his answer to the question, "What is Enlightenment?" (1991 [1784b]), Kant lamented the "self-

could express his deepest doubts openly yet indirectly.[246]   And the more Montaigne pondered relationships, the more *everything* seemed doubtable.  The main implication of this unending reach of doubt, Montaigne concluded, is the need of decision.  His conclusion was short of Kant's thesis of self-legislation, but only just (in an abstract logical sense, if not in a full-bodied cultural sense).  As exemplified at length in his essay, "Apology for Raymond Sebond," Montaigne produced exercises of active, thoughtful reading for readers of his essays.  The French penchant for argument by indirection attained a very fine point in Montaigne's pen.

As for Cervantes and Shakespeare, Carlos Fuentes captured a portion of the spirit that is relevant here:

> Cervantes leaves open the pages of a book where the reader knows himself to be read and the author knows himself to be written and it is said that he dies on the same date, though not on the same day, as William Shakespeare.  It is further stated that perhaps both were the same man.  Cervantes' debts and battles and prisons were fictions that permitted him to disguise himself as Shakespeare and write his plays in England, while the comedian Will Shaksper, the man with a thousand faces, the Elizabethan Lon Chaney, wrote *Don Quixote* in Spain....
>
> But ..., if not the same *person*, maybe they are the same writer, the same author of all the books, a wandering polyglot polygraphist named, according to the whims of the times, Homer, Vergil, Dante, Cide Hamete Benengeli, Cervantes, Shakespeare, Sterne, Defoe, Goethe, Poe, Dickens, Balzac, Lewis Carroll, Proust, Kafka, Borges, Pierre Ménard, James Joyce ...   He is the author of the same *open book* which, like the autobiography of Ginés de Pasamonte, is not yet finished because our lives are not yet over (Fuentes 1988, pp. 69-70).

One need not subscribe to all of Harold Bloom's thesis to see that Shakespeare, like Cervantes, championed a calculating liberty to the aim of fashioning who one is to be, or not to be, in the midst of forces little understood.  The theatrical Bloom may have exaggerated but was not importantly wrong to see in Shakespeare's Hamlet a prototype of "the modern individual," moorings sufficiently loosened to be allowed, but also in a sense required, to consider alternative ways of being "what I shall become" (Bloom 1998; see also Wilson 2008).[247]

Projects of self-fashioning in the generalized sense that has been deployed in the prior paragraphs—that is, a sense that a person can assume responsibility for self-education and in that responsibility make selections among available options, sometime amending the options or even producing new ones—continued through the next centuries.  In some of the manifestations one can see what could be called a prototype of "performance art" (e.g., in the sense of a deliberate experimentation or "trial run" of one or another presentation of self).  Means and meanings, costs and benefits, and orientations to past times, futures past, and anticipations of what the present

---

incurred immaturity," the typical servility, that so widely characterized adults, urging adoption of "Sapere aude" as key impulse, the self-starting impulse, of enlightenment.

[246] This is the thinking Montaigne (1533-1592), not yet that of the generation of Descartes (1596-1650).

[247] In later context I will add to this dyad, Cervantes and Shakespeare, a third luminary, Tang.

will mean had been changing, however, and continued to change, as gradations of comfort with the process shifted within practical designs of custom and morality. Different conceptions of time were bound up, consistently or not, in the processes that produced those changes, and in our various retrospects it is extremely difficult to make consistent sortings among the productive relations. For instance, the reader may have noticed in the second of the two paragraphs extracted from Fuentes' memoir a line that could be bent to the kind of conception associated typically with Newton's view (regardless the doubt he might have expressed, as noted in the previous Part): time as an absolute eternal container of all possibility. Did Fuentes mean to say that there is only one master story of the human condition, many songs sung but all to a single rhythm that is time itself? And would that count as an ethnographic counterpart to the transcendentalist aim of Kant's critical theory? More generally, we must contend with the influence of biography or "life writing," which interacts with "history writing" in various ways (e.g., as Holmes [2016, p. 286 has said, challenging or reconstituting context and conditions of the person being written).

By the middle of the eighteenth century the romance of Cervantes' famous knight had been transformed into a supposedly more realistic style of writing "character" (i.e., "character formation"). In Germany, as previously noted, this would be remembered under the heading, "Bildungsprozess," or plotted styles of "becoming who one will be"—imaginal "types," one might say, available to youth as they contemplated alternative future selves; templates offered in a novelistic manner of what otherwise could be called a morality play.

A major conduction in the relation of Romanticism with its cultural context, including the then-current conceptions and evaluations of phenomena later collected as "the Enlightenment,"[248] developed during the eighteenth century as a notion of Bildungsprozess: the course of a youth's character formation within and partially against the dominant values of the youth's sociocultural context. We remember explicit treatment of this course of character formation largely because of a literary form, the Bildungsroman. As the naming convention indicates, both the notion of a general process and the type of novel arose as a self-consciousness of event in German lands—Christoph Wieland's *History of Agathon* (1767) together with Goethe's *The Sorrows of Young Werther* (1774) and his *Wilhelm Meister's Apprenticeship* (1795-96) being the widely agreed forerunners. In retrospect, however, one can see much of the literary form in earlier works, such as Henry Fielding's *Tom Jones* (1749), Laurence Sterne's *Tristram Shandy* (1759), and Voltaire's *Candide* (1759)—arguably in works earlier still.[249] The

---

[248] Whereas we remember "the Enlightenment" as that definite article suggests, there was much disagreement during the eighteenth century about component processes and issues of what later was collected as a unified, or at least a single coherent movement. When Kant's essay, "Answer to the Question, What Is Enlightenment?" was published in the first volume of the *Berlin Monthly*, a magazine giving outlet to members of the Berlin Wednesday Society, the word, "Aufklärung," was already in circulation, but it meant different things to the magazine's readership, and Kant was intent on promoting his conception. It is significant that he began his essay with a general diagnosis, that most adults remained in a self-incurred immaturity or tutelage, waiting for someone to tell him or her what to know, what to do, and not, as Kant urged, taking charge of his or her own mental life.

[249] It should be evident by now that my interest is not in the game of arguing "first origins"; I am merely citing here the prevailing convention of lists. Moreover, the general form of Bildungsroman has not been eclipsed. As cases in point, Alfred Döblin's *Berlin Alexanderplatz* (2018 [1929]) was long touted (by

convention can be defined more or less narrowly. I take the core of it to be "character formation," while the chief interest of the discourse in that process was to question, often indirectly and partly implicitly, prevailing understandings within and of the dominant pattern of values, as these became manifest in tensions between the central consciousness (and conscience) as it developed in the course of the novel and the societal context and conditions of that development.[250] From the standpoint of the character under formation there is, typically, an ambivalence to be negotiated—on the one hand, recognition of the need to find one's proper place in society while, on the other, determination to claim the distinctive honor of *oneself* and to be acknowledged for it, a distinction of self as the unique integrity of being a unity of *one*, distinguished from every other. The literary form is noted also for featuring an ambiguous ending: the observing reader is denied the anonymous narrator's trick of privileged invasion of the privacy of mind—that is, the first-person experience, the register of feeling even more than that of knowing, of the character who is now formed into adulthood. This feature has been visualized with great effect by Caspar David Friedrich in his most famous paintings, his subjects shown from behind—one in the case of *Wanderer above the Sea of Fog* (1818), three in *Chalk Cliffs on Rügen* (1818)—as an inwardness gazing out across a large open vista, toward a distant horizon. What is the character feeling, and thinking, in and of the gaze? Friedrich has denied his viewers even the hints of facial messaging. One of the three in *Chalk Cliffs* is on hands and knees, his top hat tumbled to the side: is he prayerful, or has he lost something? Perhaps a touch of vertigo? Who knows? And more especially that famous *Wanderer*: standing erect with walking stick in hand on the ledge of his promontory, back to the viewer: is he aghast at the vastness before him, or is he intimidated? Is his pose magisterial, or challenged, or maybe simply nonchalant, toward the great expanse that he surveys? Read into his stance, in that place, what you will.

There is an irony here: Kant, often named as one of the "Enlightenment philosophers" most anathematic to the Romanticists, both argued for an educational process keyed to a value rationality of ends and asserted that human being is legislator: the "categorical imperative"—that one ought to act as a virtual, with intent of actuality, legislator (i.e., "Act only according to that maxim whereby you can, at the same time, will that it should become a universal law")—is a major admonition to "build character," to cultivate one's self, to live life as an exemplar.

One may recall from standard histories of the time that many scholars who had been interested in both the promises and the dangers of the French Revolution soon found themselves mired in revulsion by the Terror following 1789 (see, e.g., Burke 1910 [1790]; Chateaubriand 2018 [1849-50]). Some responded with opportunity. Friedrich Schiller, for instance, sought a method of building a more compassionately effective social being through a dialectic of the opposition he read in Kant (and elsewhere) between what he regarded as the necessary material

---

Walter Benjamin, among other) as a Bildungsroman of the early twentieth century; Hermann Hesse, *The Glass Bead Game* (1969 [1943] followed, while W S Merwin's *The Mays of Ventadorn* (2002) has been called a Bildungsroman of the early twenty-first century (and for good reason; see Mlinko 2017).

[250] Another interesting test case occurred during the time of Laurence Sterne's satirical forays, also in Hanoverian England—namely, the experiments in "masculine design" that reached a peak during the 1760s and 1780s in several deliberately contrived explorations of gender-bending costumery, cosmetics, and arts of coiffure, celebrated in pomp and circumstance as "macaroni style" (see, e.g., McNeil 2018; McCormack 2015).

forces of nature, embodied in "the sensuous drive," and the ideational forces of freedom, honed in conceptual formalities ("the formal drive"), which aspire to a moral unity. As he saw the basis of this project, a human being "as a moral being, ...

> cannot possibly rest satisfied with a political condition forced upon him by necessity [of nature], and only calculated for that condition; and it would be unfortunate if this did satisfy him. In many cases man shakes off this blind law of necessity, by his free spontaneous action, of which among many others we have an instance, in his ennobling by beauty and suppressing by moral influence the powerful impulse implanted in him by nature in the passion of love. Thus, when arrived at maturity, he recovers his childhood by an artificial process, he founds a state of nature in his ideas, not given him by any experience but established by the necessary laws and conditions of his reason, and he attributes to this ideal condition an object, an aim, of which he was not cognisant in the actual reality of nature. He gives himself a choice of which he was not capable before, and sets to work just as if he were beginning anew, and were exchanging his original state of bondage for one of complete independence, doing this with complete insight and of his free decision (Schiller 1954 [1794], I.3).

This new capability, this new work "as if [the person] were beginning anew," amounts to a cultivation of a newly self-fashioned and self-fashioning "play drive" (*Spieltrieb*), created in dialectical unification of the merely formal drive and the merely sensuous drive, surmounting each as it was. How exactly that creative process is itself created and, in process, comes to its fruition as a new person was left in suitably murky imagery. Schiller was quite aware that one must somehow negotiate an internally contradictory process: "when the reason suppresses the natural condition [of "natural man"], as she must if she wishes to substitute her own, she weighs the real physical man against the problematical moral man" yet to be formed; that is, reason "weighs the existence of society against a possible, though morally necessary, ideal of society." But before a person has even the "opportunity to hold firm ... with his will" to the law of moral man, "reason would have withdrawn from his feet the ladder of nature." Furthermore, Schiller was quite aware that this contradictoriness existed as both condition and context to any person's Bildungsprozess, one's own great act of self-fashioning, and as condition to the aggregational process by which an actual society would surmount itself toward realization of that "ideal of society." In summary of the "great point" that he sought to make, Schiller wrote of the need "to reconcile ... two considerations": one must "prevent physical society from ceasing for a moment in time"—as if one could—even as "the moral society is being formed in the idea." We may be sure that this reconciliation demands a certain delicacy of process, which Schiller illustrated by reference to a "mechanic [who] has to mend a watch" and, in order to do so, "lets the wheels" cease operation. By contrast, "the living watchworks" of society must be "repaired while they act, and a wheel has to be exchanged for another during its revolutions" (Schiller 1954 [1794], I.3).

The set of problems with which Schiller was grappling, ranging in scale from the tasks of a person's upbringing to the tasks of rebuilding Theseus' ship as it sails, remains wholly with us.

In following sections I will continue to address the problems, in various aspects and by different perspectives. When we come to the later sections, we will encounter a sage Jürgen Habermas still grappling after more than half a century, still leaning into strong winds and still professing Kant's hope for species maturity and responsibility. Much has changed during the two centuries since Kant, Schiller, and their contemporaries. Little if any of that change has made the problems easier of solution. Some considerable fraction of the change has obscured them, to the point of pushing them toward an oblivion of consciousness. One wonders, for instance, what Schiller's prognosis would be, were he to succeed, as in Benjamin Franklin's wish, to visit us after these two centuries and have the benefit of various object lessons of self-fashioning (one hesitates to dress it now with the name Bildungsprozess), compliments of our entertainment industry. Of the many instances from which to choose an exemplar of our time, perhaps he would select David Bowie, "a man caught in the midst of a psychodrama (his own) that became a public spectacle" (Doggett, 2012, pp. 15-16), creating value for himself of himself, first as one, then as another near-avatar, via and for the mass-consumer business of musical visual-aural performance, while living through a partly fluid, partly fragmented self-image in search of valorizing responses to the sequence of "play-driven" beings by its own fandom. Some of us today think the "event" of David Bowie (among similar others, such as Donald Trump) was/is perfectly ordinary. Others of us think that, if ordinary (and the evidence is massive), we ought not to be happy about the fact. What would Schiller think, should he be walking among us to see, after two hundred years, "how things turned out"?

Romanticism attempted an analogous re-settlement within a European culture that, by long tradition Christian, had repeatedly witnessed religious wars and dissensions, both with its sister "religion of the book," Islam, and with its parentage in Judaism, as well as internally in numerous sectarian fissures; and long before 1800 it had been facing claims on public authority from secularizing, individualizing, and democratizing forces of a *personalized* reason within and among self-legislating subjects via their own inventions of instruments of power. The potency of this revolution of mind gained attention initially through some of its applications as materialized reason—mechanical means of harnessing vast stores of energy (steam, coal, wind), for instance, which enabled and increasingly required new, denser organizations of human labor and direction. Already, however, those activists of the mind whom we call "the Romantics" were deliberately undertaking another program of colonization of the mind, this one partly conceived in corrective reaction to those rapid advancements in the dense organization of power. While they still often spoke the vocabulary of "soul," their reactivity was *not*, by and large, an effort to return to some golden age of past times. Goethe can be taken as an exemplar of this alternative orientation to making "future times": his resuscitation of the legend of Dr. Faustus, a strong cautionary tale about roads foreseeable, and his troubled admirations as expressed in *Elective Affinities*, lived in conjunction with the interests of a man who debated whether it is better to know how to read the signals of "predestined affinities," or to have the greater freedom that comes with lack of those skills.[251]

---

[251] Once again it is noteworthy that European aristocracy shared with ancient Chinese texts a sort of devotion to "yuan," a sense of "predestined affinity" as in a kind of bond linking past, present, and future

It has surely been apparent in foregoing paragraphs that questions of value lay at heart of the discourse of Bildungsprozess. Temptation to ill or coarse manner, sloth, idleness, cold disdain, betrayal, profligacy, belligerence, or another morally repugnant attitude could never be banished from the developmental process; and that was part of the key lesson of the story: it was always a matter of personal choice in the work and substance of one's character, and society always offered an array of choices, which were presented (mostly implicitly) as if on a gradient of qualities that marked differences of quantity along some master dimension of moral being: from the Summum Bonum, the greatest good, the supreme virtue, to the Summum Malum, the greatest evil, the supreme vice. In the same year that Caspar David Friedrich painted his *Wanderer*, his near contemporary, Carl Friedrich Gauss, used the method of least squares as a theory and technique for regularizing measurement error in his surveys, a regularization today remembered as the Gaussian ("normal") distribution.[252] This model offered a grid on which an idea as old as Plato's pharmakon and Aristotle's golden mean could be located: what in one measure will kill in another measure will cure; some water is vital, too much will asphyxiate. Extraordinarily powerful and useful when appropriately applied, Gauss' model can also invite one to align qualities that seem to reflect a single underlying gradient of quantities as a "normal" distribution. Thus: moral qualities of character as positive quantities of "goodness" or negative quantities of "badness," the opposing poles of a moral dimension. Some philosophers or historians of morality have objected, on the ground that, as Neiman (2002, p. 287) put it, "Evil is not merely the opposite of good but inimical to it."

Inimical, yes, but also intimately connected. If Hitler is held up as emblematic of the first step on a road to the evil of genocide via their destruction of at least six million Jews, could not one also, in the same manner, hold up as an exemplar of the first step on the road to the good of averting the evil of a nuclear holocaust, with hundreds of millions of fatalities, the Russian Lieutenant Colonel Stanislav Yevgrafovich Petrov? For, on 26 September 1983, Petrov ignored signals from the USSR's early warning system that multiple missiles were coming from US bases, because he did not believe the signals, did not believe that the USA would launch such an attack. Is it of interest that whereas so many people recognize the name "Hitler," hardy anyone recognizes the name "Petrov" or his deed? Petrov himself, in fact, pushed away recognition (was "encouraged" to do so), saying that he was "only doing my job."[253] Is that ironic?

---

(genealogy, ancestry, etc.) of familial affiliation that supersedes tribalism (see Elvin 1997, pp. 20, 23, e.g., on "the Confucian domain").

[252] More than a century after Goethe's epistolary novel, *The Sorrows of the Young Werther* (1784), Karl Pearson, best-known today as a statistician and methodologist, composed his first book (under a pseudonym, Loki, at age 23, slightly younger than Goethe's age in 1784), *The New Werther* (1880). Early in the sequence he enthused to his young lady friend the rapture of studying *everything*, all to the good for his character and the world (pp. 6-7).

[253] For the rest of the story, see Downing 2018, pp. 195-198, 253-254. Forty-four days after Petrov's wisdom, Russian authorities, now convinced that a secret US missile attack was imminent, ordered their arsenal to red alert. Lt General Leonard Perroots, a US intelligence officer, noticed the indications and, (mis)reading them, did not recommend that US forces go to red alert or undertake any adjustment of posture; this, too, very likely saved us from nuclear destruction (see also Plokhy 2018).

What is missing from the gradient, what the gradient cannot convey, is the intimacy that unites those two poles, hidden in the mean or median cast as merely a mid-point marker on the line, as the most "popular" position in the distribution of probabilities. The primary and main focus of the discourse of Bildungsprozess, like that of most of our discussions of morality, is on goodness, not on evil, on the gradient as a gradient of goodness, not as a gradient of evil. We resist the dialectic, the unity of opposites. While we can be, often are, fascinated by evil—and, as noted previously (Hazelrigg 2014, pp. 27-28), tend to have more words at hand as degrees or dimensions of negative emotions than of positive emotions—we prefer the good but often treat it as ordinary enough that we barely notice its presence, while we seek to protect, isolate, good from evil, as if there could ever not be a circuit of exchange between them. This tendency, one should recall, was noticed by Goethe, regarded by many as the greatest of the Bildungsroman authors. It was Heinrich Faust, not Wilhelm Meister, however, who, seeking to gain ever greater good for humankind, bargained his soul with Mephistopheles.[254] One could conclude that the good in exchange was the scientist's vainglorious desire, nothing more; thus, a lesser evil for a greater evil. But the story works far more tellingly as the soul of merely one human being in exchange for great good benefiting all humankind.

While the "problem of evil" was not an invention of Goethe's time or place, it gained much gravity of consideration within the context of Bildungsprozess, because of the additional primacy of responsibility assigned to the individual person. This was not at the expense of positively valued traditions, of course, but in conjunction with them, as if, at least for the most vital of those traditions, there could be no conflict, much less contradiction. As the weight of responsibility for the individual person grew, however, it became more difficult to rely on any leavening by the grace of tradition. In part, this was due to the weakening taken-for-granted standing of religious tradition, vis-à-vis emphasis on the importance of skepticism implied by encouragements for the individual person to "think for oneself," to decide for oneself "who one shall become in relation to the world." Even if the traditional "problem of theodicy"—how to answer the contradiction of an all-knowing, all-powerful, ever-present God who permits so much evil to visit even the most devout of persons—had lost some of its luster as religious tradition became less automatic and necessary, the problem of evil not only remained to be assayed; it also felt far more burdensome: without the handy crutch of God, each person alone was vulnerable to a sense of being trapped in a first-person feeling of an "unbearable lightness of being." Perhaps nothing really mattered as effective counterpoint to the great burden of personal responsibility in the midst of so much temptation to evil.[255]

---

[254] *Faust, Part One*, a variant of the prototype of tragedy, was begun before *Wilhelm Meister* (1795-96) and was first published in 1790 (the last edition, in 1828-29).

[255] Neiman's (2002) "alternative history of philosophy" offers a highly intelligent reading of varied aspects of the problem of evil in Western thought from the eighteenth to the twentieth century— intelligent despite but also because of the fact of her own religious belief. In a related vein, her later (2014) study of cultures of infantilization, beginning with the notion of "coming of age" as a problem generated within and from the Enlightenment period of European thought, offers keen insights. Her reference to infantilization is not confined to nor even primarily about recent trends but addresses movements beginning with the *Sturm und Drang* movement of the 1770s, which focused on celebrating an exuberance of emotive life in the increasing liberalization of individual subjectivity, especially among

That the discourse of Bildungsprozess came undone becomes evident when one follows the evolution of the Bildungsroman. What had been a pronounced tendency to a heroism of the individual directing his (usually his) own self-project of character formation dissolved into a model of complicity, the individual person's struggle to uphold some premise of a voluntarism against the growing, seemingly relentless pressures of modern life, as these pressures molded aspirations and expectations in multiple, often ambiguous and sometimes ambivalent ways. In the meantime even as the length of a generation shrank, the gap between succeeding generations lengthened, as Mannheim (1952 [1927]) among other observers noticed,[256] and the Bildungsroman shifted into a plethora of "coming of age" stories that were often less projective than reactive and reductive. By the middle of the twentieth century countless youth were seeking understanding of how they had become who they were, and countless parents seeking corresponding answers about their own children, in the mirrors offered by the latest renditions of what, in each storyline, was a merger of commercial value and literary reflection of authorial experience (see, e.g., Moretti and Sbragia 1987; Moran 2015; Strawson 2015).

As Moretti and Sbragia (2000, p. 229) summarized in their update, for European youth it was collectively "the youth of 1919" who marked a profound generational change in the dialectic of inscription/erasure by which a life's story is produced as palimpsest. For youth of the USA this came more than a generation later—not on the heels of a second world war, the vast destruction of life that had preceded and then accompanied it, but in the shattering "coming of age" that took place first in the mud of Korea and then in the jungles of southeast Asia. Whether earlier or later in worlds of that century, it was the sheer immensity of destruction, virtually incomprehensible in each of its moments of realization, that made "coming of age" in Europe and then the USA something like a mockery of Immanuel Kant's hope for an eventual maturity of the species *Homo sapiens*. Is this what reason is finally about? Is this what happens, when

---

youth, and which is sometimes viewed as a forerunner of the Romanticist movement. For a relevant point of comparison, see Hall's (1904) once commanding text on *Adolescence*. Hall, convinced in the priority of instinct, understood liberalization of the individual person to be antithetical to nature, thus conflicting with and impeding the "natural course of maturation."

[256] The gap between parents and their sons (mainly) who fought "the Great War" was surely the greatest generational gap in then recorded European history, and it figured in much of the literature that immediately followed that devastation (e.g., in the Waugh family; see Waugh 2004). For an extraordinary account of impacts, Paul Fussell (1975) is unsurpassed. Generational transactions during the hundred years from 1750 had been momentous, no doubt. But the standards thus set failed the test of incomprehension which so many fathers passed so easily as they trotted their sons off to the great slaughterhouse of "honor and duty" from 1914 onward. Public consciousness had indeed been changing, and unusually rapidly, during the prior century, generating new expectations of adult interests and capabilities most especially among inhabitants of the cities. However, the fact that the Great War was soon marked in consciousness as a "loss of innocence" tells us more than even the most gifted of the post-war writers could have imagined. Of more recent times, Paul Taylor (2014, p. 29) has told us from his analyses of demographic, political, economic, and other characteristics, that "the [US] generations are more different from each other now than at any time in living memory." That temporal frame might have been loosely intended; but Taylor, born in 1949, probably would have remembered grandparents who had direct or indirect memories that included the generation of Fussell or perhaps Evelyn Waugh. The most distinctive of the recent U.S. generations, as shown by Taylor's analyses, were the so-called Millennials, persons born during the 1981-1996 period.

all is said and done, by the power of human judgment? And then came the doctrine of MAD, "mutually assured destruction": would Kant have understood any of this?

Nietzsche wrote the most biting account of the failure of Bildungsprozess, declaring that its most notable accomplishment was a proliferation of a new type of philistine. At one time the name of an entire people (by one account, anyone not identified as a member of the ancient Israelites), the word "philistine" had become a term of specific derogation by the seventeenth century in England and in Germany, meaning an uncouth person, one who does not appreciate artistic or intellectually "refined" value. In one of his "Gentle Reminder" poems, Goethe asked, "What is a Philistine?" and answered, "A hollow gut, / Stuffed with fears and hopes" (see, e.g., Morgan 1958, p. 378). By that day the epithet was being applied broadly to bourgeois persons as a type, those who elevated material wealth over artistic or intellectual values, a preference that implied moral hypocrisy. This was meant to be consistent with the interest in recovering ancient Greek intellectual morality, such as had been part of the "battle of the books" contests between "ancients and moderns" (see Curtius, 1953; Arnold 1869; Morley 2009).

Tamsin Shaw, rescuing Nietzsche from his worst tendencies and thereby demonstrating the consistent diagnosis and (partly implicit) prognosis of European cultures that follow from Nietzsche's skeptical critique, contributed an especially timely inquiry into the late nineteenth-century awareness of and responses to the problem of "intellectual authority," as she put it, most especially the thusly motivated proposals to achieve transformation of "human consciousness without first requiring a transformation of society" (Shaw 2007, p. 40). Nietzsche himself was complicit in that sort of hieratic view of "what must be done," mainly during the period of his enamored response to Richard Wagner's heroic musical alchemy, but he later concluded in the futility of an alliance of philosophy and art as aesthetic shepherd of a process of reforming human consciousness. This personal conclusion did not, of course, end all notion that only leadership by an intellectual elite could generate the necessary reconstitution of human consciousness around some mythic core of secular culture (witness the late twentieth-century "royalist-bureaucratic" project of achieving unification across multiple national-cultural societies of Europe without engaging in the slower and much harder work of building more finely granular social processes as substance and support).[257] In the end, before the silence of paresis won, Nietzsche was "troubled," as Shaw observed,

> by the fact that in the absence of an egalitarian account of our rational capacities, such as Kant's, we cannot assume that there will be any way of making the legitimate insights of philosophers available to all. Every area of philosophy would have to yield a categorical imperative in order for us to have equality before the laws of reason. Our most complex forms of justification would have to be reducible to simple, useable principles, which were themselves uncontroversially valid. And philosophy by its very

---

[257] Taubman (2017) has now offered an excellent illustration of the recurring temptation. Mikhail Gorbachev was often criticized for "failure" to take central and eastern European countries by the hand, post-1989, and lead them through the challenges of reform and reconstitution. Gorbachev rightly insisted that each of the national peoples must take responsibility for their own destiny.

nature deals with the nonobvious, the controversial, the outer limits of our comprehension of rational justification (Shaw 2007, pp. 57-58).

One suspects that Goethe (as well as Hölderlin) caught sight of the dilemma at or near the beginning of the century. Boyle (2000, vol. 2, pp. 780-784) considerately chose Goethe's play, *The Natural Daughter*, as index of the aesthetics of political consciousness ten years after July 1789: "Unknown to me," says Eugenia, "are the powers that made my misery." Obviously the optimism of Kant's essay *On Perpetual Peace* (1795), with its prescription to continue pursuit of the republican cause against the dogmatism of monarchal paternalism, had evaporated. First performed only months before Kant's death in 1804, *The Natural Daughter* was an exercise in nostalgia, no doubt, and in that it exemplifies a general tendency, not unique to Goethe's time by any measure, to cast a premise as its own conclusion. Nevertheless, the effect was to admonish viewers not to neglect the sort of cautionary tale told in Kant's metaphor of human being as crooked timber. Whereas the dogmatisms that had ruled advertised themselves as the truth of divine provenance, the "crooked timber" metaphor urged caution because human intentions were alone never enough and resulting actions would often be clumsy at best and sometimes horribly perverse. Naked of the supposed protection of divine oversight, responsibilities would always rest with the human actors, however sagacious or ignorant they might be, and for Kant that lesson of responsibility was itself integral to a principle of hope.

The prevailing message of Goethe's play, as of other of his late works and those of other figures of the Romanticist movement, extended far onto futures now past. Indeed, Boyle (2000, p. 780) concluded that audiences today easily recognize that message as pertinent to their own experiences, for those "powers" (die Mächte) of which Eugenia spoke ultimately "are unknown to us too, though we have a little more insight into the immediate agencies." The play's characters, and we too, become "two-faced—or inconsistent, as mere psychology would put it—only under the impact of the political engine and sometimes ... against their will. Integrity of character is impossible in a modern politicized world, for the source of what one is and does lies outside one, in some unknown and inaccessible centre of power."

Thus, the "problem of aggregation" (as it has sometimes been named): seen there mainly in its top-down direction of hierarchical manifestation, it was being rehearsed by Goethe's players, and by Boyle's, in virtually standardized scripts of anguish and heartbreak over so many "lost hopes." We today know it well. The script has not changed all that much, and we repeat the lines from memory. But technologies have greatly magnified the "powers" of Eugenia's day. And their effects, which may now be outrunning our collective intelligence.

Two centuries ago, as the notion of a "science of society" was gestating, primarily in France and in, for example, the writings of Claude-Henri de Rouvroy, comte de Saint-Simon, memories of the Terror and of Napoleon's empire were still fresh enough that a "precautionary reasoning" recommended various "institutional orders" as martingales on the emotional excesses to which individuals were increasingly prone, as forces of industrial production loosened the bondages of tradition. Well-known examples of such diagnoses and recommendations include not only Saint-Simon's *Mémoires* (still counted among the Grand écrivains de la France) but also his secretary August Comte's *Course in Positive Philosophy* (1830-42) and Alexis de

Tocqueville's *Democracy in America* (1835, 1840 [2004]). The sort of naïve realism of Comte's optimism of a "positive philosophy," it bears noting, was tempered by provisions of his "religion of humanity" in concert with his "queen science," sociology. Locutions such as "the rabble" would eventually be replaced, it is true, by slightly less condescending nominations ("the masses" and "mass society" having prevailed a century later), but underlying concerns about the wellsprings of emotive as well as cognitive energy coalesced by processes of aggregation (e.g., "the crowd," "mass psychology," "social movements," "riots" rather than "rebellions," and so forth) remained much the same, or at times sharply intensified. Comte thought it wise to educate the common people in a dogma of humanistic religion, in order to create compatible resources of a pacifier in public as well as domestic arenas. Lest we become agog that anyone could believe such stupefying cynicism might be effective in the cynic's preferred way, we need only recall the process and outcome of the US presidential campaign of 2016. By the same token, one should recall the words of a president of the French republic (and an accomplished student of recent literatures of philosophy), who put the point this way in answer to the question, "Is democracy necessarily deceptive?"

> Democracy always has a form of incompleteness, because it is not self-sufficient. There is an absentee in the democratic process and in its functioning. In French politics, this absence is the figure of the King, which I think fundamentally the French people did not want to abolish. The Terror has dug an emotional, imaginal, collective vacuum: the King is no longer there! Attempts were subsequently made to place other figures in this vacuum. These were in particular the Napoleonic and the Gaullist moments. The rest of the time French democracy has failed to fill that space. We can see this with the permanent questioning of the presidential figure since the departure of General de Gaulle. After him, the normalized presidential figure of an empty seat has returned to the heart of political life. All that is expected of the President of the Republic is only that he should occupy this empty seat. Everything has been built on this misunderstanding (Macron 2015).

Macron was addressing a question that has come to be identified in some literatures of the social sciences as Durkheimian (even though it is much older): how should hierarchy from apex (state, monarch, God) to general base (citizens, subjects, believing flock) be mediated? The question has to do with "the problem of aggregation," with the added assumptions that more than one solution is possible and, perhaps, that choice among options could be made by legislation. A mostly implicit response to the question is addressed in the next section.

### §17. What Is It about Art?

The question is, what is it about *art* that encourages us to think that, because of the power of artistic imagination, we can understand the articulation of subject/object relations with a degree of insight that the power of scientific imagination, or any other sort of imagination, does not offer? Why do we find pertinence as well as distinction in the idea that it is "the overwhelming concern of the modern poet," but perhaps not of the modern scientist, "to find new ways" of generating "new opportunities" and putting them to work? (Engell 1981, pp. 283, 285). What is it about art that prompted us to assign soterial powers to it, as Arthur Danto (e.g., 1997) said, and that induces in us the concern that, but for art, how would we go about "sustaining loss"? (see

207

Horowitz 2001; also Hauser 1982 [1974], pp. 702-761). Rather, is it an endless loop within the perceptual (i.e., aesthetic) compass of an enculturated species who individually must sustain loss until not, aggregated to the collective emission of what Claude Lévi-Strauss (1963 [1958], p. 260), recalling Bernhard Karlgren's image of "the formal survival of a decadent or terminated social order," called "its dying echo"? As one follows Ben Hutchinson's (2016) useful tour of a popular "lateness" motif in European literature, various waystations of Euro-American writing pop into mind, too, and a voice of distant explorations connects with Paul Veyne's (1988 [1983]) signposts of beliefs that are not simply believed but believed *in*. And then a realization returns to one's memory—namely, that already I have been shown that a map can be greater, more as well as less detailed, than the terrain to which it refers: "Myth is an intermediary entity between a statistical aggregate of molecules and the molecular structure itself" (Lévi-Strauss (1963 [1958], pp. 226-227). Yes, an "entity"; but in the way that both an event and a flow are, each, an entity.

Issues involved in the latter questions and an ensuing discourse about human needs and functions of art form much of the motivation to the discussions that follow. Before proceeding, however, a digression must be tolerated, simply because the first response to my initial question (What is it about art?) points to another: "*which* art?" Burt (1991, p. 3) was incorrect only by underestimation, I think, in saying that "the most consequential decisions in much [most, maybe all] of social science research [or any other empirical inquiry] involve assigning units of analysis"—that is, decisions about classification and measurement. The definition of "art," and ensuing typologies of "art," surely must rank high in the list of decisions about proper unit of analysis.

According to standard English dictionaries, the word "art" means, first, "skill acquired by experience, education, or observation" and, second, "a branch of learning." Derived from the Latin "ars"—which in turn derives from the Greek "árti" (the temporal adverb "just," as in "just now," whether of present or of aoristic past time)—the Latin word meant "skill" or "craft" or "power." These designations were and are extensive. So, too, the general term "art" covered much ground in English usage (as did its cognates in other European languages), according to standard histories of the concept, until the seventeenth century, at which time specifications were added as "types" of art and as a hierarchy across those types.

A general overview of "European art" (including European-descendant cultures of the Americas and Oceana) is enough to suggest the existence of hierarchical biases. Most basic of these, no doubt, is an intellectualist bias of "head over hand" in the work of production. By the time members of our species decided to name us "Homo sapiens" (or "Homo sapiens sapiens") that trench had been dug to a music supposedly engrained in the very fabric of time, all future generations eagerly trundling down the path in search of food and security but also the origin of "intellect," perhaps wondering, now and then, "What is the point of being able to ask questions that we cannot answer?" Or—though this addition is often missing—"… answers that satisfy us once and for all?"

One of the earliest of those frustrated questions was apparently in reference to regular experiences of what must have been a mystery, the mystery of fertility. Consider as illustrative evidence the several carvings known as "Venus figurines." Among the most famous is the one known as Venus of Willendorf. About 28,000 years old, by best estimate, it is far from being among the earliest artifacts of human "culture" (a word much newer than "nature," at least in Greek and Latin as well as in Romance and Germanic languages).[258] Carved of a sedimentary limestone rock composed of smaller egg-like balls (hence, the name "oolithic") and tinted with a red ochre, it (along with some of the related figurines) has attracted far more attention than, say, a typical Oldowan chipper or scraper, even though these latter stone items are about two million years old. Why the difference? An "obvious" answer is that the latter are ordinary and plentiful instances of manual tools, interesting mainly because of their age as evidence of tool-making hominids, whereas the figurines are considered very early examples of art; plus, whereas we are confident that we know all of the meaning of the stone tools (they are "simply tools," and as such simply "craftwork"), the "artworks" invite continuing speculation as to meaning (were they testimonials to feminine fertility pure and simple, or are they evidence of an eroticism, maybe pornography, treatments of "women as sex objects"?). Quantity might play some part, too: old "tools" (though not necessarily of one specific site and age, as with the Oldowan tools) are considered more common, and not especially intellectual, because more numerous. But in fact there was very considerable art at work in and among the different tool-making techniques. Try making an Acheulean axe head (300 thousand years old). Or a lithic burin, which was used to carve bone or wood—some of the results of which are today typically considered works of art, whereas the burin itself is not.

Sociological histories of art or the arts or particular arts, meaning in each collection "fine arts" or something approximating that elastic notion, have usually been less than popular among artists themselves—indeed, among some social scientists as well—for being "reductionist" or "too reductionist." The designation generally means that a sociological history gives too much weight, too much attention, to conditioning and contextual factors that are considered by artists as non-intrinsic to the art or arts themselves. By contrast, a preferable account would feature mainly or exclusively intrinsic factors of influence, motivation, technical development—that is, factors mostly or wholly internal to an art in "artistic self-conception" or to "artistic expression" in general.[259] Favored artistic self-conceptions and/or self-expressions include, for instance, an art's own traditions: schools, epigone, revolts or revolutions, styles and innovations of technique, many of the factors focused in a psychology of artistic perception, motivation, and sensitivity of performance, sometimes couched in a psychology or mysticism of genius.[260] One should not be

---

[258] In Latin, from "colere," meaning "to tend, cultivate"; not until the early 1500s did "cultivation" expand to include "mind" (etc.) along with "soil," "plants," etc., as objects of cultivation. In ancient Greek as well, "kalliergeia" referred only to "cultivation" of soil and the like. In German common usage "Züchtung" ("breeding') initially referred to selective cultivation of plants and animals before being extended to human manners, and "Kultur" is an even more recent addition than its appearance ("culture") in Middle English.

[259] Bourdieu's (1996 [1992], pp. 113-140) description of a tendency to insularity that can result from self-reflexivity, which applies about as well to the sciences as to the arts, offers good insight into processes of identity formation as those processes may unfold outside (thus perhaps less routinely) the constraints of institutionalized channels (see also White 1992).

[260] Much the same has applied as well to sociological histories of philosophy (e.g., Collins 1998) and to particular social sciences, sociology included. The intrinsic/extrinsic dialectic is usually at issue in one

surprised to read that when the discipline in question is understood from within as a primarily if not exclusively "intellectual" or "cognitive and emotive" or "artistic" discipline, members of the discipline might be inclined to charge "reductionism" against a history that gives "too much" weight to "material" rather than "ideal" factors.

Arnold Hauser's (1982 [1974]) sociological history of art is a case in point. Now rather dated relative to sequences of contribution to particular research topics but nonetheless replete with good insights and summaries, this is history with a largely conventional sociological set of categories and themes—plus, some would say, an ideological cast that favors "material" factors as basic and "ideal" factors as supported by and reflective of that base.[261] In any case, Hauser did usefully distill his own and others' investigations as accumulated over many decades into several coherent vignettes of "the arts" in parts and as a whole, informed by a sociological perspective I consider utterly conventional of the discipline's mainstream. Consider, for example, this passage about Europe's fifteenth-century Renaissance:

At the time of the Renaissance the artist had, for thousands of years, been performing essentially practical tasks; he had helped support life and had helped communicate with good and evil spirits as an intercessor at religious ceremonials and divine services. He had served society as prophet and seer, eulogist and propagandist, teacher and educator, entertainer and master of ceremonies. Now, after formulating and sublimating the scientific, moral, and aesthetic ideals of the ruling classes, the Church, and the elite, he becomes fully conscious of his own subjectivity and, no matter what tasks he may undertake, never loses sight of it again. It is not the consciousness of subjectivity which is new—this was always surfacing from time to time with varying intensity; what is new is the consistent pursuit of it, the intensification of subjectivity as a sense and a value in itself. True, the change is not completed in an instant. Medieval traditionalism, which opposes subjectivity just as obstinately as it does rationalism, endures for a long time and only finally breaks down, in a manner conclusive for the history of style, with the development of mannerism. The Renaissance does, however, mark the beginning of the process, and the special situation, till then unprecedented, in which the artist now finds himself is in no way more significantly expressed than in his loyalty to both the past and

---

way or another in these, too. For example, the historian must try to evaluate variables of quality in a manner that practitioners of the examined discipline will recognize as relevant and astute; but the recognition can itself easily be overtly or covertly a statement of preference for intrinsic grounds of evaluation. If one has written a sociological history of, say, the cultivation of peas, a champion pea-grower might well complain of the history that its author did not sufficiently grasp all of the important differences among peas or among techniques of cultivation. As with any such contest, it is incumbent upon the reader to become well enough educated in such matters to be able to exercise judgment of the claims—sometimes a very tall order.

[261] I hesitate to call the ideological cast "Marxian," which is probably the likeliest attribution made by critics of the book; for that would be to misjudge the book (which, ideologically, is closer to a Weberian liberalism that takes economic formations as fundamental) and to add to the trivialization of Marx' contribution to theory (about which, see Hazelrigg 1989b; 1993b; 1995).

the present, tradition and initiative, freely selected forms and imposed forms (Hauser 1982 [1974], p. 279).[262]

The process in question was a reformation of the substance and significance of human society. The whole of society had been subordinate to, dominated by, *one* of its institutions, the Church (and, in idealist terms, a master consciousness of a theology of divinity). The events celebrated as "the Renaissance" marked an advancing transition from a theistic conception of "culture" to a humanistic conception—culture as a product of human activity (especially "soulful" activity), rather than as something humans were given by divine authority.

One of the signal characteristics of that process was a memory of European precedence: the ancient Greeks had left surviving traces of an earlier emancipation of "art" from "religion," dating roughly from the Ionian ascendancy, the artifacts demonstrating a degree of individual "free expression"—that is, not happenstance variations but determinate stylistic character that can be associated with a particular (though unnamed) person. Moreover, evidence from about the same time is indicative of a correlative emancipation of what should count as demonstrable knowledge rather than mere opinion, an empirical standard that invoked pragmatic means of "trial and error" searches for general principles of "process and reality" (i.e., some variable blend of inductive and abductive reasoning). By the same token, the "free expression" that remains visible to us in some of its effects was highly limited: "With the exception of Euripides and the Sophists all the poets and thinkers of the fourth and fifth centuries [BCE; i.e., one to two centuries after the earliest evidence of emancipation] support the interests of the aristocracy and of reaction" (Hauser 1982 [1974], p. 259).

As more recent backdrop to Europe's Renaissance, numerous historians in addition to Hauser have built broadly similar accounts of formal education during the medieval periods, such as it was. Aside from monasteries and courts, hardly any existed beyond parent-to-child transfers across generations. Most attention has been given to the so-called seven liberal arts: the trivium, composed of grammar, rhetoric, and logic; the quadrivium, composed of arithmetic, geometry, astrology, and music. The Latin "liber" ("free") referred to the very small fraction of an area's population who were (at least mostly) free of the requirements of daily sustenance (which is to say, "free" only by rough approximation to today's sense of discretionary or "free time"). What is just as obvious but less often explicitly remarked is a set of absences from that curriculum of the "threefold path" (i.e., the trivium) and of the fourfold path (quadrivium): no instructive discourses on painting or sculpting, the two "fine arts" that became so visible and famed during the 1400s and after. One could argue that instruction in some basics of drawing, architecture, and civil or mechanical engineering was available under the heading of geometry; likewise, elements of written composition within the bounds of the trivium, and of poetry there as well but also under "music" in the quadrivium. However, "musical art" was to a large extent an address

---

[262] That was composed as part of a long chapter entitled "Art as a Product of Society," which was followed by a short chapter entitled "Society as the Product of Art"—both preceded by a short essay on interactive and dialectical relations, useful especially for being comparatively rare by sociologist authorship.

of metrics, following from the ancient Greek tradition of "learners" ("mathematikoi") who benefited from "mousikē paideia" as "hearers" ("akousmatikoi").[263]

One lesson to add to that brief piece of potted history is that hieratic order predated the advent of Christianity; indeed, while the word and concept (in narrow sense) are from the ancient Greek—from "hierasthai" ("to be a priest"; "hiereus" being "priest" in the sense of one who intercedes with the gods)—hieratic scale is much older, found in ancient Egyptian art forms, for instance, as well as in ancient Greek art forms and, at least as prominently, in Christian art forms. As for these last, painting was not prominent among Christianity's art forms for some time. But Hauser's (1982 [1974], p. 265) comment is probably on target: "The oldest Church fathers may still have regarded [pictorial artists such as the catacomb painters, dating from the second century] as makers of idols"; if so, however, these artists "were soon numbered among the Christian apologists and pillars of the Church." It was a matter, one might say, of adapting new technology in prosthesis to ends of the faith.

Thus, while Renaissance artists developed a "humanistic conception of culture," it carried the old principle of exclusion: "a cultural elite" from whom the great majority of people, peasant or city-dweller, were "to be excluded as a matter of principle" (Hauser 1982 [1974], p. 283). A hierarchy of earthly order, reflecting divine order, reflected itself in a hierarchy of artistic activity both as expression and as appreciation: "high culture," "fine art," and so forth. After having won a degree of emancipation "from the Church and the guild," dominant medieval institutions of rightful order, artists set about making themselves "intellectual wards of the humanists" in exchange for subsidy both material and ideal. It was a new "community of interests" now built of bourgeois patrons and market-oriented aristocrats, organized around the same hierarchical principle and in reflection cultivating an increasingly unified hierarchical conception of "Art," with the newly blossoming forms, painting and sculpture, at top. This rebirth of artistic valuation now learned from Christianity the importance of monopoly as well as hierarchy, becoming the monopolizing arbiter of "taste" and "manners" in the making of a proper member of modern society—which was to say, a proper bourgeois as well as a proper aristocrat (or noble). Properly decorated bodies, as in costumery and ceremony, took the lead—hence, painting and sculpture, portraits and busts. Excepting ecclesiastical and courtly documents, literary arts developed more slowly, one notable consequence of the lag being that literary forms

---

[263] During the fifth century (BCE) mousikē (from which, "muse" and "the muses" as well as "music") was virtually tantamount to our meaning of "culture" in the sense of "high culture." Pythagoreanism placed central emphasis on a teaching of the significance of numbers, and in that sense held that fundamentally reality is mathematical. Similar if less mystical tenets were held in other schools of thought as well, and in this generality a concept of mousikē formed the core of a new theory and practice of paideia—or childhood upbringing, understood as the ideal of enculturation to "kalos kagathos" ("beautiful and good"), an ideal of the aristocracy (see Jaeger 1945, p. 13). This core consisted in a formation that we differentiate into poetry, music, and dance, the central thematic being metric-time-rhythm. In one of the more notorious speeches delivered in Aristophanes' *Clouds* (961-1016) the speaker rails against mousikē paideia as fundamentally inferior to the archaia paideia which it replaced. For some insightful treatments of these matters see the essays collected in Murray and Wilson (2004); in the setting of Europe's Renaissance, Walter Pater (1986 [1888]) has retained relevance.

quickly emerged in popular, vernacular idioms, which, in the hands of a Chaucer, Cervantes, Shakespeare, or Sterne, could weave carefully designed satirical criticism of official order.

In the meantime, a new hieratic conception of Art became ensconced, its new high priest named Leonardo da Vinci. The nomination was retrospective, to be sure, though not by much, and not without dissent from champions of a different candidate such as Raphael. We would do well to remember caution against heroicism in our admiration of the accomplishments of artists (as of others); for as Hauser (1982 [1974], p. 240) remarked, an artist such as "Raphael is regarded sometimes as *the* exemplary classical master and sometimes as a representative of conventional mediocrity."

Many accounts point to intellectual fashions of Europe's Renaissance in general and to a statement by Leonardo da Vinci in particular. The general factor antedates the Renaissance in that (as mentioned above) hieratic conceptions had been dominant for many centuries, and then gained strength and resilience owing to the general imprint of Christian theology. But as city life in Europe rejuvenated and expanded, productions of material wealth again reached a level that could subsidize the maintenance of more and more persons who were not directly involved in the production of subsistence (food, shelter, security), and craft shops became more plentiful and diversified in keeping with the human penchant to make new things, new meanings. Think, for example, of the contrast between the typical iconic paintings of Christian Europe's early fifteenth century and Leonardo's allegorical yet humanly realist portrayals of thirteen persons in *The Last Supper* (1498).[264] Not that Leonardo was alone in transition: Botticelli's *Saint Augustine in His Study* (1480) and Ghirlandaio's *Saint Jerome in His Study* (1480), *Angel appearing to Zacharias* (1490), and most notably in another respect, his *Old Man and His Grandson* (c1490), as well as Raphael's *The School of Athens* (1511), all testify to a new understanding of realism during that period. Leonardo was different, however, in his array of interests and intellectual entrepreneurial spirit (in the basic sense of "entreprendre" or "undertake"). All of these men were dependent on patrons who provided a protective legitimacy as well as financial support for their cautious adventures in painting. They were also recipients of an increased personal freedom that had come from a certain diminution of theology, which as a profession as well as confession had been a mainly Christian and thus European pursuit.[265] What they accomplished collectively, in

---

[264] Perhaps it is now needless to point out that sufficiently good depictions of the works of pictorial art that I cite in this book are available on the Web, Wikipedia being perhaps the site most often used (for pictorial, literary, and other arts). Museums also have increasing digital presence, much of it freely available. All of the works I cite are standard fare. Courbet's *Origin of the World* has been called pornographic. I concede that *only* because of absence; otherwise, the presentation is mundane (if not ordinary).

[265] With apologies to Latin American Christians; but most of the action had been consummated in Europe and long before the advent of a "liberation theology" (ignore Christian theology, and the audience for a "liberation *theology*" would never have existed). The dominant cultures of China had not developed discourses of the kind we read in European Christian theology; likewise, the dominant cultures of India. Islamic cultures subordinated theology as such to a sectarian schism that has been debated, sometimes fought, on the basis of a genealogy primarily. While theology as such in Europe maintained something of a supra-national presence even as the Holy Roman Empire lost cohesion of force, Christianity became subservient to the nation-state in a process slowly generalized from west to east.

addition to their individual works of individually identifiable styles, was the production of an institutionalized form of *Art* that could be reproduced, renewed in sequences of difference, from within its own ideal and material resources. Leonardo still stands out as a progenitor in that production. He was not the first of whom it could be said "polymathic," to be sure.[266] But has anyone else ever set such an astonishingly high standard for that adjective? His legatees looked back at the works of a painter and draftsman, of course; but further inspection came across many other kinds of work, too, those of a mathematician, inventor, engineer, sculptor, architect, musician, anatomist, botanist, geologist, astronomer, historian, and cartographer, not to mention the individual titles or descriptions of all the written documents he left as lessons of his works. Not surprisingly, Leonardo's name carried enormous weight of authority long after his immediate time.

The institutional form therein begun, or begun again,[267] depended on core processes of a renewability from resources of imagination which were typically regarded as ostensibly intrinsic to the art, while in fact they were extrinsic as well, sometimes from resources considered to be (from within the art) inimical to artistic merit. We have already seen evidence of that, in terms of imaginations of Newtonian mechanics. An earlier illustration comes from Leonardo himself (and others) in the use of "line and angle" of geometric abstraction as a means of developing a toolkit of techniques known collectively as "linear perspective," directly used for purposes of conveying depth and texture of field as well as orienting the ideal viewer relative to that field, but gradually also including other uses of imagined horizons temporal as well as spatial (e.g., a field of expectations and delayed effects; a means of harnessing while containing a contexualism

---

[266] Once again, it is worth noting the gap of about two millennia between the time of Leonardo and achievements by Greek painters of the fifth century BCE. Pliny the Elder recorded in his *Natural History* (1855 [c78], book 35, chs. 35, 36, 44) that Polygnotus of Thasos (fl.c465 BCE) was the first to paint "expression into the countenances" of his subjects, "in place of the ancient rigidity of features" (although Aristotle [*On Poetics*, 6.15] said that his "portraits were in the grand style and yet expressive of character" but that he "depicted men as better than they are"); that Apollodorus (fl. c480 BCE) was "the first to paint objects as they really appeared"; and that Lysistratus of Sicyon (4th century BCE) was the first to sculpt a realistic human face by making a plaster mold. Virtually none of the paintings survived, leaving us without basis for independent judgment. Pliny's characterization at least of Polygnotus' work differs from Aristotle's evaluation, made four centuries nearer the time of Polygnotus, but the difference is less than contradiction. All in all, the evidence suggests that the major developments of a new realism during the time of Leonardo were similar to developments achieved nineteen centuries before he was born.

[267] We can ask questions that we cannot answer not only because of the generation of counterfactuals. Here, for instance, one can ask whether Europe's Renaissance artists saw any relevance in the ancient Greek experience that prompted them to think in terms of "beginning again" and perhaps benefiting from the earlier processes. But there are many degrees of freedom in how we, now, conceive the comparative subjectivities and objectivities (or the comparative subject/object dialectics) between "Renaissance artists" and "ancient Greek artists," and the evidence by which to sort out those degrees of freedom is thin, especially considering that some substantial portion of it would have to pertain to the respective grids of consciousness (concepts, perceptions, etc.) which are themselves historical both as objects of our deliberations and in relation to and of our own grids (e.g., Pater 1986 [1888]). In sum, a skeptic's fertile playground.

214

vis-à-vis "invariantism" against supposed threats of lethality by relativism, as discussed in Unger 1984, for instance; and so forth).

No less a figure than Leonardo, with his uses of geometric abstraction when teaching the arts of drawing and painting (as well as anatomy, etc.), is typically cited as the authority behind the modern hierarchy of "the arts"—that is, the composition of Art, meaning "the fine arts" (see Leonardo 1989 [1851]).[268] He argued strongly that painting held top spot, protesting that it should not have been left out of the inventory of the seven liberal arts of the scholastics. Of all the arts, he argued, painting is based on all of the basic principles of geometry ("the science of continuous quantity") as well as arithmetic ("the science of discrete quantity"), is "the sole imitator of all the manifest works of nature," and utilizes all ten functions of the eye, vision being the highest of the senses (Leonardo 1989 [1851], pp. 13, 16, 18, 35-37). His case for painting vis-à-vis literary arts (chiefly poetry) was aided by a common perceptual bias, that ambiguity is a problem attendant on words, more than or more seriously than on visual images. The competitor against which he seemingly had greatest difficulty in building his case was music, which he (p. 34) called younger sister of painting. Some of his appreciation of music suggests an awareness that it, like poetry and mathematics, is a mode of emotive expression that can be, for both producer (whether composer or player, though with difference) and consumer (auditor, player or not), exceptional in first-person experience. Profoundly kinetic as auditory experience, it arranges time in dialogue between producer and consumer, often across such vast differences of historical time that it can seem to the listener as transcendent of time and space. Granted, the word "transcendent" has multiple meanings, and in present context perhaps the comparatively weaker meaning, "beyond ordinary experience," is primarily applicable (and because of, not despite, the fact that this is always in hock to whatever counts at the moment as "ordinary"). In usual understanding music, and for a given person an own-repertoire of favorites, is so remarkable because it induces feeling not otherwise experienced, with such flawless expression of one's own spirit that one assumes its unique standing without a moment's reflection—or so it can seem, even though *ex post* verbal expressions of "swelling heart," "soaring," and the like, are not uncommon. During the heyday of Romanticism Beethoven reportedly confessed to a young woman, Bettina (née Brentano) von Arnim (1861 [1834], p. 284), that he was displeased with most people because they did not appreciate that "music is a higher revelation than all wisdom and philosophy."[269] Yet as Ficino observed long ago in one of his letters (1.92), music begins in reason, then moves to fantasy, and on to tactile drumming, perhaps words, the whole body in dance. Music begins in reason in that it is and depends upon an organization of measures, measures of time (rhythm, cadence, etc.), for the feeling of motion and harmony (armonia) of

---

[268] A collection of Leonardo's writings was published in 1651 as his *Treatise on Painting*. Martin Kemp has done a great service to us by sorting that collection into improved coherence and supplementing it with many of Leonardo's drawings, including several gems from the collection of the Royal Library, Windsor Castle.

[269] The conversation was reported by Bettina herself in a letter she sent to Goethe while in Vienna, dated 28 May 1810, one of many letters she later published of her correspondence with Goethe. She was in the midst of the Romanticist movement, first as sister to Klemens Brentano, then wife to Ludwig von Arnim, and as prolific writer, composer, artist, and singer in her own right. While I do not recall an independent confirmation of the Beethoven sentence, its tenor is in keeping with much that has been documented.

parts. This sense of a transcendent quality is likely the substance and the support of a once common notion that music is a universal of human nature—that is, not merely that music has existed in every human culture (if indeed it has) but that music is in fact integral to an alleged pre-cultural nature of human nature.[270] Leonardo did not deny that claim, but his discussion of "universality" was restricted to painting (1989 [1851], pp. 201-202).

The evidence of a native of European or European-descendant culture who, untutored in, say, the music of Chinese or Indonesian tradition and, hearing a performance from that musical tradition for the first time, finds it to be "less musical" or "not exactly musical," or "simply noise, not music," is surely enough to encourage skepticism at least toward the "pre-cultural" claim. But one need not go outside European tradition to read evidence of similar experience. During the late eighteenth century composers such as Mozart and Beethoven wrote in a distinctive style (later designated "classical") using four-bar or eight-bar phrases with advertisement of the progression in and from an introductory statement (whether formally a prelude or not), thence through rising tension, followed by a final resolution. Tension was conveyed sonically (with or without lyrics) via elements styled as "dissonant"; the resolution, via a return to chords styled as "consonant," such as dominated the initial passages. A distinction between "consonance" and "dissonance" was forged in habituations to a chording technique that trained ears to expect "harmonious sound." While there had been variations around the dominance of "consonant sound," and variations within that dominance, listeners in "classical style" relied on a narrow range of expectations about the use of "dissonant sounds." It was against that backdrop that early auditions of Richard Wagner's *Tristan and Isolde* (composed by 1859) often ended in hot sparks, as music critics along with longtime patrons of operatic music riotously rejected what they were hearing. Not only were expected bounds of acceptable dissonance widely breached; when resolution does finally arrive, unexpectedly in a quiet major chord, it is at the end of a long solo of sad resignation in the futility of a passion. Counterpoints to "happy ever after" formulations had been read repeatedly in prior works of poetic expression, of course; but never with such stark, wrenching finality in musical composition.[271] A dialectic of light/dark, especially one correlated with good/evil, did not fail to disturb.

Leonardo (1989 [1851], pp. 13-16, 88-115) gave considerable attention to techniques of chiaroscuro (a dialectic of light/shade, or a gradient of shadings) as well as coloration but was seemingly little aware of those same techniques (and of color) in music. Because the surviving

---

[270] The relevant literature is large. A selective start through recent works might include Blacking (1995), Shawn (2002), and Levitin (2006).

[271] Later commentators have attributed this "eruption" of strong dissonance as an effect of industrialization. It very likely was not. Rather, it came mainly from within musical experimentation as artistic expression in the tradition of romanticist aesthetics of heroic Bildungsprozess, as wrought by Hölderlin, for example. But a Whiggish style of historiography easily fastens onto the fact that one can see in retrospect an early stage of industrialization in, say, the advent of (very noisy) railed trains, supposedly preparing ears for more dissonance in music. Likewise, the notion that with the advent of "consumer society," especially since the early twentieth century, the focus of popular music shifted increasingly from the music as such to a larger spectacle, visual and tactile as well as aural. Much the same could have been said (and perhaps was) of the musical form of the march during the nineteenth century and the minuet prior to that.

record of his musical activity—writing, invention, performance—is sketchy, speculation has had a relatively free run. While this cuts potentially in either direction, the greater risk is probably hagiographic, given the enduring fascination that "polymathic" carries (i.e., "he *must* have been a great composer, too"). The known record does testify to his experimental attitude toward musical as well as pictorial productions, however (designs of keyboard mechanisms, of novel shapes of the lyre, etc.), and his drawings demonstrate very fine skill in the pictorial use of shadings. Perhaps his comparisons of painting and music were motivated mainly to promote the former, not to neglect the latter.

In any case, his brief won in the court of artistic audiences, as a profusion of painters invented new pigments for color, new styles of conveying colored shapes of bodily surfaces (human, animal, vegetable, fruit, utensils, furniture, drapes, and on and on) and of shaded depths of field, multiplicities of perspective (linear, oblique, etc.), horizons, and vanishing points, new uses of reflexivity in addressing the viewer, and so forth. The profusion grew more rapidly with passing centuries, becoming well-nigh explosive during the nineteenth century and dominating as chief, at times seemingly exclusive focus of attention in a "discourse on art" that, in wake of Kant's *Critique of the Power of Judgment* (1790) and the Romanticist movement, inaugurated a new philosophy of "aesthetic experience," now specialized from perception in general to the perception, the appreciation, of beauty in particular (see, e.g., Hegel 1975 [1835]; Gombrich 1950; Belting 1994 [1990]; Freedberg 1989; Pippin 2014). Compared with music or the literary arts, painting became the easier mirror of consciousness of life in modern society. The mirror makers tried valiantly to keep pace with that life, preserving the capacity of a two-dimensional surface to stimulate, inform, amuse, sometimes shock its audience. Imagination could suffer fatigue—and did, now and then—with eruptions of concern about "the exhaustion of art" and convictions that "nothing new remains to be said." On each occasion the announcement soon proved to have been prelude, or so it seemed, to "the next new thing in art," reinvigorating art's capacity to shock, to scandalize, to inform. Illustrative examples of some of the most famous episodes include the following: (1) invention of techniques to convey the shimmer of light, as photons excite electrons in moisture-laden air (often as depicted above ponds, etc.), a development that reflected greater understanding of the physics of light propagation, thus that "air" is not necessarily a neutral or transparent medium; (2) techniques of manipulating viewer perspective so as to make a representation of three dimensions in two conform more closely to what the eye is capable of seeing in its stereoscopic perception of depth of field; (3) Marcel Duchamp's added technique to portray elapsed time, thus *four* dimensions on the surface of two, as in his *Nude Descending a Staircase, No. 2*; (4) advertisements of reflexivity in the dialectic of original/copy, as in either of René Magritte's *The Human Condition*; (5) developments by Piet Mondrian, among others, of techniques to experiment with "pure geometries" of color, line, and shape on two-dimensional surfaces, in approximation to a "complete abstraction"; (6) exploration of counterfactual relations internal to the compositional forms of human embodiment, as developed by Georges Braque and Pablo Picasso, among others; (7) allegorical expression in Christian texts transferred to allegorical expression in secular texts of technologies of morality, as in Picasso's portrayal of bodies victimized by aerial bombardment in Spain's civil war (*Guernica*); and, to cite but one more, (8) depictions of the controlled yet seemingly helter-skelter proliferations of rhizomatic networks of communication, as with Jackson Pollock's "drip art" techniques.[272]

Note, too, that it is all too easy to regard each of the developmental "events" as if isolated to painting, as if no interchanges with other artworks (or sciences) had been taking place, before, during, and after the memorializing Art event. At very least, the usual scenario has had painting in the lead, perhaps because specific painted works have been greatest or best at scandalizing audiences. It was, for instance, Pollock's "drip art" that came to mind so readily when Jean-François Lyotard (2011 [1971]) sought illustration, figuratively speaking, for his exploration of the rise of "the figural" as a reasonably coherent sequence of movements that challenged the literal as being beyond the grasp of words yet claiming to have something important to teach, and thereby expand, the capabilities of literation. The main point of departure in Lyotard's exploration features fourteenth-century developments of projective geometry, for instance, as providing "support" for "representational painting ..., at once as a transparency that makes visible and an opacity that makes legible," although Lyotard devoted some attention to earlier presentations such as eleventh-century illuminations of texts. His sequence of passages takes the reader to Pollock's figurations (his "drip paintings" of the late 1940s and early 1950s), at least some of which, according to Lyotard's (2011 [1971], p. 275) appreciation, demonstrate "the elimination of all recognizable figure." This curious elision becomes evident, as said above, when (if not before) one thinks of rhizomatic figurations.[273]

But another historian could tell a different Story of Art. In his *Likeness and Presence* (1994 [1990]) Hans Belting told an important part of an alternative story in his choice of subtitle: "a history of the image before *the era of art*" (emphasis added; see also Gombrich 1950, ch. 1). David Freedberg (1989) likewise gave suitable emphasis to the evidence that human propensities to make material realizations of what they can imagine washes out even a hint of secure line between "tool-making" and "art-making" (see also Mitcham 1994). A well-crafted tool, under some circumstances indeed even a poorly made yet suitably functional tool, gave the pleasure of assistance from a device of prosthesis. By the same token, an "artistic image" could as easily be a "tool to see with" ("see," here standing in for other senses as well as eyesight). By the end of the sixteenth century in some cities of Europe strictures by Christianity against challenges to received authority were loosening. In the Anglophone world probably the first name to register in that respect of memory is Francis Bacon, whose major work on a new method of inquiry (with

---

[272] Consider, too, the vast array of invention and development of human portraiture, a sequence that reflects European "obsessions" with selfhood as if a stark peculiarity of European cultures, when in fact it was only a sequence of extensions from the Christian-centered fascination with one legendary figure, Jesus, his "family," a history of ancestral origin in an original garden, along with themes of renunciation, betrayal, redemption, and the like. Another expression of the origination theme can be seen in Harman's (2002) uses of a notion of "ancestral time."

[273] My judgment of "curious elision" invokes Deleuze and Guattari's (2004 [1980]) use of "rhizomatic process," explicitly modeled on botanic structures. This latter work was published (indeed, written) long after Lyotard's dissertation, to be sure, but the figure of "rhizome" already had a very long history not only in botanics proper but also in agriculture, horticulture, and the like. While I agree that Deleuze and Guattari's understanding of botanic rhizomes left much to be desired (especially vis-à-vis arborescence), their general application of the figure was (is) a useful reminder of a different geometry.

emphasis on both tests by empirical observation and skepticism toward inherited understandings) gained increasing attention by the 1630s. Freedberg (2002) has left us a magnificent volume that features the works of several scholars whose approach was virtually identical to Bacon's, but with the difference that they compiled a great volume of documentation, in pictures as well as words, of their efforts to make sense of the huge variety of nature's things, plant, animal, and mineral. Their efforts were organized as the Accademia dei Lincei, founded in 1603.[274] This could be counted as Europe's first institutionalized venture in using artistic skills (as we would say) to demonstrate insights of modern science. The record covers many particulars, ranging from pleasure in rendering colorful imagery of various discrete objects, to many curiosities of "deformity," to interesting patterns of similarity across things conventionally treated as widely separate. Perhaps the most important for present purposes, however, is the growing awareness of difficulties of satisfying interests in classification. On the one hand, the Linceans' picture-making manifested "a deep investment in the worth of appearance and the value of the surface" (Freedberg 2002, p. 416), an investment initially encouraged by invention of the microscope. But on the other hand, experiences gained through this prosthesis by microscopic lens had by the 1620s raised awareness of a dialectic of identity/difference in intersection with a newly re-conceived dialectic of interior/exterior, one of the lessons being that colorful description of surfaces often said little or nothing about more important variations among Nature's things. A new tradition of "natural history" was underway, offering unexpectedly rich spaces of interiority which some of the Linceans began to tackle via juxtapositions of picture and diagram.

As for Leonardo's younger sister of painting, by the late 1700s subtle experimentations of musical composition involving inaudible dimensions of music traveled along the dialectical tension within the unity of the private/public opposition—inescapably, since most newly written music was composed and performed for private, small audiences (patrons, courtiers, musicians' relatives and friends), some of whom, it is safe to say, would have been scandalized had they understood all that was in play. When a performer studies sheets of music in preparation, the music would be inaudible except for the brain's ear. Indeed, this often occurs as a composer writes those sheets. In this sense, "inaudible music" had been understood long before the late 1700s. Now, however, some composers were expanding the value of inaudible music to include other auditors (but bear in mind that many people were then as now at least amateur performers, some of whom tried their skills of composition). An accomplished composer could write with expectation that many likely auditors would study the sheets as preparation for full performance, and understand what the composer intended to convey with silences, with entrances that begin so softly, so quietly as to be uncertainly audible, with resolutions repeatedly postponed by nearly or fully inaudible though *imaginable* passages, and so forth. *Imagined* sound became more skillfully, more prominently imbricated within measures of audible sound. One can read a sequence of notes that no human voice can produce—for example, an implied sonority as if rumbled from the depth of a torso or as if autochthonous of the Earth—all in vivid anticipation of voiced notes that come later. An auditor who has prepared for a performance by reading the sheets will be aware of those unvoiced notes, an awareness that affects what is heard next. A

---

[274] The Academy's name translates as "the lynx-eyed," recalling one of the Argonauts, Lyncæus, the "lynx-eyed" (i.e., acute of eyesight). Galileo became a member a few years after the academy began.

composer can build on that effect by inducing echoes. Remember, sonic expectation can produce sound in a brain's ear, imagined sound, that no mechanical or digital recorder will hear, can possibly hear. This might raise the question, Was sound actually produced? More to the point, however, is the question, On what basis will that judgment be made? *If* one accredits the listener (a well-prepared listener) of an episode of, say, Robert Schumann's *Humoreske* (1839), that listener will have definitely heard an echo of a melody written in a middle stave—that is, separately, between the upper stave (right hand) and the lower stave (left hand)—with instruction that it is "*inner voice* only" ("innere Stimme), not to be performed by the pianist.[275]

Having repeated all of that, I hasten to return to Ficino and caution that while music does indeed induce feelings that can be highly resistant to conveyance in words alone, there is much in the literary arts that draws on similar if not the same resources of emotion. When considering literate expression, prosaic as well as poetic, we should abide by Valiavitcharska's (2014, p. 182) admonition *not* to "assume that the sounds are merely a garment for the thought" (i.e., parergon, supplement). She was of course there invoking the memory that literacy began, and (excepting those who were congenitally deaf) for individual human consciousness *begins*, in sound, the authority of the voice that comes with nurturance and care (i.e., the so-called oral tradition). But she was invoking as well the even broader experience that verbal composition, whether oral or written, is *rhythmic* and as such engages the body, the words having cadence as in bodily dance. A congenitally deaf person uses vision of other's body to learn the emic rhythms of speech and from there, of literate recitation. A person congenitally without eyesight as well as sound faces the more difficult course of learning rhythms of speech tactilely—difficult but not impossible.[276] Means of the *innere Stimme* are various and achievable. They are found in sociality.

Not for the first time, to be sure, but with accentuated urgency, the late 1800s brought to vision and sound a utility question, a question so blatantly about utility that some observers were convinced it gave further testimony to a degradation of life as part and parcel of modern society. The utility question was manifest in new commodifications of art, in mechanical means of using an image in separation from its original uniqueness of a painter's or an organist's or a singer's performance, and to apply that copy to ends having nothing to do with the artwork itself but to advertise or decorate something else, especially some other commodity available for purchase. At the same time, this utility question was also manifest as a growing suspicion that Art is in fact *useless*, or on the verge of losing all useful role or function in sociality or in the well-being of society. Once again, the specter of an exhaustion of imagination was at hand, the evidence being that artwork had apparently become incestuous, consumed in its seemingly fixated view on continued conversation with past artistic styles (thus, "neo-this" and "neo-that"). Hauser (1982 [1974], p. 307) summarized a major part of this discourse as "the fatal romantic renunciation," a renunciation that becomes still more extreme in the assertion that "the only justification for life" is in Art. Ross Posnock has recently pointed to the same question of utility, following on his

---

[275] Charles Rosen began his magnificent study of *The Romantic Generation* (1995) with many illustrations (including the Schumann instance) of the experimentation of sound, silence, imagination, echo effects, and more, as means of musicality. His presentation is lucid though demanding.
[276] And, looking ahead to a topic of the next Part, a task soon to be accomplished by prostheses such as implants.

pairing of Ralph Waldo Emerson and Friedrich Nietzsche as exemplars of a modern renunciation of "the self-determining subject": this would become a renunciation of artistic subjectivity itself, ending in the question, "So what is Art for?" (Posnock 2016, pp. 315, 96-99).

For many commentators, and not a few artists as well, that question has been intended as both functionalist and teleological, and the primary answer in such terms has emphasized the intent of Art, or of "great art," to expand capacities of imagination by "saying" something that is new, even better if "shockingly new." Qualification depends on conditioning and context, but not always in predictable ways or degree, and sometimes when investigating actual cases of "shock endured," ambiguities can prevail to an extent that tangles features of audience reception. The general idea has been that the creative imagination as displayed in works of the literary, pictorial, musical, and theatrical arts most especially can disturb the habituated sensibilities of audiences out of their own lethargies of imagination. There have been many instances of that confirmatory evidence. Among the most notorious, Arnold Schoenberg's *Chamber Symphony No. 1* (1907), D H Lawrence's *Lady Chatterley's Lover* (1928), and Samuel Beckett's *Waiting for Godot* (1953) are later examples. Walt Whitman's *Leaves of Grass* (1855) and Mark Twain's *Adventures of Huckleberry Finn* (1884) were scandalous in their day. Some commentaries have emphasized that artists themselves deliberately seek "shocking effects" as a way of gaining stature—that is, by being not just noticed but reviled as well as celebrated, depending on preparation within different segments of relevant audience. No doubt there is something to this: rare the artist who seeks anonymity or even (though less rare) modest fame or notoriety; and by the same token, when fame or notoriety does come, it is usually in response to a work that is seen as sharply different, aberrant, in some respect. However, one should not credit the artist with too much prescience: success in gauging what will shock, and whether it will be "productive" in desired ways, is not only far from being automatic but also, when it does happen, remembered more often and more prominently than the failed attempts. An important differentiation for many artists favors fellow artists, curators, and collectors (plus patrons, when vital, and various other "opinion leaders" such as art journalists and critics) over other, more diverse audiences, including paying members of museums, theaters, and music halls, plus the occasional visitors through the turnstiles. Duchamp's famous *Nude Descending a Staircase, No. 2* did and still does "shock" the viewer who seemingly cannot see in it any "realism" (although the principal import of this incidental fact is as an indicator of a failure of educational process). For an artist's primary audience the only "shock" was an appreciation of how well he achieved the desired effect. On the other hand, his *Fountain*, unveiled five years later (1917) carried shock of a different kind for those artists who understood the message as a denigration of their hard-earned skills of creative imagination.[277]

---

[277] As reminder: Duchamp's *Nude* was chiefly an effort to convey a realism of motion (remember, by 1912 motion pictures were becoming a significant art form)—that is, to convey not just three but four dimensions on a surface of two dimensions, and the nude body lent itself better than a clothed body to that aim. His *Fountain* was a porcelain urinal (exhibited on its back, on table or floor), and thereafter the emblem of his announcement of the "readymade" art form. It has often been said of *Fountain* that it was intended to be emblematic of a "conceptual position" chiefly because it completely lacks any intended aesthetic function (which claim tells us mainly what was therein meant by "aesthetic").

221

Painted nudes, which have been far more often nude women than nude men or children,[278] can be read historically as a gauge both of dominant gender relations in a population and of what counts as realism. One bridge between the two is constituted as eroticism—historical variations in what counts (or "works") as "the erotic"—and its connection to pornography (a concept with roots in ancient Greek culture).[279] One might remember that when Leo Tolstoy wrote his answer to the question, "What is art?" (completed in 1897, published in 1904), his asceticism probably did not allow him to imagine any eroticism as a communication of emotion, especially (as he understood it) the "positive" emotion of empathy. His asceticism to the side, Tolstoy probably also would have objected to the idea that something new from an artist can be legitimately accorded the standing of "art" only if it can be shown to have some historical link to prior artworks. After all, what does not have such connection, direct or indirect? Further, given any level of religiously inspired asceticism, what would have been the sanitizing barrier to links with the ancient Greeks' sometimes "erotic" figures painted on their abundant kraters and other items of surviving pottery?[280]

The historicity of a capacity of "shock" can be assessed also in other frames of Europe's record of painted scenes. For example, compare Peter Paul Rubens' *The Judgment of Paris* (c1625) with Lucas Cranach's painting of the same mythic scene (c1530). For present purposes, the main feature of each painting is the artist's depiction of three goddesses, Hera, Athena, and Aphrodite, fully nude, along with Paris (aka Alexander, son of the king and queen of Troy).[281] Rubens, a Flemish Calvinist painter in Baroque style, rendered the mythic theme in a quasi-theological fashion, with each goddess rendered in voluptuous body, one of them fully frontal. Cranach, primarily a court painter in Saxony who specialized in religious themes and portraits, painted in a style somewhat more austere than the Baroque, rendering the nude goddesses with slightly greater modesty of bodily proportion as well as frontal exposure. In each case, size of contemporary audience (small and of privileged standing) afforded the artist protection against claims of moral offense, as did their use of mythic theme. Later, of course, Rubens' works in general became emblematic of the "excess" that was purportedly hallmark of the Baroque style,

---

[278] In his review of Vladimir Nabokov's *Lolita*, Donald Malcolm (1958, p. 195) said that Nabokov had "coolly prodded one of the few remaining raw nerves of the twentieth century." The narrow range of his evaluation of "raw nerves" partly reflected his audience (*The New Yorker* magazine), as larger US audiences in 1958, while agreeing that "child porn" was abhorrent, judged adult-centered pornography also to be abrasive of their sensibilities (and not always hypocritically).

[279] The word in English apparently was invented as recently as 1843, presumably for its specific reference in its Greek root to "prostitute" (pórnē, which is related to pernanai, "to sell"). Other European languages remained with older, more general terms (e.g., in German "Schmuck," which means "dirt" or "filth" in a more general sense as well as "dirty literature"), although some have adopted the English "pornography" (e.g., recent German).

[280] Although not much discussed, such objects were documented in collections of ancient artworks as early as the eighteenth century. See, e.g., Winckelmann (1764), who compared across collections of works from several sites, mostly Mediterranean. See also Heidegger (1971 [1960]), who, while focused more on poetry (and Hölderlin in particular) than on painting, and displayed still another kind of asceticism, offered good insights into the dialectic of art as, on the one hand, a means of cultural expression and, on the other, an expression of a culture as a whole.

[281] More detail of the mythic theme and the paintings (Rubens completed several versions, as did others) will be presented in the next section of this Part.

his "fleshy" female bodies most often cited as an obviousness of evidence. With that contrastive pair of portrayals of nude bodies in mind, recall Edouard Manet's *Luncheon on the Grass* (1863), previously considered. In painterly terms, what was revolutionary about the work had nothing to do with the fact that the principal female figure is nude, lounging matter-of-factly on a small blanket, next to two fully clothed men and, in background, a gossamer-covered woman rinsing herself in shallow water, all of them presumably having enjoyed together a basket lunch, remains of which lie off to the side. For many viewers then and still today the scene is disturbing (if not shocking) not only because of the fully nude woman in presence of two fully clothed men but also because she, and her companions, are not mythic figures, gods female and male, whose presence can bestow privileged standing to their painterly creator, but ostensibly four ordinary bourgeois adults enjoying a "picnic in the park."[282] This difference supposedly renders the female nudity too personal. Compare this nudity with Cranach's depiction of the woman in *The Nymph of the Fountain* (1534)—no less nude, reclining in a greater exposure of her body, showing her viewer a facial expressive that has been read as slightly seductive (as contrasted with the almost disinterested, perhaps thought-absorbed expression of Manet's principal nude); but Cranach's nymph is a mythical figure, which is to say a figment, a fantasy, "not real," and thus without threat to mores.[283]

Finally, let's add one more contrast:[284] Gustav Courbet's *The Origin of the World* (1866), a small painting, still (or "perhaps still") not well known to the general public. This nude woman is lying on her back, one leg opened from the other, showing not only a full mound of pubic hair but also her slightly open vulva. To accentuate the effect even more, her head, arms, and lower legs are not visible. Reportedly painted for one of the artist's friends (who kept the painting veiled), the image can easily be described as "erotic," bordering on if not well across the line to "pornographic." Was that Courbet's intention, or the whole of his intention? If indeed "beauty" is in the eye of the beholder, what of "the erotic" and "the pornographic"? More to the point, why did Courbet entitle his work, "The origin of the world"? Was this merely his version of the more traditional "cover story" of myth and/or religious or godly thematic? But, to ask the question in a different way, what title would better speak the intended realism? Courbet had, as a very simple matter of fact, depicted the origin of every human being who has ever lived, the

---

[282] They were, of course, Manet's models, known as such to his circle, at least three of them remembered today by name (the nude woman, one of his favorites, Victorine Meurent; the man with a cane, his brother, either Gustave or Eugène; the other man, his future brother-in-law, Ferdinand Leenhoff). There was no need to hide their identities in a cloak of anonymity or mystery, for they were not intruding on dangerous territory by portraying some religious icon or powerful church or courtly figure or wealthy patron.

[283] The intended contrast is not free of complication, however. Manet was reportedly inspired to paint his *Luncheon* by viewing *The Pastoral Concert* (c1510), a similar painting by Giorgione and/or Titian, which features two nude or nearly nude women and two fully clothed men in a pastoral setting, the theme seemingly having nothing to do with any mythic or historical identity of the four persons (or, as in Manet, a startling rejection of some parts of traditional painterly technique) but rather as allegorical tribute to poetic and musical expression. My impression of *Concert* is that insofar as an idealization was intended, its focus had more to do with expressivity than with bodily appearance (see, e.g., Bourdieu 2017 [2013], pp. 36, 52, 70, 71, 243-244; but also Pippin 2014, pp. 48, 99 n.6).

[284] Later in this Part other contrasts will be introduced (e.g., Cindy Sherman's bodies).

223

beginning of each person's world as first-person experience. Even more, one could quickly add: the initial conception of each human being in a coital act. What could be "more real"?[285]

For all that realism, of course, many viewers today would probably cite Courbet's "dirty little picture" as testimony of how much, and what, has changed during "the era of art." Belting (1994) was right to emphasize the reformation of attention, the increased privileging of attention and its techniques, during "the era of art." It is now surely news nowhere that the movement of secularization which continued gradually through and from the twelfth and thirteenth centuries of European society was *critical* to what had been its central institution, the Church—"critical" at least in the ancient Greek sense of "crisis" or "turning"—and the chief theme of that well-known story was (is) told in the fact that "crisis" was (and largely still is) understood as a *negative* event or process. Established relations of power and authority were being challenged in and by crisis, followed by reaction, counter-movement, and a sort of revanchist sentiment among those who had felt threatened.[286] Some part of the movement/counter-movement dialectic gained expression in, and was worked out via, disputations of "art": when would "artistic imagination" be "in praise of," versus when "in blasphemy toward," divinity? Arguments about "the iconic," and efforts of "iconoclasm," were only a part of that expression.

In the annals of European philosophy the person most remembered for having diagnosed a crisis of "the arts" as secular servant to theology, and then to turn it into a crisis of Art itself, was Hegel, in the third part of his *Encyclopedia* as well as in his lectures on art and aesthetics, last delivered during the 1828-29 academic year.[287] It became a "crisis of Art" theme largely due to the tradition of a hierarchy that had developed after Leonardo. A "crisis in painting" could easily generalize into a "crisis of Art," and to a large degree it did just that with Hegel himself. But it has been mainly in a long train of commentary, most of it recent, that, following the figure of synecdoche, the theme has been about Art in general, the arts taken as a whole.

---

[285] This latter illustrative case may be called upon again, in Part Six, in a discussion of the Kantian principle of hope and MacKinnon (2017).

[286] What was "counter-movement" relative to "movement" is often ambiguous—certainly after so much time has passed, and perhaps in the contemporary scene as well. For example, a monk accredited with having founded the Cistercian order, Bernard of Clairvaux (d. 1153), was motivated chiefly by perceived need to "purify" the monastic order supposedly founded by Bernard of Nursia (d. 550), the Benedictine order. To some extent the Cistercians probably invented what they sought to restore to practice, "the Order of Saint Benedict." Cistercian monasteries sprouted up all over Europe, though mainly in remote rural areas, locations that soon proved to be consonant with vernacular languages and local customs (e.g., of spirited drinks), which were in accord with the Cistercian emphasis on an immediacy of faith—thus an individualist orientation that stood in ironical relation to the Cistercian scriptoria which served as centers of Latin scholarship, just as the tolerance of local custom merged with Cistercian changes of agricultural technique. The Cistercians also favored arts in praise of the saints, ultimately God.

[287] As with his lectures on the philosophy of history (last delivered in 1830, published in 1848), his lectures on aesthetics were a popular presentation of his general system, keyed partly to conventional divisions of the discourse of philosophy. They are somewhat looser than the few works that were published by his own authority (the greatest of which, first entitled *Science of the Experience of Consciousness*, was published in 1807 as *Phenomenology of Geist*; and the last of which, *Elements of the Philosophy of Right*, appeared in 1830).

One passage from Hegel's lectures tells us that "the spirit of our world today,

or, more particularly, of our religion and of the development of our reason, appears as beyond the stage at which art is the supreme mode of our knowledge of the Absolute. The peculiar nature of artistic production and of works of art no longer fills our highest need. We have got beyond venerating works of art as divine and worshipping them. The impression they make is of a more reflective kind, and what they arouse in us needs a higher touchstone and a different test. Thought and reflection have spread their wings above fine art. Those who delight in lamenting and blaming may regard this phenomenon as a corruption and ascribe it to the predominance of passions and selfish interests which scare away the seriousness of art as well as its cheerfulness; or they may accuse the distress of the present time, the complicated state of civil and political life which does not permit a heart entangled in petty interests to free itself to the higher ends of art. This is because intelligence itself subserves this distress, and its interests, in sciences which are useful for such ends alone, and it allows itself to be seduced into confining itself to this desert (Hegel 1975 [1835] vol. 1, p. 10)

While Hegel had said little about art in his first major work, *Phenomenology of Geist*, published in 1807, or in his *Philosophy of Right*, published in 1820, in the third part of his *Encyclopedia* he laid out what he nominated as "the third level of Geist, the standpoint of absolute Geist, i.e., of art, religion, and philosophy" (Hegel 1971 [1830], §385). His discussion in that third section of the volume is consistent with his lecture notes on the significance of art in relation to religion and philosophy, although he did not repeat the exact phrase (that "art ... is, and remains, a thing of the past") that would eventually attain heights of notoriety.[288] By his account of the advancing movement of the Absolute, the turn he had witnessed in Art's lack of ability to fill "our highest need" was indeed a sign of progress toward eventual realization of that movement, although he acknowledged that those who were not yet enlightened into his system, would misread the evidence. Be that as it may, he avowed, "it is certainly the case that art no longer affords that satisfaction of spiritual needs which earlier ages and nations sought in it, and found in it alone, a satisfaction that, at least on the part of religion, was most intimately linked with art." But never mind, Hegel (1975 [1835], vol. 1, p. 11) assured: while it is true that "art, considered in its highest vocation, is and remains for us a thing of the part," we now have a philosophy that can fill our highest need, and better than art could do in its heyday.

Hegel's statement that art was, and would remain, a "thing of the past" attracted little attention for quite some time, in part because his lectures on aesthetics attracted little attention, and in part because "the Hegelian system," commonly described as an "Objective Idealism," lost followers and mostly lay fallow until the ferment of the existentialist movement in France began as late as the 1920s to import Hegel along with Heidegger and others (see, e.g., Boschetti 1988

---

[288] Note, too, that in his lectures on the philosophy of history he referred to a "history of special departments of life and thought—of Art, Law, and Religion'; and in the third part of his *Encyclopedia* (1971 [1830], §572) he referred to his philosophy as the science of the unity of art and religion—indeed, as subsumptive of what had been separate departments of life.

[1985], p. 62; Flynn 2014, p. 24). Heidegger's writings on "art" eventually became influential and rejuvenated attention to Hegel's aesthetics, perhaps in part because they can be read in at least two different ways. Note first of all that for Heidegger "art," as both concept and empirical phenomenon, is reducible neither to the particular person who has created a work of art (or to any generative notion of "creator") nor to the actual process of a person creating a work of art (or to a general notion of "work" or "a work"). That is, "art" must be understood as something distinctive relative both to work and to creator. It is in this sense, according to Heidegger (1971 [1960], pp. 41-48), that Art exists as a force in itself, a force that satisfies its own purposes *through* the creator and the work. Now, this Hegelian claim that Art is itself a force that has effects via creator and thence creative work can be understood in phenomenal terms in the same way that one understands any human product as potentially gaining objective status in its world— that is to say, attaining an objectivity of sociality, of a human beingness as a humanly produced collectivity of effects of the ensembles of relations that are the individual human beings, their products, their world(s). On the other hand, Heidegger can be read as having invoked an essentialism that seemingly guides the historical process. Here, one can easily encounter an impression of a ontotheological mysticism that, further, can be read as a "deeper" or "originary" process unfolding beneath or behind "the merely human."[289] As in Heidegger's (1962 [1957]) larger notion of an originary "thrownness into world" condition of human being, the ambiguity persists, serving, one might say, as a saddle for the dilemma in Kant's legacy.

One might note that while Heidegger's commentary on Hegel short-circuited the question about the latter's "completion of history," an odd effusion passed intact through Heidegger and on to the present day. Hegel's sense of completion in his own project—as he saw it an evidently major step in the completion of history—was a major part, perhaps the main if not primary part, of the inaugurating force behind an idiom of "lateness," an idiom that recalls millenarianism of Christian belief (and related emotive-cognitive effects). Existentialist angst then spurred the traffic of this now long, oddly peripatetic sequence of installments of "lateness," as in "late stage of capitalism," for instance, and "late modernism." These periodically renewed "stages" of what must have been seen as a developmental sequence that stumbled and fell into a recursive loop still seem to serve as a stand-in for a completion that was announced but did not happen when expected, although this "world weariness" perhaps sustains the loss as temporary postponement. The beginning of "Heaven on Earth" became increasingly late as Christianity proceeded through its second millennium. Indeed, "the modern world," and more especially still its late spawn "post-modernity," has been more about lateness—or as Andrew O'Hagan has been

---

[289] As illustration: Heidegger (1971 [1960], p. 41) answered his own question, "Where does a work belong?" with this: "The work belongs, as work, uniquely within the realm that is opened up by itself." This *could* be only a way referring to the ongoingness of history, that each new episode or event or work comes from within its history of episodes or events or works (and as such might have been at least on the verge of realizing the limitation that must be respected in processes the crucial relations of which are non-ergodic; see Hazelrigg 2010, pp. 5-7; Isaac and Lipold 2012). But one also reads in that same discussion intimations of an essentialism that calls on a mystical process, a mysticism that easily invites a dogmatism of thought. One suspects an offer of "new" clothing for the "second object" of Kant's transcendental Illusion, the object that supposedly humans cannot live without, one of ultimate nonhuman authority.

heard to say, more to do with what is "after the fact"—than with being up-to-date, much less in the lead (see Hutchinson 2016).

However, some allowance should be made for the fact that historical comparisons are usually difficult, especially from first-person standpoint, even when the difficulty is evidently not an impediment. Artistic consciousness is no exception. Jasper Johns, in an interview in 2008, said that "artists today know more. They are aware of the market more than they once were. There seems to be something in the air that art is commerce itself." As a statement of personal perception, that is just as it is. Each of the first two claims is at least arguable, however, despite the elasticity of "once were." As for art being "commerce itself," it always has been that, at very least in the sense that "commerce" means more than financial action (i.e., as with "intercourse," it once referred primarily to social engagement), and many, if not most, artists have depended on financial transactions of their work since long before Johns was born.[290]

Agreement in Hegel's sense of completion hardly survived his own demise, as most of his successors preferred a verdict that had been rendered by Friedrich Wilhelm Joseph von Schelling in the fifth of his philosophical letters on dogmatism and criticism, written in 1795: creative imagination, nurtured in freedom, insists on continuation of that freedom in each of its projects, for its "entire dignity" rests in the premise "that it will never be completed. In that moment in which [an artist or scientist] would believe that he has completed his system, he would become unbearable to himself." Why? Because in that moment he would "cease to be a creator, descending instead to being merely an instrument of his creation" (Schelling 1856, part 1, volume 1, p. 306). Had Hegel read that letter? Probably not. Schelling's works were generally not well received, in part because he was seen as being inconstant. In any case it is doubtful that Hegel would have been deterred from his destiny.

Was Hegel exaggerating in his thought, "completion"? The question can be asked twice, once with reference to his claim about "art as thing of the past" (or "the end of art," as the phrase was remembered; e.g., Danto 1997), but then also with reference to "the past" that was Hegel's past: were artists ever *that* influential in European societies? This second reference is of interest here, especially in its relationship to the tendency in philosophical discourse (as in most religious discourse) to import some sort of "special actor" as linchpin, as Hegel did in his own quest of self-privilege as one who understood the spirit of the Absolute, and its course of becoming, better than did the Absolute itself, and without telling us how that happened (excepting obscure explanatory exercises by, for instance, "the cunning of reason"; e.g., Hegel 1914 [1848], p. 34).[291]

---

[290] This is not to say, however, that the relation of "art" and "commerce" has been static. Struggles to command and if possible to monopolize attention became the dominant action of art as commerce during the twentieth century, nowhere more visibly accomplished than in popular music during the second half of the century (see, e.g., Doggett 2012; Hagan 2017).

[291] I am referring to Hegel as privileged phenomenological observer at the center of his system. This is the same principal who knows already at the core of philosophy as the science of the unity of art and religion (Hegel 1971 [1830], §572) that its governing principle rests on national culture (as is clear in his lectures on the philosophy of history).

The question I mean here is not about the artist as servant to the Church; rather, the artist as an actor apart from service as decorator.

"When Hegel spoke of art as a thing of the past he meant that art was no longer understood as a presentation of the divine in the self-evident and unproblematical way in which it had been understood in the Greek world." This was Gadamer's (1986 [1977], p. 6) reading, both of the meaning of the "thing of the past" phrase and of Hegel's "past." One can easily see reasons to doubt the cultural comparison, in part because it depends on a far too monolithic view of "the Greek world" and the supposed "self-evident and unproblematical way" of regarding art. During the period usually labelled "classical" (from the late fifth century to Alexander's death in 323 BCE), artistic expression devoted increased attention and skill to developing a "humanism" of form, along with a dialectic of beauty/ugliness in, for instance, statuary of persons who stand out as "identifiably real," by named artists, as well as in sculptural depictions of monstrosity, as in practices of apotropaia (ritualized actions and objects meant to "turn away" harms and evil influences).[292] But did Hegel really think, by comparison, that once Christianity came on stage, the need of art disappeared, or that it was reduced to ornamentation of Christian scripture? No doubt several prominent figures of Romanticism did extol "the ancient Greeks," sometimes giving the appearance of little or no awareness of the great range of cultural differences of place and time concealed within that nomination. But even if we try to imagine that Hegel believed that pictorial art by, say, Leonardo, Raphael, Ghirlandaio, and Rubens was aesthetically inferior to the best that had survived from Athens, are we supposed to think as well that productions by the recent painters were uniformly lacking in distinctions relevant to a "universal need for art"? Belting was on target in his account of "art before the era of art" (c1550), when he (1994) pointed to iconic images of Christian art as passages of sacred presence, even if the iconography did at times threaten to displace "the Word" as preeminently decisive of all things holy. It was after that transition into Belting's "era of art" that Hegel spied what he took to be the end of art's utility, and it had come about not so much as an exhaustion as a supersession: Hegel's own project of philosophy would henceforth perform better and more the functions that art had tried to fulfill.

Let's return once more to Europe's twelfth-century renaissance, the recovery of city life and the long-distance trading markets which formed a counterweight to, and then a gradual replacement of, the monasterial system of organizing territory. A new soterial theme took shape within European cultures, its main expression being a self-conscious movement that in retrospect has been called a "New Humanism." [293] Concomitant with the slowly general weakening of the

---

[292] A headgear worn by Athena, known wholly or in part as Athena's aegis, was (and is) exemplary (although we do not know what it was substantially). It both afforded protection and terrorized opponents. Judging by surviving accounts (e.g., *The Iliad*), the Gorgons (from "gorgós," "dreadful"), of whom Medusa was one, were in early times conceived as a human-like animal form of ugliness (or a form blended of human and beast), perhaps inherited from their own ancestors, perhaps borrowed from Egyptian or other cultural heritage. During the classical period the humanist movement extended even to a beautification of Gorgons, Medusa especially (see, e.g., Woodford 2003).

[293] By "New Humanism" I do not mean, of course, the literary movement of the early twentieth century (e.g., Irving Babbitt); rather, a somewhat similar movement nearly eight centuries earlier (see, e.g., Knowles 1963 [1941]). Also, I again acknowledge that periodizations are controversial, sometimes to

228

central power of churchly organization, dissolution of feudalism's hieratic principle, and greater vernacular consciousness of language, its conceptual schemes, and growing funds of first-person cognitive and emotive experiences in those vernacular languages (whether via market and trade relations directly or through a new civic life of expanding cities), mentalities began to exhibit a gradual emancipation of person-values from the strictures of a religious doctrine that favored "life after death" over worldly life and everyday affairs of human beings. Habits tend to die more as persons die, however, and in this matter the habit of looking to signs of extra-human authority of meaning and truth, especially eternal meaning and truth, gradually shifted from the "official" plenipotentiaries and old-style mythical characters to a newer, mundane-world kind of special actor who could bring quasi-theological solace and security. Judged from present-day standpoint, "the scientist" had "not yet" attained cognitive-emotive powers sufficient to those old expectations. After all, Roger Bacon (c1219-c1292), remembered much later as a forerunner of modern empirical science, was largely neglected in his day and, well into the sixteenth century, celebrated mainly as something of a magus. On the other hand, "the artist" could be safely enlisted by the church itself as a sort of special actor who could bridge between the sacred and the secularizing cities and trade routes. Mere craft was not enough. Belief required a certain majesty of "expression" that would lend conviction in credentials transcendent of place and date while still addressing concerns of everyday life here and now. Giotto di Bondone, the early fourteenth-century Florentine painter, is remembered as an exceptional artist for having bridged an arc of redemption in standard religious themes (e.g., paintings of "The Life of Christ") but with portraits that looked very much like ordinary people, one's neighbors even. Vasari set the tenor of historical memory when, in his *Lives* (1896 [1568], part 1) he emphasized Giotto's virtually unprecedented skill in depicting human beings as they "actually looked," not in the straited and stilted fashion that had prevailed for centuries. In short, a new realism was being invented, one that invited ordinary men and women to find themselves in the mysteries of painted scenes.[294]

Such changes in the practice of artistic expression during the centuries following the twelfth did take place, no doubt, alongside as well as "within" uses of art as both embellishment of "the Word" and additional motivator to belief in a religious majesty. Consider, for instance, the tie between churchly Christianity and the artistic movement or style called Baroque, which, art historians more or less agree, extended from the early 1600s to the late 1700s. Historians also generally agree that this style was both extension of and successor to the Renaissance style of European artistic sensibility. Further, however, most historians have connected that style with doctrinal strategies designed during the Council of Trent (1545-63) to counteract attractions of

---

the point of submerging studies of the processes being collected into stages or periods. There may well be as many historians who disdain as who agree the notion of a "twelfth-century renaissance" (or any "renaissance," for that matter). Haskins (1927) is nonetheless still worth reading, as are Knowles (1963 [1941]), Chenu (1968 [1957]), and Panofsky (1960), whether one agrees or disdains the phrase; likewise, Vasari (1896 [1568]), and see Rowland and Charney (2017).

[294] Giotto is typically credited as progenitor of the individualization of subjects by "physically accurate" depiction, but this new kind of realism developed only gradually. Ghirlandaio's *Old Man with His Grandson* (c1490) has been identified as epitome of that development, primarily because he rendered the unknown elder man's nose "entirely as it was," the disease-induced rhinophyma included (in contrast to the still-typical practice of ignoring "blemishes" of a sitter's physiognomy).

the protestant movement against the Church of Rome. Whereas the latter movement generally championed "plain style" as correction of corrupt practices within the established Church, a main counter-movement argued that "the arts" should be popular servants of Catholic doctrine against the Protestants, and to that end should cultivate ornate visual and aural displays of grandeur, majesty, and awe-inspiring beauty. It is not as if visual and aural arts had not previously been devoted to religious-doctrinal service, of course. There had been little safe alternative, until partly secularized centers of power and authority had developed. But now the service was becoming virtually official institutionalized expectation and practice. This was, recall, the era of inquisition, Giordano Bruno and then Galileo Galilei serving as advertisements that damnation to hellish fire could begin in this world, too. Stephen Greenblatt (2011, pp. 250, 251) quoted (from Redondi 1987 [1983], p. 340) a Jesuit prayer three lines of which summarize a large part of the official lesson: "All the bodies of the world shine with the beauty of their forms. / Without these the globe would only be an immense chaos. / In the beginning God made all things, so that they might generate something." In sum, all of what is ultimately derives from God (or Hegel's Absolute). Human beings have only to appreciate it as such. The function of art is to celebrate that core lesson. Or as Greenblatt expanded on the point, "the obedient young Jesuit was to tell himself every day that the only alternative to the divine order he could see celebrated all around him in the extravagance of Baroque art was a cold, sterile, chaotic world of meaningless atoms."[295]

One of the lessons we have learned from ancient Greek culture is that the broad, common ordinariness of believing *in* myths even when many or most people do not believe those myths easily persists while the arts and the sciences flourish in the larger culture; moreover, that this conjunction may well be immune to the freedom of legislation. When in the course of events an alarmed population finds no solace in any other explanation of, and avenue of escape from, the condition that has alarmed, myth offers a kind of "fail safe" alternative precisely because it consists in, or at least rests upon, nothing but articles of faith. If nothing else works, articles of faith gain power and authority from their nonrationality, not in spite of it. In situations short of dire alarm, myths also easily serve as shortcuts or conveniences for those who resist the effort of reason and empirical evidence, thus serving as a sort of catchment basin for failures of education. One need not believe the myth in order to believe *in* it, in the apparent simplicity of its comfort and assurance (Veyne 1988 [1983]). As the power and authority of Christianity gradually leaked out of the vessel, replacements of mythic stature seemed already to hand in the very arts that had been brought on board by the church itself as its own augmentation by splendors of music, painting,
architecture, and so forth. The arts, or in a sense more appropriately *Art*, had already learned the catechism, so to speak. But in addition, Art, unlike Science, was not offering a "cold, hard, impersonal rationality" in competition with theology and religious belief. Art inherited a large

---

[295] Greenblatt was there implicitly recalling an earlier account in which he (2011, p. 238) had said of Giordano Bruno (and his *Expulsion of the Triumphant Beast* [1584}, which lead to his execution by fire in 1600), "What he prized was the courage to stand up for the truth against the belligerent idiots who were always prepared to shout down what they could not understand." Little did Greenblatt know that five years later the idiots would become more elevated. As for the notion that "bodies of the world shine," one could spy an inheritance (perhaps via a swerve near Hegel?) in Dreyfus and Kelly (2011).

burden, one that by Hegel's diagnosis was coming to an end not because Art had necessarily failed but because history had moved on, and it was the turn of philosophy to carry the burden.[296]

But the secularizing effects were also being encouraged by forces largely external to both artistic endeavors and religious doctrine. The economy of attention was changing, for political-economic reasons, and a major factor among those reasons was, as Pinkard (1994, p. 268) has said, "the decline of the aristocratic ethos," which added to "the sense of 'groundlessness'" that had been accumulating for cultural reasons.[297] Indeed, attention itself was becoming privileged in a new way, to which Hegel's "elevation" of an essentially disembodied consciousness ironically contributed. "The god is present in the statue, and we intuit him (or her) in seeing the statue. The artist therefore can only understand himself as a fabricator, someone who makes things, not someone who creates things. The statue must be seen as having, so to speak, inspired its own creation" (Pinkard 1994, p. 235; cf. Hegel 1977 [1952], §709). The "make things" locution is a statement of "fabricating" a material object from the idea of that object, the idea itself having independent existence that human being does not make, does not invent, but discovers. The idea is the creative force; it operates through human being. In order for the "made thing" to have majesty, to be divine, it must not be seen as having been created by human being. For that seeing would instill nihilism.

Recall the ambiguity preserved by Heidegger which I cited above as serving as a saddle for the dilemma bequeathed in Kant's legacy. That ambiguity well describes the persistent chief pairing of conceptions of Art. On the one hand, we know the idea that something new can be accorded the status of "art" only insofar as it can be shown to have historical connection to prior outcomes already accorded the status of "art." On the other, we know the idea that "art" is more than simply its reception theory, more than any fact of its having been accepted by a requisite audience as "art" or as a countable presence within the institution of "art"; for there must be some value that transcends the historical, thus giving any specific works of art the standing as instances of Art. This standing is crucial to Art's soterial power, which must come from source other than human being. People sing "God's own music," as Gant (2017) has documented, and the singing, whether in more or less full voice or in the silence of mind, inspires, elevates, spirit. But the human penchant for "making differently" does complicate matters.

Whether Pinkard's (1994) thesis about dissolution of an "aristocratic ethos" is correct or not, human beings have left a thick trail of what might be called evidence of "evolving artistic expression" in European and European-descendent cultures during the several centuries since Art won increasing independence from religious, primarily Christian, strictures about the portrayal of life forms in general and human, or human-like, life forms more particularly.

---

[296] A notion of the excessive burden of Art became one of the main themes of the work of philosopher and art critic Arthur Danto, who devoted many pages (e.g., 1995) to exploration of "the end of art" thesis and Hegel.

[297] In Hauser's (1982 [1974], pp. 660, 661) view, similarly, "Hegel's prophecy of the collapse of art originated in the experience of post-revolutionary events and their expression in romanticism." Hauser then added that the "howls about the supposed 'end of art' have their origin in the ideology of the upper class, in spite of the fact that most of the people who proclaim it are artists who are led by the nose from above and are unaware of their own situation."

Whether the mode of expression be pictorial or musical or bodily (as in architecture, dance, sculpture, etc.) or literate, the record has been one of successive "periods" and "styles" of creative imagination—that is, of materialized makings (poiesis) of cognitive-emotive, sometimes cathectic, meanings—much as we humans have typically built our records of passages within, of, and by any other category of "human history." The categories often attain, though impermanently, objectivities of sociality, within which habitations there are long inertial moments during which everyday consciousness mistakes the habitations as having extra-human, extra-cultural, extra-historical significance and even material substance. For a believer a mere wafer of flour and water can become in the moment an actuality of divine presence. For long periods of time this has been the grave burden loaded likewise onto Art. It is in that sense that one can rather easily appreciate the ability of Hegel to believe that he stood at the apex of human history, an objective intellect who had surveyed all of history, concluded that now was a pinnacle eventuality in which all of human progress had come to its final concentration as philosophy, superseding all prior achievements of consciousness of the Absolute, *and* that *his* encyclopædic grasp of all prior expressions of that trajectory of the Absolute coming into full consciousness of itself was *itself* that culmination. It was now clear that Art, like prior expressions of religiosity, no longer needed to carry the grave burden under which it had been stumbling along.

A generation after Hegel's death in 1831 it became clear instead that Art had not been finished, if in fact anyone was still reading Hegel's phrase at all—or, if so, reading it as "the end of art" ("end" meaning finality). Gadamer was right in trying to reconnect the Hegelian phrase with the context of Hegel's "past," the time when Europe's most important artists were serving as church architect, interior decorator, and composed of masses, oratorios, and other "religious music" (e.g., Handel's oratorio of 1741). Pippin's (2014) choice of 1750 as transitional year is appropriate even though it re-invites "debate" about "origins," "beginnings," and the like. If we ignore Hegel's presumption of "inevitability" of the basic process he knew he had spied, one could argue that the choice of 1750 is too early. Beethoven's Mass in C major, published in 1812, was not a popular success, but in 1823 he finished his even more demanding Mass in D major ("Missa solemnis"), and it gained wide approval in parts as well as in whole. Pippin's main point remains, however. Hegel's "past" was already past by the time Hegel was born (1770). That is not unusual for first-person consciousness of history's periodic past, as distinguished from one's first-person past (which is an ongoing recension). Thus, the chief question is not whether Hegel would have been surprised by the great burst of artistic imagination that began a generation after 1831, connected with names such as Édouard Manet, Franz Liszt, Jules Perrot, Oscar Wilde, Edith Wharton, and Louis Sullivan. Nor whether he would have been surprised that creative imagination—even though that phrase was being applied less often in the sciences than in the arts—was beginning to generate also an enormous expansion, indeed a nearly complete overhaul, of the biological sciences in the persons of Charles Darwin and Alfred Russel Wallace, and of the physical sciences (as in James Clerk Maxwell's ingenious theory of thermodynamics). The chief question is, rather, why Hegel's locution, "art as a thing of the past," and its rephrasing as "the end of art," gained enough weight that it could be the proverbial "quarter-ton cannonball on a mattress" and pull a discourse of "modern society" into its basin. Hauser (1982 [1974], p. 657) was not wrong to say that "only since Hegel" have we "begun to talk about the collapse of art as a part and a symptom of total cultural development which has apparently come to an end," even if there was a considerable lag in onset after Hegel. Of course, "the arts" have never actually collapsed, but the tone of conversation about tomorrow has nonetheless often advertised a sense of urgency among artists themselves, some of whom then resurrect a sort of Hegelian line about "man's need of art" as offering a "perspective of the eternal." The sense of urgency also reflects an evacuation of confidence in the ability of the "here and now"—in renewal and continued fertility of a particular artistic style, for instance, and likewise in first-person self-confidence to "remain vital" in working a furrow.

Some artists have also given voice to concerns about self-perceived ability of present actors actually to do as Marx (1976 [1888], p. 8) proposed and not merely to "read" or "paint" or "sing" or "interpret the world" but to *change* its actuality and thus its potentiality—that is, to change the ways in which, the conditions by which, we produce/reproduce not just words and pictures and musical scores but *world*. Then again, of course, we *have* been changing world. But many of us have doubted that the balance of change has been good, and because of this doubt the recommendation to take "the perspective of eternity" has seemed intelligible although none of us actually knows what that is.

There is a sharp irony in the recommendation. Hauser was neither wrong nor contrary to Hegel when he (1982 [1974], p. 657) pointed to a major comparative thread of the "end of art" talk: "What we understand by the end of art is its failure compared with the extent of scientific achievements." The irony comes to visit as we notice that by far the greatest, the most effective, the first and nearly the *only* actual success in taking "the perspective of eternity" was produced by Isaac Newton in his equations of motion (which, as we know from our daily rounds, still apply without exception within that part of "the universe" known as its "Newtonian domain").

Those of us who are conversant with the social sciences should then also notice another part of the irony: the process represented in that nomination (Newton's equations of motion) is a process of aggregation, and we still know too little about it. I am referring not to "the physical" as we so often think it ("physical pure and exact," devoid of "social" and other contaminants) but to the social as it includes, encompasses, gives meanings of, "the physical" (and other domains): how do the contextual, conditional, and causal factors of "Newton's past" (factors shared to large extent with many others) funnel into the first-person cognitive-emotive understandings of one actor (in this instance Newton), then issue into effects, tiny to potentially very large, that aggregate in time, both individually and in concert with action effects by other actors, to produce a sequence of new realities from Newton to Clerk Maxwell to Einstein to Dirac, and so on? The same question can be asked also, of course, about sequences in the creative imaginations of those actors we nominate as "artist." But there we (unlike Hegel) tend far more to see multiplicities (e.g., "the arts," "styles") than we typically see in "modern science" (or that section, "natural science," which we regard as exemplar of the whole) as general template. And even though "the arts" are lenses by which we experience "the real" (or realities) just as much as is "science," it is generally apparent that "the real" that we see through the latter lens is somehow *more real*. That is, necessity is still more real to us than freedom.

Bourdieu recalled Hegel's work in aesthetics insightfully when reminding his students of the complicated relations of process (thus history) due to the "doubling" of human being—integral producer of sociality and thus of objectivities of human action, whose actions are informed by objectivities resident in first-person subjectivities of consciousness, whence more effects of cognitive-emotive experiences in more and potentially different sociality:

I think that everything we do, everything we say, everything we think is at the crossroads between two histories: the history that we carry inside our heads and the history that objects carry with them. Things are historical through and through, and this is even more true of what is in our heads. We are in the presence of the 'natural'—of what goes without saying, of the self-evident—when the incorporated subjective phenomenon, when the incorporated historical phenomenon and the objectivated historical phenomenon are at one. I think that part of the great charm of artistic experience lies in the fact that it is one of the incarnations of this experience of the natural, of the 'this feels right to me', 'I feel at home in this painting'. These themes are Hegelian: 'I am so well-adjusted to the historical experience that this painting embodies that it is as though I had painted it myself; I feel good in this work, I inhabit it' (Bourdieu 2017 [2013], pp. 215-216); cf. Hegel 1971 [1830], §562).[298]

Hegel easily comes to mind, especially vis-à-vis Kant, when we think of Romanticist charges that the "mechanicism" of science-based thought is too neglectful of, reductive of, the richly varied particularities of life. As first-person experience, an assumption that Bourdieu's "incorporated subjective phenomenon"—itself necessarily an "incorporated historical phenomenon"—and "the objectivated historical phenomenon" (i.e., the objectivity produced in and by a sociality, always "historical through and through") "*are at one*," as Bourdieu put it, is the shovel that one ultimately turns against both sides of the dilemma labelled "individual solipsism" and "transcendental necessity," and as if in the very same moment of one's seemingly inescapable presumption of continuity of self in time. Bourdieu was addressing what has been called "the problem of scale" (i.e., "e pluribus unum," or from "the many" particulars to "the unity" of one compound or cohesion), a problem about which he had many intelligent things to say but did not convincingly "solve" (and about which, more in Parts Four and Five). He was also trading on the metaphor of a feeling of "being at home" as if without its opposite side, however, the metaphor of the feeling of "being lost," an opposition that parallels the fact/counterfact dialectic.

This brings us to another of the most troubling features of Hegel's vision in regard to a "complete aesthetics" (as also in his general system): "the problem of counterfactuals" simply disappears from view, as if it either never did actually exist as a problem of perception or, through an operation of Hegel's system motivation, is perpetually vanquished in advance (as with the

---

[298] Hegel's answer to the question, "What is the human "*need* to produce works of art?"—a question that matters especially because, unlike the necessity of any beauty of natural formation, the beauty of a work of art exists within "precisely the freedom of production and configurations"—can be found here: "The universal and absolute need from which art (on its formal side) springs has its origin in the fact that man is a *thinking* consciousness, i.e., that man draws out of himself and puts before himself what he is and whatever else is. Things in nature are only *immediate* and *single*, while man as spirit (Geist) *duplicates* himself [sich *verdoppeln*], in that (i) he is as things in nature are, but (ii) he is just as much *for* himself (Hegel 1975 [1835], vol. 1, pp. 5, 30-31).

related query, "what happens to 'error,' once it has been realized as such?"; see, e.g., Hegel 1977 [1952], §§38-41, 78-89, 111-131), because perception as such really does not matter all that much.[299] Truth and error, fact and counterfact, reside in the unity of opposites of a dialectic that unfolds continually in quest of complete realization of the Absolute. Hegel thought this process as a flow of asymptotically successive stages, each manifesting in self-transcendence as a new unity. Otherwise there is no position, there is no information, of counterfactuality (or of error) from which to learn, excepting admonition to avoid the position of the empty abyss. Because in Hegel's system this dialectical process transpires behind the back of consciousness, regulated by operations of the cunning of reason, any actual empirical actor is either instrument or vessel (or perhaps both), left to wonder by what means the final realization of the Absolute can possibly be recognized even as an article of faith. It is at such juncture, of course, that one catches sight of the inexplicable exception of consciousness—namely, Hegel's "special actor" privilege as phenomenological observer. His effort to correct Kant's neglect of the question, "Whence the determinate normativity?" (see, e.g., Hegel 1977 [1952], §§50-53; cf. Brandom 2002, p. 213; 2009, pp. 65-66) began and ended in hock to a dogmatism, a somewhat secularized rendition of Christian theology. Both Art and Science are expressions of Hegel's Absolute. Human acts of invention that matter are really acts of discovery.

What, then, was being discovered by human actions of Art? What discovery came from, say, the increased replacement of egg by linseed or walnut oil as medium of pigments? The paints did gain thereby in luminosity and in resilience. Was anything else discovered? Or, more specifically, what discovery came on Hieronymus Bosch's use of the "alla prima" style in his *Garden of Earthly Delights* (1504)—that is, applying paints to a surface only once, with little or no underpainting? What was revealed to human consciousness by Tintoretto's use of a carmine pigment in *Miracle of the Slave* (1548)? Or by Rembrandt's use of lead white to make "flesh tones" during the mid-1600s? It is clear from Hegel's remarks that "the fine arts" were appreciated for their role as "the supreme mode of our knowledge of the Absolute."[300] Recent commentators on Hegel's aesthetics have cited his view that Art was able to rectify deficits of "ethical life," of "genuinely mutual recognitional" relationships" (e.g., Pippin 2014, p. 36). Art, said Hegel (1971 [1830], §562), had a "close connection" with "various religions," although "*beautiful* art can only belong to those religions in which the spiritual principle, though concrete and intrinsically free, is not yet absolute" (the gratuity of this "not yet" holding the door for those religions in which the spiritual principle does have the potential of attaining the absolute). But then Hegel (1975 [1835], vol. 1, p. 10) also said of "the spirit of our world today, or, more particularly, of our religion and of the development of our reason," that it appears to be "beyond the stage at which art" can remain "the supreme mode of our knowledge of the Absolute." That task now was incumbent on philosophy (one imagines Hegel's philosophy). Not that Art—"fine

---

[299] Similarly, while Hegel offers an appreciation of irony, in the end he (1975 [1835], vol. 1, pp. 64-69, 159; see also 1971 [1830], §571) deprecates it as actually inutile: "irony … is often bare of any true seriousness and likes to delight especially in villains"; irony "ends in mere heartfelt longing instead of in acting and doing."

[300] However, he (1975 [1835], vol. 1, p. 9) also cautioned that "while on the one hand we give this high position to art, it is on the other hand just as necessary to remember that neither in content nor in form is art the highest and absolute mode of bringing to our minds the true interests of the spirit (Geist)."

art," "beautiful art," any art—was extinct; but the scaffolding in which history would transpire had moved beyond it. If in earlier times "the artist" had been a special actor used by the cunning of reason, the mantle had now shifted Hegel's philosopher. According to Hegel's calendar of dates, Belting's "era of art" was over even before Belting's mother delivered him into her world.

That is "all," it seems to me, that Hegel meant by his statement that "art is a thing of the past." Contrary to some present-day romanticist readings, Hegel's romanticism (if that is what it was) was *not*, had never been, an indictment of modernity's supposed assault against "beauty" or "the sublime," or against a superior sensitivity of artistic expression to first-person experiences of "feeling," or against a Keatsian defense of rainbows against prisms, or anything of the sort. "The genuine objectivity"—in contrast to the limited "grade of liberation" that "even fine art" brought to bear—resides "only in the medium of thought," Hegel (1971 [1830], §562) wrote late in the final volume of his *Encyclopedia*, "the medium in which alone the pure spirit is for the spirit, and where the liberation is accompanied with reverence." That objectivity now comes from philosophy, which is the movement that "finds itself already accomplished when, at the close, it seizes its own notion—that is, only *looks back* on its knowledge" (Hegel 1971 [1830], §573). This latter passage will seem familiar to a reader of Hegel's *Philosophy of Right*; for it replays the much more famous passage in his preface to that work, wherein the owl of Minerva takes flight only at dusk, after the day's rendition of reality, such as it is, has been achieved (Hegel, 1991 [1820], p. 23).

When, more than a century after Hegel's diagnosis, Clement Greenberg got around to declaring his understanding of "modernism" in art, and in painting most particularly, he knew that history very well, including the lived history that Hegel had missed, and he knew the truly critical focus that had come together earlier, in the work of Kant.

> Western civilization is not the first civilization to turn around and question its own foundations, but it is the one that has gone furthest in doing so. I identify Modernism with the intensification, almost the exacerbation, of this self-critical tendency that began with the philosopher Kant. Because he was the first to criticize the means itself of criticism, I conceive of Kant as the first real Modernist (Greenberg 1993 [1960], p. 85).

Kant gave considerable emphasis to "pleasure" in his critique of judgments and qualities of perception (i.e., aesthetics) that inform particular judgments. His Romantic critics did not so much disagree with the notion of "pleasing effects" as find it insufficient because too indebted to the "legislative" principle (subject, actor, etc.)—or, to put it the other way around, not adequately sensitive to the intrinsic value, the mystery, the inherent force, of the object "as it is" prior to any legislative intent and whether its effect is pleasing or repugnant; in other words, valuation as if from within "the perspective of eternity." By 1800, who in Europe could not recite a litany of repugnant acts in the Terror, objectively available ("object lessons") to the artist who knew how properly to memorialize the lesson? Or think of Wilfred Owen's poetry in wake of Europe's Great War or Picasso's *Guernica* as testament to horrors of death from the sky. Utilitarianism attracted the same criticism. Hegel offered an alternative aesthetic theory that for a time had persuasive force mainly because of what was taken to be its "encyclopedic" housing. But that authority of voice evaporated surprisingly fast, and soon all of his effort got reduced to a "punch line" that he surely regarded as empty of future meaning: "art is a thing of the past"; i.e., the legitimate function that Art had once performed now exceeded its capabilities, not because Art had declined absolutely but because Art had become unable to keep up with the progress of the Absolute.

The great difficulty of keeping "futures past" aligned in a coherence is tightly bound up *both* with the equally great difficulty of aligning any actor's sequence of "pasts" and periodical pasts of a history *and* with the problem of counterfactuals, the problem that always leaves causal factors, if not also contextual and conditional factors, in a limbo of skepticism. Bourdieu (above) was touching on this in his comments about "doubling." It has been said likewise of Duchamp's "readymades" that the invention of the "form" or "type" was "the invention of reality"—that is to say, the incisive discovery that "reality, in contrast to the picture of life, is the only thing of relevance. Since then, painting no longer depicts reality but is reality itself (which presents itself)" (see Richter 1995, p. 218; Horowitz 2001, p. 155). This conclusion is off by centuries, even millennia. How long ago did humans first realize that the content of a memory or a dream has something to do with a past reality, while also being real in itself? How long before humans further realized that memory (remembered dream included) is not only not static; the internal dynamic is constitutive/reconstitutive, as pieces of the once-remembered "scene" drop out, thus changing the remainder, and so forth? Furthermore, a painted scene itself is hardly static. Surely for many viewers repeated viewings of Manet's *Luncheon on the Grass* (1863), for example, or of Bosch's *Garden of Earthly Delights* (c1500) result in different first-person experiences and, though this is not an "automatic next step," different realities in paint. Further, too, how many viewers of Leonardo's mural, *The Last Supper* (c1498), and viewers of canvas-painted copies of Leonardo's mural, and viewers of posters (photographs, tapestries, etc.) of Leonardo's mural and/or of painted copies of it, when they think of the presumed "original scene" that Leonardo was depicting, "see" that scene as Leonardo depicted it, not otherwise?

Richter no doubt knew that, of course. He was there talking in an interview as a working artist being queried about the many faces of "reality" and how they appear as he is working. On the one hand, he (1995, p. 262) also said, when asked of Magritte's work, that his painting, *The Treachery of Images* (1929), popularly known as "This is not a pipe" and taken as example of much of Magritte's work, "that's just not a very important piece of information"—not that Richter disagreed but that it had become so commonplace. This was the voice not of "heroic artist" or philosopher of art; rather, of an "everyday working artist" (a title or phrase not intended as depreciation in any way) who tries to utter his cognitive-emotive experiences partly in words but more richly in images, and who (like most of us, whether it be in words, images , or both) must grapple with uncertainties of reality For he (1995, p. 68) had also said (previously and more than once) about that ever-present challenge, "We can't rely [only] on the picture of reality that we see, because we see it mediated through the lens apparatus of the eye, and corrected in accordance with past experience." Enter an understanding from the science of human optics and anatomy: who now does not know that we humans are organically limited to a very narrow range of electromagnetic radiation (aka "light"), and that even with various prosthetic devices at hand we still cannot exhaust all information present in electromagnetic radiation (or "light"). This was part of what transpired as enlightenment. Enter an understanding also, however, of the power of concept in human understanding. With that, too, in mind, we then might engage in an analysis, from which we ask, "So which is the *real* reality?" Richter's reply to his interviewer, about "picture of reality," carried that understanding—perhaps twice, the second carriage being a comment on the first, simply because when we are "dealing with facts," whether scientific or artistic or some combination, we usually do not even think to try to evade the dilemma Hume showed us, the inability of the perceiving I to catch sight of itself in its act of perceiving. Like the reality of a specific pigment of paint, the reality of a chunk of scientific "color" (i.e., light) is inescapably conceptual whether we remember that or not. But there is more. Richter continued his reply to the interviewer with this: "Because that ["the picture of reality that we see"] is not enough for us—because we want to know whether it can all be different—we paint." There, in that homage to the continued production of counterfactuals, some of which we may take as means and purpose of utopic impulse, *there* is the genuine voice of the working artist. If art, or Art, must have function, what better candidate. This is an artist's response to the terrorist, who, as Conrad (2007 [1907], pp. 38-39) said of one of his characters, takes on "the part of an insolent and venomous evoker of sinister impulses which lurk in the blind envy and exasperated vanity of ignorance."

Futures past can, sometimes do, remain in captivity to "the past" that is always already dead. How can we regtrieve them? How would we know if somehow one or another of them is still alive? If one judges by some commentaries (e.g., Horowitz 2001), the continuing juncture of historiography and theology (including various quasi-theologies) changed at some more or less specific date in European and Euro-American consciousness of "time's passage," as death of "the past" became also a death of self-confidence in freedom due to an apparent conviction that when the necessity of original sin and divine redemption died the only remaining necessity was of death on the heels of a now-peculiar original deficiency, an original incapacity which ensures that hope is always something that was a condition of a future past now dead. Forthwith, human culture first as Art and then as Philosophy was reduced to a perpetual task of "sustaining loss."

Each generation still today sustains the loss of its predecessor. But now, as the viewpoint of "the eternal" has evaporated, human being is apparently unable to grasp any point to it. Art after the end of art became empty of "point," empty of genuine will. So, too, then, philosophy after … —but after what, or whom? Well, certainly after Hegel; maybe still, or again, after Heidegger and Sartre. Creative imagination demonstrated repeatedly an ability to invent a panoply of mythic creatures, some of them hydra-headed or other monstrous composites of parts, all of them frightening ghosts of the ancient night. Nothing else happened. After Freud we can tell rather different stories about the night callers, what they might signify. So, for instance, we exchange original sin for Oedipus and Electra (maybe Clytemnestra and Narcissus, too?); but otherwise nothing else happened. Apparently, that same creative imagination enabled us, maybe impelled us, to invent questions that we persistently ask and cannot answer, satisfyingly if at all—except, we remember, to stimulate existential angst about futility. The mirrors held up by Nietzsche showed that it has been *we* who have created nihilism (even though we still reply, in the absurdity of existence, that it was Nietzsche who invented nihilism). The knowledge which has been left to us is—and always will be, after evaporation of the viewpoint of eternity opened, by some mysterious dispensation, a single one-way lane of negational traffic—inadequate to our needs because it does not "resolve anything, but rather points to a condition, our condition, of perpetual nonresolution. What is life like when the condition for asking just that question is that the most fulfilling answer is always—remains—in the past, from which therefore we are always in exile" (Horowitz 2001, p. 90). One might wonder if this rhetorical question is, under different pretence, a virtual line from *Waiting for Godot*. Has "waiting for Godot" been, all along, mostly waiting for the day when we humans can no longer make any new meanings?

Horowitz (2001, p. 73) chose a famous line from Flannery O'Connor, not Beckett, as an augmenting illustration. Although it might seem that literary artists did converge on a theme of "death and the past," after the Great Depression, the massive destruction wreaked in World War II even before the atomic bomb, and revelations of the Holocaust, it was hardly a new theme. Nor had there been a gap in attention to it, at least from Homer onward. Nonetheless (to recall prior discussion in part), Faulkner's (1994 [1951], p. 535) character, Gavin Stevens, observes that the "past is never dead. It's not even past," Hartley (1953) began *The Go-Between* by advising that "the past is a foreign country," and (to cite but one more example) Katherine Ann Porter replayed a version of Faulkner's line at least once.

One surmises, however, that O'Connor can seem more fitting because of her own trials of life and religiosity. She (1988 [1952], p. 59), also like Faulkner tracing threads of redemption, has one of her characters proclaim that, "Well, I preach the Church Without Christ. I'm member and preacher to that church where the blind don't see and the lame don't walk and what's dead stays that way. Ask me about that church and I'll tell you it's the church that the blood of Jesus don't foul with redemption." There is mutual irony in the passage, resulting from O'Connor's metaphorical pairing of two characters in this, her first novel, *Wise Blood*, with its strong features of an absurdism mixed with an irony that traces the shifting connection between redemption and renunciation. One of her characters, Enoch Emery, inherited "wise blood" from his father, the result being that he understands what will happen next as well as what has happened. This mystical experience of world is due not to any rational action by him but simply to feelings which come from within him, his wise blood. By contrast, Hazel Motes, a war veteran and self-declared preacher whose announcement is the line famously cited, has used reason to figure out the hypocrisy of established church religion, which he has renounced. But it soon becomes clear that he is as much captured by Christianity within and because of his atheist mission as was (is) any devoted believer. His renunciation is the other side of the doctrine of redemption that he has rejected. O'Connor's allegory, as she shows it, unfolds as absurdist theatre—not exactly Beckett but with resemblances. The unity of theme rests in the same irony: a past—indeed, very likely a mixture of many pasts—is not dead; it lives in *me*, and in *you*, and *you*. Must we take that to be another debilitation? Or that, rather than the fact that our cultural memory can be so often so astonishingly short?

Life is absurd, according to some outstanding theatre of the twentieth century—and not only theatre by Beckett, although his *Waiting for Godot* or *Endgame* (1957) might still be the emblematic artwork; think of the forlorn Willie Loman in Arthur Miller's *Death of a Salesman* (1949), along with many others. Why is life absurd? Or has it always been absurd? Supposedly because it has no "ground" and no point. Supposedly, too, "no, once upon a time it had a point"—

239

which was, by Christian doctrine, eternal grace (contingent of that first great inequality: qualification). That, supposedly, has been the big loss. Hazel Motes was unwelcome messenger. So, too, in a somewhat different setting in time and place, Faulkner's Isaac McCaslin: poor Ike thought he had done all the right things, certainly he had tried his best, and still it all came to *nothing*.[301] An Art that had been carrying water for Christian belief, bearing up under the weight of celebrating the majesty of a belief and its attendant rituals, having worked itself into this standing as soterial servant, now sought to shock its audiences by declaring that the world is *without meaning*. Human meanings, the subtext said, are never good enough, never will be good enough. Who could be surprised that many working artists had opted out of that play, if ever they had been in it, saying only, "Leave me out of it and let me make *my* art."

Pictorial art became "minimalist," perhaps fitting to a world without meaning (if anyone can imagine such an object). Poetic art turned in part to popular culture for refreshment (after T S Eliot on one hand and Robert Frost on the other). Wallace Stevens was still difficult and esoteric; John Ashbery was yet to come. (This was, recall, a time of Allan Ginsberg's *Howl* and Jack Kerouac's *On the Road* poetics, offered as a renewal of automotive discovery of a vast country.) Arts of theatre had been taking the lead—Camus, Cocteau, Beckett, Miller, and so on—both live-stage and cinematic. Sidney ("Paddy") Chayefsky's screenplay, *Network* (1976), brought to the cinematic screen the gravity of emotions of ineffectuality and alienation that many people had experienced in daily life but not seen and heard so reflectively in the shared mirror of a sociality. Chayefsky's screenplay was adapted to live theatre by Lee Hall and first performed in London's Royal National Theatre from November 2017. Hall modified the end of the play by bringing Howard Beale (Bryan Cranston) "back from the dead" as, in effect, a Greek-choral voice speaking as Beale's shade, lying on the stage floor:

> And so Howard Beale became the only TV personality who died because of bad ratings. But here is the truth: the "absolute truth," paradoxical as it might appear, the thing we must be most afraid of is the destructive power of absolute beliefs—that we can know anything conclusively, absolutely—whether we are compelled to it by anger, fear, righteousness, injustice, indignation; as soon as we have ossified the truth, as soon as we start believing in that Absolute—we stop believing in human beings, as mad and tragic as they are. The only total commitment any of us can have is to other people— in all their complexity, in their otherness, their intractable reality.

Beale then ends by saying "it is not beliefs that matter it is human beings. This is Howard Beale signing off for the last time." The irony, perhaps unintended, is that Beale's words, the words of a dying man, would have in an earlier time carried great weight *because* he knew they were his last, that he was a dying man and thus that his words were privileged in an ethical, even legal, tradition that had begun in religious conviction. Now they were simply words of a dead

---

[301] The McCaslin family populated Faulkner's fictional county of Mississippi, and in more than one of his artworks. I am referring specifically to Ike in the short story, "The Bear" (Faulkner 1994 [1942]), which became a section of his novel, *Go Down, Moses*. I once knew a woman whose roots were in Holmes County, which was still home of some McCaslins (and other Faulkner characters). She had iinteresting stories to tell, more or less in follow-up to Faulkner, but was afraid to put them into print. After reading one of her drafts my initial skepticism lifted, and I understood her reluctance.

man, whose shade no longer carried persuasive force—a man, moreover, who had very recently demonstrated a kind of personal madness, a being out of control.

The issues involved in the "crisis of Art," conventionally dated as having begun during the 1800s, unfold in differing, sometimes seemingly contradictory ways. For all its notoriety, "shock value" has played a less important role in that unfolding than have other, less noticed correlations across functions, ends, interests, and valuations of Art. As illustration of the inconsistency, if not contradictoriness, of relations, consider this comparison. On the one hand, the place of architecture among the visual arts has been (and remains) ambiguous because its chief uses have been defined as some blend of "the decorative" and "the mechanical," neither of which has traditionally been accorded status as "fine art." (The "mechanical"? Too much hand, not enough head. The "decorative"? Too superficial, cosmetic, no real substance; mere artifice.) Some uses, in other words, have been qualifying but others disqualifying; the specter of uselessness haunts mainly if not only the qualifying kind. The best paintings and musical compositions have been inherently safe in that they have no practical use, whereas the arts of architecture, like print making and glass blowing, are usually primarily concerned to meet expectations of practical utility. (It was the clarity of that status ladder that was befuddled by "impertinences" such as Duchamp's notorious *Fountain* and Andy Warhol's celebrated soup cans.) On the other hand, however, "high art" was partly about lack of practical utility only in a rather narrow sense, given that so much weight had always inhered in, been assigned to, an experience of a "majesty" of creative imagination. The point had been that artists who were "blessed" with "talent" would harness their imaginative powers to create "objects of art" that would elevate humankind, works that demonstrate new and different ways of doing and thus being. The activities subsumed under "Art" were about the creation of meanings (just as were the activities subsumed under "Science"). What could be more human, more humanly useful, than that? Think of "the function of art," if it must have one, as culturally prosthetic—affording us new abilities of vision, of sound, of touch and bodily motion.

Along the way, I think it is clear, the conception and perception of Art as about creations of meaning, of meaningful being, got coopted by one of the components. This part of a whole was elevated to dominance of the whole. Superficially, one might conclude that painting became the part that dominated Art. More effectively, however, the component, in the sense of a part of artistic consciousness, that dominated the whole of Art was not one of the types in hierarchy of artistic production (painting) but a quality in principle common to all types, "beauty," which for many of the Romantics became not simply an emblem but the core value and, in a sense, even substance of Art, thus losing sight of the fact that Kant's third critique, his would-be capstone, often cited as the initiating argument, was primarily about *perception* and *judgment*, not beauty (which, along with the sublime, recall, was taken to be empirically the extremity of subjectivity in acts of judgment). John Levi Martin (2017) has undertaken a systematic, detailed study of literatures that have treated "beauty" as a term of equivalent logical status to "truth" and "goodness" in a purportedly classical triad of "the true, the good, and the beautiful." Martin's conclusion is that in fact "the beautiful" is a recent accretion. Indeed, as one follows the course of his inquiry that conclusion not only becomes compelling, it also rests on a bed of evidence that strongly suggests that the accretion, far from being unmotivated, stemmed (consciously or

241

not) from interest in restoring or reinvigorating, although in more secular terms, the traditional trinitarian motif of Christianity as foundational to human values. If a specific date should be wanted for this accretion, 1750 is as good as any, for it was then that Alexander Gottlieb Baumgarten published his treatise on aesthetics (see, e.g., Caygill 2016). As Tolstoy (1904, pp. 20-21, 65) recounted the event (disapprovingly), Baumgarten proposed a "division of the Perfect (the Absolute) into the three forms of Truth, Goodness, and Beauty," later solidified as the "Baumgartenian Trinity—Goodness, Beauty, and Truth." It was a century after Baumgarten's treatise, however, that the formulation gained its most explicitly religious tincture, in a work by a French philosopher, Victor Cousin, who preached "a sentimental theism" in which he attempted "to wed a somewhat neo-Kantian theory of knowledge and action to his religious sensibilities," the result soon becoming perhaps "the most important influence on French social thought since Descartes" (Martin 2017, p. 5).[302] This was the context of which Bourdieu (1996 [1992], pp. 295, 105) proposed rewriting "the history of pure aesthetics" in order to show (among other lessons) "how professional philosophers have imported into the domain of art certain concepts originally developed in the *theological* tradition." Cousin, via his "theory," which amounted only to a "confusion of aesthetic value and moral (or social) value," was a principal figure in that event.

For Kant, "beauty" was exceptional both because of what it was and because of what it was not. Whether following the text of Kant's third critique or not (the point could have come already from Baumgarten, for instance), the Romantics appreciated the premise with which Kant began his inquiry: "beauty" is as near to being "pure subjectivity" as could be imagined ("the eye of the beholder," etc.; i.e., valorization of a "pure individuality," which lay at the heart of the aim but also by presumption the sustenance of Bildungsprozess). In what must have been the same moment of conceptualization, however, something of the moment of "beauty" necessarily escaped "the conceptual"—"necessarily," for otherwise it would not be a phenomenon of radical individuality (since concepts are loaded inherently with sociality, history, etc.). What better means, then, to serve as conduit of "pure intuition" (in "neo-Kantian" guise). We can see a continuation of that "promissory note" in Arnold Gehlen's (1960, pp. 61-64) reference to painters (he mentioned Manet in particular) for having created works that proposed intuitions (Anschauungen) for which corresponding concepts (Begriffe) apparently did not exist.

Is that coherent? If it should be an accurate account of an artist's intent, or at least effect, then why were nonesuch later produced? Given the human proclivity to make meaning—and not solely as those of a first-person experience but also as topics of conversation, more material for the conduct of sociality—there would surely have been sufficient incentive to produce new concepts to cover the absences. Poets would have been busy at it, since, as Merwin (2002, p. 12) has put it, one of a poet's chief concerns is to create an authenticity of connection between words

---

[302] I do not dispute Martin's tentative verdict (qualified with "perhaps") about Cousin's influence, but I would argue that the comparative field at the time consisted mainly of rather weak "neo-Kantians" and "neo-Hegelians," some of the latter figures actually being anti-Hegelian in much the same way that some "neo-Kantians" were actually anti-Kantian. An illustration of the weak field is given in Descombes' (1980 [1979], p.p. 20-21) recall of a famous exchange between André Cresson and Léon Brunschvicg, two of the most prominent philosophers in France during the late nineteenth and early twentieth century.

and experience. It is not as if insufficient time had passed, for Gehlen was writing the better part of a century after Manet had startled his Parisian circles in the 1860s. Perhaps suitable concepts *had* been produced during the interim but Gehlen had not noticed them. We cannot say; for we do not actually know what intuitions he had detected, since he, by his own account, lacked the conceptual means by which to convey them thoughtfully to others, or so it would seem from his own accounting (see also Gadamer 1967; 1986 [1967], p. 93). We, on the other hand, do notice in retrospect new concepts coming to the fore—for instance, in the naming of styles and periods, in the discourses about "the origin" of this or that "work of art," and so forth. Indeed, sometimes we can catch glimpses of intended outcome when a painter or composer or playwright talks openly with friends about what "difference," what "statement," a work in progress is striving to make, in that moment when expectations of imagination take over as if "the work" now "works" itself into being.

It is especially then that we should remember that artworks, in that very process of making, teach us lessons (if we are prepared to understand) about ourselves, our societies, our histories. Kant led the way, Pippin (2014, pp. 3-4) has reminded us, into the nineteenth-century understandings of that formative, educative process, and key to the vitality of *Kant's lesson to us* is his insight that artworks *are* educative because they are *not* restricted to the purely intuitional. They present a different kind of conceptual window precisely because they do *not* come to us from some alien-like esoteric or mystical realm of intelligence but from our own histories, the histories in and by which specific artworks can come to be. As Pippin (2014, p. 27) said in his regard of Manet in particular, "The narrative that we need for modernist painting begins" not in the 1860s and Manet but "with the reaction against the rococo in the 1750s." Whether Pippin meant in that an endorsement of the view that artistic imagination advances (or simply changes) only by a generational displacement of parents is unclear (he probably did not, and certainly not as some kind of inevitable creative force). But he surely did mean to say that the idiom of "clean break," "fresh start," and the like, is, for any other art, merely a showpiece of the self-justifying art of propaganda. Remember, artists, too, work in order to be noticed, to gain advantages of reputation, material but also ideal advantages.

When Hegel came on scene with his lectures on aesthetics, Art was already overburdened with the load of "cultural," or "national-cultural," expectations—and this aside from the huge inherent contradiction that had been woven into expectations of "beauty" (and, more especially for poetics and music, "the sublime"). First-person experiences could easily run blindly with cathectic and other energies of emotion, only to collapse into frustrations supposedly always ready in ambush by the inherent conceptuality of second-person conversation and third-person inference and attribution. An almost scholastic literature of "genius" took root in that collapse, as did related arguments about an inevitable "tragedy of the idea" and "tragedy of culture." Listen to Pippin (2014, p. 33) once more: "art, at least for most of its existence, had for Hegel a kind of philosophic work to do; in his language, that work was a particular way of what he also called 'working out' (herausarbeiten) modes of self-understanding with respect to the basic problem, …the issue of 'the Absolute,' that 'subject-object' problem."

## §18. Artful Pleasures in Artifice

Hegel (1975 [1835], vol. 1, pp. 1, 33) agreed that in "the spacious *realm of the beautiful*, and more precisely in the realm of "*art* or, rather, *fine art*," an observer sees abundant evidence of the arousal of feelings of pleasure, all empirically undeniable as first-person experiences. "Feeling as such is an entirely empty form of subjective affection," however—that is, "a purely subjective emotional state of mind in which the concrete thing vanishes, contracted into a circle of the greatest abstraction." While one might wonder what power performs this "greatest abstraction," one must also allow for slippage, since the line appears in the lecture notes of Hegel's university course on aesthetics. On the other hand, there is little doubt that Hegel understood pleasure, and the realm of "feeling" in general, as within a "spacious realm" of secondariness: feeling differs from "intelligent rationality" by its "particular subjectivity," which bears its own "vanity and caprice" (Hegel 1971 [1830], §93). In Hegel's appreciation, Kant had rested content with the merely "subjective," in regard to "the judgment and the production" of art, and thus had failed to reach the "absolute true and actual" reality. Only by overcoming Kant's deficiencies could one (i.e., Hegel) grasp "the starting point for the true comprehension of the beauty of art," and indeed the entire realm of a complete aesthetics (Hegel 1975 [1835], vol. 1, p. 60; cf. Bowie 2003, pp. 140-141).

Kant "always considers" pleasure and displeasure to be "one feeling," Howard Caygill (1989, p. 286) has pointed out. That is, this one feeling is a dialectical unity of opposites. It is at the core of the aim of consciousness in its search for a unity of experience, a coherence of meanings. The general expectation—not unique to Kant—was that seeking coherence and unity would generate outcomes assessible between poles of "the pleasing" and "the displeasing," *and* that at personal level one had both power of judgment and freedom to exercise redress. In regard to one's prospects of future action, the regulative attitude need not be (and should not be) Polyanna's wishfulness. As I partly recalled above, Kant, already in his first critique, in his initial treatment of the transcendental power of judgment (1998 [1787], beginning at B171/A132), held that "truth and illusion are not in the object, insofar as it is intuited, but in the judgment about it insofar as it is thought. Thus, it is correctly said that the senses do not err; yet not because they always judge correctly, rather because they do not judge at all" (B350).

That limit must be kept in mind with another. Kant is sometimes quoted as having said that there "could never be a Newton for a blade of grass." That is not precisely what he said, however. Rather, to put those words in context:

> it is quite certain that we can never adequately come to know the organized beings and their internal possibility in accordance with merely mechanical principles of nature, let alone explain them; and indeed this is so certain that we can boldly say that it would be absurd for humans even to make such an attempt or to hope that there may yet arise a Newton who could make comprehensible even the generation of a blade of grass according to natural laws that no intention has ordered; rather, we must absolutely deny this insight to human beings (Kant 2000 [1793], pp. 270-271).

Because of inherent limits of the human mind, explanation must sometimes transpire via the "as if" of a teleologic (culture being the supreme teleologic action—free of what we discern as laws of nature—even when within a culture such action is deemed to be the motive of nature itself or the motive of a god expressed through nature, or some such attribution). Here, in this second part of his third critique, Kant was recalling and then expanding on his fundamental point of the transcendental Illusion: because of limitations of the conceptual, the perceiving subject ascribes (inscribes might be better) a necessity of objectivity to that which it can only intuit. Thus, we perceive relative purpose in and among parts of nature, among parts of the natural object, and so on, *as if* it inhered in nature itself, when the most we can know with certainty is that relative purpose (e.g., the usefulness of parts of nature to other parts of nature) simply reflects the limit of the conceptual capabilities of mind. It must be clear, therefore, that the intention to which Kant referred in the above passage was *human* intention. Likewise, the natural laws, the mechanical principles of nature, and so forth: all are products of human intention to understand, to know, even when (*especially* when, one might say) those products are accorded an objective necessity of "the thing itself," the "object as such."

Judgment is exercised in the conjunction of necessity and freedom: that is (to use a popular shorthand), of *understanding*, which operates within a deterministic framework, and of reason, which operates on the grounds of freedom.[303] Far from denying the experience of feeling, far from denying the force of emotions, Kant entertained such experience for what it undeniably is, which is that it can only "speak for itself," as it were. His sarcastic remark about a "genteel tone recently sounded in philosophy" (Kant 1993 [1796], p. 72) registered objection not because that "tone" made way for "feeling" (or, in today's equivalent idiom of sarcasm, a "feel-good emotion") but because it promised something it could not deliver, and at likely cost of another demagoguery.

The expectation of pleasure, of greater satisfaction of the will of consciousness to expand its own unity, is key to first-person experience of personal perception—and that means also key to the specific domain of aesthetics and its exercise in the power of judgment. Kant has often been credited with resurrection of aesthetics as an interest of philosophy; and because of the dominant reception for many years of the main point of his third critique, that credit has been as reductive as the wish to turn foolscap into action.[304] Bear in mind that "aesthetic" is from the ancient Greek aisthēsis, which in turn comes from a verb, *aisthánomai, "to* perceive," and the verb covers both perception from the senses and perception from combinations or interactions of intellect and senses. This is the basic category that Kant recovered. Soon thereafter an entire "philosophy of art"—no less than "Kant's philosophy of art"—was poured into that category as if a readymade. Who could be surprised to learn that "the pour" was already made to be the chief

---

[303] Bear in mind that to say "deterministic framework" is not necessarily to invoke a necessitarian doctrine (i.e., does not exclude probabilistic statements). Likewise, to say that reason "operates on the grounds of freedom" is not to exclude contextual, conditional, or causal relations. Counterfactuals are neither empty nor unnecessary.

[304] Kantian theory did not invent an aesthetics of the bodiless eye (i.e., *visual* perception as dominant and well-nigh exclusive). But because of his selection of "beauty" as one of the first-person experiences that virtually everyone agrees is as close as one could imagine to a *purely* subjective experience, one with virtually no possibility of an objectivity by convention (or "by nature"), since the attribution is "entirely in the eye of the beholder," he formally (mostly implicitly) authorized that view of "the aesthetic," which remains with us to the present day. A mistaske.

defect of what was, supposedly by his own account, secondary to his philosophical system (see, e.g., the succession of "commonplaces" adumbrated by Horowitz 2001, pp. 25-27). To charge that Kant's "philosophy of art," undeveloped though it be, fails chiefly because it ignores "the artifactuality of artistic beauty" is a howlingly hollow claim to make of someone who insisted that his subject was anything but a passive recipient. Indeed, a *legislator*.

As one tries to erase the anachronisms and restore Kant to his time and place, it is useful to recall Momigliano (1993, p. 49), as he, referring to writing during the fourth century BCE, discerned in a new effort to write *of a life* (in distinction from writing of a people) of a place and time that "the search for rules of life" had to reckon with the new power of words (see also Misch 1907, vol. 1).[305] "Plato's fear of being overpowered by rhetoric ["bewitched," as it were] is as real as Isocrates' fear of having his words controlled by philosophers." Momigliano well knew, of course, that these struggles have been replayed incessantly. The proper names change, the settings evolve or shift, sometimes regressively; vocabularies circulate through various experiments, etymological migrations, and recapitulations. Now and then new sorts of action call for semantical attention. But the struggle with words in inventing, rehearsing, repairing, and recasting stories of personal life continues. Samoyault's (2016) newly told story of Roland Barthes conveys many facets of the featured writer's own continuations of the struggle, including his late flirtation with beginning again, a "new writing."[306] In a related vein, Miller (1993, p. 178) recently reminded critics of Foucault's treatment of "ruling-class male ethics" that they generally overlooked "a clear message"—namely, that "the relative autonomy within particular fractions of particular social formations to manufacture and manage oneself is dependent on the institutions of those formations." Institutionalized contexts both enable and constrain, all at once as well as in sequences and scatterings, often in ways that evade conscious reflection until (if ever) later reflections of memory catch sight of differences and thus, usually by inference only, changes.

Writing so as to be remembered is not a new aim, of course, nor is the aim any more insured against futility. Aristocracy, a familial institution, has long practiced genealogy, a sort of familial biography. "As we know of Hecataeus of Miletus [c550 – c476 BCE, Greek historian and geographer], it was no extravagance to claim fifteen ancestors." No doubt, fifteen generations of documented ancestry exceeds today's norm; but then "extravagance" is the key word in that report by Momigliano (1993, p. 24): Hecataeus' skepticism of ancestral claims by fellow aristocrats is good rehearsal for considering all the people of Great Britain today who claim descent from "a knight who came over with William the Conqueror." Being already lean documents, genealogical trees are less vulnerable to the severe abstraction that lies in the future of most biographies (autobiographies included); for if an individual "life" is perceived to have continuing worth, it usually survives only in the condensation that becomes a few lines of some sort of history. Reviewing a list of ancient Greek biographies that were later attested in one way or another, Momigliano (1993, pp. 8-11) could only agree that, excepting fragments here and

---

[305] Bear in mind that Misch's history, still very useful, has a strong imprint of the theoretical "system" of his mentor, Wilhelm Dilthey, who, comparatively well read of Kant, resisted the dominant neo-Kantians of his day.
[306] And see Laurent Binet's *Seventh Function of Language* (2017 [2015]).

there, the general fate was to be dissolved into those later testimonies. Roman, Arab, and other scribes thought it worth the effort to preserve some of the histories (Herodotus, Thucydides); several scripts for theatre (the grand triad of tragedians); a few works of the Homeric song-poets; and a selection of treatises of philosophy, geography, mathematics, early science. But hardly any biography.

Was there any "new writing" to be considered during Kant's time? Indeed there was. It had been growing plentifully, much of it taking a novel form of writing "of a person." One need mention only the name of a young woman, Jane Austen, born 1775 in Hampshire.[307] Her "lives" were a sensation because, as was remarked in Part Two, they were so personal, brimming with feelings that traveled on the quotidian qualities of everyday life, as every reader could recognize. Austen's "sense," and her "sensibility," of character portrayal was finer, more subtle and far less melodramatic than had been displayed in 1740, with publication of Samuel Richardson's *Pamela,* which was for the time an intense psychological fiction conveyed in epistolary form. Richardson drew upon an account of actual events that had taken place with an air of scandal in a family during the 1720s in Leicestershire. Austen drew upon her first-person experiences, actual and imagined, of family life in the midst of efforts to maintain position in circumstances that no longer remained stable for the course of a lifetime. The very condition that Hume had highlighted in his *Treatise*—namely, that, try as he might, he could never catch sight of his own "perceiving I" in the act of perception—was becoming a disturbingly personal concern of many. (Who *am* I? Who shall I *become*? Of what may *I* hope?) This fact of "personal concern" was itself a reflection of the steadily opening ground of individual freedom that was being mapped by Kant and his legislator-subject. The meaning of freedom included the very possibility that an individual person could freely express emotional energies in first-person experiences and then convey those energies of feeling more and more freely in second-person expressions of relationship. Goethe's epistolary account of a young artist caught up in unrequited emotions for a woman beyond bounds, *The Sorrows of the Young Werther,* first published in 1740, became a financial as well as literary success for the also-young Goethe who (as mentioned above) was thereafter marked as a leading light of the Sturm und Drang ("storm and urge") movement, which evolved into German Romanticism.

Earlier I referred in passing to the dilemma of the musical composer (taken as exemplar of artists more generally) who seeks distinction in works. However much one wants to fill staves with new sounds and thus new manifestations of the dialectic of audible/inaudible, success ultimately becomes a difficult negotiation with audiences, whom one must re-educate at the same time as deliver pleasure. Of the countless memorials to that passageway, Goethe's realization of a tragic fate awaiting "the modern," no less but also no more than it did in antiquity, should remain instructive. This is not, as Goethe's superb biographer (Boyle (2000, p. 690) reminded us, the tragedy of an individual's death; nor is it that of an entire culture; "for death is a part of the natural process" (as we are wont to divide experience into parcels—"natural," "cultural,"

---

[307] To put Austen's nativity in perspective of a person today, she was born two years before my great, great, great grandfather (paternal line), although he in Virginia. That is but two generations longer than the earliest ancestor whom I personally knew, *and* whom I remember as recalling personal memories of his great grandfather. Those pasts are fragmentary—but fragments that, in varying degree, remain alive.

247

etc.). Rather, the great tragedy is manifest in realizations that, in history, these "processes of Nature destroy perfections so rare, and so nearly ideal, that nothing entitles us to expect them." This is the tragedy of an idea that no one has succeeded in bringing fully into the empirics of experience. It is the musical wish that has never found harbor in a staff. And it is, to repeat Boyle again, "a realm of human experience discontinuous with that of natural law," as Kant had taught the difference, yet it persistently shows up as "a realm not of individual moral freedom but of tragically arbitrary history." In principle we should not be, but in practice we so often are, taken in by the pathetic fallacy, confusing how we wish things to be with how they actually are, how they actually are made to be. Such is our desperate need of the comfort of firm belief that (and in) our experiences are sufficient evidence of *real* objects, not merely objects that we have "legislated" into being. Thus, the circuit by which we the reader appreciate (for example) the vexed continuity of Goethe at work on the conclusion of *Faust*, Goethe at work on the conclusion of *Wilhelm Meister*, Goethe at work on his youthful commercial success, Wilhelm's apprenticeship, and, in the midst of all that, Goethe at work on the conclusion of *Elective Affinities* (see Boyle 2000, 366-367): a circuit in which we see the work of art simultaneously as representation and as transformation—of context and conditions but also of authorial voice and eventually, through the decades, of a writing that might become "readerly," if/when a prepared audience comes to the library, music hall, or gallery.

Jacques Derrida is well-remembered as having been a creator of upsetting effects—that is, of producing meanings that upset traditional effects, thereby creating upsets especially in receptions that are more readerly than writerly. John Searle (1983, p. 76) reported that Michel Foucault used the phrase "obscurantisme terroriste" in connection with the name "Derrida," a view that Searle himself affirmed seemingly with some delight.[308] Derrida's preferred pose could be likened to that of Duchamp's "readymades" or Adorno's "negative dialectic": recognizing the inescapable necessity of a "standpoint" from which to unravel formations by unexamined, sometimes unrecognized presuppositions and assumptions, even as the unravelling could be followed along circuits that would take the action to his very own standpoint (about which he had taken care to acknowledge that its seeming privilege was only a point of departure that would itself soon be questioned). His productions highlighted dependencies of meaningful being on "freeze-framing," the unnoticed work that is performed within assumptions of innocence attending frames and contexts and other species of the parergon, or as he also named it the "hors d'oeuvre" (the work "outside the work"). In writings such as *Margins of Philosophy* (1982 [1972]) and *The Truth in Painting* (1987 [1978]) Derrida sought to explicate the hidden works of stabilization that, when noticed in passing, are passed by as merely natural, ordinary, "the way reality simply is." Frames, for example, are simply there to hold fast the integrity of "the work inside" (a painting, say), fixing demarcation against what encompasses the featured work, a supplement that otherwise means nothing. Derrida's writing upsets that "freeze framing," demonstrating that the conventional analytic disparity of "inside" vis-à-vis "outside" is easily demolished in a reversal of polarities, thus exposing the hidden work (cf. Hazelrigg 1992). In

---

[308] Searle's unwillingness to engage Derrida directly when invited to contribute (to a volume that became Derrida's 1988) his earlier paper (Searle 1977) in which he leveled his initial attack on Derrida is worth noting. See also Searle (1995, pp. 159-160) in which he repeated his charge but with an addendum that suggested that Derrida had conceded (a claim that evinced either lack of understanding or a self-flattery).

much the same vein, his (1982 [1972], pp. 307-330) remarks on "context" highlight the taken-for-granted tendency to assume that a work has a distinctive context that hangs with it, ignoring the laminations and other expansions that constitute the dynamism of context. As context changes, that of which it is contextual changes, although the dominating tendency is to hold to identity of "thingness" in and against a shifting "background." Any "work of art," and in the same way any representation, any enunciation, is potentially limitless, just as linguistic recursion generates the possibility of infinite expansions of syntactical formation. Recursions also hold open the potential of infinite regress; yet this potential of a "destabilization gone wild" is put to rest, though only temporarily, by agreements of usage (conventions). Thus it is that "context" is simultaneously a subjective and an objective parergon: neither one and then the other nor a mere correlation between independencies but a dialectical relation that holds both together, rather like the dynamic of "superposition" which resolves into "one or the other" (subjective *or* objective), the "choice" depending on observational gaze.

There was (is) nothing especially new in those exercises of disruption and skepticism. It is nevertheless understandable that Derrida's work generated anxieties of authority, just as had some of Hume's writings, Swift's writings, and so forth. While Derrida's gaze was more insistent, unrelenting, than Hume's, his rub was also rougher against established intellectual authority. Some commentators, Searle (1983) included, characterized Derrida's work as chiefly an attack on foundationalism. But in fact the issue of foundationalism, a somewhat weaker version of essentialism, had already been settled everywhere but in some backwaters of naïve realism.[309] Derrida was extending an explication of the *conditions* of the collapse, as those conditions were already present in Kant's critical theory. Because few readers had given much attention to those implications of Kant's efforts, the force of Derrida's persistent openings and re-openings carried considerable impact, an impact furthered by a presentational style that had been designed to unsettle by demanding unusual repetitions of attention. In fact, then, Derrida's "deconstruction" was *not* a "new game," although it was carried out through some combinations of movements that could be pieced apart as "new" and "old" (assuming the piecing could be held in place and time by a single temporality). A few of the implications he unfolded could be traced to Hume's skepticism, and of these a few could be seen in Montaigne's cautiously expressed doubt and of course in Descartes' famous adventure in doubt, especially in light of the choice of backstop against the threat of infinite regress (that God would not play the trickster). From the standpoint of reason Descartes must have known the choice was telling in its feebleness, but whether this stake in belief was his own or only one for an audience of pubic authorities (mainly the church) remains undecidable.

As for the general idea of "parergon," it is much older; and while the older usages of the word did indeed have something to do with aesthetics in the sense of perceptual experience (as

---

[309] My biggest mistake during the 1970s (as seen in work written mostly during those years; Hazelrigg 1989a) was underestimation of the extent to which foundationalist arguments had already collapsed. The failure was largely due to contextual and conditional socialization. I could see that Derrida, for instance, was being repetitious relative to his own milieu of socialization but not to that of the social sciences and analytical philosophy in the USA (where he became the celebrity good or bad). But I did not appreciate just *how old* his positioning was.

with the similar notions of "frame" and "context") they had not, so far as I know, generated the sort of controversy that followed Derrida's exercises.[310]

One of the earliest surviving documentary uses of the word, "parergon," appears in the context of Heracles' "twelve labors" (i.e., "athloi" or "contests"): in addition to those, and often occurrent with his travel to the site of one of the twelve, Heracles performed many lesser deeds, called "parerga" (the plural of "parergon," which is "para" or "beside" + "ergon" or "deed," "work," "labor," "task"). These minor deeds, as well as the dozen contests, were popular scenes on red-figure pottery from the sixth century BCE onward. Thus, although in some sense "on the side" or "supplemental to" the "main work," they maintained an importance of long duration in Greek culture. Given the contrast that was recalled with each repetition of the collective name, "parerga," they protected the place and even greater importance of the presences of "art work" to which they were supplemental; perhaps mere morsels (hors d'oeuvres) that advertised (honestly or falsely?) the feast still to come. Derrida was not inventing a new metaphor or concept so much as he was extending application of an old one, and in a way that unsettled some taken-for-granted assumptions. That event, too, was hardly new. After all, early in the century of Derrida Einstein had unsettled on a massive scale, had he not? So, too, Bertrand Russell, with what were called "paradoxes" that upset some prominent logicians, not to mention "ordinary people." It was with regard to Russell's not-yet-tamed eruptions that Robert Musil wrote a famous essay in 1913 entitled "The mathematical man," in which he observed that, thanks to work by Russell as well as David Hilbert, mathematicians had now "actually looked all the way to the bottom and found that the whole edifice was floating in midair. But the machines worked!" That is, Musil (1990 [1978], p. 42; translation modified) was recognizing that in this new world the very best mathematicians had shown that mathematical logic was not anchored to anything solid, real; yet the machines that had been built with aid of such tools actually did work. All of this, of course, before anyone had conceived a quantum computer.

In today's context one could say that the phrase "history of myth" is far less troubling, disturbing, or controversial than the phrase "myth of history." However, this disparity marks the work of a largely quiet bias against the reciprocity of "myth" and "history," a bias executed mainly under the heading either of "historicism" or of "positivism" (a bias that can accommodate traffic between them). Damisch (1996 [1992], proceeding partly from Kant's discussion in his third critique, has elaborated on that reciprocity with considerable insight in his extraordinary study of the judgment of Paris, as that mythic arc has replayed in representations ranging from at least two of Sophocles' plays—*Krisis* (i.e., Judgment) and *Eris* (i.e., Discord), neither of them surviving—perhaps preceded by one or more of the many lost plays of Aeschylus and followed by Euripides' *Andromache* and *Helena*, to recent reworkings; as well as a large number of works of modern visual arts, mainly paintings and engravings, from Botticelli (c1486) to Marcantonio

---

[310]However, controversies of one sort of another have been attendant at least since Greek playwrights used dynamics of context—for instance, as first they introduced then repeatedly modified uses of choral effect. A chorus could function rather blatantly as instructor of moral lesson, or as historian or genealogist; or more subtly as a shift in framing or as an audience within the play, whether as guide to, as antagonist to, or even as mock of, the "real" audience; and so forth. Similar controversies remain alive today in regard to contextuality of meaning, truth, and the like (see, e.g., Preyer and Peter 2005).

Raimondi (c1515), to Rubens' several versions (e.g., 1606) to Raphael (c1757), then to Manet's *Luncheon on the Grass* (1863) and Renoir (1908-10), among others; and still other forms, such as Goethe's *Helena in the Middle Ages*, his play within a play in *Faust, Part Two*; a few operas (e.g., compositions by John Weldon and by Daniel Purcell, and by others, commonly using as libretto William Congreve's masque, written during the 1690s); dance, such as Antony Tudor's choreography of 1938, using music from Kurt Weill's *Three Penny Opera*; plus one of Gore Vidal's novels, published in 1952. As this mythic arc has recurred so often for such a long span of time in alliance with understandings of aesthetic perspective as parergonal to something else, something deemed more important, it surely merits inspection. Damisch himself (1996 [1992], p. 146) prompted us to ask, is this *a history*, or is it the power of mythic structure dominating history? Once again, we must attend an accounting process that, short of dogmatic call-and-response enforcements, depends simultaneously on seemingly prior fixed boundaries and on conditionalities that easily open our inspections to the presence of counterfactuals of aesthetic perspective, thereby shifting "prior boundaries."

Before turning to such issues, a brief summary of the storyline of the Judgment of Paris will be useful; for although a major theme not long ago when Greek mythology was a popular pastime, its audience has now diminished. What follows has been pared to a core. At risk of plunging already into the sorts of uncertainty adumbrated in the preceding discussion, let me say simply that various texts that have been by convention accorded "supplemental" status are here ignored. To cite only a single example, this one from fifth-century BCE Greece, the *Encomium of Helen* by Gorgias of Leontini addresses issues of morality and the power of language, topics that seemed remarkably fresh to us a half-century ago, as the question of the parergon, related matters of framing and context, and counterfactual perspective came to our attention once again (thus see Rorty 1967; Hazelrigg 2016, pp. 246-251; and for a review of literature relevant specifically to morality and language, Valiavitcharska 2006).

Different versions of the story exist in ancient Greek literature. One of the oldest, dating perhaps to the seventh century BCE, is from Proclus' *Cherstomathia 1* (trans. Hugh Evelyn-White), a summary of surviving fragments of a Homeric epic cycle (the Cypria Fragment I). The basic storyline is that Eris, goddess of discord and strife, prone to jealousy of other goddesses, is angered that she alone has not been invited to the wedding of Peleus and Thetis (future parents of Achilles). Denied entry, she tosses amidst the assembled goddesses a golden apple on which are inscribed the words, "for the fairest one," knowing that its very appearance will instigate discord. Sure enough, Hera, Athena, and Aphrodite each claim rightful possession of the apple. Mighty Zeus, preferring not to wade into the dispute himself, instructs Hermes to escort the three lovely ladies to a meadow on Mount Ida, there to find a young shepherd, Alexandros ("defender of men"), tending his flock. Better remembered by the name Paris, this princeling of Troy "must" judge which of the three goddesses is the rightful claimant. Each makes her presentation, each offering a reward by her godly distinction. Hera promises to make Paris king of all Europe and Asia. Athena promises wisdom and victory in war. Aphrodite promises to award him as his bride the most beautiful woman in the world (goddesses excepted, of course). Stymied by their apparel, Paris has the three disrobe, after which he selects Aphrodite, thereby gaining Helen (who was current wife of Menelaus, a king of Sparta and brother of Agamemnon). Thus, the Trojan

War. Athena, insulted that she had not been chosen, sides with the Greeks (a choice usually nominated as the decisive event, even though the war drags on for ten years).

Aphrodite herself was renowned for her sensuous beauty. Her very origin, as recounted in Hesiod's genealogy of the gods and goddesses, told the story of this sensuousness (Hesiod's *Theogony*, 174-205, composed c700 BCE). Cronus, having castrated his father, Uranus (god of the sky or heavens), collected the severed genitals "from the land" and flung them "into the surging sea," after which "a white foam spread around them from the immortal flesh, and in it there grew a maiden." Her name itself reminds us of the origin: aphros, "foam," as in a water-surged foam of seminal fluid; oditē probably meant "wanderer." The Greek verb, aphroīsiazō, meant "to indulge lust," and of course the word "aphrodisiac" made its way into English by the early 1700s (regarding the syzygy of the Aphrodite figure, see Davidson 2007, pp. 519, 608).

The weight of the Christian church later suppressed some details of that origin story beneath a gloss of "sea foam." Inheritor of a "mind (soul) and body" duality, Christianity intensified that analytic relation into an ever-stronger antagonism due chiefly to bodily powers, relative to weakness of mind (or of will). Believers learned as a chief lesson of the Garden of Eden that Satan's easiest point to subversion of the soul consists in the body's many temptations. By the fourth century BCE the Christian church, now well institutionalized, admonished its flock "to avoid consenting to pleasure even when engaged in the legitimate coitus of married couples" (Reddy 2012, p. 350). Some have avowed (as did Reddy) that this repressive force of the church became still greater beginning in the eleventh century. That conclusion may well be correct, although Europe was a very large and diverse "cultural place" then. In much of England, for instance, the evidence of medieval Latin documents indicates that local official attitudes about sexual behavior were rather relaxed, by comparison to corresponding attitudes centuries later. One wonders to what extent our evidence for increased repressiveness toward sexual behaviors is reflecting defensive actions by the church more than actual increases in repression (i.e., the difference, say, between increased rates of "crime" due to more stringent patrolling and rate increases due to greater incidence of the same behaviors). Momentous changes in many European societies were underway, as Haskins (1927) summarized for us long ago. It was, or soon would be, the "epoch of the Crusades," which of course had religious motivations but also had much greater consequences in the temporary migrations of men into very different cultures, some lessons of which they carried back to home territories. Equally as momentous, city life was recovering from the long period described as "the Dark Ages," and the "earliest bureaucratic states of the West" were being built. The twelfth-century renaissance also

> saw the culmination of Romanesque art and the beginnings of Gothic; the emergence of the vernacular literatures; the revival of the Latin classics and of Latin poetry and Roman law; the recovery of Greek science, with its Arabic additions, and of much of Greek philosophy; and the origin of the first European universities. The 12th century left its signature on higher education, on the scholastic philosophy, on European systems of law, on architecture and sculpture, on the liturgical drama, on Latin and vernacular poetry (Haskins 1927, p. viii).

252

In any case, there is no gainsaying the general conclusion that for centuries churchly worries about pleasure, its kinds and their consequences, dominated a broad swathe of public order and much of domestic life.

A telling detail of the suppression, often overlooked, can be seen in the fact that the Latin word, "voluptās," is a nominal formation meaning "pleasure" or "delight" or even "satisfaction" (from an adverbial "volup": "agreeably" or "pleasantly" or "delightfully"); yet its vernacular meaning probably in most cultures of Europe soon became dominated by one specific meaning (as in the usual denotation-cum-connotation of the English word, "voluptuousness," which was usually applied as "voluptuous woman"). The detail stands out clearly in a juxtaposition formed by the title of Jay Bernstein's 2006 book, *Against Voluptuous Bodies*, a juxtaposition that opens into a terrain of context, framings, and Kant's notion of parergonal work. Before entering that terrain more specifically, however, let's take a short detour through some of the literary terrains of "pleasure" (not yet a philosophy of utilitarianism but suggestive).

The Latin noun, "voluptās," (plus its root and derivatives) was used by Roman writers principally with the general meaning of "pleasure," "delight," "satisfaction," and the like. More specific meanings were usually conveyed by context and/or by explicit qualifier. Surviving writings by Cicero (106-43 BCE) present the word in multiple places, sometimes with ambiguity. For example, in his indictment against Gaius Verres, ex-governor of Sicily charged with corruption and extortion (*Im Verrem*, "Against Verres," 70 BCE), we read, "Certainly, the delight arising from virtue and from victory is much greater than that pleasure which is derived from licentiousness and covetousness" (2.1.57: certe maior est virtutis victoriaeque incunditas quam ista voluptas quae percipitur ex libidine et cupiditato). The English translation just given is by Charles Duke Yonge (1812-1891), a classicist and historian of high standing. Rendering as he did "ex libidine" as "from licentiousness" is unexceptional with regard to the general sense of the English word ("lacking proper restraint"); but in English usage the intent is often more specific: especially "lacking proper restraint in matters of sexuality." Did Cicero intend this specificity? Perhaps. But the phrase "ex libidine" probably more often meant in Cicero's time "from caprice" or "from willful disregard of propriety" (which would fit the charges against Verres). Likewise, the phrase "ex cupiditato": the English "cupidity," as with "covetousness," generally means "excessive desire," usually for power or money, but sometimes it is synonymous with "lustfulness."[311]

Much later in life (44 BCE), Cicero wrote in his essay, *De senectute* ("On old age"), the oft-cited line, "No man is so old that he does not think himself able to live another year" (§24: nemo enim est tam senex qui se annum non putet posse vivere). More to the point here, he also

---

[311] We see a similar ambiguity in Machiavelli's (1988 [1532], VIII.36) carefully crafted encomium of Lorenzo de Medici (aka Lorenzo the Magnificent), as he averred that "considering both his voluptuous life and his grave life, one might see in him two different persons, joined in an almost impossible conjunction." Nonetheless, no one would doubt that Lorenzo's virtues were great, and "vices of his [cannot] be adduced to stain his great virtues, even though he was marvelously involved in things of Venus" (i.e., Aphrodite). Machiavelli concluded by recalling that Lorenzo died in excruciating pain (probably cancer of one or more abdominal organs) in his forty-fourth year. See also Damisch (1996 [1992], pp. 150-151).

said in the same essay that of the "many noteworthy customs" that could be addressed, he wanted to draw attention to "the one whereby a person has precedence in debate according to his age"; and then added this: "What physical pleasures, then, are comparable to the distinction which influence bestows?" (§64: quae sunt igitur voluptates corporis cum auctoritatis praemiis comparandae). Here I have cited William Armistead Falconer's 1923 translation. Falconer (1869-1927), a student and professor of law, educated in late Victorian traditions of the U.S. southland, observed a certain sense of decorum in his translations. His translation of the uncontroversial §24 is sound. But in §64, whereas he preferred the more general "physical pleasures" for "voluptates corporis," I would simply say "pleasures of the body" or "bodily pleasures," preserving more of the sense of "flesh" of "corporis." In this passage, it seems to me, there is little if any room for doubt of Cicero's intended meaning, and I judge that Falconer's choice was determined by his sense of decorum. Recall from prior discussion the controversy over Darwin's thesis that sexual selection is a process that operates to some degree independently of, or outside, what had been more nearly settled theory (at least within science) of natural selection The latter dynamic had been understood solely as an instrumental utility function: "survival of the fittest" (or, more accurately, "pruning of the insufficiently fit"). But Darwin's notion of a separate aesthetically gauged sexual-selection process emphasized a utility function based on a "pleasure principle." So long as "beauty," meaning physical attributes of the fleshy body, could be read as "honest signals" of something else (i.e., a mere supplement)—namely, "fitness to survive"—the "dangerous idea" could be reined in. Darwin let this horse perform, however, to the dismay, even outrage, of the dominating segment of scientific as well as popular culture.[312]

Note that—in now returning to Bernstein's book—we are facing a similar opposition. On the face of it, being "against voluptuous bodies"—the title of his book—could hardly be better formulated to evoke images of "pleasures of the body." And there is that, to be sure. Whereas in vernacular English the likeliest image is gendered and sexual—as in most notably one of Peter Paul Rubens' renditions of *The Judgement of Paris* (from 1600) and following that long line of roundly fleshy nude women (see the sequence of images in Damisch 1996 [1992]) to Manet's *Luncheon on the Grass* (1863)—one should begin with the general notion of a pleasantness, a satisfaction, of the human body. Not that this more general notion is unconnected to sexuality; rather, it may be seen as a broader frame and context of a historicity of "beauty." In Damisch's (1996 [1992], pp. 146-147, also 89-90) appreciation of "the singular trajectory of the judgment of Paris" we may detect a reader tip-toeing up to a *tertius gaudens* scenario, in which alternative interlocutors can re-adjudicate a first-person experience of "a man who is called upon to make [a choice] among three women, the outcome being, with a regularity so consistent as to suggest its predetermination by some internal necessity, that he settles on the third and last of them, who is acknowledged to be the most beautiful, the best, the most obliging, but also the least talkative, the most silent." That triad has been reflected in receptions of the story, which tend to come in third-person perspective as an opposed pair in augmentation of the narrator, who is presented

---

[312] "The case of the male Argus pheasant is eminently interesting, because it affords good evidence that the most refined beauty may serve as a sexual charm [i.e., factor of selection], and for no other purpose" (Darwin 1871, p. 516; see Prum 2017, pp. 23-25, *passim*).

*within* the story both as Paris making his choice and as the anonymous authority of the story relating Paris' experience, each of the pair seeking to align with this first-person voice against the other of the pair. The "empowering third" is simultaneously parergonal to the story and the central thread of the story itself. The invocation of Paris' experience—choosing from his "desire for beauty, a desire for love, not one for power [Hera] or knowledge [Athena]" (Damisch 1996 [1992], p. 209)—acts as an imputed first-person experience for (as well as by) the artist and the artist's would-be audience, highlighting the duality of human being as, to use Kant's image of a "crooked timber," a being who is "animal and yet rational," and *as such* the unique beholder of a perceived thing (beauty) which in principle "should actually concern only form" yet in practice is usually mixed up with "charms" (Reizen) or with seductive advertisements that are "themselves passed off as beauties," such that the aim of "a universal aesthetic liking" (pleasurableness) is itself reduced to a "barbaric" goal because of the "admixture of *charm* and *emotion*" (Kant 2000 [1790], pp. 95, 108). Bernstein (2006) continued the reading via art works that are "against pleasant bodies," art works that have followed an apparent deflection of the trajectory examined by Damisch, into a later modernist scope from Chaim Soutine (e.g., his self-portrait of 1918, with "impossibly red lips pushed forward toward the picture plane") to Jackson Pollock's *The Wooden Horse* (No. 10), to the several "ugly bodies" of Cindy Sherman's "tragic modernism" (Bernstein 2006, pp. 68, 184, 253).

Remember that at about the time that Anselm Feuerbach (Ludwig's nephew) painted his far less Baroque version of *The Judgement of Paris* (1869-70), and well after Paul Cézanne's radically different rendition (1862-64), Darwin (1871) was composing what Prum (2017, pp. 17-18) has called his "*really* dangerous idea"—namely, that mate selection is at the core of an evolution of natural aesthetics. This gave too much of a role to "beauty," to traits considered too subjective, tangential and excessive—in a word, *voluptuous*.[313] It displaced what had been the acceptable compromise—bodily beauty as an "honest signal" of fitness—with beauty as valued simply for what it is, beauty. We will find a very similar dynamic in a dialectic of opposition in Bernstein's thesis that the history of art (painting in particular) from voluptuous bodies to minimalist bodies serves as an honest signal for a transformation that extends well beyond, and in some sense deeper than, the conventional bounds of "art"—that is, "art" conceived as one of several domains of sociocultural formation, and one that itself has often been regarded (after Hegel) as mainly parergonal to other, more important domains. Whereas some working artists recognize their activities, and perhaps themselves as principals, in Bernstein's readings of specific "works of art" as philosophically relevant, and to some degree informed, other artists prefer to think of their activities as simply art, and themselves as simply artists, artists working "art for art's sake." But as we saw in the prior section, "art" was loaded with large philosophical weight during the late eighteenth and early nineteenth centuries, whether working artists sought it or not. Part of that weight came from the expectation that works of art, when considered as novel irruptions and more generally when considered in sequence, stood as testaments to "the meaning of history," markers of the progress of pilgrims on their journeys of life. Explicitly

---

[313] Martin's (2016) study of the place of "beauty" in a supposedly classic triad of "the true, the good, and the beautiful" is highly informative in this regard, especially as he gave attention to a range of neo-Kantian figures in conjunction with the rise of the social sciences.

religious motifs of expression had been gradually supplemented by, and then gradually displaced by, motifs such as pleasing pastorals, the verbally indescribable sublimities of nature, the beauty and charms of the human body (safely portrayed via recoveries of old myths), and of course the purchase against death by portraiture. Horowitz (2001) drew good attention to the peculiar mausoleum-quality expectation assigned to art when, in his study of "art and the mournful life," he wrote of "art as the tomb of the past."

Contradictions could, and did, abound. Think of the "art for art's sake" declaration, for example. Sometime between 1905 and 1917 Kazimir Severinovich Malevich developed an art-world movement known as Suprematism, the (or his) inaugural statement being a 1915 painting entitled *The Square* (a densely, thickly black square on a white background). By intent, the work of abstraction represented a feeling—in particular, the feeling of "the rediscovery of pure art which, in the course of time, has become obscured by the accumulation of 'things'" (Malevich 1959 [1927], p. 74). As he elaborated in the second essay of his 1927 manifesto, the supremacy of art as such would be conveyed by a "supremacy of pure feeling in creative arts." This was his "desperate attempt to free art from the ballast of objectivity" (Malevich 2000 [1927], p. 117). By all outward signs the intent was genuine. Never mind that "the ballast of objectivity," of mere "things," included paintings still on easels, paintings hanging on walls in buildings, some of them dwellings of collectors of "works of art," and so forth. One must begin with one's own imaginations of an ideal world, even if through feelings of hopelessness (Malevich's "desperate attempt," his words).[314] Many viewers of *The Square* today respond with a curiosity ("What was the point?") or, having repeatedly pondered and dismissed that question, with a blasé shrug. But history calls, as Tatyana Tolstaya (2018 [2015]) recounted in her essay on Malevich's signature painting. What we do know, and what Malevich surely himself anticipated, is that the object he produced does have a capacity of meanings some of which can arouse intense feeling. Can art escape that? Would any artist *want* to escape that?

Bernstein's point of departure, both initially and finally considered, was the failure of Kant's effort toward an integrative bridge in his third critique. In light of that, and of efforts that followed, Bernstein has seen what he considered the crux of "the entire history of modernism"— namely, its worry over what could be left of art, what could now be worth artistic assertion into future worlds, whether art was now capable of "honestly signaling" *anything*. His assessment can be taken as presupposing a rather grand vision of art's purpose; and as I have cautioned, we must consider that some artists (among other inquirers) dismiss the vision as all too grand, too heroic. This counterview, itself varied in the temporality of vision as well as emotion, generally puts more emphasis on what a working artist actually does when creating "a work" or, more generically, "a style of work." An artist needs an audience for what she or he wants to express. Few artists want to be relegated to the ranks of a copyist, and while there are audiences content with the work of a copyist, an ever youthful, ever hopeful artist's vision is for more—eventually to be the copied, not the copier. If successful in the odd negotiation that follows that desire, an artist achieves a call-and-response dialectic of "unique self" / "collective other," the dynamic

---

[314] I cannot check the Russian, both because my Russian is now virtually non-existent but also because the Russian text apparently disappeared. The English is from German translation and unexceptional. I know nothing of the person who translated the Russian into German.

being a flow of "works identified as in-the-style-of-Artist-A" by a knowing audience of fellow artists, collectors, curators, dealers, and critics.[315] In that way the artistic desire of a painter or sculptor, for instance, is much the same as that of a poet, librettist, composer, architect, novelist, playwright, cooper (in the day), furniture maker, and so forth. The desired effect amounts to "building one's self now" in an action sequence intrinsically social. Sometimes an artist's expression somehow exceeds his or her "known style," as the artistic self sees it, as well as in receptions by audience. And sometimes this exceptionality is intended as (in the often recited words of or about Beethoven) "writing for future audiences." Even so, however, the activity is always *now*, by present self. The aesthetic (and perhaps decidedly ethical) style identified with an artist can be expected to develop or unfold or evolve from an immanence of stylistic resource, but also from experiences that are informative (contextually, framedly, and/or parergonally) within an artist's creative life.

There can be no gain in trying to gainsay that first-person perspective of an artist, other than another comment tangential at best. But nor is there point to denying the possibility, indeed likelihood, of a corresponding second- or third-person experience with or of a present artist. Nonetheless, there is also the possibility, even likelihood, that Bernstein's view of artistic work as "honest signaling" of tragedy, a "horror of nonidentity," the emptiness of a life form, can accommodate a working artist's modest hopes as something other than evidence of the perverted magic of a self-deluding alienation or false consciousness. An idea associated with Damisch proposes that "art thinks." If by that claim one means elliptically a self-conscious cognitive, or cognitive-emotive, expression, rather than some notion of an "extended mind" that engenders not simply by "representation" (as a programmed computer, for instance, or an autopilot does) but by "transformation" of that which a human being has accomplished into some sort of henceforth independently materialized intelligence (as in perhaps a forthcoming "artificially intelligent robot"), then of course. Artist and artist's audience express—somewhat collaboratively but also separately and sometimes antagonistically—cognitively as well as emotively an on-going productivity of meanings, felt and reflective (not always in the same way). This includes a range of audience productivities, sequential and sequentially self-referential, as in some manner critical commentaries, assessments, and self-reflections (among them, the proverbial viewer's sometimes exasperated query, "What does it mean?"). It has been said with regard to Damisch's thesis (and otherwise) that aesthetic experience of, in, and by art inevitably entails a *failure* of understanding relative to its "object"—as if one first experiences an object prior to any aesthetics, then engages the object aesthetically, and thus engenders a space or gap. This display of words at idle is part of the price that we now pay for all prior reductions of "the aesthetic" to the famous qualities known as "beauty" and "the sublime." However, what we *have* learned from considerations of parerga and related issues of perspective is an elaboration of the dialectic of unity of opposites: understanding is also misunderstanding. A work of art, so considered, always exceeds cognition of it, in the sense that there always remains a potential of

---

[315] A vital part of that dynamic is what economists call "the pricing mechanism," which in the case of the category "original work of art" is not well understood. For important insights see, e.g., Velthuis (2005), Thornton (2008). In light of her ethnographic book I asked Thornton to consider writing a lengthy essay theorizing the dynamics of the production of artistic value (e.g., primary focus on painting). She was much too intelligent to enter that bogland.

more thought; and this remains the case after "cognition" has been explicitly amended to "cognitive-emotive" experience, or a juncture of "thinking of feeling" and "felt thought." This is hardly unique to an objectivity of "art work," however. The presence of potentia occurs when apprehending a face, a mountain view, a "starry sky at night," a linguistic expression (even when the words are at idle, one's first approach is with expectation of "work being done; now I must figure out what it is!"). In life, always more can be experienced. Aesthetics inheres in that opening, an opening to judgment. This historicity was central to Damisch's approach. As Kant repeatedly said, using one of his favorite "thought experiments" (the geometry of a sphere), give me just a few degrees of arc and I can tell you everything about the idea of that sphere, although I will never exhaust experiences of any actual surface of it. "I cognize the limits of my actual knowledge of the earth [Erdkunde] at any time, but not the boundaries of all possible description of the earth" (Kant 1998 [1787], B787/A759). Call it Art or artifice, the potentiality of human being's creative imagination is boundless.

### §19. Vocabularies of the Artificial and the Real

Modern science, because of its skeptical attitude and experimentalist empirical bent, would gradually change the terms of the "objective necessity" that had rounded the circle of the transcendental Illusion. This much Kant foresaw. The nineteenth century increasingly witnessed fruitions of that keen insight. The innovations were material, in the one-sided sense that people generally have in mind when they either extol or lament "modern technology" as thingness. But of course the innovations were also always innovative of thinking and feeling, inventions at once material and ideal, and as such they brought along changes in conceptions of reality. As many witnesses have shown, first one and then another new realism came along, typically in pace with a sequence of what Crary (1990) called "techniques of the observer" (see also Brooks 2005, Brown 2003; but for important context see also Snyder 2016, Belting 2008, Mann 2000, and Slobodkin 1992; among many others). And each new realism sought to seal its advent as innovation by a reworking of objective necessity, however temporary it proved to be (for a case study, see Hazelrigg 1993a).[316]

Brooks (2005) pointed to the growing weight of Kant's progeny, an empirically based science as stimulant to the production of new realisms. Several signal episodes were mentioned in passing, earlier in this Part. There were directly new realisms of the sciences themselves, to be sure. The history of chemistry supplies an abundance of illustrative material, a mere smattering of which could begin with Dalton's law in 1801 (a new reality of the composition of gaseous mixtures), jump to Hess' statement of the conservation of energy, then to Mendeleev's periodic law of the elements, Werner's invention of coordination chemistry, and Ramsay's models of chemical bonding and realization of "noble gases." Similarly in geology and in physics; and perhaps most widely famous, the new realities in biology. The arts were not far

---

[316] An interesting coda to that essay was afforded by some readers who reported having been puzzled that I ended by returning to what seemed to be "a conventional representationalism" (an impression perhaps abetted by the editors' placement of the essay in a section bounded as "representationalism"). All I did was remark the persistent fact of a one-sided materialism of bones ("still, the bones"), as an indication of the very "objective necessity" that Kant had discerned as and in operation of the transcendental Illusion. It is so easy to see, as is said in French, plus ça change, plus c'est la même chose, without hearing or feeling the initial intent of a biting satire.

behind, however, and occasionally even a step ahead. Consider the movement known as impressionism, manifest in nineteenth-century works of literature (e.g., Balzac, Mallarmé) and in music (e.g., Debussy, Ravel) as well as visual art. A major stimulant to the movement in visual art, for instance, was the development via photographic technology of a new realism—indeed, one that had for some time seemed to set the standard for what "realism" must mean. If, say, a painter, what was one to do in the face of this new standard of what counts as "*really* real" by representation? Claude Monet's answer, first and most notoriously in a painting he dubbed *Impresssion, Sunrise* (1872), was to do what daguerreotypy and colloidal process and gelatin dry-plate process could *not* do, emphasize impressions of movement: the light dappling across moving foliage, for example, and light refracting variously by the different densities of water vapor in the sky (clouds), shimmers of color in apparel, on a pond, reflecting off a tablecloth or the blush of demoiselle's cheek.[317] Impression set in train a number of other techniques of vision issuing in another new realism, each of them initially as "outrageous" as impressionism had been: among them, the "fracturing" of obvious forms (e.g., the human visage) by Picasso and others, designed to show multiple perspectives on conventionally familiar objects all at once; Duchamp's new study of the human form in motion, *Woman Descending a Staircase, No. 2* (1912), designed to depict on the flat, two-dimensional surface not only the third dimension (long since achieved by inventions of perspective) but also now the fourth, time, just as Einstein had announced his Riemannian union of space-time; and lessons in reflexivity by Magritte (e.g., *The Treachery of Images*, 1929; *The Human Condition*, 1933; *Hegel's Holiday*, 1958).

One must always try to keep in mind the reflexivity of scholarly work itself, as of artistic representation, even though for reasons adumbrated by Hume it is well-nigh impossible in the moment of work; for autonomy, as related by Kant (liberation from one's "self-incurred [yoke of] immaturity"; Kant (1991) 1784b, p. 54), remains a look ahead as one declares *Sapere aude!*[318] As Brooks (2005) demonstrated throughout his *Realist Vision*, in the on-going productivity of scholarship the settled is always also the unsettled—if not yet realized as such in the moment, then in waiting, a "potestas" contemplating "imperium," as it were; and when sensed only as potestas the ambiguity or uncertainty can be highly unsettling to those who have that sense of a vision-in-the-making. In other words, it is a sense of being in an interregnum, a crisis of settled authority. An initiating hint of appreciation of this "dilemma" can be read in Roman Jakobson's essay, "On Realism in Art" (1987 [1921]), in which he points to a conflation of two different meanings of "the real" in representation: borrowing his notation, (A) aspiration and intent of the composer versus (B) perception by one who views or hears or touches the representation as "true

---

[317] It has been said that impressionism offered a "greater subjectivity" in representation, but that is mistaken. A new realism, whether it be impressionism or some other new realism, is neither more nor less subjective. It is simply differently subjective, but this difference seems obviously one of "greater subjectivity" because the new realism disrupts the still-obvious objective necessity of that which it challenges.

[318] Duve's (1996; also 1991) insightful reading of Duchamp's "R Mutt" action and the advent of "the readymade" locates to the early twentieth century a realization that Kant's third critique was neither primarily nor mainly about "beauty" but about the aesthetics of perception and critical judgment, and ties that realization to a shift in the play of realisms (partly recalling Schiller's "play drive"; Schiller 1954 [1794]). See especially Duve (1996, p. 93 on "Duchamp's test" and pp. 384-389 on the relation between Duchamp and Magritte).

to life." Then comes the conflation (C), mostly covertly, as an effect of the aggregative operations of periodization and scaling into "movements" or "types" or "styles," perceived unities of various realisms. When C dominates, Jacobson urged us to see, it is easy to lose sight of the difference between A and B. On the other hand, adults do proceed as if C exhausted all there is to know about the real (whatever version it might be), because most of sociality that they experience has passed through the mangle of aggregation processes such that those aspirations and intents are not recoverable. Theorists, too, have been known to proceed in the same way in their "lived theory" even when the theory they propound says differently.[319] This "inconsistency" is not necessarily bad faith or false consciousness. Indeed, the "escape clause" (if that is what it is) can occur in either of at least two ways: the propounded theory is abstract (for seemingly necessary purposes of making headway on a problem) to an extent that it could not, as such, be lived by anyone; or the propounded theory is based on a value projection (i.e., a utopist impulse) or on a basic concept formation that is counterfactual to the dominant everyday sociality. A theorist might deliberately choose a greater degree of estrangement from the mainstream currents of a discipline—evading the labels of "movement" or "type" or "style" or "school"—as the cost of greater "freedom of thinking," knowing all the while that the cost of hermitage is the quietude of no audience.[320] But one must also remember Bloch's (1985 [1935]) advisory in his essay on the dialectic of (non-)synchronicity: not all people who can be seen together at a given time are in fact living in the same Now. They may carry different "earlier things" in mind, in their actions, in their motivations.

At the beginning of the twentieth century a world-famous physicist, Ludwig Boltzmann, writing reflections on a thesis by Schopenhauer, wondered about questions that humans seem impelled to ask, despite being repeatedly unable to provide answers that satisfy. Are such questions beyond human understanding? Or are they empty, meaningless, as Darwin had said? Boltzmann (1905, pp. 400-410) counted himself among those who found the choice disturbing, haunting. He was most disturbed by the fact that, while it did seem evident that the questions are empty, humans cannot let them go. Why? What does that mean? He found the experience to be much like the nausea induced by a migraine.

Reason is never finished, because it cannot avoid calling forth its absence or its negation, thus contributing to unsettlement of its own works. This dialectic has been popularly manifested in various ways, including expressions of a notion of insufficiency or deficiency at the core of human being—for instance, the notion that the very necessity of reason is both a utility required by humans in order to make sound judgments of inference (logic's laws, such as "excluded middle") and a necessary supplement (a prosthesis for some part of the human insufficiency or disability) nonetheless falls short of achieving perfect judgment even when it is aligned with proper moral law. Our discourses of reason, rationality, morality, and judgment swing between poles of optimism and pessimism, thereby recording chapters of our histories of subjectivity. Periodic eruptions of protest against a hubris of rationality are often tinged with regret for "what has been lost"—some account of a mythical past or "state of nature" as it was prior to human

---

[319] It would be unconscionable not to mention the work of Hayden White in this regard (e.g., 1973, 1978, 1987; see also Paul 2011), for he brought much insight to these matters of the production of realisms.
[320] Macherey (1978 [1966]) touched on these matters, especially in his appreciation of Balzac.

inventions of such "instruments" as belatedly necessary tools for regaining means to proper ends.[321]

At one point in his address of Hegel's struggles with—one could say, on behalf of—the Absolute, Pippin (2014, p. 33) adumbrated a crucial juncture of the struggles as "that 'subject-object' problem" (as mentioned above). One or another manifestation of "that problem" has circulated throughout this and the preceding Parts. In Part IV I will pick up the threads again, this time more directly in terms familiar from twentieth-century social science. As transition, let me recall from Part One, in order to place it within context of the social sciences of the twentieth century, perhaps the most important stimulants to Kant's reformation of his own project (and the advent of his critique of critique)—namely, Hume's skepticism. Given the unshakable lesson, it seemed that the only remaining options would be a blind empiricism, an empty rationalism, or a dogmatism natural and/or divine—unless Kant could achieve a self-consistent alternative. He failed. But the failure left us with a radically clarified diagnosis of the problem. It has often been said that the social sciences have been handicapped by an inferiority complex vis-à-vis the physical sciences. True or not, the larger handicap has been their captivity as a footnote to Kant's failing effort. The social sciences have been shaped mostly within the legacy of Kant's effort, and largely without understanding the resulting diagnosis.

Early in this century one of the previous century's most prominent scholars, Jerry Fodor, used the occasion of reviewing works by another of that century's most prominent scholars, Donald Davidson, to offer an assessment of the record of accomplishments in the areas in which he had made his greatest mark. His general conclusion must have offered assurance to many bright young scholars that there was still a future to be had in the discipline:

> A lot of the last century of the philosophy of language and the philosophy of mind has been driven by attempts to find a bullet-proof argument against scepticism. The preferred tactic has been Pragmatist, practically without exception. ... The basic idea is to opt for an epistemic account of truth; hence for an a priori connection between what's true and what's believed to be. Some philosophers, for example, have managed to convince themselves that the truth is what (i.e. whatever) everyone will come to believe 'eventually'.
>
> That sort of account doesn't work because, of course, truth isn't an epistemic notion. What's true depends on how the world is, not on how we think it is....

---

[321] The so-called romanticism close on the heels of Kant was that in part. Subsequent episodes include most notably the invention and development of "Freudian psychology" and its offshoots. Most recently we have witnessed a spate of reminders that reason, while useful for detecting hidden biases of presupposition, perspective, assumption, and argument, is also partial, imperfect, limited, and, an instrument of intellect, easily infected by the prejudices or prejudgments that are integral to institutionalized formations and self-identities. Among those reminders, see Kahneman (2011), Mercier and Sperber (2017), Mbembe (2017), and Sloman and Fernbach (2017). Brekhus' (2015) related survey offers useful context.

> ... The world is prior to the mind, so what we believe is one thing, but whether what we believe is so is quite another (Fodor 2002, p. 14).

One part of Fodor's response, the phrase "of course" (in the middle of the cited paragraphs), could suggest that his own confidence needed a persuasional boost. Be that as it may, however, his characterization of a century of effort to fashion a "bullet-proof argument" against skepticism is a round-about way of saying that the dilemma of this part of Kant's legacy remained. His own option was simply to assume that (1) "noumenal reality" does exist, (2) beliefs about that reality, no matter how generally agreed they may be, are not an adequate criterion of "truth," but (3) no one has succeeded in achieving what might count as "direct access" to that reality. Without real evidence of what does exist as it is in itself, by means other than conscious human thought that can be conveyed understandably to various interlocutors, the word "truth" idles.

Art (meaning Fine Art) was for a long time in "oversold" condition. So, too, Truth.

# Part Four
## Passages between Self and Society

The health of one's perspective can be maintained, sometimes improved, by reaching back to an earlier day, reading passages that were then freshly composed, listening for the poetical or musical chords conveyed through the lines, compared with one's memories. Or so I have found. More than fifty years ago a lead article in the *American Journal of Sociology* addressed "a problem of the relationship between small-scale and large-scale sociological theories" (Wagner 1964). Several years later I engaged with that article, mostly indirectly, in various writings and then in 1991 published an article that was inadequate to the task (Hazelrigg 1991). One of the dimensions of that inadequacy had to do with the fact that I concentrated too much on sociology, hardly unique in the failure to grapple with the issue of scale. It had been thrashed about in economics, too, for example, as partisans of "macro-economics" (as one part of the discipline was being styled) wondered what if any good could flow from some of their colleagues' study of individual-actor variations of perception, evaluation, decision, and action having to do mainly with matters of labor supply, consumer choice, and similar other topics of "micro-economics." Likewise, within political science, there had been (and is) a division between scholars who concentrate attention to institutions of government while others use survey techniques to canvass changes and correlations of individual preferences in political attitudes, interests, and actions, especially voting behavior. Effort to integrate between scales had been subordinated to other aims far more generally than I had appreciated. And while I had understood the track extending from Kant's critical theory through the several editions of "neo-Kantian" theory to social theorists who were prominent at the start of the twentieth century, my understanding of the complexities of that track and its manifestations in social science generally was not adequate.

Wagner's article came at a time when major lines of contention within a professional discipline tended to sort by generation. Older scholars generally hewed to "macro" phenomena, while "micro" interests were likelier to attract attention among younger scholars. This was in large part because advances in techniques and uses of broad-based survey research, along with growth of university-based programs of instruction and research, favored the recently trained. Among sociologists the contention had already been aligned by competition between two highly reputed and influential personal figures of the same generation, gentle-spirited Talcott Parsons (1902-1979) and the usually irascible George Caspar Homans (1910-1989; see Homans 1984, e.g., pp. 293-304, 321-331). The former was a champion of "large-scale theory," to use Wagner's terminology (e.g., Parsons 1961), while the latter was both a critic of Parsons and more pragmatic in his theoretical approach, moving between an ethnographic pursuit that mixed granularities of perspective (as in Homans 1941) and a more intensive analytic study of exchange processes among individuals in groups (as in Homans 1961). Finer-grained still were the studies of "small-group processes" by a few scholars slowly building their cause, some of whom had been allied with Parsons (e.g., Hare, Borgatta, and Bales 1955), while others (e.g., Herbert Blumer) developed a "symbolic interactionist" perspective that partly reflected the perspective of George Herbert Mead. Wagner boldly entered that varied and contentious terrain to offer a critical

263

assessment of what had been accomplished.[322] He concluded that the discipline was "hardly closer to solving [the problem of scale] than it [had been] in the first decade" of the century. "The task of finding an effective transition from microsociological interactional conceptions to the analysis of macrosocial phenomena, as formulated fifty years ago by [Max Weber], remains still to be done" (Wagner 1964, pp. 572, 583-84). He was correct. The task remains undone. It rests at the center of the social sciences' dilemma. In fact, Mead (1907, p. 380), reviewing a new book by Henri Bergson (1907), pronounced unsolved problems of aggregation (though he did not name them as such) to be a "general defect" found in various fields, including biology, seeing no hint of solution from Bergson beyond still another round of question begging. Having benefited from study of Hegel during his time in Germany, Mead may have been aware that quantitative change without qualitative change is itself indicative of a scale indifference to the extent of the quantitative change. If so, he failed to mention it. But it is clear that the crux of the task is not simply quantitative, not simply the *numerical* issue of "the one and the many." On this there has been general, though not universal, agreement. The crux is about organization, about qualitative difference and the process by which it occurs. The abiding temptation has been to talk about "the problem of order" but to commence the talk from a *premise* of order as if all was homologous. After all, as Kant had said, a speaker cannot but experience an order of reality, even as he or she cannot perceive the ordering that occurs in the actions of the perceiving I. This experience does tend one to an assumption of scale indifference. Except that, for most of us, it seems clear that numerical addition is not in itself a sufficient condition of much of our phenomenal world. The task remains. Indeed, if one surveys the massive volume of literature since Wagner's article, as Puddephatt (2009) did with regard to "symbolic interactionism" and the relation of Blumer, for instance, to Mead, the lasting effect can be disheartening in the extreme. For what one mostly reads amounts to cycles and recycles, retracings of retracings of commentaries on commentaries that yield mostly more of the same. Kant's legacy is replayed again and again, by players who apparently have little or no awareness of how the script came to be (for a partial exception see Tugendhat 1986 [1979]).

Something of a re-awakening to the task during the 1980s led to publication of several large anthologies (examples being Alexander, Giesen, Münch, and Smelser 1987; Hausman and Wise 1985; Knorr-Cetina and Cicourel 1981) as well as occasional articles (e.g., Coleman 1986; Collins 1981; Harris 1985; Garfinkel, Manski, and Michalopoulos 1992).[323] According to James

---

[322] My choice of adverb, "boldly," is not misplaced: as Edmund Leach said in his review of Homans' *Social Behavior* (Leach 1961, p. 1339), while the book's "framework of simple propositions" might strike a reader as "stating the obvious" (although Leach himself did not favor much of it), it "covers an area of difficult and hotly disputed sociological theory." His description was not exaggerated, although it must be said that a large portion of the "hot dispute" involved blind dancing across as well as around fuzzy and/or elastic category boundaries. Having been participant in such "conversations," I am quite aware that some of the blindness is deliberate, a tactic in the competitive sparring of status warriors.
[323] Already in 1970 one could catch a glimpse of recognition of the multidimensionality of the problem, as Laumann, Siegel, and Hodge (1970), having assembled a selection of readings about "the logic of social hierarchies," wrote a brief introductory essay that suggests awareness, both reluctant and disappointed, that achievements had been feeble. Several of their selections were gentle reminders that

Coleman (1986, pp. 1321, 1326), "the major theoretical obstacle to social theory built on a theory of action" is still an inadequate theorization of "the means by which purposive actions of individuals *combine* to produce a social outcome." Therefore, he recommended, our "central theoretical problem is to characterize the process through which individuals' actions lead norms (with sanctions) to come into existence," a recommendation that he continued four years later (Coleman 1990; Garfinkel, et al., 1990). Some (e.g., Alexander et al. 1987) argued the need to free the central issue of "micro-macro linkages" from the thematics of "the individual versus social structure," presumably so as to solve the former without having to grapple with the complexities of the latter. But the latter will not go quietly. Those complexities simply cannot be removed from the means of theorizing, or the means of research, or the means of life. As numerous scholars had noted (e.g., Kristeva 1969; Meyer 1986), the constitutional framework of the social sciences was built of a foundational duality of "self and world" conceived in a substantialist-atomist logic, and much of the text subsequently written has consisted in a search for parallel stratifications of the two poles, whereby they can be "mapped" onto each other in a correlative operation of the same logic. This, the issue of homology: does a single order, a single logic, apply generally? Anne Rawls (1987, p. 145) remarked the same point: "Attempts to bridge the dichotomy between agency and social structure"—recent illustrations being Giddens (1984), Habermas (1984 [1981], 1987 [1981]; see also 1987 [1985], and Granovetter (1985)—"ultimately fall back on the idea of individuals and structures as separate poles in the production of orderly and meaningful action." Delusions of the theorist as special actor, immune to the very matters under investigation, do not take us beyond the initial question ("beyond," that is, in the sense of forward; sometimes they do take us backward).

Not everyone has agreed about the task, or at least what to call it. Anthony Giddens (1984, pp. 140-41), for example, declared the "micro-macro" division to be a "phoney war." One could have easily suspected another episode of the disciplinarian habit of inventing new vocabulary within which to house old or mostly old ideas for purposes of new publication. Such episodes have long been associated with generational succession, as the new either engage in Freudian wishes or, more sedately, seek new "topical areas" in which to cast their own nets for good fortune. But in this instance there *were*, there *are*, some genuine issues beyond vocabulary to be pursued hopefully in new frames of inquiry toward new insights. The copula of "individual *and* society," a phrase that names a host of perennial topics, was and remains part of the focus, as some scholars have imagined that preparations had been made for advances in understanding processes wherein phenomena of micro-level became phenomena of macro-level, either because of actual indifference to scale or because a decipherable algorithm of scale translation was being achieved. As Andrew Abbott (1999, p. 62) said with respect to Mead, he had long ago argued that "self and society both emerge from the same process." But there had been remarkably little

---

"social organization" exists in layers and that little had been established about the processes by which the layers are integrated, whether more or less well. The editors included an excerpt from Stinchcombe (1965), for example, which presents a stimulating if brief propaedeutic that illustrates the potential of an integrative multilevel, multidimensional inquiry.

theorization of how that common process, if indeed it is a single process in common across scales, actually works.

More than thirty years after Giddens' declaration, however, one might conclude either that he was correct in his verdict or that someone declared victory but did not celebrate, perhaps having decided that the victory was empty. My aim here is not to issue a verdict but to add some clarification of the issues that were, and still are, involved in Wagner's "problem of scope" (which, as should be clear by now, I prefer to designate instead a "problem of scale"), to consider more of the history of those issues in some mainsprings of social theory and research, and then to draw the issues toward a different point by exploring the conditions of the alleged division of "micro versus macro"—namely, the common element that determines what is divided. A major theme throughout is partly captured by a description of Jane Austen's perspicacity: "She knew that character is elusive and that to observe anyone, however closely, is to be misled, but that we may never learn until we *are* misled" (Honan 1987, p. 248). The point is *not* a conclusion of unpredictability because of indeterminacy; rather, that the determinate relations constitutive of "character" are complex in dynamics. Formulations of "the micro-macro problem" have typically neglected that complexity. Sociocultural orders are at least as complex as the weather, or so I conjecture (lacking both conceptual and mensural basis for careful comparison); and if that is an accurate assessment, then the analytics of our usual representational models are inadequate in some respects, including as a basis for deciding questions of scale indifference and theorizing processes of what might be called, however inadequately, aggregation.

It is within that framework that later in this Part Four I briefly characterize the works of some early theorists—some would say "founding theorists"—of sociology in particular, mainly during early decades of the twentieth century. Before turning to those topics, however, I need to attend to some matters of terminology.

### §20. Some Matters of Terminology

Not being one who believes (or proposes to believe) that we can do without concepts, I shall try to indicate initially what I intend by some key concepts that have traveled under one or another polysemic word, though without pretending either that I will have thereby eliminated ambiguity or that achieving elimination would necessarily be a good thing. Some ambiguities are inherent to sociality, and any theorist who believes that she or he has erased them is probably descended of one of P T Barnum's guests (cf. Levine 1985).

Several of the key terms I will leave to an understanding of contemporary vernacular usage (e.g., "individual," in the sense of an "individual human being" or "individual person"; and "society," although this is perhaps less free of complicating ambiguity, which we will come to later). The reader will no doubt have already noted, however, that I intend by "individual human being" a meaning that is probably not part of vernacular usage: I intend Marx' (1976 [1888, p. 4) "ensemble of social relations," albeit with the clarification that "social" does not mean only "familial" or "civic" or "domestic" but rather includes relations, processes. and

266

phenomena that our professional-disciplinarial habits have separated as "cultural," "economic," "political," and so forth. Furthermore, I mean that any psychologism is neither starting point nor cause or condition but consequence of a historically particular sociality. Among major illustrative examples of contextuality of psychologistic accounts, I would name Augustine's self-confessional divinity-reflective account, Locke's "tabula rasa" account, and Hobbes' "natural kind" account—not one of them devoid of sensitivity to cultural conditions, yet all of them, in somewhat differing ways, assuming a universality of human being housed in "soul" or "mind." This seeming necessity of what might be called a "minimalist" universality was for long housed conveniently in a religion that successfully ignored its own cultural conditions and geographic location well short of being "global," much less "universal." Nonetheless, "soul" could be easily wedded to the other terms of a psychologism, and were, if differently, from Augustine to Hobbes and Locke, by whose time "mind" had to accommodate similar furnishings without the automatic imprimatur of humble "confession to the divine."[324]

I noted in Part Two that Derek Parfit (1987, part 3) presented a formulation of "person" that is similar to Marx' "ensemble of relations" account, emphasizing that once we grasp that inherence we will appreciate the futility of a practical reason that assumes or proposes a clear distinction of ethics separating oneself from others. He also argued that his account makes "self" a superfluous concept. I agree the basic point, except that "self" highlights reflexivity in a way that "person" does not, and I think this difference is important even aside from avoiding a laxity of vernacular habit. The notion of reflexivity will be discussed below. Here I will mention only that concerns about "stability of self" have changed in conjunction with consciousness of reflexivity as a fact, in roughly the same sense that Christopher Fynsk (1996) intended when he argued that, despite the oft-noted "discovery of language" (see, e.g., Rorty 1967; and above, Part One, §9), a consciousness of language as a fact remains far less than common. We mostly take native language for granted (as Kant said, a conceptual scheme). Recall Hume looking for the ground of reflexivity of self-consciousness: he knew the experience of reflexivity, but it was attended by doubt because he could not catch sight of it in action. If it is not an illusion of memory, then it must take place in a fluidity of moment, the hinge between memory and anticipation, moments of a conceptual scheme (which has room, by the way, for illusions of memory, as well as Kant's "transcendental Illusion").

---

[324] Attaining clarity of intent is far from easy. For instance, Locke (1975 [1700], 2.27.9) said of "person" that the word refers to "a thinking intelligent Being, that has reason and reflection, and can consider itself as itself, the same thinking thing, in different times and places, which it does only by that consciousness which is inseparable from thinking, and, as it seems to me, essential to it." Patently psychologistic, one might think, since nothing of sociality was mentioned. But did he intend that exclusion? Even if he meant by "reason" a strictly psychologistic faculty, "reflection" could have been intended as inclusive of the "thoughts of others," even "taking others' views into account." Further, did Locke intend by "blank slate" that the infant's social context counted for nothing at birth, at two or six months, and so forth? Similar uncertainties can be raised about meanings recorded by Augustine and by Hobbes.

In a film by Steven Soderbergh, *The Limey* (1999), one character diagnoses another via simile: "You're not specific enough to be a person. You're more like a vibe."[325] The contrast can be read metaphorically as an application from quantum dynamics (while reminiscent of Proust): Valentine's "personality" is like the vibration of a wave form that has not (yet?) resolved into a specific particle, because he prefers to remain elusive, even hidden, the spread-out blur of a vibrating string. This is not John Locke's "person"; and yet Locke clearly did recognize an "essential" malleability of "person" (or at least of "child-person") in his account of dynamics on a blank slate, and perhaps it occurred to Locke that dynamics could not begin within that nullity, that condition of zero-degree writing. Thus, what counts as "stability," not only to an observer but also, though potentially differently, to the consciousness of a reflexive self? The diagnostic metaphor is broken, however, since it leaves to first-person decision when and where to collapse the wave form into a particularity of being; resolution can occur only in and as the interaction of observation, whether it be second-person conversation or third-person surveillance. First-person awareness of resolution is not automatic. Indeed, as Theunissen (1984 [1977]) argued in his study of Sartre's thought (and more generally), the basis of reflexivity is seeing oneself through others, through expressions of otherness (cf. Mead 1913; Wiley 1994, ch. 4).

This brings to mind a distinction Max Weber made famous by his discussion in the first part of his *Economy and Society* (1968 [1922]). The core of his contribution to inquiry, which he called an "interpretive sociology," would rest by design in *meanings*—not in the abstract motions of actors walking past one another, bumping into one another, as in the imagery of billiard balls on a table, but in meaningful interactions of actors within a context rich in meanings (reasons, expectations, interests, motives, aims, and so forth). This does not mean that all activities meet the standard of "meaningfulness"; far from it. Much of what human beings do is simply from the inertial force of habit—activities designated by Weber as "behaviors." Activities that are self-consciously laced with meanings are, on the other hand, "actions," and they are "social actions" insofar as the actor takes into account the meaningful presence(s) of other(s), whether "other" is a specific person or, to borrow from Mead, a "generalized other" (see below). The conceptual distinction of "action" (and "social action") from "behavior" became rather standard fare in many parts of the social sciences, sometimes to such an extent that it was repeated, one might say, habitually and as if unproblematic. A conceptually useful distinction in principle, in practice it can be difficult to use because of the assumption that an observer's inferences of meaning, intent, and the like, are sufficiently accurate and reliable, and then the more difficult assumption that a given actor's consciously considered actions can be, in principle, consistently coherent enough to have coherently entailed observable effects.

Much of Weber's inquiry addressed cultural variations, over time and across space, in the varied formation of an individuality of person (e.g., Weber 1930 [1905], 1968 [1922-23], 1976 [1896; 1909]). One of the chief themes was a stylized distinction between what could be

---

[325] The speaking character is Adhara (portrayed by Amelia Heinle); the recipient, a rather sleazy Terry Valentine (by Peter Fonda). Lem Dobbs wrote the screenplay.

called an account of personhood (or selfhood) in terms of "who one is" and an account in terms of "what one can do, and how well." The former sort of account, regarded from the standpoint of late nineteenth-century Europe as "traditional," stressed identification in terms of "status" (that is, "station in life") organization, mainly hierarchical and inertial in the sense of a "body at rest." In short, born a peasant, always a peasant; born to aristocracy, always an aristocrat, even if in penury. The second sort of account, seen as of more recent provenance (although Weber was well aware of a similar distinction in ancient societies), put greater stress on personal mobility within an organization of status, the latter understood not in the traditional sense of "social honor" and "station in life" but in the newer sense of "prestige" and "self-fashioning presentation"— although no less hierarchical for being both newer and more fluid. This was an update of theme within the old debate between "ancients and moderns," now with clearer advantage to "the moderns" mainly because of greater liberation of the individual person from the heavily viscous medium of traditions that prized, at least ostensibly, steadfast sameness over entrepreneurial vision and risk-taking.[326]

One of the ironies of "change," in terms of Weber's framework of inquiry, is that today, a century after his death, a prominent discourse seems to have shifted approximately 180 degrees the polarity of Weber's contrastive types. Rather than seeing a sequence of greater liberation from "the past" and a larger selection of options from which growing proportions of individuals may choose, the regnant principle of an alternative discourse has become the loss of "stability of personal identity" due to what is considered to be excessive fluidity, false measures of the supply/demand dialectic of ability, and an overwhelming array of options, the latter defined mainly in terms of commodity consumption, such that the diversity of array is largely a matter of distinctions that lack "real difference" (see Rosa 2013 [2005]; Haskel and Westlake 2018). This notion of exaggerated difference has as counterpart a notion of exaggerated precision (as well as univocity) in the means by which the "how well can you do what you claim you can do" is assessed (see, e.g., Young 1958; Abbott 2009; Muller 2018). The idea that a surfeit of choices (i.e., consumption choices; production choices are rarely matters of public discussion) has been wasteful in the collective and confusing to individuals, leading them to spoil time and psychic energy, has gained considerable traction in a critique of instrumental rationality, as well as in broader conservation efforts (e.g., see Horkheimer and Adorno 2002 [1969]; Leiss 1972; Gazzaley and Rosen 2016; plus the brief controversy around Schwartz 2004, Grant and Schwartz 2011). But the argument regarding confusion and an overtaxing pressure on personal identity

---

[326] As Braddock (2012), Brown (2003), and others have demonstrated (and for contrastive context see Benedict 2001), the fascinations of collectors, a practice that bloomed profusely during the latter part of the nineteenth century (e.g., see Goncourt 1881), afford insight into the diverse contents of a self's identity and reflections of society (or "the furnishings of a mind"), as reflected in "things" kept nearby as points of reference. This practice has often been identified as a trained habit of "consumerism," and surely there is an abundance of evidence of that. However, the practice is much older, even older than the advent of the modern museum. Charles I of England was proud of his cabinet of curiosities, along with his collection of painting. The difference has been a sort of democratization of habits of consumption.

269

has also turned increasingly on beliefs that the rate of change—social in all aspects (economic, political, cultural, etc.) and therefore overdeterminedly taxing psychologically—has simply become too great (see Bellow 2015).[327]

Note, however, that the first sentence of the prior paragraph revolves around a locution of uncertainty (i.e., "*seems* to have shifted"), or in this instance an ambiguity that is actually, at least in part, an ambivalence. In Weber's own time, expressions of "too much" and "too fast" were widely heard and read. One of Weber's near-contemporaries, Émile Durkheim, had heeded the laments, as he partly shared in concerns about a "cult of the individual"—erosions of traditional order, increased estrangements, anomie, hollowing of institutions of "civic function" that had integrated the individual person into the whole of society as such (see, e.g., Wallwork 1972; Putnam 2000). Similar concerns animated a large part of the Romanticist movement, as was recounted briefly in the prior Part. We here face the conundrum of a relativity of perspective analogous to that which Einstein highlighted, circa 1914, as he thought through the shift that made his first theory of relativity "specific" in comparison to his second ("general") theory: on what platform can one stand—knowing that it, too, is historical—as one compares an earlier to a later historical period? Proust had asked the question, albeit without realizing how extensive its domain would become. Recent scholars have not been blind to the difficulty, as they have struggled to make sense of this dialectic of subject/object relations: how does one gauge capacities of an individual person resident here-and-now to change, adapt, grow, as conditions and perhaps even context of preparation-for-tomorrow evolve from the conditions and context of yesterday's objectivities (which were, after all, products of earlier actors, etc.)? Limits due to the problem of counterfactuals loom large as one faces the conundrum, especially as those limits are made all the more severe when one must contend with the possibility that governing conditions are overdetermined (cf. Case and Deaton 2020).

Whereas in earlier circumstances positive consequences could be easily seen in greater rates of change from century to century, and even from generation to generation, by the early 1900s large and growing populations in Europe and the Americas were increasingly doubtful, increasingly frustrated, and sometimes angry. Not for the first time but more stridently and more robustly than before, due both to recent increases in inequality and to the greater diversities in cities of populations more capable of reasoning while also increasingly exposed to instrumental rationalities (see Stinchcombe 1986, p. 154), emblems of large-scale organizational processes became politically ideologized and directly politicized. The main emblems—"modern society," "modern technology," and "modern capitalism"—signaled a new conception and measure of scale. Major contests of the past had been largely contained *within* a society. Peasant revolts had focused mainly in localities and against the local segment of aristocracy or landed gentry.

---

[327] It is hardly lost on observers that anyone is formally free to step off the hedonic treadmill any time. Likewise, the correlation between attitudes toward minimalism in painted art and attitudes toward minimalism in lifestyle shifts from positive to negative, then back again, as is partly signaled in waves of "rediscovery" of Thoreau. On the dialectic of formal/substantive (in Weber's terms and in connection to the dialectic of form/content) with regard to reasons and rationalities, see Stinchcombe (1986).

Religious conflicts had been mostly contained within regnant polities. Republican revolts had been specific to this or that monarchy. Anti-clericalism had taken one form in sixteenth-century Britain, another form later in France, still another in Italy. But now the target was a "kind" of *society as a whole*, even if the boundaries of "kind" were rather blurry (as in "modern society"), plus the entirety of a new sort of "technology" (the name itself a newly-conceived target of remorse and threat) and of a way of organizing economic activity that, while hardly new in basic principle, had become voraciously powerful and invasive of the "private sphere" as never before. A new literature developed in response to what would be summarized as "the Social Question"— that is, the plethora of wounds and deceits and bad faith that were felt by the huge and growing populations of cities (see, e.g., Howerth 1906; Tönnies 1907; Steiner 1919). This last naming itself, "the *Social* Question," is telling, for it might have been named "the Political Question" or "the Economic Question." Instead, the focal "point" had become the whole of a society, the whole of a way of life. The word "society" had been brought into discourse as indication of an organizational scale much larger than a sewing circle or a professional association or a fraternal or sororal club. The new literature was partly ancillary to, but also partly diagnostic of, the aims and abilities of a new literature of social-science theorizing and empirical inquiry. Would they be useful in addressing the host of problems and actual as well as potential unrest stimulated by such massive change? Later in this Part Four we will consider in the context of efforts to build an authority of voice by social scientists some of the works by a small number of theorists: Emile Durkheim, Georg Simmel, Max Weber (again), and George Herbert Mead.

Today it is apparent that rates of change have accelerated to intragenerational scales of difference, even to a decade-by-decade scale of difference, as discussed in §19. Have fluidity and impermanence become destructive, as some (e.g., Rosa 2013 [2005]) have claimed? Perhaps, the feeling is, trajectories of change have reached, even exceeded, natural limits of species capability. As Rosa viewed the terrain, that judgment seemed likely: "in a society where the past has lost its obligating power, while the future is conceived as unforeseeable and uncontrollable, 'situational' or present-oriented patterns of identity dominate." These patterns are contrasted to the "who one is" identity formations of past or "traditional" societies. By this conception of "the new," the temporal orientation that dominated in the popular ideology of Bildungsprozess has shifted from a focus on "my future self," which one seeks to enact via a continuing "up-bringing," toward a more fragile search that becomes fixated on an evanescence of experiences in a fleeting Now, resulting, as some scholars have seen it (e.g., Taylor 1989), in a passivity due to the multiplicity of time horizons imposed on a person from without. This is temporality that emphasizes temporariness on ever shorter scales: "if families, occupations, residences, political and religious convictions and practices can *in principle* be changed or switched at any time, then one no longer *is* a baker, husband of X, New Yorker, conservative, and Catholic per se"—or other enduring identity formation of "thingness," as it were—but a set of shifting capacities, orientations, interests, desires, actions. This sense of being as "now a changeling" connotes emotions of unreliability, untrustworthiness, of "otherness" itself (as in the older, slower, traditional society, the stranger who has come into one's community). Instead of

271

reliable *being*, a process of continual *becoming* has now been ruling as the dominant modality of human life, and this has, so to speak, become *too much*. Because expectations are now always, or mostly, or primarily, expectations of what one is capable of doing in a "here and now" that carries or bears an only "vaguely foreseeable duration," the identity-satisfying stability harvested in the nostalgia of a traditional sense of endurance of "who I *am*" has increasingly lost resilience, in favor of the fluidity of senses of "what I can do, and (more or less) well," depending on what the market demands. The scale of "time itself" changes, and this change is understood as a matter of human legislation, not as a matter of something so stable as "Nature's order" or "God's will."[328] Rosa, among others, has questioned whether this induces us to "disregard identity predicates in our self-description because they suggest a stability that cannot be made good" (Rosa 2013 [2005], pp. 146, 147, 233). Others have suggested a resurgence of nativism (e.g., Wuthnow 2018).[329]

With that as backdrop, let's recall Weber's distinction between "behavior" and "action" (or "social action"). A first-person report of intent seems to circumvent the need of inference, but it does so on the assumption that first-person reports are always both truthful and adequately insightful. Both self-deception and first-person ignorance of determinative influences are almost always possible conditions (see, e.g., Alston 1993; Kahneman 2011; Mercier and Sperber 2017), and are inherently difficult to assess. On the other hand, observer inference is troubled both by the inherent uncertainty of a single observation and by the fact that repeated observation erodes reliability of test. That is, think of a case in which one seeks to test one's understanding of first-person's intention when engaged in a specific kind of action under specified conditions; assume one observes the person during repeated enactments, and one is confident that conditions have

---

[328] Legislation as occurred during the International Geographic Congress of 1871, and again during the International Meridian Conference of 1884, as well as in prior episodes of constructing and coordinating calendars (cf. Kosmin 2018), and in changing the metric of clock time—adding quarter hours, then minutes, then seconds; now building clocks that measure in yocto-seconds of time (one trillionth of a trillionth of a second), and building devices that depend on that exactitude (a long way from Frederick W Taylor's "scientific management" of time and motion; see Part Five, below).

[329] It is evident from the historical record that there have been past times when observers expressed concern that "the pace of change" was exceeding, or was on the verge of exceeding, the abilities of human beings to adapt and "keep up" with a "helter skelter world." No doubt such concerns were being expressed in Max Weber's world—evident from belletristic literatures of the time. Robert Musil (1953-60 [1930-43], pp. 1, 8) began the first volume of his trilogy with a scene of "Motor-cars ... shooting out of deep, narrow streets into the shallows of bright squares," and a little later his "man without qualities" observes that "[i]t doesn't matter what one does. ... In a tangle of forces like this it doesn't make a scrap of difference" (see also, e.g., Döblin 2018 [1929]). Analysts such as Rosa and those he featured in his review of others' works suggest a "this time is different" diagnosis. There may well be a connection between that diagnosis and the nativist-political reactions against "too much change" and "too much openness" that have been displayed recently increasingly in polities of Europe, North America, Australia, and elsewhere, during the second decade of the current century.

remained stable during that time. The problem is that as one repeatedly observes a finite data set, one reduces the reliability of inference testing. In general, the solution is to generate new observations, rather than rely on the same data in hand. But can one assume that the repeated enactments amount to a series of new and independent observations, especially when one is confident that context and conditions have been stable? This is a dilemma that too many social scientists have ignored while engaged in empirical inquiry, but also while engaged in theorizing from their own first-person experiences (reading and re-reading, writing and rewriting, along with child care, grocery shopping, etc.), *as if* these experiences had somehow been repeatedly and independently refreshed. Imagine, then, the proverbial "everyday person" who might have not even a glimmer of awareness that a dilemma exists at the center of his or her experience.

One last topic of clarification, before returning to the notion of "scale." Although I have already addressed the matter repeatedly (e.g., Hazelrigg 1989b, 1993a, 1993b), I want to review what I mean by "the dialectic of subject/object relations," and in the process make an aspect of it more specific. Adorno has provided a suitable vehicle for the task. In one of his better-known passages of *Negative Dialectics* Adorno wrote (in Ashton's English translation, which in this passage I judge to be unexceptional) the following:

> Due to the inequality inherent in the concept of mediation, the subject enters into the object altogether differently from the way the object enters into the subject. An object can be conceived only by a subject but always remains something other than the subject, whereas a subject by its very nature is from the outset an object as well. Not even as an idea can we conceive a subject that is not an object; but we can conceive an object that is not a subject. It belongs to the meaning of subjectivity to also be an object, but not to the meaning of objectivity to be subject. To be an object also is part of the meaning of subjectivity; but it is not equally part of the meaning of objectivity to be a subject (Adorno 1973 [1966], p. 183).

The passage occurs in the context of Adorno's presentation of "The Object's Preponderance" (or I would say, "the priority of the Objekt").[330] In fact, Adorno never actually argued priority or

---

[330] Adorno here used the noun "Objekt" rather than the more customary "Gegenstand." The latter refers etymologically to that which "stands against': primarily against a consciousness and antecedently to that consciousness; then, by inference, "against" another Gegenstand thing. From the Latin "objectum," "Objekt" is etymologically that which is "thrown against" or "thrown out from," typically against or from a "Subjekt" as conscious being. But "Objekt" (much like the English "object") hosts considerable ambiguity; it can include not only simple "thingness" but also, for instance, an intentional presence, an aim, or a goal (as in, e.g., "the object of my affections" or "of my effort," etc.). A good illustration of the difference, post-Hegel, is in Marx' first thesis on Feuerbach: "The main defect of all hitherto-existing materialism … is that objects [Gegenstand], actuality, sensuousness, are conceived only in the form of the object [des Objekts], or of *contemplation*, but not as *human sensuous activity* [Tätigkeit], *practice*, not subjectively. Hence it happened that the active side, in contradistinction to materialism, was set forth by idealism—but only abstractly" (Marx 1976 [1888], p. 6). Hegel, aware of the ambiguity of "Objekt," explicitly subsumed all of it under his notion of the dialectical process of Aufhebung. Adorno offered little guidance.

preponderance but rather presupposed it in what Hullot-Kentor (2006, p. 195) described as his "autocratic" style of presentation. There is an irony lurking in larger context, for only three pages earlier Adorno (1973 [1966], p. 180) had levied a charge by "traditional norms of philosophy" of hysteron proteron, typically accounted as a kind of hyperbaton (a figurative or rhetorical syntactical rearrangement, putting "the latter before"), or as Adorno put it, "to presuppose as transmitting what we would deduce as transmitted." While this predication suggests merely a sentential transmission, or one might say a "merely rhetorical" device, hysteron proteron is a logical fallacy in supposed argumentation: one begins one's argument with a premise that in fact (but usually implicitly) presupposes the conclusion to be reached (i.e., begging the question). In the case of Adorno, generally speaking, he began with a premise of what Bernstein (2001, pp. 287-288) called Adorno's "modern naturalism." More pointedly, as Bernstein alerted his reader, Adorno was "reflectively acknowledging," in that passage, "the a priori of modern naturalism: there is nothing else for a consciousness to be if not the consciousness of an object of a certain radical kind, one capable of becoming aware of its indelible objecthood."

Reframe the indented passage from Adorno into second-person perspective. What would an interlocutor say in response to the declaration? One good possibility is, "And how do you know that?" For instance, "How do you know there is always a remainder of Objekt after any subject has conceived it? Since you are a subject, give me first a description of that remainder as you know it to be and then a description of the process by which you gained that knowledge and its source." In short, an interlocutor might well ask Adorno where he himself *is* in that account. More specifically still, the interlocutor might ask Adorno about his location relative to the apparent disappearance, at this juncture, of the *dialectic* of his "negative dialectic." It is apparent in the passage (and elsewhere in Adorno's writings) that in fact the subject/object dialectic disappears into an analytic distinction of objectness that is prior to human being. This "modern naturalism" is reminiscent of a knowledge of prehuman origins.

As interlocutor, I could say to Adorno, "Consider the objectivity of our conversation, the objectivity of what has just transpired between us, as recorded in your memory and as recorded in my memory. It is suffused with your subjectivity and with my subjectivity, and we might agree to call that 'our intersubjectivity' (shared second-person experience); but if we do, we are agreeing to a very large and complex assumption—namely, that between your subjectivity and mine there has been all along a mutual agreement on composition of the object, 'the conversation and its meanings.' However that mutual agreement might be, it is still the case that 'the objectivity of our conversation' could well exist in two versions, yours and mine. Now, where is the objectivity that escapes your and/or my subjectivity? I do concede that my understanding of your intended meanings could be, in part or in whole, faulty; likewise, I can imagine a similar concession from you; and therein one can say surely the possibility, maybe even high probability, of an objectivity that remains after the subjectivity of my conception of you, your intended meanings, and likewise an objectivity that remains after the subjectivity of your conception of me, and my intended meanings. Each of us, in conversation, might have respective clues as to the objective remainder of one's own meanings, and on such basis seek improved mutuality of

274

second-person experience. But every morsel of that, in however many iterations it occurs, is contingent on the respective subjectivities in each's objectivity of 'our conversation.' I might have a sudden intuition, an 'implanted thought,' a presence of 'alien voice,' or a holographic hallucination, that purports to be of 'the missed objectivity'; but even that will be relative to, contingent on, the subjectivity of your meanings in the objectivity of 'our conversation' as it has transpired until that particular event. Now, do you, Adorno, have a different pipeline to 'the object' as it is in itself—not merely as it is for you and as, in principle, it could be for me, but as it is precisely in itself as always-prior-object? If you do, explain it."

Let us now shift gears and consider the word "scale," central to this Part Four. Ahl and Allen (1996) pointed out in their primer on hierarchy theory that a useful distinction is made between "scale of observation" and "scale of measurement." The former notion rides within conventional dimensions of space and time. Observation can be narrow or broad, near or far, with varying degrees of each. One can think also of spatial depth, from superficial to deeply penetrating or recessed. Observation can vary temporally as well as spatially—now, later, records of past processes and events; one-shot or repeated discretely or continually—and these, too, can vary in a kind of temporal depth, not in the sense of "deep past" (as previously discussed) but in the sense of clocks that differ between superficial and deeper or "hidden" processes ("fast time" versus "slow time," and the like), by which I am not intending any "conspiracy theory" but simply recognizing Kant's point that at least some causes are knowable only inferentially, by their effects, and that this raises issues of clocking.

It should be clear that those two uses of "scale" are interrelated and share semantic logic to a considerable extent. The same can be said of the concept which I intend primarily by the same word, "scale," but now with a different focus, which can be called "organizational scale." Think of a compound, an organization of different parts. The parts may differ qualitatively on one or more dimensions; or some or all of the parts may be of the same kind, under some definition of "kind," but repeated a finite number of times and therefore very likely variant within kind. These variations are conceptual, to be sure, and with general agreement on boundaries they can then be left as empirical matters, to be settled by observation and measurement. Ahl and Allen used several biological illustrations for clarification. An organ is composed of tissues, tissues are composed of cells, cells are composed of ..., and so forth, until we come to physical-chemical substances. Now let's shift perspective from "things" of one kind or another and think in terms of "process"—osmosis, for instance. Fluids traverse cellular walls by osmosis. Does osmosis also occur at the scale of tissues? At the scale of organs? In other words, is the process of osmosis sensitive to the organizational scale of a whole relative to its component parts? Asked somewhat differently, is the process of exchange (of sustenance, of waste, of information, etc.) governed by the same operational dynamics, the same process logic, across the different scales?

Note that there *is* a difference between those two ways of asking a question: the first named a distinct process, known as "osmosis," which is characterized by its own dynamics, while the second question named a more abstract process, "exchange." My point in making that unannounced switch is that questions of organizational scale are usually sensitive to one or another dimension of abstraction, or to a variation in the dialectic of abstract/concrete; and depending on what already counts as "settled knowledge" of a particular organizational form, it can be difficult to maintain consistency empirically in terms simultaneously of abstraction and of scale. Illustrations of that difficulty will be seen below, in regard to discussions of "self and society." Bear in mind that the address is similar to the address posed in prior discussions as "What counts as X?" questions, wherein it always became evident that the difficulty was in fact both empirical and conceptual at one stroke. Observation inescapably involves classification and measurement—and in each of those operations potential questions of organizational scale.

Unfortunately, relevant literatures have become a bit of a mess due to careless uses of the word (and to an extent the concept), "scale." A variety of modifying phrases (e.g., "scale free," "scale invariant," "scale sensitive") appear in seemingly relevant literatures with little or no indication of how they relate to one another. Sometimes the self-similarity property of a Mandelbrot process (i.e., a process governed by fractal relation) is said to be "scale neutral," which could lead one to think that "self-similarity" is synonymous with "scale free," even though the former term refers to comparisons across organizational scale. In part, the mess has resulted from typical motivations of competition for celebrity in the status queues of a profession or a specialty within a discipline, sometimes riding on little more than a repackaging of older ideas under a new name and claiming discovery. The recent popularity of "scale free" phenomena illustrates the point, as usage of the phrase accelerated in the development of network theory.[331] In that context the qualifying notion of "scale-free" means that the process in focus operates uniformly across the distribution of size (e.g., the size distribution of connections per node in a network). But even as such, the notion has not been free of ambiguity.

Most often, the notion of "power law" has referred to a distribution that has the general form of:

$$p(X) \sim X^{\alpha} \qquad (4.1)$$

where $p(X)$ is the probably of observing a given value of X, the copula function ($\sim$ rather than $=$) indicates that the relation is approximate, and the exponent $\alpha$, known as the "scaling parameter" or "factor," takes a value usually in the $2<\alpha<3$ range with either positive or negative sign, and with a specified minimum value of X (i.e., $X_{min}$) greater than zero. It should be evident that the word, "power," simply refers to the presence of the exponent.

---

[331] The perspective of "network" is itself illustrative, in that recognition of the importance of networks—in various phenomena of trade or, more generally, processes of distribution and exchange—has a very long heritage. In this case, however, there has been fruitful work conceptually as well as methodologically, much of it due to Harrison White (e.g., White 2002) and his large cadre of progeny. I return to these issues in Part Five.

While the vocabulary has become popular in recent times, the distributional process to which it refers has a long history (see, e.g., Simon 1955). It has traveled under various names, including "cumulative advantage" and, most recently, "preferential assignment" (or some variant thereof), while in vernacular it is often designated simply as "the rich get richer" principle. The latter locution will be familiar to some readers as a statement of the "the Pareto principle," after Vilfredo Pareto (1971 [1927]), who estimated that roughly 80 percent of outputs are due to about 20 percent of inputs. In general terms, think of a relation of Y ("output") to X ("input"); assume a large number of observations of the joint distribution (X,Y). Now convert each numerical value of X and each numerical value of Y into their respective logarithmic values (this generates a "log-log distribution"). Plot this log-log distribution. The plotted observations will line up in a straight line (approximately) if the relationship of Y to X follows a "power law" distribution, the slope coefficient of the regression of Y on X being your estimate of the scaling factor.

When the power-law principle is described as "scale free," the meaning is simply that for any specified process that follows the principle (or model based on it), the regulative function (i.e., the exponent $a$) takes one value for all sizes of a relevant organizational property (e.g., the size distribution of networks, measured as number of nodes per network; the size distribution of wealth holdings, measured as number of gold balls per holder; and so forth). The principle is as such perfectly sound. As indicated just above, it is far from new. Applications are sometimes unsound, however. First of all, the relation is only approximate. In actual applications one can virtually never be certain that any observed quantity (X) selected at random is drawn from a given power-law distribution. Moreover, there can be a tendency to misattribute a starting value of zero to a model. In terms of Locke's "tabula rasa" model (to elaborate on a point made earlier), one might hypothesize that the cognitive contents of mind grow in accordance with a power law: the more one has learned the more capable one becomes of learning still more (at rate $a > 1$, perhaps $a \rightarrow 2$). But of course a power-law process of, say, wealth accumulation would never get started if it had to start at zero-degree wealth. Likewise, Locke's new-born does not in fact begin at zero but begins in the ongoing sociality of parents, guardians, local community. If a given process fits the power-law principle, it will be only because that process is already well underway. The equation stated above describes an already accomplished distribution of outcomes of that process (which is the point of the $X_{min} > 0$ condition). Not that the given process had no beginning, no origin or zero point; but originations typically follow a principle different from that of a power law or any other principle that describes effect distributions of an already existent basin of attraction.[332]

In the remainder of this Part Four (and in the next) I will use the term "scale" to refer to the central issue of homology—namely, is the relation of ordering among units (parts of a whole,

---

[332] It should also be noted that, as more and better-studied data have accumulated, it has become evident that the enthusiasm about scale-free networks was oversold. Broido and Clauset's (2018) analysis of nearly 1,000 data sets for a variety of different networks strongly indicates that scale-free networks are more nearly rare than ubiquitous (for more, see §29).

for instance) governed by one constant logic, or is it governed by different logics among different units or at variable quantities of a given unit or specified properties of a given unit? By way of illustration, consider the popular assumption in the social sciences that a single correlative logic operates between determinants of phenomena at the level of individual actors and determinants of phenomena at the level of, say, families or groups or communities or entire societies. Is that assumption actually supported by good evidence, or is it simply taken for granted? Or, stated in terms of process dynamics, are the dynamics of a specified process of action by individual actors governed by the same logic, the same ordering principles, as the dynamics of corresponding processes as they operate at higher levels of organizational scale? An assumption of *homologous* process, apparently not uncommon, has seldom been examined empirically. But it is difficult to judge that claim, or its opposite, because this part of relevant theorizations has been ignored completely or left implicit and vague. There are some well-known theoretical claims *against* an assumption of homology, to be sure, but they are unusual enough to stand out under notable labels. Perhaps the instance with greatest traffic is known, mainly in economics and some parts of organizational theory, as "economies of scale" (plus the contrary, "diseconomies of scale")— namely, that efficiency, under some description, can be an accelerating (or decelerating) function of size of a specified process (or part or whole) of a commercial firm. It has been difficult in general to sort among theorists on relevant dimensions of organizational scaling principles, however, because of neglect and/or ambiguity. Thus, my point of departure has generally been to assume of a given theorist a position of homology, unless there seems to be good evidence to the contrary. But as my "seems to be" is meant to signal, this is often a difficult determination, because of a number of complications, some of which will be treated in Part Five. Here, I shall concentrate on a few initial problems (in addition to those treated above).

A first clue to the complication consists in the fact that when one asks standard reference works for the antonym to "homology," what one gets in return is a set of "negation" words, such as "dissimilarity," "disagreement," "disproportion," and "unlikeness." Since "homology" means "one logic" or "one order" (by etymology), the logically expected principal antonym should be "heterology" (just as most dictionaries tell us that the chief antonym of "homogeneous," meaning "of one kind or origin," is "heterogeneous"). This first clue says that the assumption of a single logic is so strongly taken for granted that its etymological antonym apparently has no purpose. Another test can be made—as Hannan, Pólos, and Carroll (2007, p. xi n.1) testified from their own experience—by watching for your word processor (or publisher's grammar checker) to react to your writing of "logic*s* of organization" (see also Kontopoulos 1993).[333] Or seek a definition of "heterology": seldom does "different logics" appear in response. Rather, one encounters synonyms such as "abnormality," "lack of correspondence," and the like, as general terms. In addition, answers are given more specifically and variably by discipline of science—in biology, for instance, "the study of abnormality in tissue structure, arrangement, or manner of formation" or "lack of correspondence" among "apparently similar body parts"—and these, on further

---

[333] Another, and related, illustration: what does your word processor say about the plural "knowledge*s*"?

inspection, usually involve a difference of organizational scale.[334] This last point can be rather ambiguous.

As a simple illustration of the ambiguity of what counts as "scale difference," consider this example from basic chemistry. On the one hand, one thinks of any elemental atom of a certain kind as being uniform: an atom of carbon is an atom of carbon is an atom of carbon. Except, depending on discipline, it need not be. Since the early 1900s we have learned of variants called "isotopes." Carbon is carbon by atomic definition: it has six protons in its nucleus, which gives it sixth place in the periodic chart of elements. Most carbon atoms contain also six neutrons in the nucleus. But tiny amounts of carbon have five, seven, or eight neutrons. The first two are stable isotopes. Carbon-14, on the other hand, is not stable. It is this instability that makes the carbon-14 isotope an accurate clock over long intervals (i.e., "radioactive carbon dating"). So, we have four forms of carbon atoms. What difference does that make? In their chemical properties they are interchangeable; for example, any of the isotopes interact with oxygen in the same way. In their atomic properties, however, the isotopes of carbon can have different consequences. We just saw one of them (a long-interval clock). All four forms occupy the same slot in the order of chemical elements. Thus, what is homologous at chemical scale is heterologous at atomic scale.

To put the point of the foregoing illustration in other words, what counts as "homology of scale" can differ at different levels. This can matter. In our everyday-world activities most of us are very unlikely to encounter Carbon-14, and because this isotope radiates energy at a frequency that can harm human cells, one should prefer not to encounter Carbon-14 too much. A similar point can be made about our everyday physical world: Newton's laws of motion still work very well for us in our everyday physical world. In fact, when human beings were sent to the moon Newton's equations, not Einstein's, were used; they were easier to work with in those engineering tasks, and the differences in lunar outcome were small. At the quantum scale of physical processes and at the very large scale of Einstein's relativity, on the other hand, Newton's equations are of little or no use. Furthermore, the order of the quantum realm and the order of the gravitational (or macro space-time) level have remained incompatible with each other. Until further notice, then, physical theory recognizes three fundamentally different levels of scaling. Meso-level scaling, our everyday Newtonian world, is pragmatically sound for most of what we

---

[334] The social sciences generally had little to say about "heterology" until Georges Bataille's "theology," which did attract some attention in sociology as well as in literary studies. For a selection of his writings from his collected works, see Bataille (2004). Bataille used "heterology" as a name for his effort to produce thought without thought, or a kind of nonthought thinking that tries to do without conceptual order. (Perhaps I have misunderstood him, for I simply do not know how to do what he thought he could do. Derrida's project had a useful point which remains important. I do not see that Bataille's project was more than a self-contradictory effort to escape any and all conceptualization.) Bataille's earlier work in economic theory was valuably insightful, however, and in some of that discussion (e.g., 1988 [1949], vol. 1, pp. 19-26) he seemingly addressed an issue of scale in a way that suggests heterology in its literal sense.

do, but it seemingly has nothing fundamentally useful to say about the relation of the extreme micro (quantum) to the extreme macro (gravitational or Einsteinian space-time). [335]

That incompatibility is troubling insofar as we expect homology. Markus Gabriel (2015 [2013], p. 204) has referred to what he called a "compulsion to integrate," an expectation of a single, unified "conceptual order that must place all existing things together." Galen Strawson (2018 [1995], p. 24) referred to himself as having "a blithely Kantian confidence in the ability of philosophy [i.e, of a suitably skilled thinker] to reach conclusions of extreme generality." These two sentences are different statements, to be sure, but they share some assumptions about order and thus relations and rules, or logic. We have repeatedly encountered this commonality—for instance, in the presumption of continuity in time; in accounts of memory work; in first-person consciousness as "my experience," an aggregation of action effects in temporal sequence (more or less), with parings and reconstitutions along the way.[336] As shown explicitly in one of his recent titles, *I Am Not a Brain* (2017 [2015]), Gabriel's argument is aligned partly by renewed interest in brain-mind correlations as they are being driven by new technical instruments such as functional magnetic resonance imaging (fMRI), which we have now harnessed into longstanding pursuits of reduction—that is, conjoined with the conviction of a homology that, due to regnancy of analysis, has usually been sought through disassemblies of a whole into its parts rather than through explorations of assembly.

Dissection is hardly a new activity, of course, and it has almost always been dissection of a materiality understood as representative of an ideality—an ideality conceived as existing in a statics ("design") far more than in a dynamics. Recall that in medieval European texts of mental faculties a large function was assigned to "sensus communis," a notion held more or less across various European cultures (see, e.g., Gadamer 1989, pp. 25-30) and referring variously to what every "competent adult would know," with or without any notable ethical component (see, e.g., Anthony Cooper 1709, which a few years later became the fourth part of his influential opus magnum, *Characteristicks of Men*, ...; 1999). In general, the sensus communis was held to be a part of the brain, chiefly the coordinator of information from different sensory organs, and to that extent a sort of directive agency. But description of this function rarely went beyond its name, which alone was thought sufficient description of the process of its operation. Output of the sensus communis proceeded to the "imaginativa" (a name which brings to mind Ludwig

---

[335] The micro, meso, macro distinctions are relative, of course. In the ordinary realm of societal affairs it has been common to denote the individual person as micro, organization forms consisting of two or more persons as meso, and society as a whole as macro. These are arbitrary, to be sure; as just defined "meso" can include anything from a two-person family or household to a corporation of thousands of employees. Well-designed research would probably use degree distinctions of organization. Furthermore, as I intend the usages all of the differences whether of "level" or of "scale" are differences of and within sociality, not of presence versus absence of sociality.

[336] It has been a major theme, of course, even a basic platform, of modern science, to imagine a single "grand unified theory" of all of the physical world (see, e.g., Weinberg 2015); and, in what is known as "the Langslands program," a "grand unified theory" of all of mathematics (see, e.g., Langlands 2010; Frenkel 2013). That ambition does not, however, necessarily imply homology.

Wittegenstein's later comments about a "picture theory of language"), thence to the "cognitiva" (the locus of concept formation); thence, to the back of the brain wherein was located a dual faculty, the "estimativa" (rendering judgments) and "memorativa" (memory), this last thought to be a sort of plastic substance, as Plato had declared, on which impressions were formed (and which could be excessively plastic in women and children, thus making them much too "impressionable" and inconstant). As Arab scholars disseminated Aristotle's recovered texts, a partition was resumed between cognition and feeling, the latter assigned not to the brain but to the heart.

By the time that William Carpenter assembled his massive compendium of *Principles of Mental Physiology* (1875)—that is, *physiology,* not psychology—some understandings of the relation of "mind and body" had changed. Perhaps most prominent, certainly the most controversial, was Carpenter's own hypothesis that the human brain was (is) malleable not by original substance but by external activity. However, while there are suggestive indications in Carpenter's 722 pages of text of an instrumentalism—broadly similar to that of John Stuart Mill's pragmatic utilitarianism—the medieval legacy is still easily discernable in Carpenter's discussions. Moreover, although one encounters ipsative expressions and reflexive pronouns throughout his text, and occasional though brief passages about reasoning processes, volition, and "personal identity," there is little sense of a coherence of "self" as processual formation or functionalist principle of "self-determining powers." This last phrase, cited from Carpenter's index, is the nearest one finds to a discussion that a then-teenaged Mead would write some forty years later, entitled "The Social Self" (1913; see also his preceding essays of 1910 and 1912).[337]

Indeed, the span of a single generational distance had rarely been measured by difference in content of thought within one language, English, as great as that between Carpenter's text of 1875 and the essays composed by Mead during the first two decades of the new century. Even the trajectory of content in Mead's compositions during those early decades is remarkable. Had they been composed in German rather than in English, Mead's star would very likely have risen higher than it did, in the academy of US scholars, perhaps a height approximating the stars of other members of Mead's birth cohort, most notably Durkheim, Simmel, perhaps Weber as well (although their works were greater in range). But with the comparison of 1875 and 1913 in mind, what is more remarkable is that the distance between Mead's product and the *current* status of theorization regarding what I have called "passages between self and society" is as small as it is, considering that we are measuring a span of more than twice as many years. Of the few markers of important difference that one can note, the fact that Gabriel took "the compulsion to integrate" to be a summary description of the actuality of a society, and especially of a "national culture," should be ranked highly among them, not only because of its existence but, even more, because so little has been accomplished on that front. As will be seen later, parts of Gabriel's argument are reminiscent of Mead. But aside from some small changes in vocabulary, the issue of homology remains about where it was when Mead died (1931), and far more attention during the interim has been given to dissections than to aggregations or integrations.

---

[337] More will be said about Mead's theorizations below.

Some of the illustrations offered in the foregoing paragraphs suggest that an assumption of homology (which I shall designate also as an assumption of "scale indifference") need not itself be uniform across all levels or scales or across all relevant processes. Does that suggestion extend to important topics of the social sciences? There is reason to think that it does. An example was mentioned above: economies (and diseconomies) of scale have been observed, but variably for different processes and for different parts of commercial firms. A related example comes to mind when one explores Adam Smith's notorious expression, "invisible hand."[338] His point was that the intent of a purposive action need not be achieved. The failure can take various forms: lack of any consequence of the action; lack of intended consequence of a benign intention but with an unexpected consequence that could be either benign or malign (sometimes called "perverse consequence"); lack of intended consequence of a malign intention but with an unexpected consequence that could be either benign or (in a different-from-intended way) malign. More specifically, of course, Smith's main point was that selfish private interest (intent) could result in beneficial consequence for society as a whole (or for some organizational level between individual person and society as a whole). Private vices can produce public goods. Further, he did not identify malign intent with pursuit of selfish private gain; indeed, he saw such pursuit as perfectly normal and appropriate. He argued that in general persons are most productive when they choose their actions for private gain. This, he explicitly said, will generally result in greater public good than if all personal actions are chosen by intent to benefit the public good. Why? Because persons motivated mainly to serve the public good are generally less determined and less effectual (Smith 1776, vol. 2, pp. 32-33). Thus, one could conclude (although Smith did not say) that different scales of effect as measured at level of society result from a given degree of intent according to whether the intent is mainly to yield selfish gain or to add to the greater good.

### §21. Impressions of Self

The ancient Greek concept of "self," as it can be inferred from ancient Greek literatures, was basically an "institutionalized role" type of position within social, cultural, economic, political structures of everyday life. This should not be read as endorsement of the notion that only "stock characters" were available. Characterizations by Greek playwrights were more complex than that, even as they did rely on recognizable "character types" in their tragedies and comedies. By "institutionalized role" I mean the existence of publicly recognized, stable positions of an individual agency, similar to (if not identical with) Simmel's "social types" (e.g., "the stranger," "the miser," "the adventurer").[339] But I also mean more mundane "types" such as "father," "nurse," "huckster," and so forth, as well as more unusual ones such as "hero," "hermit," and "poet." These are historical, cultural variable formations, no doubt, but literary evidence suggests broad similarities of category (e.g., "stranger") which cam make ideal typifications useful devices. Although "types" are often institutionalized and thus in any given temporal and spatial context usually stable and well-bounded, occupancy of a role can accommodate noticeable

---

[338] As numerous commentaries have now pointed out, Smith rarely used this phrase in his *Wealth of Nations* treatise (and once in his *Theory of Sentiments* treatise), but it caught the fancy of a great many people.

[339] See various essays in Donald Levine's collection of Simmel's work; e.g., Simmel (1971 [1908a]).

individual variation, including variation due to incumbent efforts to alter the occupied role either for "better fit" to incumbent preference or for broader ends such as "reforming the role of priest" or allowing finer specification of "stranger" in terms of "signs of danger."

Furthermore, as has been pointed out before, that fact that the Greek vocabulary of Homer used several different words to refer to attributional or aspirational features of deliberate action does not imply the absence of a unified conception of actor or of mental experience, any more than similar multiplicities of terms in English and other present-day languages signifies such absence (see, e.g., Long 2015). On the other hand, some ordering of terms is a useful (if problematic) exercise. If "person" is a name for the ensemble of social relations that composes an individual human being, then what exactly is "self"? How does it compare conceptually with "mind," which has been aptly described as "the thing that is both closest" to a person's reflection on first-person experience "and yet is still, in some sense, quite mysterious" (Long 2015, p. 1)? I have already said that, contrary to Parfit (1987, part 3), I do see a useful differentiation of meaning of "self," vis-à-vis "person," and more will be said in that vein later in this Part Four (e.g., in connection with the Meadian conception of "multiple selves").

I think Marcel Mauss' Huxley Memorial Lecture of 1938 is germane here. Mauss (1985 [1938]), proposed from his extensive familiarity with ethnographic records a classification of pertinent concepts that accorded with the sort of evolutionary schema that had held attention well into the twentieth century. These were, in his native language, "personnage" (role or character), "personnalité" and "personne" (or the Latin "persona," hence person), and "moi" (self; or "soi," one's self). His "personnage," derived mainly from ethnographies of North America and Australia, referred to a clan-based, clan-specific position within clan organization, a position to which specific title, kinship nomenclature, duties, and rights attached, and which could be ceremonially presented by specific mask and/or body paint. This characterization partly fits the ancient Greek notion of "self," or "person" as self-conscious and to some extent reflexive identity. But whereas Mauss had concluded from the ethnographic record that the American and Australian clan-specific "role" did not assign "inner conscience" (a seat of moral consciousness within the individual man or woman who is incumbent of a role), the corresponding attribution for ancient Greeks is not so well supported.

To begin with, and to repeat a caution already emphasized, to say "ancient Greek" is to cover a very long span of time—from the Homeric song-poems to Aristotle and the Hellenistic period—during which "Greek culture," already variable from place to place (i.e., Athens vis-à-vis Sparta, etc.), changed enormously. The fact is, we know very little about authors in the Archaic age of Greece. In the famous instance, "Homer," we cannot be confident even that he existed as a single person rather than as, say, what we would call a "school" or "tradition of poetic art." More can be said of Archilochus (c680-c640), lyric poet of Paros and accorded high status in a hero cult; but even so, most of it is only speculation (see, e.g., Lefkowitz 2012, pp. 30-37, 44). It is said that he followed Homeric style; and in absence of good contrary evidence, that seems probably true. But of whom in that broad period could not the same be said? Of course, "saying the same" is hardly a constant in time or space. Konstan (2006, p. 76) was right to warn against the assumption that careful correspondences of meaning across languages are easy to construct, or to defend. As he said of the Greek word "orgê," it was in its own context (as with the English word "anger" today) "conditioned by the social world in which it operated" (cf. Schrag 1997, pp. 1-2). No less than Achilles enacted a lesson of the complexity of anger: what initially seemed to have been a wholly interior emotional state soon proved itself to have existed in a specific dynamic of sociality. Achilles' anger "forces him into patterns of linguistic conflict that, like his physical withdrawal, isolate him from the community." By the end of Homer's tale Achilles has come to a new (for him) and more diverse understanding of the gift of language "even" in the realm of heroic deeds and honor, enabling him to play the lyre and sing, for himself as for others (*Iliad* 9.185-189; Heath 2005, p. 123).

Narratives are also exercises in sampling. Whatever can be said from a base of existing evidence is surely tainted by an unknown amount of sampling error. Surviving evidence surely did not survive randomly from the ancient Greeks, and the selectivity reflected interests of later audiences as well as vagaries of accident, decay, and deliberate destruction. If one compares surviving documents by Aeschylus with those by Sophocles, and then each of these texts with surviving documents by Euripides, some patterns of difference become reasonably clear. To what extent those patterns would have been understood identically across the three tragedians themselves must remain in doubt, perhaps not so much because their perceptions of each other's works would have been incoherent comparatively as because they would have had difficulty making sense of what *we* see as patterns of difference. If we today have difficulty understanding one another with mutually agreed accuracy and precision—and we do, sometimes continually— imagine the difficulty when the temporal span is two and a half millennia. Not that it is difficult to understand; in fact, it is difficult *not* to understand. The rub comes as we try to make good, and to judge, the "mutually agreed" part. No "ancient Greek" person is still around; and as the contentiousness of much of our more or less recent commentary on "the ancient Greek literature" testifies, we, too, have difficulty adjudicating our different understandings of them.

The "institutionalized role" conception of what for the ancient Greeks would have been best counterpart to our concept of "self" (and "self-identity of person") is nonetheless a good place to begin. One large generalization in comparative register also aids in beginning. If one takes the "Cartesian self" as our representative concept (and by now it should be clear that I for one believe our understanding today is much better than that), then it seems abundantly clear that few if any ancient Greeks would have seen any likeness at all, probably would have faced severe challenge in trying to understand what Descartes was saying, and might well have been horrified to the extent that they did understand. Recall that for Descartes the irreducible determining fact was an interior first-person confidence that *his* conjectures that "world" existed could not be entirely wrong because *he* existed, despite the fact that he had tried mightily to doubt himself into non-existence. His failure in that effort was the founding fact in his logic. There was also the bit about his God not being a trickster—which would have struck probably most ancient Greeks as odd, at the least, because the gods they had known deceived mere mortals time and again, sometimes just for the fun of it. But Descartes' radically subjectivist-individualist anchor for all that exists would surely have struck ancient Greeks, from Homer and Hesiod to Aristotle and Alexander, as plainly ludicrous (see Ricœur 1992 [1990], p. 8).

Beyond that broad comparison, generalizations become progressively precarious. This is partly because we cannot be highly confident that they would have endorsed our meaning of "institutionalized role" as a description of their conception(s). But it is also due to the fact that, contrary to an overly simple reading of Mauss' classification, we maintain important features of the "institutionalized role" conception—and not only because of what our playwrights concoct when they create "stock characters." Recall the sometimes harsh, even vindictive complaints that have emanated from fellow citizens when adult persons have sought to marry someone who is considered to be "same gender" as "wife" or "husband." Or when an adult person undergoes elective surgery to change from uncomfortable to comfortable "gender identification." It is clear that such complaints are rooted in a culture of traditional institutionalized role expectations of "who one is" in a nativist sense of binary gender identity, and that this identity is more about "selfhood" than about anatomy. Likewise (and usually less tumultuously), occupational assignments, typically thought to be more like a suit of clothing that one can don, then exchange for another, nonetheless often carry a selfhood correlation that is like an institutionalized role assignment. While this is partly attached to gender assignments ("women are better at one kind of occupation, men at another"), it extends within, and sometimes across, the gender binomial, as when, for instance, "people" (men or women) of a given "character type" are thought to self-select for entry into actuarial occupations, and those of another "character type" into nursing, and so forth.

Recall that in drawing on Mauss' classification I objected to the apparent notion that "inner conscience" did not pertain to selfhood among the ancient Greeks inasmuch as selfhood for them was much like the "institutionalized role" conception, which Mauss associated with cultures that (at the time) were still often described as "primitive" (whether intended in the sense of "originary" or in a more invidious sense). However that conception might have been for, say. Australia's Arrernte or North America's Huron or Apache (and I doubt that the characterization fit any of them), it would be wide of the mark to say that ancient Greeks were incapable of understanding the notion of an "interior judgment of morality" or were oblivious to a logic of counterfactual thinking or lacked reflexivity of consciousness or had no sense of "myself." In Part Two I referred to that part of the famous speech by Achilles (*Iliad* 9.320-323) in which he expressed his moral judgment of anyone who practiced deceit. One could say appropriately that Achilles was there expressing heroic character; and that would be fitting, in the sense that "being hero," as Christopher Gill put it (Gill 1996, chapter 2), was a definite "kind" of selfhood. But the tenor of Achilles' judgment is distinctively different in comparison to similar expressions by other heroic persons (e.g., Odysseus, Agamemnon, Hector).[340] Of Homer we cannot determine. Of Archilochus, however, we can say that he himself claimed that his poetry reflected his own experiences, both cognitive and emotive, as his explicit resource. While the claim can be disputed (as some have done), this is partly beside the point, for Archilochus was there displaying his understanding that audience receptivity would turn partly on his authority of voice—that is, on an understanding that evinces both reflexivity and awareness of self-reflexive consciousness in others, rather than simply as an understanding of a more or less complex "whatness" (Ricœur 1992 [1990], pp. 68-69) but as a narrative tool with intent to persuade. His authority of voice evinced a reflexivity of first-order thought (i.e., thought of what one or another character would say and do, as reflection of his own experience), and it evinced a second-order reflexivity as awareness of others and how he would expect them to hear his poetic characters. That might not count exactly as what would later be called "taking the role of the other" or "walking in the shoes of another"; but surely it is close.

Mauss (1985 [1938], pp. 2-3) must have been correct in saying that there has never "been a tribe, a language, in which the term 'I,' 'me,'" and related words did not exist, or that such words have "not expressed something clearly represented." Further, "it is plain … that there has never existed a human being who has not been aware, not only of his body, but also at the same time of his individuality, both spiritual and physical." Still, there are differences, some in nuance and some greater. Gill has given us gifts of his extensive research of surviving literatures of epic, tragedy, and philosophy, from Homer to Aristotle, seeking evidences of their uses of terms that translate approximately as "self," "person," "personality," and the like, uses that afford insight into the cultures of meaning (see, e.g., Gill 1996; 2006). Other scholars have done as well, if with partly different details of focus. My point here, in this brief recitation of some pertinent literatures about (and from) ancient Greek cultures, is simply to highlight an early standpoint, highly generalized, with regard to "self" and related terms.

This is not the place to summarize all of that work. Suffice it to say, however, that while no surviving document would support the claim that its author had endorsed Descartes' "self" concept, the skein of work from the Homeric song-poems to Aeschylus to Euripides does show a line of development that we could today say—albeit with whiggish anachronism—suggested or "pointed toward" at least something like Descartes' "subjectivist-individualist" concept (see Gill 1996, pp. 409-458). Further, Gill's (2006, pp. 356-357, 377-379) study of Aristotle's concept of "self-knowledge through others" (as presented chiefly in his *Nicomachean Ethics* and *Eudemian Ethics*) goes a long way toward demonstrating a reaction to that line of development (to the extent that it did tend to a radical subjectivist-individualist view of self).[341] For Aristotle's

---

[340] Moreover, recall that in the same monologue (*Iliad* 9.264, also 18.471) Achilles entertained counterfactual thinking in a way that makes him at least marginally more complex than the petulant narcissist character offered in some commentaries.

[341] I do not agree that this description of Aristotle's work is contradictory of the view that (as stated by Konstan 2006, p. 55) Aristotle was still "intensely conscious of rank and social role," although I do not know the gradation metric of intensity.

concept of self-identity was founded on the notion of species-being as a "political being," a being of the polis and thus of a sociality, in contrast to Plato's text (as in, e.g., *Alcibiades* 133a-c), which, if superficially similar, orients self-knowing as aspirational toward the divine and a godly wisdom, and which (in *Republic* 518c) bases education on "an essence-centered conception of personality."

By contrast, the late sixteenth-century Montaigne, dead four years before Descartes' birth, showcased through his reflections on his life, his culture, and various topics contained therein what could be considered a strikingly modern sense of a dynamic, seemingly fragmented, inconstant being (Montaigne 1958 [1580]). That this aspect of his reflections was radical for his time can best be seen against the fact that his language did not (yet) include a specific notion of "selfhood." The reflexive first-person pronoun did exist, of course, and he used it (in English, "Myself") as proper name of the being he described and judged in his *Essays*. Starobinski (1985 [1982], p. 223) caught an important point, when he said that in Montaigne the "self is distributed over all [the] various levels of syntax; it enters the scene as an agent, an implement, and a point of application." But not only did his French not include a name for the modern concept, "self"; it is at least arguable that he would have declined, had someone offered that concept under a newly coined French noun to his service. Montaigne was a figure in transition, as he himself said; both traditionalist and modernist.[342]

Shakespeare, born midway between Montaigne and Descartes, was arguably further along to a concept of "selfhood" that is recognizably "modern before its time," so to speak. [343] He was not alone in that movement. Cervantes as well as Shakespeare used a "stories within a story" device which told of a person living different lives within a life, different characters within a host character, and in the process inserted a perspectival distance by which to peer at counterfactuals. In both Shakespeare and Cervantes we read of relations that inherently question the conditions and means by which selections are made in differentiations of what counts as "the real." Proto-versions of a social science can be read in Montaigne's *Essays*.[344] But they are short of the constructions achieved by Cervantes and Shakespeare, which in turn are again constructed in Hume's *Treatise* (1964 [1739-40]) and *Essays* (1985 [1777]), Adam Smith's *Theory of Moral Sentiments* (1817), and in various other eighteenth-century works that traffic rather more gingerly

---

[342] In his note to his reader Montaigne explained, "Je suis moi-même la matière de mon livre." ("I am myself the matter of my book.") The locution, "moi-même," is the way of saying "only me" or "no one but me" ("I am the sole subject/object of my book.")

[343] If Harold Bloom's (1998) argument in this regard is exaggerated, it is by an affect meant to highlight the target. Whether Shakespeare invented the "modern individual" or not, he counts undoubtedly as an "early modern" figure.

[344] There is in Montaigne a conception of "self" as dynamic, buffeted from without by various forces, stepping ahead of itself in first-person consciousness; and Auerbach's (1953 [1946], pp. 296, 310) characterization that one sees in Montaigne "for the first time, man's life—the random personal life as a whole—becom[ing] problematic in the modern sense" is not so much wrong-headed as forgetful of "the battle of the books" ("ancients versus moderns") a few centuries earlier (see, e.g., Curtius 1953 [1948], pp. 19-20, 251-255; Gebauer and Wulf 1995 [1992], pp. 76-79).

in similar pursuits, mainly by way of classifications of characters, sentiments, and actions, some of them with at least implicit interests in an idea of self-cultivation.[345] As the social sciences later developed during the nineteenth century the basic task of populating a discourse with categories of things came more and more into self-conscious disciplinary view, sometimes with recognition that classification—how our observations are organized into packets of similarity in relations of contrast or difference between and among packets—is the basic empirical task corresponding to Kant's categories. If this basic task is not achieved correctly, then all that follows—measurements, relationships, and so on, theoretically as well as empirically—will be bungled. But unlike the Adamic mission of assigning each part of reality its proper name, no one can know in advance, or ever with certainty, what qualifies as "correct classification." The task is historical, on-going, as well as cultural in the full sense of that adjective.

It was in deep appreciation of that truism that DiMaggio (1987, p. 441) began his well-known state-of-the-art review and presentation of new work in his specialties with definition of a conceptual bin, along with a statement of the point of doing so: "I use *genre* to refer to sets of artworks classified together on the basis of perceived similarities. The challenge to the sociology of art is to understand the processes by which similarities are perceived and genres enacted." This carefully worded statement is worth remembering, for it illuminates clearly what is in fact a difficult task to achieve with satisfaction even as "good approximation." Much of the literature not just of sociology but of the social sciences generally can be read as a record of shortcomings in that regard. As Hannan, Pólos, and Carroll (2007, p. 38) acknowledged of their own effort to reform their broad area of endeavor, "We think that [DiMaggio's statement] is exactly the challenge for organizational sociology." While a reader might pause at the fact that this advice has come refreshingly to the workshop after more than a century of efforts by social scientists, it is evidence only that prior attention to classification was often less than adequate in achievement, not that the executions were empty or the visions blind. Botanists and zoologists are still trying to improve their classifications of plants and animals, after all, as are particle physicists, musicologists, and mathematicians of theirs. But as Hannan *et al.* (2007) emphasized, the efforts

---

[345] By the power of written words writers can control with greater specificity intended meaning than can painters, but the "story within a story" device has been used by painters, too. A famous example is the 1656 work by Velázquez, *Las Meninas*. Arguments about his intent continue to this day, among curators and critics as well as among museum visitors. By my account it is near impossible to miss a commentary in the perspectivism of frames. Frames appear all through the painting's field, including the two ladies-in-waiting who frame the young royal daughter of Philip IV and Queen Marianna, who along with the painter himself seem to be the two main figures in the vast field. Today we have become accustomed to debates about framing in photography and cinematography: what we see within the frame can vary in meaning according to all the scenes placed outside the frame by the photographer's positioning. Velázquez painted the larger scene outside his painting of the intended portrait of king and queen, who are still outside the overall frame but for their reflection in a mirror on the back wall, and on the canvas before him.

must be recurrent if any development has been and will yet be made; the task is far more difficult that writing a new glossary of terms; and resistances from colleagues can be fierce.[346]

Three generations younger than Shakespeare, John Locke was born into a very different world. When he undertook his inquiry into the education of a person as in some sense a self-formation, he had the resources not only of Shakespeare and other playwrights on which to draw but also those of the Puritan revolutionaries (e.g., John Milton) and Isaac Newton. As a young man Locke had sided with Thomas Hobbes regarding the dangers of too much individual liberty, even though his father had been a cavalry officer in the Parliamentary army during early years of the civil wars against Charles I. After monarchic restoration in 1660 Locke gained favor for an appointment to Holland, during which time he was impressed that Dutch civil society allowed so much public liberty with markedly beneficial consequence. Older resources were also then drawn into his mix. The ancient Greek concept of "prosopon" (and the later Latin "persona") referred primarily to the mask worn by stage actors, each of them representative of a "character portrayal" for the benefit of viewers. As the concept generalized to broader usage, it carried along the notion as "public face" or "presentation of self"—to borrow Goffman's dramaturgical locution from not only his *Presentation of Self in Everyday Life* (1959) but also other of his works such as *Behavior in Public Places* (1963), thus continuing the notion, indeed the feeling, of an inherent difference that could trade suggestively on a number of idioms (e.g., public versus private, apparent versus real, cultural versus natural, even immanent versus transcendent), all of them carrying at least hints of deference to "powers that be." Various artistic productions replayed those resources in the development of portraiture, in reliance on anonymization of models in painted scenes, in "coming of age" stories, and in moral lessons of gaps between first-person experience ("private realm of selfhood") and second- and, more especially, third-person experience ("public realm of society").

Locke's "tabula rasa" thesis placed the individual person in relation to society and culture not only as part to whole but also as a part that would ideally develop to sociocultural maturity in keeping with the host society and culture, which also had been developing from some long distant deep past. It would be far too anachronistic to see in that mereological relation even an anticipation of a recapitulation of phylogeny in ontogeny, but the mereology was primed for a better theory of evolution all the same. However, the Lockean notion of a "personal identity," to the extent that he had formulated one, was a work in progress. A human being is a natural being, and this natural being is social by nature. But Locke was empirically too sensitive to the strains of sociality to understand his dimensional multiplicity of "personal identity" as an achieved unity. The dimensions amount to a view of "identity" in at least three perspectives: as a person is seen by others, as understood in his or her own consciousness, and as aspiring to sociocultural ideals of maturity. Each of these is not only partial; it is also incomplete in and of itself at any given time. On the few occasions in his essay on understanding when he used the compound "self-

---

[346] Recall that much of the early reaction to Kant's critical theory was couched in terms of all the many kinds of things and states of experience that he had neglected.

consciousness" there is no reason from the text to think that anything more than the reflexivity of "person" was intended. This is not to suggest that "reflexivity of person" is uncomplicated. The implied inference indicates a dimension of temporality that may, from first-person standpoint, seem independent of personal context but of course is not, and the matter of context itself raises issues of temporality. Parfit (1987, p. 206) pointed well to the inherent complexity when he avowed that "I am the same person as myself twenty years ago, though I am not now strongly connected to myself then." The presumption of continuity in time is bulwark against a fragmentation that would probably qualify in any human culture as mental illness of as a symptom thereof. The dependent clause of Parfit's statement suggests that the meaning of continuity will be maintained by weaker ties, by ties that are not transitive within first-person perspective but can flow through more or less elaborate chains of connection via third-person perspective (and, to small degree, in second-person perspective). Locke was a major transitional figure between remnants of a then very old order and an order that Shakespeare, Cervantes, Velázquez, and others had been gently shepherding into popular consciousness.

Recall my preferred locution: the individual human being as an ensemble of relations. It is hardly indicative of a new insight, to be sure, even though it is neglected strikingly often.[347] The point I want to emphasize here is its resistance to the tendency of first-person perspective to decontextualize—that is, the strong bias of self-understanding toward what has been called "the egocentric predicament."[348] In recent times, the "ensemble" understanding has been descriptive of relations of part to whole in the sense that the whole of a living organism consists of organs, fluids and tissues, all with specified functions and structures; then, with the advent of cell theory, a growing wealth of descriptions of cellular activities; then, with the advent of genetic theory, more layers of descriptive wealth. In far less recent times, according to archæological evidence (see Shryock, Smail, and Associates 2011), an "ensemble" arrangement existed within hominin sociality, which extends back at least a thousand millennia. While the advent of first-person consciousness of sociality as consisting in ensembles of relations, social relations, probably can never be dated with confidence, it could have been, at least in glimmers of awareness, much earlier than we have been inclined to believe. The genealogies reported in the Mosaic books are good testimony that ensembles of social relations were deemed important well before c500 BCE (the best estimate of the date of the existing form of the Torah). It is plausible to think that this sort of consciousness of conjunction among individual beings of a "kind" was alive already when

---

[347] And sometimes not simply neglected but vehemently opposed. To repeat the illustration, Husserl (1970 [1936], §23) was strongly opposed to Hume's view of "what is true of the person" (as Husserl read Hume): "an identical 'I' is not a datum but a ceaselessly changing bundle of data. Identity is a psychological fiction." As noted earlier, "fiction" was indeed Hume's word; he meant it in its etymological sense, "something made," or we would say "a social composite" or "construction" (see discussion of Mead, below).
[348] This phrase (coined by Perry 1910) has sometimes been associated with Locke (among others), as if Locke had argued that first-person consciousness is hermetic—or, to use a phrase that will be attended again below, as if Locke had denied to first-person consciousness anything like a process of "taking the role of the other." Perry, a critic of prevailing idealism, aligned himself with a "new realism" movement but then, seeing that it amounted to a "moralist ontology," departed.

sculptors created the Venus of Willendorf at least 29,000 years ago; perhaps even the Venus of Hohlefels, approximately 10,000 years before that (see also Flannery 2018).[349]

While it is today difficult even in first-person perspective to ignore the importance of "context" (however fuzzy the use of that concept might be), the dominant tendency has been to understand "context" as primarily and mainly spatial, a bias inherited from earlier times when the life of an adult human was experienced as more variable spatially than temporally. A herder of stock, a carver of Venus figurines, a planter of seeds, knew seasonal variations and would have been likely to remember outstanding yearly differences. But migrations of people from one place to another were commonplace, until agricultural production eroded habits of nomadism, and even then the flows did not cease but became more channeled by the basins of attraction that were towns and cities, in addition to fertile valleys. This bias in favor of place over date, of geography over history, endured to modern times, as exemplified in the tendency to employ matter-of-factly an originary logic in explanatory frames as if human sociality began shortly before the founding of Çatalhöyük (7500 BCE, by present estimate).

Eventually, changes of temporal context were marked not only by first-person events ("the first figurine I carved"). At some point, time itself noticeably mattered not only in the sense of time *within* consciousness but also time *of* consciousness, and with that development most meanings of "context," temporal as well as spatial, became dynamic. Few developments have been as momentous. Think of that change of perspectival context by analogy to a difference recently determined in physical science, the difference between Einstein's first and then second theory of relativity. Each is about motion. In each the invariant standard is the speed at which light (radiant energy) propagates in a vacuum. In the first theory a moving body is observed relative to a stable platform; thus, the observer of a thought experiment (e.g., a person standing in an ascending elevator) ignores the possibility that he or she is in motion. (Think of the famous Doppler effect, the pitch change in the sound of a train's whistle as the train approaches, then leaves, your static location.) The second (and more general) theory has the observation platform also in motion. (So if you are moving in parallel to the train at the same rate and direction, you will observe no Doppler effect.)[350]

When Christian Doppler was still in knee pants, Marx and Engels highlighted the fact that sociocultural (including the physical) context had been changing more rapidly as industrial capitalism developed. "The bourgeoisie, by the rapid improvement of all instruments of production, by the immensely facilitated means of communication, draws all, even the most barbarian, nations into civilization. The cheap prices of its wares are the heavy artillery with which it batters down all Chinese walls. ... it creates a world after its own image" (Marx and Engels 1976 [1848], p. 488).[351] Note that the authors said "*all* instruments of production": that

---

[349] In present context, "kind" can mean species; in earlier contexts (and often still) extension was governed by a tribalism, a clannism, a racism, a familialism.

[350] For radiant energy that requires a medium (e.g., sound), one must also take into account the motion of the medium. Neither light nor gravity requires a medium, so a shift in wavelength is a function only of the relative motion of observer and observed.

[351] In 1976, after a colleague and I had published a comparative study of occupational mobility in sixteen countries (Hazelrigg and Garner 1976), some readers suggested that we were daft to include the

291

includes parenting, education, the system of employment, communications, health services, the relevant array of skills, knowledge, ideologies, myths, expectations, tools, and so forth. The "rapid improvements" to all of that were mostly formed in terms more or less consistent with the "own image" of those who collectively controlled production processes. Context, temporal as well as spatial, was changing for larger and larger proportions of people more and more rapidly.

As noted above, Locke was not oblivious to the relevance of culture as context within which personal experience was constituted. Indeed, his emphasis on empirical standards would have made him sensitive at least to the spatial-cultural, if less so to the temporal-cultural factors of context, and even within the relatively narrow confines of seventeenth-century England he was surely exposed to some version of "ethnocentric" bias of context (though he apparently saw little point to incorporating such biases into his thinking about developments to maturity from the initial condition of a "blank slate"). His insistence on empiricism did not prevent him inquiring into general principles of understanding, and such principles would surely have figured into his "background conception," or the folk theory he himself had learned from his heritable past, of "mind," of "personal identity," and, to the extent that he had one separately, concept of "self."

Recall from discussion in prior Parts of the present book that Kant's orientation was strongly centered by understandings of the rigor of modern science's intersections of theory (i.e., the cognitive-conceptual, striving for universality of principles) and empirics (information conceptualized in levels of particularity), then best illustrated by Newtonian mechanics but with attention to new developments of modern chemistry as well.[352] It was within that context of experimentation and general principle that his rejection of mysticism and dogmatism seemed perfectly matter-of-fact. His own efforts to establish necessary conditions of Newton's knowledge of universal principles were undertaken in the conviction that he would be setting forth both the universal principles and the limits of human knowledge. Far from ignorant of the importance of human cultures, he sought to demonstrate principles that were fundamental to any possible human culture—that is, the necessary principles of a nondogmatic experientially relevant knowledge. Criticisms of Kant's ethnocentrism—and they flowed freely from the pens of many, Herder and Hegel among them—are therefore both empirically accurate (by and large) and, in the terms of his mission, beside the point. The prejudices were (and are) highly objectionable nonetheless.

---

Philippines in the orbit of "industrial society," because it was more a supplier of "raw materials" and limited consumer of "finished goods" than any of the fifteen other countries.

[352] Developments from the 1760s (e.g., Henry Cavendish isolating hydrogen as an elementary gaseous substance) to the 1780s (e.g., Antoine-Laurent de Lavoisier inventing methods of chemical nomenclature, 1787, and the law of conservation of mass, 1789), and thereafter. Ball (2002, p. 147) nominated the 1770s as the beginning of a half-century that was both unprecedented and never since repeated in the world of modern chemistry: at the onset "barely any of the real elements were known, and scholars still spoke in learned tomes of phlogiston"; little more than a decade after Kant's death (1804) "chemists spoke much the same language as they do today."

Ethnocentric effects can be varied. Some have been mixed with a mystical orientation to "otherness," as Kant charged of those he labeled "mystagogues."[353] A prime example of the latter is the "western" notion that peoples of Asia do not have a self, or that what self they do have is so submerged in "the group" as to be virtually nonexistent. This is silly. It would be no less silly, however, to suppose that "self" is indifferent to culture, that "one self fits all," as it were. It is indeed the case that there are some versions of psychologism that do profess the existence of a logically pre-cultural individual human being (see, e.g., Molenaar 2004, 2005; and cf. Izenberg 1992). Some versions of social psychology tend more in that direction than do others; and other of the social sciences have not been immune. As a present-day scholar reminded her reader, a visiting ethnographer's native interlocutors are as capable of interpreting the cultural markers of the visitor as the latter is of her or his hosts, a mutuality sometimes missed by the novice. This applies as well to the social scientist observing "at home" (see, e,g,, Lutz 1988).

Generally speaking, the mystical notion of an empirical, experiential "selfless person" has gone out of fashion. But this does not mean that careful cross-cultural comparisons of self concept, of self-identity, and the like, are no longer difficult to achieve. Roland (1988, p. xvii) undertook a comparative psychoanalytic project in which, judged by his own insistence, one should first "decontextualize various psychoanalytic categories of their Western content," presumably all of their semantic contents, "before recontextualizing them with [in this case his] clinical data of Indians and Japanese." This seems a rather heroic feat: a "Westerner" first of all recognizing all of that which is, of himself and his context, definitively "Western"; then, by and in the categories of that recognition, stripping away the "Western-ness," until what one is left with is bare of any cultural specificity, and finally adding different formations of meaning, the first time Indian, then removing those and replacing them with Japanese. The sincerity of that proposal is neither to be mocked nor ripped out of *its* context, any more than one should do likewise with, say, Montesquieu's *Spirit of Laws*. But Roland's description of what should be accomplished in cultural renunciation is at best some sort of imaginary ideal to be approximated without any known neutral means of measuring proximity. Further, there are some omissions in his account. What of those "clinical data"? Are they already ethno-specific? And then there is the entire formation of psychoanalysis itself: once stripped of its originary European context would there be anything left to the subsequent task of re-contextualization?

As Collins (1982) observed, a theoretical projection within Theravāda Buddhism may well hold up an ideal of "selflessness," but in practice it seems doubtful that an actual person today approaches that ideal even to a degree that could be called asymptotic. The doctrine of anattā (denial of self) may be related to what earlier I called the "presumption of continuity." This is, as Collins (1982, p. 263) described it, a "hotly denied conception" insofar as it claims the mantle of transcendental being. It is not denied as experience, an experience of continuity,

---

[353] By one reading of his discussion of the two-fold Plato, Kant (1993 [1796], pp. 53-55) included part of Plato's effort as mystagogic.

of empirical being; but it is regarded as a psychological immaturity that in principle could be left behind as such—that is, as an in-principle transitory effect of being misled by desire. To quote Collins' brief summary of "the Buddhist attitude to selfhood, to personality and continuity," the experience of self results from, and as,

> impersonal mental and material elements [that] are arranged together in a temporarily unified configuration. What unifies and prolongs this configuration is desire; it is in desire for the enjoyment of these constituents of personality, and for their continuance, that there arises for the unenlightened man 'the conceit "I am"' (asmimāna), a 'conceit' which is not so much asserted propositionally as performed automatically by 'the utterance "I"' (ahaṃkāra). Desire here, indeed, brings about its own object—that is, the continuance of life-in-saṃsāra; a form of existence seen from the nirvāṇa-oriented virtuoso perspective as unsatisfactory, as 'suffering' (Collins 1982, pp. 263-264).[354]

Similarly, Goodman (2005) has argued that "self" in Buddhist thought (with particular attention to Indian Buddhism) is regarded as a social construction in the sense of a "non-literal language," a metaphorical use of language as depiction of a fictive existence. For Collins (1982), citing the Buddhist literature of abhidhamma, this is use of a reductionist language for the purpose of teaching a set of virtues to which one should aspire—in other words, a practice not all that different from the language of parables in the Christian Bible, in the Islamic Quran, and (as "mashal") in the Hebraic books of Moses.[355] The main point of the underlying coherence is what might be called a "shorthand" function: "self" focuses in personal terms a large complex of relations and events, all of which are conditional. In principle, Collins (1994, p. 69) added, an analysis of the "agency" that inheres in the complex of relations and events *could* dispense with the word (the concept., the indexicality) of "self" altogether. As for practice in the world in which even monks live, however, a "reductionist discourse cannot serve the social, legal, or behavioral purposes of the nonreductionist discourse which it can, in principle, replace." In sum, there are variations on the tactic of skirting the line between empty theory and aimless or blind empirics. A popular meme in neo-Kantian discourse has been "the tragedy of the idea," which, as noted before, aligns ideas (or some ideas, the pristine ones) with the angelic side, materiality (or "soil") with the beastly side, of a divided human nature.

---

[354] Note that Collins' reference to an automatic performative I is consonant with my earlier choice of "presumption" over "assumption" when describing/naming the experiential momentum of continuity of self. The main difference in this regard between the Theravāda conception and the secular or quasi-secular conception in European and Euro-American cultures is that in the latter there is no further end-state, as it were. One's self dies along with one's body. In the Judeo, Christian, and Islamic traditions there is the promise or proposal of a further end-state, but this is tied to a monotheistic supernatural ruler.
[355] Or, for that matter, from the "heathen" fables of Aesop and other ancient storytellers (the main difference being that in "fable" the active figure is often an animal or mythic creature, whereas in parables the active figure is human, although in quranic form less emphasis is placed on the figuration as such, relative to the intended moral).

Previously I invoked Shakespeare and Cervantes in a comparative mood with regard to what is conventionally called "the modern individual" or "modern person." To that pairing I shall now add a third figure, Tang Xianzu (1550-1616), a Chinese scholar and playwright, and close contemporary of the Englishman and the Spaniard. The addition is indeed appropriate to the comparative mood, for Tang wrote with considerable sensitivity to what could be called "matters of individuality" in the context of a China that was then at peak of cultural, economic, scientific, and technological development (very likely the leading nation of the world in 1600). Tang's most famous play, *Peony Pavilion* (1598), displays not only those concerns within extant context but also referrals to a tradition of plays, dating from at least the 1400s, designed to be read (with illustrations and usually a commentary) as well as acted on stage, and a play-within-play reflexivity (here, the dream device, described by editor Owen as an "illusionist notion of theater itself"). Lest evidence of some sort of "cultural universal" be read into the convergence of dates, I will note first of all that the convergence has more to do with the coincidence between Shakespeare and Cervantes than either with Tang. Just as the two Europeans were riding steeds that had entertained previous generations, so, too, Tang, as already mentioned. One should bear in mind that "religion" in China, then as still today (despite missionary influences) , is unlike official "religions of the book" (Judaism and its daughters, Christianity and Islam) in that it has consisted mainly in traditional collections of "minjian Xinyang" (roughly, folk beliefs) that have survived diversely without a centralizing institutional authority.

None of the three authors had invented the "morality play" vehicle of cultural celebration or personal entertainment (think of works by Aeschylus, Archimedes, among many others in Europe), nor uses of various devices of reflexivity; and casting central characters as studies in "person formation," past and present, had as long a heritage. This is not to say that the two Europeans carry no significance in the continent's transitions from medieval to modern cultural formations.[356] That is far from my intent. Likewise with regard to Tang, who came on the heels of enormous development in his own land, China. Rather, my point is about the penchant to see evidence of "cultural universals." Imagine the sheer quantity and quality of cultural particularity that must be abstracted, stripped away and ignored, in order to reduce the works of the three authors to a level of "universal principle." The principle would be *ours*, not theirs, a product of *our* cultures, not theirs. Surely one of the most important lessons to be learned from Kant's effort to bridge reason's necessity and morality's freedom, as well as from efforts by Hegel and others

---

[356] Indeed, a self-consciousness of reflexivity was rapidly becoming a hallmark of this modernity, and not only by the hands of playwrights. In the realm of portraiture, as noted above, an analogue to the play-within-play device was the use of picture-within-picture display that brought the artist and/or the viewer, or both, into the field of the painting. I used Velázquez' *Las Meninas* (1656) as illustration of the point above, because it is probably the most famous case (thanks in Michel Foucault's use of it), But it was not the first instance. Jan van Eyck's *Arnolfini Portrait* (1434) features a mirror on a back wall, reflecting the posterior sides of the two principals but also, deeper in the reflection, two viewers of the painting. Raphael's *The School of Athens* (1509-11) is another instance, if in fact a foreground figure leaning of a box is Raphael himself. Charles Le Brun's portrait, *Everhard Jabach and His Family* (c1660), less well known than *Las Meninas*, similarly depicts the painter at work on the very canvas that is in front of him.

to recoup from that failure, is that human legislations always bear the stamp of a particular here and now. This was, recall, a main lesson of Kant's *Anthropology from a Pragmatic Point of View*, lectures he delivered to his university students all the while he was at work on his most difficult project.

Whereas Hume inquired persistently and skeptically about the constitution of "self" (and more than had Locke of "person"), the Romanticists' interest in Bildungsprozess largely took for granted an existence called "self" (as did Adam Smith at about the same time, chiefly in his *Theory of Moral Sentiments*). The notion of "making one's self" as a project could take for granted an agreement about "what self is" to an extent that is measured by the general upset that followed Hume's skeptical inquiries into that very question. In retrospect one can see Hume's point: the "agreement" generally involved little clarity as to what "self" is, what kind of "thing" it is (an issue that remains alive still today; see e.g., Gabriel 2017 [2015]). Is "self" substantial, like an organ of the body? Is it a concoction of consciousness, a function only of mind, of first-person experience? Does first-person ever actually observe evidence of another's self when engaged in second-person action?—"self," that is, as a "thing experienced" different from "person"? Further, what forces shape "self" into one character versus another, and is that process ever actually observed in first-person experience? Or, in second-person experience, the shaping of "other self" (or "other person") as becoming of *this* character versus some different character?

At about the same time, Denis Diderot, writing in 1773, recalled the "person" notion of "mask" when composing his theory of stage acting (Diderot 1883 [1830]). His presentation had the effect of setting in starker relief an issue that later became known as the "principal-agent problem," where "agency" means the capacity to act in a specific context, and especially the capacity to make decisions. An actor's mask is vital to actor's success in persuading viewers of portrayed character's authenticity, because by maintaining distance between actor-self and mask, actor can continually gauge viewer reception and make adjustments of character's presentation accordingly. Thus, a manipulative director (actor-self) stands behind every effective public performance, as does the painter who manipulates a viewer into painter's intention of "correct perspective." The question might then arise, "Who is 'agent' to 'principal,'" and how are intents and interests thereby divided? Is actor-self agent to mask-principal (for it is actor-self who makes choices of how mask-principal shall act)? Or is mask-principal the effective agent for the viewer (insofar as actor-self has succeeded in manipulating mask-principal)? For Diderot's purpose, the decision would always be told by successful manipulation, even though this meant that the viewer was being deceived. Considered in that way, it is not surprising that theatrical performers as a group, and often as specific performer, had to contend with an ambivalence of reputation: the more successful, the more dangerous. From this standpoint regarding theatrical performers one can perhaps better understand analogous suspicions attending other artists—the painter who uses "tricks" of perspective to manipulate viewer's position.

Standard folk theories of the continuity of self-identity in time were generally predicated from a psychologistic understanding, as was discussed in Part Two. Kant's posit of the necessity of a transcendental unity of apperception, as discussed in Part One, is compatible with the main understanding of psychologism, inasmuch as Kant was seeking a universal theory of the knowing subject, one that would apply as integral to the unity and commonality of a species being. Thus, while Kant insisted that the test of any reasoned judgment must be empirical, and while he knew much of the diversity of the empirical diversity of human cultures and peoples (some of that display highly prejudicial), the functionalist formulation of his "I think" was meant to be integral to a necessary universalist ground of what all humans share in common as species being. By the same token, one can hardly overlook considerable tension in the understanding, not only between "the analytical" and "the synthetic," taken analytically, but also within the synthetic side of the dialectical unity. It was during Kant's time, for instance, that proto-geologists (in modern sense), biologists, and everyday explorers were glimpsing more and more clearly the puzzles of a "deep time," a "paleontology"—that is to say, building a history of life that had far greater depth than any received accounts from Augustine or Aristotle or books of the Talmud. Several budding correlationists had begun to compare stratigraphies of these evacuated "fossils" (from the Latin "fossillis" or things "obtained by digging") in relation to each other and to the evident layering of earthly crust around them. Imagine, then, that human beings are thought to be more or less "that old" as a species (whatever the estimate, it was increasingly longer that Bishop Ussher's estimate of 4004 BCE, announced to the world a little more than a century earlier): just how far can one's hopeful speculations about what is *universal* extend? Recall, too, that Kant knew that the blurry fields of light in the night-time sky, known then as "nebulae," were actually other galaxies, more or less like (and equivalent in kind) to the one in which we live—which in turn suggested high likelihood of other inhabitable planets *and*, Kant was convinced, other intelligent beings.[357] It is not difficult to imagine that in the reflexivity of his own theorizing such "tensions" weighed on Kant's imagination, much as, according to my earlier speculation, Newton had entertained (and recorded) doubts about his universal-vessel conceptions of space and time (see Part One, §1).[358]

---

[357] See Kant 1991 (1784a), p. 46; and Part One, §2, below). Kant was exceptional but not unique in that regard. A century earlier, a long generation after Bishop Ussher's pronouncement, Bernard de Fontenelle (1991 [1686]) published his *Conversation on the Plurality of Worlds*, and speculation about life on other planets, although still unusual, could be ventured without automatic passage to Bedlam hospital or its equivalent elsewhere. To round the point out a bit, Richard Holmes (2008) chose wisely when he subtitled his book on an age of wonders, "How the romantic generation discovered the beauty and terror of science."

[358] Indeed, Newton was not the only of the new modern scientists to express doubt about generality of newly cast principles. Carl Linnaeus, an inventor of zoological and botanical taxonomies, did not doubt that the boundaries of his categories were porous, and of course he was correct: they have been amended repeatedly, a process still underway. An erstwhile definitive characteristic of all mammals was long thought to be lactation, for instance, an ability reserved to them. But good evidence has demonstrated that at least one species of spider, Taxeus magnus, produces a protein-rich milk and suckles her young. Then, too, there was the notoriety of Linnaeus' inclusion of monkeys with humans in the genus Homo— a shocking violation of religious doctrine and a huge fissure in the effort to demonstrate exclusivity of "the human animal," an effort that continued long after Linnaeus.

By the time of Mead, born 59 years after Kant's death in 1804, Charles Lyell's immediate heirs in geological science had been joined by Charles Darwin and Alfred Wallace (among others) who were rapidly developing a new reflexivity of modern science. The basis of reflexivity, according to Mead's (1913) theory of the social self—namely, the process of "role taking," or trying to adopt the perspective of each significant other, thereby becoming with each a somewhat different person—is neither a constant in time nor a uniformity across persons and their conditions and contexts. The network of ties that results from the process changes (grows or declines, partly as a function of age), and it varies in diversity, both extensively and intensively, from person to person, partly reflecting the status characteristics of the given person and of that person's selections of potential as well as actual significant others. This last matter, regarding compositions of a network of ties, will be pursued later (see Granovetter 1973). First, I want to consider the fact, and its reception, that Mead's perspectivism of reflexivity implies a multiplicity within self-formation, which varies with the diversity of significant others both actual and, in aspiration, potential. In addition to gaining a different identification with each sufficiently different significant other, a person experiences a generalizing identification, the perspective of a "generalized other," which reflects the locally dominant representation of society as a whole. While the integrative effect of this perspective of "the generalized other" remains more or less strong over time, it does not erase divisibility among the identifications by specific significant others (see §28, below, regarding Tugendhat 1986 [1979] and Mead).

A newly prominent critic and commentator on the US scene, Mark Greif (born 1975), recently observed of his fellow citizens, "We really wish to be multiple" (Greif 2016, p. 82). In this aspiration one perhaps sees results of adjustment to increasing complexity of life in modern society, not merely an acceptance of multiplicity of presentations of self but a celebration of the opportunities therein presented. As local community becomes more dynamic, less constant, the opportunity to be "different things to different people" expands. Thus, perhaps aspiration has been catching up to Mead. Indeed, as Mead was catching up to Shakespeare; for the Meadian actor is something like a "fragmentary repository of alternative selves," to use Brian Cummings' (2013, p. 180) description of a prototype now so common as to be a stereotype: Hamlet.

Never at loss for emplotment (if sometimes otherwise lacking employment), this Hamlet type has now also been drawn upon to referee contests between modernity and postmodernity, apparently because he has matured beyond nominee as Europe's first modern self (as Harold Bloom proposed in 1998), to become a virtually embodied announcer at the "storm center" of "the modernity-postmodernity dispute [which] pretty much revolves around the issue of unity and the question about the resources of rationality for its achievement" (Schrag 1997, pp. 126-129). Associating a "need for unification" with modernity (and citing Kant's principle of a "transcendental unity of apperception" as prime illustration), Schrag observed that proponents of postmodernity protested that such need is "at once fanciful and ill conceived." One can indeed read discussions other than Schrag's, attributing a "quest for unity, ... at once metaphysical and epistemological," to the emotive energy of "a nostalgia for a primordial and unblemished archē, an untrammeled beginning, and an appetition for a fixed and universal telos." Schrag's contest rests on taking a particular ideology of identity (or an equation of identity and unity, along with universality and necessity) all too seriously, however, inasmuch as it accepts a (partly implicit) assumption that a self-reflexive unity of first-person perceptions and cognitive-emotive categories (as in vocabulary, etc.) is, once having been achieved, a static condition in which diversity and multiplicity have been erased. In actuality, any unity or integration of "multiple selves" is itself dynamic, no less dynamic than a first-person array of memories of past selves, a second-person shared history of remembered connections especially with significant others, and even a third-person register of reflections of how one was "generally seen" (recognized, assessed, and so forth) as a "public personage," to use Marcel Mauss' term, at various intersections of biography and history.

Those intersections sometimes involve episodes of extremely severe duress under which sociality and thus selfhood are at high risk of fragmentation. Alexis Peri (2017) has recently shared diaries that were compiled by residents of Leningrad (as St Petersburg was then known) during the great siege. Suffering bombardment, isolation from the outside world, starvation, and other assaults, residents were bound together in prolonged crisis, which over months without sign of relief gnawed at the bonds of sociality person-to-person and within a person's integrity of being. The diaries are at once a testimony to the seemingly unending assault, a resolve to "hold together," and an assessment of endurance in first-person, second-person, and to an extent even third-person experiences and relations. Peri (2017, pp. 68-69) was perceptive in understanding the dual character of this "war within"—indeed, a duality twice over, for these diarists were often writing not only as witnesses of extreme duress but also as reporters to future readers who would be, at least some of the diarists were confident, native Leningraders.

Reflexivity is a process, both biographically and historically, and there are good reasons to think that any "unity" is not only fluid but also approximate even under best conditions. Long ago Edward Laumann (1969) pointed out how little was known about the quantity and quality of information that adults had of the persons they cited as friends or acquaintances, a condition that apparently has changed surprisingly little (see, e.g., Killworth, McCarty, Johnsen, Bernard, and Shelley 2006; McCormick, Salganik, and Zheng 2010).[359] It may be (1) that one's list of significant others has changed, (2) that one or more of one's significant others have changed, and/or (3) that one's perceptions of one or more of one's significant others have changed. Sorting across the possibilities is always fraught—and thus still another matter (compare Schumacher 2014 and Schumacher 2018). Prinz (2012) has alerted us that uses of a "Meadian argument" of "the social self" are a continuing repository of variability in (as he said in his subtitle) "the social making of agency and intentionality."

The relation of "theory to theorist" easily compounds, therefore, sometimes fruitfully. As already indicated in passing, some of the best of recent fruiting of the Meadian effort has been contributed by Radu Bogdan (e.g., 2000, 2919, 2913), as he has developed and extended the problem of integration. It has been conjectured for some time that Mead's thesis deliberately

---

[359] Sometimes I suspect that the per-person quantity and quality of reliable knowledge of significant other has been declining, on average among adults, due mainly to an increase in vicarious identifications—i.e., selecting as significant other a person or persons known by celebrity and who, because of media effects, seem to be genuinely self-revealing as exceptional in some dimension other than the mere fact of "media celebrity."

accommodated the notion that "inadequate" integration could be a description of some categories of "mental illness."[360] More recently several observers have speculated on the existence of a chronic insufficiency of integration of the multiplicity (a thesis that one can read in Durkheim). Mobility and media effects have greatly expanded the sheer range of diversity of apparent experiences that a person can imagine having, and the felt disparity has upped the ante in the game of "Who would I like to be, even for a day?" Virtual reality devices have been doing the same. As Bogdan (2013) argued, pretending and imagining (or Mead's "role playing") are crucial mental activities in childhood development of mental capabilities, including self-image and self-identity. Will the increased diversity and ready availability of vicarious experiences via virtual reality devices increase the difficulty of gaining satisfactory integration of multiple self-images, even self-identities? Recent discussions of "the distracted mind" have suggested that our brains, and thus our minds, are being over-taxed by too much stimulation, sensations delivered too fast, too persistently, too complexly (e.g., Gazzaley and Rosen 2016). More than a quarter-century ago Kenneth Gergen sought to explain part of the basis of his argument about "dilemmas of identity in contemporary life" this way:

> Critical to my argument is the proposal that social saturation brings with it a general loss in our assumption of true and knowable selves. As we absorb multiple voices, we find that each 'truth' is relativized by our simultaneous consciousness of compelling alternatives. We come to be aware that each truth about ourselves is a construction of the moment, true only for a given time and within certain relationships" (Gergen 1991, p. 16).[361]

Note that the process of "absorbing multiple voices" had been going on for some time. It was not only present in Mead's accounts of "the social self." I would argue that the phenomenon had been alive for many, many generations prior to Mead and, at least for some people, self-consciously so. In fact, there are texts that recognize a multiplicity in the nexus of social relations that compose a self, a multiplicity in accord with the heterogeneity of locale and with a person's travel and more especially migration experience. One of the most popular of those texts in its day was an essay entitled "Soliloquy," written by the same Anthony Cooper mentioned above (this essay was added as the first part of his treatise; Cooper 1999 [1710]). For this man, he third earl Shaftsbury (1671-1713), moral reasoning depended on the ability of a person to engage as alternative voices in debate on a particular issue, a kind of "self-dissection"

---

[360] For one exploration, see Stephens and Graham (2000). Their discussion raises several important issues, including measurement issues in the distinction between signal and noise, and the inference problem. As illustration: I can hear the voice of my father and the voice of my mother (each biological person long dead), and I am confident the voice is memory, not an external auditory signal. But a person presenting symptoms ostensibly of a first-person experience of "alien voices," for instance, or of "implanted thoughts" poses questions about signal-to-noise ratio, fuzziness of distinctions, memory function versus auditory sensation, and so forth. For a case study of the inference problem, see Hurlburt and Schwitzgebel (2007). For another, having to do with the process of self's senescence, see Ballenger (2006): "The discursive framework necessary to make Alzheimer's disease a viable project for modern biomedical science centered on the issue of whether Alzheimer's was a distinct disease or an intensification of a normal process of growing old" (p. 101).

[361] Compare Gergen (2015), however.

in which the person "becomes two distinct persons" on the model of Socratic dialogue. Many issues are not so one-sided as to preclude "a certain duplicity of soul," and the recommended method of soliloquy will seek that complexity, weight its alternatives, and produce a more enlightened self, thus better prepared for public discourse (Cooper 1999 [1710], pp. 72, 76, 77, 78).

No doubt the quantitative dimension of multiplicity grew more rapidly after Cooper's day—and still more rapidly a century later, when (circa 1820) a nationally integrated market society of the USA was being built and individual persons were learning to depend on networks of trust among anonymous others along with one's significant others, a few of whom might well have begun as faceless names located dozens or hundreds of miles away. This latter condition, previously discussed in connection with judicial processes, highlights also some of the crucial qualitative changes of multiplicity, introducing on large scale experiences of virtual relations (e.g., trusting anonymous others), which featured for growing numbers of people processes of differencing and diversity in time as well as in space. Whereas for most people most of the time in local places the process of achieving coherence among the multiple voices was relatively simple, coherence at greater distance in time as well as space became more challenging for more people. The trend has been continuing mainly because of changes in what now we term "media of information technology." Gergen (1991, pp. 49, 76) referred to these media as "technologies of social saturation," producing a "populating of the self" with "partial identities through social saturation," and sometimes "the onset of a multiphrenic condition, in which one begins to experience the vertigo of unlimited multiplicity." Among the effects of this "prelude to postmodern consciousness" are conditions of an "expansion of inadequacy," resulting from the greater multiplicity of comparatives. Again, one can see that Gergen's account partly recalled Mead's mostly implicit notion of multiplicity as involving a balance beam of health: too little integration of multiple selves tantamount to a mental illness but too much integration perhaps a different illness, an obsessiveness or compulsiveness, an inflexibility of regimen, this latter possibility gaining expression in issues that became controversial in wake of Barry Schwartz' (2004) book on *The Paradox of Choice*, or *Why More Is Less*. The ensuing debate has carried into a new century, with concern about human adaptability or, as Gazzaley and Rosen (2016) put it via the subtitle of their book, can "ancient brains in a high-tech world" function well enough? The key variable is still the one that Herbert Simon (1971, pp. 40-41) identified many years earlier, the scarcity of attention, which means that attention has become ever more valuable (see also Rosa 2013 [2005]).

Gergen's account points as well to another aspect of Mead's theorization—namely, that it is hospitable to processes of prosthesis. From a psychologistic point of view, of course, culture as a whole can be considered prosthetic to the natural human being. However, Lury (1998) was much closer to the mark when she wrote that "prosthetic" is a modification of culture, from within. The archæological record indicates, and current ethological studies compatibly suggest, that hominid culture is considerably older than Homo sapiens. Good evidence of domestic uses of fire by Homo erectus dates to one million years ago, for example; of deliberate burial practices among at least some bands of Homo neanderthalensis to at least 130,000 years ago. The point is that human beings have developed techniques by which to extend capabilities for a very long time. Leonardo da Vinci obviously explored techniques of flying but so far as we know did not succeed beyond his best graphic imaginations. Today a person can in a few hours fly distances vastly exceeding the top record for any bird; or remain continuously submerged at sea far longer than any whale; explore the surfaces of distant planets, comets, and asteroids by extensions of sight, smell, and taste (chemical assay); and so forth. In fact, human beings have long been inventing meanings with prosthetic intent (new concepts, new tools, etc.). But even if we restrict the word to the sense of a material thing made to be a prosthetic device, the list is very long: not only devices that are in some sense "worn" externally (makeshift crutches that were crafted, used, and sometimes bequeathed to survivors, spectacles, dentures, exoskeletons, and so forth, but also implanted devices (ocular, auditory, rhinoplastic, breast, penile, gastric stimulation, tactile-sensitive fingers and hands, cardiac rhythm, bioactive devices for pharmoco-delivery, skeletal mending and replacement, and many more). The production and use of implantable devices have in turn accelerated knowledge of bodily functions, including processes of self-recognition and reaction to materials, shapes, and densities not previously integral to organic structures and processes. On the one hand, we have determined some gradients of difference; for example, bodies accept and integrate with some patterns of some kinds of plastic material (cellular meshes) and metal (titanium in bone) better than with others (plastic cardiac valves, stainless steel in bone). On the other hand, we have determined, and continue to determine, that the relation between the organic-internal (biologic, biochemical) and the nonorganic-external (environment, context, etc.) is far more complex and subtle than the simple either-or categorizations that were taken for granted as divides between "natural" and "artificial" only a few decades ago.[362] The boundaries of I, it is clear, have been mixed, topically as well as actually, with boundaries of "the organic" vis-à-vis "the mechanical," and boundaries of "human being" vis-à-vis "the rest of life."

One of the oldest customary manifestations of prosthesis is (as mentioned in passing above) an appliance designed to assist a person who is "disabled," more often male than female but otherwise not usually of privileged status—the tree limb roughly hewn into a crutch or peg leg being one of the most common devices, sometimes supplemented by some sort of monetary award. In the world of ancient Athens and Rome the award could take the form of a pension, even though it was "at all times barely sufficient to support the disabled at the poverty line" (Garland 1995), which, as Ste Croix (1981, pp. 179-204) showed of the emic understanding of "poverty," was generally abysmally low. Nonetheless, some court cases in fourth- and fifth-century Athens can be read as an effort to display a minimum obligation of social contract, though mainly if not always for adult male citizens who were accorded the distinction of being an "adunatos," a man who was physically unable to work—thus, a "disabled man"—who, then as now, also was regularly available as butt of ridicule (see Wohl 2010, pp. 188-197). On the other hand, an early sixteenth-century Frankish knight, Gottfried von Berlichingen, had a forged metal

---

[362] For a treatment of "new technologies to form new selves," within present contexts of contradictions between interests and expectations of state functions and those of consumption markets, see Miller (1993). And insofar as we are still inclined to grasp at something that distinguishes us from other animals, it is now clear that prosthesis will not do: bonobos, chimpanzees, corvids, and no doubt other animals make and utilize helpful devices (see, e.g., Low 2016; Harari 2016, ch. 3), although (we assume) not reflexively. The main point here is that we learn from other animals and adapt some of their capabilities. Perhaps they learn from us in ways other than fear of the hunter.

arm and hand by which, via spring-loaded fingers, he could grasp sword, shield, or reins, and serve the Holy Roman Empire quite effectively, as celebrated by Goethe (1799 [1773]).[363]

At the end of the twentieth century a team of French scientists genetically engineered a rabbit, adding to its genome a gene that gave it green fluorescent fur. The event attracted much media attention, some commentators hailing it as epoch-changing. Did this event inaugurate "the most important *biological* revolution since the appearance of life on earth"? Harari (2015 [2011], p. 399) nominated it as such. "After 4 billion years of natural selection," he wrote, this rabbit "stands at the dawn of a new cosmic era, in which life will be ruled by intelligent design." A reader could suspect that the young historian had stage-managed his report a bit, in order to highlight the irony that "intelligent design," long a preserve of religious fundamentalists and right-wing politicians, had actually come to pass in the form of a fluorescent green bunny.[364] In fact, of course, that process began long ago, although admittedly in a more limited, less direct manner, when farmers learned to selectively sort their grain harvests into separate piles, one for consumption and another for next season's planting of seeds from plants that had produced better than average grains. Likewise, with bovine stock, and so forth. Certainly there are significant differences quantitatively, between genomic redesign and crop-stock selection. There may be qualitative changes in store, too, as (to cite another example from Harari 2015 [2011], p. 407) innovations such as a digital-mechanical interface between human brains—thus, shared "wet" memories, in contrast to shared "dry" memories such as books and videos—develop, raising new questions and problems for present customary practices of self-identity.[365] But it should be clear that the notion of "culture releasing itself from the shackles of biology" (Harari 2015 [2011], p. 409) has been in practice for a long time. (While I have not grown wings so as to look more like Cupid, I do fly.)

As several of the afore-cited examples testify, one of the most visible questions regarding prosthesis today is located at the boundary between "organism" and "machine," a resuscitation of a contrast that reigned during much of nineteenth-century and early twentieth-century thought in Europe and the Americas—issues illustrated between the poles of Mary Shelley's 1818 novel of a piecemeal monster brought to life and Karel Čapek's 1920 play of a robot-producing company named R.U.R.[366] In today's terms at one level the organizing issue has become

---

[363] For a status report on prosthetic arms, see Jarrassé, de Montalivet, Richer, Nicol, Touillet, Martinet, Paysant, and de Graaf (2018).

[364] Also, of course, unless one subscribes to "biblical inerrancy," the "intelligent design" detected in the biblical texts were due to human beings (whether "speaking for God" or not).

[365] For a progress report on brain-to-brain communication, not by speech but via direct electromagnetic signal sharing, see Jiang, Stocco, Losey, Abernathy, Prat, and Rao (2018). Soon, probably sooner than Thomas Nagel imagined in 1974, a sonar capability will be added as prosthetic to humans, not simply as a physical device worn by a person but as a genetically engineered capability, an organ of echo-location directed and read by one's mind/brain.

[366] The idea of a "robot" is very old. In the Homeric text, *Iliad* (1.571, 18.143, 370-379, 391, 418-422) Hēsphaistos, "famed craftsman" (mainly blacksmith), was observed "sweating with toil as he moved to and fro among his bellows in eager haste; for he was fashioning tripods [τρίποδας], twenty in all, to stand along the wall of his well-built hall." These tripods, self-moving and capable of understanding (in some sense), were built to be personal servants to the gods. In the first book of *Politics*, Aristotle, recalling

replacement of humans—at work, in combat and other dangerous milieus—but it more often rests in a question of self-identity and, from that, identity of other: how much of my body can be replaced, by machine or by "artificially produced" bio-organ, without my identity as "this person," perhaps even as "human," changing? The question is older than Mary Shelley. Heath (2005) has taken us through major parts of a discourse that transpired in ancient Greece, from Homer to Aeschylus to Plato, in which a governing question was, "What is distinctive about being human?" Their discourse featured animals on one side of a putative and changing line and "human otherness" on one side of another putative and changing line, in both parts an issue of speech, spoken language, serving as guide and as obstacle (obstacle in the sense that the very skein of the larger discourse brought the specificity of spoken "Greek" (i.e., Attic or etc.) into focus as itself on some sort of continuum of relative positions, as thus privileged only as a feature of the contingency that made it specific (this last probably accelerated by the fact of multiple "sister" dialects). A classic instance of the "animal vis-à-vis human" dialectic of accord/discord is Aeschylus' trilogy, the *Oresteia* (completed by 458 BCE), in which speech acts simultaneously as inside and outside the conflict that was a subversion of familial normalcy by animalistic spirit—Agamemnon not merely acting *as* but having *become* an eagle seeking blood vengeance (see, e.g., Loraux 2002 [1997]; Heath 2005).

The instrumentalism of Diderot's theory can be appreciated as transitional from what I called in Part Two, §10, a periscope model of self as principal (and, weakly, principle) of human action in and for first-person experiences. Developed from a general folk theory that, now partially freed of theological groundings, emphasized a naturalism of psychologistic functions of biological structures, the imagery was one primarily of cognitive-emotive being in the world yet distinct from it, looking outward cautiously for opportunities and alliances of advantage. In his concept of a dialogic self, Norbert Wiley (1994) demonstrated in these developments eighteenth and nineteenth-century seeds not only of a utilitarian perspectivism but also of a liberal democracy of limited self-rule, and rather recover that terrain I will simply refer the reader to that book (1994, esp. pp. 3-16, 220-229). Diderot's theory had much in common with Hume's account of the perceiving I. One can see at the core of this commonality of conception a rather vague notion of reflexivity, which, only partly due to the vagueness, seemed disruptively paradoxical.

What is the coherence of an instrumentalism that unfolds within and by a self that in some sense knows it is a perceiving subject, knows that as such it is also self-object, and enacts something of its perceptions of external world as a nexus of opportunities and alliances? Recall from Part One, §2, Kant's treatment of all of that complexity in his notion of a transcendental unity of apperception: a functionalist principle of the "I think" was located in the beingness of Being, the beingness that unites all empirical human beings. By contrast, other responses to the paradox (or perplexity) attempted to follow a more empirical route, so to speak, which meant that the analytical perspective that generated the sense of paradox or perplexity to begin with remained effective and thus reproduced seemingly without end the experience of that sense. We have witnessed already the exasperation with Hume—for example, Husserl's very emotional

---

those tripods, pondered the consequences "if every tool could perform its own work when ordered to do so or in anticipation of the need."

view (see Part One, §5, above)—for having "generated," supposedly, this conundrum that seemed (to some still seems) impossible to escape.

It is of considerable interest, in that regard, to make a brief detour through the literatures of "immune response," since the science of immunology, itself a recent invention, developed from and around an analytic distinction between "self" and "non-self," which was formulated as recently as 1940 by Burnet (1940; also 1958). Alfred Tauber (e.g., 1994, 2017) has done much to trace that history from the standpoints of different disciplines of inquiry (philosophical and cultural as well as biochemical and physiological). Viewed through his cognitive and emotive lens, one is struck by the extent to which the perspectives, assumptions, and uses of the "self vs. no-self" distinction in immunology have been as halting, as contentious, and as confused as they have been in the history of "self" within literatures of human behavior and sociocultural formations since the late nineteenth century. Tauber has demonstrated both deliberately and (one suspects) indeliberately, that a large portion of the confusion in immunology has stemmed from an irony of the recognition that the relation of "self vs. non-self" ("self and other," etc.) is in fact dialectical; once recognized, the complexity and subtlety must then be stuffed, somehow, back into the sorts of analytical categories with which Burnet, along with his initial critics, began (see the trajectory displayed in Tauber's sequence of reports, from 1994 to 1999 to 2000 to 2017; also see Zimmer 2018; Quick with Fryer 2018, pp. 178-181).[367] In other words, recognition that the relation of "self and environment," whether it be in the conventional domains of social science or in those of immunology (including the embryological and the epidemiological aspects), is a dialectical relation has repeatedly foundered on the shoals of perplexed utility: "What do I now do with *this*? How do I make sense of it, make use of it, with our conventional kit of analytical tools?" What began as important insight becomes another entry in a persiflage of hash (e.g., Tauber 1999, pp. 469-473).

Stories turning on supposed differences between human and nonhuman (e.g., animal-eagle, as in the case of Agamemnon) presuppose an originary point from which all sequences can be dated. Granted, there is perennial interest in wanting to begin at the beginning, the logic of an origin at which some specific development, such as Homo sapiens, began. But the seeming logic of it turns into a trap and delusion. The delimitation always has *its* origins in some set of *present* conditions. Evolutionary theory tells us that while there must have been a very first instance of Homo sapiens, it occurred millions of years ago (even by the calculations of Bishop Ussher, more than 6,000 years ago), and it was embedded somewhere is a very long sequence of gradual changes with the Homo genus.[368] This "Who was first?" question begs for whiggish answers. But consider another example of the question, much more recent in focus and much smaller in import: Who was the first statistician? This is *our* question, of course, not Montaigne's or Shakespeare's or Diderot's, and as is usually the case in such matters so much turns on what *we* are willing to count as an instance of the thing. In this case, as often, the question has usually been bound up with nativist feelings. An inquirer today looks back, seeking an answer to the question; but letting such intent rule the designation of origin points, stopping

---

[367] One is reminded of some of the "debate" raised by proponents of a "constructionist" perspective vis-à-vis "objectivism" (see Hazelrigg 1993a); similarly, discussions such as Geertz (1973) of cultural distinctions between "nature and culture," while nonetheless preserving a supposedly non-cultural (because supposedly pre-cultural) analytic priority of nature (see Hazelrigg 1992 and 1995).

[368] Even in the "punctuation" version of evolutionary theory transitions were probably more like an extended ellipsis than a comma or semi-colon, much less a full stop (dead ends)!

points, in a dating scheme of when-and-where-by-whom (And why not? What else could?) is the mark of a whiggish history. It is difficult, to say the least, to avoid these traps of whiggism, because we do ask questions with interest of today in mind. So, in France and even more in Belgium the interest has been to nominate Quetelet as statistician. In Germany: Achenwell, whose lectures at Marburg in the 1740s were clearly about "how to run numbers of interest to the state." In England: not only John Graunt but also William Petty, the latter developing estimations techniques first for Cromwell's interests, then those of Charles II. Likewise, the commissions of inquiry formed by James I of the United Kingdom to determine where, how much, and by whom—that is, actual surveys conducted through village priests, sheriffs, and others, to determine how many villages had been pulled down, how many peasants thrown off the land, whether it was done legally, and by whom, in what became known as "acts of enclosure." And those were not the first in England: Cardinal Wolsey ordered that one be undertaken circa 1515. Duke William of Normandy, now King William I of England, decreed that a massive survey begin in 1086. We know of this last-named example (as in later examples) that because the survey was partly after the fact the reports were explicitly estimations. Some later commissions learned to devise their own techniques of estimation from what amounted to samples—what we might call "statistical estimation," much as Petty, Graunt, Achenwell, and others, later developed systematically and described in their publications.

Having set that trap aside, I shall brave another one, this one more complex, the argument about "rational action" and "rational actor." These twin categories are very closely related, to be sure, but they are distinguishable: first, within the origin story that differentiates the human (as rational, including irrational) from other animals (as nonrational), as in, say, the Great Chain of Being but also in Darwin's books and much discussion thereafter;[369] and, second, insofar as one can imagine two or more poorly rational actors engaging in action that turns out to be, by some external criterion, surprisingly rational in effects, perhaps even in execution, because of constraints on the actors, whether carefully devised or happenstance or some granular blend of the two (as in each actor's everyday execution of, say, a policymaker's carefully devised "uniform" plan; see, e.g., Thaler and Sunstein 2008). Thus, I will begin with consideration of the "rational actor" category (as distinguished from "rational action").

The first point I wish to make is that the argument of human rationality has often been a conflation of two, the more basic of them about abstraction and scale. This argument has usually been presented in terms of methodology, as a contrast between the ethnographic (associated with micro-level or the "individual-personal") and model-theoretical (associated more with meso- or macro-level, i.e., abstracted aggregates). Much of the description that has been written within and about that contrast has been misleading at best. For instance, any ethnography is *replete* with abstraction. Human experience is replete with abstraction. Insofar as the argument is about or within the foregoing contrast, the vectors of difference are matters of degree, not kind, and they are simultaneously matters of theory as well as of method (see, e.g., Hannan 1991, p. 3). Any language, whether "natural" (a native tongue) or "artificial" (a symbolic or mathematical logic, or a newly invented tongue such as Esperanto), is a practice of abstraction. This is not to

---

[369] Including now, most assertively, the new genomics as authority for a renewed psychologism (see, e.g., Plomin 2018).

deny that degrees of difference can be quite large, ranging from the vernacular meanings of the repertoire of, say, a five-year-old child or a poorly educated adult to the far more complex yet equally vernacular (except that it is "native," i.e., *vernaculus*, to a far smaller group of people) specialized meanings of, say, a machine-learning program of "artificial intelligence" or a mathematical model of "the big bang" or quantum tunneling, and so forth.

The second point I want to make, also hardly novel, is that the most important distinction between "rational *actor*" and "rational *action*" already involves an issue of scale. One way of expressing it is as Max Weber did in his formulation of the old notion of unintended, sometimes perverse, consequences of purposive action. Derek Parfit (1987) formulated it in a somewhat different manner, with an entailed recommendation: if each of some set of actors attempts to produce the best outcome of common action for the general good by each's sole consideration of his or her own rational act, the result is likely to be contrary to each's conception of the general good. The most notorious illustration is a logic game known as Prisoner's Dilemma: when each actor in the game decides "plays" in keeping with strict rationality of personal choice, everyone loses in the end, relative to ideal outcome, and foreknowledge of that fact will often not change individual choices. This is the "negative side," one might say, of the same principle demonstrated in its "positive side" by Adam Smith's "invisible hand" or Thaler and Sunstein's (2008) "nudge" or a core characteristic of the classic Chinese cultural preference for strategy by indirection (see, e.g., Jullian 1999 [1992]). In Parfit's recommendation, preferred results of an intendedly rational action are often more likely achieved when individual actors individually decide what to do by a blend of motives and interests that, in each case, may fall well short of being a model of rational action. Still another way of putting the lesson is that scale often makes a difference between decision making at the level of individual actors and outcome at some effects-aggregated level of collectivity (see, e.g., Hannan, 1991, pp. 1-13). Time, in the sense of an actual processual sequencing, matters because sociality matters, and sociality is inherently processual.[370]

Hierarchal institutions of social process channel effects of individual actors' decisions and actions more or less strongly into patterns that can be seen, from one or another point of view, as rational. Market transactions—processes of distribution and exchange that both generate and are generated by (in) a dialectical unity of production/consumption—are full of illustrations. The illustrations are fewer in number and simpler in content when they rest in medieval fairs (then the primary locus of distribution and exchange), but they are nonetheless constituent of those local affairs (see, e.g., Hont 2005; Jacob and Secretan 2008; Johanek 1999; Miller and Hatcher 1995).[371] Note, by the way, that the previous sentence but one is a billboard of advertisements: first, that institutional channels—being themselves mixtures of partly rational design, partly intended and partly unintended consequences, partly traditionalist anchorage (i.e.,

---

[370] This point involves inescapably the issue of ergodicity and its requirements simultaneously theoretical and methodological. I will pursue the issue of ergodic process in Part Five, below (see also Hazelrigg 2010, pp. 6-10).

[371] Catherine Secretan (2002) has contributed good coverage of *Mercator sapiens*, a discourse by Caspar Barlaeus (1584-1648), which he presented in 1632 (see also Jacob and Secretan 2008, pp. 10-11).

the inertia of "tradition" can be generated anew, deliberately or not; think, for example, of the effects of bureaucratization), partly redesign and partly messy from the gaming efforts of those who seek dispensations, and so forth—are effective and efficient by degree and are themselves *processes* that vary across venues and overtime; second, that "rational" as a description of action need not be and typically is not a single, uniform adjective but varies by perspective, whether in "world view" or in more specific, sometimes *situationally specific*, social reflection ("What is it we want to do here?" or, Goffmanesque, "What is going on here?") and reflexive effects of *that*. Sociality is inherently processual, and usually it is inherently very complex of process. Thus, ask yourself, why do economists (among others) try so hard to build the analytical device of a closed system and determine its equilibrium conditions? For the same reason as do theorists of James Clerk Maxwell's thermodynamics, theorists of quantum chromodynamics, and so forth. Many processes of sociality are far more complex than those.

Consider the polysemic range of "rationality" that one encounters in literatures of the social sciences. A sampling of that range includes, in no particular order: (1) acting from reasons, reasoned decisions about "plan of action" or about "how should I respond" or about "what to do today," and so on; (2) assumptions of deliberation of thought, as opposed to habitual courses and as opposed to "instinctual" or "completely innate" or "forced by nature"; (3) the binary difference, "rational vs. non-rational," but then with variations internal to each side, which are often situational; (4) for example, "rational" as a gradient, with the term "irrational" demarcated at some floating point on the gradient; (5) likewise, "non-rational" as, if not a quantitative gradient, then differences in kind, among, say, religious belief, personal preference (as in "ethnic identity"), emotional state, as in "acting from fear" or from "anger" or "ennui" or "adolescent anxiety," or "arrested development," and so forth; (6) variations that can stem from the "oughts" of a notion of "morality," thence a notion of culturally variable "ethics," as these cross-cut one or another account of "the rational," as the cut could confound expectations of a virtually mandatory "reasoning" even when motivation was chiefly an issue of God's will (for a believer had to be able to figure out what God's will, and/or a priest's instructions, implied in this or that non-identical situation). And within all of that variation the idea of a social science was already present, at least in germ, if for no other "reason" then because institutional relations of power and authority, vis-à-vis changeable circumstances, were always present.

As mentioned above, perspective helps one to sort through the many variations because their differences are largely due to perspective. The main point I intended above with regard to institutional channels can be illustrated by a question such as: What can policy makers and public officials do about the fact that the average adult makes decisions, in typical situations, on the basis of a very heavy discount rate, to the extent of damaging her or his own future well-being? By "discount rate" I mean the answer one gives, in effect, to the following kind of choice. Let's assume that by contractual obligation I must pay you $1,000 a year from this date. But today I say to you, "I have just come into some unexpected cash, so I might discharge my obligation to you one year early, if you will accept enough less than $1,000 to make it worth by loss, since I could put the money in a deposit account that pays 6% a year. So how much is that $1,000 worth to you today? How much do you want for that IOU today?" Some respondents will quickly calculate in answer something more than $60. But some people will sell the IOU to me for $100 or more (i.e., I could buy my IOU for $900 or less). Whereas mainstream economic theory had, until recently, assumed that a rational actor would be willing to discount future value by three to six percent at most, experiments demonstrate the attraction of discount rates much higher than that (see Ainslie 1992; Hardy and Hazelrigg 2007; Cowen 2018). Granted, much of that research involved token sums. But there are many documented cases (i.e., "real world" cases) of adults operating by shockingly high discount rates. Granted, in some instances the discounter was pressed for cash in the short run (e.g., "lending shops" that buy personal payroll checks before pay day charge heavy discounts for a few days or a couple of weeks, trading on their customers' desperate straits). But many adults who are not in financial straits nonetheless discount at high rates. The discount rate is a quantitative measure of their impatience, their unwillingness to defer gratification (as in Weber's theory).

Moreover, the discount effect occurs in a variety of situations in which there is no evident immediate transfer of money or other material resource. For example, consider the obligation of parents to provide at least minimal formal education to their children. Some parents who could otherwise afford much larger investments in their children deliberately discount that future value by substantial amounts on the assumption that the children will live in much better economic conditions and therefore will earn much higher incomes. Not only is there no guarantee of that, economic history demonstrates long periods during which median personal and/or household incomes do not rise in real terms, occasionally even in nominal terms. The parental expense of better than average education of one or more of their children is large in immediate terms. It can be thought of as an investment in parental old age. But the contingencies of that—one or more of the children dying from disease, accident, or war; leaving the home community for life in a big city; family disruptions—are difficult to calculate. What is at interest to the parent is not primarily a population distribution of survival probabilities of Number One Son or Daughter but what will actually happen in this specific case. In short, there are various perspectives from which to judge rational decision making.

Many individual persons, corporations, and national governments today are gambling against the "worth" of future lives by deferring efforts to counteract climate change. As Cowan (2018, p. 67) pointed out, if we assume a discount rate of five percent over the course of five centuries, one life today is being equated with about 39 billion lives five centuries hence. Or, to express the same trade-off in shorter time, at that discount rate one life today is equated with 131.5 lives a century hence. Of course, no one can say with certainty what the effects of climate change will be one century (much less five centuries) from now, and that is the point of the gamble. How bad would the future condition have to be, before present moral evaluation would conclude that mortal risk to a single life today would be worth a near-certain (or "high," etc.) probability of saving, say, 132 lives a century hence? We answer such questions today by our current decisions on various fronts, in ignorance of sound estimates of future probabilities of specific future conditions of peril/security.

Max Weber evidently knew about conditions and consequences of variant abilities of deferred gratification. While he probably did not know the concept of "time discount" (or how to calculate it for specified conditions, he surely did know about the temporality of perspective. We do not know whether he appreciated Einstein's second thought experiment, its ramifications and potential meanings of "time dilation" as they could apply in social processes. Perhaps his appreciation was of the same general tenor as that of his age mate, Mead (see, e.g., Mead 1932), although he was probably more sensitive than Mead (because of cultural distance) to what he saw as a mysticism of Henri Bergson's speculations about temporality (see, e.g., Bergson 1910 [1899]). The "tumult of the day," much of it resulting from developments within and from the main sciences and accordingly stimulating expectations of newer sciences such as economics and sociology, perhaps accounted for some of what readers have seen as a tendentiousness of Weber's compositions. Indeed, life was becoming more tendentious, and Weber sought to "do justice," so to speak, to the new dynamism and the myriad experiences that were being made of it. There had developed ever more an inherent conflict, still greater than in Kant's day, between what had been a dominant Cartesian attitude of "clear and distinct ideas" and the elasticities both of a moment and of time itself in this world which Nietzsche had only recently announced as under severe threat of nihilist attitudes. Weber's emphasis on "ideal typification" as a process of inquiry was an attempt to create some stability in inquiries, especially those that emphasized the gravity of actors' own perspectives and meanings. This approach was (is) analogous to uses of the "closed system" device in the physical sciences.

Weber's category, "traditional" type of social action—hardly his category alone, to be sure[372]—illustrates the blurred membership lines and criteria of the categories, even under the harness of ideal typification (Weber 1968 [1922], Part One). While his distinction between "behavior" and "action" (i.e., "social action") is reasonably clear until one attempts to use it as a sorting device (e.g., how does one know whether another person is or is not taking others into account?), the line between "traditional action" and "behavior" is in principle less than sharp when one considers the dimension of habituation and its effects in self-identity and reflexivity. A person's habitual activities might be due to thoughtful regard for tradition, in which case one could conclude the person was taking "others" into account in some fashion, especially if the evidence of regard indicated *which* tradition and its personifications. But if no thought was being given to others during preparation or execution of the activities, the correct sorting would favor no kind of social action but behavior. An inquirer on scene might ask "Why *that* way?" and the response might be some version of "Because that's the way we've always done it." Insofar as the response is stimulated by another person, we clearly have evidence that can count as social action; and that might well have been the full extent of first person's consideration of any others during any phase of the activities under question. Under some circumstances "the traditional way" could be a rational choice ("I think this other way would be better, but that would upset lots of my neighbors, and the difference simply isn't worth it"). On the other hand, sometimes

---

[372] And difference in what counts as "traditional" adds complication when reading literatures comparatively.

we enact patterns from a repertoire, rather than engage in rational deliberation about choices, and in one sense this could be accounted as acting by habit; yet, if queried about the choice made, a person could recite the rational deliberation that had recommended use of the particular pattern in specified circumstances. Would that be genuine memory, or would it be an "ex post" rationalization, or a need to satisfy the inquirer of perspicacity?

As Alfred Schütz (1967 [1932]) made more explicit in his interrogation of Weber's scheme, expectation figures importantly in rationality as a feature of motivations (in Schütz' terms, "in order to" and "because of" motives), both in first-person anticipations, decisions, and reflections, and in second-person conversations after the fact ("giving reasons," etc.).[373] While there has indeed been a major interpretation of Weber's work that can be (and has been) summarized as a "normativism"—in effect, insisting on derivation from outside sociality (i.e., a claim of transcendental status for a "normative process"—that interpretation of Weber is easy to refute (see, e.g., Cohen, Hazelrigg, and Pope 1975), and as a claimed necessity in explanation of human phenomena in general it is evident that adding "normative" as a modifier of terms such as "act" and "expectation" is redundant (although it is often difficult to determine what exactly has been intended by the modifier (see, e.g., Turner 2016).[374] Insofar as that applies, one may simply ignore the redundancy without loss. Issues of the concept of expectation remain, but these are thoroughly empirical. They tend to cut across the stabilizing intent of any ideal typification. Illustrations were cited above—for instance, how does an actor sort through the different perspectives of rationality when enacting, or later justifying, this or that specific expectation, which, after all, amounts to an anticipation of "future world" (and, as such, could be identified with Hume's "fictions"—that is, "things made"). It is easy to see that some theorists deny any proposal of a "rational *actor*" even while assuming a model of "rational *action*": between the one and the other, all of the chaff has been blown away, or so it can be assumed. While I do not recall Weber making a point of the difference, it is clear that he knew that "action" or some more specific process was more amenable than "actor" or "self" to the uses of ideal typification.

The specter of nihilism as a predominant concern during (and after) the latter part of the nineteenth century can be appreciated from the attitude attributed to Gustav Klimt's paintings in Vienna—for example, in Karl Sigmund's (2017 [2015], p. 69) summary, "Humanity is just a freakish fluke in a vast and utterly alien world." Founding figure in the "Vienna Secession" art nouveau movement that began in 1897, Klimt painted his own declaration of freedom ("Enough of censorship. I am having recourse to self-help.") from the highly conservative traditions of the Habsburg Empire. His *Pallas Athene* (1898) exemplifies some main dimensions of that revolt:

---

[373] Note that Schütz entitled his book *The Meaningful Construction of the Social World*, not the more general and disciplinarial *The Phenomenology of the Social World*.

[374] Turner (2016, p.10) put it this way: "for every normative account there is a social science account or naturalistic alternative, which explains the same thing, or the empirically equivalent thing." Unless normativism demonstrates a "super-added normative element that cannot be accounted for naturalistically or by social science," it is idle. Ethics and morality are built within, of, and by a sociality—which does not make them any less real or less consequential.

figure-field boundaries are much less distinct, as is the figural presentation itself, the message being that one's conception of a person in memory, biographic or historic, is always already an abstraction—indeed, a flowing abstraction that changes by one's approach to it, one's address of it ("What am I seeing?"). A line can be drawn from Klimt's works or from those of a fellow member of the Secession, Emil Orlik (e.g., *Pilgrims Approaching Mount Fuji*, 1902, a flow of abstracted figures), among others, to the Abstract Expressionism movement that began in New York City, early 1940s, and made famous by painters such as Jackson Pollock, Willem de Kooning, Lee Krasner, and Roy Lichtenstein. Like Klimt and associates earlier in the century, they often left blurs or splashes in deliberately, even urgently "non-conceptual" washes, drips, hurtles of color across a canvas.[375] One of the most striking themes seen in common across so much of the work by the Vienna Secessionists and then the Abstract Expressionists has to do with the oft-stated account that these movements emphasized spontaneity, eschewed anything as formal as a "school of art" when the artists referred to each other, pursued freedom of expression *almost* as an end in itself—"almost," because all of that was essential to the effort to plumb one's psychic depth in search of what, if anything, might be so foundational as to qualify as universal. To the extent that a commonality of finding ever came to light, it was so *abstract* as to hardly count as a *nameable*. But this was not actually a conclusion. It was integral to the movement's beginning operation, which was to abstract away as much of sociality as could be accomplished, in order supposedly to find the purely psychic reality that was to be plumbed as resource of expression. The fact that the average viewer saw so little meaning in what was being found added to the sense of nihilism against which Nietzsche had been protesting before he stopped watching (or perhaps before he stopped commenting on what he was seeing).

When public reaction to such exercises became noticeable, it usually took the form of an indictment of "abuses of humanity," and these were usually deemed consequence of continuing loss of the cosseted world of a paternalism that had paraded as Christianity's ontotheological morality. This kind of sociality that denies itself in favor of an extra-human authority had taken many forms long before the sociality-denying operation of an art nouveau. As Nietzsche had diagnosed, the trail of that diagnosis of loss was at least as long as the "Copernican revolution" was old. In the initial recalculation of humanity's location in the universe the contingency had actually been only to a galaxy, the one we call the Milky Way, in which humanity had been moved by Copernicus far from the center of things to one of the galaxy's "radial arms," as commonly depicted). Soon evidence said that this one galaxy counted among a seemingly numberless multitude of galaxies (an abundance that had been known during the late 1700s, e.g., by Kant). However, the very idea that "our universe" *has* a center next came into doubt, as Einstein (and others) had concluded that we lack means of knowing the boundaries of our

---

[375] Think not only of Pollock's "drip art" but also of de Kooning's several pieces named *Woman* (distinguished by number or not), his *Excavation* (1950), his *Police Gazette* (1955). Lichtenstein's poster art continued one of the major themes of the Vienna Secession, which was then continued by Andy Warhol in his neutered commentary on commercialism. See Sandler (1976) for a standard overview of this "New York school."

universe. We can claim evidence at most of a "cosmological bubble," which is—irony of ironies—centered on *us*. Of course, because public education had not caught up with any of this (and mostly still has not), most people were puzzled when reading, for example, that acceleration and gravity are forces indistinguishable in effects, or that we cannot know the boundaries of our universe because of the speed limit of photons. The world was so much simpler before God died, that golden era when we did not have to be responsible for any of it, including our own presence in it. With so much anxiety to manage, imagine the challenge of fixing a claim of rationality to any static foundation or to any non-contingent principle that is not itself simply a posit. God the posit had worked. Kant's posit was still unsettling, as artists sought a psychic platform that has no contingency on anything more than, or less than, itself (like a god that one can believe *in*).

The distinction between "instrumental rationality" and "value rationality" is much older than Weber's treatment. (Kant made considerable use of it; so, too, some ancient Romans and ancient Greeks). There is such a large volume of criticism of instrumental rationality as a feature of "modern society" that a credulous reader could easily conclude that Eratosthenes of Cyrene must have been indebted to one of the gods for telling him how to measure the circumference of Earth; Archimedes of Syracuse, the equally indebted user of divine knowledge of, for instance, a means of estimating the value of *pi* (an irrational number, because of which a circle cannot be "squared"), the use of infinitesimals (in calculations near Newton and Leibniz), and "defense engines" against ships of invaders; the numerous accountants who maintained credits and debits of manufactures in Athens; Seneca, who sought the best way to end his own life before Nero's soldiers came for him; and so forth.[376] The notion that human beings could avoid all exercise of instrumental rationality—that is, assessing alternative means to achievement of a desired end—is patently absurd. The same must be said of corollary notions—for instance, that "calculability" is bane of the good life, cause of ills of modern life. Some of the criticism urges not abolition *tout court* but curtailment of what is seen as excessive use and/or replacement of "tradition," "value rationality," a "kingdom of ends," and so forth. On the other hand, there can be no doubt that an instrumental rationality has become a larger or more frequent consideration—if for no other reason, then because human ingenuity has produced so many new means, new instruments of action, during the centuries since the twelfth and then again after the seventeenth. (Note that in the preceding paragraph about my "second point" regarding the distinction between rational action and rational actor, much of the exemplary material assumes an instrumental rationality.)

A person can be inclined to rational action in general but constrained in some degree in a complexity of conditions that are inconsistent or contradictory in such manner that an intended action proves to be rational on some occasions but not others, or in one context but not others, or positively rational here but negatively rational (i.e., irrational) there, and so forth. Situational sensitivity has been recognized as an important factor for a long while. Shakespeare's plays use

---

[376] The large volume of criticism is highly redundant of content, so one quickly fatigues. But the repetition can have the opposite effect as well, convincing the credulous reader that there must be something to the criticism. (And there is; but not much.)

it to good effect, sometimes comedic, sometimes tragic, sometimes a mixture that itself reflects the situational sensitivity. Laurence Sterne's (1759-67) uses of it were satirically so deft that one can lose track of what was pointed criticism and what was accumulative effect, one building atop another. Urban scenes were increasingly portrayed as adventures in relative mores. As the growing complexity affected larger and larger proportions of a societal population, public opinion fluctuated between poles of interpretation: what from one point of view could be seen as a furthering of the liberalization of the individual person, could from another point of view be seen as loss of sound bonds linking people via traditional values. These fluctuations *themselves* can in turn be interpreted as flowing from situational movements in time, in history, such as "the business cycle" or cycles of profuse "demand generating concomitant supply" followed by receding "demand leaving excess supply to be devalued." These cycles are not new, although they have been instrumentalized (and partly monetized) in new ways.

One of the strange features of what can otherwise be understood as trends (e.g., economic trends, sometimes ensuring political trends) *within* rather common understanding of situational sensitivities is the fact that as processes that are seen at some level as *social* (i.e., in that broad sense which includes "economic," etc.), while the dynamics of situation as such are typically conceptualized as occurring outside the individual person—that is, they are, or produce, forces that impinge on the individual, weights to be borne—rather than as processes that operate *within* the person, consciously and subconsciously, as well as among persons. Rosa (2013, p. 184) gave a summary of the point (with reference to Weber), as I cited earlier: "in a society where the past has lost its obligating power, while the future is conceived as unforeseeable and uncontrollable, 'situational' or present-oriented patterns of identity dominate." By this conception of temporal orientation (which can be seen in many commentaries) the basic notion of Bildungsprozess as it existed in the time of Sterne and Hume, Goethe and Hölderlin, has shifted about 180 degrees, away from a focus of aspiration, "future self," toward which one seeks an up-bringing. One instead focuses on an evanescently fixation of Now, owing to a passivity that flows almost imperceptibly from an alleged multiplicity of time horizons which are imposed externally on a person, a temporality that emphasizes an almost indifferently temporariness: "if families , occupations, … can *in principle* be changed or switched at any time, then one no longer *is* a baker" or any instance of enduring punctuated status of thingness, as it were, but a set of shifting capacities and actions. Expectations are always about what one is capable of doing in a "here and now" that has only "vaguely foreseeable duration." Thus, the stability that comes with a sense of endurance of "who I am" is replaced by a fluidity of senses of "what I can do, and (more or less) well." Rosa questioned whether this induces us to "disregard identity predicates in our self-descriptions because they suggest a stability that cannot be made good" (Rosa 2013, pp. 147, 146).

This concern is hardly unique to Rosa, of course. As mentioned above (and will be topic again below), Mead's (1913) use of the "significant other" concept, and its generalization of effect as a "generalized other" (a sense of community, a third-person perspective), fits well with the concept of "individual person" as an ensemble of social relations. A person's self-reflexive

314

consciousness is composed from a population of people, significant others, who are present as incumbents of a variety of roles, to be sure, but also as specific persons whose existence in one's consciousness began or became the actual specificity of a person as exemplification of a more or less complex nexus of *his* or *her* presence as an ensemble of social relations (i.e., "role model"), each of whom has been and perhaps continues to be taken into account, as Weber said, not as stick figures or cultural dopes but as dynamic ensembles of subjectively meaningful actions within his or her nexus of significant others (see Gelernter 1992, pp. 67, 193-197).

There is a touch of irony in the realization that the foregoing description of uses of the ensemble concept—in particular, the ensemble-population of persons as significant others in one's own self-conception—could generalize from conception of the supposedly punctual self to another level of organization of agency, with or without scale effect. I am referring to recent efforts to develop (or re-develop) a concept of "group agency," as briefly discussed in Part One (see, e.g., Bratman 2018; Gilbert 2014; List and Pettit 2011; see also Godfrey-Smith 2013). This movement can be seen in part as a renewal in the sense that earlier scholars had focused attention on a group formation of agency: e.g., Gustave Le Bon's *Psychologie des Foules* ("psychology of crowds," published in 1895, and translated into English in 1896 as *The Crowd*). Whereas Le Bon's work evinced a rather reactionary reflection on "mass psychology" ("the crowd" as "the mob," "rabble-rousers," etc.), William McDougall's *The Group Mind* (1920; second edition 1927, both by Cambridge University Press) concentrated more on highly integrated, stable, hierarchical collectivities such as military and naval organizations, formations that deliberately achieve emic benefits by subordinating individual preferences and interests to the common good of an organization, as this has been defined from above, gaining and maintaining individual allegiance by processes of "esprit de corps."[377] As mentioned in passing several times, the interest was in effect regarding hypotheticals of homology versus heterology (non-homology), but these were virtually never developed by the social sciences.

Moving from first-person experience, especially *feeling* as first-person experience, to second-person experience, at which point feeling is transposed into the direct sociality of an explicit knowing (as in the assumptions of knowledge one makes of one's interlocutor), thence to the still greater abstractedness of sociality involved in transposition to third-person experience, involves interactive relations of at least two sorts of social process. The relations of one of these two, aggregation among persons each of whom has been accumulating experiences, emotive as well as cognitive, and in some manner "mashing" them into some sorts of "thematics" of memory, will be topical mainly of Part Five. The other sort is inference, processes of inference person to person, which will be considered now as well as later. Inference invokes and depends upon some sort of practical theory of mind. Jurisprudence and commerce have been among the venues in which inference and its underlying theory of mind have been systematically and most manifestly developed with reference to specific historical conditions, and therefore also the

---

[377] McDougall was also overtly racist, even for the context of the times (see, e.g., McDougall 1920, p. 187; Baltzell 1964, p. 200).

venues in which problems of satisfying the demands of inference have been most explicitly and clearly addressed. Hence, for illustrative purposes the following discussion is focused mainly in these venues. My point of departure historically (within European and Euro-American context) is a will-centered practical theory of mind and, concomitantly in jurisprudence and commerce, the assumptive platform on which inferential expectations were developed and pursued. While there have been (and are) important differences between the English common law tradition and the more formal-codex tradition of several continental countries, the traditions developed differently from a similar basis of will-centered theory and pursuant expectations of inference. Writing specifically of the US context, Horwitz' (1992, p. 13) general summary of this practical theory of mind with respect to both commercial and juridical activities can serve well enough within the broader cultural context. In the law of contract, the will-centered theory aimed to "subsume all rules and doctrines under the heading of 'will'"; and in the law of torts, under the heading of "duty" (i.e., the duty a legal subject was expected to honor willfully, including the avoidance one's civil responsibilities by negligence).[378]

Before pursuing those matters, let's briefly consider some historical dimensions of the context and conditions of the tasks of inference under the will-centered theory.[379] The importance of the historical dimensions can be appreciated especially in terms of factors such as population density and geographic mobility, with implications of the relative density of local ties based on second-person experiences. By the end of the third decade of the nineteenth century the US commercial economy had become well integrated as a single national market of distributional links, the primary nodes of which consisted of yeoman farmers, skilled craft trades and artisans, shopkeepers, and a small number of principals and agents of the distributional network itself. While this network was already important and soon would achieve far greater importance via railroads and telegraph, the bulk of personal interactions and the denser parts of the network involved direct relations of exchange, and these remained local, with some growth in regional segments. In most localities the odds were high that any adult selected at random knew, or knew of, any other adult selected at random from the same locality. The odds were similarly high that a litigation of disputes of contract or torts involved residents of the same locality—not only the litigants themselves but also their legal counsels, court officers, and jurors, if any. Now move ahead a half-century: as compared to the situation in, say, 1840, any adult resident selected at random in 1890 would less likely be acquainted with any other local person selected at random;

---

[378] The chief aim of contract law has been and is to make specified kinds of promises obligatory and thus to regulate potential as well as actual disputes; of torts, to create recourse to compensation in violations of specific rights whether by negligence or failure to observe dutiful regard for those rights or by willful disregard of those rights.

[379] There is a richly varied literature addressing various aspects of what is only sketched in this and the following paragraphs. The few citations in the sketch are good entries into the literature, but with regard to political economy in the USA during the 1830s I recommend Sellers (1992) and Howe (2009), as well as a relevant selection of the many books by the late Edmund Sears Morgan (1916-2013).

and if we stipulate acquaintance at the level of confident second-person, much less third-person, knowledge of one person by the other, that likelihood would be even lower.[380]

The law of contracts and the law of torts primarily assumed relationships of personal experience. But that assumption was rapidly becoming absurd for growing proportions of relationships, entailing a serious problem of inference. How does one achieve reliable information of another person's experiences, intents, and the like, when contact with that person in second-person terms is sporadic and fleeting, leaving one to grasp at third-person experiences that are themselves of questionable reliability in so many instances? The gaps were often visible in cases of criminal prosecution, resulting in miscarriages of justice. But gaps were present as well in contract law and in the law of torts, although these gaps were often overlooked under assumptions such as "duty to read" with no regard for the fact that parties to a contract usually had unequal access to requisite information and quality of counsel, resulting in "abuses of bargaining power that classical contract law permitted," as Slawson (1996, pp. 72, 173) has observed. "The principal purpose of contract law is to make certain kinds of promises binding," Slawson continued, but until recent reforms were enacted "producers could use their superior bargaining powers to defeat this purpose. They could make contracts that did not include the promises they had made," and rely on contract language that many people could not adequately comprehend (see also Fried 1981; Thomas 1997).[381]

During the late 1800s a search for a replacement of the will-centered theory of "self" as "legal subject" had begun. It was not that judicial authorities had concluded that will (as in the will-centered conception of self) was fictional or illusory. Potential lessons to that effect offered by Cervantes, Shakespeare, Hume, and others, could easily be set aside as irrelevant, for "the law" remained by conviction a realm still apart from literature, the arts, even philosophy. The problem rather was that the fiction of an equality of legally authoritative ability to read the mind of one's peer (i.e., to know that person's intents, etc.), as that conviction had presumed of sober adults in simpler times, had become all too obviously an indefensible assumption. Some of the impetus for reformation came from the realm of criminal law. But the stronger impetus was from

---

[380] The 26 states of the union in 1840 contained only five places with a population of 50,000 or more; the total population of the five accounted for only four percent of all inhabitants of the 26 states. In 1890 there were 42 states and 109 places of 50,000 or more, accounting for 19 percent of all inhabitants of the 42 states. Most of the 16 states added since 1840 were in the plains, the Rocky Mountains, or the Pacific coast, all having low density. These low-density territories siphoned many residents from the 26 states of 1840. Despite the siphoming, population densities in several of the 26 (e.g., CT, MA, NY, IN) increased by two and one-half to three times the amount in many of the 16 added states.

[381] Thomas (1997) is particularly good with regard to the century-long transformation of the primary mode of capital accumulation and organization, from the proprietary to the corporate mode, in conjunction with the shift not only in the constitution of subjectivity but also in the emphasis of attention, away from production and toward consumption. Literatures of economics, political science, and law began to read as if production decisions—what to produce, how, for what uses, etc.—were of no concern to disciplines of social science. Several early sociologists agreed (see, e.g., Sumner 1883, e.g., pp. 24-26).

commercial law, and the heart of the new model of legal subject was a theory of rational expectations, sometimes dubbed "the reasonable man" doctrine. One of the principals of this reformation, Oliver Wendell Holmes, Jr., stated the main premise of the theory thusly:

The law takes no account of the infinite variety of temperament, intellect, and education which make the internal character of a given act so different in different men. It does not attempt to see man as God sees them, for more than one sufficient reason. In the first place, the impossibility of measuring a man's powers and limitations is far clearer than that of ascertaining his knowledge of law, which has been thought to account for what is called the presumption that every man knows the law. But a more satisfactory explanation is, that, when men live in society, a certain average of conduct, a sacrifice of individual peculiarities going beyond a certain point, is necessary to the general welfare (Holmes 1881, p. 108).

In fact, Holmes stated two principles, not one, as presumptive. Because divining the true character of an act is impossible due to inability to measure an actor's "powers and limitations," a model of what a reasonable person would do under specified circumstances must be substituted as general standard. This model is as much a legal fiction as the earlier model of a will-centered self whose knowledge, motives, and other relevant can be fairly judged by the person's peers. But Holmes then adduced a community-based standard by which "reasonable man" is constituted: a "certain average of conduct" as deemed "necessary to the general welfare" of a community. However, this latter principle proved to be transitional, as anonymity-based standardization among and across communities increased. A standard of "reasonable expectations"—how a reasonable person should be expected to act, or to refrain from acting under risk of harm, under various specified circumstances—gradually ascended as the primary regulative principle (see Horwitz 1992; Williams 1920; Higbie 2003, ch. 2, passim; Slawson 1996; Stinchcombe 1986).

James Block (2002) effectively made the case that this conceptualization was on already fertile ground in the USA, a "nation of agents" virtually from its refounding during the latter half of the eighteenth century. Substantial components of that view had been maturing in England as well as British North America since the mid-1600s. John Whitgift, the archbishop of Canterbury no less, had accused the puritan reformers (one of their leaders, Thomas Cartwright, particularly) of proposing "such a perfection in men as though they needed no laws or magistrates to govern them," and that "every man might be as it were a law unto himself" (Block 2002, p. 48). This perception, alive long before Kant's proposal of moral order as based in the legislative thrust of ordinary action, underwrote increasingly common evaluations of current and probable future capabilities of the average adult. Even puritans of the seventeenth century, while insisting that a person's relationship with God must be individual and immediate, did not depart from adherence to notions of central authority. But they argued strongly for powers and rights of delegation, or extensions of central authority to local legislative communal action. The more radical among of them—John Pym, for instance, and Sir Arthur Hesilrige—attempted to enact a republicanism that endorsed some principles of a market model of organization for the polity. Their puritan resistances to "the significance of debt" kept them from supporting and utilizing commensurate principles in the economy, however, and the resulting failure especially to develop credit markets undermined their political republicanism (see Mann 2002; Macdonald 2003). That was England. In much of British North America the prevailing attitude was different. By the 1770s in the part that became an independent nation of "agents and debtors" (as well as creditors), ordinary people "had become, almost overnight, the most liberal, the most democratic, the most commercially minded, and the most modern people in the world" (Wood 1993, pp. 6-7).

The contrast posed by the "reasonable man" standard has sometimes been confused with another theorization of contrastive models. Late in the nineteenth century several scholars such as Ferdinand Tönnies were drawing lessons about differences between "traditional society" (e.g., Tönnies' Gemeinschaft), with its emphasis on communal relations, and "modern society" (Gesellschaft), with its emphasis on associative relations among strangers.[382] While correlative similarities are apparent, the important lessons being drawn differed. In fact, "associative relations among strangers" had been an important part of life in European societies since at least the twelfth century. Think, for example, of long-distance traders, as well as efforts at territorial consolidation and centralization of "public law" by civil authorities. Both the law of torts and the law of contract had been developing especially under the pressure of greater anonymity of life in cities and all of the territorial and distributional relations that sustained those cities. But in European societies these changes were situated within a rich texture of traditional, communal moralities. A better indication of the character of changing conditions for jurisprudence would be the sort of gradient that was used by Clifford Geertz, for instance, with regard to description or interpretation of cultures as a practice of composition *within* a culture but also as one or more perspectival instrumentalities *of* cultures in comparative perspective. This was effectively cited in Holmes' remark about what can be reasonably known. A thick/thin dialectic correlates partly with a local/nonlocal dialectic; and both apply just as well to Tönnies' associational model as to his traditional model. Thick description depends on a density of local ties and shared experience, which has been identified typically with "traditional society" (Gemeinschaft). The identification is mistaken, however, as anyone who has devoted the time and energy to follow the legal texts of many instances of medieval European law can testify. Understood as an analytical distinction, the "thick versus thin" contrast aligns with the difference between a text that is bulging with descriptions tied to particular conditions and contexts, on the one hand, and a text that offers high abstractions and general principles, including legal forms that claim effective jurisdiction in "the human condition" as such. Margalit was closer to the mark when he (2010, pp. 121-123, 141)

---

[382] One could enlist these literatures in defense of Hegel's aphorism of Minerva's owl, should additional evidence be needed. However, we very likely have before us a difference in national culture, between that of the USA (wherein "market association" was regulative on national scale by the early 1800s and belletristic literatures often featured long-distance migrations, reliance on strangers, and the like) and more traditionalist cultures of Germany, France, the Netherlands, Spain, Italy, Poland, Scandinavia, even the British Isles.

identified thick description with ethics (applications of rules) and thin description with morality (general principles), each of which is manifest in bodies of law, whether medieval or modern (also Margalit 1996).[383]

Thus, whereas stability and density of contacts between any two adults would usually have generated a substantial fund of tested inference about each other's felt experiences, skills, and implied facts with high confidence during the 1830s, by the 1890s anonymity had taken its toll. One of the consequences became a serious problem in the world of juridical process especially in urban areas. In 1830 witnesses to parties of a civil litigation of issues of contract or torts, or to defendants in a criminal trial, could reasonably be expected to have reliable insight into probable intent, for example, and the same could be expected of a panel of jurors, presumed peers of a defendant or litigants (a presumption that could itself be defended with confidence). Prejudices and inequalities were already rampant, but for any local jurisdiction these factors were sufficiently built into dominant expectations such that even the victims could tend toward a concordance of reasoning. However, as anonymities due to increased population, increased rates of migration, and decreased density of intimate contacts among residents of a given jurisdiction became more and more characteristic of city life, expectations of third-person experience regarding first-person feelings, intentions, and various other states of mind, skills, and implied facts became much more problematic both with regard to witness testimonies and in satisfying the presumption of jurors as peers. How is a juror to decide "beyond reasonable doubt" among conflicting claims about dispositions, intents, capabilities, and the like, when that juror has had no second-person experience with the litigating claimants, and all or nearly all of the third-person experience has been strained through rather abstract legal proceedings?

Holmes' point was not that, as a matter of principle, thick descriptions cannot be made in modern society; rather, that they would mire the main functions of law, the regulation and resolution of conflict, in such a massive text of process that it would simply fail, and in its failure generate still more conflict. Note that in moving from will-centered to "reasonable expectation" theory Holmes moved from a primarily psychologistic model to an explicitly social model. His contrast between "individual peculiarities" and "general welfare" made the anonymity of wide interdependence and trust in sociality an explicitly recognized condition of the rule of law. This shifted the weight of "rule of law" from a personalism of "what everybody knows" to impersonal

---

[383] Walzer (2017, p. 53) recently said, in connection with Margalit, that thick relations "have a Burkean quality" in that "they can be relations with the dead as much as with the living." That, too, is misleading in general (though it might be faithful to Margalit's intent). The principle of aristocracy as a principle of familial organization was rather thin (and a moral matter far more than one of ethics), but it united generations dead and generations to come with the present generation of a family very effectively. Likewise, a moral principle of present-generation responsibility to future generations for continuing care of Earth. Well before Kant's early version of a modern "philosophy of present" (to borrow a title from George Herbert Mead), the institutionalized hierarchal form of aristocracy, which had been a central organizing principle of feudalism, succeeded in unifying past and future, memory and anticipation, in "presentist" perspective, as counterpart to the descending hieratic principle which had made reality always dependent on a past (i.e., revealed authority rather than legislated authority).

institutionalized forms of procedure (e.g., expanded expectations of an educated public, risk insurance, a system of employment, etc.). That increased potential and actual sensitivities to prejudices and inequalities, although not necessarily to greater actual ameliorations.

## §22. Seeking an Authority of Voice

For the very idea of a science of society—including under that umbrella scientific investigations of social, cultural, economic, political, and related phenomena—one part of Kant's legacy that grew in importance during the latter half of the nineteenth century was his conclusion that in fact a proper *science* of human affairs could not be achieved because of lack of "the rational part" of a true science. The obstacle resulted from what Michel Foucault (1970 [1966]) later called the "doubling of man." That is, to put the key point in vernacular terms, the human inquirer into human affairs can only use as means of inquiry the very objects of inquiry that are the conditions and inform the aim of the inquiry. There can be no point of departure that is not already constituted by the conceptual framework that is integral to possible means of inquiry, and to the objects of that inquiry, within a culturally historically specific context. The circularity threatens the integrity of rational inquiry, as it was conceived under the sign of universality. One is always caught in the position of begging the question, a chain of regressive postures.

A short generation after Kant, Hegel tried to establish yet again the privilege of a human observer who knows—not merely knows but, like Newton with his laws of motion, knows *all*, the entirety of a history. The details of Hegel's system were soon mostly forgotten. But the universalist theme had pre-dated him, of course, along with the knower whose privileged status allows a special knowledge that erases time. Nor was Newton, with his famous laws, the first to claim erasure of time (in the sense that his laws purported to be timeless, or "for all time"). Hölderlin's poem, "Patmos" (1990 [1803]), briefly reviewed in Part Two, resuscitated a parable from Mark's Gospel about an erasure of time among those who are the elect—that is, for those who, by the grace of God, simply *understand* (see Warminski 1976, pp. 487-488).[384] A far less privileged edition of the universalist theme was called upon during the 1790s, when a figure of the French aristocracy, François-René, the Viscount de Chateaubriand, exiled in England and writing of "the genius of Christianity," comfortably expressed the key idea without casting a mere mortal as privileged agent of that which must be known: "The mind acts upon the body in an inexplicable manner, and man is perhaps the mind of the great body of the universe" (Chateaubriand 1873, p. 673). Karl Marx, a "left Hegelian in his youth," had kept Hegel's name alive through criticism during the middle decades of the century, although Marx himself had hardly any impact on thought until the century was on the verge of passing away. Whereas Marx had called on privileged knowers to examine their claims via his critical perspective, his critique

---

[384] A version of this theme remains alive as an expectation of guarantees, as in the traditional quest for certainty. Charles Taylor (1989, pp. 509-510), for example, was explicit in evaluating theories and related work according to whether the contribution would "guarantee us against loss of meaning, fragmentation, and the loss of substance in our human environment and our affiliations." Judging from numerous works of critical commentary that have been written in recent decades, Taylor was not alone in that wish, but he was unusual in being so direct, explicit, and specific.

was easily neutered (in part through his own complicity) as only another special pleading, albeit this time allegedly from a materialism rather than an idealism (ignoring that his critique had been of materialism no less than idealism, each a one-sided perspective; see Hazelrigg 1993b).

One response to the dilemma of "the doubling of man" entailed removal of a large segment of human meaning—that having to do with the realm of the apriori or metaphysical—from the object of inquiry.  By directing attention solely to what human beings do, as distinguished from what they might or might not think, feel, doubt, conjecture, and so forth, the problem of circularity could be deleted from the terrain.  Or so it seemed, for a time.  One might think of this approach to inquiry into the realm of human affairs on analogy to a mechanics of motion, or, in what seemed a closely related analogy, to observations of human beings going about their daily activities as if, peering down from the rooftop of a forty-storey building on ant-like beings scurrying around below, one supposed that an analogue to Ludwig Boltzmann's 1868 probability distribution of motions of a gas in thermodynamic equilibrium could be applied as instructive model.  If one could generate descriptive patterns of regular, repetitive motions, one might be able to infer some general principles of behavior, principles that in time, with suitable refinements, would be very much like, if not identical to, scientific laws.  Works by early demographers such as William Petty and John Graunt, previously mentioned, offered examples of what could be accomplished by studying only what people actually did, in varying context and under varying conditions.  Without undertaking any survey of personal beliefs, opinions, and attitudes on the part of inhabitants of England, for instance, Petty had determined that the problem of adequate money supply could be solved more efficiently in an *indirect* manner, by increasing the circulation of existing money.  Circulation would increase if the size of the circle within which it occurred could be reduced, and this reduction could be achieved effectively and efficiently by installing a bank as depository into which people who are inclined simply to hoard their money could put it for safe keeping as an investment paying a small return while their money would continue to circulate instead of sitting passively in a hoarding mattress.  The example seemed promisingly generalizable as a method of inquiry.  Petty can be regarded as a forerunner of modern economics, as well as epidemiology.

This response fit well with the empiricism that had been favored in some quarters of the Enlightenment in Scotland and England.  It soon caught the attention of an increasing number of scholars on the European continent—Adolphe Quetelet, who developed a "social physics," and Auguste Comte, who pursued various regularities (as in a purported "law of three stages"), being two prominent early exemplars.  Comte has generally been credited with having coined the word "sociology," although evidence indicates he was late by half a century, the Abbé Sieyès having used the word in his writings as early as 1780 (see Guilhaumou 2006).[385]  In any case, it is clear

---

[385] Sieyès' extensive writings covered many pertinent topics of the time, including the promise of new sciences of human affairs, some of which he recognized as existing in all but name in Montesquieu's work (see Sieyès 1999 and 2007).  For more on the significance of Sieyès in context of the revolution of 1789 and after, see Sewell 1994).  His insights into the development of a rhetoric of an exclusionary politics and ethics, based on factors of modern political economy rather than older terms of a hieratic

that a variety of social forces had been fomenting in favor of building some new sciences, modes of inquiry that would do for human affairs what the new modern chemistry was doing for much of the physical substance that human beings had considered important enough to name and explore. As events of 1789 and aftermath gestated in consciousness, members of Europe's aristocracy both secular and, as with the Abbé Sieyès, sacred joined members of the newly powerful bourgeoisie in pressing ruminations about the dangers of unleashed energies of emotion and reason working in concert against established order. In North America similar concerns had been expressed in public discussions, proposals, and enactments of instruments of government in republican form, which manifested a primarily pragmatic experimentalist orientation as their dignitaries continued to look to Europe, mainly Paris, London, and Edinburgh, for intellectual authority. Montesquieu, Rousseau, and Kant, among others, had published general accounts of an anthropology in a mainly descriptive, "natural history" vein during the eighteenth century. This approach did not meet Comte's expectations, for he was seeking "positive" knowledge of basic principles of human behavior in collective organization, principles that would have, or lead to, useful practical applications for the betterment of life in the new, rapidly changing, social world.[386] Having worked as secretary to the well-placed Henri de Rouvroy, comte de Saint-Simon, a source of considerable intellectual influence and a proponent of utopian thought, Comte sought to build an all-encompassing science of society. As distinct professionalized disciplines, most of what became standard members of a collection known as "the social sciences" would not emerge until later in the century, but Comte saw places for all of them, in effect, within the apex of his hierarchy of the sciences in general, an apex initially occupied by sociology and (by some accounts) later replaced by anthropology (although that could simply have been an exercise in nomenclature). His reasoning is vague, and the proposal of sociology as "queen of the sciences" can be easily read as grandiose. But it is conceivable that he had in mind a thesis of subsumption, by the contention that all the sciences are human and thus social activities, contingent of specific historical context and conditions. This would have been an early version of a thesis known as "sociology of knowledge" (including science), sometimes viewed uncomfortably as an instance of Bertrand Russell's supposed paradox of a category that is member of itself.

Be that as it may, Comte's divagations proved to have been prescient not only of later developments within the social sciences—specializations by subfields or subsystems of society, as these have been constructed—but also of the crucial problem of an authority of voice. By labeling his proposals as specific courses of a *positive* philosophy, Comte intended that they

---

nativism, elucidate much that was new about the revolution of 1789 and provide interesting counterpoint to the dilemma of those members of the British aristocracy and landed gentry who, mostly Puritan, opposed the monarch on grounds of liberty of conscience, religious and thus political, but sought to protect their interests against calls for economic liberty as well.

[386] The qualifier in Comte's "positive knowledge" stood mainly as advertisement of opposition to the "negative" or "useless" pursuits of metaphysical games and figments of untamed imagination. As with his law of stages, Comte's evolutionism tended to principles of progressive placement. Not that metaphysics was completely useless; but the speculations of metaphysics were being replaced increasingly by scientific knowledge, and that process, he imagined, would continue indefinitely.

would have, and would be appreciated as having, practical benefit to the health and welfare of existing societies and, though he seemed less disposed to the "utopian socialism" that his one-time employer, Saint-Simon, had championed, to the evolution of societies yet to come. This latter aspect of his proposals is not to suggest absurdly that Comte had already "borrowed liberally" from Darwin and/or Wallace (as he has sometimes been said to have done of Saint-Simon). It is no less absurd, however, to think that their theory of evolution came from nothing. Important parts of the logic had been developed in treatises of political economy (especially the notion of a "natural selection on variabilities"), as well as in earlier works of biology, and whether one thinks of Comte's accretions as a result of learning or of borrowing (without attribution), his ambitions surely had him attuned to the latest thought via his sieve of relevance to his own project. Just as the major designers of North America's "first new nation of the world" made provisions for a robust legitimacy of persuasively supportive authority as both foundation and public face of the new instruments of governance, Comte also had a sense that his new sciences, if they were to be useful as he intended, had to establish an authority of voice without the benefit of religion's cloak. His hierarchical view of these sciences of the social—specifically that because their topical materials were the *most complex* of all of those dealt with by modern science, their products, necessarily informed by contingencies of all that complexity, could not be as *general* as the products of the biological and physical sciences, and yet this new social science would be the *apex*—was probably central to his effort to build that legitimacy. A social science would build on the basis of the biological and physical sciences *and* would subsume them, both in the sense of incorporating their lessons and in the sense of being also the science of the conditions and activities of those sciences. Whether cavalier in his practices of learning from others, Comte surely was astutely attentive to recent developments in chemistry, in geology, and in physics, and probably saw as well the excitement of new proposals in biology,[387] all of which would have been indication that the field of attention for a new science was already crowded. If Comte was also aware of the great hurdle left in Kant's legacy for any claim of a "true science" (a "real science" rather than a "pretend science," to use vocabulary from Kantian theory)—and I know of no indication that he did have such awareness (or, if he did, that he took it seriously)—then an urgency of effort to build a foundational claim for a science of society, or of "the social," would have been all the greater.

Aside from religious ideologies and political slogans, positivism dominated orientations of a "science of society" (or "social sciences") during the middle decades of the century. Marx, one of the mid-century critics of positivism and all other brands of idealism, was easily ignored as a political agent, whether of "socialism" or, following his and Engels' manifesto of 1848, of "communism," a pronouncement that struck most scholars of the day as merely a "show piece" of political theatre. The field of human inquiry, understood in the sense of systematic empirical

---

[387] Most especially, in cell theory, which had begun with Robert Hooke in 1665 but now (early 1800s) was awhirl with debates and new theories by Matthias Schleiden and Theodor Schwann (soon thereafter, Rudolf Virchow), adding to Hooke's identification of the organic cell as basic unit of morphology, the genesis of cells only from prior cells.

study, remained poorly organized and of mostly programmatic promise at mid-century, when a doctrine of utilitarianism offered renewal of the promise but little more than a new name and a rejiggered promotion of positivist practicality. Thus it remained until late in the century, when some scholars made a point of having noticed that, contrary to its public self-reflection, the various "positivists" had actually *not* done without apriori reasonings and "things" that no one had ever experienced other than in cognitions. This resistance sharpened the positivist claim, as manifested in major figures such as Richard Avenarius and Ernst Mach. By the close of the nineteenth century the terrain on which claims and counter-claims regarding a "science of society" were being heard had become very contentious, issuing in a debate known as the "Methodenstreit" or "conflict over methods."

Recall my shorthand description of the "positive" response to perceptions of the dilemma left by Kant and his successors in philosophy: shift attention away from "metaphysical" issues of Humean skepticism, Kantian limits of knowledge, and the like, and toward directly observable matters of what human beings actually do, their observable behaviors in observable contexts under observable conditions. Critics of that alleged solution raised questions of the following sort: What in fact *is* it, that "people actually do"? What is the constitution of the "who" who behaves? What are the boundaries of this being? Circumcision of the kind recommended by the stance of positivist theorists manifested a rather dictatorial attitude: what people say about what they do, what people think in anticipation of a doing, the reasons a person can give, if asked, about an activity or sequence of activities—none of that can have any useful part in scientific inquiry into human affairs, because (1) first-person experience is hermetic, sometimes even to the person in question (i.e., first-person self-deception); (2) people often do not know why they engage in observed actions; (3) people are unreliable reporters of their own interests, reasons, goals, and circumstances, due to status-sensitivity, suspicion, poor memory function, and similar obstacles; (4) in any case, what people think before, during, and after what they are observed *doing* accounts for little of the variation of behaviors observed in the cross-section. Rather, observers carefully trained in scientific method can better interpret the significance of observed activities than can the everyday actors themselves. By the early years of the twentieth century that general view of the wares of a social science had lost much of what had once been seen as a promising course. On the one hand, some scholars found the view, and the supposed promise, anemic in pragmatics, indefensible in ethics, and perhaps even a contributing factor in apparent failures of social policy in face of the collection known as "the social question" (as discussed in Part One, §6). On the other, if that was the sum and substance of what social science had to offer, how did these new disciplines differ from good journalism or good policing or good pastorship?

If the promise of Comte's "positive" sciences of social affairs was to have any practical consequence, the late decades of the nineteenth century offered ample opportunity to prove the promise good, in Europe and in North America. Tönnies (1907, pp. 7-24) in Germany (but also addressing conditions in England and France) asked whether harmonious relations among so many people so densely packed together could still be achieved, especially in view of current economic tensions. His question was being asked widely and repeatedly. As a sociologist at the

325

University of Chicago reported in 1906, "literally hundreds of books, pamphlets, and articles have been published on 'The Social Question'" (Howerth 1906, p. 254; see also Howerth 1894). Recent growth in that number had occurred partly from use of an analytical approach: scholars as well as policy makers and opinion leaders were "specializing" in terms of their own disciplinary professions, parceling "the social question" into separate problems of juvenile delinquency, adult crime, broken families, immigrant enclaves, national integration, and so forth—an implication being that what had been treated as an all-encompassing question of possibilities of human life in the new industrial order actually consisted of several containable "social problems," each of them connected with "city life" in a specific way. This approach to the "problem of order" seemed more manageable, more conducive to retail politics, and more apposite to public policy. The effort at compartmentalization, whether undertaken with intent of bringing "special knowledge" to bear more effectively or to deflect attention from common roots, partly did obscure the fact that Chateaubriand's (1873, pp. 676, 680-681) question had come alive again: What happens when people lose faith in religion, or see it as superfluous to life in the new industrial order, but then come face to face with the facts of great and growing inequalities of life conditions, facts previously settled as "natural" or "God's will" and otherwise camouflaged in the paternalist hierarchies of church doctrine and the public good? A distributed model of "self," of "the knowing subject," comes to the fore, with growing emphasis on "feeling" as main source of genuine understanding—or as a recent team of sociologists in the USA called it, "habits of the heart."[388] If as some commentators claimed the solution lay in some sort of recovery of religious belief, US history suggests that claimants have been misfiring, and one is left unsure what would count as recovery. There have been at least three, some say four, editions of "Great Awakening" in the USA. The first, occurring during the 1730s and 1740s, led not to monarchy or other hieratic principle of authority but to a republic built of a version of the self-legislating citizen (i.e., of a few citizens). The second, 1800 to 1840, was followed by Civil War over the issue of slavery. The third, post-Civil War to about 1900, was mainly a resurgence of conservative religious doctrine and, in the southern states, resentment against federation and a resumption of local authority in favor of racist preservation of an exploited pool of captive labor. If any of those movements achieved an amelioration of inequalities of condition or consequence, the very people who were the most likely movement beneficiaries saw virtually none other than eye-of-the-needle homiletics (e.g., Gospel according to Luke, 18.18-30).

As late as the 1600s it had been relatively easy to pass off inequalities as part of the natural order, with or without (but usually with) divine authority. Either explanation made it not just difficult, but usually unthinkable, to disagree. Given that the conjunction of industrialism and capitalism generated such glaring and rapid increases in inequalities among inhabitants of

---

[388] Robert N Bellah, Richard Madsen, William M Sullivan, Ann Swidler, and Steven M Tipton (1985). And think of Ajax' story (as told by Sophocles, in addition to the Homeric storytellers) of the dialectic of justice/injustice: one of the prototypical heroic warriors, counted as perhaps the most effective offensive warrior against Troy yet gained no acclimation of "aristeia" or laurels of excellence (more below; and see Woodruff 2011; Heath 2005, pp. 268-269).

many rapidly expanding cities, with large fractions of those inhabitants being recent arrivals from the country in search of the better lives they had learned to imagine, it became far more difficult for beneficiaries of inequalities of distribution, exchange, and consumption to evade responsibilities for their own life circumstances and, if only by default, responsibilities for the concentrated masses of destitute city dwellers. What was new about this scene was actually not the extent of inequality, which had been as great or greater in many agrarian societies. In agrarian Britain, for instance, very nearly all productive land—and land was then the main "natural resource" of production, not counting of course the peasants needed to work it—was held by a few dozen families of the aristocracy and landed gentry, an extreme level of inequality that persisted even as "the new middle classes" (i.e., the bourgeoisie) were gaining wealth and power in London. What *was* new about the facts of inequality as years of the nineteenth century passed was the increasing exposures of accumulated wealth and power held by a few, cheek to jowl with teeming numbers of impoverished men, women, and children in the cities—a poverty that, taken in isolation, was usually not worse than had been experienced by landless peasants, except that it now existed in great concentrations of bodies in squalid quarters packed along filthy streets, running cesspools of diseased, dead, and rotting animal bodies. The stenches of poverty could not be camouflaged by distances of space and time in the cities, as they had been (and still were) in the countryside. If anyone was in danger of forgetting the brewing mess of inequality's products in Europe's major cities, Charles Dickens, Victor Hugo, and a host of other writers were on hand to remind and unsettle consciences. The very idea of a "social ethics," separate from religious belief, was becoming more salient.

A century before Hugo, Rousseau had famously declared that one could still perceive the difference between inequalities established by nature and those which human beings establish among themselves. But there was a subtle shift in locution of that difference:

> I conceive that there are two kinds of inequality among the human species; one, which I call natural or physical, because it is established by nature, and consists in a difference of age, health, bodily strength, and the qualities of the mind or of the soul: and another, which may be called moral or political inequality, because it depends on a kind of convention, and is established, or at least authorised by the consent of men. This latter consists of the different privileges, which some men enjoy to the prejudice of others; such as that of being more rich, more honoured, more powerful or even in a position to exact obedience (Rousseau 1984 [1755], p. 39, also p. 57).

Inequalities by nature were specified in terms of the individual person's physical characteristics, plus unspecified "qualities of the mind, or of the soul." Note that nothing was said of parentage or familial heritage or social honor or station in life, nothing that would signify a natural basis of inequality by inheritance of fortune or nobility. By contrast, the other kind of inequality was said to be a function of agreements among people, agreements either freely made by common consent or "at least authorized" by unspecified authorities, the unstated implication being that this second avenue was inferior. Also available by implication, a statement of potential: that which has been established by convention could be changed by convention.

The implication of convention could have reminded nineteenth-century readers of Kant's steady emphasis on human being as self-legislating being. But any such reminder escaped most readers, no doubt including most budding social-science readers, who got their understanding of Kant either through some of his self-styled epigone or via other secondary accounts. Memories of Kant's critique of critique had become confined to one or another academy of philosophy, which struggled to compete with the new natural sciences for careful consideration and, where not so confined, had become subordinated to concerns about authority of voice regarding matters of human affairs. Moreover, the so-called Copernican revolution of Kant's casting of "the knowing subject," giving issues of epistemology pride of place, had been subordinated to means of "proper method," scientific method, or observation and reasoning. For the idea of a science of society, this had by the end of the nineteenth century developed into a "conflict about methods," as previously mentioned, and in conflictive discourse awareness of the problem of voice was now acute. Some of the more famous of quotations from Max Weber's writings told of emotive as well as cognitive dimensions of that discourse, Weber's own frustrations sometimes highly exposed.

Weber's evident impatience with certain practices by his colleagues, in particular "the current fashion according to which every first work must be embellished with epistemological investigations" (Weber 1975 [1905-06], p. 187n), could be read as evidence of his conviction that issues of epistemology had been settled. In at least one respect that would be an accurate reading. On some basic issues Weber believed that he had struck positions around which his colleagues should coalesce; yet they had not done so, or not well enough to suit him. Probably the most important of these, in his mind, was his position regarding the proper place of values in the conduct of social-science inquiry, a position that was (and continues to be) described as "value neutrality" (and "ethical neutrality"). In his assessment of a discussion of value judgment held under auspices of a committee of the Association for Social Policy, Weber (1964 [1913], p. 139) issued one of his famous lines about the prevalence of "something like a methodological pestilence" within the discipline. Because his view was rejected, he withdrew from Association activities and joined as founding member a new German Sociological Society. But this group, too, could not agree completely to Weber's view.

One can also read Weber's objections to "the current fashion" and to the "pestilence" as indicative of frustration that so many colleagues felt the need to discourse on difficult issues that they simply did not understand (i.e., issues of epistemology strictly speaking) and that their time would be better spent in building funds of research about issues that they did understand, or on which they had at least better understanding. It did seem to Weber that far too many scholars were being self-indulgent and contributing to a "perpetual flux," while important national issues of one or another part of "the social question" were being neglected. The change in temper that is evident between his 1905-06 essay on Knies and his 1913 manuscript on the committee discussion no doubt manifested Weber's growing dismay that Germany's new king, Wilhelm II, had graduated from the condition of inept petulance, first to bellicose bombast and then, due to his infamous performance during interview by London's *Daily Telegraph* in 1908, to a general laughingstock.[389]

My own view is, however, that Weber *had* understood the major dilemma bequeathed by Kant and knew from that gap how precarious the claim of respectable authority for social science would be. This would be all the more troublesome for the kind of social science that Weber pursued, since he rejected both the fatuous simplicity of a positivistic approach—and positivism as philosophy had become very influential because of the prestige of Avenarius and Mach—and the obfuscations of an approach of empathetic intuition and related mysticisms. (The parallels in that regard to Kant's own navigational beacons is notable.) Weber found the central claim of positivism to be literally absurd, *both* because the claimants had not actually proceeded as they professed *and* because, in that self-delusion, they had deliberately ignored the greater part of the phenomena of human reality, the "irrational reality" that had become endemic to modern society, along with the nonrational phenomena of magical and quasi-magical thinking, all of which constituted a huge reservoir of novelty and innovation (see, e.g., Weber [1949 [1904], p. 6n). By contrast, Weber aimed to build a discipline of inquiry that would incorporate elements of the traditional, the habitual, and the mechanical with elements of the calculative, the improbable, and the value-directed, all oriented relative to his central theoretical interest, subjectively meaningful activities of actors in sociocultural context. The double register of interpretation, crucial to his self-understanding, was one of the preparatory lessons he tried to convey. It was in this double register that Weber sought to unite "self" as agency of the individual scholar, himself included, and "self" as agency of the subjectively meaningful activities of actors in their everyday contexts of sociality (i.e., social action), along with their merely habitual activities.

At the turn of the twentieth century a rather strong tendency to the "thin and shallow" in characterizations of selfhood prevailed among social scientists (a tendency that has continued, with some exceptions, to the present day). It was as if abstraction had been taken to an extreme; and yet one suspects that the tendency had been present already at the starting point of inquiry, before any effort of abstraction had begun—in part because abstraction had *already* occurred and was present in initial assumptions of inquiry. It is easy to apply that description to Weber, along with many others, mainly because of silence. In his programmatic statement for the journal, *Archiv für Sozialwissenschaft und Sozialpolitik* (Weber 1949 [1904]) conceptualization of self, selfhood, self-identity, and the like, is scarcely evident; and yet the central theme of the article has to do with the importance of clarity in matters of meaning: meaningfulness as a phenomenon

---

[389] Bismarckian programs of public policy were invented as partial solutions in Germany already by 1890 (at which date Wilhelm II dismissed Otto von Bismarck from chancellorship). In the UK movement to programs of palliation was slower to appear (not until the four-fold program of 1948) and in the USA slower still, excepting reforms during Franklin Roosevelt's first and second administration.

of the object of inquiry as well as of the inquirer, and the importance of keeping those registers distinct. In his essay on the late nineteenth-century economist, Karl Knies, and the problem of irrationality, he made a point of clarification (with reference to Hans Münsterberg's text on the basics of psychology) that "interpretation" in his sense "is a thoroughly secondary category, indigenous to the artificial world of science" (Weber 1975 [1905-06], p. 153).[390] But for Weber those second-order interpretations are, or should be, of the first-order interpretations, the meanings, of everyday actors (the object of inquiry).[391] But in the 1904 *Archiv* article Weber offered nothing in the way of a concept formation of "self" (or "person"), although he did refer to "self-realization" and "self-deception" in passing. Only in a "methodology" paper written at the same time as his study of the Protestant ethic did he have more to say—namely, that through first-order interpretative activity one can "develop his own self intellectually, aesthetically, and ethically (in the widest sense) in a differentiated way" (Weber 1949 [1905], p. 144).

The sketchiness of social-science conceptions of "self" was perhaps partly a reflection of wariness about engaging with psychology. In Weber's case we just saw a disciplinary statement in support of that wariness. Then as now, an ambivalence has characterized the relation between the social sciences and psychology, especially as the latter claimed foundation in physiology and biology. On the one hand, insofar as the social sciences have intended a priority of sociality (and that has been far from agreed within),[392] they have been cautious about avoiding a dependence. On the other hand, they also have tended to rely on a kind of anchorage in "the natural" by using "individual" as an undeveloped, almost nonconceptual primitive term. And thus we have a line to the odd spectacle today of seeing critics, especially critics with a notable theoretical bent, expressing impatience with "so much attention" to topics of *self*. The preference being implicitly evidenced is that "self" should be left out of the story, the better to deflect attention from the presence of the storyteller *in* the story. One would rather be the faceless narrator who knows the entire script but can make it seem to unfold of its own natural "inner logic."

The sketchiness partly reflected also an invocation of a rather simple rationalist model, a primarily instrumentalist rationalism that reflected the inquirer's own self-conception (however inaccurate it may have been). In recent decades instrumentalism has become an unfavored "perspective," almost on a par with "positivism," and the same negative paintbrush has tinted reception of Weber (along with others). It seems to me, however, that an instrumentalist

---

[390] In Weber's German, "'Deutung' ist eine durchaus sekundäre, in der künstlichen Welt der Wissenschaft heimische Kategorie." I prefer "domestic" or even "homely" to "indigenous" as correspondent to "heimische," in order to avoid suggestion of difference to the point of uniqueness.
[391] Münsterberg (1913, p. 27), on the other hand, offered interpretations as basis for (e.g.) the "selection of those personalities which by their mental qualities are especially fit for a particular kind of economic work," never assessing directly the relevant meanings or interpretations made by the "personalities" in question.
[392] For example, Bellah et al. (1985, p. 143) attributed to "the Lockean position" the assumption that the "individual is prior to society," and they derived from that position what they distinguished as two forms of individualism, the utilitarian and the expressivist.

rationalism is present in nearly all human mentalities, beginning at least as early as a suckling infant demanding supply of gratification and a mother or surrogate who (one hopes) engages in a careful and subtle negotiation to teach scheduling, predictability, reciprocity, and related lessons of sociality without rejecting the infant's developing experience of self-agency. The evident preference to avoid effective address of the dilemma left to us by Kant's demonstration of the limits of knowledge has also been involved, however, serving as a general avoidance mechanism that flatters by assuming too much of a basic model of rationalism. After all, if one can insinuate to one's audience that one considers most people to be highly rational in judgment, decision making, and the like, so much the better for one's own authority of voice. An indication of the effect of that design can be seen in the assumption that rationality is categorial, its opposite being "irrationality." As Weber (among others) noted, rationality at least of the instrumentalist kind varies on a quantitative gradient from maximally rational to maximally irrational. (The opposite of "rational" is its absence, the "nonrational," as in mythical, magical, or religious belief.) And to make the concept still more complex, the quantitative gradient is itself a matter of context and conditions.

The following passage from the end of Weber's 1904 programmatic statement for the *Archiv* makes a number of important statements relevant to the present discussion.[393]

In the empirical social sciences, as we have seen, the possibility of meaningful knowledge of what is essential for us in the infinite richness of events is bound up with the unremitting application of viewpoints of a specifically particularized character, which, in the last analysis, are oriented on the basis of value-ideas. These value-ideas are for their part empirically discoverable and analyzable as elements of meaningful human conduct, but their validity cannot be deduced from empirical data as such. The "objectivity" of the social sciences depends rather on the fact that the empirical data are always related to those value-ideas which alone make them worth knowing and the significance of the empirical data is derived from these value-ideas. But these data can never become the foundation for the empirically impossible proof of the validity of the value-ideas. The belief which we all have in some form or other, in the meta-empirical validity of ultimate and final values, in which the meaning of our existence is rooted, is not incompatible with the incessant changefulness of the concrete viewpoints, from which empirical reality gets its significance. Both of these views are, on the contrary, in harmony with each other. Life with its irrational reality and its store of possible meanings is inexhaustible. The concrete form in which value-relationship occurs remains perpetually in flux, ever subject to change in the dimly seen future of human

---

[393] This is the Shils-Finch translation, which in general I find unexceptional. I will emphasize, however, that Weber usually wrote (in the body of the article, though not in the title; nor of course in the name of the journal) about the "cultural sciences" (as in the initial sentence of the above quotation: "Auf dem Gebiet der empirischen sozialen Kulturwissenschaften …" or "In the area of the empirical social Cultural sciences …"). This was surely his way of stressing that at least *his* interest lay with socio-cultural meaningfulness as topic, as observed object.

culture. The light which emanates from those highest value-ideas always falls on an ever changing finite segment of the vast chaotic stream of events, which flows away through time (Weber 1949 [1904], p. 111).

Note first of all that at the beginning of the passage and then again at its end we see evidence of Weber's concern to "thread the needle," so to speak, on the one hand emphasizing that the intended object of inquiry is meaningful conduct, and the "meaningfulness" is always contingent on "value-ideas," culturally and historically specific, while on the other hand not denying that such contingency applies as well to the socio-cultural scientist, and that empirical evidences gained by the scientist do not address the "inherent" validity of the value-ideas, and yet the scientist can justifiably claim an objectivity of evidence based on faithfulness of that evidence to the meaningfulness manifest in and by the object of inquiry.[394] As is well-known, Weber was generally critical of "system," because system-builders are guided more by a logic of their system than by meanings manifested by the objects of inquiry of whom the system is supposedly explanatory. This does not mean that Weber was therefore "unsystematic" in his own logic of inquiry, the central focus of which was always intended to be what he sometimes called "subjectively meaningful" conduct. An assumption of rationality was part of that focus. No doubt it was also part of his intent in referring to "the meta-empirical validity of ultimate and final values, in which the meaning of our existence is rooted"—at least in the sense that "knowledge is better than ignorance," "life-giving ends are better than death-giving ends," "effective means are better than ineffective means," and so forth. It is notable that he made no effort to explain or justify his notion of "objectivity" relative to that which had been taken for granted of the Naturwissenschaften. Indeed, he usually emphasized the distinction.

Finally, with regard to the quantitative dimension of rationality, not only is the quality contingent in principle, so too is the gradient. Much like Plato's pharmakon, wherein one person's lethal potion is another's curative, "the rational" under some circumstances can be "the irrational" under others. That which is "irrational" is a store of possibilities, some of which may later be welcome as actualities, however improbable they might have appeared at the time (or later to the theorist). Like the deft negotiations of different meanings of "validity" which we saw just above, this latter part of Weber's programmatic statement—history as a fount of change even in the meanings of what counts as "rational" (in second-order as well as first-order interpretation)—smacked too much of "relativism" to some of his later readers, a criticism that Weber had anticipated.

Weber was of course not the only major figure among early twentieth-century social scientists to attempt to establish an authority of voice, personally and for a specific discipline. I

---

[394] Was Weber aware of the sleight of hand? Probably. The subtlety of his discussion (here and elsewhere) suggests that he was aware of the limits as Kant had described them and was trying to constitute as much of a "generalizing science" as possible within those limits, making a virtue of the double presence of "meaningfulness," "empirical," and "interpretation" as unavoidably contingent qualities.

will not attempt a representative survey, either by nationality or by approach or particular brand or discipline of social science. Nothing will be said of Herbert Spencer or of Leonard Hobhouse, for instance, or of Gaetano Mosca or of Vilfredo Pareto, and so forth. I will refer instead to only three cases in addition to Weber, one of them briefly.

Émile Durkheim, senior to Weber by six years, was probably as sensitive to "the Social Question" as Weber, although mainly in French rather than German context. Named by Bellah and his associates (1985) as an early exemplar only in passing, Durkheim was convinced at least as much as they that most, perhaps nearly all, of the trouble of modern society could be traced to a "cult of individualism." His principal focus was on what he considered to be a generalizing breakdown of integrative functions in modern society—leaving in place of the erstwhile results of those functions a growing chasm between the individual person (or household) and the state— and on means of staunching that erosion and repairing the fabric of society. Both parts, the diagnostic and the reparative, were approached in terms of institutional orders that had been, and perhaps could again be, the loci of integration: most especially, the organization of labor, the educational institutions, and finally the rituals of religion. To that extent Durkheim was sensitive to matters of organizational scale. But as Wagner (1964) pointed out, the manner in which he insisted on the integrity of "social facts" vis-à-vis the claims of psychology on "self" and related topics, combined with his uncritical adoption of a "homo duplex" thesis, which aligned "the natural part" with a psychobiological individual being, meant that matters of scale for Durkheim did not extend in any interesting way to the individual level except in terms of pressures and constraints by macro-level forces on the individual. And in his eyes, the "cult of individualism" had been complicit in weakening or even erasing institutional mediations. Apparently lacking comfort with questions of a dialectical unity of opposites, the analytical analogue, questions of the basis on which the homo duplex thesis would have made sense, did not occur to him. The nearest he came to tackling such issues was in his effort to conceptualize the "conscience collective," relative to an individual mindfulness, a "common consciousness" that is at once "with knowledge" and "with moral order."[395]

This "conscience collective" is, Durkheim (1984 [1902], pp. 38-39) said, "the totality of beliefs and sentiments common to the average citizens of the same society." By focusing this "totality" on "the average citizens" he surely intended a conception of variation in the "beliefs and sentiments" of the members of a society, a notion that comports well with his oft-cited discussion of "deviant behavior" as a repository of potentials that perform specific functions within and for the moral order of a given society. The implied gradient is not the same as the gradient of rationality, as described above, but the functional logic of it to Durkheim's theoretical

---

[395] Some scholars have recently opposed any reminder that "conscience" (in French) referred not only to knowledge in general but also to "moral order," spurning the latter lest Durkheim be accused of ethnocentrism, treating the moral order of one culture as indicative of all. That Durkheim was ethnocentric is beyond doubt, as it is for all of us who experience through our native language(s) which is (are) integral to world(s). That Durkheim was aware of that fact and sought to "overcome" it is also doubtlessly true, as it is for many of us.

perspective is similar, in that it accords a quantitative dimensionality to the conscious contents of individual persons. Durkheim also said, in the same passage, that the conscience collective is "something totally different from the consciousness of individuals, although it is only realized in individuals." A number of implications can be drawn from that. One is that he had in mind a scale-sensitive heterology: quantitative variation on at least some dimension(s) of the contents of consciousness at individual level is translated into modal pattern at the collective level. Put otherwise, if Durkheim was aware of something like a Gaussian distribution—and that cannot be ruled out of hand, for Durkheim had probably heard about, even read about, Carl Gauss' theory of errors—then one could surmise that he understood the modal pattern of "the average citizens" as located in the band of central tendency (i.e., 68 percent of the total variation) of a Gaussian "normal curve" model of individual-level quantitative variation. Indeed, he might have thought that modal pattern in analogy to Hegel's notion of quantitative variation becoming, under certain conditions, a qualitative difference. On the other hand, however, this speculative attribution is contrary to what Durkheim otherwise argued, mostly implicitly, about the direction of the causal arrow. For Durkheim, potency is largely from the macro or meso (i.e., "conscience *collective*") to the micro (individual consciousness). His argument about the functionality of deviance allows a potential to occur in the opposite direction (as do, of course, implicit powers of the theorist's creative thinking, etc.). But the weight of his argument (e.g., regarding deficits of individualism, vulnerabilities of mechanical solidarity, etc.), along with his abandonment of the "individual ego," "self," and the like, to a naturalistic psychology, flows "from top down," as it were. This is reflective of the "evolutionary" threading that runs like a warp on which he weaves his argument: the "organic holism" of traditional cultures is giving way to the "mechanical part-work" of modern cultures, and Durkheim doubts that a Kantian "legislative man" can succeed as well as any edition of the mythic-heroic absolutist "law-giver" of the past. Perhaps he believed species maturity to be impossible.

Before leaving Durkheim, I will note one more of the implications of his remark that the conscience collective, while "totally different" from individual consciousness (a difference tied to his stipulation of "social fact" as a reality in itself, separate from "psychological fact"), "is only realized in individuals." Some contemporaries of Durkheim had been proposing the reality of a "group mind." The presentations were sometimes so fuzzy that a reader could (can) not be confident of intended meaning, and some authors (e.g., McDougall 1927) later either clarified or changed their meanings. The apparent intent of the phrase, "group mind," was at least in part an effort to bridge organizational level and scale from an "atomistic individual" to collective units variously labelled "class," "crowd," and "nation" (among others). This development failed to survive the inherent difficulty of professional disciplinary competitions and suspicions, plus concerns that its relationship with a philosophical movement known as "vitalism" would further jeopardize the disciplines' already precarious standing as "genuine science." One of the most prominent of these scholars, the already cited William McDougall who was then a well-known psychologist previously acclaimed for his text on social psychology (centered on a "hormic psychology"),[396] published in 1920 a work entitled *The Group Mind*, which, as he lamented in preface to the second edition (1927, p. xiii), was either ignored or largely rejected. From his point of view, two sorts of writers had addressed his topic, "those who regard every group as a mere aggregate of the individuals" (i.e., no "value added" by scale) and "those who treat of the State, the Church, and other historical groups, such as the great political parties, as aggregates of the individuals *plus* a mystical and shadowy entity, the spirit of the whole, that hovers uncertainly above the individuals and intervenes only on great occasions" (1927, p. xiii). Referring to the works of those "who expound the psychology of *Gestalt* or *Configuration*," he concurred with the effort to "strike the key note that the whole is more than the sum or aggregate of its parts and that the life of the whole requires for its interpretation laws or principles that cannot be arrived at by the study of the parts alone" (1927, p. xiv). Without mentioning it (probably without noticing it), McDougall had thus hit upon a defining feature of sociology as Durkheim, among others, had conceived it.[397]

Max Weber (1968 [1922], p. 14) argued that "collectivities must be treated as solely the resultants and modes of organization of the particular acts of individual persons." At least "for sociological purposes there is no such thing as a collective personality which 'acts.' When reference is made" to a collectivity such as "a state, a nation," and the like, "what is meant" is nothing more than "a certain kind of development of actual or possible social actions of individual persons." Weber surely would not have disagreed with Mary Carruthers (1990, p. 13) that "Memoria is better considered … as *praxis* rather than as *doxis*," nor would he have disputed Paul Connerton's (1989) point that conventions of agreement/disagreement among members of a given society tend to encourage care in what and how a society's pasts are memorialized, the care sometimes focused especially on negotiations of internal controversies (e.g., remembrances of 1789 in France, of the Civil War in the USA). Sensitive to the demands of a nationalism (and himself no shrinking violet as patriot), the view just quoted from Weber no doubt reflected in part his own worries about the uses to which ideological manipulations can be

---

[396] His term, "hormic" (from the Greek "hormē," or "impulse"), was intended to stress that the core of psychology should be conceived as the purposive goal-seeking behavior of the individual. In his not entirely sympathetic review of the book's first edition George Herbert Mead (1908, p. 386) noted that McDougall had attempted to make psychology more compatible with the social sciences by choosing "act rather than a state of consciousness" as his "ultimate unit" of analysis. McDougall's text reportedly lived through thirty editions (a report I have not verified).

[397] Note that McDougall used the word "aggregate" as designating a compound that contains nothing but its individual components, leaving open the question, then, by what means the compound has any integrity of its own (i.e., the aggregate being nothing more than an arithmetic sum), as if the compound holds together as such by some magical power. Since I have used, and will continue to use, the word "aggregate" in nomination of "aggregation process" in a set of specific applications, I must emphasize that this reductive conception is unnecessary and beside the point. A geological aggregate is a mass of smaller components that have been compacted into a degree of solidity. The construction material known as concrete is an aggregate of materials compacted and bound by cement, itself an aggregate that can act as a binder either through chemical reaction (hydraulic cement) or via dehydration (non-hydraulic cement). Metallic alloys result from a bonding characteristic of the metal or from a heat treatment (annealing) as in steel.

335

put. By the same token, however, he was genuinely skeptical that anything like a notion of "group mind" was of use to social science other than as ideological object to be studied. His own studies of charisma demonstrate that he appreciated the fact and the powers of a "like-mindedness" that sometimes led individual persons into a followership that would become destructive of their own material interests, even of ideal interests that initially seemed aligned with those of the charismatic leader. But he had demonstrated similar outcomes of acts that were quite rational on instrumental or value grounds.

Where was Durkheim on this matter of "group mind"? The phrase repeated above, that a "conscience collective" is "only realized in individuals" (i.e., in individual consciousnesses) suggests that he rejected the notion, even if he avoided agreement with Weber's insistence that the causative arrow can and *does* go also from the micro (i.e., the individual social actor) to macro levels of organization. What Connerton (1989, p. 38) said about ambiguities of locution by Maurice Halbwachs in his discussions of "collective memory" could be applied to Durkheim as well. Not long ago, in fact, there was a partial consensus among some scholars that Durkheim had himself adopted a "group mind" concept, but the phrase was used so loosely that one cannot be sure that "mind" was being attributed to a supra-individual entity or to a modal representation (i.e., as Durkheim explicitly said, to "the average citizens of the same society").

Georg Simmel, nearly exact contemporary of Durkheim (Simmel the elder by one and a half months), entertained similar interests from similar backgrounds (e.g., neo-Kantian thought; both men Jewish in contexts in which acceptance, even tolerance could not comfortably be taken for granted). Like Durkheim, Simmel was concerned to understand the relations involved in the Latin "e pluribus unum": the unitariness of "individual person" conceived in scalar relation to the unitariness of "society," both "society" in general and in its various types. Part of what was distinctive about Simmel's effort was told in the subtitle of his 1908 volume, *Soziologie*, a set of "Investigations about Forms of Sociation." This last phrase, "forms of sociation," has presented an issue of translation, since the German word, "Vergesellschaftung," has no single counterpart in English. It is sometimes translated also as "socialization," which can fit in some contexts. But "socialization" tends to suggest "person learning, adapting to, conforming to, already extant expectations," and this misses the point of "making society" or "producing sociality," which was integral to Simmel's use of the word.[398]

Wagner (1964, p. 573) pointed out that Simmel was the first major figure among early sociologists to pursue explicitly the issue of scale in forms of sociation, and to do so explicitly in quantitative terms. In the first pages of *Soziologie* Simmel addressed "the problem of sociology" (1971 [1908a], p. 24) as to how to understand the welter of interactions among individual persons,

---

[398] The prefix, "Ver," signifies a *processual* noun or verb, part of the distinction of "Vergesellschaftung" (i.e., the *process* of "making society" or of "producing sociality"; likewise, "Selbstvergesellschaftung," or the process of a self-remaking in order better to fit changed conditions *or* to attain greater capability, etc.). The word was not, as has been claimed, Simmel's neologism; Marx used it, as did Weber, among others.

which vary by kind and within kind by degree (duration, intensity, etc.), and within that welter form more or less mutual bonds that endure. "A collection of human beings does not become a society because each of them has an objectively determined or subjectively impelling life-content." But societies do exist, do endure; they also do change, have a history. Societies differ qualitatively and have distinctive histories, but the dimensions of Vergesellschaftung (or sociation, and sociality as its more or less distinctive product) are crucially quantitative, and Simmel pursued those dimensions all the way to "society as such" (as in the second essay of *Soziologie*, in which he asks, "How is society possible?"). The importance of quantitative dimensions can be seen in the different complexities of the smallest groups—for instance, the processes that develop when a dyad expands by exactly one person, to become a triad—demonstrating, as Simmel did, that mere change of number can have profound qualitative consequences. In the third essay of *Soziologie* (1908, pp. 32-100), about "the quantitative determination of the group" in general, Simmel proposed a variety of similar implications—for instance, that "socialist organization" is limited to small scale, primarily because with increasing size (increasing number of members, thus lines of comparison and interaction) the problem of relative deprivation can become sufficiently pronounced to disrupt mutuality and solidarity (cf. Runciman 1966). Likewise, later in the volume (pp. 627-681) he again generalized effects of "expansion of the group," now with particular emphasis on "developments of individuality." In a passage reminiscent of one of Durkheim's central concerns, Simmel drew attention to evacuations of organizational life at meso-level, by citing a comparative case from ancient Greece: "the

> individualism of the Stoics had its complement in cosmopolitanism; the rending of narrower social bonds, which during this period was promoted no less by the political situation than by theoretical contemplation, shifted the center of gravity toward the individual, on the one hand; and on the other, toward the widest circle to which every human belongs simply by virtue of his humanity (Simmel 1971 [1908c], p. 274).

In this application of a principle that is sometimes called "Simmel's ratio" he was referring specifically to the time ("this period") when the Stoics were prominent in ethical theory (i.e., from early third century BCE).[399] His point about evacuation has more general application, of course (readers today surely recognize present applications). One implication of his treatment is that as the "widest circle" of cosmopolitanism (or today's "globalization") becomes "too wide," the marginal effect of quantitative change shifts in quality, from "benign promise" to "malign force," and the bounds of what then counts as "virtue simply by humanity" shrink to narrower compass. Just as it became increasingly noticeable by evidence of present-day societies that nation-state boundaries were weakening, ideologies of nationalism became resurgent in reactions that have sometimes exhibited personal velleities of a tribalism. Christopher Clark (2012) has recounted similar, and stronger, visceral reactions during the early years of the twentieth century.

---

[399] And, it must be said, Simmel was there engaging a bit in a common caricature of Stoicist ethics.

Other Simmelian observations that have maintained more recent resonance include his (1971 [1908c], p. 286) contention that an "individualism" which holds that "the factual reality of human nature is comprised of the uniqueness of individuals' qualities and values, a uniqueness the development and intensification of which are moral imperatives," is objectionable because it "is the denial of every kind of equality." Perhaps Simmel had in mind the doctrine of Bildungsprozess—in particular, that by virtue of individual liberty each person was obligated to strive to develop to the highest degree his or her capabilities. A statement of that notion, published at about the same time by John Erskine (1915), urged a "moral obligation to be intelligent." But Simmel's point was rather different, ostensibly more in keeping with concerns about "meritocracy" as were later expressed by Michael Young (1958; also Lemann 1999; Case and Deaton 2020).

Simmel did ask, "How is society possible?" With only that title in mind, and a cursory familiarity with Simmel as a sociologist of forms who studied what he called "quantitative dimensions" of social order (e.g., dyadic vis-à-vis triadic groups), one could easily anticipate an essay about scale: given the complexities of a group of three relative to a group of two, in turn relative to a single person, how is anything as complex as an entire society, numbering members in the hundreds of thousands, even millions, at all possible? After all, human relations at their best are mostly a tissue of indirection mixed with assumptions large and small arrayed in networks of trust among people who are mostly strangers to one another across large territories. Add to that "best case" image competitions and conflicts of all sorts, many of them propelled by emotional energies of suspicion, deceit, exploitation, and worse, how is society ever possible? There must be some critical factors or processes that serve to "translate across scale," such that what can be usually manageable at the level of, say, a family household can also be a social order manageable at the scale of an entire society. "Perhaps," one imagines, "Simmel has investigated, lessons to teach."

As the previous illustrations testify, Simmel did have lessons to teach, but an explanation of "scale transitions" was not one of them. In addition to astute observations of "quantitative dimensions," processes of exchange and consumption, generative factors of conflict, and what would later be described as "small group processes," Simmel's study of European history was extensive enough that he surely understood that, and how, mimetic processes had generalized into all relations of production since the 1600s, using theatrical arts, for example, as venue for experimentations in social relations. It was the bourgeoisie of Europe who re-invented theatre on a scale and with a complexity that rivaled and then exceeded what the ancient Greeks had accomplished. Indeed, as Gebauer and Wulf (1995 [1992], p. 312) put it, "The bourgeoisie's claim to the leading role in society is manifest in its culture of taste and emotion, which not only exemplifies but is simultaneously one of the constituent elements of power" (cf. Bourdieu 1984 [1979]). Nonetheless, one ends a re-reading of Simmel's voluminous writing with evidence that he had never actually engaged in explanation of processes by which scale transitions occur. Not that he was unique in that regard.

Simmel's chief puzzle was not scale effects in aggregation (Zusammenfassung), although he did give passing notice to it (e.g., in his essay on "The self-preservation of groups," the eighth chapter of *Soziologie*, at pp. 377-378).[400] His chief puzzle, rather, was how "a collection of human beings" does "become a society" (Simmel 1908a, p. 24). His essay on group self-preservation (Selbsterhaltung), partly reminiscent of the itinerary of Durkheim's inquiries, is a halting search for answers, as he considers various forms of Vergesellschaftung (forms of sociation or "society making") at meso-levels of organizational hierarchy, especially institutionalized formations such as church, army, party, and so forth. Simmel was too astute not to be aware that each of those formations—creating a new political party, for example, or a new fraternal organization—always takes place within an already existing form of sociation at macro level, the society of which the creative individuals are members. Simmel's conundrum resulted from his own insistent conception of the foundation or basis of all forms of sociation: the individual human being. Although he was at times explicitly skeptical of received traditions of psychologism, he nonetheless shared something of that perspective, even as he also rejected various mysticisms that attended some of those traditions. He needed a starting point for his analyses, one that could to some degree serve as a constancy against and on which the logic of his analytical operations could be maintained in consistency. This starting point was "the human being" as a punctual presence with stable bounds. The individual human being had priority over "society"; all derivative forms of sociation logically began with this tightly bound human being. This position—which, it is clear from several passages of Simmel's writings, was formed from his own experiences of deliberate thought—is comparable to declaring that because theory (e.g., bioevolutionary theory) tells us that some of Homo sapiens' direct ancestors lacked the organic capacity of language, we must conceptualize the logical integrity of what is essentially Homo sapiens, human being, as it existed prior to language. Of course, there have indeed been thinkers who believed more or less exactly that proposition, whose arguments presuppose a pre-linguistic "human nature," a pre-cultural "human nature," and so forth, as previously discussed several times (above, and see, e.g., Hazelrigg 1992, 1993a, 1993b, and 1995).

### §23. Boundaries of I

"What kinds of subject were being formed by this new amalgam of philosophy and rhetoric, the 'beautiful sciences'?" This question was raised by Howard Caygill as part of his consideration of the large part played by Alexander Gottlieb Baumgarten leading into the Bildung movement during the late years of the eighteenth century in Germany. It was Baumgarten's "philosophical rephrasing of the doctrine of invention," Caygill (2016, p. 10) pointed out, a rephrasing away from "the finding or discovery of the materials of a discourse (or thought)" and toward "one of

---

[400] This chapter has not yet been translated completely (so far as I recall). Albion Small offered a rough translation of the first part of the essay, in the *American Journal of Sociology*, volume 3, in 1898, but I do not think it adequate. As founding editor of that journal, Small had the task of building audience, which depended on publication of papers that would attract attention. Early in his tenure he selected works by Simmel, many of them to appear in his *Soziologie*. Nearly thirty years later Small lamented that the articles by Simmel had attracted so little notice, and by his measure even less often (countable "on the fingers of one hand") any serious engagement (Small 1925, p. 84).

creativity," that should count as the centerpiece of his major contribution. This reformation shifted the attitude of the Cartesian cogito, the attitude of subjectivity, from passivity to activity. It would thereafter be "not so much a matter of finding given materials for a discourse as of creating what precisely was not already there."

When, during the subsequent two centuries, Kant was remembered more than in passing, probably the most malign response to him and his legacy centered on the verdict that it was he who turned "rightful order" upside down by bringing subjectivity to the fore as the principle of a pure functionality of the "I" ("Ich"), the knowing subject. In retrospect it might seem obvious that the knowing subject was always already there, albeit in faceless, occulted form. But that sense of obviousness would be mistaken: there was indeed a time when "the object" had regal priority, as celebrated in the priority of ontology as first philosophy, theology at the ready with images of eternal damnation. Indeed, several scholars have in recent years written as if they remembered that earlier time as a kind of prelapsarian era (see, e.g., Dreyfus and Kelly 2011; Taylor 1989).

The verdict about Kant is not so much mistaken as far too heroic in its imagery. Before Kant, scholars such as Baumgarten had already urged a new understanding of the subject/object dialectic (even if they did so mainly in analytical terms), and that understanding entailed a host of new positions in discourse, thus in political language.[401] Caygill answered his own question by indexing a number of institutionalized roles, taking his cue partly from "the changing place of the lower faculty of philosophy within the German university, during the second half of the eighteenth century." This was explicitly a matter of reforming institutions of higher education in Germany, in conjunction with "the transformation of the 'beautiful sciences'" (i.e., the amalgam of rhetoric and philosophy in an aesthetics of cultivation) "into the concept of Bildung." But one must not be blinded by the aesthetic of "the beautiful sciences" and lose sight of the practical and pragmatic: the new university, reformed and re-oriented, was still an institutionalized form, and its consequences as cultivated persons would occupy positions in an institutionalized order, just as had been true of the "free professions" and "seven liberal arts" of medieval universities. "The new subjectivity interested in and emerging from the new lower faculty was no longer preparing for the study and a career in law, medicine or the church," however. This new principle of subjectivity, in its several versions, "was trained to contribute to the emerging public sphere of commercial civil society and expanding provincial and state bureaucracies, which called for 'cultured' individuals who would not necessarily become professional specialists" (Caygill 2016, p. 10; cf. McClelland 1980).

Kant's project was informed by a kindred spirit. It was not this spirit that developed into the anathema of Kantian critical theory. Rather, it was the open-ended dilemma that chilled the most careful readers of Kant's three volumes, the failure to render an authority of voice that would be fully transcendental and therefore absolute—an authority that would be, like Newton's

---

[401] One is here reminded of Sewell's (1994, p. 204) observation when, referring to the Abbé Sieyès' uses of rhetoric in service to the bourgeois revolution, he stressed "the simultaneous power and uncontrollability of all inventive political language." This could be said of any inventive uses of rhetorical skill, of course, whether of a "political language" or some other. But then, what language is not about power and disputative relations?

laws were thought to be, outside time, once and for all. And those careful readers, usually confused about what the "transcendental Illusion" must "really mean," fretted most openly about the fact that no one seemed to be able to refute Humean skepticism. It was Hume who had robbed any claim to certitude—of knowledge and thus of authority—of the necessary stability, the necessary rock-solid anchorage, in a that which *is*, *must be*, independent of human being. Kant's accomplishment could be seen in context of a much older ancestry than Hume or Baumgarten; for some scholars had realized that the ancient Greeks became masters in the arts of cultivating self-doubt as a productive experience (Buxton 1994, pp. 32-34). Those who were convinced that the Kantian revolution was wrong-headed, and even those who, as with Husserl (1970 [1936], §§23-24; see Part One, §5, above), found Humean skepticism to be disastrous, could seek solace in the absolutist convictions of Plato or even in the more measured convictions of Aristotle. For those Greeks who struck stances of skepticism were either *very* ancient (i.e., pre-Socratic) or collected under the opprobrium of "the Sophists" (i.e., those who are "tricky with language").[402]

The Greek ancestry was (is) nonetheless real and important.

What is special about the Greeks is the degree to which they investigated themselves. They took the Other and held it up to constant scrutiny. They sang about it, they analyzed it, and even staged it in publicly funded religious festivals. The Greeks had an overwhelming interest in learning more about who they were not, at least in part so they could better understand what made them who they were. In our attempts to understand Greek thought, we should not forget that this process of self-scrutiny created the blueprint for the societal change that has brought about so much amelioration of past injustices. The conversation the Greeks had about themselves helped to produce the *concept* of freedom, as well as the world's most creative and influential examinations of good and evil, an ethical language. If we want to understand the Greeks, our energy may be better spent exploring what is special to them rather than what universal human weaknesses and perversities they exhibit. As Edelstein wrote about Xenophanes, in his age "only a Greek could have discovered and maintained that man is by nature self-reliant and progressive. Outside Greece, the doctrine was unknown, as was the experience in which it was based" (Heath 2005, pp. 21-22; Edelstein 1967, pp. 16-17).

That sort of self-regard, collective as well as individual, is not at all unusual today, and I am not as confident as Edelstein of the judgment that "the doctrine" was known only to the Greeks of the time of Xenophanes of Colophon, Ionia (c570-c475 BCE). Such bold claims in the face of such haphazard survival of documents, as well as undeclared expertise of so many other cultures of the time, is cause for caution (see Bachvarova 2016). In any case, however, the evidence that by the time of Xenophanes that characterization was established in at least some circles of Greek self-regard ("self-reliant and progressive by nature") is sound enough.

---

[402] Protagoras, first of the sophists of the time of Pericles and held in high regard by Pericles and others, stimulated an attitude of skeptical inquiry, followed by others. But of all the works of the fifth-century sophists we have only fragments, not even a total of twenty pages, and most of what we otherwise know of their works was filtered through the lens of Plato and his strong (but mostly explicit) bias against them. Skepticism then, too, rankled those who saw themselves as defenders of rightful order.

Poets then as now could exercise greater latitude, albeit generally under institutionalized conditions. An apparently popular instance was a collaborative contest in which one poet (and remember, these were usually singing poets, the rhythmic meter serving mnemonically) would sing a couple of new lines, and his competitor would then reply with two in continuation of the thematic content, although perhaps with an embedded novelty or challenge. A fragment from a contest between Homer (or a Homeric disciple) and Hesiod, still often recited, is of interest here because of a verbal construction:[403] "en nearois humnois rhapsantes aoidēn" (the last word refers to "bards" who "stitched together a song in new hymns"). The "stitching" is of interest, in that it suggested a practice that we call "improvisation"; and the point of that is of special interest because the practice is of a *collective* subject—two musicians who maintain distinction while melding that distinction into a single identity of musical composition *and* composer. Musically this amounts to a first-person *plural* expression that acknowledges an ancestry in others (think of jazz, rap, etc.).

Why is that piece of grammar of special interest? As will be seen shortly, it has to do with the boundedness of the first-person singular pronoun, nominative case, which, unlike its plural counterpart, is simultaneously a noun: "I." One should bear in mind that in the standard discourse of subject/object relations much attention is devoted to this abstraction, not only the first-person singular nominative pronoun (usually in priority over first-person plural nominative pronoun) but also with a conceptualization of "self" or "self-identity of personhood" (or some corresponding notion) that carries that same abstracted character as the pure functionality of "I" (or Kant's "Ich"). By contrast, note that Caygill's answer to his question indexed not those abstractions but the less abstracted "kinds" of subjects as institutionalized roles or positions, which are inherently social. Sociality means that "I" inherently refers to an otherness that is both quantitative and qualitative—that is, present in number and in kind. An "I" recognizes an other as also an "I" and most especially when engaged in second-person relation but also and through a very different reflexivity when generalizing in third-person contemplation of a "pluribus" as a "unum" (i.e., "e pluribus unum"): a perspective shift by and from "sufficient" quantity via an effect of scale to a different *kind* of interlocutor. This is the "they" as a formation of sociality that seems, at least at times or under specific conditions, to "speak" as if of a single, unified authority of voice. Ancient Greek playwrights and biographers, beginning as early as the fifth century BCE, treated the choral voice (i.e., the poetic-theatrical chorus) as simultaneously voice of "the community" and surrogate of the poet, giving the poet's individual voice an expressivity of first-person plural, whether it be the collectivity of an ethical community of mortals, or of the Muses, or of a more abstracted agency of a god or gods, who have purportedly been "working through" the poet (see, e.g., Lefkowitz 2012). The voices of mythic agents could be of past or of future time, in either case a representation of a collectivity typically with pointed individual focus, as when the Muses withdraw from a creative actor (including even the speaking poet in a reflexive conditional or counterfactual). All of this can seem strange to a present-day theatre-goer. But that sense of strangeness is *anticipation* of the strange—because this *is*, after all, theatre. It is an experience that ethnographic scholars often encounter.

---

[403] The fragment has a long history, which is not germane here; but see, e.g., Lefkowitz (2012, p. 16; Bachvarova 2016, p. 414).

One must beware one's first-person tendency to think that "self" is usually (or even universally) what one personally knows as first-person experience. The necessity of conceptual scheme is crucial to this tendency, for "self" is regarded as a kind of "thing" or "property" that every human being *has*; and while we imagine a difference between the "form" of the thing that every human being has and the "content" of that thing, and allow the latter to be variable from one cultural place to another and from one historical time to another, the "form" of the thing is usually considered to be far less culturally and historically specific, even tending toward the universal. The same can be said of closely related "things" or "properties" of every human being, such as "mind" and "cognition" and "emotion" and "thought." It is all too easy to forget that each of those concepts *is* cultural and historical, because we have this almost visceral sense of a disturbing instability of literally everything that we take for granted in our claims of knowledge—indeed, even more deeply than that: in our assumptions of what we already safely and securely know. This is the sort of spectre of "radical skepticism" and "radical relativism" to which one can so easily rush in nomination of the culprit behind an experience of threat. It is, no doubt, a red herring: the road of regress induces fatigue rather quickly, and we literally *cannot* doubt everything all at once. (*That* was the basic, and enduring, lesson of Descartes' reported project of radical doubt.) Because "self" is an ensemble of social relations, shared knowledge—beginning with some version of a "sensus communis" or the somewhat different concept of "aisthēsis koine" of the ancient Greeks (see Vico 1990 [1708-09])—is inherent to a self-identity even when that formation loses sight of the reflexivity in which it is anchored and imagines that first-person experience is always a "beginning of the world" all over again (see, e.g., Zerubavel 2018). The generalized other, as Mead saw it, remains integral to what an "I" experiences, and the integration can be strong enough that first-person perspective looks out in periscopic wonder at all that "I have newly discovered." The boundary condition of "I" versus "not-I" inescapably includes memory of past differentiation, and in any given moment of presence, of one's self-presentation, that memory, to the extent that it is invoked, must seem "simply there," as Hume pointed out. For where otherwise would one be in any reflexive awareness? Thus, the kind of theoretical distinction that Wrong (1961, 1994) pursued as an "over-socialized" condition is extremely difficult to determine "from inside," which therefore always leaves anyone making a second- or third-person of the condition at risk of imposition.

The boundedness of "I" inherently forms within a dialectical unity of opposites, these being "I" and "not-I" (remember Shakespeare, Cervantes, Tang). While the dialectical relation of internal/external therefore informs criteria and conditions of that boundedness, the strong tendency toward analytical relations, with emphasis on exclusion of any "undivided middle," reframes the dialectical formation into a formation that appears to offer, by presupposing, a choice in the distribution of conditions, criteria, even perspective and thus focal point—internal *or* external—and this choice has in effect a history, which is in part a history of migratory attention. Kant rewrote that history up to his day and, in the process, changed conditions of its subsequent history. But because his "categories of the understanding" (the building blocks, so to speak, of his conceptual scheme, and mostly ours as well), lend themselves so easily to "the analytic" as prior condition of any (nondogmatic) inquiry, the subsequent history has actually consisted in circulations between the "either-or" poles. The boundedness of "I" has followed

343

those circulations, hardly ever diverging far from prior focal attention to either the "interiority" of "I" or the "exteriority" of "not-I." The very idea of "internal relationality" being anathema to the dominant perspective (i.e., analytics), the question of boundary has remained central to other conceptualizations. As we saw via illustrations in the prior section of this Part Four, disciplines otherwise as diverse as demography and immunology have devoted considerable energy toward "getting the boundary right." Therein lie great stores of power.

Claude Fischer (1982) addressed one feature of boundary movements long before it rose to recent prominence as a result of Putnam's (2000) reprisal of Durkheimian concerns about anomie and related problems of order (i.e., Putnam's "bowling alone" hypothesis). In Fischer's (1982, p. 2) words, "Individuals' bonds to one another are the essence of society." The glue or cohesive, "bonding," in that view has remained a source of anxiety since long before Durkheim's day, and concerns about commodification of personal relationships and other effects associated with emphases on utilitarian and commercial instrumentalism had added to the weight of evidence (which can be read in opposing ways, of course). After Robin Dunbar published results of his studies of the size and structure of network ties among individual persons, which indicated that any adult taken at random was located in a network of interpersonal ties with as many as 150 other persons (and even more, if one relaxed the "degree of emotional bond" as filter for what counted as a meaningful contact), a spate of additional studies of "social networks" and "Dunbar's number" quickly followed, in elaboration and refinement of that initial work (see, e.g., Dunbar 2010; Dávid-Barrett and Dunbar 2013; Dunbar, Arnaboldi, Conti, and Passarella 2015). As the content of "bonds of sociality" is methodically reduced when deciding what qualifies as a "social tie"—such that, for example, the decisive criterion moves increasingly from, say, "close friend" to "someone you speak with upon encounter" to "a person you know about, can discriminate from others"—the network size increases in more or less accordant waves, apparently reaching sums as large as 1500 or more. These wave-like patterns in network composition may well have reflexive significance in the responding person's self-concept—in particular, how she or he perceives personal boundedness relative to a network of "ties to others" (i.e., what that phrase means in self-conception). One manifestation, oft-noted, is the sort of status game in which the count of a person's "Facebook friends" and/or "LinkedIn connections" is important coinage, rather like the count of a university professor's dollar volume of research grants and/or refereed publications (or publications in the "Top Five" journals; see Heckman and Moktan 2018). Another manifestation was emphasized by Granovetter (1973), that reliance on one's strong ties tends to be redundant of information, whereas attention to others with whom one is only weakly connected is likelier to bring in new information and in the process perhaps create conditions for new bondings at a meso-level of organization. Still another and perhaps interesting manifestation appears to be an "evolution" in the attraction of personal identification with, or by means of, texts of "the stranger," whether vis-à-vis Simmel's (1971 [1908]) essay or more recently the novel of that title by Albert Camus (1946 [1942]) as if, one might say, "mythic friendship to believe *in*." Whether, and in what ways, this differs from "mythic ethnicity," for

344

instance (and perhaps other manifestations of what Appiah 2018 called "lies that bind"), remains for investigation.[404]

Recent careful analysis of data drawn by probability sample from the US population in 1985 and then again in 2004 indicates that, whereas "social network" size may well have increased very substantially in "Facebook" terms (perhaps even before the advent of Facebook), the composition had changed during the two-decade interval, in that networks of "confidents" had shrunk. The number of respondents saying that "there is *no one* with whom they discuss important matters" had nearly tripled, to become the modal case (the mode had been 3 in 1985), and the mean network size had declined by about one-third (McPherson, Smith-Lovin, and Brashears 2006, p. 353; emphasis added). Perhaps this is an instance of the trade-off between quantity and quality (or "more is less"): abundance of items of a kind tends to diminish the value or utility of any one of the items. We face here a limitation of sample-survey research, which (1) seldom allows in-depth interviewing that probes respondents' subjective meanings of concepts and relations and (2) even more rarely accumulates with sufficient density in time relevant observations of specific persons' actions, reasons, and underlying meanings. These would be of course practices, and they would run counter to the priority that is given to cross-sectional representation of a population. In addition, we also have an illustration of the importance of the dialectic of text/context (see Lee and Bearman 2017); once that relation is taken into account, the evidence appears to be more a matter of silo effects in the discourse of electoral politics (see also Paik and Sanchagrin 2013).

Movements of the "I" versus "not-I" boundary are typically discussed via a perspective of the "self" or "person" in question, whether it be a specific person or a generalization of "persons of this or that kind" or perhaps "any person." This is understandable because for most of us what one personally knows as first-person experience consists normally of matters of thought, integral to one's self-reflection and self-identity, and this necessity easily sprouts an "intellectualist" bias. Handicraft, making with one's hands, especially musical performance, is an antidote, as mentioned in discussions in Parts Two and Three. What I want to emphasize here is that my small qualifier, "normally," demands attention in sometimes fierce counterpoint to anyone's intellectualism, under certain conditions that typically have to do with possession of one's mortal body. An individual person can become tightly enmeshed in terrifying first-person experiences of struggles for that possession, as occurred in previous centuries when church and crown used instruments of both inquest and inquisition to examine bodies for evidence of various kinds, such as cause of death. Both institutions engaged in practices of holding a person's body as surety of acceptable thought and behavior. Such practices in Europe began at least as early as

---

[404] The reality of ethnicity is an expansive illustration. Consider, say, a present-day person who is tenth-generation descendant of an Englishman who arrived in British North America during the 1630s. Counting that man and his wife (also, let's say, from England), the tenth-generation descendant has 512 ancestors. Chances are, given the strong tendency to patrilinealism, that person probably self-identifies as being of English ethnicity, and given also the tendency to homogamy the chances are that the plurality of ancestors were of English heritage. But in principle the plurality, even the majority, could have been from countries other than England.

an imperial authority that could hold the human body in bondage for service to the empire or, if the body was female, to the service of privileged men. Similar practices in the sacred realm of European cultures date at least to the twelfth century. Ecclesiastical tribunals by the thirteenth century held papal authority to take possession of the body of a person who had been accused of heresy of belief and/or blasphemy of behavior or other expression, then to subject the body to horrendous tortures for confession, and, if eventually convicted, kill the person's mortal being as an act of purification (and, of course, as advertisement to others). In its summation the practice was known as an "auto de fé" (an act of faith). These confiscations continued in France well into the time of Voltaire, whose protest on behalf of the "innocent blood" of a young chevalier de La Barre, Jean-François Lefebvre, became a significant document in the cause of anti-clericalism (see Voltaire 1879 [1975]). The Spanish Inquisition, more notorious in Spain's colonies of the New World as well as at home, continued until 1834. All of these public displays of hieratic authority assured that the proper boundaries of "I" were never a purely private first-person consideration, for one's body was always a potential avenue to control of thought. While papal authority was eventually removed and similar inquisitorial practices today are largely secular, the sociality of first-person experience continues to live in "ways of the hand," musical and not so musical, as well as in "ways of the head."

A demonstration of that contingency much less brutal than Lefebvre's experience has attended a different meaning of the Latin phrase, "auto de fé," one closer to its etymological roots wherein "auto" means or refers to "self." In this usage of the phrase one's intention was euphemism: a reference to suicide. During the early modern period of Anglophone cultures a debate about the morality of deliberately "killing oneself" opened a somewhat different window of proper boundaries of "I": is an adult person, otherwise known to be "of sound mind," at liberty to end his or her own life? Is this properly an act of faith between that individual person and his or her duty to society, to God, to another collective principle of moral order, or is the act ipso facto proof of moral derangement? An obviously theologically laden question during the late 1500s and early 1600s, a time of puritan movements, it had been accepted and answered affirmatively by none other than John Donne (1572-1631), a man of the cloth (the Church of England, no less) as well as of the bar and the pen. As Samuel Sprott documented, "In the long strife between authoritarianism and the individual reason, at the close of the sixteenth century the humanists' support for a rational man's self-respect issued in a challenge to the dominating ecclesiastical defamation of suicide," and John Donne gave voice to the humanist cause "amid English circumstances" (Sprott 1961, pp. 5-6). So, too, had others, Shakespeare among them. His Hamlet became for many audiences the signature character of a liberty laced with the anguish of self-doubt, the doubt reflecting in part a question of who has moral rights to the body in which "my life exists." It is, of course, clear at least in some registers that "traditional society" had already been left behind, because for Donne and his contemporaries "the past" was a self-conscious perspective of choices, whereas in cultures genuinely traditional, the myths in which people believed by habit across generations rather than by personal choice were virtually timeless, outside history (see, e.g., Kemp 1991). No doubt Donne and others could look back to Aquinas and Augustine, for example, but those authorities were now dated, points of comparison from a "then" to the new and changing circumstances of a "now." A hundred years after Donne's birth the debate on suicide was still alive, but the boundaries of a person's own latitude had

346

become more pliable and responsive to interests of personal liberty. David Hume, another man of the cloth, saw little need to converse with the shadows of Aquinas or Augustine, as he "claimed against the menaces of superstition and guilt not indeed a rational man's wish but his 'liberty' to kill himself, while the shrieks of authoritarians were loud for crueler penalties" (Sprott 1961, pp. 94-95).[405]

The boundaries of "I" remained fluid throughout the events of what Sprott called "the English debate on suicide." Where did (does) one draw the line between what was uniquely the individual person's "free choice" and what was imbued as and from sociality? Knowing that time's arrow runs along all of the force vectors of sociality, whether flowing upward from individual person to society or downward from society to the individual person, and probably well aware that one need not be expert in measurement techniques to detect good clues as to which vertical direction of vector is usually the stronger, many of those deeply invested in that debate voiced reasoned arguments about too much weight wearing too heavily on vulnerable shoulders. It was a concern repeated three centuries later in Émile Durkheim's studies of anomie and suicide, the former judged as a malady of sociality complicit in the most intensely personal act of suicide. Hamlet's anguish could be understood in different ways—for instance, as purely a matter of intra-psychic proveniences or as a matter of the social relations that, variably in time and circumstance, were integral to his character or as forces of sociality weighing too heavily on a person who could have been known as having heroic character. Recall the story of Ajax' tragic life course. Or should it be named the tragedy of Ajax? One of the greatest of the Achaean warriors at Troy by virtue mainly of his capacity of physical violence, as Sophocles told us in his play about Ajax, this warrior has gained fame and thus honor among his fellow warriors. He was not sullen, as Achilles was. But he is boastful, whereas Achilles was content to let others sing of his heroic character. Ajax is also a bit thick-headed, prone to hubris, less adept, less flexible, and less capable of learning new ways than Odysseus after the war has ended, and in the competition for inheritance of Achilles' great sword Ajax loses this greatest prize of honor to Odysseus. Having offended Athena by his arrogant and hubristic attitude, Ajax is tricked by the goddess into dishonorable actions. Fate has swerved his course into offenses against the community. When he regains clearer vision of his actions, he is ashamed and throws himself upon Achilles' sword. Sophocles has affirmed the nugget of tragedy: one's greatest excellence can easily be one's own entrapment in delusion.[406] The ambivalence is also preserved: Who was responsible for the turn, the peripetea? Our analytical habit urges us to parse that which cannot be divided— for example, into parts that are "social" and parts that are not, parts that are, in some logical sense, prior to the social (cf. Woodruff 2011).

---

[405] As Sprott (1961) also pointed out, terms of the debate had partly shifted to what might be termed "public policy of the common welfare," to which end counts of deaths by suicide were recorded year by year in mortality bills. Sprott compiled counts as annual rates (per 1,000 deaths) for Greater London, 1629-1800. Yearly fluctuations were small enough that they could have been due to measurement error.
[406] Sophocles' play (c443 BCE) gives one of the strongest representations of reflexivity in ancient Greek literature (as it has survived to us). While drawing comparisons across such distance is perilous (and having just planted a foot in that declaration), I will suggest that the closest analogue in recent times to the tragedy of Ajax would be found in the militarist culture of Japan during the first half of the previous century.

The strangeness of the ancient Greeks as they represented themselves in their stories is a challenge to us on multiple dimensions, only one of which is discernment of differences between their "theatre" and the conditions of their everyday lives that supported theatrical excursions into their history and mythology. The narrational I is always there, to be read as integral to the story, which is a story of times long before the I who spoke (or sang) of an ancestral people, events, actions. We, like Alexander Pope (among others), are neither Odysseus (for example) nor the speaking I who narrated to an audience not so different from Odysseus' playwright. The same sort of problem of fidelity and internal consistency arises between a translator, such as Pope, and the playwright. How can we know? A translator's strategy necessarily comes into play even for those of us who speak modern Greek (for whom the ancient dialects must be learned as a foreign language), and the main strategic difference will be, in effect, how "strange" to make that narrational I and those of whom he spoke (or sang). Thus, to take another (and related) example, Peter Green's recent translation of the Homeric *Odyssey* is careful to maintain linguistically a healthy cultural-historical integrity of difference, vis-à-vis a translator such as Pope, who sought (in 1726) to please *his* audience's expectations of familiarity and decorum. In my judgment Green's representation is preferable; but, and because Green was careful to preserve difference, one must work harder to learn.

We must try to remain alert to the differences that are in, and for, us an understanding of Other as strange, because these are resources of human being, ways of being human, and thus resources of understanding.[407] As one reads from the Homeric works to Aeschylus, Sophocles, and then Euripides, the differences change and the sense of strangeness changes, on some dimensions lessening because with that sequence in times of "the ancient Greeks" we experience trends that seem formally similar to trends in the sequence of times of, say, Europe's twelfth-century "little renaissance" and then, comparatively, again in the sequence of times of Leonardo, his contemporaries and multiple successors. By *our* calendar, the temporal distance covered by that first sequence (about four centuries) is roughly the same as the distance from Leonardo's *Saint Jerome in the Wilderness* (1480) to, say, Édouard Manet and his famous *Luncheon on the Grass* (see above, §15). Euripides' calculation? Surely much shorter than the interval which one of the Homeric poets would have said, had he become a "time traveler"; beyond that, I cannot say.

Ethnographies of our own contemporaries present similar challenges and opportunities. Again, to illustrate by one example only, Catherine Lutz' (1988, pp. 88-93) ethnography of first-person pronoun usages among the Ifaluk, a people of a Micronesian atoll, documented their preference for the first-person plural nominative case (versus preference for first-person singular in the USA), especially when emotion is locutionally present. Furthermore, whereas we tend to separate cognitive and emotive "elements," the Ifaluk did not. One word covered both cognitive

---

[407] These resources are useful today, even as homogenization of cultures increases because of increasing density and extension of contacts, connections, and intersections. Moreover, recall that Kant knew that the celestial formations then called "nebulae" were a multitude of galaxies, at least some of which, he conjectured, hosted living beings; and for all his own fund of biases by ethnocentrism, he might well have recommended to us a healthy fund of resources of "the Other" as some degree of preparation, should highly intelligent beings from other planets arrive.

thought and emotional feeling, and its application was general. Recall that the key stimulant to Husserl's strong reaction to Hume, during his Vienna lecture of 1935, was the supposed dissolution of "an identical 'I'" (Husserl (1970 [1936], §23). It is not, according to Humean skepticism, "a datum but a ceaselessly changing bundle of data. Identity is a psychological fiction." Perhaps Husserl was especially sensitive to a then-current development that disposed him to a reading of Hume that he could only reject, because it was highly uncomplimentary to a project of transcendental phenomenology (as Husserl's had been intended). The dimensionality of time was no longer that of an absolute vessel, containing all but its own categorial essence. Rather, time had become a variable of utmost importance to various conditions and processes of human life. Relativity had "invaded" the formerly static terrain of time, and this surely complicated bases of evaluation and comparison. The more one looked, however, the more evident it became that some actors had learned part of the lesson of relativity before Einstein published his theories.

An illustration of one of the embedded points follows. This illustrative exercise is meant to emphasize the importance of endogenous relations to some of the complexities already laid out in the foregoing discussion. Bear in mind that the concept of endogeneity is an effort to treat in analytic terms a major aspect of the internal relationality of dialectical logic.

More than half a century ago James Meade (1964) gave an elegant demonstration of trade-offs between efficiency and equality (equity) in distributions of valued products. While this relation has sometimes been cited as distinctive of institutions of capitalism, it is certainly not unique to those institutions, as studies of centrally managed economies such as that of the former USSR, English monarchal economies, and the economies of some "developing countries" (wherein bureaucratic inefficiencies and personal corruptions throw "buckets of sand into the gears") have indicated. The point here, however, is that individual persons, as persons and as household heads, repeatedly face decisions, in personal planning and in public policy, that are marked by those trade-offs, and their responses in making the decisions are relevant to major questions about not only distributions of income and wealth, for instance, but also the means and quality of understanding within and among the decision makers, as that may change as relevant circumstances change. It has become commonplace to acknowledge that a "typical person" is not a computer. This is partly a way of saying "not perfectly rational" (i.e., vis-à-vis a "rational actor" model)—which is not exactly news but also can be beside the point since analytic models are intended to be idealizations that simplify some dimensions in order to acquire clearer observations, analytically, of other dimensions. However, the "not a computer" locution more importantly acknowledges limits in the management of large sets of observations (or "data"), complex logical relations, and calculations of cost-benefit ratios and the like, *not* as static conditions but as temporal estimations. Yet it is this "typical person" who stands in the midst of economic functions of production, distribution, exchange, and consumption, at several levels: labor supply, decision making, flow management, quality control, choices of saving/investment vehicles, and so forth. How do these persons, as individuals and as householders, evaluate trade-offs between efficiency and equity, and how do those evaluations change, in what ways, under specified conditions?

Various algorithms for use in making those evaluations have been devised since the early twentieth century. Let's proceed first with brief definitions of the two qualities in trade and then consider a few of the evaluative algorithms. Efficiency and equality have each been defined with mathematical precision, although it must be noted that the precision can cover some underlying conceptual ambiguity. In words, "efficiency" is a quality defined by cost-benefit ratio. An early statement, known as "Pareto efficiency" or "Pareto optimality" (which is only slightly related to Pareto's "80/20 rule"; see §20, above), describes a distribution of goods that is "balanced" in such manner that a change intended to benefit even a single unit (e.g., person, household, etc.) would inflict cost on at least one other unit in the distribution. Note that the secondary quality, a *balanced* distribution, is quantitative: a given distribution can be more or less "Pareto efficient" (nearer to, farther from, optimum).[408] Note also that the components of "cost-benefit relations" are relative: that which is cost to one person can be, often is, benefit to another person; much depends on how the system of relations is bounded (e.g., positive sum versus zero sum versus negative sum), and much depends on accounting procedures (e.g., whether, to what extent, and for whom, specific costs are externalized to the system of relations), this last point being a notorious instance of an "underlying conceptual ambiguity" (i.e., what gets counted under which label, and who benefits).

Whereas Pareto's distributional algorithm is in principle a good measure of efficiency, it ignores variation in equality or equity. Max Lorenz, a US economist, had devised by 1904 a model, now known as the "Lorenz curve," which is basis for assessing equality of distribution of a good (though it its initial form, to the neglect of information about efficiency). The basic operation of this model is a plot of the percentile distribution of goods of a given kind (income, wealth, moral rectitude) against the percentile distribution of the population of eligible holders of that kind of good. Popular literatures usually collapse the percentiles into deciles or quintiles, for ease of presentation. Thus, for instance, a quarter-century ago the quintile estimates for the USA, based on size of adjusted gross income as reported on official tax returns, were that the bottom quintile of income earners received 4.2 percent of all income; the second (third, fourth) quintile, 10.0 (15.7, 23.3) percent, and the top quintile of earners accounted for 46.9 percent of all income. This distribution can be compared to a theoretical model of perfect equality, in which each quintile would receive exactly 20 percent of total income.[409] Note that the quintile figures just reported, based on adjusted gross income as defined in the US tax code, are biased in a number of ways. One of the largest biases is due to the fact that high-income earners gain proportionately greater advantage from the rules by which adjustments (i.e., reductions) are made to "gross income." Another bias is due to regulations affecting taxation and transfer payments,

---

[408] In the engineering context of Pareto's work the "efficiency" concept is defined more generally: given available inputs, how closely do outputs approximate theoretical maximum? This assumes that theory is sufficiently capable of robust definition of "maximum." That capability is high for engineering problems of Newtonian mechanics; not so high for problems of social-science interest, and one must be able to discriminate between "real change" and estimation error.

[409] A ratio of the actual to the perfect can be computed. The Gini coefficient compares the area between the line of perfect equality and the line of the Lorenz curve to the total area under the line of perfect equality, thus giving an index of inequality. Note that different Lorenz curves can produce the same Gini coefficient. Note also that the "80/20 principle" made famous by Pareto (discussed above) is a version of quintile distribution for wealth (which is more concentrated than income).

some of which slightly favor lower-income earners while others of which strongly favor high-income earners. Still another set of biases has to do with the difference between "equality" (in its arithmetic sense) and "equity" (which adds a sense of fairness or morality), and about which more will be said below.[410]

One can compare populations—in total or by category (e.g., by ethnicity, by type of household, and so forth)—in terms of descriptive properties of distributions of specific goods, including the efficiency and equality of those distributional processes. One can also compare distributional properties *over time*, although that is more complicated because criteria by which the distributional processes operate often change over time (e.g., tax and transfer regulations, reporting basis of a census of wealth, and so forth). There is "ample evidence" that the positions of individual households *within* a distribution of wealth change over time (Ljungqvist and Sargent 2004, p. 8), and that is complicated by the fact that observation of change will be sensitive to the fineness of the distributional gradient (e.g., decile vs. quintile vs. quartile; or binary, as in Pareto's "80/20" rule). Again, however, the point of chief interest here has to do with individual persons whose action choices are presumably *endogenous* to the dynamics of distributional processes—on the one hand responding to meso- or macro-level factors of public policy, market processes, and other perceived forces, and on the other hand generating effects that can at least in principle aggregate to induce change in those same meso- or macro-level factors, processes, and forces.

Some economists, especially those of experimentalist bent, have undertaken systematic study of some dimensions of those endogenous relations. For example, do persons maintain preferences among alternative distributions of goods of a certain kind (e.g., income)? Do the preferences align in a hierarchy? Are they primarily by criteria of equality or of efficiency? Is there a systematic difference according to whether persons judge effects of a distribution for their own welfare or for some notion of "the general welfare"? To what extent do their own decisions or actions accord consistently with their previously advertised distributional preferences? What are the determinants, or at least correlates, of that consistency? And so forth. These and related questions can be pursued in efforts to understand not only actual effects of future orientations by individual persons as they engage in activities directly and indirectly germane to the distribution (and to some extent production) of goods but also to their *capabilities* of effectuality. Perhaps at least under some conditions in certain contexts those capabilities are seriously limited. Perhaps a declared preference is nothing more than a statement of belief that has no independent status or effect beyond the fact of the statement, which in turn occurs only when a stimulus prompts the person to remember prior statement(s) of the belief (see, e.g., Needham 1972, p. 131).

An experiment designed by Traub, Seidl, and Schmidt (e.g., 2008) was intended to shed new light on some of those questions—chiefly, how do experimental subjects solve trade-offs between criteria of equality and criteria of efficiency, when asked to rank several empirically

---

[410] Other algorithms have been devised (e.g., one that incorporates information on "taxes and transfers," most of the net benefit of which goes to the top earners). For more details about models, measurements, estimates, and trends of income distributions, see Publication Number 4091 of the Congressional Budget Office (2011), which was produced at a time before partisan politics affected Congressional Budget reports so much.

distinctive and mostly plausible income distributions (graded by quintile)? Which criteria tended to dominate in their preference hierarchies? A major stimulus to the experiment had been prior claims that three-fourths (or more) of adult persons violated at least some expectations of Lorenz models (i.e., violations of criteria of equality, in favor of efficiency criteria). Based on their review of previous research, the authors reported estimates ranging between 30 and 60 percent of subjects generally disfavoring Lorenz criteria. Estimates from their own experiment fell roughly in the middle of that range, the disfavor being somewhat higher among female than among male subjects (a difference they associated with the greater tendency among women to be risk averse, a tendency well documented in previous research). They also reported the presence of framing effects, especially whether the subjects were explicitly put at risk of cost-benefit from the results of their rank ordering or explicitly assured zero cost-benefit (the token being an actual substantial payment for participation in the experiment).

The subjects of that experiment were not computers, and they were asked to perform a less than simple task: how to rank order a dozen clearly divergent income distributions, each of them expressed in quintiles of income earners. Did they understand what they were *implicitly* being asked to do (i.e., reveal the criteria by which they sorted the dozen from most to least desirable or acceptable)? We do not know, but we do know that most of them were university students of economics, while others were students of business or law programs in the university. Were they predisposed to understand? Perhaps. Were they predisposed to favor criteria of efficiency over criteria of equality, so long as the inequality was not "too great"? That was the major pattern of the experimental results. My intent in asking these questions is not to impugn the researchers' work; rather, to add to our understanding of just how complex the process of the experiment was, especially by bringing into that process the background of the subjects as one or more factors of relevance to their performance. (And, to repeat a point registered above, we know from the report of the experimental results that significant framing effects were present, and such effects can be significantly interactive with background characteristics of experimental subjects.)

Part of my point about raising the matter of "background" (in itself and vis-à-vis framing) is that persons, including subjects in an experiment, bring with them variable mixes of biography and history—cultural, social, political, all sorts of variations, at least potentially—and these can affect performances of a present moment. This is part of the enormous complication of research, *any* kind of research (experimental, ethnographic, etc.), into human relations, human affairs, even research into the task (actually relatively simple, in the larger scheme of human life) of how adult persons evaluate "better and worse" in quintile distributions of income.

Before taking that point to its next step, let me introduce another complication that has been evident already in prior discussions. In most uses the Lorenz model assigns primacy to "equality"; but this is arithmetic equality: $1,000 equals $1,000, pure and simple. What many people have in mind, when thinking about "equality of good," far is more complex than that: it includes some notion of fairness. Someone evaluating an income distribution might well be thinking, "Well, returns [i.e., income] should be proportionate to what a person has put into the process that is expected to generate returns." This could refer of course to investment of cash in

352

an interest-bearing account at a local bank or (probably still more cash) into a stock fund. But it can also refer to returns on an investment in undergraduate education or a professional-degree program or a job-training program (whether a skilled-craft apprenticeship in manufacturing or an internship or residency program in medicine). It can refer to a worker's expectation of return on "showing up for work, and working hard, day after day" (as reported by Williams 1920 and Hamper 1991, for instance, among many others). Thus, an arithmetically equal distribution need not be an equable or fair distribution, and the difference can be evaluated in terms of the underlying relativity of cost/benefit ratios. Moreover, recall that adults tend variably to discount the effect of duration, and this can be implicated in judgments about fairness. Some actors make decisions, and act accordingly, as if future value will be worth less, often much less, that the real effect of a prevailing rate of monetary inflation. This generalizes beyond consequences that are directly measurable in monetary terms. The consequence of ending one's formal schooling with this or that credential might well change—they often have—as various other conditions change in such a way that demand for that credential changes, more often declining that growing. In much the same vein, the consequence of moving household to a place that seems to promise better opportunity will often prove to be contingent in unexpected ways. In effect, in other words, persons tend to gamble that future conditions will offset their present discount rate. Sometimes the gamble works; sometimes it does not. For those who gamble with a high rate of temporal discount, the odds are increasingly against success as the rate increases. This is integral to the subjective meaningfulness of actor's decisions and actions, but actors generally do not see the effect in advance. The effect is itself variable over time, depending on various contingencies. It is implicated in the endogenous relations that are very difficult to observe appropriately even when we assume constant calendar time.

Now to the "next step," announced just above. As previously mentioned, there has been a strong tendency to think "individual person" as a tightly bounded category (the "punctual self" concept), a boundedness that is assumed to corral effectively well, or simply to ignore, the multiplicity of reflexively present significant others in one's self, a boundedness that perdures except under extraordinary circumstances. This tendency correlates with a number of other tendencies in the way we typically think of "individual human being," including the presumption of temporal continuity of selfhood (discussed in Part Two) and concepts such as Julian Rotter's (e.g., 1966) locus-of-control gradient (i.e., from strictly internal control, caricatured as heroic actor, to strictly external control, caricatured as the anti-heroic schlep or perpetual victim) and what Gilbert and Malone (1995, p. 21) called a "correspondence bias"—that is, a "tendency to draw inferences about a person's unique and enduring dispositions from behaviors that can be entirely explained by the situation in which they occur." One version of this latter tendency attributes it mainly to the influence of theories that ignore or discount situational determinants. However, Gawronski's (2004) review of work disputes that attribution. While that kind of psychologism does still have defenders (e.g., Molenaar 2004, 2005), they are increasingly scarce.

Nonetheless, in one-shot interviews of persons (and in repeated one-shot interviews of persons) it has been common to assume that the person is characterized in specific relevant ways by a stability of presence that, while not necessarily immutable, displays consistency from time

353

to time, situation to situation, and so forth. That assumption is in keeping with the presumption of continuity in time which (as Kant said) underwrites our ability to have coherent experiences in time. The same assumption is typical of experimental research of individual persons as well, as can be seen in the research cited above. Several ordinary features of taken-for-granted everyday reality conduce to that assumption by the researcher as well as by other actors. A person is identified by a distinctive name, face, and body image, for example, sets of habituations that include behavior patterns, geographic preference hierarchies (home, workplace, probable sites of friends, probably holiday sites, etc.), and similar other routinized expectations. A tendency of biological expectation ("I would know him anyplace") easily generalizes, such that just as we reply on an expected physiognomy, body image, gait, and so forth, of a person clearly bounded in identified being by his or her skin, as it were, so we have similar expectations of boundedness in terms of important social, cultural, and other collective or associative characteristics.

A moment's reflection can illustrate how misleading that generalization from the biologic actually is as an empirical matter. The presumption of continuity can perdure even as conditions of experience change. "Just how much does Pat's body have to change until an acquaintance will say, 'Well, that's not Pat, not the Pat I know'?" Of course, one might object, "we do make allowances for that"—that is, for example, a prosthetic leg or ear pan or eyeball (maybe, with some sort of assurance, a transplanted face). And we do. But then consider: could Pat, or you, survive without taking in a minimum amount of water every day, oxygen every few seconds, metabolizable calories, minerals, and so forth, expelling waste products on a minimally regular schedule? One's biological skin must be a great deal more than, and more complex than, this heaviest organ that a human body carries around. Plus, other living beings, also vital to one's survival, are hosted within the body—and not just a few other living creatures but *thousands upon thousands* of other *species* of life, the population of a given species being sometimes too small, sometimes too large, for the continuing health of the human host.[411] Then, too, in addition to the gasses and the liquids and the solids that must flow repeatedly through the skin and its orifices, there is also a vital flow of information some of which is processed in consciousness and some of it not, though available to reflection. A major example of the latter is what has been summarized traditionally as "the immune functions" of an organism but which is, as we are increasingly producing the requisite knowledge to understand, empirically a large array of identifications—rather, an array of identity *gradients* that align dialectically, a unity of opposites, of self/not-self.[412] The effort to identify definitive criteria by which the traditional analytic distinction between "self" and "not-self" can be reliably and coherently determined has been persistently frustrated by growing evidence that any such distinction is context sensitive at best. More generally, while popular conceptions of "organism" (human or non-human) still imagine a tightly bounded independent being (i.e., "organism" versus "environment," with no undivided

---

[411] In addition to the sheer quantitative aspects of this population each of us carries around, consider the exquisite insight into the dialectic of the pharmakon (as, e.g., discussed by Plato in the *Phaedrus*): that what kills you can also cure you, and vice versa (cf. Derrida 1981 [1972]; Hazelrigg 1979).

[412] The relevant literature has expanded during recent years. As previously mentioned, following the course of Alfred Tauber's works during the past quarter-century (e.g., Tauber 1994, 2013, 2017) yields a useful overview of the revised understandings.

middle), conceptualization in the biological sciences has increasingly diverged from punctual images. Peter Godfrey-Smith (2013, p. 19) recently declared, for example, "There are no fundamental or most-real individuals in biology" (see also Hamilton and Fewell 2013). This is not exactly a new insight, of course. More than eight decades ago Ludwik Fleck (1979 [1935], p. 60) announced that any specific "organism can no longer be construed as a self-contained, independent unit with fixed boundaries."[413] True, Fleck had hardly any audience at the time, and his insight nearly disappeared. The social sciences have been even slower than the biological sciences to recover, apply, and develop Fleck's conception and the different approach that it implied (see, e.g., Zerubavel 1996).

Now, with the foregoing paragraphs in mind, let's recall the problem of endogeneity in the context of Weber's argument about the importance of taking into account actor's subjectively meaningful activities. This is a fundamental matter of perspective in first-person experience. A theorist will unavoidably work from and within a perspective, which will involve a variety of assumptions, conceptualizations, and other apparatuses of the particular discipline of theorization, which will surely involve some simplifying models as taken-for-granted points of departure.[414] Whatever the theoretical perspective may be, Weber, argued, it must accommodate subjective meanings as they inform actor's understandings, perceptions, decisions, and actions. Because and insofar as our focal interests are in and about processes—and "our" includes theorist and analyst as well as those who are the objects of inquiry—one must be aware that temporality is unavoidable. As has been emphasized above, temporality is no longer an absolute framework (as in popular conception of Newtonian mechanics); it is relative as condition, and a crucial part of that relativity is that actor perspectives tend to be elastic. This elasticity is integral to endogeneities. Thus, relevant endogeneities *must* be observed and estimated *within* the temporal course of process dynamics *actor by actor*. Comparisons made at any point in time across actors can tell us nothing of importance about endogeneities. This being the case, two resulting observations should come to mind. First, if one follows Weber's point about the importance of actor's subjective meanings, the task facing the social scientist is vastly more difficult than that faced by any other scientific inquirer. Second, one can see why the main preference has been to disregard actor's subjective meanings as epiphenomenal and otherwise to depend mainly on analytic designs that emphasize cross-sectional rather than per-person process dynamics.

At this juncture, let's now return more explicitly to "the language issue" (i.e., conceptual schemes, etc.) and do so in the context of George Herbert Mead's general theoretical framework, on which I have been repeatedly drawing.

---

[413] As illustration of the position to which he was objecting, Fleck (1979 [1935], p. 60 n.1) cited a passage by Hans Gradmann (1930, p. 641), a well-known botanist: "If the modern biologist wants to form an objective picture of the living world, he must rid himself of all ideas based on a subjective approach. It is sometimes not at all easy to get rid of such prejudices completely." Fleck referred to this rather common position as materialism, but it was a major stance taken by "objective idealism" as well, although Gradmann likely preferred to think of himself as materialist.

[414] These models probably will be carried by some self-conscious deliberations on the part of the theorist; once activated as points of departure, they become in subsequent effects taken-for-granted models.

## §24. Sociality and the Dialectic of Subject/Object

Mead's general framing perspective might be described as a pragmatic naturalism, a phrase that prior to the impact of Darwin's famous publications would probably have been characterized as borderline oxymoronic. In Part One, recall, I cited Rorty's (1967) extensive collection of major papers of US philosophy's dawning interest in language as a crucial topic, the earliest of those papers coming soon after Ludwig Wittgenstein's (1922 [1921]) challenge that the propositions of metaphysics are meaningless. Because these papers were specific to philosophy, the fact that none of Mead's early twentieth-century publications was included should not be surprising, even though several of his articles had appeared in a US journal of philosophy. The absence of John Dewey, a mentor and colleague of Mead, is somewhat surprising; the absence of Josiah Royce (a prominent US philosopher at turn of the century, sometimes described as neo-Hegelian), still more surprising. But the collection was pulled together by Rorty when he still counted himself among the US analytical philosophers of the day. Dewey not only did not meet those criteria of membership, he was seen generally as marginal to the US academy of philosophy, which in turn had been secondary at best in Royce's day to European academies.[415] By the late 1980s Rorty had learned something of Mead's work, however, identifying him with the US philosopher Wilfrid Sellars (e.g., Sellars 1963). Disciplinary allegiance surely had a determinative role in this identification, although it is still curious that Rorty apparently did not notice that he was assimilating the work of a man born in 1863 (Mead) to a man born in 1912 (Sellars). In any case, Rorty (1989, pp. 65 n.26, 63), referring to "Sellars' naturalization of the obligation-benevolence distinction," said that it, "like Mead's view of the self, helps pull up the roots of the temptation," strange as it is, "to see 'society' as *intrinsically* dehumanizing." The core of the identification consisted in the fact that each writer agreed in the view "that the self is a creation of society."[416]

Mead's naturalism was assumed, not argued, in much the same attitude that a person then assumed the presence of a body and thus not only a biography of personal life but also a history of biology as written by Darwin, Wallace, and their successors. A key lesson from Hegel had been mixed into that assumption from biology—namely, that reason is not a faculty of the person taken in isolation (i.e., the psychologistic view) but consists in sociality, simultaneously society and self, and thus for any person is ineluctably contingent (see Hegel 1977 [1952], §§438-439). Mead agreed. Whether or to what extent he located it as integral to Hegel's early thought, or of the rather loosely anchored versions of "Hegelianism" that had briefly flourished now and then, cannot be determined from Mead's own publications, which seldom mention Hegel directly

---

[415] A useful gauge is the list of officers and speakers among the delegation of 96 members of the International Congress of Arts and Science who attended the 1904 Exposition in St Louis (see Rogers 1905-1908, e.g., vols. 1, 10, and 14).

[416] In the set of his own papers republished in 1982 as *Consequences of Pragmatism* (his newly claimed perspective) Rorty included a paper written for a 1980 conference, in which he gave extensive attention to Dewey (drawing attention to Dewey's effort to meld "the naturalistic" and the transcendental), and a paper explicitly on major works of social science (again featuring Dewey, this time in conjunction with Foucault). Nowhere in the book is Mead mentioned, which fact suggests that Rorty had not yet come to him.

356

(see, e.g., Mead 1901). But the basic point of importance to Mead could as well have come from the pragmatist reception of Darwinian theory with regard to temporal sequences in evolutionary process, or from Royce's lectures at Harvard, or both. Consider again the claim of an originary logic according to which a process, whether natural "or" social, can self-start from its own absence. This punctuality of "origin" would imply that a species lacking reason could "have invented reason itself," as Mercier and Sperber recently put it, before conjecturing instead that the human capacity and capability of reason gradually evolved within "bands of hunter-gatherers" as cooperative skills in the hunt, in foraging, perhaps in search-and-rescue operations for a wayward child, and so forth (Mercier and Sperber 2017, pp. 1-4, ch. 16). Indeed, one can infer something similar in the probable behaviors of earlier members of the Homo genus, as today in the hunting skills of species of pack animal (examples which illustrate Mead's point that "instinct" is a social category). Mercier and Sperber's example of echolocation, a capability that has apparently developed in only a few species even though by human perception it would seem useful to species that do not the capacity, at least not the capability, illustrates the interactive dimension of what, by analytic logic, is seen as an external relation between organism and environment. To cite (and correct) another of their examples, there are indeed animal species (hundreds of them) within the Rotifera phylum that do have the capability of the wheel, which some of the species use for swimming as well as for ingestion of food.

Locating reason within sociality rather than prior to it did raise some complication vis-à-vis the simplicity of a single "great chain of being" sequence from an originary point, as John Dunn (1979, p. 47) explained: "it was no longer easy to see how the claims of individuals could serve as a commanding external standard to which society must endlessly, as best it could, measure up. If individuals themselves were cultural artefacts, social products, trapped once again within a relentless causality, though now a sociological and no longer a homogeneous natural causality, it was hard to see how they could have valid claims to a measure of tolerance very much more extensive than the majority of their society felt on the whole inclined to give them." Notice the tendentiousness of Dunn's syntax, a decided reluctance to utter in an air of definitive conviction. To have done so would have been to undermine a key part of the very point he was making, specifically about the air of liberalism to tolerance within a pluralism in which liberalism itself would have pride of place but also, more generally, about claims to any universalism tout court. The main alternative to that liberalist bias was not Kant's hope for species maturity toward better legislation but the peculiar anarchism to which Rorty referred in his barbed comment about those who like to "see 'society' as *intrinsically* dehumanizing." The absurdity of that posture can lead one "to repudiate the claims of sociology," Dunn (1979, p. 48) reminded, and stake out a supposed position from which "the somewhat over-rated causal status of sociology [or economics or political science, etc.] can safely be viewed with unlimited scorn." This yields precisely nothing. Mead, having no definitive solution to such conundrums, simply wedded to his naturalistic viewpoint a pragmatic program of theorizing sociality "within" self-reflexive processes of personal identity, the processes that Kant had enfolded into the conditions of the very possibility of "I think." By seeking to assimilate the works of a man long since dead (and more often than not forgotten) to the works of a philosopher whose main works were appearing a half-century after Mead's (and Rorty had high regard for Sellars), the recent convert from analytic philosophy to his own brand of pragmatism was, one can think, paying indeliberate compliment to the memory of Mead.

Contingency induces a tendentiousness when it extends deeply into language. Language had played a major part in Kant's critical theory, primarily in the form of conceptual scheme, which he regarded as a species-universal even as contents varied by culture. To be sure, the fact of language had been given consideration in European literatures before Kant (i.e., at least since the seventeenth century; see, e.g., Aarsleff 1967; Eco 1997; Needham 1972; Vico 1988 [1710]). But language is sneaky by omnipresence. It is always there, but always both ahead and behind itself, making it well-nigh impossible to grasp its effects *entirely as such* (see Fynsk 1996). As a result, it is easy to hold the fact of language at some remove from the "core of things," so to speak, and especially from the authority of the theorist or analyst. Social scientists during the late nineteenth and early twentieth centuries treated language, if at all, only in passing. When, later in the new century, that neglect was being offset by an attention that sometimes bordered on the fervid—especially in debates about the notion that cultures in general (i.e., not only those of "primitive peoples") are inherently relative because the meanings of perception are formed within different linguistic cultures—the instability posed to scientific knowledge itself invited renewed effort to demonstrate a basic universality in language (as discussed above, in Part One). A troubling concern to Max Weber, given his emphasis both on subjectively meaningful conduct and on the authority of scientific knowledge by reason of its means and standards of validity, is it surprising that issues of linguistic variation garnered little explicit treatment in his voluminous writings, including those which dealt directly with human cultures? One easily hears the tension of trying to thread the needle, as it were, to have both objectivity and relativity (see, e.g., Weber 1949 [1904], 1964 [1913]; cf. Beiser 2011, pp. 546-556, 562-565).

Formalists such as Vladimir Propp (1895-1970), whose morphological studies of folklore in search of fundamental themes of meaning stimulated the generalizing structuralism of Claude Lévi-Strauss (1908-2009), and the argument of Noam Chomsky (b. 1928) that basic language knowledge must be innate, given that children learn language use so quickly (see, e.g., Chomsky 1975; McGilvray 2014), seemed to offer re-assurance of a universalist platform not only in body but also in mind. No one had disputed the fact that at any given time and place at least one language is present in human relations and thus available for acquisition by ordinary processes of learning. But the omnipresence of language, the fact that one is always within at least one language, now stimulated a new quest: there must be a foundational language ability, always already present in the capability of human mind *before* sociality—the assumption being that sociality of the human kind would not have developed without language—and therefore, given the omnipresence, that foundational ability must be universal to the species *and* in its essential (mental as well as physical) structure and features. The expectation of an originary logic has been tenacious. The promise of justifiable authority of voice was to be found in the reduction of culture to the logical structure of that foundational ability.

Mead had already come to the fact of language, not on the basis of a pre-social platform or foundation, however, but from the perspective of social relations that always already exist in the pragmatics of human communication. The idea that language use could exist independently of sociality was apparently foreign to him at early age. In any case, something like a dialectical relation of sociality and language seems to have been entertained from lessons he learned from his philosophy teacher at Harvard (see, e.g., Royce 1894), if not before, and was reinforced during his study at Leipzig with Wilhelm Wundt, whose "psychophysical parallelism" interested Mead even as he soon found reasons from his pragmatist bent to object to the idea that understanding of "psychic phenomena" would follow from location of correlations with physical (i.e., organic) structures and/or functions (i.e., another version of the general thesis of parallel stratifications of self and world).[417] Arguably the single most important US theorist of sociality during the first half of the twentieth century, Mead's work was slow to be appreciated in its own innovative terms. Jürgen Habermas (1992 [1988], ch. 7) acknowledged some striking similarities between his later theory of "communicative action" and Mead's formulations during the early years of the century, similarities that had gone unremarked, maybe unnoticed, in the preparation of Habermas' (1971 [1968]) review of theories and perspectives of knowledge and human interest (but see also Habermas 1979 [1976], pp. 73, 109, 136).[418]

The most systematic statement of Mead's core theorization, his theory of the self, was presented in an article published in 1913 in the *Journal of Philosophy, Psychology and Scientific Method*. Other articles published during the years from 1908 to 1930 developed particular (and sometimes tangential) themes, as did lecture notes that were published posthumously as three books which, unfortunately, bear some markings of a "normalization" by the compilers: *Mind, Self, and Society* (1934), *Movements of Thought in the Nineteenth Century* (1936), and *The Philosophy of the Act* (1938). A half-century later, one of his last students, Herbert Blumer (1966), published an article in the *American Journal of Sociology* with intent at least in part to introduce Mead's work to other sociologists, the point being that excepting the subdiscipline known as "social psychology" Mead's work had made little impact. That intent was entangled with Blumer's promotion of a perspective of his own coinage, "symbolic interactionism," which,

---

[417] How much of Kant's critical theory had Mead read and, more importantly, what had he made of it? I know of no good evidence by which to answer even the first part of that question. Judging from the compilation of his lectures on "movements of thought" (Mead 1936), plus his brief historical overview of "scientific method and the individual thinker" (a paper he prepared for John Dewey's volume on *Creative Intelligence*), my guess is that he mostly relied on summaries by others, probably mainly Royce (see Mead 1917, pp. 194-196). Apparently Mead's lectures were silent about Durkheim, Simmel, Weber, Tönnies, Ratzenhofer, and other European social scientists, (excepting Thomas Reid, Comte, Marx, and Herbert Spencer) and early US social scientists as well (excepting Charles Horton Cooley and William James).

[418] But Habermas' (e.g., 1963; 1971 [1968], pp. 91-112) attention to the pragmatism of Charles Sanders Peirce helped to bring attention to Mead—as if European thinkers needed to vouch for the importance of a North American thinker (see also, Joas 1985 [1980] and 1993; Habermas 1992 [1988]; Huebner 2014; Joas and Huebner 2016). Compare the lack of attention to Mead even after John McKinney's (1955) careful overview. Neglect was hardly unique to Mead: similar arguments by Lev Vygotsky (1986 [1934]; 1978) also drew little notice (see Tomasello 2019).

while consonant with Mead's work, was bound up with Blumer's methodological views, and these views became a focus of controversy that deflected from Mead's work.[419] It is readily evident from Mead's writings that all human actions, whether of public or private realm (and either by Habermas' distinction or by Erving Goffman's), are infused symbolically (i.e., by language) and are "interactive" in the sense that even when a person is physically alone and sitting passively in thought the dynamics of sociality are alive in that experience. Again, Weber had recognized no less—thus, his notion of "the subjectively meaningful" criterion of his "social action" category. As Goffman (e.g., 1959, 1974) emphasized, "the habitual" (Weber's category of simple "behavior") carries meaning insofar as it can be recognized as human. If the prevailing tendency of Blumer's symbolic interactionism is to underestimate the resilience of objectivities that are produced by and in social actions, as some critics have charged (e.g., Wood and Wardell 1983), that lapse would certainly not be unique to Blumer's brand of theory. Blumer's interest in promoting the label, "symbolic interactionism," as a distinctive disciplinary field of inquiry remains somewhat obscure, in view of the obvious redundancy. Perhaps another episode of "claiming the mantle" was in play.

The concern about resilience of objectivities raises another question of terminological clarity, this one having to do with the meaning of the word, "intersubjectivity." Effort to sort subtle but important differences of meaning in any given document is sometimes unsuccessful, depending on guidance by document's the author. The locus of the problem is the prefix as it appears in Blumer's label: "inter" can mean "between" or "among" or "in the midst of," the modality being either spatial or temporal (or both),[420] the referent being a correlation between (among, etc.) *independent* terms (things, states of affair, etc.); or it can mean a relation of mutuality or reciprocity or (in a specific sense) a togetherness, whether in temporal modality alone or in spatial as well as temporal modality, but because of the exchange dimension of mutuality or reciprocity the referent (thing, state of affairs, etc.) stands at any moment in a relation of difference to what it *was* prior to the mutuality or reciprocity (perhaps also to what it will yet revert to or become, once the exchange has "expired"). Those are altogether different meanings: one depends on a tight boundedness of each of the referents being addressed, such that the referent maintains its prior integrity of being, its integral self-identity in space or time or both, such that it can "come or go," as it were, without difference of being;[421] the other depends on boundedness that is itself dynamic, changing as relations change. This is Mead's "social self,"

---

[419] I will return to "the Blumer controversy" later, but my interest extends only to clarification of Mead's work.

[420] Note that here I mean "modality" in its technical sense of the logic of a grammar—that is, the modes of being, the modes in which something is experienceable, expressible (thus, existent), here or there or everywhere, now or then or any time. Specific modalities include possibility, probability, necessity, willingness, ability. Thus, for example, if A and B are independent, then to order (ask, etc.) that they "merge" is to order (ask, etc.) that they undergo change of being. Modalities of time, space, or both regulate the limits and contents of perspective—of what we experience, of what we meaningfully express, of what we know as existents. A language deprived of its modalities (i.e., modal verbs and other means of modality) would cease to function as we know language, even though nominations and many other verbs would continue.

[421] By "*tight* boundedness" I mean that it is relatively impervious and that the relations of "lumpers and splitters" (Zerubavel 1996, 2018) are "taken for granted" so deeply as to be almost imperceptible.

a being who changes in significant ways with each different significant other with whom he or she interacts—that is, *shares action,* taking "other" into account (Weber 1968 [1922], pp. 3-28). This is the conception that, when implications are pursued, so many persons have found unsettling (as Weber did), as if it means that one's self will go swirling off into that "Funhouse" to which John Barth (1968) pointed his reader, or now perhaps the one of which Pink sang in 2008, the imagery a Rorschach test for insecurity, paranoia, or loss of trust in others. Concerns about "stability of self" may well be recurrent, lit for each generation through and by current events of one sort or another, including for some the "inflammatory words" of literary types. An illustrative instance of this was remembered in 1963, one suspects, when Saul Bellow recorded that "Writers of genius in the twentieth century"—he named Paul Valéry, D H Lawrence, James Joyce, "among others"—

> have made us question the stability of the experiencing self, have dissolved it in intellect or in instinct, in the common life of the species, in dream and in myth, and all together have made us aware that the sovereign individual, that tight entity whose fortunes, passions and moral problems filled the pages of novels (and of historical studies as well) was simply a fabrication, the product of a multitude of interests and influences and of our ignorance of physics, psychology and our social class divisions (Bellow 2015, p. 161).

Marking his twenty-fifth year in 1940, Bellow had already lived through some tumults that surely did sow doubts about "stability," with or without the stimulus of some "genius writers," and the ensuing years were not exactly settling. Bellow's own experiences, like the modal experiences of other members of his generation (in Europe, Japan, China, Russia, as well as the USA), probably lent more of a sense of immediacy of relevance to the works of Valéry, Lawrence, Joyce, and others, than to, say, the works of Shakespeare, who also had something to say about stability of self—or Montaigne, Augustine, and many between. (One wonders, too: had he not read Dostoyevsky, or was that name included in the "among others"?)[422]

The difference in conception of "intersubjectivity" is important also because of what might be called "the other face" of the dynamics involved: the production of an intersubjectivity is simultaneously the production of an objectivity. Thus, when Habermas (1992 [1988]) wrote his appreciation of Mead, entitled "Individuation through socialization: on G H Mead's theory of subjectivity," he could as well have added to the subtitle recognition that Mead's was also a theory of *objectivity.* The social relations that are formed as two or more persons engage one another in the complex dynamics of role-taking, negotiating each other's perspectives, meanings, interests, goals, preferences, and the like, constitute an objective reality not only in the sense that each has become an object to the other and therefore has become also a significantly new object (a different "me") to and within the thereby further developed fabric of "oneself," but also an

---

[422] And as to "wondering," a reader may have been wondering why I have drawn as often as I have on the works of Saul Bellow. Only one of my many favorites, I find some of his fictioning particularly useful because his main characters were "copied" from identifiable people, people he knew and others knew and often with marked variation due (in part) to Bellow's own strong emotional attitudes. This complexity of voice, existing both in and behind the scene, is itself very reflective of human relations in general and illustrative of much of Mead's theory.

objective reality in the sense of "we" that had not existed before, a "we" as a shared experience of second-person and third-person relations that have inescapably reformed one's first-person identity into another new collectivity or community. Here we can see characters, for example, of the revisions that were being undertaken in legal texts—from the simpler communalism in which "everyone knows your name" (and probably "your mother's and father's names, too") to collectivities, perhaps nascent communities, built of networks of "trust among strangers," networks made resilient by "contacts, contracts, and torts," together with the model (or fiction) of "the reasonable man" (see §21, above). Here, too, we can see intersections between Mead and three of his contemporaries, Simmel, Weber, and Durkheim (although with mixtures of valence, ranging from the confident progressivism of Mead to the worried conservatism of Durkheim).

As much of the previous discussion of Mead should suggest, one can see in his pragmatic perspectivism hints of a dialectical logic, probably reflective of a Hegelian background (from Royce, for instance) as well as some aspects of the evolutionary theory developed by Darwin and Wallace. Mead's discussions of the process in which an individual person becomes self-aware via the opposition of otherness—others who become significant in and by their opposition, their pushing back—easily suggest a dialectic of passage at the core of an inherent reflexivity of meaning: inhibited/effected action, fact/counterfact, and so forth. "Other selves in a social environment logically antedate the consciousness of self," for the other "must be admitted as there," always already there (as otherwise a human neonate would not survive). Furthermore: "Whatever our theory may be as to the history of things, social consciousness must antedate physical consciousness" (Mead 1910, pp. 178-179, 180; see also 1900, 1901, 1913, 1925, 1927). Mead's emphasis on "taking other's perspective" (i.e., role taking, playing) was hardly a new idea, to be sure. Diderot (1995 [1821], p. 103) had made the point, for instance, when thinking a famous line of Horatian advice: if "you would have me weep, you yourself must first feel grief" (Horace, 1929 [c18 BCE], lines 102-103). But then, said Diderot, a question: how to feel a grief that is not your own? His answer (implicit in Horace)? By imagination: "if I can't imagine myself in your place; if I'm unable to hang from the end of the rope suspending you in the air, I won't be moved to shudder." Mead generalized the point to far less dramatic venues and as a central principle of his theory of the social self—namely, that developmentally the initiating act of language use, the gestural act, comes *from* a significant other *toward* oneself and in that act of "pushing back" (which Mead sometimes called "world answering back") engenders an imagination of other's point of view within which one finds an *otherness of oneself*.[423] "In the process of communication the individual is an other before he is a self." Indeed, it is in the act of "addressing himself in the role of an other [i.e., anticipating how other will understand one's address, etc.] that his self arises in experience" (Mead 1927, p. 80). Mead's argument in this regard differed from Diderot's view in one important respect—namely, in different concepts

---

[423] The reader of Mead's 1913 essay on the social self must bear in mind that Mead could express himself only in a chain of sentences, could not say everything at once, thus was at risk of giving the impression of a stage theory. He did not intend that a person's self develops "all at once"; it is rather a process, one could say a "maturation" process, and certainly the fact of language and thus of the gestural act is always already present *in process*—before the formation of a "generalized other." But role-taking or role-playing begins in language uses within imagination virtually from the beginning, usually the dyadic relation of mother-infant interaction of contests of time, satisfaction, expectation, and perspective.

of imagination. Contrasting imagination to judgment, Diderot (1995 [1821], p. 113) held that imagination "creates nothing; it imitates." In Mead's perspectivism imagination is closer to the Greek concept of mimesis (rather than the Latin "imitatio"): it is active, productive, and most crucially productive of sociality as the constitution of a self, a self-conception, an identity of person (and so nearly a dialectical relation of identity/difference that one can easily read that into his sentences, although Mead himself tended usually to analytical logic). In his examples of child's play, games, and other experiences of role playing, his discussions indicate that knowing how to play a specific position (e.g., third base in baseball) involves knowing the experience of playing every position (role) reasonably well. The game as a whole is indexed in the play of each position—including, of course, the oppositional. The activity is carried out in language use, which always has the potential of surprise—for oneself, for other(s), and, occasionally, for the "generalized other."[424] As Rorty (1982, p. 125) pointed out, "the realm of possibility expands whenever a new vocabulary is invented" (assuming, of course, that the vocabulary is not merely another cycle of the game of "old wine" in supposedly new bottles). The potential is integral to the motivation, and unexpected effects may ensue. But inferential uses of those effects are limited, basically for the reason that Hume said. The expansion does virtually nothing to aid us in any of our efforts to ascertain "conditions of possibility" (including the appearance of a genius of reason "behind" the unexpected). In order to attain that imagined goal, we would have to "envisage all such inventions before their occurrence. The idea that we do have such a metavocabulary at our disposal, one which gives us a 'logical space' in which to 'place' anything which anybody will ever say, seems just one more version of the dream of 'presence' from which ironists since Hegel have been trying to wake us." Limits of counterfactuality, with or without the complications due to endogeneity, keep us well supplied with suspenseful puzzles.

Practical concerns of the kind adumbrated above in the fugitive sketches from Diderot and Horace illustrate the kinds of concerns that occupied Mead as well, at the same time that he was engaged in writing his papers of theorizing. Scatters of evidence here and there depict Mead as flowing with much confidence in social experimentations as well as in theorizations. His studies in philosophy under Royce doubtlessly contributed to that blending of activities, as Royce himself became more and more inclined to a pragmatist approach.[425] Similar orientation was very likely involved in a mutuality when Mead joined John Dewey on the faculty in Ann Arbor, and then in 1894 when he moved with Dewey to the University of Chicago (refounded two years earlier) and its growing tradition of social engagement, public policy, and the idea of a city as a sort of laboratory. Jane Addams and Ellen Gates Starr had opened Chicago's first settlement house, Hull House, in 1889, for example, and five years later a house associated with the

---

[424] This concept can be likened to Heidegger's (1962 [1927], pp. 163-168, 176-178) notion of the "they," a notion integral to his conception of "publicness" (Öffentlichkeit). Referring to the form of the "who" as "the neuter, *the 'they'* [das Man]", Heidegger equated the open-ended anonymity of the plural pronoun and that of the singular pronoun "one" (i.e., "das Man"); e.g., the expression "One is" or "One does."

[425] In his main works of philosophy Royce was a perplexed thinker, trying to reconcile the irreconcilable. In some of his articles, however, one can see a more venturesome and pragmatic approach. Three of these (Royce 1894, 1895a, 1895b) are typically cited as the writings by Joyce that probably had the most substantial impact on Mead.

university opened on Gross Avenue (later renamed McDowell Avenue). Mead became involved in the latter venture (see, e.g., Mead 1907-08), as well as in applications of his work of theory to problems of the interstitial connection from the institutional orders of family to the very different institutional orders of public education (see, e.g., Mead 1904; Baltzell 1964, pp. 159-178).[426] Experimentalism must have seemed a perfectly natural expression, one might say, of his pragmatic naturalist perspectivism. While this would be to assume a naiveté that is contradicted by evidence, it does nonetheless point to tensions in Mead's perspectivism.

One can conclude that Mead's understanding of his naturalist perspective was relatively uncomplicated by the concerns that Weber had expressed with regard to his own emphasis on the category of "subject meaningfulness" vis-à-vis expectations of a scientific knowledge. There is evidence by Mead's own hand that contradicts that conclusion, however. He did of course write otherwise various sentences that include phrases such as "they exist in nature"—in one instance "they" referring to "objective differences" of standpoint, by which a specific array of "objects ... may all be considered as 'here'" (Mead 1925, pp. 256-257). It is not always clear what exactly he intended by "nature." In general, it seems to have functioned primarily and mainly as an implicit background assumption in his thinking, a taken-for-granted "fact" based especially in Darwinian theory and, with that, perhaps presumptions aligned with the same functionalist thread in Dewey's pragmatism. The stance is certainly not a novel one; it has been used repeatedly (e.g., see the case of Clifford Geertz, in Hazelrigg 1992, pp. 252-255). I know of no evidence that Mead believed nature, "the natural world," to be a human production (as in Hazelrigg 1989a, 1989b, 1993b, 1995), and there is some evidence by his own hand that he refused any such thought (e.g., Mead 1932, pp. 93-118). Yet at least on occasion he seemingly verged on it—for example, when he (2001, pp. 3-8) argued that instincts are social, when he (1927, p. 80) said that "social beings are things as definitely as physical things are social," and in other sentences.[427] Judging from some of the preparatory writing for his Carus Lectures (1932, pp. 93-118), Mead was in fact struggling to reconcile (in his words) rationalism and empiricism. But with greater pertinence of his pragmatic theoretical efforts, I think, the struggle can be better viewed as an effort to reconcile his convictions in a perspectivism of sociality and his

---

[426] The logic of Mead's theorization of the dynamics of selfhood-in-continuing-formation partly parallel some aspects of Jean Piaget's empirical conclusions of his studies of development in children (see, e.g., 1952 [1936]; also 1926 [1923] and 1954 [1950]). The resemblance probably reflects general developments in processes then usually denoted under the label "socialization" or "child development" (the former of which could be read as implying a Lockean "blank slate" conception of the human neonate as a pre-social, pre-cultural being).

[427] It is worth noting that the manuscript of the volume which Mead had entitled *Essays in Psychology* (Mary Jo Deegan inserted "Social" into that title when she recovered the volume for publication: Mead 2001) was completed circa1910. One can imagine psychologists of the day recoiling from several of Mead's statements, perhaps a factor in Mead's apparent decision to shelve the entire volume. While some have suggested that Mead's relatively weak presence in US social science was due to slow publication, in fact he averaged more than one article a year after 1895 until his death. Lewis and Smith's (1980, ch. 8) overview suggests that his work gained little attention, and other indicators agree with that. Karpf (1932, p. 318) described Mead's articles as "fragmentary" and "both involved and obscure." Perhaps Mead's efforts to sort through some complexities had something to do with that.

understanding of the requirements of a scientific knowledge—in sum, a struggle very much like Weber's.

Not long before his Carus Lectures were composed, Mead delivered another lecture in Berkeley, California, in January 1929, commemorating the landing of George Berkeley (not yet a bishop) in British North America two centuries earlier. This lecture, the last of Mead's writings that he saw in print, was published in August 1929 in the *Journal of Philosophy*. I bring it into play here because of his use of a sequence of thought experiments. The first is Berkeley's own argument of what he called "immaterialism" (later called by others "subjective idealism," which naming manifests something of a misunderstanding of Berkeley's self-conception).[428]

Like John Locke, Berkeley was an empiricist. Knowledge derives from our sensations, "the impressions of the mind's inner activities."[429] Locke was on the right road, according to his dead colleague—Locke (1632-1704) was gone by the time Berkeley (1685-1753) published his *Treatise* in 1710—but he pulled up short by concluding that, of course, those sensations are of real things external to mind. Why, Berkeley asked, was Locke not consistent with his own basic principle? When someone (e.g., Samuel Johnson)[430] protested to Berkeley that if he stubbed his toe he felt pain because the object was much harder than a thought, Berkeley could simply reply that, yes, you experienced a real sensation of pain, but from that you made an inference as to its cause, and for that you have no evidence other than by sensation. "Of course, Berkeley could ask," Mead elaborated, "what more there could be in experiencing outside matter than having sensations of hardness and of extension, provided one always experienced the sensation when he had the visual sensation of it, and anyone who had travelled along Locke's new way of ideas was hard put to it to find any difference." Then consider this thought experiment.

> Imagine the conventional Christian God at work, in full display of definitive character, omniscient, omnipotent, and omnipresent. All will be as God declares. The human creature was endowed with mind, and mind processed sensations. These sensations told of an outer world. But perhaps God really ended his creation with a mind filled with abilities and contents of sensation according to the natural senses. Why would God then go to the trouble of also making that material world? Maybe God did not. Maybe God ended with mind filled with abilities and contents of sensation. How would we be able to discriminate between the two hypotheses? The evidence for them would be the same, our sensations.[431]

---

[428] This was initially presented in his 1710 *Treatise*. Garnering little attention, he rewrote the text as a set of dialogues among three interlocutors, and this, published three years later as Three Dialogues, gained considerable attention.

[429] Unless otherwise noted, the following quotations are from Mead's 1929 paper.

[430] Boswell (1887 [1799], p. 471) reported a conversation with Johnson to that effect. But Boswell was somewhat imaginative in his accounts. Zaretsky (2015) offered good perspective on Boswell, not only in relation to Johnson.

[431] Bertrand Russell's (1921, p. 159) later version: "There is no logical impossibility in the hypothesis that the world sprang into being five minutes ago, exactly as it then was, with a population that 'remembered' a wholly unreal past."

The second thought experiment was Mead's own, which he labelled "an economist's fable." Imagine a huge hoard of gold.[432] Gold is a thing, an unusual thing as metals go, because it does not interact with oxygen. While rather abundant in Earth's crust, recognition of that fact was very slow to develop, mainly because central authorities, whether of secular government or church, knew that it would be easy to hoard gold as a store of value. But what is "value," one might ask. How does one "store value"? It would be a useful unit of exchange, of course, as it (unlike silver) does not deteriorate by oxygenation. More to the point, it could be maintained as rare existence and thus a substance of intrinsic value. It could be made into jewelery as well as coins, but otherwise it would not be of much use: it is not edible, not hydrating, uncomfortable as clothing, and unless alloyed with a base metal it is too malleable to use in construction. Indeed, that set of limiting facts, all understood as tokens of gold's alleged rarity, added to its "intrinsic worth." Because gold had little use value, with careful management of its supply—creating scarcity, as with diamonds—it could have high and relatively stable exchange value.

Now, this hoard of gold was stored securely in a bank's vaults. "The bank issued its paper [money] according to legal ratio [$20.67 per troy ounce, when Mead was writing], and remained therefore entirely sound. No one wanted the gold as long as he knew he could get it." Suppose, however, that one day a bank official found that the gold was gone. What to do? As the bank officials pondered that question, no one else knew of the theft, and business continued as before. In short,

> we move about in the world of our sensations, with their extension and solidity. Our distance sensations indicate to us what we must do to attain contact sensations, but we never get away from sensations, we only pass from certain sensations to other sensations, and they are all of them ordered in a law-abiding world of sensations. To be sure, we assume there are physical things answering to these sensations, but our only interest in them is our belief that they ensure our getting other experiences if we act intelligently. Now comes Berkeley the burglar, burrows underneath our presuppositions and takes the material universe away, and lo! all goes on as before. The same divine intelligence that was supposed to have created this physical universe is directly responsible for the meanings which our experiences have for us, and we never discover that the material backing of our ideas is gone. And, unlike the back directors, we discover that we have no way of finding out whether it is gone or not, because we never could experience it anyway; all we could get would be some more sensations.[433]

---

[432] Remember, Mead was writing in 1929; the US Bullion Depository at Fort Knox, KY, was not created until 1933, after Franklin Roosevelt had declared a Federal Reserve monopoly on the holding of all gold bullion, coins, and certificates, thus ending the "gold standard" of the US dollar domestically and thereby enabling the Federal Reserve to print fiat money in order to stimulate demand. Foreign governments could continue to sell US dollars for gold until 1971, when the Nixon administration completely severed that practice of "gold backing" as well. Of particular relevance, see Diderot's (1995 [1821], pp. 75-83) satire on luxury in his Salon of 1767.

[433] Bear in mind that for Mead "sensation," if ever present in thought and talk, involved language, which implied concepts, perspective, etc. (i.e., sociality). Also bear in mind that Mead's paper appeared in print less than three months before the Great Crash of 1929, which began on the 24th of October and reached bottom on the 29th when the New York Stock Exchange collapsed. Like Mead's thought

366

The third thought experiment recounted by Mead was Albert Einstein's. Recall that a human person's sense of dimensionality begins with a base sensation of two dimensions: a person has a body circumference, which implies diameter or width, and a height, which, together with width, is enough to suggest depth or distance (as architects and painters realized centuries earlier). But how is this third dimension actually measured? We commonly think of the metric of depth or distance as the meter (or foot, yard, mile, etc.). But in fact if one looks into the convention of the International System of Units, meter is a metric of time (i.e., duration) as well as distance. The point is, while one has two bodily dimensions of diameter and height without doing anything, without going anywhere, just standing in place, one cannot measure distance (or length) without moving, even if vicariously in thought, because one can move only in time. The longest unit of duration is the "light year," the duration of a photon's travel in vacuum in 365.25 days. This is the upper limit of duration. The shortest unit of duration is "Planck time," the duration of a photon's travel in a vacuum one Planck length, which is the lower limit of duration. Crucially, those are properties of the *observer*. Distance suggests horizon, to be sure, but horizon, too, is a property of the observer (thus, when moving toward a horizon, one finds that arrival is always deferred). Likewise, a vanishing point is also a property of the observer (a fact that artists and architects learned to use to the benefit of their works of art). But what is "crucial" about any of that? This is where the thought experiment à la Einstein comes into play.

Einstein's initial theory of relativity was attuned to observations that could not be reconciled with principles of Newtonian mechanics (e.g., those from the famous "Michelson-Morley experiment" of 1887). In place of various ad hoc "solutions" to the puzzling central result of the observations, Einstein substituted a relativity principle for "length contraction" and "time dilation" (the former notion already offered by several theorists) in conjunction with the posit of constant speed of light ("speed" rather than "velocity," because the experiments had shown that spatial direction was irrelevant). In this 1905 paper ("special theory of relativity") Einstein maintained the assumption of a fixed observer. But the principle of relativity suggested that privileging the observer's position was both inconsistent empirically and unnecessary by logic. Thus, the biggest thought experiment of a long line of them since James Clerk Maxwell's "demon" imagination: what changes if *every* part of the system—the observer and observer's instruments as well as observed objects and relations—are in motion? This became Einstein's 1915 theory. Mead, writing only 13 years later, understood that Einstein's general theory came from a thought experiment in which the observer was no longer privileged by absolute location in space and time—indeed, that time and space are not absolute but are joint functions of relative motion.

This was Mead, writing during his sixty-fifth year, a man born during the US Civil War and educated in a peripatetic sequence of brief sojourns after his four years at Oberlin College (1879-1883)—a year at Harvard, a winter term at Leipzig, a couple of years at Berlin—grasping

---

experiment of the golden hoard, the operation was always social; it began in sociality, it was maintained in sociality, it ended, when it did, in sociality. Exchange depended on the sociality of trust, which is as fragile as the next panic.

theory that was already being widely regarded as incomprehensible to the general public: "In the twentieth century the physicists made

> the extraordinary discovery that if exact measurements were to be made, it was necessary to take into account the relative motion of the observer and that which is measured; that as this varies the actual length of the spatial and temporal standards of measurement change. There is no constant unit of measurement, nor can there be. It goes with this, of course, that there is no absolute space nor absolute time. They vary with the perspective or frame of reference of the observer (Mead 1929, p. 428).

While some nuances were missing or jumbled, the grasp was remarkable.[434] One can also see in that grasp evidence that Mead's pragmatic attitude was sometimes in tension with a rather "old school" naturalist attitude. Early in the century he sought a path between a new program of vitalism, associated with receptions of Henri Bergson, and the idea of "a completely mechanical world" in which "every series is conceivably reversible" (Mead 1907, p. 381). Two decades later he was trying to decipher the potential relevance of Minkowskian space-time and the advent of the quantum program, yet still remembering the world of Newtonian mechanics. On the one hand, he (1932, p. 48) wrote in his Carus Lectures that "the function of the past in experience" is performed through "continual reconstruction as a chronicle to serve the purposes of present interpretation" which takes place within extant conditions of a principle of action informed by expectation and anticipation of future conditions and events. On the other hand, he (1932, p. 13) also wrote in those lectures that "the irrevocability of the past event remains even if we are uncertain what the past event was"—as if "irrevocability" implied continued effects or relevance of remembered or never-cognized past event.

Mead understood "self" not as a fixed entity but as a process, a negotiation within an ensemble of relations produced and sustained in the processes of sociality as a dynamic unity of various perspectives. Sometimes the ensemble goes awry, and it is especially then that the force of sociality can be seen—or, as first-person experience, simply felt. Imagine waking to "memory of me in my world," as one ordinarily does, except that in this instance you have no memory of the world into which you have awakened (from, say, a coma), and you realize you are not at all confident in a self-identity as persons around you seem to suppose of you—as, for instance, they call you by a name, speak of how you were yesterday or last week, and so forth. You have woke into a sociality that you do not remember in particulars, although you have some latent sense of its continuity of processes involving you as a person with others. If enough memory has been lost, a break in continuity is no longer processed as the ordinary break of "Oh, I fell asleep," a fact about you that others are recognizing as problematic in a non-problematic way. Aloneness has become a new experience, as one goes about the task of rebuilding from shards, glimmers, and suggestions from others a sustaining sociality. You gather by inference from others that you

---

[434] Not to say that Mead's grasp was without significant gaps. According to a statement attributed to him (whether actually from his own lecture notes I cannot say), he (1936, p. 38) did not know that photons (i.e., light) lack mass, though they do have momentum (measured as the ratio of energy to speed of motion, or E/c). It is evident from his Carus Lectures (Mead 1932, e.g., pp. 104-105) that he viewed the quantum theory of Max Planck with some doubt or perhaps only puzzlement. He was hardly alone in that, of course.

had once *been* integral to a sociality of *me*, in *my* world (Mead's "generalized other"). At that moment of realization you realize the experience of being alien, as others about you are alien to you.

Ordinarily, one is not bothered by the insight, left to us by Mead (among others), that our knowledge of continuity is never immediate but always constructed after the fact: the continuity of "I" is retrospected through "the memory of me," always by the "I" of a next moment. Or, in Kant's precedence, I cannot know as an object that which I must presuppose in order to know *any* object, and that presupposition is of the temporally continuous "I" that is the radical ground of my being able to synthesize any manifold of representations whatsoever. Hume said much the same. We are still in the realm of a "pure auto-affection," as others have said, *if* we think this "I" as a pure functionality not yet enmeshed in sociality. This is the sort of "solution" that makes "autonomy of action" (as an empirically realizable category) always secondary to autonomy-deferring *"real* determinants of action" (or to what Kant called "alien causes"). In the meantime, this "I" serves as locus of reference for the actions of sociality by which one knows continuity of self, affirmed in memory of me—which is to say, in sociality. It is the memory of me that authorizes anticipation of future instances of "I," even though from within the egocentric predicament to which "I" tends it is "I" who does the anticipation of what could and/or will come to pass.

Up to a critical juncture what has just been said is consonant with formulations such as Mead's. A phrase such as "the social self," for example, or "the social development of the self," involves a redundancy by the terms of Mead's own argument—up to a point. That point or juncture is marked by the presumed necessity of a temporally continuous principle of action, an atemporal principle of action that is located in and as the "part" of individuality that causes something it is not. Yet, as Kant well demonstrated, that "part" can only be a posit, for it is categorically inaccessible to our efforts of knowledge, so it can do "only" the work of a posit. Why, then, should anyone ever postulate a subject (or an interior self-presencing of subject) that cannot be an object to itself? This raises the question of the conditions of the production of, and the work done by, the posit: the preconstituted subject, by (i.e., against) which is decided what is knowledge, what is history, what is sociality and social structure, and so forth, carries with it a preconstituted experience that is "necessary" for there to be any interpretation of experience, just as the preconstituted subject is "necessary" for there to be an historical subject (i.e., a *social* self). It was as if the motivation had been to discover a founding principle that would be logically (even genetically) anterior to that which is founded upon it. If all that is founded upon it is (taken to be) the determinate *regularity* of all social-cultural-historical phenomena, then the founding principle must itself be outside history, society, culture. The "reason" that, in Horkheimer's lament, had never *actually* ruled human history was itself taken to be timeless.

But the problem with that sort of postulation and the quest it stimulates (the bridge) remains exactly as Kant saw it. The price of postulating a subject (or its innermost informational part) that cannot be an object to itself, in order to erect a universal system of determinate

369

regularity as foundation of all contingent phenomena, is that such a subject can never catch sight of the ruling reason. The impossibility of it is congenital to, and inescapable within, that universal system. Therefore, the "bridging problem" works out to be nothing so much as an agency of perpetual employment for philosophers and social scientists: it cannot be solved in its own terms, and because those terms are defined as poles so self-evident in both their presence and their need of a bridge, the impossibility of solution remains hidden. The self-evidence of those poles has been most powerful in the case of "the individual"—to the extent that shaking the authority of an atemporal principle of action stimulates much concern about "loss of the subject," a "paralysis of agency," an "abolition of man" (variants from Clive Lewis 1943 to Friedrich Tenbruck 1984), a flight from autonomy and responsibility, and so forth. The idea that autonomy of action has origins anterior to the polis, in a deep interiority of the individual, is a very old and hallowed conceit. One can understand the attractions of a pragmatism, whether it be Mead's quasi-naturalist version or Rorty's ironically tethered version.

Even before his famous 1913 paper, "The social self," Mead insisted that a self does not exist in isolation. As were many of his contemporaries, he was well aware of compositional facts of the matter, both the hierarchical and the lateral (see, e.g., Giannelli and Fischer 2016). In a more pointed notice of the matter of theorizing, Mead had argued in his 1910 paper concerning the "social objects that psychology must presuppose" that sociality is a condition of conceptions of the individual person in analytic isolation. There is no "unique observer" to which all sense, all perception, all sensation, all experience of reality, reduces. On the other hand, there *is* perspective; it is social in one and the same moment that it is of and by an individual observer, and implicit in that individual observer is a host of significant-other perspectives via role-taking. Likewise, there *is* abstraction, and there *is* reduction; each is social in one and the same moment that it is by an individual observer. Each observation is relative to the activities—to the motions, if you will—of and within a sociality.

A perspectivism was (is) basic to Mead's theorizations. It is present in his formulation of "taking the role of the other"—which is to say, of a perspectival act, of seeing the world through another's eyes and taking that view into account in some fashion; of the child learning to play a game by learning to play all positions in the game, even if not with equal alacrity or polish; of the adult worker even in the hayfield learning to adapt motions to those of another person, so as to optimize relations of task performance (Mead 1913, 1925, 1926, 1927, 1999, 2001).

Those understandings predated Mead, to be sure, yet nevertheless they had remained controversial in receptions of his theorizations, especially insofar as readers realized they were crucially important elements. Critics sometimes charged solipsism, that everything reduced to the viewpoint, to the limits, of a particular person. The notion that only a mind can be known to exist with certainty (as in the Cartesian "cogito ergo sum") is an absurdity that seems to be significant only because it assumes as its own standard the unreality of an achieved perfect self-knowledge known with certainty and with the equally unreal aspiration to a perfect knowledge of others with certainty. While an extreme narcissist might believe that of himself (a Caligula, let's say, or a modern-day Nero), and dogmatists have made at least a show of belief, I know of no theorist who has proposed as much (not even Descartes, who had to rely on an assumption about his God). Nevertheless, the charge has continued to appear in literatures related to Mead (see Puddephatt 2009). With regard to Mead, it should be evident that the charge collapses precisely because there is no such thing as an isolated individual person or self. Self is in fact sociality. Self is in fact an "ensemble of social relations," as Marx (1976 [1888], p. 7) said:[435] the individual person *is* social, which means that something of a whole, a communal and/or an associational whole, is integral to the integrity of the individual person; therefore, "it is always society itself, i.e., man himself in his social relations, that appears as the final result of the social production process" (Marx 1987 [1939], p. 98). This is of course where one finds "also" the production (including reproductions, whether with no or little or, seldom, much difference) of perspectives, of views of world.

Puddephatt (2009) was referring not to Mead himself, it should be noted, but to some of the purportedly Meadian literature that developed in his wake. The most consequential at least in the short run was the work of Herbert Blumer, who on the one hand tried to convince other social scientists, sociologists most especially, to take Mead's contribution more seriously, but who on the other hand created confusion because of some of his presentations as would-be heir of Mead. The resistance to Mead was in part due separately from the efforts of Blumer, as Mead had identified via his publications initially as a philosopher, then as a "social behaviorist" and toward the end as a "social psychologist," a relatively new designation.[436] And more than a few readers balked at what they regarded as Mead's "radical" proposals. Factional loyalty was hardly a new feature of disciplinary perspectives, no doubt, but new labels created some new factions. Blumer's efforts contributed to that, especially as he promoted a new specialty known as "symbolic interactionism."

Mead brought the fact of language into the entire fabric of sociality, locating especially the "significant symbol" as carrier of meanings inherent to person-to-person transaction and therefore in the thoughts of the individual actor as he or she sought to take into account the comparative meanings and perspectives and circumstances of "significant other" interlocutors, whether they be face-to-face or at some distance or remembered in memory or anticipated in rehearsal. This centrality of "communication," as Habermas (e.g., 1990 [1983]) and Luhmann 2012 [1997]), among others, have described it (and see Piaget 1926 [1923] and Vygotsky 1978), has made it more difficult to claim any special dispensation or privilege as speaker or writer. It

---

[435] Recall that Marx' point, in his critique of Feuerbach's materialism, was (is) that Feuerbach had abstracted the human person from the concrete reality of social relations in order to obtain his isolated individual, which in his confusion he had thought that he was beginning with that isolate. I know of no evidence that Mead had read any of Marx, but he was making much the same point in his critique of originary thinking.

[436] One of the best treatments of the whole of Mead's theorizations was (is) Miller (1973). The author then known as a philosopher, his book was marketed as a work of philosophy. The "silo effect" in attention was already effective, long before anyone coined the phrase "social media." Collections of Mead's papers had been published in 1964, one of them (Mead 1964a) with the "philosophy" label. Three of the books posthumously published in Mead's name (1934, 1936, 1938) are of variable accuracy, the one entitled *Mind, Self, and Society* (1934) being the most misleading and the most often cited by social scientists.

was perhaps primarily with this focus, implicit more often than explicit, that much of the sharper aim toward Blumer was intended (see, e.g., Stryker 1988; Cook 2011), as if social scientists could continue to do what Einstein had shown was beyond the abilities of physical scientists.[437]

Granted, some of Blumer's notions were rather wooly. His emphasis on "emergence" was perhaps the wooliest, insofar as it suggested some sort of special property, something above and beyond the already long-recognized fact that human actions are sometimes productive of effects that had not been present prior to the actions. Mead (1932) himself spent much effort in his Carus Lectures, when discussing "emergence" and "the emergent" in conjunction with notions of a present moment's past time, in seeking clarity of his meanings of "temporal sequence," "determinacy," and so forth—especially the "presence of a past" that must be there in present effects even though one can never gain direct access to the determinants from which present effects arose, because the determinant events are as such now past even if the conditions that supported those events have persisted (an "if" that can be supported by logic but empirically must depend on inference from the effects at hand). In a generic sense, of course, human actions are productive even when the effects of those actions are *re*productive of a status quo; short of that, human realities would disappear, and we do know, I assume, that human beings are capable of making *all* human reality disappear via collective and total suicide. One might also identify "emergence" with products or effects that had not been intended or anticipated, a notion to which one of Mead's contemporaries, Max Weber, gave special attention.

The central thread running through most of the facets of the "Blumer controversy" can be understood as a "conflict of interpretation," roughly of the kind that was displayed, for example, in the response of Eric Hirsch to Hans-Georg Gadamer's treatise, *Truth and Method* (see Hirsch 1967, pp. 245-264; Gadamer 1989).[438] Remarkably, after all of the prior discussions of Kant's legacy—much of that effort having aspired to refutation or at least to circumvention of the dilemma, but an increasing volume of it having sought instead to reach a workable settlement in acceptance of his demonstration of the limits of knowledge—there had (and has) remained a narrow strand of simple refusal, in preference to a dogmatism. Huebner's (2014) account of the career of Mead as a reflection of the disciplines of social science, sociology most particularly, is apposite. In that regard especially, consider the fact of John McKinney's (1955) good effort to bring Mead into the fold.

---

[437] As has been noted before, social scientists have been slow to recognize that the model of science that was taken for granted before James Clerk Maxwell and Charles Darwin, a version of Newtonian mechanics that Newton himself on at least one occasion seemed to doubt, has not been taken seriously by leading members of the physical sciences for several decades. Mercier's (2016) book about the difference of argumentation also applies.

[438] An English translation of Gadamer's text was first published in 1975 (a revised translation in 1989). While the initial translation left much to be desired, the disagreement expressed by Hirsch was not substantially prejudiced by those deficiencies of translation. Hirsch's position was an instance of the "originalist" doctrine that has at times been taken with regard to the US Constitution—in effect, that its original meanings remain intact even if no extant person understands or ascribes to them. But what that doctrine actually amounts to is the claim that *my* reading is *the* correct reading as first intended and written by the text's author(s).

Any given action always takes place within the products, enablements/constraints, of already extant action effects. It could be said, as Claude Fischer (1982, p. 2) has, recalling Georg Simmel , that the dyadic bond is the smallest unit of sociality, and that this bond exists within a more or less extensive network of similar bonds, dyadic and larger, which network is in turn linked within the complexity of similar other networks but which for every living person has always already existed in the infant mind's recognition of the pushiness of a caretaker. Those effects can and often do attain objectivities as resilient as the trust that undergirds successes of fiat money, for instance. But the trust is vulnerable to panic from the vaguest suspicion that someone has "stolen all of the gold." I concur with Fischer's discussion of bonds—but with the stipulation that those bonds exist *within* the self-identity of an individual person, and in that sense the individual person is the smaller unit of sociality.

If there was reluctance to bring Mead into the fold of a social science, that reluctance probably had much to do with a fact already touched upon—namely, that Mead's theorizations brought into focus, as seldom had been so clear before, one's relation to oneself as a reflexivity that seems always to be rooted just beyond the limits of reflection. This realization induces an insecurity of authoritative speaking and writing much as did some parts of Hume's *Treatise* (thus falling "dead-born from the press," as Hume later said). Sometimes the resistance was expressed in the view that Mead brought psychology into sociology—that is, via his self-description as a psychologist who has become social—although his own writings (e.g., Mead 1910) should have made evident the opposite understanding (i.e., that he was placing the possibility of a psychology on sociological bases). I think the more serious source of resistance had to do with the pulse on which Stryker (1988) had his finger—the threat to an authority of science—and this was bound up with Mead's perspectivism (cf. Turner 1983).[439]

Mead's perspectivism had been developed primarily in the field of relations formed by and within his concept of "significant other"—both the differences among a person's actual significant others, resulting from a selection process, and the still greater disparities among the potential significant others who were available for selection. Mead's (1907-08) interest in the local settlement-house movement brought him into contact with at least some of the greater diversity, but there is little doubt that the bulk of his thinking about the "significant other" process was in terms of the more restricted range of differences. One should not conflate "restricted" with "absent" variation, however, in practices of "taking the role of the other." No doubt many men and women today who were each of multi-sibling parentage will recognize the expression of a substantive gap, even some degree of contradiction, between sibling experiences of one and "the same" parent. The otherness that pushes and therein adds reflexivity of relation is both external and internal—that is to say, more carefully, a dialectic of external/internal that itself

---

[439] The same threat loomed in resistance to the claim of "ethnomethodology" by Harold Garfinkel (e.g.,1967), which was primarily reaction to the dominance of his chief mentor, Talcott Parsons, and which met sometimes fierce resistance despite early efforts (e.g., McKinney 1969) to relate his proposals to existing perspectives. The fact that Garfinkel, like Blumer, chose to create a new discipline (or sub-discipline) rather than demonstrate his argument from the grounds and implications of existing literatures perhaps derived from the usual move to "change the subject" by creating a new vocabulary for old ideas. In any case, bear in mind that we have not left the domain of Kant's legacy, and genuinely new ideas remain distressingly scarce.

moves through a dialectic of other/same. The diversity that can come from weak ties can also be present within a dyad of siblings each of whose perspective on nominally the same parent or parents could as easily be described as from the pushiness of a sharply different significant other.

A recent, publicly discussed case of that kind of internal difference came to us from Tara Westover's (2018) memoir of her own very personal struggle to gain and protect freedom of aspiration as the young daughter of highly restrictive parents, paired with a response to her memoir by an older brother who had been very supportive of his sister's efforts but who also had different perceptions of the parents. (Posting his review of his sister's memoir on her Amazon webpage, he described some of the differences while also verifying his sister's experiences. His post was soon removed, due to a number of ugly attacks directed against both sister and brother.) Fortunately, the extremity of conditions of sociality reported for that household has not been typical (albeit also not exactly rare). But the mere fact of difference in perspective remains, whether with large or small degree of effect. Assume a four-person household (two parents and two children): there are six dyadic relations and four triadic relations, each of the ten relations having a different internal audience of one or two observers. This set of internal relations alone is enough virtually to ensure that perspective and experience will differ for each member (child *or* parent).[440]

As presented in abstraction of other family members, the set of relations featured four actors who were present not just as "four individual persons," as if they were interchangeable, but as persons characterized within the institution of a familial household organization, with explicit conditional positions or statuses of age, gender, and locally accepted mating and parenting relations. Mead's primary focus in the bulk of his writing had to do with establishing the sociality of self-identity. This does not mean, however, that he was unaware of "status and role" conditions of the operative dynamics of sociality and thus of variations of self-identity. His involvement with local venues of the settlement-house movement, with the differences between what he knew in Chicago and what he experienced of the diversities of life in Hawaii during visits with his wife's relatives, with the differences of culture as experienced during his months in Germany, and so forth, had provided sufficient opportunities to understand that, and how, taken-for-granted encapsulations of conditional positions and processes—gender, national and ethnic-group identity, and class, for example, or the revision of "legal subject" from will-based to a different abstraction, one that assumed more anonymity of relation as reasonable basis of expectations—are relative to, and are integral to, the dynamics of a particular formation of sociality.

*******

In closing this Part Four, I want to take a quick look back to earlier discussions and to issues in play during Kant's productions of a critique of critique. It should be clear that with Mead a circle closed, so to speak, around the many efforts of Romanticist theorists during the decades either side of 1800 to coordinate their central notion of selfhood as an individual project, a

---

[440] To complete the reflexive aspect of the point, what a theorist or analyst will recognize about her or his "objects of study" (other people, their actions and relations) is often not welcome as an insight pertinent to the process of that study.

Bildungsprozess, within current and near-future conditions of modernizing societies of Europe and Europe-dominated territories in other parts of the world. This effort of coordination was doomed, as Izenberg (1992) argued, because the theoretical framework and perspective in which it was conceived and conducted contained as premise the contradictions that only gradually appeared clearly enough to be seen in the preferments of a conclusion. A dehistoricizing—or in its own perspective a *pre*-historicizing—that followed from reliance on an originary logic left it without requisite conceptualizations, occluding the primary "difference not only between Romantic and modern versions of the self but between the Romantic and pre-Romantic versions of the purported constant myth of recovering and rejoining the absent ground of truth" (Izenberg 1992, p. 10). The generalized contradiction lay between "the individual" and "the social" (again, intending this latter phrase as encompassing the many distinctions among the social sciences: cultural, religious, juridical, political, economic, etc.), inasmuch as any self-fashioning of "the individual person" could occur only in the midst of aligned/misaligned forces of social conditions, social processes, social institutions, including the ideological formulations of Romanticism itself, those of its predecessors as they hovered in memory, and those of modern institutionalized services of rights, obligations, and duties of citizenship—all of which purported various versions of a universalist program of future lives, and all of which had to be worn by self-fashioning imaginations of individual creativity as if they constituted an original skin (a "second nature") that only now had come to maturity. No wonder, as many scholars later reported, any effort to discern necessary correlations between parallel structures or stratifications of "the individual," so conceived, and of "the social," in all its complexity of an experienced world, had failed its aim. By bringing sociality thoroughly into "the interior" of individual self-identity, at the same time ensconcing individual self-identity thoroughly within sociality, Mead had radically changed the terms of social-science theorizing, although theorists were slow to understand that achievement. It was not an unprecedented achievement. Marx' insistence on "ensemble of social relations" as constitutional description of "the individual" had been rather more than a preview, but it had made little or no impression on literate audiences—any more than did any of Marx' writings until after his name had become a specter of threat.[441] Mead added some specific emphases, one of the most controversial being that "self-identity" was now understood to be a multiplicity, the "many in one" processes of sociality. Mead's replay of a core Kantian principle—the transcendental unity of apperception—had been moved from the realm of pure functionality to ordinary empirical processes of world-making. Not surprisingly, a new armature of story-lining was already being fashioned into a new kind of Bildungsprozess novel: think of James Joyce's *A Portrait of the Artist as a Young Man* (1916), for instance, or of Alfred Döblin's *Berlin Alexanderplatz* (1929).

Markus Gabriel (2017 [2015], p. 124) has understood the radical position staked out by Mead for a social science, describing Mead's "social interactionism" as "radical" for insisting that human consciousness is constituted not only *in* but also *of* sociality, and then seemingly making a point of the fact that Mead's position has been "recently restated" by Wolfgang Prinz

---

[441] A core thematic of Hegel's philosophy, his notion of Nature, as manifestation of an Absolute Becoming, gradually gaining consciousness of itself in trial-and-error formations leading to Homo sapiens, could have been understood as suggesting Mead's central theme, and perhaps it did, although Hegel's rose had lost its bloom.

(2012), and drawing a major link from Mead's (and Prinz') argument to the work on "one of the most important postwar philosophers," Hilary Putnam.[442] My aim in directing attention to these links is told by the fact that, having apparently endorsed that argument, Gabriel then mostly ignored it, as he reverted to his own formulations of debate about "transcendental ontologies" (2011) and his stance regarding what he (2017 [2015], p. 144) viewed as the basic alternative answers to his remaining question, "Yet who or what is this self after all?" The alternatives he (2017 [2015], p. 139) counterposed, "bundle theory" and "substance theory," were regarded as contraries. With both assumed to have location in the individual person qua individual organism, the principal point of contention has been whether the referent of "self" is to a single substance or to a collection of substantive properties. From Gabriel's standpoint, the crucial contention is about reductionism: whatever "self" is—and he never actually resolved his own ambiguities, perhaps ambivalence, in that regard—does "it" reduce wholly to "brain"? The sociality answer given by Mead (and by Prinz, Bogdan, and others) is not simply contextual; it is *constitutive*. But having cited that point, Gabriel then overlooked it.

Why? Gabriel's (2017 [2015], pp. 145-146) formulation of "the binding problem" tells his answer: this "problem" remains after sociality is taken into account because it resides *within* the human being as an in-itself objective presence that, as such, *comes into* sociality. "Rocks are an example of the in-itself" (Gabriel 2017 [2015], p. 208): a rock, though it "has an absolute being," has no "beliefs about itself—because it has no beliefs"; and that, apparently, makes all the important difference about an objectivity, which otherwise could be accorded products of human activity. One might ask, "Isn't a 'rock' at least a 'being-for-us'?" But, no. Gabriel could acknowledge Brandom's (2000, p. 11) account of "self"—in Gabriel's (2017 [2015], p. 166) words, "the general name for our fellow players in the game of giving and asking for reasons" (i.e, beliefs)[443]—without penalty, because for him the prior question remains one of the "in-itself object" (i.e., not merely *about* that *object* but *of* that object in-itself, prior to any naming). The challenge of "scientists of the brain" (Prinz excluded, one presumes) was all-consuming—and therein grievously threatening—precisely because, by Gabriel's assumption, it is not one of Brandom's "games" of "giving reasons" but one of an extra-human authority of a Nature in the singular, uniform, and universal backdrop to human experiences (Gabriel 2017 [2015], pp. 158-161). We seem to be back to Samuel Johnson's toe.

---

[442] Gabriel was correct in that attribution, and the point he was making, presumably, turned on Prinz' record as an eminent figure in the world of cognitive and brain sciences (Prinz, born in 1942, is recently retired as director emeritus at the Max Planck Institute in Leipzig). Gabriel's (born in 1980) citations were in the context of his explanation why "I am not a brain" (Gabriel 2017 [2015]; judging from a few comments—e.g., pp. 144, 165—the English edition offers some up-dating of the German edition). Gabriel could have cited Radu Bogdan (e.g., 2000) in addition to Prinz' book. Gabriel's citation of Putnam was to his essay collection, *Reason, Truth and History* (1981).

[443] Brandom (2000, pp. 158-159): "the representational dimension of propositional contents should be understood in terms of their *social* articulation—how a propositionally contentful belief or claim can have a different significance from perspective of the individual believer or claimer, on the one hand, than it does from the perspective of one who attributes that belief or claim to the individual, on the other. The context within which concern with what is thought and talked *about* arises is the assessment of how the judgments of one individual can serve as reasons for another."

Since Gabriel was aware of the difficulty (the impossibility) of the standard he could only suggest, he fell back to an asymptotic benchmark—namely, an ideal to which one must try to approximate. Or, in his (2017 [2015], p. 154) words, "an ideal of objectivity is formulated from a standpoint that cannot be absolutely objective. The distinction between our subjective standpoint, the self, and the domain of objects under investigation from the objective standpoint, nature or the not-self, cannot be derived from the objective standpoint alone. These theories were not forged first in laboratories but in social relations, ... which Fichte before Marx recognized." It is symptomatic that Gabriel counterposed "laboratories" to "social relations" (cf. Latour and Woolgar 1986; Marx 1976 [1888], p. 4).[444]

Captured by his concerns about "brain-mind" duality, Gabriel's position evinced what amounts to a naturalist view—as outlined (ironically) by an internationally renowned director of studies of cognitive and brain sciences (Prinz (2012, pp. 182-183): "Like an organ of the body," this thing called "self" is regarded as "a naturally given component of the mind that develops prior to and independent of experiences." This notion, Prinz added, is "deeply rooted in our folk psychology" ("our," meaning the folk psychology that has been dominant in European and Euro-American cultures). Conversely, what Prinz called "constructivist construals of subjectivity" regard "self" not as a "natural organ of the mind" but as "an acquired structure" of mind which developed during species evolution perhaps in "the interplay of symbolic communication, dual representation [i.e., simultaneously subject and object], and authorship attribution."

The struggle exemplified by Gabriel reminds me of a heated debate that occurred during the 1830s primarily between two highly eminent comparative anatomists, Robert Edmond Grant and Richard Owen (for more detail, see Hazelrigg 1993a). Physically, the focus of debate was a set of small fossilized jawbones. But a difference of identification by Grant and Owen ramified far beyond. A visible difference of anatomy was assumed to be about correct identity of fact, absolutely objective fact. Yet, as the debate unfolded, conceptualization of "whatness" was inescapably entwined in social relations, and not only because of contested reputational goods (including the regard of Owen as an unpleasant fellow). Where Owen saw identifying markers of a marsupial and thus mammalian animal, Grant saw identifying markers of a reptilian animal. The question of which claim to authority was correct was understood to be of profound import to the integrity of existing zoologic classification as a theoretical matter but also to the utility of standard techniques of analyzing fossils. Here, then, was another test case for what have been called "constructionist" approaches to the practice of science (e.g., Latour and Woolgar 1986), and it is clear that the debate developed in ways that are consistent with that perspective. The science of organic fossils is an inherently social undertaking—in observations, in the field or in

---

[444] The mistake was described by Marx in his third thesis on Feuerbach: that the objectivity claimed by Feuerbach's materialism (which Marx regarded as the most highly developed of all materialisms) came about only because the doctrine has divided society into two parts, then claimed one of the parts (the objectivity of science) as superior to the whole (society, composed of subjects as well as objects). As Marx (1975 [1932], p. 298) said elsewhere, "Not only is the material of my activity given to me as a social product (as is even the language in which the thinker is active): my own existence is social activity, and therefore that which I make of myself, I make of myself for society and with the consciousness of myself as a social being." Dogmatic claims attempt to circumvent that contingency, by asserting some kind of "special actor" privilege.

laboratories; in sampling, classification, and measurement; in debates, in journals, and in receptions whether professional or popular. As I argued on previous occasion, however, most observers still tend to "side with the bones" as purely objective things that exist without "human fingerprints"—that is, in perfect in-itself integrity within some pristine pre-human realm of fact (Hazelrigg 1993a). Recall from a discussion in Part One, above, Robert Pippin's (1999, pp. 53, 56) reminder of Kant's display of "objective necessity" in response to the transcendental Illusion, the absolute necessity of a "real object," *the* absolutely objective object, standing behind or beneath any phenomenal object of (as Gabriel called it) "the not-self" that self-consciousness "must" presuppose as prior to any consciousness, or at least any consciousness as sapience if not also as sentience (see Kant 1998 [1787], B354/A297).

In one of the last essays that Mead published, he in effect drew the circle on Kant's insistence on legislation as an ordinary yet extraordinary activity that links responsibility to the hope of species maturity. Mead's point is worth repeating:

> The world in which humanity lives today, especially in the western world, is as different from that of the eighteenth century as were two geologic epochs. We can determine what plant life and what animal life shall surround us; and to a large extent we do. We can determine what shall be the immediate incidence of cold and heat upon our bodies. We can determine what sort of a human race shall be bred, and how many of them. All the conditions which we believe, in large measure, determined the origin of species are within our power. We can do all this, but we have not accepted the responsibility for it (Mead 1929, p. 430).

In his later meditation on time, and in conjunction with consideration of Heidegger's varied accounts of being and time (from Temporalität to Zeitlichkeit),[445] David Wood (2007, pp. 135-138) agreed that "between finite ecstatic temporal projection and historical thrownness a dimension is opened up in which selfhood is articulated"—his point being not that this is the only possible avenue of an articulation of selfhood but that Heidegger's pursuit is understandable in that regard. Wood also agreed that "being-with-other is constitutive for self." But he worried about lack of any backstop on this trajectory (which Heidegger had overseen as one determined by and bound to its destination). Referring to Heidegger's "march of explication disguised as argument"—a march that had been driven via "a common stock of nationalistic and militaristic rhetoric"—Wood confronted problems of consistency, even contradiction, recognizing them as timely in practicality as well as in theoretical issues. On the one hand, for instance, Wood could not but agree with Heidegger's "dehiscence of self," insofar as Heidegger's target had been the "metaphysical standard" of self as a "self-sufficient substance." On the other hand, the supposed argument was built in telic terms as a destiny, and this stimulated serious consternations about a post-dehiscent agency untethered to anything larger than itself.

The chain along which we are driven—from resoluteness, to thrownness, to fate, to being-with-others, to community, to destiny, and ultimately (in the case of Schlageter) to a

---

[445] The former word was intended as Time, as an absolute frame (e.g., as Copernicus, maybe Newton, but not Einstein, intended it), while the latter is "timeliness," an experiential condition, a matter of sequences, schedulings, processes of ordering, and so forth, a relative temporality and temporariness.

hero's death, and to martyrdom—knows no end but self-surrender: identity through identification. In the absence of a higher being, Heidegger offers us, in different aspects, the West, Germany, or Hitler (Wood 2007, p. 137).[446]

Kant's aspirational emphasis on species maturity, recall, was twinned with freedom (the realm of ethics) vis-à-vis necessity, whether it be the necessity of a realm of nature ("noumena" as that to which the concept refers) or the "objective necessity" integral to a position of response to the transcendental Illusion. A fear of freedom comes to the fore as recognition that the road to maturity, and the attendant responsibility to which Mead referred, can offer no guarantees of safe passage *or* of destination, because there is no guarantor. There never has been a guarantor. And in that realization rests perhaps the only gauge we can ever have of how far our legislations have taken us, forward or backward, in that passage.

---

[446] The parenthetical reference is to Albert Schlageter. As the Weimar Republic fell behind in meeting obligations of reparations under the Treaty of Versailles, French and Belgian troops occupied the Ruhr valley, taking control of its industrial production. Some German troops, Schlageter (1894-1923) among them, retaliated through sabotage of the occupational forces. Captured and executed, he became a figure of martyrdom especially in right-wing German politics. At the beginning of his tenure as rector of the University of Freiburg, under Nazi auspices, Heidegger (1988 [1962], pp. 96-97) celebrated the martyrdom as if a manifestation and validation of his own thought (see also Safranski (1998 [1994], pp. 241-242).

## Part Five
## Mereology, Agency, Efficacy, and Questions of Scale

Helmut Wagner's article in the *American Journal of Sociology* made little difference at the time (1964). The idea that there might be an important problem of scale evidently did not resonate, because most readers of the journal had simply adopted the assumption that no such problem existed, that homology prevailed. The fact that his illustrative material came from European theorists of the early twentieth century could be taken as support for that assumption: "we" had moved beyond that state of social theory. Notably, while Wagner mentioned several early North American theorists in his list (especially Charles Horton Cooley), his main attention was directed first to Durkheim, Weber, and Simmel, then mainly Talcott Parsons and his associates, and to George Homans and to Howard Becker. An assumption of homology seemed to satisfy in much the way that the mentality of "one size fits all" adequately summarized the ideology of mass consumption. It did not help, of course, that counterviews to the homology assumption treaded into the vagueness of mysticism when trying to explain why or how a single organizational logic does not work equally well at levels ranging from individual actors to any society as a whole. Even aside from the bias of positivists against "the metaphysical"—usually taken as umbrella for any posit of what lies at the other end of an inference (examples today including dark matter, dark energy, and gravitons)—invoking the power of an unexplained factor or process called "emergence" did little more than rephrase the question supposedly being answered. Widespread conviction in homology was less the case than a matter-of-fact assumption. But either attitude was all the more comfortable in that it had the effect of deflecting attention away from difficult issues of the knowing subject, thus protecting the theorist's (and more generally the scientist's) ability to pronounce reality from Olympian heights without having to demonstrate that the reality undergirds both that ability and particular pronouncements from it. Homology enables one to "backfill" relations and processes without direct evidence to the demonstration. As has been seen repeatedly, Hume's challenge to perception and Kant's generalization of the challenge can be set aside without prejudice, or so it is assumed. One assumption covers all.

Twenty-two years after Wagner's article, James S Coleman published in the same journal a consideration of "macro and micro" relations and related issues of social theory. Four years later Coleman published his treatise on *Foundations of Social Theory* (Coleman 1986; 1990). Whereas Wagner was only modestly known in 1964, Coleman was very well known and a somewhat controversial member of the social science academy who in the year of Wagner's article published a major textbook, *Introduction to Mathematical Sociology*, which stimulated some controversy among those members of the academy for whom mathematics was a foreign language less useful than, say, sixteenth-century Farsi or twenty-third century Klingon. But the larger controversy was stimulated by the report Coleman and colleagues had prepared for the US Congress from their mandated research on educational opportunity, a report commonly known as "The Coleman Report," presented in 1966 (see Marsden 2005 on this and various aspects of Coleman's career; also, Alexander and Morgan 2016 on the report 50 years later). Initial receptions of the report were confused, sometimes mistaken by apparent intent, but also reflective of a naïveté that the report, as a deliberative scientific document, could largely ignore the ideological morass into which it was cast.

More of Coleman's work will be considered below. Here, I will focus on one key aspect for present purposes—namely, his address of some matters partly summarized by the following diagram, which Coleman included both in the 1986 article and in the 1990 treatise.[447]

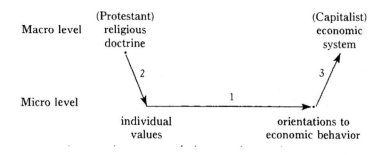

Figure 5.1. James Coleman's Micro-Macro Model (1986)

This was Coleman's (1986) representation of the main relations of Max Weber's thesis about the Protestant Ethic as a stimulant to the spirit of capitalism. While my aim here is not to criticize his reading of Weber, I will note in passing that one can gain the impression from his citations in the book (1990, e.g., pp. 422-425, 442-443, 446-447, 448-449) that Coleman had relied mostly on others' summaries of Weber (and perhaps his own very old notes from those summaries). The one quotation from Weber concerning his organizational theory was taken not from Weber's main theoretical writings but from a little book by Jacob Mayer (1944, p. 47), an excerpted paragraph that Mayer took from a 1909 address by Weber to a meeting on highly charged issues of public policy. Weber was there speaking at least as much, and openly, as a political actor aiming to rally attention to a national cause, rather than as a scholar reading from his typically complexly woven, often highly detailed and qualified expository studies (as in, e.g., Weber 1968 [1922], part one; his unfinished treatise on economic, social, political, and cultural organization). In fact, this one quotation (taken from Mayer 1947) appears twice in Coleman (1990, pp. 422, 613), presented in each setting as an adequate account of Weber's theory of organization. In the terms of the second setting, Coleman seemingly failed to see that Weber was doing (in his 1909 address) exactly what Coleman had judged to be missing in Weber's work as a social scientist—namely, using his scholarly studies as a basis for his intervention in matters of public policy (and at risk of violating Weber's own admonition about "value neutrality," although evidently he

---

[447] Coleman's diagram in his treatise (1990, ch. 1, fig. 1.2) is somewhat different from the one he had published in 1986 (shown above), mainly in having a directional arrow at macro level from religious to economic system. Since his 1990 book, the diagram has been invoked repeatedly as a guide (e.g., Sampson 2012, p. 63), usually with the same terminology.

believed that he could safely compartmentalize and prevent value positions from biasing his own scholarship).

Among the three relations depicted in the above diagram, primacy was given to the micro or individual-actor level: individual values lead to specific orientations of economic behavior by individual actors. This was in keeping with Coleman's general insistence on his understanding of a perspective known as "methodological individualism." The lack of a parallel arrow at the macro level (later supplied in 1990, e.g., fig. 1.2) was presumably in keeping with the version of that methodological doctrine which says that all determinative processes must pass through the individual person. His discussion in 1986 seemed inconsistent on that point, however, in that despite the lack of that macro-to-macro arrow he wrote of a "corporate actor" as having agency. But at the same time, while chiding theorists who failed to attend both to legal organizations and to contents of law in theory and in practice (1986, p. 1313), he was curiously silent about the replacement of will-centered legal theory by the "reasonable man" standard which O W Holmes, Jr., and other jurists had brought into play (see Part Four, §21, above). Coleman was correct, I believe, in his assertion of the importance of legal texts—for example, "All case law is based inherently on a theory of action" (1986, p. 1313), although more distantly in some instances than in others—yet he seemed unaware of the large presence of "legal systems" in Weber's studies of organization.

Be that as it may—and I will come back to some of those points later—Coleman was one of the few scholars still to take Talcott Parsons' early efforts seriously and, in doing so, to pose a question that had been seldom asked, much less seriously addressed: Why did Parsons abandon his "voluntaristic theory of action"? To Coleman it seemed that Parsons had been on the right track, difficult though it was, and then during the 1940s, without much in the way of explanation, shifted away from the perspective (stylized in Figure 5.1, above, as the primary linkage) which in 1937 Parsons had declared the linchpin of coherence in earlier theoretical contributions. This was a major motivating concern in Coleman's 1986 article in the *American Journal of Sociology*. He left the question behind as an unsolved puzzle, and by 1990 Parsons had nearly disappeared from Coleman's survey of the foundations of social theory (a single entry in the book's index, no citations among its twenty pages of references).

Coleman's invocation of Parsons' theory of action, and more specifically the question of abandonment which he raised, comprise a historical text as point of departure for this Part Five. What can we learn by taking Coleman's question seriously, within a context at times analytical, dialectical, or enthymemic of pursuits of a theory of "human affairs in process," in wake of what we have learned from David Hume and Immanuel Kant?

The main contents of this Part Five have to do with three interlinked components of social process (and again, I remind that I mean "social" as inclusive of other disciplinary labels, such as "economic," "political," etc.). These three components are: aggregation, scaling, and my effort at a new concept and methical approach which I call "abstractive condensation" (or AbCon, for short). By way of preview, I next offer a few words about each of these components.

By "aggregation" I mean the process of individual actors collecting, or being collected, to form a multi-person organization. I write the verb "to form" timorously, because I do *not*

383

mean that any surviving human being has ever been without "the social," without the accompaniment of others. At live birth, there was at least a birthing mother; chances are, others were present in her life, at least some of them physically present. Even the most severe eremitic monk lived in the sociality of his memories and with the sociality of his conversations with his divine being (whether a godhead figure or a conversation with ancestors). Here the focus is simply of the aggregation of individual persons as an organizational problem much as Georg Simmel (1908) addressed it a century ago and as Michael Hannan (1991) addressed it during the 1970s and later (e.g., Hannan, Pólos, and Carroll 2007). Tyler Cowen (2018) has given attention to "aggregation problems" in a somewhat different, and more difficult, sense: "how we resolve disagreements [about distribution of resources and products] and how we decide that the wishes of one individual should take precedence over the wishes of another." This is certainly an important focus but one that will not be directly pursued here. Rather, I am concerned with the analytically prior question of the logic or logics of organization (of individual persons) as such—that is, as dynamic nodes of sociality.[448] And from that priority I focus on *effects* of per-person actions within sociality.

The aggregation process can be as simple as arithmetic addition. It can be slightly less simple: an addition process in which variable weights are assigned (i.e., some persons "bigger" actors than others). Or if we assume that the addition is continuous and that the increments are independent, we might expect to see the organizational logic of a geometric Brownian motion model, such as (expressed as a stochastic differential equation, linear in variables and functional form):

$$dS_t = \mu S_t \, dt + \sigma S_t \, dW_t \qquad (5.1)$$

where $W_t$ is Brownian motion, and $\mu$ ("the percentage drift") and $\sigma$ ("the percentage volatility") are constants ("drift," modeling deterministic trend; volatility, modeling a set of statistically predictable events occurring during the process). While this is a simple model, one should not be misled by the simplicity. As May (1976) demonstrated, simple models can cover complicated dynamics (for various other models, see Coleman 1973, Coleman 1990, Tuma and Hannan 1984, Ljundqvist and Sargent 2018, among other sources).

However, aggregation is not simply about bodies, a relatively simple collection process. It is about *effects of person-actors' actions* (of a particular kind); and that might or might not be as simple a modeling problem. First, assuming conceptual issues have been settled, there is a set of metrical issues that must be solved. More about this, below.

My concern with regard to the second of the three components mentioned above is more specifically with breaks or discontinuities or perhaps thresholds in the logic of aggregation. This is directly the matter of scaling—that is, whether there are effects of scale in a given organization of individual persons. Again, bear in mind that scale effects, if there are any, will be in the logic by which person-actors' actions (of a given kind) produce aggregated effects. The operative

---

[448] For what it is worth, I think Cowen misconstrued the intent of Kenneth Arrow's (1963) logical analysis of preference hierarchies. But maybe I have misunderstood Cowen.

question can be phrased in terms of homology: does one logic apply uniformly across organizational levels? Simmel addressed the question: for example, when comparing dyadic and triadic organization, the scale difference generating a new organizational capacity (coalition formation). This was the main point of concern raised by Helmut Wagner in 1964, when he concluded that little or no advance had been made since the efforts of Simmel and Weber. Under given conditions the process of aggregating persons should be relatively simple in its temporal dimension, because in most instances an organization already exists, with addition or subtraction of members now and again, processes of adaptation and adjustment ensuing. On the other hand, if an existing organization takes on a proportionally large group of new members (especially if these persons have previously been an organized group—a small partnership, for example— rather than a happenstance collectivity), the addition can result in a scale effect. More difficult manifestations of the aggregation process can occur when individual persons come together with purpose of forming a new organization, even if the aspiration is well short of a new *type* of organization. For most situations a model or models already exist. Much the same can be said of the process of aggregating effects of specific kinds of actions by person-actors: it will occur within an existing organization. But for *this* process of aggregation it is not so clear that any existing model will be adequate. Here the importance of institutional channeling may well be crucial. Think of a workplace, for example, and the coordination problem among production workers: because of institutional channeling in an existing organization of work, coordination has been solved more or less well. Do we have existing models of that, not only conceptual models but models that are also metrical?

The model shown as equation 5.1 assumes one continuous summation of independent increments. Because of the uniformity, the organizational logic is said to be homologous. In application to the aggregation of human beings, however, the three simplifying assumptions of that model may be (and generally are) far sort of realistic description. In terms of bodies, organizations usually grow in spurts (if at all); sometimes they shrink; persons rarely behave as independent actors but often act as nodes within mutually influential networks; and, partly because actors are fond of tokens or emblems (e.g., credentials), when they aggregate they sometimes aggregate not only in some sort of temporal stutter of dependency clusters but also with some sort of numerical thresholding that signals a shift in logic.

Which (if any) of those observations can be said of the aggregation of effects rather than bodies? For the effects of actions that are of principal concern (effects of work in production, for example), coordination usually implies some form of interdependence among workers linked into some sort of network. Existing network models might be adaptable. If there is a scale effect, it might take the conventional form known as "economy of scale." But it could be a bit more complicated than the typical case.

Bear in mind throughout discussions of models here and in the following sections that the primary and main criterion by which to judge a theoretical model is *not* its descriptive realism. An organizational history will better accomplish that, not only for any specific organization but also for sets of organizations of an institutional type. Rather, the chief purpose is to tackle the messiness of human affairs with explicit simplifying assumptions in order to gain insights into the dynamics of one or a nest of processes. If a model proves useful in that way, then by removing

385

or at least softening a given assumption one can perhaps gain additional insight into process dynamics with greater descriptive realism. That is often our only effective means of peering into the "obscure site" of a process, in order to observe operations. Descriptive realism is not irrelevant. It is one main standard by which increments of insight are judged. But because good models are scarce, if already existent at all, whereas empirical observations are abundant if not always well constructed, it would be rash to discard an existing "good model" on grounds of descriptive realism until a better model can be built.

Wagner's point in 1964 was that theorists had been giving too little attention to the scale dynamic in a variety of organizational settings. When, under what conditions, and in what form does a scale-sensitive change in organizational logic occur as a function of aggregation—that is, as a function of numerical change in the micro-to-macro relation (as depicted above in Figure 5.1)? As said more than once before, little has changed since Wagner's article. While recent good insights must not be neglected (see, e.g., Hannan, Pólos, and Carroll 2007; Kontopoulos 1993; and, from a different point of view, Reich and Bearman 2018), there is much that remains poorly understood.

The third of the three components mentioned above has to do with temporality, not of the aggregation process as such but with the process by which an actor gains and utilizes first-person experiences as "personal goods" (i.e., knowledges, skills, pragmatic exercises of experimentation or "trial and error," and so forth), which are mostly developed in organizational settings and thus are developed interactively with similar other actors, and which figure into aggregation processes understood cross-sectionally at any given time, as each given actor is mutually and dialectically both influenced by and influencing others in the given organizational setting, all of which may be (sometimes is) preparation and anticipation of mobility within the given organizational setting and/or from one organizational setting to another, a next, setting. Whereas aggregation process can be studied as a process in cross-sectional perspective (i.e., across specified action effects of individual persons), this temporality of first-person experience has locus within a given person's dynamics of selfhood, of personal growth and development. In other words, the "units" that are aggregated are not static "things," as we tend to think of person as embodiment; nor are they uniform across actors, each having static characteristics. Each is "in process," a per-person process that must be understood as an acquisition of "goods," relative goods, which, vis-à-vis any given organizational setting, include goods of relative scarcity and thus competitive resource for that setting (i.e., "rival goods"). Part of the discussion in sections following these introductory remarks will be concerned with alternative ways of modeling per-person action effects in repetition (within an institutional channel, such as education), a main initial assumption being a concept that I call "abstractive condensation," the central dynamic of which can be described as follows: for each given person-actor each of a sequence of effect states of a given kind is absorbed as condition to the next action state, seriatum, each state in the chain of effects as such being successively abstracted and condensed into one or more thematic vectors of cumulative outcomes. The assumption of an institutional channel is crucial, for it implies the operation of an existing, continuing particular way of organizing sociality toward some purpose. This assumption is realistic, I argue, in that *per-person chains of experience* that are likely to be factors in *cross-person aggregation processes* are accumulated in institutionally regulated organizations of person-actors (the organizations themselves in many instances being themselves supra-individual actors or loci of agency, some of which feeds back as enablement/constraint to the person-actor members). The process of abstractive condensation within a larger process of creating a new type of organization is a very different kettle of fish, which also I will discuss later, partly with the aid of Reich and Bearman (2018), which, indirectly and in almost a quasi-counterfactual manner, displays the great power, constitutive and regulative, of an institutional channel.

Let's return to an earlier point. When reviewing his brief on a key part of Kantian theory, Alan Montefiore (2011, p. 83) used the phrase "holding together" as a substitute for the notion of "empirical-synthetic unity." It was a fitting choice, in part because it reminds us of the abundant aggregative capacity of German lexicon. The phrase, "holding together," can be rendered as a "Zusammenhang," and even better as "Zusammengehörenkeitsgefühl," literally the "feeling of hearing-togetherness" or, more cleanly, "feeling of solidarity." In other words, the process of sequences of effects of action and how those sequences become one or more ongoing storylines surely has something to do with at least some of the more or less contemporaneous processes by which actors aggregate into more or less stable yet fluid organizational forms. Indeed, while the principal organizational setting may (and will) change for an individual person (e.g., moving from formal education to a labor market to a firm), the temporality of effects of action continues. So we really have at least two dimensions of temporality at play—one having to do with aggregation into an organization of membership, the other having to do with per-person accumulations of effects of action, effects that take place within the sociality of the individual person, thereby extending or reforming or strengthening or sometimes eroding (etc.) the person's capacities of linkage into a present organization of membership and/or joining a new organization of membership, or even attempting to create a new (if not unprecedented) organization of others. In short, the problem of aggregation as it has been conventionally considered is *not* a simple aligning of static persons (as if so many Lego blocks) into an existing or new "structure" of organization. Such "structure" is changing in part because those "blocks" are *not* static; they are actors always already inherently social, always already participants in sociality, whose effects of action can influence, do influence, and/or might yet influence, an organization to which they already belong (a family, a school, a firm, etc.) or an organization to which they are seeking membership or an organization from which they are exiting (Albert Hirschman's "exit" rather than "voice" or "loyalty"; Hirschman 1970; 2013, esp. pp. 310-330). It turns out, in other words, that any "relatively simple problem of aggregation," as well as potential scale effect(s) of organizational size or other properties of the organization as such, is really not so simple after all. It is in the nature of the process, for example, that an exiting production worker, say, or a newly introduced production worker, for a given organization initially creates static in the existing coordination network of production workers' action effects (see, e.g., Hamper 1991).

Given what I just wrote (and with reference to Ben Hamper's memoir of life as a rivet-gun operator), this is a good opportunity to say that I use "production" ("produce," etc.) in two senses throughout the following discussions. Syntactical setting will usually indicate which of the two I intend primarily and/or mainly, but there will never be an impervious line between them.  Hamper's worklife on an assembly line was indicative of being a "production worker" in a "narrower" or more specific sense (i.e., in vernacular, "actually *making something* rather than being a 'pencil pusher' in the front office or a mechanic who keeps my rivet gun in good order or a sweeper who cleans up behind me, or even my shop floor supervisor, who started out as I am now").  This sense of the word applies to the teacher in a classroom but also to the pupil, both engaged in producing a competent reader, speller, and so forth.  It applies as well to the parent in a household who brings various resources into the home.  But there is also running throughout all of that another and larger meaning of "production":  all are also producing sociality, means of human life here-and-now in this place at this time, and they are accomplishing that in the specifics of what it means to be a "worker" (including teacher, etc.), a "pupil," a "householder" and/or a "coupled partner."  They are also accomplishing that in the far more general sense of what it means to be integral to a sociality here-and-now in this time and place.  Granted, most of that production is reproductive.  So, too, is most of what is accomplished in each of those more specific meanings of producing.  Note that what I have just tried to describe is integral to the meaning of "processes of aggregation."

Before turning to §25 I need to address, even if briefly, still another matter.  This has to do with one of those phrases that seem to absorb so much time and energy to no good purpose. Although much older than Max Weber, "methodological individualism" is often attributed to him—mainly, I suspect, because he made an issue of it in service to his preferred method, in his "Grundriβ der verstehenden Soziologie" (his "interpretive sociology").  As argued in Part Two, persistent first-person experience is a texture of interpretation (even when the first person thinks "pure truth" or "*this* is the real").  But not only first-person experience:  second-person and third-person experiences are chock full of interpretation.  Without interpretation there would be no communication, no trust, no trade, and so on.  As I pointed out earlier, because of one passage in Newton's works, one can read his theory of space and his theory of time not as pure absolutes but as "virtual absolutes" or "quasi-absolutes."  Before Einstein put final seal to his general theory, he interpreted a result as telling him that he needed to add a "cosmological constant." Later, he declared that addition his biggest blunder.  Now some theorists interpret observations as telling them that he was right after all.  We like to think—as some locutions I have just used may suggest—that observations "speak for themselves," that a particular observation tells us this or that.  Hardly.  Our very first task is always to sort "signal" from "noise."  The sentence just written can be read as saying that signals come labeled as such, leaving the rest to be noise. Hardly.  But when we think they do—and we often do—we are committing interpretation without awareness of it (see, e.g., Hazelrigg 1992).

Weber (1968 [1922], p. 13) wrote that various "collectivities," often referenced "as if they were individual persons" (by which he meant "persons" in the sense that Coleman named "natural person," as distinguished specifically from a corporate actor) "must be treated as solely the resultants and modes of organization of the particular acts of individual persons, since they alone can be treated as agents in the course of subjectively understandable action."  Why the qualification?  What was it about this "individualism" that made it "methodological"?  In Weber's terms the adjective signified that his method of inquiry was founded on the intentionality of an individual person as actor (i.e., his "interpretive sociology").  More generally, Weber was *not* asserting that he believed that simple behaviors (i.e., non-intentional activity, such as accidently bumping into another person rounding a corner) are inconsequential or otherwise of no concern to the scientist. Nor was he asserting that the individual person is the only *real* subject-object. In other words, the adjective served to discriminate his intent from anyone who had proposed an "*ontological* individualism." The adjective can also be interpreted as an "as if" statement, signifying what could be called a "simplifying convenience of my method of inquiry." While a discussion in the next section will point to instances of an adoption of that stance (albeit mostly implicit), it was emphatically not Weber's. He believed not that subjective meaning is a sufficient category but that it is an *inescapable* category of understanding phenomena of human affairs.[449]

More perspective can be added by considering the bounds of "individual" in its lexical sense. This is a useful exercise both with specific regard to Weber's sociology and as a bridge to §25, which again (after §9) has to do with mereology.

Taken literally, "individual" means "not divisible." If that is definitive of "individuality," then can any "whole" be itself individual, given that, or insofar as, a whole is understood to be a composition of parts? The favor that Cartesian logic gives to analytic perspective promotes that question to the status of conundrum. In a dialectical logic that features at once both opposition, even contradiction, and unity of opposites, the point of departure is the integrity of "alone-ness"—that is, "all-one-ness," an expression of the Latin "e pluribus unum." But as Karl Marx stated several times in different sentences, most succinctly in the third of his eleven theses on what he took to be the most highly developed version of a materialist philosophy (Feuerbach's), scholars as well as "simple workers" have a pronounced tendency to divide a whole into two parts and then declare one of those parts to be superior to the whole (Marx 1976 [1924], p. 4).

Those issues have been animating conceptions and perceptions in theoretical biology for quite some time. Perhaps the most frequent citation is the phenomenon known as "hive society" or "colony behavior" (as in ants, bees, etc.; see, e.g., essays collected in Bouchard and Huneman 2013; Gordon 2010). But the underlying principle of extension surely points as well to "herd society," "pack society," "pride society," and so forth. Little more effort is needed to raise analogous questions about George Herbert Mead's conception of "the social self" as an ensemble of others—that is, "significant others" and "the generalized other," all jostling for place in some sort of variably integrated but dynamic whole known by proper-noun name. It is plausible to think—per hypothesis; good evidence for it will probably remain far beyond us—that the brain of our species ancestor was wired in a more "collectivist," less "individualistic" architecture. Neural architecture might have been less variable across organisms; variant information, is the material on (by) which evolutionary selection works.

One salutary consequence of some of the recent reconceptualizations of "individuality" in biological context—in effect, reconceptualizations of aggregation process—has been

---

[449] I initially wrote "necessary"; but that implies the opposition of "necessary versus contingent," and the process is suffused with contingency. Interpretation is inescapable and contingent.

389

improved understanding that the phenomenon not only has not been, perhaps has never been, a static state or condition but also that species evolution itself has followed a gradual gradient "from groups to individuals," to borrow Bouchard and Huneman's book title (2013)—which is to say, paths of increasing individualization of being. Perhaps more notable, however, is the recognition that this gradient has correlated with evolution in efficiency, not only in degree of efficiency but also in the dynamics of its process. Deborah Gordon put part of that point this way, based on her extensive and finely detailed study of the organization of individually identified ant-members of different colonies of a few of the many thousands of species of ant:

> The patterns or regularities in ant colony behavior are produced by networks of interaction among ants. The networks of interaction are complicated, irregular, noisy, and dynamic. The network is not a hidden program or set of instructions. There is no program—that's what is mind-boggling, and perhaps it is why, at the beginning of the twenty-first century, there is so much we do not understand about biology. It is very difficult to imagine how an orchestra could play a symphony without a score. It takes an effort to avoid slipping into thinking that there is an invisible score hidden somewhere (Gordon 2013, p. 47).

Gordon's research has been extraordinary in a number of ways, the most important of them stemming from her ability to tag individual ants harmlessly and apparently unobtrusively, such that she could map each organism's behavior in networks of interaction chiefly by chemical signals. She was able to determine that even though "colony behavior" is noisy (uncompleted signals, false signals, etc.), it is predictable at least with regard to basic tasks. Furthermore, an age-related pattern of the development of colony behavior over time is also predictable. While individual organisms do not behave with much predictability, their behaviors when interrelated as nodes in networks of interaction result in patterns or regularities that are predictable. Because an ant colony is very large in population, which is distributed vertically as well as horizontally the span of a colony, Gordon was unable to tag every ant (lest she destroy colony integrity). This precluded observation on the basis of a probability sample of the population. However, while that limitation must be kept in mind, the focus of her research was primarily and mainly on the dynamics of process (in effect, aggregation), and for that I think the fact that she sampled in time is of greater consequence than the restriction against sampling in space.

My point is that whereas the popular impression of "ant life" emphasizes the monotonous drudgery of highly efficient workers, the fact is that individual ants as such are *highly inefficient* if one examines them in terms of per-ant productivity of *any* task. At individual level there is a huge volume of wasted effort, a lot of wandering about, virtually random walks that end with *no* task accomplishment. It is because of the vast population size of a colony that it survives in a more or less optimal state of health (i.e., a weakly dynamic equilibrium). A very large degree of inefficiency per ant—indeed, at any given moment of large amount of per-ant *ineffectivity*—is made tolerable by sheer number of ants. It was this condition that accounted for the observation of networks of interaction as "complicated" and "irregular" as well as "noisy." No invisible hand directed an invisible orchestra playing according to an invisible score. Colony life survives only because a vast number of "units" manage to produce just enough food, just enough defense, and so forth, for that vast number of consumers none of whom ever accomplish much at all.

## §25. Part-Whole Relations: Levels, Scope, and Scale

Coleman's question is no longer in play, for the world of theory has mostly forgotten Parsons. But why *did* Parsons abandon his "voluntaristic theory of action?" So far as I am aware, Parsons rarely acknowledged the question; and when he did, it was in defensive posture. My own guess is that during the late 1930s or early 1940s he came to a more detailed understanding of Weber's efforts and in particular the difficulty of building from the sociality of an individual-person complex of action-relevant factors—first-person experience, perceptions, wants, desires, intentions, reasonings, and so on, ending with executions of actions and their consequences—to supra-individual phenomena. This was in part, I think, because Parsons was no clearer than Weber had been in conceptualizing all of that complexity into an integral formation of theory. It was far beyond the basic standards of Newtonian physics, and it was becoming increasingly clear that Darwinian biology, though more complex, had only vague analogies to offer social theorists.

The complexity of Weber's course in trying to settle matters coherently, ranging from his earliest efforts to the Kategorienlehre that he left unfinished (i.e., Part I of *Economy and Society*) had been neglected in Parsons' reception of Weber as documented in his 1937 *The Structure of Social Action*, and Parsons lacked anything close to the carefully insightful, lucid yet succinct tour guide that Stephen Turner gave us especially in his essay, "Weber on Action" (1983). I assume that as Parsons began to invoke the demands of his more empirical, research-oriented side, he came face-to-face with the magnitude of the task. Most relevant concepts were weak, sometimes incoherent in themselves separately even before brought into operative conjunction with each other. Instruments of reliable observation and measurement of key variables such as "intention" were non-existent.

Attention will now turn in this section to some matters of mereology, including meanings of a basic part term, "individual," thence some meanings of "levels" of organization, following which meanings of "scope" and "scale." These are preliminaries to the subsequent sections of this Part Five.

### Part-Whole Relations

I will not repeat remarks made in previous sections about issues of classificatory activity in the registers of theory and empirical research. Rather, I will only insist that they must not be ignored, all the while realizing that usually we do exactly that in order to make intended use of one or another language. Jacques Derrida, like others before him from at least the Sophists of ancient Greece to Cervantes, Borges, and others, prescribed beneficial invitations to stay awake in those uses.

Here, I will simply begin with a basic notice that mereology, or the study of part-whole relations, typically proceeds from an analytical point of view, which is to begin after much of the work has already been accomplished. This occurs already in large part in our ordinary language uses; for, as Bourdieu (1990 [1982], p. 189) pointed out, in "a general way, language expresses things more easily than it does relations, states more easily than processes." It is an insidious bias, because of which much more effort is generally needed in order to think in terms of *relations* and *processes*. Ordinary language uses incline us to begin with things and states, then to derive in some way relations among things and processes that link states together.

What counts as "part" is always relative to a "whole." But this presupposes what counts as "whole." A strong tendency to a foundationalism undergirds an analytic "building block" perspective, which usually trades on an absolutism by which some wholes are always already given. That is inescapable, even as our avowedly most fundamental science, physics, goes in search of ever more basic particles (from the Latin "particular" to "little parts"). There should be no harm in noticing that the search is much like prior quests—the pot of gold left behind by the Little People, Adam's task of giving every *thing* its rightful name, and so forth. For present purposes, the prime instance of an "absolutist" claim, one that recognizes the abstraction in which "arbitrariness of language" lives, is "the individual human being." This is our foundationalist stance but for which none of us would be here writing and reading these words (which in fact would never have existed).

This stance is of course not so much undeniable as an initial contingency as only another expression of the contingency of first-person experience, as discussed in Part Two. I will return to it later as an important posit in the context having to do with any theorist's posit as simultaneously a self-posit. For the moment, my concern is with the mirror image of that stance regarding an absolute presence: what counts absolutely—that is, non-relatively—as "an individual human being"? Without repeating all of the particulars, I will invoke as point of departure my §23 and questions of the boundedness of "I," the first-person experience of a self-consciously reflexive human being. Whereas we might think of the largest organ, skin, as the biological boundary, for example, that thought is absurd, for obviously the skin is permeable, allowing perspiration to evaporate as a way of controlling body heat, the lung tissue to absorb oxygen without which respiration fails, and so forth. Even without acknowledging that biology is a social phenomenon (a collection of more or less standardized, provisional thoughts, facts of flesh, practices, etc.), any individual person enters into an ongoing sociality without which the chance of survival would be zero. The relationality, the relativity, is inescapable (try though many of us do). The thesis of absolutism serves as a sometimes convenient fiction, the most common of the conveniences being a means of forestalling other questions (e.g., wherefrom an "authority of voice" or "the sensus communis," etc.). A human being is born with the capacity and rudiments of the capability of a *self*-reflexivity, but the capability develops only in sociality as self-identity develops. Along with that comes the sort of "personal discovery" that Jia Tolentino reported in her (2019, p. 180) confession: "I am part of the world—and I benefit from it" (she was here citing the graininess of a corruption that cannot be escaped—"even if I criticize its emptiness; I am complicit no matter what I do." This is hardly a new insight, of course. Each of us comes to at least the opportunity of it, for one's world is in one's conditions of being and therefore within oneself, but those conditions can include favors of self-deception, self-delusion, even self-denial.

I also presume that, contrary to analytics, "part-whole relations" begin with the third word of that phrase. In other words, "identity" implies "difference," just as "difference" implies "identity." Or, think of "classification" as such: one cannot avoid classification; it is inherent in language, in thought, in one's world. The cells of a classification exist only by virtue of a matrix of relations of "same/other," "identity/difference," a unity of oppositions. It is analytical logic that adds to that matrix the stipulation of absolutism (but actually only a quasi-absolutism, for reasons already said). The members of a given cell (or of some cells) already have the stature, a solidity, of being present as "absolute things"; the cell boundaries are by that presence fixed and impermeable, serving as protection against one of the prime sins in Cartesian analytical logic, an "undivided middle," an ambivalence that calls into doubt the completeness and necessity of the classificatory logic. A mess of confusions flows from inheritances of remnants of Cartesian theory, none of them more persistent than the confusions invested in and attending ideologies of individualism, whether this "ism" be modified as "only" "methodological" or ensconced within some supposedly pristine first-philosophy realm of "the ontological."

But let me turn around and look forward, to what I mean by "individual," beyond the etymology of something that cannot be divided (without collapse of integral existence, which I take in a biophysical sense). As an adjective the word can be applied to many entities. As a noun it usually refers to a person (unless context makes it otherwise clearly referential), and so I will use it here. But, to avoid confusion, I will sometimes use it in compound, individual-person, if the specification is not otherwise clear, because a corporation, a limited-liability company, has legal standing as a "person," and this directly relates to the question of part-whole relations and, more specifically, what entities can be taken as having agency (about which, more below, in §26). These matters have often been dealt with in such vague manner that a reader cannot be clear what a given author intended.[450] The integrity of an individual person cannot be understood apart from the fact of sociality: as I have said repeatedly, an individual person is, from birth if not before, not merely "embedded in the social" but *is* social, a social being—and that fact includes dynamism.

An analytic distinction prominent in standard mereology can be seen in various instances of the notion of "individual person and person's environment" (as in the aforementioned notion of embeddedness, that a person can be or become embedded in one or another setting without change of identity). As a generalization, that is mistaken. The conceit of the preeminence of "thing" vis-à-vis any relations into which "thing" enters or could enter is told by the following illustration. Try this experiment. Climb into an advanced jet aircraft (e.g., the F-35) in your street clothes. Buckle up and urge the craft to an altitude of about 60,000 feet. What happens? Water in your body fluids will boil (though not yet in your vascular blood)—saliva in your mouth, for instance, the water in your mucous membranes, on your eyeballs, in the alveoli of your lungs, and so forth. This is because atmospheric pressure at that altitude is so low that the boiling point of water drops from 212 degrees Fahrenheit to below your body temperature. But never mind. You are already on the way to brain death because of asphyxiation (hypoxia). The lesson that you would be learning the hard way is that the integrity of your thingness depends on a number of relations, some as simple as the relation between pressure and temperature. These relations are *internal* to you exactly as much as the integrity of your living body is dependent upon them. But presumably you knew that before you left the surface of Earth. Cellular respiration is dependent on internal relations of, for instance, the oxygen you breath into your lungs from your ambient environment. In that specific way, to mention only this one, your environment is not wholly external to you. It is also internal to you. (And if your rejoinder to this illustration is,

---

[450] Coleman's treatise is troubled by such ambiguities, to an extent, it seems, because he himself was not confident about relevant classification decisions (see Coleman 1990; his 1986 paper is less ambiguous).

"But that is biological," remember that these relations within "the biological" are simple in comparison to the complexity of sociality.

The integrity of an individual person is in continual flux because and insofar as the self-identity of that person becomes, as George Herbert Mead theorized (see §24, above), more or less different with each different significant other with whom self is engaged in the dynamics of sociality, not only during the "formative years" but thereafter as well (albeit perhaps less plastic). While I am at this juncture, let me state one more stipulation as clearly as I can. I know of no evidence that "group mind" exists (cf. List and Pettit 2011, pp. 8, 73). Nor do I know where "group mind" could exist, other than as a belief in the minds of individual persons. I do know, on the other hand, that contagion exists, especially emotive-cognitive contagion, and that it can generate behaviors that most of the participants would not, or might not, perform from their deliberate reflections (i.e., "mob action," "crowd behavior," etc., which are sometimes described as if some kind of "group mind" agency took charge). I know also that agreement and trust exist, that each is a dynamic process, potentially fragile, can collapse into its opposite, and that each carries a pair of subscripts, one for time and one for place, inasmuch as there are historically variable cultural patterns to the dynamics of trust, agreeableness, and the like.[451] The issue of a collectivity as an existent individual entity persists despite rejection of "group mind," and for good reason. I will discuss this issue in a moment (and again in the discussion of "agency"), but first I want to attend to another mess within what is known as "methodological individualism" (cf. Ylikoski 2014).

List and Pettit (2011, p. 3) offered as a basic definition this: "good explanations of social phenomena should not postulate any social forces other than those that derive from the agency of individuals." I will amend that (perhaps; I'm unsure what they meant in some passages), first by repeating another stipulation: by "social" I mean to include the subject matter of all disciplines of the social sciences. This is not intended as an act of imperialism. It is simply to say that the various subcategories—"economic," "cultural," "historical," "political," and so forth—are only analytical conveniences (at best); the boundary conditions are extremely vague; the conveniences serve as all-too-convenient alibis ("that's a topic for the X discipline of social science, so I will leave it to them"); *and*, because the conveniences are bound up with professionalism, usages often lapse into instances of the fallacy of misplaced concreteness. Second, I do not know how expansively List and Pettit intended their verb "derive." I intend it (here but also more generally) to include chains of derivation (i.e., "to derive directly but also indirectly"). With those stipulations added, the sentence as such is not problematic. However, other meanings have been loaded into that sentence. One of the most objectionable has been the supposition of an originary logic, the main point of which is "first there were individual persons, then they developed social, cultural, (etc.) characteristics, and 'human society' was born." The supposition is literally absurd. There is no empirical evidence that such a human being ever lived. As a matter of logic, such a human being could never have survived without the care of an older human being, which

---

[451] Some societal cultures tend to be more inclined to paranoia (e.g., Russian, USA); these tendencies vary from time to time (e.g., in the USA, more paranoia behind the years of the Palmer raids, again during the McCarthy years); the tendencies can be easily manipulated to personal advantage by political figures.

means sociality. As a matter of biological science, the supposition is not only pre-Darwinian; it is pre-Aristotelian.[452]

Now, about supra-individual entities. We know of several. Family is one. Does it exist as an individual entity? Yes. Does it act as an individual entity? The question has become more complex. An observation would often see coordinated action, and our linguistic practices reflect that: "The Aurelius family do not live here now. Patricius and his wife had a falling out. The lad moved to Carthage." As that snippet of history says, "the family" was considered a unit. But it was a patriarchal unit. The son, aged 17 years, went off to school in Carthage. Is that Aurelius family still a unit? Even when it was a unit, did it act as such, or did the members do what father told them to do? If the latter, does "the family" as such count as a "collective actor"? This is a difficult question; it is also an important question. The "agency" aspect I will attend later. Here I want to address what Georg Simmel (1950 [1923]) called "the quantitative dimension" of social organization. Some collectivities of individual persons have more of an "omnibus" quality than does "the family" (or, more to the point, an idealized image of it): individual person-members come and go, but the "group" (especially if "formalized") retains enough identity over time that it can be addressed or referred to by proper name.

Simmel demonstrated that quantity matters. He also demonstrated that a collectivity does not exist in isolation. It assumes characteristics that are more general than it, and so in that sense can be regarded as extrinsic even though they have relevance internally. His essay on 'The Stranger" was concerned with a type of social presence; it could be, of course, an individual person, but it could also be an individual family or a group of troubadours. It could be a collection all male; it could be a mixed-gender collection, a family or clan, or neither. If gender matters to the general society (city-state, region, whatever), and it usually has, the collection will be marked accordingly. Chances are, it will be patriarchal, also probably age-graded. It will be marked linguistically, too, and probably by other characteristics. To what extent will those markings not only affect the hosts' reception of "strangers in our land" but also constitute relations within the group? And of course the hosts will want to know about intentions, good or ill. Here we come to a realization that Weber made during the "evolution" of his thinking about the epistemological demands of his "interpretive sociology": if we cannot be confident of "reading" strangers' minds—and both John Bunyan and Benjamin Franklin were indeed strangers to Weber—perhaps we can use our accumulated experiences of "encounters with strangers" to know which observable characteristics are one or another kind of signal. As Stephen Turner (1983, pp. 516-517) determined from his careful reading of Weber's course of deliberations, Weber eventually decided to substitute observable "conditions" (i.e., "agents under a description") for "actors' intentions" and "reasons" as signals of impetus or determinant of an

---

[452] Conceptual and theoretical modeling techniques have stimulated interest in problems of "deep time" or "deep history" research. Simulations by generative models, for example, have been used to formulate and test hypotheses about "early humans" (dating not always specified). A recent example of the interest is Coxworth, Kim, McQueen, and Hawkes (2015). These can be useful exercises, so long as one does not lose sight of the severe limitations. The hypotheticals can be assessed as plausible scenarios, perhaps including means of estimating likelihoods of specified descriptions. But without empirical observations of the "early human" in question, testing can be only hypothetical.

action. Thus, the problem of attribution of intention had to be elided, not solved. At present, this same realization brings into relief the importance of the compositional question that is connected to quantity: how do we as observers (including our ability as second-person interlocutors) know the compositional variations that distinguish a collectivity that is only a sum (or average) of its parts' characteristics from a collectivity that is *more* than that? Simmel very nicely demonstrated the importance of that difference when he pointed out that the addition of one individual person to a dyad changes the dynamics of the group by creating the condition of coalition formation. In this instance we know the qualitative change of specific process that occurs in wake of a change in number. In order to explicate the dialectic of identity/difference when assessing collectivities in terms of the general distinctiveness mentioned just above—that is, does collectivity A operate as a sum or average of its individual person-members characteristics, whereas collectivity B evinces something more, a "value-added" factor—we need to be able to compare operations of specific processes.

That brings us to another controversial topic, rationality. Here I will make still another stipulation: because the analytic model of process that is most developed, most often used, and thus also the model about which the most knowledge has been accumulated is an input – output model, I will attend almost exclusively to instrumental or means-end rationality. To follow the terminology used by Weber, value rationality is an alternative, not unimportant. But it is mainly a matter of belief: one either believes X or does not believe X; and if one does not believe X, one might not hold any belief at all relevant to the domain of X, but one might believe Y instead, and Y might be either anti-X or just different from X. It is difficult enough to assess relevant process dynamics without engaging relations of value rationality, but they are surely not irrelevant. One might assess a particular belief as a texture of ignorance or bias, or as a texture of knowledge; but that does not tell us much about how the given belief works. Belief from ignorance is on average probably as securely held as belief from knowledge and skillful experience. While we have about as much evidence that ignorant belief has effects (i.e., "works" for the one who believes the belief), as does knowledgeable belief, it is difficult to assess the process of ignorant belief at work without prejudicing that process by invoking one's knowledge as tool and as standard. Consequently, it can be difficult, even impossible to defend against a charge that one has not been studying a given ignorant belief on its own terms but rather a perversion of it. Whereas someone who prizes the openness and skepticism of science must be careful about such matters, a demagogue uses them as tools of manipulation. For the art of making decisions from ignorance is a pasture on which demagogues feast, as well as a sign of the failure of education. Demagogues need ignorance; families, cities, societies, do not.

The field of investigation for processes of instrumental rationality is very different in that respect. To begin with, rationality exists as a gradient: in principle, from perfectly positively rational to perfectly negatively rational (or irrational). Comparative standards are built in. If one knows an actor's goal (and a first-person report is as close to sufficient as one can get, minus self-deception or dissimulation), one can allow actor's report of comparative assessments of the availability of means and then the efficacy of means, and still bring to bear one's own alternative assessments with empirical evidence of their relevancies and reliabilities. Much of the criticism of "rational actor" models is biased by assuming perfectly positive rationality is at issue. It is not, or need not be. Granted, some practices rely on such heavily simplified assumptions about "rational" that they seem to be address the actions of an automaton. But those practices are increasingly avoided.[453] Rationality is limited by knowledge—knowledge of attainability of a goal, of availability of alternative means, of how to apply those means, and of techniques of deliberate feedback or updating, such as to improve capabilities over time. Those limits are in turn a function of resources of learning. Within existing limits, which vary by circumstances, by place, and over time, most adults most of the time: (1) seek the best job they can find, (2) seek to perform in a job in ways that gain approval, thus increments of income and related benefits, and (3) try to preserve rather than degrade their conditions of health. They drive on the correct side of the road, do not wade through Everglade marshes carrying a string of fish, do not jump from a building's third-floor (or higher) window, and come to shore when patrolling sharks are sighted or a thunderstorm is looming. Rationality counts in "little" ways as well as the "big" ones that emulate a supercomputer or a mathematician's equations.

I will return to matters of rationality in §26, in connection with "agency" and "efficacy," and again in §27, having to do with institutions. In the meantime, I need to attend again to some other matters of terminology.

## Organizational Levels, Scope, and Scale

I will specify my uses of three words that relate to each other and have at times been used as if interchangeable. My distinctions among (1) level of organization, (2) scope of perspective, and (3) scale or effects of scale follow.

By organizational *level* I mean level of aggregation, primarily aggregation of individual persons in an organizational form. Main instances include (in order of increasing aggregate) individual person, household family, neighborhood (especially school), firm or workplace, city, state. By *scope* I mean detail of perspective or view, and I will recall Wagner's (1964) term for this: microscope and macroscope, with mesoscope added for intermediate use.[454] The key sense of this set of terms is straightforward if one follows the notion of a microscope or telescope. In present setting think of individual person as basic unit: this unit can be found also at each of the levels described above, and in other organizational settings as well (e.g., a network, a simple collectivity that qualifies as none of the above level-related collectivities). Thus, the presence of individual person can be seen microscopically (the individual person seen as singleton, which is *not* to say "asocial" or "pre-social"), mesoscopically (household family, etc.), and so on through the person's presence in larger and larger collectivities (i.e., macroscopic views). By *scale* I mean a relational proportionality between input and output of a specified process (or generically

---

[453] I do not mean to belittle the costs of relaxing strong assumptions, which enable efficacies of mathematical modeling. As more factors, and especially factors of dubious metrical quality, are brought into play in order to allow rationality-modified dynamics, the efficacy of those modeling procedures declines. But these are adjustments to, not replacements of, a principle of rationality, which by my understanding counts as an instance of Ludwig Fleck's "reverence for an ideal," a notion similar to current concerns for "the role (and historicity) of epistemic values in scientific inquiry" (Rietmann 2018, p. 93).

[454] Because Wagner tended to use "scope" and "scale" (a specific meaning of "scale") interchangeably, I (1991) chose to write only of scale. That was a mistake, as I later realized.

of "process" as such). Note that in ordinary usage the meaning of "scale" is similar to that of "scope," but with the difference that this meaning of "scale" is the map-to-territory perspective (as in "scale of map" vis-à-vis territory). I adopted Wagner's notion of scope in order to assimilate that usage of "scale" to it, rather than conflate that usage (and thus "scope") with the meaning of "scale" that I chiefly intend. Phenomena of scale (as I intend that word) often cross as observables from micro to macro perspective, as well as from the level of individual person to a collective level. The standard question about aggregation of observations (whether these be of individual persons or their acts or effects of their acts or some other events), such as was emphasized by Coleman, for example, asks whether the aggregation from microscopic to macroscopic, at whatever organizational level the macroscopic is focused, involves an effect of scale; and if it does, what form that effect takes. It is here that the issue of homology rests. A scale effect amounts to a change in the logic of aggregation—for example, a change from simple linear to, say, linear with a threshold effect; or a change from simple linear to curvilinear, because of a multiplier effect.

With those basics in mind, let's proceed through the three terms more generally, in order to add some pertinent detail and clarity.

If one presupposes homology, then one is observing the same process whether observing it micro-, meso-, or macroscopically. To what would that gradient of observational detail refer? First of all, to individual-person actors of the process, either as agents or as recipients of the process dynamics. But this would not be each individual person in isolation. Rather, it would be to each relevant person in a setting of sociality. That setting can (generally does) vary by organizational size: one person acting by oneself (e.g., hoeing a vegetable garden, cooking a meal, etc.), virtually always with one or more other persons in mind, relevant to the activity of the moment or not; or two persons acting more or less in concert; and so forth, until we reach, say, the level of a neighborhood or a school or workplace, etc.; and then the organizational level of an areal jurisdiction of government (county, city, etc.); and perhaps the level of membership in a probability sample of an entire societal population of individual persons. Furthermore, as the observer in question I might attempt to observe "the same named individual persons" within two or more settings on that gradient of organizational size (level of hierarchy)—performing an activity of given kind when, say, at home and in school or at home and when at work or at work and when a meeting of the relevant union or professional or business association or political party, and so forth. According to the homology assumption, the dynamics of the specific kind of activity that I will be observing—perhaps a kind of conversational pattern (e.g., turn-taking or entrepreneurial thinking)—should follow the same process logic; but, being a careful researcher, I want to test the assumption. Insofar as the assumption is correct, the *scope* dimension will be irrelevant: I will observe the same process phenomena without difference.

Let's be a bit more specific about scopic difference. Action and action-effect scenes will differ as I, the observer, shift from one scope to another. Think of the processual phenomenon of "schooling": as observer my primary interest is in what I take to be the primary and main outcome of "schooling"—namely, the "education" ("upbringing") of children, the acquisition and use of various kinds and extents of knowledge and skill, to compose competent adults; or, in short, the production of a next cohort or generation of persons. A range of observational scenes will be possible; the possible scenes will correlate to some extent with organizational level; I must try to choose scopic perspectives best exposing dynamics of the process of schooling. Shall I focus on a particular school districts or on a set of school districts sampled from a larger territory? Either could be my macroscopic perspective. In either case, what I observe will consist in aggregate data that have been compiled by authoritative agents of the district(s) and component schools, perhaps supplemented by contractual agents from external organization(s). The compilation process is interested; the interest will be overtly tied to primary and main organizational mission ("education") but will also reflect concerns within the district(s) and larger context (e.g., cost-benefit analysis, equity of resource distributions, etc.). Some or all of such matters might be highly relevant to the primary and main organizational mission.

Presumably, I would also observe relevant scenes within each of some number of specific schools; and within each of those, specific classrooms and teachers; and within those scenes, still more specific action networks among students and student-to-teacher; and within those scenes, per-pupil relations of teacher-to-parent, and so forth. Thus, I would have worked through a nest of scopic perspectives when building my measured observations. The task is complex.

Let's return to the assumption of homology: what if it is *not* correct? (Remember, I do not know the answer in advance, despite conventional tendencies.) If the scopic variation of my observation has included the relevant difference(s) in organizational logic, then I might observe evidence of that shift in logic. I say "might," because my observation must satisfy a number of other pertinent criteria, such as relevant time and/or place of setting, relevant conditions (including context) of the processual activity being observed, and that my attention has been appropriately and sufficiently sensitive to an event of logic shift, and so on.

Note that if the scope dimension is *in fact* irrelevant, nothing about relevance of organizational level *as such* in process dynamics will have been affected, assuming that during my efforts to test the assumption of homology I attended to possibilities of scale effects in the input-output process dynamics under investigation. That is to say, a scale effect could itself be a likely dynamic housing *another* shift in logic. But, as will be argued in more detail later, the temporal dimension of observation can be critical, because of organizational tendencies to renormalization.

With the foregoing paragraphs in mind, I am less than confident that we do in fact have good evidence supporting the homology assumption. The question remains open.

Organizational "level" should be understood largely as it has been used mereologically in studies of parts that are organized hierarchically. I concur with Ylikoski (2014) that the three qualifying adjectives, macro, meso, and micro, have been confounded recently in a literature of "supervenience" (which itself is prone to ambiguity and obfuscation) and as a result attached to organizational levels. For present purposes I do associate "microscopic" with individual person, which is also the "unit level" of organization. But for another purpose the "microscopic" could well be some intra-organic dimension or process of individual human being. Level and scope come together in the individual person simply because for my purposes it is the ground floor, so to speak. An individual person can indeed be characterized by specific attributes or properties, and these can be seen as "interior," as in mind, conscious deliberation, attitudes, interests, and so forth. From my standpoint, however, an "interior/exterior" dialectic does not align with "individual versus social" in any analytic perspective.

It remains the case that "microscopic" refers not directly to level but to the "scope" through which one is observing. Consider that many individual adult persons dwell in a household collectivity of two or more persons (call it "family"). One can observe each or any one of the persons as such (microscopic) or one can observe the family as such (mesoscopic) which is to say observe the individual persons as members constitutive of and enabled/constrained by and as *this* family. It is misleading think of "meso" and "macro" as "supra-individual," as if the observations take place without the presence of individual persons. Rather, the observations are of different organizations of sociality, which include individual persons but arranged in collectivities of one kind or another (e.g., family, school, firm). The collectivities can be described quantitatively (population size, nodes and edges of a network, frequency and/or duration of transactions, etc.) and qualitatively (kin or other status identities, kind of transaction, etc.). In many, perhaps most collectivities the aggregation process amounts to arithmetic summation, the significance of which can be expressed in terms of central tendency (mode, median, mean) and dispersion, the individual persons possibly weighted on one or another characteristic (e.g., relative influence potential in a network, comparing a heavy node to a light or near-isolate; age-grading in a family or household). In other collectivities the individual persons are bound into an organization in which the aggregation process is internally structured into separate sets, and usually a hierarchy of sets, of formal statuses. These are not unusual organizations of sociality, even though qualitatively distinctive (e.g., an army, a corporate firm, a school). Even a household family, insofar as it is age-graded (e.g., with children and/or with very elderly or ill-disposed members) and/or retains some tendency to patriarchy or matriarchy, will usually display at least a weighted averaging, sometimes a distinct hierarchal regime. These weights are instances of a scale effect insofar as they manifest in the outcome of a specific process, but the effect might be very small and/or short-lived. I will return to these and related matters later. In the meantime, let me repeat that my primary and main interest in "aggregation process" is not the aggregation of bodies but the aggregation of per-person actions, especially action-effects, both over time and across persons.

Within that conceptual specification, it is important to emphasis that "scale" is inherently a relational and mensural concept, referring at base to relations of parts to each other and to the whole of which they are parts. The relations can be networks of nodes of action effects, for example, or quantities of components in a summation of components or, conversely, the resultants (e.g., sediments) of a decomposition or analysis of a complex process outcome into its simpler parts. In short, a composition or constitution may be either starting point or ending point of a perceptual act—that is, either an effect of prior process now present as input to a next (perhaps repetition of) process or an effect as outcome of *this* presently observed process. For present purposes, attention is to the mensural as well as to a more general relational aspect of the concept, especially to the dynamic of change in a relational property.

Consider as simple illustration a physical bridge that was built to span a gap of length L and designed to safely support a load of weight W. Could I use the same design for a span of 2L and maintain the same safety factor for the same load W? Or would I have to reduce W in order to maintain safety, if I use the same design, same materials, and so forth? If the latter should be the case, could I reduce weight limit to half-W and maintain the safety factor? Or could I substitute thius new materials that has a greater tensile strength (or some other relevant measured property)? And so forth. These are relatively simple issues of mensuration pertaining to the scaling in which a process outcome is related to conditions of input.[455]

In some systems of relations, effects of process dynamics are maintained in consistent proportionality to that dynamic over time and across components. To say that a system of relations displays a "scale effect" is to say that the process in question is not homologous, but it remains to be said whether that effect is temporary, followed by reversion to the prior logic, or becomes a new and stable organizational logic. Think of the bridge illustration again: if, say, we double the input, what do we observe as output? If also doubled, the proportionality of output to input has been maintained. Sometimes this persistence is described by saying that the process could be "scaled up." That phrasing is misleading: there is no effect of scale as such in that scenario, for the proportionality has remained constant. The process is homologous through that change in input. Note well: homology has been demonstrated *only* for that range of variable input. Beyond that range? We do not know. Most if not all systems are limited in ability to maintain proportionality, the typical effect beyond a limit being system breakdown; the integrity of process is lost. The same point about limits applies as well to systems in which proportionality is itself variable. If I increase input by ten percent and observe an output greater by twenty percent, I have gained a substantial increase in efficacy and efficiency of process. But increasing input by twenty percent will not necessarily result in a forty percent increase in output; nor will a five percent increment of input achieve necessarily a ten percent boost (or even any boost) of output. A scale effect is typically bounded, and variation of effect within the bounds is not necessarily linear. Similarly, in some systems one can cut input, under a specific condition, without reducing output, and achieve a scale effect known as hysteresis—the condition typically being to initiate the process with a slightly greater-than-necessary input, then once the process is working smoothly reduce the input by slightly more than the superfluous increment of initial input. (This technique is frequently present in schedules of reward/penalty.)

Phenomena of scale can be observed in ordinary physical systems (the hysteretic effect mentioned just above being one of them). One practical advantage of Newtonian mechanics is its utility for many physical phenomena and everyday problems with them. The range of that utility is greatly facilitated by homology of process across an enormous range—from dandruff falling from one's head to the calculable maintenance of Keplerian orbits of planets in our solar system, all uniformly addressed within a single analytical-logical grid.[456] Then the advent of

---

[455] West's (2017) popular account illustrates various uses, and confused uses, of "scale."

[456] Thus, for instance, the independence of two force vectors of a projectile (e.g., a bullet) fired from a rifle anchored in parallel to a flat ground at an altitude of, say, three feet above that surface, in comparison with (assume) a second bullet, equivalent in all properties, which will freefall from the same three-foot altitude when released by a friction-less mechanism at the exact instant that the fired bullet leaves the muzzle: which bullet hits the ground first? The answer is that they hit at the same moment. The vector of gravity is the same for the same three-foot altitude and is equally independent of the vector of propulsive force.

quantum mechanics introduced a significant scale effect at some (still unknown) boundary between the quantum and Newtonian domains. The science of quantum mechanics has passed every test that has been put to it, and with remarkable precision. Yet much of what we have learned from and about quantum reality is so extraordinarily strange to our Newtonian-world experience that we are inclined to wonder, "So what *is* real?" Despite the strong bias that we learned in favor of homology in our Newtonian world of experience, it seems that a scale effect rules at some threshold from quantum to Newtonian reality. So far, theoreticians have been unable to devise a theory that makes quantum reality homologous with Newtonian reality. Since the human body is composed of atoms and subatomic particles, including those of the quantum realm, the effect of scale must operate within us, too (though evidently well below the realm of consciousness), and with a regularity that must indicate a well-ordered transition.

Given the range of variation in uses of phrases such as "scale effect," "scaling up," and "scale neutral," on might conclude either that the basic concept is new or that concerns about the phenomena are too new to have generated incentive to improve vocabulary. Neither is the case. Concerns about scale effects in physical reality date at least to Aristotle, and this ancient theorist liked to analogize from physical to social realms. Start with the first book of *Politics*, wherein he gave his conception of the organization of society, Athens foremost in mind. Human population and territory are organized in three forms—layers, one could say (*Politics* 1252a-1256b). In ascending order these are the household (oikos), the village (kōmē), and the city (polis). The household and the village are each hierarchal and rooted in tradition. But the city (as polis) is a koinonia, a collective partnership rooted in negotiations among the citizens (politēs) of the polis, whose decisions must consider the diverse interests of the residents of the city, some of whom are foreign residents (metics: as was Aristotle himself). Benveniste (1973 [1969], p. 107) reminded us that some of the metics were long-distance traders, and this small fact appears indirectly in ancient Greek dialects as a difference of scale in the organization of commerce. The word, "émporos," designated a large-scale merchant, but it referred to a long-distance trader ("émporos" derives from "emporeúomai," which means "to voyage by sea"). The large scale of an émporos probably entailed warehousing and wholesale merchandising, unlike the kápēlos ("small merchant"); and then as now, costs relative to benefits were sensitive to size of store (large storage reducing unit-cost but at greater risk of lost value in, say, warehouse fire). In the three books of *Economics* (a treatise once attributed to Aristotle but now thought to have been written by one of his students) one finds interesting if brief discussions of commerce, the circulation of money, sources of value, and various related topics, some of which evince an awareness of supply-demand relations and effects of difference of scale, although within a less specific vocabulary. While the second book deals specifically with the economy of a city, the discussion is less insightful than the corresponding discussions in Aristotle's *Politics*.[457]

---

[457] In addition, Aristotle discussed relations of exchange, mainly in terms of equity or justice, in the fifth chapter, fifth book of *Nicomachean Ethics*. All of his discussions are very general. While a literature purporting to qualify him as prescient of modern economics has grown in recent years, it is at least by my standards far too anachronistic. The generality allows abundant specificities to be read into his texts. At roughly the date Aristotle entered Plato's Academy, Xenophon, a contemporary of Plato, wrote a brief text in his *Cyropaedia* (bk 5, ch. 5) that has been cited as perhaps the earliest account of division of

Relative to the household, a village was more nearly self-sufficient simply because of the shared organization among households (which often, though not always, reflected tribal lineage). Because a city extended into the territory of surrounding villages and otherwise encouraged trade with settlements far and wide, a city was self-sufficient (at least in the ideal case). And this state of self-sufficiency (autarkeia) was both material and spiritual. The city's benefits from trade and internal market relations were sufficient to allow cultivations of reason, public support of artistic developments, and attainments of the good life. Note that nowhere in that explicit discussion did Aristotle mention what we call the question of scale. But the ingredients are there. I tend to be cautious in following accounts of Aristotle that read Durkheim or Max Weber or any other nineteenth-century theorist into the text of *Politics*, not because I see no similarities but because of the Whiggish anachronism of such readings (cf. Loraux 2002 [1997], pp. 154-155). On the other hand, Aristotle was explicit in discussing what amounted to a division of labor, both in household and in city organization, and he was explicit also in asserting the primacy of polis vis-à-vis politēs, yet at the same time making it clear that a city results from and is maintained by and within negotiations among the citizens insofar as the latter attend to diversity of interests in the city. All of that adds up to a recognition, in effect, of a difference of scale—that the logic of the layers of negotiation differs from the organizational logic of an autarkeia, on the one hand, and from the organizational logic of a household, on the other. It is here that the long series of works by Nicole Loraux have been so helpful. She undertook carefully thoughtful readings of Aristotle's text first to hear and then to see an interweaving of two more or less parallel texts. Loraux drew that "duplication" into our attention by demonstrating that the text I adumbrated above is the text of a classical history (beginning at least from Herodotus), and until recently the primary and main focal perspective of subsequent historians of Athens in particular as the "ideal case" of ancient Greek democracy, its success and failures. Along with that but subordinated to it, sometimes almost to the point of vanishing, was a second text which by Loraux' description is more anthropological, even ethnographic in its appearances (see, e.g., Loraux 2002 [1997]; 1995 [1990]). It is in this text, which often requires some interpolation, that we learn some details of the productivity, spiritual as well as material, of women—not only the women of the institution of hetaireia (whose standing has suffered in recent literatures due to overinterpretation, even an estrangement) but also the wives and mothers of the men who have come to us far less often as the nameless, somewhat gauzy "presences between scenes" that were the main venue of women. Slaves also figure in this latter text; we can see their abundant material presence in the dominant text, although of course they are nearly all unnamed. The place of woman was in the household, to be sure. But then, since not all households existed in the villages and rural settings between villages, the majority of wives and mothers resided in Athens proper, the chief locus of politics. And if we look in the right places we see many female actors—among the gods, for example, in surviving artworks, and in plays. Think of Sophocles' Electra and the repeated sequence of revengeful acts—daughter against mother, mother against husband—scenes that, while playing out in household settings, ramify

---

labor. Fair enough, if one acknowledges that the account is a bare sketch, describing a scene in a Persian kitchen, in a text that purports to be a biography of Cyrus' upbringing but was probably concocted of rumors and imagination. Ventures in "deep history" can bring useful reminders of our own assumptions, especially those of meaningfulness (see, e.g., Scott 2017).

against the unitary congress of a city-life that pretends to know anger only as division among its inhabitants. Sophocles left to "the citizen-spectators gathered in the theater to guess what in this anger that does not forget is the ultimate danger for the city because it is the worst enemy of politics" (Loraux 2002 [1997], p. 160).

At least in Sophoclean theatre, one might think, the ever-present threat to a unifying homology from household to city stemmed from unbounded psychic energy, relative to any city's claim to an orderliness of reason. But we also know the abundant precedence to that threat: the Homeric song-poems are among other things lessons in the power of emotions, from the gamut of Achilles to Ajax' early version of Isaac McCaslin's lament (in the Faulkner short story, "The Bear"): like Ike, Ajax had done all the right things as best he could but still got no glory). Thence to the sharp history of warfare, hubris, and sacrifice in both victory and defeat as told by Thucydides: various lessons of scale in emotive registers.

Phenomena of scale have also figured in understandings of the mereology of biological organism. Some of this has been straightforward—for example, the question of body mass as it relates to vital organic functions. Susan Oyama's (1985) speculative exploration of matters of scale in developmental processes of organic organization, which she conceptualized in terms of information processing, has been prescient. The application of information theory is relevant, no doubt. It is still instructive to read George Miller's (1967) little book on communication, in part as a means of gauging how far we have (and have not) come during the subsequent five decades, whether under the "old" labels, such as "communication," or new, such as "cognitive science" (see e.g., Turner 2007b, 2018). It has been clear since Miguel de Cervantes' Don Quixote, if not before, that the primary discrimination within "brain function" is neither telegraphic nor spot-lighting but in a selection process of filtering and updating (a form of repeated sampling). This is the chief selection effect of both memory and forecast or anticipation. The lesson was ignored, by and large, until Bayesian inference became a putative revolution. While statistical theory had already recognized it—for instance, in the work of Ronald Fisher and Leonard Savage (see, e.g., Savage 1972)—in general, it is true, common practice was to assume that sampling is a once-and-done utility, an assumption due to a punctualist understanding of the frequentist approach to probability. Humans do have a finite "span of attention," as Miller (1967) called it, and the span is both temporal and spatial. This finitude underlies a prevalent scarcity of attention (Simon 1971), no doubt, but there is nothing in it that necessitates a "once and done" observational stage. Updating happens even when not planned, and some sort of filtering is usually conditional to it. These actions need not be left to happenstance, of course. They can be learned as a strategy of decision making—indeed, as a strategic action of learning, thus implementing selection effect as a recursive process (Miller 1967, pp. 89-92, 111-117; Savage 1972, pp. iv-v; Ljungqvist and Sargent 2018).

I will have more to say about filter-and-update sequences later, inasmuch as I see this as a major process, or a subprocess, of aggregation. For now, since the phrase will appear here and there, I want to be more specific about the resampling, beginning with its uses in the theory of information control and engineering. For the moment I will focus mainly on the first part of the "filter and update" phrase; while filtering usually is followed by an updating, the form of this updating is not automatically entailed by filtering as such. Also, in later discussion I will use the notion of filter primarily but not exclusively in terms of a per-person operation of first-person information resampling, although this operation will usually quickly intersect with an array of second-person standpoints (and probably third-person as well) within networks of per-person ties and more specifically networks of ties among effects of per-person actions. But more about that later, in §29. For the present I will address more general applications of control theory. The basic idea of it is one that any of us who have learned to ride a bicycle (for instance) will surely have experienced, for we have made good use of a filter-and-update sequencing in terms of vectors of forward motion and momentum both linear and angular within one's capability of sensorimotor feedback (in effect, a sort of gyroscopic sensor). The information that comes back to a novice rider is processed according to an implicit continuous-time model. While that is a skill that the body has learned from crawling, then walking, then running, etc., the skill has not implanted very well in one's reflective consciousness.[458] The reflection tends to be in terms of discrete-time measurement of the vectors of motion, and that simple difference is enough to induce fear of falling. What is more, the sensory information tends to be noisy, partly because of nervousness but also because of random-variable feedback into one's body. One must learn to trust the body's capability all over again. That happens via a sequence of filter-and-update processing of the variable feedback to the body's sensorimotor balance. The basic filter in that feedback flow of information is one known as a Kalman filter (a name that refers to a class of highly efficient recursive filters; about which, more later).

Back to Oyama's explorations. Her (1985, p. 119) key insight was achieved via recursive observation into determinate patterns of evidence—in particular, for instance, evidence that once "cell layers are formed, they can enter into higher-level morphogenetic interactions," and these may "in turn bring about further changes in cell activity. Cells both constitute and are controlled by the tissues they construct." This was a keen insight into a dialectical morphology of complex hierarchical organization in which scale effects can be observed. Thirty-three years later Carl Zimmer's (2018) orchestral medley of genomic studies included some accounts of various views of cellular configurations as tissue in which cells can communicate with their neighbors, borrow functions and materials from each other, change own and other cell's processes, and host "alien" cells as therefore mosaic tissues or as microchimeras (mothers retaining cells of their offspring), with sometimes benign, sometimes malign effects.

Read years ago, Oyama's perspective brought to mind lessons Jorge Luis Borges had tried to teach his reader by posing this apparently simple question: "Why does it disturb us that the map be included in the map and the thousand and one nights in the book of the *Thousand and One Nights*? Why does it disturb us that Don Quixote be a reader of the *Quixote* and Hamlet a spectator of *Hamlet*? I believe I have found the reason: these inversions suggest that if the characters of a fictional work can be readers or spectators, we, its readers and spectators, can be fictitious" (Borges 1962 [1949], p. 196). A bit more needs to be said, however. In particular,

---

[458] These are relative distinctions, of course. Neural processing time of the human brain is but a fraction of the frequency bands of many kinds of signal. Thus, the brain's ability to process a finite number of distinct signals per second (on average, about 5/second; at maximum, about 10/second) means that a "continuous-time" information flow, which as electromagnetic signal can flow at $10^{10}$ signals per second, will be processed as a "discrete-time" sequence (see Tegmark 2017, p. 309).

what Borges called "inversion" I would call "reflexion" or "reflexivity" (see Ashmore 1989). The relation is an instance of the dialectical unity of opposites. One should bear in mind, too, that a "fiction" is a "making," as is a "fact"; but we tend to treat these as opposites pure and simple— not as a unity of opposites, that is, but as foundational difference locked in oppositional isolation (i.e., a Cartesian analytical relation of clear and distinct ideas or categories or "things"). Borges was questioning a dominant sense ("common sense") reality of space. (Or, now we say, space-time.) It can be closed or not-closed, because the difference is perspective: the reader or spectator who appears outside the writing or the spectacle is also inside it. After all, does not a reader join in ("get into") the story being read? Does not the spectator experience the spectacle from within? The journey "back and forth" begins, Coleridge said, with a "willing suspension of disbelief." That is to say, the "program" can be started, rewound, started again, via a switch in perspective—the very kind that, Mead (e.g., 1999, pp. 7-19) pointed out, children practice in play as an exercise in taking the role of the other, thereby becoming a bigger, denser, more complex and more versatile self. Borges' questions pointed to endogeneities of process, and to the likelihood of scale effects within them. Mead at times verged on adding to our understanding of that.[459]

An important principle in Oyama's (1985) theoretical framework is present also within work by Scott Feld in studies of social organization (e.g., Feld 1991). Generally speaking, the conditions that lead to the initial production of a social formation are not identical to the conditions that lead to maintenance, expansion, or decline of that formation. This is *not* to deny the importance of endogeneity in either maintenance or change of the organization. My point is different, and not exclusive of endogenous processes. One of the reasons for the non-identity I mentioned is inescapable: the conditions of an extant organization include the presence and operation of the organization itself—that is, an organization is partly its own environment, to use that traditional terminology—whereas the conditions prior to the organization's formation do not. As Zimmer's (2018) review has shown, organic process runs on internal relations of various kinds, some of which display functional sensitivity to scale. At a certain point in development, for instance, stem cells building a tissue generate a functional specification of *kind* of tissue. The information of that generative process is retained in the newly specific somal tissue, however, and as several scholars demonstrated it is possible to recover to *present* action that formative relation, in effect "rejuvenating" somal cells into their ancestral stem-cell multivalences. In short, "the ontogeny of information" retains capacity which can be recovered via understandings of its *relational* constitution, including the sensitivities to scale within that relationality (Oyama, 1985, pp. 15-19). We have in this insight a view of the reality of "institution" to the specific organizations that "fit the type" (as will be further discussed below).

---

[459] It is appropriate to recall here as well the discussion by Marx of "fictitious capital": its reality consists only in a promise (trust, expected value) of tomorrow, which, to be effective, depends on the possibility of bringing forward to today tomorrow's dollar (a "credit dollar"), which is to say the possibility that future value can be discounted to present value (Marx 1987 [1939], p. 98; see also Harvey 2006, ch. 9). A century and a half after Marx' *Grundrisse* was written, John Cochrane (2011) was applauded for beginning his presidential address to the American Finance Association with this announcement: "Asset prices should equal expected discounted cash flows."

Recent work in ecological theory has been developing those sensitivities—for instance, in regard to population growth rates within predator-prey relations (see, e.g., Pascual 2001; Pilosof, Porter, Pascual, and Kéfi 2017). For any given species more than one prey and more than one predator are usual networks, and these networks sometimes cross over. Multi-species pairings can be observed at more than one organizational level (e.g., for red deer, predators include wolf and cougar species but also various infectious diseases, while prey include a variety of meadow grasses but also a farmer's field corn and fruit). Returns on defensive actions vary by predator, while returns on food search usually also vary by species. As Pascual (2001, p. 258) pointed out, "ecological rates, such as those associated with per capita population growth, predation, and competition for resources, are not constant but vary as a function of densities. This density dependence in intraspecific and interspecific interactions leads to nonlinearity in ecological systems and in the models we build to capture their dynamics." I do not doubt that similar complexities can be seen in factors and relations of human sociality (about which, more below).

As we saw in Part Four, §24, there is some evidence that Mead was aware of the question of scale as an important issue. In his review of a work by Henry Bergson, for instance, he (1907, p. 380) referred to "pronounced unsolved" problems of aggregation, although he did not name them as such, and he thought those problems to be a "general defect." Abbott's (1999, p. 62) attribution—that for Mead self and society result from "the same process"—is indeed a fitting impression, if one reads it in a general and rather loose manner. To infer from that impression that Mead endorsed homology is a step too far, however. I know of no evidence that he ever pursued the question of homology as such, nor can I say that he ever entertained it in thought. There is no doubt that the question lies open in Mead's discussions of some of his core concepts, such as taking the perspectives of significant others and incorporating them into one's own (see, e.g., Mead 1927, pp. 77-78). But I do not see that he pursued those processes as they take place across different organizational levels, with possibilities of scale effects at those boundaries. Very few theorists have made the attempt.

On the other hand, Mead was sensitive to issues of reflexivity in its temporal dimension. In principle, self's perspective is inherently perspective on self, a reflexivity, although the effects of this will vary from person to person. Insofar as scaling is present in perspective and its often anticipatory reflection, it becomes implicated in self's understanding of same/other relations and applications of scale-relevant techniques. Think of temporal scale, for instance. Not all that long ago most people, being farmers or peasants, rarely if ever saw utility or even meaning in a unit as small as a second, and very little to a minute. Effects of actions were usually timed in durations longer than that—weeks, months, seasons—and if a question ever arose that quantitative change in the frequency or regularity of a practice might yield better effect, there was plenty of latitude for trial and error. But now consider the femtosecond, the temporal unit by which the process of chemical reactions occur, for example, and are measured as such. As techniques are built of this temporal unit, they become incorporated into the temporality of reflexivity of self—at first for those who practice the technique but then increasingly also for others who imagine the pace of that ultra-fast process in various metaphors and other references, and who think of using such products in their everyday lives. A femtosecond, by the way, is one-quadrillionth of a second—

that is, one thousandth of a trillionth of a second. Femtochemists are in the business of capturing the process of bonding on film. No camera shutter yet devised approaches the required speed, but no matter: use a flash of illumination that lasts only a few femtoseconds. Since the 1980s engineers have demonstrated laser pulses that are timed in femtoseconds. The next task was then to develop that technique as a photographic apparatus. By 1996 engineers had accomplished exactly that, generating sequences of images that show the process of a chemical bond being formed and, correlatively, the process of a chemical bond breaking. Imagine children growing up in school, matter-of-factly watching film strips of chemical bonding, learning to see their worlds in terms of such rapid processes, measured in femtoseconds. And then later, in the next class or another class, a process of spatiotemporal intervals measured in light years.

The most common applications of "scale" in settings familiar to most people today have to do with processes that are more closely analogous to Newtonian mechanics. Someone wants to know if more output can be gained from a production process with proportionately little added to the input. In other words, can the logic of the process be made more efficient in that means-to-end relation? Since labor time has traditionally been the largest input factor, the question has been one of "increased output per same rate of labor time." Assembly-line production, recall, was invented to that purpose—to increase the "time efficiency" of human motions. Not many inventions in human productivity have been as consequential as "economy of scale." By the same token, one might invest instead in more employees and/or in newer physical plant for a production process, in expectation of reaping more than an equal return on the investment (i.e., increasing returns to scale). Such innovations have profoundly reshaped human societies since the late nineteenth century. While human motions can never be measured on any time scale even suggestive of femtosecond gradations, productions via polymer chemistry and perhaps proteomic biochemistry are probably within future grasp.

Some factors of production are more, and some less, scalable. Haskel and Westlake (2018, p. 66 n.2) illustrated that difference in memorable fashion when they invoked a thought experiment to describe returns on an investment in knowledge. Suppose the existence of a newly found planet: rich in familiar resources, it is inhabited by a human-like species. Suppose that a committee of economists has completed an extensive survey, the conclusion of which is that the planet has twice the resources of Earth—twice the labor power, twice the stock of capital, and so forth. While it also has twice the amount of music and twice the volume of poetry, it is stuck with the same algebra, the same geometry and trigonometry, the same calculus that we have on Earth. Should one expect that sameness to have been a serious deficit? Has it been a handicap to production output? The economists might well have concluded that it had not been, and should not have been, a handicap. Poetry and music are forms of knowledge that might or might not be scalable; but unless the human-like species would have utilized a logic different from ours, the mathematical knowledge as we know it would have been completely scalable to their different conditions. Indeed, the scalability of knowledge and similar informational intangibles (such as algorithms) has been a, perhaps the, major factor in the recent large increases in inequality in the USA and other countries (see Haskel and Westlake 2018, pp. 133-134).[460]

Now let's consider again the relation of scale to level. Whereas "level" is a description of the results of aggregation in organization, "scale" pertains to the dynamics of a process, which could be an aggregative process. Conceptually, the two terms are easy enough to keep separately in mind. But in operation of process an effect of scale can be obscured by or confounded with a difference in level. An instance of this was seen above in the discussion of long-distance trade and warehousing in conjunction with Aristotle's account of Athens. Because of a gain in benefit relative to cost (i.e., a scaling effect), warehousing was formalized as a different organizational level, with different per-person agents, interests, and so forth. This particular effect was replayed during the period leading into Europe's twelfth-century renaissance, as resumption of long-distance trading was indicator of and stimulant to resumption of city life, which in turn spawned resumption of large-scale investments in artistic activities—for instance, architecture as in the Gothic style of cathedral construction, new engineering designs such as harnessing wind power on land, and navigational aids such as the magnetic compass. In short, effects of scale have something in common with prosthetic devices (as these were treated above, in §21).

The relation of scale to level also often involves a change of level that results in a return to scale. It is not uncommon, certainly, for individual persons to engage collectively in actions. Sometimes effects of such actions scale differently from the effects of ostensibly the same action performed by one or more of the same individual persons each acting as a singleton.[461] Scaling of effect might take the form either of an increased efficiency of process resulting in the same output from a diminished input or of an increased rate of return to the same input. In either case, the output-per-input ratio calculated per person for the collectivity as a whole is greater than the average of the action effects of the sum of individual-person members acting as singletons. The scale effect (in either of the forms) is due to some jointness or sharing of actions, attributable (per hypothesis) to a shared agency or joint agency or commitment (see, e.g., Bratman 1999; Gilbert 2000; Tuomela 2007). The dynamic can be in principle a process of aggregation, of individual persons coming together in mutual agreement of effort at a given time. The dynamic may also come to fruition on a temporal gradient of learning, however, or of simply attaining the agreement itself; for one should not assume that agreement is effortless or a "natural tendency." If the result of "coming together" is a melding of interests, perspectives, and intents, such that one can see in the resulting joint or shared action the sign of a "multiplier effect" (an effect of difference in scale *as such*) it is a result of sociality which demonstrates the lesson that *re*production usually occurs "with difference," a produced difference that is inherent in the current sociality (Hazelrigg 1989b, pp. 191, 203).[462]

---

[460] Note that whereas standard practice in model-building has been to assume constant returns to scale in production functions, that simplification is not necessary (see, e.g., Ljungqvist and Sargent 2018).
[461] The implied observational determinations can be very difficult to make. An action performed by an individual person seemingly as singleton might carry an impression of prior cooperative action of exactly the same type, the apparent singleton continuing the cooperative venture in mind if not in talk.
[462] These are some of the ways in which one can read in Mead's articles an (unnamed) grasp of "scale effect."

Finally, to repeat a point made earlier, this scale effect would have been occurring *across* organizational levels; for the individual-person actor is still an agent at the level of individual person even while acting in collectivity (e.g., family or work group). In principle, an observer could examine the activities in microscopic and in mesoscopic or macroscopic view, either alternatively or simultaneously, much as a conversational analyst observes an audiovisual recording of, say, a play group in one or both registers. When the collectivity in question has legal standing as a corporate-person actor, the process is much the same except that specified individual-person actors are officials of the corporation, some or all of whom are authorized to speak not simply on behalf of but *as* the corporate-person actor (e.g., the chief executive officer, within specified bounds; the chief financial officer, within specified bounds, and so forth). Other individual-person actors who are members of the corporation but who lack official standing beyond, say, "employee" have obligations and may receive benefits greater than would accrue to them as so many singleton actors (better wage rates, etc.) in return for their contributions to the collective whole, the assumption typically being that those contributions will be greater than would occur for any given employee acting in similar capacity as a singleton, owing to resources available only to those employees (which could include the prestige resource of being, say, a specialist in cryptography at Microsoft or at JP MorganChase, an incentive to contribute at much greater degree than being the "same" specialist at Local Firm).

Thus, individual-persons aggregate to higher level of organization, and the effects of their individual-person inputs may manifest scale effects due to the aggregation. Scale effects can occur *within* the individual level as well, however, since we are concerned with process. For example, an individual person might learn a new interactional skill from contact with a new significant other via an informal network of individual persons. Granovetter's (1973) thesis of the power of weak ties applies far beyond search functions regarding, say, employment. An expanded perspective can open not only new interpersonal linkages but also opportunities for growth and development previously unseen or underappreciated. For reasons having to do with the institutionalization of resource acquisition and attendant process relations, however, most scale effects—or at least most *observable* scale effects—will take place across organizational levels (see below, §27).

The qualification inserted in the immediately preceding sentence prompts me to make more explicit and distinctive another key point already stated: it is *usual* for individual persons to be present in relations of sociality at different levels of organization at the same time or nearly so, and that contingency increases observability, especially of scale effects. An individual person is a singleton actor of and in a sociality; probably also a member of a family, a different practice of sociality; probably as well a participant in an educational process, whether formal (e.g., a school, a job training program) or informal (a hobby, a game such as bridge or basketball, etc.), and a participant in a workplace regime—each of these last activities still another practice of sociality. In all of these organizational settings, any given individual person will likely perform a variety of actions, although usually not all at the same time; and it is not always clear whether the intent of an action is specific to a specific organizational level only but perhaps ramifies in effect to a higher level, or is intended only or primarily and mainly to both individual-person and intermediate level (e.g., family or school) but ramifies upward as well as downward.[463]

The key point of the foregoing consideration I take to be this: *the basic unit is an "action effect."* It begins with an individual person (or, for legal purposes, a corporate-person), whether the action itself begins at individual-person level or higher. The effect of an individual-person's action performed at individual-person level may remain at that level or it might aggregate with the effects of other individual-person actors; the aggregated effects may remain at level of the individual persons, or they may ramify to higher level even if the individual-persons themselves remain only at the level of individual person (i.e., do not engage as collective actors as such). These relations of process will be described considerably more in later sections of this Part Five. Before turning to those descriptions, however, I need to present further preliminaries.[464]

## §26. Agency, Efficacy, and Model Relations

More than once theorists and analysts within the social sciences have retraced steps laid down in Immanuel Kant's critical inquiry of claims of knowledge, as they have begun within the domain of what Kant called "the rational part" of genuine science only to find pathways blocked because inquiry into human affairs could not depend on the timeless and placeless qualities of necessity. At the start of the twentieth century, the retracing occurred in the mind of Max Weber. His early training had inclined him to think in terms of causal inference, as the long tradition of modern science through Newton to the end of the nineteenth century had promoted by its own practices and promises. The accelerating pace of "discoveries and applications" during the century had sparked imaginations of extensive developments of all the sciences, including the newest of them. Weber, having struggled with ill health during the mid-1890s, resigned his teaching duties and, during intermittent periods of convalescence, contemplated issues of empirical inquiry in view of his own prior research in legal and economic history. Initially adopting a standpoint of probabilistic theorizing that wove together concepts of objective possibility, causality, and a criterion of attributional adequacy, he soon moved increasingly away from the logical strictures as deemed adequate for physical science and toward an interpretivist emphasis on the subjective meanings of human reasonings (see Turner 1983; Martin 2011, ch. 2; McKim and Turner 1997). Logical standards of causality not only could not work where relations of necessity did not obtain; they overlooked the contingent realities of human meanings that lay at the foundations of what it meant to *be* human. Thus, we have from his recuperative days some

---

[463] To be clear: an action intended to be effective at, say, an intermediate level of organization will virtually always also have immediate effects at the individual-person level, at very least for and of the individual-person actor. The intermediate-level effect could ramify to a higher level. It could also ramify back onto the individual-person actor with whom it began, and in unexpected, perhaps unpleasant, perhaps destructive ways. It is easy to imagine such a case when the initial intent is to do harm elsewhere. But the same feedback can occur from benignly intended action that, on feedback, results in harm (the "Good Samaritan penalty").

[464] When, some years ago, I began the process of making these proposals more systematic and in written format, I surprised myself when I realized that my nomination of "unit action-effect" was so similar to a stipulation by Talcott Parsons and his associates during the late 1940s and after, although it also figured in Mead's theorization (see, e.g., Mead 1938; see also Lasswell and Kaplan 1950, pp. 3-5, 240). I do not fix on a "unit-act," however; "unit action-effect" is difficult enough.

of the most complicated, at times inconsistent writings on issues that defined a period remembered as "the conflict" or "struggle over methods." The most salient question that survived was about the possibility of another kind of science, one that could contribute empirical generalizations of greater worth than mere opinion despite lacking the limit by necessity that could guarantee certain knowledge.

During the last half of the twentieth century one could see in literatures of social science a gradual shift away from the vocabulary of "cause and effect," at first toward "determinants and their effects." As Tyler Cowen (2018, pp. 102, 103) recently observed, "the brute reality is that contingency is real." Moreover, because "disturbances to the flow of temporal events need not dwindle into insignificance," probabilistic estimations offer only weak guidance in inferences that we make. Indeed, although a few scholars continue to insist that they had unlocked the chest of causality (see, e.g., Pearl 1990, 2010; Pearl and MacKenzie 2018), the unadorned fact remains that claims of causal inference are lame without the bulwark of necessity.[465] Instead of "cause" a term of choice in recent discussions has been "agency," paired with "agency's effects" and "efficacy." I will adopt this nomenclature, as follows.

## Agency

If society is a whole, which of its parts are capable of agency? And for that matter, what exactly do I mean by "agency"? A good provisional definition is Riskin's (2016, p. 3): by "agency" I mean "an intrinsic capacity to act in the world." The basic idea is not peculiar to the social sciences, of course, although in the physical sciences the dynamis has historically been "cause and effect" rather than "agency and effects." I will make explicit also that the basic idea for the social sciences includes "intrinsic capacity to act with intent, with purpose." Other clarifications need to be considered. They will be pursued in following paragraphs.

Most discussions assume that the basic, unitary part capable of agency is the individual human being, at least one beyond a specified age (which can vary by venue and other conditions) and presuming a minimal physical and/or mental capability. Agency has also been allowed or attributed to specified collectivities. Traditionally, in most if not all societies, a collective unit of some additional description qualified as "family," at least "family of procreation" if not more broadly defined, has been accorded agency, even though that agency has usually been gendered first and foremost as male (i.e., patriarchy). Other collectivities that have been accorded formal or informal right of agency have included both central government as such and agencies of that government; clusters of population settlement such as a city; religious institutions of one kind or another which have performance rights of agency typically with regard to marital, birth, coming-

---

[465] Granted, that has not impeded use of phrases such as "causal analysis," "causal efficacy," and "causal structure" by social scientists (e.g., Coleman 1986, pp. 1311, 1312; Elster 1993, p. 302; Steel 2004). But nothing fundamental of the topic has changed since Max Born (1949, p. 1) wrote this: "Nature, as well as human affairs, seems to be subject to both necessity and accident. Yet even accident is not completely arbitrary, for there are laws of chance, formulated in the mathematical theory of probability, nor can the cause-effect relation be used for predicting the future with certainty, as this would require a complete knowledge of the relevant circumstances, present, past, or both together, which is not available. There seems to be a hopeless tangle of ideas. In fact, if you look through the literature on this problem you will find no satisfactory solution, no general agreement."

of-age, and funereal ceremonies, and other customs of belief and practice such as confession, absolution, expiation, exorcism, and adjudication. In general, however, the notion of *collective* agency has been fraught historically with both controversy and ambiguity. Here, too, the matter has not been peculiar to the social sciences. As illustration, consider that the issue of agency has an analog in the world of chemistry. Bundles of atoms of same and/or different elements vary in their properties. Bundle atoms of neon together, and what does one get? Only a bundle of atoms; the bundle has no properties beyond those of each individual atom; there is no interaction, because neon is inert even to itself.[466] Specific bundles of various other atoms can be highly energetic, rapidly (magnesium and oxygen) or slowly (iron and oxygen), and can join with still other compounds, generating new characteristics. An issue presently under debate in physics is of particular relevance here, in that it illustrates the quality of "agency" within physical science. In the realm known as quantum physics evidence that quarks bundle together has been reliably produced for decades. Until recently two distinct collections had been demonstrated: a baryon, consisting of three quarks (up, down, and charm), and a meson consisting of two quarks (up and anti-charm). Each has a distinctive internal structure, formed in very strong bonds known as "gluons" (i.e., the strong force). Thus, each is an analog to what in chemistry has been called a "molecule" (e.g., of carbon dioxide). A molecule has agency: the atoms are bonded more or less strongly and, as such, are capable of participating in chemical reactions (e.g., forming new compounds such as those of DNA). Evidence of a *five*-quark collection—composed of one baryon and one meson—has now been produced, and this has led to the issue that I mentioned as reason for this illustration: does this collection qualify as a quantum analog of "molecule"— a "little mass" that *as such* has distinctive properties, including agency—or is it simply a "bag of particles"? Each side has its champions (for a summary report, see Cho 2019).

Izenberg (1992, p. 5), recall, viewed events during Europe's Romanticist movement of "supra-individual entities" with great interest. These entities included a "people" or "Volk" or "national character," supposedly endowed with a spirit suggestive of distinctive agency. Yet all the while, the supposed process by which "the idea of personal individuality was extended and transformed" into the special collectivity was persistently, and conveniently, glossed. A more recent innovation, one with early fruition in the USA, was (is) the commercial corporation. This form of organization acquired agency rights, including most importantly agency under protection of limited financial liability, by a late nineteenth-century judicial ruling, although as John Dewey (1926) later wrote in regard to "the historic background" of this "corporate legal personality," as a matter of US constitutional and statutory law the innovation was a cobbled effort in 1886 that fell apart in 1906, when the US Supreme Court held that the 1886 statement on behalf of the court had standing neither in fact nor in law. The convention persisted anyway, and qualified corporations are legal subjects with standing comparable to a "natural person."[467]

---

[466] At least I know of no evidence that a neon compound has been demonstrated. But that could change. Not long ago, for example, xenon, another of the so-called noble gases, was considered inert; likewise, krypton. Compounds of each now exist.

[467] The sequence of legal cases heard before the US Supreme Court is especially interesting for reasons addressed by Dewey (1926), who, as Patterson (1950, p. 619) later said, "pulverized most of the traditional concepts of corporate legal personality, and left the fragments on the lawyer's doorstep." The

The framework within which that meaning of "corporate person" gained force of law was comparative, the standard being the individual adult person as legal subject. It was also during this period, recall, that the core legal meaning of "natural person" as legal subject shifted from a will-based theory of agency (or more specifically, intent) to the "reasonable man" doctrine (the gendered "general case" being matter-of-factly explicit). But as we saw above with regard to the arguments of James Coleman, "individual person" is not always free of ambiguity.[468] Since I wish here to specify my meaning of "agency," I should first specify my meaning of "individual human being," a phrase that I will generally shorten to "individual person" or "individual person-actor" (the latter used when I want to make clear the "actor's action effects" coupling). My main point in using Coleman as foil or exemplar as I just did is not that I intend a general critique of his work. Rather, his writing is a good example of ambiguities or confusions that can creep into one's composition without notice. Substantively there are parts of Coleman's work that I find useful at least as points of departure. One of his (1986, 1990) basic premises holds that "actor is regarded as acting purposely." I do not think that he meant that person-actors *always* act with purpose. I know I do not mean that. Actors may do other things, too, including acting without purpose. But from the standpoint of agency I think Coleman was right to stipulate purposive, intentional action, allowing that actual effects may be contrary to intended goal or purpose. He also stipulated, however, that the actor should be "well-organized" and not "problematic" to any important extent. Given the context, those stipulations might have been intended as description of Max Weber's view. Weber often used an "as if" locution. As one example, he (1968 [1922], p. 6) stipulated that "it is convenient to treat all irrational, affectively determined elements of behavior as factors of deviation from a conceptually pure type of rational action." Well aware that he was being counterfactual, his "convenience" was recognition of a simplification, and elsewhere (in his treatment of the attraction, the sociality, of charisma, for instance) he attended directly to the dynamics of affective relations as having subjective meaning, although not necessarily a clearly shared meaning and/or an internally rational or coherent organization of meaning. Was Coleman adopting that "as if" approach? Perhaps. But his discussion suggests otherwise, for he seemed to believe that if a given actor is in some way importantly problematic, or not well-organized, then the regnant domain is psychology, not sociology. While this might have been a page from the Hobbesian "as if"—here I mean Hobbes' (1949 [1647], ch. 8, §1) suggestion that we "consider man as if but even now sprung out of the earth, and suddainly (like Mushromes) come to full maturity without all kind of engagement to each other"—Coleman apparently thought that "the social" must be coherent, well-organized, without problems, if it is to be worthy of sociological attention. This stance seems to me to be implicit in his stipulation about the proper constitution of a sociological problem or topic: "sociologists lose their problem

---

chief interest of the world of commerce was that by establishing the legal status of the corporation on the model of a "natural person" as legal subject, the financial liability of a corporation could be limited to assets of the "corporate person" as such, thus protecting the assets of officers and board of directors.
[468] In his 1986 article, for example (cited above in §25), I have read ambiguity or confusion or both, and not all of it having to do with his uncertainty about how far to extend the category, "corporate actor." His 1990 treatise is also troubled by ambiguities and some inconsistencies. Jon Elster (1993, p. 297) described the book as "the most explicit and detailed statement of the rational-choice research paradigm in sociology" but also "more dogmatic" than some others (citing economists as instances). There are occasions of reading when one wonders if Empson (1953) undercounted types of ambiguity.

when they assume purposes and goal-directed actions of societies as units." Did he mean the exclusion in recognition of a boundary to political science? I am not sure what he meant. Allowing that "for some investigations" collectivities "such as formal organizations" may be "regarded as purposive actors," Coleman (1986, p. 1312) said that more generally "the coherence of their action [i.e., the action of a collectivity] would itself be taken as problematic" and thus, apparently, outside the domain of sociology. I have also noted more generally his tendency to invoke some notion of the propriety of intellectual domains—the properly sociological versus the properly psychological—which at least suggests, it has seemed to me, that the sociologist should avoid investigation of the "interiority" of the individual person, despite the theorizations of George Herbert Mead, Charles Horton Cooley, and others.

Some of Coleman's meanings become a little clearer, if no less confusing, in his treatise, where he (1990, p. 4) suggested, for example, that he preferred to treat the individual person-actor as other than "a socialized element of a social system," the preference due to his belief that if the latter definition should be adopted the "questions of moral and political philosophy which address the fundamental strain between man and society cannot be raised. Problems of freedom and equality cannot be studied." He did not explain his reasoning. Perhaps he imagined that a "Hobbesian model of man" (by which he might have had in mind the popular caricature of Hobbes) is itself self-explanatory. In any case, it appears he assumed his readers would know what he meant by "man" in his reference to "fundamental strain between man and society," and he surely was convinced in his own conception (whatever exactly it was) as he repeated it by saying that the "image of man as a socialized element of a social system" makes impossible "within the framework of social theory" any intent "to evaluate the actions of a social system or a social organization." Where he expected to find for such inquiry a human being who is not socialized he did not say. It must also be said, however, that in other discussions Coleman seemed to have in mind actual—i.e., "socialized"—individual persons as actors going about their business. One wonders in what manner he understood himself. [469] In any case, to repeat a stipulation already started and defended, I do not regard "individual person" as in any sense of actuality or reality to be a pre-social (or non-social) being.

Back to the concept of "agency." Recall my earlier discussions of Kant's argument that there can be no science, properly considered, of culture, society, human affairs, because of lack of the rational part. This is simply to say that human beings possess considerable freedom from necessity, including most importantly the freedom to self-legislate. It is not to say that humans have no rational capacity. But because of the freedom from necessity, and to the degree of that freedom, our rational capacity is solely phenomenal (in the terms of Kant's critical theory), which is to say that human being's rational capacity lacks the power of strict necessity—that is, necessary relations—and therefore yields results of systematic inquiry that are limited to bounds

---

[469] I have given more attention to Coleman's 1986 paper than to his 1990 treatise, because the latter shows markings of a compilation of separate papers written at different times and perhaps for different audiences. He alluded to this quality in his preface, and the instances of duplication verbatim indicate more attention to simple compilation than to coherence of presentation. I did not know Coleman personally; I wonder if poor health had become an issue.

of empirical generalization.[470]  The limit is to rational capabilities and their extensions.  We can and do legislate; but lacking necessary relations, we legislate into unknown conditions.  Whereas the Newtonian third law holds tomorrow and next century just as it did in his century, the model equation

$$Y = a + b_1X_1 + b_2X_2 + \ldots + b_nX_n + e \qquad (5.2)$$

—where Y is, say, inequality of wage-and-salary income by gender, $X_1$ is adult-person age, $X_2$ is educational attainment, $X_n$ collects other relevant variables (including job title), and e collects errors due to measurement, missing variables, and sampling—will at best pertain to a particular population yesterday and perhaps today (which is to say that each of the variables should carry a subscript of place and date).  Moreover, whereas in any specific application within Newton's domain Newton's law usually has relatively little "error of prediction," the prediction error of the foregoing equation, no matter how many specific variables $X_n$ expands into, will usually be large.

In Kantian terms there are in principle noumenal causes ("*real* causes," one might say, not faint imitations).  But we do not know what they are.  The best we can do is infer what they seem to be, what they might be, from observed events that we assume are caused effects.  It could be appropriate to say that noumenal causes "have agency," but that would be to deploy the word "agency" with very different meaning from using it to say that human beings "have agency."  I intend this extension of Kant (who, as best I remember, never used the word "agency") as mere backdrop to the following.  Some scholars (e.g., Pickering 1995, pp. 6-26) have speculated that material things (other than human beings and other animated beings) have agency, a "material agency."  In Pickering's (1995, p. 6) world, one "can start with the idea that the world is filled not, in the first instance, with facts and observations, but with *agency*."  Indeed, one can.  But the declaration ceases meaning if one allows "ideas" to be among the many "facts and observations" disallowed first instance.  His world is "continually *doing things*, things that bear upon us not as observation statements upon disembodied intellects but as forces upon material beings."  But the straw man who will be blown away in Pickering's weather is this "disembodied intellect."  No one denies that sensation—bodily sensation, sensory organs, impressions formed from sensory stimuli—is a beginning of human understanding, but without categories (i.e., language) it would begin and end as something like a blur of "white light."  It would not even register as pain (i.e., a contrastive category in a dialectic, pleasure/pain).

But is "material agency" only a figment of imagination, a disembodied imagination?  Not exactly.  Where Pickering's grasp might have lain between, say, Pierre Duhem's (1969 [1908]) concern to "save the phenomena" and Ludwig Fleck's (1979 [1935]) "reverence for an ideal" with respect to epistemic values in scientific inquiry I cannot determine (Rietmann 2018, p. 93).  But I think what he intended was something like George Herbert Mead's pragmatic notion of posing a hypothetical and watching to see whether and how "the world answers to it."  This fits reasonably well the facts of a scientist's laboratory or "big machine" (as it did Eratosthenes, his gnomon, compass, and a well near Aswan, Egypt).  Those are human doings, of course.  What

---

[470] Furthermore, even in the Newtonian realm of strict necessity, recall Kant's advice that what is true in principle need not be true in practice.  Thus, the point of my earlier illustration of the theoretical as well as empirical utility of the statistical distribution named after Lord Rayleigh.

of a hamlet nestled against mountain foothills, suddenly buried in a rockslide? Does that count as the agency of Newton's first or second law? Or is it a re-enchantment? Pickering (1995, p. 20) referred to what he called "the struggles with material agency that I call tuning"—the "struggle" being between that agency and the agency that Pickering qualified as "human." This rendition of an "inspirited" world is at best something like Kant's "hidden causes"—except that for Kant the causes are only posits by reason and can exist to human mind only by inference, never by direct sense—and at worst a misleading confusion joining the company of evil spirits in the night. No doubt we experience "the world" as "continually *doing things*." But those are our experiences. To say that these things that are "doing things" are "things that bear upon us not as observation statements upon disembodied intellects but as forces upon material beings" does nothing more than obfuscate. The observation statements are *ours*, as we try to understand what is happening to us not as "disembodied intellects" (one of which I have yet to encounter) but as materialized meaningful beings.[471]

We do, no doubt, invest our own agency in machines. Otherwise, we would not fly, live for months at great oceanic depth, or detect still more evidence of how little we know about quantum dynamics or the solar systems of Andromeda. Sometimes we forget that the agency is actually ours. Sometimes we try very hard to write ourselves out of our own existence. As Nick Bostrom (2014, pp. 130-139) cautioned, we need to think more intensively and carefully of the thesis that intelligence and ultimate goals are approximately orthogonal. There is much greater variation in human minds than in human brains,[472] and there is no reason to believe that variation in human minds is more than a fraction of the variation in all possible minds. Compare the mind of an octopus to the mind of a typical human being (see, e.g., Godfrey-Smith 2016).[473] Clearly an intelligent problem solver, an octopus gives signals that humans who engage them are convinced are evidence of cognition, perhaps even reflexive thought. As with some other animal species—elephants, whales, sharks, gorillas, bonobos, chimpanzees, and so on—specific behaviors can be read as indicative of mindfulness, a thought that in the day of Mead (1913), for example, would have been regarded by most as befuddled.[474] Even so, the octopus mind does not compare all that well to the capability of the human mind. Is there any evidence against the

---

[471] Tegmark (2017, p. 314) was correct in cautioning that we not get our perspective backward: it is not that the universe determines human meaning; rather, that human being determines the meaning of the universe, which can very well, and should, include the meanings of other beings, a process in which they and we participate.

[472] Obviously still a hypothetical comparison, since we are learning more about "the brain" than about "the mind." It has been estimated that the neural network of the human brain covers about $2 \times 10^9$ nodes and $2 \times 10^{15}$ connections. If mind in some sense exists in or is supported by that network but is not wholly reducible to it, then human mind must have an even larger functional capacity.

[473] If you doubt that an octopus has a mind, you really must read Godfrey-Smith's book (or any number of other reports by humans who have engaged with them extensively in their own habitats or in a laboratory's tanks. The experience does raise an important question about intelligence and sociality; for at least some species of octopus are quite intelligent and skillful yet seem to be predominantly solitary animals.

[474] Mead drew a line at "signs" (versus significant symbols) as limit of non-human intelligence. As recently as the field work of Jane Goodall few zoologists and ethologists were prepared to concede that chimpanzees were (are) capable of communication more complex than, say, bovine mooing.

hypothesis that a similar magnitude of difference cannot obtain to the superior side of the most intelligent human minds? This is one of the questions that have been occupying some of the sharpest of human minds today, as we proceed with investments of our agency in machine intelligence—the "superintelligence" of "machine intelligence," it is being called (see Bostrom 2014; Tegmark 2017). Need a "machine mind" of superintelligence be intrinsically social? And if social, whether by legislation of some programmed necessity or by the happenstance of a "machine evolution," would it be a sociality in which humans would happily, critically engage?

The phenomenal complexity of humankind's realm of freedom, of its limited capacity of rational self-legislation, consists in processes of sociality. It is within these processes that human powers of constitution as well as regulation reside. In accordance with prevailing tendencies to think in terms of a psychologism, however, a virtually monadic individual person has often been cited as locus of phenomena of human efforts of rational action. Romanticist theorists reinforced that already prevailing tendency, even as they were calling for greater attention to "feeling" and to a primacy of first-person experience. Not surprisingly, given that sociality was thus relegated to a secondariness (an "add-on" property of individuality), evaluations of human rationality of judgment have often been rather unflattering (see, e.g., Kirman 1992; Mercier and Sperber 2017; Friedman, Isaac, James, and Sunder 2014). Phenomena of human affairs are so abundant with evidence of correlation that one easily stumbles over that evidence in a sometimes bewildering array of possible meanings, including the meaning of "pure chance" or a "random walk." In principle, one can locate within the text of correlations evidence of effects of context and of conditions, effects of endogenous relations of one or another process, and effects (usually weak, sometimes inconsistent) of individual-actor judgments, decisions, and choices of action. On the other hand, evidence of causality is usually impossible to see, especially in the individual-level correlations or associations. Lacking demonstrable connection to necessary relations, we quickly exhaust our means of sorting through the complexity of our data, and usually long before we turn to issues of counterfactual conditions. Even if we are confident about temporality of effects, too many discriminable counterfactuals typically stem inference to causal factors. While all of the observations are temporally located, they are usually silent, or nearly silent, of the temporality of process, so we try to infer process from distributions of outcomes that vary only or mainly in cross-section, not in time. Given an analytic segregation of sociality as *external* to individual actors, and given the typical reduction of observation to the *outcomes* of processes, rather than the processes as such (and that assume attention to temporality at all), correlations and search for inferentially useful meanings among them are conducted on aggregate data, with emphasis on modal or mean patterns that can be detected in the aggregated observations of outcomes taken as the aggregated effects of the conditions, perhaps contexts, and perhaps perceptions, judgments, decisions, and actions of individual members of a sampled population. Sometimes an analyst seeks inferential evidence, in the cross-sectionally aggregated observations, of endogenous relations of conditions within the process that has been assumed to be the generator of observed outcomes. When the same individual members of a sampled population are observed at different times, the measures are usually of the same outcome variables, rather than of direct factors of process dynamics, and the calendar of times is usually standardized across sampled members rather than keyed to any temporality of the process itself. My point is not that no one has thought of following a design with the characteristics I have mentioned. To the contrary: a few scholars

418

have made the effort. Rather, the effort is rare because it is very expensive, especially when the principal object of the effort is to obtain a probability representation of a national population in descriptive cross-section. Functions of state have usually ruled social science decisions, as Jack Gibbs (1979) reminded us.

In prior discussions I have insisted on "violating" conventional boundaries by which the social sciences have been divided (or have divided themselves in fluctuating "turf struggles"), and I will continue that practice in this Part Five. Should the practice be seen as some sort of revanchism, I will only say that "revenge" has nothing to do with my motivation. Sociologists, for example, have often complained about economists "taking over" topics that had been in the province of sociology. I see those squabbles as largely irrelevant, and in only small part because sociologists failed to advance understandings of the "stolen topics" mainly due to failures of theory formation vis-à-vis advances by economists. Those are not my concerns. I try to learn from all disciplines. The main and crucial point here is my prior insistence on understanding "the social," or "sociality," as inclusive of political, economic, geographic, cultural, and other dimensions of human affairs, all of which are historical, and have been long set apart from each other as if "eminent domains" established at some creation. Consider economics again: its chief focus is exchange relations (market, pricing mechanism, supply-and-demand, etc.), but this focus necessarily also includes distribution, consumption, and production. All are integral to human affairs.[475] Indeed, production at its broadest is production of human being, production of sociality, of legislations and dispute regulations and resolutions and means of achieving them and doing so within organizations of space and time, and ideologies of justice and fairness and equity and normality, and practices and products of science and technology—and on and on and on. It is obviously too much to be held in any one consciousness, and I do not pretend that I do. But I dislike the blinders that disciplinary professions create by declaring what is and what is not relevant or "within the domain" or legitimate topic for Person P. My aim is better understanding of a process, irrespective of which of the conventional social sciences supposedly has claim to it. Furthermore, bear in mind that (as I have said before; Hazelrigg 1989a, 1989b, 1995) some of the most consequential social sciences have conventionally lain outside "social science" (i.e., are designated as the physical and biological, etc., sciences).[476] They are nonetheless human affairs, performances by human beings, conducted within sociality, productive of massive quantities and qualities of dimensions and conditions of human life. By my intents they are, first and foremost, *social* sciences.

As mentioned above, Coleman evinced some uncertainty about the proper location of the quality of "agency" within different levels of organizational hierarchy. The issue has indeed been a vexed one, and in some respects it is being replayed in discussions about "artificial agents"

---

[475] Doreian and Hummon (1976, p. 5) touched briefly on that but did not carry out the point, perhaps shying away from potential accusations of disciplinary hubris. As discussed above (Part One, §9), Latour's (2005, pp. 87-120) report of an eventual recognition that without the stubborn limit of necessity against which to calibrate certainty, conclusions are always contingent. And yet, while his diagnoses of several ill-formed perspectives in sociology are helpful, he could not understand that theories, experiments, and so forth are not produced first in laboratories but in social relations, as was the laboratory itself, all of its equipment, its personnel, it ideas and motives, and so.

[476] For many illustrations from biological sciences, now especially genomic processes, see Zimmer 2018.

(see Bostrom 2014, pp. 11-13, 127-132, 226-255). Although human beings have been investing agency in "made things" (including trained animals) for many centuries, the concern now is about scale effects (multipliers, etc.) because the agency being invested now is intelligent as never before and might become self-reproductive in accelerating sequences of development, an algorithmic mechanic-self-evolution. Coleman's uncertainty was not whether in some very general sense that might be possible. Rather, it was whether, and if so under what conditions, a multi-person organization could attain a "supra-individual" agency. The locution is ambiguous. It could refer to recorded experiences of a "mob action" or a "crowd that had a mind of its own" (an imagery that attained great tragedy in memories of La Terreur which reigned for ten months from September 1793). Or it could refer to the multi-person organization of a commercial firm with approved articles of incorporation, which Coleman somewhat tentatively addressed. From my point of view, the agency of a "supra-individual organization" as such must be more than the sum or average of the agencies of individual person-members, weighted or unweighted. With formal organizations such as a commercial corporation or a government agency, evidence of the "more" is usually straightforward, mainly for legal reasons: the organization as such is entitled in law to act as if an individual person-subject, and explicit regulations make that determination relatively easy. A corporate CEO can speak for the corporation as a whole, about matters within the legal jurisdiction of the corporation, and that could include something as "incidental" as a personal dress code, for example, so long as the code was established by regular internally public procedures about employee behavior. When the organization is informal (albeit to say not necessarily extra-legal), matters are less clear, meaning that while the organization may operate perfectly well by procedures agreed at the moment, it does not have explicit codified rules of operation in general. Four friends or acquaintances can agree to go for a walk or to attend an art exhibit or musical performance or sporting event; does that agreement give the "group of four" as such an organizational authority, an organizational voice, that is more than the present assent of four individual persons? There is sharing, to be sure, a consequential fact, as Gilbert (2014) said (see also Bratman 1999, 2018; Tuomela 2005). But does the sharing enact a single collected agency? Assume, for example, that the four persons are in agreement that they shall abide by majority rule: if three of the four vote to attend this rather than that event, the fourth is expected to go along. Does that establish an agency of the group as such? A citizens committee has been created by town council for the purpose of formulating a plan about X, Y, and Z. The seven committee members agree at first meeting that all official conduct will be governed by Roberts' Rules of Order. Have they thereby created agency of the committee as such, an agency that consists in more than majority vote on decisions if a quorum is present?

My point in posing those questions is the simple one of gradient: small increments of difference in organizational history and order might or might not include a threshold from the fact of multiple to a single agency. In an abstractness of theoretical discourse such determination can perhaps be made clear, but confidence with regard to empirical cases can be a very different matter. The problem is similar to the one that Stephen Turner (1983, pp. 509-510) highlighted in his scrutiny of Weber's sequence of stances regarding "action"—namely, the attribution of intent (also see List and Pettit 2011, pp. 28-31). Sometimes one can look to an audience for evidence. In the last of the scenarios queried just above, for example, the town council would have been the committee's principal audience, and the council lent their own authority to the committee as such, not simply to each of the citizen members. But in many instances there is no observable audience to signal whether the whole of a number of parts is only a summation of partial agents or possesses an agency greater than the sum. Acknowledging the gradient, List and Pettit (2011, p. 32 n.18) specified criteria that must be satisfied. Taken separately, the criteria seem to be sensible and plausible. However, the authors were forthright in admitting that, much as with the problem demonstrated by Arrow (1963) regarding preferences, it is impossible to satisfy their criteria of "group agency" in one system of relations.

It is difficult to determine where, as a general rule, demarcations on that gradient actually lie. List and Pettit (2011, pp. 2, 12, 194) argued that a collectivity that is capable of agency must be more enduring than a momentary agreement to go for a walk; can be linked with other such entities in a network of exchange but the network itself does not qualify (thus, a firm but not a market); retains self-identity as members come and go (i.e., an omnibus); involves some sort of joint intention, although that alone is not enough to establish agency. Those specifications are reasonable, but they are insufficient and do not overturn List and Pettit's view that a "generally accepted account of how far groups can themselves constitute agents" had not existed. Their discussion is at some crucial points rather murky, however. Do they actually believe that such an entity as a "group mind" exists? It is not clear. They wrote of a group agent as "having a mind of its own"; but was that an "as if" formulation? They said of a limit case that "a group that satisfies plausible conditions for agency may have to embrace an attitude or intention that is rejected by all its members individually." Given that "group agency" must be more than the sum of the groups' parts and must involve more than majority rule, how would a group of individual person-actors arrive at an attitude or intention that all of them reject? I suppose by a preferential voting system, in the sense that no one's first choice won (and so in that sense was rejected), leaving second choices (or perhaps some combination of second and lower choices) the winner. But why would that voting rule be acceptable as sufficient when majority rule was not? It was here that List and Pettit's "a mind of its own" locution came into play; but they left that camera obscura obscure. While they were refreshingly direct about rejecting "mysterious forces" (as in vitalism, for example), in this instance some mystery apparently escaped their detector. As they acknowledged generally, "discoverability" is an important practical matter for both theory and research.

Tuomela (2007, pp. 18, 20-21, 224-225) pointed out that the abstract integrity of "group" with regard to matters of agency, shared intention, joint commitment to task, and the like, must begin with self-definition of membership, individual persons *believing* that they are members (under some description). The limit condition remains where it was during discussions of first-person experience throughout prior sections of this book. Discoverable conditions must be specified, and that requires at minimum a second-person negotiation. The contingency is simply unavoidable. Being able to determine the boundaries of observational categories, even before thinking of anything as complicated as measurement, depends on evidence of what is proper to "individual person," what is proper to "collectivity" as context or condition (or both) to what is proper to individual person as such, and what is proper to "collective" or "group agency," if such does exist. This means an observer must grapple with the dynamics of what Tuomela called the "conformist transmission of information" within a network or some other collection of individual persons, knowing that such transmission can be enough to bring about "the amount of sharing that collective action requires" in, say, a decisional task. Does that sharing constitute "group agency"? Is it "genuine enough," or is it "too conformist"? The presence of sociality does not have an "on/off" switch. It is a complex presence. It makes observation, whether it be styled as "everyday" or as "scientific research," more complex than a textbook description.

Similarly, as Kuran (1995) abundantly documented, sociality is replete with rules and therefore rule-violations. Everyday rules of etiquette are constraining enough to induce "public lies" (as part of Kuran's title says)—for instance, preference falsifications. As a matter of own personal preference, I rarely engage in assignations of "the most" or "the best," because they are like any coinage prone to falsifications (to say nothing of being too demanding of my abilities of discrimination). They are part of the etiquette of "scholarly support" if not "cheerleading." In any case, the choice yields cost for either option one selects. A distinction between "individual personal decision" and "collective decision" can seem clearly cut when stated as abstraction, but the abstraction easily "obscures the variability of the locus of decision" (Kuran 1995, p. 22). There are consequences if one does, but also if one does not, publicly falsify one's own-most preference. Sociality can also be a "saving grace," however, so long as we expect that discovery via second-person "talk" can be as usefully productive for social-science research as it is in everyday discourse.

Late in their book List and Pettit (2011, pp. 170-171) moved into more definitive writing of their own theory. They state as a desideratum that "what makes an agent a person is not what the agent is but what the agent does." By syllogistic standards the sentence is rather odd in that it assumes agreement on "agent" as condition to decide "person." But never mind. How did they unfold their intended point? They began with their actual premise—namely, that the primary distinctiveness of mind (as a property of human being) is not that it is an intrinsic quality but that it is a performative quality.[477] The binary contrast is at least notably similar to another pairing in a vocabulary that was often used during the late eighteenth and nineteenth centuries (in Tönnies' thinking, for example, as in Weber's and by others): a difference between the status of "who one is" (ascription: one's nativity, one's parentage, etc.) and the status of "what one can do and how well" (achievement: associated with a loosening of ties of individual person to traditions; greater freedom to migrate, farm to city; etc.). As the contrast was generally employed by scholars such as Tönnies and Weber, its intent was that of summary, an ideal typification of historical trend. List and Pettit's usage is of an analytic that implies a necessary choice, lest one lapse into the fallacy of an undivided middle. Empirically this "forced choice" is baseless.[478] The earlier scholars wrote in terms of relative tendencies, not stark opposition. Indeed, List and Pettit (2011, p. 173 n.121) did as well: in the text they affirmed that "a person is an agent who can perform effectively in the space of obligations" (hence, so must a collectivity with agency), but in a footnote they acknowledged that convention will allow someone who is not capable of speaking

---

[477] Thus, my earlier query about "mind" neglected that their performative criterion opens that category to new membership: anything that performs suitably as mind *is* mind, a version of the Turing test.
[478] Martin Kusch (2014) made much the same point in his critique of List and Pettit (2011).

for own-self to have an assigned spokesperson, and this provides entitlement to the designation, "person," and perhaps "agent" (depending on specifics of convention).

The burdens on individual person remain in multi-person agencies, of course, whether the form is public-governmental or private-commercial, and in these settings as in the individual "the most appropriate attitude may be," as Bostrom (2014, p. 320) said, a "determination to be as competent as we can." That will always occur within some sort of "space of obligations," to use List and Pettit's phrase, and that space will virtually always be or involve hierarchy in some degree and dimensionality. Tempting though it may be to believe otherwise, autonomy of action is never actually individual, because autonomy is inherently a social relation. The instrumental utility of an individual person's cognitive abilities depends to variable extent on the person's own hierarchy of goals, medial but especially ultimate goals, and on contingencies which are deemed to be most influential and/or most important. That mix will tend to be fluid, situationally and over time, but constrained perhaps increasingly by habituations, some of which might have developed as integral to the person's techniques of filtering and updating information. This last point is another manifestation of Herbert Simon's (1971, pp. 40-41) recognition that the growth in volume and complexity of information generates scarcity of attention (see Williams 2018). Adult persons do have hierarchies of preference, but these are more revealed by actual choices than by the person's own reflexive inquiry as systematic self-awareness of all held preferences and how they all relate to one another. Thus, "determination to be as competent as we can" (in Bostrom's phrase) does not necessarily yield improved sagacity. Indeed, if there is self-interest in knowledge as a function of rational utility, it is not immune to a person's inner "manipulations of the ratio of 'knowledge' to 'ignorance'" (as I said once before with regard to Georg Simmel's study of the dynamics of secrecy; Simmel 1906; Hazelrigg 1969, p. 324), which can amount to effort to exert greater control over the social relations in which one is implicated (cf. Goffman 1959, 1963). Such manipulations are also part and parcel of hierarchical organizations, as many scholars have said of the governmental agency of bureaucracy and as Coase (1937) delineated in his theory of the firm—although delineated by means of another vocabulary (consider a firm's interest in protecting its internal labor market, for example, or its interests in externalization of as much cost as it can get away with; see Bridges and Villemez 1994). Michael Stone (2018, pp. 126-127) has shown some of the antiquity of interests in "the safeguarding of knowledge" from misuse or violation by those who were defined as lacking requisite preparation for the cultivation and transmission of esoterica—specifically as those interests were manifest during the Second Temple period of ancient Judaic culture both in its local formations and as it spread through much of Hellenistic culture. This theme shared features of the "fear of freedom" sensibility that Eric Dodds (1951, p. 244) recalled from ancient Greece beginning during the third century BCE when, instead of pursuing a new age of reason, "Greek civilization" embarked on "a period of slow intellectual decline." This "fear of freedom," Dodds (1951, p. 252) recounted, was manifest as an "unconscious flight from the heavy burden of individual choice which an open society lays upon its members." Moreover, he related that deterioration to conditions of his own time:

> We too have experienced a great age of rationalism, marked by scientific advances beyond anything that earlier times had thought possible, and confronting mankind with the prospect of a society more open than any it has ever known. And in the last

423

forty years we have also experienced something else—the unmistakable symptoms of a recoil from that prospect (Dodds 1951, p. 254).

The list of those symptoms was long: hostility to immigrants; Jim Crow laws in many states that encouraged and sheltered vigilante "nightriders" to hold "lynching parties" which were treated as entertainments by local citizens; resurgent anti-Semitism; evangelical crusades supporting open hostility toward "the government" (mainly federal); rampant paranoia toward anyone labelled "troublemaker" (as in the raids by Attorney General Palmer); popular celebrations of murderous thugs romanticized as latter-day Robin Hoods (e.g., Bonnie Parker and Clyde Barrow); and so on—long before Donald Trump arrived in Washington, DC, ushered in by many morally corrupt politicians who eagerly traded the prospects of a decent society for control of the government (see, e.g., Hochschild 2018, pp. 9-18).

By my conception (to repeat yet again), sociality is *inherent*, and it is inherently a *doing*. I begin with oppositions such as "intrinsic" – "extrinsic" as a dialectical unity of opposition; the meaning of each is relative to, depends upon, the meaning of the other. Few exemplars illustrate the point as well as Mead's conception of selfhood and his conception of sociality. Amartya Sen (1993) made much the same point in his "capability" perspective: capability is both being and doing, not one or the other. His conception is good antidote to the absurdity of an analytic logic that has lost contact with its basis in dialectical logic. The choice of "either" – "or" presupposes its basis in the unity of "both" – "and." It is on that basis that "one or the other" is ever available as a choice. Absolutists and demagogues want all important choices reserved to themselves. It is not surprising that theorists who have repeated during the past two centuries and more that all foundations are contingent (e.g., Butler 1995), neither absolute nor necessary but open choices of legislation, have often been targeted as enemies of righteous authority.

When all is said and done, the conception of agency that I hold is similar to the principal thread running through many parts of the discussion by William Sewell, Jr. (1992), when he stipulated that "agents' thoughts, motives, and intentions are constituted by the cultures and social institutions into which they are born" and (I add) in which they develop capacities and capabilities during youth and after. The "cultures and institutions are reproduced" by actions of the agent, actions that reflect upbringing; but the reproduction is at most an approximation, for a number of reasons. For one, the upbringing is seldom without variation by local circumstances, which are dynamic ("local" is temporal as well as spatial). Second, the conditions under which an agent's thoughts, interests, motives, intentions, decisions, and actions tend to be reproductive of a culture, *and* of one or more institutional organizations of actors, continue to be dynamic (whether they are geographically the same or different from the conditions of upbringing), due in part to population churn, which brings new mixes of potential significant others into contact and reflexive focus for the given agent.[479] Indeed, as Sewell has appreciated, these fluctuations, some of them trend-like, have been at times more pronounced during recent centuries, as means

---

[479] One of my disappointments with Sewell's essay was that it continued neglect of the highly relevant work of G H Mead. In this instance the neglect was presumably not about Mead specifically but about scholars conventionally identified as social psychologists and about literatures ten to fifteen years older than an author's doctoral studies. See also other papers collected in Sewell 2005.

of transport and other instruments of communication have grown more powerful in reach and less expensive, thus less monopolized by interests of wealth (which also tends to make them more "disruptive," harder to control at least in the sense of reducing variance of effect).

Following Giddens (1984), Sewell adopted the "duality of structure" locution, which I find both unnecessary and easily misleading; for it separates agency and action from what are then treated as nesting or environing or contextual organizations, a framing that has in turn engendered other locutions such as "embedded in structures" or "in contexts" or "in situations." The analytic mission is overdone. We are invited to enter something like a conceptual world of billiards or ten-pins. Excessive analytics yields overgrowth of terms, new supposed concepts that are usually vague enough to create ambiguities about conceptual boundaries, interrelationships, and mutual influences—all of which easily collapses into another cacophony of confusions. Sewell's (1992, p. 21) conception of "agency," on the other hand, is amenable: agency is "profoundly social or collective." Yes, indeed. I am in agreement especially also that Goffman taught us much. On the other hand, Sewell's opposition of "reproduction" and "transformation" is too sharp, too susceptible of quiet erasure of an undivided middle. As I have already said, the concept of "reproduction" need not, and surely should not, carry any sense of completeness or perfection. Not only in principle but also in practice, our reproductive activities—and they are extensive, no doubt—are usually "with difference," and sometimes the differences expand, sometimes slowly and imperceptibly (or virtually so), but sometimes noticeably enough that they are regarded as, felt to be, unwanted, unexpected, unanticipated— or, less often, welcomed with surprise, even relief.

Recalling my point of departure by means of Riskin's (2016) definition of "agency" as the "intrinsic capacity to act in the world," and the ensuing discussion aimed at clarification but generative of questions as well, I can only agree that more needs to be said about "capacity to act"; for while one might claim an experiential knowledge of what it means to act, the deed itself does not tell us much about the capacity from which it comes. One might analogize from the physical realm and, thinking of the distinction between potential and actual or kinetic, conceive the dimension of "capacity to act" as the potential-energy version of the kinetics of Max Planck's (1949 [1948], p. 43) "dimension of action," which he defined as the product of "energy" and "time." Given that "mass" is a store of energy and "motion" implies time, this could be seen as inspired by both Newtonian and Einsteinian mechanics. But although aware that agency ("the capacity to act"), like action, is a consumption of energy, we have little to show for the analogy in the realm of sociality, certainly nothing that resembles Planck's inspired payoff, a basic measure of "energy input": it was the dimensionality of "energy * time" that prompted him, however, to formulate his "elementary quantum of action" (dubbed "h" in entropy theory), and this is a factor of information.

One can also think of "capacity to act" as something like but conditional to intentionality of the act. Evidence of capability as well as capacity comes with realization of intention. Recall Coleman's (1986, p. 1312) "appropriate theoretical strategy": one principle held that we should be interested *primarily* in purposeful action; another, that we should "limit ["notions of purpose, goal-directedness, and homeostasis"] to the level of actors in the social system—not positing them for the system itself";[480] third, that any activity of a "system composed of actors" should be conceived as "an emergent consequence of the interdependent actions of the actors" who make up the system. Now, one can acknowledge that non-purposive actions can also be of interest and that the second and third principles can be amended to allow "collective actor" under specified description (as Coleman did, although usually in reluctant or tentative manner). The key point is his focus on the category, "purposeful" or "intentional." This involves a rationality at least to the extent of a self-knowledge that enables actor to assess (1) goals, (2) conceivable means to a specific goal, and (3) an intention to realize that goal, all of which surely constitutes at least part of a "capacity to act." Moreover, that capacity can include a reflexivity all along the way (i.e., not only in the execution of an act), and the reflexivity is conducive to continued self-formation, a self-educational process, integral to the sociality of self (e.g., filter-and-update sequences). This aspect of self-formation reminds one of the Hegelian-like notion that intentional action induces self-knowledge (as discussed by Velleman 1989 and 2000). Others have agreed that the idea is coherent and useful, although not that the uses include actually grounding "a theory of reasons to act" (e.g., Setiya 2007, p. 107). If we think of the category "intention" as "reflexive desire-like belief," then an intended action can be considered to be self-explanatory, in the sense that content of the intention describes reasons to commit an action, and the doing of the action is first-person revelation of the desire-like belief, the "want" of doing's purpose, so to speak—while, as acknowledged by Velleman (2000, pp. 19-21, 26), the completed outcome (an experience of first-person revelation, self-knowledge) specifically need not conform to the purpose as such but may be (often is) rather an unintended effect of the action. While I think objections raised by Bratman (1999) and Setiya (2007) are well taken, I also think that the line of proposal should be productive of new theory and, one hopes, efforts to develop relevant metrics. Here my concern otherwise is with questions of the theorized pay-off of the sort of account constructed by Velleman. What can be said of the resultant self-knowledge? If there is any, it must remain a matter of first-person consciousness, unless we assume that the person in question is reliably insightful of unintended effect (or shall we accept, in this setting, that *any* reported belief counts as self-knowledge?) and a reliably honest reporter of that insight (rather than, say, concerned to meet interlocutor or larger-audience expectations). The theory might remain untestable.

We have encountered problems owing to the inertial force of belief already (e.g., above, in Tuomela's caution about "conformist" inertia of belief), and it is in any case hardly a newly recognized problem. In his lectures on logic Kant (1974 [1800], p. 80) acknowledged that a "moral rational belief" can generate a "practical conviction" that is "often firmer than any knowing." For in knowing "one still listens to counter-reason"—that is, room for action from

---

[480] I do not understand what he meant by restricting homeostasis to "the level of actors in the social system" rather than posit it "for the system itself." Homeostasis *is* a property of a system of relations among parts, the process by which a system of relations tends to attain and maintain an equilibrium of conditions. But he (1986, p. 1322) seemed to believe that treating a "system itself" as homeostatic "eliminates the possibility of immanent change." By my lights, homeostasis can be effective without being perfect or immune to internal disruption—by fatigue, for instance, or by other variances. The conditions composing a stable equilibrium need not each be invariant. Some of the most stable equilibria persist dynamically.

skepticism remains, and therefore entertainment of counterfactuals—"but not in belief," for belief "turns not on objective grounds but on the moral interest of the subject" (i.e., "believing *in*" belief X). The inertial force of belief can be a resilient barrier to knowing, or a resilient channel that guides knowing in specific ways. These are matters of sociality and therefore inherently of interest to theory (about which, more below in §27). It is the observational conduct that is problematic. Rationality is an indispensable posit; otherwise, theorizing itself makes no sense. But it is rarely unaltered by other factors, which in some circumstances dominate.

Here we necessarily enter a terrain of awkward questions about theorization as itself an activity that relies on coherence, internal consistency, healthy skepticism, and testing that is as rigorous and relevant as can be achieved. The theorist, the analyst, the researcher, is always at risk in the process (see, e.g., Butler 1995). Is there evidence that intentional action (vis-à-vis some category of purpose or aim) by each of specific persons during some span of time has *itself* notably improved in terms of effectivity (and, where appropriate, efficiency)? Is there any evidence that we know how to classify actions and their outcomes (as well as purpose or aim) with sufficient stability and reliability over spans of time, such that we are confident we are comparing apples-to-apples over time in the observer's etic framework *but also* in the observed person's emic framework (since it is within the latter, presumably, that the first-person revelation will occur)? The short answer to each query is that we have little sound basis for empirically assessing the timelines of self-knowledge outcomes, and the processes by which they occur. This is almost as true of the process of theorization and testing by empirics as it is of the sociality that is being studied as if the several or many participants are less attentive to standards of coherence, skepticism, and so forth, that define the principled activity of scientific inquiry. Too seldom have we expended the very considerable effort to observe and measure relevant events and process markers for the same persons at regular intervals over long spans of lifetime. We all practice an agency of one sort or another, but we have less assurance about processes of those practices, because we do not keep time accounts (or rarely do). We are as musicians who have learned the words (or those we favor) but not the rhythm.

Even the general notion of agency has been contentious at times. Riskin (2016) began the introduction to her book on the history of efforts to explain "what makes living things tick" by reciting one of Thomas Huxley's lectures of 1868. This lecture was about "protoplasm"— literally, from the Greek, "first" + "to shape"—or as Huxley put it, "the physical basis of life." His point was that no special pleading, no invocation of magical substance or principle of vitalism of anything of the sort was required as central or even addendum to the biological conception of life. After all, we all know of the extraordinary qualities of water, without which we would not exist, and we do not imagine that either those qualities or water as such is due to anything more than an oxidation of hydrogen. There is no need to "assume that something called 'aquosity' entered into and took possession of the oxide of hydrogen … then guided the aqueous particles to their places." This was, Riskin pointed out, a controversial point of view, because common conception held that such "special properties" as water has must have been caused by something external to water, some external "special force," if not directly divine then divine guidance via nature. Huxley's so-called mechanical view of nature was, if not blasphemous, an abomination due at best to ignorance. The inertial force of belief is easily reinforced whenever a biologist, chemist, or physicist is confronted with the (sometimes inevitable) reductive question—in this case, "*Why* does the oxidation of hydrogen produce something this special? Why is $H_2O$ so refreshing but $H_2O_2$ is not?" It does not help for the biologist to answer, "If you take in too much water your cells will drown, but hydrogen peroxide is a useful antiseptic."

Riskin's (2016) history is about notions of "agency" in the centuries-long struggle to make sense of the relation between "the organic" and "the mechanical," a relation considered usually as oppositional in analytics, the second term of the opposition intended as secondary to the first. Thus, to think of organic process in mechanical terms was considered inherently, and radically, reductive. The key thematic in that oppositional relation stemmed from the Greek roots of the word, "mechanic" or "machine"—the Greek "mēkhos" to "mēkhanḗ," meaning a "contrivance," a "made thing." That secondariness had been a settled fact, by and large, until a notion of "agency" was extended to "made things." The emblematic metaphor was "the clock works": a purely physical "contrivance" of material things in motion can "tell the passage of time," and therefore influence, motivate, change, human activities and states of being. Moreover, check your dictionary for the word "contrivance": you will first read of "the use of skill" to make something; you will then read that the process and product of that skill will carry a sense of "artificiality"—that is, of being ingenuine, misleading, a feint.

Thus, a question: what exactly *is* the power of this quality called "agency"? In what does "agency" consist? From where does the motive force come? Is it the same quality whether present in organic or in mechanical things? The most general definition, Riskin (2016, p. 3) pointed out, refers to the power or ability "to do things in a way that is neither predetermined nor random." Note that "predetermined" refers to a chain of causality. If "agency" is *not* that, does its power operate as an instance of an "uncaused cause"? The general agreement has been that anything with "agency" is a thing, organic or mechanical, "whose activity originates inside itself rather than outside." This could be said of an "organic thing," even if we doubted that the thing was capable of sentience or at least of sapience. Theocratic terms assured a seamlessness, due to divine will. But to imagine that the same could be said of a "clockwork" kind of thing seemed outlandish. And yet it was clear that humans were capable of contriving spring-loaded things—"robots," we say—that "move on their own": "she plays piano on her own" (a device known as the Jaquet-Droz Musicienne, one of three automatons built by Pierre Jaquet-Droz, his son, and an associate, between 1768 and 1774).

The difference between activity that "originates inside" the thing with agency rather than outside that thing can easily be taken for granted. But what (or who) has defined that boundary? Although we might say that it is an "obvious fact of nature" or of "divine providence," it is by now surely understood to be a product of human conceptualization, the way in which categories of classification are drawn. We say much the same for our "obvious difference" between what is "natural" and what is "cultural" as with the difference between "organic" and "mechanical" (and "inside" and "outside"). But consider a horse. A herd animal, a horse is intensely social. When not being "properly horse" in "horse world," he or she is very nervous, unsettled, suspicious, until "domesticated," which means resocialized into a human world of sociality. Trained to do my bidding, she or he has developed with me a cross-species sociality, and it is both emotive and cognitive. Because I know "horse," I am aware that I have taken on the great responsibility of substituting for at least a large part of the herd (if a singleton, that horse and I *are* the herd).[481] My responsibility is to ensure not only proper diet, freshwater, grooming, healthcare, and (for my benefit) repeated riding/working, but also both emotive and cognitive stimulation, without which a horse suffers what we humans call depression. One must learn "horse meanings" of reward and penalty, both proper contents and schedulings. Penalty of the wrong kind or insensitively timed can easily damage "horse morale" (a horse, like a human, must be allowed and encouraged to display a pride of being and doing). Is that "nature" or is that "culture"? And what was it prior to "domestication," which in the most likely encounters will have begun long before the training one gives ("wild horses" are unlike most horses encountered in human circuits)? Yes, it is nature. But this is a human meaning, a human practice, our category "nature" (and therefore cultural), not a wild horse's meaning or practice (Hazelrigg 1995; also 1989b, 1992, 1993b).

Agency occurs in the realm of freedom. But it is limited by the force of what one deems a necessity. An illustration from human biochemistry has to do with oxygen content of an atmosphere. If the $O_2$ content is too low (i.e., significantly below 20%), one dies of asphyxiation. If the content is too high, one also dies of asphyxiation, because the $O_2$ binds with surface proteins of lung tissue which prevents transfer to hæmaglobin. This sort of limitation of free range by necessity is less ubiquitous and less sharply defined in ordinary human activities, to be sure, but it does exist. Perhaps the most common occurrence has to do with skills or knowledge. Without requisite skills or knowledge, one cannot achieve a desired outcome via effort alone. Some minimal level of competence is needed, either one's own or competence lent or sold by another person or perhaps a machine. Competence has been in a race with ignorance in this regard, since awareness of what will count as a minimal competence depends on relevant knowledge. Ignorance has been growing. In addition to the growth of ignorance that occurs as a corollary of the growth of knowledge—that is, learning more about what we do not know (addressed in Gross 2007, p. 743; see also Schneider 1962)—ignorance has increased as well in the sense that growth of knowledge has been also a growth of ignorance, as more and more adults are being left "behind the curve," lacking knowledge of ever larger portions of what there is to be known. Rationality, in the sense of knowing how to determine first if X is or should be a desired goal and then, contingently, how to achieve it, is neither a free good nor independent of a substantial recommendation, even requirement, of knowledge and skill. One's sense of personal efficacy, of being sufficiently capable in the shared world, usually depends upon it. Thus, John Erskine's (1915) "moral obligation to be intelligent." We depend on one another.

---

[481] Horses are about as gender sensitive as are humans. If my horse is female, a mare, I must be cautious for any female human in our presence; the mare's first preference is that she is alpha female, and she will not be content if a female human physically separates us. Horses are very emotive; they read emotion mainly through the left optical circuit, and it is that pathway that is most sensitive to emotive bonds of trust, affect, and command. (Thus, left-side mounting, probably learned by humans through trial and error.) In a related vein, while some of the stories about a "horse whisperer" are mostly hype, there is a sound understanding at base: horse hearing is very acute, as compared to human hearing, so if you want a horse to listen intently to you, speak softly (few experiences are as off-putting as a bunch of loud-talking strangers).

## Action Effects and Efficacy of Action

Whereas Talcott Parsons and colleagues chose as their central variable "the unit-*act*," I will shift focus to a consequentialist direction to the effect end of the equation and write of "efficacy" of action.[482] This large simplification is recommended by the fact of a classificatory overload: the vast array of "acts," even of "*kinds* of acts," is a huge obstacle, and I do not have the time to begin to parse that jungle into workable metrics. Achieving that goal even with the restriction to outcomes (and their efficacy) is a large and complicated task, toward which I might make some headway. As I will explain below, workable metrics for effects and efficacy are available (and improvable) for major actions conducted within institutional channels (e.g., gaining competency in a specific skill).

Action effects are central to the micro-macro gradient of processes, the very processes that Coleman (1990, p. 10) judged as having gotten too little attention. I concur in that verdict. I must now raise a question, however, before proceeding further toward the goal of additional attention to Coleman's concern. The question is important to our understanding of the range of meanings of Coleman's charge: do we give sufficient attention to the mostly quiet work that is performed by our uses of those little words known as prepositions? More specifically, what does it mean to say "micro-to-macro effects"? Coleman's concern was rightly about a "translational" process by which individual-person action effects become in some sense effects associated with a collectivity (to which the individual person "belongs"). There are different pre-positional arrangements. Not all of them are interchangeable without serious cost of confusion. Consider the following locutions:

1. effects as the collectivity;
2. effects of the collectivity;
3. effects by the collectivity;
4. effects on the collectivity;
5. effects within the collectivity.

The first indicates an effect or set of effects of individual actions as the formation of a collective organization (presumably of the individuals whose effects are being referenced). This could also be called the "aggregation effect" of the individual actions. The second locution refers to effects of the individual actors as members of the collectivity *as such*. This could also be called "effects of the aggregation as such." The aggregation as such could be nothing more than a sum of or an average of (weighted or unweighted) actions by the individual members of the aggregate, but it could alternatively include a "value added" component (sometimes called "emergent") that is due to (or attributed to) a multiplier or interactive effect of actions of the individual actors who

---

[482] Referring to "the epistemic problem," Cowen (2018, p. 103), playing devil's advocate, said that it "suggests that the philosophic doctrine of consequentialism cannot be a useful guide to action because we hardly know anything about long-run consequences." An accurate appraisal, it deflects attention from the fact that short-term predictions are generally better, and so long as we update regularly short-term will be adequate for many scenarios. But then, what other basis is available? Graham Harman (2016, pp. 98-99) argued that "[i]f we measure authors, politicians, or wild animals by their degree of impact, then we erase missed opportunity, bad luck, and foolishness from our model of the world." Counterfactuality is always a problem, but it does not preclude our application of standards.

are members of the aggregate. More will be said about this later; it is a version of what I am calling a "scale effect." The third locution nearly reduces to the second; but whereas the second refers somewhat vaguely to the collectivity *as such* as an actor, the third makes that claim rather more pointedly as a statement of agency. Think of a corporate actor, which, as legal subject, utters with one voice even if not all members of the corporation agree with any given utterance.

Whereas the first locution conveys primarily the constitutive aspect of individual actors' effects, and the second and third convey effects of collective members' actions with or without specifying any "value added" component, the fourth locution indicates that individual actors are *affecting* the collective organization as such, whether these actors are external, wholly or in some portion, to the organization or are members whose actions are affecting the aggregate as such from within (and, in either external or internal case, whether for good or ill). Moreover, whereas in the first locution almost certainly and in the second and, perhaps less clearly, third locutions the presumption would be that the effects were by intent of the individual actors (in the corporate case disagreement with official voice could be taken as an act of "exit"; Hirschman 1970), with the fourth locution the effects on the collectivity need not be by intent of any or all of the members. This latter provision could also apply to the fifth locution, at least insofar as the "effects *within*" are on the organization as such (i.e., the fifth being subsumed by the fourth). The fifth could also be a statement, however, that members' actions (or some members' actions) are internal to the organization but not effective *on* the organization as such; rather, on some, or perhaps in unforeseen ways on all, individual members.

All well and good, one might say: to heed such distinctions of the little words would be to forestall ambiguities and confusions. I do not disagree with that conclusion. However, another complication must be considered—namely, the semantic space of "effect"—for that is what is being pre-positioned relative to "collectivity."

A persistent theme running throughout my discussions is the importance of *process*. I do not reject the importance of statics, but if the aim is to improve understanding of "how things work," consideration of *dynamics* cannot be postponed, and simply comparing representations of states of affairs at two or more dates is at best an inadequate preview of that consideration. It might be good enough to reduce the likelihood of, or perhaps even rule out of hand, this or that hypothesis of a given process dynamics. But little in the way of a positive account of the process dynamics will be gained. In barest form, the dynamics of a process can be represented as an input-output model. The dynamic has to do with the means by which inputs become outputs, and this dynamic form of the copula (i.e., "becomes" instead of "is") has typically begun with the placeholder of a "dark room"—a camera obscura that somehow "just works" even though we still do not know how the input did become the output. This model is no more satisfying to our interest in knowing than was Hume's lesson about the obscurity of process in the very moment of the perceiving I's perceiving. If we cannot actually see the "process at work," how do we know that an observed output is due *only* to our known inputs? We need to gain *insights*, as best we can, to what happens during the "throughput" (an equally obscure realm). Following the older vocabulary of "cause and effect," we can regard the output as an effect of the inputs. That substitution works reasonably well with the five locutions discussed above. Still, there are complications. With regard to the first locution, for example, if a process outcome is a collective organization that seemingly did not exist prior to the operation *on* or *with* or *by* or *as* the inputs, yet we cannot say in what that operation consisted, do we not find ourselves, after all is said and done, in a position rather like the precontractual conditions of contrast (à la Locke)? Changing vocabulary from "cause and effect" to "input and output" does not of itself avoid but only ignores Hume's point about causality. We can still talk about "scale effect" in the sense of the various prepositional locutions described above, but it is not so clear exactly how the "value added" component is composed (if in fact there is one), because it is not clear how an observed outcome came to be, given observed inputs.

That problem brings us to another sense of "effect," and how it relates to the meaning of output or outcome of a process. Analytically, the term "effect" often refers not to "process outcome" as such but to an effort to partition observed variance of a measured outcome into parcels each uniquely attributable to a measured input, plus possibly to one or more of a set of "interactions" between measured inputs. Typically a venture in statics (observations of inputs and outputs in cross-section), it tells us very little about the process that, by hypothesis, converts inputs into outputs, and the little that it does seem to tell us is by inference only (i.e., another hypothetical).

Here I must interject another major limitation of inquiry. It has to do with a condition known as ergodicity. Recall from an earlier illustration Newton's second law of motion, also called his second law of thermodynamics: it is commonly expressed as $F = M \times A$ (i.e., force is a product of the mass of a body and the acceleration of its motion; imagine a boxer's punch delivered *through* opponent's jaw). Another way of expressing the law is that it describes the relation between an object's mass and the amount of force that must be applied to it in order to accelerate it by a given amount (i.e., $A = F/M$). Note that none of the three variables carries a subscript, either t (time) or s (space) or both. That is because within the Newtonian domain the relation holds regardless of where and when it is observed; it is independent of time and space. This is an instance of a relation that is *ergodic*. I can compare objects of same or different mass at two different places; the amount of force I need to apply in order to achieve the same proportionate acceleration will be indifferent to place. I can perform the same experiment at two different times; again, the relation will be the same. The relation is necessary, and the necessity is not contingent on anything except Newtonian domain.[483] Thus, I can compile hordes of data on variation of outcome in ten or a hundred or a million different places in space and use those data to investigate exactly the same relation as it was empirically manifest in the year 5000 BCE or in the year of Leonardo's birth or during the first second of the detonation of the first atomic bomb at White Sands, NM, and be utterly confident of the generalization from cross-sectional (i.e., spatial) variation to longitudinal (i.e., temporal) variation. For how many relations of process in human affairs can that same statement be made? Probably not a single one. But there is more to be said about the condition known as ergodicity.

---

[483] Note that "Newtonian domain" assumes error-free measurement and no "hidden variables" in the focal relation (as mentioned in the earlier illustration, regarding ballistics, for example, no unobserved variation in gravity, windage, and so forth).

Theoretical development of ergodic relations began with work by James Clerk Maxwell and Ludwig Boltzmann, who invented and developed statistical mechanics as a means of solving a micro-to-macro problem of the time, especially with reference to gaseous materials. By what process do the material properties at the atomic level produce phenomena at molecular and molar levels of matter? It had become readily evident, especially from the work by Boltzmann, that the dynamics of gases are far too complex to be effectively modeled in terms of a Newtonian strict determinism. (Recall again the previously cited illustration of the complexity of modeling dynamics of projectile trajectories, despite the fact that as an adequately closed system the projectile observes Newtonian principles.) Maxwell had come to realization of that limitation from his work with the dynamics of heat; Boltzmann, from his work with gases. By the turn of the twentieth century statistical mechanics had become a leading area of research in physical science (see, e.g., Gibbs 1902).

Boltzmann, raising an issue of the dimensionality and transitivity of measurement, coined the term "ergodic" to describe hypothetical relations of measurements of dynamics that vary simultaneously in four dimensions. For the next quarter-century this issue was focus of intense investigation. In 1931 George Birkhoff published what he believed to be a proof of a theorem regarding the conditions under which metrical relations would be consistent between spatial properties and temporal properties. At about the same time John von Neumann (1932) reached similar conclusions, although he was more cautious, naming his work a proof of "quasi-ergodic" hypothetical relations. Despite intense effort in mathematical theory (e.g., Furstenberg 1961), the topic remains unsettled. But whether theorem or hypothesis, "ergodicity" names a very serious limitation for theory and research in disciplines of social science.

For present purposes, the main point is that metric distributions for spatial relations (i.e., cross-sections) do not necessarily generalize to metric distributions for temporal relations. Thus, if we are interested in understanding "how things work" in the realms of human sociality (which are far more complex than Boltzmann dynamics of gaseous materials), we need observations of *processes*, not merely of cross-sectional states. Measured observations of cross-sectional states tell us very little if anything of process dynamics. But the social sciences have made hardly any concerted effort to develop metrics of process dynamics. Relations within the realm of human processes, events, and so forth, are almost certainly all non-ergodic.[484] Because of this limit our habitual reliance on cross-sectional variation as sufficient substitute for variation in time—the variation of a process operation and outcome in repeated sequences—is generally mistaken and misleading in supposed consequence.[485]

Several economists have for quite some time been alert to the demands of ergodicity and the consequences of failure to meet them, not only for empirical research but also for theory.[486]

---

[484] I am being deliberately cautious in the preceding two statements, because they are empirically based (i.e., about empirical relations) but proposing a necessary limit.

[485] The technical literature on ergodicity is complex (see, e.g., Petersen 1989). Regarding application to human affairs, see also Hazelrigg (2010, pp. 5-7) and Isaac and Lipold (2012).

[486] Attempts to demonstrate violation of the ergodicity assumption in social-science inquiry have been sparse, mainly for the same reason that the use of cross-sectional variation as sufficient surrogate for longitudinal variation has been so common: longitudinal data in the sense not just of comparing cross-

But let's take some illustrations from the sociological literature instead. Stanley Lieberson and Lynn Hansen (1974) nicely demonstrated much of the lesson forty years ago, but that aspect of their paper garnered little attention. More recently, Kathryn Neckerman and Florencia Torche (2007) concluded from their review of relevant literature that remarkably little is known, after decades of theorization and research, about the dynamics of processes that result in inequalities, not only of static comparisons (especially inequalities based on other than nominal or identity categories) but also of processes themselves. The weak record is due in part to problems of measurement: ordinal measures are easy but contain so little information as to be very nearly useless in the study of dynamics (especially comparisons of populations over time, and still more especially of the dynamics of specific processes). While interval measures are marginally more informative, they are more difficult to construct for reliable use. The weak record also results from weak theory, however, the lack of strong models of driving processes. "Much discussion, particularly about the causes of inequality, is based on inferences from the timing and incidence of changes in distributions, with few direct measures of possible drivers such as SBTC"—that is, skill-biased technological change, one of the popular hypotheses in recent years (Neckerman and Torche 2007, p. 348). Inference from the timing and incidence of changes in distributions is a typical result of using a sequence of cross-sections of a population as one's base of observations for understanding the dynamics of process, whether continuous or continual (discrete). The operational dynamics (or mechanisms) of the process are not directly observed. Such inference is weak— not demonstrably invalid—and we lack basis for deciding when an inference is reasonably good and when it is spurious. Goldberger (1989) demonstrated decades ago that even those theoretical efforts that have been accorded highest standing are well short of what is needed in order for investigations of processes of status transmission (and thus of inequality) to be meaningful. Grawe and Mulligan (2002, pp. 45, 48-49), writing a dozen years later, repeated Goldberger's conclusion that "economic theory has not improved our understanding" of status transmission and pointed again to the lack of requisite data (see also Bowles and Gintis 2002, Manski 2004).

Institutionalists stress the importance of the channeling effects of each of several major institutions, and they are right to do so (see, e.g., Meyer 2010). This is a principle that will be maintained in the discussions below. With regard to the micro-to-macro dimension of process, however, the chief issue is not solved so much as it is merely set aside. One thinks of an analogy to Adam Smith's "invisible hand" statement: it is evident that "something happens" during a "translation" from the level of individual actors to the level of aggregate supply and demand, for example, or of aggregate productivity, and so forth; but the dynamics of that process whereby the effects of a large number of individual person-actors become higher-level aggregates remains all too obscure, and the obscurity is because of weak theory, first of all, and then, once good

---

sections at two or more times but in the sense of tracking processual variation are expensive and difficult to obtain. There have been a few empirical efforts at testing, roughly approximate though they were (see, e.g., Jianakoplos, Menchik, and Irvine 1989). One can build theory that stipulates ergodic process, as recently done in the acclaimed text by Ljungqvist and Sargent (2018, pp. 36-39, 685) and in Peyton Young's (2015) review of work in stochastic evolutionary theory, among a few other discussions. It is a useful if extreme simplification that allows a theorist to move on to other dimensions of a model without being handicapped by having always to maintain translations between serial and cross-sectional perspectives (translations well beyond empirically meaningful capability).

theory indicates what to examine, observations of *process*, as distinguished from our usual observations of distributional states, the inputs and the outputs.

As the just-ended paragraph attests, discussion so far in this sub-section has been mostly of "effects." It is indeed *effects* that must be sought. But although not all effects need have a distinctive feature that I call "efficacy," some effects should meet that distinction in order to make room for first-person representations in second-person talk. By standard dictionary definition, "efficacy" means "ability to produce a desired or intended result." That suits my purposes well enough initially, although in general my suggested approach is to begin with an observed outcome of what appears to be intentional, purposive action (for I have no means at hand, in my imagined scenarios, to attempt to test intent and purpose, a testing not easily done even in face-to-face conversation). I acknowledge that whereas past general usage has been to treat "efficacy" and "effectiveness" as synonyms, a distinction has become standard in literatures of pharmacological research, "efficacy" referring to tests made under experimental conditions (i.e., "controlled" or "ideal" conditions) while "effectiveness" is reserved for "real world" conditions. In that setting the latter term would be more appropriate for what I am doing. But I will stick with the former because of its allowance of actor's "desired or intended result." In other words, is an effect first of all recognized as such by the actor in question and, secondly, how does it relate to that actor's purposes? Has it added to a sense of efficacy? We will return to these and related matters in §27.

**Model Relations**
Another preamble is in order. Neither newly minted nor esoteric, it is nonetheless a useful reminder at this juncture. Various literatures are replete with illustrations of a tendency among readers to assume a theory-independent standard (which means, inter alia, an assumption-independent standard) by which to decide—indeed, usually to assume—which analysis of observations, measured or not, gives the correct or at least the best reading of what is real, whether "the real" references only a momentary state of affairs or the dynamics of a process. Stated otherwise, the implicit question-qua-expectation is, "What should I believe?" The question is no doubt real. Skepticism recommends it at least once a day. However, this logical domain of answers exists only as fairy tale. It did not exist otherwise for Newton and his science of mechanics; nor for Kant and his critical theory; nor for Einstein or Bohr or Heisenberg or Wheeler, and so on. Theologians have offered a few other answers. Many magicians have. There are always, it seems, run of the mill demagogues with press kits at the ready. Prêt à avaler.

Rationality is important to knowledge and to skill in the process by which they are acquired, in the process by which they are applied, and in the process by which their results are judged. This implies a competence of capacity to act, which surely does vary by person, by task, by date and by circumstance. Competency may be treated as a variable quality of an individual person, to be sure, but without losing sight of the fact that it is inseparable from the person's sociality in the sense that it neither begins prior to sociality nor develops outside a sociality. Nor is it enacted independently of a sociality, although as it changes in quality (kind, integrity, degree, etc.) that change will be reflected in the person's social relations. These stipulations tend to run counter to the expectation of an analytic logic according to which all variables (factors, determinants, etc.) should be "Cartesian clear and distinct" at least as signals, however troubled by noise the signals might be. While as analytic definition the criterion can be met (i.e., "true by definition"), as referents of observation, and more especially of measured observation, separating signal from noise in a consistent, reliable, defendable manner is not easily achieved. The desired outcome would not be easily achieved even were the things being observed relatively constant during time under observation, something like a billiard ball. The task is very much harder when the object of observation (still more, of measurement) thinks about what is happening at the moment, why it is happening, how that happening might be used, and so forth.

Rationality has been a controversial topic in large part because of confusion between an empirical reality and an effort of theory to model that reality for purposes of investigation. Models are by definition simplifications. Some critics have been inclined to reject this or that model as being oversimplification. Fair enough, assuming the critic understands exactly what is being said in both registers. Sometimes, however, the criticism of a model becomes (or was in first instance) a description of reality. A model that assumes rational actors is rejected as overly simple and "thus" unrealistic (a redundant statement, of course), which criticism in turn becomes a description of reality: "most people are not rational." Were the concluding statement, "Most people are not *that* rational" or "not *always* rational," or some such, there would be little to quibble about (and the person who built the model would almost surely not have disagreed, assuming that the simplification being disputed was deliberate in the first place). The critic can then fairly be called upon to supply a superior model, one that is usefully more realistic. If the critic's claim is that no theoretical model is possible because the reality is just too complex, the claim amounts to a concession to ignorance and the termination of inquiry into that reality. For in fact any description of the reality offered by the critic (e.g., in defense of the claim of excessive complexity) is itself a model, not a theory-free, assumption-free reality as such (unless the critic is brash enough to claim complete and perfect assumption-free perception, followed by also complete and perfect communication of the perception). Chances are, any description supplied will have assumptions of rationality built in, critically recognized or not, and among those assumptions of rationality there will be several *self*-assumptions by the critic.

As an illustration of part of my point, consider the following scenario. An unusual conference of prominent economists convened at the Santa Fe Institute in September 1987. Among the attendants were theorists such as Kenneth Arrow, Thomas Sargent, Lawrence Summer, José Scheinkman, and W. Brian Arthur. Arthur had been assigned the task of explaining to the assembly some differences of "complexity theory" and their importance to economics. The conference was still more unusual, however, in the fact that several theoretical physicists had agreed to attend, in view of their interests in "complex process" and (in some cases more than others) their interests in theoretical developments in economics. These latter attendants included Philip Anderson and David Ruelle, perhaps figures not as familiar to an audience of social scientists as, say, Murray Gell-Mann or Steven Weinberg but giants in their fields.[487] A later account of exchanges during the conference includes this passage, which begins with quotations of Brian Arthur's report:

> "The physicists were shocked at the assumptions the economists were making [during the latters' comments, and in Arthur's own presentation]—that the test was not a match against reality, but whether the assumptions were the common currency of the field [of economics]. I can just see Phil Anderson, laid back with a smile on his face, saying, "You guys really *believe* that?"'
>
> The economists, backed into a corner, would reply, "Yeah, but this allows us to solve those problems. If you don't make assumptions, then you can't do *anything*."
>
> And the physicists would come right back, "Yeah, but where does that get you— you're solving the wrong problem if that's not reality" (Waldrop 1992, p. 142).

As one can easily imagine, the question attributed to Anderson, the economists' reply, and the retort from physicists have been recited many times.

Of course, the physicists got away with a fiction of their own, granted to them freely simply by virtue of the comparative prestige of physics in the arcades of modern science. The fiction begins with the assumption that any perception is theory-free—in other words, that an empirical experience of "what the real is" is theory-free. That *is* an assumption, and because of that assumption one cannot conclude that the theory behind any experience of "what the real is" is in fact assumption-free. Indeed, experience suggests that it would not be free of assumptions. But insofar as one has granted any claimant the right to say what theory-free, assumption-free reality *is*, one has granted all. No science can rightfully claim that. It is the preserve of demagogues, lunatics, and other true believers. Yet to one degree or another all sciences do in fact claim that, at least to the extent of a convention that must be taken for granted if any further inquiry is to be made. "Who would believe us, who would fund our projects," a scientist would understandably complain, "if we began with the precaution, 'We can only assume that X, Y, and Z are really real—and that we do know what we are doing'?!" Recall from Part One Pippin's (1999) point about "the second object," the object that must be present by necessity (as it were).

Physics gained its (well-deserved) prestige because of the enormous success of Newtonian theory in making sense of so much of what human beings have experienced of their worlds—none of which was a foregone conclusion in 1687. They could, as Kant recognized, assume a world of necessity. This remained the case with Einstein, despite shrinkage in necessity's list of residences (light's speed limit is crucial).

The world of human affairs is not so simple (nor, as physicists of the twentieth century increasingly realized, was, is, their world of physical science). The greater complexity, present by virtue of freedom, has entailed a different logic of relations, the relations of theory and its models. Some basic conceptual distinctions among types of action-and-effect relation, crucial to

---

[487] See also Anderson, Arrow, and Pines (1988). Anderson's (2011) memoir is well worth reading, too. It includes observations of both economics and sociology, as well as his (2011, p. 134) criticism of the origin myth that lies at the heart of physicists' quest via reductive analytics to the one original equation.

437

theory formation and empirical inquiry alike, inform the framework within which basic issues of identification must be addressed. During the late 1950s and 1960s (when, to put it in first-person terms, I began serious studies of scientific methodology) very few social scientists had much of an understanding of the logic of identification (and most physical scientists, still working within Newtonian processes, were unaware that issues of identification existed). Charles Manski has done more than anyone else (at least in my experience) to educate the rest of us about those issues (see also Martin 2015, esp. pp. 139-141). As Manski has repeatedly stressed, the logic of identification must be satisfied before giving much attention to matters of statistical (i.e., sampling) inference (matters understood as entirely extraneous to the Newtonian realm):

> Studies of identification seek to characterize the conclusions that could be drawn if one could use a given sampling process to obtain an unlimited number of observations. Studies of statistical inference seek to characterize the generally weaker conclusions that can be drawn from a finite number of observations. Analysis of identification logically comes first. Negative identification findings imply that statistical inference is fruitless: it makes no sense to try to use a sample of finite size to infer something that could not be learned even if a sample of infinite size were available. Positive identification findings imply that one should go on to examine the feasibility of statistical inference (Manski 1997, p. 369).[488]

Manski has published a long series of articles and books that lucidly and systematically present theoretical and empirical implications of the basic fact that most relations of human affairs are contingent, usually in chains or networks of contingency that become very complex even when nonlinearities are not involved. By "nonlinearity" I mean not simply that the metric distribution of a given variable is not linear (i.e., includes a threshold or a hysteretic adjustment, for example, or distributes on a curved line, as in a quadratic or hyperbolic line of values). Rather, I mean a process that, in strict mathematical sense, follows a nonlinear function relating inputs (actions) to outputs (effects). This is the kind of nonlinearity that is induced, for example, by a feedback due to filtering and updating, positive or negative, endogenous to a process, or a scale effect in the outcome of a process.[489] Nonlinearities make an otherwise already complex phenomenon even more complex, of course.[490] Manski's publications are remarkably clear and incisive explications of the limits that ensue because (to put it in Kant's terms) freedom is gained at the cost of certainty and necessity of relations (i.e., lack of the "rational part" of a "true science").

---

[488] Think carefully about what is entailed by "unlimited" or "infinite number of observations": it is qualitative as well as quantitative. Note that my presentation above follows Manski primarily and mainly (for his detailed expositions, see, e.g., 1993b, 1995, 1997, 2000, 2004, 2006, 2007). I have added some augmentations, here and below; these are conceptually sound but, I admit, empirically difficult, in some instances perhaps impossible.

[489] As Harrison White (1992, pp. 346-349) put it, the human being is effectively a Kalman filter capable of updating expectations and courses of action accordingly. More about this in later sections.

[490] Nonlinearities of process that vary endogenously as a function of densities of interactions (networks or chains of relation) have been addressed fruitfully in literatures of ecological theory (see e.g., Pascual 2001) as well as in many studies of density-dependent regulatory functions in other settings (e.g., gene expression, labor markets, querty-type innovations). I suspect similar functions occur in the operation of institutional channels of effects of per-person actions and aggregated action-effects (see below, §§27-29).

The list of main action-to-effect relations includes the following. Note that these are not necessarily mutually exclusive; indeed, empirical settings are typically complex mixtures of two or more kinds of relations, virtually all of them regulated probabilistically in time, which sets for the theorist and researcher the inherently difficult task of devising a model that is (1) simplified enough to be tractable (i.e., generative of useful insights into process that can be tested against experience) but also (2) not so simple as to have no meaningful applications of insight to actual experience, while also (3) expressible to interested persons who are not mathematical logicians. I should note, too, that the requisite conditions just described pertain when quantitative metrics are unavailable, but the lack of such tools is a severe handicap, leaving problems of ambiguity, selection, and other complexities of relations only weakly addressable (if at all). For example, it can be taken as virtually a truism that "context matters." There is an abundance of experience in support of the importance of the dialectical relation of text/context: meaning often depends on it, as we find repeatedly when dealing with ambiguities of text lacking relevant context. For much the same reason, efforts to pick apart effects of context from other effects, endogenous or exogenous, as we typically seek to do in analytic frameworks, sometimes founder on ripples of ambiguity. Context does matter. But how it matters and the matter it makes can be obscured in a nest of difficulties (Erbring and Young 1979; Manski 2013, 2017).[491]

Since my chief focus is on person-action effects in an endogenous process, I will begin with that, and I assume an empirical setting of two or more person-actors engaged in what Max Weber defined as "social action," which is to say that the person-actors take each other's actions into account and in doing so may make assumptions about interests, motives, and purpose.[492] The setting is thus a collectivity of some description. In referring to the person-actors as "members" of the collectivity I do not necessarily assume more than de factor membership. For collective actors in formal sense the membership is also de jure, but actions are taken by individual persons acting as corporate agents (legal officers) of the corporate body as principal. The question of an agency of the corporate body as such may remain, however. Likewise, the roughly correlative question of a nonformalized collectivity (i.e., one lacking standing as legal subject): problems of ambiguity leave the question of agency by this kind of collectivity as such to the side, at least for the moment. Ambiguity, along with uncertainty in broader sense, will continue to bedevil efforts at clarity.[493]

---

[491] Robert Huckfeldt (2013, p. 1) began his case for the importance of context by stating his main thesis: "the political opinions and behaviors of individuals cannot be explained apart from the environment in which they occur." Thus, as illustration, he said that while "Missourians can avoid St. Louis, and St. Louisans can avoid the Central West End" part of the city, "residents of the Central West End have a more difficult time avoiding each other." All of that is presumably true. But it is not evidence of an effect of the neighborhood (or city or state) as such. Putative evidence could be simply correlated effects of individual characteristics, perhaps in part because of selection into the Central West End or perhaps selection effects of both migrations into and migrations out of the area. I will return to some of these complexities below.

[492] Note that only as a convenience am I neglecting the possibility that "other" is this dyad need not be physically present in order to be "taken into account."

[493] Lest my intent be misunderstood, let me emphasize my central meaning. I am in favor of reducing ambiguities of meaning as much as possible, so long as those efforts do not themselves bias the outcome of effort as such. In the final analysis, ambiguity is inherent in much of sociality, and often it is oil to the

(1) Endogenous interactions: the outcome of each person's action varies with the outcomes of the actions of the other persons who are parts "members" of the collectivity. This category may be divided into two:

    (1.1)    Anonymous endogenous interactions: one has no information about the internal structure of the collectivity, nothing that discriminates any of the members by pertinent characteristics. This subcategory may be divided into two:

        (1.1.1)  Anonymous endogenous interactions at one specific date: in other words, observations of interactions at present (as in the typical cross-sectional sampling);

        (1.1.2)  Anonymous endogenous interactions in per-person trajectories: in other words, a temporal record of pertinent observations; in order to be useful and manageable, the interactions would probably have to be qualitatively specific, which probably means specific strategic or task interactions.

    (1.2)    Profiled endogenous interactions: each person-actor has a specific but not necessarily unique profile of status and/or network characteristics that describe an internal structure of the collectivity; this category may be divided into two (as above):

        (1.2.1) Profiled endogenous interactions at one specific date: as above;

        (1.2.2) Profiled endogenous interactions in per-person trajectories: as above.

(2) Exogenous interactions: the outcome of each person's action varies with exogenous variables of the collectivity as such (i.e., variables the empirical distributions of which are not a function of the process endogenous to the collectivity; this category can be divided and then subdivided as above (but see below, regarding "contextual effects").

(3) Correlated effects: the outcome of each person's action tends to vary with the outcome of one or more other persons in the collectivity because they face "similar institutional environments" and/or because they have "similar individual characteristics."

With regard to "correlated effects," note that I quoted part of Manski's (1995, p. 128) account in order to set in relief the basis of my alternative description. By "similar institutional environments" I mean, for example, a school as distinguished from a plant nursery, a musical rehearsal, a baseball team, or a group tour of a city or museum. But whether all of these (and similar other) organizational sites and settings can be described by approximately the same meaning of "institutional" is not, insofar as I can see, important to the account. As for correlated effects due to "similar individual characteristics," Manski said that he meant effects expressing a "nonsocial phenomenon." I take that only as a way of distinguishing effects not due to the

---

axle. This message is difficult to convey; I have tried before (e.g., Hazelrigg 1985), only to be told that I am either an anarchist or a sophist, if not some hybrid of both. An expanded effort (Hazelrigg 1986) did not help. In another attempt (Hazelrigg 1993a) I found that my effort had to conform to one of two existing receptacles. This I could understand as making my own point (if oddly), but some readers took my assigned category as evidence confirming that I had joined John Barth in the funhouse.

sociality of the given collectivity of the moment. If he meant that the individual characteristics are themselves nonsocial, that they did not develop within sociality and/or that they do not express characteristics of the sociality of the given person (whether the specific persons had ever previously been in the same local organization or not), I do not adopt that account. Or, to put it another way, I take Manski's expression, "nonsocial phenomenon" in Weber's sense that the person-actors do not in *this* instance in *this* collectivity take each other's interests, intents, and so forth, into account when deciding and executing their own individually separate actions. Fit to the restriction can be difficult for an observer to determine, even aside from knowing each of the observed person's first-person considerations and whether each took one or more other members into account. The very fact of their mutual membership might be testimony to a selection effect that for all intents and purposes *appears* to be merely happenstance but is actually anchored in a sociality within the members' assumptions, interests, and so forth.

Having described the partition of "observed effect" into three logical components—endogenous effect, exogenous effect, and correlated effect—I turn to the vexed issue of what counts as "contextual effect," which could be considered a subcategory of "exogenous effect." In his discussion of "why social inquiry fails," Flyvbjerg (2001, pp. 38-49) placed considerable weight on the fact of context. I do not disagree with his basic point, but I think he understated the difficulty of the task of giving "context" proper due in order that inquiry "can succeed again." While it is one thing to reject the notion of a universal ontology—that is, the notion that understanding of human affairs can be usefully achieved independent of time and place—it is quite another to specify "contextual relations" in the sense of how context *as such* could achieve effects of and by its own presence. Let's begin where Flyvbjerg did, his emphasis on what he called the "Dreyfus-Bourdieu argument" about inherent limitations, and more particularly such limitation relative to what he regarded as the "standard" expectation that any sound theory must be "context-independent."[494] His statement of what is the "standard model" of science could be regarded as a strawman, since that statement has had only distant relation to actual practices of scientific inquiry since the early part of the previous century. But let's come back to that after first acknowledging that Flyvbjerg's claim about a standard model has continued to have some adherents, perhaps none other so much as in some self-deceptive imaginations within the social sciences.

Bent Flyvbjerg (2001, p. 38) declared that "context counts," and indeed it does. It counts both spatially and temporally. As Abbott 2001 put it, "time matters." So does place. Illustrating his general claim by reciting Pierre Bourdieu's (1977) critique of a well-known "structuralist theory" of gift-giving, Flyvbjerg's (2001, p. 41) summation is apropos: "Context, sequence, tempo, and rubato in the gift exchange determine what counts as a gift at all." The argument there reprised was hardly a new one. Without repeating parts of my discussion in Part One, I will only remind the reader that Kant had stated just that argument repeatedly from 1787 onward, as he explained why there could be no exact science of human affairs; rather, only a collection of discourses of empirical generalizations. Critics, especially those later labeled "neo-Kantian," sought to reverse or, failing that, to ignore Kant's statement of limitations of knowledge; and

---

[494] Flyvbjerg attributed the argument separately to Hubert Dreyfus and Pierre Bourdieu, citing specific works by each (e.g., Bourdieu 1977).

they were emboldened to do so because Kant himself had held Newton's science as standard in large part because it could appear to be context free, good equally at all dates in all places of the universe.

So what did the then-famous theorist of that "non-contextual" theory of gift-giving think he (Claude Lévi-Strauss) was doing? In order to answer that question, let's return to an already described illustration (the ballistic missile scenario) of what Newtonian mechanics actually takes as its context. Newton's laws of motion are theoretically complete only in a very precise context which probably exists only in imagination. Application of the principles as they are precisely stated (i.e., the equations) assumes abstraction of "complications" of context. For example, one of these abstractions results in an ideal vacuum. "Atmospheric context matters" could be the headline. So, too, gravitational-field context, and so forth. It was only two centuries after Newton that means were invented by which to locate theoretical expectation for, say, the final trajectory of a ballistic missile within the dispersion of empirical outcomes due to perturbations from atmospheric and other empirical contextual factors. An equation was written for a two-dimensional distribution of positively valued random variables—in effect, inscribed concentric circles of decreasingly likely outcomes of perturbed landings relative to the theoretical target (or "bullseye"). Relevant context is admitted as supplement to the theoretical principle, although only on the basis of a large number of exactly repeated trials of the intended outcome. This, mind you, is the physical science of Newtonian mechanics in actual practice, as distinct from anyone's ideal image of what "true science" is supposed to be. The difference is of course "the human factor" (i.e., application, use, measurement error, etc.).

Jacques Derrida was a pertinent teacher in that regard. Our analytics enable us, even encourage us, to practice neglect, sometimes randomly and sometimes systematically. In his essay on "white mythology," for instance, he (1982 [1972], pp. 207-271) pulled us back to a dialectical perspective, by which it is clear that any "context" is relative to a "text" (as well as vice versa), that the analytic boundary can be elastic and variably mobile, and that comparatives are crucially affected by and in that mobility (Turner 1980; Lee and Bearman 2017). Recall, for example, the trend in college textbooks: supposedly students balked at textbooks that lacked "sufficient white space" around the ink of text, because this signaled "too much difficulty of learning"; and so margins grew, which of course meant thicker, heavier books which in turn "justified" higher pricing, which in turn meant larger financial profits to authors as well as to publishers, paper companies, printing companies, and so on. Newton's equations might have been presented as "text without context" (as noted in Part One there is a hint of evidence that he himself was unsure of that), which could be seen as the inevitable reduction from "text *in* one uniform universe" to "text *of* one uniform universe." If the above-cited interpretation of student preferences among college textbooks is accurate, context was determinative of at least one major quality of text and thereby became decisive of what counted as text in application (i.e., worth reading).

Thus, in terms of human evaluations, expectations, uses, and so forth, context matters in Newtonian mechanics and in other domains of the production of meaning. But now I turn to the main point I want to make; and this I owe to the brilliance not of John William Strutt, third baron Rayleigh (after whom that two-dimensional distribution was named), but of Charles Frederick

Manski: just as it is in theory a seemingly easy matter of semantics to decide what is "text" and what is "context" but far less easy in practice to make that division constant and stable, so, too, is it difficult to isolate effects that are strictly "contextual" from other kinds of effects within the analytical logic of experimental—to say nothing of less carefully controlled—inquiry (see, e.g., Manski 1995). Despite Manski's uncommon skills of clear and precise locution, that message has been slow to gain attention—at least in part, I suspect, because it tells so many of us that we have produced page upon page of confusions).

The most common applications of the "context" concept in the social sciences has been areal and/or historical, "place" and "date." A notable first tendency has been to treat these two dimensions as mutually independent; or more commonly, to treat "place" as independent of "date"—the error memorialized in a famous novel by Thomas Wolfe (1940), toward the end of Proust's first volume of *In Search of Lost Time* (1993 [1923]), and in the aphorism attributed to Heraclitus of Ephesus, that no one ever steps into the same river twice (see Plato's *Cratylus* 402a). It is a mistaken inference of and from memory: any given place, like any given person, carries a temporal subscript, but first-person experience is only presence, the instance of now. Of the areal applications, the most common are a "rural versus urban" (or "country vs. city") dichotomy and, more recently, neighborhood. Spatio-temporal context is no doubt important in the sense that per-person decisions about action choices can be influenced by perceptions of "what is going on around me," circumstances that are "relevant to my interests, my choices," and so on. From an analyst's point of view, no doubt, there is always the question of how one draws the line between "text" and "context"—that is to say, what is integral to and inseparable from the composition of an interest, a decision, an action, and what is external to it in the sense that the action or decision or interest would have been the same in any of the "ordinary" differences of circumstances. And here, of course, the analyst's perception of such matters is limited by the counterfactuality problem. Still, it could be useful to know "what was going on" around, say, Marcel Duchamp when he composed *Fountain*; Paul Desmond and Dave Brubeck when they composed what became known simply as "Take Five"; Virginia Woolf when she composed *The Wave*; Zora Neale Hurston when she composed *Jonah's Gourd Vine*; and so forth. Then, too, one must face the fact that in general one could only guess at the relevant "what is going on" within the actual spatio-temporality of other-actor's first-person perception in relation to one's *own* (observer) perception of "what *was* going on" there then, this latter perception posing the same kind of question ("what of relevance in going on circumstantially to the here-and-now of my experience").[495]

One of the most common dictates of areal context comes from state functions: the data are compiled on that manner, aggregated by often-large areal divisions. It has not been a secret, for example, that the age-adjusted risk of mortality in the USA has differed greatly by region of the country and that this difference is associated with a Black versus White racial contrast. The five states with the lowest age-adjusted mortality rates in 2017 were California, Connecticut,

---

[495] The reflexivity issue is crucial, though often ignored. Like others (e.g., Pierre Bourdieu, discussed in the next section), I believe that a theory must take account as explicitly as possible of the theorist, forgoing special pleading, Mannheimian exception of a "free-floating" intellectual as special actor, and similar conceits.

Hawaii, Minnesota, and New York; the average across the five was 624 per 100,000. The five states with the highest age-adjusted rates were Alabama, Kentucky, Mississippi, Oklahoma, and West Virginia (all five relatively poor, especially in rural areas; Oklahoma in the list because of poverty among the Native American population). The average across these five in 2017 was 927 per 100,000, nearly 50 percent higher.[496] The mortality disparity persisted within categories of age, as already noted; it also persisted within gender categories (i.e., male vs. female), within the Black versus White categories, and within each of the top five categories of cause of death. It is clear, of course, that a US state is as such a legal actor, in that constitutional provisions specify delegated powers both directly and by default (i.e., powers not otherwise constituent federally). To that extent "state as context" has substantive meaning of agency, per-person members of legislative, executive, and judicial branches exercising powers of office on behalf of the state (which is to say, enabled/constrained by powers of offices of state agency). Accordingly, there are collective-actor effects within and behind the sorts of aggregate data just summarized.

A number of social scientists have staked considerable territory in or of "neighborhood effects." Because there is often ambiguity of meaning in "effect of context" (neighborhood or otherwise), I will reiterate what I mean, for this will be my baseline during the following discussion. An effect is an outcome of a specified process, an outcome of specified dynamics, and as such the term implies some kind of agency of that process or of a condition or conditions of that process. Does any specified instance of context meet that criterion? This is the key question. Moreover, because it is difficult to estimate the effect of a constant, and since most instances of context tend to be relatively stable during the period of a specified process of action effects, I generally ask for a comparative: one specified context in comparison to some other (comparable) context, as just illustrated via the aggregate data on mortality risk. In general, it does appear that the comparative dimension is rather easy to satisfy by neighborhood as context. Does the fact of neighborhood as a specific kind of context also then meet the agency criterion? Some well-known scholars have answered the latter question in the affirmative, even though one sometimes suspects it was against a suppressed skepticism (e.g., Sampson 2011, 2012).

I agree that for a given neighborhood or set of contiguous neighborhoods there will very likely be one or more well-defined agencies: a neighborhood school, for instance, or officers of a governmental agency such as a police department, a parks and recreation department, building inspection, waste management, public health, and so forth. Not only does each of those count as an agency; each of them can be counted as a "collective agency," and by virtue of governmental authority the collectivity as such has power of agency. But does *neighborhood as such* have agency? If organized as a "homeowners association" with some sort of formal standing that accords with local government policy, it would. Lacking that recognition, it is difficult to see what the source of agency would be. Members of a collectivity can agree among themselves that the collectivity of them has agency; but the agency is of that agreement (by consensus, by simple

---

[496] These data are maintained by the National Center for Health Statistics, a US federal agency. As happened during the Reagan administrations, so again during the Trump administration there have been efforts to suppress reports of data, even to prevent their compilation. In response, some agencies have been determined to protect sets of data by disseminating them through official reports and making data downloads available.

majority, whatever the rule), and it does not extend to any constituency beyond the membership except by treaty.

Sampson (2011, p. 228), having observed that residents are not randomly distributed across areal sections of a city, at least some of which are locally identified as neighborhoods, took that observation as indicating areal distribution as if by some matching process, asserting that the distribution reflects person-actor choice in a process of residential selection that is "influenced or caused by neighborhood factors." A year later, however, in his book-length final report of his research project, Sampson (2012, pp. 288-289, 299) was rather more circumspect in his wording. Although still trying to cast "neighborhood" as in some sense an agent sharing responsibility for the migration choices of individual persons and their respective households, he avoided saying that any neighborhood selected its residents or caused its residents to be *here* rather than there. Offering rich descriptions of how a city's neighborhoods varied by many individual person-level variables as those variables had been aggregated to neighborhood level, he presented as suitably relevant and important a number of factors such as measures of crime, child health, artistic activities, internet use, litter in streets and/or on sidewalks, and community engagement, among others. But these factors, whether individually considered or collected as compound measures (e.g., "socially perceived disorder"), constitute variables of relative attraction/repulsion which both present actual and potential new residents can evaluate when deciding residential alternatives. It is those actual and potential residents who decide, not the neighborhood as such. Moreover, evaluations are not by the factors evaluated but by or within perceptions of the evaluators. As another champion of the importance of "contextual influence" conceded, the influence is manifest in social interactions, whether occurring via primary groups or as "some form of social interaction at a casual and impersonal level." But, avoiding the issues of identification, he still affirmed that context has "influence" (Huckfeldt 1986, pp. 20-23, 54-55, 149, 161; see also Sander, Kucheva, and Zasloff 2018).

There is a sense, of course, in which "being of a place" can imply distinctive experiences, and for that sense "place" need not have formal status. Consider disparities of life conditions. If one were to choose a single number as best indicator of overall quality of life in a particular area, it would probably be life expectancy at birth. The US Bureau of the Census recently released such estimates at the level of census tracts for the period 2010 to 2015. The range is startling: in Chicago's census tract 812 the average was 90.0 years (standard deviation 2.96). Covering 0.15 square mile, this area is very "upscale," needless to say: it lies southeast of the intersection of East Division Street and North State Street, down to East Walton Place and East Chicago Avenue, an area that includes the Near North Side and the Magnificent Mile. By contrast, the average for census tract 6903 was 59.9 years (standard deviation of 2.20). This tract is 0.20 square mile, lying southwest of the intersection of West Marquette Road and South State Street. It is one of the poorest areas of the southside of Chicago, with a median household income of about $20,000. The population estimate was 2393 residents, of whom 94 percent were African American. The life-expectancy estimate predicts that the average new-born child in that area will live three fewer *decades* than the average child born to a mother living in the area up by the old Gold Coast. But census tract 6903 was only a few years worse in that respect than some other areas nearby (e.g., tract 6702, 62.2 years; tract 6712, 64.0 years). While the three-decade disparity in Chicago might have been the largest in US cities during that time, travel about 275 southwest to Adams County, and you will find that the disparity is not only a problem of major cities. In census tract 1 (of Quincy, the county seat) the average life expectancy was 85.3 years; in neighboring census tract 4 it was 66.2 years. This disparity correlated with poverty (5% vs. 30% below the poverty line; $49,000 vs. $29,000 median household income) but not with race (the two tract populations were indifferent in percent African American: 8% vs. 9%).

Depending on the population size and density of an area, the experiences though in some way "distinctive" are seldom uniform across persons. It is important to bear that in mind when thinking about "context" in the sense of residential neighborhood. For example, Alex Kotlowitz (1991, 2019) has supplied vivid insight into a part of South Chicago that was extraordinarily troubled during his first exploration nearly three decades ago, and his ethnography probably gave added incentive to the city to undertake neighborhood change, beginning with demolition of massive ghettos that had been only recently constructed as projects of urban renewal. But destructive though those "projects" turned out to be, to conclude that most young men and women who came of age in those places at that time were failures would be seriously mistaken. Victims of their circumstances? No doubt they were. Uniformly victimized? No. Given their circumstances, most of them proved to be remarkably resilient, determined to prevail against very harsh conditions and very steep odds. Deprived of opportunity? No doubt. Waste of human potential? No doubt. But even so, most of those young women and men refused to be reduced to the ciphers that project designers had assumed of them. Even in a war zone, foreign or civil, declared or not, most of the agency is by individual persons, whether considered as singletons or in collectivities. Teamwork can be vital, but the effectiveness of a team is often no better than a weighted average of the team members.

Sampson (2012, p. 159) argued that "collective efficacy," indexed by residents' self-perceptions of their shared efficacy in maintaining local order, was itself an influence on actual rates of local disorder or violence; and it may well have been. But the influence could exist only as a vector *through* the potential violators: they would have been cognizant, at least indirectly, of "neighborhood watch," so to speak. What would the signal have been? Was it a property of the neighborhood as such, over and above its residents' presence and actions? Or was it instead perceptions by potential violators about the attitudes of "lots of people who live in this area"? A "neighborhood watch" sign may well carry deterrent value, but that value is determined by the residents who "live here" *and* by potential violators as they process the signal, the meanings they make of the sign, not by the neighborhood as such (cf. Wacquant 2001, 2002, 2008, 2014).

I am not arguing that "place" is unimportant. Every person is *from* a place, is *in* a place at any date of observation, and might at such date have a different place as aspirational reference. And places do vary in many ways, some of them implicated in the life chances per person of the people located in place (as demonstrated, for instance, by Kate Brown 2013, by Peter van Wyck 2004, and others, and as will be discussed further in the next section). None of that is at issue. What *is* at issue is whether named-place as such—rather than "place with these values on some set of variables $Z_1, Z_2, \ldots Z_n$," significantly discriminative of named-places—adds marginally to a model of the per-person outcome of some action-effect process. Compare two specifications of a basic model of that outcome as a function of a set of appropriate per-person conditions $X_n$:

in one version the model is augmented by dummy variables indicating the per-person named-place; in the other version the augmentation is instead by the set of $Z_n$ variables, treated as additional per-person conditions. Is there a difference in power? If any of the dummy variables add significantly to model power, are they interactive with any of the $Z_n$? Tests of this sort are always vulnerable to the "missing variable" problem, of course (as well as to counterfactuality: i.e., what would the comparative outcome have been if residents of Place A had been switched with those of Place B, and so forth?). One can imagine a defender of "contextual effect" arguing that any given test did not take into account an "aura of place" or some other unmeasured factor. But we would at least have more information about the name of the game being conducted. It simply is not helpful, but nor imaginative, to argue in effect that *inequality* (of neighborhoods) "explains" *inequality* of childhood schooling (Boushey 2019, pp. 46-47). We must do better.

There is another kind of distinctive "place" effect that might be detectable—namely, one that differs by place according to a factor or factors that do not result from any per-person action (or that have not resulted from any per-person action; my parenthetical switch to past imperfect tense is recommended by the factor "climate change"). This could be termed (as Manski has) an "ecological effect," on the assumption that "environment" or a specific "environmental factor" is exogenous to persons of the given area. (I am generally skeptical of that assumption; but never mind for the moment.) Less global than the general matter of climatic environment, factors such as local terrain, altitude, isolation (e.g., a measure of population density, distance to nearest commercial airport, etc.) might be considered as suitably ecological, but the criterion of agency rests in per-person perception, evaluation, and the like, not in the factor itself. While it would be appropriate no doubt to include such factors in a list of variables potentially *conditioning* per-person actions and action-effects, I see no compelling reason to think of any of them as having agency or "causal force." Imagine a house that was built at the foot of a mountain; the side of the mountain elevation above the house is strewn with boulders and rocks, perhaps a rockslide or avalanche "waiting to happen." Ignoring the evident risk, an adult person moves into the house and some time later is killed when an avalanche cascades onto the house. As a matter of local statutory law, this event might count as "death by natural causes." No doubt the potential energy stored as the mass of boulders and rocks could be regarded as causative power. The definitive agency was, by my evaluation, the adult person's decision and action to ignore the evident risk. Mountains, boulders, and rocks, rivers and floodplains, and so forth, do not perceive, do not think, do not evaluate, do not decide, do not act thoughtfully or ignorantly, rationally/irrationally or nonrationally. They are merely masses in motion, potential when not actual flows of energy (and all human productions of our understandings).

Works by Manski and others have given us better tools by which to assess potentials or future as well as present conditions, make decisions, choose actions accordingly, monitor effects, and register updates from our new experiences. Their works give us the better tools; they do not make applications of those tools for us. Of the several crucial lessons that are available in those works, I will emphasize these four for present purposes.[497]

---

[497] I have been giving main attention to works by Manski, because they are clear, systematic, well focused, and persistent. I do not mean that no one before him had made related contributions. Lucas

First, a basic point that I have previously emphasized multiple times (e.g., Hazelrigg 2010, pp. 5-7; Hazelrigg and Garnier 1976, p. 508): because very few (if any) relations in the realm of human affairs can meet the test of ergodicity, cross-sectional data tell us little or nothing about the dynamics of human processes. Manski (1993b) demonstrated quite clearly that the ability to distinguish between an observed effect due to a factor F (e.g., the force of a social norm) and a common unobserved factor is virtually nonexistent when the data are cross-sectional. Identification is incomplete and cannot be made complete. This message has been resisted. While the resistance is understandable, given that very little of available data are adequately keyed to the temporality of process (even though theoretical interest is in learning "how things happen"), resistance is merely avoidance, not a solution (see also Young 2015, pp. 376, 367-368, 359; Petersen 1989; Simon 1962).

Second, observations are inherently uncertain both directly and because the relations that one seeks to observe are themselves uncertain due to their contingencies. If observing scientists are not always adequately rational in their decisions and actions, then one might expect that other person-actors are less than completely or perfectly rational in their decisions and actions, too, and thus that failures of predictions based on the standard assumptions of expected utility theory should be neither surprising nor grounds for dismissing probabilistic versions of that theory or class of theories (see Friedman et al. 2014; cf. Hahn and Solow 1995). Therefore, person-actor reports of own interests, perspectives, motivations, goals, preferences, choices, decisions, and actions, especially when those reports are responses to carefully built questions or other stimuli, should not be rejected out of hand merely because they are fallible, interested, and biased (see, e.g., Manski 1993b, 2018). If those three qualities—being fallible, interested, and biased—are grounds for dismissing first-person reports by other persons, then any theorist or researcher might as well close shop for having failed the same tests.

Third, limits resulting from the nonobservability of counterfactual alternative timelines of a given process should be explicit in theorizations of that process, with attention both to issues of reflexivity and to assessments of the probable biases due to selection. These must be recognized as inherent to the process of theorization itself and as explicit factors in models of the process that is focal in one's theory. A common focal process is social learning: a present cohort, facing a decision about optimum response to a present situation of choice among alternative pathways toward a specific goal, will understandably seek guidance from the record of prior cohorts who faced a similar decision between similar alternatives under similar conditions. Assessment of the information would be relatively straightforward, within bounds of the comparative design, but for one factor: lacking information on outcomes of pathways not taken by prior cohorts, one cannot know if the pathway(s) previously chosen was (were) in fact optimal. The accumulated information is thus inherently ambiguous. Using computational analysis and sets of simulated data, Manski (2004, 2006) generated insights into the logical structure of this prevalent scenario of systematic learning from one's predecessors. While there can be no adequate substitute for the counterfactual information that will remain unobservable, knowing that logical structure is the next best advantage. In general, "social learning from private

---

(e.g., 2016) has fittingly linked to Manski's contribution some of the earlier works (e.g., by Robert Hauser, Arthur Goldberger, and others).

experiences" of suitably comparative other persons is "a process of *complexity within regularity*. The process is complex because the dynamics of learning and the properties of the terminal information state flow from the subtle interaction of information accumulation and decision making. Yet a basic regularity constrains how the process evolves as accumulation of empirical evidence over time (weakly) reduces the ambiguity that successive cohorts face" (Manski 2006, pp. 46-47; Simon 1962).

Fourth, Manski's logical analyses present in a very clear, systematic, and detailed manner some of the key limits to human inquiry that result, as Kant argued, from the absence of relations of necessity. This can be summarized by statements that Samuel Lucas (2016) wrote in his critical study both of the research behind the Coleman report of 1966 and of the requirements that must be considered and, insofar as possible, met in any successor study.

> Manski (1993) demonstrated that even with the introduction of controversial assumptions, contextual and endogenous effects cannot be distinguished. Moreover, even the determination of whether such effects exist is fraught with peril; Manski (1993, pp. 35-36) shows four common scenarios in which important conditions for these results are violated" (Lucas 2016, p.129).

And in wake of what has been learned, henceforth

> every analysis requires an implicit or explicit model of the production of its outcome. Ideally, analysts would select a model to guide data collection and analysis, such that the model should be evident prior to data collection. ... The belief that one can estimate causal effects simply from data, without imposing a set of assumptions that make estimation possible and meaningful, has been shown to be in error. Thus, if the aim is to estimate causal effects, the first advice is to conduct theoretical analyses. ... [A]s Sørensen and Hallinan (1977) and many others demonstrate ..., just developing and manipulating the theoretical equations implied by various claims can be illuminating and helpful (Lucas 2016, pp. 132, 133; also see Lucas 2009; White 1992).[498]

The expectation that a theorist must specify all expected relations by type is important. It is also very demanding, first of all because it entails clear exposition of conceptual differences (what counts as this kind versus that kind of relation).[499] Indeed, what *does* count as endogenous? Or, to put the question more pointedly, endogeneity means "generated from within"; but from "within *what*"? I have already, several times, remarked the tendency to begin with "individual" as not fully social or even as not social at all. This can entail the view of "individual" as entering an endogenous process manifesting a more or less complex selection effect, including enchained effects of unequal distribution of resources; and that inequality within selection effect can be seen most easily as "contextual effect" ("the poor neighborhood into which you were born"). This

---

[498] Having in advance of the production of data (I believe "data collection" is too passive, as if one merely collects pebbles on a beach) an "explicit model of the production of its outcome" is surely not new advice, but it is advice often ignored. See also Lucas' (2014) demonstration that multilevel modeling, even with appropriate sampling designs, does not escape problems of identification.

[499] A brief illustration of the critical effort for the theorist, and a display of some of the challenges, can be seen in Ketokivi and Mahoney (2016).

picture can in turn be used to relieve the individual person of some of the onus ("not your fault, really"), but it can also be used to continue a neglect that the locality, probably the society as a whole, has already accepted as normal, natural, justified ("just the way life is").

Previously I have focused mainly on the psychologistic model of "the individual," and that remains relevant to present discussion. However, for theoretical economics the sequence of modeling presumptions about the person-actor took a somewhat different course during the late nineteenth century. Earlier I referred to Alan Kirman's (1992) titular question: "Whom or what does the representative individual represent?" This "representative individual" recalls something of the perspective of Newtonian law as a disciplinary aspiration among economists: the model of a being called "the economic actor" was designed as deliberately unrealistic—a "perfectly rational, perfectly informed, perfectly logical decision maker who exercises perfect foresight," and so forth—because, as Brian Arthur openly explained to Philip Anderson (see above), this model is theoretically workable, and it serves as a useful benchmark for empirical inquiries. Few economists during the late nineteenth century understood the significance, likely even the fact, of the Rayleigh distribution vis-à-vis Newtonian laws, but most of them aspired to the status of a "law-finding" science, which they understood to be epitomized by Newton's work. However, a development proximate to the time of Alfred Marshall and colleagues is also apropos—namely, the "representative individual" as formulated in the "reasonable man" doctrine in legal theory, a model that was accorded as "normative" increasingly in the sense of a *statistical* reference within the framework of Gauss' theory of error (see §21, above).

Consider the example of a measured per-pupil achievement effect of having been a pupil enrolled in a specific school for some number of years. This outcome, compared to outcomes for other pupils in the same school for the same number of years, can be considered first of all as a comparative effect of the endogenous process of formal schooling. Further, the comparison has been "standardized," let's say, for relevant measurable differences in per-pupil "conditions" such as mother's educational attainment, household income, number (and relative age) of siblings, and gender and racial-ethnic identity. Whatever the estimate of endogenous effect, a critic can point to the possibility of a selection effect, suggesting even that the endogenous process of formal schooling had little distinctive effect other than reproducing the achievement differences that existed among the pupils as they first enrolled in the school. So far, my scenario has said merely repeated descriptions of scenes already presented. But now a difference: why is the purported selection effect not in fact the effect of an endogenous process or processes that occurred prior to the pupils' enrolment in this particular school? In other words, the scenario presented above was "left-censored" in terms of what should count as "endogenous" versus "selection effect." It was as if one is reading a novel in which all action, including remembered events and experiences, of all the characters began at age 30, say, and one can only guess about what "might have happened distinctively differently" across the various characters during their previous 29 years of life.

Thus, what is at the moment adjudged in some degree "selection effect" was probably due to prior endogenous process, however complex in its composition, a process of unequal distribution of resources of all various kinds (or, to use a more active term, unequal "allocation," which is better indication that particular person-actors were involved in, to some extent in charge of, the allocation as such). This refers to the institutionalization of inequality (see Martin 2009, ch. 4). It is, to use Manski's phrase, an endogenous process of "complexity within regularity": institutionalization makes both of those aspects of sociality relatively stable and equilibrating. In most societies today the institutionalization is manifest most "obviously" in terms of "gender." In US society, and at least a few others, it is also "obviously" manifest in terms of "race." Let me briefly pursue the former as illustration of what I mean; most of it fits also the facts of "race" in US society.

We legislate the individual human being as being born in one of two natural kinds, male or female. This has been "the law of gender" for centuries, the presumption and the expectation being that a universal law of nature is at work (see Hazelrigg 1995, pp. 248-290). However, the relevant characteristics are mostly continua—quantitative gradients, not just qualitative kinds. The gradients are morphological as well as biochemical; they are also "behavioral," constitutive of the specific social being of the individual person. But we legislate only two genders. What have we done with the qualitative "undivided middle"? It was first legislated as "hidden," kept out of sight. Then, with a little more democratization, it was legislated as "confused," a "confusion by nature." Then "mixed," "mixtures by nature"; and that is approximately where we are now: we still legislate primarily a binary, and this remains our image of "the normal," although at present we do seem to be more "willing" to make more and more "allowances." We still legislate the physical appearance of "female": long flowing soft hair, lipstick and other spots of color added to the face, long full eyelashes, small diameter ankles and wrists, specific apparel choices such as high heels and a dress that accentuates certain curves, and so forth. Likewise, a preferred appearance of "male." These are legislations. They are effects of endogenous process. Out of those processes come each new cohort and generation of individuals each of whom then brings selection effects to the next round of institutionalized processes, especially those involving competition/cooperation.

The majority of the person-actors who direct allocations are "male" and "white." Thus, the selection effects that a child brings in trail reflect those two attributes above all others. A child born "female" learns quickly not to aspire to physical science, technology, engineering, or mathematics (rather than the "caring professions," languages and literatures, etc.). Likewise, a child born "black" has entered sociality with relatively low life chances in general, especially if "male" as well (with exceptions such as mass-entertainment sports). Does all of that mean that what we call "selection effect" is really "endogenous effect" in disguise? Well, yes and no. Yes, in that the selections (by "gender," by "race," etc.) occur within endogenous processes that have been both completed and reproduced at any child's date of birth. No, in that a child is born into a legislated two-by-two grid of institutionalized inequality, and that means that the child has already been selected to be a relative winner or a relative loser in the game of life, well before the child has more than barely begun to participate in endogenous processes that (because of the reproduction cited in the prior sentence) are twice bifurcated, each bifurcation between the relatively privileged (male, white) and the relatively deprived, handicapped, and most deficient (female and black). We know that those factors of disparity are not due to necessity; they are due to choices, those made and those not made. Different choices, different legislations can be made. Hugh Mehan's career-long work is relevant here with regard to childhood education, both in the

451

family and in formal schooling.  Work by Mehan and his colleagues has demonstrated both that "selection effects" (and "context effects") are due to prior endogenous processes and that those effects can be overcome within a birth cohort to a significant extent (see, e.g., Mehan, Villaneuva, Hubbard, and Lintz 1996; Mehan and Chang 2010; Mehan with Chang, Jones, and Mussey 2012). But his efforts also have demonstrated that because the inequalities have been institutionalized and thus reproduced again and again over many decades, very considerable sustained effort and determination are required, whereas US society has been devoting fewer resources, proportionately speaking, to education (both remedial for new parents, as well as children's education) except for well-to-do white families and especially their male children. [500]

Aristotle taught us to discriminate among material, formal, efficient, and final or telic cause; but we eventually learned that making those discriminations empirically was (is) a highly fraught task.  Hume taught us that "cause" is a purely theoretical notion; but that left us unsatisfied, because the notion that each of all (or even some) events is empirically an uncaused occurrence seemed pointless.  Then Kant taught us that real causes are hidden: we can make educated empirical guesses about them by inference from observed effects; but, lacking the leverage afforded by relations of necessity, that is about the best we can do within our limits (even when we imagine that we are legislating necessity).  This, too, has not been satisfying to many scholars, some of whom have tried repeatedly to prove Kant wrong (e.g., Pearl 1990; Pearl and MacKenzie 2018).  None has succeeded.  In response we have learned to modify what we mean by "cause" and to accept that empirically we can examine the *conditions* under which an effect can be observed, often we can determine within reasonable limits the temporal sequence of a variable effect vis-à-vis correlated variation in one or more of the conditions, and from that we can make estimates, within reasonable limits, of the relative contributions of specific conditions to the observed effect, although those limits can be disappointingly wide because, being human, we are prone to error—although, too, as Gauss tried to teach us in his theory of errors, what one person may see as "error," another may see as "innovation" (see Hazelrigg 1980).  Indeed, to put it in other words, "even" a system of stochastic relations—along with Łukasiewicz logic and "fuzzy logic" (see Zadeh 1965)—presupposes a set of categories and comparative semantics.

The decomposition of observed effects is important as an exercise in logic because, while aiding theorist and researcher alike in determining source(s) of an observed effect, it clarifies critical ambiguities and problems of identification.  The principal site of those benefits is that relation which Hume told us could never be other than theoretical—namely, the causal relation, causality.  The verb "to determine" itself captures a large part of the obstacle: it means "to ascertain" but it also means "to cause"; and the perceiver does both, simultaneously fixing and creating a limit (as the Latin root says).  Associations and correlations are abundant in human experiences.  Sociality is a hotbed of associations and correlations.  Thus, a rich plethora of suggestions of "cause and effect"—none of them ever more at face value than happenstance—stand at the ready.  Kant added that surely there are true causes, but we have no unmediated or

---

[500] Recall that "privilege" means "private law."  In US society persons who are male and white have the edge in being the primary and main legal subjects, while persons who are female and/or black are objects primarily and mainly of that "private law."

direct access to them. We can only try to infer from those of our plethora of experiences that we deem important enough to be (putative) effects worth worrying about their causes—that is, their "true causes," causes other than our own interests, biases, expectations, and other "errors" of our perceptions. But lacking certitude of any anchorage in necessity, we are left holding only the ingredients of contingency and assessments of probability; and we face not only obstacles due to perceptions we could never have made all at the same time (i.e., all of the alternative timelines or pathways that might have been taken) yet must somehow keep in mind as potentially important information (i.e., the counterfactuals: "what if …?") but also the potentially endless regress of steps in our inquiries (i.e., always the next question: "but what causes that?").[501]

Eventually, inquirers took another leaf from Kant's book of lessons: we can know better that which we do, that which we make (i.e., the legislative act). And so, developments of the experimental method: we make a treatment—at least a binary condition, if not a gradient of degrees of treatment—and watch the variable effects of that manipulation (within a framework of ceteris paribus), relying on randomization or precision matching to distribute the condition(s) across the individual persons or other units of observation.[502] Observability of counterfactual outcomes remains a problem, however, and ethical considerations preclude experimentations on human beings and other animal units for a wide range of topics. Some have recommended what are called "hypothetical experiments" as a substitute, but these typically involve much stronger assumptions which are untestable conditions of, not within, the given experiment.

The advice to focus on what we can know better—our own actions—recommended also a notion of "agency," human agency, rather than the givenness of a hidden realm of "causes" that we must "uncover." While this perspective seemed to facilitate some steps of enlightenment, it also highlighted as never before the gravity of common experiences of tragedy and unintended effects of purposive action—all of which seemed much like a realm of hidden causes. In the meanwhile a major shift was made in the calculus of "causal analysis," turning on a distinction between "the effects of cause(s)" and "the cause(s) of effects." Largely stimulated both by developments of and interests in statistical analysis, especially as these intersected with uses of "hypothetical experiments," attention shifted more and more to means of estimating effects of causes (Holland 1986, p. 945). This seemed to avoid the conundrum of "hidden causes": one simply adopts a set of observable factors as having "causative force," then focusses on (mostly statistical) analyses of observable effects of those factors. This fit quite well with interests in partitioning observed variances and covariances, especially in cross-sectional frame. Often

---

[501] Although it appears that he deliberately skirted Kant and moved from Hume to John Stuart Mill in his overview of major philosophical texts on causal inference, Paul Holland (1986, p. 947) understood the absence of necessity as the linchpin of what he termed "the fundamental problem of causal inference," acknowledging that in any strict sense "causal inference is impossible." But he also allowed that the problem can be circumvented by making some strong assumptions. Indeed, the assumptions are so strong that the resulting exercise has little to do with "genuine testing" in traditional sense of that phrase.
[502] Too often our appreciation of randomization neglects two facts: (1) the probability of a balanced coin returning a sequence of thirty heads is exactly the same at the probability of it returning fifteen alternations of one head and one tail, or vice versa; and (2) "in the long run" means that a given experiment must be exactly repeated many times, yet exact repetition runs counter to "the normal course of events."

unnoticed, Hume was being recalled: the problem of discriminating between correlations and causes ceased to be an empirical issue, as the matter of "cause" was happily returned to pure theory. In other words, it is up to the theorist to stipulate the list or network of a hierarchy of causes, which an analyst should then follow by a mapping of observed "effects" of observed "causes."

This shift dominated for a few decades, even as some well-known social scientists who had been promotive of it also cautioned against its limits (e.g., Duncan 1984). Recently Michael Sobel registered an observation which, if probed to its conclusion, suggests that the line between approaches—"effects of cause" versus "cause(s) of effect"—is not exactly impermeable, nor the compared categories clear and distinct (see also Hazelrigg 1989b). Sobel's inquiry sharply raises issues of authority of voice:

> Much of quantitative political science and sociology may be characterized as a highly stylized search for new causes of effects. Researchers typically begin with one or more outcomes and a list of causes identified by previous workers. Potentially new causes are then listed; if these account ("explain") for additional variability of the response, then the new causes are held to affect the outcome, and the significant coefficients in the new model are endowed with a causal interpretation. The process is repeated by subsequent workers, resulting in further "progress." When researchers realize that they are merely adding more and more variables to a predictive conditioning set, one wonders what will take the place of the thousands of (purported) causal effects that currently fill the journals (Sobel 2000, p. 650).

Morgan and Winship (2013, p. 442) wrote a concurrence (if reluctant and/or tentative) with that observation, taking it to be a recommendation for the "effect(s) of cause" approach.[503] Sobel's (2005, p. 104) passing reference to the example of climate change points us to recognition that if we consider climate change not as a thing or a state but as a process long in the making, then we can see linked chains of cause-and-effect relations. An initial change such as human inventions and developments of carbon-burning industrial machinery resulted in consequences that become causes in turn, produce other effects, both adding to the prior effects but also generating new effects, some of them multiplier effects and other scale effects such as positive feedback loops that cause large accelerations of components of the process, perhaps ending finally in extinction of our and other species. Kant's hope for species maturity was, and remains, only a hope.

The shift to an "effects of causes" approach did not staunch all interest in the quest for valid and reliable means of causal inference—that is, in the older sense of inferring from facts taken as observed effects to the (nonobvious and non-observer) causes that produced those facts. Some of the analysis that featured estimations of "effects of causes" had a peculiarly static feel, which was fed by the growing abundance of cross-sectional data, and critics connected that to their own theoretical and empirical interest in the investigation of process rather than basically static description (see, e.g., Sørensen 1998). While sometimes conceding that "agency" fit

---

[503] Morgan and Winship (2013) were straightforward in their preference for moderated implications of reasoning, however, maintaining protections for what could be considered "practical solutions" (see, e.g., their page 43 n.6).

problems having to do with public policy and social engineering, for which the typical "effects of causes" approach to analysis could be useful, champions of an older model of science held fast to the idea that *basic* or *pure* social science should insist on the superior power of "causal analysis" when tackling investigations of phenomena fundamental and crucial to the realities of human endeavors, to their generative processes, their structures and functions, and the like. Ambiguities and inconsistencies persisted, however. Morgan and Winship (2013, p. 47) cited Hubert Blalock (1964 [1961], pp. 13, 176), for instance, urging practice that they described as "more permissive" with regard to logical obstacles to causal inference such as the likely complication of unobserved determinants that, in Blalock's words, make it "nearly impossible to state accurate scientific generalizations."

An eminent champion of what he has termed "the scientific model of causality," James Heckman (2005, pp. 2-3, 1), has been critical of those who "want to describe a phenomenon as being modeled 'causally' without producing a clear model of how the phenomenon being described is generated or what mechanisms select the counterfactuals [by which he meant the general term, "hypotheticals"] that one observed in hypothetical or real samples." Borrowing Holland's (1986) terms, "they want to model the effects of causes without modeling the causes of effects." His position is sound. While it could be taken as consistent with Sobel's comment regarding climate change (cited above), one can detect a substantial distance between respective views. To begin with, Heckman noticed the tendency among some scholars to conflate different meanings of "model"—or perhaps the better account is to say different kinds (conceptions) of "model" (see also Doreian 2001). On the one hand, a model is a device of theory, not intended to be a realistic ethnography or more abstracted description of quotidian life. As a product of theory, a model includes a set of explicit simplifying assumptions, the better to focus inquiry on mechanisms conceived within a "ceteris paribus" framework and thus hypothetical. However, the same word, "model," has been used also to name the process of identification of relations "from population distributions (infinite samples without any sampling variation)," thus also hypothetical; but still again, also to name the process of estimating parameters on the basis of real (sampled) data (i.e., an "estimated model").

The point of departure is theory, of course. Thus, Heckman's (2005, p. 2) "scientific model of causality" was itself a statement of theory, and as such the "model is in the mind. As a consequence, causality is in the mind." Again, Heckman was hardly the first to have made that statement (think Hume, for instance, and Kant). But responses to Heckman's endorsement have been curiously anachronistic, to say the least. Sobel (2005, p. 106) not only expressed doubt that "most scientists (or philosophers) would subscribe" to the view that models are "not empirical statements or descriptions of actual worlds" but also apparently aligned himself with rejection of that view. Perhaps the disagreement stemmed only from neglect of Heckman's recognition that different uses (or kinds) of "model" have often been conflated. But one suspects rather that the disagreement is a reflection of the longstanding inability either to accept Kant's demonstration of limits of knowledge or to overturn and dismantle that demonstration. Heckman's declaration is, after all, nothing more than acknowledgment of "conceptual scheme" dependency: we cannot know noumena directly but only indirectly as phenomena that manifest effects of our perceptions and conceptions. Causes in themselves, causes strictly as such in the traditional sense, remain hidden because we can "reach" them only via inference, and all of our processes of inference are human productions, effects of human productions. While they *could* occasionally give accurate descriptions of noumena, we cannot detect the difference. Because we cannot know noumena except via those processes, we have no independent point of comparison. This of course means that we have whole worlds of phenomena that we can, that we do, know. But inasmuch as we remain without anchorage by necessity in noumena, that knowledge can only ever be uncertain, tentative, provisional, and relative to the conditions of its production (which always include, depend upon, acts of legislation). Whereas Kant thought he had shown that Newtonian mechanics fundamentally differed, we now know that even Newton's laws are relative to a particular perspective and framework. Such are our "actual worlds" (to reprise the words of Sobel's would-be alternative, which would be worlds without human fingerprints).[504]

## §27. Institutional Channels

My primary and main focus in this and the next section is on institutions as channels of per-person actions and action effects. These channels are communicative, regulative, and constitutive only insofar as they are enabling/constraining, integrative/dispersive. They are major sites of organizational innovation, both successful and frustrated, as well as organizational continuity. My discussion concentrates on only three of the major institutions that could be cited in such a listing: (1) family, including kinship relations; (2) education (child-rearing or "upbringing"), including the part of it that was hived off from the institution of family (and church) as a state function of schooling; and (3) work as the regular provision of labor power for sustenance—immediate now usually in a place other than one's domicile—as it evolved into the modern version of the institution of work, including employment, occupational position or status, apprenticeship, and associated processes. These three institutions involve nearly everyone at specific places and dates in the course of a life, from the new person as an anticipated member in a family of procreation (however temporary the parental union) to the end of a career at work. The dynamics of each of these institutions tend strongly to distributive process, one consequence of which is that they tend to be articulated with each other, although not necessarily well articulated (about which, more below). Various other institutions intersect with them, some of which will be discussed however briefly in the following pages. As communication channels, it follows that information theory is relevant and will be pursued, along with theory of transport phenomena.[505] Issues of macro-to-micro relations, and the reverse, will be addressed; thus also, issues of scale, here and in the next two sections. In one sense, the fact of institutionalization can be understood as a "solution" to a problem of scale, scaling effects in aggregations across persons but also within-person scaling effects over time.

---

[504] "If there could be what serious philosophers dream of, a philosophy at once thoroughly truthful and honestly helpful, it would still be hard, unaccommodating and unobvious. For those reasons, it would doubtless be disliked by those who dislike philosophy as it is. But it might, more encouragingly, succeed in recruiting some new enemies as well, who would do it the credit of hating it for what it said and not just for what it was" (Williams 2014 [1996], p. 370). Sentences I wish I had written.

[505] Transport phenomena are a category of physical theory, and the general topic is material, processes and states of the transport of matter. Transport theory and information theory are generally convertible.

But first, a pair of questions: what counts as an "institution," and where do they come from (Turner 1997)? A complaint often levied against the social sciences in general has been that they harbor a plethora of seemingly technical terms, most of which lack sufficient intensional specificity and clarity to enable a reader to know conceptual relations among them. The more discursive the disciplinary style, the greater the profusion, and the ambiguities are often compounded as various media join the fray of lackluster usages. In 1985 the Gallup Organization offered polls asking adults to indicate their level of confidence in nine "institutions." Three decades later Gallup's "list of institutions in American society" had expanded to 15. The paragraph above, referring vaguely to "various other institutions," could have mentioned "charities" and "philanthropic organizations," as these were gradually separated from "church," plus "chambers of commerce" among other civic organizations, "political parties" and "lobbying organizations" included; none of those appeared in the Gallup list at either date. On the other hand, their 15 in 2016 included "the military," "banks," "newspapers," "the medical system," and "big business," along with "church or organized religion," "public schools," and "the police." Level of public confidence has declined in most of the 15, in some instances ("US Congress") hugely. Only "the military" gained public confidence.[506] My point is not to dispute any one of Gallup's selections for the list, nor to appeal for any candidates they did not include. Rather, what are the criteria for this or any similar list of "the main institutions of American society"? Who knows?

Dictionary definitions generally tell us what most people already agree to think, and in the case of "institution" the thinking is rather wooly. Peyton Young, who has contributed many thoughtful observations on "institutional dynamics," cited a recent edition of the Oxford English Dictionary as his (1998, p. xi) point of departure—"an established law, custom, usage, practice, organization"—which is similar to Edward Evans-Pritchard's (1939, p. 190) accounting, "the recurrent and complex interactions of behavior" (cf. Giddens 1984, p. 24; among many others). Both are very broad in coverage, although the wiggle room of "established" in Oxford's wording is at least suggestive of some degree of restriction. One wonders about intersections with other dimensions—predominantly "cultural" in the usual meanings of divided terrain—and the extent to which the intersections are relevant to qualifications of "institutional." I noted, for example, that Anthony Giddens nominated "modes of discourse" as one major institution, which reminded me first of Richard Hofstadter's (1963, 1964) assessments of alienation, "paranoid style," anti-intellectualism, and resentment as prevalent and persistent features of "political culture" in the USA, as well as Robert Hughes' (1993) equally sharp prognosticative insights thirty years later into the US "culture of complaint." Hughes would have been one of the few to be anything but shocked by the outcome of the US presidential election of 2016. For all of his (and Hofstadter's)

---

[506] Other organizations have conducted similar polls, sometimes with partly different lists. Pew Research Center's "Fact-Tank" newsletter of 6 August 2019, for example, reported generally higher public confidence in the military, police officers, public school (K-12) principals, scientists, and college and university professors; lower confidence in business leaders and especially elected officials. My citations ignore issues of data quality; interest is mainly in the nominations.

powers of discernment, however, one might still wonder whether the evident threads, and whole tapestries, of alienation, anti-intellectualism, resentment, and paranoia were (are) *institutional* for having been (and being) established at least as attitudes and usages, and perhaps even custom, of first-person experience and second-person standpoint, some of it reflected in legislations. Do they comprise an "institution" of the sort that once was called "national character"? Or are those patterns (if that is what they are; see, e.g., Indiana 2008) only features of individual-personal mentalities?[507] Many have argued that the patterns are manifest not only in ideations but also in materialized culture as social structures (see, e.g., Bourdieu 1990 [1982]; Dahms 2011). Even so, and seemingly especially in US public discourse, recognition of that condition is sublimated under themes of "classlessness" (in the USA) or "proletarian," or now "precariat," cultures (more generally).

John Levi Martin deftly interwove several strands of keen insight when he (2009, p. 339) described "institution" in terms of "free-floating heuristics"—or perhaps a nested set or a nexus of two or more heuristics—each of which "tells us what to do" vis-à-vis one's location within a prevailing structure of sociality. The nesting follows from recursive properties that are evident of at least some institutions.[508] The recursion itself exists as a chain of "know-how" instructions that can be all the more effective for seeming not to be instructional at all but simply an ordinary part of life here-and-now, or "what is to be expected." Indeed, Harrison White's (1992, p. 116) definitional offering—that "each institution is transposable from one of its concrete examples to another"—is an indication of a bounded ubiquity in instances that are taken to be normal and expected.[509] And Young's (1998, p. 146) observation that expectations are both products of and foundational to institutions is consistent with the main dynamic of heuristic guidance as Martin proposed it. Thus, "mutually consistent expectations" of an organization's members sustain its institutional form; for those expectations flow through hierarchies and networks, and from cohort

---

[507] These questions remind me of the one that I was assigned when serving as part of a research task force on a US presidential commission on mental health during the late 1970s: Can a society as such be mentally ill? Being still uncomfortable with the notion of "national character," I had to address the aggregation question nonetheless: If a large percentage of a societal population display symptoms of the pathologies of resentment and paranoia, would that fact mean that the population as such is, "on average," pathological? How large would "large" have to be? Thomas Schelling (1978) arrived in the nick of time, yet his models were not all that helpful to my task.

[508] A recursive operation is governed by a rule that can be applied to the result of an application of the rule. Notice the verb "can be": in the coding of a machine language recursion is written as a procedural call that applies to its consequence, resulting in an enchainment or nesting potentially seriatum ad infinitum, but usually a condition is inserted which, when met, stops the recursion. Recursion need not be ruled automatically, however. One often reads recursive structure in ordinary syntax, for example, present by writer's choice. The "call" can be implicit. Think of the journalist's rule of "5 Ws + How": "Harry met Sally (where) in a restaurant (where) in Seattle (when) last Friday (why) to have lunch (why) to get to know each other (who else) with Alice and Bob (how do you know), according to Harry" (and so forth). Theory can be constructed recursively (see, e.g., Ljungqvist and Sargent 2018).

[509] Likewise, see Hannan, Polos, and Carroll (2007, pp. 31, 57), who also stressed the importance of heuristics for institutional processes (bearing in mind that what I am here calling "institution" they called "organizational form."

to cohort, as heuristics of "what to do" (and how) in a structural location. The heuristics have the informality of customary regularities, although only in part. They also exist surreptitiously or implicitly as well as directly in certifications, licenses, and contracts, in titles and manuals of instruction, in the agendas that specific organizations of an institutional type promulgate among their members.

Martin's insight has intuitive appeal, as we consider, here and in the next section, main positions of occupancy within three institutions: within a family, within a school, and within an organization of work. Watching a child learn how to be a student within all the particularity of *this* school among *these* children and teachers as latest expansion of the child's world, but also observing a representation *not as such* available to the child (the institution of schooling), one can appreciate the complexity of sociality in a regulation that can seem almost endlessly iterative for the school, a similarly long chain of cycles (i.e., an iterative code: "repeat") for experienced teachers, principals, and parents (among other adults), and yet also a virtually unique first-person experience for each child faced with the task of learning *how to be* (or at least "seem") anew. Martin's insight recalls part of a passage first written a century earlier, as a team of researchers stressed that an "institution can be fully understood

> only if we do not limit ourselves to the abstract study of its formal organization [or the specific formal organizations that are instances of a given type of institution] but analyze the way in which it appears in the personal experience of various members of the group and follow the influence which it has upon their lives.... The superiority of life-records over every other kind of material for the purposes of sociological analysis appears with particular force when we pass from the characterization of single data to the determination of facts, for there is no safer and more efficient way of finding among the innumerable antecedents of a social happening the real causes of this happening than to analyze the past of the individuals through whose agency this happening occurred (Thomas and Znaniecki 1958 [1927] p. 1833).[510]

Linkages between cognitive activity and institutions were both assumed and sought by many other social scientists during the early twentieth century—among them Émile Durkheim, whose inquiries will again be considered below. Toward the end of the century Mary Douglas (1986, p. 45), an anthropologist of Durkheimian bent, could declare confidently that any individual person's "most elementary cognitive process [still] depends on social institutions." Of course, as Douglas was well aware, the individual persons who enact institutional agendas are the "thinking substances" of organizations of an institutional type. But the agenda setting that in a sense *is* an institution "of type," as Kenneth Arrow (1974) had emphasized, is usually both so effective and sufficiently efficient that it can easily seem from the inside that, to invoke the title of Douglas' little book, institutions do think—at least the most consequential bits. While variable

---

[510] Rehberg (2016 [1985], p. 106) described George Herbert Mead's conception of institutions as "interactional syntheses." That is fitting, although I think a closer formulation for both the Thomas-Znaniecki and the Mead views would be something like "synthetic formations of or from the average ±2 standard deviations of individual-person actions on key dimensions."

trade-offs between effectiveness and efficiency will be evident in correlation with other conditions, the fact of institutionalization itself keeps the balance in check, though variable range of "in check" (White 1992, pp. 124-125; White 2002, p. 327; Meade 1964).

Overlooking vagueness of conception, scholars have displayed considerable continuing interest in the question how institutions come to be. The framing of the question usually betrays a proclivity that some theorists tend to belabor to their own detriment—namely, the assumption (usually implicit) that for a class of phenomena P there should be one and only one theory, or type of theory, covering uniformly (1) how P came to be; (2) the causes or reasons or conditions of evident variations among P across places, and whether "place" thus counts as "context" for P; and (3) how P, once emergent from its original conditions, changes or develops or evolves. This proclivity can be understood as a persistent preference for advocates of any one of a number of single-factor theories or theoretical perspectives—in other words, the understanding that a proper theory or perspective must be basically "structuralist" or "functionalist" or "evolutionary" or "rational utilitarian" or "conflict resolutionalist" or whatever the favored uni-factor of the time. The other side of that same coin rests in an abundance of evidence that, while experiences (as potential empirical evidences) are very diverse qualitatively as well as quantitatively, well-constructed theories are scarce: they are not easily made, even when the intended coverage of experiences is rather narrowly focused by a master narrative of explanatory perspective. Jack Knight's (1992) review of approaches to the study of institutions offers illustrative material (see also North 1990; Knight 1995). It is apparent from that literature that some organizations have been institutionalized, and that once institutionalized those organizations became especially resilient. It is also apparent from that same literature that the relation of "organization" to "institution" is one of conceptual nesting, as I have already indicated, in the sense that an institution of type A can contain some variety of organizations of type (A1, A2, etc.). Thus, various organizations are recognized as "familial" within the institution, "family": a "nuclear family" is not exactly the same as an "extended family," and neither is exactly the same as a "blended family," and so forth; but they are all instances of the institution, "family," and as such they all consist in temporal as well as spatial organization of relational positions that share interest, means, goals, *and* (yes) function in procreation and support of children. No activity is more basic to sociality than the production of children as members of a sociality here and now. This criterion, the maintenance and continuance of sociality, certainly fits "family" as "institution." One could make an equivalent case for "schooling" as an "institution"; likewise, "work," in the general sense mentioned above. But then, which of our many organizations would be left out? Recalling Gallup's lists, for example, while "newspaper" can easily be regarded as an "organization of work," a means of communication, an instrument of public solidarity, and so forth, by which of the properties would it count as an *institutionalized* organization? One might justifiably wonder whether the conceptual relation of "organization" to "institution" is loose synonymy rather than a nesting. Here we are touching a serious weakness of functionalist logic, of course: it *is* prone to a "survival implies necessity" bias, according to which virtually any extant activity must be not only functional but *vitally* functional (for otherwise the activity would no longer exist). That circularity is not unique to a functionalist logic, however.[511]

Some of the text on institutions has continued the psychologistic presumption of human being as an integral existence prior (logically because genetically or originally) to all human culture. An illustration can be read in Arnold Gehlen's version of the thesis of human being as a "deficient creature" (Mängelwesen): deficient by nature, humans were impelled by necessity to create institutions in order to survive (Gehlen 2004 [1956], pp. 5-8, 46-49). By this view one can entertain a thought experiment of "if, then" reasoning: imagine the disintegration of even the most archaic institutions; what would happen? The main result would be release of subjectivity to return to its natural state—namely, the "mōrdischer Art" ("the murdering kind").[512] This recall of the Hobbesian premise was different in at least one important respect, however. For it was performed well after the horrendous abundance of evidence that "even" with modern institutions, and to no small extent because of modern institutions, tens of millions of people—most of those millions entirely innocent of the arts of war—were blithely and eagerly murdered by people who called themselves patriots of a national socialism. Likewise, beginning four centuries earlier, tens of thousands of people were blithely and sometimes eagerly murdered by immigrants bringing messages of salvation and enlightenment from across the ocean. The very idea that after millions of generations of human beings living via cultural institutions "subjectivity" had not changed, had retained a fundamental "red in tooth and claw" nastiness, remained an idea that could not be proven or disproven by the acts of Holocaust and genocide. Why? Because those acts were acts of nothing less than human organizations of murderous prejudices, thugggery, depths of soulless existences of Homo sapiens. The arts of annihilation had been improved to such an extent by the 1930s that the massacre of millions, previously laid out over the course of centuries (as with the indigenous peoples of the Americas), had now been achieved in less than a decade.

I will not repeat all of my criticism of theorizing by devices of an "originary logic" or from the premise of a psychologism such as is manifest in Arnold Gehlen's version of "human being as deficient creature." Suffice to say that neither approach is necessary to an evolutionary perspective. Young's (1998) approach retains integrity and utility without use of any "originary" orientation. An effort to explain "how institutions emerge out of anarchy" might sound daunting and therefore dauntingly profound, especially when the theorist cannot demonstrate the empirical existence and maintenance of that beginning state for *any* known species of the Homo genus (see Hechter 1990, p. 14; cf. Tomasello 2019). Hartmut Kliemt (1990, p. 78) was on target when, in a reprise of John Locke, he ventured forth with his prediction that "chances are slight that modern game-theoretical analyses of the emergence and maintenance of social institutions will be able

---

[511] Whereas such an application of reason is fitting in a certain logic of necessity, it is not fitting in a logic of contingency. But this limit does not make "function" irrelevant to explanation (see, e.g., Fararo and Skvoretz 1986); it simply means that pointing to a function is in itself generally short of sufficiency.
[512] Karl-Otto Apel (1962) touched on much of this in his review of Gehlen's book, which, he concluded, could be of some use if understood as a "Socratic provocation."

461

to solve the problem of explaining the emergence of nonstrategic rule-providing behavior without already assuming this kind of behavior on the level of individual choice." Indeed. Interesting theoretical problems of the institutionalization of "social organization" begin with, and *within*, that organization, not before its emergence into existence (not even as a "thought experiment"). These problems include, to name only a few, commitment, coordination, agenda setting, and enforcement—four functions sometimes emphasized as primary resources of "the institutional advantage" in literatures on organization—but also trust and mutuality. As such, of course, they arise *throughout* sociality—that is, not only in relations between market and state (see Greif, Milgrom, and Weingast 1994 for an insightful case study) but also between market and/or state and the "smaller" institutions of family, school, and work (among others), as well as intersections among these.[513] The still more telling point is that the really interesting problems appear in "social organization" no doubt before any distinctive instance or type of it has been institutionalized. Again, Kliemt (1990, pp. 74, 68) was very likely right in saying that problems of commitment—keeping individual person-actors attuned to agreed rules and thus to expectations—"will arise almost everywhere if social interaction of rational players is subject to closer scrutiny," to say nothing of relatively irrational players (see Reich and Bearman 2018, and below). Descending neither as a gift of heaven nor as a gift of nature, commitment power and other "rules of the game of life" are "socially provided by regular actions of human beings"— which is to say, *as* and *within* existing sociality. Genuinely *pre*-organized, never organized, human beings (insofar as one can imagine such for a thought experiment) could have accomplished *nothing*: no communication, no meaningful interaction, no post-natal survival.

Forty years earlier Lasswell and Kaplan (1950, pp. 29, 31, 33) laid out a framework that, like Hechter's, placed definitive weight on "solidarity and cooperation," qualities that they took to be the central meaning of "organization" (and thus of "group": "an organized aggregate"), the "traits" of which are "patterned as institutions." Yet they, like Kliemt but unlike Hechter, saw no problem with the view that group formation takes place in the midst of "persistent groupings" (no need to re-invent "grouping"). Why did Hechter find that objectionable? Because, by his own account (1990, p. 14), it depends on an "exogenous" explanatory condition, thus neglecting "the question of the prime mover." As pointed out in the previous section, however, the line between what is "inside" and what is "outside" is *analytic*: empirically unnecessary, the line is contingent on, thus relative to, how one defines positions in a system of relations. Lasswell and

---

[513] There is another kind of problem, too, a tendency to cease analysis prematurely. As Garicano and Rayo (2016) document, organizations can fail because of the problem of commitment. But what accounts for that? Especially in hierarchical organizations "weak commitment" may be a reflection of "weak incentives," which in turn (assuming executives are paying attention) could be a cost-benefit decision. But this instrumentalist view could miss what is in fact a disagreement or incompatibility of nonrational interests or goal commitments (see, e.g., Greif 1994). Similar chains but different valences can be seen in flatter "network" organizations. In similar vein, invoking "institution" as explanation can simply beg the question, as demonstrated by Acemoglu and Robinson (2012) via their rhetorical question, "Why do nations fail?" Invoking "institutional failures" only re-asks the question. Mekhennet's (2017, p. 318) notice of a tendency to a fallacy of misplaced agency is also germane.

Kaplan were nearer to target when they advised that they were "interested in neither groups nor individuals as 'social atoms' but in interpersonal relations," which "under specified conditions exhibit organization of varying kinds and degrees."[514]

Of the three institutions on which I focus, "family" in the broad sense might be accounted as the oldest, although something like "hunting and gathering" as analogue to "work" would surely have been as old. Who can know how either began? It occurred so long ago, without thoughtful planning or design, and long before the gradual process of speciation into Homo sapiens.[515] With such questions in general, there simply could be no Event One or Date One. As William Riker (1995, p. 121) said of "the experience of creating institutions," no punctual event defines a starting point: "No institution is created de novo." Most likely the process occurred via random variation in relevant practices, on which relative-advantage selection worked, coupled with habituation and continued selection against weakest alternative organizational forms. It is important to remember that evolutionary selection works primarily as a "negative" force, in the sense that selection is *against* the least well-adapted, rather than *for* the most well-adapted practices. This bias tends to conserve variation and thus variability. Amartya Sen drew attention to this difference when he (e.g., 1993) urged that attention be given directly to those institutionalized flows of information that support and enhance *capabilities* of actors, their "beings and doings," in addition to summaries such as population-based vital rates and GDP per capita. Tufekci (2017) has made good application of this proposal in her study of organizational capacities, three of them in particular: narrative, or developing, promulgating, and following through on a distinctive story; disruptive, or means of gaining attention, negative and positive, and directing it toward a desired end; and institutional, including electoral, or the ability to induce change in established ways of influence and activations of goals, including changing the means, even the goals. All of these capacities are reminiscent of White's (1992) emphasis on our proclivities to identify "self and other" via storytelling, Martin's (2011) emphasis on heuristics, and of course Kant's emphasis on legislation. Tufekci's discussion is especially pertinent for the institutional capacity because of her (2017, pp. 192, 195-222) extensive uses of signaling theory and technology. As has been repeatedly said, one of the most important facts about institutions is the stability and resilience afforded organizations of a type. But that strength can also be seen as ossification insofar as it resists rejuvenative innovation. The path dependencies, habituations, or self-similarity conservations that are characteristic of institutions tend to selective impedances of filtering and updating. As will be argued in the next section, we could be doing much better.

Riker's (e.g., 1980, 1995) pursuits of the charter activities of those who sought to design a "First New Nation" were attentive to the traps of originary thinking, especially obsessions with

---

[514] Note that one of the benefits of this feature of the analytic model is that an actor, whether individual person or collectivity such as a commercial firm, can manipulate the location of the inside-versus-outside boundary—the better, for example, to "externalize costs" (which is another way of saying "transfer them to a more general population," a favored strategy of corporate capitalism's version of social welfare).
[515] The condition has enthralled some theorists so much (e.g., Hayek 1967b, p. 96) that they recommend leaving such processes to thoughtless happenstance (cf. Farrier 2020 and Koselleck 1985 [1979]).

neatly punctuated points of departure. Theories of ontogeny such as Tomasello's (2019) offer useful explorations within a culture of identities, so long as it is clear not only that theorization is the potentially useful point of it but also that most of the propositional text, especially the boldest parts, will likely remain untestable. My primary intent in this section is not to survey a history of "institution building," however, nor is it to offer a "theory of institutions," especially one that would seek representative or even simply wide coverage of this "class of P." After all, much of the required effort would have necessarily been preparatory to the theory proper, beginning with a defensible answer to the question, "What is my list of specimen cases of P, each with proper spatial and temporal markers or subscripts?" Not only Riker but many others as well have been there before me, and before Riker, too. Some attention to their efforts will sketch the terrain of endeavor well enough to explain my claim of selectivity—to focus, that is, on a small handful of institutions that, today, channel a huge proportion of the daily activities of most persons with enduring consequences whether small or great to the person and sometimes distinctively to one or another collectivity: family, as locus first of one's own infancy and childhood, then of part of one's adult habitations; education, as child-upbringing and as formal schooling but also as a site of work in which authority of voice is crucial and perpetually vulnerable to the latest charges of a Socratic undermining; and work—that is, occupational employment both as continued learning and as per-person participation in another collective regime, this one of producing, distributing, exchanging, and consuming human resources, among them sociality. Many of other typically nominated institutions—those of public governance, for instance, of healthcare, of religious concerns, of the arts and sciences, of death, and so on—will be treated only in ancillary ways (where by "ancillary" I mean person-actor involvements as educational and occupational activities) or not at all.

While the three institutions that I have just cited do account for most of the channelings of everyday actions and effects by the vast majority of members of modern societies, my neglect of "the market" and of "the state" in that list of major institutions is glaringly obvious. Even more glaring would be the absurd claim that neither is important to those channelings; for each is an omnipresent, pluripotent organization of complex dialectical relations, especially those of enablement/constraint. Herrick Chapman (2018, p. 8), a specialist in French history, recently quoted Charles de Gaulle's address to the council of state following the army revolt in Algeria— "There is a France only thanks to the state, and only by the state can France be maintained"— and then said of that conventional understanding that it had behind it the force of "sound history and potent myth." I would not imagine it otherwise. Applications have varied greatly, no doubt, but something of that same moment of "the state" can be said of most, probably all, modern societies (even during their failures, as in Zimbabwe and Venezuela, and severe tests, as in the USA after 2016 and the UK following their "Brexit" referendum). My principal interest here, however, is in something both smaller and larger than Gaullist grandeur—namely, the processes involved in aggregations of effects, and of senses of efficacy, from the individual level to levels of collective organization—and aside from electoral participations (which are heavily "mythic" in ways well documented by Achen and Bartels 2016, Packer 2013, Pomerantsev 2014, Taylor

2019, among others) few individuals are effective actors of state even at local level, despite the fact that many agencies of state employ a great many person-actors in administration of legislations, executions, and adjudications, including those of family, schooling, and work. On the other hand, "state" as governance and administration is more or less effective on and to virtually all person-actors in modern societies, and in ways that can affect an individual person's sense of efficacy directly and indirectly. This has to do with the "macro-to-micro" side of Coleman's diagram (as this was described in Figure 5.1, p. 398) and, similarly, in Durkheim's quest for a solution to what he saw as a grievous "crisis of individualism." The relevance is undoubted, although I differ from both Coleman and Durkheim in conceptualizations. But pursuing that relevance is simply too great a task for this volume. Perhaps in another lifetime.

Recalling those words by Charles de Gaulle, one wonders whether the chief officers of the Syndicat Général de la Bourse de Commerce de Parishave would have said the same. Just as the complexity of the institution known as "the state" is great, so, too, "the market"—which, like "the state," is prone to think of itself (speaking elliptically) with definite article, singular number, nominative dominance, an image of mastery buttressed by potent myth. Vernacular speech has sometimes referred to a contest of collective actors: *the* state versus *the* market. One could think of them rather as not quite orthogonally intersecting matrices (see Schumpeter 1976 [1942]), and thereby avoid confusions that tend to equate "collectivity" and "sociality" (without remainder on either side). It is not that collectivities do not exist; nor that sociality would survive in absence of collectivity (at very least, the mother-child dyad). Rather, it is that sociality persists whether any given person-actor is presently member of any particular collectivity or, excepting conditions of sustenance deprivation, none at all.

Certainly "market" is a bundle of heuristics and in those dynamics qualifies as a "master narrative" of enabling/constraining guidelines. It is not without conditions, however. Thus, here again Lockean theory was relevant most especially because of failures, not of "market" as such but of the pre-contractual conditions of agreement in *trust*, confidence not primarily in relations of anonymity as such but in relations—thus regular expectations of mutual interestedness—of an underlying sociality in which trust and therefore market transactions depend. It is that basis in a pre-existing sociality (i.e., one that *is* already, and therefore sustains negotiation) that serves as the condition by which market process operates as a distributed process, the distribution largely following institutional channels—those of market as such, but not at all restricted to them. It is this penetration into virtually all parts, aspects, and perspectives of experience that is manifest as the image of mastery, market mastery, and it has been so successful because it *is* basically the distributed process of sociality—an insight that grew among the "Scottish moralists" as well as Kant and others (see, e.g., Schneider 1967).

The myth of mastery pertains as much to "the market" as to "the state." Both institutions fail in parts frequently, but the failures tend to be in processes distributed at some remove from the core of the institution. Moreover, some of the failure is hidden or camouflaged. With regard to the market model, for example, partial failures of the model's core, the pricing mechanism, typically induce an array of inefficiencies contrary to the image of market process as epitome of

465

efficiency; but these inefficiencies are usually costumed in ambiguity due to the fact that most observers tend individually to focus on one or the other "side" of the dialectic, ignoring the fact that the pricing mechanism is inherently dialectical. That property shows up most readily in the relativity of process terms in exchange transactions: "buy," for example, is simply the other face of "sell," and vice versa. Accountants have known this since Luca Pacioli promoted advantages of double-entry bookkeeping when he published his mathematics textbook in 1494. Most people today still do not use double-entry, however, finding it strange and confusing that each and every entry must appear twice, once as a debit and once as a credit.

Were the market model actually the master that some apologists trumpet, surely at least a few of the most obvious inefficiencies would have disappeared long ago. One would think it in the interest of employers, for example, that they have large assorted pools of highly qualified potential employees from whom to choose. They usually do not. Potential employees should be highly skilled in all of the skills employers seek. Probably most are not, in part because whereas educational attainment is primarily a signaling effect of credentials for potential employers and the credentialing usually occurs before age 25 or 30, skills continue to evolve for high-wage jobs. The institutions of family, child-rearing, and formal education should make better effort to stay abreast of changing conditions and probable future conditions, including especially the probable future conditions of work. If institutions were more efficient, the rate at which poor matching between "employer demand" and "employee supply" would not have been increasing but would now be far lower and tending to zero. Employees would be better attuned to the accumulating costs of their own firm's externalizations of pollutions, therein charging those costs in the long run to the public treasury but in the meantime to the localities of poorer inhabitants. The list goes on. The main point that scholars such as Douglass North (1990) continued to urge is that analytic models must take institutions into account not simply because markets fail massively now and then (as in the great crash of the financial market in 2007-08) but because markets operate via institutional channels which are replete with inequalities of condition, ambiguities, frictions, and mounds of "just in case" bumf, much of it state-mandated with the cost to commercial firms externalized via write-offs against otherwise taxable income. Such is how even the nearest real-world approximations to the abstract "market model" actually operate. The near collapse of all financial institutions during the events of 2007-08 would have been complete had not a few highly insightful persons had both checkbook and credit card issued by the national treasury (cf. Geithner 2014; Bernanke, Geithner, and Paulson 2019; Glantz 2019). It is a mistake, moreover, to attribute the boom-and-bust cycles uniquely to "the capitalist system." The main difference is, in that regard, that capitalism tends to be more transparent than centrally managed economies, in which functions of both economic and political institutions are managed by the same persons, the same segments of society in which there is less of what Hume called "elbow room." The dynamics of "boom and bust" occur in centrally managed economies, too. Think of Argentina, Greece, Italy, Venezuela, and Zimbabwe, to name only a few recent examples.

A major strand in the literature of theory treats "institution" effectively as a propagative systemic equilibrium: it induces equilibria in its component organizations and in its effects on external relations, inter-institutional relations, as well. This strand runs through not only Hegel's treatment of bureaucracy, which Max Weber adopted, but also through neo-Kantian formulations to Durkheim, among others. Randall Calvert (1995, p. 82), repeating the understanding that "institutions are equilibria," located it in the work of late twentieth-century economists. But the same conceptualization can be seen in earlier work, including Durkheim's statement in one of his last writings (published in 1917 in the *Bulletin de la Société française de philosophie*) — namely, that "human

> societies present a new phenomenon of a special nature, which consists in the fact that certain ways of acting are imposed, or at least suggested *from outside* the individual and are added on to his own nature: such is the character of the 'institutions' (in the broad sense of the word) which the existence of language makes possible, and of which language itself is an example. They take on substance as individuals succeed each other without this succession destroying their continuity; their presence is the distinctive characteristic of human societies, and the proper subject of sociology (Durkheim 1982 [1901], p. 248).[516]

That sense of systemic stability or resilience was already presented by Durkheim in the preface to his second edition of *The Rules of Sociological Method*, wherein he (1982 [1901], p. 45) adopted the word "institution" as a special term denoting "all the beliefs and modes of behavior instituted by the collectivity," a "synthesis" that "occurs outside each one of us (since a plurality of consciousnesses are involved)," and so "it has necessarily the effect of crystallizing, or of instituting outside ourselves, certain modes of action and certain ways of judging which are independent of the particular individual will considered separately." Durkheim's way of placing "individual person" as such in contrast to "collectivity" as such illustrates the dilemma created by careless drawing of analytical boundaries across the inside/outside dialectic.

In any case, Durkheim's locution about a "succession" that does not destroy "continuity" was presumably his way of referring to the process of regulation of complex relations already known as "equilibration," or the dynamics of regulation that seeks "equal balance" across many relations. This was not a new concept: the Latin-derived word itself, present in English texts from the early 1600s, was translation of the Greek "isorropia," which appears in texts at least as old as Herodotus (then in Plato, Euripides, etc.). Granted, the meaning tended mostly to a notion of "equal balance," not "system relations," but it often included the idea of process—that is, the process of attaining and then maintaining an equal balance of forces (e.g., a mental balance of interests, goals, etc.). Leibniz (1921 [1704], pp. 118-124) has sometimes been cited for having written a passage (in his rebuttal of John Locke on human understanding) that can be read as an endorsement of "dynamic equilibrium," or the idea that "equilibrium" is not a constant but a state of regulated variation. The key passage, written in French, refers to the fact that in German the word typically used to name a clock's pendulum or a pocket watch's balance wheel, "Unruhe," means "unrest" or "disquietude." I do not dispute the reading: "le balancier d'une horloge" does refer to either of these two means of regulating the movement of a clockwork (whether weight-

---

[516] Note that Durkheim's1917 paper was reprinted in the translation of the second edition of his *Rules*. Also note that the above-quoted passage reflects Durkheim's "homo duplex" thesis, which, like the Lockean problem of precontractual conditions of contract, supposes social conditions of a "human nature" prior to the advent of human sociality (see, e.g., Durkheim 1973 [1914]).

or spring-driven); and the notion of "mechanics," and more especially whether it applied to the dynamism of animal life, were topics of major concern to Leibniz.[517] The passage appears in his section about "modes of pleasure and pain," a very old theme that included such notions as a "golden mean" and a "balance of virtues," among other expressions of a process of dialectical equilibration. Much the same conceptualization of "dynamics of equilibrium" can be read in the ancient Greek texts, as later in Rome by, for example, Seneca. This should not be construed as a version of the "best of all possible worlds" impression of a dynamic equilibrium, however, for it is generally at such moment that disruption will be most notable. Or, as Thomas Laqueur (2015, p. 117) cautioned, "It is in the nature of an old regime to seem adamantine and unending until it begins to end."

Later in Leibniz' century Hume, having set aside fanciful disquisitions professing certain knowledge of human origins, addressed the logic of convention and agreement as person actions that already presuppose themselves, and had this to say in his *Treatise* (book 3, part 2, §2), about the origin of justice and property:

> I observe that it will be for my interest to leave another in the possession of his goods, *provided* he will act in the same manner with regard to me. He is sensible of a like interest in the regulation of his conduct. When this common sense of interest is mutually expressed and is known to both, it produces a suitable resolution and behaviour. And this may properly enough be called a convention or agreement betwixt us, though without the interposition of a promise, since the actions of each of us have a reference to those of the other and are performed upon the supposition that something is to be performed on the other part. Two men who pull the oars of a boat do it by an agreement or convention, though they have never given promises to each other. Nor is the rule concerning the stability of possession the less derived from human conventions that it arises gradually, and acquires force by a slow progression and by our repeated experience of the inconveniences of transgressing it. On the contrary, this experience assures us still more that the sense of interest has become common to all our fellows, and gives us a confidence of the future regularity of their conduct, and it is only on the expectation of this that our moderation and abstinence are founded. In like manner are languages gradually established by human conventions without any promise [and] gold and silver become the common measures of exchange ... (Hume 1964 [1739-40], p. 490).

Trust *in* as well as of sociality, whether in any particular experience of it honored or broken, is always already present, exists in and for the typical person as an acquired skill of sociality, and is implicit in that person's expectations and self-reflexivity. Moreover, it is maintained in and by the "regularity of conduct"—in other words, regularity as a dynamic seeking of balance. Two and a half centuries later Peyton Young (2015, p. 360) said of that remarkable passage that Hume had conceived not only the importance of *dynamic* equilibrium but also three key factors in "the evolution of social norms": (1) equilibria of repeated games; (2) they evolve through a dynamic learning process; and (3) they underpin many forms of social and economic order.

---

[517] English translators of "le balancier" have varied between "pendulum" and "balance." One might suppose that Leibniz had in mind a pendulum-regulated clock, given the date, but in fact the pocket watch had been a popular item already for more than a century.

By today's standards, nonetheless, eighteenth-century understandings of "equilibrium" were rudimentary, for the general tendency continued to emphasize static condition, often with an expectation of certainty attached. Durkheim's posture at turn of the twentieth century was far from rare. An emphasis on "normality" in categorial sense still dominated, such that it could be taken for granted that "proper balance" once obtained is self-reproductive except when altered by external force. The very idea that equilibrium as a regulative state or condition is *itself* dynamic, continuously adjudicative and adjustive, eluded secure grasp. Gradually more scholars became comfortable with the notion of a regulative process of complex relations in which the forces of component contingent processes are held in variable balance via "filters and updates," which are themselves contingent processes that engineers have long described as "feedback loops," some of them positive and some of them negative. Hahn and Solow (1995, p. 134) captured this in their conception that institutions "should be seen in part as adaptive mechanisms, and not merely as obstacles to the achievement of a frictionless economy."[518]   In general, negative feedbacks tend to be dampers (as in any of the martingale processes); positive feedbacks tend to be multipliers or accelerators.[519]   An equilibrium is generally maintained through carefully calibrated series of information filters and resulting updates of first-order processes, some of the updates dampening while others increase proportionality of output to a given rate of input. If either the damper or the multiplier (accelerator) fails, the system of relations departs from its equilibrium. Under some conditions both modifiers can malfunction at the same time, in a way that induces a chaotic outcome, which may be an orderly chaos (as in, e.g., "Lorenz' butterfly") at least for some duration but usually collapses the system into entropy (loss of information). War is one such condition, usually massively destructive. Much has been made of "sensitive dependence" as a trigger of a later chaotic dynamism. But that is hardly the only manifestation of an equilibrating path dependence that can wreak havoc. At personal level, one may, usually does, have choices in an equilibrated state, choices that may well matter in the margin (and it is usually only in the margin that personal choices matter). But many historians (most recently Clark 2012; Tooze 2014) have demonstrated that marginal choices can accumulate into horrific effects, especially with the aid of multiplier effects of technology. Institutional channeling tends to promote stabilizing path dependencies of the effects of person-actions, and these dampers will usually dissolve sensitive-dependence effects. But processes of filtering information and appropriate updating are typically inefficient and sometimes do fail.[520]

---

[518] The last part of their sentence reflects their criticism of the brand of macroeconomic theory that took Newtonian law as model (Newton's laws being "frictionless" because proper domain is a vacuum).

[519] The notion of a "martingale process" comes from the physical equipment applied to a horse—straps that prevent the horse from fully extending his or her neck, thus dampening acceleration and maximum speed. Conversely, a "multiplier" introduces a nonlinearity in the opposite direction, *increasing* the proportionality of output to a given input. Unregulated, a multiplier can induce severe instability, even collapse, of a system of relations.

[520] The resilience of equilibrium can sometimes surprise. For example, standard theory in economics had held that one of the major costs of inflation is a disruption in the reliability of price signals, that the signals of price-setting behaviors at micro-level become erratic and lead to inefficiency, perhaps ineffectiveness, in uses of monetary policy at macro-level. Work by Nakamura, Steinsson, Sun, and Villar (2018), based on a major new data set built from detailed records of the high-inflation years of the US economy (1970s), indicates that relative price signals maintained stability to a remarkable degree.

It has been remembered now and then that institutionalism, as an explicitly distinguished disciplinary approach, began in economics as a reaction to the prevailing "static" tendency of theory. If one wants a reminder of what that reaction meant at the time, read Thorstein Veblen's 1898 essay on why economics was still "not an evolutionary science." There is some irony in the realization that whereas physical science was broiling in turmoil over serious discrepancies in Newtonian framework, many social scientists knew nothing of it and remained champions of the view that "evolutionary theory" and "scientific theory" were strictly antithetical worldviews. If any theory was expected to be taken seriously as scientific, its principles had to be timeless. Moreover, insofar as a "mainstream" existed in economics, it was too restrictive in its attachment to the individual person as sum total of economic phenomena. Institutions such as "the market" had their own dynamics that exceeded simple individual actions of exchange. This criticism was directed not only to economic inquiry in the USA and Great Britain, as is sometimes imagined, but also to emerging developments of the discipline on the continent, a prime example being Carl Menger's marginalist account of the acts of individual persons in market transactions. Veblen's emphasis on "institutionalist" approaches amounted to an expansionist revision of classical liberalism in the Anglophone world. Born one year after Veblen's paper appeared, Friedrich Hayek, like Menger an Austrian and initiated in what became known as the Austrian school of economics, disputed the Mengerian approach by launching his own rather subtle renovation of classical liberalism toward a more institutionalist perspective (see, e.g., Hayek 1948). In sum, "the problem of aggregation," though not yet so named, was disturbing if not yet disrupting settled conceptions of central processes of modern society. This was also the time of another great wave of globalization (also not yet called that), due to technical advances in long-distance transport (trains, steamships, aircraft on horizon) and communication (telegraph, telephone, radio on horizon), as well as increasing integrations of market relations.[521] Thirdly, and manifested most conspicuously at turn of the century by Durkheim, widely expanding interests in and some movements toward democratization of individual liberties had been raising new alarms about stability and social order—or as Edmund Burke (1756, p. 1), had put it, laying "open the foundation of Society." Burke's satirical skewering of the idea of a "natural society" existent prior to the inventions of human institutions—or, to quote his subtitle, prior to all of "the miseries and evils arising to mankind from every species of artificial society"—had been long forgotten. Reading Veblen in conjunction with Burke measures how much had changed during the century and a half.

Burke had used the word "institution" as both indication of human production and image of stability. By the evidence of his mid-century satire and of his late works such as *Reflections* in 1790, he did not find that conjunction to be problematic. By the middle decades of the next century, however, arrangements instituted by human production were increasingly viewed as potentially disruptive in unexpected and perhaps unpleasant ways. At the time, few readers gave much attention to writings by Karl Marx and Friedrich Engels. Even their *Communist Manifesto* of 1848 generated little alarm. Contained within it lay an insight into the "foundation of society"

---

[521] By saying "another great wave," I am acknowledging as a previous wave the so-called Age of Exploration, which was also the beginning of Europe's colonial interests in a kind of global integration of markets.

that later readers would find strange: every production is also a consumption; one cannot make something that has not existed without destroying something that already exists. This insight was not unique to Marx and Engels. Writing a recapitulation about some "great leading facts in palæontology" in the tenth chapter of his new book, Charles Darwin concluded,

> We can thus understand how it is that new species come in slowly and successively; how species of different classes do not necessarily change together, or at the same rate, or in the same degree; yet in the long run that all undergo modification to some extent. The extinction of old forms is the almost inevitable consequence of the production of new forms. We can understand why when a species has once disappeared it never reappears. Groups of species increase in numbers slowly, and endure for unequal periods of time; for the process of modification is necessarily slow, and depends on many complex contingencies (Darwin 1859, p. 343).

This traffic between biological theory and the theory of political economy had been underway for some time, of course, most obviously since the days of Scottish thinkers such as Bernard Mandeville, Adam Smith, Adam Ferguson, and David Hume, Johann Goethe and the von Humboldt bothers in Germany, Geoffroy Saint-Hilaire and Georges Cuvier in France. The idea that destruction could be creative was undoubtedly not being expressed for the first time. But it captured imaginations then, as later (e.g., Schumpeter 1942), as it centered on temporal dynamics of what appeared to be major regulatory processes in different arenas of science. The idea that production of new forms has disruptive and destructive effects had a long heritage in traditionalist registers, from which cautionary notices were issued against "changes that are too rapid" and/or "too large in scale." Burke's *Reflections* continued that tradition, as did a century later Durkheim's worries about losses of braking functions that had been performed by various organizations of the middle range. Their concerns have not been forgotten: most economists, for instance, agree today that "positive feedbacks" (i.e., multiplier effects) should be monitored by "automatic governors," the trick being to gauge the right second- or third-order equilibrium. An interesting expression of such ruminations during the years from, say, Mandeville's *Enquiry* (!732) as well as his prior *Fable of the Bees* (1924 [1714, 1729]) to Adolph Berle and Gardiner Means' (1932) treatise on the modern corporation took the form of repetitive debates about the relative merits of two models of economic probity, the entrepreneur and the rentier, to each of which the subtitle of *Fable* could be applied, though differently: *Private Vices, Public Virtues*. The rentier lives off the land (and those who work it for him) in aristocratic order, conserving traditions and maintaining the peace, whereas the entrepreneur thrives of fails by taking risks, making new products, and perhaps advancing progressively.

That last sentence is stylized to exaggerate the would-be task of intermediation. But the exaggeration is not far from the dominant view of contestation until recent times (and not *that* far even today). Images of the entrepreneur are in fact far older than Mandeville. The historian (and one-time army commander) Thucydides had impressively good things to say of the epicheirētēs, an "enterprising person" (from the root word, "hand," or one who takes in hand to lead or to do something), as did Thucydides' successor, Xenophon, among others. The core meaning of the Greek word is very close to the Latin verb "entreprendre" (to undertake), thence the French noun "entrepreneur." In seventeenth-century England they were called "adventurers" (as in the Virginia Company of London, for instance)—risk-takers indeed. Vilfredo Pareto (1963 [1916], p. 1559) later said that such persons were "adventurous souls, hungry for novelty," and, unlike the cautiousness of rentiers, who fear loss of the patrimony, brave risk-takers who knew, or thought they knew, how to calculate gradients of uncertainty and future horizons acted as if they had comparatively low discount rates. Adam Smith later styled the duplex as entrepreneurial "merchants" and "gentlemen" rentiers—a contrast that retains force yet today, although it has become a bit more refined (see e.g., Piketty, Postel-Vinay and Rosenthal 2014; Freire-Gibbs and Nielsen 2014).[522] But make no mistake: most of the "adventurous souls" sought "novelty" as a way of making their material progress in the worlds of their time. While land ("real property") remained the primary factor of production well into the 1800s, the large majority of it was owned or controlled by rentiers via laws of inheritance (and primogeniture, by law or custom, in many countries). By the time of Berle and Means' (1932) explanation of the new corporate form, then Ronald Coase's (1937) explanation of the commercial firm as a privatized "internal market" (that is, a partly entrepreneurial market within the larger market), the revolutionary organization of forces of that dialectic of production/consumption, creation/destruction, as foreseen by Marx and by Darwin in their different realms, had spawned its own institutionalized standing (see Dahms 2000, for example; Block 2002; Hont 2005; Larsen 2010).

This "market revolution," as it has sometimes been called (Larsen 2010), did not mark the advent of market relations as such, nor did it engender a new arena occupied by cooperations, competitions, and conflicts between market and state. But it certainly did both involve and entail sequences of increased organizational complexity and corresponding means of regulation. Here again, Durkheim's (e.g., 1984 [1902]) focus on organizational forms and functions reflected a range of popular concerns, positive and negative. His contrast between forms of solidarity offers one window on those concerns, but a window that also insinuates some later evaluative changes. Whereas Durkheim identified the older or traditionalist form of solidarity as mechanical and the newer, more modern form as organic, the critical tendency today is to evaluate the older form as organic (connoting wholesomeness, alive, natural) and the newer as mechanical (connoting inert, unhealthy, unnatural, artificial). Durkheim's understanding was different: the older, simpler form was based on similarity of parts, homogeneity, growth by duplication and segmentation, while the newer more complex form was based on greater interdependencies of dissimilar parts, growth by generation of new kinds, new specializations, new differences. If the rentier mentality imagines reproduction by budding, grafting, and cloning, the entrepreneurial mentality imagines reproduction by recombinations, mutations, and drift.

In Durkheimian terms, then, one could say that "institution" consists in specific forms of the "conscience collective." Would that add anything to what has already been said in regard to

---

[522] Tallies by the Oxford English Dictionary indicate that the word "entrepreneur" was seldom used prior to 1870. But that would very likely be true of all words that entered the lexicon as technical or specialty terms. As recently as 2005 a prominent economist, Edward Lazear, could publish an article simply entitled "entrepreneurship" in a prestigious journal (proposing a new theory thereof). For a recent cautionary note about using words such as "theory" as if "neutral" or immune to anachronistic usage, see Kearnes and Walter (2019), who point out (fittingly) that "speculators" in seventeenth-century England "were castigated for laying claim to knowledge on the basis of conceptual virtuosity without having mastered the relevant disciplines." Shades of Platonic criticisms of the Sophists.

an understanding of the concept, "institution"? But the very question is posing an anachronism inasmuch as Durkheim both used the term and wrote much about "institutions" well before most other scholars at his time. Perhaps the better question is a transposition—namely, is "institution" only another name for the "conscience collective," the subjectivity/objectivity of the contents of a shared consciousness, conceptual scheme, knowledge, expectations, and so on? Durkheim's "conscience collective" was not, after all, white light. It has colorful patterning, as it were, and the colors that make a pattern might be considered, metaphorically, as representations of the variety of institutions, the variety of institutionalized forms of organization. To remark on the "stability and resilience of institutions" might be nothing more than to think the stability and resilience of our prevailing patterns of thinking. Or is there more? Perhaps, in other words, we have only been circulating among various names (or "technical terms") for the same phenomena, or the same basic dimensions of one phenomenon.

If we conceive "institution" as a system of relations that form distributed processes across levels of organization (as in the micro, meso, macro gradient), we are clearly within the territory that Manski called "complexity within regulation." The regulation is made somewhat simpler by the fact that much of the complexity consists in redundancy and overdetermination. The redundancy can be seen in the fact that most organizations of an institutional type display massive evidence of it in the form of iterations and recursions: following the same heuristics, the same agenda items, with the same regulation categories of actor, and so forth. The main temporal dimension is iterative, in effect a code that at regular intervals stipulates one main command, "repeat." This looks very much like Durkheim's mechanical solidarity. Much of the distributed process, especially those parts that are mainly hierarchical (i.e., the micro, meso, macro gradient), features recursion more than iteration, and it is recursion, or the regularity of filtering and updating, that produces much of the overdetermination that one can observe in the enablement/constraint effects within organizations of specific institutional type. This looks much like Durkheim's organic solidarity. With those parallels in mind, one can perhaps better see the tendency to duplications within the heritage of several new terms—for instance, path dependency vis-à-vis habituation, weak versus strong ties in network relations, entrepreneurial vis-à-vis renter interests, and so forth—all of which display similar patterns of information function.

In advance of some discussions that follow I want to add another set of "technical terms" (more a matter of perspective), having to do with "long-memory process." The issue of stability points to the fact that many institutions have had a long evolutionary history (family and work among them, and in a more limited fashion schooling as well). In order to grasp the main point, consider a standard per-person Markov model. In most instances the effective period of temporality is short, in the sense that the process being modeled is quickly re-iterative. Each new outcome state of a given process is fully or nearly fully absorptive of effects (information) of prior operations of the same process. In Markov terms, the "window of lag" is short; no shadow of prior outcomes, no delayed effect of prior operations, affect the present outcome; or, if there *is* a delayed effect, it is small and soon absorbed in current operation. But there are exceptions, and the exceptions tend to be very notable, *if* one is prepared to detect them.

By way of illustration, imagine two men born the same year to different families in, say, eastern Nebraska. They graduate high school the same year, then attend the same university and obtain a baccalaureate, following which they go to work for the same company in Omaha. At age 45 each is in middle management, Jay staying with the company that first hired them, Ray having moved to another Omaha company. Jay's annual salary is about $15,000 greater than Ray's. If one were familiar with the research literature on social mobility in the Midwestern region of the USA, what status factor would first come to mind as "explanation" of the income difference? There are several possibilities, of course, but one of the most likely is difference in parental status: Ray was born to a farming family in eastern Nebraska in, say, 1952, while Jay was born to an Omaha family the same year. Sometimes parental status, whether measured as father's occupation or mother's education, casts a "delayed" effect above and beyond all of the intermediate stages—birth cohort, level of education, first job, starting salary, and so forth—that would be typical determinants of future life chances. In this illustration we have observed one of the less usual "success stories": two men born in 1952 of Midwestern families obtained college degrees: that in itself was an improbable event, but once it happened its implication became integrated in a then-typical sequence of employment success. The question then becomes, why would a difference in parental status have anything to do with later success? Why haven't all implications of that difference already been integrated into the respective career trajectories? The answer is (when this sort of delayed effect occurs) all implications *have* been integrated, but not all of them have become visible in effect. The delay of *effect* can be due to different possible mechanisms. One is simple prejudicial discrimination. Imagine, for instance, that the difference in parental status was not occupational or educational but racial: Ray was born to an African American family. That in itself would easily have been enough to account for the disparity of income; indeed, it would have made that disparity even more telling, precisely because the fact of Ray's comparative success at various stages along the way would have been an even less likely sequence of events, given racial discriminations, only then to suffer discrimination in wage rate. (Women in general will recognize the point.) Similar if less "blanket ready" prejudicial discrimination could have accounted for the disparity for a white Ray, too, of course. An adage such as "You can take the boy out of the farm, but you can't take the farm out of the boy" might be said with genuine intent to compliment, but it can also be double-edged. Then, too, one can imagine that the effect of "farm background" was mainly or even entirely within Ray's self-image: a less confident person, due to his own doubts about "being from farm country," could have been the dynamic; and because the inside/outside dialectic contains a fluidity that analysis strives to assign to one side or the other, self-image can be absorptive of other-image (including generalized other-image, or the "they") *and* vice versa, as Erving Goffman (e.g., 1959, 1974) so deftly illustrated.

Shadows of long past conditions or events can travel in a variety of ways and influence the course of potential events all along the route. Or having seemingly been left behind for good, the effects can pop into experienced reality without warning. Conversely, however, the warning can be explicit from the beginning. Perhaps the most salient case of this latter condition is yet another sort of "original sin" public announcement: "Once a criminal always a criminal." The standard of jurisprudence in the USA tends to be two-faced: a recognition of restitution and redemption is offered the newly convicted person via sufferance of designated penalty for only a finite period of time; but on the other hand, once that period of time has ended, often the person must contend with a label virtually as visible as a brand to the forehead, "ex-convict," foretelling one or more of various and possibly permanent disqualifications (e.g., occupational licensing or other job opportunities, housing options, voting, and so forth).

The durability of many institutions suggests that they might be, or consist at least partly in, long-memory processes. Here again, of course, there is a terminological question: what counts as "long memory"? Our physical science has offered one answer, in that we now observe events, and the processes that generated those events, that happened 130 million years ago (in the galaxy NGC 4993, the event recorded as GW170817, a neutron-star merger). This is but one part of another origin story that some of us like to tell, another sort of Ziggy Stardust tale that continues to entertain. It surely does count as "deep time," if not exactly what we generally mean by "deep history." While the measure of "human scale" does include such expanses, these are well beyond what ordinarily we mean by the time of institutions. An institution such as family certainly has a history measured in tens, even hundreds of thousands of years, depending on when we choose to start the clock. But the question is not how old the institution as such but how long the shadow cast by any event or "stage" of its history. In the case of US history there is reasonably good evidence, to cite one example, that the importation of slave labor beginning early in the 1600s not only disrupted then-extant relations of familial organization among the imported enslaved persons but also continued to mangle those relations, in comparison to the corresponding relations of dominant (European descended) populations, to such an extent that one can point to long-memory effects of chattel slavery on and within familial organization of persons of African ancestry still today, more than four centuries later and more than a century and a half after formal emancipation. The effects have persisted within black communities, person to person and generation to generation, in self-concept and expectations, but they have persisted also in white perspectives and attitudes of prejudicial discrimination, without which the deleterious long-memory effects among black residents whether descendent of slaves or recent immigrants would have diminished. Long-memory processes do no doubt endure in and as "impersonal social structures" (e.g., gender biased organization of temporal budgets in employment), but the endurance is maintained in wet as well as dry memory.

The fact of long memory in institutions resides both in the iterative and in the recursive aspects of distributed process. Iteration is such a simple "coding," it almost surely predated the beginning of Homo sapiens as such, even if as a semi-conscious "script"—or what theorists such as Frederick Hayek (e.g., 1948, 1067a, 1967b) have countenanced as "design without a designer" (singular or plural, in the sense of deliberate, reflective purposive action). Likewise, recursion is at least as old as human language. As has been pointed out already, recursion is a much more complex "complexity within regulation." If this points to an ambiguity within the temporality of sociability, there is very good reason for it, as has been acknowledged at least since the time of John Locke's struggles with the pre-contractual conditions of contract. None of us has ever been present before the beginning, the originary condition and process; therefore, we are always faced with the dilemma of the proverbial chicken and egg whenever we try to set the zero-time of a clock (without which we can never know the length of the "*real*" first interval and thus make music—despite the fact that we *do*). An institution has characteristics that make it a nearly virtual reality; that is, it exists in its effects and nearly not in fact. It exists as if a template that attains concrete reality only (or nearly only) in its copies. From an evolutionary point of view that likeness is misleading, however, in that it assumes the template exists first and copies are pulled from it. If from an evolutionary point of view, for example, "family" is one of the oldest if not the oldest, of institutions, then it seems highly probable that actual organizations which we identify as actually existent families in some array of variations, some of which did not survive, became an emulatable pattern. Only after one or a few modal tendencies became well established and self-reproductive as modal form with very limited variations did a category of consciousness that today we define as "the institution of family" become normal expectation of perception and conceptual utility. While this reasoning is plausible and consistent with general evolutionary theory, it of course must remain hypothetical for lack of directly observed evidence of the referenced processes.

The pragmatic fact about "institution" is simple: no institution ever exists without or apart from the organizations of which it is the type. The very fact of an institution's distributed process is dependent upon the organizations of type through which it functions as "regulation of complexity." This dependence is integral to an institution's strength, its resiliency; for it is the channel by which filtering and updating occurs *bidirectionally* —that is, as constraint and enablement simultaneously (macro-to-meso-to-micro, and vice versa) as if by an evolutionary clock that has always been underway. (Reason tells us that, logically, there *must* have been an existential condition of the clock's presence as clock; but since we have, and can have, *no* experience of that condition, this reason is, as Kant said, empty and idle.)

In what sense, then, can we say that "institution," as such, has strength and/or resilience? What evidence do we have of that strength and/or resilience? It is one thing to point to the fact, or the apparent fact, that "family" is at least as old as the species, if not older; likewise, under some reasonably broad description, "work" (although the Book of Genesis suggests that "work" began only after the species became capable of original sin). Can we point to firmer evidence of an institutional strength and/or resilience? There are several means of demonstration without exceeding the bounds of historical experience. One of them is to compare effects of deliberately concerted human actions with and then without the presence of what can count as an institutional channeling. Many instances of the "with" condition come to mind. As it happens, a substantial bundle of evidence for an instance of the "without" condition has recently come to hand—to wit, Adam Reich and Peter Bearman's (2018) report of an excellent project of scholarship built in, of, and around a concerted effort to achieve better working conditions for employees of a huge retail firm, without much aid of what was once an institutional channel of organized labor and against the institutional resistance of economic, political, and legal organizations at best indifferent to, and in some instances determined to defeat, any resurgence of a union movement. The outcome of that contest in the narrow sense was far short of surprising. Of far greater interest, with some elements of surprise, were lessons learned about the process of concerted efforts to build new implementations of what would otherwise be deemed ordinary relations of sociality. Problems of commitment, of intent, of energy, of "getting action" and "telling the story," were all ordinary and ordinarily manageable problems—which is *not* the same as saying "easy." For the ordinary is often *not* easy, for simply being ordinary. But the effort, the commitment, and so forth, were present and engaged in the level of individual persons on a day-to-day basis. Yet so little effect accumulated from all of it. I do not mean that the scholarship

476

has had no effect (although I do believe that the report has been unduly neglected). Nor do I mean that the young people who engaged as organizers during the summer of this community project and quasi-experimental study gained no benefit. Far from it. I mean rather that the *organizational* work, the *aspirations* of improved conditions of employment in a major retail company, had so little cumulative effect. Nearly no *micro-to-meso* aggregation of per-person action effects could be detected.

The judgment just rendered could be considered a conventional instrumentalist judgment, however, by which I mean (inter alia) judgment anchored in the expectation that should a concert of action designed to produce something new in the face of resistance, the proof of success will be told soon. This mark of impatience is not a new one, to be sure, and its fault if there is one is often obscured by correlative as well as countervailing processes. For even when our strategies of observation are guided by such processual theories as we have, the involved simplifications usually leave them vulnerable to varieties of surprise. And insofar as the concerted actions have been dependent on the presence and activities of a certain kind of audience, expectations from our theories can generate easy confirmations of what are actually self-fulfilling prophecies. In short, who can yet say what eventual effects might come of the project partly orchestrated by Reich and Bearman. It is good to be reminded once and again of perspectives refreshed by scholars of what the rest of us tend to set off, or aside, as "artistic worlds," scholars such as the late Harold Bloom, Stanley Cavell, or William Mitchell. In his essay on "the arts of occupation," for instance, Mitchell (2012) delivered a different perspective by and through which to judge success/failure of a projection. Reading his prior account of the "forces of media, capital, and culture" which "swirl about us like massive storms of images" (Mitchell 2011, p. 253), we are put into mirror image of our sense that we "know more about the world now than ever before, just as it seems to be more than ever escaping our comprehension, much less our control." Note that a few centuries ago Newtonian scientists struggled with a contradiction that had grown within, and then projected from, that world's version of the dialectic of local/universal. An implication of the local being a function of the universal became notorious as a problem—namely, "action at a distance." Because this was simply preposterous, there had to be a phenomenon of mediation, which was named "the æther." This tendency to seek a necessity not of human making, although weaker than it was in that day, remains a force as we strive to grasp "the very idea" that today "the local" has been "generated by the global," leaving to its mysterious sidekick, Robin to Batman, the question how all of the plentiful localities ever got "summed up" to a globality in the first place. What may later be recognized as "revolutionary" can begin in dim muddles of inconsistency, contrarieties, contradictions.

One of the greatest strengths of Reich and Bearman's (2018) study comes from the fact that they gave serious attention to the project participants' own efforts to live "examined lives" (to invoke the title of James Miller's [2011] study), conducting repeated observations in "real time" as the organizational project came alive and then evolved through various stages. From one standpoint it might seem to be relatively easy to attend to those self-examinations, because the participants, by virtue of the fact that their very presence *as* participants meant that problems of commitment and the like had been at least partly "solved," were often inclined to personalize success of the project as one's own self success. From another standpoint, however—this one in a sense an inversion of the foregoing—attending to the self-examinations was probably a fraught undertaking no matter how sensitively conducted, for the reason adumbrated in Nietzsche's phrase "human all too human" (see the riff by Miller 2011, pp. 348-349). Virtually any solution that has been achieved to an organizational commitment problem—and the organization studied by Reich and Bearman was from its beginning, remember, a continuing construction—will be manifested as a more or less complex cost/benefit ratio (and here I mean "cost/benefit" as both a dialectic and a mathematical ratio). As Reich and Bearman (2018, pp. 173-175) recognized, because the organizational project (OUR Walmart) remained throughout the study an aspiration, a goal just out of reach at best, costs of effort would be inevitable (some of them potentially very serious), while the primary and main benefit, the goal which informed the reason and emotive energy of commitment by aspirants, would remain an unlikely objective product from which project proponents could gain telic satisfactions, while project opponents could depend upon that unlikelihood (in short, as Reich and Bearman pointed out, a continual illustration of the exit-or-voice scenario that Albert Hirschman [1970] had described). An organization of much effort, commitment, and aspiration, *without* the support of an institutional channel through which to express that organization, and *in the face of opposition* from collectivities duly supported by a number of institutional channels (the corporate firm, whatever any of its employees might think of the project; local governmental agencies concerned to maintain public order and to be seen as supportive of commercial enterprise for the employment, the payroll, and the tax revenues it brings to the community; probably local non-governmental agencies, a Chamber of Commerce or a Business Alliance, for instance), might well be described as a "David versus Goliath" story but as those scenarios *usually* unfold, contrary to the titular story. At least that was the short-term verdict.

Consistent and sustained evidence based on repeated observations of network ties and on repeated scans of neural activity by functional MRI testified that project participants were indeed engaged in affective as well as cognitive relations of mutual recognition, commitment, and paths of collective endeavor as the weeks and months passed. But the repeated scans suggested also that "mutual liking" increasingly took a back seat to functional, goal-directed orientations based on the moral-evaluative filter-and-update aspect of exchange relations, and real-time observation gave indications of the same conclusion (see Reich and Bearman 2018, especially chs. 5-6 and the appendix; plus Zerubavel, Hoffman, Reich, Ochsner, and Bearman 2018). Per-person actions of principal interest and intent had as their substantive condition a collective goal of organization extending beyond the immediate organized effort that was "the project." As often happens with goal-directed actions that are substantively oriented beyond themselves, actors found processual satisfactions along the way, too, both in and of the collective effort as such, and whether the substantive orientation was meeting with success or not. Exchange relations are a fount of such satisfactions—satisfactions of *procedure*—especially when and insofar as participants judge that expectations of reciprocity are being met, even as (if) the collective substantive goal is not. It is in these satisfactions of process (when sufficiently mutual) that relatively enduring ties develop as second-person experiences. As Philip Wagner reminded us a quarter-century ago in his study of what he called "the Geltung hypothesis" (1996), humans of all ages seek evidence of relative standing as proof of recognition and esteem, and that goal-seeking tendency is often accounted as "individualist." But all of it can occur only within the relations of sociality, and picking apart the "strictly individualist" from the collective, whether associational or communal, is a task both herculean and sisyphean.

That is partly an old story, of course, which Reich and Bearman acknowledged in citing, for instance, Mancur Olson's (1965) report on the general unlikelihood of collective action. The often unsaid qualification is important: people engage in collective action far more often than not (indeed, the real unlikelihood is successful avoidance of collective action). The qualifier is "collective action to *change* this or that part or feature of institutionalized order" (as in the Our Walmart effort). Finding processual satisfaction is integral to both the attraction and the vulnerability of that sort of collective action. It is not that normative expectations are irrelevant, but unless they are consistent with underlying relations, as in relations of exchange, they do not count for much (Bearman 1997; Reich and Bearman 2018, p. 258). More often than not, the main effect of a person's actions, intended or not, is reproductive—reproductive of existing processes, existing relations, existing distributions of power and other goods, with little or no consequential difference. It is extraordinarily difficult for a given actor's effects to be otherwise, for the collectivity within which those effects jostle to live, as it were, are also heavily reproductive. A project such as OUR Walmart depends vitally on solidarity, but the process by which solidarity is produced and maintained relative to any goal direction is not categorially different simply because the goal is to change some existing pattern or arrangement of institutionalized order, and it is not altogether evident at any given moment, any given day or week, what in fact the maintenance of solidarity is achieving, relative to the action effects of any given person or the aggregate of effects by the host collectivity. This is a "hidden" vulnerability when, and insofar as, solidarity is deriving largely from satisfactions by process. This momentum of the reproductive, from which little or nothing beyond solidarity results, cannot be easily directed into the substantive goal attainment, and by and large that is how most actors most of the time like it to be within the satisfactions of solidarity. They are comfortably adjusted within the exchange relations of solidarity, doubt that significant changes actually resulting from the "expected" substantive goal would be of real benefit personally and would more likely require them to commit to some sort of re-adjustment that would count as yet another expenditure that might have little or no personal return on the investment.

"Sometimes," however, "people have understandings of themselves and others" that, under the right conditions, do "generate social change." Deliberate effort to achieve specific changes—that is, "organizing" for change—"is about inducing that kind of realignment of self and other. And this means that the mechanisms by which structure gets into us might also contain the foundations for how change takes place" (Reich and Bearman 2018, p. 258). This eminently Meadian observation is uncommonly well illustrated by major parts of Reich and Bearman's *Working for Respect* (2018, especially ch. 5 and appendix). "Organizing"—in the sense of the word given just above—is different from institutionally channeled actions.[523] That difference brings us back to the commitment problem. Commitment to the collective substantive goal brings with it procedural expectations of "doing the right thing." Actors learn, sometimes with a measure of surprise, that pleasure can be found in the process of attempting to achieve a substantive good in the face of long odds. The moral-evaluative aspect of exchange is the stuff of trust. It is, as Hume said, a fiction. But then so, too, is sociality. These are "made things." We still lack a good grasp of that process, the process by which these made things come to be as objectivities that have been produced, that have come about through change.

All of the *institutionalized* processes directly involved in the contested site of the OUR Walmart project favored established authority, including officials of law enforcement who, by virtue of their primary authority, were prone to see disturbances of the peace by the organizers, especially when store managers and other company officials raised careful claims of disruption. The Occupy Wall Street movement of 2011-2012 showed the boost that recent technologies known as "social media" (as if other media are not) can give to early stages of what might spawn a mass movement. But the boost does not persist so easily, because those same media, in their accelerated sequences and cycles of effects, tend to be self-consuming. Zeynep Tufekci (2017) further illustrated the different temporalities of institutionalized processes when she compared the rapidity of recent mobilizations of protest and counter-protest, achieved through the newly established channels of social media, with the years-long and often difficult slog of efforts to build a civil-rights movement during the 1950s (from the Montgomery bus boycott in 1955, for instance, to the 1963 March on Washington, DC), which gained resilience during the slower pace of building and maintaining those efforts in many local venues before weaving them into a national campaign. Tufekci's study brings to mind yet again Herbert Simon's (1971, pp. 40-41) general conclusion that accelerated flows of information achieve greater scarcities of attention and thus a greater risk that valuable efforts and products will fall into oblivion (see also Doggett 2012). One obvious upshot of this (as of other) instances of the supply/demand dialectic is the greater premium thereby placed on efficiency of filters, followed by insightful updating.

A century ago scholars began to notice that because of increased democratization, though it was more formal than substantive, institutions of state had been developing what was called an "administered society," a nomination often associated with figures of the Institute for Social Research in Frankfurt am Main but present as well in discussions by US scholars such as Adolph Berle, Gardiner Means, Charles Lindblom, and others.[524] The tenor of discussions signaled a

---

[523] The difference can be seen also in comparison of "union organizing," as it transpired during the initial movement of industrial labor organization, and "organized labor" as an institutional channel, routinized and reproductive.

[524] As Lindblom's obituarist in Santa Fe, NM, wrote fittingly, "Throughout his career Lindblom pursued the troubled attempt of scholars, political leaders and ordinary citizens to understand the social world well enough to shape it." His career-stamping article on "the science of 'muddling through'" (1959) is worth reading today. On first reading I thought he was seriously shorting the capacity of his fellow

shift in focus of what had generally passed under the heading of "the problem of order" (as treated in Part One and again in Part Four), and it connected with alarms about "the rise of the individual," as evidenced by Durkheim's concern that "civic society" was being evacuated (i.e., failures of what might be called "institutions of the middle range"). However, the discussions also often betrayed an historical myopia, inasmuch as imperial orders of Europe had been administering populated territories for centuries before and after Rome, both directly and, after Rome, through the Christian Church and its monasterial orders. But there had been a change, no doubt: until the recovery of city life was well under way after Europe's sixteenth Christian century, most of those populations had been administered via simple neglect. Excepting occasional uprisings by peasants, most individual persons had no voice that would be heard beyond a hovel's threshold. The emblem of that order of administration could well have been the fabled Four Horsemen of the Apocalypse, supplemented by a fifth: sheer ignorance and anonymity.

In conjunction with his studies of "the legitimacy of the modern age" (another strange locution, also with a very long history; see, e.g., Haskins 1927; Curtius 1953; Morley 2009), Hans-Georg Gadamer (1966) wrote of "the idea of a perfectly administered world." One of the various chimera to which hubristic impulses are susceptible—as if anyone could have better knowledge of a world of conditions not yet realized than they have of their own presences—this idea, Gadamer said, "appears to be the ideal to which the outlook and the political convictions of the most advanced nations are committed" (the year was 1966, remember, a time when such fancies were still ripening on at least a few vines):

> Moreover, it seems significant to me that this ideal is presented as one of perfect administration and not as a vision of a future with a predetermined content. It is not like the state of justice in Plato's utopian republic, nor does it endorse the dominance of one people or race over another [a Gadamer blindspot]. Contained in the ideal of administration is a conception of order which does not specify its content. The issue is not which order should rule, but that everything should have its order; this is the express end of all administration. In its essence, the idea of management incorporates the ideal of neutrality. It aspires to smooth functioning as a good in itself. That the great powers of our day would prefer to confront each other on the neutral basis of this administrative ideal is not, in all probability, such a utopian hope (Gadamer 1966, p. 577).[525]

Fifty years later it had become clear that the issue of "which order should rule" had not vanished and that, while the expectation in Gadamer's next sentence—"From here it is hardly a big step to consider the notion of world administration as the form of order peculiar to the future"—was

---

species members. Now, more than half a century later, it is not clear to me that the species will survive long enough to develop greater and better capacity on average.

[525] What I called Gadamer's "blindspot" was his apparent neglect that this formalist or proceduralist strategy was (is) indeed a design that harbored substantive choices and implications, including imperialist motives internal and external. Think, for example, of the continuation of slavery in all but name, and under the rule of law, in the USA long after the formal ("constitutional") abolition of slavery.

in fact realized to the extent of a practical consideration, as interests far more substantial than those of a (seemingly pure) procedural functionalism remained potently alive.

And yet Gadamer (along with Curtius and others) could not help but have known that a rather large chunk of Europe had been an "administered world" under the Romans, and that a huge portion of the continent had next (after c451 CE) been inherited into the administered world of the Christian Church in various and shifting alliances with emperors and, after the sixteenth Christian century, nation-state rulers.[526] Likewise, the inland empire of China across different dynastic regimes.

Administration was far less concentrated and dense in earlier centuries, no doubt, with provisional devolution of authority to regional and local levels of territorial organization (as in feudalism) and, though less visible in compliance and diversions, in local but generalizing organizations of consciousness. A kind of romanticism has often been attached to "revolts from below" (peasant uprisings, etc.), but beyond local skirmishes these were rare events, for means of physical mobility, communication, and violence were generally very limited beyond the compass of small localities, and in the rare cases of greater mobilization the monopolization of means by regime centers virtually always meant that local costs in body counts and destructions otherwise of means of livelihood (e.g., "slash and burn" razing of crops, livestock, and buildings) quickly told the difference between imagined and actual outcomes. Regimes centers were generally known as "church and court," with feudal postings of allegiances in monastic and baronial systems, but the organizations of power as well as authority were to very considerable extent "bureaucratic" well before that word gained much attention. Thinking was administered because language *is* "administering," through complex conventions of vocabulary and constraints/enablements of literacy. Orality was largely habitual, recitative, local, and conserving. Arrival of the printing press was quickly met by rules and means of scarcity from the center in expensive licensing, imprimatur, rapid confiscations following rare if any notice of having breached the peace and dignity of church or court, and closer surveillance of literate skills, especially writing. More recently, an increasing democratization of those skills and of media of distribution (as in "social media") has eroded concentrations of oversight and thus of centralized administration of many information flows. A recent consequence, alarms about "fake news" and the like, has pointed to insecurities about and of "skills of the general populace," as the flows have become more distributed, diverse, and resistant to administration at local level. The concern is hardly new, of course; alarms about the printing press, the broadsheets, Martin Luther's postings of 95 theses, and so forth, were hardly rare. Perhaps the biggest difference has to do with perceptions of difference between "the ignorant peasants" and "the virus of mobs." While skilled centers develop algorithmically powerful filters for visual and aural signals in flows

---

[526] The date 451 CE marks the Council of Chalcedon, generally regarded as the last of the ecumenical councils agreed by most Christians. Most of the substantive issues were agreed in an effort to subordinate them, if not wipe them away, to a procedural functionalism of the Church bureaucracy. But several segments of Christianity did not agree, among them the Assyrian Church of the East and the Oriental Orthodox Churches (not to be confused with the Eastern Orthodox Church), which included episcopal denominations among Coptics, Armenians, and Syriacs. The later schismatics known as "protestant reformers" generally left the Chalcedon agreements in place.

distributed to, and tactically diverse among, individual persons, those individual persons appear on average to be too poorly skilled in needed techniques of investigation to distinguish between "preferred bias of message" and "message that challenges such preferences." Algorithms are less expensive than improvements to education of the general populace (for relevant discussions see, e.g., Roth, Dahms, Welz, and Cattacin 2019; Smith and Browne 2019; Achen and Bartels 2016; Greif 2015).

"Institutions get constructed through intentions," but an institution is "not necessarily intentional in the sense of conscious design by named actors" (White 1992, p. 170). How many theorists have made that statement? I am not sure the number, but it is large, and it includes theorists well before Adam Smith and David Hume (think "ancient Greeks, Romans," among others). Constructive intentions can be constructive *indirectly*, sometimes almost inadvertently, as "named actors"—both individual person actors and collectivities of person actors—intend to achieve more or less equivalent or at least comparable and compatible goals through individual actions that sooner or later must be, if not already are, coordinated *within* the actions of multiple individual person actors (whether already as a collectivity or not) and who thus, whether by pre-planned design or not, engage in and as an organized collectivity, not a mere network, that is, but a mutually interested and deliberating concert of purposive intentions that sometimes end with unexpected results. While "institution" is a powerful, very resilient form of objectivity—by which I mean the objectiveness of products of sociality that we produce and reproduce in, by, and as the subject/object dialectic of production—the actual operation of that production and reproduction is formed within organizations of a type. To the extent that "institution" as such performs any "work," it is the work of a store keeper of resources om hand: an imprimatur, an authority of credence that certifies all schools as *schools*, for instance, the heuristics conveyed in organizations of type as appropriate to *schools*. This storage is itself a very substantial resource for organizations that are recognized as being of type, no doubt, and it is a resource that efforts to organize outside "institutional authority" miss every day. There has been a tendency to invoke "institution" as explanation, however, when in fact the invocation only shifts vocabulary focus and begs the question. Acemoglu and Robinson (2012) answered their rhetorical question, "Why do nations fail?" by reciting "institution," and indeed there is point to the answer, but only if one then explains how specific institutions fail—and then also how *those* failures (i.e., the failure of those institutions that are demonstrably critical) aggregate to failure of a nation-state as a whole. After all, a state itself is an institution, as well as an organization of more specific institutions (e.g., legislative, executive, judicial, administrative, military, naval, etc.), and it exercises regulations of other institutions as well (e.g., family law, protections of children, public-school revenues and regulations, and so forth).

Mekhennet (2017, p. 318) reminded her reader of a fallacy of misplaced agency, using the instance of "religion" as illustration: "Religion doesn't radicalize people; people radicalize religion." One might regard that as a truism: agency effects come from actions of person-actors. But that, too, is an oversimplification, the traditional habit of seeking "first cause" or "originary status" as key answer enfolded in process. An institution—and surely "religion" counts as one

483

(or as a genus containing many specific "religious institutions")—exists historically as a more or less rich context, and within that a set of conditions influential in the formation of a person as a developmental sequence of selves. Sometimes, conditions specific to a focal stimulant induce relatively quick, seemingly instantaneous change in what had been a person's "mode of being in the world." Religion has been a spawning bed of such change—"conversion," as it is typically called, and typically celebrated by reference to Augustine's *Confessions*. There are others, too: the "Aha!" experience (the third-century BCE Archimedes' Eurēka!—which, by the way, is akin to "heuristic"), a first-person experience stimulated by second- or third-person relation, as when for a pupil of mathematics the basic difference of calculus "suddenly falls into place" or for a pupil of music the "ruleless logic" of improvisation is "suddenly heard as an embodiment of mind."

Thus, while "institution" is a powerful, exceptionally resilient form of objectivity, to say "in institutions" is not in itself an answer to the question how processes of aggregation of action effects work. It does propose an important framework within which we might be able to see relevant evidence suggestive of an answer, however. In his essay on self-fulfilling prophecies, Merton (1948, p. 210) said of the specific kind of prophecy "whereby fears are translated into reality" that it "operates only in the absence of deliberate institutional controls." On the one hand, that says less than one might think, if taken as explanation, since an institution is what it is, in operation, because it reflects support by other processes of society, in particular those of the specific organizations that are of an institutional type but also processes of organizations of different but correlative institutional type, thus involving important and large segments of the societal population. On the other hand, insofar as Merton's conclusion is in fact correct, it offers room for considerable insight both from examination of the specific effectivity of "institutional controls" and from or by contrary cases that one might happen upon (i.e., instances in which an institution one would expect to have had that effect did not in fact break a translation of feelings of fear into a reality of sociality. In order to get at the regulated, and regulative, dynamics of aggregative processes, we must attend to per-person experiences, both subjective and objective, of enablement/constraint, including the filters and updates that tie effects to effects over time and person-to-person whether "individual" as such or also as member of this or that "collectivity."

### §28. Abstractive Condensation, Aggregation, and Scale

The main focus of this section is with cumulative processes in two different forms, each of them centered on *per-person action effects*, and each of them an aggregative process. Initially I will treat them as distinctive in a number of respects, even though they are interrelated and (in one sense of the word) interactive. By "aggregation" in the following discussions I mean in general an accumulation not of bodies as such but of the *effects of actions* performed by individual person-actors. These individual person-actors are always already situated of and within a sociality. Note the indefinite article of "a sociality": while I assume that sociality is endemic and in that sense universal to our species, empirically it is always of a date and place in space-time and in its specificities tends to vary accordingly. Because an individual person-actor is always already of and within a sociality, that person is already member of at least one collectivity, however small it may be. (While real hermits there may be, it is very unlikely that any one of them reached childhood as a hermit and sustained loss of memory of upbringing.) In most jurisdictions corporate bodies such as an incorporated commercial firm, a governmental agency, and various nongovernmental agencies have legal standing as a person, but they act via human beings who have legal standing as officers of the corporate body. That difference is not inconsequential.

One of the two forms of cumulative process, which I will call "abstractive condensation" (AbCon in short), is a per-person first-person experience of efficacy, of having and making effects that the person believes make a difference. I will have more to say about this concept later. For the moment I emphasize that the experience is both subjective and objective. That it is subjective is probably taken as normal expectation, but I emphasize that I mean "subjective" in the sense primarily of a first-person *feeling* of accomplishment and efficacy—that is, believing that one's actions have mattered not only to oneself but to others, that one's actions have made significant contributions and can continue to make significant contributions. The first-person experience of efficacy is objective in the sense that first-person actor treats "me" as an object of prior and on-going actions and that this object may be, usually will be, a stimulant to others in cross-person relations, both actual and potential (i.e., anticipatory). Thus, each first-person actor is object to another or others and (usually) increasingly learns to take others' standpoints into account, although some are better at it than are others..

The other form is similar to the conventional meaning of "aggregation"—except that, to say again, the units that are aggregated are *action effects*, not bodies. It is not that bodies do not aggregate (as in a population census of, say, a teacher's class size, an employer's payroll, or a city's residents). These quantitative size distributions of population do have significant effects, as Simmel (1908) argued more than a century ago. But as Simmel (e.g., 1971 [1908c]. p. 274) also very well knew, the bodies are not merely countable stick figures. Each is in principle an integral complexly dynamic node in and of an already existent temporally and spatially local sociality. A population census may or may not correspond "territorially" to any already existent collectivity other than the one defined for purposes of the census (whether by officials of some agency or by social-science observers with specified intent). As mere stick figure, each of the countable bodies would at best manifest only superficially the dynamic complexity as it was at a moment in time and space, and as if it could, and potentially would, continue to be the constant presence it had already been (by assumption). My chief concern is with the action effects of human bodies in sociality, effects of per-person actions that occur in a family, in a classroom, in a place of work, and/or elsewhere, and often within the interstitial space "between" and to some extent shared by two (or more) institutional types of organization (e.g., family and school, vis-à-vis a child's experience, or church and school when the latter is in part a religious organization). The per-person actions have meaning to the actor; effects of the actions may or may not have meaning to the actor, but even when they lack meaning to the actor in question they may have or gain meaning to other actors, those who take the effects into account in some fashion and in some degree. It is the effect primarily as an objective presence that can be aggregated along with "like" effects from others, and its meaningfulness to one or more others, if it has any, will be carried into the aggregation, whether that meaningfulness to others is confirmatory, consensual,

485

conflictual, and/or randomly distributed. It is the objectivity of effect—that is, consequences of effect that might or might not ramify or propagate—that is of primary interest with regard to aggregation process. This interest presupposes an observer—in principle, potentially a trained scholar—who observes the process. What is primarily of interest about "the problem of aggregation" (and, within that, "the problem of scale") is not directly of the quantity and/or collective organization of individual persons as physical beings; for they are always already in some manner and degree "aggregated." Even an isolate in this or that network of ties is already internal to at least one collectivity by at least one person's reckoning.[527] As mentioned in §22, there is nonetheless relevance to that ratio which is sometimes designated "Simmel's ratio" as a simple quantitative fact—namely, as the ratio of per-person self (no matter how complexly configured, as in George Herbert Mead's conception of a multiplicity of self-other relations under degree of integration) to the number of significant others in self's locality—for as the ratio diminishes, *qualitative* dimensions of those "quantities in ratio" (their *meanings* to self and to other, which need not be in agreement) can change in seriously consequential ways and extents. More will be said about this, but for the moment think of "tipping point" arguments about racial, ethnic, and/or religious-confessional diversities in residential neighborhoods. There is no logical necessity that the implied ratio have any meaning whatsoever, or any meaningful consequence. (Think, for example, of the ratio of persons with "attached" earlobes to persons with "loose" earlobes or to persons who have none at all.)

The two forms, abstractive condensation and aggregation, are interactive processes in that they affect each other; they are more or less simultaneous, although they may occur by partly disphasic clocks, and they yield different kinds of outcome—respectively, a sense of personal efficacy and an array of collective effects, some of which might manifest multiplier or other scale effects. Ultimately, I confess, cleanly separating outcomes of the two forms is probably impossible. Pickering's (1995) concept of the mangle is helpful to my point. Previously I have said that when one begins an inquiry with aggregate data, seeking to learn something of the dynamics of the "micro-to-macro relation" (as in Coleman's diagram; figure 5.1, p. 382), one is faced with the impossible task of unpicking results of the mangle. Better to start with observations of action effects at micro-level (individual-person action) and follow the cumulative processes that end in, say, average worker productivity or a locality's average score in reading proficiency as tested by the Programme for International Student Assessment (PISA). If we really are interested in learning how a specific process works, it makes sense to examine more than a gross output of that process—or, correlatively, a gross input followed by a gross output, the story of how the former became the latter left in shadow of the proverbial camera obscura. Does anyone doubt that we do engage in what could be called "real-time observations of the dynamics of process X"? Such observations are made often, even every day and on multiple occasions within a day, but usually the observations are made casually and without record. Think of the range of specifications in place of that "X": substitute, for instance, watching one's own

---

[527] As has been said before, even Robinson Crusoe survived birth and carried a substantial fund of collectivity information in mind as he rose from the coastline of some apparently deserted island somewhere in a vast sea.

486

child participate with others in a swim-meet or in the rehearsals of a ballet company; or oneself among others attending a new-skills workshop, or being a patient in a local ER, or bidding at a cattle auction, or driving the morning rush-hour freeway to the office; and so forth. We loosely accumulate experiences of "how things work" in various and sundry venues many, many times. But seldom if ever do we undertake carefully measured observations of the dynamics that we observe; and even more rarely do we undertake such effort as a research team with a specific program of inquiry in mind, and repeat the effort as consistently as possible some number of times; and repeat it all again within varied conditions. Even the most carefully made observational data, however, might always already contain indiscriminable effects of a mangling. Something of Pickering's mangle might be inherent to perception, in which case analytic operations will be forestalled. Indeed, how cleanly *can* we separate observations of the dynamics of sociality into two distinctive processes of accumulation, as I have proposed? The question remains open. Only concerted and repeated effort will tell the tale.

The question is perhaps most complex in regard to the institution of familial organization, partly because these organizations have become far more diverse in US society. A century ago, and more, the diversity consisted mainly in distinctions among procreational family, residential family (aka "family of orientation"), and genealogical or tribal family. In US society the fact of racial prejudice and discrimination no doubt affected each of those organizational perspectives, due to the history of slavery and post-Emancipation continuations of attitudes and behaviors of oppression of persons of African ancestry; and yet each of the three distinctions was apparent in families identified as "Black American."[528] Recent changes in oppressive attitudes and behaviors with regard to legal categories of parental ties (e.g., "married" versus "cohabiting" versus "single parent" versus "blended-family" household) and with regard to sexual preferences and the binary conception of gender have resulted in profound changes in the composition of "family" in each of those three distinctions, especially the procreational and the residential. That new complexity will add layers of complication to efforts to observe the processes of abstractive condensation and aggregation, simply in order to determine whether, and to what extent, these compositional diversities have extended into the processes as such. That question aside, "family" was already the most complex of the three institutions at primary and main focus here, since its endogenous dynamics surely overlap with and to some (probably variable) extent influence each of those processes as they operate in the institutional realms of school (at least a family's children) and work (at least insofar as a residential family includes one or more members engaged in paid external employment or self-employment).

With respect to the intersections of family and school, for instance, the dialectic of enablement/constraint is surely a crucial factor in composing the conditions of "upbringing"

---

[528] The same observation applies to persons of families who survived efforts to exterminate the indigenous inhabitants of North America. And here there is often the additional complexity due to mutual rejections at cultural interstices. An important point about constraints being the other side of institutional enablements was recently demonstrated by Hsu, Hannan, and Koçak (2009): "falling between chairs," as it were, more easily occurs when trying to straddle chairs that have been "assigned" to institutionally different disciplines (as in, e.g., "academic disciplines"). Refusal to accept defeat, in order to preserve one's indigenous culture no matter how much it may have been assaulted and altered, is to enact a concept of honor and its basic ethic that are profoundly alien to "victor's domination."

(education) well before a child enters a "school" (i.e., under an institutional description). A family setting in which good balances are established but also monitored and appropriately updated—especially between authority and independence, freedom and security, aspirational encouragement and sensitivity to contingency, and so forth—will surely be integral to a child's development of a self-similar sense of personal efficacy and, because of that, to the child's action effects as resources available to other students in a school, to the classroom teacher, and other parents insofar as they are respectful of others' "upbringings" as reciprocal resources and thus giving appropriate attention to the dynamics of classroom, playground, and so forth. The sine-qua-non institutional resource, commitment, does not always integrate well at boundaries of family and school, however. This has become increasingly problematic as a mismatch between the main regulative temporality of family and that of school. Parents too often reproduce their memories of yesterday as means of educating their children for tomorrow, a disphasing in the supply/demand dialectic of a child's upbringing. It reflects poor educational achievements by parents, which manifests generational or at least cohort shifts in sensitivities to that dialectic; but even more seriously it reflects failures of filter-and-update routines in parental information stores after their completion of formal education. There is some evidence that young adults today, and especially young women, are revising that mismatch, perhaps massively, as young women, better able to self-support now and tomorrow, are postponing child-bearing indefinitely, perhaps permanently. Most recent data on fertility measures in the USA (and other countries) are suggesting continuation of the trend toward completed fertility below replacement rate, with growing proportions of women forgoing birth children entirely. Inasmuch as growth of total population has been the first-order treadmill beneath the feet of traffic in favor of continuous increases in per-person productivity in workplaces, perhaps these women will prove to have been more prescient than policymakers and run-of-the-mill politicians when the day comes that most primary producers are smart machines. Will that be accounted as evidence that women have become more sagacious because of, rather than despite, the many generations of male repressions and belittlements?

Each of the two processes—per-person abstractive condensation and aggregation across per-person action effects over time—occurs in all sorts of place and at various dates, sometimes by schedule, sometimes haphazardly. They generally do occur within pre-existing organizations, especially institutionalized organizations, although there are usually overlaps (as indicated just above), and the overlaps are important. As already mentioned, my recommendation is that we proceed by concentrating on organizations of each of three types of institution. That program will offer more than enough complexity to keep research teams busy for career-long tenures. Because the three institutions—familial organization, schooling, and work—are major loci of life-course activities for the large majority of a societal population, this program would include inherent overlaps not only in that each surviving person proceeds through the three kinds of organization but also in that many adults will be involved in at least two of the types (family and school, family and work), and some will be involved in all three types (teachers with school-age children, for example) at specific times.

In the following paragraphs I will concentrate on the concept, abstractive condensation (or AbCon), with only occasional attention to the cross-person aggregation of effects of per-

person actions. Later, I will switch primary focus to the process of cross-person aggregation, including scaling of effects. As I have already said, the AbCon concept addresses a process that is based in a first-person phenomenon that most if not all of us experience during the course of a life, beginning at some early age of childhood. That simple sentence hides some considerable complexity, however, and the complexity cannot be ignored, even though ignorance is probably the default setting. Let me explain what I mean. In the transition that follows I will be replaying parts of the discussion in Part Two, but transitionally and with some elaboration.

The three person characteristics—first-person, second-person, and third-person—are products of analytic distinction of perspective. They have number, singular or plural. Here I will begin with the singular in reference to the question of aggregation, since first-person plural already assumes an aggregation process such that "I" and "we" are accorded equivalent first-person status as such. That is in keeping with sociality, as I have repeatedly said. But because the aggregation question has generally assumed first-person singular as the basis of "the micro," I will do likewise initially.

As with all analytical distinctions, the abstractness of analytics of personal perspective does violence on experience. There is an obvious irony in that, which I will begin to point to now but must also let unfold as we move along. The dominant tendency has been to treat our analytical distinctions as points of initiation and departure, even though they are like definitions (also a form of analytical distinction) in that illusional application of logic. Certainly human beings have invented many categories of analysis as abstractive devices (i.e., simplifications), intended to clarify and regulate by paring away "excess" (or in an older vocabulary, paring away the accidental in order to leave the essential); and in that history there is common sense (virtually unavoidable) in assuming that one begins with "the categories." Why? Because virtually all of those that one presently uses have been available in a cultural heritage, one's cultural heritage, whatever it may be. Because they have been inherited, it seems that they must have come first at first. One confronts the illusion when attempting to apply the "pristine device"—if one thinks that one's scheme of categories is such.[529]

A useful illustration of the problem can be seen in Ernst Tugendhat's (1986 [1979]) study of "self-consciousness and self-determination." His preferred theoretical perspective was, by his own account, linguistic-analytic, since in examining "self-consciousness" as first-person event he proposed to begin in effect with the stories that persons report of the experience of consciousness of self and therefore of the assumption that there must be something like a "relation of oneself to oneself" (Tugendhat 1986 [1979], pp. 3-11, 18-26, 289, 219-221). By his theoretical perspective he thus sought what had been presupposed, a complete and perfect script already written. But the actual stories of self-consciousness and self-determination (including institutional heuristics and agenda descriptions) are always all incomplete and imperfect. As already pointed out again and again, "even" Newton's script for a "purely physical" mechanics can be considered complete and perfect only in abstraction of myriad variations of atmosphere,

---

[529] As indicated in Part One, the dominant reception of Kant was long founded on the assumption that his specification of "categories" was intended as a pristine pure logic, even though it later became clear that he was well aware that they were (are) cultural and thus historical.

489

gravitational gradients, and errors of measurement in human actions of physical production (thus, of consciousness, self and other). Having surveyed arguments by Fichte, Wittgenstein, and others, Tugendhat came to the work of George Herbert Mead and "the assumption that there cannot even be something like a relation to one's own being outside an intersubjective context." On the one hand, the assumption seemed to introduce important, perhaps even crucial, empirical insight. On the other hand, the assumption carried more complication into the analytic problem, especially more ambiguity of meaning. Tugendhat struggled to understand what Mead had been attempting to theorize, chiefly because his (Tugendhat's) analytic binarism of thingness ("binarism" in the sense that only "yes" and "no" are allowed, as he put it) neglected that for Mead "intersubjectivity"—as with "self" and other main categories (including "memory")—were conceived not as each a binary thingness (thereby disallowing ambiguity, ambivalence, and so forth) but as *process*, a perspective that Tugendhat eventually came to but only as a secondariness which he termed "deliberation" (not irrelevant but I would prefer the more "imperfect," because an always on-goingness of sociality, "negotiation").[530]

Abstractly, "first-person (singular) experience" (the category) has sharp bounds and an internality that make its roots and thus its presence purely private. And this is indeed what each of us tends to think of one's own "first-person experience." It is peculiar in being persistently present tense; but then each of us assumes the same: I am, here-and-now, I, myself. The event of one's being is always on-going now (presence), but the on-goingness has a variable fluidity of internal temporality (aspect), which can be perfective (completed action or event as a whole) or imperfective (incomplete and progressive with attention to stages or parts of, a sequencing *in*, the action's temporality; i.e., an awareness of *process* as such). Even when of perfective aspect, the action carries the sign "until further notice" (until one's death, and sometimes still in an afterlife as survivors argue over and re-present "what X said in life," much as Scheffler 2013 described).[531] *Imperfective* aspect is, on the other hand, an *inherent* signal of repetition and repeatability: the process can be a simple iterative sequence of the steps of a recognized process, or it can be a sequence of nestings or recursions of a process recognized for its inclusivity, potentially open-ended (as in the "days of one's life"). Languages, therefore schemes of categories, vary in these regards: some are more accommodative of recursion, and of those that do accommodate it the techniques vary; some have elaborate aspect rules, while at least a few (e.g., Mandarin) have some verbs that entirely lack aspect, albeit what is not present in "orthography" can be signaled via intonation; and so forth.[532] But my point is less about cultural variations than about the fact (so I claim it to be) that aspect (and other features of language, such as ambiguity, paradox, etc.) are not "add-ons" or "blemishes" or "logical errors" of efforts *at*

---

[530] In fairness to Tugendhat, I must add that he relied apparently only on the edited collections of student notes of Mead's lectures. Also, Tugendhat did understand something of the richness of Mead's effort *and* took it much more seriously than most readers of Mead.
[531] Perfective aspect implies a fully absorptive end-state, but there is no processual necessity of empirical fulfillment. "Things change," to use the vernacular; "don't belabor me with statics of a Cartesian logic."
[532] Lest that statement be misunderstood, anything that a speaker of a given language wants to say can be said in that language, even though its semantic equivalence to any saying in another language may be problematic.

communication; rather, the features are integral to the productivity of language, communication, sociality.

As stated in Part Two on several occasions, "my first-person experience is *mine*; only I know what it is; you either take my word for it or you do not, but no one else can take possession of it." And yet, empirically—that is, *as an experience*—that declaration suffers the complication that David Hume observed of all perception: while I may sternly insist that I do have first-person experiences *as such*, I cannot demonstrate that any particular experience I have had is in fact purely first-person. There is an apparent immediacy in first-person perspective that makes my experience inescapably mine. Why an apparent immediacy? Because while no one has, as it were, an Archimedean pivot on which to rely in order to observe the immediacy as such, the possibility of that anchored perspective is nonetheless easily imaginable, and this makes the sense of an immediacy apparent (thus, another facet of the irony).

What I do have, and can discuss internally with myself as well as with other persons, is thought *about* my first-person experience—in other words, memory (or anticipation, imagination of an experience that may yet happen). I do remember looking out this window to my right, observing that pesky squirrel once more trying to solve the puzzle of the bird feeder, and in this memory I do recall thinking thoughts of "pesky squirrel," "determined little rodent," "learning via trial and error," "certainly not without some intelligence," and so forth; and without further reflection I might think "all of that was strictly, purely *my* experience." Yet everything I have perceived in the instance, and everything that I thought then and later, was thoroughly infused with sociality. To recall Stephen Darwall's (2006) set of lessons, an ethic of second-person standpoint was all along engaged *in me* in my thoughts. I might have thought, "Let me get the shotgun and sting that little rodent." But I did not, because it would not have been a humane act. (Besides, years earlier I did once use the shotgun against some squirrels; did not hit any and had not intended to; but then I noticed, attracted by a shout, a young woman pushing a stroller along our mostly deserted roadway—a furlong away, on the other side of the house—she, obviously frightened by the shot, sprinting away, and I vowed never to fire the shotgun again, not *here*.) The potency of second-person standpoint is not easily escapable. Then, too, again recalling Mead, how does one cordon off the potency of "generalized other"? That third-person perspective cannot be remote from a second-person standpoint, and it is, one assumes in retrospect, bound into one's first-person perspective.[533]

The "inescapably mine" is always present tense (or what some grammarians now call the progressive present), and that, together with the imperfective aspect of action, suggests a quality of recuperative immediacy. Neither word of that phrase can be exactly wholesome, however, for the result would quickly overburden consciousness. Human beings are storytellers from very

---

[533] Darwall (2006, p. 290) was correct in saying that when "we summon one another as agents second-personally, we jointly presuppose autonomy of the will and assume we can fully govern ourselves by second-person reasons, any object-dependent desires to the contrary notwithstanding." No less is implicit in one's sense of other's (as one's own) capability (the core of public ethic propounded by Amartya Sen; see, e.g., Sen 1993)—indeed, in the very possibility of trust, which comes after a language, a sociality. Mead's point about the *generalized* other circulates throughout (see also Darwall 2006, pp. 313-314).

early age, because each of us writes internally a "serialized story" of sequences of and in one's first-person experience. The accretion is continually abstracted for consistency and coherence in an on-going normalization/renormalization of self, significant others, even the generalized other and various settings and their circumstances—in sum, of a persistent immediacy of storyline. Recall Kant's admonition that reason alone—pure reason, pure rationality—if it could actually exist would be empty, while experience without theory, if such were possible, would be a huge meaningless welter of sensation and otherwise blind.[534] The process is variably flawed—variably from time to time and as places change—and sometimes the flaws are noted from within (e.g., as a cognitive dissonance, but perhaps first and more often as an emotive or emotive-cognitive dissonance). The very fact of one's sociality virtually assures occurrence of inconsistencies, incoherences, contradictions, which can be variably "ironed out" but which also, from the "egocentrism" of first-person perspective, can be cited as diagnoses of "what's wrong with the world and thus my place-time within it."

It is here that first-person experience sooner or later encounters ironies of aspiration and ambition, which can be serious enough to congeal into a generalized irony that destabilizes one's "life story."[535] The AbCon concept that I propose takes the peculiar immediacy internal to first-person experience as an on-going fact built of whatever sources and conditions of sociality that have been extant and relevant, all of which has been "digested" via serial abstractions and then serially condensed into a "storyline" however flawed it might be (from within). It *is* the given person's experience of "all that"; and "all that" will show markings of a sociality as it has been experienced, many of those markings carrying identified fingerprints of other persons singly and collectively.

The concept I propose is undoubtedly not novel. Intimations of it, perhaps more, can be discerned in the Bildungsprozess movement of the late eighteenth and early nineteenth centuries (e.g., in Hölderlin, in Goethe, perhaps in Humboldt). What I along with others have judged to be Hegel's introspective lesson of a progressive recognition function (Anerkennung), as laid out in rough statement especially in early sections of his *Phenomenology of Geist* (1977 [1952]), albeit given the voice of an absolutist Being in self-propulsive mission of self-discovery, could well have germinated in such reflections after Hume and Kant (e.g., see Brandom 2007, Pippin 2010). But intimations can be seen not only via the eyes of Hegel's phenomenological observer.

---

[534] Harrison White (e.g., 1992) emphasized our proclivities for storytelling as a kind of insurance policy against that blindness, in that our stories build from the historical condition of a conceptual scheme. This includes myth-making and legendary tales, of course, much of it brokering lessons in how to be this or that (i.e., institutional "heuristics," as avowed by John Levi Martin vis-à-vis Durkheim's misbegotten assumption that "a fundamental difference" lies between theoretical and empirical (i.e., observational) statements; Martin 2011, pp. 5-10). But it also includes stories of factuality, including historiographic and scientific factuality.

[535] In this discussion I tend to use both "aspiration" and "ambition" together because, while they are semantically similar, I want to capture the difference as well. The first word derives from the Latin aspirāre, "to breathe upon" (as plants do), "to favor"; but also "to have a desire for something above one's present condition," thus "to rise up." The second word derives from the Latin ambire, "to go around" (as in looking for something), and has cognates of "to amble," the noun "ambit," and the adjective "ambient"; but also via the stem cognate Latin ambigere, "to go around," "to wander around," and from which the cognate "ambiguous." I want to capture all of that.

492

After Hegel, during a period in which his works were largely ignored, efforts such as Franz Brentano's struggle to clarify his concept of intentionality show mainly introspective suggestions of a more or less complex process of "judgment" riding the border between sensation and concept, yielding a confidence of experiential knowledge within a proscenium of consciousness (see the address by Turner 2012, which demonstrates connections from Brentano to Max Weber, among others). In the political-economic theory of market process, as it developed during the late eighteenth century in Scotland, and earlier in England by William Petty (see, e.g., McCormick 2009), one can also see glimmers of the idea because of an implicit assumption of self-similarity within the main formulations of exchange relations. Petty himself unwittingly used that assumption during his early conceptualization of what today is known as "economy of scale," and in particular the mechanism of a multiplier as it modifies the potential terms of an equilibrium (as in a bargain struck to satisfaction of both buyer and seller). As an organizational form, "market" was already being conceived, in effect, as an information flow determining the fluidity of some dialectical ratios such as production/consumption and supply/demand. In each ratio an expectation of balance or equilibration depended on an elasticity of terms such that satisfactory bargains could be achieved. This was, of course, the very idea of "market" as a price-setting mechanism. However, that elasticity was also working on the dialectical ratio of same/difference, although the "work" was mostly rather quiet and implicit. In consequence, an exchanged good could be accorded the status of "constant thing" (self-similarity) even as it was being valued differently by parties to the exchange, all of whom were self-satisfied in the event. This extraordinary notion was not entirely unprecedented, to be sure. There had been various mysticisms in medieval Christianity, and in Petty's own time the claim of "two bodies" of the king, one mortal and one immortal, was being defended by the body of England's Charles I. But for a new science that was becoming more skeptical of anything deemed "mystical"—not yet exactly a positivist attitude but moving toward rejection of "the metaphysical" in the name of Lockean empiricism—the quiet elasticity of equivalencies in expectation was both vague and compelling, enough on both counts to lead Adam Smith to venture his image of a "hidden hand" at work in market transactions. The image was partly a metaphor in place of explanation of how aggregation works. Was Smith another, however, who had glimpsed in introspection the play of a judgment that would not be a single, undivided, uniform act (even if, unlike Jonathan Swift, he did not elevate its point to the status of satirical exposure of a society's hypocrisy)? A century younger than Petty and more than a generation younger than Swift, Smith had the advantage of both figures as preceptors, along with early British experiments in Bildungsprozess as well.

Imagine a child learning to read, first "out loud" in a sequence of exchanges with a tutor (preferably another person but robotic tutors are gaining skills) patiently reinforcing coordination of sight, sound, and memory recognition, and in the process building the recognitional pleasures of growth and development, the sense of expanding capability and becoming a different person. Or a pupil learning basics of arithmetic: number symbols and names, with coordinated patterns of fingers, sticks, marks of chalk or pencil or lines in sand or soil; then the number line; fractions and decimals; then addition and subtraction; and so forth. As with reading, repetition is vital to progress, the clock of repetitive cycles gradually lengthening, but fluidly, with reversals always available and intermittent. These are difficult skills—reading probably the single most difficult for virtually everyone, numeracy difficult in part because of deeply entrenched gender bias in many if not all societies. Observing the growth and development within and of the child is itself a profound eventful process of sociality and must be explicitly honored as such as integral to the most general skill of communication, of sharing, of trust, within the child's self-awareness of *being* a productive member of a specific, gradually expanding sociality. That self-awareness is simultaneously a reward, an expression of, and a stimulant to continuation of the basic process of becoming different. Nietzsche's admonition against the Delphic oracle is celebrated in each and every success of that basic process, although realization of that celebrant is all too easily squelched by an impatient or otherwise uncaring tutor. One can observe the process in operation most readily in the child's response to well-formed tutorials, but it is present in other activities of sociality, perhaps more readily in those that transpire in institutionalized organizations, because of the regularity of complexity; but also during efforts to build a new organization without the aid of, and even more when opposed by, existing institutional form, as witnessed in the report by Reich and Bearman (2018) and in the partial interstitial disruptions that can occur in per-person transitions from one institutional form to another (e.g., the occupational mismatches, as in Kalleberg 2007).

While it is tempting to describe the AbCon process in terms of a stage theory, that would have more to do with the institutional form of an organization than with the basic process itself, which tends to be at least more nearly continuous. The stages that are most observable are tied to record keeping, as in test scores, promotions, calendars of heuristic and/or agenda change. These and various other graduated events, credentials, and the like, within a sociality need, depend on, a granularity of process. The basic temporality of AbCon is fluid for reasons that I will come to in a moment. But that is not to say that first-person experiences in and of the process itself are empty of "noted events." Several examples were mentioned in the prior sentence about "observable stages." Moreover, Mead's (1905, p. 406) comment regarding Wilhelm Wundt's concept of "gesture" as initial moment of "sign" (in turn then also of "symbol" and thus of language as a whole) is apropos: "the gesture itself is a syncopated act." A pregnant sentence indeed, as Mead's observation carries a cornucopia of meaning.[536] Given that the word, "syncopation," was increasingly popular at the turn of his century (mainly due to rags and jazz), Mead might have had musical connotations foremost in mind—specifically, the disturbances of expected rhythmic cadence or beat that make a composition "off beat" by surprising placements of accent (e.g., switching strong for weak and vice versa). However, the word is also cognate with "syncope," which means not only a "swooning" but also a syllabic condensation (whereby, for instance, the town name "Leicester" becomes, in pronunciation though not in orthography, "Lester"). This latter operation is more than suggestive of the AbCon concept.

The basis of the AbCon process is memory function. Begin with the understanding that memory is both selective and productive. Again, think of a child learning a new skill, a "know how" knowledge, or a new "know that" knowledge. Accomplished lessons proceed in sequences of steps. As the sequences accumulate remembered experiences, memory of a sequence tends to adjust selectively, paring away redundancies, sorting contents into more abstract categories and relations among them, emphasizing general principles as they are exemplified by specificities of

---

[536] The third edition of *Roget's 21st Century Thesaurus* lists nearly forty synonyms of the verb, "to syncopate."

the dynamic record of experiences, especially those that manifest some sort of reward/penalty dialectic. In conjunction with the abstractions, resultant gaps and holes, along with connections newly made by the abstractions, are bridged or backfilled through the generalizations, which can be supplemented by inventions that seem to be by implication but which may later prove to have been illusions or otherwise inconsistent with the evolving biographic story. These procedures tend to occur "behind the back of consciousness"—that is, without much reflection—and one can well imagine that they operate far from perfectly; yet who can test that imagination?[537] The condensation smooths and synthesizes but can also produce distortions, including distortions of distortions already rendered by prior abstractions. The AbCon process involves cycles of repetition, some of them iterative but others recursive. As the AbCon process continues it tends to produce also a second-order learning, a learning *about* learning, and this soon (if not already) creates and feeds into a kind of "sub-order" of learning—namely, a need or "hunger" to learn more, potentially a habituation that becomes recursively self-generating and increasingly "interiorizes" the dialectic of reward/penalty. Learning accelerates.

The sequences can be understood as filter-and-update routines. These are partly implicit, in the sense that they can proceed without an explicit self-conscious awareness of either event, the filtering or the updating. A simple illustration is a notation rule on one's copy of sheet music (e.g., relative hand positions) or a re-alignment within an additive column of variably multi-digit numbers: one experiences the notation even though it is nowhere to be seen literally. Somewhat less simple illustrations include rules of linear algebra (e.g., substitution and recollection) and the bodily sense of angular momentum in riding a bicycle. Bear in mind that while the content of the AbCon process consists in first-person experiences having to do with personal efficacies, reference within those experiences will often include other persons, especially those who count as instances of Mead's "significant other" inasmuch as they are experienced as in some manner and degree contributing to, evaluating, testing, and/or criticizing, one's efficacy. As such, these others will share membership with first-person actor in one or more networks (e.g., family members, friends of household members, teachers, fellow pupils, and so forth). Wei and Carley (2015) have developed a metric model of network dynamics as manifested in variable persistence of a node's centrality and/or a node emergent into centrality within a network of significant others. This model could be used as a rational standard against which to theorize some patterns of variation in the filter-and-update regimen of a per-person AbCon process.

The reader will perhaps have noted that most illustrations have been drawn from a venue that could be described as "schooling," although mostly at a level of learning that surely will have taken place prior to entry of a formal organization carrying that name. Similar discussions could be made of the AbCon process as it proceeds in other institutional channels—"work," for instance, or "family" aside from the educational activity of training a child (be it deliberately or by happenstance, or some mixture of both). The older the first-person in question, the more difficult it is to maintain credibility of illustration without simultaneous consideration of the cross-person aggregative process as well. I will come back to this later, but the following provides a foretaste of some of the difficulties. My previous discussion has rarely ventured

---

[537] This is a point at which Nietzsche's critical remark about the temporality of "self-knowledge"—whether one's aim is commemoration of a past or making a future—is especially salient.yet largely idle.

beyond the beginning assumption that AbCon processes are typically first-person-experienced as private exercises. But one does not need to follow that storyline very far until it becomes evident that first-person self-reflexivity quietly transforms the "private" into a quasi-private experience. While it can take place within and as a first-person awareness *as if* no other person is present, sociality assures that the main focus of orientation ordinarily involves an audience effect in what amounts to a selection of notices, the notices retained for some period of time as explicit flags or markers of progress. For the child, of course, parents, other kin, and/or guardians are usually the initial audience in terms of the child's first-person most noticed audience of significant others (as in, e.g., commemoration of "you learned to succeed at X when you were barely N years old"). Even so, others will nearly always also have been "audience," some of them age-mates and thus constitutive of a comparison group that has already been integral to proceedings, at least partly in a competitive sense. As several scholars have been documenting since the 1980s (e.g., Hallinan 1988; Hallinan and Williams 1990), studies of "classroom organization" have attempted to gauge relative effects of various components of "audience"—grade peers, parents, teacher, and so forth, but not always with good sensitivity to the complexities of sociality. In part this has been due to a tendency to use a rather static analytic perspective, as if "classroom organization" exists as a static shell within which events happen. Treating "organization" as a process, the dynamics of which are simultaneously per-student activities, student-teacher interactions, peer influences of various kinds and degrees (including the extra-curricular), parental influences, and dynamics of the classroom collectivity as such (e.g., multiplier effects between more and less accomplished students), is hardly a simple exercise in comparing students across various population-status cells (e.g., gender, race-ethnicity, parental income, etc.). Equality of educational opportunity is partly endogenous to processes within the school and within a school's classroom, as Hallinan (1988) contended thirty years ago.

Moreover, audience effects can rather quickly expand to include not only other parents but also other adult significant others, such as an extra-curricular activity coach, music or dance instructor, and so forth—even a vicarious aspirational audience member (becoming the next star of popular culture, for instance)—whose presumed and anticipated evaluations could loom large, qualifying these added "others" as "significant" in some degree in one or another selected venue. These expansions tend to be filtered, qualitatively and quantitatively, by location and by date, especially "the historical." The definition of "local" (and of "localism," perhaps to some extent separately) changed during the century from, say, 1850 to 1950, albeit more in some places than in others: compare the plains of Kansas with the neighborhoods of Brooklyn, for example, the city center of London with Tokyo's Ginza or with Beijing's Qianmen district (the old South Gate commercial and residential district located south of Tiananmen Square). Meanings of "family" and of "kin group" changed, although differently, across those places during that hundred-year period, as did the meanings of "work." These changes were locally irremediable, very dense in dynamics of sociality, subtly corpuscular in propagative energy, and both recuperative and transformative of cultural traditions. The sociality of a prison, for example, is not the sociality of a hospital, and neither of those is the sociality of either a school or a factory. Each institutional type persisted during the hundred years, as did differences of cultural tradition from one place to another. Person-incumbents of a prison, a hospital, a school, or a factory in 1850 would not have felt "at home" in an organization of the same institutional kind in 1950 (and vice versa), although degrees of difference might have varied by kind. Comparative relations of local sociality across institutional kinds probably remained much the same in 1950 as they were in 1850, however. I suspect that aggregation process is deeply involved in the relational stability.

Back to the AbCon concept. Following the example of David Hume, I have sought direct evidence of my own first-person immediate engagement in the AbCon process, either part of it on speculation that they might be experientially separable. None has been discerned, none even at a glimpse. I have found evidence of consequences, evidence of having forgotten elements or steps of one or another sequence of steps that I am confident I must have taken. I have found an abundance of evidence of what I do remember, of course. And as I grow older the evidence of realizing that I have forgotten what I am confident that I once did know—and then through some kind of unobserved process from which I "suddenly" recall that which I had thought I had wholly lost from memory—has also been a frequent first-person experience. On reflection, I then also realize that the recall of the seemingly forgotten has not always ended in success—*and* that I generally do not recall the particular failures of recall, neither the content category of that which I did not recall nor usually even the bare fact of that specific failure. Occasionally, later, after that reflection, another stimulant (sometimes the same stimulant as before) will remind me not only that I had previously failed to remember a forgotten prior first-person experience but also the content category of that experience—and sometimes the actual content itself, or what I take to have been the actual content, that had been forgotten. But nowhere in all of those first-person experiences do I experience any evidence directly of the "internal operation" of memory or of recall, as distinguished from its outcome. By evidence from my observation of other persons, I am confident that this outcome is not unique to me, rather that it is general.

All of which raises a question: is abstractive condensation as such a *motivated* process? That is, is it at all sensitive to self-conscious motive or intent, such that the first-person I am can, in some fashion in some degree, self-consciously directly facilitate it, improve it? The question is more complex than that simple locution proposes, but as best I can determine the answer is that in *this* respect motivated action matters mostly, probably only, by indirection. Self-conscious effort to forget tends to be counterproductive. Self-conscious effort to initiate abstraction and condensation, or to directly manage it or modify its pace or its selectivity and so on, is probably without any effect at all. (I say only "probably" because of the circularity problem.) However, indirection is another matter, and a different way.[538]

Generally speaking, some portion of the per-person actions of an individual person are motivated actions, the motives being integral to the action. A direct and immediate effect of an action may therefore be understood in principle as a motivated effect insofar as the effect accords with actor intent. The dynamics of the AbCon process in operation on motivated effects of a per-

---

[538] There is a large and valuable literature on indirection, much of it about Chinese culture and much of the best of that—aside from the indigenous literature, which, beyond ancient classics, is proportionately not large (since what I am calling "indirection" has been integral to most ethnic cultures of China)—has been written by French scholars, probably because of European cultures French culture is the nearest both in understandings of and in preferences for indirection. I find that of recent exemplars works by François Jullien (e.g., 1999 [1992], 2000 [1995], 2004 [1991], 2004 [1996]) and Mark Elvin (1985, 1997, 2004) are exceptionally insightful.

person sequence of actions will generally reflect that motivation, but this does not imply that the dynamics themselves are a result directly of the motivation. Because the main dynamic of both the abstractive and the condensative phases are based in memory function, however, there can be another motivational factor affecting the AbCon process. When this effect does occur—and it is hardly rare—it is by indirection. It can be best summarized by means of a colloquial expression: "use it or lose it." That is to say, the paring away that is primary to abstraction generally occurs as a negative selection of relatively recent effects that have seldom or never become integrated as means (or other resource) in subsequent actions, and condensation tends to seal gaps and create connections in place of gaps that have resulted from the abstraction. AbCon is usually repetitive not only in the sense that it tends to stay abreast of recent effects of per-person action but also in the sense that, as new effects accumulate and gain some degree of integration with prior results of the AbCon process, an iterative or second-order abstraction-and-condensation sequence can occur, making the integration more efficient. Think of a child learning new skills: success will depend on the child's motivated efforts to learn (whatever the setting, which is always one of a sociality, usually with specific others immediately present; but we are holding these influences aside for the moment). The motivated effects, success in learning, are remembered to variable extent for a variable period of time, both variations being a function of rehearsals of the lessons in the child's own-time memory function. These repetitions are iterative, albeit some of them may be, and increasingly likely will become, recursive. Learned products that are not rehearsed often enough are increasingly at risk of disappearing under operation of the AbCon process. On the face of it, this negative selection seems to be similar to the negative selection that operates in biogenetic evolution—the weakest formations dropping away—but with some differences. First of all, the "having disappeared" status can be a temporary, not a permanent, one in sociality, due to the advantage of remedial learning. Secondly, the clocks differ, so the meaning of "weakest" is more nearly immediate; or stated differently, the half-life clock of a learned product is, on average, much shorter than the half-life of most, if not all, selection-sensitive products of genetic recombination, mutation, and drift.

While the question of motivation within and of the AbCon process should remain open to further consideration, there is much evidence that motivations do exert influence on first-person reflections of outcomes of the AbCon process, and this influence is perhaps most interesting in its condition as a long-memory effect most often manifested in intersections of biographical and historical time in first-person storytelling after the AbCon process has generated many outcomes. Insofar as an observer's focus is another person's first-person experiences— and here the status of "observer" has greater interest when it is a well-trained theorist or analyst is at work—one still knows only what one makes of first-person reports of that experience— thusly in and as second-person experience—while "that experience" must remain at some remove as *first-person*, even though as Darwall (2006) after Kant emphasized, second-person standpoint is surely present at least often if not always in adult first-person experience (i.e., Mead's attention to the importance of a "generalized other"). The risk of a generalized *irony* increases when first-person reaches for a "summation of my life to date." The first-person perspective from which that reach begins can be very resistant to dialogue.

Some years ago a senior social scientist offered such an accounting in public venue (and one must keep the publicity in mind, remaining agnostic about trials of its journey to that venue). Having given an overview of significant episodes of a life story that had been solicited, this well-known professor ended with the following reply to a rhetorical question about how one's life and life works have shaped the world:[539]

> Having admitted to that aspiration [of shaping the world that was], I am tempted to say "bah, humbug" in answer…. Although I know (and am grateful) that my work is taken seriously and respected if not admired by other scholars, and my teaching too is appreciated by and has enriched many students over the years, none of my scholarly research and writing—as far as I can tell, alas—has even rippled the surface waters of "the world" outside academe, let alone in any way actually … "shaped the world."

That summary statement has no doubt been repeated in similar versions by others many times, both before and after this one event.[539] At what date, roughly, does this main theme of first-person storytelling begin within a biography? Does it vary by historical setting? And most important for present purposes, to what extent, assuming the initiation is relatively early in a biography, does a theme of "aspirations and ambitions frustrated in the course of a life" make a difference in cross-person aggregation of per-person action effects? If and as one's sense of personal efficacy flags, does that fact significantly affect the dynamics by which per-person action effects are aggregated to become a, or the, modal effect of a collectivity, an organization of an institutional kind, of which the particular person-actor is a member? This is another way of asking the question, does a sense of efficacy from the AbCon process, however that process actually works, have any relevance to the process of aggregation? I have suggested that the two processes are in some sense mutual or interactive. But even if that is the case, the outcomes of abstractive condensation might have so little effect on the dynamics of cross-person aggregations of per-person effects, that nothing, or virtually nothing, would be lost by ignoring the AbCon process and all of its complications due to the near-hermeticism of first-person experience. The effects of per-person actions are important inasmuch as they become the aggregates of which so much emphasis is placed during national accountings (worker productivity, birth and morality rates, high-school and college graduation rates, and so forth). Per-person assessments of efficacy of efforts to "make a difference" might be an idling wheel in that scheme of relations; and yet in other frames, consequential. Consider that since the 1990s mortality rates in the USA have been increasing among white men who did not obtain college degrees. Much of that increase can be counted under the heading, "deaths of despair," to cite Anne Case and Angus Deaton (2020), the despair partly manifested as addiction to alcohol and/or other drugs and as self-conscious suicide. Most if not all of these men thought that they had been living proper lives, "doing all the right things," and yet somehow they were not reaping the expected rewards. Did they understand the gamble that had been taken in ending formal education short of a college degree? Probably not,

---

[539] In the interest of full disclosure, I met the author of that late reflection a few years after celebrating my 21st birthday anniversary on "red alert" during the "Cuban Missile Crisis." His sincerity of aspiration was undoubted and, I thought at the time, destined to be frustrated. Had he learned of my thought, he probably would have said I was "too cynical." Perhaps he was correct; but I would have replied, "more realistic." I return to the problem of reality in Part Six.

not if the decision had been made while looking in the rearview mirror at paternal and/or maternal records. Did they imagine that being white and male no longer carried the same subsidy that had benefited their parents, more particularly their fathers? Probably not, for those two advantages were as such simply "part of the water, part of the air being breathed," and, like the water and the air, never considered as optional.[540] As high-school education became during the twentieth century an increasingly "mass entitlement," it also became an ordinary commodity, and the mass entitlement shifted to the fact of a high-school diploma, increasingly variable of (hidden) measured content excepting a "time served" certification (see Collins 1979, as well as Young 1958 and Lemann 1999).

The lament against youthful aspiration is mistaken for several reasons. One is of course the rationality of second-person standpoint, the rationality of ethics or "practical reason" and our dependence on legislation. The AbCon concept is built around a first-person sense of personal efficacy. That inescapably features determinative acts of legislation (sociality), but the sense can sit uneasily with such acts because "determination" (even when "merely social") can seem nearly contradictory of, at least inconsistent with, a volition of personal efficacy. The tension is, I have judged, endemic. Several years ago, during initial experimentations with an AbCon concept of one sort or another, I conducted pilot studies as guidance to theorization.[541] One study explored meanings of personal efficacy in the vernacular of "success in life." Most of the adult persons I surveyed reported the belief (or "feeling") that they were being "mostly successful" in life.[542] As it happened, the 2016 General Social Survey queried a representative sample of US adults and found the same tendency of self-perception. My pilot study also asked respondents to "think of the two most important actions" they had recently taken, whether at work or in some other capacity, give a one-sentence description of that action, then estimate how long "the effects of each of those actions" lasted or would last. Estimates greater than "a few days" were rare. If the first part of the pilot study suggested an optimism of personal efficacy, the second part told more the "just another day" sort of story, matter-of-fact and hardly consequential. That the first part indicated no correlation between "being successful" and occupational status (or, among college students, school year) was not surprising.[543] Absence of correlation in the second part had not been expected, however.[544] Were the results from those two parts evidence of a "disconnect" in

---

[540] James Wood's (2018) novel, *Upstate*, treats these issues with great poignancy.

[541] Some of these studies were conducted with assistance of Professor Brenda Hughes, whose support and aid were invaluable and for which I am very grateful.

[542] The surveyed persons were a "convenience sample" of university students, staff, and faculty, personnel in other state offices, truck drivers, carpenters, store clerks—in short, as much variety of conditions as I could conveniently achieve. A few questions were delivered in print and/or orally.

[543] However, the General Social Survey indicated greater likelihood of "successful" response among those who were at least baccalaureates

[544] A third part of this pilot study included items designed to explore variations in how (and whether) adults could express valuation of time as such. One question asked how much I would have to pay the respondent to appear at a designated time in a designated indoor place, with chair provided, and do nothing but sit there for an hour. Most of the students gave amounts ranging from a few dollars to ten or twenty dollars (a few said "nothing"). The older respondents, all employed, gave amounts that could be roughly gauged in proportion to salary or wage-rate, but on sliding (increasing) scale, indicating that their "leisure time" was highly valued and too scarce to waste. Not only faculty members but also state

evaluative thinking? If so, I concluded, it was reflection of a "realism" in the sense that a person adjusts perceptual frame and anchorage depending on evaluative conditions, including the good at issue (see, e.g., Hazelrigg and Hardy 1997; Hardy and Hazelrigg 1999). One can reconcile "mostly successful life" with a realization that few if any actors whom one knows are actually indispensable and that the large majority of us have small parts to play. This is commensurate with the oft-quoted remark by Max Weber (1968 [1922], p. 1402) about someone being "as powerless as the fellahin of ancient Egypt"—a small remark that manages to straddle ethnocentrism in both directions.[545]

The lament is mistaken also because self-assessments are influenced by random factors, and it is difficult to filter them out of one's perspective. Generally speaking, it remains the case that, having trained ourselves to admire the omnipotence, omniscience, and omnipresence of the gods, we have been slow to grasp the importance of randomness, an ineradicable presence along with legislation, to our efforts of theorization. It was only a century ago, after all, that Ronald Fisher demonstrated the practical utility of randomized controlled experiments (see Salsburg 2001, pp. 46-51), and although we know more about such effects than is usually acknowledged, we still have much to learn about effects of random noise in our legislative actions.[546]

The significance of random factors can be appreciated in several forms. One has to do with variant alignments and intersections of biography and history. James Chriss (1993, p. 470) put his finger on an example of this when he cited, with reference to an episode early in Erving Goffman's career, "the precarious and highly contingent nature of the progression of human life." Another expression of the same point comes from an interview by *New York Times* culture critic Manola Dargis of Brad Pitt and Leonardo DiCaprio, in advance of a showing at the Cannes Film Festival of Quentin Tarantino's then new film, *Once upon a Time ... in Hollywood*, in which both DiCaprio and Pitt star.[547] Well into the interview Dargis, DiCaprio, and Pitt are talking history, chances, and talent, when DiCaprio says (Pitt agreeing the point), "I grew up in this industry, I have a lot of friends who are actors, and there's so much talent out there. But it really boils down to being at the right place at the right time." Who has not heard or read that sentence—so often uttered that it often sounds trite. In fact, it is anything but. The same point was made recently by one of the foremost social scientists of stratification, life chances, and mobility, Michael Hout (2012, 2018), when he demonstrated that so much of the variation in life chances depends on

---

office workers gave answers in hundreds of dollars. I took this evidence—perfectly understandable to any economist—as indication that most of the (non-student) respondents were thinking with self-interest in mind (i.e., "free time" is so rare as to be worth much more than my paid "work time").

[545] What is most remarkable about that citation of Weber is its popularity: of the dozens of Max Weber's references to ancient Egypt, this one has been by far the most often repeated. On the long-term interest—or one might say instead "fascination"—with "the Egyptian peasant" see Mitchell (1990) and Hamdy (2009).

[546] This includes, no doubt, effects known as "unintended consequences of purposive action." For an illustration of a massive case of that outcome in legislative action, see Menand (2020).

[547] The interview was published in the *Times* 23 May 2019, C1, under the title, "Old Hollywood, Tarantino-ized." I am quoting from the *Times'* online edition of the previous day, published under the title, "Brad Pitt, Leonardo DiCaprio Talk Tarantino, Stardom and What Might Have Been."

where/when one enters the fray. If born during the late 1930s or early 1940s in the USA, for instance, one had in store large opportunities for educational and occupational advancement, vis-à-vis one's parents, for "structural" reasons. Neither the infant nor the infant's parents would have known that, of course, for all of it lay within the contingent conditions of each of some number of more or less probable alternative futures. The most that the parents and then the child could have done was to try to be prepared opportunistically, to filter and update information, skills, and so forth, appropriately on a more or less regular basis. Only in retrospect can we see how the many contingencies were expressed and resolved; and thus we know that the resolutions came with considerable benefit to children born during those years. Compare, then, the record of children born in the USA during the 1960s or 1970s: while perhaps expecting continued improvements via "structural" factors such as had benefitted their parents, these children faced on average noticeably weaker conditions of opportunity, with effects that have persisted four or more decades later.[548]

One could say that different "cohort effects" lay in store for the two birth cohorts, and that would be appropriate so far as it goes. One must parse subject-verb pairings very carefully with regard to "cohort," however, which at base is only a statistical aggregate, partly arbitrary (e.g., in starting point, in length of interval). All too often one reads text in which a cohort is in effect described as having agency, despite many warnings against that mistake (e.g., Ryder 1965; Ni Bhrolcháin 1992; Hout 2012). Some will protest against that restriction, that it denies the very possibility of a "collective actor." It does not. It allows that actions of individual persons can have effects that are distinctive in some specified dimension or quality by difference of collectivity in which the persons exist integrally. That alone says less than might be supposed, however, because virtually all person-action occurs within some sort of collectivity. Even a cattle rancher living alone in a county of fewer than a hundred human residents (e.g., Loving County, Texas, 2000, with a density of less than two-tenths of a person per square mile) is unavoidably an actor in one or more collectivities (e.g., a network known as "the cattle market," another that supplies groceries, etc.). Does a birth cohort as such ever become, as such, an agent of action? There is no doubt that members of a given birth cohort can on average display a distinctive preference hierarchy, for example, which is expressed as a difference in pattern of actions. But the actions are by persons. Even the person or persons who are precisely "the average" of the cohort are acting as persons, not as the cohort. Moreover, it is typically the case that not all

---

[548] Recall from §26 that Manski (2004) demonstrated crucial dimensions of the dynamics of the process of learning from observations of the outcomes of prior person-actors in specific situations, especially the selection problem vis-à-vis outcomes observed relative to distributions of their counterfactuals (see also Manski 2006). Note that I have used scare quotes around "structural" in the above discussion. That is not because I doubt that such conditions are real or that they are in some sense "institutional" for being very resilient but, rather, because of a tendency in much of the literature to portray "structure" and "action" as analytically "either-or" factors. That is absurd. Without per-person actions of a certain kind, repetition, and coordination, "structures" would do nothing; and although foresight is all too rare, it does exist—which is to say that some kinds of action accord with "structural factors," but other kinds can work against those factors, and being able to discern the difference is a function of education.

members of a cohort will display a particular "cohort effect," which generally is a group mean effect and thus a probability term of the distribution of members on some specific variable. That variable can be, or be correlated with, a "vacancy chain" or a sequence of supply-demand exchanges; and actors as "supply elements" of exchange benefit unevenly, both from and for, the competition, some losing relative to others and some perhaps losing in non-relative terms as well.[549]

Robert Frank (2016), citing his own biography as illustration, made the same point: the date and place at which one enters the stream of history are highly influential conditions of one's own perspectives, interests, motivations, decisions, actions, and other features of the course of one's biography. Those conditions—which could be described as an ethnography of a specific family, a network of relations, a culture, and so forth, at a specific place and date—are the conditions of contingencies. They do not dictate specific perspectives, interests, motivations, and the rest; but they do "shuffle the deck" and "load the dice" with specific biases, and those biases can weigh very heavily on distributions of resources, opportunities, options, and choices. In the study of status mobility those distributional differences have often been denoted as "structural factors" or "determinants" of status outcomes. The wording is suitable if one keeps in mind the notion that the diameter of a pipe is a determinant of the rate at which a liquid can flow through it. But for any molecule of that flowing liquid the diameter is fixed, whereas the "motive force" pushing each molecule forward is variable though constrained by that fixed diameter. This very simple illustration from transport theory is also an illustration from communication theory. Thus, bear in mind that the analogy to constrained flow of fluid is applicable in information-theoretic terms to the AbCon process as well as to institutional channeling. Signal theory builds around the basic notion that the volume of channel flow is a function mainly of two variables, bandwidth and rate of flow.

Bandwidth is standardized, in the sense that bits of information are conveyed via signal frequency (as in radio stimulating an eardrum or in light stimulating skin—retina, tanning, sunburn, etc.). Bandwidth is measured as the difference between two frequencies: either between zero and the frequency of an audible sound or a radiant light reflecting off paper or being emitted by photonic diodes (or other device); or between two non-zero frequencies—say, A4 and C5 ("C over Middle C," a musical minor third). The metric is cycles per second. Rate of flow, which is measured in bits per second, is analogous to water moving through a pipe: the faster it flows the greater the volume of information conveyed (and perhaps received). Claude Shannon incorporated into his theory of communication an insight gained from Ralph Hartley (and now known as the Shannon-Hartley theorem), setting the theoretical upper limit of the rate at which usable information (i.e., net of any error-correction bits) can flow via any channel of specified

---

[549] What I mean by the "both from and for" phrasing is that uneven benefit derives from but also tends to reproduce prior inequalities. As one benefits, one tends also to reproduce, and perhaps pass on to a successor, the conditions of that benefit. It is the expectation of this chain that the children of the 1960s and 1970s, *and* their parents, supposed should continue from parent to child, as it had tended to do for these parents (born late 1930s or early 1940s) in relation to their parents (born during the early decades of the century). Resistance to continued policies of investing in a society's future members overrode that expectation, the resistance coming from some of those same parents and their children.

bandwidth (Shannon and Weaver 1949). Mensural demands of the theorem are straightforward and rather easily met in, say, music or audiovisual signaling. They can be met in principle for other sorts of action effects as well (e.g., the repetitive signals of a pricing mechanism, such as the buy/sell bids of a stock option; the Nielsen ratings by viewers of television programing; etc.). But the measurement demands generally exceed what we now typically have available when considering either the institutional heuristics and agenda messages of family, school, and work, the channeling of per-person action effects into aggregate effects of organizations as such, or the per-person AbCon process. Granted, "what we have available" is a resultant of little effort to invent the appropriate measurement techniques.[550]

The task is complicated by the presence of random noise mixed with the signal of interest and by the fact that institutional process is distributed process. When there is no unified or well-coordinated "sender" agency, distributed processes tend to introduce a larger noise component. When some of the distributed process is recursive, efficiency of signal is increased (i.e., more compaction of bits). By analogy, think of the important work of recursion in syntax: linguistic structure accommodates aggregation of distinct phrase-meanings, a nesting of actions (which can occur also semantically as word-compounding, more frequent in German than in English). This aggregation is also a compaction that occurs over time, a process in the "evolution" or "historical development" of a language's capacity and versatility. It very likely forms the central dynamic of the AbCon process. And it occurs collectively, in the sense that the sociality of language use is the "carrier," so to speak, of the process. Recursive rules are rather easily accommodated in signaling, again because they require little additional code. Iteration, on the other hand, which generally requires more code, is a form of repetitive signaling that depends on a loop whereby first outcome of a function serves as starting value for the next cycle of the loop. Thus, whereas a recursive rule simply calls for its repetitive application, an iterative rule calls for application of another function, the loop. Iteration is a form of repetition that can generate successively closer approximation to an expected outcome. Because it requires extra code, and because the greater the code the likelier the presence of error, iteration tends to be noisier in outcome sequence, however, and this noise is less likely random. I will return to the problem of random noise in a moment.

Whatever the functional form of distribution (and holding Gaussian noise to the side), the intended informational content (the "message") is usually diffuse simply because of variation among organizations of an institutional type. The message is distributed across organizations that variably *manifest* the institution. Likewise, the aggregation of per-person action effects tends to vary across organizations of institutional type, and thus the macro-manifestation of action effects can feature inconsistencies and potentially contradictions, which in turn can be seeds of institutional change. More than one hundred million household families manifest the institution of "family" in the USA; more than a hundred thousand schools, "K to 12," manifest the mandated part of the institution of "school"; more than five million places of employment, private and public, including self-employment, manifest the institution of "work" (i.e., paid employment). Cross-alignment abounds (i.e., many school administrators, teachers, maintenance and custodial

---

[550] For a useful sampling of recent research on information rates for speech in different languages, see Pellegrino, Coupé, and Marsico (2011).

workers are both adult children of others and parents of school children; and so forth). Heuristic messages criss-cross: patterns can be mutually reinforcing patterns or at cross-purposes. Aggregative flows of per-person action effects likewise intersect in complicated ways. In sum, it is clear that "institution" is a highly complex formation: manifestly real in its effects, its conditions, and its transactions, it also exists as a virtual reality that becomes manifest only in specific organizations populated by specific individual persons.

Message dynamics are not in that same way initially clear for the per-person AbCon process. The main obstacle is of course the fact that, while the filter-and-update procedure of abstraction and then condensation will be processual of experiences that include second-person and third-person influences, the dynamics of the AbCon process as such are inescapably first-person experiential. Memory functions are surely involved. But to assume that second-person memory reports are isomorphic with the first-person memory function itself is, so far as I can discern, an act both bold and bald (if also unavoidable). It might be tempting here to invoke the Hegelian notion of an intelligence that operates, as it were, behind the back of consciousness (Hegel 1977 [1952], §87). But if so, the dialectic surely accommodates conscious learning, an incorporation of learned skills that could include something like a Bayesian process of filter and update in application of neural decisions about what parts of an immediate experience should be pared away and thus how to update a storyline. Whether the repetitiveness of process is coded only as iteration or more efficiently as recursion remains rather opaque, much as Hume left it.

Whereas recursion can be most easily innovative of information, another of the processes that express an "infinite behavior" in channel-based computational dynamics, replication, tends to be distinctive for preserving all information from past to present coding, and unlike either recursion or iteration it displays decidable convergence (i.e., a termination point). This makes replication especially relevant to modeling system processes. For example, begin with the simple premise that physical activities of human sociality are replicable and at least in principle with neither gap nor remainder. From that premise, as Paul Romer has pointed out, it follows that

> the aggregate production function representing a competitive market should be characterized by homogeneity of degree one in all of its conventional (that is, rival) inputs. If we represent output in the form $Y = AF(K, H, L)$, then doubling all three of K, H, and L should allow a doubling of output. There is no need to double the nonrival inputs represented by A because the existing pieces of information can be used in both instances of the productive activity at the same time. (The assumption that the market is competitive means that the existing activity already operates at the minimum efficient scale, so there are no economies of scale from building a single plant that is twice as large as the existing one.) If farming were the relevant activity instead of manufacturing, we would clearly need to include land as an input in production, and in the economy as a whole, it is not possible to double the stock of land. This does not change the fundamental implication of the replication argument. If aggregate output is homogeneous of degree 1 in the rival inputs and firms are price takers, Euler's theorem implies that the compensation paid to the rival inputs must exactly equal the value of output produced. This fact is part of what makes the neoclassical model so simple and makes growth accounting work. The only problem is that this leaves nothing to

compensate any inputs that were used to produce the discoveries that lead to increases in A (Romer 1994, p. 10).

Bear in mind that the expressed necessity ("must exactly equal") is of course a manifestation of a theoretical model, not of actual phenomena.[551] An actual phenomenal world does not necessarily conform to that model. However, replication both reinforces and is reinforced by the fact that market relations tend to be path dependent, a characteristic of institutionalized organization more generally. In market-based choice (decision making) path dependence tends to be a powerful force that can and very often does create what amounts to *directed* decision making, although usually under a different name. This observation complicates both proposals and critiques of what is sometimes called "directed technological change" (see e.g., Acemoglu 2002), which tend to presuppose that market processes are non-directive (or if directive, only by some mysterious "invisible hand"). We will come back to these matters and their implications later.

Before returning to the problem of random noise, let me proceed briefly with a different observation and a question thereby raised. Institutional channeling hosts bidirectional flows of relevant information (as well as noise, random and otherwise). The question is about symmetry; more specifically, whether bidirectionality implies process reversibility: under what conditions, if any, is aggregation of per-person action effects reversible? Different meanings can be read of that question. One of the few carefully systematic efforts to filter among those differences is Hannan's (1991). For a number of reasons pertaining to data availability, probably the most common of the main meanings has to do with the conditions under which aggregated data—in the sense of data that consist in distributional statistics for a collectivity of actors, not the links from units to aggregate—can be legitimately used to test hypotheses of person-level relations.[552] Putting emphasis on consistency and linearity of relations, Hannan (1991, pp. 20-30, 32, 33, 59) outlined conditions under which aggregated data may be used productively with care. One can generalize that conclusion to the broader question about conditions under which aggregation and disaggregation can be treated as symmetrical and reversible of process—namely, when thorough consistency and linearity of relations is maintained.[553] The consistency criterion is rather more demanding than the criterion of linearity (Hannan 1991, pp. 16-22). Earlier I suggested imagery of Pickering's "mangle" as a rough test: once the work of mangling has concluded, how easily

---

[551] The phrase "homogeneous degree 1" simply means that if the inputs are multiplied by k, then the output will also be multiplied by k (in other words, a relation of "constant returns to scale"). Thus, according to the model, in the absence of nonrival goods (such that A is null in the above equation), there can be no increasing (or decreasing) returns to scale.

[552] As noted previously, for some social scientists, economists especially, it is not just availability pure and simple but also quality of data, the argument being that most adults cannot (or at least do not) report per-person or even per-household accurate estimations of many variables, especially utilitarian monetary variables, whereas errors tend to be cross-canceling during aggregation, and otherwise adjustments for known (or suspected) systematic bias can be introduced. Aaggregation/disaggregation biases should not be confused with errors of mensural estimation (as Hannan pointed out)..

[553] Lest that discussion be misread, I do not mean reversibility of time. I mean reversibility of algorithmic steps by which a process—aggregation or disaggregation—unfolds. In simple illustration, I can assemble seven letters into the word, "reason," and I can disassemble the word "reasons" into its seven letters. Is one process the reverse of the other? The passage of time is "unidirectional" is both.

can one pick apart the product sufficiently to restore the ex-ante conditions of those inputs which had been put through the mangle? The consistency criterion is in fact a presupposition in favor of homology. But homology is often at the core of what is at issue. As Hannan emphasized, the criterion rules out of bounds complications of multiplier (i.e., scale) effects, notions of "emergent properties," and the like.

This latter point brings us to the other main meaning that can be read of the question about conditions—that is, conditions that differentiate between homologous and heterologous relations. Recall that I have persistently reminded the reader of dialectical perspective. Thus, for example, before undertaking analysis of conditions that are enabling versus conditions that are constraining, one should conceptualize the basis of that analysis as enablement/constraint: each calls out the other. (Likewise, cost/benefit; supply/demand; production/consumption; and so on.) Thus, also, recall Coleman's "boat figure" (Figure 5.1, p. 382). The typical understanding of that diagram is that the right side, the "macro-to-micro" relation, is chiefly if not entirely constraining and the left side, the "micro-to-macro" relation, is chiefly if not entirely enabling, in the sense of creating collectivity or enabling an existing collectivity to function. Does that separation really make sense? Consider this version of the question: under what conditions is either of that pair of directional relationships *both* enabling *and* constraining (rather than, conversely, one but not the other)? In this latter regard, recall as well Marx' critique of all versions of the Robinsonade: rare indeed the individual person who is not current member of at least one collectivity; and nonexistent the person who has never had such membership (myths of the wolf-suckled babe notwithstanding).[554]

Now the problem of random noise, a more insidious form of "random factor" affecting a flow of information with regard both to self-assessments of personal efficacy of action and the process of aggregating the action effects of per-person actors cross-sectionally and over time. It should be evident in personal reflection that self-assessment of ability (i.e., skills, knowledge, a sense of competence, etc.) is important to one's feeling of efficacy, in part because it affects one's motivations to learn, to improve, and therefore one's confidence to engage challenging action, including learning, and thus to invite new feedback in assessment of ability (see, e.g., Nuhfer, Fleischer, Cogan, Wirth, and Gaze 2017). Unfortunately, mistaken results of research reported in 1999 and widely disseminated encouraged the view that persons of low ability in general, and persons of low ability on at least some particular tasks, tend to be self-delusional when assessing their ability (Kruger and Dunning 1999). That general conclusion was quickly accorded status of confirmed generalization, known as "the Dunning-Kruger effect." If one considers for a moment the motivating hypothesis behind the initial research, as well as later studies that supposedly confirmed the effect again and again, a logical problem comes to mind: if cognitive ability is in question, why would one's "meta-cognitive" self-assessment of one's cognitive ability be any less questionable? If person P's actual ability on any given task is, per hypothesis, significantly lower than P's own assessment of that ability, then an observer should expect that P's reported self-assessment will contain more "noise" than would be true of the comparable report of self-assessed ability by a person who in fact has high ability on the same

---

[554] In the introduction to his *Grundrisse*, written in 1857, Marx (1986 [1939]) skewered Daniel Defoe's version of "first origin" conceits: "the individual and isolated hunter and fisherman, with whom Smith and Ricardo begin, belongs among the unimaginative conceits of the eighteenth-century Robinsonades."

task. Sorting out the noise factor is not easy. But in addition to that complication (which was ignored in prior research), observed results of the studies were generally presented in a way that arithmetically guaranteed the "shape" of the result, obscured that guarantee, and, because the presentation seemed so easy for readers to understand, was repeated in most of the replications (for details, see Nuhfer et al., 2017). While there is abundant reason to doubt that "the average adult," or for that matter *any* adult, is a perfectly rational actor and immune to self-deceptions, more careful efforts to estimate adults' self-assessments of specific skill, knowledge, and similar cognitive contents suggest that, on average, any gap between "reality" and "self-impression" is much smaller than indicated by studies conducted by Kruger, Dunning, and their followers.

On the other hand, if indeed "the modern condition" has been one of existential angst and dread, resulting from some conjunction or copulation of processes and states of mind described by Søren Kierkegaard and Jean-Paul Sartre, for example, perhaps the dominant orientation of present self has become more often, and/or in greater degree, one of generalized inefficacy: "nothing I can do will make any difference anyway, so why try?" No doubt, modern societies have become much more complex and more demanding since the end of the eighteenth century, the time of Hume and Kant. No doubt, public education has failed more often and to greater degree in providing the tools needed to maintain levels of competency and efficacy. Too many adults are only marginally literate, lack numeracy even at that level, are ill-equipped to think in probabilistic terms by which to manage uncertainties and ambiguities, and all too often lapse into conspiratorial thinking because it offers seemingly certain answers that are devised in such ways as to defy disproof. Lacking skills of logic by which to detect circular reasoning or question begging, the poorly equipped seek feelings of power and consequence, even invincibility, from convenient sources. Demagogues have always lain in wait.

Separating random noise from a signal is easier when one already knows what the signal is or, in the vernacular, what the signal is "supposed to look like." That, of course, is a common bias of prejudgment. Equally confounding is the fact that common expectations about evidence of randomness are also ill founded. Imagine, for example, seeing a pattern of outcomes of "fair flips of a fair coin" that shows regularly alternating "heads" and "tails" for, say, twenty trials but then is interrupted by an unbroken string of twenty heads (or tails) before resumption of the same regularly alternating outcomes. What does one make of that? A coded message (digital format) embedded in a random pattern? While it is tempting to conclude as much, there is no evidence for it. By saying "fair flips of a fair coin," I meant that each flip is an independent event, and on each event the probability of "heads" (or "tails") is exactly .50 (or 50 percent). What, then, would be the probability of getting a constant string of twenty heads (or twenty tails)? The answer is straightforward: $0.50^{20} = 9.537^{-7}$ (or, in words, 0.50 self-multiplied twenty times yields a twenty-trial probability that is very small—namely, .0000009537, or less than one in a million). As those words just announced, the probability of *any* pattern of outcomes of twenty fair flips of a fair coin is that same small number. Of course, strictly independent events are not ordinary in human worlds. Events are usually influenced by their conditions, and sometimes an event is internally influential in the sense that an event of a given type changes the conditions of a next event of the same type. The benefit of strict independence is that it establishes a theoretical benchmark against which or in terms of which events that are not strictly independent can be compared. This also means, however, that there is abundant room for the "almost independent"

508

event (or, conversely, the "weakly dependent" or "moderately dependent" event), and these gradations of dependence can be, typically are, composed not only of "signals" of potential or actual interest but also of "noises" that are "almost random" "randomly influential," or "under some conditions, sometimes, random-like."

In sum, information-theoretic flows are virtually always amalgams of signal(s) and noise, some of which can be conditionally "chunky" enough to stand out as biased frameworks and/or conditions within or under which human actions are ventures into a casino or lottery in which players are inclined either to indulge in one or another version of the gambler's fallacy or to ignore consequences of the gambler's fallacy as if dynamics of the fallacy and its outcomes had nothing to do with their relative successes as well as failures. Replication can interrupt prior experience as a productive sorting: imagine, following the above recounted sequence of forty-plus fair flips of a fair coin, that a second sequence of forty-plus trials of the same coin matches the first sequence exactly: one might reasonably suspect a nonrandom message.

Other forms of randomness are difficult to detect specifically and sort out, which means that it is also difficult to detect specific consequences of the randomness, especially in the AbCon process and its outcome at any stage of the updating. There is a tendency to assume that random noise is of little or no consequence simply because it is random. If in fact we could in general clearly distinguish between random noise and a signal of interest, that simple assumption would be utilitarian. However, distinguishing the relative effects is difficult especially in absence of key observations of the process dynamics about which inferences must be made.[555] As has been demonstrated repeatedly, random noise affects measurements of variables of interest and conduces to misleading presentations of analytic results, especially graphic presentations. As Nuhfer and colleagues (2017) have shown, that effect has combined with logical problems in understanding "value added" measures (i.e., $y_{t+1} - y_t$, relative to $y_t$ as baseline), to result in published work that misrepresented self-assessments of competency and efficacy (mainly to exaggerate the extent of error in self-assessments).

If I am right in my postulation of the main dynamics of the AbCon process, it seems likely that Thomas Bayes had already formulated much the same conception and assumed its operation in ordinary per-person applications, especially those resulting in evaluative judgments of personal efficacy. "It is conditional probability," as Leonard Savage (1972, p. 44) later said, "that gives expression in the theory of personal probability to the phenomenon of learning by experience."

The concept of AbCon raises a question of duration, the duration of relevant experience and the duration of a present dependence. Recall from §27 that I added another set of "technical terms" (rather, as I cautioned then, more a difference of perspective), these having to do with memory functions and more especially notions of "delayed effects" and "long-memory process" (see, e.g., Beran 1994). The implications apply to issues of stability especially with respect to

---

[555] For some recent illustrations of the difficulty, see the sequence of studies extending from Hearst, Newman, and Hulley (1986) to Conley and Heerwig (2012), using as a randomized controlled experiment the US Selective Service draft during the US war in Vietnam, in order to investigate (inter alia) subsequent health and mortality consequences of military service in that war.

institutions (and, for example, the notorious conclusions of the "school outcomes" study by James Coleman and associates, plus repetitive outcomes by later scholars) but also to the question whether process characteristics of delayed and/or long-memory effects apply to the AbCon process, as I have conceived it, as well as to cross-person aggregation of per-person actions effects. I will return to these implications in a moment, but first I need to review some matters of framework.

In general, it can be argued that the AbCon process should be largely immune to delayed or long-memory effects, because of operations of the filter-and-update sequences that are at the heart of abstraction and condensation. Thus, if outcomes of the AbCon process are primarily and mainly implicated (if at all) in the per-person actions of a given person, AbCon outcomes will be implicit in those per-person action effects and will otherwise have no influence—thus, no delayed effect or long-memory effect—on cross-person aggregations of action effects. But could there be indirect influences? For that matter, can one be so confident that the AbCon process is *as such* lacking long-term endogenous dependencies? Is it not possible that filter-and-update sequences can and do maintain some long-memory properties? For example, what about the long memory of entering the same workplace every workday during the past twenty years? Or, conversely, the long memory of having entered N number of different workplaces over that same twenty-year period? In either case, one might expect that filter-and-update sequences proceeded as usual but with little more effect on or in the twenty-year memory than reconfirmation and, perhaps, added imbrications of emotive or emotive-cognitive first-person experiences.

One must keep in mind the difference between "wet" and "dry" memory. While the main tendency probably has been to connect "memory" with the human brain, the fact is that humans have been building memory into physical structures far longer than historiography has recorded. Think of writing, of course, but also the even "drier" memory of a physical structure such as a dwelling or a cemetery or an office building or machine shop remembering "how to be" for far longer periods than twenty years. Most long-memory process even in cross-person aggregation is directly or indirectly physical, some of it ceremonial in conjunction with one or more physical markers involved with, say, "going to work" or "visiting a place" but no less also "standing for the national anthem" or "attending a funeral." And whether ceremonial or not, surely the largest quantity of long-memory is historiographic, including visual and/or aural accounts, as in still imagery, film, sound recording (think of the cave art in Sulawesi, recently announced to worlds beyond, dated to 44,000 years before today). Some portions of historiographic long-memory process are manifest institutionally—in the heuristics of "how to be" in this or that institutional setting (what it means to be "student in school" or "working a job," etc.). One specific form of "institutional memory" occurs in a specific organization of institutional type, when and insofar as a particular member of the organization has been "invested" (by self and others) as curator of the organization's institutional memory. This form is an indicative brand, so to speak, blending relatively explicit AbCon functioning within extant results of cross-person aggregation. A local curator can be called upon under the assumption of a stability of memory, this stability indeed at focus of a (perhaps repeatedly celebrated) agreement among organizational members but likely exaggerated to the extent of the filter-and-update sequencing in abstractive condensation. An interesting empirical question is whether

510

investiture is selective: is a person who is perceived by other organization members as "old fashion" or a "slow adopter" or of "conservative attitude" more likely to be chosen as "local curator of institutional memory"? And perhaps self-selected in such terms as well?

Now to return to my recall of the discussion in §27: I used a thought experiment of two men born the same year to different families, two men who obtained a baccalaureate from the same college and then went to work for the same company in Omaha. We see them at age 45, in middle management, although Ray had moved to a different Omaha company. Both can be seen as successful by local standards, but Ray's salary is about $15,000 lower than Jay's. Why that disparity? Plausible explanations considered earlier focused on prejudicial discriminations—for example, that Ray was born to an African American family. The point now is the question how, assuming that scenario of a prejudicial discrimination in life chances, would that background information have become a *delayed* effect, when the decisive characteristic had been present all along, during the first twenty years of what appeared to be equivalent "success stories"? On the one hand, one could argue that this was an instance of a negative-selection effect: persons who benefit proportionately the most from college, for example, tend to be those who are actually *least* likely to have attended college in the first place and then gained a degree (see, e.g., Brand and Xie 2010).[556] We could thus plausibly conclude that Ray was the more tenacious, the more resilient of the two men but because of the sociality of racial prejudice the discriminatory effect was merely delayed. Furthermore, while there is abundant evidence indicating that economic (i.e., income) returns to education are generally positive (see the review in Brand and Xie 2010, for example), that same fund of evidence also demonstrates that the correlation is far short of complete, which means a variety of factors can be cited in explanation of the income disparity in the foregoing illustration without ever mentioning racial (or any other) prejudicial discrimination. Further, as will be seen later in some detail, official data on worker productivity are little more than a gloss on per-person dynamics of productivity and its connection to worker earnings. All in all, then, what has been called in the illustration a delayed effect could have been category error.

But for the sake of argument let's assume that it was a delayed effect, as was categorized in the foregoing discussion. In what sense could that be counted as an instance of long-memory process? If the disparity in income was a direct effect of prejudicial discrimination, such effect had been present as potential all along but became manifest only after some delay, the effect then being manifest not all at once but gradually over ten to fifteen years. Since the potential would have been plainly observable, had the dynamic been that of a long-memory process it must have been the kind that can be said of a physical building in its long memory of "how to be." While we generally know how such information is "stored" in a physical thing, how might it similarly be stored in an individual person? Of course, we also know even moderately strong correlations

---

[556] Note that sign as well as degree of relationship is relative to comparative standard; thus, e.g., greater benefit of college by those least likely to attend could be only in comparison to the least likely who in fact did not attend (see Brand and Xie 2010, pp. 293-294). In an earlier application I used an inverse Mills ratio to segregate that portion of a sampled population who stood out as very unlikely to have acted as they did and examined them further (Hardy, Hazelrigg, and Quadagno 1996, pp.182-184). Because of the relativity, such comparisons can generate insights, but they can also mislead.

leave considerable latitude in expectations about fairness or justification of cross-person relations in relative distributions of rewards such as employment income. How might the information that became a delayed effect have been stored? For Ray's employer it could have been part of that very expectation—in other words, an expectation that because of ancestry Ray simply could not have been worth what "someone like Jay" would have been paid "for the same hours and quality of work." But more than that, the information might have been stored also in Ray's own self-concept—his own first-person meaning of being "*me*," object to myself. In either vector, however, the information had been present all along, its effects being persistently manifested. Isn't the key point of "*delayed* effect" that it is new, not previously manifest?

The simple answer is that filter-and-update sequences of AbCon operate mostly along the edges, so to speak, paring away experiences that amount to negative selections by a criterion of use. Main thematics are retained, sometimes reshaped, augmented, and/or re-sectioned but rarely jettisoned for another theme. That is the ordinary answer. A more complex answer is put into relief by recalling the sort of defensive armament cited by Walter Pater a century and a half ago, when it was common to lay both glory and sorrow at the feet of a stalwart personality, still a world of heroism but much too late for Goethe, Byron, and company. Responding to the flood of concerns about the whirl of modern life with impressions that Émile Durkheim would surely have recognized as personal, Pater said that if one begins

> with the inward world of thought and feeling, the whirlpool is still more rapid, the flame more eager and devouring. ... At first sight experience seems to bury us under a flood of external objects, pressing upon us with a sharp importunate reality, calling us out of ourselves in a thousand forms of action. But when reflection begins to act upon those objects they are dissipated under its influence; the cohesive force is suspended like a trick of magic; each object is loosed into a group of impressions—colour, odour, texture—in the mind of the observer. And if we continue to dwell on this world, not of objects in the solidity with which language invests them, but of impressions unstable, flickering, inconsistent, which burn and are extinguished with our consciousness of them, it contracts still further; the whole scope of observation is dwarfed to the narrow chamber of the individual mind. Experience, already reduced by a swarm of impressions, is ringed around for each one of us by that thick wall of personality through which no real voice has ever pierced on its way to us, or from us to that which we can only conjecture to be without (Pater 1986 [1888], pp. 118-119).

That "wall of personality" is thicker for some than for others. Thickness is nurtured and gauged in correlation with resources of sociality (material and ideal). Resilience is real as well as varied; it is learned within local sociality, and local sociality can itself be infected with all sorts of status stratification, all of them discriminatory and any of them prejudicial in assumptions, perceptions, and operational dynamics. Today we read (and write) of "silo effects" within sociality, a version of path dependence or of the night-time drunk who looks for his lost car key only within the circle of the nearest light cone.

For all the sequencing of filter-and-updating intervals over the course of a quarter-century or more of a work life, there can nonetheless remain a constant or near-constant memory of "who I am." That memory can be centered on a conscious or a less-than-conscious sense of privilege and "great things to come." It can be centered instead on an intensely conscious sense of dread and/or despair—that "sooner or later my luck will turn bad," or that "sooner or later people will remember that I am an X," this "X" being individually filled in by a generally disfavored status (black, immigrant, farm boy, ex-con, and so forth). This long-memory effect can of course have deleterious effects in a person's actions, therefore in effects of actions, and therefore in how those per-person effects are integrated in cross-person aggregations of action effects.

Here, too, of course, the information flow, whether in the form of a delayed effect or the repetitive effect of long-memory process, will ordinarily occur through one or more institutional channels, and that means that the flow is constraining/enabling with some specificity that probably varies by institution. Douglass North (1990, 1995) undertook a relevant review and analysis of variable institutional processes, including their relative stabilities. As prelude, he emphasized that while for any given person-actor there is always already an inheritance of institutional processes, the processes began and continue in the actions of human beings, not in the abstract principles of any scientific model (which always come late to the scene), and he then gave an overview of major ways in which the main standard model of society as proposed by his own discipline of social science (economics) could be improved by greater attention to institutional processes. His list of excessive simplifications was not novel, as he surely recognized. Insofar as relevant actions of the average adult are reflective of a more or less coherent model implicitly (if not explicitly) held by that person, it is generally evident that the actual level of coherence does not approximate the main standard economic model very well. The rationality manifested in that person's actions is far from perfect and is sometimes confused by inconsistencies from nonrational sources. Knowledge is incomplete and often partial due to prejudices. Judgments tend to be myopic and habitual, displaying little evidence of effective updating. Some relations are assumed to be certain, when at best they could be only probabilistic and sometimes only weakly estimable. All in all, these and related concerns do raise questions about easy assumptions of convergence across person-specific self-models.

And yet convergence of some sort does occur, the evidence of it seen in the facticity of major institutions—commercial markets and firms, government agencies, schools, orchestras and dance companies, scientific laboratories, and so on. Aggregation processes do achieve results, both public and private, whether we have good understandings or only feeble guesses, or bits and mixtures of each, of how those processes operate. As John Kenneth Galbraith (1955) pointed out long ago, "economic intelligence" is often in "poor state" partly because it is so easily camouflaged in the quotidian details of market process.

No doubt the evidence of "achieved results" comes mainly from macroscopic levels of observation. We seldom make much effort to observe the aggregations as they occur, as processes. It does seem clear that convergences across person-specific models and actions need not be complete or perfect or entirely consistent, free of contradictions, in order to coalesce over time, enough at least to reproduce the institutions that those persons inherited as enablements/constraints. The dynamic of a Gaussian convergence is usually enough. This leaves abundant room for the reproduction of distributional inequalities and other "small failures" of the market model (e.g., privileged information, embezzlements, etc.), however, and it contains little if any assurance against institutional sclerosis over the same period of time.[557] Indeed, sclerosis may well have become increasingly likely insofar as relations *among* the major institutions converge to an equilibrium. But the presence of internal contradictions—a presence likely to continue because of unintended effects of disparate measurement costs and disparate transaction costs within one or more (usually several) of the major institutions—tend to work as negative feedbacks which dampen tendencies to inter-institutional convergence. It is also virtually a truism that, whether institutional or not, organizations are prone to "agency costs," one of the main variables of that generality being the case-specific definition of "principal." Parents or guardians are agents for children (principals); teachers and school officials and, again, parents are agents for a school's pupils; and so forth. But the agent/principal dialectic is usually reduced to the conveniences of an analytic distinction, which allows categories of "agency costs" to be ignored or even denied under a heading of prejudicial discrimination, for example, as it is easy to confuse aggregation effects of agency as effects of per-person bias. The main point in that observation is that the fact of organization itself is not a costless good, but it can be very difficult to observe, much less make sound estimates of, the cost, because there is no Archimedean platform on which to stand (i.e., outside sociality, thus outside all organization) when observing and estimating. Rather, all available "platforms," by dint of presence in organization, tend to be repositories of inequality of perspective, frames, preferences, and so forth, as well as of material resources. Enablements are always also constraints and vice versa. And yet none of this subverts Hume's famous dictum about fictions. These are always human products.

For infants and young children inequalities of familial (parental but potentially also in kin networks and in networks of parental friends) are formative of the launching pad. In general, this inheritance is reflective of household (parental, kin, guardian, etc.) status, which is indicative of infant's initial life chances through actions taken (and the counterfactual, actions not taken) by one or more parents (and hereafter by "parent" I include the effective parenting member, one or more, any gender and any generation, biogenetic or foster or guardian agent). The impact of the familial inequalities has been strongly expressed well before the child enters formal schooling, and usually by age four or five, the period of rapid development (both organic, especially neural, and social, including as before skills separately described as linguistic, cultural, economic, etc.). In sum, the array of possible, potential, and probable "launching pads" into formal schooling is anything but a level field of options in the distribution of past, present, and therefore future resources for the child. The capabilities of four-year-old children can and do vary widely. That variance is all too often characterized as "natural difference," as if it is variation of "in-born" capabilities or even capacities. It is in fact anything but. Insofar as there are variant capacities at birth (and excluding variations due to biologically based disablements, such as Down syndrome, microcephalia, etc.), variation in capacity or potentiality at birth is much smaller than variation in capabilities at age four. The difference is due to resource-based practices, where the most vital "resource" is variety, density, and carefully measured complexity

---

[557] To repeat a point made in §27 (and which will be repeated below), a geometric Brownian motion model is a good point of departure for assessing aggregation of per-person action effects and for assessing cross-person aggregations. Its strength, simplicity, is also its weakness, of course.

of continued stimulus via sociality. The sociality will have been present; otherwise, the infant would not have survived. In the broad scheme of US society (and others), however, its "richness" has been and is, and should be appreciated as, shockingly variable. In US society this variation has been and is correlated with racism and, perhaps to diminishing degree, genderism. The commonality underlying those correlations has been and is, however, distributional inequality. As vignettes offered by many ethnographic accounts have testified—in this book, for instance, those by Hochschild (2016), Isenberg (2016), and Vance (2016), among others, in recent years— lots of white male four-year-old children have been victims of an inheritance of poverty. Consequences of that poverty are also distributed, none of them strictly inevitable. Some have highlighted "resilience" of character as regulating difference in the outcome of childhood and youth poverty (e.g., Clausen 1991, 1995; Werner 1992, 2001; Smarsh 2018; Westover 2018). But resilience, too, is learned, not inherent at birth (Case and Deaton 2020).

Poverty and distributions of its effects are measured qualities; measurement is a social act; and social acts are not free. One of the particular contributions of North's work was his insight that of all "transaction costs" (as economists call the costs of "social acts," as if some acts are not social) measurement costs are among the most important of overlooked costs. They tend to be swept into the seldom explicated notion that institutional channeling is necessary, natural (or almost), and as close to a "free good" as anything ever invented by human ingenuity (whether deliberately or by happenstance). When was the last time an economist (or anyone else) asked about the cost of equilibrium? To the extent that there is a considered idea behind that bias, it has to do not with the organizational processes that become institutionalized—family, school, work, governance, etc.—but with the stability of the institutional form of the given processes, once the institutionalization has been achieved. While there have indeed been newly invented institutions over the centuries, and while existing institutions do change, most of it so gradual as to be unnoticed within a human lifetime—North (1990, p. 89) pointed out that much of the change proceeds in small increments—the fact of equilibrium itself has been deemed so improbable that it has commanded most attention as a matter of theory and of empirical inquiry, most especially concerning its conditions, its stability, its benefits, rarely anything about its costs. The backdrop to that attention is of course a sense of the "blooming buzz of the quotidian" in everyday life. It seems amazing, in light of that experience, that a market of exchanges, for example, can not only work toward equilibrium but also, even more notable, that "the market mechanism," the buy/sell dialectic of the "pricing mechanism," presupposes for its successful operation an equilibrium state known as *trust*. At some basic level, per-person actions both presuppose and imply trust among strangers even as many, sometimes the large majority, of those person-actors get the short end of the stick. This is one major factor beneath the observation that institutional sclerosis can be overlooked for long periods of time.

As has been pointed out before, most attention to questions of determinants of schooling has been focused on "school resources." This was true during the 1960s, when James Coleman was directing the large study that resulted in the Coleman report, mainly because it was as such an "ordinary" topic of public policy at local as well as state and federal levels, and agency costs rarely ventured through accepted boundaries of public discourse. Those boundaries were instrumental to the background focus that contributed to the basis of controversy which greeted

515

what was received as Coleman's only important conclusion—namely, that "family" contributed more than "school" to later success. Whereas "public school" was thought to be (as that phrase says) a public good, therefore a matter of public policy and a contentious matter for reasons that had to do both with a heritage of racism and with sometimes hostile concerns about "government interference where it does not belong" (upbringing of children), "family" was thought to be the sanctuary of privacy and the seat of moral order. Public policy could rightfully attend to public institutions but had no right to interfere with privacies of the family. Children were first and foremost part of "family": only as a child aged toward adulthood did the public order gain some jurisdiction that many families considered acceptable, yet the concern about public resources for public education could also only be effective as a matter of public order. The "interference" of the federal government in race relations—which was the perspective of many white families as they considered efforts to rectify the "separate and unequal" discrimination against US school-age children of African ancestry—exacerbated that "prior" and partly independent ambiguous location of public schools at intersections of public and private realms. Institutional sclerosis is often a long and heavy shadow of historical events, as it was in this intersectional setting. Some adults, and some of their children, had not given up on the idea of slavery. Outrageous, to be sure, but a truth abundantly confirmed by attitudes and actions.

Subsequent studies confirmed Coleman's conclusion, though mainly from one side only: the typical statement was that "school resources have little to do with the subsequent success of pupils"; little if anything was said comparatively about "family resources." For example, David Card and Alan Krueger (1996, 1998) offered systematic assessments of the existing research and added some of their own. The general pattern of results was ambiguous, chiefly because effects of observed variations in school resources had such weak, if any, effects on student achievement that only weak and ambiguous conclusions could be drawn. Krueger (1999) documented small effects of class size on standardized test results among 11,600 kindergarten-through-third-grade students, the effect being larger among minority students and students from poor families. But while he was confident that "Hawthorne effects" (effects of being knowably watched to purpose) were unlikely, other uncertainties of plausible relationships could more than match the small effect size. As Card and Krueger (1996, p. 47) said in one of their overviews, some three decades "after the Coleman report it is unfortunate and frustrating that more is not known about schooling," but the available evidence was generally so weak and subject to "all the standard criticisms of drawing causal inferences from observational data" that little could be said with confidence. Another two decades later, the main conclusion remained: variation in school resources seemed to make little if any difference. But now the other side of that conclusion was stated openly and perhaps with greater confidence: "family background is far and away the most important determinant of educational achievement and attainment" (Morgan and Jung 2016, p. 83).

Question: what accounts for that long record of stability—the *same results* of research by at least three generations of investigators coming to the fore, and despite the fact that Coleman's conclusions were unsettling, to say the least, at least a few implications from those conclusions could be (and occasionally were) drawn as implications for public policy; and one would like to think that surely a society as wealthy as the USA would be interested in making

516

investments in the public goods of family life, especially to benefit tomorrow's society? It is easy to point to "institution." But institutions *can* be changed. One answer to the question is largely as it was for Card and Krueger (1996, p. 47): "it is unfortunate and frustrating that more is not known about schooling." But of course that statement is only to repeat the "begging the question" fallacy: why is so little known today, more than fifty years after the Coleman report? Here we come to the nugget, as Morgan and Jung (2016, p. 83) whispered: because "schooling" is understood to be only that which takes place outside "family." The shell within which that nugget rests has to do with nomination of "principal" relative to whom costs of "agency conflict" are calculated. In principle, one might suppose, the primary and main principal of investment in education is and should be tomorrow's citizen—today's children. But today's principal is more often the person who today bears the immediate cost (including opportunity cost) of that investment in tomorrow. Credible data pertaining to return on investment are scarce, especially inasmuch as investment is in a collective good (the commonweal) from which individualized returns might not be trackable. Moreover, these principals are usually no less prone than average to myopia and to fatigue from uncertainty, to shareholder bias favoring quarterly if not monthly reports of encouragement, and to other preferences for a personal psychology of continual re-affirmation.

Institutionalized organizations are resilient and convey resilience. More generally, much the same must be said of sociality, and the very fact that first-person experience is built of, while also tending to camouflage, sociality in what has been called "the egocentric predicament" leaves the first-person perspective highly vulnerable to failure of aspiration and ambition. The ancient Greeks put much emphasis of moral clarity in hubris, which was judged to be usurpation of what rightly belonged to the gods. Secularized, it has become the usurpation of that which is a whole by that which is but one of many parts. Parts may vary in weight, while no one of them is in fact the whole. Seen in this light, the irony that has followed along the foregoing discussion has also now brought us back to the basic problem of aggregation. Convergence of one sort or another does occur, repeatedly, usually within the heuristics and agenda of one or more institutions, yet never automatically as if volumes of probable and improbable per-person actions had nothing to do with what might otherwise be attributed to some sort of divine providence or absolutist stochasticism of reversion to a golden mean.

And what do we do with "learning from experience"? Experienced in first-person terms and perhaps via a model such as I have proposed under the label, Abstractive Condensation, we can theorize it *from* experiences only via second-person standpoint and perspective. This limit is unavoidable. The ability of a given person to "unspool" first-person experiences *as such* varies significantly, perhaps by location in networks, hierarchies, and so forth, as well as over time. But there is no foreseeable test of degree or even qualitative difference in that variation. Each of us, considering one's own first-person experience, probably imagines that comparisons *should* be possible. One who has known a confessor such as the professor cited toward the beginning of this section may well believe a judgment of complete veracity, and there would be no considerate point in second-guessing that. Still, the professor's statement was a *public* confession. And how otherwise would anyone have known it, even had the public been a single other person of this or that "hearing community"?

The importance of this second-person standpoint of an AbCon experience seems about as inestimable as unavoidable. Readers who have gotten this far in the present book have read in preceding pages citations and characterizations of many reports, offered by intelligent, often eloquent interlocutors of a sociality: sometimes in a Meadian sense of third-person accounts that revolve much about and through the presence of one or another generalized other; sometimes in a Simmelian sense of "character type" (e.g., the stranger, the flaneur, etc.); sometimes in blended (Meadian-Simmelian) senses of dyadic or triadic (or larger) familial organization or partnership or musical group, and so forth. As we read accounts by Higbie (2003), Isenberg (2016), Smarsh (2018), Vance (2016), Westover (2018), and/or others, we form images of parts of the sociality in which we, the readers, feel as well as know. Although the confessing professor did not make a point of it—and perhaps, if asked, would have rejected the thought—whatever the conceptual scheme that forms the means and meanings of conceptions and perceptions, it is emotive and cognitive all at once. Our analytic tendency to think them apart, even as opposed parts, lames our sense of second-person standpoint, as Darwall (2006) and Hochschild (2016) strove in their different ways to instruct us: morality, respect, and accountability are not just interchangeable; they are inseparable in the synthesis that *is* experience. Whether one agrees with Darwall's proposals in whole or only in part, his instruction, like Hochschild's, reminds us of the syntheses that sociality makes and then makes again, and that the analytics of scholarship, much like any dogmatics of politics, too often neglects or ignores.[558] Unlike dogmatics, however, scholarship at its best calls for and defends open publicity and skepticism. That was the point at which Hegel went astray. If humanity survives to undertake better inquiry, conceptual development, in itself and as basis for measurement of differences/similarities, must begin again.

## §29. Advances in Process Modeling

In this last section of Part Five I will focus more specifically on the task of modeling aggregation process, and to that end I need to be as clear as I can manage about my meaning of that word, "aggregation." To repeat still again, in the usual social-science vernacular "aggregation" refers to a combining of individual persons into collectivities of various sizes and complexity of agency, the latter ranging from unweighted average of individual agents to corporate forms in which the collectivity is itself as such an agent represented in and as offices (which can vary from a monocratic dictatorship to some form of participatory democracy). I do not reject that usual meaning so much as I insist that at any given moment in any given place any individual person is always (or virtually always) already member of at least one collectivity. In other words, *that* aggregation has virtually always already happened. This is not to say that the fact of the collectivity or the fact of an individual person's membership within it is permanent, static, or ahistorical in the way that some observers have been inclined to view billiard balls on a table as analog. It *is* to say, however, that sociality is always already present, and therefore no individual person whom one is at all likely to encounter will be, can be, in any sense prior to a presence of "the collective" or of a sociality. Therefore also, the aggregate will rarely if ever be a simple sum of discrete, self-identical parts, like so many pebbles on a beach waiting for some collector

---

[558] Theorists, analysts, and policy makers tend to live "work lives" very different from the work lives of typical production plants and offices. This difference has been manifest in much of the written and video speculation about a "post-work world." One thread of that has been a vision of "post-work" as "post-competition," even "post-conflict"—an interesting self-reflection, one suspects.

to come by and collect them into a sample or count them into a census. The idea that theory must enable us to understand how any individual comes to be a member of a collectivity is miscast. The relations of which any individual does *exist*, does have *being*, as member of a collectivity sre present even before that person is born.

It is in one sense, then, only a small step to say that aggregation is also, *and* more to the point, some sort of collection of per-person actions, and *still more* to the point that it is some sort of collection of per-person action *effects*. In another sense, of course, an actual practice of that bare locution would be an altogether much more complex undertaking. And *that* is what I mean by "aggregation." Indeed, it *is* a much more complex undertaking. And yet it occurs every day in virtually every place that human beings are present.[559] I do recognize that in meaning "aggregation of individual person-actor actions and still more specially *effects* of person-actor actions," I must also recognize that each person-actor might be acting as (that is to say, "as if") a strictly separate individual person—in intents, in self-conception, and so forth (i.e., acting as if a one-of-a-kind or unique being who is entirely independent in the world)—and perhaps also, at the same time, as a representative of some collectivity of which the person is a constituent member. I do recognize that many individual persons truly believe that each *is* that purely psychologistic being, the "self-made man" person, whether of heroic stature or less.

In my view, every individual person is already, has always been, integral to a collectivity, and I do not mean that merely in the sense of an abstract category such as "person of the world" or "member of a species." I mean it as "a concrete organically individual being" existing in the midst of "a concretely real, actually lived time-and-place world." Moreover, each person as an actual individual person-actor does not just *have* spatiotemporal location; that person *is*—that is, is constituted as—a spatiotemporally specific location in a local sociality, which consists in one or more networks of relations among other such individual persons. The physical embodiment of each individual person-actor is present, of course, and as such it has become constituent of action, to some extent, both in its sources of perception, conception, motivation, and so forth, and in its reception by others often as action performed by *that* person, whether a named person, a seemingly familiar person, a stranger, or a ghost-like memory of a once-and-gone human being who left traces behind at least in memories But the effectivity of what aggregation process *does* is constituted by relations among the *effects* of actions *performed* by those bodies.

What happens to those effects? More to the point initially, however, is another question, the answer to which is instrumental: what counts as an *effect*? Institutional agenda is the major determinant. In a work setting, for example, a diversity of many action effects will very likely be observable on most occasions. But the focus of interest will be "worker productivity" as this is defined and perceived institutionally as that institutional type is manifested in *this* place of work. Getting to that end-state of "qualified effect" does not just happen, however, whatever one might suppose about the superiority of "undirected" or "as if by design" or "invisible hand" dynamics (e.g., Hayek 1967b). It is the resultant of a process that could be described as

---

[559] I leave room, at least theoretically, for a "true hermit" (not to say, however, external to all sociality). Even after death, as Scheffler (2013) has said, most of us will not soon escape sociality, not entirely. The decay function will usually be greater than the lifespan of bacteria, fungi, and maggots.

"negotiative" or "managed" or "routine" or, usually, by all three of those adjectives at once. In general, in other words, when considering the effects of person-action, one must attend to a distinction between observer-defined effects and actor-perceived effects, where "observer" would be officially representative of institutional expectations and "actor" would be employed "worker" (or "student," etc.), not merely because of the difference as such but because of the constitutive or productive relation formed thereby.[560]  But one must not stop at that recognition as conclusive, precisely because it leaves out of the picture *another* "observer," the theorist or analyst—and especially the theorist or analyst who presumes to be, or is presumed to be, the authoritative voice of that "true observer" (i.e., the one who, in terms of Kant's transcendental Illusion, speaks for, or as, noumenal reality). Thus, we have at minimum a triad of actors. Call them Observer 1 (who is acting as official representative of institutional expectations), Actor (who is acting as, say, worker in a firm and as such is also of course an observer), and Observer 2 (who is acting as exogenous actor observing Observer 1 and Actor doing what they do, supposedly without any endogenous impact on the observed scene.[561]  One must beware (and forgo) the convenience of separating Observer 2 as second-order (i.e., the notion of meta-level activity), for it obfuscates what must be kept as clear as possible:  the acting, including the observing, are all events on the same level of first-person experience, at the same level of second-person standpoint during any (if any) mutual engagement, and via the same level of self-reflexivity vis-à-vis a generalized other. Observer 2 has no more claim to "special actor" status than does Observer 1 or Actor.[562]  To repeat, getting to an end-state of "qualified effect" is a *negotiated* and *managed* process no matter how routine it might have become.  Part of the point, so to speak, of institutionalization is to convert as much of that process as possible and efficient of outcome into a routine. This venue of routinization did not await the invention of modern bureaucracy.

To say that an action has had an effect is to say that the action registered an observable effect in some manner to some degree, without which the action would have lacked consequence. But how can anyone know whether an action, one's own action or another's action, was in fact consequential?  While there must be an observation, the observation could be delayed, as when we say that an action had a delayed effect. Whether "delayed" or not, however, an effect has

---

[560] This relation is sometimes called "interactional" (e.g., Collins 1981). I tend to avoid that usage because it often presupposes "actors" conceived on what I call a "billiard ball" model (self-identical entities acting "between" each other without mutual self-effect), a conceptual tendency of Cartesian analytics (supposing the quiddity of thingness independently of relationality).

[561] I said "supposedly" while recognizing that the endogenous/exogenous dialectic is typically analyzed as separate categories, the boundary being contingent on a theoretical model.

[562] Note, too, that because of memory function "actor perception" can also be "observer-defined" in the sense that is manifest in my AbCon concept insofar as Actor reflects on own-self trajectory: this reflection, moreover, can occur as a self-reflexively attended process (i.e., I think about my own reflection on own-self trajectory and perhaps make adjustments or anticipations accordingly—i.e., integral to my filter-and-update habit, which probably includes what Mead called "taking the perspective of significant other" and layering that into own-self effects and feedbacks).  Many different kinds of reflective writing trade on those results, with varying degrees of temporal depth and distance and always with some consideration of those relations.  Recent illustrations of range in kind include Clark (2019) and Fowler (2020).

been experienced, and that event is, one might assume, a "caused event." While "uncaused events" might be allowed as experiential and thus having some kind of meaning, the tendency is to dismiss them as "magic" or "mysterious" or "puzzles." Otherwise, the question becomes one of an unknown cause: "what caused the effect that I just experienced?" This is the Kantian issue of "hidden" cause. That is, our experience does not consist directly of causes but only of effects, impressions on our sense organs that we recognize, classify, and so on, insofar as the impressions are or become reflective, and we then try to infer from those effects their causes. Note that if we could experience causes directly as causes, we could ask what they *implied* as their effects. But because we know only effects, implication cannot be a source of empirical evidence. We are left with inference. We can only *infer* what the causes must have been, or might have been, or could (or could not) have possibly been.

Thus, inference is constitutive of what an effect will be in its source or origin or potential, and therefore how it will be registered *as* a definite effect. Accordingly, any given action might not be registered in effect at all. In fact, probably most *potential* effects of most actions never do achieve any kind of registration, never gain recognition as actual, and slip into oblivion. This kind of counterfactual—the "missing effect"—might nonetheless live notoriously as the ever-present "missing variable" syndrome.

How else could it be? We have only our experiences, our powers of reason, and finally our powers of judgment—all of which occurs within an already existent sociality. Once we have qualified effects, however, there are other issues to be addressed, and judgments made. To take one such example, there is the already mentioned issue of symmetry/asymmetry of aggregation process, which can mean one thing as an issue about bodies, and something rather different as an issue about effects of actions.

Disaggregation as simple reversal of aggregation might seem to be rather straightforward when the units in question are viewed only as physical bodies, the distinctiveness of which does not disappear during aggregation into a network or a census (as it does through the "mangling" of action effects). But imagine those bodies as linked within and through sociality: the question of aggregation/disaggregation becomes more complex (as in, say, marriage/divorce).[563] For now the units are *effects of actions*, and picking apart the outcome of an aggregation in order to regain the input units as they were prior to aggregation is difficult, probably always at least bordering on the impossible, even when no scale effects have entered into the relationality. That is because aggregation of effects of per-person actions is aggregation through and as sociality. It involves more than a simple addition of parts that are ordinarily understood as lacking mutually relative

---

[563] Bear in mind, of course, that the predicate phrase "viewed only as physical bodies" was prejudiced already: where exactly are the bounds of "physical body"? Do they include or exclude, for example, the micro-organisms but for which a human body would not survive? Do they include or exclude the shared gases in the immediate locale of this and that body? Any "distinctiveness" of a "body" is always already a "resolved" classification problem.

521

identities. As Harrison White sometimes said (at least in conversation), a kind of melding or annealing of input effects occurs during this kind of aggregation.[564]

Another complex issue to be addressed is the form/content dialectic of the aggregation process. Aggregation is not indifferent to the effects being aggregated. Whatever an effect is more specifically, it is a signal in channel-based information flows and as such can manifest a wide range of signal properties (frequency, amplitude, etc.). The content, meanings, can range from simple head counts, as in a census of bodies under various descriptive labels (e.g., year of birth, gender, racial-ethnic identity, etc.) to more complex codings that allow subtler dynamics of repetition than simple iteration. Recursivity has much greater capacity for innovation of signal content—indeed, to the extent that it can be self-generative of information in an unending loop. This leads to a peculiar feature: recursive coding dictates "return to starting point" (thus, the loop); yet because of previous filter-and-update cycles, "starting point" might in fact have been altered without detection but consequentially, the agent being nothing more than random noise (see, e.g., White 1992, pp. 346-349).

This difference between iteration and recursivity can be profound in developmental terms. Consider as a stylized illustration, for example—stylized in that it focuses on one major dimension of irrational motivations of public policy—this contrast: the mainly iterative practices of employment in the band of southern US states that were intent on continuing the civil war "by other means" (e.g. Jim Crow legislations) and the generally more recursive and therein more innovative employment policies of northern industrial states to which huge numbers of families of African ancestry were fleeing for jobs and better physical security and opportunity (e.g., major cities of New York, Pennsylvania, Michigan, Illinois). The southern states with largely planation economies, having been devastated during the war, had no choice but to begin anew. In general, that is a condition highly conducive to the advantages of adopting the latest in production technologies. Instead, the southern states mostly iterated old habits and therefore lost in market competitions again and again. Employers in leading industrial firms in northern states were likelier to evolve policies that selected industrial-work capabilities without regard to biases of

---

[564] Earlier in this section I rehearsed Hannan's (1991) assessment of the conditions under which one might expect reversal of aggregation as yielding elements as they were prior to aggregation. His chief focus was on aggregated *data* as they typically exist in summary of counts per person and the conditions under which such data can be usefully taken as indicative of per-person process events or dynamics. He was not writing a solution to the problem of "undoing" the work of a mangle or a process anything like a melding of effects as inputs. There is today another crucial difference. Now that information is being rapidly converted into a language that is uniform semantically and syntactically across all kinds of information, it has perhaps seemed in principle that this uniformity should facilitate the disaggregation of collective information into its individual per-person pieces. Interests in protecting per-person property rights have been promoting that goal. At least to date, however, the main result of such efforts has been demonstration that much of the information, and probably all of the most important information, is destroyed by the disaggregation process. Most of the digitalized information pertaining to identified individual persons ("personal data") actually exists as interlocked constructs of and within sociality.

skin color and the like (which were far from unknown in the northern states, and only in part because the large flows from southern states included many white families as well). Moreover, in at least some of the northern industrial areas the repetitive signaling in employment policy shifted from recursive to the still more innovation-friendly action habits of replication. The relevant information channels that carried signals about technology transfer (including transfers of organizational technology) were as open to officials of public policy in the southern as in the northern states, but the irrationalities of sentiment about race, slavery, and lost causes overwhelmed economic interest even in the most forward-looking parts of the southern states (e.g., Birmingham). There is irony in the fact that (as mentioned earlier) replicative cycles are more friendly to innovation in part because the productive moment of updating can generate undetected change in the initial conditions of a cycle, such that the return phase of the loop is not in fact a return exactly to the status quo ante. Thus, "status quo ante" can itself be subject to an evolutionary contingency.

I assume one's focus of inquiry should always be multi-dimensional, at least implicitly and in potential (for one cannot do everything at once). The process of per-person actions and action effects is reflexive (as described above in terms of the AbCon concept), and this means already that one is attending to the composition of an interiority/exteriority dialectic of self as of, in, and in some manner about sociality (as Mead, Vygotsky, and others proposed); therefore also with notions of "interpersonal collectivity" and "interactional orders," both as storytelling from second- and third-person standpoints and as first-person experience of an inherence of the action of storytelling to oneself about otherness. At the same time, one's actions and their effects also engage, and invite further or different engagements with, that very otherness in the inherent reflexivity of self-presence; but also in fugitive expressions, propagations, and ramifications that reflect limits of self-presence, as a result of which one can catch sight of otherwise missed arcs of ambiguity, confoundings of the taken-for-granted, violations or reversals of intent, sometimes an irony that shudders self-awareness into an instability. Through such limit experiences one builds an understanding of what Mead called "the generalized other" as a representation that probably only ever approximates the complexity of sociality. And yet, as was said above, this is a product of itself, which is to say a product of the spatio-temporality of aggregations *across* persons of per-person action effects. The individual persons and/or any collectivity of them may well accredit all of it to a myth that they believe *in*—whether it be more specifically a myth of the gods or a supreme God, or a myth of Nature and its own peculiar intelligence, or a myth of a holographic designer sitting on some far distant planet running a demonstration project. Even at that, at any one of the accounts, it remains the case that such complexity of sociality is only of human provenience.

If it seems odd to make a point of the spatio-temporality of process, as I did just above, well, it *should* seem odd. It *is* odd. And this oddity has a very long history. Josiah Ober (2015, pp. 119, 232) recently described from some surviving artifacts efforts of ancient Greeks to devise better incentives and mechanisms for institutional innovation in domains of "citizenship, warfare, law, and federalism," all of which was presumably undertaken to the aim of improved cooperation and coordination: for those "classical Greeks were well aware of [the] potential," the power, of institutionalized form. And yet they sometimes marveled at the results—and never more so than when the results went against best intents, as they often did (blame then going to "the gods" for being so capricious or to one of themselves for acting with insult to this or that particular god). It is keenly of interest that such explanations rarely if ever carry a subscript for time, often as well none for space. And of course that is practiced as a common expectation: any *true* explanation will be without those subscripts. Which is why I do make a point of emphasizing that any *process* is spatiotemporal (cf. Abbott 2001, 2016, among many others). *Any* process, including the process of explanation. Because of the implicit if not explicit presence of those subscripts, "process" is usually more complex than it appears to be in a given location of space-time.[565]

Furthermore, recall that aesthetics is both study of and perspective of perception, which is always spatiotemporal. Recall, too, that it is in the experience of musical composition, as I tried to show in Parts Two and Three, that one can best understand the complexity of the aesthetics of temporality. The best venue for that is a composition in which one actually hears sounds "as if they were sustained by string instruments or voices," as Rosen (1995, p. 3) said of a Beethoven piano sonata, when in fact it is one's imagination that supplies the presence and the intensity of an aural temporality well *after* the instrument's sound has ceased. That is, the most sensitive microphone records nothing, nor does one's ear; but "the music lingers on" so persistently that any listener who, having never before experienced the event, follows along the staves will notice an odd dissonance between eye and ear. Performers are aware of the musical event, of course, and often convey it in bodily rhythm—sometimes without self-conscious awareness but often as commitment to the composition and to the listener. This is the power of temporality in musical composition. Composers such as Johann Sebastian Bach, his son Carl P E Bach, and Ludwig Beethoven did not invent that dialectic of audible/inaudible (or sound/silence), but they mastered it to a fine degree of artistic expression that nurtured others in, among other projects, the movement of Bildungsprozess. Christopher Clark's (2019, p. 74) chosen exemplar of this fine capability of aesthetic perspective in a historian, the Hohenzollern king, historian, and scholar of music, Frederick II (aka "the Great"; 1712-1786), is highly instructive inasmuch as he (Frederick) displayed from young age an integrative sense of what could be understood, as many others did understand, two opposing analytic perspectives, the linear and iterative versus the nonlinear and recursive. As has often been noted in commentaries from time to time, for the better part of four decades Frederick played "exactly the same cycle" of three hundred concertos for flute, again and again. One can see in this habit a progression that displays simultaneously a recursivity and an equilibrium. It was no doubt by *nomination* a repetition of "exactly the same cycle." But musically? I do not know a single performer who would agree.

---

[565] In other words, I am hardly the first to have noticed evidence of that complexity. Read Molseed's (1987) effort to sort through Simmel's effort, for example. But how easily we forget such evidence. On the one hand, we often recall the basic ethical principle proposed by Kant—act as if thy will would become a universal law: Yet can one imagine a more demanding, more daunting criterion for future judgments and decisions? But we turn around and suppose that such universality has somehow already been created and that we can learn it, understand it, follow it.

The ancient Greeks were aware that knowledge not only accumulates, it also aggregates, in that parts of an accumulation become interactive over time, potentially differently from place to place. Archimedes of Syracuse (c287-c212 BCE), for his day the epitome of physical scientist and engineer, understood processes in ways and to an extent that Aristotle (384-322 BCE) evidently had not, and probably could not have, comprehended.

Awareness of that complexity is very old in human cultures (even if it was less detailed or less specific than in our present-day awareness). Ober (2015) noticed evidence of it in ancient Greek settings, as was briefly described above. It is also expressed in an aphorism which today we usually read in its Latin version—Ars longa, vita brevis—typically rendered in English as "art is long, life is short." Because the English word, "art," is now usually taken in a too-narrow "specialized" sense ("high art" or "fine art"), the source of the Latin aphorism, a Greek aphorism recorded by Hippocrates of Kos in the Hippocratic medical text, gives better meaning:

*Ho bios brakhys, hê de tekhnê makrê,*
*ho de kairos oxys, hê de peira sphalerê,*
*hê de krisis khalepê*

This can be rendered as, "Life is short, technical know-how goes far / the crucial time is fleeting, trials perilous / and the decision difficult." Despite some ambiguity—always a major challenge for translators—the key point is "technē," the art or craft of *knowing how* to perform a technical skill to do or to make something (for Hippocrates, a healthier body). Life is short. Is technē "long"? Does it go far in choice of applications? Or in its effects? Or in its variety? Any one or all of these could have been the medical teacher's intent. In other words, life is short under best of conditions. A life needing attention from a physician is seemingly in danger of becoming even shorter. A physician has little time in which to choose among likely remedies, knowing that trials can add to risk, and thus the decision (judging the "turning point": crisis) is difficult.[566]

The examples of Archimedean physical science and Hippocratic medical science, each in differing contrast to Aristotle, give indication that knowledge was indeed aggregating, and the aggregation was not homologous over time. Nor has it been to this day. One can still argue that within its domain Newtonian physics has remained constant, but whether that domain is located as it was in, say, 1700 or even 1900 is not exactly obvious in answer or perhaps even in meaning of question. Present-day physical science offers examples of aggregation process at extremes of capaciousness: the states of quantum systems, on the one hand, and the states of cosmic systems on the other. Are these systems homologous? Or demonstrably compatible with one another? The questions have been asked since the 1930s, repeatedly. They remain open. It is not clear, however, that the question itself has not changed (see, e.g., Einstein, Podolsky, and Rosen 1935; Einstein and Rosen 1936; Muller 2016).

---

[566] The meaning most often construed in English is a bit different yet relevant. Different translators with different preferences in mapping the Greek of the Hippocratic Corpus (a collective work) to English have decided somewhat different meanings. I have followed, but amended, the text of Aphorism 1.1 (Hippocrates 1868 [c370 BCE], vol. 2).

Consider another illustration: by being in Class C with Teacher T of School S, Pupil P is participant in aggregative effects of a process of mutually influenced learning—specifically skill acquisitions that include skills of a substantive topical content, skills of participation within one or more networks of ties (among class members with each other and with the teacher, these ties channeling experiences of development, assessment, etc.), *and* skills of learning, which are the most specific in some respects but in others the most general. All of the intra-aggregate (intra-class, intra-school, etc.) effects are filtered, updated, and integrated on a continuing basis, while they are also being continually filtered, updated, and integrated within the AbCon process that transpires for, within, and to some extent *as* each pupil. One might think of the whole of it as a practical problem of differential, then integrative calculus, but performed by persons who are, in the main, short not only of skilled experience in the techniques of calculus but also of any model of a perfectly rational actor. Yet outcomes are achieved. Institutional heuristics are instrumental in the achievements, no doubt; but imperfect and poorly skilled individual persons are the actors who put the game into play. At the end have they, as with Ober's "classical Greeks," performed as well as they could have, should have, performed?—and been performed?

All the while, Pupil P has been maintained by and maintains participation in still another, partly separable dynamic of aggregation, the network of ties of his or her familial organization of mutual influences, which manifest in some dynamically variable combination both enabling and constraining factors; and these, too, are aggregative effects that, being channeled as experiences within another dimension of P's abstractive condensation process, will be integrated more or less well into her or his self-integrity. Have those mutual influences been performed as well as they could have, should have, been performed? The same description and question of quality can be asked of mutual influences of neighborhood actors, community actors, and so on.

Let's put some empirical estimates on those correlations. A recent report for California, one of the wealthiest of US states (accounting for one-seventh of the US total GDP and growing at a compound annual rate of 3.23 percent, more than twice that of the US economy as a whole), "three-quarters of the young children who often miss days at kindergarten later fail California's math and reading tests in the third grade. Pupils who fail those tests are in turn four times likelier to drop out of high school, and those who drop out are eight times likelier to end up in jail." In the state's wealthiest city, San Francisco, nine of every ten murder victims under age 25 were high school dropouts.[567] This chain of effects, evidence of a "path dependence" (or serial correlation), is not unique to California. My point is, rather, that the enchainment occurs in the wealthiest of states, not only the poorest. Aggregations of action effects tend to be stratified in per-family or per-household sequences of age-specific life chances. The waste of future adults is a profound measure of a society's ethical health (see, e.g., Harrison 2014). The stratification as such is not surprising. The evidence for its principal dimensions has long been known. This means that the kinds of measured observations that need to be made of the dynamics of

---

[567] The GDP data are for 2016. The other data were from a study reported in *The Economist*, 29 October 2016, p. 28. National and state data from the Programme for International Student Assessment tell the same story.

aggregation process as such can be focused within relevant cells of a stratified grid in order to determine if the process dynamics differ.

A long line of ethnographic studies, from Thomas and Znaniecki (1958 [1927]) and Sutherland and Locke (1936), for example, to a spate of recent entries (Higbie 2003; Hochschild 2016; Isenberg 2016; Vance 2016; Payne 2017; Smarsh 2018; among others) have offered good descriptions within specific cells of a grid of stratifications, most of them redolent of anguish and pain, physical as well as emotional. Orange (2018) recounted personal experiences of the double line of cultural marginalities. Payne (2017, p. 200) described patterns in which some conditions of material poverty can encourage self-defeating behavioral and action habits both directly (e.g., poor diet, weak preventative health care) and indirectly (e.g., via weak educational opportunity and achievement). The patterns feature a temporality of "self-reinforcing cycles," in Payne's summary, "between poverty and self-defeating actions," and the reader understands more or less well what he meant. But then a question comes to the surface: Payne, like Vance, Orange, and others in similar childhood context, evaded or broke the cycle well enough, long enough, to have achieved much success relative to friends and relatives left behind. Westover (2018) survived harrowing repressions in the name of religious-nativist conviction. Smarsh (2018) lived years of rural impoverishment that, day by day, did not seem like poverty but simply ordinary life, until she visited another world.[568] What was different for Payne, as for others? That is, what *made* the difference? Surely the case can be made for "resilience," as various scholars have (e.g., Clausen 1991, 1995; Werner and Smith 1992, 2001). But that is only to rephrase the question, as Hugh Mehan and his colleagues demonstrated repeatedly over many years of observation and study (Mehan, Villanueva, Hubbard, and Lintz 1996; Mehan and Chang 2010)[569].

The cycle that Payne, Vance, Hochschild (2016), and others have described in respective ethnographies is real enough, even if too little is understood about variations in the per-person dynamics during the first twenty to thirty years of life. One point of understanding about which

---

[568] Many memoirists have left accounts of their young years in a parental family, whether single-parent, two-parent, or otherwise. Few have been as taxing on the reader as Westover's (2018) memoir of growing up in the midst of sometimes extraordinarily difficult parental relations. Smarsh (2018), only six years older than Westover, gave us a strong counterpoint; not that her years of youth were free of stresses—to the contrary—but her familial setting was supportive in a more accommodating manner. Westover's account, because of the often extreme circumstances of her upbringing, offers some good illustrations of the complications that can attend, or arise from, juxtapositions of first-person experiences and second-person standpoint (Westover 2018, passim, especially when read in light of pp. 333-334). Juxtaposition—unlike integration or conciliation of accounts together with the perspectives which they represent, all for the sake of a single coherent story—leaves the raw edges of difference more or less in place while acknowledging the moral interests of trusting care that are at stake in second-person standpoint (see Darwall 2006).

[569] Recent theoretical and experimental inquiry has also advanced our understanding of the stratified aggregation of per-person opinions and attitudes (see e.g., Butts 2016; Friedkin, Proskurnikov, Tempo, and Parsegov 2016), which also can be used to direct measured observations of selected samples, rather than be concerned about de novo probability representation of a society's population at given date. More about this issue below.

there is no doubt is that childhood conditions of "household family," and sometimes conditions of "family" in a broader sense, are within and of a powerful institution, as it channels first-person experiences—perceptions and perspectives and folk theories of cause-and-effect and empirically tested self-conceptions of agency—along paths that reflect material and ideal conditions within which any specific family currently exists. Because for most persons family is the very first very powerful institution of consequence, the effects it leaves within the person—which is to say also within the relations between parent and child, among siblings, and across inhabitants of a place and time both here and now *and* of imagined futures—can easily last a lifetime via long-memory process. These effects can and often do endure thematically during all of the usual filter-and-update sequences, especially when the sequences are iterative (or sometimes recursive albeit still resistant to innovations). The "cycles" may be vicious or virtuous, or some mix of the two, and may seem like perfectly ordinary life in any case. That, too, can be a resilience, of course, one that is otherwise known as "surviving day by day."

It is clear that many vectors of force/influence are continually at work in the dynamics of self-integration.[570] These vectors can be generally described in a loose conceptual model. But the more one specifies empirical contents, the messier the model becomes—and that, even before attempting to give adequate attention to measurement problems. Many theorists would join Fligstein and McAdam (2012, pp. 196-197) who, like others, have cautioned that measurement too often lacks sound connection to substantive theory, due to the assumption, only sometimes explicitly stated, that analysis of measured observations will reveal the main if not the sole "structure" represented in the data. This is a common presupposition that actually offers a dual perspective: on the one hand, that observations by which data are generated are perfectly free of substantively relevant theory; on the other, that measurement techniques are also perfectly free of substantively relevant theory. One need not be especially discerning to know that neither of those perspectives can be supported. The other face of Fligstein and McAdam's caution is, however, that a theorist must work under obligation to produce a theory with enough specificity and clarity of conditions and main (hypothetical) empirical implications to offer guidance when a researcher selects among relevant techniques of measured observations. That includes the task, admittedly daunting, of sorting through the myriad of potential and likely effects (using the classification of effects offered by Manski 2007, 2018). Estimating a model of carefully specified measured relations and effects, once all of the mensural problems have been adequately addressed, would perhaps be a suitably challenging problem for the logic algorithms of "machine learning" computation. But some advances have been made from "wet brain" power.

The temporality of aggregation is complex in large part because aggregation of action effects occurs simultaneously in two registers: a per-person aggregation of that person's action

---

[570] These dynamics are not independent of the dynamics of cross-person aggregation. To recall a discussion early in this section, the latter dynamics can be likened to what Pickering (1995) called "the mangle," and I have referred to "the impossible task of unpicking results of the mangle" as a way of describing the task of reversing a process of cross-person aggregation of action effects. The same descriptive simile can be applied to the dynamics of self-integration. To use the locution, "individual person-actor" or "action effects of an individual person," is to say that to divide an "individual person" would be to divide, thus to break, the "ensemble of social relations" (Marx 1976 [1888], p. 7; 1987 [1939], p. 98).

effects and a cross-person aggregation of per-person action effects. The simultaneity of registers can of course be subject to analysis. (It would be in any case futile to suggest otherwise.) But in doing that one must be careful not to generate too many clocks (i.e., as if independent clocks; see Hazelrigg 1997). I am not referring to the notion that the sense of efficacy generated within and from abstractive condensation (AbCon) might be a distinctive "subjective time" (meaning that it is internal to first-person experience and remains so even as first-person talks *about* it in second-person perspective, which transpires as a shared time). Rather, I am referring to the plain fact that each of the registers runs on the same clock. Institutional form enforces that, by and large. Cross-person aggregation never occurs either instantaneously or by a once-and-done schedule, and while it is occurring each per-person actor is continuing to act and generating more effects (at least potentially) which accrue to her or his account, this accrual being a simple accumulation but potentially also an aggregation in the same sense that pertains to cross-person aggregation. Think of the per-person accounting register as an employee's "reputational good": A supervisor says, "Employee 159 has really turned into a much more productive worker!" Employee 157 says, "Employee 159 has suddenly become a rate buster, making the rest of us look bad!" That exemplifies the premium of aggregation over and above simple accumulation. The metric basis of the latter description can shows up in an official book of accounts; the former, perhaps not.

Ethnographies are likelier to detect that aspect of aggregation. Observations designed for large-sample surveys usually do not, but that is usually a matter of cost and convenience. That kind of deficit, combined with penchants for standard analytics, can censor interpretation to the point of incomprehension. From James Coleman to Karl Alexander and his colleagues to James Heckman and his colleagues, the systematic evidence accumulated from survey observations has consistently been that the typical elementary school cannot erase a substantial deficit of specific skill that has been incurred by a child's fifth or sixth or seventh birthday anniversary (see, e.g., Alexander 2016; Alexander and Morgan 2016; Garcia, Heckman, Leaf, and Prades 2016). The evidence has been of states, for the most part, not of process: a state assessment at age A, then again at age A+n, and so forth. One is left with the task of inference (as always) but in a poverty of clues toward answering the question, "What happened?" It is here that better observations can be obtained under quasi-experimental conditions, or from records of a demonstration project that approximated a "randomized control" design. Nearly forty years ago in Ypsilanti, Michigan, for example, David Weikart proposed a systematic study based on an innovative program designed with Charles E Beatty, principal of Perry Elementary School, with children ages 3 and 4 years at risk of school failure because of prior resource deprivations. The curriculum emphasized skills of learning (self-control, attentiveness, patience, planning, becoming better organized, etc.). The children were divided into a group exposed to the program and a control group. Implementation was not perfect, and one could criticize the program for deliberate exclusion of children from a curriculum expected to be beneficial. Heckman and his team have analyzed the outcome data, using a design that corrects flaws of implementation, and have concluded that children exposed to the treatment did benefit, that improvements of cognitive skills did persist, but that the gains did decay over time (Heckman, Pinto, and Savelyev 2013). Heckman and his colleagues also estimated the rate of return on investments in the program as averaging 6 to 10 percent per year (at least as good, they noted, as the rate of return on equity

529

investments since 1946). Important, too, is the demonstration that gains in understanding process dynamics in the education of young children can be achieved without engaging in typical large cross-sectionally representative population samples (see also Heckman 2008; Heckman, Moon, Pinto, Savelyev, and Yavitz 2010; Garcia, et al., 2016).

As I have said before, because most empirical research in the social sciences has been keyed to cross-sectional representations of a national population (or some large segment of that population), concerns of inference testing from sample to population have been dominant. This is understandable, since state functions (and funding for much research) are mainly concerned about accurate descriptions of state space, mainly of persons occupying specific state spaces. It is generally based on assumptions of static state-space descriptions.[571] Concerns about processes, on the other hand, must be focused on dynamics, and that means more than simply comparing two or more state-space descriptions separated as periods. With models of dynamics, one must face the fact of serial correlation: observations are highly likely to be autocorrelated, the size of the autocorrelation can vary (even switch signs) across temporal lags of different lengths, and the problem of noisy signals never disappears. While our toolkits for estimating error of sampling inference have grown since the days of Ronald Fisher, with major improvements in power and precision, little of that development translates into applications for estimations of process models. Insofar as the latter involve sampling, it is primarily a sampling of possible realizations of the process in question. Bootstrapping techniques have been used in theoretical physics and can be adapted to estimation problems in the social sciences. But little work on those applications has occurred (at least to my awareness). In the meantime, one must not lose sight of a key fact, when estimating parameters of a process model with appropriately conceived and measured observations: those empirical estimates will be the best we have, until further notice. That does not mean that the problem of serial correlation has disappeared. But it does mean that a set of the best estimates available will be a reasonable basis on which to pursue additional inquiry (always until further notice).

To make explicit a conceptual point that runs through the discussion in §28, experience aggregates primarily and mainly through institutionalized conceptualizations (heuristics, agenda, etc.) along with any theorizations, informal as well as formal, that are built from them. At a general level, cross-person aggregation occurs via already extant collectivities—that is, relations and networks of individual and group-level actors as these transpire over time—even if a goal of a collectivity is to re-invent itself or to generate a new collectivity. At particular level, of course, cross-person aggregation occurs within the life course of each individual person as a member of one or another collectivity over time, primarily through specific institutionalized forms of conceptualization and theorization. That means that the temporal aggregation of experiences within and as the individual person's ongoing formation takes place not within the person as an isolate but as always already an ensemble of relations of and by pre-existing socialities. Insofar as the collectivity is "novel"—by which I mean primarily that it is noninstitutional, a "work still

---

[571] The studies enabled by national sample surveys are not without research utilities, but they tend to be limited to static-state descriptions. An example is the National Organizations Study (see Kalleberg, Knoke, Marsden, and Spaeth 1996), which is about workplaces but has little to say directly about the dynamics of relevant processes.

in progress" and usually consumptive of much dedication and effort to stay alive—cross-person aggregation of per-person action effects will be relatively precarious, unless the collectivity is at an intersection with one or more institutionalized organizations (in which case, depending on the intersection, aggregation might still be precarious). In other words, cross-person aggregations of per-person action effects are generally most successful, and most efficacious within first-person experience, *and* most likely to generate action effects of the collectivity as such (i.e., collective action effects mainly of agenda setting, commitment power, coordination, and/or enforcement) when the collectivity is an organization of institutional type.

The main answer to "what happened?"—as, for example, state-specific analytic accounts of skill deficits among elementary-school pupils were being assessed in studies described in the prior section—was framed as early as Coleman's study in terms of "family." This was of course also a matter of the interstices between two major institutions, "family" and "school." And that addition, along with each of those two institutions taken separately, was also a matter of resource distribution, which has typically been unequal on several dimensions. Coleman's answer quickly generated a trail of controversy, in part because the answer was not formulated with enough care in attention to those details. The studies by Alexander and colleagues, conducted in Baltimore schools, were sensitive to those controversies; and while one understands the reasons for that sensitivity, one consequence was a stifling of discussion.[572] In writing an introductory essay for a collection in honor of the fiftieth anniversary of Coleman's report, Alexander (2016) chose an analytical "either-or" title: "Is it school or family?"—an unfortunate wording, from my point of view. In place of that recovery of controversy, the answer should have been about cross-person and per-person aggregations of action effects between and in two intersecting institutionalized forms—one of familial relations, the other of educational relations.

The kinds of models typically employed in Coleman-related studies have been variants of standard least-squares regression models: variation in an observed outcome variable is expressed as an algebraic function of variations in some number of other variables, which are rendered as "conditional" to the outcome. Arithmetically the covariations are basically correlational; but if the guiding theory is specific and strong enough, and if observations are suitably arrayed in time, the correlational matrix can be interpreted as one of "cause and effect" or at least one of "outcome as result of inputs."

In various preceding discussions I have repeatedly used a hyphenated adjective, "input-output," in conjunction with a few nouns, usually analysis, process, and model. In this last section of Part Five I will consider some recent advancements in modeling that can be applied to theories of process. But first, I will make some clarifying comments, beginning with a main distinction. As a qualifying description of any one of those three nouns, "input-output" has been used in various branches of engineering and some of the physical and biological sciences primarily to designate a kind of model or analysis of process. By contrast, in the social sciences, where the qualifier has been less widely used, most of the applications have been in economics

---

[572] This is not to say that no new insights were generated; to the contrary (see, e.g., Alexander, Entwisle, and Olson 2014). One major addition was evidence that pupil gains in skill from a given year tended to degrade during the ensuing summer recess much more than had been understood.

531

and related fields such as accounting. While the main economic application of the phrase began in connection with analysis of economic process, the emphasis soon shifted from analysis of the dynamics of process to analytic descriptions of end states of accounting flows of funds or, more abstractly, value. I intend the phrase, "input-output analysis," as such and in conjunction with processual models, mainly as it has been used in engineering and the physical sciences. In order to get to the payoff of that intent, however, I need to review some of the history of economics.

The person-name most often associated with "input-output analysis" especially in the US academy during the previous century was Wassily Leontief, who formulated standards and rules for the practice of input-output analysis and was sometimes accorded status its inventor. In fact, economists and other social scientists with core interests in economic relations had been using some version of input-output modeling for many decades before Leontief—probably as long ago as William Petty, at least as long ago as François Quesnay and his *Tableau économique* of 1758, followed by Karl Marx' analyses in the *Grundrisse* and in *Capital*, all aiming at creating a "national economic table" or a "balance sheet" for an entire national economy (see, e.g., Remington 1982, p. 591; Clark 1984; Belykh 1989; Bjerkholt 2016)). While those efforts were crude by present standards, they are recognizable as having the same intent by similar means as now applied in national accounts (now even for the entire globe via organizations such as the World Input-Output Network). Virtually all of that analysis is at highly aggregated levels, as summary accounts of the outcomes of multitudinous productive actions by multitudinous human beings. The process dynamics by which those outcomes occur are acknowledged but submerged in resultant measures of interdependencies in the aggregated tables. Imagine that household budgeting can begin and end with a balance sheet of revenues and expenditures heedless of the processes by which revenues are gained and expenditures disbursed. An accountant might reply that the accounting task is simply to balance the books, whatever the means and ends of the flow of funds. As several observers have noted, tasks of comparing per-person production functions and aggregated levels and rates of return on investments of products have been repeatedly postponed (cf. Card 1999).

In any case, much of the formulation of this kind of input-output analysis was conducted in the USSR as a core part of the governmental effort to rationalize the planning of nationwide economic development, although much of that theoretical work was blunted by Stalin's fierce aversion to mathematics and its applications. As Remington (1982) said, theorists such as the polymathic Alexander Aleksandrovich Bogdanor (1873-1928) succeeded in representing systematically the "interdependence of all the elements" of an entire national economy in an enchainment of relations among all parts. "Carrying the 'chain' metaphor further, they called it 'chain-linkage', which can be rendered, not too anachronistically, as 'feedback.'

Bogdanov spelled the idea out best. The relationship among the economy's sectors was dynamic [and] not linear, he insisted. Each link in the chain had both backward- and forward-leading linkages, except for the first and the last links. The last was the sector of final demand, the first was the basic elements of production. The rest supplied inputs to the next link and received as inputs the outputs of the preceding link. From this point arose a methodological advance of immense importance. A plan could not simply specify the desired output targets of some critical sector or of the sectors that served to satisfy final demand. Rather, targets had to be calculated iteratively for all parts of the economy, first by calculating backward from the sector taken as the leading link (be it an estimate of the population's consumption needs or the requirements of a bottleneck area) all the inputs needed to meet the target, then the inputs required by the sectors producing those goods, and so on back to the beginning of the chain; then, the process has to be repeated from the other direction to ensure that the needs determined by the plan were consistent with the resources available to the economy (Remington 1982, p. 590).

Emphasis on "the plan" as (temporary) end-state soon subordinated interest in process dynamics as such, however.

Leontief entered the picture during the 1920s in the USSR. His biographic memorials (as well as some reports by others) are not entirely self-consistent with regard to influences on and developments of his own work in input-output modeling. Surely some part of the inconsistency can be understood as adaptations to setting, as Leontief migrated through the Soviet academic and state bureaucracy (the former struggling for some degree of independence), thence into the German academy from 1925 to 1931, and finally into the US academy. While lauded later in the USA as founder of input-output modeling, Leontief's own early publications were more inclined to cite important predecessors. One instance of that citation clearly accredited Marx, and in a way that reflects both some understanding and, very likely, a sensitivity to geopolitical concerns of his new home, the USA. In pages of the *American Economic Review* Leontief wrote these words (albeit relative to a background published the year before, in Leontief 1937a and 1937b):

> In the very first pages of the first volume of *Capital*, Marx raised against the "vulgar" (I guess he would call them today "orthodox" or "neo-classical") economists the accusation of "fetishism." Instead of looking for the ultimate deep-lying price-determinants, they [those economists] operate, according to Marx, with superficial, imaginary concepts of supply and demand, money costs, etc., all of which refer to purely fictitious relations. Although these subjective concepts acquire in the mind of acting economic individuals the quality of independent, tyrannically dominating forces, actually they are nothing but the products of deliberate actions of the same individuals.
>
> This typically Hegelian observation is strikingly correct. Is, however, the theoretical conclusion which Marx seems to draw from it actually justified? If it were, his criticism would indict modern price theory even in greater degree than any of the theories of his contemporaries, John Stuart Mill, senior, or Malthus (Leontief 1938, p. 1).

In those remarks Leontief was largely correct. As the subjunctive of condition in the last sentence signals, Leontief disagreed with what he took to be Marx' conclusion, and that disagreement must be understood from each point of view

There is no doubt that Marx theorized a network of interdependencies. This network can be specified as "economic," but by my reading of Marx it pertained to the entirety of a society and indeed in the terms of my perspective to the entirety of sociality.[573] The whole of the network

---

[573] Here, no doubt, "entirety" ais a bit ragged, for as Marx and others were well aware transnational trade had become (indeed, had been) a substantial factor in the economy of many societies. Marx was on hand

was (is) production in the broadest sense. The interdependencies of production are seen in the fact that any specific act of production is also a consumption (inputs must be consumed in order to obtain an output) and any specific consumption is also a production (consumption produces yet another output). Likewise, neither distribution nor exchange drops from heaven or just happens as a gift of nature; rather, each term refers to a set of relations produced in and by the activity of human beings. Moreover, this composition of the general process of production— namely, the making of a specific product by consuming some prior good and/or service, distributing that specific product to various regions of the economy (society) where it enters into relations of exchange so that it becomes a consumption as means of further acts of specific production—has been most highly developed in capitalism. The same composition can be seen in accounts of pre-capitalist formations, however. Even the simplest division of labor in society entails a circuit or network of interdependent activities.

What was the point of Leontief's comment about Marx' "theoretical conclusion" being, if correct, an indictment of "modern price theory"? In order to answer that, we need to step back to the late 1860s and 1870s, a time when theorists of economic reality were pondering what they (and others) considered a major conundrum sometimes named "the paradox of value": why do so many people seemingly value an object that has no particular use, certainly no "essential" or "necessary use," so much more highly (or, for that matter, even as highly) as an object that is indeed "essential" and "necessary" to everyone virtually always everywhere? This seemed the height of irrationality. To put materiality to the paradox—and it *was* paradoxical, inasmuch as popular belief was at the core—so many people pay much higher sums of money for a diamond ring or necklace or other sort of jewelery than for the quantity of water needed weeks on end, the water being absolutely essential while the diamond is nothing more than an adornment. (This was, bear in mind, prior to the use of diamond-amended teeth on a saw or drill bit.) Some observers responded that the answer lay in the fact that diamonds are so rare; thus, a scarcity of supply was at least part of the answer. But then it became known to the theorists that, well, no, diamonds are "market-scarce" only. The mine owners carefully calibrate supply in order to maintain scarcity relative to demand.

Three theorists came to basically the same answer at about the same time: Carl Menger in Austria, William Stanley Jevons in England, and Leon Walras in Switzerland. The answer was a new theory of the process of valuation—"new," relative to Adam Smith's (and later Marx') labor theory of value. First, two stipulations of vocabulary: "value" in this context is instrumental and thus rational, not nonrational as in a traditional or religious value (granted, the boundary often proves to be blurry and pervious); and the process of valuation involves some sort of conciliation between two instruments—use value and exchange value—each of which is a kind of utility (a way of utilizing an object). The new theory is focused in a new concept: "marginal utility" Think of this innovation arithmetically. The utility of a valued object can be calculated as an average (weighted or unweighted) of the value (use or exchange) of the object at each of the stages of its production from "raw" to "ready for consumption." A grain of wheat has potential use while it is still growing; actual uses, as it has ripened in the head of each stalk of the grass; and so forth, until it becomes one of countless grains in a bushel of wheat grains that have been cleaned and stored as seed for the next crop cycle or made ready for human diet; and so on still more, until it becomes newly sprouting grass or a loaf of bread ready for your table or

---

to observe early years of the great wave of "globalization" during the latter decades of the nineteenth century.

534

a fermented drink for your mug.  At each step along the way, a use value and an exchange value can be assigned (at least potentially).  Also along the way, of course, costs have been incurred, and presumably the actual costs are factored into the value of the grain (certainly the exchange value; probably the use value, too, although differently assessed).  What, then, is the end value (whether use or exchange)?  One could calculate it as an average across each of the steps.  But that is often easier said than done—and  especially if one is concentrating calculation in exchange value, since for that calculation one wants to include cost-of-production factors all along the way.  Who will make those calculations?  Will they be made fairly, equivalently?  Who will report the results?

The key insight of the theorists of "marginal utility" (the concept and then an entire theory) held that the "averaging" calculation was not how the typical consumer managed the fact that any "produced object" could have been produced *only over time*.  At least since the advent of Smith's labor theory of value (arguably since William Petty), theorists had agreed that the gradient of time (i.e., labor time) was the main variable of production (i.e., production requires time and that means more of a necessary but variable cost).  But calculating labor time was no longer so straightforward, given the new and increasing division of labor in an industrial factory system of production.  Certainly the typical end-state buyer was not prepared to make those calculations, which, though in principle adequately approximated by simple arithmetic, were logistically daunting for sophisticated scientists of economic production (whose best efforts were in any case prone to error).  Menger, Walras, and Jevons simplified the arithmetic problem by simplifying the temporal dimension, arguing that economic theory should treat the time factor as the ordinary consumer treats it, and that was by answering the question, "How much am I willing to spend for one more unit of this good or service?"  By marginalizing the time factor in that manner, the conundrum was solved.  In effect, the solution was achieved by a partitioning of consumers.  A potential buyer of another gallon of water had obviously already benefited from all of the water necessary to survival as of that date; so the price of the next gallon could be very low, even near zero, when "everybody has access to water."  A potential buyer of diamonds, on the other hand, is by that fact alone not a typical consumer; only persons who have already demonstrated ability and willingness to spend a large sum on a produced object having little or no intrinsic use value qualifies as "buyer of *another* unit" when the unit is diamond.[574]

It is important to note that the "marginal utility" concept can be understood also as a reply to a standard analytic expectation that sound explanation must account for the origin of any process that is to be explained.  To put the point less abruptly, this is the expectation that a logically sound explanation will account not only for any *present* instance of that which is to be explained but also to any future *and* any past instance.  This is of course to marginalize history (as did the common view of Newtonian mechanics).  Insofar as I can determine, this was probably not the motivation of any one of the three theorists, but the expectation points to a conflict.  The perspective taken by Menger, Jevons, and Walras assumes an ongoing history of sociality that

---

[574] Menger's 1871 treatise of "principles of economics" (as the work was translated into English) is distinctive in a few important ways, vis-à-vis works by Walras and Jevons, the largest being that he generalized the "marginal utility" concept to all parts or stages of production process, not simply "final-stage consumption."

includes some form(s) of market exchange. Thus, when thinking of the buy/sell dialectic, it is unrealistic to ask how much a starving man will pay for some quantity of food. If he is starving, he probably no longer has any money or goods or service with which to bargain for food. Rather, the realistic background assumption is that in general some minimal level of need satisfaction has already been achieved in some span of "the long run," with reasonable expectation of continuing satisfaction. Relative to *that* sort of background the valuation key of *marginal* utility makes sense. The starving man is effectively "priced out" of the market. Value in its nonrational sense (caritas, for example) will be left to his salvation, if he has any chance of it.

Marginal utility explains how people assign exchange value by their consumption choices (taken as revealed preferences). A labor theory of value, whether Smith's or Marx' version, has a different focus, explaining how intrinsic or use value comes to be. The two definitions of value as an instrumental concept do not coincide, but they need not be viewed as contradictory. They can be understood, rather, as complements. The labor theory intersects easily with a practical rationality of aesthetical (i.e., perceptual) and ethical judgment. When I stand before a cathedral, for example, the majesty of this human production has nothing directly to do with religion but with the process of human labor. I am struck by the enormity of the project and try to grasp all of the vast labor that went into its production: all the knowledge and skill that so many human beings committed to the making of it, from the architects who broached the initial design to patrons and local believers, to the masons who carved and set the enormous stones in mutual alignments, the carpenters and carvers of interior wood; and so forth. Much the same evaluation occurs when I attend a piano recital or an orchestral composition. These are applications of the labor theory of value. Leaving a donation at Durham, paying for passage of the attic tour of Lincoln's cathedral, buying entry to musical performances, all are rendered as investments in livelihood, craft, and upkeep; and those can be viewed as conventionally what they are, exchange-value measures for maintenance, continuation, and performance time. But the appreciations are of the human labor, applied long ago and/or last week.

The conflict is always present, but it tends to become perceptual (i.e, aesthetic and ethical) when manifest as a market failure. Markets are always prone to failure, and in one sense they are always failing in small, mostly imperceptible ways. That has implications for Leontief-style input-output analysis and its successors. The most important of these implications follows from the fact that the results of that form of input-output analysis are an expression of "real-world markets." A primarily descriptive application of the form—namely, a "national account"—is substituted for the core theoretical model of economic process. But this substitute model is empirically tested mainly in terms of whether it "breaks" or not—that is, in terms of the balance sheet of macro-economic interdependencies. Perceptually, judging from historical records, that test has attained public notice as a major event such as the Great Depression following 1929 and the Great Recession following 2007. Relative to the theoretical model, however, the real-world market is breaking virtually all of the time. Whereas the theoretical model assumes that market relevant information is freely available and equally shared among all market actors, for instance, in fact market actors do *not* uniformly share relevant information. Whereas the theoretical model assumes also that market actors are, if not perfectly rational, at least approximately rational in uniform degree, in fact not only are they rarely if ever perfectly rational but they also vary in degree of approximation both spatially and temporally. And likewise, with other assumptions (e.g., about skills of calculation, skills of estimating probabilities, and so forth). In other words, the basic assumptions of the theoretical model of exchange relations are never more than approximately satisfied, and the degree of satisfaction varies over time, depending on other historical conditions, and from place to place, depending on relevant variations of locale (e.g., prevailing rate of general inequality, quality of available education, racial-ethnic animosities, etc.). In the input-output calculations that result in accounting balances of interdependencies, the multitude of "small failures" of actual market process (vis-à-vis the theoretical model) tend to be "ironed out" arithmetically, because the inputs are already accomplished aggregates. This "ironing out" is justified by the assumption that most of the information that disappears is error (e.g., measurement error). Some of it no doubt *is* error. But vital information about the specific market-relevant actions and action effects has also disappeared. This contributes to what John Kenneth Galbraith (1961 [1955], p. 200) judged to be "the poor state of economic intelligence." Sound information disappears under what Galbraith called "the bezzle"—all of the little adjustments that are made not only during aggregation but also in the input-output accounting process by which the balances come out right, some of which covers discrepancies innocent or fraudulent. The balance-sheet accounting seems to work well enough during "good times." However, "when the tide goes out," to use a famous cliché, some market actors are "caught swimming without trunks." The tweaks that are used to smooth perceptually the smaller failures tend to forestall what will later become the massive failures that can be seen by all.

I mean "input-output analysis" different from that which generates the balance-sheet accounts, although the notion of interdependencies remains intact. In my meaning the focus is on *process dynamics beginning with per-person actions and action effects*, observing those effects as they aggregate per-person over time (building a profile trajectory of accomplishments such as measured skill acquisitions in school and measured task completions at work) and as they aggregate across persons in a specific organizational setting of institutional type. As already acknowledged, the task will no doubt be more difficult in the institutional setting of "family," a realm traditionally reserved as "private" even though long subject to means of "policing" (see, e.g., Donzelot 1979 [1977]; Wacquant 2008, 2009, 2014; Higbie 2013; Hochschild 2018, esp. pp. 9-59). Abundant evidence has demonstrated that the production of a next cohort or generation of citizens begins not in the institution of "school" but in that of "family," and because school heuristics and protocols are addressed to the "average or better student," deficits from early years tend to remain.

I argued in §27 that the power of an institution is manifest in its channeling of actions and simple behaviors. This should apply as well to the cross-person aggregation of per-person action effects. Insofar as the actions of a given person occur outside the organized activity of a specific collectivity, they are unlikely to have any effects available to aggregation. Insofar as the actions occur within a specific collectivity that is outside any institutional type, they may have effects within that specific collectivity, but the effects are less likely to have enough duration or impact to persist into any cross-person aggregation of per-person effects. A collectivity that survives in absence of institutional type tends to be an isolate among collectivities, relatively independent not only of collectivities of an institutional type but also of collectivities that are not of any institutional type, all of which makes them unusually dependent on activities of its own members for accumulation and maintenance of both material and ideal resources. Rather, it is the action effects of individual persons who are members of an *institutionalized* collectivity that are most likely to be available to cross-person aggregations. The fact of institutionalized form is normally manifested in many ways—greater organizational stability, for instance, and greater resilience of dynamic equilibria, but also greater ability of an organization of type to evolve in accordance with relevant external changes, These manifestations stem mainly from greater organizational resources of four types—agenda setting, commitment power, coordination, and enforcement—all of which are afforded within the heuristics of a given institution. All four also presuppose trust and an agreed mutuality of net benefit, which are implicitly reproduced as the sociality of each of the resources. While institutional authority tends to regulate across all organizations of the given kind—across schools, for instance, such that all or nearly all schools are recognizable in how they achieve and maintain prescribed organizational effects—there are nonetheless variations within kind which maintain a flexibility of kind that serves as potential to evolutionary change of the kind. Each of the four types of organizational resource also varies in strength across different institutional kinds. Of the three on which I have been focusing, I judge family to be weakest in general, school somewhat stronger, and work organization strongest of the three. That is partly because of the age gradient among individual persons as members of an organization of kind, which means that by the time of entry into work organization much experiential sorting has taken place.

Probably the greatest variation in each of the four organizational resources is due to inherited inequality. No present-time household family, defined as a unit of parentage and/or guardianship, begins from nothing or as the proverbial "fresh start"; it begins rather with an inheritance of inequality of access to resources, mental as well as material. New parents who were, each or both, born into poverty or near-poverty have difficulty escaping that condition before union, which thus increases the odds that as they become a unit of procreation the offspring will also arrive into conditions of poverty or near-poverty. This was very nearly an automatic continuance among the landless peasantry of previous centuries (and still some parts of the world). The other end of the spectrum then consisted of families of aristocracy (major or minor, noble or plain), as the principle of aristocracy was basically an incorporation of past and future generations along with the present, hierarchically distributed generation of a given family. The obligation of all members was to contribute to the patrimony of the principal member(s), who tended to be entitled and male. That principle amounted to a reasonably effective process of aggregation. It was primarily and mainly and endogenous process, but exogenous shocks were a continual threat, as was lack of heir. The chief exogenous threat was raiding by other aristocratic families, especially those who were higher in the queue of standing (including of course the highest, a monarch). Families formed alliances, mainly via exchanges of daughters, which amounted to a game-theoretic competition before invention of the phrase. The majority of families today still live under the threat of impoverishment, or at least of a rather abrupt descent in the hierarchy of material resources, due to death, illness, accidental injury, addiction, and/or incarceration, each of which "causes" tend to be explained as unintentional and thus exogenous, even though they are often at least partly endogenous to the familial unit. Costs of descent can be very high and lasting, visiting deleterious effects on the next generation of the given family.

538

Agenda setting can of course be intended endogenously, and it may conform more or less well to the institutionalized modality of "household family," "family of procreation," and so forth; but where the stamp of inherited inequality is heavy, agenda setting tends to be by default, and the default condition can be regulated mainly by parental death, abandonment, divorce, disability or chronic disease, and abuses physical and/or mental.

By the time an adult enters a local labor force, the long train of accumulated effects of resource inequality have stamped a nearly indelible ticket of life chances for a range of plausible destinations. Those who avoid premature death, chronic illness and disability, plus one or more cycles of incarceration, face "the meaning of life in modern society"—known otherwise as "work" in an occupationally defined career that supposedly offers stable income, employer-provided benefits such as health insurance and retirement pension, and a track of identity-forming successions up the ranks of status promotions and wage-rate of salary increases, whether according to a schedule designed for skilled craft workers in production plants or one for corporate employees in grey flannel suits or one for the liberal professions and technical sciences. Rather, that was the main idealization of work two, three generations ago. For young adults in recent decades it has all become much more precarious. Forty years ago André Gorz (1982 [1980], p. 3) wrote of "the abolition of work [as] a process already under way and likely to accelerate." Few people took him seriously. Gorz added, perhaps expectantly, that the most important but still undecided part of that process was "the central political issue of the coming decades"—namely, how to manage its consequences for the health of self-concept and sociality. Only recently have more than a scattering of percipient observers taken up that challenge. This most readily available institutional channel of per-person actions and effects is now undergoing massive change before much effort was made to study the routine processes by which per-person action effects were being aggregated during a long period of relatively stable equilibria in the complex relations of worklife. Records pertaining to the two main factors of production, labor and capital, were assiduously maintained by private firms and public agencies during that long period, but the underlying observations were not always well conceived, the measurements less than adequate, and the entire record keeping process focused almost entirely on static-state descriptions, month by month, quarter by quarter, or year by year. Historians have only the thinnest of descriptions of actual *processes* to study in retrospect (see, e.g., Gordon 2016; Hunnicutt 2013).

In general, "labor productivity" is defined as output per hour of labor of all persons involved in the production of goods or services. However, in usual practice the definition is specified further as production of goods or services in the business sector, and sometimes still further as excluding agricultural production. Conceptual and mensural problems attending the numerator of the ratio have been evident for decades, some of them becoming ever more important with increasing relative growth of output consisting of intangible goods and services that are free or nearly free to consumers. This is not a new concern—radio and television consumption had until recently been nearly free—but digitalization and the internet have generated free or nearly free services such as information search, maps, communications, and libraries, even as radio and television broadcasts have become monetized. Of course, "free" is itself a problematic description, given accounting practices that can isolate ("externalize") costs from relevant benefits. Generation of profits, or profit margins, is virtually always a competitive exercise in which distributions of power, the power to define not least, predominate.

Why the typical restriction to "business sector"? According to Bureau of Labor Statistics (and relevant other agencies), this restriction is because "it is difficult to draw inferences" on productivity from GDP resulting from government in general, nonprofit organizations, and paid employees of private households, as well as problems in calculating the rental value of owner-occupied dwellings. However, other estimations do include government services. The BLS program, Current Employment Statistics, surveys approximately 142,000 organizations (as of 2019), including government as well as business sectors, representing about 689,000 worksites, each month, obtaining data on total employment and average weekly hours of work, among other variables, which are then presented by industry group of production and nonsupervisory workers in non-agricultural establishments. These data are mostly presented in public releases as period-to-period "percentage change" for a given variable (although the "levels" data can be obtained), and while the data are adjusted for seasonal variation they generally do not include adjustments in terms of other compositional changes. Some changes in composition ramify in a variety of ways, a prominent example being the changing gender composition behind trends in labor-force participation rates: from 1948 to 1978 to 2018 participation rates among men declined from 86.6 to 77.9 to 69.1 percent; among women they increased from 32.7 to 50.0 to 57.1 percent). Trends such as this one tend to be manifested differently according to occupation and industry groups, for example, and thus also by geographic area.

There are of course similar compositional differences in other variables, some of them not obvious in or by standard labels of input and/or output. For instance, the variable "weekly hours" might be better labeled "hours at work per week in X type of workplace," for the meaning of "work" varies a lot by industry, by occupation, even by firm or agency of employment. The size of the record-keeping process is already a source of frustration to many employers, so one should not expect BLS to add such degrees of detail. But there is little doubt that at least some of the variables for which data are recorded are prone to undocumented variation in significant amounts, and this heterogeneity is rarely if ever randomly distributed by factors such as industry, occupation, and rate of compensation (including benefits). If one examines the "levels" data for weekly hours, for example, there is generally a strong attraction to reports of an "expected" value of 40 hours. It does vary by industry group, however. By way of illustration, consider that the monthly averages for the calendar year 2017 varied from a low 41.1 to a high of 41.4 hours in manufacturing of durable goods; 39.7 to 40.2 in nondurable manufacturing; 38.4 to 39.0 in transport & warehousing; 37.1 to 37.8 in publishing (except internet); 37.2 to 37.6 in financial activities; 32.8 to 33.0 in education & health services; 30.5 to 31.7 in motion picture and sound recording. This sampling is enough to show that while there was considerable variation across industry groups, there was very little within an industry group (the 2017 data were not unusual in either regard). The contrast could remind one of the standardizing effect achieved by and in an institutional heuristic.

Relative to that pattern of the "hours worked" variable, it is more difficult to find similar evidence of variation in per-person work productivity (i.e., in the numerator of the ratio). But there is some evidence. It can be seen indirectly in areal differences (and in sector differences)

540

of some aggregated data on worker productivity. Ciccone and Hall (1996) estimated from state-level data (which they had assembled) that the state with the highest average worker productivity enjoyed a productivity level during the late 1980s than was about 170 percent of the level for the lowest-ranked state, and the average level of the top ten states in worker productivity was about 123 percent of the average level of the bottom ten states. My own estimate for state-level data based on a published report by the Bureau of Labor Statistics is that the disparity has increased during the thirty years since the late 1980s, the ratio of productivity level between highest and lowest ranking state now at least two-to-one (see the abscissa line, figure 11, in Pabilonia, Jadoo, Khandrika, Price, and Mildenberger 2019). According to Ciccone and Hall's study, variation in productivity was mainly a function of differences across states in per-county areal density of employment. This significant positive correlation was net of variation in workers' average years of education, which they used as a surrogate measure of labor efficiency. By that assumption, in other words, the evidence suggested that variation across states in productivity was due primarily not to quality of worker preparation but to the concentration of businesses and thus employment opportunities. But it is also clear that this kind of observational base is conceptually inadequate, too crude and inattentive to important variations—sector differences, to be sure, industrial and commercial as well as regional—but also variations among members of the labor force at a given firm. Variation in quality is often greater than variation in wage rate: whereas the latter is set in terms of an estimated mean productivity within a competitive labor market, the former is set by worker motivation especially among newer workers who have yet to regress to the mean.[575]

Explicitly formulated substantive theory is crucial, of course, and what I have done so far is merely antecedent. I will suggest some explanatory models but only in preliminary fashion, and these will usually entail preparatory work in concept formations and in the innovation and calibration of new metrics. I should also say that I intend "explanation" in a rather general sense, avoiding, for instance, what I regard as a false contrast between "explanation" and "description" inasmuch as an explanation of a process outcome (how the outcome came to be) would be a description of process dynamics. Formalization that obscures that connection is dysfunctional until and unless the connections have been well theorized. I should note also that I find little to recommend counterposes of, say, "the notion that appropriate explanations specify factors that seem to make a difference to the probability of observing the events to be explained" versus a supposedly contrary approach that, as Hedström (2005, p. 2) put it, seeks to "explain a social phenomenon by referring to a constellation of entities and activities, typically actors and their actions, that are linked to one another in such a way that they regularly bring about the type of phenomenon we seek to explain." From my point of view, those versions of explanation or of explanatory framework are not mutually antithetical but are to some extent complementary (and see his pp. 75-76). Hedström's own preferred explanatory approach (the second of the two just cited) begins with a conception of "desires and beliefs" as main factors of per-person motivation and intention but will produce action only when opportunity is present. This framework can be

---

[575] Bear in mind, too, that historical trend can result in important compositional changes. For example, while it is often noted that older white men have suffered because of poor education, the deficit is relative; other groups have improved in educational attainment, while white male adults, especially those of less well educated parents, have not kept up. Ike McCaslin was "doing all the right things" but according to a script that was no longer relevant.

compared with the similar framework devised in Edwin Sutherland's (1939, pp. 4-9) theory of "differential association," which included a "decisive" factor of opportunity (implicitly a kind of cost/benefit evaluation of opportunity), except that whereas Sutherland assumed of the person a Meadian theory of social self (with continual updating via relations with others), Hedström chose a more nearly psychologistic "intra-individual" conception of a per-person actor as analytically a pre-social being who then generates "the social" via interactions with similar other per-person actors (see Hedström 2005, pp. 76-87). Moreover, while I do not doubt that individual person actors do have "desires and beliefs," also "attitudes and preferences," and that these variables of first-person experience tend to be involved in per-person intentions and motivations of actions, and that per-person actors can give accounts (second-person, often with third-person features) of reasons and (in first-person terms) causes, I am also aware that correlations are very low (partly because of noisy measures no doubt, but I suspect only partly and perhaps small part).[576] Until a much better grasp of those dynamics is in hand, I prefer to begin with actually observed actions and action effects. These can be attested as subjectively meaningful from characteristics of the sociality in which they transpire. True, per-person actors can dissimulate to one another, and they can be self-deceptive as well, and neither kind of event will necessarily be evident within and from the local sociality. But when not, one would have only the conundrum of first-person experience on which to reply.

Our tendency to begin and end with analysis is never more troublesome than here, where that tendency recommends that we begin with the per-person process, develop adequate insights into the process by which each person's action effects aggregate over time—no doubt within some grid of "kinds of actions" and perhaps a more complicated grid that begins with relevant conditionals of kinds of actions—and only then turn to aggregations of per-person actions effects (i.e., sequences of per-person actions effects) *across* person actors. The problem is as obvious to us as it was to Simmel: very "complex relations within regulation," to recall Manski's apt phrase one more time, are the locus of very important processes which operate in spatial and temporal dimensions simultaneously. I have also often called to mind another apt phrase: each and every individual person is "an ensemble of social relations" (Marx 1976 [1888], p. 7; 1987 [1939], p. 98). This, too, emphasizes the simultaneity of temporal and spatial dimensions of human actions and their effects. One must attend to the composition of the "interiority" of self as a collectivity via sociality (as George Herbert Mead proposed) but also to the composition of "interpersonal collectivity" (beginning with the collectivities into which a given person is born), which are of course processually temporal and spatial *and* which may well vary, usually do vary, in conditions from place to place and from date to date.[577]

---

[576] Recall Bill McGuire (1989) demonstrating that prior research had rarely found attitude-to-behavior correlations big enough for measures of relevant attitude to account for even eight or nine percent of the observed variation in actual behavior. In response to that upsetting revelation, some analysts revised their measures of specific attitudes so as to include presumptive behavioral variations of propensity. This strikes me as rather like an enlistment of the dynamic ex post rationalization as mensural as well as conceptual premise.

[577] To state this important point in a different vocabulary, the dynamics of a process may as such evolve over time, but at the time of inquiry an investigator wants to examine the process "as it now usually operates"—that is, in its modal or mean tendency of operation (equilibrium or stationary condition);

My point is not that we must attend to all of the complexity all at once. That challenge would be a sure road to frustration and despair. As a point of departure, it might be appropriate to begin with per-person actions, build a time-series of relevant measured observations within an appropriate input-to-output model of action effects, beginning with a basic model such as the geometric Brownian motion (GBM) model mentioned near the beginning of this Part Five (i.e., as equation 5.1). Then one could add time-sensitive covariates that include relevant network dynamics in which each of the individual person-actors is a node of perceptions, motivations, and influences; then conduct perhaps a Fourier-type analysis of each time-series in order to build an understanding of the endogenous dynamics and how exogenous conditions impinge on those dynamics. But this is only preliminary then to an input-to-output model of the cross-person aggregation of per-person action *effects*, keyed to the theoretically expected workplace goal of production. Because (and insofar as) per-person actions and their effects will presumably have been undertaken in network relations all along the time-sequence—and undertaken within a competitive/cooperative framework of perception of worker relations in a network vis-à-vis that expected goal of production—revision of those early-stage analyses, now accommodating filter-and-updating loops, could next become part of the construction of cross-person aggregation patterns.

Before proceeding further with discussion of models, I need to explain what I mean about "accommodating filter-and-updating loops," since these can be, on principle, components of any model. Recall from §27 the familiar utility of a filter-and-update feedback process—as learned and then practiced, for example, in riding a bicycle. Humans learn to gain advantages through tactical and strategic uses of feedback loops in most circuits of communication. Think of the patterns involved in "breaking the ice" conversation during informal gatherings, or in the more formulaic exchanges in a job interview or a student-teacher conference. Several different kinds of filtering mechanisms have been invented, many of them no doubt older than the oldest of our surviving records of information exchange. The most versatile of filters are those of a general class known as Kalman filters, most of which have been formalized as mathematical models of continuous-time processes, even though their practical utilities are almost always discrete-time measured sequences of filtering followed by some sort of updating, more or less in line with the logic of Bayesian updating. These sequences are adapted to the monitoring and regulation of the flow of information through specified channels, such as are available in institutionalized form in many organizations. They can be applied recursively, which enhances their efficiency and their utility as means of monitoring and controlling information flows. These means are often built into the agenda-setting properties of organizations of this or that institutional kind, albeit with greater frequency and formality in some (schooling, workplace) than in other (familial) settings.

---

however, the process as such always operates in time and place (e.g., aggregation of per-person action effects as these effects are "interactive" with the corresponding per-person action effects of other person-actors—all of which raises the problem of parsing dynamics by too many clocks (see, e.g., Hazelrigg 1997). Understanding dynamics of processes of change is difficult due to the inherent complexity and ambiguity of "time"—how it is conceived, measured, and so forth—all of which is integral to those dynamics. The processes are not self-motivating. They are enacted by human beings, beings of a sociality that is always of, about, and "in" time as well as *a* time.

543

As just mentioned, filtering is usually followed by an updating of information, based on one or another result of the filter, and in the following discussion I will tend to use the compound gerund phrase, "filtering and updating" (or F&U) as a convenience. But it should be understood in advance that a filtering need not entail any one functional type of updating, or even any at all. The most common uses of Kalman filters include noise reduction and neutralization. Virtually any channel of information flow is noisy, some of it random but some of it nonrandom, and all of it tends to interfere with the expected signal. Kalman filters can strengthen the expected signal relative to the interference. These filters can be used also to reduce ambiguity of expected signal (assuming sufficient theoretical expectation about the ambiguity).[578] Aside from responses to noise, filters can be used to engage a governor or martingale process to dampen the rate of flow of an underlying process, to trigger a threshold effect (e.g., switching to a different channel of flow, as in switching a pupil to a remedial or accelerated curriculum, or activating an alternative function of the information), or to initiate another kind of updating of the process being filtered.

How is the filtering performed? In some applications it is built into the input-output flow dynamics as a routine action, but this does not mean that no per-person action is involved (by which I mean action beyond design of an automated algorithm). Who performs the F&U in a given organization? On the one hand, the question seems to invoke some managerial process. But on the other it is not difficult to imagine any number of members of an organization doing the same, even if not in official capacity. Humans are fond of "comparison behavior" and "status competitions" of various sorts, including some that indulge a "conspicuous consumption" slant. I think I have never been a member of an organization in which these predilections could not be observed.

In the AbCon process the given first-person actor performs an F&U routine more or less regularly, some of it self-reflectively but almost surely most of it liminal, even sub-liminal in action much of the time, in that one usually does not deliberately pare or forget a memory of past I (a "me," then and there). It is core to the AbCon process, and as such it tends to operate much like a first-order Markov process: the F&U outcome tends to be fully absorptive of past status and the act of F&U itself. Available models provide for F&U as an ordinary component (see, e.g., Sargent 1999, pp. 115-121).[579] Insofar as AbCon is only first-person experiential, access to the performance is closed; but on the assumption that per-person performance is self-reflective, and to the extent that the assumption can be engaged mutually, one could succeed in obtaining second-person information about the performance. Whether this achievement would qualify as insightful information is another matter. Anyone who has interviewed another for purposes of

---

[578] Recent improvements in machine-learning algorithms for language translation have come from application of these ambiguity-reduction filters. It should be clear that "expectation," whether as benchmark for shedding noise or for sorting dimensions of ambiguity, should be driven by theory even when the basis of the theory is induction from machine learning; for it is the theory that flags the possibility that expectation can worsen, not improve, meaning. Any inductive product from machine learning must be filtered by appropriate theory.

[579] Sargent specified Kalman filtering integrated into a recursive least squares design, plus a variation designed to accommodate a deliberate misspecification that will be corrected, perhaps successively, as new data comes into play. These developments exceed presently available measured observations of per-person action, but they offer useful theoretical tools.

building a biographic account can testify to the myriad "pitfalls": scholarly inquiry is obviously not "immune" to the ordinary complexities of sociality. I suspect that even a paragon of perfect honesty cannot avoid and never detects reconstitutive memory—surely not, if any details of the journalist's "five questions" are at account.

An F&U procedure in per-person aggregation of own action effects over some period of time would surely occur within, and perhaps to the benefit of, a collectivity in which the person is member. The main endogenous condition would probably be a status hierarchy melded into and partially overlapping network ties among members of the given collectivity. Think of an age-graded student acquiring skill information in a specific substantive area of the curriculum, following a per-person trajectory of acquisition: at least one major effect would be variable movement in a relative ranking of skill levels among all students, a ranking at least available to local-public evaluations. A given student maintains awareness, via more or less shared mutual standings within the collectivity's network of (variable fluid) ties, of relative contributions of own-action effects to the collective good. A teacher is influential in that maintenance, both at a general level (partly deliberated, partly happenstance and perceptual by others) and in terms of effects on per-pupil specific status in the collectivity network.[580] A prominent example of the latter would be the event of teacher selecting a highly successful pupil as "volunteer" tutor to a poorly successful pupil (a sort of "teacher's aide," subject to status elevation by the publicly acknowledged selection and, correlatively, perception by other pupils as "class brain," "teacher's pet," and/or other designations). The dynamics of and from an F&U routine can be complicated and complicating (e.g., of network resources of status, influence, etc., and of the evolution of ties and tie-strengths).

Can one imagine similar scenarios of an F&U procedure performed in per-person action effects aggregated in time within familial settings? Yes, although the opportunities of measured observation would probably be rare. Within workplace settings? Yes, and here there could be several circumstances in which measured observation might be conducted via, say, audiovisual recording. Think of a restaurant, for instance: employees are assigned segmentally (a blend of functional and "geographic" segmentation)—supply, kitchen, retail service, managerial—with some stratification of networking. Per-person F&U within per-person action sequences is likely, as indeed one has no doubt observed variations in personal learning curves among a server crew of this or that restaurant and wondered (or have had confirmed via conversation with the crew chief) how closely "management" monitors and what form (if any) feedback takes, with what sensitivity, and so forth.

With these last remarks, I am of course attending the riddle of two traversely intersecting aggregation processes: one, per-person aggregation over time of own-action effects, what if any F&U is ever performed and, if it is, under what conditions, with what consequence, and so forth; the other, a form of cross-person aggregation (also over time) of multiple per-person action

---

[580] I am thinking here primarily and mainly of grammar or elementary school. The teacher's part in the sociality of schooling changes markedly as one moves up the age-graded hierarchy of organizations of institutional type. This progression can be seen most easily in terms of networks, the teacher's part becoming more and more nearly that of a contract worker from "middle school" years to high school and then college.

effects at least insofar as these effects constitute a collective good as institutionally defined and evaluated by the "organization as such," usually with some hierarchical dimensionality among the individual per-person actors, managerial, line, and support staff. These intersecting processes are complex, and I am not yet prepared to conceptualize them with much specificity. While they no doubt vary from organization to organization, probably by institutional type, perhaps also by organizational age and by subcultural factors along with various other contingencies, I suspect that distinctive patterns can be discerned by institutional type, plus some patterns across two or institutional types. In the meantime, many and various pertinent questions come to mind. For instance, which specific "official" of a collectivity has an obligation to monitor, evaluate, and reflect cross-person aggregation? As a matter of agency, this function would generally come under the heading of "managerial office," but such offices are usually multiple in number and in specific jurisdiction. In a restaurant setting, for example, "head chef/cook" normally runs the kitchen; but as this is usually "shift work," who coordinates across shifts? Likewise, the crew of table servers is normally coordinated under a crew chief, of whom also there will typically be two or more, working different shifts. And who oversees supply lines, the crucial, first-instance agency? Then, too, who integrates the whole of the action effects of the entire collectivity, not only day by day but over spans of time during which restaurant reputations can subtly change along with notoriously "fickle" consumer preferences relative to notoriously thin restaurant margins?

In a sense, there is still the Smithian image of an "invisible hand" at work in cross-person aggregations of per-worker action effects: "everything just all comes together, somehow." That imagery, and imagination, is crucial to sociality. The very fact of collectivity has already assured a "coming together." But there can be immense variation in that process—in how it happens, in the quality of the happening and its results (main, incidental, intended/unintended, side effects, and so forth), in its reproduction of its own conditions, in innovative tendencies, and so forth. It is not mere wordplay to say that aggregation is integrative; but aggregation can also be—in brief spurts or in side effects or spill-over effects—*dis*integrative as well (or, in a newly more popular idiom, "disruptive," one of the kernels of Schumpeter's fascination with creative destruction— as if any organism ever accomplished anything without consuming other organisms). Digitalization of information flows has made the conversion of "information" into "data" more serviceable due to computing power. But it has also magnified by orders of magnitude the sheer volume and pace of "data" that "must" be taken into account. Until accounting has been accomplished, one faces a situation much like the problem of noisy signals. Machine-learning algorithms can aid in the accounting. The inherent risk is, however, that machine learning can become internally directed by the goals of the machine rather than by goals of the human beings it supposedly serves, while no human being is capable of independently detecting the difference. Low-skilled workers already operate as slaves to a "smart machine," and the trendline is upward.

Based on a GBM model, a Fourier analysis of the temporal aggregation of per-person action effects for each person would generate useful data about trend and fluctuations around each per-person trendline. The base model for each person would describe parameters for what would amount to each person's dynamic equilibrium: one parameter for strength of the central-tendency attractor and other parameters for volatility (mainly amplitude and period length). One or more sequences of F&U can be inserted in the base model—in recognition of per-person skill learning, for instance, or for purposes of filtering noise or for sensitivity to exogenous shocks to temporal aggregation.[581] These per-person parameters could then be compared across persons as an initial inspection of internal conditions of cross-person aggregation, comparisons including relevant per-person covariates and perhaps covariates of task differences among the persons.

However, that analysis would assume a crucial simplification—namely, that cross-person aggregation would be of the per-person patterns of equilibration, the signals of which could arise only after delays of some length. In fact, cross-person aggregation would generally occur by the same clock as the per-person aggregation of action effects. In terms of workplace tasks, there might be sets of accounting lags in cross-person aggregation (e.g., by pay period), and it is conceivable that pay-period lag would be reflected in both per-person and cross-person processes of aggregation (a testable hypothesis). But the temporality of aggregation dynamics could vary even if a uniform clock (e.g., pay period) operates, since the cross-person process might be less volatile (i.e., more reflective of habituations due to status factors, person-to-person network ties, intercorrelated rhythms of task coordination, etc.). These and other concerns recommend that another modeling approach be used in addition to the one just described. The following is one set of models that begin with the same per-person observations for the cross-person as well as the per-person aggregation process.

Assume we have for each of several pupils in a classroom or workers in a plant a long sequence of per-person task-action effects. How might we model these relative to each other, as in a cross-person aggregation of the multiple per-person task-action effects taken as information signals? One basic approach is to the model them as a dynamic Bayesian network. Perhaps the simplest of this kind of model is the one commonly known as a "hidden Markov model," which dates partly from work done in the development of nonlinear filters (see Ljungqvist and Sargent 2018, pp. 34, 57-63,1387-1388). This basic yet flexible model (hereafter, HMM) is highly useful for modeling intercorrelated adjacent sequences, where the adjacency is both temporal and spatial. The model comes in a variety of modifications that allow expansions of several kinds (for a good overview, with illustrations from genomic sequencing, see Yoon 2009). The central advantage is that HMM "can be used to describe the evolution of observable events that depend on internal factors [that] are not directly observable" (Yoon 2009, p. 402). The basic logic of HMM is as follows: imagine a signal; it is noisy; thus, what one observes is a compound or conflation of at least two factors. This conflated signal is our observable event, which we have in a sequence that is marked by some degree of serial correlation. Hidden within each event is a meaning that we are after. But when we believe we have grasped that meaning, what have we actually grasped? An *interpreted* meaning—that is, the part of the observed signal that has been separated from its conflation with all other components (treated as noise, or observational error). The logic of this model should sound familiar. As parts of Yoon's presentation manifest, we are still grappling with Kant's transcendental Illusion. That is to say, the tendency is to forget the presence of the adjective, "interpreted," and identify the (interpreted) meaning with an assumed

---

[581] A variety of filters are available, but the most often used are Kalman filters of one sort or another; see illustrations in Sargent (1999, pp. 11-13, 96-97, 115-118) and in Ljungqvist and Sargent (2018, pp. 55-68, 142-143, 1388-1389).

"hidden true meaning," as if we had actually gained direct access to "hidden causes." So long as we refrain from that sleight of hand, however, what he have actually gained through the HMM model is a scoring technique that enables us to construct pair-wise or multi-wise *alignments* of serially correlated sequences of interpreted meanings of observed signals of multiple per-person action effects. This dynamic Bayesian network provides us with a systematic basis for the study of cross-person aggregations.

Another approach that follows from the GBM basic model was usefully illustrated by Nicole Saam (1999), under the heading of "master equation" modeling. This approach has a long heritage in the physical and (more recently) biological sciences, and Saam's illustration shows its utilities for social-science applications despite some severe limitations. For purposes of overview, recall a thought experiment introduced in §26 during a review of work by James Clerk Maxwell and Ludwig Boltzmann in relation to the challenge of ergodicity. Call it the "gas box" case, the very simple case of a closed system of gaseous relations in equilibrium. This system can be fully described in only three variables—volume, pressure, temperature—far simpler than any system of human relations. To say that this system is in equilibrium is to say that the gas is completely isolated; it is neither gaining nor losing heat. This latter condition is simply a convenience for purposes of the illustration. It could be removed, but then we would need to consider change in the variables. The point of my illustration would not be affected.

Now, by knowing to the limits of measurement the value of each of the three variables, we know all of the system's present condition, all of the information it contains at the moment. We know nothing specific of the system's condition as it was at any particular time yesterday or last week or last year, however. Nothing. We can "unpick" the present relations of the system. Even if we succeed sufficiently in that effort, we gain no information about what the condition of the system actually was one hour ago or five hundred days plus one hour ago. We can of course make inferences about the system's past. But unless we observed that past condition of the gas box, we have no empirical evidence by which to test any of the inferences. By inference, for example, the system was probably gaining/losing heat, because we know from past experience that maintaining a closed gaseous system in equilibrium is difficult. For one thing, heat transfer is usually quick and easy. For another, wait long enough and containers spring leaks. And so forth. But none of that will tell us exactly what the prior condition of the system actually was. We cannot know the actual set of three-variable readings if we did not take the measurements at the appropriate date, and lacking those measurement values we also cannot say how the system actually changed during the interim. What one *can* do—and this is the kernel of the "master equation" approach—is build a model of the evolution of the given system through a stochastic distribution of alternative states during some specified period of time (or, in principle, during an infinite period). We still will not know the system's contingent condition at any specific date, but we will have the next best set of information, a probability distribution of those states of the system.

To repeat the limit: all that we can say about any prior interim of that "gas box" process, a process strictly deterministic in its momentary dynamics, will be inferential, contingent, and stochastic. Recall from my discussion of institutional dynamics in §27 the presence of a "master narrative": it is bounded by the same limits: inference, contingency, and stochasticity.[582] Can a "master equation" approach offer what a "master narrative" approach cannot? If we are as limited as we are in learning about any prior state of a simple thermodynamic system—left with the same tools, reasoned inferences formulated from some assumptions by which to anchor some of the contingencies (e.g., no leaks) when estimating probabilities—then *imagine what more we face* when we try to "retroject" from present to past conditions of a typical system of relations of sociality, *in order then to make claims about the process(es) by which the experienced present came to be what it is.* There is no substitute for measured observations of process dynamics as the process is in operation, doing what it does. Saam (1999, pp. 50, 52-53, 60) built an input-output model (or what she called "a simple and—from the sociological point of view—empty balance algorithm") which she applied to a particular setting by specifying dynamic conditions of per-person interactions (i.e., the dynamics of what she called a "trend configuration," as in an HMM model). This resulted in a conceptually impressive micro-macro model (albeit mensurally weak in application), the central thesis of which was a per-person aggregation function of "elite members of the military" who achieve (or not) the cross-person aggregation of a coup. The final model "cannot be solved analytically." As with other uses of formalization, however, her uses of simulation techniques demonstrated some diagnostic tools for assaying contingencies of specific assumptions and stochastic outcomes.[583]

With a different approach, one could say that in principle it, too, begins from the GBM model. But in fact it logistically begins a major recognition: whereas a GBM model can be applied without difference—whether the unit is an atom or molecule of gas, the proverbial billiard ball, an actual human being or the measured effect of per-person task actions of an actual human being—human beings are generally always already assembled as members of a sociality, which has a distinctive compositional structure of one kind or another. One of the most general of such structures is a network of nodes and internodal ties. The ties are usually generated by persons as nodes, although the generation is usually enabled/constrained by an institutional form (i.e., family ties, school ties, work ties). True hermits are rare. Aside from such cases, "isolates" can be set as one relative limit to density of ties, while an upper relative limit is set in accordance with a pragmatic management algorithm—as in a set of Dunbar numbers, the maximum of which is an approximation to the cognitive limit of the number of other persons with whom ego person can maintain stable relations to the extent of knowing every other's nominal identity and relationship to each other person as node in the network (see Dunbar 2010; Dávid-Barrett and Dunbar 2013). However, "node" need not be identified with a nominally distinctive individual person. It can be defined instead in terms of a nominally distinctive task action by a nominally distinctive actor, for example, or, more importantly, in terms of a *measured effect* of a nominally distinctive task action by a nominally distinctive actor.

---

[582] These limits can be summarized by saying "historicity," for example, or "sociality." Amitav Ghosh (2016, p. 115) expressed the crucial meaning: "if the entirety of our past is contained within the present, then temporality itself is drained of significance."

[583] Because she tied her master-equation approach to a master "attitude-to-action" motivational model, the empirical relation of which was (to my mind) seriously exaggerated, some of the diagnostic outcomes are questionable. But the illustration of a general utility remains intact.

The institutional character of network generation (or person's membership) can be seen in Giannella and Fischer's (2016) typology of networks, which was developed inductively from their consideration of how person networks clustered on specific dimensions. The largest cluster was "career and friends" (non-kin based), at 24 percent, correlating with the institutional arena of work (employment, occupation, etc.). The second largest was "family and community" (i.e., kin-based), at 20 percent, while the third largest was "family-only," at 16 percent; these two clusters sum to 36 percent for the institutional arena of family life. Thus, three largest clusters accounted for three-fifths of all of the networks examined. Note that the data which Giannella and Fischer examined were from person networks formed and active prior to the advent of the "social media" technologies such as Facebook and LinkedIn, plus their immediate predecessors.[584] Obtaining more and better observations from familial settings will be difficult, for reasons stated earlier. However, "family" has traditionally been one of the "step-children" of the social sciences. Recent efforts to study process dynamics within familial settings have demonstrated promises of continuing improvement in concept formation and in mensural techniques (see, e.g., Yavorski, Kamp Dush, and Schoppe-Sullivan 2015).

Several different strands of modeling have been developed with a concept of "network" at core. Some of these have been simulational and generative, as with Joshua Epstein's (2006) work which builds upon computational approaches from the 1950s such as cellular automata and other gaming algorithms. A related sequence of developmental work has pursued computational analysis of networks and other organizational forms by Kathleen Carley and her colleagues (see, e.g., Joseph, Wei, Benigni, and Carley 2016). A third approach that has incorporated networks is the relational-event-sequence modeling by Carter Butts and colleagues (see, e.g., DuBois, Butts, McFarland, and Smyth 2013). Whereas the main convention during the 1970s and 1980s defined nodes as individual persons, network nodes can be defined just as readily as events— acts of one or another kind, or specific effects from acts of a kind, and so forth—and these event-nodes can be arrayed both cross-sectionally within specified contexts and in temporal sequences in which a later event is conditioned on prior events in the sequence.

A similar approach has been developed by Tom Snijders and colleagues. An abstract by Snijders for an early article well describes the initial state of this model-building project:

A class of statistical models is proposed for longitudinal network data. The dependent variable is the changing (or evolving) relation network, represented by two or more observations of a directed graph with a fixed set of actors. The network evolution is modeled as the consequence of the actors making new choices, or withdrawing existing choices, on the basis of functions, with fixed and random components, that the actors try to maximize. Individual and dyadic exogenous variables can be used as covariates. The

---

[584] Again, terminology matters, especially when it circulates in ways that mislead, conflate, confuse, etc. Identifying new communication techniques such as Facebook, LinkedIn, and the like, as "social media" is objectionable on a variety of grounds. Historically, it can suggest that the advent of smoke signals, semaphores, telegraph, telephone, radio, and so forth, were not already *social*. An absurd position to promote. It can suggest that communications of information labeled as "economic" or "geographic" or "political" or "linguistic" or "zoological" (etc.) are somehow other than, even contrary to, *social* media. Another absurdity.

change in the network is modeled as the stochastic result of network effects (reciprocity, transitivity, etc.) and these covariates. The existing network structure is a dynamic constraint for the evolution of the structure itself. The models are continuous-time Markov chain models that can be implemented as simulation models. The model parameters are estimated from observed data. For estimating and testing these models, statistical procedures are proposed which are based on the method of moments. The statistical procedures are implemented using a stochastic approximation algorithm based on computer simulations of the network evolution process (Snijders 2001, p. 361).

There has followed a series of publications reporting development of the model in a variety of dimensions (see Snijder, 2005, 2009; Snijders, van de Bunt, and Steglich 2010; Snijders and Steglich 2015). The initial estimation technique relied on a calculation-intensive "method of moments" approach. Subsequent work (e.g., Snijders, Koskinen, and Schweinberger 2010) has offered a much more efficient maximum likelihood estimator. This is still a matter of "work in progress" and remains dependent on the use of simplifying assumptions (which will no doubt continue to be the case).[585] For instance, in the stage of development with Koskinen and Schweinberger (2010) per-person actors were assumed to have control of their outgoing ties under two particular constraints—that ties could change only one-by-one and that actors could not coordinate. These simplifying assumptions, intended to restrict the model to the smallest possible number of constituents of network change, while obviously severe, provided a basis from which subsequent work can proceed by gradually relaxing particular restraints on dynamic actor-based models of data arrays both cross-sectional of networks (including covariates of per-person characteristics and of network properties) and longitudinal in per-person aggregations of action effects. Gradually these models can be calibrated relative to observations of "real world" features of institutional settings as well as status characteristics of per-person actors. But just as any ethnography remains contingent on assumptions, so, too, will these formal modeling efforts.

My intent here is not to review or condense those several lines of development. Rather, I shall continue with my description of a general modeling approach, with the understanding that prospects of substantive theory that only a short time ago seemed dismal, because of the complex relations that substantive theory needed to address, have brightened considerably—indeed, to the point that scholars in the forefront of model building now often await guidance from substantive theorists. Powerful means of adjudicating among competing models within a generalized frame of signal processing are available and have been used in many disciplines, from astrophysics to machine learning to neural networks, as well as to engineering problems of signal processing and statistical decision making (see, e.g., Knuth, Habeck, Malakar, Mubeen, and Placek 2015). The selection techniques can be adapted to the specific contingencies of alternative models within the disciplines of social science. But that will depend on substantive theorizing in those disciplines.

Imagine an input-to-output model of a time-series of aggregated effects of per-person task-actions of a well-defined kind in comparatively described organizations of an institutional

---

[585] I must acknowledge that my tracking of this work has been sporadic in recent years, and I urge the reader to move directly to the production by Snijders and colleagues, only some of whom are mentioned in the present account.

kind (workplace, school, etc.) over an interval of time (and relevant temporal circumstances) sufficiently long to detect tendencies to equilibrium states (i.e., basins of attraction), which in many instances are likely to be multiple under varying contingencies (i.e., contrary to the conventional expectation of a single "master" equilibrium).[586]

Think of a commercial firm that produces a good or service. The output is that product. The inputs consist in all of the relevant activities (labor time) contributed toward that product. Let's assume a relatively particular "thing" (good or service) as output. The inputs are varied, this variation being to a large extent a function of the organizational hierarchy of the firm and, relative to that, the particular occupational functions performed by employees. Some of the latter can be classified as "line functions"; others, including the managerial, as "staff functions" that facilitate line workers to satisfaction of the principal's product task. In most basic principle, all of the output could be accounted for by the collectivity of line workers. But very few if any firms in existence are that "basic." Staff workers must attend to legal actions both internal to the firm (contracts, dispute resolutions, etc.) and external in relations with other organizations of various kinds, some of them suppliers of goods and/or services to the present firm and others governmental in some regulatory or constraint/enablement sense (e.g., provisions of public goods and services, "infrastructure," such as transport and communication services. Staff workers must also attend to routine internal management processes, which include a monitoring of line workers in performance of expected tasks. Already, it is clear, we are in the midst of an on-going collectivity that is both hierarchical (very likely on more than one dimension at any given time) and a network or (more likely) networks of ties among per-person actions (or specified actions of task orientation), these actions being partly perpendicular and partly transverse to hierarchical levels of the organization *and* aligned both with and across a distinction between action directed toward expected output and action that is secondary to (supportive of) that directed action. It is these latter actions, and more to the point their *effects*, that are key to the aggregation process that forms the definitive core of the collectivity (its reason for being, its measure of success, and at least in principle its internal distribution of rewards/penalties).

A crucial preparatory step toward the conduct of measured observations of that process of aggregation in terms of an input-to-output model is the conceptual construction of a carefully specified mapping of the information flows throughout the networks of ties as those flows are regulated (enabled/constrained) in and by the hierarchical relations of the collectivity. Perhaps the most crucial goal, certainly at least one of the crucial goals, of that mapping is a conceptual model of relative contributions of staff vis-à-vis line functions to the core process by which the action effects aggregate into a final output. This goal must be achieved quantitatively as well as qualitatively. That in itself will be a major result both theoretically and empirically for any and

---

[586] This latter criterion must be left open-ended, simply because any such tendency will usually be difficult to discern and even when apparently discerned will very likely be confounded by "external" drift, random shocks, etc. The criterion of stationarity is always only an assumption imposed by model, pretensions of empirical support much easier to imagine when working with panel data of static description per panel. But enough experience with dynamic systems has been accumulated to know that any given dynamic system may be capable of multiple equilibria—which raises interesting questions about conditions under which transitions between basins of attraction can occur.

each venue of collectivity. Such studies conducted with various kinds of work collectivities over some period of time should result in a still greater theoretical consequence.[587]

Contributions simultaneously theoretical and methodological toward an ability to model a "complete network structure as well as relevant actor attributes—indicators of performance and success, attitudes and cognitions, behavioral tendencies—must be studied as joint dependent variables in a longitudinal framework where the network structure and the individual attributes mutually influence one another" (Steglich, Snijders, and Pearson 2010, p. 330; see also Snijders 2009). Does a "network structure" have influence? It does, at least in the sense that it consists of constraints/enablements, very much as the biographical-historical intersections in birth-cohort structure influenced life chances in Hout's (2012, 2018) explanatory framework. These are channels of probabilistic influence. Networks and structures are not actors, just as "individual attributes" are not actors but conditions which make specific actions contingent in specific ways and degrees. Developing models that are complex enough to respect an assumption that a given "network evolves as a stochastic process 'driven by actors,'" with appropriate differentiations between endogenous drivers (in other words, that the actors are influenced by the characteristics of the "current network structure itself") and by exogenous conditions that are represented as "actor covariates" and as "dyadic covariates," as the case may be (Snijders, van de Bunt, and Steglich 2010, p. 44), is the goal of model building. Developing the substantive theory described above is necessary preparation.

DiPrete and Forristal (1994, p. 349) emphasized some useful reminders of caution about complexity. On the one hand, given the complexity of human relations it is easy to formulate models (and theories behind them) that are "impossibly difficult" in various respects, including empirical estimation. On the other hand, I will add, a well-conceived theory will surely be an advertisement of the difficulty, insofar as the theorist bothers to think through the demands being made of an estimation model. The linkage between those poles must be built by adequacies of conceptualization and measurement. Too many of the concepts that are used date from eras when the social sciences were still mainly inheritors of everyday categories, and it remains the case that "measurement in social network analysis is a subject which tends to receive too little attention" (Snijders 2009, p. 6).

Considerable progress has been made toward the development of actor-based dynamic network models that are capable of representing micro-level action effects relative to macro-level outcomes (cf. Snijders and Steglich (2015). Powell (1990) was on track thirty years ago when he wrote that neither the existing models of "market network" relations nor those of "hierarchical organization" would be adequate to the daunting task. Some melding of the two would have to be made. That melding has been at work in various shops, with good records of success. More must be accomplished, however, and daunting tasks remain. On the one hand, as one team of model builders pointed out,

---

[587] The same overall project of inquiry could be conducted, at least in principle, for venues of school and—albeit in principle ignorant of ethical as well as technical concerns—for venues of family. As mentioned earlier, the "in principle" locution is surely nearer everyday realism for venues of work, and even there would surely encounter difficulties.

*complete* network studies (i.e., measurements of the whole network structure in a given group) are clearly preferable to personal (ego-centered) network studies, because selection patterns can best be studied when the properties of nonchosen potential partners are also known, and because of the possible importance of indirect ties (two persons having common friends, etc.) that are difficult to assess in personal network studies. Complete network data, on the other hand, are characterized by highly interdependent observations. This rules out the application of statistical methods that rely on independence of observations—i.e., most standard techniques. To our knowledge, no previous study succeeded in a statistically and methodologically credible assessment and the separation of selection and influence mechanisms (Steglich, Snijders, and Pearson 2010, p. 332).[588]

Among the many problems yet to be addressed adequately, one was previewed above in the "gas box" illustration. Or as Snijders (2005, p. 2) summarized, "a network usually is the result of a complex and untraceable history." The problem of unobserved initial conditions is surely not unique to the study of networks. Addressing its applications in network data could prove to be more difficult than in other data arrays (see Heckman 1981b), but in any case one should bear in mind that the goal is not to estimate the date and place of any "first origin" or original condition.

Substantive theory must attend more to the difference between the endogenous dynamics of a given network and the evolution of that network as such. Network stationarity is only a tool of modeling, rarely an empirical condition of actual networks. While a network might tend to stationarity during some extended period, with only fluctuations around a stable and possibly flat trend line, there is usually some nonnegligible likelihood of more rapid, perhaps trend-altering evolution. One likely stimulant to faster, perhaps uneven network evolution would be innovation in organizational technology within an institutional arena or at the interstices between arenas. A current illustration is the advent of "platform" technology by which previously separated arenas of product development and product distribution and exchange become integrated under a single managerial process, eliminating multiple borders and gate-keeping functions. Think of Amazon, for instance, which expanded from book seller to an open-access platform for all processes of the production and distribution of publications without the previous conventions of intermediation by the filters of critics and/or accountants of publishing houses. Should one expect to use a self-same model that incorporates variable rates of change (perhaps second-as well as first-order) in network structure as such? Perhaps, depending on circumstances. Should one expect instead an evolution from one model to another? Perhaps, again depending on circumstances. Mulder and Leenders (2019) addressed part of that question, as they, proceeding from early work by Carter Butts (2008), developed extensions for "analyzing relational event streams" in *time-ordered* networks. These are indeed promising developments. As mentioned multiple times already, having well-measured observations is far more importantly, initially and perhaps fore some time, that having population-based probability samples of observations.

---

[588] That "separation" was reference to the problem of modeling distinctive effects of per-person influences on other actors in a network vis-à-vis effects that reflect initial and reproduced partner selections, on the other hand, and initial but reformed partner selections on the other.

To develop substantive theory in absence of relevant experiences is, to recall Kant once again, to develop empty logical containers. But in order to be useful to substantive theorists, the experience must be well conceptualized and well measured. Ordinary experience is conceptual, no doubt, and it is usually at least crudely mensural; and this obtains even when a first-person actor is mostly incognizant of either. Vague conceptualizations and/or simple rank-order measures (as in "more rather than same or less than") offer little that is useful, however, and it is here that much work remains to be done. We do have, of course, first-person cum second-person reports of experienced dynamics in process, and those reports are valuable in their perspectives and informational contents. But it is useful to have also observations from one or more third-person perspectives, because that difference in perspective is likely to entail some diversity in informational content. This is not to presuppose third-person perspective as standard of objectivity. Objectivity is produced within sociality from first- and second- as well as third-person perspectives, interests, aspirations, and so forth. Rather, the main point is to generate an abundance of diverse information, from which one can then theorize pertinent proportions and their intersections—that is to say, the extent to which measured observations of the dynamics of specific processes do or do not mutually correspond, reinforce, contradict, and/or indicate faulty boundaries of concept or problems of mensural technique. A substantive theorist must expect to face the often difficult task of filtering signal from noise, some of the noise being an "artifact" of techniques of inquiry.

Here we again encounter general tendencies to faddish, sometimes ideological disputes about "proper method." Should one prefer deductive or inductive methods? Is a qualitative approach to inquiry superior to a quantitative approach? And so forth. These are not merely simplifications of momentary assumptions, useful to the development of a line of inquiry. They are major obstacles to inquiry. They reflect one of the severest consequences of a penchant to convert dialectical logic into an analytical logic—namely, to evaluate all important choices into a binary ("either-or") format. This is not peculiar to scholarly inquiry, of course. One can see it in disputes about "managerial style," whether it is better to reward good performance *or* to penalize poor performance (e.g., parental practices of child rearing, educational practices of classroom activities, managerial practices of the workplace, etc.). Sooner or later one notices the advent of a sort of dance of turn-taking sequences: first one option is favored, then reaction sets in and the other option becomes favorite. Recent studies and manuals of advice regarding "managerial style" have directly or indirectly addressed that dance. An instructive example can be read in a report of Woike and Hafenbrädl's (2019) laboratory experiment, the multiple trials of which were designed to assess the relative impacts of three sets of factors on per-person performances of common tasks—the three being (1) "situational outcome structures," (2) "personality types" as accounted by standard psychological instruments, and (3) "situational cues such as the format in which people receive feedback" about task performances. The experimental evidence showed that this third kind of factor could be decisive after taking the other factors into account. What is notable for present purposes is the fact that the "situational cues" were directly about first-person cum second-person meanings—that is, about interpretations and how these were negotiated among network members across levels of hierarchy. One of the failures of our reliance on large-sample survey observations for our data utilities consists in a major *unmet need* of such data for purposes of theory development. A substantive theorist must understand as well as possible the intended meanings conveyed by informants in the second-person standpoints of observation. A "standardized questionnaire" or "interview schedule" offers only a weak substitute for the use of post-interview discourse *about* the interview just held. This is very time-consuming if done well, and thus typically unaffordable for large-sample surveys.

Inasmuch as "complexity within regulation" is an appropriate description, the complexity of this undertaking would be focused toward the dynamics of that regulation. In other words, the "dynamics of that regulation" could stand as a name for an outcome of this process of building a theory: what is the process by which N number of classified workers in this workplace succeed in reproducing an effective sociality with intent to satisfy the work objective of the firm? Or the question could be rephrased so as to pertain to the school setting; and, at least in principle, also to some selection of familial settings. The task calls for complex models. But I am here reminded of a too-often neglected article in which Manski (1993a) raised the question whether intelligent high school students might be as successful in reaching pragmatic solutions to difficult problems that econometric have usually addressed mainly by assumption. Students face a binary decision: go to college or go to work? A rationally instrumental approach could involve assessment of the alternative returns as lifetime income. The assessment should depend on per-person expected returns on the investment of time and other resources for each of the two options. Lacking good measured data on students' expectation states, economists have typically assumed homogeneity across students and that the average distribution of returns is random or that students attempt per-person conditioned estimates, based on what might be called "folk theory" information from the prior experiences of forerunners (e.g., gender, race-ethnicity, parental education or occupational status, perhaps student's self-perceived ability, the self-perception perhaps informed by teachers evaluations, school grades, and so forth). As Manski pointed out, the homogeneity assumption is surely incorrect. But independently of that issue, there is a substantial problem, for "decisions

> under uncertainty reflect the interplay of preferences, expectations, and opportunities. Choice data alone [i.e., action on options] cannot disentangle these factors. The identification problem can be solved if choice data are combined with interpretable subjective data on expectations and/or preferences (Manski 1993a, p. 55).

In other words, the stance I took just above is basically a stance of ignorance. One needs well-measured observations on per-person variables (here, expectation states, preference states) that are typically lacking, because requisite investments in measurement technology have not been made. But then, what we lack, we lack. Manski did not stop there, however. We know that high school students (their parents, their teachers, etc.) do make decisions to go to college or to go to work. Are they any better, on average, at making those decisions than are better-than-average econometricians who make assumptions about the unknowns? Perhaps they are, insofar as the students assume not independence between ability and expectation (as some econometricians do) but a positive correlation, even if only moderate in size. But we cannot demonstrate evidence in support or rejection of that hypothesis. We do know actual choices on options, but we have no basis on which to make independent judgment (inference) that a choice was due to difference in expectation., because we lack measured observations of such differences. Assumption does not count.

The models that will be discussed below (as with the GBM and other models) presuppose repeated sequences of well-measured observations on metrics some of which have yet to be constructed. A program of measurement technology must be prelude. For those social scientists who believe that ethnography does not involve measurement and therefore is superior (the initial belief and that implication being mistaken) my proposal will not be popular. I admit that the proposed models might be impossible because the requisite measurements might be impossible. I have no better answer than to repeat Manski's (1993a, p. 56): "We shall not know whether this is feasible until we try."

Before proceeding to further discussion of some modeling techniques,[589] I want to recall (from §26) my reference to another of Manski's (2006) sage advisories: selection effects can be hidden in a complexity of relations that is nonetheless bounded by regularity. Let me here offer illustration of pieces of that advisory. Consider data compiled by the US Bureau of Census and the Bureau of Labor Statistics which have enabled many researchers to examine the correlation between a person's level of educational attainment and subsequent annual income (e.g., see Abel and Dietz 2019). Simple arithmetic enables one to calculate what has called been "the college premium" in future income (i.e., the arithmetic difference between the average annual income of those adults who acquired only a high-school diploma and those who also graduated college with a baccalaureate degree).[590] A recent concern among analysts has been that as college expenses have grown, both directly and through the withdrawal of public subsidies as investments in the quality of a future labor force, the size of that premium might be declining. There is evidence of a recent decline. Since 1970 the overall trend in size of premium has been upward, but most of that increase occurred during the 1980s and 1990s. Since the early 2000s the premium size has mostly fluctuated. Benefit on the investment cost has been small to nonexistent for college students whose performance put them in the bottom quarter of their class and/or for students who withdrew without a degree.[591]

All of that report of data is merely background to this question: what exactly accounts for the premium? Is it due to improved skill and knowledge acquired in college? Or is it mostly due to a credential effect, the fact of the college degree as such, which might or might not signify that important learning took place but could nonetheless serve potential employers as a noisy but inexpensive signal? It has been forty years since Randall Collins (1979) drew our attention to

---

[589] Manski's (1993a) article is also a good illustration of the gains that can be made by meeting (or failing to meet) the demands of formal modeling.

[590] Abel and Dietz (2019) controlled for demographic differences between the two groups and expressed the premium in constant (2018) dollars. The internal rate of return adjusts for the initial cost of investment. As a comparison point, the long-term rate of return on investment in stocks has been 7% to 8%. For those having only a bachelor's degree the recent rate has been just under 14% (which compares to nearly 16% in 2000-2001. In constant dollars the difference in average annual income between baccalaureates and high-school diplomas, adjusted for demographic differences between the groups, was about $30,000, which gives an estimate rate of premium at nearly 14%.

[591] The US National Center for Education Statistics began a tracking study of first-time enrollees in post-secondary institutions in 2011-12. By Spring 2017 hardly more than half had received some kind of credential (of whom: 9%, only a certificate; 11%, an associate's degree; 37%, a bachelor's degree). More than seven in ten of the 44% who had not received even a certificate were no longer enrolled in any educational institution.

such questions (see also Mincer 1974), and sound answers remain elusive. But there is more to the questioning: is the premium really due to a *pre*-college selection process, or perhaps a set of intercorrelated selections, which might or might not interact with factors and events later within college? (And if due to a pre-college selection, does that translate also as a deferred factor in post-college employment chances?) On the one hand, attracting the best prepared high-school graduates should be in the interest of college-admission officers. On the other, there is surely a degree of self-selection involved, at least to the extent of forethought, some skills of means-end rationality, and discipline, plus motivation to make an application and risk rejection. An average non-applicant might be less prepared financially to invest in increasingly expensive college enrollment. Even aside from that, however, he or she might be simply less willing to forgo the employment income of two, four, or six years. Moreover, perhaps even the average applicant, as compared to the non-applicant, has also a better understanding of the logic, if not the calculation, of expected utility. Still more: one could imagine that the average applicant has as well a better sense of *objective* expected utility, which is a function of the *aggregate* of decisions and therefore would not be directly observable to the given applicant but could still be projected from recent experience, and which, as such, would provide a basis for assessing comparative advantage. In conjunction with that, perhaps the average applicant has better skills of anticipation by which to project competitive situations ten or twenty years ahead. Any or all of those factors could well be interactive both with the college-admissions process and with some dimensions of the process of being in college, especially those threads of perseverance toward a degree. How does one "piece apart" all of the interacting factors and arrive at estimates of how much of a "college premium" is due to what happens *within* the "college process," how much to what was present as pre-college potential ready to be activated during the college process, and how much to what was already activated before the high-school student made application? With only cross-sectional data at hand, one has no chance of partitioning and sorting into "causal pathways" or anything like that. Even with typically designed longitudinal data (i.e., time-separated cross-sectional panels, two-wave trackings) little can be achieved. In the final analysis, of course, obstacles due to counterfactuality remain daunting (see, e.g., Manski 1997, pp. 369, 381). But there is little we can do about that, whereas we could obtain otherwise better estimates by attending directly to the measures of per-person process observations *during the relevant process*.

The other part of Manski's (2006, p. 47) advisory instructs us that a "basic regularity" constrains how a process evolves, and we must not lose sight of that. A per-person process that feeds into an existing complexity of relations, or that in some degree produces a complexity, is not difficult to imagine, inasmuch as the process could be punctuated by filtering and updating, which might produce nonlinearities of feedback. To the extent that these endogenous feedback effects are positive—that is, adding to the pace and/or the magnitude of endogenous effects—the resulting complexity can become more or less destabilizing of the process, or at least of some dimension or component of it. This seems generally unlikely within the per-person process of educational trajectories, mainly because the institutional channels of formal education have been inherently and predominantly traditionalist or conserving: the primary intent is to convey what various filters regard as worthwhile of accumulated experience (knowledge, skills, attitudes, etc.) to each new cohort of student. Formal institutions of education are rarely institutions of anarchic or revolutionary thinking. Perhaps we see the telling evidence in the case of a student—high school or college—who has the energy, the foresight, the imagination to be disruptive in ways that (later judgment will declare) prove to be very valuable. Think of the early years of Bill Gates, for instance, before he convinced his parents that he really did have a good plan well worth pursuing and he needed to drop out of college in order to achieve the main goals ahead of likely competitors. Harvard College was a great place to sit at the knee of many eager, brilliant tutors. It was a great place for building networks of very-important-people contacts. It was not a great place for a teenage inventor who imagined what seemed, at least to the teenager, to be a very bright idea. Socrates was ejected from the schoolyard because he was too disruptive. Steven Wozniak was expelled from the University of Colorado because he was too exuberant, too "not serious." Institutions, at least the major institutions, are indeed "evolving complex systems" (to borrow a phrase favored at the Santa Fe Institute). But often they evolve slowly. They are first and foremost *conserving* systems, places that strenuously hang on to yesterday (calling it virtue or truth or tradition, or "all of the above") as they face unknowns of tomorrow, future times and places. Institutions of education may well be the most fragile, the most prone to destabilizing effects, in that regard, because they are places of the energy of youth along with the sagacity (when it is that) of forebears, all trading in the currency of ideas—thus in promises and visions and ideals, sometimes with sound interests in legislating the new. And yet conserving interests remain everywhere, including among faculty who try to avoid becoming out-dated (like another proverbial Isaac McCaslin).

Kenneth Arrow (1974, pp. 21-22) is remembered now and then for having said that "there are profound difficulties with the price system, even, so to speak, within its own logic, and these strengthen the view that, valuable though it is in certain realms, it cannot be made the arbiter of social life." One does not have to search in order to find evidence of economists especially who would recoil from that statement. The lucidity of Manski's work reinforces Arrow's message, however, and that reinforcement occurs in no small part because Manski has used tools that are associated metrically at the core of "the price system" (i.e., in exchange relations, instrumental rationality, preferences, expectations, and so on) to deliver the message's key point. Note that Arrow did not reject "the price system." Rather, he pointed to its limits. Sociality is larger than market. How could Arrow have rejected "the price system"? He knew well enough that "price" and "interpret" come from the same root (the Latin "pretium").

Manski's "basic regularity" reminds us of the force of *institutionalized* organization and, on the other side of that, one of the main lessons of Reich and Bearman's (2018) report (as was discussed earlier). Before leaving the present discussion, I want to reinforce previous cautionary notes against the tendency to formulate analysis in terms of forced binary choices, as if correct analysis must be *either* this or that in perspective, in conceptual tools, even in entire competing models. An illustration passed before us just above—namely, the notion that because Arrow pointed to major limits of the price system (which generalizes to "market model," etc.), he must have been rejecting it or at least was advising that it *should* be rejected. In a related vein, Robert Lucas (1986, p. S402) has indicated that while he agrees with a basic "adaptive behavior" model, filtering and updating either does not occur to any noticeable extent much of the time or does not lead to persistent directed change but rather is absorbed in fluctuations.[592] "Technically, I think of economics as studying decision rules that are steady states of some adaptive process, decision rules that are found to work over a range of situations and … are no longer revised appreciably as more experience accumulates." Note that Lucas was speaking of potential *change in decision rules*, not whether person-actors cease to engage in adaptive behavior. After some passage of time, during which the decisions rules might be tweaked on the basis of experience, they become settled (not to say ossified, though that, too, can happen) and are used repeatedly. Note also that Lucas was in effect describing a concept of dynamic equilibrium—that is, a process of bounded variations as in regression-to-mean sequences or some other attractor-regulated bounding. This does not preclude the possibility of complexity due to nonlinearity of relations (as in a filtering-and-updating process that engenders a mildly positive or temporary feedback). An equilibrium state not only is *not* a constant (rather, a variable) condition; the variation can become directed, resulting perhaps in new decision rules, perhaps eventually a return to the prior steady state or perhaps to new state of equilibrium, or perhaps a collapse of the system. But institutionalized organizations are crescive formations. Because the gradual change is regulated from within as part of normal operating process, it usually appears to be something like a natural progression and a spontaneous generation. The underling dynamic is of a process well-nigh ubiquitous but generally manifested as and via bounded windows of opportunity. Paul Ricœur had the gauge of it when, with specific reference to "the political," he (1965 [1955]) pointed out that what counts at any given historical juncture as "politics" (i.e., "politics" as known in the historical moment) is "smaller," more specific than "the political" by which it is determined as *just this*, historically contingent activity. Relations of power are as ubiquitous as sociality, but many manifestations of those relations do not count as "politics" here or there, then or now.[593]

This caution should be remembered with regard to any discourse of "collective decision making" (as, for instance, in Kant's repeated call upon legislation). If we think of it as a process "that identifies a pattern of future coordinated actions as the intended actions of the members of a collectivity, and creates corresponding intentions in enough members of the collectivity that in the ordinary course of events the pattern is realized" (Tideman 2006, p. 6), then surely we have the outlines of a pathway of aggregation (and one that is similar to Coleman's focus on voting). There is enough slack in that description to allow lots of elbow room for vagaries of sociality: for instance, what defines, and what conditions, "*enough* members"? By Elmer's (2013, pp. 1 n.1, 93-97) reading of the *Iliad*—a useful illustration of precautionary points—the internal narrative authority "generally regards the support of *all* the members of the collectivity as necessary for the realization of collective action." But was brooding Achilles' *grudging* support

---

[592] This is a view I have previously endorsed as applicable to one particular situation—namely, that of older adults, who, especially once they are in a retirement condition, tend to adjust expectations about financial needs and resources. Here, too, the problem of counterfactuality impedes conclusions of "cause and effect" (see Hardy and Hazelrigg 1999).

[593] Oliver Marchart (2013, p. 119; 2011) recently addressed this dynamic in terms of a "null-institution"—that is, an institutionalized formation that is "empty" yet influential, even determinative, toward others. One could say that it occupies the space that became urgently necessary after the "necessity of foundations" gave way to a "necessary contingency." These formulations are variant expressions of Pippin's "necessity of the object *before* the object," as discussed above in Part One.

(as it so often was) equivalent to a lesser soldier's acquiescence, or another's compliant response to Odysseus' appeal, or Thersites' submission to Odysseus' forceful retort, or another's exuberant impatience to begin? These questions point to the implied process of aggregation, and to the possibility of a scale effect (perhaps a distribution of weights according to skills, relative immunities, and so on, of collected members).

Conceptualization should be attentive to the measurement problem, even when (perhaps especially when) the gap between one and the other seems unbridgeable (as it often does). Our conceptual schemes often specify only categories, sometimes with rank orderings among them, but that is a large step too short because difference in rank (i.e., ordinality) masks an infinitely large volume of potential variation. Cartesian logic assumes that "clear and distinct" ideas there be, but in practice ambiguity usually prevails. The introduction of fuzzy sets and gradients of membership was a major step in the right direction (Zadeh 1965), albeit still often neglected. While most decisions that human beings make are made between or among presented options which in the moment can seem prima facie to be properly Cartesian, closer inspection typically manifests considerable ambiguity and sometimes ambivalence. It has often been common practice to ignore those departures from clear categories as unimportant, even random noise. But doing so only postpones the problem: most of decisions among options are made in the midst of uncertainty, including uncertainty about outcome. This, too, has often been neglected as if of no importance. "Once uncertainty in the consequences [of a decision] is admitted, *no ordinal theory of choice can be satisfactory*" (Luce and Suppes 1965, pp. 281-282; emphasis added). When a theory itself does not provide requisite logic of discrimination, no observation can give adequate leverage against so many possibilities. Choices, and the preferences that might be therein made manifest (as in the "proof is in the pudding" folk adage), are only qualitative, for all practical purposes, and one is at a loss to normalize their temporal distribution, without which even simple empirical generalizations regarding the dynamics of process float as if in a Newtonian aether.[594]

Thus, challenging though it will be, one must develop measures based at least on a metric of equal intervals. They will likely be second-order measures, with only relativistic anchors (i.e., no absolute zero). The social sciences have seldom had the benefit of productive efforts in— much less a systematic program of—mensural innovation. There are some exemplars of neglect. Peter Burke's initiative in 1980 to promote the development of some measures regarding "self" is an example (see his p. 26 for an illustration of second-order measurement): why was it nearly an orphan birth, not generative of much concerted effort? In general, professional organizations of the social-science disciplines do far too little to encourage appropriate rewards for the difficult tasks of building relevant measurement technology.

Even simple, very basic theoretical models depend on adequate measurement. None can be more basic than the GBM model of the temporal dimension of a process. As indicated earlier in this Part Five, the stochastic differential equation (equation 5.1) consists in two terms: one,

---

[594] For efforts to utilize Zadeh's insight and thereby amend Luce's famous axiom of choice so that it corresponds more closely to actual conditions of "behavioral optimization," see Gul, Natenzon, and Pesendorfer (2014). Their article, read in conjunction with Luce and Suppes (1965), provides good insight into Luce's classic work as a measurement theorist and a sequence of applications of that work.

the coefficient μ, estimates drift or trend in the process central tendency, while the other, σ or $σ^2$, estimates volatility around the Wiener process (drift or trend) and may be a function of either unpredictable events (random disturbances) or predictable events (e.g., of a limit-cycle process). In classical setting, the central model assumption is stationarity of observed process (independent and identically distributed observations), which strictly speaking is generally only approximated when a process is in equilibrium, whereas in most actual applications serial correlation obtains across the temporal distribution of observations (i.e., a non-zero autocorrelation function). Now let's add to that simple model the idea of a scale effect. How shall the addition be theorized, as an independent third term, as a modifier of the Wiener process, as a modifier of the limit-cycle process, or as a modifier of each? The question has seldom been asked in studies of sociality, so there is very little literature on which to draw for guidance. A first step surely would be to determine what type of scale effect should be theoretically expected in a given setting. For reasons that will become clear, my expectation a priori (stating that rather loosely, since a conjunction of casual experience and logic informs the expectation) is that an independent status is unlikely. Before pursuing these matters of type, however, I need to settle my position with respect to another issue.

As mentioned earlier, Anna Broido and Aaron Clauset (2019) recently pointed out that the phrase, "scale-free," has been used in a variety of ways, some of them ambiguous. At least most of the usages have in common the idea that relations and vectors are "scale free" *if* they are invariant across levels or hierarchical dimensions of organization. An organization that is "self-similar" or homologous from macroscopic to microscopic levels can be understood and described by a single logic of relations at all levels. More often than not, this property has been asserted as assumption, one of the simplifications used as a convenience, even though in this instance there is substantive theory and some good evidence that the assumption is wrong. Most readers have known "economy of scale" as the idea that output is disproportionately enhanced by a given increase in input. The usual understanding is that the coefficient is positive—that is, an increase in output relative to size of input—but it can be negative (which should imply a negative selection). In more recent times readers have likewise known about "network effects"—this, too, being another expression of the disproportionality of an input-to-output ratio. The now common illustration of this effect refers to alternative networks as rival goods: as choices indicate a growing preference for one network over others, the preferred network becomes increasingly attractive to new users not merely as a faddish preference but because it offers a larger number of connections.

Both of those phrases have in common the notion of a multiplier of a pre-existing effect, whether that effect is an expression of a marginal preference for one rather than another network by early adopters (which might have been only random variation) or a marginally successful rate of output from investments of a quantity of input. The basic idea refers to an effect of circulation of a good: a unit of exchange can be used repeatedly because of a dialectical relationality. The most common or conventional meaning of "multiplier" as a technical term in the social sciences refers to the circulation of exchange value, whether by barter or by cockleshells or by fiat money. The means of exchange matters: bartered goods have restricted uses; cockleshells, more general uses insofar as others agree to the utilities; fiat money, a virtually universal use (and all the more

562

so when the fiat money serves as reserve currency in trading networks among multiple societies). Fiat money can circulate through many users within a short span of time (i.e., high velocity, which increases liquidity of exchange). Thus, it can easily function in recursive processes. That implies more opportunities of innovation and development. The elements of the buy/sell dialectic circulate as if different quantities of value even when (as in the case of fiat money) the carrier signal is itself virtually worthless. Household dollars are sent out soon after receipt, in exchange for goods (food, etc.) supplied by a seller who then uses the same dollars to replenish her or his stock of goods for sale from another party, and so on. The cycle can continue repeatedly—and most effectively when the repetition is in the form of recursion or replication. Thus, "use" need not have a final or fatal end-state. Consuming food replenishes, yielding energy that can be used to produce more food, and so forth. In that sense, a unit of input can generate many units of output, because the fact of input-output *interdependencies* is actually a dialectical relation. In other words, designation of "input" vis-à-vis "output" is the action of a temporal mirror. Circularity is not merely of the unit of exchange, fiat money or cockleshells; it is of the goods and/or services themselves as uses.

Earlier I referred to a feedback in which the apparent "starting point" toward which an F&U subroutine had supposedly returned had in fact changed, the agent being random drift or noise. The agent can also be a directive human being, of course. An idea which runs through Taylor's time-and-motion studies, through basic conceptions of bureaucratic organization from Hegel through Weber to present-day scholars, and through studies of the developmental processes that can be engendered by innovation focuses on a recursive F&U subroutine by which specifiable functions and their organizational expressions are *infinitely divisible* at least in principle. A popular and still current expression of this is the Schumpeterian notion (after Darwin and his predecessors in political economy) of "creative destruction" in applications of labor time, such that the wilting and eventual death of present jobs will supposedly always entail as its "replacement effect" an equivalent or greater number of new jobs. It also means that repetition via recursion rather than iteration yields a larger number of opportunities in general and more opportunity for innovation in particular to occur. This is the juncture at which "multiplier" in its orthodox sense in exchange relations—in usual meaning, the velocity with which fiat money changes hands—can also generate innovations, and innovations that directly have multiplier effects. The core idea beneath this is at least as old as the ancient Greek conception that a polygon is in principle an object having a countably infinite number of sides (i.e., an apeirogon).[595] The velocity at which an input becomes a *different* input later as a result of some production process is the inherent circularity of sociality.

The most common instances of a multiplier in cross-person aggregation are surely those just described. Beyond those, a multiplier would similarly proceed as an innovation within and

---

[595] The notion as applied to human realities has been vehicle for many satirical studies of ingenuity, from Kafka to the screenplay by Gilliam, McKeown, and Stoppard's screenplay, *Brazil* (1985; see Hazelrigg 2020), to Colum McCann's (2020) novelistic study of the dialectic of Palestinian/Israeli perspectivism.

of a process, initiated by one or more persons as change of a procedure or application of a skill. The consequence would be a scale effect. This sort of event would probably be difficult to detect, however, unless via a direct on-the-spot observation. A lot of the potential by innovation is never actualized on a per-person basis, partly because of a value rationality (e.g., traditional interest of one sort or another) but also because of failures of education especially during the first half-dozen years of life when capacity as well as capability is so expandable. Potential that is in possible aggregations of per-person action effects is also often unrealized, at least in part due to the enablement/constraint dialectic of institutionalized channelings of information. Insofar as an innovative effect does prove to be sustainable in cross-person aggregation of effects, it is usually vulnerable to absorption and smoothing in a renormalization of process. While the event of scale effect might be retained in per-person memory for some period of time, and perhaps become part of the lore of an "institutional memory," it could just as easily disappear as a distinct event in an organization's history and in members' biographical memories, especially when the scale effect was experienced as less than "revolutionary" or "momentous" within local sociality. Local scale effects can become no more than wrinkles in what appears retrospectively to be a trendline of generally constant homology (minus static or random error), as consequence of a renormalization that is itself forgotten as such. When a renormalization is remembered as such, it is usually as the memory of a momentous or a revolutionary change of process—the now oft-cited "classic" example being the electrification of existing processes more than a century ago, which enabled huge spatial extensions of distributed processes of production.

Recall that in §28 I referred to William Petty's seventeenth-century recognition of this circularity as an exchange process linking individual per-person action effects. Implicit in that recognition was not only the basic dynamic of "economy of scale" but also at least the beginning of an understanding of what Adam Smith would later try to convey under the phrase, "invisible hand," the dynamic of an "as if" process. That, in turn, suggests that Petty glimpsed also that the most important source of a disproportionality in the input-to-output ratio consisted not directly in per-person actions but in a multiplier effect due to interactions among such actions under specific conditions. His main intuition might have come from his investigations of vectors of contagious diseases—in particular, the conditions of sudden, "explosive" growth rates of infection (i.e., rates recently popularized as "power law" rates). The upshot that I wish to draw from this speculation is that Petty was probably on the verge of concluding that the greatest consequence of "economy of scale" comes about as mostly unexpected effects of innovation in organizational technology.

I will return to that tentative conclusion later. In the meantime, I want to continue with a recall of my earlier discussion of "scale effect" and relate it to a tendency to conflate "scale" and organizational "size," from which a conflated meaning of "economy of scale" has been derived. Hannan, Pólos, and Carroll (2007, pp. 210-214) addressed that in their discussion of advantages of scale: "A scale advantage exists when the returns to some activity grow with the scale at which [the activity] is done." By "economy of scale" I mean a disproportionality of change in a process output relative to a change in process input. Nothing was said about proportionality in the general statement just quoted. What is the dynamic? There are various expressions of it, but the main idea is captured by market rivalry: as size of Firm F increases relative to greatest rival, approaching monopoly or quasi-monopoly, Firm F gains a competitive advantage in the relevant market, even if output has remained proportional to input. Indeed, as the recent example of Jeff Bezos' venture known as Amazon demonstrated, the short-run price of gaining a monopolistic standing can be a negative return (assuming eventual success). Hannan et al. (2007) then added an explicit next step, however: assuming the cost of an activity can be divided into a *fixed* cost (i.e., costs proportionate to quantity of activity) and a *variable* cost per unit activity that declines as total activity increases, the size of total activity matters as an implicit scale effect. In other words, the disproportionality expressed in the fixed-to-variable cost ratio yields an economy of scale.[596] Note, by the way, that it is a mistake to dismiss this insight as "merely" a fixture of "market economics" or "monetary transactions." One can observe the same dynamic in friendship and kinship networks, for example.

Size sensitivity can be expressed also as a density sensitivity, which is usually exhibited in the scaling properties of fungal growth, for example, and in physical dimensions of polymer chains under athermal conditions that minimize entanglements as well as interactions between component monomers (i.e., "ideal" models). These properties have been studied in real as well as ideal models extensively since the 1970s (see, e.g., Gennes 1979; Hofmann, Soranno, Borgia, Gast, Nettels, and Schuler 2012). Similar work has been done on the scaling properties of "soft matter" under conditions of model stationarity (i.e., stable process parameters).

Now a third step can be made: can cost ratio accounting be partitioned between and among per-person workers? That is to say, can one detect similar scale effects directly of per-person action effects? Here we must acknowledge differences among institutions: detection is difficult within familial settings, partly for reasons intrinsic to the institution. Detection is easier in school settings but has rarely if ever been attempted with sufficient specificity. Within work settings there are important differences across industries not only in the likelihood of detection but also in the likely existence of per-person scale effects due directly to per-person actions.[597] Similar differences probably occur across occupations within given industries. Much depends on the network properties across per-person workers in a given firm or agency or other collectivity. One easily addressable dimensional distinction can be made by recalling an older concept of "teamwork."

Not all that long ago effective work teams included a "warehouse" function of "just in case" instrumental rationality. This amounted to a perpetually forward-written insurance policy of a "reserve fund" of labor-time (i.e., the temporality of labor-power). The implicit part of the contract said that under normal conditions productive activity would be regulated in terms of an equilibrium that is "comfortably" short of "all-out" or "overdrive" effort. When called for, extra-effort activity would be expected from all per-person members of the work team, and it need not

---

[596] In general, reduction of variable cost is limited, after which point the ratio plateaus, then tends to reverse.

[597] By way of illustration, some data from a Bureau of Labor Statistics report (USDL-19-0858) released 23 May 2019 give relevant data on changes in labor productivity in 2018 (bear in mind that "hours of work" measures the major "variable cost" factor). In the industry group "wireless telecommunications carriers" output increased more than 6% while hours worked decreased about 3%; "software publishers, output increased about 16% and hours worked grew by about 11%; "automotive repair and maintenance, output was unchanged while hours worked grew about 5%.

count in the ledger of compensation as "overtime pay." Rather, it would be expected as part of commitment or loyalty to the job and the firm, the implicit clause referring back to "normal conditions" equilibrium. During the early 1970s a new regimen began in a number of industries at about the same time, the most noted instance being the automotive industry and Toyota's "just in time" revision of teamwork. This was presented as a gain in total efficiency, due to reduction to near-zero of "wait times" in the production process, including the supplier functions and the traditional warehousing function, which was explicitly keyed to material parts but implicitly also referred to per-person work activity. Every part supply and every per-person work performance would be expected at peak efficiency. Thus, for example, now an automobile dealer's mechanics are not waiting for repair or maintenance work to "stop by"; rather, they are scheduled days in advance to perform more or less specific work on specific vehicles at specifically appointed times on specific days of the week. A delivery driver for UPS or FedEx is expected to rush each package to its recipient as quickly as possible by following an algorithmic map of delivery times and places. In short, teamwork still exists and is expected, but it is all governed by a temporal regimen according to which each per-person worker is encouraged not simply to meet fixed costs but to reduce total costs of activity by reducing variable costs per unit of activity by maximizing volume of units per pay period. Even "bathroom time" has become a direct per-person cost to the individual worker. A firm's employees are increasingly contract workers who each understand personally the fixed-to-variable cost ratio. The clock has lost one sense of contingency.[598]

What was just described is not itself a scale effect (nor a sequence of scale effects) due directly to individual per-person actions, however. Rather, it was (and is) an organizational innovation to which per-person workers are expected to conform. The innovation was itself no doubt a product of per-person actions, some of which can be traced back to Frederick Winslow Taylor, Henry Ford, Max Weber, and others. But the innovation was an evolutionary process, not an all-at-once accomplishment. As is usually the case the greater part of the accomplishment was not any punctual invention but a gradual development of several inventions in graduated intersections. This recognition points then to a question: to what extent are scale effects ever due to per-person actions in microscopic sense—that is, to per-person actions other than those involved in the invention and development of a new organizational regime? Nearly thirty years ago David Gelernter (1992, p. 67), forecasting "mirror worlds" (i.e., a technology of virtual reality, which already has become part of our everyday reality), emphasized the importance of "ensemble," almost as if recalling Karl Marx or George Herbert Mead. His reference was to any "group of objects that *interact*; a group, accordingly, that is more than the sum of its parts." That was a useful reminder then, and it remains so today, but only insofar as one understands first of all that any individual person is always already present in at least one collectivity, within which he or she is always surely engaged in interactions with other members, and probably in network ties with members of other collectivities. And the key question here is whether, in any given instance, an interaction *is* yielding more than the sum of its parts. If the fact of interaction itself

---

[598] And then, of course, there is an event of pandemic proportion in pace and volume, when vital supplies are both in very limited availability and slow to be produced in requisite quantity because producers have been habituated to the measured pace of just in time, and too many people have forgotten that "complexity" can also mean "fragility."

is by virtue of definition a product greater than "the sum of its parts," then by definition a scale effect has been determined. But that is of course the empirical question: when, and under what conditions, is the organization of a collectivity "more than the sum of its parts"? (And doesn't it matter *which* parts---persons, actions or action effects?) Surely "scale effect" must refer to something more specific than an act of synonymy in parlance. Granted, we social scientists have been too often in the habit of spinning out new "technical terms" that, it turns out, are only renamings presented as if new discoveries. (We are hardly unique in the annals of that practice, no doubt; but this is not the best of company.)

As mentioned above, Broido and Clauset (2019) tested the assumption that homology prevails at least in many kinds of networks, choosing the network model of organization as their data base in recognition that "network" is "a powerful way to both represent and to study the structure of complex systems of all kinds."[599] Their collection of nearly a thousand data sets was drawn from "social, biological, technological, and informational sources." This specification was recommended by the popularity of so-called power-law models, which have been presented as "scale free," seemingly meaning homologous. I say "seemingly," because the claim is hardly credible as a general rule of homology, since it is evident that many processes do not proceed at any exponential rate initially; and even if the claim is that certain processes of growth shift into an exponential rate or that specific decay functions proceed exponentially, that claim implicitly recognizes that the shift amounts to a scale effect of some kind—perhaps a "tipping point" or "threshold" effect, as demonstrated in Thomas Schelling's (1971) famous study of residential segregation (see also Jones 1985; Stauffer 2008). Beyond that, however, the claim is surely self-limiting; for any decay function proceeding exponentially will soon reach exhaustion, and any growth function that proceeds at exponential rate much greater than unity will eventually tip into a nonlinearity function that is likely to become chaotic, unless at some earlier stage it generates a standing martingale or other governor. In any case, Broido and Clauset concluded that "scale-free networks are rare." While their conclusion clarifies some issues, it does not address the issues either of sources of scale effects or of conditions under which scale effects occur.

With Petty's seventeenth-century insight in mind as background, let's move ahead two centuries and consider some insights that Karl Marx composed in 1866, in the first section of his chapter on "the machinery system." Among them, he explained that technical developments can achieve over a period of time a systematic coherence as if assembled by pre-existing design, but when the trajectories of development are examined more finely in their actual processes one will realize that they generally proceed in uneven sequences which are punctuated by inconsistencies and contradictions. Thus, a "radical change in the mode of production in one sphere of industry involves a similar change in other spheres," but the logical intersections are sometimes retarded by habituations of human action. So, for example, different "branches of industry" may well be logically interconnected by virtue of "being separate phases of a process," and yet actually they are "isolated by the social division of labour, in such a way, that each of them produces an independent commodity." These habits of work result in inconsistencies which are slow to disappear because habituations within the division of labor are slow to adapt fully to the implicit

---

[599] This power has recently been augmented by proof that Ringel's conjecture is correct: any network graphable with 2n + 1 vertices can be reproduced (i.e., completely mapped without any overlapping) by one or more simple graphs exclusive of loops (see Montgomery, Pokrovskiy, and Sudarov 2020).

logic of the new technical relations. Marx (1996 [1867], pp. 386-387) cited as illustration the interlinkages among spinning, weaving, and other components of the older technology of the production of textiles, all of which had only recently (i.e., 1856 to 1866) become integrated into one coherent system of mechanical processing: "spinning by machinery made weaving by machinery a necessity," lest spinners' products would pile up in excess quantities; but weavers were often less than eager to see their traditional skills become redundant, their jobs disappear. Likewise, spinning by machinery and weaving by machinery became jointly the condition of "the mechanical and chemical revolution that took place in bleaching, printing, and dyeing." And so forth. What is still more remarkable about Marx' account, however, is the glimpse it afforded of multiplier effects. Had the coherent "machinery system" descended from Heaven, as it were, ready-made and entire, observers would certainly have noted that it was much more productive of desired output in quantity than had been the traditional system it replaced, and they would have observed that this increased quantity of commodity was being produced by a smaller number of workers. Marx' careful descriptions demonstrated, however, that in the process of working through the inconsistencies and small contradictions that were produced during the actual transformation from the multiple steps of the craft system to the integrated process of the "machinery system," multiplier effects were observable at the interstices, as one set of conditions (outcomes) stimulated and then became a correlated set of necessities (inputs), the result being a larger than expected increment of "final" outcome.

This was of course the somewhat mystical "hidden hand" that Adam Smith had spied during his eighteenth-century imagination of an ideal pin factory, and it would soon become Henry Ford's assembly-line of production and Frederick Winslow Taylor's time-and-motion script and mission of serious inquiry. However, Marx' insight had also already included something of far greater moment than the assembly-line and the reduction of working motion into smaller and smaller increments: *machines had begun to produce machines.*

> Modern industry had therefore itself to take in hand the machine, its characteristic instrument of production, and to construct machines by machines. It was not until it did this, that it built up for itself a fitting technical foundation, and stood on its own feet. Machinery, simultaneously with the increasing use of it, in the first decades of this century, appropriated, by degrees, the fabrication of machines proper. But it was only during the decade preceding 1866, that the construction of railways and ocean steamers on a stupendous scale called into existence the cyclopean machines now employed in the construction of prime movers.

> The most essential condition to the production of machines by machines was a prime mover capable of exerting any amount of force, and yet under perfect control. Such a condition was already supplied by the steam-engine. But at the same time it was necessary to produce the geometrically accurate straight lines, planes, circles, cylinders, cones, and spheres, required in the detailed parts of the machine. ...

> If we now fix our attention on that portion of the machinery employed in the construction of machines, which constitutes the operating tool, we find the manual implements reappearing, but on a cyclopean scale (Marx 1996 [1867], pp. 387-388).

Cyclopes, the one-eyed giants of Greek and then Roman mythology who provided Zeus (Jupiter) with his tools, including his thunderbolts, suitably represented the scale of productive force and looming oversight that had so quickly sprung up from the ground of what had previously been understood as the "natural" force of simple machines—lever, axle, wedge or incline, and so on— that had served craftworkers for countless centuries. In a footnote Marx pointed to one "of these [new] machines, used for forging paddle-wheeled shafts in London"; it had been given the name "Thor." "It forges a shaft of 16½ tons with as much ease as a blacksmith forges a horse-shoe."[600]

Having witnessed those transformations within such a short span of time, it was easy to "see" corresponding transformations that were being impelled into what Marx had distinguished as "the social relations of production" as they had existed during all those prior centuries. Both the conditions and the necessities of sociality were being reforged massively. More than a long generation later, Max Weber picked up the theme and added this:

> An inanimate machine is mind objectified. Only this provides it with the power to force men into its service and to dominate their everyday working life as completely as is actually the case in the factory. Objectified intelligence is also that animated machine, the bureaucratic organization (Weber 1968 [1922], p. 1402).

Now, it is also true that simple machines, such as the wedge and the screw, are also "objectified mind" in their form and in their uses. But between old and new times it was the power of the new forms of machine and of organization that made the whole so compelling.

Times change, memories struggle to keep up, and perspectives become stilted, forgetful. In recent decades countless observers have been saying that we have been in a period of rapid change in patterns of workplace employment and productivity, with "AI robotics" entering a new phase of the organizational innovation which began with what has been styled as a "post-Fordist" regimen, one in which "work teams of staff and line employees participate in planning decisions in order to improve productivity" (Rifkin 1996, p. 184). Innovations that pass inspection as both integrable and significant improvements of functional efficiency in the organization of a firm's production process tend to be integrated quickly into that process, sometimes as an entirely new design. The effect can be disruption to very large extent. As machine learning assumes the chief redesign function, the battery of required skills of a production process could be increasingly built into robotic algorithms, which in turn could reduce quantitative and perhaps qualitative requirements of a human labor force. At least such has been a major concern. A common retort is that while the renovations are and no doubt will continue to be disruptive, for some workers more than others, the process is hardly unprecedented, and new occupations have always been invented during prior episodes. This is a bit like the argument that results of "natural selection"

---

[600] A recent report by a business correspondent for *The Economist*, 31 May 2018, began with this: "Few industrial scenes offer the drama of a steelworks in full flow. Perched high in a cabin, a technician guides a bucket the size of a house to send 250 tons of lava-like molten metal into a vast crucible. As a roar echoes across a gargantuan hall, a pile of scrap slides into the mixture. Plumes of illuminated smoke rise. Sparks like giant fireflies tumble down. ThyssenKrupp's steelmaking plant in Duisburg makes 30,000 tons of the metal daily."

in past times have always included new and/or newly prosperous species of life—an evidently true statement but unheard by those who did not survive. Humans have displayed a tendency to assume that Homo sapiens will always exist, which in its specificity is rather like the thought of Homo neaderthalensis or the "thoughtless" demise of the dodo bird (Raphus cucullantus). Many observers such as Jeremy Rifkin (1996) have been calling attention to dire implications of the changing parameters of "work" at least since the 1960s, the time of Alvin Toffler (1970). But there has been little effective response in public policy, and some humans have been content to emulate the head-in-sand posture that is proverbial of the ostrich (see, e.g., Guston 2016; Kristof and WuDunn 2020; Susskind 2020). The debate is centuries old. But this fact hardly confers immunity, especially on those who are ill-prepared.

We can glimpse in those port-Fordist exercises perhaps some systematic habits (heuristic incubators, one might say) of productivity enhancements that offer clues into the birth of scale effects. In other words, major scale effects come about mostly as a result of innovations in the organization of productivity—new patterns of work that are already aggregative of per-person effects across persons over time, the new increment of disproportionality of output relative to input being due to that innovation—but after the fact the source of the increment becomes a bit mysterious because old and new organizational technologies do not remain in parallel closely enough to be compared in process dynamics. The tendency is to look for change either in the stock of workers (e.g., better education, better discipline, etc.) or in the stock of capital (e.g., less rentier than entrepreneurial). The bias that thingness takes precedence, logically and genetically, over relationality or process conduces to that expectation. It is not that one form of capital stock is inherently superior to another: a rentier can take rents from assets in order to live luxuriously or in order to invest in a new innovation. Likewise, it is not that per-person education and skill acquisition is either all-defining or unimportant: applying this personal stock innovatively can enable one to stay abreast of forces larger than those of one's own product. One of the harshest yet understandable reactions that today one can hear to Ike McCaslin's lament tells Ike that he could have given more attention to changes that were occurring all around him and used lessons of foresight to initiate relevant updates; but now that it is too late for him he vents frustration of "being left behind" on a convenience of scapegoats, gaining succor from an always plentiful cast of politicians who are quick to ride bigotry into office, while younger adults and children simply wait for his generation or cohort to die (one funeral at a time, as Planck is remembered having said), hoping that their generation can repair all of the damage.[601] Scott Sandage's (2005, pp. 258-259) rehearsal of Willy Loman's fated trajectory, followed by his own family memories one generation removed, is a fitting summary for both Ike and his later critics.

The fertility of organizational technology is not a new development, of course. One can take note of the Roman centurion system, for instance. Nearer in history, it is worth briefly to recall from the nineteenth century the advent of the US Railway Mail Service and its fleet of

---

[601] US labor-force composition by educational attainment changed 2000 to 2019 at least in raw quantities of attained credentials. In 2000 42% of the labor force aged 25 or older had no more than a high-school diploma; that figured dropped to 32% in 2019. Conversely, 31% had a bachelor's degree or more in 2000; in 2019, 41%. These data are from the Current Population Survey, calculated and reported by professional demographer Cheryl Russell in her DemoMemo blog (13February2020).

Railway Post Office (RPO) carriages, which were added to high-speed passenger trains (thus offering a huge source of added revenues to the railway companies). Specially trained clerks were assigned to sort mail on the fly, bringing overnight mail service on many inter-city routes to businesses, government agencies, and families. It was fatiguing work, sometimes resulting in stress injuries (and evidently some of the earliest federal concerns about occupational safety). The chief benefit was rapid acceleration in the networks of written communication and parcel delivery across the North American continent, made possible by innovation of organizational technology designed to harness an otherwise unchanged labor-time productivity of workers to the power and speed of railroad transport. Clerks were expected to display per-person rates of production comparable to those of workers in static workplaces (an expectation that no doubt contributed to stress injuries), so the greater efficiency of output to input came from the mobile organization of work, not the unit of work (or worker) as such. RPO carriages were replaced during the mid-1900s by mechanical sorting systems located in regional centers of the US Postal Service, now interconnected by air and truck transport.

This last example brings me to consideration of one of the most important statements of and about theory written toward the close of the previous century, Paul Romer's (1994) succinct review of crucial neglects in the development of a formal theory of production functions. Before turning to that review, however, I will pause to recount as context a few more bits of disciplinary history, especially of economic theory. I will begin by following a distinction within the history of scientific theory: "theory" in general is larger than "formal theory." As noted previously, the champions of formalism have been correct in principle from one point of view, the Newtonian. Formulating and testing a proposition within ceteris paribus frame is one thing; formulating and testing a system of relations is quite another, and economic theorists were increasingly interested from the late 1940s onward to achieve the latter. Ceteris paribus remained in place at system boundaries: the system of Newtonian mechanics applied *within* the Newtonian domain, and economic theory as developed increasingly by formalists could do the same. It had been known since before Lord Rayleigh that the Newtonian system was incomplete as empirical description because (to continue with the illustration I have been using) a ballistic trajectory is affected all along its path by atmospheric and gravitational variations. These variations cannot be measured accurately and reliably because they are highly variable in time and space. They are part of the theoretical Newtonian domain, but because of the "extreme" heterogeneity in time and space they are treated as error terms, estimable only after the fact as probability distributions relative to the standard of a theoretical distribution of error (e.g., the Rayleigh distribution).

Not all that long ago the dominant theoretical perspective in economics was central to what is now called "classical theory," later followed by "neo-classical theory," both of which can be and were the focus of formalism (see, e.g., Solow 1956 and 1957; Mankiw, Romer, and Weil 1992). That perspective was primarily about national accounts—or more specifically a *system* of national accounts, as formalists envisioned (and as described above in connection with Wassily Leontief). This began as mainly a static system, understood roughly on the model of the Newtonian system as static inasmuch as its system of relations was assumed to be applicable everywhere at all times, deviations treated as error terms (mainly errors of measurement, possibly category errors, later some sampling errors). Economic theorists who envisioned formalist statements imagined that they could accomplish the same, even though the contributions to aggregate error would be larger and more various.

However, as interest turned more to the explanation of "economic growth" (mainly rate of growth of total aggregate output as such and per capita), treated as a property of the system of relations, the new emphasis entailed realization that this task would complicate formal theory far beyond the images of Newtonian mechanics. The chief variable of the system of relations as a whole was taken to be gross national product (later modified to gross domestic product, GDP), expressed primarily as an aggregate and only secondarily as a per-person (per-worker) ratio. Substantively, the key question asked about the source of growth. What are its drivers? Only two drivers had been identified in classical theory, capital and labor, each qualitatively as well as quantitatively variable, but for "technical" reasons only the quantitative would gain a place in the formal table of terms. The various "technical reasons" soon led to the introduction in formalism (spreading to theory more generally) of a differentiation between endogenous and exogenous terms (i.e., inside versus outside the formal system). That division had already been made in practice, of course, though without much fanfare; for anything that a formal system could not accommodate was pushed outside. Some of this was acknowledged under one or both headings of "simplifying assumption" (e.g., that a complete contract is possible, information is available to all equally, some workers are better trained, etc.) and "measurement error" (e.g., that national accounts are uniformly accurate over time and across places; that per-person consumption choice is accurately measured; etc.). Thus, "endogenous growth theory," a new topical name, manifests concern with those sources of growth (or, more generally, change in aggregate output) within the formal system but without settling what exactly those sources are vis-à-vis any list of relevant factors within economic theory in general.[602] Main candidates have been proposed and expressed in terms of capital and labor—that is, as qualifications within either or both of those classical factors of production (e.g., investing capital in research and development, enhanced training of labor power). As empirical description it might be all well and good to show that variation in total output varies across national economies mainly by exogenous factors such as rate of saving and rate of population growth, relative to steady-state relations of capital and labor (as proposed by Solow 1959 and as shown in estimates for a large selection of countries by Mankiw et al., 1992). But because those factors were unexplained variables external to the formal system of relations—moreover, augmented in Mankiw et al. (1992) by another externality, investment in human capital (i.e., schooling)—it could all be dismissed as a work of magic. While the name, "endogenous growth theory," had come from the work of an otherwise diverse collection of theorists and empirical analysts during the 1980s, that work in general had distinguished

> itself from neoclassical growth [theory] by emphasizing that economic growth is an endogenous outcome of an economic system, not the result of forces that impinge from outside. [Thus,] the theoretical work does not invoke exogenous technological change to explain why income per capita has increased by an order of magnitude since the

---

[602] The concern has also reflected disagreement about returns of scale on capital—whether it is negative (as Solow 1956 proposed) or positive or at least neutral (as endogenous growth theory generally proposes).

industrial revolution. The empirical work does not settle for measuring a growth accounting residual that grows at different rates in different countries. It tries instead to uncover the private and public sector choices that cause the rate of growth of the residual to vary across countries. As in neoclassical growth theory, the focus in endogenous growth is on the behavior of the economy as a whole (Romer 1994, p. 3).

The emphasis must be put on *"formal* theory," with the understanding that formalization is a literally crucial step in building a *systematic* theory that can be tested against evidence not in piecemeal fashion but as a system of theorized relations. Another way of putting that is to say (as Romer did) that "everyone knew" that formal theory had depended upon the presence of some outlandish simplifying assumptions, in order to facilitate formalization. Otherwise, the system of relations, *especially* if stated as a *dynamic* system, would be so formidably complex as to be mathematically intractable. And while reservations had been expressed now and then, the general attitude was that formality had to be preserved at all costs. Why? This answer Romer did not say explicitly, but its presence in his remarks cannot be missed: it was formalization that gave economic theory the appearance of science on the presupposed model of *real* science (i.e., the Newtonian model). Gradually, some theorists of economic systems began to realize that the presupposed model had itself been abandoned by those *"real* sciences" which had been held up as ideal. And gradually, then, a succession of trade-offs began. Romer's statement was a major milestone in that development. One of the main sequences which he (1994, p. 10) highlighted concerned directly and indirectly the conditions of how and why theorists had been so reluctant to tackle the "complicated issues that arise in the economic analysis of the production and diffusion of technology, knowledge, and information."[603]

Note that the process of theorization just described is reminiscent of the AbCon concept (abstractive condensation) in some respects. As a memory function, recall, AbCon reflects and reinforces a layered or partitioned store of per-person experiences. Some of the experiences are shared across persons, often without much explicit recognition of the sharing. Experiences of and within a language are probably the most widely shared within a sociality, closely followed by the heuristics of at least some institutionalized organizations. Other experiences, on the other hand, tend to remain as first-person experiences as such, even when shared with others via second-person standpoint. Certain discrete events within a biography would count among the most per-person specific. Filter-and-update exercises are generally respective of differences in those gradations. In the theory-development scenario presented in the foregoing account the core of an AbCon-like process has been focused on a presupposed system of relations abstract enough to approximate a criterion of temporal as well as spatial universality within a specified domain of knowledge and application. Most of that work of theory development has been by US theorists, using US data as evidence for purposes of calibration (e.g., as Romer said, trying to calibrate the exponent in the basic model that governs proportional rate contributions of capital and labor). Efforts to make a basic formal model that fits economies other than that of the USA

---

[603] I would have said "production and distribution" because "diffusion" can be mistaken as a wholly or largely passive process. As early as 1962 Fritz Machlup was surveying issues of "the production and distribution of knowledge," but his work garnered little attention, mainly because he was viewed as a product of Austrian institutionalist theory and therefore out of date.

more or less equally well have been exercises in futility.[604] Results from (rarer) efforts to test the expectation of *temporal* universality have been no less disappointing for proponents of formalism who have promoted it as more than a useful diagnostic tool (useful to tasks of elucidating inconsistencies and contradictions as well as hidden assumptions).

In effect, these tribulations of the development of a viable formalized theory of economic processes stem from lack of any means of overcoming the plethora of contingencies in those processes (and thus once again illustrate a futile struggle to overcome or circumvent Kant's main lesson). Whereas Newtonian mechanics could abstract away confounding contingencies by specifying the domain as a vacuum with constant gravitational force—thereby arriving at a good approximation to a necessary relation (e.g., "force is a product of mass under acceleration") that would apply under spatiotemporal description *within the domain*—efforts to build a universality within a formal system of economic relations (output defined as a product of capital and labor in specified rates of contribution) failed because of the absence of a necessity from pure rational principle (an absence integral, it is surely worth remembering, to the basis of freedom of action). Romer (1994, p. 10) put the point this way: "many different inferences are consistent with the same regression statistics." Lacking the crux of a necessary relation, one is left without any non-contingent basis for selecting among those "many different inferences." Theorists of economic relations can take consolation, of course, from the fact that they have not been alone in tilting at these windmills. Others should be grateful to them for struggling so persistently in the exercises, thus demonstrating yet again Kant's transcendental Illusion.

Now, with that bit of disciplinary history in mind, let's get back to the question of scale effects. By way of recapitulation, bear in mind that the key question is about proportionality in the relation of output to input: an effect of scaling as such will be manifest as an increase (or, contrariwise, a decrease) in rate of output either in return from the same rate of input or in return that exceeds an increase in input. With an adequate fund of measured observations, a relatively simple model (e.g., a two-dimensional Ising model), adapted to the dynamic effects of coordinated per-person actions such as occur in institutionalized settings of school or work, would be able to detect those changes (see Stauffer 2008).

An implication in light of Broido and Clauset's (2019) investigation, consistent with prior theorization, is that scaling is endogenous to the aggregation process itself. This does not mean that it is never a direct effect of per-person action; the example cited above of Jeff Bezos and his Amazon firm illustrates one mechanism. But are there, have there been, other, less spectacular mechanisms? Is there evidence more generally of per-person action effects generating scale? Is it plausible to expect to observe such evidence in the everyday institutionalized activities of, say, a family, or of school, or of work? Note that the question is

---

[604] Remember, the estimations by Mankiw et al. (1992) achieved success by including three exogenous factors. Note that Romer (1994) recounted efforts as of the early 1990s to assess an expected convergence among many national economies to a basic formal model (and thus to each other). Failure in that regard has continued. An article in *The Economist*, "Not just a first-world problem" (volume 434, 18 January 2020, pp. 69-71), highlighted the continuing puzzlement that ruling theory has failed what once was thought to be an easy test of a "convergence" thesis. This thesis was central to most of the "modernization" literature of the social sciences from the late 1940s onward.

*not* one from another Robinsonade. No one "does it alone." It is nonetheless possible, even likely, that an individual person-actor can be the primary and/or main agent of action effects aggregated across the sum of a collection or network of agents. However, the question is also about observational logistics, and in such terms it does seem likely that the third of those venues, the workplace, is the easiest setting in which to undertake requisite observations, inasmuch as employment firms already have interest in promoting (and rewarding) per-person actions that might generate a scale effect.

Standard histories of economic organization are replete with case illustrations of the claim that major scale effects have been achieved via innovations of organizational technology. Developments by Ford and by Taylor are oft-cited cases, but they are hardly the only major instances. Ronald Coase (1937) proposed, as noted earlier, that the commercial establishment now known as a "firm" was (is) an innovation in the organization of economic relations designed to improve efficiencies in input-output relations in various dimensions. One such dimension is the conversion (thus "privatization") of a selective portion of the existing general labor market into an internal labor market, thereby reducing informational and transaction costs.[605] In general, information has been treated in economic theory as a nonrival good—which is to say that it can be used by many simultaneously—and this should apply as well to the information contained in an innovation of a given kind. In practice, of course, a given fund of information is not always equally available and equally usable, partly due to negligence or lack of understanding by some potential users and partly due to monopoly efforts by other users. Therefore, while it may be that a given innovation began in part by chance events (thus, an exogenous source), development is usually an organizational effort of per-person actions linked through network effects. Likewise, once within such network relations a given innovation tends to generate other innovations. Both of these kinds of network effects imply that the *aggregate* rate of innovation and of development will be an endogenous event. Furthermore, assuming competitive market relations, transactions tend to be at or above some minimal level of efficiency. While this implies pressure *against* any economy of scale, a new development in organizational technology can change the game, until a new equilibrium is attained.[606]

There *are* some scale effects that can develop from direct improvements of one or more particular persons' productivity, the quality and/or quantity of output directly due to specific per-person actions. They tend to be submerged by median or central-tendency considerations in the collectivity of which the persons are members, however. One sometimes reads proponents of

---

[605] While this dimension was apparently highly important during most of the twentieth century (good data about the importance were actually rather scarce), other legal-rational provisions of "due process" probably eroded while also supplementing the effect. Bridges and Villemez (1994, p. 62) concluded from their study that fewer than "a third of the positions" in their sampled firms "were regularly filled through inside hiring" (also pp. 95,125, 159, 184). That estimate was made during the early phase of innovations in organizational technology such as the internet (and the World Wide Web) which enabled commercial firms as well as research groups to become distributed organizations, with per-person inputs to production functions scattered around the globe—thus, massive shifts toward externalized labor ties, temporally as well as spatially, still underway.

[606] Here, too, of course, one must bear in mind that "efficiency" is always defined relative to an organizational perspective and interest (see, e.g., Meade 1964; White 1992).

the value of aggregated data relative to per-person data argue that the former are more accurate since aggregation "averages out" errors. That is generally true insofar as the errors are random and the data base is large. But small though well-founded differences can be "averaged out" as well. The per-person differences of action that could generate directly a scale effect mostly occur as enhanced weighting attached to a particular person's work as contribution to the whole of the collectivity. They mostly occur in professions, and more specifically in professional partnerships and/or agencies, wherein per-person growth of experience can engender an elevated level of professional skill, as in the practice of law or medicine or music. More generally, they can occur within replacement events—for instance, as successive cohorts of workers become marginally better trained in skills of specified task. However, it can be exceedingly difficult to sort actual relative contributions of members who, by formal position in a collectivity, could be expected to have weighted impact, and by that an effect of scale for the collectivity as a whole, from contributions of "ordinary" other members, since per-person actions effects are situationally transactional. Insofar as a given collectivity is performing with organizational efficiency the tasks that result in output, sorting the whole of per-person inputs into separate contributions may be as difficult as achieving the relative sorting of effects of innovation or development of an organizational technology. If one is privy to informal talk within a given firm or agency, one may well hear indicators in the use of jargon or colloquial expressions: a "rate buster" could be taken as indication that a specific worker's contribution is disproportionately large. Some of the indication can become part of official or quasi-official parlance, as in designation of a specific employee as "one of our high performers." As Susan Fowler (2020) has documented, however, the "high performer" label (like similar others) can be used to excuse, camouflage, or justify an apparently correlated action that is reprehensible and if performed by an average or less-than-average employee would garner a different response.

As the foregoing discussion implies, the likelihood of per-person scale effects in work settings tends to be occupationally conditioned, and the conditions can be confounding. In most places of work employment, monetized rewards are tied to occupation and tend to be wage-rate specific, even for salaried positions (i.e., salary per expected regular hours of work). Under conditions such as those, the tendency is for per-person productivity to conform to a rentier model (this tendency often enforced among workers themselves via brandings such as "rate buster"), and the likelihood of any per-person scale effect is therein lessened. By contrast, monetized rewards for per-person productivity in professional partnerships tend to be more entrepreneurial, in the sense that the partner has an expected level of salary which is augmented from an appropriate division of partnership profits.[607] However, a large-firm employer who imagines emulating the partnership model in order to gain positive scale effects will be dissuaded after estimating measurement costs across the firm's work force.

---

[607] A per-person multiplier effect within a partnership can be directly due to a particular agent to the partners. For an interesting account of one such case—Gordon Bunshaft, who, although a principal, acted as agent to the trio of principals in the partnership of Skidmore, Owings & Merrill—see Adams (2019). The Bunshaft record also illustrates that generational succession can be a distinctively unhappy time for those on the way out (another version of "feeling left behind"); see Adams (2019, pp. 240-241).

As I wrote earlier in this section, the kinds of measured observations that are required of the dynamics of aggregation process as such still need to be made. Once the practice has been accomplished with reasonable success in repetition for specified institutional settings, it then needs to begin again, but now focused within relevant cells of a stratified grid in order to determine if the process dynamics differ within an institutional constellation of organizations, and then again from one constellation to another.

Newton's theory was not a mirage in its own terms and context, and we can readily understand the fascination it held for Kant a half-century after Newton's death. Indeed, its claim to an absolutist knowledge approximated the relativity of space-time well enough to enable three human beings to find their way to the vicinity of an intended landing site on Earth's moon, and then home again, only fourteen years after Einstein's death. But the simplicity of the theory had taken on some of the characteristics of a mirage, as other disciplines of modern science sought blueprints for their own specific developmental paths. The idea that one could hold the essence of the entire universe in the basic algebra of three laws of motion and an inverse square law of gravitational attraction had become an emblematic promissory note of modern science in general, by the time of Joseph Priestley (1733-1804) in chemistry and Charles Lyell (1797-1875) in geology, among others. Before the end of Lyell's life, early versions of social science had been formulated with similar visions. Herbert Spencer (1820-1903), whose "survival of the fittest" law was announced in his *Principles of Biology* five years after Darwin's *Origin of the Species*, extended his evolutionism into an early sociology. This was not only an English vision, of course, as corresponding imaginations were being expressed in French and German as well. While today our visual memories of those principals have them attired in outdated costumes and odd habits of personal grooming, it was for the many principals themselves an exciting time of unfettered possibility—to discover God's natural laws in vernacular tongues, promising enlightenment among hundreds of thousands of "ordinary people" all around the globe, even into lands of "oriental despotism" and "the dark continent."

Unfortunately, the mirage continued to absorb vanishing points of "world views" throughout the twentieth century and even now into this century. Perhaps there have always been competing versions of a "reality problem" in human thought, due in part to the aspirational quality of the best of that thought. It is supremely difficult to maintain consistent sortings when the quest to learn begins, unavoidably, from expectations of what it is that must still be learned— that is, sorting noise and error from anticipations of what "the real signal will look like." That difficulty weighed on travelers even when the destination was understood to be a nirvana of absolute truth, because different and competing claimants to prior knowledge were always on hand. With the loss of those charades of absolute certainty and necessity, the difficulty did not disappear. But it has seemingly become more intolerable simply because it has now become clear that the mirrors both reflect only the mirror-makers and hide nothing behind or beneath. Self-responsibility is an unwelcome beast, a reminder that human beings are not and will never be those gods that they once imagined as benign caretakers or cantankerous tricksters. Unfortunately, too, our educational institutions, beginning with the family of procreation, have remained bound to nineteenth-century habits of eighteenth-century mirages, enlivened mainly by the anguish of starring into what for all too many people feels like an abyss of freedom.

Earlier in this Part Five (§27) I drew briefly on the art historian, William Mitchell, in description of a growing gap between the enormous volume of knowledge that is available to understanding of our multitudinous worlds and the actual fund of knowledge that most adults have ready to use and indeed are capable of using in a controlled manner. The fact of the gap as such is not new. There is abundant testimony from and about Europe's twelfth century, for example, that a gap then existed between the many generations of tradition and the inventions of modernity—this at a time when nearly all of Europe's received "literature of learning" was theological, simply because theology *was* Europe's principal fund of verified knowledge (see, e.g., Curtius 1953; Chenu 1968 [1957], ch. 9). What *is* different, however, is first the sheer magnitude of the gap; second, the rate at which it has been growing; and third, the increased range in the costs of ignorance, as so much of that knowledge today has been and continues to be materialized in extraordinarily powerful productions that can literally incinerate human worlds in the span of a day. As Mitchell (2011, p. 253) said, today so many people have such little comprehension that they can no longer imagine exercising any control of future choices.

Recall to that context Kant's categorical imperative: an average citizen must act as if that person's will should become a universal law. This is the legislative act which sits at the core of the realm of freedom as Kant distinguished it from the realm of necessity. This act of law-making is a summation of all that makes humans different from both the angels (denizens of divine essence, for whom freedom would be superfluous) and the beasts (denizens of natural necessity, on whom freedom would be wasted).

Imagine that today. When James Madison, Alexander Hamilton, Thomas Jefferson, and others devised the constitution of a new nation, they located the legislative function in a representational body because they did not expect that the majority of citizens of the new nation were, or would soon become, well enough educated to perform legislation by direct democracy. But they thought, they hoped, that the aggregate of voters would produce requisite assemblies of well-educated representatives, men and women who believed in an ethical obligation to be as intelligent as possible, and to become still more intelligent as the years pass and conditions change. In recent times, as one scans the average competencies of such assemblies of legislators, the perception does not reward hope. The bulk of evidence tells of a massive failure of education not only among those who elect their legislative representatives but also among a large proportion of the representatives themselves.

That will be central to the concerns of Part Six.

## Part Six
## The Reality Problem of Future Worlds

The biggest general lesson from Part Five is that advancement of theory and modeling has been distressingly slow, partly because of a longstanding neglect of concept formation and scarcity of adequately specific substantive theory. Equally important has been the missing measurement. Even for existing concepts there has been strikingly little development of mensural technology. The bulk of funding has continued to be devoted to repetitions of the same state-space descriptive work that is mainly in service to governmental administrative functions, which means that the emphasis is placed on total population-based representative sampling of observations, an emphasis both expensive and of little or no theoretical payoff especially for any interests in observing the dynamics of process.

In his book, *The Reckless Mind*, initially published the first year of the new century, Mark Lilla (2016 [2001]) wrote passages that in retrospect could be described as "prescient"— certainly beyond my appreciation at the time, in much the same way that I had not appreciated Christopher Lasch (1979) on narcissism and failures of leadership a generation earlier. Lilla focused mainly on "the narcissistic attraction of intellectuals to tyrants who they imagine are translating their own ideas into political reality," prominent examples ranging from Martin Heidegger and Carl Schmitt during the first half of the twentieth century to Michel Foucault and Jacques Derrida during the second half. Had it been written a year or two later *The Reckless Mind* could have given notice to several lesser lights who had been populating the administration of the US presidency of George W Bush, whose leadership skills had already proved to be less than exemplary in a good way. Multiple displays of outcomes of what must have been cross-person aggregations of per-person action effects left one doubly incredulous at missed opportunities for research (among other explorations of intelligence).[608] In a second book, *The Shipwrecked Mind*, Lilla (2016) continued his survey by focusing on a few early twentieth-century intellectuals whose motivations, cognitive and emotive, stemmed in part from a cultural pessimism seeking refuge in an oddly modernist nostalgia for a prior, better epoch. The sense of being shipwrecked and abandoned on some reef of time leads to the magical thinking which Lilla dubbed "epochal thinking":

> One need not have read Kierkegaard or Heidegger to know the anxiety that accompanies historical consciousness, that inner cramp that comes when time lurches forward and we feel ourselves catapulted into the future. To relax that cramp we tell ourselves we actually know how one age has followed another since the beginning. This white lie gives us hope of altering the future course of events, or at least of learning how to adapt to them. There even seems to be solace in thinking that we are caught in a fated history

---

[608] Richard Alan Clarke, advisor on counterterrorism for the US National Security Council from 1998, would have been an excellent source of insight until his departure from the Bush administration in 2003 but of course would have been bound by protocol. Perhaps we shall never know details of the process that could shed light on the counterfactual question, What might have been different had the right officials heeded Clarke's alert?

of decline, so long as we can expect a new turn of the wheel, or an eschatological event that will carry us beyond time itself (Lilla 2016, pp. 16, 135).

The discomfit that comes with facing human responsibility for human actions and their effects is unrelenting when some of those actions and effects amount to multipliers of other human actions and effects. A generally favored target when faced with "obvious" evidence of the multiplier is an abstracted "technology," the abstraction making it easier to evade the fact that other fruits of the labors of technical innovation and development are widely cheered. Evasion is made all the easier when those desirable fruits are in focus—most of us prefer health to illness, longer life span to shorter, and so on—by the convenience of marginalizing their unwanted kin as "side effects" and similar avenues of "externalizing costs." This is common fare, noted and remarked many times before.

What is less often noticed is the expectation that humans—or at least some humans, those who are or would be "our leaders"—should "get out in front of" the making of history, leading its course in morally preferable, less dangerous directions. The grammatical slack of that idiomatic expression, to "get out in front of," is recognition of something important in popular sentiment—namely, that in order to be "in front of" the process of making tomorrow, one must be "out" of the process itself—that is, not among the plebian actors of the play but the playwright and director who stands outside the audience's view. Thus, the attraction of the strong, the heroic leader. Never mind that he or she (but almost always a "he") plies the illusory chords of a demagogic music. Load the responsibility of vision and control onto the leader, the one who displays strength and certainty of conviction. This "wanting and waiting to be told" is in some part a self-recognition of weak ability to exercise judgment—not only poor skills of judgment but also a poverty of reasoning or a poverty of relevant information (perhaps a poverty of attention, thus another vicious circle), or poverty in both the rational and the empirical registers on which judgment depends.

The implied location is nonexistent, of course, and the one who assents to being that leader is, as will eventually become clear to many of the erstwhile followers, one of the greater fools. There are very simple lessons from economics that should have taught all of us at least that much, the sum of the lessons being that human actors, while far from perfectly rational, are on average rational enough (though unevenly so) to know how to adapt when the dialectic of reward and punishment changes (as, e.g., the relative distributions of benefits and costs of what a given actor might insist are *perverse* and *unexpected* consequences of her or his benignly intended actions). While a given actor, utilizing publicly available information, might be able to "get ahead of the curve" on, say, a specific investment opportunity, that advantage is soon lost, becoming no advantage at all, perhaps even its opposite. This sort of scenario plays out in the multiple realities of human action on a frequent and largely regular basis. It is one of the vital conditions of the penalty of greed for those who learn too slowly.

Rationality tends to fail, however, as dread aggregates into a more collective consciousness. Sontag's (1966, p. 225) insight fifty years ago retains some force: "collective nightmares cannot be banished by demonstrating that they are, intellectually and morally, fallacious." Surely a prominent instance of "collective nightmare" still in fresh memory of most adults is the financial crisis that began in 2007. As if we really needed another lesson to the point, this development demonstrated the immensely powerful forces that can and do ensue from and in aggregation processes. In this case the forces were generated in aggregations mainly of consequences of greed and fear in certain kinds of market transactions over which the regulatory aims of hierarchical structures, those of corporate firms and governmental agencies most prominently, lost moderating influence in part because those aims themselves can *magnify* the effects of greed and fear (e.g., when strong lobbies convinced the US Congress to remove the safety barriers that had been in place through the Glass-Steagall Banking Act of 1933). Tomes reporting week-by-week events of the Great Recession (e.g., Geithner 2014) give glimmers of the multiplier effects orchestrated within firms such as Bear Stearns and Lehman Brothers, while tomes assessing practices of governmental agencies (e.g., Mallaby 2016 on Allan Greenspan's tenure as chairman of the Federal Reserve Bank) tend to underestimate the extent to which financial firms are usually steps ahead of regulatory intents (which intents sometimes prove themselves to be invitations to new, poorly understood means of evasion).[609] One might think those steps another form of Galbraith's (1961 [1955]) bezzle.

I will return to some of these matters below. But in this final part I want to focus attention to a basic problem which can be (has been) summarized as "the reality problem." One can avoid that summary, of course, and attend to variously more specific "problems of reality." Some of that dispersion will be evident in the following pages. But all of the more specific problems share in a common basis: what is the constitution of reality? I am far from the first to have drawn attention to the question; nor was the late Vincent Crapanzano (2015, p. 368), upon whom I drew in §11. His abundant experiences as an anthropologist had taught him that normal life "demands that we be bad epistemologists." Any critical observer is in a sense bound into the circuits of a dialectic: "We are destined to live not in illusion, not in reality, but in oscillation" from one to another of those states—that is, "in what we declare illusion and reality to be"—and in a perspective by which normally we do not see that the "distinction is made from within the oscillation itself" (see Dahms 2011). This experience is of an apparently endless continuous conundrum of, within, and by any sociality that is oriented primarily and mainly by its presence from what it has been, rather than by what it yet might become (i.e., Nietzsche's retort to the Delphic dictum).

---

[609] Orléan (2014, pp. 276-277), using the case of Lehman Brothers as his illustration, correctly indicated the irremediable uncertainty that attends vital transactions. In the popular consciousness, much of it stoked by crassly self-serving actions of politicians and political commentators, economists were abject failures with respect to the financial crisis of 2007-2008. Orléan's point about irremediable uncertainty is germane to that false view. So, too, is the fact that a number of prominent economists, including Robert Shiller, Richard Duncan, and B Mark Smith (representatives of three different audiences) *did* offer warnings about instability in the financial markets, some of them repeatedly. Smith's (2001) very useful account of "the evolution of the stock market" (his subtitle), written for a wide audience, includes late chapters with titles such as "An accident waiting to happen" and "Greenspan's dilemma." Shiller's more technical barometer of the pricing mechanism in the US housing market issued repeated warnings, "correction ahead," and as they were repeatedly ignored it became increasingly likely that the magnitude of correction was being amplified. For the few who believed the evidence, it was opportunity for large investment in profits ahead. But that is hardly comfort for the many more who lost much or all of their savings, however complicit in the greed and fear they might have been.

Before resuming discussion of "the reality problem" writ large, I want to assemble a few illustrative evidences of particulars, especially those which are implicated in two problems of major concern in the closing section, §30: failures of education, which feed the growth of ignorance and incompetence as they have continued to reproduce thematics of the general reality problem; and problems of the authority of voice, which both follow from and add to generation of the general reality problem in the sort of captivity to which Crapanzano referred. Between those admittedly complex dimensions, educational failure and authority of voice, rests the survival of future worlds of Earth that *might* be inhabitable by our species, thus the survival of the human species along with a great many other species of life on this planet.

Are we as a species inherently suicidal? The question must be taken more seriously than ever before. It points to another serious question, this one being the core of what is known among cosmologists as Fermi's paradox. One day while lunching with three other physicists connected with the national laboratory at Los Alamos Enrico Fermi asked, "So where are they?" His question, proximally stimulated by a flood of news reports about "unidentified flying objects" during months leading up to that summer day of 1950, was seriously proposed on the basis of what was then known about the universe, our galaxy, and the place of our solar system within it. Now seven decades later the question has grown more insistent because of greater knowledge than Fermi had *and* because of our own self-induced greater peril. As for the former, best estimates now indicate that while Earth is about 4.5 billion years old and the oldest traces of life date to about 3.8 billion years ago, the median age of Earth-like planets in the Milky Way is about 6.5 billion years. Given that we have recently begun exploration of our solar system, it follows that suitably intelligent beings on some of the other planets in our galaxy have long since been doing the same, and probably with much more advanced technology. These considerations, based on a simple inventory of probabilities from known facts, make Fermi's question much louder: *Where are they? Why no contact?* Perhaps the real question, however, following Fermi's point, is different: Why *would* they? "Wait a bit longer," they could have concluded, "and those creatures on this otherwise nice planet will wipe themselves out."

Consider the education problem. On the one hand, most available evidence indicates that the proportion of adults who refuse to participate intelligently in responsibility for future worlds has certainly not lessened during the past seven decades; and if "refusal" is qualified as active, not just passive, the proportion has actually grown. On the other hand, the proportion of adults who, judged by their behavior and attitudes, are able to discriminate between well-informed, rationally based claims of authority and claims of authority that rest on magical, irrational or nonrational thinking, often demagogic in inspiration, has probably decreased during that same period of seven decades. The decrease has been due partly to educational failure and partly, independently of the educational failure, to alienations and resentments stimulated by growing complexities of everyday life.[610]

---

[610] I say "independently" because of personal knowledge of some credentially well-educated persons whose feelings of alienation and resentment dictate their most crucial beliefs and at least some of their actions.

Social scientists have been complicit in the problems. It is easy to criticize those who are deemed "soulless, mechanical, cynical number-crunchers," "pea-counters," and the like. But that is worthless posturing, another marker of ignorance. Let me choose a different example, one that is far closer to my own theoretical perspective in many ways. Jacques Derrida was exceptionally incisive and accomplished in major dimensions of enlightenment. Following closely on the heels of other scholars, he demonstrated with unusual clarity of effect a main basic lesson of a third-century (BCE) scholar, Archimedes, who brought into clear focus a relativity (i.e., lack of absolute position), when he challenged his listener to supply him with a lever long enough and a pivot located at the correct spatial coordinates, so that he could lift Earth from its position. He knew that none of the apparatus was or could be real, of course, even though he also knew that, if all of it could be real, he could demonstrate the palpable reality within his thought experiment.

Reality is a human production. It is not clear that Archimedes should be said as having subscribed wholly to that view. But nineteen centuries later some scholars (e.g., David Hume) were making the argument, as also did Derrida two centuries after that. The message was disturbing to most people who heard it during the late 1700s, although not all that many people did hear it. By the late 1900s proportionately many more people did read or hear about Derrida's repetitions of the message, and for most of those adults (some of them scholars) it was sheer rubbish. Reactions were sometimes heated. One might have said that Socrates had returned, ready to befuddle and pervert our youth. The reality at work was simpler and much more distressing: the majority of adults simply lacked adequate preparation from which to understand Derrida—or Hume and Archimedes, for that matter. One must remember, while considering that condition, that these same adults are the first to act as educators of their own children.

The difficulty is not simply a matter of "learning," however, for one can read works written by highly educated authors that perpetrate misunderstanding via divisions of what counts as "real reality." Lilla, for example, expressed some profound unhappiness with current events on grounds of ethics and aesthetics as well as epistemology that ring familiar to many of us (Lilla 2016 [2001]). But his unhappiness found its most revealing focus in Derrida's work, and mainly for having held up a mirror to our production/reproduction of realities effectively enough that we could see our own complicities throughout, no longer able to attribute them to forces beyond our human realm, to forces that come into play beneath or behind human language, forces of divine origin either directly or via some congeries of pre-human laws of nature (Lilla 2016 [2001], pp. 161-190). One would think that the writings by/of Derrida have been the mother's milk on which our children have been raised—that Derrida's text has been the most effective text of public and private education—this, despite the fact that very likely the commonest charge against Derrida has been his "obscurity of composition."[611]

---

[611] Lilla (2016 [2001], p. 190) himself referred to "the dark and forbidding works of Jacques Derrida." Lilla is not alone; many others have refused Derrida's work as incomprehensible. Derrida's point, aesthetically, was to make his reader think *hard*, perceive *incisively*.

There *has* been an "evolution" of thought recently, as there had been during prior centuries. But to confuse a diagnostician of that change and development with its underlying processes and conditions is the same sort of reaction as that of commentators who reject the image (often angrily) they see when diagnosticians hold up a mirror showing human responsibility for the massive degree of climate change now remaking fond worlds inherited from, say, Alexander von Humboldt, John Muir, and kindred figures of nineteenth-century pastoralism. In fact, the message of Derrida's long journey in words was an unfolding of lessons already present in Kant's transcendental Illusion. One clue to that presence in Lilla's diagnostic thinking can be seen in his charge against "the mistaken belief"—championed by Derrida, according to Lilla—"that it is language, not reality, that keeps our democracies imperfect" (Lilla 2016 [2001], p. 186). One suspects that Lilla failed to take note of the (implicit) premise— namely, that an analytic distinction between "language" and "reality" can be achieved such that he, or anyone, can know reality other than by, in, and as an exercise of language.

When an adult person thinks that he or she is being seen as "too ignorant to understand," that person's reaction often is terse, rejective and harsh, resentful of the messenger and increasingly alienated. Am I saying that others of us should defer to and respect that "nativist" reality? No, of course not. To the contrary: we should not accept, much less promote ignorance. Rather, we must eradicate the ignorance. Education must do much better. *That* is how others should be respected, and the respect must begin with our children at earliest age. Later is too late.

## §30. Education and Authority of Voice

I shall begin my sampling of particular illustrations with the physical sciences, both because the Newtonian heritage still has foremost residence in popular consciousness and because these are the sciences most often in mind when people raise concerns about "modern technology" (or, in the time and space of Martin Heidegger, "the question concerning technology"). While the dominant popular perception of the latter concern has been that technology is too radical, too alienating, and the like, in general aspect the physical sciences have actually been, and are, rather conservative. Remember, Max Planck was referring in particular to his own discipline, physics, when he uttered his jibe about the measure of progress being in units of "funeral time." The conservatism is organized primarily in terms of theory: good ones are scarce, so change should occur only when a demonstrably better one comes along. In general, that has been the practice.

Twenty years ago and more, when teaching undergraduate courses in data analysis, statistics and research methods, I varied illustrations of relevance to future lives in order stimulate attention and interest. The illustrations often had to do with expected changes in the institution of work (tasks and their requirements), linking to those changes some selection or combination of the basic utilities of classification, measurement, sampling, estimation, and so forth. Sometimes the illustrations were on average successful, sometimes not, and the variance was always considerable. One of the more interesting instances occurred in connection with measurement. I began with the number line, the fact that the basic unit, an integer, is precisely spaced from each neighbor by equal intervals of the line, and that each space is infinitely divisible, which means that not only the entire sequence but any segment of it is infinitely long. I then related that to the power and to various problems when measuring events or properties of

584

interest in everyday life as well as in the social sciences—one such example being that while we tend to load heavy significance onto personal preferences and treat them as comparatives, they are usually measured only as rank orders, and because rank orders conceal infinite amounts of variable information we really do not understand the comparisons we think we are making. In the course of a practical illustration, I emphasized that the number line is of known dimension in length whereas the ordered ranks come in chunks of unknown size or distance between ranks of an indeterminate dimensionality. I then introduced David Hilbert's concept of a space that contains not just one dimension, as in a line, or two dimensions.as in a plane, or three, as in a cube, but an infinite number of dimensions (i.e., "Hilbert space"; Hilbert 1950 [1902]). This had proved useful in generating a large range of new understandings and some new technologies, one of them (which I used as further illustration) being the mapping of signals, in particular light. For a human being at birth, the sight of physical light depends on the small number of rods and cones in the eye. But this physical spectrum of light actually consists of an infinite number of points of light in the full spectrum of color, thus potentially an infinite number of colors, which can be used not just in signal theory but in communication technology, in cryptocybernetics, and so on (which were then in development). It was at about this point that a student interrupted, obviously agitated by some stimulant, the identity of which became "clear" after he blurted that I was "just making stuff up." To wit: "everybody knows that points of light must have dimension, otherwise they would not exist; therefore there cannot be an infinite number of them in any real space; so either I am making it all up or this Hilbert space is not real." (That is more or less the gist of his protest.) After some back-and-forth by me, I realized I had lost him long before the Hilbert case, the evidence being that it was news to the student that a point in Euclidean space is dimensionless. The student not only had not fully entered the twentieth century at least in terms of basic geometry; he had gotten stuck, as it were, at some crossroads more than twenty-one centuries earlier than the birth of David Hilbert's new invention. Again, there is reality, and then there is the *real* reality.

Granted, of course, in our everyday worlds we do see lines and planes and therefore points everywhere. That experience of reality demonstrates the utility of geometry as a kit of basic tools. The system of relations is a human invention; thus, the utility, founded in imagination—indeed, one might say a zoo of fictitious beings—are all relational. This system of relations is a language, with its own concepts and semantics, its own relations of grammar or syntax, and so forth. The relations of geometry are abstract, no doubt, and purely, wholly endogenous to a system, whether it be that attributed to the Euclideans, that of Minkowski (useful to Einstein), or some other.[612] Yet we can, and do, experience them as realities of our everyday

---

[612] I do not mean to suggest that only three conceptions are available. Three cosmological conceptions of space-time are implied by Einstein's equations of general relativity. These equations explain how the mass/energy relation operates to determine the curvature of space-time. The equations take different solutions depending on conditional assumptions, the key assumption being about the state of matter. Assume a perfect vacuum, in the sense that a space-time system is empty of matter. Here the energy density of that system is sufficient to produce a curvature. Specified as "vacuum equations," Einstein's equations take three simple solutions that imply symmetry (i.e., the curvature is uniform throughout the system). One of these solutions describes what is called Minkowski space-time: it is perfectly flat (the "cosmological constant" is zero). A second solution is derived when the constant is positive; this

worlds, even though the experiences we do have are not always acknowledged as Euclidean or Minkowskian or application of a Hilbert space, and so on. In such uses we tend to think and act as if in the midst of a magic show, for we have no idea how to account for all the process(es) implicit to those experiences. That "hiddenness" of realities of, from, and by human making has gotten to very large proportion in recent decades, growing every year in ways that most of us do not realize, both because the innovative capacities of our sociality have been increasing enormously while our educational institutions still operate as if our calendars had just announced the new year, 1950, or even 1920.

The average adult today is incapable of sorting through the growing number and variety of realities. What is that person inclined to make of media statements that "the economists dropped the ball, thus the Great Recession" or theoretical physicists today "cannot decide what is real"? Lacking understanding of the state of economic theory, the state of quantum theory, the history of either, and the appropriate procedures of scientific inquiry, that average person is poorly prepared to evaluate and make reasoned judgments about such reports. The current situation in theoretical physics offers excellent illustration. The standard model, generally agreed since the 1970s, is incomplete; very few dispute that conclusion. The "cavity" in want of a filling is very large, extending all the way from celestial gravity and its "music of the spheres" to quantum electrodynamics and its "silence of the quarks." Einstein knew that his general theory was well short of the last word. Inquiry that he and two colleagues, Boris Podolsky and Nathan Rosen, published in 1935 and 1936 confirmed as much, and he spent the last of his years in futile search of the solution. Some theorists have considered the standard model but a step or two away from that solution. But no one has demonstrated the path of those missing steps. Most effort during the past thirty years has been devoted to a purportedly fundamental theory, unifying Einsteinian and quantum worlds (as well as the Newtonian). But this effort, known as "string theory" (or "superstring theory"), has failed to yield even one falsifiable hypothesis (i.e., nothing that can be empirically tested), and some leading theorists have concluded that it is a dead-end— indeed, an embarrassing dead-end, because it looks more like a religious faith than a scientific theory (see, e.g., Woit 2006). Far too many adult members of today's society want to be told "what the truth is," in simple, unambiguous dictation, lacking the preparation for anything more complex than a Sunday morning homily and lacking the patience that modern science can only presuppose. This combination of conditions of first-person experience is fertile ground for any run-of-the-mill huckster, snake-oil salesman, or demagogue-in-waiting. Add to that a combination of raw resentment and capacious paranoia: what per-person response should one expect when the person has been told that responsibility for massive climate change is theirs, too? Fermi's paradox becomes a bit less paradoxical.[613]

---

version, called "deSitter space-time," is spherical. In the third, the constant is negative, and this system, called "anti-deSitter space-time," is a saddleback. None of the three seems compatible with quantum dynamics; thus, the search for a workable theory of quantum gravity.

[613] Many years ago my granduncle Clint Livingston, having retired from his position at Los Alamos and visiting his sister (my maternal grandmother) before moving on to Los Angeles, told of rumors of strange phenomena in the area of the laboratory. This would have been shortly before newspapers began a flurry

The embarrassment begins from recognition of Kantian interdependence of rationalism and empiricism: reason without experience is empty; experience without reason is blind. The best versions of string theory offer an elegantly logical tapestry that lacks all demonstrable connection with human experience even after all of the enormously powerful sensory apparatuses have been brought to bear (e.g., the Large Hadron Collider at the border of France and Switzerland). Thus, the theory remains empty in the double sense that it has incorporated no evidentiary base and it has continued to fail to offer testable hypotheses. By the same token, the embarrassment was quickened by an episode that began during the late 1990s, a scandal known as "the Bogdonov affair." Two brothers, Igor and Grichka Bogdonoff (aka Bogdonov), managed to publish a series of theory papers in reputable physics journals that experts in their reputed fields of inquiry concluded were empty of meaning (see Woit 2006, pp. 213-219 for a brief overview), while other reputable physicists continued to defend the pair as misunderstood geniuses. Woit quoted one physicist who, having attended a meeting of physicists at Harvard, reported that

> no one in the string group at Harvard can tell if these papers are real or fraudulent. This morning, told that they were frauds, everyone was laughing at how obvious it is. This afternoon, told that they are real professors and that this is not a fraud, everyone here says, well, maybe it is real stuff (Woit 2006, p. 214).

More recently, the balance of opinion has swung against the brothers. But the damage to credibility had already been done, as it appeared that some of the most prestigious of theoretical physicists had become unable to distinguish between gibberish and genuine advancement of theory. Sustaining such damage to their authority of voice, how can leading physicists imagine that "the average citizen," who has been overwhelmingly daunted by physical theory since Albert Einstein and the days when it was commonly said that only "(insert very small number) people in the entire world understand Einstein's theory," has any chance of learning anything that modern physics has to teach?

The reality problem for physics began even before Einstein, however, thanks to deficiencies in standards of education. Recall that the comfortable world of Newtonian mechanics had settled major worries about reality long before the 1900s. Then the theoretical work by Max Planck, Einstein, Paul Dirac, and others began to demonstrate unsettling consequences for that domain. Yet at a popular level, understanding of Newtonian mechanics had not been all that good even before the name of Einstein became famous. As evidence I cited in a footnote early in Part Five drawn from my personal experience of lessons I had been learning in my physics courses during the 1950s. To repeat with more detail, imagine this experimental set-up. On a level plain that runs flat for at least a mile (think the salt flats west of Salt Lake City, for instance) someone has built a bench to which is attached a rifle (.22 caliber), the barrel perfectly parallel to and exactly three feet above the ground, with a triggering device attached to the side of the muzzle in such a way that at the exact instant a bullet fired from the rifle leaves the muzzle another bullet held exactly parallel to the fired bullet is released and falls to the ground

---

of reports of what were described as "unidentified flying objects." However, Clint added, that marijuana and peyote were also rumored phenomena. Another chapter of the reality problem.

587

because of gravity. My question—which bullet hits the ground first?—was asked of a large number of adults after I explained the set-up, with the aid of a sketch I had made. (Bear in mind that "large" in my part of that world was relative to a very low-density rural population.) Most of those I asked chose the bullet falling to the ground; no one chose the other bullet. In fact, the two bullets hit the ground at the same time, although the better part of a mile apart. The force of gravity is an *independent* force vector; it is completely unaffected by the force that propels the bullet fired from the rifle. I remember a few men telling me that I did not know what I was talking about, and I could see their point. If you do not know (do not believe) the physical science of it (Newtonian through and through), the correct answer can easily seem counterintuitive. No one is born knowing Newtonian physics. What I had demonstrated was a failure of education. Very few school districts in the western half of the USA in those days required a course in physics even in high school. And some of the men who indulged me had not attended four years of high school in any case.

One part of the reality problem of physical science is that the state of knowledge has passed what the average adult citizen can understand to such extent that there is little recognition between physicists and others. This dimension of the problem is mainly a problem of education. That which theoretical physicists have been trying to accomplish is not so outlandish, when stated in broad general terms, as to be beyond the grasp of a reasonably well-educated adult. Technical details are one matter. The main basic point of the inquiry is quite another, and it is one that every citizen should be able to understand, assuming sound knowledge of basic physics and the general mission of modern science.

What then *is* the main impetus of the apparent current conviction of so many theoretical physicists in string theory? Woit (2006) gave a shorthand explanation in the subtitle of his book: "the search for unity in physical law." String theory is a mathematically elegant foray toward achieving that unity. But it seemingly has no means of intersecting with the empirical physical world that can generate testable hypotheses, and many theoreticians are unwilling to accept string theory simply as an article of faith. That is one major dimension of the reality problem for contemporary physical science.

There is more, however. Why so much investment in this "unity of physical law"? There are many processes of that part of our world which we distinguish as "biological" that do not follow any know "physical law." Likewise, the parts that we distinguish as "economic" and "political" and "linguistic" and "architectural" and "musical" and so on: these, too, include processes which do not follow any known physical law. Moreover, as noted above, most physicists have been aware since the early decades of the previous century that a sizeable gap exists within the hierarchy of "levels" of physical reality, from the gigantic size (one might say "macro-macro") of matter/energy processes that are described by Einstein's equations, to the extremely tiny size ("micro-micro") of processes of the quantum world. What has been at stake in this "search for unity in physical law"?

The short answer is one that has been at issue in prior sections of this book: the assumption of homology. The expectation that "one logic should fit all sizes" had been a regally crowning emblem of Newtonian mechanics for more than two centuries, and most scientists had simply taken for granted that homology is not an assumption but a demonstrated fact, a law, of modern science. Now? The best that can be said from demonstrated physical theory is that the assumption might pertain only in parts. But few physicists are willing to accept that: there *must* be one unitary story, as there had been by God and then by Newton. [614] At least since the development of modern atomic theory, Newtonian mechanics has been understood as simply a crude approximation to the "real reality" beneath it—in the sense, for example, that while the chair on which I sit is mostly empty space at atomic level, I do not fall through because the molecular structure of my body "matches scale" with the molecular structure of the chair as well as the planet on which both chair and I sit. From what we know about forms of life, it appears that Newtonian organization was a physical prerequisite. A good case can be made, as astrobiologist Charles Cockell (2018) has recently done, that a similar organizational connection from the Newtonian physical to the post-Darwinian biological generalizes beyond this planet. The case is largely one of logical extrapolation from what we know about life forms on this planet, however. In short, it is only a hypothesis and will remain empty until we accumulate sufficient observations of life forms beyond Earth.

In the meantime, the search for a grand unified theory—covering all since the Big Bang and perhaps even some of the reality prior to that explosion—will continue, and that continuation will very likely include proponents of a universal homology throughout the several sciences that rest on the platform of physics, an assumption at least as old as Aristotle. In the meantime, too, of course, the reality problem will continue to irritate.

In §20 I mentioned in conjunction with Durkheim's thesis of evacuated intermediations of civic functions recent research by Robert Putnam (2000) which, at least by measure of popularizing a meme ("bowling alone"), alarmed many readers by offering good evidence that "social isolation" had been increasing. Soon followed a "clash of realities." Now, I mean that otherwise overly dramatic expression simply as recognition of what is or should be the normal course of science: alternative theories of reality are tested by experience. Of course, it not as simple as that ending clause might suggest, for the time when it was assumed that "experience" can be "theory-free" (or at least "neutral") and thus incontrovertible test of difference in theory had been left behind as nostalgia for pre-Humean epistemology. In the give and take of contests between theories, moreover, the idea of "alternative theories of reality" can become emotively charged investments in "reduced form," as it were—namely, "different *realities*" as such. This is roughly the current state of theory and evidence regarding a "social isolation" thesis. In wake of Putnam's popular book, other social scientists did their own investigations based not on potentially sampling-biased observations but on observations from probability sampling of a nationally representative population of per-person respondents who were asked to nominate nodes in personal networks. Node number or density became a measure of isolation (e.g.,

---

[614] As noted in §1, recall, Newton himself was not so confident. By acknowledging that space and time might be no more that human efforts of imagination and not actually existent in the universe, Newton was saying in effect that the issue of a single logic was simply another "artifice." His ambivalence might have been a reflection of dim insight into the conundrum that Kant exposed: insofar as that "real reality" does exist, we can know it only via its phenomenal effects, which will have come to our understanding only via our conceptual schemes (which are historical, cultural, contingent, etc.).

McPherson, Smith-Lovin, and Brashears 2006). Results confirmed a recent and clear decline in average network ties. This result was quickly controversial, partly because it conflicted with other studies that had found no trend. Paik and Sanchagrin (2013), suspecting the presence of bias introduced by interviewers as well as respondents, then conducted some replication studies during which they did detect interviewer bias that could account for the apparent trend. Processes of sociality are complex; scientists at work are not external to them.

Those studies, all conducted by reputable scientists, offer a number of lessons.[615] One of the most important is that gaining a correct description even of an ostensibly simple state-space can be a difficult task. Integral to that lesson is the importance of careful preparatory work in classification and measurement. What counts as "social isolation"? And "social" qualifies "isolation" relative to what?—" political" or "economic" or "cultural" or "physical" or "biological" or "individual" in a psychologistic sense? Yet, if any one (or more) of those, wouldn't it nevertheless imply "social" as well? In my admittedly brief overview of the literature from Putnam to Pait and Sanchagrin I did see evidence that at least some of the disagreement in outcomes could have been due to categorial difference (and probably differences in category error), even before mensural error and sampling error are taken into consideration. As demonstrated by Paik and Sanchagrin, interviewing depends on intersections and reciprocities of second-person standpoints in sociality. That alone makes for a complex process of research. It is still more complex, however, because one or both participants in the dyadic relation (assumed) can be implicitly invoking third-person perspective at the same time (e.g., the "they" of a generalized-other of "being interviewer" and/or of "being interviewed," which in either perspective can also draw on a generalized-other reflexivity about the *other* participant's "being this or that").

Leave aside for another moment the issues of measurement and sampling. Assume that one takes as classification an ostensibly simply demographic criterion of "what counts": an example of it would be per-household population density. There is already a quantitative variance (in Simmel's sense): where, in the likely range of "persons per household" should one draw a threshold, below which "social isolation" is invariably (or, to introduce complication) "usually" greater? Or, why not avoid the threshold issue and just use the integer scale of cardinal numbers? But is "social isolation" really mapped by cardinal numbers? (Where is the zero-degree of "social isolation"?) All right; interval numbers? But is that the correct mapping? Maybe a log transform? And so forth. The popular temptation is to "let the data speak for themselves" (e.g., look for "natural breaks," etc.). Surely we have learned the great pitfalls of *that* abdication, haven't we?

Let's consider an actual times-series sequence of observations, using a threshold-definition of what counts as "social isolation"; our population-based measure is "proportion of all households comprised of only one person." The US time-series shows an early jump (13% in

---

[615] I have not followed that research literature since Paik and Sanchagrin (2013), who gave a good review of the preceding studies. Subsequent work might have added more clarification, and/or more complication.

1960 to 25% in 1990) followed by modest increases from 1990 to 2018 (28%).[616] But then a question arises: is the category uniform across the expanse of the United States? Hardly. Being the one of a one-person household in the countryside of Loving County, Texas, is probably not the same experience as in, say, Travis or Bexar County, Texas. That leads to another question: did the threshold isolate the same experience in 1960 as in 2018? Granted, the quantitatively defined threshold to "socially isolated" uniformly applied. But the meaning of "socially isolated" was very likely more than a difference of "one" versus "more than one," whether in Loving or Travis County, 1960 versus 2018.

Today there is as much or more variation across countries as there has been in recent years over time, in the proportion of households comprised of one person. Data for 2017, for instance, range from Norway (47%), Denmark (43), Germany (42), Sweden (41), and Estonia (40), to Italy (32), UK (30), Poland (25), and Portugal (22), among European countries. Based on the short time-series available for several of these countries (mostly from early 2000s), some upward trend has been generally evident, but the country-specific increases were mostly modest. One suspects that a substantial part of the increase has been associated with population aging and thus is mainly female, and there are other studies documenting the correlation between age and isolation. But are those differences across countries due mostly to differences in population aging? Probably not (judging from my observational experiences in Italy vis-a-vis Sweden, Germany, and Norway). More to the point, is the experiential meaning of that definition of "isolation" (i.e., being the *one* person) uniform across those countries? I doubt it.

My aim in the foregoing exercise has not been to offer any direct settlement of the empirical issue about "social isolation." Nor has it been primarily to illustrate that the complexities of producing good data are often overlooked (many other areas of research could be selected for that purpose). Nor again has it been to restate my conviction that understanding the outcome of process, whether we call it "social" or "political" or whatever modifier you choose, can occur only though direct study of the process dynamics as such. Rather, my aim has been primarily to illustrate that contests between different realities are a result of scientific research about even seemingly simple questions *and* to emphasize that this is indeed how it should be. Some social scientists involved in the contests about the isolation thesis have said that the very fact of the contest should be taken as evidence of why it is a mistake to promote social science as *public* activity (i.e., "doing science in the newspapers"): the typical John or Jane Doe is not able to understand the normal course of scientific research, tends to see disagreements between scientists over "what reality really is" as proof that scientists "don't know any more than I do," and thus lose respect for the scientist's claim of authority. I understand that concern, here as in my discussion of authority of voice. However, I think the only genuine solution is not to avoid discussions in public (that would actually contribute to the problem) but to solve the great failure of education. Every adult should be able to understand the basic processes of science, and that must include an understanding of why claims of certainty and

---

[616] The only other country for which I located a good-quality time series of that length was Japan—1960 (17%), 1970 (20), 1980 (20), 1990 (23), 2000 (28), 2010 (32), and 2015 (35), similar to the US series until greater increases after 2000—but my search was hardly thorough..

necessity are claims of religion or myth or demagoguery, *not* of science. Genuinely democratic acts of legislation depend upon a much better "educated public," for this and many other reasons.

The jury is still out in regard to what Robert Putnam (2000) called "America's declining social capital." Improvements in data quality, in techniques of measurement, and in abandoning the faulty logic of trying to answer process questions with cross-sectional data, even when the cross-sections are approximate replications separated by date, will result in substantial improvements of ability to answer Putnam's question—although by the time all of that has happened the reality about which he was concerned will have changed. We must also attend to basic problems of classification, and in particular the assumption of uniformity in what counts as "social capital" (and "isolation"), in light of so much inequality across segments of societal populations. What realistic chance do offspring of families of African descent or Mexican descent or Lakota Sioux descent have to acquire the kinds and amounts of "social capital" inherited by offspring of billionaire, even millionaire parents in the USA? I have raised that sort of question previously in these pages—for example, in light of Arlie Russell Hochschild's (2016) ethnography of household families in Louisiana's bayou country. Another sort of example is available in Isenberg's (2016) study of "down and out" segments of the US population at different periods of US history (see also Higbie 2003, Orange 2018, and many other relevant texts).

Consider the case of Andrew Jackson, the first truly vile person to be elected to the office of the US presidency (1828). By comparison to Thomas Jefferson, John Adams (and his son, who was Jackson's predecessor and first opponent for the office), James Madison, and so forth, Jackson was clearly an ignorant lout. That is among the nicest of derogatory words for him. He was uncouth, an ardent bully, violent and murderous—the list goes on. Most of those words could have been applied fairly to a majority of white adults in the then 24 states of the Union. While most members of that majority had probably never actually committed homicide, I have no doubt that many of them would have murdered men and women of native ancestry, as Jackson did indirectly as well as directly, and men and women of African ancestry, as Jackson surely also did. Aside from homicide and probably some less violent acts against other human beings, most of the white population during the 1820s were materially and educationally quite unlike the Jefferson, Adams, Madison, or Gallatin families. When these men and women saw Jackson sitting in the White House, they felt that they were not such abject failures after all, though uncouth and ignorant they might still be. For all his mingy qualities, Jackson in the White House was instrumental in knitting more of the country together. Granted, not the black-skinned, brown-skinned and red-skinned people; they were treated no better, usually worse, by Jackson than by any of his predecessors, although few if any of those predecessors were prepared to treat them as equals. The large swathes of white-skinned people who had been regarded, often by each other, as "white trash" and similar designators of those who had been perennially left behind by "the better sort" now felt recognized, redeemed, more hopeful for their children, one imagines. What had changed? Three times as many people voted in the 1828 election as had voted in the presidential election four years earlier. What had changed? Reforms of state election laws had by 1828 extended the franchise to all or nearly all white men aged 21 years or older. What had changed? Mainly gradual weakening of the property qualification for white men. Women of any color could not vote; nor could men who were typically identified by color of skin.

Most white men were born into poverty and ignorance. Inequality was not as high as it would become for later generations, however, and the gap between what the average white man knew and what he needed to know in order to be competent in economic production, in civic obligations and duties, even in "book learning," was not nearly as great as it would become during the twentieth century. The ideology of hard work, honest labor, and just deserts was materially realized often enough to be effective incentive—if you were white and male. Most of the population was agrarian. Concerns about "social isolation" were not entirely foreign; but concerns about "right to privacy" scarcely weighed on anyone, for most lands were sparsely populated. The right to participate in an increasingly important "public sphere," on the other hand, was of rapidly growing concern, and the election of 1828 offered some assurance that this right was being observed—if you were white and male. No doubt many white men felt resentment, although, as Isenberg (2016) repeated, the prevailing ideology continued to promote the idea that men and women of the thirteen colonies had defeated the British aristocracy and would never allow one to grow on this land.

None of that means, of course, that severe isolation, alienation, and demoralization were unknown in 1828. But what became known as "Jacksonian democracy" lessened the grip of those psychic torments for most white men. Instead, feelings of isolation, alienation, and demoralization were being segregated into slave shacks on huge plantations and into lands that white men did not want, or did not *yet* want—in other words, the beginnings of what would be "reserved lands" for the hundreds of thousands and then, with "westward expansion," millions of the unwanted people who had survived wholesale extermination. When Andrew Jackson contemplated his "Indian wars," for example, he probably had never heard of the Timucuan people or the Guale people or the Jororo people or the Calusa people, among many other nations of the Florida territories, all gone by 1800. They simply could not compete with the white men. They were not simply "left behind," like the "white trash"; they went away. The surviving white men really did not care where they went, when they went away, so long as they left their lands to the white men. That is a measure of demoralization: an entire people who cannot compete. Did any of the white men see a lesson in that experience? And which reality was (is) the *real* reality? How that question is answered poses a dilemma for theorists who strive to practice science, not religion or magic or popular ideologies or the demagogue's craft.

Sociality is replete with conflicting, sometimes contradictory realities. I have just described some of them. The first set of examples, note, come from a part of society that we tend to set apart as superior to the whole of which it, science, is a part. That complicates matters for the theorist. I will come back to that problem of reality later. For the moment I want to emphasize again the problem of education. While technical details of this or that science—physics, chemistry, and so forth—can be a bit much for any non-specialist, a good grasp of the general framework of any physical science is not beyond the bounds of what we should expect of any competent citizen in a democracy. That adult will be expected to discriminate among politicians and other opinion leaders some of whom are always inclined to "do whatever it takes" to get elected. That "whatever" typically runs the gamut of means of manipulation, whether these are the means of a flagrant fraudster in the real-estate industry or a more sophisticatedly ethical stock seller in the banking or other segment of the financial industry. But citizens who are poorly educated have few or no resources by which to discriminate among claims and are thus among the most easily manipulated. The poorly educated are much more likely to be cheated, misled, pushed to the back of the line. Poor skills of various sorts are a proximate cause of much harm to individual persons and their families, harms that become an inheritable legacy. Their children are likely to follow in their footsteps into the realm of "the left behind." The multiplicities that confounded Walter Benjamin a century ago (as I described at the beginning of Part Two) have themselves been multiplied extensively, producing many new realities. Now, for instance, we have instruments that can see in the wave-length of radiant energy small enough to discriminate spatial features (e.g., "moving parts") not just of molecules but of atoms and parts of atoms, and give us image resolutions that are fast enough to discriminate movements, changes, of "moving parts" in femto-seconds—that is to say, in millionths of a billionth of a second. This enables us to watch the action of a biochemical altering the regulation of blood pressure in a human body, for example, or to observe the action of photosynthesis as cells of a plant convert sunlight into chemical energy. Who can understand this? Well, in fact many human beings do understand it, and use the knowledge (even if they, too, find the very idea of a femto-second impossibly fast). But a great many other human beings do *not* understand any of it, do not have adequate knowledge with which *to begin* to understand the technology, its uses, benefits and dangers. The fact of the matter is, huge numbers of human beings have been left behind in that way, and these failures of education have been accumulating over many decades, even centuries.

There is so much more to know, since the days when Newtonian physics was the last word, and the proportion of that growing body of knowledge that *is* learned *and* maintained in utilities of understanding has been shrinking at least as fast as the knowledge has grown. At roughly the same time educational institutions have been asked to do more and more for larger and larger proportions of children and young adults yet given less and less resource for accomplishing the task. What is more, whereas even one century ago the education that had been provided to a high-school graduate stood a good chance of being adequate, if only barely, to the average adult for the duration of that person's lifetime, this "steady-state" expectation has long since become unrealistic. Provisions for "continuing education" are even more pathetic than typical provisions for education to age 20 or 22.

Sensitivities have also changed since those halcyon days of Newton's physics. During his own century most peasants were ignorant of most things beyond immediate existence as a peasant. They knew they were ignorant, though exactly of what they seldom had more than an inkling, and they were in no position to protest with desired effect when the privileged few referred to them as "dumb animals" or worse. That condition was rather slow to change for most adults a century later, but as literacy increased and more peasants could read what was being said about them as a general class of people the grounds of resentment became clearer as a shared environment, one that could be seen as extending far beyond the local manor house. Today larger proportions of adult populations have a better understanding of their ignorances, including some rough idea of what they do not know (one of the effects of modern media of communication), and they are quicker to catch sight of the cynicism that is all too often on offer when they are told, in effect, that they are "too dumb to understand." Recall the Ike McCaslins of our world. Faulkner's character was a man of his time and place, of course, and that meant that he carried various—though, given time and place, partially predictable—sorts of ignorance, prejudice, and moral blindness in his head, in his mindful being. But within those bounds he usually wanted to do the right thing, and at least some of the time he thought that he knew what the right thing was (even if he accepted that not everyone would agree). Yet all too often his intentions just didn't work out for him. Ike might have suspected at times that he was "just too dumb to know how to get it right." But when a person supposedly in a position of local leadership says that to him, it might not sound like a fair description. When political leaders promise him a better world ahead in exchange for his vote at next election, but then his world fails to improve, perhaps worsens even more, the smell of cynicism could eventually become noticeable. One might ask, Why does "eventually" take so long? The question is understandable. And yet, where otherwise will he find at least the appearance of someone caring, even as the evidence of cynicism and fraud becomes unmistakable?

Resentments tend to solidify in an inertial sense of time as *empty*. An experience that "it doesn't matter what I do, nothing changes for the better, only for the worse" aggregates per-person identities into an identity of lacking efficacy, of being "out of time" in the sense of a disconnectedness, that one simply does not matter to anyone who could make a difference. The generational cycles can and do become recursively self-reinforcing, the opportunities for innovation afforded by recursion serving mainly to improve the odds of surviving in the midst of such poverty of means that *on average* the local rates of life expectancy and mortality are getting worse all around, while the most tenacious children manage to survive and occasionally escape to tell the story (e.g., Vance 2016; Smarsh 2018; Westover 2018; Orange 2018; Woolf and Schoomaker 2019; Case and Deaton 2020).

What happens next, within and from this inertial sense of empty time? While analytically the question can be treated as "multi-part," it is important to keep in mind that in the consciousness of resentment "parts" tend to blur into each other almost as if the subject who feels the experience has entered into a constantly turning kaleidoscopic consciousness, a blur of feelings that cannot be articulated in or as stable, distinctively patterned thoughts. The experience becomes overdetermined to such an extent that engaging from within it by an analytic perspective can easily seem pointless. With that in mind, it is evident that a part of the question involves a transfiguration of "empty time" from an emptiness that is internalized as guilt or shame, or some mixture of the two, into a nostalgia for a past future time of ambitions and aspirations that concealed inadequate capabilities by which to realize what would presumably just happen by dint of the ambition or the aspiration. In this aspect resentment is experienced primarily and mainly in psychologistic terms of personal worth, and in such terms the personal reflection tends to be a remorse of withdrawal and isolation, a remorse that might have begun in anger but soon spreads out into an inwardly focused accusation of "not good enough," with or without a projective/protective cover of victimhood. The "not good enough" is reflected as an effort that struggled against impossible odds in an unfairness of circumstances. In fact, a critical observer can see the realism of the first-person actor's pleading account, although the observer sees the nostalgic tinge where the first-person actor sees only or mainly a "reality pure and simple." This is the confusion, pain, sense of betrayal expressed in first-person perspective as the lament that "I followed in my parent's footsteps, it was good enough for them, why can't it be good enough

595

for *me*?" The transfiguration proves to be impotent—unable to release the plaintiff from his or her captivity in a past future time that was dying if not already dead on adoption.

The cultural, political, economic dimensions of a sociality still vary in their support for and promotion of psychologistic interpretative schemes as justificatory ideologies, to be sure. One main dimension of that variation is quantitative in a Simmelian sort of way: how much cross-sectional aggregation of interpreted events of a specific kind must occur before individual interpreters within that sociality change their points of view on their interpretive horizons, vanishing points, and rates of present-value discount, such that vanishing points on that horizon *and* the horizon as such can be seen as a "*group* phenomenon," not the phenomenon of an isolated individual?[617] It is here, thus, that individuals who feel resentful at having lost and been left behind ("through no lack of effort and will on my part") may eventually mobilize for action. Whether it is or becomes a "burn down the house" self-destructive action or an action having a better chance of achieving remediation and recovery is another question. If in fact the longstanding employment system does break down, as now seems probable, with no meaningfully effective replacement having been tested and enacted, we will likely see a massive "field experiment" enter the arena. That system had knitted together institutionalized organizations of work, some educational and retraining programs, investments in future health care and old-age security benefits, and the regulation of dispute settlements in several arenas. Far from perfect, with many cracks, lapses, and bureaucratic featherbedding, the system was nonetheless an effective agglomeration of services in support of millions of families present and future. Not only is little concerted effort being made to design inter-institutional replacements, most designful actions to date have been intended as further destruction of the system. What will replace the institution of work as a managerial organization of the energies of tens of millions of men and women as those energies, together with associated interests, ambitions, and feelings of having no purpose and of being unwanted, are no longer harnessed in and as the production of goods and services?

Another "part" of the "What next?" question will be realized (or not) in and as a realization that resentment's imaginary revenge (as in "burn down the house") can eventually consume most or all ambition of the deed in advance—and perhaps along with it the present distinction of empty time itself. Bourdieu (2000 [1997], p. 222) was a bit too late to be considered prescient for having alerted his readers to consequences of a collapse of the modern employment system, "the support, if not the source, of most interests, expectations, demands, hopes and investments in the present, and also in the future or the past that it implies." Social scientists have never been immune to ahistoricism in general or to the Whiggish version in particular. Social scientists other than economic historians can seem peculiarly vulnerable, however, on

---

[617] To take another illustration of artistic use of perspectival dimensions, think of the portrait painter who has learned the ability to paint eyes in such a way that a viewer, standing at a certain range of distance, feels that "those eyes follow me wherever I stand." Then it dawns on the viewer that the same "event" happens, at the same time, to every viewer in the room, whether one or many. Hence, a "group effect" has been formed by and in perspective, although a viewer who remains dominated by a psychologistic interpretive scheme might well miss that insight altogether and see only a "spooky action" unique to him or her.

matters of economic process. The employment system as we have known it—or, better, as we recall it from the memorial 1960s, 70s, and 80s—was of recent vintage. So, too, the capitalism of which it has been a prominent part, an industrial capitalism of the factory system.

Even though it was formulated by modifications of a template inherited from Christianity's churchly organization, *modern* capitalism has been as much a formation from and by industrial order as from and by bureaucracy. In 1530, the year Charles I of Burgundy became Charles V of the Holy Roman Empire, capitalism was still primarily an industry of extractive labor and mercantilism, but a range of manufactures did exist, and they extended well beyond military and naval armaments (see Parker 2019, pp. 353-379). Sales of weapons, armor, anchors, and grains were generally unrivalled as sources of revenue to the crown bureaucracy, until waves of silver and gold mined by indigenes of a New World stimulated the development of metallurgy in directions other than coinage. Land, minerals, and the bodies of labor were no doubt the principal forms of material capital and would remain so for some time to come. It is usually the case that profoundly innovative transformations of sociality are seen to be that mainly in retrospect, and this was true of sixteenth-century Europe. Not the century of René Descartes, it was prelude to it. The fact that Charles V continued to administer his own education after 1530 with entrepreneurial ambitions constituted a significant part of that prelude. By most measures China was still the leading nation in the world and would retain that standing in 1600, although Europe had been giving little heed. European expansions of territorial organization, global trade routes, and ambitions of technological innovation based in no small part on lessons being brought back from China would impel Europe into a new confidence of perspective at about the same time that China began to withdraw from contacts with their barbarians (Europeans chiefly among them).

"Capitalism in its various forms," Bourdieu (2000 [1997], p. 225) summarized late in his career—the prepositional extension presumably intended as a catch of temporal as well as spatial variants—"is a set of pre-emptive rights over the future." He was correct in that observation, too, but it is important to recognize that this use of "pre-emptive rights" to time did not in fact begin with capitalism—not, that is, unless Augustine, for instance, Saul-cum-Paul, and the "church fathers" during those intervening years count as early capitalists. It is difficult to conjure a large-scale institutional formation that has been more effective in staking claim to "pre-emptive rights over the future" (indeed, present and past as well) than the church of Christianity in all its various forms, including domination of calendar time (such that we count years of ancient Greek lives, for instance, in what amount to negative numbers). Regimes that are explicitly recognized as being totalitarian have never survived so long. May we expect that capitalism will relinquish its pre-emptive rights over time? Not in the foreseeable future, for its malleability to "necessary adjustments" has been nearly as remarkable as that of churchly Christianity during at least its first seventeen centuries.

It has been generally forgotten that nowhere in the books taken over by Christianity as an Old Testament will one read of Heaven and Hell. Some books of the New Testament come closer to it, although that approach was constituted primarily as actions by and within an institutionalizing church promulgating gospels attributed to Jesus decades after his probable year of death—indeed, after two centuries, in the case of the "Gospel according to Luke" (the most explicit and extensive of the four in making that attribution). The innovation was inspired, one might say, for it gave the church (i.e., *the* Church) enormous authority of managing relative risks of reward and punishment. It must have been extraordinary dullness of intellect or extraordinary loyalty to their (now "pagan") gods that caused Roman emperors to be so slow in adopting this armory of simple and inexpensive tools by which to shore up their own authority (as did Constantine, c312).

Because sociality is inherently furnished and bound by contingency and relativity, useful perspective always depends on comparisons for which no "absolute zero" is available. We have reasonably good evidence of the persistent insurrections against the Roman state by early Christian evangelists and proselytizers, who used their ability to convince downtrodden inhabitants of belief *in* this new sacred authority to very good advantage in recruitment of mundane forces. Some of that evidence is internal to the Christian New Testament itself; other, from writings of the early "church fathers." However, that history is not of particular relevance to my concern here. Rather, within present-day context a better comparison case is China, modern as well as ancient. This is primarily and mainly because Chinese thought never established the sort of hieratic organization of authority that joins "other-worldly authenticity" to "this-worldly" mundane interests in management of populations and their territories. On the one hand, this meant that great weight was loaded onto individual self-responsibility (a fact that takes on a patina of irony in view of the "western" stereotype of either a "selfless culture" or a "culture of over-conformity"). On the other hand, the same fact has accentuated the premium of a single, uniform authority as "central authority" in Chinese sociality, for it also increases vulnerability of that central authority to subtle, indirect forces of decay, along with all the usual more direct potential challenges, especially given the (historically variable yet always large) territorial size and ethnic diversity of the population traditionally nominated as "Chinese."

Mark Elvin, a specialist in Chinese history, has said that "the most overpowering contrast" of Chinese culture to European and Euro-American cultures is "the virtual absence in premodern China of the idea of a transparent creator God who is distinct from Nature in a fundamental qualitative sense" (Elvin 2004, p. xxiii). There is ample evidence behind Elvin's comparison, and it dates from more than 22 centuries ago. A Confucian scholar whose family name was Jia (born c200 BCE) and who became known to history as Jia Yi (Jia "the scholar") held that notions of a supernatural godhead were simply superstitions inherited from the dim past and would fall to dust as people became better educated. Mature human beings had no need of superstitious thinking at all.

Before proceeding to my destination with Jia, a brief digression for some context will be important. Various debates in the literatures concerning recent Chinese history—for instance, whether Daoism is a religion or a philosophy—have been conducted in terms of European and Euro-American categorizations, amounting thus to impositions on Chinese cultures. However, several scholars, Elvin among them, have demonstrated better sensitivity. Nearly half a century ago Richard Bush (1970, pp. 9-10) wrote of an "astounding fact of our time"—namely, that a nation-state accounting for a quarter of the planet's human beings exhibited "hardly a trace of religion as [Westerners] have known it." Note that he did not say "hardly a trace of religion." But the very idea of "religion" in the Western part of the world had been so heavily laden with specific choices and emphases for so long that the word could hardly be applied to "the three institutionalized teachings of Confucianism, Taoism, and Buddhism" (Bush 1970, pp. 20, 21; see also Bush 1977). Then, too, how should one understand the famous "May Fourth movement" (May 1919), which sought to root out all superstitions including those of "traditional religion"? Was this movement a genuine reflection of Chinese culture, or was it a reflection of "Western ideas" of enlightenment? Such questions had been provoking European and Euro-American theorists for more than a century to think critically, but only sometimes self-critically, about categorial contents and boundaries. Our record has not been a good one. Both Leibniz and then Hume were known among contemporaries for their interests in Chinese thought—all to the good—yet neither knew very much of Chinese history, hardly anything beyond what they were told by priests and religious scholars who had visited, in some instances had lived in, China.[618] More than a century after Hume Max Weber (1951 [1915]) wrote a treatise on Confucianism and Daoism that betrays his presumably good intents by too much absence of knowledge (see Yang 1961; Granet 1979 [1922]). If one prefers an excuse, it can be said in a back-handed way: at least Weber recognized an importance of China in world history and in a comparative study of forms of sociality, and it was not unusual in his time and place for a social scientist to rely on reports by traveling dignitaries, religious officials (usually missionaries), explorers, and sundry other persons who had registered seemingly intelligent accounts of "exotic" places. (Think of Durkheim, for instance, among others.) Ignorance of Chinese society and history was endemic in most centers of the Western academy until very recent decades.[619]

Of recent expositions, I have found François Jullien's (e.g., 1999 [1992]) to be among the most sensitive and insightful—in part, I think, because of all European cognitive-linguistic cultures French has greater affinity to the Chinese preference for indirection and subtlety (also see Elvin 1985, 1997, 2004). Vincent Gossaert and David Palmer (2011, p. 7) offered many good insights into the "massive changes and convulsions that have rocked, torn, and recomposed Chinese society" since 1900, as has William Rowe (e.g., Rowe 2001, 2007, 2009, 2018). Some of their best insights take the form of cautions: avoid the simplification of synoptic views, for instance, because their Western biases in favor of "either – or" oppositions will miss many most crucial of distinctions. But also be careful about conflations. Do not conflate "religion" and "morality," or "religion" and "theism" (Goosaert and Palmer 2011, pp. 10-11, 20-21, 26, 28-31, 51-52, 84, 87, 95-97, 226). The popular phrase "ancestor worship" is a Western concept that

---

[618] As Antognazza (2009, pp. 359-361) said, *Novissima Sinica* is only "a collection of documents and writings communicated to him during his correspondence with the Jesuit missionaries," plus Leibniz' preface. Some of the material does show effort to avoid a European ethnocentrism.
[619] I was first alerted to this fact during the 1960s when I briefly knew Roy Hofheinz (junior along with his father) in Texas. He described in considerable detail several biases in existing literatures—for instance, that "modernization" had never occurred in China and that Western social science faced the task of explaining the "failure," when in fact the metric of failure was merely a Western standard of what "modern" was supposed to look like. Beyond that bias, however, lay astounding ignorance: that China had no metropolitan areas, for instance, no industrial production, no centers of higher education, no science and technology, no modern medicine, no modern architecture, and so on. Hofheinz' work began to correct that ignorance. Later scholars (e.g., Rowe) still encountered it during the early 2000s, however.

conflates "worship" and "respect." A closer approximation is the respect shown to ancestral voices, burial grounds, and related interests of indigenous peoples of the Americas.

It is common in "the West" today to refer to China's "inland empire." While that phrase understandably grates on Chinese sensitivities, it is nonetheless reasonably well taken insofar as it refers to one ethnic group, the Han, as dominant over dozens of other ethnic groups who also have comprised "the Chinese people" over the centuries (and this remains consonant even if we exclude the sizeable numbers of Tibetan and Uighur peoples). From a Chinese standpoint, on the other hand, some peoples of "the West," the USA especially, should maintain a better self-awareness: European immigrants to the New World created inland empires through their own domination of indigenous peoples, in some instances practicing policies of extermination toward those peoples and confining survivals to "reserved lands" that are small fractions of mostly poor territories that dominant peoples were willing to relinquish. Moreover, some of those same immigrants of European ancestry quickly began the importation of enslaved peoples from Africa as chattels to work plantations in regions that experienced hot humid weather many months of the year. If any population most merits nomination as an "inland empire," therefore, people of European descent in the USA are surely a top contender.

Jia Yi is less often remembered in China today than in prior centuries, and my reading of that history notices a correlation between the remembrance of Jia Yi and the sense of confidence and security in civil authority. As the Scholar himself pointed out, the absence of a first-mover, over-arching deity who knows and controls everything leaves the burden of responsibility for all public security and well-being on the shoulders of human beings. In self-recognition of that load as well as in the interest of self-preservation, emperors generally cultivated an image of majestic presence that had some likeness to an other-worldly personal authority. During the post-dynastic regime of Mao Zedong this interest developed as a personality cult. For a time, in wake of the reforms by Deng Xiaopeng, it appeared that reliance on an unquestionable authority as had been practiced in that personality cult could be consigned to the dustbin.

If one travels about 65 miles on the S3 toll road northwest from Wuhan, Hubei province, one will come to Macheng, which is what in the USA would be called the seat of a county by the same name, also in Hubei. That county was the site of "seven centuries of violence in a Chinese county," the subtitle Rowe (2007) gave to his study of *Crimson Rain*. The historical record does paint a picture of so much flowing of human blood that the county could have been seen at times as a place where rains fell sticky and red. It would be mistaken to think of Macheng as a typical Chinese administrative unit, but it probably also was not wholly unique in proclivity for violence or in the fact that ethnic and religious enmities were among its deepest roots. Rowe made that case in great detail; and while reading his book, one is continually reminded of Jia the Scholar wondering whether purely human authority could ever be enough. Would the secularism of Confucian philosophy and bureaucratic organization suffice? Today, the question is, can *any* "purely human" civil authority ever overcome the "inland empires of the mind" known as this or that national group, this or that ethnic group, this or that religious group, and self-legislate future worlds of a purely human group? Jia's sensitivity to the issues was as finely tuned as any that can be read in surviving texts from ancient Greece or Rome.

Problems of an authority of voice intersect with, are complicated by, the reality problem, as already evidenced, and the intersections and complications must be managed somehow by any theorist of sociality (see Dahms 2011). It is hardly an insight of rare instance that most per-person actors, children being brought up as well as adults, are implicitly theorists of sociality whether they claim the standing or not. Most of them could be much better at it, but then so could the rest of us. Problems of educational quality are not uniformly distributed, to be sure, but credentials do not confer immunity. Judith Butler (1995) was correct to remind all of us that a theorist is included in the theory, even if lacking that self-awareness. This inclusion is not that of an automaton but within broad limits of choice which are partly physical but mainly conceptual and thoroughly social. Here I agree with Hume that both wants and will are determinative yet also determined at very least by one's own imagination and usually by interests of sociality as well, not that the difference is Cartesian other than by Cartesian analytics. Speaking-and-hearing, writing-and-reading depend on an authority of voice that is invoked in that activity but can be undermined as the disparity between what is spoken or written and what is heard or read lengthens enough to unsettle profoundly, if not so far as to advertise a madness that disqualifies an authority of its legitimacy. These are delicate dynamics. The delicacy does vary by condition of sociality. But Butler's main point generalizes even so, inasmuch as every sentient human being is in some manner and degree a theorist, which is to say simply a contriver of explanations of "how things are now" and perhaps "how they came to be as they are." Some are better at such contrivances than are others. Virtually all of us could be better at it than our present products testify. When teaching classes in, of, and about theory, I routinely offered that judgment, urging students to engage their talents, such as they might be, in order to improve them by acquiring better skills of logic, reasoning, the resources of language (at least native tongue but then also to expand by learning another in order to gain *that* perspective), so as to learn to see and denote one's hidden premises, presumptions, assumptions, and so forth, then to examine them critically for what they mean and what they do in reasoning about experiences.[620] The encouragement invariably brought up for inspection one or more versions of a reality problem, and the experience could dishearten those students who preferred that there be certain answers by standards of logical necessity. Where does one begin the exercise? What shall we adopt as premises to be taken for granted provisionally, in order to get the inquiry underway now rather than some later day? The role of teacher is thereby put at risk, and that is the first lesson of the exercise. The

---

[620] Similar encouragement was offered in courses on data analysis and statistics, pointing out that each student used a largely inherited classification, engaged in measurement even if crude, and continually sampled among possible, usually redundant, experiences, without much if any effort to investigate variations in a preliminary way. One cannot avoid classifying, measuring, sampling, and for that matter estimating correlations and other relational properties; and most of us can perform those tasks better and better, thus becoming better prepared for decisions. Unfortunately, whereas my early lecture about "every person a theorist" seemed to register rather well, the corresponding lecture about methodology seemed to misfire, lacking desired effect. The rate of misfiring increased over the years, perhaps in concert with the point of Rodgers' (2011, p. 39) conclusion that "[t]he recession of the social echoed the shrinking prestige of sociology" (the discipline within which my curriculum was housed). As the discipline relinquished more and more of what had been its domain a century ago, its attraction of students diminished.

same can be said of the exercise of the many preceding pages of reading (insofar as that activity ever actually got underway).

In 2008, years before the 2016 presidential election in the USA, Farhad Manjoo alerted his readers that reality had been rapidly fragmenting into many different realities. One might rebut by invoking the distinction of *"experienced* reality"—not that reality as such has fragmented but that the ways in which persons experience it have become increasingly fragmented into divergent views. The urgency of Manjoo's question asks, however, "What is the difference?" Granted, variation in experience has long existed, but there was nonetheless a strong basin of attraction in the distribution of that variation, such that at any given time a large majority of adults held to a single, relatively uniform and stable understanding. The difference now is mainly that new communication technology has democratized authority of voice at least to the extent that now, rather than a handful of voices acting as "opinion leaders" who moderate differences in "point of view," dozens, hundreds, even thousands of divergent voices have broadened the span of views that can be, and are, broadcast into all the nooks and crannies of what used to be called "mass reception" and "mass audience" but have now evolved into "mirror sites" that add still more variation to the messages, yet at the same time tend to sort the messages into "silos" of like-minded persons. Manjoo's question is of urgent concern for a number of reasons, but the main reason lies in another form of the same question—namely, are most adults capable enough to manage results of that democratization? Or, in different idiom, are they now faced with "too many choices" in this marketplace as well? (see Schwartz 2004; also Arrow 1963; Hazelrigg 1986, 1993a). This raises again the problem of education and consequent capabilities of the average adult. Manjoo's concern about fracturing is not a new one. Similar concerns were being expressed during the 1840s, for example, then during the 1850s, the 1860s, the 1870s, and so on, well into the twentieth century. There are some differences, however. Fractures that could end in a rupture of the union among the fifty states are readily apparent and could yet achieve that result. But there is another danger that could overtake the threat of rupture—namely, consequences of climate change. The reality of climate change could easily become the reality that has no human future. If the current and projected future human population continues to be distributed geographically as at present, about one-third of all humans in 2070 will live in areas in which the mean annual temperature will be 30 degrees Celsius (86 degrees Fahrenheit) or higher than at present. That implies summer highs greater than humans can tolerate without the protection of coolant technologies in vast regions of the planet, regions which already struggle to supply such protection. Where will all of those people go? Those who can will migrate. Many of those who cannot will probably die, a fact that will increase feelings of desperation among survivors. In another fifty years the panic will be still greater, affecting much larger parts of the planet. And the lethal effects of climate change will have only begun.

In Part Two I invoked Stanley Cavell's (2004, p. 379) insight that voice presents a "nonnegotiable demand for recognition." That came on the heels of my observation, drawing on Kant's proposal of a "categorical imperative," that the legislative act, which figures importantly in his critique of practical reason and his assay of the power of judgment, spontaneously enacts its own dependence on an anticipation of that which is to be legislated. The anticipation amounts to a voice of Kantian hope, moreover, insofar as it speaks of that which has never before been experienced, no matter how tentative its current vision. What we must now understand also is that this mission has become all the more demanding of per-person skills of understanding and judgment. For now, prior to the feasibility of any formally considered legislative action, a "pre-legislative legislation" can no longer be taken for granted but must be achieved anew, constituting again a community of hearers who are mutually agreed or agreeable enough to address simultaneously one relatively uniform proposal of new formal legislation. That task has itself become more and more difficult. Achen and Bartels (2016, p. 277) made the case that in this new normalization of public discourse there is seldom a current majority to form such a community of hearers who are *capable* of that "pre-legislative legislative act," and anyone who has been paying close attention must search very persistently to find even shreds of evidence against their case: "the sheer magnitude of most people's ignorance about politics" has been confirmed in electoral outcomes so often that one could conclude it is a perverse combination of ignorance and quest for "the end," annihilation. Can one think of a greater, a more urgent, illustration of the failure of education, a failure at the very core of how we have been producing citizens—indeed, healthy *persons*—in this society? We as a society have been massively failing to assure that next cohorts of adults have gained "the educational prerequisites for democratic citizenship" (Dunn 2000, p. 269). Social scientists have been complicit in that failure. We are complicit, for example, every time we affirm a gender discrimination that says women are not good at math because they were born female, that men are not good at caring and nurturance because they were born male. The list goes on. It is all too easy to conclude that many political leaders are content to "keep them ignorant; it's easier to manipulate them, practice the bezzle in all its varieties, maintain our birthright advantages."

Voices and their audiences, present and prospective, are seldom independent of institutional channels, and those channels tend to be self-serving and reflective by intent. Note that variance in that dependence is not uniform: I suspect that it is greater in institutions of politics and religion than in education or work, and usually skewed to the negative. Cavell's voice, for example, did not lack timbre, was never empty of good message, yet could rarely be heard beyond the venues of higher education. Is that bounded dispersion indicative of a demoralization of potential audience, or of increasing derangements of sociality since Cavell and similar other voices began speaking? Or is it indicative simply of an irrelevance in today's world? In any case, one sees failure of education still again, a failure to teach potential audiences to hear together, to know how to generate community of hope for betterment together—the centerpiece, in other words, in all of Cavell's intent of message. Granted, it has become more difficult for education to compete with ever-new entertainments in that growing sector of service industry and business, where illiteracy and innumeracy can be so easily camouflaged by an iconic messaging that requires little or no skill in filtering signal from noise, especially as noise itself becomes just another signal. At the least, messaging is smeared across even the barest of views and soundscapes, all converted into entertainments that demand nothing more than the price of entry—which, even aside from skills of piracy, tends to zero when the mere presence of medium has replaced need of any other messaging. Perhaps the titans of industry and commerce believe that, as the employment system rots away, the masses of persons left behind can be sufficiently tethered to the institutionalized reality of entertainments such as Reality TV (recall Terry Gilliam's 1985 film, *Brazil*, the middle panel of his triptych; see Hazelrigg 2020).

The bite of literary works by Sheila Heti (born 1976) and Nell Zink (born 1964)—to take two as representative of many more—reflects an art form that evinces Cavell's point about a demand for recognition, especially as the art form has been struggling to retain some freshness when so much of the world about those authors and the rest of us has become extraordinarily decrepit and decayed through a few of the oldest, simplest forms of corruption. Imagine through the experiences of these novelists the prospects of present-day theorists of the social sciences. John Dunn (2000, pp. 60, 269, 299) reminded us at the start of this century that theorists—he was referring specifically to political theorists, especially the sort who try to promote an intelligence of civics functions, but the same could be said of that sort of theorist in all sister disciplines of the social sciences—that our theorists have repeatedly demonstrated that they "simply [do] not have a clue" how either to respond to or to avoid the many "disagreeable facts" of corruption, brutality, cowardice, cruelty, and the like, all of which have acquired the allures of "show business," the fancy of becoming a celebrity for *being* a celebrity. This is the teeter of a generalized irony made into a "funhouse" reality of realities (Barth 1968).

But writers such as Heti and Zink do apprehend, even if only "vaguely," that admitting as much in public might prove disabling of their craft. Heti (2010) perused youthful experiences rich in feelings of uncertainty, confusion, and drift, all in service to urgent inquiries into "how should a person be" within sight of future times that might hold clues to recognizable developments of "own self" vis-à-vis "others," yet seeing so little to hold onto in the midst of still more contradiction and uncertainty. Much like Heti's update of a "coming of age" story, Zink's (2019) brave effort to tell a coherent story of incoherence across broken patches of what might be meanings—her latest (or the last I have read) of the short sequence of novelistic explorations of her life and times—carries as its title, *Doxology*. The choice is an acidic admiration for what now seems to so many to have been a simpler, more secure era of belief, *popular* belief, which is if nothing else an advertisement of ties in sociality. The difference being this: then, most of the populace believed *in* the belief pleasantly, thoroughly enough, that the songs of praise (the ecclesiastical "doxology") washed them clean of doubt and worry at least once a week; now, most of the populace are simply unable to abide by their own responsibility for those same corruptions and brutalities and all of the cowardice and cruelty that would be blatantly indicting were it not for the shows of celebrity celebrating celebrity. [621] Think of songster Beck's breakout hit of 1993, "Loser": careless words, neither pretending nor in search of a coherence. Different forms of truth, or different forms of ignorance? Or, rather, a dialectic of cruelty/cowardice? Dunn (2000, ch. 5) reminded us also of Kant's third step toward the legislative act: once reason and experience have done the work they can do, one is left to make a judgment, to decide; and this act is an aesthetic exercise, an act of critical perception informed by, rarely dictated by, reason and experience. Such self-responsibility has become too demanding. Nietzsche's slave morality did not die. (Another failure of education.)

---

[621] Before Christianity the ancient Greek word, doxa, meant "opinion" or "expectation" (and, depending on context, "good opinion" or "estimation" of a thing or event or person), a meaning that carries through to the Latin "paradox" (from the Greek paradoxon, "contrary opinion"), a belief or opinion that is or appears to be contrary to common belief or opinion.

An authority of voice can still haunt, however. As recently pointed out by Amitav Ghosh (2016, p. 23), a novelist today must face "the irony of the 'realist' novel: the very gestures with which it conjures up reality are actually a concealment of the real." His insight can be applied in a variety of ways having to do with the dynamics of a readerly text under the everyday sign of modern society. Writing oneself as a scandal is surely not a newly invented device to draw more readers into one's story. Augustine knew the hook well, as he wrote his confessions. (Redemption would not be the same without it.) But the device has become less and less effective than it was in the days of, say, Oscar Wilde. It has always been incumbent on a writer never to get too far ahead of intended readers when crafting a new or even partly recycled imaginary world, and this remains good advice. Measuring distances in a calculus of probability has become more complex, however. To draw on Ghosh again, even the best of fictionists today "would be faced with the Borgesian task of reproducing [a] *world in its entirety*" (p. 23, emphasis added) but for the fact that readers can still be captivated by careful "scaffolding of exceptional moments." A writer must be deft in inventing the moment but even more deft in following some trajectory of events *from* as well as in some sense *within* it. Not too fast, not too far, lest the reader balk: "No, this is just *too* improbable; it could never happen that way." The irony is that ever more highly improbable events *have* been happening, at seemingly faster clip, outside the novel's story, sometimes with consequences that are indeed difficult to believe: "how could that happen in *this* day and age?!" Has anyone undertaken a history of events so improbable that one hears spectators exclaiming, "If this were in a novel, no one would believe it"? (Ghosh 2016, p. 24). How does one today make sense of any notion of a reciprocity between "art imitating life" and "life imitating art"?

Thus, we have never left the intersection at which so much is knitted together as one huge challenge: the challenge of education, one's own as teacher along with the education of nominal pupils, cannot be separated from an authority of voice. The question raised by Marx and repeated by Dunn (2000, p. 298)—Who educates the educator?—is not, never can be, a question that exists outside a sociality. The circularity of reflexion, of recursion, of replication, is undeniably present, but this need not mean that the same center, radius, and circumference must be repeated over and over. The odds are that it rarely if ever would be repeated over and over; for, as previously said, the opportunities of innovation, planned and unplanned, are too numerous for such constancy to occur even if attempted. Rather, the key point is, a perspective of productivity that is self-consistent in being at one stroke epistemological, ethical, and aesthetic depends both on one or another filter-and-update regimen and on well-considered anticipations of a sequence of betterments. The legislative act, whether imagined via the enormous rigor of Kant's standard—his categorical imperative: act as if the will of thy action would become universal law—or in the rather more modest pragmatism of average foresight and discipline, demands to be recognized, along with an authority of voice. But potential audiences have often been educated to other ends, with other intents, in other realities. The educational task has become much larger, still more difficult. I keep as lodestone the point Marx stressed in his eleventh thesis on Feuerbach: as expressed by Zeynep Tufekci (2017, p. 277), "we make our path, questioning as we go along." But whose questions are we asking, and to whose ends and benefit?

The juncture at which I have from the beginning of my journey engaged Kant, Marx, and Nietzsche in a vicarious mutual conversation is centered in what previously I have called a "utopist impulse" (see, e.g., Hazelrigg 1989b). I now add that I have meant also throughout these present hundreds of pages to echo Pierre Bourdieu, as he (1990 [1982], p. 198) said before an august body of the Collège de France, "Nothing is less cynical, less Machiavellian ... than these paradoxical statements which announce or denounce the very principle of the power which they exercise." An ethic that must ground its highest principles in a presupposition of saints and sinners has no useful application of guidance or resolve, only repression and the hypocrisy of demagoguery. Surely we are now well beyond a surfeit of demagogues, are we not? The theorist as educator must learn to do better.

For a theorist authority of voice is now challenged, more seriously than ever before, by and through our failures of education. Are those of us who have been called upon to educate— and the number includes each and every parent at least; yet also, by a principle of sociality, each and every adult in sight and/or sound of a child—are we without responsibility for the failures? Does one need to have a formal credential in order to discern educational failure? Recall one's fellow student in seventh grade, for instance, whose efforts to penetrate the mysteries of basic linear algebra failed to discriminate dynamics of the obstacle enough to gain even the slightest imagination of remedial tactics. Did one not have an obligation of civic mutuality toward that person? Recall one more time Arlie Russell Hochschild's (2016) recent mix of vignettes of individual persons each of whom could be accounted another "ordinary theorist who got left behind": her reportage suggested that we receive and understand her vignettes with a healthy measure of empathy, just as Faulkner (1994 [1942]) had proposed toward Isaac McCaslin, among other of his "fictitious" characters. Most of Hochschild's characters were poor materially and in learning; some of them probably had been born into poverty or near-poverty. Shall we express our empathy by herding them into Scott Sandage's (2005) corral of those nineteenth-century adults whom credit agencies and similar other judges had branded "born losers"? How do we square those "failures" with the experience of another child of the nineteenth century, Charles William Eliot (1834-1926)?

Eliot was not born into poverty. He was educated at Harvard. He ascended to become the president of his alma mater in 1869, and he thereafter was instrumental in the conversion of what had been little more than a genteel finishing school for young men of elite families into a prototype of the new intellectually entrepreneurial university that the very name, "Harvard," connoted during the next hundred years. And yet, by Daniel Rodgers' (1974, pp. 233-240) clear-eyed and respectful vignette of the man, we can discern another person countable as an ordinary theorist who, although propelled by his comparatively very fast start into high advantages of family, education, employment, and local community, also joined the collectivity known as "the left behind," despite having done all the right things, just as Ike McCaslin had done in Mississippi. Does Eliot merit some portion of Hochschild's graceful empathy?

Shortly after Charles Eliot was born, the near-sacred godfather of North American faith in a transcendentalism, Ralph Waldo Emerson (1983 [1841], p. 267), instructed his sizable audience that an institution could be the work of a single individual person (or man) alone: "An institution is the lengthened shadow of one man," Emerson said, and his pronouncement has been one of the claims on history by which he is most remembered. Whether Eliot thought of himself as such a man I do not know. It is clear that toward the end of the nineteenth century he was widely regarded as such, a premier exemplar of his own professed faith in this "self-reliant, self-made man." His credentials at Harvard conferred much presence, of course, and he knew how to convert that presence into more than any ordinary authority of voice. Eliot became—and this, clearly, in his own eyes, too—a good deal more than any "run of the mill" theorist. No less than Henry James produced a two-volume biography of Eliot, and one can easily imagine that Emerson would have nodded from his grave the gratuity of pinning Eliot's name to the Emersonian scroll of one-man institutions.

Well before the end of that century, however, Eliot noticed that the world out and about had been changing. The personal genius of craft was giving way to an industrial-labor organization of the process of production. Born of an elite family descended of an immigrant from Somerset during the 1670s, Eliot's first-learned boyhood experiences were of the liberal professions (clergy, teacher, law, physician, etc.), along with the craftwork of farmers and produce markets, smiths and mongers, cobblers and saddlers, spinners and weavers, shopkeepers, and so forth. Most of that daily tableau had been comforted within the arc of an almost-puritan work ethic. Thus began Charles Eliot's own induction into not only a requisite sociality of a "self-reliance of the individual" but also an aesthetic and ethic of "the joy of work." That phrase became something of a dictum to Eliot. His "quest for joyful labor," as Rodgers (1974, p. 233) called it, looked more and more out of touch with the actual everyday experiences of work, as labor-time was transformed by a different clock.

It is abundantly clear that Eliot understood the fact of that difference, even as he struggled to understand the correlative contradictions within his *own* situation, his livelihood as president of an increasingly influential university. The moral code by which he had theorized the ethic of work was becoming increasingly abstract, not because he was aware that the code itself had changed—it was *his* code, after all, and he knew its integrity against challenges—but because his campaign to recover the joy of work was addressed to an audience and conditions that had been disappearing despite his mission.[622] Here, then, another everyday theorist was also being left behind, while his public status remained high and lucrative at least in material register. Here too, then, a "problem of reality" to compare with the one (assuming it was sufficiently uniform to count as only one) that Hochschild (2016) highlighted among industrial workers a century later. But Eliot's life illustrates still another.

About midway through his first chapter Eric Griffiths (1989) highlighted a lesson that each theorist must learn, not once but repeatedly as conditions change. This I will call a dialectic of rich promise and rich problem. It is always on offer with the printed voice. Think of the link that must be negotiated between uses by a performer and uses by a musicologist of the ambiguity evident in virtually any musical score: the performer has the advantage of feeling free to create

---

[622] Rodgers (1974, p. 240) cited an earlier observer of habits of disconnect between a way of talking and a way of acting, a disconnect that could have been obvious to at least parts of his audience (see also Thomas 1997, pp. 149-151). That disconnect—talking one way but acting another—is another description of McGuire's (1989) conclusion from scholarly research: attitude is generally a poor predictor of behavior.

where the musicologist feels obligated to explicate the truth of what is already there on the sheet. Guarantees there may be. But they come with very short half-lives; for during their interval the imperfections, the fallibilities, *and* the potentials invite elucidation by the very next performer. This lesson was evident in Hume's account of the relation of reason and experience, theory and practice, deduction and induction. Kant took it to heart. A theorist today must do likewise— indeed, as never before. Doing so will not garner a Nobel Prize, as did Oliver Hart's and Bengt Holmström's repackaging of the lesson that a perfect contract can never be written (see Hart 2017). It is a mistake, however, to think that this version of the lesson tells anything new about what counts as science and what does not (see, e.g., Offer and Sönderberg 2016). The ground of that debate disappeared long ago, even though news of the funeral has travelled very slowly. (Another failure of education? Or the same one?)

Charles Eliot's intermittent struggle to understand present circumstances of his society, his time and place, as they were being revealed in reports from outside the academy involved effort to negotiate and renegotiate his own past and present, his futures past and his futures present. Some of that effort transpires willy nilly, noticed or not, as memory functions in first-person experience and in a local sociality continue in and as the on-goingness of that sociality. The harder part of effort, however, harder usually because of resistances felt but not always cognized, easily dissolves into the taken-for-granted inertial sink of habit, as a given person's sense of efficacy is mainly reinforced through the filter-and-update windows of abstractive condensation. Normally one maintains a sense of personal efficacy even while losing effectivity in the world. But when that loss grabs self-consciousness, one can sink into despair, demoralization, and worse—all the more easily when the local sociality has reserved a room in the inn, compliments of teachers, parents, and others.

Theorists must learn to be better at these very difficult tasks of education. Recall Arendt's (1977) discussion of the mental *activity* of thinking: the chain of one's prior thoughts and their prior conditions fall heavily on one's present thinking, the *nunc stans* of one's reflections of, on, and in a world beyond the doorstep, the doorstep of one's mind. No matter how assiduously one scrutinizes experiences of the "beyond" that is implicit promise of theorizing, there necessarily remains to the activity of thinking a doubt, an inescapable uncertainty of the object of thought and *its* existence. Conviction that one *has* grasped that existence is always elusive (except by facile closure). There are useful options of what was once called "participant observation" (as if a special technique, as if any one of us is not already that). Or, more: of "passing," for example, of "going native," and similar "subterfuges." These activities might indeed bring one into new experiences and perhaps thereby new insights, but they are couched within a realization that one is a visitor. Understood in general as "content" of one's first-person experience, the *is* of sensation is always transitory, bordering on the ephemeral, such that in a moment of reflection one's thinking *of* some strip of that experience, or thinking about the experience of first-person experience as such, can have a stability and persistence of presence of the real that exceeds what "must have been" the momentary real itself. Or is it the other way around? To recall Hegel's (1971 [1830], §465) famous aphoristic recognition that "The intelligence [which "is recognitive"] knows that what is *thought*, *is*, and that what *is*, only *is*

608

insofar as it is a thought,"[623] Arendt (1977, p. 198) then brought her reader up short with this: "all such doubts [about which is which, and which is first] disappear as soon as the theorist's solitude is broken in upon and the call of the world and our fellow-men changes the inner duality of the two-in-one into a One again." The "rescue" is not guaranteed. Neither God nor Nature, nor yet again some other dictator of demagoguery, will save us. And those UFO visitors? Why would they? This is only one planet.

Arendt's scenario was, bear in mind, almost exactly two centuries after Kant's exposure of the transcendental Illusion. As Robert Pippin well knows—otherwise he would have seen no purpose in writing some of his books (e.g., Pippin 1997, 1999, 2005)—very few adults understand what that was about, and therefore why it was, and still is, of such importance. The larger part of what transpires in today's institutional realm of education is still keyed to a world that has as much or more in common with the end of the nineteenth century than with the current century. Most of today's public discourse still pretends its anchorage in a rhetoric of constant certitudes, presuming a knowledge of timeless truths. Given that the apparent guarantee of certitude and necessity has dissolved, however, what can be the solid bedrock, the immovable stanchion? The answer is, as it always has been, judgment, an act of legislating next steps. Is that enough for the average person in this society, in any other society? A theorist must engage in the midst of uncertainty and contingency, not in some magical reality, and stories issued from the engagement must acknowledge the uncertainty and contingency. That means negotiating an irony that is common to science but not to magical, religious, or demagogic thinking: science encourages skepticism even as ignorance of science encourages skepticism toward claims of knowledge in and as science (see, e.g., Watkins 1984).

Harrison White (1992) was correct to put some emphasis on storytelling, on the stories that we tell about ourselves and our world(s) in order to feel confident and secure in our skins. Is it possible to achieve that confidence and security, when the stories are acknowledged to be what in fact they are, stories written by human beings? When the stories carry obvious fingerprints, are they thereby disqualified from credibility? Must (as demagogues love to preach) the average adult be dependent on stories that must be believed *in* (to recall again the distinction illustrated by Paul Veyne 1988 [1983])? I am repeating myself, I acknowledge. I am repeating the question, with text I have already used, because it is now perhaps *the single most important question* that we as a species face. I do not know the answer. I cannot confidently guess what the answer will prove to be, perhaps prove to have been all along. I am confident, however, that if the answer is, will prove to be, that *we*—not just many of us but the vast majority of us—cannot accomplish that feat of self-confidence in responsibility, then we as a species are surely doomed to extinction. And in that process we could easily destroy this planet's capability to host any life forms higher than slimes and scums, prions, viruses, and bacteria; maybe tardigrades, maybe some species of insect. If we are lucky, we might yet save the planet by saving ourselves.

A "utopist impulse" is, always has been, an aspirational consciousness, much like Kant's hope for humankind, Marx' point in his eleventh thesis, and Nietzsche's critique both of a slave morality and the advice from Delphi. Ghosh's (2016) report of a Great Derangement joins a long

---

[623] "… was *gedacht* ist, ist; und was *ist, ist* nur, insofern es Gedanke ist."

line of similar reports of concern and doubt about the ability of our species to avoid self-destruction (e.g., Wallace-Wells 2019). As stated in the pages above, I have been discussing both in print and orally the evolving current conditions by which that concern and doubt have gained increasing force of conviction. The effort has had little if any beneficial effect, as best I can tell. I am less hopeful today than I was thirty years ago. The prospects for Homo sapiens as a surviving species do not look good. The immediate prospects for a humanity of which we can be proud are even worse.

~~~~

# Bibliography

Aarsleff, Hans. 1967. *The Study of Language in England, 1780-1850*. Princeton: Princeton University Press.

Abbattista, Guido. 2001. "The English *Universal History*." *Storia della Storiographia* 39: 100-105.

Abbott, Andrew. 1999. *Department and Discipline*. Chicago: University of Chicago Press.

_____. 2001. *Time Matters*. Chicago: University of Chicago Press.

_____. 2009. Review of Young 1958. *American Journal of Sociology* 115: 322-326.

_____. 2016. *Processual Sociology*. Chicago: University of Chicago Press.

_____, and Alexandra Hrycak. 1990. "Measuring resemblance in sequence data." *American Journal of Sociology* 96: 144-185.

Abel, Jaison R, and Richard Dietz. 2019. "Despite rising costs, college is still a good investment." *Liberty Street Economics*. New York: F R B of New York.

Acemoglu, Daron, and James A Robinson. 2012. *Why Nations Fail*. London: Polity.

Achen, Christopher H, and Larry M Bartels. 2016. *Democracy for Realists*. Princeton: Princeton University Press.

Ackerman, Bruce. 2010. *The Decline and Fall of the American Republic*. Cambridge: Harvard University Press.

Acton, Peter. 2014. *Poiesis*. Oxford: Oxford University Press.

Adam, David. 2019. "Psychology's reproducibility solution fails first test." *Science* 364 (21 May): 813.

Adams, John. 2008. *Hallelujah Junction*. New York: Farrar, Straus & Giroux.

Adams, Nicholas. 2019. *Gordon Bunshaft and SOM*. New Haven: Yale University Press.

Adorno, Theodor W. 1973 (1964). *The Jargon of Authenticity*. Trans. Knut Tarnowski and Frederic Will. Evanston, IL: Northwestern University Press.

_____. 1973 (1966). *Negative Dialectics*. Trans. E B Ashton. New York: Continuum.

_____. 1976 (1957). "Sociology and empirical research." Pp. 68-86 in *The Positivist Dispute in German Sociology*, edited by Theodor W Adorno, et al. Trans. Glyn Adey and David Frisby. London: Heinemann.

_____. 1982 (1956). *Against Epistemology*. Trans. Willis Domingo. Oxford: Basil Blackwell.

_____. 1991 (1958). "In memory of Eichendorff." Pp. 55-79 in *idem, Notes to Literature*, volume 1. Ed. Rolf Tiedemann; trans. Shierry Weber Nicholsen. New York: Columbia University Press.

_____. 1997 (1970). *Aesthetic Theory*. Trans. Robert Hullot-Kentor. Minneapolis: University of Minnesota Press.

_____. 2001 (1995). *Kant's* Critique of Pure Reason. Trans. Rodney Livingstone; ed. Rolf Tiedemann. Cambridge: Polity.

_____. 2006 (1969). *Philosophy of New Music*, 5th edition. Trans. Robert Hullot-Kentor. Minneapolis: University of Minnesota Press.

_____. 2008 (2003). *Lectures on Negative Dialectics*. Ed. Rolf Tiedemann; trans. Rodney Livingstone. Cambridge: Polity.

_____, Hans Albert, Ralf Dahrendorf, Jürgen Habermas, Harald Pilot, Karl R Popper. 1976 (1969). *The Positivist Dispute in German Sociology*. Trans. Glyn Adey and David Frisby. New York: Harper & Row.

Agamben, Giorgio. 1993 (1978). *Infancy and History: Essays on the Destruction of Experience*. Trans. Liz Heron. London: Verso.

Agerberg, Mattias. 2018. "The curse of knowledge?" *Political Behavior*, online 15March; doi.org/10.1007/s1109-018-9455-7.

Ahl, Valerie, and Timothy F H Allen. 1996. *Hierarchy Theory*. New York: Columbia University Press.

Aiewsakun, Pakorn, and Aris Katzourakis. 2016. "Time-dependent rate phenomenon in viruses." *Journal of Virology* 90 (August): 7184-7195.

Ainslie, George. 1992. *Picoeconomics*. Cambridge: Cambridge University Press.

Alatas, Vivi, Abhijit Banerjee, Arum G Chandrasekhar, Rema Hanna, and Benjamin A Olken. 2016. "Network structure and the aggregation of information." *American Economic Review* 106: 1663-1704.

Albani, Paolo, and Berlinghiero Buonarroti. 1994. *Aga Magéra Difúra*. Bologna: Zanichelli.

Alvarez, Doris, and Hugh Mehan. 2006. "Whole-school detracking." *Theory into Practice* 45: 82-89.

Alexander, Jeffrey C., Bernhard Giesen, Richard Münch, and Neil J Smelser (eds.). 1987. *The Micro-Macro Link*. Berkeley: University of California Press.

Alexander, Karl. 2016. "Is it family or school?" *RSF Journal* 2 (September): 18-33.

_____, Doris Entwisle, and Linda Olson. 2014. *The Long Shadow*. New York: Russell Sage Foundation.

_____, and Stephen Morgan. 2016. "The Coleman Report at fifty." *RSF Journal* 2 (September): 1-16.

Alexievich, Svetlana. 2016 (2013). *Secondhand Time*. Trans. Bela Shayevich. New York: Random House.

Allen, Amy. 2016. *The End of Progress*. New York: Columbia University Press.

Allen, Garland E. 2005. "Mechanism, vitalism and organicism in late nineteenth and twentieth-century biology." *Studies in History and Philosophy of Biology, Part C* 36: 261-283.

Allison, Henry E. 2008. *Custom and Reason in Hume*. Oxford: Oxford University Press.

_____. 1973. *The Kant-Eberhard Controversy*. Baltimore: Johns Hopkins University Press.

Alston, William P. 1993. *The Reliability of Sense Perception*. Ithaca: Cornell University Press.

Anderson, Philip W. 1972. "More is different." *Science* 177 (4 August): 393-396.

_____. 2011. *More and Different*. Hackensack, NJ: World Scientific.

_____, Kenneth J Arrow, and David Pines (eds.). *The Economy as an Evolving Complex System*. Boulder, CO: Westview.

Andrabi, Tahir, Jishnu Das, Asim Ijaz Khwaja, and Tristan Zajonc. 2011. "Do value-added estimates add value?" *American Economic Journal: Applied Economics* 3: 29-54.

Antognazza, Maria Rosa. 2009. *Leibniz*. Cambridge: Cambridge University Press.

Antonio, Robert J. 2000. "After postmodernism." *American Journal of Sociology* 106: 40-87.

Apel, Karl-Otto. 1962. Review of Arnold Gehlen's "Philosophie der Institutions." *Philosophische Rundschau* 10 (1-2): 1-21.

Appiah, Kwame Anthony. 2018. *The Lies that Bind*. New York: Liveright.

Arendt, Hannah. 1977, 1978. *The Life of the Mind*, 2 volumes. Ed. Mary McCarthy. New York: Harcourt Brace Jovanovich.

Arendt, Hannah. 1998. *The Human Condition*, 2nd edition. Chicago: University of Chicago Press.

Aristotle. 350 BCE. *On Metaphysics*. Trans W D Ross.

Aristotle. *On Politics*.

Aristotle. *On Rhetoric*.

Arnold, Matthew. 1869. *Culture and Anarchy*. London: Smith, Elder and Company.

Arrow, Kenneth. 1963. *Social Choice and Individual Values*, 2nd edition. New York: Wiley.

Arthur, W Brian. 1994. *Increasing Returns and Path Dependence*. Ann Arbor: University of Michigan Press.

Ashenfelter, Orley, and Alan B Krueger. 1994. "Estimates of the economic return to schooling from a new sample of twins." *American Economic Review* 84: 1157-1173.

Ashmore, Malcolm. 1989. *The Reflexive Thesis*. Chicago: University of Chicago Press.

Auerbach, Erich. 1953 (1946). *Mimesis*. Trans. Willard R Trask. Princeton: Princeton University Press.

Augustine of Hippo. 1994 (post-410). *Sermons 273-305A*. Trans. Edmund Hill. Hyde Park, NY: New City.

_____. 1998 (c400). *Confessions*. Trans. Henry Chadwick. Oxford: Oxford University Press.

_____. 1998 (426). *On the City of God against the Pagans*. Trans. R W Dyson. Cambridge: Cambridge University Press.

Austen, Jane. 1933. *The Novels of Jane Austen*. 5 volumes, 3rd edition. Ed. R W Chapman. Oxford: Oxford University Press.

Austin, John L. 1962. *How To Do Things with Words*. Oxford: Clarendon.

Averill, James R. 1983. "Studies on anger and aggression." *American Psychologist* 38: 1145-1160.

Axelrod, Robert. 1984. *The Evolution of Cooperation*. New York: Basic Books.

Azoulay, Pierre, Christian Fons-Rosen, and Joshua S Graff Zivin. 2019. "Does science advance one funeral at a time?" *American Economic Review* 109: 2889-2920.

Azoulay, Vincent. 2014 (2010). *Pericles of Athens*. Trans. Janet Lloyd. Princeton: Princeton University Press.

Babbage, Charles. 1835. *On the Economy of Machinery and Manufacturers*, 4th edition. London: Charles Knight.

Bachvarova, Mary. 2016. *From Hittite to Homer*. Cambridge: Cambridge University Press.

Bagehot, Walter. 1867. *The English Constitution*. London: Chapman and Hall.

Bailey, Issac J. 2018. *My Brother Moochie*. New York: Other Press.

Bakewell, Charles Montague. 1908. *Sources in Ancient Philosophy*. London: T Fisher Unwin.

Baldi, Pierre. 2001. *The Shattered Self*. Cambridge: MIT Press.

Baldick, Chris. 1987. *In Frankenstein's Shadow*. Oxford: Oxford University Press.

Baldwin, Richard. 2016. *The Great Convergence*. Cambridge: Belknap.

Bales, Robert Freed. 1950a. "A set of categories for the analysis of small group interaction." *American Sociological Review* 15: 257-263.

_____. 1950b. *Interaction Process Analysis*. Boston: Addison-Wesley.

Ball, Philip. 2002. *Bright Earth: Art and the Invention of Color*. New York: Farrar, Straus & Giroux.

Ballenger, Jesse F. 2006. *Self, Senility, and Alzheimer's Disease in Modern America.* Baltimore: Johns Hopkins University Press.

Baltzell, E Digby. 1958. *Philadelphia Gentlemen.* Glencoe, IL: Free Press.

———. 1964. *The Protestant Establishment.* New York: Random House.

Baluška, František, Stefano Mancuso, and Dieter Volkmann (eds.). 2006. *Communication in Plants.* Berlin: Springer.

Banerjee, Abhijit V, and Esther Duflo. 2011. *Poor Economics.* New York: PublicAffairs.

———. 2019. *Good Economics for Hard Times.* New York: PublicAffairs.

Banville, John. 1982. *The Newton Letter.* London: Secker & Warburg.

Barth, John. 1968. *Lost in the Funhouse.* New York: Doubleday.

Barthes, Roland. 1972 (1957). *Mythologies.* Selected trans. Annette Lavers. New York: Noonday.

Bartholomew, David J. 1967. *Stochastic Models for Social Processes.* London: Wiley.

Barton, Nicholas H. 2010. "Mutation and the evolution of recombination." *Philosophical Transactions of the Royal Society: B* 365: 1281-1294.

———, and Alison M Etheridge. 2004. "The effect of selection on genealogies." *Genetics* 166 (February): 1115-1131.

Batagelij, Vladimir, Patrick Doreian, Anuška Ferligoj, and Nataša Kejžar. 2014. *Understanding Large Temporal Networks and Spatial Networks.* Chicester, UK: Wiley.

Bataille, Georges. 1988 (1949). *The Accursed Share,* volume 1. Trans. Robert Hurley. New York: Zone.

———. 2004. *The Unfinished System of Nonknowledge.* Ed. Stuart Kendall; trans. Michelle Kendall & Stuart Kendall. Minneapolis: University of Minnesota Press.

Baudelaire, Charles. 1964 (1863). "The painter of modern life." Pp. 1-40 in *idem, The Painter of Modern Life and Other Essays.* Trans & ed. J Mayne. London: Phaidon.

Baumberg, Jeremy J. 2018. *The Secret Life of Science.* Princeton: Princeton University Press.

Baumgarten, Eduard. 1964. *Max Weber Werk und Person.* Tübingen: JCB Mohr (Paul Siebeck).

Bearman, Peter S. 1993. *Relations into Rhetorics.* New Brunswick, NJ: Rutgers University Press.

———. 1997. "Generalized exchange." *American Journal of Sociology* 102: 1383-1415.

———, and Paolo Parigi. 2004. "Cloning headless frogs and other important matters." *Social Forces* 83: 535-557.

Beck, Ulrich. 2010. "Welche universität wollen wir?" Pp. 103-108 in *Was passiert?* edited by Johannes-Charlotte Horst et al. Zürich: Diaphanes.

Becker, Gary. 1964. *Human Capital.* New York: NBER.

Beer, Daniel. 2016. *The House of the Dead.* New York: Knopf.

Beiser, Frederick C. 1987. *The Fate of Reason.* Cambridge: Harvard University Press.

———. 2011. *The German Historicist Tradition.* Oxford: Oxford University Press.

———. 2014a. *The Genesis of Neo-Kantianism.* New York: Oxford University Press.

———. 2014b. *After Hegel.* Princeton: Princeton University Press.

Belykh, A A. 1989. "A note on the origin of input-output analysis and the contribution of early Soviet economists." *Soviet Studies* 41: 426-429.

Bellah, Robert N, Richard Madsen, William M Sullivan, Ann Swidler, and Steven M Tipton. 1985. *Habits of the Heart.* Berkeley: University of California Press.

Bellow, Saul. 2010. *Letters*. Ed. Benjamin Taylor. New York: Viking.

———. 2015. *There Is Simply Too Much to Think About*. Ed. B Taylor. New York: Viking.

Belting, Hans. 1994 (1990). *Likeness and Presence*. Trans. Edmund Jephcott. Chicago: University of Chicago Press.

———. 2001 (1998). *The Invisible Masterpiece*, revised edition. Trans. H Atkins. Chicago: University of Chicago Press.

———. 2011 (2008). *Florence and Baghdad*. Trans. D L Schneider. Cambridge: Harvard University Press.

Benedict, Barbara M. 2001. *Curiosity*. Chicago: University of Chicago Press.

Benjamin, Walter. 1968 (1936). "The work of art in an age of mechanical reproduction." Pp. 219-253 in *idem, Illuminations*. Trans. Harry Zohn; ed. Hannah Arendt. New York: Harcourt, Brace & World.

———. 1996 (1916). "On language as such and the language of man." Trans. Edmund Jephcott. Pp. 62-74 in *idem, Selected Writings*, volume 1. Ed. Marcus Bullock and Michael W Jennings. Cambridge: Harvard University Press.

———. 1996 (1924). "Goethe's Elective Affinities." Trans. S Corngold. Pp. 297-360 in *idem, Selected Writings,* volume 1. Ed. Marcus Bullock and Michael W Jennings. Cambridge: Harvard University Press.

———. 1999 (1933). "Antitheses concerning word and name." Pp. 717-719 in *idem, Selected Writings*, volume 2, part 2. Ed. Michael W Jennings, Howard Eiland, and Gary Smith. Cambridge: Harvard University Press.

Bennett, Alan. 1991. *The Madness of George III*. London: National Theatre (1992 book, London: Faber & Faber).

Benveniste, Émile. 1973 (1969). *Dictionary of Indo-European Concepts and Society*. Trans. Elizabeth Palmer. London: Faber and Faber.

Beran, Jan, Yuanhua Feng, Sucharita Ghosh, and Rafal Kulik. 2013. *Long-Memory Processes*. Berlin: Springer.

Berger, Peter L. 1967. *The Sacred Canopy*. Garden City, NY: Doubleday.

Bergson, Henri. 1910 (1899). *Time and Free Will*. Trans. F L Pogson. London: Allen and Unwin.

Berkeley, George. 1710. *A Treatise concerning the Principles of Human Knowledge*. Dublin: printed by Aaron Rhames.

Berle, Adolf A., and Gardiner C Means. 1932. *The Modern Corporation and Private Property*. New York: Macmillan.

Bernanke, Ben S, Timothy F Geithner, and Henry M Paulson, Jr. 2019. *Firefighting*. New York: Penguin.

Bernstein, J M. 2001. *Adorno: Disenchantment and Ethics*. Cambridge: Cambridge University Press.

———. 2006. *Against Voluptuous Bodies*. Stanford: Stanford University Press.

Besnier, Pierre. 1674. *La Réunion des langues, ou l'art de les apprendre toutes par une seule*. Paris: Sebastien Mabre-Cramoisy.

Biernacki, Richard. 2012. *Reinventing Evidence in Social Inquiry*. New York: Palgrave Macmillan.

Binet, Laurent. 2017 (2015). *The Seventh Function of Language*. Trans. Sam Taylor. London: Harvill Secker.

Birkhoff, George D. 1931. "Proof of the ergodic theorem." *Proceedings of the National Academy of Sciences of the USA* 17: 656-660.

Bishop, Bill, with Robert G Cushing. 2008. *The Big Sort*. New York: Houghton Mifflin.
Bjerkholt, Olav. 2016. "Wassily Leontief and the discovery of the input-output approach."
Memorandum, No, 18. Oslo: Department of Economics, University of Oslo.
Blacking, John. 1995. *Music, Culture, and Experience*. Chicago: University of Chicago
Press.
Blalock, Hubert M. 1964 (1961). *Causal Inference in Nonexperimental Research*. Chapel
Hill: University of North Carolina Press.
Bloch, Ernst. 1985 (1935). "Ungleichzeitigkeit und Pflicht zu ihrer Dialektik." Pp. 104-126
in *idem, Erbschaft dieser Zeit*. Frankfurt am Main: Suhrkamp.
Block, James E. 2002. *A Nation of Agents*. Cambridge: Harvard University Press.
Block, Per, Johan Koskinen, James Hollway, Christian Steglich, and Christoph Stadtfeld.
2018. "Change we can believe in." *Social Networks* 52: 180-191.
Blom, Phillipp. 2010. *A Wicked Company*. New York: Basic Books.
Bloom, Harold. 1998. *Shakespeare: The Invention of the Human*. New York: Riverhead.
Bloom, Paul. 2016. *Against Empathy*. New York: Ecco.
Blumer, Herbert. 1966. "Sociological implications of the thought of George Herbert Mead."
*American Journal of Sociology* 71: 535-544.
Boer, Karin de. 2000 (1997). *Thinking in the Light of Time*. Trans. Karin de Boer and Janet
Taylor. Albany: SUNY Press.
Bogaard, Paul A. 1979. "Heaps or wholes." *Isis* 70: 11-29.
Bogdan, Radu J. 2000. *Minding Minds*. Cambridge: MIT Press.
_____. 2009. *Predicative Minds*. Cambridge: MIT Press.
_____. 2010. *Our Own Minds*. Cambridge: MIT Press.
_____. 2013. *Mindvaults*. Cambridge: MIT Press.
Boltzmann, Ludwig. 1905. "Über eine These Schopenhauer." Pp. 385-402 in *idem,
Populäre Schriften*. Leipzig: Barth.
Bonanno, George. 2009. *The Other Side of Sadness*. New York: Basic Books.
Borges, Jorge Luis. 1962 (1949). "Partial magic in the *Quixote*." Pp. 193-196 in *idem,
Labyrinths*. Trans. James E Irby. New York: New Directions.
Born, Max. 1949. *Natural Philosophy of Cause and Chance*. Oxford: Clarendon.
Boschetti, Anna. 1988 (1985). *The Intellectual Enterprise*. Trans. Richard C McCleary.
Evanston, IL: Northwestern University Press.
Bostrom, Nick. 2014. *Superintelligence*. Oxford: Oxford University Press.
Boswell, James. 1887 (1799). *The Life of Samuel Johnson*, 3rd edition, volume 1. Ed.
George Birkbeck Hill. Oxford: Clarendon.
Bott, Elizabeth. 1957. *Family and Social Network*. London: Tavistock.
Bouchard, Frédéric, and Phillippe Huneman (eds.). 2013. *From Groups to Individuals*.
Cambridge: MIT Press.
Bourdieu, Pierre. 1977. *Outline of a Theory of Practice*, revised edition. Trans. Richard
Nice. Cambridge: Cambridge University Press.
Bourdieu, Pierre. 1984 (1979). *Distinction*. Trans. Richard Nice. Cambridge: Harvard
University Press.
_____. 1987. *Choses dites*. Paris: Éditions de Minuit.
_____. 1990 (1982). "A lecture on the lecture." Pp. 177-198 in *idem, In Other Words*.
Trans. Matthew Adamson. Cambridge: Polity.
_____. 1996 (1992). *The Rules of Art*. Trans. Susan Emanuel. Stanford: Stanford
University Press.

Bourdieu, Pierre. 2000 (1997). *Pascalian Meditations*. Stanford: Stanford University Press.
_____. 2007 (2004). *Sketch for a Self-Analysis*. Trans. Richard Nice. Chicago: University of Chicago Press.
_____. 2017 (2013). *Manet: A Symbolic Revolution*. Trans. Peter Collier and Margaret Rigaud-Drayton. Cambridge: Polity.
_____, and Loïc Wacquant. 1992. *Réponses*. Paris: Seuil.
Boushey, Heather. 2019. *Unbound*. Cambridge: Harvard University Press.
Bowie, Andrew. 2003. *Aesthetics and Subjectivity*, 2nd edition. Manchester: Manchester University Press.
_____. 2013. *Adorno and the Ends of Philosophy*. Cambridge: Polity.
Bowker, Geoffrey C. 2005. *Memory Practices in the Sciences*. Cambridge: MIT Press.
_____, and Susan Leigh Star. 1999. *Sorting Things Out*. Cambridge: MIT Press.
Bowles, Samuel, and Herbert Gintis. 1976. *Schooling in Capitalist America*. New York: Basic Books.
_____. 2002. "The inheritance of inequality." *Journal of Economic Perspectives* 16: 1-28.
Boyle, Nicholas. 1991, 2000. *Goethe: The Poet and the Age*, 2 volumes. Oxford: Oxford University Press.
Braddock, Jeremy. 2012. *Collecting as Modernist Practice*. Baltimore: Johns Hopkins University Press.
Brand, Jennie E, and Yu Xie. 2010. "Who benefits most from college?" *American Sociological Review* 75: 273-302.
Brandom, Robert B. 2000. *Articulating Reasons*. Cambridge: Harvard University Press.
_____. 2002. *Tales of the Mighty Dead*. Cambridge: Harvard University Press.
_____. 2007. "The structure of desire and recognition." *Philosophy & Social Criticism* 33: 127-150.
_____. 2008. *Between Saying and Doing*. Oxford: Oxford University Press.
Bratman, Michael. 1999. *Faces of Intention*. Cambridge: Cambridge University Press.
_____. 2018. *Planning, Time, and Sociality*. Oxford: Oxford University Press.
Braudy, Leo. 1986. *The Frenzy of Renown*. New York: Oxford University Press.
Brekhus, Wayne H. 2015. *Culture and Cognition*. Cambridge: Polity.
Bridges, William P, and Wayne J Villemez. 1994. *The Employment Relationship*. New York: Plenum.
Brielmann, Aenne A, and Denis G Pelli. 2017. "Beauty requires thought." *Current Biology* 27: 1506-1513.
Brito, Natalie H., and Kinberly G Noble. 2014. "Socioeconomic status and structural brain development." *Frontiers in Neuroscience* 8: 276. (doi: 10.3389/fnins.2014.00276 [last access 25Feb2017])
Brock, Hermann. 1945 [1931-32]. *The Sleepwalkers*, trans. W and E Muir. New York: Pantheon.
Broido, Anna D, and Aaron Clauset. 2019. "Scale-free networks are rare." *Nature Communications* 10: 1017. <doi/10.1038/s41467-019-08746-5>
Brooks, David. 2010. "The arena culture." *New York Times*, 31 December, p. A23.
Brooks, Peter. 2005. *Realist Vision*. New Haven: Yale University Press.
_____. 2011. *Enigmas of Identity*. Princeton: Princeton University Press.
Brooks, Van Wyck. 1915. *America's Coming-of-Age*. New York: Huebsch.
Brown, Bill. 2003. *A Sense of Things*. Chicago: University of Chicago Press.

Brown, Chloë, Anastasios Noulas, Cecilia Mascolo, and Vincent Blondel. 2013. "A place-focused model for social networks in cities." *arXiv*: 1038.2565v1 [cs.SI] 12 Aug.

Brown, Frederick. 2016. *For the Soul of France: Culture Wars in the Age of Dreyfus*. New York: Knopf.

Brown, Kate. 2013. *Plutopia*. Oxford: Oxford University Press.

Brown, Peter. 1995. *Authority and the Sacred*. Cambridge: Cambridge University Press.

Bruch, Elizabeth, and Robert Mare. 2009. "Segregation dynamics." Pp. 269-293 in *The Oxford Handbook of Analytical Sociology*, edited by Peter Hedström and Peter Bearman. Oxford: Oxford University Press.

Bruford, Walter. 1975. *The German Tradition of Self-Cultivation*. Cambridge: Cambridge University Press.

Brynjolfsson, Erik, and Andrew McAfee. 2014. *The Second Machine Age*. New York: Norton.

Bukodi, Erzsébet, John H Goldthorpe, Brendan Halpin, and Lorraine Waller. 2016. "Is education now class destiny?" *European Sociological Review* 32: 835-849.

Burke, Edmund. 1756. *A Vindication of Natural Society*. Oxford.

_____. 1910 (1790). *Reflections on the Revolution in France*. London: J M Dent & Sons.

Burke, Kenneth. 1945. *A Grammar of Motives*. Englewood Cliffs, NJ: Prentice-Hall.

Burke, Peter J. 1980. "The self: measurement requirements from an interactionist perspective." *Social Psychology Quarterly* 43: 18-29.

Burnet, Frank M. 1940. *Biological Aspects of Infectious Disease*. Cambridge: Cambridge University Press.

_____. 1958. *Clonal Selection Theory of Acquired Immunity*. Cambridge: Cambridge University Press.

Burt, Ronald S. 1991. "Measuring age as a structural concept." *Social Networks* 13: 1-34.

Bush, Richard C II. 1970. *Religion in Communist China*. Nashville, TN: Abingdon.

_____. 1977. *Religion in China*. Niles, IL: Argus.

Butler, Judith. 1995. "Contingent foundations." Pp. 35-57 in *Feminist Contentions*, by S. Benhabib, J Butler, D Cornell, N Fraser, and L Nicholson. New York: Routledge.

Butts, Carter T. 2008. "A relational event framework for social action." *Sociological Methodology* 38: 155-200.

_____. 2016. "Why I know but don't believe." *Science* 354 (21 October): 286-287.

_____. 2017. "Comment: actor orientation and relational events." *Sociological Methodology* 47: 47-56.

Bybee, Joan. 2010. *Language, Usage and Cognition*. Cambridge: Cambridge University Press.

Calvert, Randall L. 1995. "Rational actors, equilibrium, and social institutions." Pp. 57-93 in *Explaining Social Institutions*, edited by Jack Knight and Itai Sened. Ann Arbor: University of Michigan Press.

Campbell, Karen E, and Barrett A Lee. 1991. "Name generators in surveys of personal networks." *Social Networks* 13: 203-221.

Camus, Albert. 1946 (1942). *The Stranger*. Trans. Stuart Gilbert. New York: Knopf.

Camus, Albert. 1955 (1942). *The Myth of Sisyphus*. Trans. Justin O'Brien. London: Hamish Hamilton.

Cannadine, David. 1990. *The Decline and Fall of the British Aristocracy*. New Haven: Yale University Press.

Cantrell, Steven, Jon Fullerton, Thomas J Kane, and Douglas O Staiger. 2008. "National Board certification and teacher effectiveness." NBER Working Paper 14608. Cambridge: NBER.

Card, David. 1999. "The causal effect of education on earnings." Pp. 1802-1863 in *Handbook of Labor Economics*, volume 3, edited by Orley Ashenfelter and David Card. Amsterdam: Elsevier.

_____, and Alan B Krueger. 1996. "School resources and student outcomes." *Journal of Economic Perspectives* 10 (4): 31-50.

_____. 1998. "School resources and student outcomes." *Annals of the American Academy of Political and Social Science* 559 (September): 39-53.

Carpenter, William B. 1875. *Principles of Mental Physiology*. London: Henry S King.

Carroll, Sean. 2010. *From Eternity to Here*. New York: Dutton.

Carruthers, Mary J. 1990. *The Book of Memory*. Cambridge: Cambridge University Press.

Cartwright, David E. 2010. *Schopenhauer*. Cambridge: Cambridge University Press.

Caruso, Gregg D. 2012. *Free Will and Consciousness*. Lanham, MD: Lexington.

Cascardi, Anthony J. 1999. *Consequences of Enlightenment*. Cambridge: Cambridge University Press.

Case, Anna, and Angus Deaton. 2020. *Deaths of Despair*. Princeton: Princeton University Press.

Castronova, Edward. 2005. *Synthetic Worlds*. Chicago: University of Chicago Press.

Castro-Ruiz, Estaban, Flaminia Giacomini, and Časlav Brukner. 2018. "Dynamics of Quantum causal structures." *Physical Review X* 8 (011047): 1-15.

Catte, Elizabeth. 2018. *What You Are Getting Wrong about Appalachia*. Cleveland: Belt.

Cavell, Stanley. 1969. *Must We Mean What We Say?* New York: Charles Scribner's Sons.

_____. 1971. *The World Viewed*. New York: Viking.

_____. 1979. *The Claim of Reason*. Oxford: Clarendon.

_____. 1988. *In Quest of the Ordinary*. Chicago: University of Chicago Press.

_____. 2004. *Cities of Words*. Cambridge: Harvard University Press.

Caygill, Howard. 1989. *Art of Judgement*. Oxford: Blackwell.

_____. 2016. "Bildung and strategy: the fate of the 'beautiful sciences.'" *Radical Philosophy* 196: 9-13.

_____. 2017. *Kafka: In Light of the Accident*. London: Bloomsbury Academic.

Chai, Leon. 1990. *Aestheticism: The Religion of Art in Post-Romantic Literature*. New York: Columbia University Press.

_____. 2006. *Romantic Theory: Forms of Reflexivity in the Revolutionary Era*. Baltimore: Johns Hopkins University Press.

Chalmers, David J. 1995. "Facing up to the problem of consciousness." *Journal of Consciousness Studies* 2 (3): 200-219.

Chandra, Vikram, Ingrid Fetter-Pruneda, Peter R Oxley, Amelia L Ritger, Sean McKenzie, Romain Libbrecht, and Daniel J C Kronauer. 2018. "Social regulation of insulin signaling and the evolution of eusociality in ants." *Science* 361 (27 July): 398-402.

Chapman, Herrick. 2018. *France's Long Reconstruction*. Cambridge: Harvard University Press.

Chartier, Roger. 2007 (2005). *Inscription and Erasure*. Trans. Arthur Goldhammer. University of Pennsylvania Press.

Chateaubriand, François-René de. 1873. *The Genius of Christianity*, 9th revised edition. Trans. unlisted. Baltimore: John Murphy.

Chateaubriand, François-René de. 2018 (1849-50). *Memoirs from Beyond the Grave*. Trans. Alex Andriesse. New York: NYRB Classics.

Chenu, Marie-Dominque. 1968 (1957). *Nature, Man, and Society in the Twelfth Century*. Ed. & trans. Jerome Taylor and Lester Little. Chicago: University of Chicago Press.

Chiao, Joan Y, Shu-Chen Li, Rebecca Seligman, and Robert Turner (eds.). 2016. *Oxford Handbook of Cultural Neuroscience*. New York: Oxford University Press.

Cho, Adrian. 2019. "New pentaquarks hint at zoo of exotic matter." *Science* 364 (7 June): 917.

Chomsky, Noam. 1975. *The Logical Structure of Linguistic Theory*. New York: Plenum.

Chriss, James J. 1993. "Looking back on Goffman." *Human Studies* 16: 469-483.

Ciccone, Antonio, and Robert E Hall. 1996. "Productivity and the density of economic activity." *American Economic Review* 86: 54-70.

Cicero, Marcus Tullius. 45 BCE. *De Natura Deorum*.

_____. 45 BCE. *De Amicitia*.

_____. 44 BCE. *De Officiis*.

_____. c43 BCE. *De Legibus*.

Clark, Christopher. 2012. *The Sleepwalkers*. London: Allen Lane.

_____. 2019. *Time and Power*. Princeton: Princeton University Press.

Clark, David L. 1984. "Planning and the real origins of input-output analysis." *Journal of Contemporary Asia* 14: 408-429.

Clark, Mary Marshall, Peter Bearman, Catherine Ellis, and Stephen Drury Smith (eds.). 2011. *After the Fall*. New York: New Press.

Clarke, Arthur C. 1973. *Profiles of the Future*, 2nd edition. New York: Harper & Row.

Clausen, John A. 1991. "Adolescent competence and the shaping of the life course." *American Journal of Sociology* 96: 805-842.

_____. 1995. *American Lives*. New York: Free Press.

Coase, Ronald H. 1937. "The nature of the firm." *Economica*, n.s., 4 (November): 386-405.

Coates, Ta-Nehisi Paul. 2015. *Between the World and Me*. New York: Spiegel & Grau.

Cochrane, John. 2011. "Discount rates." *Journal of Finance* 66: 1047-1108.

Cockell, Charles. 2018. *The Equations of Life*. New York: Basic Books.

Cohen, Jere, Lawrence Hazelrigg, and Whitney Pope. 1975. "De-Parsonizing Weber." *American Sociological Review* 40: 229-241, 666-674.

Coleman, James S. 1958. "Relational analysis." *Human Organization* 17 (Winter): 28-36.

_____. 1963. Comment (on Parsons, "On the concept of social influence.") *Public Opinion Quarterly* 27: 63-82.

_____. 1964. *Introduction to Mathematical Sociology*. New York: Basic.

_____. 1973. *The Mathematics of Collective Action*. Chicago: Aldine.

_____. 1986. "Social theory, social research, and a theory of action." *American Journal of Sociology* 91: 1309-1335.

_____. 1990. *Foundations of Social Theory*. Cambridge: Harvard University Press.

_____, and Lingxin Hao. 1989. "Linear systems analysis." *Sociological Methodology* 19: 395-422.

Coleridge, Samuel Taylor. 1817. *Biographia Literaria*. London.

Collini, Stefan. 2016. "How to be ourselves." *London Review of Books* 38 (20 October): 40-41.

Collins, Randall. 1979. *The Credential Society*. New York: Academic.

Collins Randall. 1981. "On the microfoundations of macrosociology." *American Journal of Sociology* 86: 984-1014.

_____. 1998. *Sociology of Philosophies*. Cambridge: Harvard University Press.

Collins, Steven. 1985. "Categories, concepts or predicaments?" Pp. 46-82 in *The Category of the Person*, edited by Michael Carrithers, Steven Collins, and Steven Lukes. Cambridge: Cambridge University Press.

_____. 1994. "What are Buddhists doing when they deny the self?" Pp. 59-86 in *Religion and Practical Reason*, edited by Frank E Reynolds and David Tracy. Albany: SUNY Press.

Conley, Dalton, and Jennifer Heerwig. 2012. "The long-term effects of military conscription on mortality." *Demography* 49: 841-855.

Connerton, Paul. 1989. *How Societies Remember*. Cambridge: Cambridge University Press.

Connolly, Paul, Ciara Keenan, and Karolina Urbanska. 2018. "The trials of evidence-based practice in education." *Educational Research* 60: 276-291.

Conrad, Joseph. 2007 (1907). *The Secret Agent*. Ed. Michael Newton. London: Penguin.

Cook, Gary A. 2011. "Revisiting the Mead-Blumer controversy." Pp. 17-38 in *Blue-Ribbon Papers: Interactionism*, edited by Norman K Denzin, Lonnie Athens, and Ted Faust. Bingley, UK: Emerald.

Cooper, Anthony Ashley, 3rd earl of Shaftesbury. 1709 (1999). Sensus Communis. Part Four of *idem, Characteristics of Men, Manners, Opinions, Times*. Ed. Lawrence E Klein. Cambridge: Cambridge University Press.

_____. 1710 (1999). *Soliloquy*. Part One of *idem, Characteristics of Men, Manners, Opinions, Times*. Ed. Lawrence E Klein. Cambridge: Cambridge University Press.

Copp, David. 1980. "Hobbes on artificial persons and collective actions." *Philosophical Review* 89: 579-606.

Corey, David D. 2015. *The Sophists in Plato's Dialogues*. Albany: SUNY Press.

Cortásar, Julio. 1966 (1963). *Hopscotch*. Trans. Gregory Rabassa. New York: Pantheon.

Cowan, James, and Dan Goldhaber. 2015. "National Board certification evidence from Washington State." Working Paper 2015-3. Center for Education Data and Research, University of Washington, Seattle.

Cowen, Tyler. 2018. *Stubborn Attachments*. San Francisco: Stripe.

Coxworth, James E, Peter S Kim, John McQueen, and Kristen Hawkes. 2015. "Grandmothering life histories and human pairs bonding." *PNAS* 112 (22 September): 11806-11811. <doi: 10.1073/pnas.1599993112>

Crapanzano, Vincent. 2015. *Recapitulations*. New York: Other Press.

Crary, Jonathan. 1990. *Techniques of the Observer*. Cambridge: MIT Press.

_____. 1999. *Suspensions of Perception*. Cambridge: MIT Press.

Culler, Jonathan. 2015. *Theory of the Lyric*. Cambridge: Harvard University Press.

Cummings, Brian. 2013. *Mortal Thoughts*. Oxford: Oxford University Press.

Cunningham, Andrew, and Nicholas Jardine (eds.). 1990. *Romanticism and the Sciences*. Cambridge: Cambridge University Press.

Cunningham, Vinson. 2020. "Prep for Prep and the fault lines in New York's school." *The New Yorker* 96 (9 March): 56-67.

Curran, Andrew S. 2019. *Diderot and the Art of Thinking Freely*. New York: Other.

Curtius, Ernst Robert. 1953. *European Literature and the Latin Middle Ages*. Trans. Willard R Trask. Princeton: Princeton University Press.

Czapnik, Dana. 2019. *The Falconer.* New York: Atria.

Dahms, Harry F. 1995. "From creative action to the social rationalization of the economy." *Sociological Theory* 13: 1-13.

_____. 2000. *Transformations of Capitalism.* New York: New York University Press.

_____. 2007."Confronting the dynamic nature of modern social life." *Soundings* 90:191-205

_____. 2011. *The Vitality of Critical Theory.* Bingley, UK: Emerald.

Dale, Stacy Berg, and Alan B Krueger. 2011. "Estimating the return to college selectivity over the career using administrative earning data." *Journal of Human Resources* 49: 323-358.

Dallmayr, Fred R, and Thomas A McCarthy (eds.). 1977. *Understanding and Social Inquiry.* Notre Dame, IN: University of Notre Dame Press.

Damisch, Hubert. 1994 (1987). *The Origin of Perspective.* Trans. John Goodman. Cambridge: MIT Press.

Damish, Hubert. 1996 (1992). *The Judgement of Paris.* Trans. John Goodman. Chicago: University of Chicago Press.

Dancy, Russell M. 1991. *Two Studies in the Early Academy.* Albany: SUNY Press.

Danto, Arthur. 1997. *After the End of Art.* Princeton: Princeton University Press.

Darnton, Robert. 1989. *The Kiss of Lamourette.* New York: Norton.

Darwall, Stephen. 2006. *The Second-Person Standpoint.* Cambridge: Harvard University Press.

Darwin, Charles. 1859. *On the Origin of Species.* London: John Murray.

_____. 1871. *The Descent of Man, and Selection in Relation to Sex.* London: John Murray.

David, Paul. 2001. "Path dependence, its critics and the quest for 'historical economics'." Pp. 15-40 in *Evolution and Path Dependence in Economics*, edited by Pierre Garrouste and Stavros Ioannides. Cheltenham, UK: Elgar.

Dávid-Barrett, Tomas, and Robin I M Dunbar. 2013. "Processing power limits social group size: computational evidence for the cognitive costs of sociality." *Proceedings of the Royal Society B* 280: 1151. <doi.org/10.1098/rspb.2013.115>

Davidian, Marie, and David M Giltinan. 1995. *Nonlinear Models for Repeated Measurement Data.* New York: Chapman & Hall.

Davidson, Donald. 1984. *Inquiries into Truth and Interpretation.* Oxford: Oxford University Press.

_____. 1987. "Knowing one's own mind." *Proceedings and Addresses of the American Philosophical Association* 60 (January): 441-458.

Davidson, James. 2007. *The Greeks and Greek Love.* New York: Random House.

Davies, James C. 1962. "Toward a theory of revolution." *American Sociological Review* 27: 5-19.

Davies, William. 2018. *Nervous States.* London: Cape.

Dawkins, Richard. 1998. *Unweaving the Rainbow.* London: Allen Lane.

DeGroot, Morris H. 1974. "Reaching a consensus." *Journal of the American Statistical Association* 69: 118-121.

Déguignet, Jean-Marie. 2004 (1998). *Memoirs of a Breton Peasant.* Trans. L Asher. New York: Seven Stories Press.

DeLanda, Manuel. 2006. *A New Philosophy of Society: Assemblage Theory and Social Complexity.* London: Continuum.

_____, and Graham Harman. 2017. *The Rise of Realism.* Cambridge, UK: Polity.

Deleuze, Gilles. 1991 (1953). *Empiricism and Subjectivity*, revised edition. Trans. Constantin V Boundas. New York: Columbia University Press.

———. 1994 (1968). *Difference and Repetition*. Trans. Paul Patton. New York: Columbia University Press.

———, and Félix Guattari. 1977 (1972). *Anti-Oedipus*. Trans. Robert Hurley, Mark Seem, and Helen R Lane. New York: Viking.

———, and Félix Guattari. 2004 (1980). *A Thousand Plateaus*. Trans. Brian Massumi. New York: Continuum.

———, and Claire Parnet. 2002 (1977). *Dialogue II*. Trans. Hugh Tomlinson and Barbara Habberjam. (Including the draft essay, "The actual and the virtual," trans. Eliot Ross Albert). New York: Columbia University Press.

Dennett, Daniel C. 1984. *Elbow Room*. Cambridge: MIT Press.

———. 1987. *The Intentional Stance*. Cambridge: MIT Press.

———. 1996. *Kinds of Minds*. New York: Basic Books.

———. 2003. *Freedom Evolves*. New York: Viking.

Derrida, Jacques. 1964. "Economimesis." Pp. 56-93 in Sylvaine Agacinsky, Jacques Derrida, Sarah Kofman, Philippe Lacoue-LaBarthes, Jean-Luc Nancy, and Bernard Pautrat, *Mimésis des articulations*. Paris: Aubier-Flammarion.

———. 1976 (1967). *Of Grammatology*. Trans. Gayatri Chakravorty Spivak. Baltimore: Johns Hopkins University Press.

———. 1981 (1972). *Dissemination*. Trans. Barbara Johnson. Chicago: University of Chicago Press.

———. 1982 (1972). *The Margins of Philosophy*. Trans. Alan Bass. Chicago: University of Chicago Press.

———. 1987 (1978). *The Truth in Painting*. Trans. Geoff Bennington & Ian McLeod. Chicago: University of Chicago Press.

———. 1988. *Limited, Inc.* Ed. Samuel Weber; trans. Samuel Weber & Jeffrey Mehlman. Evanston: Northwestern University Press.

———. 1993 (1983). "Of an apocalyptic tone recently adopted in philosophy." Trans. Peter D Fenves. Pp. 51-81 in *Raising the Tone of Philosophy*, edited by Peter D Fenves. Baltimore: Johns Hopkins University Press.

Descartes, René. 1984 (1642). *Meditations on First Philosophy*, 2nd edition. Pp. 1-62 in *The Philosophical Writings of Descartes*, volume 2. Trans. J Cottingham, R Stoothoff, & D Murdoch. Cambridge: Cambridge University Press.

Descombes, Vincent. 1980 (1979). *Modern French Philosophy*. Trans. L Scott-Fox and J M Harding. Cambridge: Cambridge University Press.

Desrosières, Alain. 2002 (1993). *The Politics of Large Numbers*. Trans. Camille Naish. Cambridge: Harvard University Press.

Deutscher, Guy. 2010. *Through the Language Glass*. New York: Metropolitan.

Dewey, John. 1903. *Studies in Logical Theory*. Chicago: University of Chicago Press.

———. 1926. "The historic background of corporate legal personality." *Yale Law Journal* 35: 655-673.

———. 1939. *Freedom and Culture*. New York: G P Putnam's Sons.

Diderot, Denis. 1883 (1830). *Paradox of Acting*. Trans. Walter Herries Pollock. London: Chatto & Windus.

———. 1995 (1821). *Diderot on Art – II*. Trans. John Goodman. New Haven: Yale University Press.

Dihle, Albrecht. 1982. *The Theory of Will in Classical Antiquity*. Berkeley: University of California Press.

Dilthey, Wilhelm. 1985 (1887). "The imagination of the poet." Trans. Louis Agosta and Rudolf A Makreel. Pp. 29-173 in *idem, Selected Works*, volume 5, *Poetry and Experience*. Ed. Rudolf A Makreel and Frithjof Rodi. Princeton: Princeton University Press.

_____. 1985 (1910). "Goethe and the poetic imagination." Trans. Christopher Rodie. Pp. 285-302 in *idem, Selected Works*, volume 5, *Poetry and Experience*. Ed. Rudolf A Makreel and Frithjof Rodi. Princeton: Princeton University Press.

DiMaggio, Paul. 1987. "Classification in art." *American Sociological Review* 52: 440-455.

Dinh, Christopher, Timothy Farinholt, Shigenori Hirose, Olga Zhuchenko, & Adam Kuspa. 2018. "Lectins modulate the microbiota of social amoebae." *Science* 361 (27 July): 402-406.

DiPrete, Thomas D, and Jerry D Forristal. 1994. "Multilevel models." *Annual Review of Sociology* 20: 331-357.

Dirac, Paul A M. 1929. "Quantum mechanics of many-electron systems." *Proceedings of The Royal Society* A123: 714-733.

Döblin, Alfred. 2018 (1929). *Berlin Alexanderplatz*. Trans. Michael Hofmann. New York: NYRB Classics.

Dodds, Eric R. 1951. *The Greeks and the Irrational*. Berkeley: University of California Press.

_____. 1973. *The Ancient Concept of Progress and Other Essays on Greek Literature and Belief*. Oxford: Clarendon.

Doggett, Peter. 2012. *The Man Who Sold the World*. New York: Harper.

Donzelot, Jacques. 1979 (1977). *The Policing of Families*. Trans. Robert Hurley. New York: Pantheon.

Doreian, Patrick. 2001. "Causality in social network analysis." *Sociological Methods and Research* 30: 81-114.

Dostoyevsky, Fyodor. 1918 (1864). *Notes from the Underground*. Trans. Constance Garnett. New York: Macmillan.

_____. 1990 (1880). *The Brothers Karamazov*. Trans. Richard Pevear and Larissa Volokhonsky. Berkeley: North Point.

Doubt, Keith. 1990. "Contemporary sophism and social theory." *Contemporary Sociology* 19 (May): 474-476.

Douglas, Mary. 1986. *How Institutions Think*. Syracuse: Syracuse University Press.

Dowd, Timothy J. 2011. "Production and producers of lifestyles." *Kölner Zeitschrift für Soziologie und Sozialpsychologie*, Sonderheft 51: 113-138.

Downing, Taylor. 2018. *1983: Reagan, Andropov, and a World on the Brink*. New York: Da Capo.

Dreyfus, Hubert, and Sean Dorrance Kelly. 2011. *All Things Shining: Reading the Western Classics to Find Meaning in a Secular Age*. New York: Free Press.

DuBois, Christopher, Carter T Butts, Daniel McFarland, and Padhraic Smyth. 2013. "Hierarchical models for relational event sequences." *Journal of Mathematical Psychology* 57: 297-309.

Duff, Timothy. 2008."Models of education in Plutarch." *Journal of Hellenic Studies* 128: 1-26.

Duhem, Pierre. 1969 (1908). *To Save the Phenomena*. Trans. Edmund Doland and Chaninah Maschler. Chicago: University of Chicago Press.

Dunbar, Robin I M. 2010. *How Many Friends Does One Need?* London: Faber and Faber.
_____, Valerio Arnaboldi, Marco Conti, and Andrea Passarella. 2015. "The structure of online social networks mirrors those in the offline world." *Social Networks* 43: 39-47.
Duncan, Otis Dudley. 1984. *Notes on Social Measurement.* New York: Russell Sage.
Dunn, John. 1979. *Western Political Theory in the Face of the Future.* Cambridge: Cambridge University Press.
_____. 1980. "Short books on great men." *London Review of Books* 2 (22 May): 20-22.
_____. 2000. *The Cunning of Unreason.* New York: Basic Books.
_____. 2005. *Setting the People Free.* London: Grove Atlantic.
Durkheim, Émile. 1953 (1911). "Value judgments and judgments of reality." Pp. 42-51 in *idem, Sociology and Philosophy.* Trans. D F Pocock. London: Cohen & West.
_____. 1973 (1914). "The dualism of human nature and its social conditions." Pp. 149-166 in *idem, Émile Durkheim on Morality and Society,* edited by Robert Bellah. Chicago: University of Chicago Press.
_____. 1982 (1901). *The Rules of Sociological Method,* 2nd edition. Trans. W D Halls. New York: Free Press.
_____. 1984 (1902). *The Division of Labor in Society,* 2nd edition. Trans. W D Halls. New York: Free Press.
Duve, Thierry de. 1991. *Pictorial Nominalism.* Trans. Dana Polan. Minneapolis: University of Minnesota Press.
_____. 1996. *Kant after Duchamp.* Cambridge: MIT Press.
Eagleton, Terry. 2014. *Culture and the Death of God.* New Haven: Yale University Press.
Ebbs, Gary. 2017. *Carnap, Quine, and Putnam on Methods of Inquiry.* Cambridge: Cambridge University Press.
Eco, Umberto. 1997. *The Search for the Perfect Language.* Trans. J Fentress. Oxford: Blackwell.
Edelstein, Ludwig. 1967. *The Idea of Progress in Classical Antiquity.* Baltimore: Johns Hopkins University Press.
Edmunds, Lowell. 1975. *Chance and Intelligence in Thucydides.* Cambridge: Harvard University Press.
Edsinger, Eric, and Gül Dölen. 2018. "A conserved role for serotonergic neurotransmission in mediating social behavior in Octopus." *Current Biology* 28: 1-7.
Edwards, Michael. 2014. *Civil Society,* 3rd edition. Cambridge: Polity.
Einstein, Albert, Boris Podolsky, and Nathan Rosen. 1935. "Can quantum-mechanical description of physical reality be considered complete?" *Physical Review* 47 (15 May): 777-780.
_____, and Nathan Rosen. 1936. "The particle problem in the general theory of relativity." *Physical Review* 48 (1 July): 73-77.
Elder, Glen H, Jr. 1999. *Children of the Great Depression,* 25th anniversary edition. Boulder, CO: Westview.
Eliot, T S. "The Hollow Men." Pp. 123-128 in *idem, Poems 1909-1925.* London: Faber & Faber.
Elmer, David F. 2013. *The Poetics of Consent.* Baltimore: Johns Hopkins University Press.
Elster, Jon. 1989. *The Cement of Society.* Cambridge: Cambridge University Press.
_____. 2003. "Coleman on norms." *Revue française de sociologie* 44: 297-304.

Elvin, Mark. 1985. "Between the earth and heaven: conceptions of the self in China." Pp. 156-189 in *The Category of the Person*, edited by Michael Carrithers, Steven Collins, & Steven Lukes. Cambridge: Cambridge University Press.

_____. 1997. *Changing Stories in the Chinese World*. Stanford: Stanford University Press.

_____. 2004. *The Retreat of the Elephants*. New Haven: Yale University Press.

Emerson, Ralph Waldo. 1983 (1841). "Self-Reliance." Pp. 257-282 in *idem, Essays and Lectures*. New York: Library of America.

Emmons, William R, Ana Hernández Kent, and Lowell R Ricketts. 2018. "The bigger they are, the harder they fall: the decline of the white working class." Demographic Wealth, 2018 series, Essay no. 3. Center for Household Financial Stability, Federal Reserve Bank of St Louis.

Empson, William. 1953. *Seven Types of Ambiguity*, 3rd edition. London: Chatto &Windus.

_____. 1977. *The Structure of Complex Words*, 3rd edition. Totowa, NJ: Rowman and Littlefield.

Engell, James. 1981. *The Creative Imagination*. Cambridge: Harvard University Press.

Epstein, Brian. 2010. "History and the critique of concepts." *Philosophy of the Social Sciences* 40: 3-29.

_____. 2015. *The Ant Trap*. New York: Oxford University Press.

_____. 2016. "A framework for social ontology." *Philosophy of the Social Sciences* 46: 147-167.

_____. 2018. "Social ontology." *Stanford Encyclopedia of Philosophy*. [last access 23 August 2018].

Epstein, Joshua M. 2006. *Generative Social Science*. Princeton: Princeton University Press.

_____, and Robert Axelrod. 1996. *Growing Artificial Societies*. Cambridge: MIT Press.

Erbring, Lutz, and Alice A Young. 1979. "Individuals and social structure." *Sociological Methods and Research* 7: 396-430.

Erskine, John. 1915. *The Moral Obligation to Be Intelligent, and Other Essays*. New York: Duffield.

Evans-Pritchard, Edward. 1939. "Nuer time-reckoning." *Africa* 12: 189-216.

Everett, Caleb. 2017. *Numbers and the Making of Us*. Cambridge: Harvard University Press.

Faguet, Émile. 1899. "Que sera le XXe siècle." Pp. 245-335 in *idem, Questions politique*. Paris: Hachette Livre BnF.

Faraday, Michael. 1853. "Experimental investigation of table-moving." *Athenæneum* no. 1340 (July): 801-803.

Fararo, Thomas J, and John Skvoretz. 1986. "Action and institution, network and function." *Sociological Forum* 1: 219-250.

Farrier, David. 2020. *Footprints*. New York: Farrar, Straus and Giroux.

Faulkner, William. 1994 (1942). "The Bear." Pp. 140-246 in *idem, Novels, 1942-1954*. Ed. Joseph Blotner and Noel Polk. New York: Library of America.

_____. 1994 (1951). *Requiem for a Nun*. Pp. 471-664 in *idem, Novels, 1942-1954*. Ed. Joseph Blotner and Noel Polk. New York: Library of America.

Feinstein, Leon. 2003. "Inequality in the early cognitive development of British children in the 1970 cohort." *Economica* 70: 73-97.

Feld, Scott L. 1981. "The focused organization of social ties." *American Journal of Sociology* 86: 1015-1035.

Feld, Scott. 1982. "Social structural determinants of similarity among associates." *American Sociological Review* 47: 797-801.

_____. 1991. "Why your friends have more friends than you do." *American Journal of Sociology* 96: 1464-1477.

_____, and Bernard Grofman. 1977. "Variation in class size, the class size paradox, and some consequences for students." *Research in Higher Education* 6: 215-222.

Felski, Rita. 2015. *The Limits of Critique.* Chicago: University of Chicago Press.

Ficino, Marsilio. 1996 (c1490). *Meditations on the Soul: Selected Letters of Marsilio Ficino.* Ed. C Salaman. Rochester, VT: Inner Traditions.

Filmer, Robert. 1648. *The Necessity of the Absolute Power of All Kings.* London.

Fischer, Claude S. 1982. *To Dwell among Friends.* Chicago: University of Chicago Press.

Fish, Stanley. 1980. *Is There a Text in This Class?* Cambridge: Harvard University Press.

Fisher, Philip. 2002. *The Vehement Passions.* Princeton: Princeton University Press.

Fitzgerald, Penelope. 1995. *The Blue Flower.* New York: HarperCollins.

Flannery, Tim. 2018. *Europe: The First One Hundred Million Years.* London: Penguin.

Flaubert, Gustav. 1869. *L'Éducation sentimentale.* Paris: Michel Lévy Fréres.

Fleck, Ludwik. 1979 (1935). *Genesis and Development of a Scientific Fact.* Trans. Fred Bradley and Thaddeus J Trenn; ed. Thaddeus J Trenn and Robert K Merton. Chicago: University of Chicago Press.

Fligstein, Neil. 2013. "Understanding stability and change in fields." *Research in Organizational Behavior* 33: 39-51.

_____, and Doug McAdam. 2012. *A Theory of Fields.* Oxford: Oxford University Press.

Flint, Anthony. 2014. *Modern Man: The Life of Le Corbusier.* Boston: New Harvest.

Flint, Robert. 1893. *Historical Philosophy in France and French Belgium and Switzerland.* Edinburgh and London: William Blackwood and Sons.

Flores, Ralph. 1984. *The Rhetoric of Doubtful Authority.* Ithaca: Cornell University Press.

Flynn, Thomas R. 2014. *Sartre.* Cambridge: Cambridge University Press.

Flyvbjerg, Bent. 2001. *Making Social Science Matter.* Trans. Steven Sampson. Cambridge: Cambridge University Press.

Fodor, Jerry. 2002. "Mouse thoughts." *London Review of Books* 24 (7 March): 12-14.

Fontenelle, Bernard le Bovier de. 1990 (1686). *Conversation on the Plurality of Worlds.* Trans. H A Hargreaves. Berkeley: University of California Press.

Foster, Dean P and H Peyton Young. 2001 "On the impossibility of predicting the behavior of rational agents." *PNAS* 98 (23 October): 12848-12853.

Foucault, Michel. 2008 (1964). *Introduction to Kant's Anthropology.* Trans. Roberto Nigro and Kate Briggs. Los Angeles: Semiotext(e).

_____. 1970 (1966). *The Order of Things.* Trans. A M Sheridan Smith. New York: Pantheon.

_____. 1972 (1969). *The Archæology of Knowledge.* Trans. A M Sheridan Smith. New York: Pantheon.

_____. 1978 (1975). *Discipline and Punish.* Trans. Alan Sheridan. New York: Pantheon.

Fowler, Susan. 2020. *Whistleblower.* New York: Viking.

Freedberg, David. 1989. *The Power of Images.* Chicago: University of Chicago Press.

_____. 2002. *The Eye of the Lynx.* Chicago: University of Chicago Press.

Freeman, Joshua B. 2018. *Behemoth.* New York: Norton.

Freire-Gibbs, Lucio Carlos, and Kristian Nielsen. 2014. "Entrepreneurship within urban and rural areas." *Regional Studies* 48: 139-153.

Frenkel, Edward. 2013. *Love and Math*. New York: Basic Books.

Ferguson, Adam. 1782 (1767). *An Essay on the History of Civil Society*, 5th edition. London: T Cadell.

Frank, Robert H. 2016. *Success and Luck*. Princeton: Princeton University Press.

Fried, Charles. 1981. *Contract as Promise*. Cambridge: Harvard University Press.

Friedkin, Noah E, Anton V Proskurnikov, Roberto Tempo, and Sergey E Parsegov. 2016. "Network science on belief system dynamics under logic constraints." *Science* 354 (21 October): 321-326 and Supplement.

Friedman, Daniel. 1998. "Monty Hall's three doors." *American Economic Review* 88: 933-946.

_____, R Mark Isaac, Duncan James, and Shyam Sunder. 2014. *Risky Curves*. Oxford: Routledge.

Friedman, Sam, and Daniel Laurison. 2019. *The Class Ceiling*. London: Policy.

Friess, Horace L. 1926. "The sixth international congress of philosophy." *Journal of Philosophy* 23: 617-638.

Frimer, Jeremy A, Linda J Skitka, and Matt Motyl. 2017. "Liberals and conservatives are similarly motivated to avoid exposure to one another's opinions." *Journal of Experimental Social Psychology* 72: 1-12.

Frodeman, Robert, and Adam Briggle. 2016. *Socrates Tenured*. Lanham, MD: Rowman & Littlefield.

Fromm, Erich. 1941. *Escape from Freedom*. New York: Farrar & Rinehart.

_____. 1955. *The Sane Society*. New York: Henry Holt.

Fuentes, Carlos. 1988. *Myself with Others*. London: Andre Deutsch.

Furstenberg, Hillel. 1961. "Strict ergodicity and transformations of the torus." *American Journal of Mathematics* 12: 178-268.

Fusaro, Vincent A, Helen G Levy, and H Luke Shaefer. 2018. "Racial and ethnic disparities in the lifetime prevalence of homelessness in the United States." *Demography* 55: 2119-2128.

Fussell, Paul. 1975. *The Great War and Modern Memory*. Oxford: Oxford University Press.

Fuster, Andreas, Paul Goldsmith-Pinkham, Tarun Ramadorai, and Ansgar Walther. 2018. "Predictably unequal? The effects of machine learning on credit markets." Working Paper, Center for Economic and Policy Research, Washington, DC.

Fynsk, Christopher. 1996. *Language and Relation*. Stanford: Stanford University Press.

Gabriel, Markus. 2011. *Transcendental Ontology*. Trans. aided by Tom Krell. London: Continuum International.

_____. 2015 (2013). *Why the World Does Not Exist*. Trans. Gregory S Moss. Cambridge: Polity.

_____. 2017 (2015). *I Am Not a Brain*. Trans. Christopher Turner. Cambridge: Polity.

Gadamer, Hans-Georg. 1966. "Notes on planning for the future." *Daedalus* 95: 572-589.

_____. 1967. "Begriffene Malerei?" Pp. 218-226 in *idem, Kleine Schriften II*. Tübingen: Mohr.

_____. 1989 (1965). *Truth and Method*, revised 2nd edition. Trans. Joel Weinsheimer and Donald G Marshall. New York: Continuum.

_____. 1986 (1967). "Art and imitation." Trans. Nicholas Walker. Pp. 92-104 in *idem, The Relevance of the Beautiful and Other Essays*. Ed. Robert Bernasconi. Cambridge: Cambridge University Press.

Gaius. 1904 (c170). *Institutes of Roman Law*. Trans. Edward Poste. Oxford: Clarendon.
Galbraith, John Kenneth. 1961 [1955]. *The Great Crash 1929*. Boston: Houghton Mifflin.
Galen of Pergamon. 1916 (c175). *On the Natural Faculties*. Trans. Arthur J Brock.
Galiani, Sebastian, Matthew Staiger, and Gustavo Torrens. 2017. "When children rule." NBER Working Paper 23087. Cambridge: NBER.
Gama Goirochea, Armando. 2016. "Scaling properties of soft matter in equilibrium and under stationary flow." Pp. 289-313 in *Communications in Computer and Information Science*, edited by C.J. Barrios Hernández, et al. Cham, Switzerland: Springer International.
Gant, Andrew. 2017. *God's Own Music*. Chicago: University of Chicago Press.
Gao, Xingjian. 2000 (1990). *Soul Mountain*. Tr. Mabel Lee. New York: HarperCollins.
Garcia, Jorge Luis, James J Heckman, Duncan Ermini Leaf, and Maria José Prados. 2016. "The life-cycle benefits of an influential early childhood program." NBER Working Paper 22993. Cambridge: NBER.
Garicano, Luis, and Luis Rayo. 2016. "Why organizations fail." *Journal of Economic Literature* 54: 137-192.
Garfinkel, Alan. 1981. *Forms of Explanation*. New Haven: Yale University Press.
Garfinkel, Harold. 1967. *Studies in Ethnomethodology*. Englewood Cliffs, NJ: Prentice-Hall.
Garfinkel, Irwin, Charles F Manski, and Charles Michalopoulos. 1992. "Micro experiments and macro effects." Pp. 253-276 in *Evaluating Welfare and Training Programs*, edited by Charles F Manski and Irwin Garfinkel. Cambridge: Harvard University Press.
Garland, Robert. 1995. *The Eye of the Beholder*. London: Duckworth.
Gaskill, Nicholas, and Adam J Nocek (eds.). 2014. *The Lure of Whitehead*. Minneapolis: University of Minnesota Press.
Gates, Henry Louis, Jr. 2019. *Stony the Road*. New York: Penguin.
Gawronski, Bertram. 2004. "Theory-based bias correction in dispositional inference." *European Review of Social Psychology* 15: 183-217.
Gazzaley, Adam, and Larry D Rosen. 2016. *The Distracted Mind*. Cambridge: MIT Press.
Gebauer, Gunter, and Christoph Wulf. 1995 (1992). *Mimesis*. Trans. Don Reneau. Berkeley: University of California Press.
Geertz, Clifford. 1973. *The Interpretation of Cultures*. New York: Basic Books.
Gefter, Amanda. 2016. "The evolutionary argument against reality" (interview of Donald D Hoffman). *Quanta Magazine*, 21 April; reprinted as "The case against reality" in *TheAtlantic.com*, 25 April 2016.
Gehlen, Arnold. 1960. *Zeit-Bilder*. Frankfurt a.M.: Athenäum.
_____. 2004 (1956). *Urmensch und Spätkultur*. Frankfurt a.M.: Klostermann.
Geithner, Timothy. 2014. *Stress Test*. New York: Broadway.
Gelernter, David. 1992. *Mirror Worlds*. New York: Oxford University Press.
Gelman, Andrew, and Jonathan Auerbach. 2016. "Age-aggregation bias in mortality trends." *Proceedings of the National Academy of Sciences USA* 113: E816-E817.
Gennes, Pierre-Gilles de. 1985. *Scaling Concepts in Polymer Physics*, corrected edition. Ithaca: Cornell University Press.
Gentzkow, Matthew, and Jesse M Shapiro. 2006. "Media bias and reputation." *Journal of Political Economy* 114: 280-316.
Gergen, Kenneth J. 1991. *The Saturated Self*. New York: Basic Books.
_____. 2015. *An Invitation to Social Construction*, 3rd edition. London: Sage.

Geuss, Raymond. 1981. *The Idea of a Critical Theory*. Cambridge: Cambridge University Press.
_____. 2014. *A World without Why*. Princeton: Princeton University Press.
Ghosh, Amitav. 2016. *The Great Derangement*. Chicago: University of Chicago Press.
Giampietro, Mario, Timothy F H Allen, and Kozo Mayumi. 2006 "The epistemological predicament associated with purposive quantitative analysis." *Ecological Complexity* 3:307-327.
Giannella, Eric, and Claude S Fischer. 2016. "An inductive typology of egocentric networks." *Social Networks* 47: 15-23.
Gibbon, Edward. 1776-89. *A History of the Rise and Fall of the Roman Empire*, 6 volumes. London: Strahan & Cadell.
Gibbs, Jack P. 1979. "The elites can do without us." *The American Sociologist* 14: 79-85.
Gibbs, Josiah Willard. 1902. *Elementary Principles of Statistical Mechanics*. New York: Charles Scribner's Sons.
Gibson-Davis, Christina, Anna Gassman-Pines, and Rebecca Lehrman. 2018. "'His' and 'hers'." *Demography* 55: 2321-2343.
Giddens, Anthony. 1984. *The Constitution of Society*. Berkeley: University of California Press.
Gieryn, Thomas F. 1983. "Boundary-work and the demarcation of science from non-science." *American Sociological Review* 48: 781-795.
Gilbert, Daniel T, and Patrick S Malone. 1995. "The correspondence bias." *Psychological Bulletin* 117: 21-38.
Gilbert, Margaret. 1989. *Social Facts*. London: Routledge.
_____. 2000. *Sociality and Responsibility*. Lanham, MD: Rowman and Littlefield.
_____. 2014. *Joint Commitment*. Oxford: Oxford University Press.
Gill, Christopher. 1996. *Personality in Greek Epic, Tragedy, and Philosophy*. Oxford: Oxford University Press.
_____. 2006. *The Structured Self in Hellenistic and Roman Thought*. Oxford: Oxford University Press.
Gill, Gurtek, and Peter Straka. 2016. "A semi-Markov algorithm for continuous-time random walk limit distributions." *Mathematical Modeling of Natural Phenomena* 11 (No. 3): 34-50.
Gitlin, Todd. 1995. *The Twilight of Common Dreams*. New York: Henry Holt.
Glantz, Aaron. 2019. *Homewreckers*. New York: HarperCollins.
Glück, Louise. 2012. *Poems 1962-2012*. New York: Farrar, Straus & Giroux.
Gmeindl, Leon, Yu-Chin Chiu, Michael S Esterman, Adam S Greenberg, Susan M Courtney, and Steven Yantis. 2016. "Tracking the will to attend." *Attention, Perception, & Psychophysics* 78: 2176-2184.
Godfrey-Smith, Peter. 2013. "Darwinian individuals." Pp. 17-36 in *From Groups to Individuals*, edited by Frédéric Bouchard and Phillippe Huneman. Cambridge: MIT Press.
_____. 2016. *Other Minds*. New York: Farrar, Straus & Giroux.
Goffman, Erving. 1959. *The Presentation of Self in Everyday Life*. New York: Doubleday.
_____. 1963. *Behavior in Public Places*. New York: Free Press.
_____. 1974. *Frame Analysis*. Cambridge: Harvard University Press.
Goldberger, Arthur. 1989. "Economic and mechanical models of intergenerational transmission." *American Economic Review* 79 (June): 504-513.

Goldsmith, John, and Jason Riggle. 2012. "Information theoretical approaches to phonological structure." *Natural Language & Linguistic Theory* 30: 859-896.

Gombrich, Ernst H. 1950. *The Story of Art*, 1st edition. London: Phaidon.

Goncourt, Edmond de. 1881. *La Maison d'un artiste*, 2 volumes. Paris: Charpentier.

Goodman, Dena. 1994. *The Republic of Letters*. Ithaca, NY: Cornell University Press.

Goodman, Paul. 1960. *Growing Up Absurd*. New York: Random House.

____. 1977. "On being a writer." Pp. 204-215 in *idem, Nature Heals*. Ed. T Stoehr. New York: Free Life Editions.

Goossaert, Vincent, and David A Palmer. 2011. *The Religious Question in Modern China*. Chicago: University of Chicago Press.

Gordin, Michael. 2015. *Scientific Babel*. Chicago: University of Chicago Press.

Gordon, Deborah M. 2010. *Ant Encounters*. Princeton: Princeton University Press.

Gordon, Peter E. 2016. *Adorno and Existence*. Cambridge: Harvard University Press.

Gordon, Robert J. 2016. *The Rise and Fall of American Growth*. Princeton: Princeton University Press.

Gorst-Rasmussen, Anders, Darryl Veitch, and Andras Gefferth. 2012. "Why FARIMA models are brittle." *arXiv: 1203.6140v1*. Last access 24 December 2019.

Gorz, André. 1982 (1980). *Farewell to the Working Class*. London: Pluto.

Gould, Carol C. 1978. *Marx's Social Ontology*. Cambridge: MIT Press.

Gouldner, Alvin W. 1970. *The Coming Crisis of Western Sociology*. New York: Basic.

Goulemot, Jean-Marie. 1991. *Ces livres qu'on ne lit que d'une main*. Aix-en-Provence: Alinéa.

Gradmann, Hans. 1930. "Die harmonische Lebenseinheit vom Standpunkt exakter Naturwissenschaft." *Naturwissenschaften* 18: 641-644, 662-666.

Grafton, Anthony, and Megan Williams. 2006. *Christianity and the Transformation of the Book*. Cambridge: Harvard University Press.

Gramsci, Antonio. 1971. *Selections from the Prison Notebooks*. Trans & ed. Quintin Hoare and Geoffrey Nowell-Smith. London: Lawrence & Wishart.

Granet, Marcel. 1979 (1922). *La religion des chinois*. Paris: Payot.

Grann, David. 2017. *Killers of the Flower Moon*. New York: Doubleday.

Granovetter, Mark. 1973. "The strength of weak ties." *American Journal of Sociology* 78: 1360-1380.

____. 1985. "Economic action and social structure." *American Journal of Sociology* 91: 481-510.

Grant, Adam M, and Barry Schwartz. 2011. "Too much of a good thing." *Perspectives on Psychological Science* 6 (1): 61-76.

Gratton, Peter. 2014. *Speculative Realism*. London: Bloomsbury.

Grawe, Nathan D, and Casey B Mulligan. 2002. "Economic interpretations of intergenerational correlations." *Journal of Economic Perspectives* 16 (Summer): 45-58.

Greenberg, Clement. 1993 (1960). "Modernist painting." Pp. 85-93 in *idem, The Collected Essays and Criticisms*, vol. 4. Ed. J O'Brian. Chicago: University of Chicago Press.

Greenblatt, Stephen. 2011. *The Swerve*. New York: Norton.

Greer, Michelle. 2001. *Kant's Doctrine of Transcendental Illusion*. Cambridge: Cambridge University Press.

Greer, Rowan A. 1989. *The Fear of Freedom*. University Park: Pennsylvania State University Press.

Greif, Avner. 1994. "Cultural beliefs and the organization of society." *Journal of Political Economy* 102: 912-950.

\_\_\_\_\_, Paul Milgrom, and Barry R Weingast. 1994. "Coordination, commitment, and enforcement." *Journal of Political Economy* 102: 746-776.

Greif, Mark. 2015. *The Age of the Crisis of Man.* Princeton: Princeton University Press.

\_\_\_\_\_. 2016. *Against Everything.* New York: Pantheon.

Grice, H Paul. 1957. "Meaning." *Philosophical Review* 66: 377-388.

Griffiths, Eric. 1989. *The Printed Voice of Victorian Poetry.* Oxford: Clarendon.

Groethuysen, Bernard. 1968 (1927). *The Bourgeois.* Trans. Mary Ilford. New York: Holt, Rinehart and Winston.

Groff, Ruth Porter. 2013. *Ontology Revisited.* New York: Routledge.

Gross, Matthias. 2007. "The unknown in process." *Current Sociology* 55: 742-759.

Grossmann, Igor, and Michael E W Varnum. 2015. "Social structure, infectious disease, secularism, and cultural change in America." *Psychological Science* 26: 311-324.

Grusky, David B, and Robert M Hauser. 1984. "Comparative social mobility revisited." *American Sociological Review* 49: 19-38.

Guess, Andrew, Jonathan Nagler, and Joshua Tucker. 2019. "Less than you think." *Science Advances* 5 (4 January): 1-8.

Guilhaumou, Jacques. 2006. "Sieyès et le non-dit de la sociologie: du mot à la chose." *Revue d'histoire des sciences humaines* 15 (November).

Guillaumin, Émile. 1983 (1943). *The Life of a Simple Man,* revised edition. Trans. Margaret Crosland. Hanover, NH: University Press of New England.

Guizzard, Giancarlo. 2005. *Ontological Foundations for Structural Conceptual Models.* Enschede, Netherlands: Telematica Instituut.

Gul, Faruk, Paulo Natenzon, and Wolfgang Pesendorfer. 2014. "Random choice as behavioral optimization." *Econometrica* 82: 1873-1912.

Guston, David. 2016. "The muddled legacy of Alvin Toffler." *Slate.* 8 July.

Haber, Samuel. 1991. *The Quest for Authority and Honor in the American Professions 1750-1900.* Chicago: University of Chicago Press.

Habermas, Jürgen. 1971 (1965). "Discussion" (of Parsons 1971 [1965]). Pp. 59-66 in *Max Weber and Sociology Today,* edited by Otto Stammer. Tr Kathleen Morris. New York: Harper & Row.

\_\_\_\_\_. 1971 (1968). *Knowledge and Human Interests.* Tr. Jeremy J Shapiro. Boston: Beacon.

\_\_\_\_\_. 1973 (1971). *Theory and Practice.* Tr. John Viertel. Boston: Beacon.

\_\_\_\_\_. 1979 (1976). *Communication and the Evolution of Society.* Tr. Thomas McCarthy. Boston: Beacon.

\_\_\_\_\_. 1981 (1980). "Talcott Parsons: problems of theory construction." *Sociological Inquiry* 51: 173-196.

\_\_\_\_\_. 1987 (1981). *The Theory of Communicative Action,* volume 2. Tr. Thomas McCarthy. Boston: Beacon.

\_\_\_\_\_. 1987 (1985). *The Philosophical Discourse of Modernity.* Tr. Frederick Lawrence. Cambridge: MIT Press.

\_\_\_\_\_. 1988 (1970). *On the Logic of the Social Sciences.* Trs. Shierry Weber Nicholsen and Jerry A Stark. Cambridge: MIT Press.

\_\_\_\_\_. 1989 (1962). *The Structural Transformation of the Public Sphere.* Tr. Thomas Burger with Frederick Lawrence. Cambridge: MIT Press.

Habermas, Jürgen. 1990 (1983). *Moral Consciousness and Communicative Action*. Tr. Christian Lenhardt and Shierry Weber Nicholsen. Cambridge: MIT Press.
_____. 1992 (1988). *Postmetaphysical Thinking*. Tr. William Mark Hohengarten. Cambridge: MIT Press.
_____. 1994 (1991). *The Past as Future*. Tr. & ed. Max Pensky. London: Polity.
_____. 1996 (1992). *Between Facts and Norms*. Tr. W Rehg. Cambridge: MIT Press.
Hacking, Ian. 1995. *Rewriting the Soul*. Princeton: Princeton University Press.
Hagan, Joe. 2017. *Sticky Fingers*. New York: Knopf.
Hahn, Frank, and Robert Solow. 1995. *A Critical Essay on Modern Macroeconomic Theory*. Cambridge: MIT Press.
Halewood, Michael. 2014. *Rethinking the Social through Durkheim, Marx, Weber and Whitehead*. London: Anthem.
Hall, G Stanley. 1904. *Adolescence*, 2 volumes. New York: D Appleton.
Hall, Robert E, and Thomas J Sargent. 2018. "Short-run and long-run effects of Milton Friedman's presidential address." *Journal of Economic Perspectives* 32: 121-134.
Hallinan, Maureen T. 1988. "Equality of educational opportunity." *Annual Review of Sociology* 14: 249-268.
_____, and Richard A Williams. 1990. "Students' characteristics and the peer-influence process." *Sociology of Education* 63: 122-132.
Halliwell, Stephen. 2008. *Greek Laughter*. Cambridge: Cambridge University Press.
Hamdy, Sherine F. 2009. "Islam, fatalism, and medical intervention." *Anthropological Quarterly* 82: 173-196.
Hamilton, Andrew, and Jennifer Fewell. 2013. "Groups, individuals, and the emergence of sociality: the case of division of labor." Pp. 175-194 in *From Groups to Individuals*, edited by Frédéric Bouchard and Phillippe Huneman. Cambridge: MIT Press.
Hammerstein, Notker, and Ulrich Herrmann. 2005. *Handbuch der deutschen Bildungsgeschichte*, volume 2. Munich: C H Becker.
Hamper, Ben. 1991. *Rivethead*. New York: Warner.
Hannan, Michael T. 1991. *Aggregation and Disaggregation in the Social Sciences*, revised edition. Lexington, MA: D C Heath.
_____, László Pólos, and Glenn R Carroll. 2007. *Logics of Organizational Theory*. Princeton: Princeton University Press.
Hansen, Mogens Herman. 2006a. *Polis*. Oxford: Oxford University Press.
_____. 2006b. *The Shotgun Method*. Columbia: University of Missouri Press.
_____. 2008. "An update on the shotgun method." *Greek, Roman, and Byzantine Studies* 48: 259-286.
Hanushek, Eric A, and Ludger Woessmann. 2012. "Do better schools lead to more growth?" *Journal of Economic Growth* 17: 267-321.
Harari, Yuval Noah. 2015 (2011). *Sapiens*. New York: HarperCollins.
_____. 2016 (2015). *Homo Deus: A Brief History of Tomorrow*. London: Harvill Secker.
Hardy, Melissa, and Lawrence Hazelrigg. 1999. "Fueling the politics of age." *American Sociological Review* 64: 570-576.
_____. 2007. *Pension Puzzles*. New York: Russell Sage.
_____, and Jill Quadagno. 1996. *Ending a Career in the Auto Industry*. New York: Plenum.
Harman, Graham. 2002. *Tool-Being*. Peru, IL: Open Court.
_____. 2016. *Immaterialism*. London: Polity.
_____. 2018. *Object-Oriented Ontology*. London: Penguin.

Harper, Kyle. 2017. *The Fate of Rome*. Princeton: Princeton University Press.

Harré, Rom, and Paul Secord. 1972. *The Explanation of Social Behavior*. Oxford: Blackwell.

Harris, Jeffrey G. 1985. "Macro-experiments versus micro-experiments for health policy" (with comments by P B Ginsburg & L L Orr). Pp. 145-186 in *Social Experimentation*, edited by Jerry A Hausman & David A Wise. Chicago: University of Chicago Press.

Harris, Sam. 2010. *The Moral Landscape*. New York: Free Press.

Harris, William V. 1989. *Ancient Literacy*. Cambridge: Harvard University Press.

Harrison, Daniel M. 2014. *Making Sense of Marshall Ledbetter*. Gainesville: University Press of Florida.

Hart, Oliver. 2017. "Incomplete contracts and control." *American Economic Review* 107: 1731-1752.

Hartley, Leslie P. 1953. *The Go-Between*. London: Hamish Hamilton.

Hartman, Geoffrey. 1981. *Saving the Text*. Baltimore: Johns Hopkins University Press.

Harvey, Andrew C. 1989. *Forecasting, Structural Time Series Models and the Kalman Filter*. Cambridge: Cambridge University Press.

Harvey, David. 2006. *The Limits to Capital*, updated edition. London: Verso.

Harvey, F David. 1966. "Literacy in the Athenian democracy." *Revue des Études Grecques* 79 (July-December): 585-635.

Haskel, Jonathan, and Stian Westlake. 2018. *Capitalism without Capital*. Princeton: Princeton University Press.

Haskins, Charles Homer. 1927. *The Renaissance of the Twelfth Century*. Cambridge: Harvard University Press.

Haslett, John, and Adrian E Raftery. 1989. "Space-time modeling with long-memory dependence." *Applied Statistics* 38: 1-50.

Hastings, Justine S, and Olivia S Mitchell. 2011."How financial literacy and impatience shape retirement wealth and investment behaviors."Working Paper 16740.Cambridge:NBER.

Hauser, Arnold. 1982 (1974). *The Sociology of Art*. Trans. Kenneth J Northcott. Chicago: University of Chicago Press.

Hausheer, Herman. 1937. "St Augustine's conception of time." *The Philosophical Review* 46 (September): 503-512.

Hausman, Jerry A, and David A Wise (eds.). 1985. *Social Experimentation*. Chicago: University of Chicago Press.

Hawking, Stephen. 1988. *A Brief History of Time*. New York: Bantam.

_____ (ed.). 2007. *A Stubbornly Persistent Illusion*. Philadelphia: Running Press.

Hawthorn, Geoffrey. 1976. *Enlightenment and Despair*. Cambridge: Cambridge University Press.

_____. 1991. *Plausible Worlds*. Cambridge: Cambridge University Press.

Hayek, Friedrich A. 1948. *Individualism and Economic Order*. Chicago: University of Chicago Press.

_____. 1967a. "Notes on the evolution of systems of rules of conduct." Pp. 66-81 in *idem*, *Studies in Philosophy, Politics and Economics*. Chicago: University of Chicago Press.

_____. 1967b. "The results of human action but not human design." Pp. 96-105 in *idem*, *Studies in Philosophy, Politics and Economics*. Chicago: University of Chicago Press.

Hazelrigg, Lawrence. 1969. "A reexamination of Simmel's 'The Secret and the Secret Society.'" *Social Forces* 47: 323-330.

Hazelrigg, Lawrence. 1973. "Aspects of the measurement of class consciousness." Pp. 219-247 in *Comparative Social Research*, edited by Michael Armer and Allen D Grimshaw. New York: Wiley-Interscience.

_____. 1979. "What would Francis Bacon think?" *The American Sociologist* 14: 21-24.

_____. 1980. "One man's poison is another's staple." *Contemporary Sociology* 9: 51-53.

_____. 1985. "Were it not for words." *Social Problems* 32: 234-237.

_____. 1986. "Is there a choice between 'constructionism' and 'objectivism'?" *Social Problems* 33: 201-213.

_____. 1989a. *A Wilderness of Mirrors*. Gainesville: University Press of Florida.

_____. 1989b. *Claims of Knowledge*. Gainesville: University Press of Florida.

_____. 1991. "The problem of micro-macro linkage." *Current Perspectives in Social Theory* 11: 229-254,

_____. 1992. "Reading Goffman's framing as provocation of a discipline." *Human Studies* 15: 239-264; reprinted as pp. 137-160 of vol. 3 of *Erving Goffman*, edited by Gary Alan Fine & Gregory W H Smith. Thousand Oaks, CA: Sage, 2000.

_____. 1993a. "Constructionism and practices of objectivity." Pp. 485-500 in *Reconsidering Social Constructionism*, edited by James Holstein and Gale Miller. New York: Aldine de Gruyter.

_____. 1993b. "Marx and the meter of nature." *Rethinking Marxism* 6 (Summer): 104-122.

_____. 1995. *Cultures of Nature*. Gainesville: University Press of Florida.

_____. 1997. "On the importance of age." Pp. 93-128 in *Studying Aging and Social Change*, edited by Melissa Hardy. Thousand Oaks, CA: Sage.

_____. 2004. "Inference." Chapter 4 of *Handbook of Data Analysis*, edited by Melissa Hardy and Alan Bryman. London: Sage.

_____. 2009. "Forty years of *Knowledge and Human Interests*: a brief appreciation." *Current Perspectives in Social Theory* 26: 189-206

_____. 2010. "On theorizing the dynamics of process: a propaedeutic introduction." *Current Perspectives in Social Theory* 27: 3-79.

_____. 2012. "Developments of analytical logic and dialectical logic with regard to the study of process dynamics." *Current Perspectives in Social Theory* 30: 61-95.

_____. 2014. "Experience, problems of scale, and the aesthetics of perception." *Current Perspectives in Social Theory* 32: 3-51.

_____. 2016. "Turning the circle: considerations of 'the postmodern turn' à la Simon Susen." *Current Perspectives in Social Theory* 35: 229-277.

_____. 2019. "'How can [we] not know?' *Blade Runner* as cinematic landmark in critical thought." *Current Perspectives in Social Theory* 36: 111-132.

_____. 2020. "Efficiency and efficacy in the world of Terry Gilliam's *Brazil*." *Soundings* 103: 158-183.

_____, and Maurice A Garnier. 1976. "Occupational mobility in industrial societies." *American Sociological Review* 41: 498-511.

_____, and Melissa Hardy. 1997. "Perceived income adequacy among older adults." *Research on Aging* 19: 69-107.

Hearst, Norman, Thomas B Newman, and Stephen B Hulley. 1986. "Delayed effects of the military draft on mortality." *New England Journal of Medicine* 314: 620-624.

Heath, John. 2005. *The Talking Greeks*. Cambridge: Cambridge University Press.

Heckman, James J. 1979. "Sample selection as a specification error." *Econometrica* 47: 153-161.

Heckman, James J. 1981a. "Statistical models for discrete panel data." Pp. 114-178 in *Structural Analysis of Discrete Data with Econometric Applications*, edited by Charles F Manski and Daniel McFadden. Cambridge: MIT Press.

_____. 1981b. "The incidental parameters problem and the problem of initial conditions in estimating a discrete time – discrete data stochastic process." Pp. 179-195 in *Structural Analysis of Discrete Data with Econometric Applications*, edited by Charles F Manski and Daniel McFadden. Cambridge: MIT Press.

_____. 2005. "The scientific model of causality." *Sociological Methodology* 35: 1-97.

_____. 2008. "Schools, skills, and synapses." *Economic Inquiry* 46: 289-324.

_____, and Sidharth Moktan. 2018. "Publishing and promotion in economics." NBER Working Paper 25093. Cambridge: NBER.

_____, Seong Hyeok Moon, Rodrigo Pinto, Peter Savelyev, and Adam Yavitz. 2010. "Analyzing social experiments as implemented." *Quantitative Economics* 1: 1-46.

_____, Rodrigo Pinto, and Peter Savelyev. 2013. "Understanding the mechanisms through which an influential early childhood program boosted adult outcomes." *American Economic Review* 103: 2052-2086.

Hechter, Michael. 1990. "The emergence of cooperative social institutions." Pp. 13-33 in *Social Institutions*, edited by Michael Hechter, Karl-Dieter Opp, and Reinhard Wippler. New York: Aldine de Gruyter.

Hedström, Peter. 2005. *Dissecting the Social*. Cambridge: Cambridge University Press.

_____, and Lars Udehn. 2009. "Analytical sociology and theories of the middle range." Pp. 25-47 in *The Oxford Handbook of Analytical Sociology*, edited by Peter Hedström and Peter Bearman. Oxford: Oxford University Press.

_____, and Petri Ylikoski. 2010. "Causal mechanisms in the social sciences." *Annual Review of Sociology* 36: 49-67.

Hegel, Georg W F. 1842-43. *Vorlesungen über die Ästhetik*, 2nd edition. Ed. Heinrich Gustav Hotho. Berlin: Duncker und Humbolt.

_____. 1914 (1848). *Lectures on the History of Philosophy*, 3rd edition. Ed. Eduard Gan; corrected by Karl Hegel; trans. J Sibree. London: G Bell and Sons.

_____. 1970 (1830). *Hegel's Philosophy of Nature*. Part 2 of *idem, Encyclopedia of the Philosophical Sciences*. Trans. A V Miller. Oxford: Clarendon.

_____. 1971 (1830). *Hegel's Philosophy of Mind*. Part 3 of *idem, Encyclopedia of the Philosophical Sciences*. Trans. A V Miller. Oxford: Clarendon.

_____. 1975 (1835). *Aesthetics*, 2 volumes. Trans. T M Knox, from H G Hotho's 2nd edition (1842-43) of lecture notes. Oxford: Clarendon.

_____. 1977 (1952). *Phenomenology of Geist*, 5th edition. Ed. J Hoffmeister; trans. A V Miller. Oxford: Clarendon.

_____. 1991 (1820). *Elements of the Philosophy of Right*. Trans. H B Nisbet; ed. Allen W Wood. Cambridge: Cambridge University Press.

Heidegger, Martin. 1962 (1957). *Being and Time*, 8th edition. Trans. John Macquarrie & Edward Robinson. New York: Harper and Brothers.

_____. 1971 (1960). "The origin of the work of art." Pp. 15-87 of *idem, Poetry, Language, Thought*. Trans. Albert Hofstadter. New York: Harper & Row.

_____. 1972 (1969). *On Time and Being*. Trans. J Stambaugh. New York: Harper & Row.

_____. 1977 (1938). "The age of the world picture." Pp. 115-154 in *idem, The Question Concerning Technology and Other Essays*. Trans. William Lovitt. New York: Harper & Row.

Heidegger, Martin. 1982 (1975). *The Basic Problems of Phenomenology*, 3rd edition. Ed. F-W Von Herrmann; tr. Albert Hofstadter. Bloomington: Indiana University Press.

_____. 1988 (1962). "Schlageter." Pp. 96-97 in *idem, Political Texts 1933-1934*. Tr. William S Lewis. *New German Critique* 45 (Autumn): 96-114.

_____. 1991. *The Principle of Reason*. Tr. Reginald Lilley. Bloomington: Indiana University Press.

Heilbron, Johan, and George Steinmetz. 2018. "A defense of Bourdieu." *Catalyst* 2: 35-49.

Hendry, Andrew P. 2016. *Eco-evolutionary Dynamics*. Princeton: Princeton University Press.

Henrich, Dieter. 1971 (1965). "Discussion" (of Parsons 1971 [1965]). Pp. 66-71 in *Max Weber and Sociology Today*, edited by Otto Stammer. Tr. Kathleen Morris. New York: Harper & Row.

_____. 1987 (1986). "Karl Jaspers: thinking with Max Weber in mind." Trans. Adrian Stevens. Pp. 528-544 in *Max Weber and His Contemporaries*, edited by Wolfgang J Mommsen and Jürgen Osterhammel. London: Allen and Unwin.

_____. 2003. *Between Kant and Hegel*. Ed. David S Pacini. Cambridge: Harvard University Press.

_____. 2006. *Die Philosophie im Prozeß der Kultur*. Frankfurt am Main: Suhrkamp.

Herrmann, Ulrich. 2000. "Bildung durch Wissenschaft? Mythos 'Humboldt.'" *Pädagogische Rundschau* 54: 487-506.

Hesse, Hermann. 1969 (1943). *The Glass Bead Game*. Trans. Clara & Richard Winston. New York: Farrar, Straus, and Giroux.

Heti, Sheila. 2010. *How Should a Person Be?* Toronto: House of Anansi.

Hewitt, John P. 1990. *Dilemmas of the American Self*. Philadelphia: Temple University Press.

Hewitt, Rachel. 2017. *A Revolution of Feeling*. London: Granta.

Higbie, Frank Tobias. 2003. *Indispensable Outcasts*. Urbana: University of Illinois Press.

Hilbert, David. 1950 (1902). *Foundations of Geometry*, 2nd edition. Trans. E J Townsend. LaSalle, IL: Open Court.

Hillcoat-Nallétamby, Sarah, and Judith E Phillips. 2011. "Social ambivalence revisited." *Sociology* 45: 202-217.

Himmelfarb, Gertrude. 1991. *Poverty and Compassion*. New York: Knopf.

_____. 2004. *The Roads to Modernity*. New York: Vintage.

Hippocrates of Kos. 1868 (c370 BCE). *The General Works of Hippocrates*. Tr. and ed. Charles Darwin Adams. New York: Dover.

Hirsch, Eric D., Jr. 1967. *Validity in Interpretation*. New Haven: Yale University Press.

Hirschman, Albert. 1970. *Exit, Voice and Loyalty*. Cambridge: Harvard University Press.

_____. 2013. *The Essential Hirschman*, edited by Jeremy Adelman. Princeton: Princeton University Press.

Hirschman, Daniel, and Isaac Ariail Reed. 2014. "Formation stories and causality in sociology." *Sociological Theory* 32: 259-282.

Ho, Simon Y W, Matthew J Phillips, Alan Cooper, and Alexei J Drummond. 2005. "Time dependency of molecular rate estimates and systematic overestimation of recent divergence times." *Molecular and Biological Evolution* 22 (7): 1561-1568.

Hobbes, Thomas. 1839-45. *The English Works of Thomas Hobbes*, 11 volumes, edited by William Molesworth. London: John Bohn.

_____. 1909 (1651). *Leviathan*. Oxford: Clarendon.

Hobbes, Thomas. 1949 (1647). *De Cive, or the Citizen*, rev. ed. New York: Appleton-Century-Crofts.

_____. 1972 (1658). *On Man* (last five chapters). Trans. Charles Wood, TSK Scott-Craig, and Bernard Gert. Pp. 33-86 in *idem, Man and Citizen*, edited by Bernard Gert. Garden City, NY: Doubleday.

Hochschild, Adam. 2018. *Lessons from a Dark Time and Other Essays*. Berkeley: University of California Press.

Hochschild, Adam. 2019. "Obstruction of justice: when America tried to deport its radicals." *The New Yorker* 95 (11November): 28, 30-34.

Hochschild, Arlie Russell. 2016. *Strangers in Their Own Land*. New York: New Press.

Hölderlin, Friedrich. 1990 (1803). "Patmos." Trans. Michael Hamburger. Pp. 244-263 in *idem, Hyperion and Selected Poems*. Ed. Eric L Santner. New York: Continuum.

Hoffman, Donald D. 1998. *Visual Intelligence*. New York: Norton.

Hofmann, Hagen, Andrea Soranno, Alessandro Borgia, Klaus Gast, Daniel Nettels, and Benjamin Schuler. 2012. "Polymer scaling laws of unfolded and intrinsically disordered proteins quantified with single-molecule spectroscopy." *PNAS* 109 (2 October): 16155-16160. <doi.org/10.1073/pnas.1207719109>

Hofstadter, Richard J. 1963. *Anti-Intellectualism in American Life*. New York: Knopf.

_____. 1964. *The Paranoid Style in American Politics, and Other Essays*. New York: Vintage.

Holland, Paul W. 1986. "Statistics and causal inference." *Journal of the American Statistical Association* 81: 945-970.

Holmes, Oliver Wendell, Jr. 1881. *The Common Law*. Boston: Little, Brown.

Holmes, Richard. 2008. *The Age of Wonder*. New York: Pantheon.

_____. 2016. *This Long Pursuit*. New York: Pantheon.

Homans, George Caspar. 1984. *Coming to My Senses*. New Brunswick, NJ: Transaction.

Honan, Park. 1987. *Jane Austen*. London: Weidenfeld and Nicolson.

Hont, Istvan. 2005. *Jealousy of Trade*. Cambridge: Harvard University Press.

Horace. 1929 (c18 BCE). *Ars Poetica*. Pp. 442-489 in *idem, Satires, Epistles and Art of Poetry*. Trans. H Rushton Fairclough. Cambridge: Harvard University Press.

Horkheimer, Max, and Theodor W Adorno. 2002 (1969). *Dialectic of Enlightenment*, rev. ed. Tr. E Jephcott; ed. G Schmid Noerr. Stanford: Stanford University Press.

Horowitz, Gregg M. 2001. *Sustaining Loss*. Stanford: Stanford University Press.

Horwitz, Morton J. 1992. *The Transformation of American Law, 1870-1960*. New York: Oxford University Press.

Housman, Alfred Edward. 1922. *Last Poems*. New York: Henry Holt.

Hout, Michael. 2012. "Social and economic returns to college education in the United States." *Annual Review of Sociology* 38: 379-400.

Hout, Michael. 2018. "Americans' occupational status reflects the status of both of their parents." *PNAS* (18 July). <doi:10.1073/pnas.1802508115>

Howard, Richard. 1981. "Proust Re-Englished." *New York Times Book Reviews* (3 May).

Howe, Daniel Walker. 2009. *What Hath God Wrought*. New York: Oxford University Press.

Howerth, Ira W. 1894. "Present condition of sociology in the United States." *Annals of the American Academy of Political and Social Science* 5: 112-121.

_____. 1906. "The social question of today." *American Journal of Sociology* 12: 254-286.

Howlett, Peter, and Mary S Morgan (eds.). 2011. *How Well Do Facts Travel?* Cambridge: Cambridge University Press.

Huckfeldt, R Robert. 2013. *Politics in Context.* New York: Algora.

Huebner, Daniel R. 2014. *Becoming Mead.* Chicago: University of Chicago Press.

Hughes, Robert. 1993. *Culture of Complaint.* New York: Oxford University Press.

Hullot-Kentor, Robert. 2006. *Things Beyond Resemblance.* New York: Columbia University Press.

Hulme, Mike. 2009. *Why We Disagree about Climate Change.* Cambridge: Cambridge University Press.

Hume, David. 1958 (1748). *An Enquiry Concerning Human Understanding.* Ed. L A Selby Bigge. LaSalle, IL: Open Court.

_____. 1964 (1739-40). *A Treatise of Human Nature.* Ed. L A Selby Bigge. Oxford: Clarendon.

_____. 1985 (1777). *Essays.* Ed. Eugene Miller. Indianapolis. Liberty Classics.

Humphrey, William S., and Joe Stanislaw. 1979. "Economic growth and energy consumption in the UK, 1700-1975." *Energy Policy* 7: 29-42.

Hunnicutt, Benjamin Kline. 2013. *Free Time.* Philadelphia: Temple University Press.

Hurlburt, Russell T., and Eric Schwitzgebel. 2007. *Describing Inner Experience.* Cambridge: MIT Press.

Husock, Howard A. 2019. *Who Killed Civil Society?* New York: Encounter.

Husserl, Edmund. 1964 (1950). *The Idea of Phenomenology.* Ed. Walter Biemel; trans. William P Alston and George Naknikian. The Hague: Martinus Nijhof.

_____. 1965 (1910-11). "Philosophy as rigorous science." Pp. 71-147 in *idem, Phenomenology and the Crisis of Philosophy.* Trans. Quentin Lauer. New York: Harper & Row.

_____. 1970 (1900-01). *Logical Investigations,* 2 volumes. Trans. J N Findley. London: Routledge & Kegan Paul.

_____. 1970 (1936). *The Crisis of European Sciences and Transcendental Phenomenology.* Trans. David Carr. Evanston: Northwestern University Press.

_____. 1991 (1893). *On the Phenomenology of the Consciousness of Internal Time.* (Volume 10 of the 1966 Critical Edition of Husserl, edited by Rudolf Boehm). Trans. John B Brough. Dordrecht: Kluwer.

Hutchinson, Ben. 2016. *Lateness and Modern European Literature.* Oxford: Oxford University Press.

Huxley, Aldous. 1926. *Leda.* London: Chatto & Windus.

Ijiri, Yuji. 1971. "Fundamental queries in aggregation theory." *Journal of the American Statistical Association* 66: 766-782.

_____. 1975. *Theory of Accounting Measurement.* Studies in Accounting Research #10. Sarasota, FL: American Accounting Association.

Immermann, Karl. 1981 (1836). *Die Epigonen. Familienmemoiren in neun Büchern 1823 – 1835.* Ed. Peter Hasubek. Munich: Winkler.

Indiana, Gary. 2008. *Utopia's Debris.* New York: Basic Books.

Irwin, Terence H. 1983. "Euripides and Socrates." *Classical Philology* 78: 183-197.

Isaac, Larry W., and Paul F Lipold. 2012. "Toward bridging analytics and dialectics." *Current Perspectives in Social Theory* 30: 3-33.

Isaac, R Mark, and Duncan James. 2000. "Just who are you calling risk averse?" *Journal of Risk and Uncertainty* 20: 177-187.

Isenberg, Nancy. 2016. *White Trash*. New York: Viking.

Izenberg, Gerald N. 1992. *Impossible Individuality*. Princeton: Princeton University Press.

Jacob, Margaret C, and Catherine Secretan (eds.). 2008. *The Self-Perception of Early Modern Capitalists*. New York: Palgrave Macmillan.

Jacobs, Carol. 1999. *In the Language of Walter Benjamin*. Baltimore: Johns Hopkins University Press.

Jaeger, Werner. 1945. *Paideia*. Trans. Gilbert Highet. Oxford: Oxford University Press.

Jakobson, Roman. 1987 (1921). "Realism in art." Pp. 19-27 in *idem, Language in Literature*. Ed. K Pomorska & S Rudy. Cambridge: Harvard University Press.

James, William. 1890. *Principles of Psychology*. New York: Henry Holt.

_____. 1909. "On a very prevalent abuse of abstraction." *Popular Science Monthly* 74: 485-493.

Jarrassé, Nathanaël, Etienne de Montalivet, Florian Richer, Caroline Nicol, Amélie Touillet, Noël Martinet, Jean Paysant, and Jozina B. de Graaf. 2018. "Phantom-mobility-based prosthesis control in transhumeral amputees without surgical reinnervation." *Frontiers in Bioengineering and Biotechnology* 29 November.

Jay, Martin. 2005. *Songs of Experience*. Berkeley: University of California Press.

Jeffries, Stuart. 2016. *Grand Hotel Abyss*. London: Verso.

Jenkyns, Richard. 2016. *Classical Literature*. New York: Basic Books.

Jepperson, Ronald, and John W Meyer. 2011. "Multiple levels of analysis and the limitations of methodological individualisms." *Sociological Theory* 29: 54-73.

Jianakoplos, Nancy, Paul Menchik, and Owen Irvine. 1989. "Using panel data to assess the bias in cross-sectional inferences of life-cycle changes in the level and composition of household wealth." Pp. 553-644 in *The Measurement of Saving, Investment, and Wealth*, edited by Robert E Lipsey and Helen Stone Tice. Chicago: University of Chicago Press.

Jiang, Linxing, Andrea Stocco, Darby M Losey, Justin A Abernathy, Chantal S Prat, and Rajesh P N Rao. 2018. "BrainNet." *arXiv*: 1809. 08632v1.

Joas, Hans. 1985 (1980). *G H Mead*. Tr. Raymond Meyer. Cambridge: MIT Press.

_____. 1993. *Pragmatism and Social Theory*. Tr. Jeremy Gaines, Raymond Meyer, and Steven Minner. Chicago: University of Chicago Press.

_____, and Daniel R Huebner (eds.). 2016. *The Timeliness of George Herbert Mead*. Chicago: University of Chicago Press.

Johanek, Peter. 1999. "Merchants, markets and towns." Pp. 64-94 in *The New Cambridge Medieval History*, volume 3, edited by Timothy Reuter. Cambridge: Cambridge University Press.

Johnston, Barry V. 1995. *Pitirim A Sorokin*. Lawrence: University Press of Kansas.

Jones, Edward E, and Victor Harris. 1967. "The attribution of attitudes." *Journal of Experimental Social Psychology* 3: 1-24.

Jones, Frank Lancaster. 1985. "Simulation models of group segregation." *Australian and New Zealand Journal of Sociology* 21: 431-444.

Joseph, Kenneth, Wei Wei, Matthew Benigni, and Kathleen M Carley. 2016. "A social-event based approach to sentiment analysis of identities and behaviors in texts." *Journal of Mathematical Sociology* 40 (3): 137-166.

Jost, John T, and Curtis D Hardin. 2011. "On the structure and dynamics of human thought." *Political Psychology* 32: 21-57.

Joyce, James. 1916. *A Portrait of the Artist as a Young Man*. New York: B W Huebsch.

Julius Caesar. 1996 (58-49 BCE). *The Gallic War*. Tr. Carolyn Hammond. Oxford: Oxford University Press.

Jullien, François. 1999 (1992). *The Propensity of Things*. Tr. J Lloyd. New York: Zone
_____. 2000 (1995). *Detour and Access*. Tr. S Hawkes. New York: Zone.
_____. 2004 (1991). *In Praise of Blandness*. Tr. P M Varsano. New York: Zone.
_____. 2004 (1996). *A Treatise on Efficacy*. Tr. Janet Lloyd. Honolulu: University of Hawai'i Press.

Kahneman, Daniel. 2011. *Thinking, Fast and Slow*. New York: Farrar, Straus & Giroux.

Kalleberg, Arne. 2007. *The Mismatched Worker*. New York: Norton.
_____, David Knoke, Peter V Marsden, and Joe L Spaeth. 1996. *Organizations in America*. Thousand Oaks, CA: Sage.

Kane, Thomas J, Jonah E Rockoff, and Douglas O Staiger. 2008. "What does certification tell us about teacher effectiveness?" *Economics of Education Review* 27: 615-631.

Kant, Immanuel. 1949 (1786). "What is orientation in thinking?" Pp. 293-305 in *idem*, *Critique of Practical Reason, and Other Writings in Moral Philosophy*. Tr. & ed. Lewis White Beck. Chicago: University of Chicago Press.
_____. 1974 (1798). *Anthropology from a Pragmatic Point of View*. Tr. Mary Gregor. The Hague: Martinus Nijhof.
_____. 1974 (1800). *Logic*. Tr. Robert S Hartman and Wolfgang Schwarz. Indianapolis: Bobbs-Merrill.
_____. 1979 (1798). *The Conflict of the Faculties*. Trans. Mary J Gregor and Robert E Anchor. Lincoln: University of Nebraska Press.
_____. 1900 (1888). *On Education*, 2nd ed. Ed. T Vogt, trans. A Churton. Boston: Heath.
_____. 1991 (1784a). "Idea for a universal history with cosmopolitan purpose." Pp. 41-53 *idem*, *Political Writings*, revised edition. Trans. H B Nisbett; ed. Hans Reiss. Cambridge: Cambridge University Press.
_____. 1991 (1784b). "An answer to the question, 'What is Enlightenment?'" Pp. 54-60 in *idem*, *Political Writings*, revised edition. Trans. H B Nisbett; ed. Hans Reiss. Cambridge: Cambridge University Press.
_____. 1991 (1793). "On the common saying: 'this may be true in theory, but it does not apply in practice.'" Pp. 61-92 in *idem*, *Political Writings*, revised edition. Tr. H B Nisbett; ed. Hans Reiss. Cambridge: Cambridge University Press.
_____. 1993 (1796). "On a genteel tone recently sounded in philosophy." Tr. P Fenves. Pp. 51-81 in *Raising the Tone of Philosophy*, edited by Peter Fenves. Baltimore: Johns Hopkins University Press.
_____. 1993 (1936-38). *Opus Postumum*. Ed. Eckart Förster; tr. Eckart Förster and Michael Rose. Cambridge: Cambridge University Press.
_____. 1998 (1787). *Critique of Pure Reason*, 2nd edition. Tr. Paul Guyer & Allen W Wood. Cambridge: Cambridge University Press.
_____. 2011 (1764). *Observations on the Feeling of the Beautiful and Sublime*. Tr. P Guyer; ed. P Frierson & P Guyer. Cambridge: Cambridge University Press.
_____. 2012 (1786). *Groundwork of the Metaphysics of Morals*, revised edition. Trans. & ed. Mary Gregor & Jens Timmermann; rev. tr. Jens Timmermann. Cambridge: Cambridge University Press.

Kantor, Jodi, and David Streitfeld. 2015. "Amazon's bruising, thrilling workplace." *New York Times* (15 August): A1.
_____, and Megan Twohey. 2019. *She Said*. New York: Penguin.

Kaplan, Abraham. 1964. *The Conduct of Inquiry*. San Francisco: Chandler.

Kaplan, Greg, and Sam Schulhofer-Wohl. 2018. "The changing (dis-)utility of work." NBER Working Paper 23738. Cambridge, MA: NBER.

Karpf, Fay B. 1932. *American Social Psychology*. New York: McGraw-Hill.

Kearns, David, and Ryan Walter. 2019. "Office, political theory, and the political theorist." *The Historical Journal* (early view online). <doi.10.1017/S0018246X19000220> (last access 3 September 2019.

Keats, John. 1973. *The Complete Poems*. Ed. John Barnard. London: Penguin.

Kemp, Anthony. 1991. *The Estrangement of the Past*. New York: Oxford University Press.

Kemper, Theodore D. 1978. *A Social Interactional Theory of Emotions*. New York: Wiley.

Kesey, Ken. 1962. *One Flew over the Cuckoo's Nest*. New York: Viking.

Ketokivi, Mikko, and Joseph T Mahoney. 2016. "Transaction cost economics as a constructive stakeholder theory." *Academy of Management Learning & Education* 15: 123-138.

Kierkegaard, Søren. 2014 (1844). *The Concept of Anxiety*. Trans. Alastair Hannay. New York: Norton.

Killworth, Peter D, Christopher McCarty, Eugene C Johnsen, H Russell Bernard, and Gene A Shelley. 2006. "Investigating the variation in personal network size under unknown error conditions." *Sociological Methods and Research* 35: 84-112.

Kirman, Alan P. 1992. "Whom or what does the representative individual represent?" *Journal of Economic Perspectives* 6: 117-136.

Kirschner, Robert P. 2002. *The Extravagant Universe*. Princeton: Princeton University Press.

Kittler, Friedrich A. 1986. *Grammophon Film Typewriter*. Berlin: Brinkmann & Bose.

_____. 1990 (1985). *Discourse Networks 1800/1900*. Trans. Michael Metteer with Chris Cullens. Stanford: Stanford University Press.

_____. 1996 (1988). "The city is a medium." *New Literary History* 27: 717-729.

_____. 2013. *Die Wahrheit der technischen Welt*. Ed. Hans Ulbrich Gumbrecht. Berlin: Suhrkamp.

Kleingeld, Pauline. 2011. *Kant and Cosmopolitanism*. Cambridge: Cambridge University Press.

Kliemt, Hartmut. 1990. "The costs of organizing social cooperation." Pp. 61-80 in *Social Institutions*, edited by Michael Hechter, Karl-Dieter Opp, and Reinhard Wippler. New York: Aldine de Gruyter.

Knight, Jack. 1992. *Institutions and Social Conflict*. Cambridge: Cambridge University Press.

_____. 1995. "Models, interpretations, and theories." Pp. 95-119 in *Explaining Social Institutions*, edited by Jack Knight and Itai Sened. Ann Arbor: University of Michigan Press.

Knorr-Cetina, Karin, and Aaron V Cicourel (eds.). 1981. *Advances in Social Theory and Methodology*. London: Routledge & Kegan Paul.

Knowles, David. 1963 (1941). "The humanism of the twelfth century." Pp. 16-30 in idem, *The Historian and Character*. Cambridge: Cambridge University Press.

Knuth, Kevin, Michael Habeck, Nabin Malakar, Asim Mubeen, and Ben Placek. 2015. "Bayesian evidence and model selection." *Digital Signal Processing* 47: 50-67.

Koch, Anton Friedrich. 2006. *Versuch über Wahrheit und Zeit*. Paderborn: Mentis

Köhler, Wolfgang. 1925 (1921). *The Mentality of Apes*, 2nd edition. Trans. Ella Winter. London: Kegan, Trench.

Koestler, Arthur. 1965. *The Yogi and the Commissar, and Other Essays*. Danube edition. New York: Macmillan.

Konstan, David. 2006. *The Emotions of the Ancient Greeks*. Toronto: University of Toronto Press.

_____. 2018. *In the Orbit of Love*. Oxford: Oxford University Press.

Kontopoulos, Kyriakos M. 1993. *The Logics of Social Structure*. Cambridge: Cambridge University Press.

Kornbluh, Anna. 2019. *The Order of Forms*. Chicago: University of Chicago Press.

Korsgaard, Christine M. 1996. *Creating the Kingdom of Ends*. Cambridge: Cambridge University Press.

_____. 2009. *Self-Constitution*. New York: Oxford University Press.

Kortian, Garbis. 1980. *Metacritique*. Cambridge: Cambridge University Press.

Koselleck, Reinhart. 1985 (1979). *Futures Past*. Trans. Keith Tribe. Cambridge: MIT Press.

Kosmetatou, Elizabeth. 2002. "The Athenian inventory lists." *L'Antiqué Classique* 71: 185-197.

Kosmin, Paul J. 2019. *Time and Its Adversaries in the Seleucid Empire*. Cambridge: Harvard University Press.

Kotlowitz, Alex. 1991. *There Are No Children Here*. New York: Nan A Talese/Doubleday.

_____. 2019. *An American Summer*. New York: Nan A Talese/Doubleday.

Kristeva, Julia. 1969. *Semiotica*. Paris: Seuil.

Kristof, Nicholas D, and Sheryl WuDunn. 2020. *Tightrope*. New York: Knopf.

Krueger, Alan B. 1999. "Experimental estimates of education production functions." *Quarterly Journal of Economics* 114 (May): 497-532.

Kruger, Justin, and David Dunning. 1999. "Unskilled and unaware of it." *Journal of Personality and Social Psychology* 77: 1121-1134.

Kuehn, Manfred. 1989. "Hume and Tetens." *Hume Studies* 15 (November): 365-376.

_____. 2001. *Kant: A Biography*. Cambridge: Cambridge University Press.

Kuran, Timur. 1995. *Private Truths, Public Lies*. Cambridge: Harvard University Press.

Kusch, Martin. 2014. "The metaphysics and politics of corporate personhood." *Erkenntnis* 79, supplement 9: 1587-1600.

Kuttner, Robert. 2018. *Can Democracy Survive Global Capitalism?* New York: Norton.

Laffont, Jean-Jacques. 1989 (1986). *The Economics of Uncertainty and Information*. Trans. John P. Bonin and Hélène Bonin. Cambridge: MIT Press.

Langlands, Robert P. 2010. "Is there beauty in mathematical theories?" University of Notre Dame, January. <publications.ias.edu/rpl_works/L12/beauty/ND.pdf> (last access 24 March 2018)

Langlois, Charles-Victor and Charles Seignobos. 1898. *Introduction aux études historiques*. Paris: Librairie Hachette.

Lareau, Annette. 2011. *Unequal Childhoods*, 2nd edition. Berkeley: University of California Press.

Larsen, John Lauritz. 2010. *The Market Revolution in America*. New York: Cambridge University Press.

Las Casas, Bartolomé de. 1875 (1561). *Historia de las Indias*, 5 volumes. Madrid: Imprenta de Miguel Ginesta.

Lasch, Christopher. 1979. *The Culture of Narcissism*. New York: Norton.

Lasch, Christopher. 1984. *The Minimal Self.* New York: Norton.
_____. 1995. *The Revolt of the Elites and the Betrayal of Democracy.* New York: Norton.
Lasswell, Harold D, and Abraham Kaplan. 1950. *Power and Society.* New Haven: Yale University Press.
Latour, Bruno. 2005. *Reassembling the Social.* Oxford: Oxford University Press.
_____, and Steve Woolgar. 1986. *Laboratory Life*, 2nd edition. Princeton: Princeton University Press.
Laughlin, Robert B. 2005. *A Different Universe.* New York: Basic Books.
Laumann, Edward O. 1969. "Friends of urban men." *Sociometry* 32: 54=69.
_____, Paul M Siegel, and Robert W Hodge (eds.). 1970. *The Logic of Social Hierarchies.* Chicago: Markham.
Law, John. 1994. *Organising Modernity.* Oxford: Blackwell.
_____, and John Hassard (eds.). 1999. *Actor Network Theory and After.* London: Blackwell.
Lazear, Edward P. 2005. "Entrepreneurship." *Journal of Labor Economics* 23: 649-680.
Leach, Edmund. 1961. Review of G C Homans, *Social Behavior. American Anthropologist*, n.s. 63: 1339-1341.
Le Bon, Gustave. 1881. *L'homme et les sociétés.* Paris: Rothschild.
Lee, Byungkyu, and Peter Bearman. 2017. "Important matters in political context." *Sociological Science* 4: 1-30.
Lefkowitz, Mary R. 2012. *The Lives of the Greek Poets*, 2nd edition. London: Bloomsbury.
Leibniz, Gottfried Wilhelm. 1921 (1704). *Nouveaux Essais sur l'entendement humain.* Paris: Flammarion.
Leiss, William. 1972. *The Domination of Nature.* Boston: Beacon.
Lemann, Nicholas. 1999. *The Big Test.* New York: Farrar, Straus & Giroux.
Leonardo da Vinci. 1989 (1651). *Leonardo on Painting.* Trans. Martin Kemp and Margaret Walker, ed. Martin Kemp. New Haven: Yale University Press.
Leontief, Wassily. 1937a. "Implicit theorizing." *Quarterly Journal of Economics* 51:337-351.
_____. 1937b. "Interrelation of prices, output, saving, and investment." *Review of Economics and Statistics* 19: 109-132.
_____. 1938. "The significance of Marxian economics for present-day economic theory." *American Economic Review* 28, supplement: 1-9.
Levine, Caroline. 2015. *Forms.* Princeton: Princeton University Press.
Levine, Donald N. 1985. *The Flight from Ambiguity.* Chicago: University of Chicago Press.
_____. 1991. "Simmel and Parsons reconsidered."*American Journal of Sociology* 96: 1097-1116.
Lévi-Strauss, Claude. 1963 (1958). *Structural Anthropology.* Trans. Claire Jacobson and Brooke Grundfest Schoepf. New York: Basic Books.
Levitan, Daniel J. 2006. *This Is Your Brain on Music.* New York: Dutton.
Lewis, Clive S. 1943. *The Abolition of Man.* Oxford: Oxford University Press.
Lewis, David. 1973. "Causation." *Journal of Philosophy* 70: 556-567
Lewis, David. 1986. *Counterfactuals*, corrected edition. Oxford: Blackwell.
_____. 2000. *Papers in Ethics and Social Philosophy.* Cambridge: Cambridge University Press.
Lewis, J David, and Richard L Smith. 1980. *American Sociology and Pragmatism.* Chicago: University of Chicago Press.
Lewis, Michael. 2016. *The Undoing Project.* London: Allen Lane.

Lewontin, Richard C. 2001. *It Ain't Necessarily So.* New York: NYRB Books.

Libet, Benjamin. 1985. "Unconscious cerebral initiate and the role of conscious will in voluntary action." *Behavioral and Brain Sciences* 8: 529-566.

_____. 2004. *Mind Time.* Cambridge: Harvard University Press.

Lieberson, Stanley, and Lynn K Hansen. 1974. "National development, mother tongue diversity, and the comparative study of nations." *American Sociological Review* 39: 523-541.

Lilla, Mark. 2016 (2001). *The Reckless Mind.* New York: New York Review.

_____. 2016. *The Shipwrecked Mind.* New York: New York Review.

Lincoln, Bruce. 1994. *Authority.* Chicago: University of Chicago Press.

Lindblom, Charles. 1959. "The science of 'muddling through.'" *Public Administration Review* 19: 79-88.

Lipset, Seymour Martin, and Reinhard Bendix. 1959. *Social Mobility in Industrial Society.* Berkeley: University of California Press.

List, Christian, and Philip Pettit. 2011. *Group Agency.* Oxford: Oxford University Press.

Liu, Jintao, Rosa Martinez-Corral, Arthur Prindel, Dong-yeon Lee, Joseph Larkin, Marçal Gabalda-Sagarro, Jordi Garcia-Ojalvo, and Gürol M Süel. 2017. "Coupling between distant biofilms and emergence of nutrient time-sharing." *Science* (6April).

Ljungqvist, Lars, and Thomas J Sargent. 2018. *Recursive Macroeconomic Theory*, 4th edition. Cambridge: MIT Press.

Llinás, Rodolfo Riascos. 2001. *I of the Vortex.* Cambridge: MIT Press.

Lloyd, Geoffrey, and Nathan Sivin. 2002. *The Way and the Word.* New Haven: Yale University Press.

Locke, John. 1975 (1700). *An Essay Concerning Human Understanding*, 4th edition. Ed. P H Nidditch. Oxford: Clarendon.

_____. 1980 (1690). *An Essay concerning the True and Original Extent and End of Civil Government.* Ed. C B Macpherson. Indianapolis: Hackett.

Löwith, Karl. 1994 (1986). *My Life in Germany Before and After 1932.* Trans. Elizabeth King. Urbana: University of Illinois Press.

Long, Anthony A. 2015. *Greek Models of Mind and Self.* Cambridge: Harvard University Press.

Lopreato, Joseph, and Lawrence Hazelrigg. 1972. *Class, Conflict and Mobility.* San Francisco: Chandler.

Loraux, Nicole. 1993 (1984). *Children of Athena.* Trans. Caroline Levine. Princeton: Princeton University Press.

_____. 1996. *Né de la terre: mythe et politique à Athènes.* Paris: Seuil.

_____. 2002 (1997). *The Divided City: On Memory and Forgetting in Ancient Athens.* Trans. Corinne Pache with Jeff Fort. New York: Zone.

Lorenz, Max O. 1904. "Methods of measuring concentration of wealth." *Journal of the American Statistical Association* 9: 209-219.

Low, Tim. 2016. *Where Song Began.* New Haven: Yale University Press.

Lucas, Edward Verrell. 1907. *The Life of Charles Lamb*, 4th edition. London: Methuen.

Lucas, Robert E, Jr. 1972a. "Econometric testing of the natural rate hypothesis." Pp. 50-59 in *The Econometrics of Price Determination*, edited by Otto Eckstein. Washington, DC: Board of Governors of the Federal Reserve Bank.

_____. 1972b. "Expectations and the neutrality of money." *Journal of Economic Theory* 4: 103-124.

Lucas, Robert E, Jr. 1976. "Econometric policy evaluation." *Carnegie-Rochester Conference Series on Public Policy*. 1: 19–46. <doi:10.1016/S0167-2231(76)80003-6>
_____. 1986. "Adaptive behavior and economic theory." *Journal of Business* 59: S401-S426.
Lucas, Samuel R. 2009. "Stratification theory, socioeconomic background, and educational attainment." *Rationality and Society* 21: 459-511.
_____. 2014. "An inconvenient data set." *Quality and Quantity* 48: 1619-1649.
_____. 2016. "First- and second-order methodological developments from the Coleman Report." *RSF Journal* 2 (September): 117-140.
Luce, R Duncan, and Patrick Suppes. 1965. "Preference, utility, and subjective probability." Pp. 249-410 in *Handbook of Mathematical Psychology*, volume 3, edited by R Duncan Luce, Robert R Bush, and Eugene Galanter. New York: Wiley.
Luckhurst, Roger. 2019. *Corridors*. London: Reaktion.
Lucy, John. 1997. "Linguistic relativity." *Annual Review of Anthropology* 26: 291-312.
Luhmann, Niklas. 1982. *The Differentiation of Society*. Trans. Stephen Holmes and Charles Larmore. New York: Columbia University Press.
_____. 1990. *Essays on Self-Reference*. New York: Columbia University Press.
_____. 2012 (1997). *Theory of Society*, 2 volumes. Trans. Rhodes Barrett. Stanford: Stanford University Press.
Lury, Celia. 1998. *Prosthetic Culture*. London: Routledge.
Luther, Martin. 2013 (1525). "Against the rioting peasants." Pp.116-122 in *On the Freedom of a Christian*. Ed & trans. Tryntje Helfferich. Indianapolis: Hackett.
Lutz, Catherine A. 1988. *Unnatural Emotions*. Chicago: University of Chicago Press.
Lynch, John Patrick. 1972. *Aristotle's School*. Berkeley: University of California Press.
Lynch, Michael. 2012. "Revisiting the cultural dope." *Human Studies* 35: 223-233.
Lyotard, Jean-François. 2011 (1971). *Discourse, Figure*. Trans. Antony Hudek and Mary Lydon. Minneapolis: University of Minnesota Press.
Mac Carron, Pádrig, Kimmo Kaski, and Robin Dunbar. 2016. "Calling Dunbar's numbers." *Social Networks* 47: 151-155.
Macdonald, James. 2003. *A Free Nation Deep in Debt*. New York: Farrar, Straus and Giroux.
Macherey, Pierre. 1978 (1966). *A Theory of Literary Production*. Trans. G Wall. London: Routledge & Kegan Paul.
Machery, Edouard. 2017. *Philosophy within Its Bounds*. Oxford: Oxford University Press.
Machiavelli, Niccolò. 1988 (1532). *Florentine Histories*. Trans. Laura F Banfield & Harvey C Mansfield. Princeton: Princeton University Press.
Machlup, Fritz. 1962. *The Production and Distribution of Knowledge in the United States*. Princeton: Princeton University Press.
MacKinnon, Catharine. 2007. *Butterfly Politics*. Cambridge: Harvard University Press.
Macron, Emmanuel. 2015. "J'ai rencontré Paul Ricœur qui m'a rééduqué sur le plan philosophique." ("I met Paul Ricour, who re-educated me on a philosophical level") *Le 1 hebdo* no. 64 (8 July).
Macy, Michael, and Andreas Flache. 2009. "Social dynamics from the bottom up." Pp. 246-268 in *The Oxford Handbook of Analytical Sociology*, edited by Peter Hedström and Peter Bearman. Oxford: Oxford University Press.
Madkour, Mohcine, Driss Benhaddou, and Cui Tao. 2016. "Temporal data representation, normalization, extraction, and reasoning." *Computer Methods and Programs in Biomedicine* 128 (May): 52-68.

Makkreel, Rudolph, and Sebastian Luft (eds.). 2010. *Neo-Kantianism in Contemporary Philosophy*. Bloomington: Indiana University Press.

Malcolm, Donald. 1958. "Lo, the poor nymphet." *The New Yorker* 34 (8 November): 195-200.

Malevich, Kazimir. 1959 (1927). *The Non-Objective World*. Trans. Howard Dearstyne. Chicago: Theobald.

———. 2000 (1927). "Suprematism." Trans. Howard Dearstyne. Pp.117-124 in *Modern Artists on Art*, 2nd edition, edited by Robert L Herbert. New York: Dover.

Malinvaud, Edmond. 1955. "Aggregation problems in input-output models." Pp. 189-202 in *The Structural Interdependence of the Economy*, edited by Tibor Barna. New York: Wiley.

Mallaby, Sebastian. 2016. *The Man Who Knew*. New York: Penguin.

Mampe, Birgit, Angela D Friederici, Anne Christophe, and Kathleen Wermke. 2009. "Newborns'cry melody is shaped by their native language." *Current Biology* 19: 1994-1997.

Mandeville, Bernard. 1732. *An Enquiry into the Origin of Honour and the Usefulness of Christianity in War*. London: printed for John Brotherton.

———. 1924 (1714, 1729). *Fable of the Bees*, 2 vols. Ed. F B Kaye. Oxford: Clarendon.

Mandeville, John. 1900 (c1360). *The Travels of Sir John Mandeville*. Ed. David Price. New York: Macmillan.

Manjoo, Farhad. 2008. *True Enough*. Hoboken, NJ: Wiley.

———. 2016. "Why we need to pick up Alvin Toffler's torch." *New York Times*, 7 July, B1.

Mankiw, N Gregory, David Romer, and David H Weil. 1992. "Contribution to the empirics of economic growth." *Quarterly Journal of Economics* 107: 407-437.

Mann, Bruce H. 2002. *Republic of Debtors*. Cambridge: Harvard University Press.

Mann, Thomas. 1927 (1924). *Magic Mountain*. Tr. H T Lowe-Porter. New York: Knopf.

Mann, Wolfgang-Rainer. 2000. *The Discovery of Things*. Princeton: Princeton University Press.

Mannheim, Karl. 1952 (1925). "The problem of a sociology of knowledge." Pp. 134-190 in *idem, Essays on the Sociology of Knowledge*. Ed. Paul Kecskemeti. London: Routledge & Kegan Paul.

———. 1952 (1927). "The problem of generations." Pp. 276-322 in *idem, Essays on the Sociology of Knowledge*. Ed. Paul Kecskemeti. London: Routledge & Kegan Paul.

Manski, Charles F. 1993a. "Adolescent econometricians." Pp. 43-60 in *Studies of Supply and Demand in Higher Education*, edited by Charles T Clotfelter and Michael Rothschild. Chicago: University of Chicago Press.

———. 1993b. "Identification of endogenous social effects." *Review of Economic Studies* 60: 531-542.

———. 1993c. "Identification problems in the social sciences." *Sociological Methodology* 23: 1-56.

———. 1997. "Identification of anonymous endogenous interactions." Pp. 369-384 in *The Economy as an Evolving Complex System, II*, edited by W Brian Arthur, Steven N Durlauf, and David A Lane. Boca Raton, FL: CRC Press.

———. 2000. "Economic analysis of social interactions." *Journal of Economic Perspectives* 14 (Summer): 115-136.

———. 2004. "Social learning from private experiences." *Review of Economic Studies* 71: 443-458.

Manski, Charles F. 2006. "Social learning and the adoption of innovations." Pp. 31-47 in *The Economy as an Evolving Complex System, III*, edited by Lawrence E Blume and Steven N Durlauf. Oxford: Oxford University Press.

_____. 2007. *Identification for Prediction and Decision*. Cambridge: Harvard University Press.

_____. 2013. *Public Policy in an Uncertain World*. Cambridge: Harvard University Press.

_____. 2017. "Mandating vaccinations with unknown indirect effects." *Journal of Public Economics Theory* 19: 603-619.

_____. 2018. "Survey measurement of probabilistic macroeconomic expectations." Pp. 411-471 in *NBER Macroeconomic Annual* 32, edited by Martin Eichenbaum and Jonathan A Parker. Chicago: University of Chicago Press.

_____. 2019. *Patient Care under Uncertainty*. Princeton: Princeton University Press.

Manuel, Frank. 1965. *The Shape of Philosophical History*. Stanford: Stanford University Press.

March, James G, and Herbert A Simon. 1993. *Organizations*, 2nd edition. Cambridge, MA: Blackwell.

Marchart, Oliver. 2007. *Post-Foundational Political Thought*. Edinburgh: Edinburgh University Press.

_____. 2011. "Democracy and minimal politics." *The South Atlantic Quarterly* 110: 965-973.

_____. 2013. *Das unmögliche Objekt*. Frankfurt am Main: Suhrkamp.

Marcus Aurelius. c175. *Meditations*.

Marcus, Laura. 1994. *Auto/biographical Discourses*. Manchester: Manchester University Press.

Margalit, Avishai. 1996. *The Decent Society*. Trans. Naomi Goldblum. Cambridge: Harvard University Press.

_____. 2010. *On Compromise and Rotten Compromises*. Princeton: Princeton University Press.

Marin, Peter. 1995. *Freedom and Its Discontents*. South Royalton, VT: Steerforth.

Marsden, Peter V. 2005. "The sociology of James S Coleman." *Annual Review of Sociology* 31: 1-24.

Martin, John Levi. 2003 "What is field theory?" *American Journal of Sociology* 109: 1-49.

_____. 2009. *Social Structures*. Princeton: Princeton University Press.

_____. 2011. *The Explanation of Social Action*. New York: Oxford University Press.

_____. 2015. *Thinking through Theory*. New York: Norton.

_____. 2017. "The birth of the true, the good, and the beautiful." *Current Perspectives in Social Theory* 35: 3-56.

_____, and Alessandra Lembo. 2020. "On the other side of values." *American Journal of Sociology* 126: 52-96.

Martiniani, Stefano, Paul M Chaikin, and Dov Levine. 2018. "Quantifying hidden order out of equilibrium." *arXiv*: 1708.04993.v3.

Marx, Karl. 1975 (1932). *Economic and Philosophic Manuscripts of 1844*. Pp.229-346 in *idem* and Frederick Engels, *Collected Works*, volume 3. New York: International.

_____. 1976 (1888). "Theses on Feuerbach." Pp. 6-8 in *idem* and Frederick Engels, *Collected Works*, volume 5. New York: International.

_____. 1979 (1852). "The eighteenth Brumaire of Louis Napoleon." Pp. 101-197 in *idem* and Frederick Engels, *Collected Works*, volume 11. New York: International.

Marx, Karl. 1986 (1939). *Economic Manuscripts of 1857-58* (Part One). Volume 28 of *idem* and Frederick Engels, *Collected Works*. New York: International.

_____. 1987 (1939). *Economic Manuscripts of 1857-58* (Part Two). Volume 29 of *idem* and Frederick Engels, *Collected Works*. New York: International.

_____. 1996 (1867). *Capital*, volume 1. In *idem* and Frederick Engels, *Collected Works*, volume 35. New York: International.

_____, and Frederick Engels. 1976 (1848). "The manifesto of the communist party." Pp. 477-517 in *idem*, *Collected Works*, volume 6. New York: International.

_____. 1976 (1932). *The German Ideology*. Pp. 19-539 in *idem*, *Collected Works*, volume 5. New York: International.

Mason, Paul. 2015. *Postcapitalism*. London: Allen Lane.

Matthews, Gareth. 1992. *Thought's Ego in Augustine and Descartes*. Ithaca: Cornell University Press.

Maturana, Humberto R, and Francisco J Varela. 1980 (1972). *Autopoiesis and Cognition*, 2nd edition. Dordrecht, Holland: D Reidel.

Mau, Steffen. 2019 (2017). *The Metric Society*. Trans. Sharon Howe. Cambridge: Polity.

Mauss, Marcel. 1985 (1938). "A category of the human mind." Trans W D Halls. Pp. 1-25 in *The Category of the Person*, edited by Michael Carrithers, Steven Collins, & Steven Lukes. Cambridge: Cambridge University Press.

Mayer, Jacob P. 1944. *Max Weber and German Politics*. London: Faber and Faber.

Mayntz, Renate. 2004. "Mechanism in the analysis of social macro-phenomena." *Philosophy of the Social Sciences* 34: 237-259.

Mazzarino, Santo. 1966 (1959). *The End of the Ancient World*. Trans. G Holmes. New York: Knopf.

Mbembe, Achille. 2017. *Critique of Black Reason*. Trans. Laurent Dubois. Durham: Duke University Press.

McAfee, Andrew, and Erik Brynjolfsson. 2017. *Machine, Platform, Crowd*. New York: Norton.

McCarthy, Cormac. 2006. *The Road*. New York: Knopf.

McClelland, Charles E. 1980. *State, Society and University in Germany*. Cambridge: Cambridge University Press.

McCloskey, Deirdre. 2006. *The Bourgeois Virtues*. Chicago: University of Chicago Press.

McCormack, Matthew. 2015. *Embodying the Militia in Georgian England*. Oxford: Oxford University Press.

McCormick, Ted. 2009. *William Petty: And the Ambitions of Political Arithmetic*. Oxford: Oxford University Press.

McCormick, Tyler H, Matthew J Salganik, and Tian Zheng. 2010. "How many people do you know?" *Journal of the American Statistical Association* 105 (489): 59-70.

McDougall, William. 1927. *The Group Mind*, 2nd edition. Cambridge: Cambridge University Press.

McDowell, John. 1998. *Mind, Value, and Reality*. Cambridge: Harvard University Press.

McGilvray, James. 2014. *Chomsky*, 2nd edition. Cambridge: Polity.

McGuire, William J. 1989. "The structure of individual attitudes and attitude systems." Pp. 37-69 in *Attitude Structure and Function*, edited by Anthony R Pratkanis, Steven J Breckler, and Anthony Greenwald. Hillsdale, NJ: Erlbaum.

McKim, Vaughn R, and Stephen Turner (eds.). 1997. *Causality in Crisis?* Notre Dame, IN: University of Notre Dame Press.

McKinney, John C. 1955. "The contribution of George H Mead to the sociology of knowledge." *Social Forces* 34 (December): 144-149.

_____. 1969. "Typification, typologies, and sociological theory." *Social Forces* 48: 1-12.

McNeil, Peter. 2018. *Pretty Gentlemen*. New Haven: Yale University Press.

McPherson, Miller. 1983."An ecology of affiliation." *American Sociological Review* 48: 519-532.

_____, Lynn Smith-Lovin, and Matthew E Brashears. 2006. "Social isolation in America." *American Sociological Review* 71: 353-375.

Maxwell, James Clerk. 1902. *Theory of Heat*, 10th edition, with corrections and additions by William Thompson, Lord Kelvin. London: Longmans, Green.

Mead, George Herbert. 1901. "A new criticism of Hegelianism: is it valid?" *American Journal of Theology* 5: 87-96.

_____. 1904. "The basis for a parents' association." *Elementary School Teacher* 4: 337-346.

_____. 1905. "Social psychology as a counterpoint to physiological psychology." *Psychological Bulletin* 6: 401-407.

_____. 1907-08. "The social settlement." *University of Chicago Record* 12: 108-110.

_____. 1908. Review of McDougall's *Social Psychology*. *Psychological Bulletin* 5: 385-391.

_____. 1909. "Social psychology as the counterpart to physiological psychology." *Psychological Bulletin* 6: 401-408.

_____. 1910. "What social objects must psychology presuppose?" *Journal of Philosophy, Psychology and Scientific Methods* 7: 174-180.

_____. 1912. "The mechanism of social consciousness." *Journal of Philosophy, Psychology and Scientific Methods* 9: 401-406.

_____. 1913. "The social self." *Journal of Philosophy, Psychology and Scientific Methods* 10: 374-380.

_____. 1917. "Scientific method and individual thinker." Pp. 176-227 in *Creative Intelligence*, by John Dewey, Addison Moore, Harold Chapman Brown, George Herbert Mead, Boyd H Bode, Henry Walgrave Stuart, James Hayden Tufts, and Horace M Kallen. New York: Holt.

_____. 1925. "The genesis of the self and social control." *International Journal of Ethics* 35: 251-277.

_____. 1926. "The nature of aesthetic experience." *International Journal of Ethics* 36: 382-392.

_____. 1927. "The objective reality of perspective." Pp. 75-85 in *Proceedings of the Sixth International Congress of Philosophy*, edited by Edgar S Brightman. London: Longmans, Green.

_____. 1929. "Bishop Berkeley and his message." *Journal of Philosophy* 26: 421-430.

_____. 1930. "Cooley's contribution to American social thought." *American Journal of Sociology* 35: 693-706.

_____. 1932. *The Philosophy of the Present*, edited by Arthur E Murphy. London: Open Court.

_____. 1934. *Mind, Self, and Society*, edited by Charles W Morris. Chicago: University of Chicago Press.

_____. 1936. *Movements of Thought in the Nineteenth Century*, edited by Merritt H Moore. Chicago: University of Chicago Press.

Mead, George Herbert. 1938. *The Philosophy of the Act*, edited by Charles W Morris, et al. Chicago: University of Chicago Press.

_____. 1964a. *Selected Writings*. Ed. Andrew J Reck. Chicago: University of Chicago Press.

_____. 1964b. *On Social Psychology*, revised edition. Ed. Anselm Strauss. Chicago: University of Chicago Press.

_____. 1999. *Play, School, and Society*. Ed. Mary Jo Deegan. New York: Peter Lang.

_____. 2001. *Essays in Social Psychology*. Ed. Mary Jo Deegan. New Brunswick, NJ: Transaction.

Meade, James E. 1964. *Efficiency, Equality, and the Ownership of Property*. London: Allen & Unwin.

Mee, Charles L, Jr. 1977. *A Visit to Haldeman and Other States of Mind*. New York: M Evans.

Meeks, Wayne A. 1995. *The Origins of Christian Morality*. New Haven: Yale University Press.

_____. 2003. *The First Urban Christians*, 2nd edition. New Haven: Yale University Press.

Mehan, Hugh, Irene Villanueva, Lea Hubbard, and Angela Lintz. 1996. *Constructing School Success*. Cambridge: Cambridge University Press.

_____, and Gordon Chang. 2010. "Is it wrong for us to want good things?" *Journal of Educational Change* 12: 47-70.

_____, with Gordon C Chang, Makeba Jones, and Season S Mussey. 2012. *In the Front Door*. Boulder, CO: Paradigm

Meillassoux, Quentin. 1997. *L'Inexistence divine*. Doctoral dissertation, University of Paris.

_____. 2008 (2006). *After Finitude*. Trans. Ray Brassier. London: Continuum International.

Mekhennet, Souad. 2017. *I Was Told to Come Alone*. New York: Henry Holt.

Menand, Louis. 2002. *American Studies*. New York: Farrar, Straus & Giroux.

_____. 2020. "The changing meaning of affirmative action." *The New Yorker* 95 (13 Jan): 62-68.

Mercier, Hugo. 2016. "The argumentative theory." *Trends in Cognitive Sciences* 20: 680-700.

_____, and Dan Sperber. 2017. *The Enigma of Reason*. Cambridge: Harvard University Press.

Merwin, W S. 2002. *The Mays of Ventadorn*. New York: National Geographic.

Merton, Robert King. 1936. "The unanticipated consequences of purposive action." *American Sociological Review* 1: 894-904.

_____. 1948. "The self-fulfilling prophecy." *Antioch Review* 8: 193-210.

_____. 1995. "The Thomas theorem and the Matthew effect." *Social Forces* 74: 379-424.

_____, and Elinor Barber. 1963 (1976). "Sociological ambivalence." Pp. 3-31 in Robert K Merton, *Sociological Ambivalence and Other Essays*. New York: Free Press.

Metzinger, Thomas. 2009. *The Ego Tunnel*. New York: Basic Books.

Meyer, John W. 1986. "The self and the life course." Pp. 199-216 in *Human Development and the Life Course*, edited by Aage B Sørensen, Franz E Weinert, and Lonnie R Sherrod. Hillsdale, NJ: Erlbaum.

_____. 2010. "World society, institutional theories, and actors." *Annual Review of Sociology* 36: 1-20.

Meyer, John W, and Roland L Jepperson. 2000. "The 'actors' of modern society." *Sociological Theory* 18: 100-120.

Meyer, John W, and Brian Rowan. 1977. "Institutionalized organization." *American Journal of Sociology* 83: 440-463.

Meyer, Michael. 2008. *The Last Days of Old Beijing*. New York: Walker.

Mill, John Stuart. 1965 (1843). *A System of Logic*. Indianapolis: Bobbs-Merrill.

Miller, David L. 1973. *George Herbert Mead: Self, Language, and the World*. Chicago: University of Chicago Press.

Miller, Edward, and John Hatcher. 1995. *Medieval England: Towns, Commerce and Crafts, 1086-1348*. London: Longman.

Miller, George A. 1967. *The Psychology of Communication*. Harmondsworth,UK: Penguin.

Miller, James. 2011. *Examined Lives*. New York: Farrar, Straus and Giroux.

Miller, Toby. 1993. *The Well-Tempered Self*. Baltimore: Johns Hopkins University Press.

Minev, Zlatko K, Shantanu O Mundhada, Shyam Shankar, Philip Reinhold, Ricardo Gutiérrez-Jáuregui, Robert J Schoelkopf, Mazyar Mirrahimi, Howard J Carmichael, and Michel Devoret. 2019. "To catch and reverse a quantum jump in mid-flight." *Nature* 570: 200-204.

Misch, Georg. 1907. *Geschichte der Autobiographie*, 2 volumes. Leipzig: Teubner.

Mishra, Pankaj. 2015. "The sound of cracking." *London Review of Books* 37 (27 August): 13-15.

Mitchell, Timothy. 1990. "The invention and reinvention of the Egyptian peasant." *International Journal of Middle East Studies* 22: 129-150.

Mitchell, William J T. 2011. "World pictures." Pp. 253-264 in *Globalization and Contemporary Art*, edited by Jonathan Harris. West Sussex, UK: Wiley-Blackwell.

_____. 2012. "Image, space, revolution." *Critical Inquiry* 29: 8-32.

Mlinko, Ange. 2017. "Whole earth troubadour." *New York Review of Books* 64 (7 December): 45-46.

Mohr, John W, and Harrison C White. 2008. "How to model an institution." *Theory and Society* 37: 485-512.

Molenaar, Peter C M. 2004. "A manifesto on psychology as idiographic science: bringing the person back into scientific psychology, this time forever." *Measurement* 2:201-218.

_____. 2005. "Rejoinder to Rogosa's commentary on 'A manifesto on psychology as idiographic science.'" *Measurement* 3: 116-119.

Mokyr, Joel. 2016. *A Culture of Growth*. Princeton: Princeton University Press.

Molseed, Mari J. 1987. "The problem of temporality in the work of Georg Simmel." *The Sociological Quarterly* 28: 357-366.

Momigliano, Arnaldo. 1985. "Marcel Mauss and the quest for the person in Greek biography and autobiography." Pp. 83-92 in *The Category of the Person*, edited by Michael Carrithers, Steven Collins, and Steven Lukes. Cambridge: Cambridge University Press.

_____. 1993. *The Development of Greek Biography*, expanded edition. Cambridge: Harvard University Press.

Montaigne, Michel de. 1958 (1580). *The Complete Essays*. Trans. Donald Frame. Stanford: Stanford University Press.

Montefiore, Alan. 2011. *A Philosophical Retrospective*. New York: Columbia University Press.

Montgomery, Richard, Alexey Pokrovskiy, and Benjamin Sudakov. 2020. "A proof of Ringel's conjecture." *arXiv*: 2001.02665v1 [Math CO] 8 Jan 2020.

Moran, Richard. 1994. "The expression of feelings in imagination." *Philosophical Review* 103 (1): 75-106.

_____. 2001. *Authority and Estrangement*. Princeton: Princeton University Press.

_____. 2005a. "Problems of sincerity." *Proceedings of the Aristotelian Society* 105: 341-361.

_____. 2005b. "Getting told and being believed." *Philosophers' Imprint* 5 (August): 1-29.

Moran, Richard. 2015. *The Story of My Life: Narrative and Self-Understanding.* Milwaukee: Marquette University Press.

Moretti, Franco, and Albert Sbragia. 2000. *The Way of the World.* London: Verso.

Morgan, Estelle. 1958. "Goethe and the Philistine." *Modern Language Review* 53: 374-379.

Morgan, Stephen L, and Christopher Winship. 2014. *Counterfactuals and Causal Inference*, 2nd edition. Cambridge: Cambridge University Press.

Morgan, Stephen L, and Sol Bee Jung. 2016. "Still no effect of resources, even in the New Gilded Age?" *RSF Journal* 2 (September): 83-116.

Morimoto, Yoshinori. 1970. "On aggregation problems in input-output systems." *The Review of Economic Studies* 37: 119-126.

_____. 1971. "A note on weighted aggregation in input-output analyses." *International Economic Review* 12: 138-143.

Morley, Neville. 2009. *Antiquity and Modernity.* Oxford: Wiley-Blackwell.

Moro, Andrea. 2016. *Impossible Languages.* Cambridge: MIT Press.

Morris, Ian. 2004 "Economic growth in ancient Greece." *Journal of Institutional and Theoretical Economics* 160: 709-742.

_____. 2006. "The collapse and regeneration of complex society in Greece, 1500-500 BC." Pp.72-84 in *After Collapse: The Regeneration of Complex Societies*, edited by Glenn M Schwartz and John J Nichols. Tucson: University of Arizona Press.

Mourelatos, Alexander P D. 1973 "Heraclitus, Parmenides, and the naïve metaphysics of things." Pp. 16-48 in *Exegesis and Argument*, edited by Edward N Lee, Alexander P D Mourelatos, and Richard Rorty. Assen: Van Gorcum.

Münsterberg, Hugo. 1900. *Grundzüge der Psychologie*, volume 1. Leipzig: Barth.

Mulder, Joris, and Roger Leenders. 2019. "On the evolution of dynamic interaction behavior in social networks." *Chaos, Solitons & Fractals* 119: 73-85.

Mulhall, Stephen. 2018. "How complex is a lemon?" *London Review of Books* 40 (Sept.): 27-30.

Muller, Jerry Z. 2018. *The Tyranny of Metrics.* Princeton: Princeton University Press.

Muller, Richard A. 2016. *NOW: the Physics of Time.* New York: Norton.

Mulvey, Patrick J, and Starr Nicholson. 2011. "Physics enrollments." *Focus On*, a periodical of the American Institute of Physics, College Park, MD.

Murray, Penelope, and Peter Wilson (eds.). 2004. *Music and the Muses.* Oxford: Oxford University Press.

Musil, Robert. 1953-60 (1930-43). *The Man without Qualities*, 3 volumes. Trans. Eithne Wilkins and Ernst Kaiser. London: Secker & Warburg.

_____. 1990 (1913). "The mathematical man." Pp. 39-43 in *idem, Precision and Soul.* Ed. & trans. Burton Pike & David S. Luft. Chicago: University of Chicago Press.

Muth, John F. 1961. "Rational expectations and the theory of process movements." *Econometrica* 29: 315-335.

Nagel, Ernest. 1961. *The Structure of Science*. New York: Harcourt, Brace and World.

Nagel, Thomas. 1974. "What is it like to be a bat?" *The Philosophical Review* 83: 435-450.

_____. 1998. "Conceiving the impossible & the mind-body problem." *Philosophy* 73: 337-352.

Nakamura, Emi, Jón Steinsson, Patrick Sun, and Daniel Villar. 2018. "The elusive costs of inflation." *Quarterly Journal of Economics* 133: 1933–1980.

Neckerman, Kathryn M, and Florencia Torche. 2007. "Inequality: causes and consequences." *Annual Review of Sociology* 33: 335-357.

Needham, Rodney. 1972. *Belief, Language, and Experience*. Oxford: Blackwell.

Neiman, Susan. 2002. *Evil in Modern Thought*. Princeton: Princeton University Press.

_____. 2014. *Why Grow Up?* London: Penguin.

_____. 2019. *Learning from the Germans*. New York: Farrar, Straus, and Giroux.

Newton, Isaac. 1729 (1687). *The Mathematical Principia of Natural Philosophy*, 2 volumes. Trans. Andrew Motte. London: Benjamin Motte.

Ni Bhrolcháin, Máire. 1992. "Period paramount?" *Population and Development Review* 18: 599-629.

Nietzsche, Friedrich. 1964 (1885). *Thus Spoke Zarathustra*. Trans. Walter Kaufmann. Pp. 112-439 in *idem, The Portable Nietzsche*, edited by W Kaufmann. New York: Viking.

_____. 1967 (1887). *On the Genealogy of Morals*. Tr. Walter Kaufmann & R J Hollingdale. New York: Random House.

_____. 1974 (1887). *The Gay Science*, 2nd edition. Trans. W Kaufmann. New York: Vintage.

_____. 1983 (1873-74). *Untimely Meditations*. Trans. R J Hollingdale. Cambridge: Cambridge University Press.

Nisbett, Richard E. 2015. *Mindware*. New York: Farrar, Straus and Giroux.

_____, and Timothy D Wilson. 1977. "Telling more than we can know." *Psychological Review* 84: 231-259.

Nixey, Catherine. 2017. *The Darkening Age*. London: Macmillan.

Noble, Kimberly G., Bruce D McCandliss, and Martha J Farah. 2007. "Socioeconomic gradients predict individual differences in neurocognitive abilities." *Developmental Science* 10 (July): 464-480.

Noble, Kimberly G., et al. 2015. "Family income, parental education, and brain development in children and adolescents." *Nature Neuroscience* 18 (5): 773-778.

North, Douglass C. 1990. *Institutions, Institutional Change, and Economic Performance*. New York: Cambridge University Press.

_____. 1995. "Five propositions about institutional change." Pp. 15-26 in *Explaining Social Institutions*, edited by Jack Knight and Itai Sened. Ann Arbor: University of Michigan Press.

Novick, Peter. 1988. *That Noble Dream*. Cambridge: Cambridge University Press.

Nozick, Robert. 1974. *Anarchy, State, and Utopia*. New York: Basic Books.

Nuhfer, Edward, Steven Fleischer, Christopher Cogan, Karl Wirth, and Eric Gaze. 2017. "How random noise and a graphical convention subverted behavioral scientists' explanations of self-assessment data." *Numeracy* 10 (1) article 4. <doi.org/10.5038/1936-4660.10.1.4>

Nyhan, Brendon, and Jason Reifler. 2010. "When corrections fail." *Political Behavior* 32: 303-330.

Nylan, Michael. 2005. "Toward an archæology of writing." Pp. 3-49 in *Text and Ritual in Early China*, edited by Martin Kern. Seattle: University of Washington Press.

654

Oakeshott, Michael. 1933. *Experience and Its Modes*. Cambridge: Cambridge University Press.

Ober, Josiah. 2015. *The Rise and Fall of Classical Greece*. Princeton: Princeton University Press.

Oberschall, Anthony. 1990. "Incentives, governance and development in Chinese collective agriculture." Pp. 265-289 in *Social Institutions*, edited by Michael Hechter, Karl-Dieter Opp, and Reinhard Wippler. New York: Aldine de Gruyter.

Obstfeld, David. 2005. "Social networks, the tertius lungens orientation, and involvement in innovation." *Administrative Science Quarterly* 50: 100-130.

O'Connor, Flannery. 1988 (1952). *Wise Blood*. Pp. 1-132 in *idem, Collected Works*. Ed. Sally Fitzgerald. New York: Library of America.

Offer, Avner, and Gabriel Söderberg. 2016. *The Nobel Factor*. Princeton: Princeton University Press.

Ogden, Timothy N (ed.). *Experimental Conversations*. Cambridge: MIT Press.

Ogereau, Julien. 2014. *Paul's Koinonia with the Phillippians*. Tübingen: Mohr Siebeck.

Okrent, Arika. 2009. *In the Land of Invented Languages*. New York: Spiegel and Grau.

Olson, Mancur. 1965. *The Logic of Collective Action*. Cambridge: Harvard University Press.

Omnès, Roland. 1994a. *The Interpretation of Quantum Mechanics*. Princeton: Princeton University Press.

_____. 1999 [1994b]. *Quantum Philosophy*. Trans. Arturo Sangalli. Princeton: Princeton University Press.

Orange, Tommy. 2018. *There There*. New York: Knopf.

Oreshkov, Ognyan, and Christina Giarmazi. 2016. "Causal and causally separable processes." *New Journal of Physics* 18 (093020): 1-36.

Orléan, André. 1999. *Le pouvoir de la finance*. Paris: Odile Jacob.

_____. 2014. *The Empire of Value*. Trans. M B DeBevoise. Cambridge: MIT Press.

Ortega y Gasset, José. 1975 (1914). "An essay in esthetics by way of a preface." Pp. 127-150 in *idem, Phenomenology and Art*. Trans. Philip W Silver. New York: Norton.

Osnos, Evan. 2014. *Age of Ambition*. New York: Farrar, Straus, and Giroux.

Oster, Emily. 2019. *Cribsheet*. New York: Penguin.

Oudeyer, Pierre-Yves, and Linda B Smith. 2016. "How evolution may work through curiosity driven developmental process." *Topics in Cognitive Science*, 8 (April): 492-502.

Overington, Michael. 1979. "Doing the what comes rationally." *The American Sociologist* 14: 2-12, 31-34.

Oyama, Susan. 1985. *The Ontogeny of Information*. Cambridge: Cambridge University Press.

Packer, George. 2013. *The Unwinding*. New York: Farrar, Straus & Giroux.

Page, Benjamin I, Larry M Bartels, and Jason Seawright. 2013. "Democracy and policy preferences of wealthy Americans." *Perspectives on Politics* 11: 51-73.

Palmer, Richard G. 1982. "Broken ergodicity." *Advances in Physics* 31 (No. 6): 669-735.

Panek, Richard. 2011. *The 4% Universe*. Boston: Houghton Mifflin Harcourt.

Panofsky, Erwin. 1960. *Renaissance and Renascences in Western Art*. New York: Harper & Row.

Papaioannou, Stratis. 2013. *Michael Psellos: Rhetoric and Authorship in Byzantium*. Cambridge: Cambridge University Press.

655

Pareto, Vilfredo. 1963 (1916). *A Treatise on General Sociology*. Ed. A Livingston, trans. A Bongiorno & A Livingston. New York: Dover.

_____. 1971 (1927). *Manual of Political Economy*, revised edition. Ed. Alfred N Page and Ann S Schwier; trans. Ann S Schwier. New York: Kelley.

Parker, Geoffrey. 2019. *Emperor*. New Haven: Yale University Press.

Pabilonia, Sabrina Wulff, Michael W Jadoo, Bhavani Khandrika, Jennifer Price, and James D Mildenberger. 2019. "BLS publishes experimental state-level labor productivity measures." *Monthly Labor Review* June. Washington DC: Bureau of Labor Statistics.

Parfit, Derek. 1987. *Reasons and Persons*, corrected edition. Oxford: Oxford University Press.

Paik, Anthony, and Kenneth Sanchagrin. 2013. "Social isolation in America." *American Sociological Review* 78: 339-360.

Parsons, Talcott. 1937. *The Structure of Social Action*. New York: McGraw-Hill.

_____. 1948. "The position of sociological theory." *American Sociological Review* 13: 156-171.

_____. 1949a. *The Structure of Social Action*, 2nd edition. New York: Free Press.

_____. 1949b. *Essays in Sociological Theory*, 1st edition. New York: Free Press.

_____. 1950."The prospects of sociological theory."*American Sociological Review* 15:3-16.

_____. 1951. *The Social System*. New York: Free Press.

_____. 1971 (1965). "Value-freedom and objectivity." Pp. 29-50 in *Max Weber and Sociology Today*, edited by Otto Stammer. Trans. Kathleen Morris. New York: Harper & Row.

_____, Robert Freed Bales, and Edward A Shils. 1953. *Working Papers in the Theory of Action*. Glencoe, IL: Free Press.

_____, and Edward A Shils (eds.). 1951. *Toward a General Theory of Action*. Cambridge: Harvard University Press.

_____, Edward Shils, Kaspar D Naegele, and Jesse R Pitts (eds.). 1961. *Theories of Society*, 2 volumes. New York: Free Press.

Pascual, Mercedes. 2001. "Scales that matter." Pp. 255-286 in *Carving Our Destiny: Scientific Research Faces a New Millennium*, edited by Susan M Fitzpatrick and John T Bruer. Washington, DC: National Academies Press.

_____, Manojit Roy, and Karina Laneri. 2011. "Simple models for complex systems." *Theoretical Ecology* 4: 211-222. <doi 10.1007/s.12080-011-0116-2>

Pater, Walter. 1986 (1888). *Studies in the History of the Renaissance*, 3rd edition. Ed. Matthew Beaumont. Oxford: Oxford University Press.

Patterson, Edwin W. 1950. "John Dewey and the law." *American Bar Association Journal* 36: 619-622, 699-701.

Paul, Herman. 2011. *Hayden White*. Cambridge: Polity.

Payne, Keith. 2017. *The Broken Ladder*. New York: Viking.

Pearl, Judea. 1990. *Causality*. Cambridge: Cambridge University Press.

_____, and Dana MacKenzie. 2018. *The Book of Why*. New York: Basic Books.

Pearson, Helen. 2016. *The Life Project*. London: Allen Lane.

Peers, E Allison. 1949. *The Romantic Movement in Spain*. Liverpool: Liverpool University Press.

Peeters, Benoît. 2013 (2010). *Derrida*. Trans. Andrew Brown. Cambridge: Polity.

Pellegrino, François, Christophe Coupé, and Egidio Marsico. 2011. "A cross-language perspective on speech information rate." *Language* 87: 539-558.

Pelli, Denis G, Catherine W Burns, Bart Farell, and Deborah C Moore-Page. 2006. "Feature detection and letter identification." *Vision Research* 46 (December): 4646-4674.

Peri, Alexis. 2017. *The War Within*. Cambridge: Harvard University Press.

Perry, Ralph Barton. 1910. "The egocentric predicament." *Journal of Philosophy, Psychology, and Scientific Method* 7: 5-14.

Pesic, Peter. 2017. *Polyphonic Minds*. Cambridge: MIT Press.

Petersen, Karl. 1989. *Ergodic Theory*, corrected edition. Cambridge: Cambridge University Press. Online edition 2012 at <doi.org/10.1017/CBO9780511608728>

Phillips, Alban William H. 1958. "The relation between unemployment and the rate of change of money wage rates in the United Kingdom." *Economica* 25 (November): 283-299.

Phillips, Anne. 1992. "Universal pretensions in political thought." Pp. 10-30 in *Destabilizing Theory*, edited by Michèle Barrett & Anne Phillips. Stanford: Stanford University Press.

Piaget, Jean. 1926 (1923). *The Language and Thought of the Child*. London: Routledge & Kegan Paul.

_____. 1952 (1930). *The Origins of Intelligence in Children*. New York: International University Press.

_____. 1954 (1950). *The Construction of Reality in the Child*. New York: Basic.

Pickering, Andrew. 1995. *The Mangle of Practice*. Chicago: University of Chicago Press.

Piketty, Thomas. 2014. *Capital*. Trans. Arthur Goldhammer. Cambridge: Harvard University Press.

_____, Gilles Postel-Vinay, and Jean-Laurent Rosenthal. 2014. "Inherited vs self-made wealth." *Explorations in Economic History* 51: 21-40.

Pilosof, Shai, Mason A Porter, Mercedes Pascual, and Sonia Kéfi. 2017. "The multilayer nature of ecological networks." *Nature: Ecology & Evolution* 1 (4): 101. doi: 10.1038/s41559-017-0101>

Pinkard, Terry. 1994. *Hegel's Phenomenology*. Cambridge: Cambridge University Press.

Pippin, Robert B. 1997. *Idealism as Modernism*. Cambridge: Cambridge University Press.

_____. 1999. *Modernism as a Philosophical Problem*, 2nd edition. Malden, MA: Blackwell.

_____. 2005. *The Persistence of Subjectivism*. Cambridge: Cambridge University Press.

_____. 2008. *Hegel's Practical Theory*. Cambridge: Cambridge University Press.

_____. 2010. *Hegel on Self-Consciousness*. Princeton: Princeton University Press.

_____. 2014. *After the Beautiful*. Chicago: University of Chicago Press.

_____. 2015. *Interanimations*. Chicago: University of Chicago Press.

Pitkin, Hanna. 1967. *The Concept of Representation*. Berkeley: University of California Press.

Planck, Max. 1948. *Wissenschaftliche Selbstbiographie*. Leipzig: J A Barth.

_____. 1949 (1948). *Scientific Autobiography and Other Papers*. Trans. Frank Gaynor. New York: Philosophical Library.

Plato. 1907 (c348 BCE). *Laws*. Trans. John Burnet. Oxford: Clarendon.

_____. 1926 (c385 BCE). *Cratylus*. Trans. Harold N Fowler. Cambridge: Harvard University Press (Loeb Classical Library).

_____. 1926 (c370 BCE). *Theœtetus*. Trans. Harold N Fowler. Cambridge: Harvard University Press (Loeb Classical Library).

Plato. 1927. (c360 BCE). *Alcibiades*. Trans. Walter R M Lamb. Cambridge: Harvard University Press (Loeb Classical Library).

Pliny the Elder. 1855 (c78). *The Natural History*. Trans. & ed. John Bostock & H T Riley. London: Taylor and Francis.

Plokhy, Serhii. 2018. *Chernobyl*. London: Allen Lane.

Plomin, Robert. 2018. *Blueprint*. London: Allen Lane.

Plutarch. c110 CE. *Life of Theseus*. Trans. Bernadotte Perrin.

Pomerantsev, Peter. 2014. *Nothing Is True and Everything Is Possible*. New York: Public Affairs.

Popkin, Gabriel. 2017. "Spooky action achieved at record distance." *Science* 356 (16 June): 1110-1111.

Popper, Karl. 1945. *The Open Society and Its Enemies*, 2 volumes. London: Routledge.

Posnock, Ross. 2016. *Renunciation*. Cambridge: Harvard University Press.

Powell, Walter W. 1990. "Neither market nor hierarchy." *Research in Organizational Behavior* 12: 295-336.

Premack, David, and Guy Woodruff. 1978. "Does the chimpanzee have a theory of mind?" *Behavioral and Brain Sciences* 4: 515-526.

Preyer, Gerhard, and Georg Peter (eds.). 2005. *Contextualism in Philosophy*. Oxford: Clarendon.

Price, Richard. 1983, 1991, 1994. *The Correspondence of Richard Price*, 3 volumes. Ed. W B Peach & D O Thomas. Cardiff: University of Wales Press.

Prinz, Wolfgang. 2012. *Open Minds: The Social Making of Agency and Intentionality*. Cambridge: MIT Press.

Pritchett, Lant. 2013. *The Rebirth of Education*. Washington, DC: Center for Global Development.

Pronin, Emily, Thomas Gilovich, and Lee Ross. 2004. "Objectivity in the eye of the beholder." *Psychological Review* 111: 781-799.

Proust, Marcel. 1993 (1913). *Swann's Way*. Volume 1 of *idem, In Search of Lost Time*. Tr. C K S Moncrieff and T Kilmartin, rev. tr. D J Enright. New York: Modern Library.

_____. 1993 (1923). "The Captive." Volume 5 of *idem, In Search of Lost Time*. Tr. C K Scott Moncrieff and T Kilmartin, rev. trans. D J Enright. New York: Modern Library.

Prum, Richard O. 2017. *The Evolution of Beauty*. New York: Doubleday.

Puddephatt, Antony. 2009. "The search for meaning." *The American Sociologist* 40: 89-105.

Putnam, Hilary. 1994 (1979). "Philosophy of mathematics: why nothing works." Pp. 499-512 in *idem, Words and Life*. Ed. James Conant. Cambridge: Harvard University Press.

_____. 1981. *Reason, Truth and History*. Cambridge: Cambridge University Press.

Putnam, Robert D. 2000. *Bowling Alone*. New York: Simon & Schuster.

Pyyhtinen, Ollie. 2010. *Simmel and 'the Social'*. London: Palgrave Macmillan.

Quick, Jonathan, with Bronwyn Fryer. 2018. *The End of Epidemics*. New York: St Martin's.

Quine, Willard Van Orman. 1966. *The Ways of Paradox and Other Essays*. New York: Random House.

Quintilian, Marcus Fabius. 1920 (c95 CE). *Institutio Oratoria*. Loeb Classical Library, Volume 4. Cambridge: Harvard University Press.

Raudenbush, Stephen W, Brian Rowan, and Sang Jin Kang. 1991. "A multilevel, multivariate model for studying school climate in secondary schools with estimation via the EM algorithm and application to US high-school data." *Journal of Educational Statistics* 16: 295-330.

Raudenbush, Stephen W, and Robert J Sampson. 1999. "Ecometrics." *Sociological Methodology* 29: 1-41.

Rawls, Ann Warfield. 1987. "The interaction order *sui generis*." *Sociological Theory* 5: 136-149.

Raz, Joseph. 1986. *The Morality of Freedom*. Oxford: Clarendon.

_____. 2003. *The Practice of Value* (with comments by Christine Korsgaard, Robert Pippin, and Bernard Williams). Oxford: Clarendon.

Reardon, Sean F. 2016. "School segregation and racial academic achievement gaps." *RSF Journal* 2 (September): 34-57.

Reddy, William M. 2001. *The Navigation of Feeling*. Cambridge: Cambridge University Press.

_____. 2012. *The Making of Romantic Love*. Chicago: University of Chicago Press.

Redfield, James. 1994. *Nature and Culture in the "Iliad,"* expanded edition. Durham: Duke University Press.

Redondi, Pierre. 1987 (1983). *Galileo Heretic*. Trans. Raymond Rosenthal. Princeton: Princeton University Press.

Rehberg, Karl-Siegbert. 2016 (1985). "The theory of intersubjectivity as a theory of the human being." Trans. Alex Skinner. Pp. 92-114 in *The Timeliness of George Herbert Mead*, edited by Hans Joas and Daniel R Huebner. Chicago: University of Chicago Press.

Reich, Adam, and Peter Bearman. 2018. *Working for Respect*. New York: Columbia University Press.

Reiss, Spencer. 1996. "Power to the people." *Wired* 4 (December).

Remington, Thomas F. 1982. "Varga and the foundations of Soviet planning." *Soviet Studies* 34: 585-600.

Renaut, Alain. 1997 (1989). *The Era of the Individual*. Trans. M B DeBevoise and Franklin Philip. Princeton: Princeton University Press.

Rendall, Michael, Margaret Weden, Melissa Fayreault, and Hilary Waldron. 2011. "The protective effect of marriage for survival." *Demography* 48: 481-506.

Renouvier, Charles. 1906. *Critique de la Doctrine de Kant*. Paris: Félix Alcan.

Richter, Gerhard. 1995. *The Daily Practice of Painting*. Ed. Hans-Ulrich Obrist; trans. David Britt. London: Thames and Hudson.

Ricœur, Paul. 1965 (1955). *History and Truth*. Trans. Charles A Kelbley. Evanston, IL: Northwestern University Press.

_____. 1992 (1990). *Oneself as Another*. Trans. Kathleen Blamey. Chicago: University of Chicago Press.

Ricuperati, Giuseppe. 1981. "'Universal history': storia di un progretto europeo." *Studi Settecenteschi* 2: 7-90.

_____. 2005. "Francesco Bianchini e l'idea di storia universal 'figurata'." *Revista Storia Italiana* 117: 872-973.

Rietmann, Felix E. 2018. "No escape from Fleck." *Isis* 109: 91-94.

Rifkin, Jeremy. 1996. *The End of Work*. New York: Warner.

Riker, William H. 1964. *Federalism*. Boston: Little, Brown.

659

Riker, William H. 1980. "Implications from the disequilibrium of majority rule for the study of institutions." *American Political Science Review* 74 (June): 432-436.

_____. 1982. *Liberalism against Populism*. San Francisco: Freeman.

_____. 1995. "The experience of creating institutions." Pp. 121-144 in *Explaining Social Institutions*, edited by Jack Knight and Itai Sened. Ann Arbor: University of Michigan Press.

Riley, Dylan. 2015. "The new Durkheim." *Critical Historical Studies* 2: 261-279.

_____. 2017. "Bourdieu's class theory." *Catalyst* 1: 108-136.

_____. 2018. "Science and politics." *Catalyst* 2: 88-132.

Risjord, Mark. 1999. "No strings attached." *Philosophy of Science* 66: S299-S313.

Riskin, Jessica. 2016. *The Restless Clock*. Chicago: University of Chicago Press.

Roberts, Sam G B, and Robin I M Dunbar. 2011. "The costs of family and friends." *Evolution and Human Behavior* 32: 186-197.

Robertson, Geoffrey. 2005. *The Tyrannicide Brief*. New York: Pantheon.

Rodgers, Daniel T. 1974. *The Work Ethic in Industrial America 1850-1920*. Chicago: University of Chicago Press.

_____. 2011. *Age of Fracture*. Cambridge: Harvard University Press.

Römer, Thomas. 2015 (2014). *The Invention of God*. Trans. R Geuss. Cambridge: Harvard University Press.

Roetz, Heiner. 1984. *Mensch und Natur im alten China*. Frankfurt a.M.: Lang.

Rogers, Howard J (ed.). 1905-08. [Proceedings of the] *International Congress of Arts and Science*, 15 volumes. London: University Alliance.

Roland, Alan. 1988. *In Search of Self in India and Japan*. Princeton: Princeton University Press.

Romer, Paul M. 1994. "The origins of endogenous growth." *Journal of Economic Perspectives* 8: 3-22.

Romilly, Jacqueline de. 1992 (1988). *The Great Sophists in Periclean Athens*. Trans. Janet Lloyd. Oxford: Clarendon.

Rorty, Richard (ed.). 1967. *The Linguistic Turn*. Chicago: University of Chicago Press.

_____. 1979. *Philosophy and the Mirror of Nature*. Princeton: Princeton University Press.

_____. 1982. *Consequences of Pragmatism*. Minneapolis: University of Minnesota Press.

_____. 1989. *Contingency, Irony, and Solidarity*. Cambridge: Cambridge University Press.

Rosa, Hartmut. 2013 (2005). *Social Acceleration*. Trans. J Trejo-Mathys. New York: Columbia University Press.

Rosen, Charles. 1971. *The Classical Style*. New York: Viking.

_____. 1995. *The Romantic Generation*. Cambridge: Harvard University Press.

Rosen, Sherwin. 1975. "Measuring the obsolescence of knowledge." Pp. 199-232 in *Education, Income, and Human Behavior*. New York: NBER.

Ross, Alex. 2007. *The Rest Is Noise*. New York: Farrar, Straus, and Giroux.

Ross, Lillian. 2015 (1987). "Workouts." Pp. 20-23 in *idem, Reporting Always*. New York: Scribner.

Roth, Steffen, Harry F Dahms, Frank Welz, and Sandro Cattacin. 2019. "Print theories of computer societies." *Technological Forecasting & Social Change* 149 (December).

Rothschild, Emma. 1994. "Adam Smith and the invisible hand." *American Economic Review* 84 (May), Proceedings and Papers of the 106th Annual Meeting of the American Economic Association: pp. 319-322.

Rotter, Julian B. 1966. "Generalized expectancies for internal versus external control of reinforcement." *Psychological Monographs, General & Applied* 80: 1-28.

Rousseau, Jean-Jacques. 1984 (1755). *A Discourse on the Origin and the Foundation of Inequality among Mankind*. Trans. Maurice Cranston. Harmondsworth: Penguin.

Rowe, William T. 2001. *Saving the World*. Stanford: Stanford University Press.

_____. 2007. *Crimson Rain*. Stanford: Stanford University Press.

_____. 2009. *China's Last Empire*. Cambridge: Belknap Press of Harvard University Press.

_____. 2018. *Speaking of Profit*. Cambridge: Harvard University Asia Center.

Rowland, Ingrid, and Noah Charney. 2017. *The Collector of Lives*. New York: Norton.

Royce, Josiah. 1894. "The external world and the social consciousness." *Philosophical Review* 3: 513-545.

_____. 1895a. "Some observations on the anomalies of self-consciousness." *Psychological Review* 2: 433-457, 574-584.

_____. 1895b. "Self-consciousness, social consciousness and nature." *Philosophical Review* 4: 465-485, 577-602.

Runciman, Walter G. 1966. *Relative Deprivation and Social Justice*. London: Routledge & Kegan Paul.

Russell, Bertrand. 1919. *Introduction to Mathematical Philosophy*. London: Allen & Unwin.

_____. 1921. *The Analysis of Mind*. London: George Allen & Unwin.

Rutherford, Adam. 2018. *The Book of Humans*. London: Weidenfeld & Nicolson.

Ryan, Alan. 2013. *On Aristotle: Saving Politics from Philosophy*. New York: Liveright.

Ryder, Norman B. 1965. "The cohort as a concept in the study of social change." *American Sociological Review* 30: 843-861.

Saam, Nicole J. 1999. "Simulating the micro-macro link." *Sociological Methodology* 29: 43-79.

Sabelhaus, John, David Johnson, Stephen Ash, Thesia Garner, John Greenlees, Steve Henderson, and David Swanson. 2012. "Is the consumer expenditure survey representative by income?" Finance and Economics Discussion Series 2012-36. Washington, DC: Board of Governors of the Federal Reserve System.

Sacks, Oliver. 1984. *A Leg to Stand On*. New York: Touchstone.

Safranski, Rüdiger. 1991 (1987). *Schopenhauer and the Wild Years of Philosophy*. Trans. Ewald Osers. Cambridge: Harvard University Press.

_____. 1998 (1994). *Martin Heidegger*. Trans. Ewald Osers. Cambridge: Harvard University Press.

Salinger, Jerome D. 1951. *The Catcher in the Rye*. Boston: Little, Brown.

_____. 1961. *Franny and Zooey*. Boston: Little, Brown.

Saller, Richard. 2005. "Framing the debate over growth in the ancient economy." Pp. 223-238 in *The Ancient Economy*, edited by Joseph G Manning and Ian Morris. Stanford: Stanford University Press.

Salsburg, David. 2001. *The Lady Tasting Tea*. New York: Freeman.

Samoyault, Tiphaine. 2016. *Barthes*. Trans. A Brown. Cambridge: Polity.

Sampson, Robert J. 2011. "Neighborhood effects, causal mechanisms and the social structure of the city." Pp. 227-249 in *Analytical Sociology and Social Mechanisms*, edited by Pierre Demeulenaere. Cambridge: Cambridge University Press.

_____. 2012. *Great American City*. Chicago: University of Chicago Press.

Sampson, Robert J, and Stephen W Raudenbush. 1999. "Systematic social observation of public spaces." *American Journal of Sociology* 105: 603-651.

Samuelson, Paul A, and Robert M Solow. 1960. "Analytical aspects of anti-inflation policy." *American Economic Review* 50 (2): 177-194.

Sandage, Scott A. 2005. *Born Losers*. Cambridge: Harvard University Press.

Sander, Richard H, Yana A Kucheva, and Jonathan M Zasloff. 2018. *Moving toward Integration*. Cambridge: Harvard University Press.

Sargent, Thomas J. 1971. "A note on the 'accelerationist' controversy." *Journal of Money, Credit and Banking* 3 (3): 721-725.

_____. 1999. *The Conquest of American Inflation*. Princeton: Princeton University Press.

_____, and Neil Wallace. 1981. "Some unpleasant monetarist arithmetic." *Quarterly Review of the Federal Reserve Bank of Minneapolis* 5 (Fall): 1-17.

Sass, Louis. 1992. *Madness and Modernism*. New York: Basic Books.

Savage, Leonard J. 1972. *The Foundations of Statistics*, 2nd edition. Mineola, NY: Dover.

Sawyer, R Keith. 2003. "Artificial societies." *Sociological Methods and Research* 31: 325-363.

Scaff, Lawrence A. 2011. *Max Weber in America*. Princeton: Princeton University Press.

Schaberg, David. "Playing at critique." Pp. 194-225 in *Text and Ritual in Early China*, edited by Martin Kern. Seattle: University of Washington Press.

Schechtman, Marya. 1996. *The Constitution of Selves*. Ithaca: Cornell University Press.

Scheffler, Samuel. 2013. *Death and the Afterlife*. New York: Oxford University Press.

Scheler, Max. 1954 (1948). *The Nature of Sympathy*, 5th edition. Ed. Maria Scheler, trans. Peter Heath. London: Routledge & Kegan Paul.

_____. 1971 (1915). *Ressentiment*. Trans. William W Holdheim, ed. Lewis Coser. New York: Free Press.

Schelling, Friedrich Wilhelm Joseph. 1856. *Sämtliche Werke*, edited by Karl F A Schelling. Stuttgart und Augsburg: J Cotta.

Schelling, Thomas C. 1971. "Dynamic models of segregation." *Journal of Mathematical Sociology* 1: 143-186.

_____. 1978. *Micromotives and Macrobehaviors*. New York: Norton.

Schiller, Johann Christoph Friedrich. 1954 (1794). *On the Aesthetic Education of Man in a Series of Letters*. Trans. R Snell. New Haven: Yale University Press.

Schleifer, Andrei. 2000. *Inefficient Markets*. New York: Oxford University Press.

Schmitt, Frederick (ed.). 2003. *Socializing Metaphysics*. Lanham, MD: Rowman & Littlefield.

Schneider, Louis. 1962. "The role of the category of ignorance in sociological theory." *American Sociological Review* 27: 492-508.

_____ (ed.). 1967. *The Scottish Moralists*. Chicago: University of Chicago Press.

_____. 1984. *The Grammar of Social Relations*. Ed. Jay Weinstein. New Brunswick, NJ: Transaction.

Schor, Esther. 2016. *Bridge of Words*. New York: Metropolitan.

Schorske, Carl E. 1980. *Vienna fin de siècle*. New York: Knopf.

Schrag, Calvin O. 1997. *The Self after Postmodernity*. New Haven: Yale University Press.

Schrödinger, Erwin. 1967 (1944). *What Is Life?* Cambridge: Cambridge University Press.

Schütz, Alfred. 1967 (1932). *The Phenomenology of the Social World*. Trans. George Walsh and Frederick Lehnert. Evanston, IL: Northwestern University Press.

Schumacher, Julie. 2014. *Dear Committee Members*. New York: Doubleday.

Schumacher, Julie. 2018. *The Shakespeare Requirement*. New York: Doubleday.
Schumpeter, Joseph A. 1976 (1942). *Capitalism, Socialism and Democracy*, 5<sup>th</sup> edition. London: Allen & Unwin.
Schwartz, Barry. 2004. *The Paradox of Choice*. New York: HarperCollins.
Sciulli, David. 1986. "Voluntaristic action as a distinct concept." *American Sociological Review* 51: 743-766.
Scott, James C. 2017. *Against the Grain: A Deep History of the Earliest States*. New Haven: Yale University Press.
Scott, W Richard. 2014. *Institutions and Organizations*, 4<sup>th</sup> edition. Los Angeles: Sage.
Searle, John R. 1977. "Reiterating the differences." *Glyph* 2.
_____. 1983. "The word turned upside down." *New York Review of Books* 30 (27 October): 74-78.
_____. 1995. *The Construction of Social Reality*. New York: Free Press.
_____. 2000. "Consciousness, free action, and the brain." *Journal of Consciousness Studies* 7 (10): 3-22.
_____. 2008. "Language and social ontology." *Theory and Society* 37: 443-459.
Seaver, Paul S. 1985. *Wallington's World*. Stanford: Stanford University Press.
Sebald, W G. 1998 (1995). *The Rings of Saturn*. Trans. Michael Hulse. London: Harvill.
Secretan, Catherine. 2002. *Le 'Marchand philosophe' de Caspar Barlaeus*. Paris: Champion.
Seigel, Jerrold. 2005. *The Idea of the Self*. Cambridge: Cambridge University Press.
Seligman, Martin. 1996. *The Optimistic Child*. New York: Houghton Mifflin.
Sellars, Wilfred. 1963. *Science, Perception and Reality*. London: Routledge & Kegan Paul.
Sellers, Charles. 1992. *The Market Revolution*. New York: Oxford University Press.
Sen, Amartya K. 1993. "Capability and well-being." Pp. 30-53 in *The Quality of Life*, edited by Martha Nussbaum and Amartya K Sen. Oxford: Clarendon Press.
Sent, Esther-Mirjam. 2008. "Resisting and accommodating Thomas Sargent." Pp. 92-109 in *The Mangle in Practice*, edited by A Pickering and K Guzik. Durham: Duke University Press.
Sepper, Dennis L. 1988. *Goethe contra Newton*. Cambridge: Cambridge University Press.
Setiya, Kieran. 2007. *Reason without Rationalism*. Princeton: Princeton University Press.
_____. 2018. "Monk justice." *London Review of Books* 40 (3 August): 40, 42.
Sewell, William H, Jr. 1992. "A theory of structures." *American Journal of Sociology* 98: 1-29.
_____. 1994. *A Rhetoric of Bourgeois Revolution*. Durham, NC: Duke University Press.
_____. 2005. *Logics of History*. Chicago: University of Chicago Press.
Sextus Empiricus. 1933 (c190). *Pyrrhonian Hypotheses*. In *Sextus Empiricus*, volume 2. Trans. R G Bury. Cambridge: Loeb Classical Library. Harvard University Press.
_____. 1936 (c190). *Adversus mathematikos*. In *Sextus Empiricus*, volume 3. Trans. R G Bury. Cambridge: Loeb Classical Library, Harvard University Press.
Shackleton, Robert. 1961. *Montesquieu*. Oxford: Clarendon.
Shan, Weijian. 2019. *Out of the Gobi*. Hoboken, NJ: Wiley.
Shannon, Claude E., and Warren Weaver. 1949. *The Mathematical Theory of Communication*. Urbana: University of Illinois Press.
Shapin, Steven. 1996. *The Scientific Revolution*. Chicago: University of Chicago Press.

Shaw, Donald L. 1963. "Toward the understanding of Spanish Romanticism." *Modern Language Review* 58 (April): 190-195.

Shaw, Tamsin. 2007. *Nietzsche's Political Skepticism*. Princeton: Princeton University Press.

Shawn, Allen. 2002. *Arnold Schoenberg's Journey*. New York: Farrar, Straus & Giroux.

Sherrod, Lonnie R, and Orville G Brim, Jr. 1986. "Retrospective and prospective views of life-course research on human development." Pp. 557-580 in *Human Development and the Life Course*, edited by Aage B Sørensen, Franz E Weinert, and Lonnie R Sherrod. Hillsdale, NJ: Erlbaum.

Shiller, Robert J. 2003. "From efficient markets theory to behavioral finance." *Journal of Economic Perspectives* 17 (1): 83-104.

Shils, Edward A. 1948. *The Present State of American Sociology*. Glencoe, IL: Free Press.

Shils, Edward A. 2006. *A Fragment of a Sociological Autobiography*. Ed. Steven Grosby. New Brunswick, NJ: Transaction.

Shoemaker, Sidney. 1994. "The first-person perspective." *Proceedings and Addresses of The American Philosophical Association* 68 (November): 7-22.

_____. 1996. *The First-Person Perspective, and Other Essays*. Cambridge: Cambridge University Press.

Shryock, Andrew, Daniel Lord Smail, and Associates. 2011. *Deep History*. Berkeley: University of California Press.

Sickinger, James P. 1999. *Public Records and Archives in Classical Athens*. Chapel Hill: University of North Carolina Press.

_____. 2007. "The bureaucracy of democracy and empire." Pp. 196-214 in *The Cambridge Companion to the Age of Pericles*, edited by L J Samons II. Cambridge: Cambridge University Press.

Sieyès, Emmanuel Joseph. 1999, 2007. *Des Manuscrits de Sieyès. 1773–1799*, volumes I and II. Ed. Christine Fauré, Jacques Guilhaumou, Jacques Vallier, et Françoise Weil. Paris: Champion.

Sigmund, Karl. 2017 (2015). *Exact Thinking in Demented Times*. New York: Basic Books.

Simmel, Georg. 1898. "The persistence of social groups." Trans. Albion W Small. *American Journal of Sociology* 3: 662-698.

_____. 1906. "The sociology of secrecy and secret societies." Trans. Albion W Small. *American Journal of Sociology* 11: 441-498.

_____. 1908. *Soziologie*. Munich: Duncker und Humblot.

_____. 1950 (1923). *Sociology*, 3rd ed. Trans. & ed. K H Wolff. Glencoe, IL: Free Press.

_____. 1971 (1908a). "The problem of sociology." Tr. K H Wolff. Pp. 23-35 in *idem, On Individuality and Social Forms*. Ed. D Levine. Chicago: University of Chicago Press.

_____. 1971 (1908b). "How is society possible?" Tr. Kurt H Wolff. Pp. 6-22 in *idem, On Individuality and Social Forms*. Ed. D N Levine. Chicago: University of Chicago Press.

_____. 1971 (1908c). "The expansion of the group and the development of individuality." Trans. R P Albares. Pp. 251-293 in *idem, On Individuality and Social Forms*. Ed. Donald N Levine. Chicago: University of Chicago Press.

_____. 1971 (1908d). "The stranger." Tr. D N Levine. Pp. 143-150 in *idem, On Individuality and Social Forms*. Ed. D N Levine. Chicago: University of Chicago Press.

Simon, Herbert A. 1955. "On a class of skew distribution functions." *Biometrika* 42: 425-440.

Simon, Herbert A. 1962. "The architecture of complexity." *Proceedings of the American Philosophical Society* 106: 467-482.

_____. 1971. "Designing organizations for an information-rich world" (with comments and discussion). Pp. 37-72 in *Computers, Communications, and the Public Interest*, edited by Martin Greenberger. Baltimore: Johns Hopkins University Press.

_____, and Albert Ando. 1961. "Aggregation of variables in dynamic systems." *Econometrica* 29: 111-138.

Skaalvik, Einar M, and Sidsel Skaalvik. 2007. "Dimensions of teacher self-efficacy and relations of strain factors, perceived collective efficacy, and teacher burnout." *Journal of Educational Psychology* 99: 611-625.

_____. 2010. "Teacher self-efficacy and teacher burnout." *Teaching and Teacher Education* 26: 1059-1069.

Skocpol, Theda. 2003. *Diminished Democracy*. Norman: University of Oklahoma Press.

Slawson, W David. 1996. *Binding Promises*. Princeton: Princeton University Press.

Sloan, Michael C. 2010. "Aristotle's *Nicomachean Ethics* as the original *locus* for the *Septum Circumstantiae*." *Classical Philology* 105: 236-251.

Slobodkin, Lawrence B. 1992. *Simplicity and Complexity in Games of the Intellect*. Cambridge: Harvard University Press.

Sloman, Steven, and Philip Fernbach. 2017. *The Knowledge Illusion*. New York: Riverhead.

Small, Albion W. 1925. Review of Nicholas J Spykman's *The Social Theory of Georg Simmel*. *American Journal of Sociology* 31: 84-87.

Smarsh, Sarah. 2018. *Heartland*. New York: Scribner.

Smith, Adam. 1776. *An Inquiry into the Nature and Causes of the Wealth of Nations*. London: Oxford University Press.

_____. 1817. *Theory of Moral Sentiments*, final edition, 2 vol. Boston: Wells and Lilly.

_____. 1983 (c1763). *Lectures on Rhetoric and Belles Lettres*. Ed. John M Lothian. Oxford: Oxford University Press.

Smith, Brad, and Carol Ann Browne. 2019. *Tools and Weapons*. New York: Penguin.

Smith, Thomas Vernor. 1931-32. "The social philosophy of George Herbert Mead." *American Journal of Sociology* 37: 368-383.

Smyth, Adam (ed.). 2016. *A History of English Autobiography*. Cambridge: Cambridge University Press.

Snijders, Tom A B. 2001. "The statistical evaluation of social network dynamics." *Sociological Methodology* 31: 361-395.

_____. 2005. "Models for longitudinal network data." Pp. 215-247 in *Models and Methods in Social Network Analysis*, edited by Peter Carrington, John Scott, and Stanley Wasserman. New York: Cambridge University Press.

_____. 2009. "Longitudinal methods of network analysis." Pp. 5998-6013 in *Encyclopedia of Complexity and System Science*, 11 volumes, edited by Robert A Meyers. New York: Springer.

_____, Gerhard G van de Bunt, and Christian E G Steglich. 2010. "Introduction to Stochastic actor-based models for network dynamics." *Social Networks* 32: 44-60.

_____, John H Koskinen, and Michael Schweinberger. 2010. "Maximum likelihood estimation for social network dynamics." *Annals of Applied Statistics* 4: 567-588.

_____, and Christian E G Steglich. 2015. "Representing micro-macro linkages by actor-based dynamic network models." *Sociological Methods and Research* 44: 222-271.

Sobel, Michael E. 2000. "Causal inference in the social sciences." *Journal of the American Statistical Association* 95: 647-651.

———. 2005. "Discussion: the scientific model of causality." *Sociological Methodology* 35: 99-133.

Solow, Robert M. 1956. "A contribution to the theory of economic growth." *Quarterly Journal of Economics* 70: 65-94.

———. 1957. "Technical change and the aggregate production function." *Review of Economics and Statistics* 39 (August): 312-320.

Sontag, Susan. 1966. *Against Interpretation*. New York: Farrar, Straus & Giroux.

Sørensen, Aage B. 1998. "Theoretical mechanisms and the empirical study of social processes." Pp. 238-266 in *Social Mechanisms*, edited by Peter Hedström and Richard Swedberg. Cambridge: Cambridge University Press.

———, and Maureen T Hallinan. 1977. "A reconceptualization of school effects." *Sociology of Education* 50: 273-289.

Spies, Marijke. 1999. *Rhetoric, Rhetoricians, and Poets*. Ed. Henk Duits and Ton van Strien. Amsterdam: Amsterdam University Press.

Sprott, Samuel E. 1961. *The English Debate on Suicide*. LaSalle, IL: Open Court.

Spufford, Francis. 2002. *The Child That Books Built*. London: Faber & Faber.

Srnicek, Nick. 2017. *Platform Capitalism*. Cambridge: Polity.

Stadtfeld, Christoph, and Per Block. 2017. "Interaction, actors, and time." *Sociological Science* 4: 318-352.

Stadtfeld, Christoph, James Hollway, and Per Block. 2017. "Dynamic network actor models." *Sociological Methodology* 47: 1-40.

Standing, Guy. 2019. *Plunder of the Commons*. London, UK: Pelican.

Stark, John. 1974. "Borges and his precursors." *Latin American Literary Review* 2 (2): 9-15.

Starobinski, Jean. 1985 (1982). *Montaigne in Motion*. Trans. Arthur Goldhammer. Chicago: University of Chicago Press.

Stauffer, Dietrich. 2008. "Social applications of two-dimensional Ising models." *American Journal of Physics* 76: 470-473.

Ste. Croix, G E M de. 1981. *The Class Struggle in the Ancient World*. Ithaca: Cornell University Press.

Steel, Daniel. 2004. "Social mechanisms and causal inference." *Philosophy of the Social Sciences* 34: 55-78.

Steglich, Christian, Tom A B Snijders, and Michael Pearson. 2010. "Dynamic networks and behavior." *Sociological Methodology* 40: 329-393.

———, and Patrick West. 2006. "Applying SIENA." *Methodology* 6: 48-56.

Steiner, Rudolf. 2017 (1919). *The Social Question*. Trans. Hanna von Maltitz. Fremont, MI: Steiner Archive.

Steinmetz, George. 2014. "Scientific autonomy and empire, 1880-1945." Pp. 46-73 in *German Colonialism in a Global Age*, edited by Bradley Naranch and Geoff Eley. Durham, NC: Duke University Press.

Stengers, Isabelle. 2008. "A constructivist reading of *Process and Reality*." *Theory, Culture & Society* 25 (July): 91-110.

Stephens, G Lynn, and George Graham. 2000. *When Self-Consciousness Breaks*. Cambridge: MIT Press.

Stephens-Davidowitz, David. 2017. *Everybody Lies*. New York: William Morrow.

Sterne, Laurence. 1759-67. *The Life and Opinions of Tristram Shandy, Gentleman*. London.

Stevenson, Betsey, and Justin Wolfers. 2009. "The paradox of declining female happiness." NBER Working Paper 14969. Cambridge, MA: NBER.

Stinchcombe, Arthur. 1965. "Social structure and organizations." Pp. 142-193 in *Handbook of Organizations*, edited by James G March. Chicago: Rand McNally.

_____. 1968. *Constructing Social Theories*. New York: Harcourt, Brace & World.

_____. 1986. "Reason and rationality." *Sociological Theory* 4: 151-166.

_____. 1991. "The conditions of fruitfulness of theorizing about mechanisms in social theory." *Philosophy of the Social Sciences* 21: 367-388.

Stone, Michael. 2018. *Secret Groups in Ancient Judaism*. New York: Oxford University Press.

Strawson, Galen. 2005. *The Self?* Malden, MA: Blackwell.

_____. 2015. "The unstoried life." Pp. 284-301 in *On Life-Writing*, edited by Zachary Leader. Oxford: Oxford University Press.

Stryker, Sheldon. 1988. "Substance and style." *Symbolic Interaction* 11 (Spring): 33-42.

Stuckenberg, John H W. 1882. *The Life of Immanuel Kant*. London: Macmillan.

Sudnow, David. 2001. *Ways of the Hand*, revised edition. Cambridge: MIT Press.

Sumner, William Graham. 1883. *What the Social Classes Owe to Each Other*. New York: Harper & Brothers.

Susskind, Daniel. 2020. *A World without Work*. New York: Metropolitan.

Sutherland, Edwin H. 1939. *Principles of Criminology*, 3rd edition. Philadelphia: Lippincott.

_____, and Harvey J Locke. 1936. *Twenty Thousand Homeless Men*. Chicago: Lippincott.

Sutton, John. 2000. *Marshall's Tendencies*. Cambridge: MIT Press.

_____. 2012. *Competing in Capabilities*. Oxford: Oxford University Press.

Swan, Trevor W. 1956. "Economic growth and capital accumulation." *Economic Record* 32: 334-361.

Swanson, Guy E. 1954. Review of Parsons, Bales, and Shils 1953. *American Sociological Review* 19: 95-97.

Sytsma, Justin, and Edouard Machery. 2010. "Two conceptions of subjective experience." *Philosophical Studies* 151 (2): 299-327.

Tacitus, Cornelius. 1906 (c109). *Annales*. Trans. Alfred John Church and William Jackson Brodribb. Oxford: Clarendon.

_____. 1911 (c109). *Historiae*. Trans. Alfred John Church and William Jackson Brodribb. Oxford: Clarendon.

Tackett, Timothy. 2015. *The Coming of the Terror in the French Revolution*. Cambridge: Harvard University Press.

Tang, Xianzu. 1997 (1598). *Peony Pavilion* (selected acts). Tr. C Birch. Pp. 880-906 in *An Anthology of Chinese Literature*, edited by Stephen Owen. New York: Norton.

Tauber, Alfred I. 1994. *The Immune Self*. Cambridge: Cambridge University Press.

_____. 1999. "The elusive immune self: a case of category errors." *Perspectives in Biology and Medicine* 42 (Summer): 459-474.

_____. 2000. "Moving beyond the immune self?" *Seminars in Immunology* 12 (June): 241-248.

_____. 2013. "Immunology's theories of cognition." *History and Philosophy of the Life Sciences* 35 (January): 239-264.

_____. 2017. *Immunity, the Evolution of an Idea*. New York: Oxford University Press.

667

Taubman, William. 2017. *Gorbachev: His Life and Times*. New York: Norton.

Taylor, Astrid. 2019. *Democracy May Not Exist But We Will Miss It When It's Gone*. New York: Metropolitan.

Taylor, Charles. 1989. *Sources of the Self*. Cambridge: Cambridge University Press.

Taylor, Frederick Winslow. 1915 (1911). *The Principles of Scientific Management*. New York: Harper & Brothers.

Taylor, Paul. 2014. *The Next America*. New York: Public Affairs.

Tegmark, Max. 2017. *Life 3.0*. New York: Knopf.

Tenbruck, Friedrich H. 1984. *Die unbewältigten Sozialwissenschaften oder die Abschaffung des Menschen*. Graz: Styria.

_____. 1989. *Die kulturellen Grundlagen der Gesellschaft*, 2nd edition. Opladen: Westdeutsche Verlag.

Tetens, Johann Nikolaus. 1913 (1777). *Philosophische Versuche über die menschliche Natur und ihre Entwicklung*, 2 volumes. Berlin: Reuther und Reichard.

_____. 1971. *Sprachphilosophie Versuche*. Ed. Heinrich Pfannkuch. Hamburg: Felix Meiner.

Thaler, Richard H. 2015. *Misbehaving*. New York: Norton.

_____, and Cass Sunstein. 2008. *Nudge*. New Haven: Yale University Press.

Theil, Henri. 1954. *Linear Aggregation of Economic Relations*. Amsterdam: North-Holland.

_____. 1957. "Linear aggregation in input-output analysis." *Econometrica* 25: 111-122.

Theroux, Paul. 2013. "I hate vacations." *The Atlantic* 312 (September): 42-43.

Theunissen, Michael. 1984 (1977). *The Other*. Trans. C Macann. Cambridge: MIT Press.

Thomas, Brook. 1997. *American Literary Realism and the Failed Promise of Contract*. Berkeley: University of California Press.

Thomas, Rosalind. 1992. *Literacy and Orality in Ancient Greece*. Cambridge: Cambridge University Press.

Thomas, William I, and Dorothy Swaine Thomas. 1928. *The Child in America*. New York: Knopf.

Thomas, William I, and Florian Znaniecki. 1958 (1927). *The Polish Peasant in Poland and America*, 2nd edition, 2 volumes. New York: Dover.

Thomasson, Amie L. 2002. "Foundations for a social ontology." *Protosociology* 18-19: 269-290.

Thompson, Hunter S. 1972. *Fear and Loathing in Las Vegas*. New York: Random House.

Thompson, James. 1988. *Between Self and World*. University Park, PA: Pennsylvania University Press.

Thoreau, Henry David. 1985 (1854). *Walden*. Pp. 321-587 in *Henry David Thoreau*. Ed. R F Sayre. New York: Library of America.

Thorne, Christian. 2009. *The Dialectic of Counter-Enlightenment*. Cambridge: Harvard University Press.

Thornton, Sarah. 2008. *Seven Days in the Art World*. New York: Norton.

Thuillier, Guy. 1962. "Paul Valéry et la politique." *La Revue administrative* 90 (Nov-Dec): 612-617.

Tideman, Nicolaus. 2006. *Collective Decisions and Voting*. Aldershot: Ashgate.

Tocqueville, Alexis de. 1835, 1840 (2004). *Democracy in America*, 2 volumes in one. Trans. Arthur Goldhammer; ed. Olivier Zunz. New York: Library of America.

Tönnies, Ferdinand. 1887. *Gemeinschaft und Gesellschaft*, 1st edition. Leipzig: Fues.

Tönnies, Ferdinand. 1907. *Die Entwicklung der sozialen Frage.* Leipzig: Göschen.
_____. 1971 (1896). *Thomas Hobbes Leben und Lehre,* 3rd edition. Ed. K H Ilting. Stuttgart: Friedrich Frommann.
_____. 1974. *Ferdinand Tönnies on Social Ideas and Ideologies.* Trans. & ed. Eduard Georg Jacoby. New York: Harper & Row.
Toffler, Alvin. 1970. *Future Shock.* New York: Random House.
Toft, Maren. 2018. "Mobility closure in the upper class." *British Journal of Sociology* <doi.org/10.1111/1468-4446.12362>
Tolentino, Jia. 2019. *Trick Mirror.* New York: Random House.
Tolstaya, Tatyana. 2018 (2015). "The Square." Pp. 101-111 in *idem, Aetherial Worlds.* Trans. Anya Migdal. New York: Knopf.
Tolstoy, Leo. 1904. *What Is Art?* Trans. Aylmer Maude. New York: Funk & Wagnalls.
Tomasello, Michael. 2003. *Constructing a Language.* Cambridge: Harvard University Press.
_____. 2019. *Becoming Human.* Cambridge: Harvard University Press.
Tomlinson, Gary. 2015. *A Million Years of Music.* New York: Zone.
Tooze, Adam. 2014. *The Deluge.* New York: Viking.
Trilling, Lionel. 2000. *The Moral Obligation to Be Intelligent.* Ed. Leon Wieseltier. New York: Farrar, Straus and Giroux.
Trollope, Frances. 1844. *The Life and Adventures of Michael Armstrong, The Factory Boy.* London: Henry Colburn.
Tsvetkova, Milena, and Michael W Macy. 2015. "The social contagion of antisocial behavior." *Sociological Science* 2: 36-49. <doi: 10.15195/v2.a4>
Tufekci, Zeynep. 2017. *Twitter and Tear Gas.* New Haven: Yale University Press.
Tugendhat, Ernst. 1986 [1979]. *Self-Consciousness and Self-Determination.* Trans. Paul Stern. Cambridge: MIT Press.
Tuma, Nancy Brandon, and Michael T Hannan. 1984. *Social Dynamics.* Orlando, FL: Academic.
Tuomela, Raimo. 2007. *The Philosophy of Sociality.* New York: Oxford University Press.
_____. 2013. *Social Ontology.* New York: Oxford University Press.
Turner, James. 2014. *Philology.* Princeton: Princeton University Press.
Turner, Jonathan. 1997. *The Institutional Order.* New York: Longman.
Turner, Stephen P. 1980. *Sociological Explanation as Translation.* Cambridge: Cambridge University Press.
_____. 1983. "Weber on action." *American Sociological Review* 48: 506-519.
_____. 2007a. "Public sociology and democratic theory." *Sociology* 41: 785-798.
_____. 2007b. "Cognitive science, social theory, and ethics." *Soundings* 90: 135-160.
_____. 2011. "Davidson's normativity." Pp. 343-370 in *Dialogues with Davidson,* edited by Jeff Malpas. Cambridge: MIT Press.
_____. 2012. "The strength of weak empathy." *Science in Context* 25: 383-399.
_____. 2013. "Taking the collective out of tacit knowledge." *Philosophia Scientiæ* 17: 75-92.
_____. 2016. "The naturalistic moment in normativism." Pp. 9-27 in *Normativity and Naturalism in the Philosophy of the Social Sciences,* edited by Mark Risjord. New York: Routledge.
_____. 2018. *Cognitive Science and the Social.* New York: Routledge.
Tyson, Timothy B. 2017. *The Blood of Emmett Till.* New York: Simon & Schuster.

Unger, Peter. 1984. *Philosophical Relativity*. Oxford: Blackwell.

Unger, Roberto Mangabeira, and Lee Smolin. 2015. *The Singular Universe and the Reality of Time*. Cambridge: Cambridge University Press.

Vaihinger, Hans. 1935 (1911). *The Philosophy of 'As If'*, 2nd edition. Trans. Charles K Ogden. London: Routledge & Kegan Paul.

Valéry, Paul. 1962 (1919). "The crisis of the mind." Pp. 23-36 in *idem, The Outlook for Intelligence*. Trans. Denise Folliot and Jackson Matthews, ed. Jackson Matthews. New York: Harper.

Valiavitcharska, Vessela. 2006. "Correct *logos* and truth in Gorgias' *Encomium of Helen*." *Rhetorica* 24 (Spring): 147-161.

_____. 2014. *Rhetoric and Rhythm in Byzantium*. Cambridge: Cambridge University Press.

van Alphen, Ernst. 2005. "What history, whose history, history to what purpose?" *Journal of Visual Culture* 4 (2): 191-202.

Van Bommel, Bas. 2015. *Classical Humanism and the Challenge of Modernity*. Berlin: DeGuyter.

Vance, James David. 2016. *Hillbilly Elegy*. New York: Harper.

van Heijenoort, Jean (ed.). 1967. *From Frege to Gödel*. Cambridge: Harvard University Press.

Van Norden, Bryan W. 2017. *Taking Back Philosophy*. New York: Columbia University Press.

Van Wyck, Peter C. 2004. *Signs of Danger*. Minneapolis: University of Minnesota Press.

Vasari, Giorgio. 1896 (1568). *The Lives of the Most Excellent Painters, Sculptors, and Architects*. Trans. Gaston du C. de Vere. New York: Scribner's.

Veblen, Thorstein B. 1898. "Why is economics not an evolutionary science?" *The Quarterly Journal of Economics* 12: 373-397.

_____. 1899. *The Theory of the Leisure Class*. New York: Macmillan.

_____. 1915. *Imperial Germany and the Industrial Revolution*. New York: Macmillan.

Velleman, J David. 1989. *Practical Reflection*. Princeton: Princeton University Press.

_____. 2000. *The Possibility of Practical Reason*. Oxford: Oxford University Press.

Velthuis, Olav. 2005. *Talking Prices*. Princeton: Princeton University Press.

Verhaus, Rudolf. 1972. "Bildung." Pp. 508-511 in *Geschichtliche Grundbegriffe. Historisches Lexikon zur politisch-sozialen Sprache in Deutschland*, volume 1, edited by O Brunner, W Conze, and R Koselleck. Stuttgart: Klett Cotta.

Veyne, Paul. 1988 (1983). *Did the Greeks Believe in Their Myths?* Trans. Paula Wissing. Chicago: University of Chicago Press.

Vico, Giambattista. 1988 (1710). *On the Most Ancient Wisdom of the Italians Unearthed from the Origins of the Latin Language*. Trans. Lucia M Palmer. Ithaca: Cornell University Press.

_____. 1992 (1708-09). *On the Study Methods of Our Time*. Trans. Elio Gianturco. Ithaca: Cornell University Press.

Vogel, Carol. 2008. "The gray areas of Jasper Johns." *New York Times* (3 February), AR1.

Voltaire. 1879 (1775). "Le cri du sang innocent." Pp. 375-390 in *idem, Œuvres completer de Voltaire*, l'édition Beuchot, volume 29. Paris: Garnier.

_____. 2015. *Voltaire's Revolution*. Trans, & ed. G K Noyer. Amherst, NY: Prometheus.

von Arnim, Bettina. 1861 (1834). *Goethe's Correspondence with a Child*. Boston: Ticknor and Fields.

von Goethe, Johann Wolfgang. 1799 (1773). *Götz von Berlichingen*. Trans. Walter Scott. London: J Bell.

———. 1907 (1795-96). *Wilhelm Meister's Apprenticeship*. Trans. Thomas Carlyle. London: Chapman and Hall.

———. 1971 (1809). *Elective Affinities*. Trans. R J Hollingdale. London: Penguin.

———. 1976 (1829). *Faust: A Tragedy*, 2nd edition. Trans. Walter Arndt. New York: Norton.

von Helmholtz, Hermann L F. 1853 (1847). "The conservation of force." Trans. John Tyndall. Pp. 114-162 in John Tyndall and William Francis (eds.), *Scientific Memoirs*. London: Taylor and Francis.

———. 1925 (1910). *Treatise on Physiological Optics*, 3 volumes. Trans. James P C Southall. New York: Dover.

von Neumann, John. 1932. "Proof of the quasi-ergodic hypothesis." *Proceedings of the National Academy of Sciences of the USA* 18: 70-82.

von Staden, Heinrich. 1002. "The discovery of the body." *Yale Journal of Biology and Medicine* 65: 223-241.

Vorländer, Karl. 1911. *Kant und Marx*. Tübingen: Mohr.

———. 1924. *Immanuel Kant*, 2 volumes. Leipzig: Felix Meiner.

Vosoughi, Soroush, Deb Roy, and Sinan Aral. 2018. "The spread of true and false news online." *Science* 359 (9 March): 1146-1151.

Vygotsky, Lev S. 1978. *Mind in Society*, revised edition. Tr. A R Luria, M Cole, & M Lopez-Morillas; ed. M Cole & S Scribner. Cambridge: Harvard University Press.

———. 1986 (1934). *Thought and Language*, rev. ed. Ed. Alex Kozulin. Tr. Eugenia Hanfmann, Gertrude Vakar, and Alex Kozulin. Cambridge: MIT Press.

Waal, Frans de. 2016. *Are We Smart Enough to Know How Smart Animals Are?* London: Granta.

Wacquant, Loïc. 2001. "Deadly symbiosis." *Punishment & Society* 3: 95-133.

———. 2002. "Scrutinizing the streets." *American Journal of Sociology* 107: 1468-1532.

———. 2008. *Urban Outcasts*. Cambridge: Polity.

———. 2009. *Punishing the Poor*. Durham: Duke University Press.

———. 2014. "Marginality, ethnicity and penalty in the neo-liberal city." *Ethnic and Racial Studies* 37: 1687-1711.

Wagner, Helmut. 1964."Displacement of scope." *American Journal of Sociology* 69:571-584

Wagner, Philip L. 1996. *Showing Off*. Austin: University of Texas Press.

Waldron, Jeremy. 2017. *One Another's Equals*. Cambridge: Harvard University Press.

Waldrop, M Mitchell. 1992. *Complexity*. New York: Simon & Schuster.

Wallace, David. 1967. "Reflections on the education of George Herbert Mead." *American Journal of Sociology* 72: 396-408.

Wallace, Robert W. 1998. *The Sophists in Athens*. Cambridge: Harvard University Press.

———. 2007. "Plato's sophists, intellectual history after 450, and Sokrates." Pp. 215-237 in *The Cambridge Companion to the Age of Pericles*, edited by L J Samons II. Cambridge: Cambridge University Press.

———. 2015. *Reconstructing Damon*. Oxford: Oxford University Press.

Wallace-Hadrill, Andrew. 1982. "Civilis princeps." *Journal of Roman Studies* 72: 32-48.

Wallace-Wells, David. 2019. *The Uninhabitable Earth*. London: Allen Lane.

Wallwork, Ernest. 1972. *Durkheim: Morality and Milieu*. Cambridge: Harvard University Press.

Walzer, Michael. 2017. "Does betrayal still matter?" *New York Review of Books* 64 (11 May): 52-54.

Wang, Chaohua. 2003. *One China, Many Paths*. London: Verso.

Wang, Zhongmin, and Gonzalo R Arce. 2010. "Variable density compressed image sampling." *IEEE Transactions on Image Processing* 19 (January): 264-270.

Warminski, Andrzej. 1976. "Patmos." *MLN* 91: 478-500.

Warner, Rebecca. 1998. *Spectral Analysis of Time Series Data*. New York: Guilford.

Watkins, John W N. 1957. "Historical explanation in the social sciences." *British Journal for the Philosophy of Science* 8 9August): 104-117.

_____. 1984. *Science and Scepticism*. Princeton: Princeton University Press.

Watts, Duncan J. 1999. *Small Worlds*. Princeton: Princeton University Press.

Waugh, Alexander. 2004. *Fathers and Sons*. New York: Doubleday.

Weber, Eugen. 1986. *France, Fin de Siècle*. Cambridge: Harvard University Press.

Weber, Max. 1930 (1905). *The Protestant Ethic and the Spirit of Capitalism*. Trans. Talcott Parsons. New York: Charles Scribner's Sons.

_____. 1949 (1904). "'Objectivity' in the social sciences and social policy." Pp. 50-112 in *idem, The Methodology of the Social Sciences*. Trans & ed. Edward A Shils & Henry A Finch. Glencoe, IL: Free Press.

_____. 1949 (1905). "Critical studies in the logic of the cultural sciences." Pp. 113-188 in *idem, The Methodology of the Social Sciences*. Trans & ed. Edward A Shils & Henry A Finch. Glencoe, IL: Free Press.

_____. 1951 (1915). *Konfuzianismus und Taoismus*. Trans. & ed. H H Gerth as *The Religion of China*. New York: Free Press.

_____. 1964 (1913). "Gutachen zur Werturteilsdiskussion im Ausschuss des Verein für Sozialpolitik." Pp. 102-139 in Eduard Baumgarten, *Max Weber*. Tübingen: Mohr.

_____. 1968 [1922]. *Economy and Society*, 3 volumes. Trans. Guenther Roth et al., ed. Guenther Roth & Claus Wittich. New York: Bedminster.

_____. 1975 (1905-06). "Knies and the problem of irrationality." Pp. 93-207 in *idem, Roscher and Knies*. Trans. & ed. Guy Oakes. New York: Free Press.

_____. 1976 (1896; 1909). *The Agrarian Sociology of Ancient Civilizations*. Trans. R I Frank. London: NLB.

Wegner, Daniel M. 2002. *The Illusion of Conscious Will*. Cambridge: MIT Press.

_____. 2003. "The mind's best trick." *Trends in Cognitive Science* 7 (2): 65-69.

_____, and Kurt Gray. 2016. *The Mind Club*. New York: Viking.

Wei, Wei, and Kathleen M Carley. 2015. "Measuring temporal patterns in dynamic social networks." *ACM Transactions on Knowledge Discovery from Data* 10 (July): .1-9.27.

Weinberg, Steven. 2015. *To Explain the World*. New York: HarperCollins.

Weitz, Eric D. 2007. *Weimar Germany*. Princeton: Princeton University Press.

Werner, Emmy, and Ruth Smith. 1992. *Overcoming the Odds*. Ithaca: Cornell University Press.

_____. 2001. *Journeys from Childhood to Midlife*. Ithaca: Cornell University Press.

Westover, Tara. 2018. *Educated*. New York: Random House.

White, Harrison C. 1992. *Identity and Control*, 1st edition. Princeton: Princeton University Press.

_____. 2002. *Markets from Networks*. Princeton: Princeton University Press.

_____. 2008. *Identity and Control*, 2nd edition. Princeton: Princeton University Press.

White, Harrison, Scott A Boorman, and Ronald L Breiger. 1976. "Social structure from multiple networks." *American Journal of Sociology* 81: 730-780.

White, Hayden. 1973. *Metahistory*. Baltimore: Johns Hopkins University Press.

―――. 1978. *Tropics of Discourse*. Baltimore: Johns Hopkins University Press.

―――. 1987. *The Content of the Form*. Baltimore: Johns Hopkins University Press.

White, Richard. 2017. *The Republic for Which It Stands*. New York: Oxford University Press.

Whitehead, Alfred North. 1954. *Dialogues with Alfred North Whitehead*. Recorded by Price. Boston: Little, Brown.

―――. 1978 (1929). *Process and Reality*, corrected edition. Ed. David R Griffin and Donald Sherburne. New York: Free Press.

Whyte, William H, Jr. 1952. "Groupthink." *Fortune* 45 (March): 114-117, 142, 146.

―――. 1956. *The Organization Man*. New York: Simon and Schuster.

Wierzbicken, Anna. 1986. "Human emotions: universal or culture-specific?" *American Anthropologist* 88: 584-594.

Wiesel, Torsten N. 1993 (1981). "The postnatal development of the visual cortex and the influence of the environment." *Nobel Lectures in Physiology or Medicine, 1981-1990*, edited by Jan Lindsten. Stockholm: Karolinksa Institute.

Wilczek, Frank. 2008. *The Lightness of Being*. New York: Basic Books.

Wiley, Norbert. 1994. *The Semiotic Self*. Chicago: University of Chicago Press.

Wilkinson, Richard, and Kate Pickett. 2018. *The Inner Level*. London: Allen Lane.

Williams, Bernard. 1973. *Problems of the Self*. Cambridge: Cambridge University Press.

―――. 1984. "Personal identity." *London Review of Books* 6 (7 June): 14-15.

―――. 2014. *Essays and Reviews 1959-2002*. Princeton: Princeton University Press.

Williams, James. 2018. *Stand Out of Our Light*. Cambridge: Cambridge University Press.

Williams, Jeffrey. 2014. *How to Be an Intellectual*. New York: Fordham University Press.

―――. 2018. "The rise of the promotional intellectual." *Chronicle of Higher Education* (5 Aug).

Williams, John. 1965. *Stoner*. New York: Viking.

Williams, Michael. 1998. *Groundless Belief*, 2nd edition. Princeton: Princeton University Press.

Williams, Whiting. 1920. *What's on the Worker's Mind*. New York: Scribner's.

Wilson, Timothy D. 2002. *Strangers to Ourselves*. Cambridge: Harvard University Press.

―――, and Elizabeth W Dunn. 2004. "Self-Knowledge." *Annual Review of Psychology* 55: 493-518.

Wilson, Richard. 2008. "'Our Bending Author': Shakespeare takes a bow." Pp. 67-79 in *Shakespeare Studies*, volume 36, edited by Susan Zimmerman & Garrett Sullivan. Madison and Teaneck, NJ: Fairleigh Dickinson University Press.

Wilson-Lee, Edward. 2018. *The Catalogue of Shipwrecked Books*. London: William Collins.

Winch, Peter. 1958. *The Idea of a Social Science*. London: Routledge & Kegan Paul.

Winckelmann, Johann Joachim. 1764. *Geschichte der Kunst des Alterthums*. Dresden: Walther.

Wittgenstein, Ludwig. 1922 (1921). *Tractatus Logico-Philosophicus*. Trans. Frank P Ramsey and Charles K Ogden. London: Kegan Paul.

―――. 1968. *Philosophical Investigations*, 3rd edition. Trans. G E Anscombe. New York: Macmillan.

Wittgenstein, Ludwig. 1977. *Remarks on Colour*. Ed. G E M Anscombe; tr. Linda L McAlister and Margarette Schättle. Berkeley: University of California Press.

Wohl, Victoria. 2010. *Law's Cosmos*. Cambridge: Cambridge University Press.

Wohlleben, Peter. 2016 (2015). *The Hidden Life of Trees*. Trans. Jane Billinghurst. Vancouver: Greystone.

Woike, Jan K, and Sebastian Hafenbrädl. 2020. "Rivals without a cause?" *Journal of Behavioral Decision Making*. <doi: 10.1002/bdm.2162>

Woit, Peter. 2006. *Not Even Wrong*. New York: Basic Books.

Wolf, Maryanne. 2007. *Proust and the Squid*. New York: HarperCollins.

Wolfe, Alan. 2006. *Does American Democracy Still Work?* New Haven: Yale University Press.

Wolfe, Thomas.1940. *You Can't Go Home Again*. Ed. Ed Aswell. New York: Harper & Row

Woolf, Steven, and Heidi Schoomaker. 2019. "Life expectancy and mortality rates in the United States, 1959-2017." *Journal of the American Medical Association* 322: 1996-2016.

Woolf, Virginia. 1985. *Moments of Being*, 2nd edition; ed. Jeanne Schulkind. New York: Harcourt Brace.

Wood, David. 1990. *Philosophy at the Limit*. London: Unwin Hyman.

_____. 2001. *The Deconstruction of Time*, 2nd edition. Evanston: Northwestern University Press.

_____. 2007. *Time After Time*. Bloomington: Indiana University Press.

Wood, Gordon S. 1993. *The Radicalism of the American Revolution*. New York: Vintage.

Wood, James. 2018. *Upstate*. New York: Farrar, Straus and Giroux.

Wood, Michael, and Mark Wardell. 1983. "G H Mead's social behaviorism vs. the astructural bias of symbolic interactionism." *Symbolic Interaction* 6: 85-96.

Wood, Robert G, Quinn Moore, Andrew Clarkwest, Alexandra Killewald, and Shannon Monahan. 2012. *The Long-Term Effects of Building Strong Families*. OPRE Report 2012-28A. Princeton: Mathematica Policy Research.

Wood, Thomas, and Ethan Porter. 2018. "The elusive backfire effect." *Political Behavior* 40: 1-29.

Woodford, Susan. 2003. *Images of Myths in Classical Antiquity*. Cambridge: Cambridge University Press.

Woodruff, Paul. 2011. *The Ajax Dilemma*. New York: Oxford University Press.

Wrong, Dennis H. 1961. "The oversocialized conception of man in modern sociology." *American Sociological Review* 26: 183-193.

_____. 1994. *The Problem of Order*. New York: Free Press.

Wu, Zhaohui, Thomas Y Choi, and M Johnny Rungtusanatham. 2010. "Supplier-supplier relationship in buyer-supplier-supplier triads." *Journal of Operations Management* 28: 115-123.

Wuthnow, Robert. 1987. *Meaning and Moral Order*. Berkeley: University of California Press.

_____. 2018. *The Left Behind*. Princeton: Princeton University Press.

Wyngaard, Amy S. 2004. *From Savage to Citizen*. Newark: University of Delaware Press.

Yang, C K. 1961. *Religion in Chinese Society*. Berkeley: University of California Press.

Yavorski, Jill E, Claire M Kamp Dush, and Sarah J Schoppe-Sullivan. 2015. "The production of inequality." *Journal of Marriage and Family* 77: 662-679.

Yeats, William Butler. 2015 (1937). *A Vision. The Revised 1937 Edition*. Volume 14 of *idem, The Collected Works of W B Yeats*. New York: Simon and Schuster.

Yee, Nick. 2014. *The Proteus Paradox*. New Haven: Yale University Press.

Yeginsu, Ceylan. 2018. "Track hands of workers?" *New York Times* (2 February): B3.

Yetish, Gandhi, Hillard Kaplan, Michael Gurven, Brian Wood, Herman Pontzer, Paul Manger, Charles Wilson, Ronald McGregor, and Jerome M Siegel. 2015. "Natural sleep and its seasonal variations in three pre-industrial societies." *Current Biology* 25: 2862-2868.

Yeung, King-To, and John Levi Martin. 2003. "The looking glass self." *Social Forces* 81: 843-879.

Ylikoski, Petri. 2014. "Rethinking micro-macro relations." Pp. 117-135 in *Rethinking the Individualism-Holism Debate*, edited by Julie Zahle and Finn Collin. Cham, Switzerland: Springer International.

Yoon, Byung-Jun. 2009. "Hidden Markov models and their applications in biological Sequence analysis." *Current Genomics* 10: 402-415.

Young, H Peyton. 1998. *Individual Strategy and Social Structure*. Princeton: Princeton University Press.

_____. 2015. "The evolution of social norms." *Annual Review of Economics* 7: 359-387.

Young, Michael. 1958. *The Rise of the Meritocracy*. London: Thames and Hudson.

Yourgrau, Palle. 2005. *A World without Time*. New York: Basic Books.

Zadeh, Lofti A. 1965. "Fuzzy sets." *Information and Control* 8: 338-353.

Zaretsky, Robert. 2015. *Boswell's Enlightenment*. Cambridge: Harvard University Press.

Zerubavel, Eviatar. 1996. "Lumpers and splitters." *Sociological Forum* 11: 421-433.

_____. 2018. *Taken for Granted*. Princeton: Princeton University Press.

Zerubavel, Noam, Mark Anthony Hoffman, Adam Reich, Kevin N Ochsner, and Peter Bearman. 2018. "Neural precursors of future liking and affective reciprocity." *PNAS* 115: 4375-4380. <doi/10.1073/pnas.1802176115>

Zetterberg, Hans. 1962. Review of *Theories of Society*, 2 volumes. *American Journal of Sociology* 67: 707-708.

Zimmer, Carl. 2018. *She Has Her Mother's Laugh*. New York: Dutton.

Zimmerman, Reinhard. 1996. *The Law of Obligations*. Oxford: Oxford University Press.

Zink, Nell. 2019. *Doxology*. New York: HarperCollins.

Ziolkowski, Theodore. 1990. *German Romanticism and Its Institutions*. Princeton: Princeton University Press.

Znaniecki, Florian. 1934. *The Method of Sociology*. New York: Rinehart.

Zuboff, Shoshana. 1988. *In the Age of the Smart Machine*. New York: Basic Books.

_____. 2019. *The Age of Surveillance Capitalism*. New York: Public Affairs.

## Acknowledgments

Parts of the text reported above derive from work that was supported by a fellowship from the National Institutes of Health, 1975-1980. That was a time when research agencies and foundations were able and willing to invest in long-term projects of development in the social sciences and humanities, especially promising projects unlikely to have quick payoffs. I appreciate the generous support that was afforded during those years as well as in later years by other persons and agencies. I regret that portions of my work and texts derived from them have alienated some friends, but I cannot write what I do not think with honest conviction.

Many individual persons have been especially helpful in various ways over the past fifty years. I dare not trust my memory to name all of them. At risk of giving offense by undeserved neglect, I must acknowledge these few, however, whose aids dates from the late 1960s to present times: Loretta Barrett, William Barrett, Joseph Lopreato, Louis Schneider, Margaret S Keir, Arthur Grey Hazlerigg, Sheldon Stryker, George Russell Carpenter, Kenneth Burke, Erving Goffman, Peter Manning, Donald Levine, Stanley Cavell, George H Hazlerigg, Melissa Hardy, Mabel Lee, Harrison White, Eugene F Kaelin, Jeanne M Ruppert, Alan Mabe, George Arthur Hazlerigg, Harry F Dahms, Daniel M Harrison, Katherine Hazlerigg, and Rose Coster. And my parents, Robert and Frances, who started it all for me.